Table 2
Selected Employment and Unemployment Data, 1948–1984
(percent; monthly data seasonally adjusted)

Year	Unemployment Rate								Average Duration (weeks)
		By Sex and Age			By Selected Groups				
	All Workers	Both Sexes 16–19 Years	Males 20 Years and Over	Females 20 Years and Over	Married Men	Women Who Head Families	Experienced Wage and Salary Workers	Black and Other	
1948	3.8	9.2	3.2	3.6			4.3	5.9	8.6
1949	5.9	13.4	5.4	5.3	3.5		6.8	8.9	10.0
1950	5.3	12.2	4.7	5.1	4.6		6.0	9.0	12.1
1951	3.3	8.2	2.5	4.0	1.5		3.7	5.3	9.7
1952	3.0	8.5	2.4	3.2	1.4		3.4	5.4	8.4
1953	2.9	7.6	2.5	2.9	1.7		3.2	4.5	8.0
1954	5.5	12.6	4.9	5.5	4.0		6.2	9.9	11.8
1955	4.4	11.0	3.8	4.4	2.8		4.8	8.7	13.0
1956	4.1	11.1	3.4	4.2	2.6		4.4	8.3	11.3
1957	4.3	11.6	3.6	4.1	2.8		4.6	7.9	10.5
1958	6.8	15.9	6.2	6.1	5.1		7.3	12.6	13.9
1959	5.5	14.6	4.7	5.2	3.6		5.7	10.7	14.4
1960	5.5	14.7	4.7	5.1	3.7		5.7	10.2	12.8
1961	6.7	16.8	5.7	6.3	4.6		6.8	12.4	15.6
1962	5.5	14.7	4.6	5.4	3.6		5.6	10.9	14.7
1963	5.7	17.2	4.5	5.4	3.4		5.6	10.8	14.0
1964	5.2	16.2	3.9	5.2	2.8		5.0	9.6	13.3
1965	4.5	14.8	3.2	4.5	2.4		4.3	8.1	11.8
1966	3.8	12.8	2.5	3.8	1.9		3.5	7.3	10.4
1967	3.8	12.8	2.3	4.2	1.8	4.9	3.6	7.4	8.8
1968	3.6	12.7	2.2	3.8	1.6	4.4	3.4	6.7	8.4
1969	3.5	12.2	2.1	3.7	1.5	4.4	3.3	6.4	7.9
1970	4.9	15.2	3.5	4.8	2.6	5.4	4.8	8.2	8.7
1971	5.9	16.9	4.4	5.7	3.2	7.3	5.7	9.9	11.3
1972	5.6	16.2	4.0	5.4	2.8	7.2	5.3	10.0	12.0
1973	4.9	14.5	3.2	4.8	2.3	7.0	4.5	8.9	10.0
1974	5.6	16.0	3.8	5.5	2.7	7.0	5.3	9.9	9.7
1975	8.5	19.9	6.7	8.0	5.1	10.0	8.2	13.9	14.1
1976	7.7	19.0	5.9	7.4	4.2	10.0	7.3	13.1	15.8
1977	7.0	17.7	5.2	7.0	3.6	9.3	6.6	13.1	14.3
1978	6.0	16.3	4.2	6.0	2.8	8.5	5.6	11.9	11.9
1979	5.8	16.1	4.2	5.7	2.8	8.3	5.5	11.3	10.8
1980	7.1	17.8	5.9	6.4	4.2	9.2	6.9	13.1	11.9
1981	7.5	19.6	6.3	6.8	4.3	10.4	7.3	14.2	13.7
1982	9.5	23.2	8.8	8.3	6.5	11.7	9.3	17.3	15.6
1983	9.5	22.4	8.9	8.1	6.5	12.2	9.2	17.8	20.0
1984	7.4	18.9	6.6	6.8	4.6	10.3	7.1	14.4	18.2

Source: Presidents Council of Economic Advisors, *Economic Report of the President* (Washington, D.C.: Government Printing Office 1985), Tables B-31, B-33.

ECONOMICS
Fourth Edition

ECONOMICS

Fourth Edition

Edwin G. Dolan

George Mason University

In collaboration with
David E. Lindsey
Associate Director
Division of Research and Statistics
Board of Governors of the Federal Reserve System

The Dryden Press

Chicago   New York   Philadelphia   San Francisco   Montreal   Toronto
London   Sydney   Tokyo   Mexico City   Rio de Janeiro   Madrid

Acquisitions Editor: Elizabeth Widdicombe
Developmental Editor: Carolyn Smith, Textbook Development Inc.
Senior Project Editor: Maureen P. Conway, Cobb/Dunlop Publisher Services
Managing Editor: Jane Perkins
Production Manager: Mary Jarvis
Design Director: Marsha Cohen

Text and cover design: Marsha Cohen
Copy editing: Robert Whitlock
Photo research: Freda Leinwand
Text type: 10/12 Malibu

Library of Congress Cataloging-in-Publication Data

Dolan, Edwin G.
    Economics.

    Rev. ed. of: Basic economics.
    Includes bibliographies and index.
    1. Economics.   I. Dolan, Edwin G.   Basic economics.
II. Title.
HB171.5.D58   1986   330   85-16072
ISBN 0-03-005447-8

Printed in the United States of America
678-032-98765432

Address orders to:

383 Madison Avenue
New York, New York 10017

Address editorial correspondence to:

One Salt Creek Lane
Hinsdale, Illinois 60521

CBS COLLEGE PUBLISHING
The Dryden Press
Holt, Rinehart and Winston
Saunders College Publishing

Credits and Acknowledgments
Print of Adam Smith, page 6, from Culver Pictures. Photo of Friedrich von Hayek, page 5, from The Granger Collection. Photo of Karl Marx, page 37, from Culver Pictures. Photo of Alfred Marshall, page 52, from The Granger Collection. Photo of John Maynard Keynes, page 199, from UPI/ Bettmann Archive. Print of William Stanley Jevons, page 503, from Historical Pictures Service. Photo of Milton Friedman, page 339, from UPI/Bettman Archive. Photo of Joseph Alois Schumpeter, page 631, from The Granger Collection. Photo of David Ricardo, page 804, from Culver Pictures. Print of Thomas Malthus, page 853, from The Granger Collection. Photo of Samuel Gompers, page 746, from The Granger Collection.

Part opening photographs: Photo of Chicago Mercantile Exchange by Roger Malloch, Magnum Photos. Painting of John Maynard Keynes by Gwen Raverat, The Granger Collection. Photo of Yap money by Susan Pierres, Peter Arnold. Photo of Argentinian hyperinflation by E. Shore, Woodfin Camp. Photo of computer assembly line by Robert A. Isaacs, Photo Researchers. Caricature of Liberty vs. Monopoly by Joseph Keppler, The Bettmann Archive. Photo of faculty strike by Sybil Shelton, Peter Arnold. Photo of McDonald's billboard in Heidelberg by Hiller, Monkmeyer.

The Dryden Press Series in Economics

Brief Contents

Detailed Contents

PART II   NATIONAL INCOME AND FISCAL POLICY

6. The Circular Flow of Income and Product   130

7. Supply and Demand in the Macroeconomy   152

8. Measuring National Income and Product   172

PART VI   GOVERNMENT AND BUSINESS

26. Antitrust Policy

638

27. Regulation

652

28. Farm Policy

668

PART VIII   THE WORLD ECONOMY

Preface

The last decade has been a productive one for the economics profession. Economists have gained a better understanding both of the world at large and of their own discipline. In macroeconomics, more is known about the dynamics of inflation and unemployment, the role of monetary policy, the determinants of unemployment, the role of expectations in shaping economic behavior, and the interaction between the domestic economy and the world economy. In microeconomics, such fields of study as regulation, antitrust policy, human resources, and income distribution have taken on a new life.

But at the same time that progress has been made, events have posed new questions. Economists continue to disagree on such matters as the effects of the federal deficit, the proper path for monetary policy, the consequences of corporate takeovers, and the reasons for differences in men's and women's average pay, to name just a few areas of controversy.

Both the rapid pace at which economic knowledge has advanced and the ongoing controversies make teaching economics a challenge. Meeting the challenge requires a special kind of textbook. First, it requires a book that brings the latest theoretical developments into the classroom and explains them as clearly as it explains established topics such as supply and demand. And second, it requires a book that emphasizes the tools that all economists use, the common ways of thinking that they employ even when they reach different conclusions.

The following pages outline the strategy used in this book to meet the challenges of teaching economics in the 1980s.

Overview

Introduction The book begins with a set of chapters that provide an overview of economics and the economy. The first chapter surveys the subject matter of economics and gives an idea of what economists do. Chapter 2 looks at the central problems faced by every economy. Chapter 3 provides an introduction to supply-and-demand analysis. The final two chapters in the introductory section explore the role of business and government in the economy. As a group, these five chapters focus on the essentials required as background for both macro- and microeconomics. After finishing this section, the student is equipped for either a macro- or a micro-first sequence.

Macroeconomics The crucial first step in learning macroeconomics is to get a picture of how the parts of the economy fit together into a whole. A set of three chapters serves that purpose in this book. Chapter 6 uses the framework of the circular flow to show how firms, households, units of government, and the rest of the world interact. Chapter 7 looks at three sets of markets featured in the circular flow: labor markets, financial markets, and product markets. The discussion of product markets provides students with an introduction to the way in which aggregate real supply and demand interact to determine the price level and the level of real output in the economy. Chapter 8 completes the overview with a discussion of national income accounting.

Having established a framework for analysis, the text moves on to monetary and fiscal policy. Chapters 9–13 explore institutions, theory, and issues in an integrated manner. Emphasis is placed on the fact that tools of monetary and fiscal policy allow the government, within reasonable limits, to control the growth of nominal GNP—that is, of GNP measured in current dollars.

Chapters 14–18 then turn to the topics of inflation, unemployment, and economic growth. The aggregate real supply and demand framework is used to show how changes in monetary and fiscal policy affect real variables. The issues of long-run versus short-run effects, of the role of expectations, of the fiscal-monetary policy mix, and of policy activism versus policy rules are all explored.

Microeconomics   The traditional core of microeconomics is presented in Chapters 19–25. These chapters give a careful exposition of the theories of consumer behavior, production, cost, perfect competition, monopoly, and other market structures.

The next group of chapters explore issues in the relationship of government to business. Chapters 26 and 27 cover antitrust policy and regulation. Chapter 28 deals with farm policy and Chapter 29 with environmental issues. Following these comes a section of four chapters (30–33) on factor markets, including a chapter on poverty and income distribution.

The World Economy   Much of the text focuses on the U.S. economy. The final four chapters provide a broader perspective. Chapters 34 and 35 cover international trade theory. Chapter 36 deals with problems of economic development. Finally, Chapter 37 looks at the economy of the Soviet Union as an example of resource allocation in a nonmarket system.

Teaching and Learning Aids in the Text

In order for a textbook to work in the classroom, it must not only contain the proper subject matter but also provide an effective set of teaching and learning aids. The teaching and learning aids in this book include the following.

Case studies   According to a time-honored principle, each generalization should receive a specific illustration and each illustration should lead to a generalization. Following this principle, case studies are used in a variety of ways throughout the book. First, each chapter opens with a short case study striking a key theme. Second, both boxed and unboxed cases are used to illustrate important points in each chapter. And third, most chapters include a case for discussion, with questions, as part of the material at the end of the chapter. In all, there are more than 120 cases in the book. For easy reference, an **index of cases** appears at the end of this book immediate after the regular index.

Readability   In this book readability means three things. First, it means a lively writing style that draws students into the subject matter. Second, it means complete control of the level of difficulty, as measured by standard readability formulas. And third, it means elimination of the "alphabet soup" style used in many texts. When terms such as *average variable cost* and *marginal propensity to consume* occur, the text uses the actual words, not a thicket of AVCs and MPCs that bewilder students.

Vocabulary   For many students vocabulary is one of the big stumbling blocks to learning economics. This book uses a four-level reinforcement technique to handle the problem. First, each new term is printed in boldface where it is first used and defined. Second, the term and its definition appear on the same page in the margin. Third, a list of new terms is given at the end of the chapter. And fourth, a complete alphabetical glossary of terms appears at the end of the book.

Graphs   For the benefit of students who may not be used to working with graphs, an appendix on the subject appears after Chapter 2. This appendix does more than just explain techniques. It also addresses the most common problems students have in working with graphs. One of these problems is the tendency to memorize graphs as meaningless patterns of lines. Another is the inability to draw original graphs when they are needed in note-taking or on examinations. The appendix warns of these pitfalls and explains how they can be avoided.

Appendixes   In addition to the Chapter 2 appendix on working with graphs, appendixes are used at other points in the book to cover topics that some instructors like to include and others do not. Examples include an appendix on investment decision making that follows Chapter 13, and the appendixes on indifference curves and isoquants that follow Chapters 20 and 21. Three appendixes present algebraic statements of the arguments in the corresponding chapters.

Chapter openings   The first-page spread of each chapter is used to help orient the student to the chapter. On the left-hand page a list of **learning objectives** appears. (These are keyed both to the summary that appears at the end of the chapter and to the study guide.) Following this there is a list of **terms from previous chapters** that the student may find it useful to review. On the right-hand page of the opening spread, as mentioned earlier, a **short case study** is used to introduce the chapter.

Chapter material   A number of learning aids appear at the end of each chapter. First there is a numbered **summary** that covers each of the main learning objectives of the chapter. This is followed by a set of short **questions for review.** The first question focuses on the new vocabulary terms introduced in the chapter, and the remaining ones are keyed to the chapter's learning objectives. Next there is a set of **problems and topics for discussion.** These give applications of topics covered in the chapter. They challenge the student to move beyond recall of the text, using graphic problems, projects for library work, provocative questions on normative issues, and so on. In most chapters this section includes a **case for**

discussion with a directed set of questions. Finally, most chapters conclude with an annotated list of **suggestions for further reading.**

The Package

This book is a part of a complete package of materials for teaching and learning economics. The text itself is available in a hardcover version covering both macroeconomics and microeconomics, and in separate macro and micro softcover versions. Each version of the text is accompanied by its own study guide, instructor's manual, test bank, and two-color transparency acetates. All three versions of the text share the computerized test banks, biannual newsletter, and interactive computer software, *Econo-Graph.*

Study guide   The study guide is the student's most important supplement to the text. Each chapter in the study guide is organized around the chapter's learning objectives. The learning objectives are followed by a **walking tour** of the chapter, which is a **programmed review** designed to reinforce the central concepts of the chapter. Then comes a set of **hands-on problems,** many of which emphasize the development of skill in using graphs. **Case studies** based on actual news items provide practice in real-world applications of economic theory. **Special boxes** warn against common mistakes. Finally, each chapter contains a **self-test** that presents items similar to those in the instructor's test bank. All problems and self-test questions are fully answered at the end of each chapter of the study guide. The answer sections include graphs where appropriate, as well as explanations of right and wrong answers to self-test questions.

The study guide has been developed and written by the author of the text, with the result that the two items are fully compatible.

Interactive computer software   Our unique, new interactive computer software package, *EconoGraph,* was developed for Principles of Economics at the University of Delaware, one of the first schools to move into the new technology of learning by using computers in the classroom. *EconoGraph* is a set of floppy disks that contain tutorials on the most important areas of theory covered in the text. It features extensive diagnostics of right and wrong answers given by the user and unique interactive graphic exercises. It is available for the IBM PC and compatibles, with graphics card. A demonstration disk is available on request from your Dryden Press textbook representative.

Instructor's manual   Each instructor has his or her own unique approach to teaching economics. The instructor's manual is a tool that assists in integrating the instructor's style with the approach taken by the book. Each chapter includes a checklist of instructional objectives, a chapter outline, lecture notes, and answers to end-of-chapter questions from the text. There is also a section entitled "What's Different Here, and Why" that will assist in converting lecture notes that were written for different texts or earlier editions of this text.

Test bank   A test bank containing 2,000 true-or-false and multiple-choice questions has been developed by Irvin Tucker and Ted Amato of the University of North Carolina at Charlotte in consultation with the author of the text. Numerous graphic questions are included. The test bank is available both in book form and in a computerized version for the IBM PC or Apple II, and for various mainframes on magnetic tape.

Transparencies   A set of 160 two-color transparencies is available for overhead projection. The transparencies include most of the graphs from the text plus graphs showing answers to end-of-chapter problems. Suggestions for use of the transparencies are contained in the instructor's manual.

Newsletter   The package of teaching and learning aids is rounded out by a twice-yearly newsletter available to all instructors who adopt the text. This newsletter contains fresh case studies and calls attention to policy changes and other events that take place between editions of the text.

Changes in the Fourth Edition

The fourth edition reflects the input of a great many users of the text at schools across the country. That input included detailed journals of classroom experience, focus groups on several campuses, and less formal feedback contributed via letter and telephone by users too numerous to list. In addition, the author benefited from the suggestions, the comments, and even the mistakes of his own students at George Mason University. Together with the help of many reviewers, the result was a very thorough revision.

Introductory chapters   Chapters 1 and 2 have been substantially reorganized and rewritten. Chapter 1 focuses on scarcity and choice as the central concepts of economics; it also surveys the subject matter of economics and gives an idea of what economists do. Chapter 2 is organized around the problems of what, how, and for whom, which all economies must solve. Capitalist, socialist, and other approaches to these problems are compared in order to emphasize their universal nature. Three new case studies have been added to Chapter 3 as applications of supply and demand. Chapter 4 contains new material on the corporate income tax and the economic effects of corporate takeovers. The public-choice section of Chapter 5 has been completely rewritten, and a discussion of flat-tax proposals has been added.

Macroeconomics   The macroeconomics section begins, as before, with a chapter on the circular flow. This is followed by a new Chapter 7 that discusses supply and demand in the macroeconomy. In addition to looking at labor and factor markets, this chapter provides a first overview of aggregate real supply and demand analysis. Moving this material to an early point in the book gives students the background needed to understand the effects of fiscal and monetary policy on the price level, real output, and unemployment.

Chapter 9, which covers fiscal policy, has been thoroughly rewritten in the light of theoretical developments and policy controversies of recent years. It supplements the traditional Keynesian analysis with the tools of aggregate real supply and demand analysis that were introduced in Chapter 7. The controversy over budget deficits receives extensive coverage.

Monetary theory and policy have also been a rapidly developing field, necessitating a reorganization of Chapters 11–13. Chapter 11, which covers banking institutions, contains new material on policies for ensuring the safety and stability of the banking system. This chapter now also covers the process of deposit creation by commercial banks. Chapter 12, which covers the supply and demand for money, has been extensively rewritten. The last section of the chapter explores the recent evolution of Federal Reserve policy in a supply-and-demand context. As in earlier editions, Chapter 13 integrates fiscal and monetary theory. It also explores problems of coordinating monetary and fiscal policy, interactions between domestic monetary policy and the foreign sector, and the contributions of monetarists to monetary theory.

The chapters in Part IV of the book have been reorganized. Chapters 14 and 15 apply aggregate real supply and demand analysis to problems of inflation, recession, and economic growth. These two chapters build on the introduction to aggregate real supply and demand that was given in Chapter 7, using a more streamlined graphic presentation than in the third edition. Spending two chapters on this set of topics allows a less condensed exposition of the basic theory while providing room for a significant amount of new material. Added topics include a section on the economics of rational expectations, a discussion of the productivity slowdown of the late 1970s and early 1980s, and an appraisal of supply side economics. Chapter 16, another new chapter, is devoted to strategies for economic stabilization. It provides additional discussion of the Keynesian-monetarist dialog and focuses on the issue of policy activism versus policy rules. The final two chapters, which cover the microeconomic foundations of unemployment and the accelerationist theory of inflation, will be familiar to users of previous editions.

Microeconomics   The microeconomic theory chapters have received a thorough going-over, with numerous new examples and case studies added. User suggestions for additional explanation have been incorporated, for example, in the section on the production function in Chapter 20. Also in response to user suggestions, an appendix on isoquants has been added to Chapter 20.

Applications of microeconomics have been updated to reflect both recent research work and policy developments. Chapter 26 notes the increased emphasis on economic efficiency and the new merger guidelines issued under the Reagan administration. Chapter 27 reviews evidence on the effects of deregulation of the transportation industry. Chapter 28, which covers farm policy, discusses trends in farm prices and the deteriorating farm credit picture. Chapter 29, which is devoted to environmental issues, contains an extended case study on the acid rain problem and policies that have been proposed for dealing with it.

The factor market chapters too have been revised and expanded. Chapter 30 incorporates new material on human capital, discrimination, and the issue of comparable worth. Chapter 31 reflects new research on the topic of what labor unions do. Chapter 33 explores the reasons for the increase in officially reported poverty in the United States in the early 1980s, and the policy controversies that this trend has touched off.

The world economy   The last section of the book, which deals with the world economy, has been reorganized. It begins with Chapter 34, which covers microeconomic aspects of international trade. This chapter uses the U.S.-Japanese agreement on restraint of automobile imports as a case study in the effects of protectionism. Chapter 35, which deals with international monetary theory, has been completely rewritten. It uses a new set of diagrams to draw attention to the importance of capital flows as determinants of foreign exchange rates. The new analytical tools are applied to the issue of the rising value of the dollar and the U.S. current account deficit in the early 1980s. There is more emphasis than in past editions on interactions between domestic macroeconomic policy and international finance.

The chapter on economic development now follows the chapters on international trade. This permits greater emphasis on the importance of trade and international capital flows as elements of the development process. The successes and failures of foreign aid are explored, and increased attention is given to the role of entrepreneurship in economic development.

The final chapter of the book deals with the Soviet economy. This chapter has been updated to reflect the problems and challenges faced by the Soviet economy in the post-Brezhnev era.

A Few Words of Thanks

I have been fortunate in getting help of many kinds from many quarters while writing this book. It is a pleasure to acknowledge that help here.

The first thanks go to my collaborating author, **David E. Lindsey.** David, my longtime friend and professional colleague, provided the theoretical inspiration and many of the technical details for the macroeconomic model that underlies this book. His post as associate director of the Division of Research and Statistics for the Board of Governors of the Federal Reserve System gives him a perch from which he can view macroeconomic policy as no outsider can. Of course, the contributions he has made are his personally and do not necessarily represent the views of the Board of Governors or other staff members of the Federal Reserve System. Credit for the strengths of the macro section of this book should go to David, while shortcomings and errors are a result of my failures to convey his contributions adequately.

Second, I would like to thank two people who made special contributions to the fourth edition. One is **Raymond E. Lombra** of Pennsylvania State University, who acted as a consultant on a number of pivotal issues. The other is **Katherine H. Dolan,** who prepared the manuscript for electronic typesetting and made many suggestions for improvements in the presentation.

Next, I would like to thank the many reviewers who commented on both the third edition and various drafts of the fourth edition manuscript and suggested countless improvements:

Stuart D. Allen
The University of North Carolina

William Barber
Henry Ford Community College

Lawrence Bates
Eastern Illinois University

Charles Bennett
Gannon University

Charles Betz
Cerritos College

Donald Bumpass
Texas Tech University

Peter Barth
University of Connecticut

Avi Cohen
York University

Richard Evans
Tarrant County College

Donald G. Fell
Ohio State University

Christopher Fiorentino
West Chester University

Frederick S. Inaba
Washington State Univesity

Arthur James
University of North Alabama

Anthony Lee
Austin Community College

Devinder Malhotra
University of Akron

John Manzer
Indiana Purdue at Fort Wayne

Allen Maury
Texas A & I University

Eugene F. McKibbin
Fullerton College

Paul Merkle
Louisiana State University

Joseph Meskey
East Carolina University

Herbert C. Milikien
American River College

Emile M. Mullick
University of Texas—Arlington

James Murdoch
North East Louisiana University

Jack Osmon
San Francisco State University

Stephen Pollard
*California State University,
Los Angeles*

Duane Rosa
West Texas State University

Jeffrey P. Ryan
McHenry County College

David E. Spencer
Washington State University

Steven Ullmann
University of Miami

Marion Walsh
Lansing Community College

Donald A. Wells
University of Arizona

Walter Wessels
North Carolina State University

Terrence West
County College of Morris

Tamara Woroby
Towson State University

Charles E. Zech
Villanova University

William Zimmer
Montgomery County Community College

My thanks also to **Dan Hamermesh** of Michigan State University, **Robert Plotnick** of the University of Washington, **John Saussey** and **Tony Petrucci** of Harrisburg Area Community College, **Eleanor Craig, Charles Link, Jeff Miller,** and **Michael Staten** of the University of Delaware, **Jim Bennett** and **Debbie Walker** of George Mason University, and the many users of the third edition who, in various ways, contributed their ideas and suggestions. **Peter Olson** of the University of Arizona class tested the fourth edition manuscript and helped make many final refinements in the presentation. I would also like to thank the following people who participated in an important Focus Group; **George Hoffer, Edward Millner, Robert Reilly,** and **John Marcis,** all at Virginia Commonwealth University.

Finally, I would like to acknowledge the contributions of Liz Widdi-combe and Jane Perkins of The Dryden Press, and those of Jere Calmes, Bob Cobb, Carolyn Smith, Maureen Conway, and Laurie Beck of Textbook Development Inc. Marsha Cohen is to be congratulated for the fine design of the book, and Freda Leinwand is thanked for the photo research.

Ed Dolan
Great Falls, Virginia
September 1985

Markets play a key role in the U.S. economy. This picture shows the trading floor of the Chicago Mercantile Exchange.

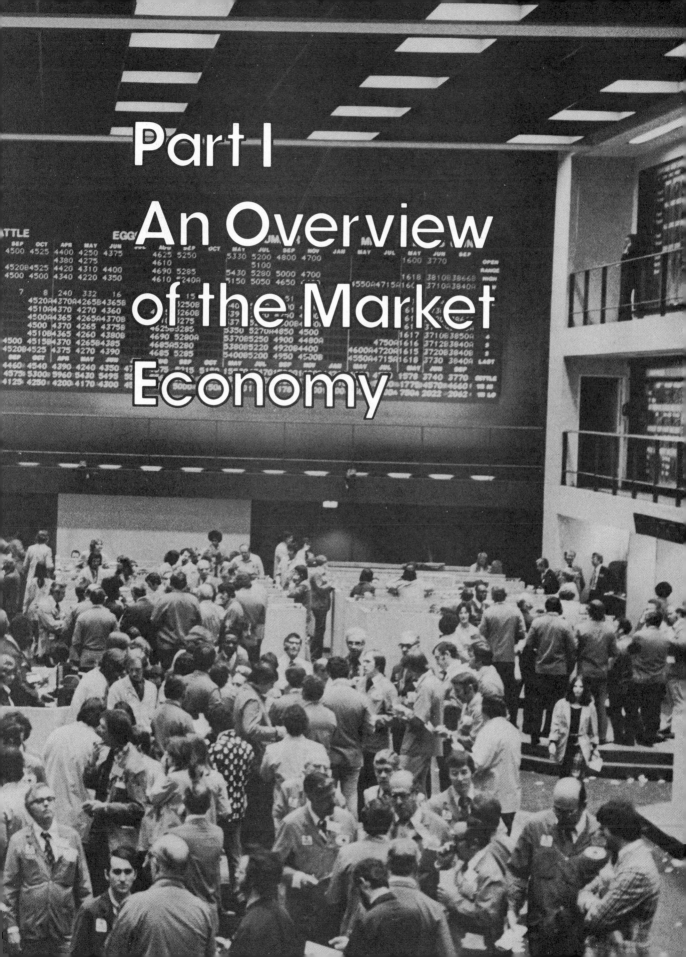

Part I
An Overview of the Market Economy

Chapter 1
What Economics Is All About

WHAT YOU WILL LEARN IN THIS CHAPTER

After reading this chapter, you should be able to

1. Define *scarcity* and *economics*.
2. Define *microeconomics* and list the units of microeconomic analysis.
3. Discuss the functions of *markets*.
4. Define macroeconomics and review recent trends in the United States with regard to *unemployment, inflation,* and *real economic growth.*
5. Explain the use of *theories* and *models* in economics.
6. Distinguish between *positive* and *normative* economics, and explain why this distinction is important.

"Dearest family, I hope this finds you well."

Ireland, 1834: In a small stone cottage a young girl reads a letter that has just arrived from America. "Dearest family, I hope this finds you well. I miss you very much, and I worry when I hear the news from home. I have a good job here. The work is very hard but I earn almost a dollar a day. I am staying at a boarding house run by a good Irish woman. We eat meat almost every night. I hope your crops were not as bad as I have heard. I am sending a little money. There is work here for Colleen, too. If she will come I can save enough to pay her way before the end of the year. I think of you every day. Your Tom."

New York, 1984: An airliner sits on a runway in the early-morning haze. There is a long line of planes ahead of it waiting to take off. In an executive-class seat Mary Garrity, Tom's great-great-granddaughter, looks at her watch. Half an hour late, and not even in the air yet. "I'll be late for the board meeting," she thinks. "I'll have to rework my schedule for the whole day. Do I dare let Wilcox handle the Garcia account? I wish I could at least make a phone call."

Scarcity
A situation in which there is not enough of a resource to meet all of people's wants and needs.

Economics
The study of the choices people make and the actions they take in order to make the best use of scarce resources in meeting their wants and needs.

What do these two stories, 150 years apart, have in common? They are both about about the ways people deal with the problem of **scarcity**. Resources are said to be *scarce* when people do not have enough of them to meet all their wants and needs. The concept is central to **economics**. In fact, economics can be defined as the study of the choices people make and the actions they take in order to make the best use of scarce resources in meeting their wants and needs.

Scarcity can take many forms. For the Garritys of 1834, the problem of scarcity took a very basic form. There were not enough potatoes in the field to feed the family. They took action, putting all their savings into a one-way ticket to New York for their son Tom. For hundreds of millions of people around the world, the problem of scarcity still takes the form of getting enough to eat. And the chance to do a hard day's work for a fair wage still attracts many of them to the United States.

For Mary Garrity, the executive of 1984, scarcity takes a different form. For her, a scarcity of time to get things done is more of a problem than a scarcity of material goods. Because there aren't enough hours in the day for all the meetings and appointments, let alone spending more time with her family, she too has to make choices. Which tasks should she see to herself? Which should she delegate to others? These two stories give us a glimpse of the subject matter of economics.

WHAT ECONOMISTS DO

A well-known member of the profession once jokingly defined economics as "what economists do." Just what is it that economists do? In the broadest sense, they study the ways in which people deal with the problem of scarcity. But as a preview of the contents of this book, let's take a more detailed look at what economists do. We begin with the distinction between *microeconomics* and *macroeconomics*.

Microeconomics

Microeconomics
The branch of economics that deals with the choices and actions of small economic units, that is, households, business firms, and units of government.

Factors of production
The basic inputs of labor, capital, and natural resources used in producing all goods and services.

Labor
The contributions to production made by people working with their minds and their muscles.

Capital
All means of production that are created by people, including tools, industrial equipment, and structures.

Natural resources
Anything that can be used as a productive input in its natural state, such as farm-land, building sites, forests, and mineral deposits.

Market
Any arrangement that people have for trading with one another.

The prefix *micro* comes from a Greek word meaning "small." **Microeconomics** is the branch of economics that deals with the choices made by small economic units: households, business firms, and units of government.

The units of analysis   In economics, a *household* is a group of people who pool their incomes, own property in common, and make economic decisions jointly. People who do not belong to such a group are counted as one-person households.

Households play two major roles in the economy: they supply inputs that are used to produce goods and services, and they consume the goods and services that are produced. The inputs supplied by households are known as **factors of production**. There are three of these. **Labor** consists of the productive contributions made by people working with their minds and their muscles. **Capital** consists of all the productive inputs created by people, including tools, machinery, structures, and intangible items such as computer programs. **Natural resources** include everything that can be used as a productive input in its natural state, such as farmland, building sites, forests, and mineral deposits. For example, the factors of production used in producing this book included the labor of the author and the editors; capital in the form of word processors and printing presses; and natural resources in the form of energy to run the printing presses and pulpwood to make the paper. In return for the labor, capital, and natural resources they sell to producers, households receive incomes, which they spend on goods and services.

Business firms are the second basic unit of microeconomic analysis. Firms buy factors of production from households and use them to produce goods and services. Firms come in many shapes and sizes. The 1980 census counted more than 16 million business firms in the United States. These range from small stores and family farms to huge corporations. Chapter 4 will discuss the role of business firms in more detail.

Microeconomics also studies the actions of units of government such as Congress, courts, and regulatory agencies. As we will see throughout this book, units of government have a major impact on the economic life of firms and households. Their decisions, in turn, are affected by events in the economy. Chapter 5 will survey the role of government in the U.S. economy.

Markets   Microeconomists are interested not only in the actions of households, firms, and units of government, but also in how those actions are coordinated. In an economy like that of the United States, **markets** play a key role in coordination.

A market is any arrangement people have for trading with one another. Some markets, like the New York Stock Exchange, are highly visible and organized. Others, like the word-of-mouth networks that put teenage baby-sitters in touch with people who need their services, do their work informally, out of sight. Whether visible or not, markets play a key role in the job of putting scarce resources to their best uses in meeting people's wants and needs. Markets accomplish this by fulfilling three essential tasks.

The first task is transmitting information. In order to put resources to their best possible uses, the people who make decisions must know which resources are scarcest and which uses for them are best. Markets transmit information about scarcity and resource values in the form of prices. If a good becomes scarcer, its price is bid up. The rising price signals buyers to cut back on the amount of that good they buy, and it signals producers to find new sources of supply or substitute less costly resources. If a good becomes more abundant, its price tends to fall. The falling price signals users to favor that good over more costly ones. Box 1.1 presents this basic principle in the words of one of the twentieth century's great economists.

The second task that markets perform is providing incentives. Knowing the best use for scarce resources is not enough unless people have an incentive to use them in that way. Markets offer many kinds of incentives.

**Box 1.1
Friedrich von Hayek on Markets and Information**

Friedrich von Hayek
(1899–   )

Friedrich von Hayek is one of the leading economists of the twentieth century. His work is wide-ranging. He was a pioneer in monetary theory and helped develop the field we now know as macroeconomics. With books like *The Road to Serfdom* (1944) and *The Constitution of Liberty* (1960), he gained a reputation as a leader in political and economic philosophy. But he is best known for his contributions to microeconomics and to our understanding of the role of markets in the economy. The following passage from his classic article "The Use of Knowledge in Society" is typical of von Hayek's insightful writing on this subject:

Assume that somewhere in the world a new opportunity for this use of some raw material, say tin, has arisen, or that one of the sources of supply of tin has been eliminated. It does not matter for our purpose—and it is very significant that it does not matter—which of these two causes has made tin more scarce. All that the users of tin need to know is that some of the tin they used to consume is now more profitably employed elsewhere, and that in consequence they must economize tin. There is no need for the great majority of them even to know where the more urgent need has arisen, or in favor of what other needs they ought to husband the supply. If only some of them know directly of the new demand, and switch resources over to it, and if the people who are aware of the new gap thus created in turn fill it from still other sources, the effect will rapidly spread throughout the whole economic system and influence not only the uses of tin, but also those of its substitutes and the substitutes of these substitutes, the supply of all things made of tin, and their substitutes, and so on; and all this without the great majority of those instrumental in bringing about these substitutions knowing anything at all about the original cause of these changes. The whole acts as one market, not because any of its members survey the whole field, but because their limited individual fields of vision sufficiently overlap so that through many intermediaries the relevant information is communicated to all.

Source: F. A. von Hayek, "The Use of Knowledge in Society," *American Economic Review* 35 (September 1945): 519–530.

Consumers who are well informed and spend their money wisely achieve a higher standard of living with their limited budgets. Workers who stay alert to job opportunities and work where they can be most productive earn the highest income they can. And profits provide an incentive for business managers to improve production methods and to tailor their goods to the needs of consumers. The importance of the market as a source of incentives led Adam Smith to call it an "invisible hand" that nudges people into the roles they can play best in the economy. (See Box 1.2.)

The third task of markets is distributing income. People who have useful skills or own scarce resources receive high incomes if they put those skills and resources to the best possible use. People who have fewer skills or resources to sell receive lower incomes, even if they make just as great an effort to use what they have wisely. Businesspeople who take risks and guess right make large profits; those who take risks and guess wrong suffer losses. In short, the market distributes income according to the value of each person's contribution to the production process—and not always in proportion to the effort required to make that contribution.

The jobs of microeconomists   To say that they study households, firms, and markets is one way to answer the question of what microeconomists do, but the question can be answered in another way as well. We can also look at what microeconomists do for a living—what kinds of jobs they hold.

Many microeconomists hold jobs in private firms. For example, an

---

**Box 1.2
Adam Smith on the
Invisible Hand**

**Adam Smith
(1723–1790)**

Adam Smith is the founder of economics as a distinct field of study. He wrote only one book on the subject, *The Wealth of Nations*, published in 1776 when Smith was 53 years old. His friend David Hume found the book such hard going that he doubted that many people would read it. But Hume was wrong.

The source of the wealth of nations, in Smith's view, is not gold or silver, as many people supposed at the time. Instead, wealth is the result of ordinary people working and trading in free markets. The remarkable thing about the wealth produced by a market economy, in Smith's view, is that it is not the result of any organized plan. Instead, it is the unintended result of the actions of many people, each of whom is pursuing the incentives offered by the market with his or her own interests in mind. In Smith's words,

It is not from the benevolence of the butcher, the brewer, or the baker that we expect our dinner, but from their regard to their own interest. . . . Every individual is continually exerting himself to find out the most advantageous employment for whatever capital he can command. . . . By directing that industry in such a manner as its produce may be of the greatest value, he intends only his own gain, and he is in this, as in many other cases, led by an invisible hand to promote an end which was no part of his intention.

Source: Adam Smith, *The Wealth of Nations*, 1776, Book 1, chap. 2.

insurance company might employ economists to study the impact of economic trends on the insurance industry and to help in designing new kinds of insurance policies to meet changing customer needs. An electric utility might employ an economist to help in preparing proposals for rate changes. A trade association that represents the natural-gas industry might employ an economist to analyze the impact of changes in government regulations. In these examples the economist is employed by business as a specialist. In other cases, people trained in microeconomics rise to positions in the firm's general management.

Thousands of microeconomists are employed by government. Government regulation of business is the source of many of these jobs. The economists who work for insurance companies, electric utilities, gas pipelines, and the like find government economists working on the other side of every issue. Government economists often work closely with lawyers in cases that have to do with regulation, equal opportunity, international trade disputes, and other issues. While the lawyer interprets the laws that apply to the case, the economist analyzes the effects on prices, markets, incomes, and jobs.

Finally, many economists work for colleges, universities, and research institutes. Most of them teach either full- or part-time. Much of the rest of their time is devoted to research on problems of economic theory. Academic economists do quite a bit of applied research too. Businesses, law firms, and government agencies often hire them as consultants rather than employing full-time economists of their own.

Macroeconomics

Macroeconomics
The branch of economics that deals with large-scale economic phenomena, especially inflation, unemployment, and economic growth.

The prefix *macro* comes from a Greek word meaning "large." Thus, **macroeconomics** refers to the study of large-scale economic phenomena, especially inflation, unemployment, and economic growth. These phenomena result from the combined effects of millions of microeconomic choices made by households, firms, and units of government. A review of the performance of the U.S. economy in the years since World War II will serve as a preview of the subject matter of macroeconomics.

Unemployment rate
The percentage of people in the labor force who are not working but are actively looking for work.

Unemployment   One of the key indicators of the health of an economic system is its ability to provide a job for anyone who wants to work. The economy's performance in this area is measured by the **unemployment rate**, the percentage of people in the labor force who are not working but are actively looking for work. (People who do not have a job who are not actively looking for work—full-time students, retired people, and so on—are not counted as members of the labor force and thus are not included in the unemployment rate.)

Even in the best of times the unemployment rate does not fall to zero. In a healthy, changing economy it is normal for a certain number of people to be out of work for a short time when they first enter the labor force, or when they have quit a job in order to look for a better one. There is some disagreement as to what the "normal" level of unemployment is. Here we will simply note that the normal level is generally agreed to lie somewhere in the range of 4 to 6.5 percent of the labor force.

Box 1.3 shows the unemployment record of the United States since 1950 in relation to this 4–6.5 percent range. During the 1950s and 1960s the unemployment rate stayed within the range that we now think of as normal. True, there were higher rates of unemployment in some years than in others. But these episodes of higher unemployment were brief. Then, in 1975, the unemployment rate jumped to 8.3 percent, its highest rate since the Great Depression. Since 1975 the rate has dropped below 6.5 percent in only two years.

Inflation
A sustained increase in the average price of all goods and services.

Inflation   **Inflation** means a sustained increase in the average level of prices of all goods and services. The most widely used measure of inflation in the United States is the consumer price index (CPI). Price stability—that is, the absence of inflation—is a second major sign of the health of an economy. True price stability means no increase at all in the average level of prices. However, many economists and policymakers would settle for any rate of increase below 3 percent per year.

Box 1.4 shows trends in inflation in the United States since 1950. Until

Box 1.3
Unemployment in the United States Since 1950

Economists do not agree on the "normal" level of unemployment for the U.S. economy, but most would like to see a rate somewhere in the range of 4 to 6.5 percent of the labor force. Rates lower than 4 percent are rarely reached because there are always people who are out of work while changing jobs or looking for a first job. As the chart shows, unemployment rates were, on the average, higher in the 1970s and early 1980s than they were in the 1950s and 1960s.

Source: *Economic Report of the President* (Washington, D.C.: Government Printing Office, 1985), Table B–33.

the late 1960s inflation stayed, for the most part, within the safe range. In fact, for the entire century from the Civil War to the mid-1960s inflation averaged only about 2 percent per year; higher rates of inflation occurred mostly in war time.

The inflation of the late 1960s was related in part to the Vietnam War, but a major change took place in the 1970s. The inflation rate dropped briefly during 1970, but it shot up again in 1973 and stayed high for a full decade. Then in the early 1980s the rate of inflation fell abruptly, much faster than many economists expected. However, the inflation of the 1970s and the fear that it may return have had a lasting impact on the U.S. economy.

Gross national product
The dollar value at current market prices of all final goods and services produced by a nation's factors of production in a given year.

Economic growth   Economic growth is a third major sign of economic health. The economy must grow to provide jobs for new workers and to provide everyone with a rising standard of living.

The most often used measure of the economy's total output is one called **gross national product** or *GNP*. To be meaningful as a measure of

Box 1.4
Inflation in the United States Since 1950

True price stability means no increase at all in the average level of prices. However, many economists believe an inflation rate of less than 3 percent per year, as measured by the rate of increase of the consumer price index, is acceptable. As the chart shows, such low rates of inflation were the rule during the 1950s and early 1960s. Inflation soared in the 1970s, however.

Source: *Economic Report of the President* (Washington, D.C.: Government Printing Office, 1985), Table B–55.

Nominal

In economics, a term used to refer to data that have not been adjusted for the effects of inflation.

Real

In economics, a term used to refer to data that have been adjusted for the effects of inflation.

economic growth, changes in GNP over time must be adjusted for the effects of inflation. Suppose we want to see how much the U.S. economy grew from 1972 to 1984. In 1972, GNP was $1,186 billion. In 1984, it was $3,661 billion, nearly three times as high. This does not mean that people's standard of living was three times as high in 1984, however. Much of the increase in GNP can be explained by higher prices. In fact, the price level was 2.25 times as high at the end of 1984 as in 1972. For an accurate comparison with the 1972 GNP, the 1984 GNP must be divided by 2.25 to take into account the change in the price level.

Economists use the term **nominal** to refer to data that have not been adjusted for the effects of inflation. The term **real** is used to refer to data that have been adjusted for inflation. In the example just given, we can say that in 1984 *nominal GNP* was $3,661 billion and *real GNP* was $1,627 billion ($3,661 billion divided by the more than twofold increase in prices over the 1972–1984 period).

The business cycle   Box 1.5 shows the growth of real GNP in the United States from 1950 to 1984. During this period the rate of growth varied around a trend of about 3 percent per year, which most economists

**Box 1.5
Economic Growth in the United States Since 1950**

This chart shows the growth of the U.S. economy since 1950. It shows real gross national product for each year (that is, gross national product adjusted for inflation) and a trend line for real-GNP growth over the whole period. A growth rate of 3 percent per year or more is viewed as healthy.

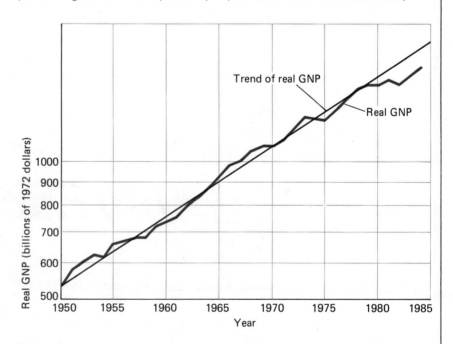

Source: *Economic Report of the President* (Washington, D.C.: Government Printing Office, 1985), Table B-2.

Business cycle
A cycle in which periods of growth of real output alternate with periods of falling output, accompanied by high unemployment.

Recession
A period in which real output falls for 6 months or more.

Recovery
A period of renewed growth of real output following a recession.

consider quite satisfactory. However, it did not follow the trend smoothly. In some years output fell below the trend, and in others it rose above the trend.

The fluctuations of real GNP around its long-term trend are referred to as the **business cycle**. As Box 1.6 shows, a typical business cycle consists of four parts. The first part, during which real GNP falls, is known as a **recession**. (Very short business downturns are usually ignored; normally a downturn has to last six months or more before economists count it as a recession.) The low point reached at the end of a recession is known as the *trough* of the business cycle. This is followed by the upturn, or **recovery**. At the end of the recovery, the business cycle reaches a *peak*, after which output turns down again and a new cycle begins.

The goals of full employment, price stability, and economic growth are closely linked. During a recession, when real output falls, the unemployment rate tends to rise. Also, during a recovery when real output is rising, the rate of inflation sometimes, but not always, tends to speed up. These are two of many linkages among economic phenomena. Macroeconomists have investigated these linkages in detail, along with others that involve interest rates, the supply of money, levels of consumption and investment, and the international value of the dollar.

Box 1.6
The Business Cycle

Over time, real output tends to grow at a rate of about 3 percent per year. However, the growth is not even. The economy tends to move in a cyclical pattern, with output sometimes falling below the long-term trend and sometimes rising above it. This figure shows the phases of a typical business cycle. The first phase, in which real output falls for six months or more, is known as a recession. After the trough of the cycle, real output begins to grow again. This phase is called the recovery. When the recovery reaches a peak, a new recession begins.

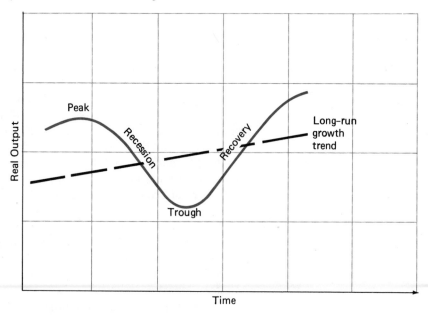

The jobs of macroeconomists   Having looked at the subject matter of macroeconomics, we can close with a brief look at some of the jobs held by macroeconomists. Like their micro colleagues, macroeconomists hold jobs in business, government, and universities.

Business macroeconomists are hired to advise managers about the impact of economic trends on their firms. This is often crucial to the survival of the firm. As just one example, take the case of the homebuilding industry. People's ability to buy houses depends on their incomes and on the interest rates at which they can obtain mortgage loans. Firms in every part of the homebuilding industry—construction, lumber, other building supplies, and so on—can benefit from knowledge about economic trends and policies. We will see shortly that it is not easy to forecast economic trends. But even when reliable forecasts are impossible, economists can help managers make plans based on a set of "what if" projections. What is true of the housing industry is true of others as well—consumer goods, banking, transportation, you name it. Businesses that do not hire economists often hire consulting firms to advise them on macroeconomic trends.

Government agencies also employ macroeconomists to aid in planning and forecasting. In addition, thousands of economists are employed by the units of government that are in charge of macroeconomic policy. The Federal Reserve System, which guides monetary policy, is a major employer of macroeconomists. The U.S. Treasury is another. The Office of Management and Budget and the Council of Economic Advisers, which advise the president, also have large economic staffs. Still other macroeconomists are found in the Congressional Budget Office and on the staffs of congressional committees.

Finally, many macroeconomists are employed by colleges, universities, and research institutes. Like academic microeconomists, they divide their time among teaching, research, and consulting.

WHY ECONOMISTS SOMETIMES DISAGREE

Economists are often the subject of jokes about failing to agree with one another. George Bernard Shaw complained that if you took all the economists in the world and laid them end to end, they wouldn't reach a conclusion. Harry Truman begged for a one-armed economist—he was tired of those with two arms because all they could tell him was, "On the one hand, . . . and then on the other hand, . . ." The noted economist Frank H. Knight, addressing the American Economics Association, once remarked, "I have been increasingly moved to wonder whether economists . . . should cover their faces or burst into laughter when they meet on the street."

One could say that economists are no worse than members of other professions. Physicists disagree about the origin of the universe. Doctors disagree about how to treat heart disease and breast cancer. Teachers disagree about the merits of new math versus old math. So why all the economist jokes?

In part, the idea that economists can't agree results from the fact that disagreements make the news and agreements don't. In fact, economists present a united front on a wide range of issues. For example, a recent survey found that more than 90 percent of economists agree on the truth of the following statements:[1]

- Tariffs and import quotas reduce general economic welfare.
- A ceiling on rents reduces the quantity and quality of housing available.
- Increased government spending or a tax cut is likely to speed recovery from a recession.

But the jokes about disagreements among economists have deeper roots than the fact that controversy is news. In the rest of this chapter we will discuss some of the main causes of disagreements among economists under the headings of theory and reality, forecasting, and positive versus normative economics.

Theory and Reality

One reason economists are said to be unable to agree is that they are unrealistic. Another old joke makes this point: A physicist, a chemist, and an economist are shipwrecked on an island, with nothing to eat but a case of canned beans. How to open the cans? The physicist suggests using a mirror to focus the sun's rays on the cans, thereby expanding the contents and bursting the cans. The chemist suggests dipping the cans in seawater until they rust through. When the economist is asked for an idea, he says, "First, let's assume that we have a can opener."

Yes, economic theory is full of "unrealistic" assumptions. It has to be, for the simple reason that economic reality is extremely complex. To take just one example, suppose an economist is asked what effect a tax cut will have on total spending by consumers. There are hundreds of millions of consumers. Their spending depends on their moods, their hopes, their fears, their health, and the weather; on interest rates, bank regulations, and what new products are on the market; on wages, fringe benefits, and lottery winnings—how long a list would you like?

But the method used by economists is not to try to make a complete list of the things that influence consumer spending. Instead, it is to try to identify the factors that have the greatest influence and to use them as the basis for a **theory**. In economics, as in other fields, a *theory* is an explanation of how facts are related. A mathematical or graphic rendition of an economic theory is called a **model**.

As an example, consider the theory of tax cuts and their effects on consumer spending. The theory says that the change in consumer spending depends on how much the tax cut raises consumers' after-tax incomes and on how long they expect the tax cut to remain in effect. In proposing a theory like this, economists don't deny that other things affect consumer spending. They simply say that of all the things that matter, it is most useful to focus on these two.

Theory
An explanation of how facts are related.

Model
A mathematical or graphic version of an economic theory.

---

[1]J. R. Kearl, Clayne L. Pope, Gordon C. Whiting, and Larry T. Wimmer, "A Confusion of Economists?" *American Economic Review*, May 1979, p. 30. It is worth noting, by the way, that the survey revealed widespread disagreement on certain other matters, such as the economic power of labor unions and the optimum level of spending for national defense.

It is clear, though, that this approach contains the seeds of many disagreements. One economist's model of consumer spending might take only the two factors just mentioned into account. Another's model might also take into account whether the tax cut affects mainly upper-income or middle-income consumers. Which theory is better? Economists try to test competing theories by seeing which one does a better job of explaining the phenomenon in question. But the tests are not always conclusive. Data on past events may not be reliable. One model may explain the events of one period better, whereas another may be better suited to the events of a different period. Before the dispute is resolved, someone else may propose a third theory that challenges both models.

Most economists would agree, however, that theories should be judged by how well they explain how events are related, not by how "realistic" their assumptions are. The economist who said "Let's assume that we have a can opener" was a bad theorist not because the assumption was silly in itself but because it produced no useful insights into the problem of getting the cans open.

Forecasting

An economic theory is a good one if it correctly explains the relationships among two or more key facts. Such theories often help us understand past economic events. For example, in later chapters we will present theories that provide useful insights into the causes of the high inflation rates of the late 1970s. But even the best economic theories are limited in their ability to help us foretell the future.

Economic theory does allow us to make statements that take the form, "If A, then B, other things being equal." Most economists would agree with the statement, "If income taxes are lowered, consumers will spend more, provided that the many other factors that affect spending don't change in the meantime." It is a short step from this sort of statement to a conditional **forecast**, which is simply an if-then statement about the future. For example, an economist might say that if income tax rates are cut by 10 percent in July 1985, total consumer spending will rise by $100 billion in 1985, $120 billion in 1986, and $145 billion in 1987, other things being equal.

Why are economic forecasts such a source of controversy? One reason, clearly, is that forecasters are often wrong. As Box 1.7 relates, forecasters have sometimes missed major turning points in the economy. They also often disagree among one another; it is not uncommon for one forecaster to be predicting recession while another predicts continued expansion.

But not all of the problem lies with the forecasters. Part of it lies with the way forecasts are reported to the public. On TV and in the newspapers, forecasts are often reported in the form "This is how it will be" rather than in the form "If A, then B, other things being equal." In addition, it is not always made clear that even when forecasts are reported as simple numbers, they are really statements about probabilities. For example, it may be reported that a certain economist has forecast that a tax cut will add $100 billion to consumer spending, when the proper way of putting it may be that there is a 90 percent probability that the tax cut will add between $80 and $120 billion to spending.

Most economists take the view that conditional forecasts, for all their faults, are a better basis for making business decisions and public policy

Forecast
A prediction of future economic events, stated in the form "If A, then B, other things being equal."

Box 1.7
The Accuracy of
Economic Forecasts

Economic forecasts—predictions of GNP, inflation, unemployment, and interest rates for the months or years ahead—are regular items of business news, and for good reason. Knowledge of future demand conditions, prices, and credit market conditions is of great value to decision makers in business and government. The thirst for knowledge about the future is a multimillion-dollar business for such forecasting firms as Data Resources Incorporated and Chase Econometrics Associates. Government agencies, including the Federal Reserve System, the Office of Management and Budget, and the Congressional Budget Office also have large budgets for forecasting.

But despite all the money spent, the track record of economic forecasting leaves much to be desired. A study by two economists at the Federal Reserve Bank of Boston pinpoints some forecasts that were especially bad:

- In 1973–1975, forecasters missed the surge in inflation and unemployment rates. They underestimated inflation by 3 to 4 percentage points and unemployment by more than 2 percentage points. At the same time, they underestimated the severity of the recession.
- In 1978–1979, they again failed to forecast a surge in inflation.
- In 1980, they underestimated the speed of the recovery from the short recession of that year. Just as they adjusted their forecasts to show strong growth in 1981, the economy fell back into recession. This left the GNP forecasts of five of the leading forecasters as much as 4 percentage points too high—the worst errors of any recent period.

In the forecasters' defense, the Federal Reserve Bank study points out that the forecasters did fairly well in the tranquil periods of 1970–1972 and 1975–1978. But that is not always good enough for decision makers in business and government. What they want is the ability to foresee turning points and unusual changes in the behavior of the economy. This the forecasters seem unable to deliver.

Source: Stephen K. McNees and John Ries, "The Track Record of Macroeconomic Forecasts," *New England Economic Review*, November–December 1983, pp. 5–18.

than whims and guesswork. For example, a maker of building supplies might ask a forecaster, "If the economy grows as much in the second half of the year as it did in the first, how will the demand for new houses be affected?" The answer might be, "A 3 percent rate of economic growth will cause housing demand to rise by somewhat more than 3 percent, if interest rates remain the same. However, each percentage point rise in the mortgage interest rate will cause about a 5 percent drop in the demand for housing." Getting an answer like this isn't as good as having a crystal ball, but it may be helpful.

At the same time, economists caution against relying too much on forecasts. In the 1970s, many forecasters projected higher oil prices throughout the 1980s. Many oil companies, banks, and even national governments got in trouble when they relied too much on these forecasts, which turned out to be wrong. This issue of how much government policymakers should rely on forecasts is especially controversial, because so much is at stake when major policy decisions are made.

Positive vs. Normative Economics

Economists, as we have seen, sometimes disagree over issues of theory. They disagree even more often when they try their hand at forecasting. But nothing produces as much disagreement as issues of economic policy. Should price controls on natural gas be lifted? Should import quotas on cars be extended? Should taxes be raised in order to cut the federal budget deficit? Questions like these tend to bring economists out of their corners ready for a real fight.

Before the sparks start to fly, however, it is worth thinking about the chain of reasoning on which policy decisions are based. It is a three-step chain that goes like this:

1. If policy X is followed, outcome Y will result.
2. Outcome Y is a good (or a bad) thing.
3. Therefore, hurrah (or boo) for policy X.

Positive economics
The part of economics that is limited to making statements about facts and the relationships among them.

The first step in this chain of reasoning is a forecast, stated in the proper if-then form. Forecasts are examples of **positive economics**—the part of economics that is limited to making statements of fact and relationships among facts.

Disputes are common in positive economics. Economists may disagree over whether facts are accurate, over how they are related, and over how they are likely to unfold in the future. But these disputes can usually be resolved by scientific methods. Repeated measurement, statistical tests of theories, and comparing forecasts with actual events are some of the ways in which the area of disagreement on matters of positive economics can be narrowed.

But positive statements of the type "If policy X, then outcome Y" do not tell us whether policy X is desirable. To make a policy decision, one must also decide whether outcome Y is good or bad. Statements of the type "Outcome Y is good" are examples of **normative economics**—the part of economics that is devoted to making judgments about which economic policies or outcomes are good and which are bad.

Normative economics
The part of economics that is devoted to making judgments about which economic policies or conditions are good or bad.

Most economists do not think of themselves as experts in philosophy or ethics. Yet economists who want to influence policy are in a better position to do so if they can point to some general principles on which their views are based. Those who base their opinion of a policy on whim or prejudice are less likely to be listened to than those who speak in terms of well-thought-out values. Calling your opponent a racist or a fascist may win cheers from those who already agree with you and boos from those who are already against you. But name calling is not as likely to win uncommitted people to your side as is an articulate explanation of your reasons for thinking that your opponent's policies will have undesirable outcomes. With this in mind, it is worth looking at some basic concepts of normative economics.

Efficiency and fairness   One standard by which economic policies can be judged is *efficiency*. In economics, as elsewhere, this means doing something with a minimum of waste, effort, and expense. (A more precise definition of economic efficiency will be given in Chapter 2.) But a policy that is efficient may not be a good one. Other standards must be used as well. Among the most important of these is fairness.

Fairness can play two roles in relation to efficiency. First, it may be added to efficiency when the choice is between two or more policies that are equally efficient—policies, for example, that differ only in terms of which groups of people bear costs or receive benefits. In such a case we might reason like this:

1. Policies X and Y are equally efficient, but they will distribute benefits to different groups.
2. The distribution of benefits under policy X is more fair.
3. Therefore, we should follow policy X.

A second use of the standard of fairness is to override that of efficiency. Many people believe efficiency should not be pursued at the expense of fairness. If both goals cannot be reached at once, efficiency should be sacrificed in the name of fairness. In such cases our reasoning might run as follows:

1. Policy X would be inefficient, but it would be more fair than policy Y.
2. Efficiency is desirable, but fairness is more important.
3. Therefore, if there is no policy that is both efficient and fair, choose policy X.

However it is used, the standard of fairness plays a major role in policy analysis. But the standard of fairness raises a problem that the standard of efficiency does not. This problem is that fairness means different things to different people. Rational debate on matters of economic policy is difficult when people attach different meanings to the same term and when they fail to make those meanings clear. With this problem in mind, let's look at two concepts of fairness that often arise in discussions of economic policy.

The egalitarian concept of fairness   One widely held view equates fairness with equitable distribution of income. The phrase "from each according to ability, to each according to need" reflects this point of view. This concept of fairness is based on the idea that all people, by virtue of their shared humanity, deserve a portion of the goods and services turned out by the economy.

There are many versions of this concept. Some people believe that all income and wealth should be distributed equally. Others think that people have a right to a "safety net" level of income, but that any surplus above this level may be distributed according to other standards. Some think there are certain "merit goods," such as health care, food, and education, that should be distributed equally, but that it is all right for other goods to be distributed unequally.

In policy debates, the egalitarian view of fairness often takes the form of asking, "What effect will this policy have on the poor?" Consider the debate over price controls on natural gas. Some people favor ending these controls on the grounds that they discourage production and encourage wasteful use of this valuable resource. But others oppose ending price controls because they believe higher prices would cause hardship for consumers in the lowest income groups.

The libertarian concept of fairness   A second widely held view links fairness to the right of people to live their lives according to their own values, free from threats and coercion. This concept of fairness stems from a long tradition in Western political thought, especially the concept of liberty as stated by such thinkers as John Locke and Thomas Jefferson.

The libertarian view of fairness puts economic rights, such as the right to own property and the right to make exchanges with others, on a par with the basic rights of free speech, a free press, and free worship. From the libertarian point of view, efforts to promote fairness should stress equality of opportunity. Attempts to redistribute income by placing a penalty on economic success or giving people unequal access to markets are seen as unfair, whether or not they lead to equality of income.

In policy debates, the libertarian point of view often takes the form of arguing that competition and economic freedom lead to a general prosperity that is good for everyone. For example, libertarian economists have been leaders in the fight to end regulations that protect business firms from competition. They have argued that when small, new airlines are allowed to compete with larger, more established ones, when savings and loan associations are allowed to compete with banks, and when natural-gas producers are allowed to compete with oil producers in an open market, the firms that serve the consumer best will be the ones that prosper.

Why distinguish?   Distinguishing between positive and normative economics and among different meanings of normative terms like fairness will not settle policy disputes. Still, viewing policy analysis as a three-step process in which positive and normative elements both play a role makes policy debates more rational in two ways.

First, the distinction between positive and normative analysis makes it clear that there are two kinds of disagreement on policy questions. We can disagree as to whether policy X is good or bad because we disagree on the positive issue of whether it will cause outcome Y, which we both desire. Or we can agree that policy X will cause outcome Y, but disagree on the normative issue of whether Y is a good thing. When the source of the disagreement is clear, the argument can be more focused.

Second, when positive statements are mixed with normative ones, they may not be judged on their merits. Reactions to value judgments tend to be much stronger than reactions to statements of fact or theory. Consider the case of tax policy. There has been much debate in recent years about the effects of tax cuts and tax increases on the federal budget deficit, on interest rates, and on economic growth. Many issues of fact and theory need to be resolved. But positive economists often find it hard to get the attention of policymakers who are distracted by charges and countercharges about "soaking the rich" or being "unfair to the poor."

This book will raise many controversial issues as it takes its tour of the subject matter of economics. For the most part, our discussion will focus on the positive economic theories that bear on these issues, although often normative considerations will be mentioned too. But a textbook can provide no more than a framework for thinking about public issues and policies. You, the reader, will have the job of blending positive theories and normative judgments within this framework to reach conclusions of your own.

Summary

1. Resources are said to be *scarce* when people do not have enough of them to meet all their wants and needs. Everyone, at all times and in all societies, faces the problem of scarcity in some form. For many people the problem takes the simple form of finding enough to eat. Even the wealthiest people face scarcity in such forms as limits on their time. Scarcity means that people cannot have everything or do everything they would like; they must make choices. The choices people make and the actions they take in order to make the best use of scarce resources in meeting their wants and needs is the subject matter of *economics*.

2. Microeconomics is the branch of economics that deals with the choices made by small economic units—households, business firms, and units of government. Households supply the basic factors of production—labor, capital, and natural resources. Business firms buy the factors of production from households and transform them into goods and services. Units of government, including Congress, the courts, regulatory agencies, and others, influence the economic choices made by households and firms. In turn, they are influenced by events in the economy.

3. A market is any arrangement people have for trading with one another. Markets play a key role in putting resources to their best uses. In doing so, they perform three tasks. First, they transmit information, in the form of prices, that helps households and firms decide which of the possible ways of using scarce resources are most valuable. Second, they provide incen-

tives, especially in the form of profits. And third, they distribute income according to the value of each person's contribution to the production process.

4. Macroeconomics is the study of large-scale economic phenomena, especially unemployment, inflation, and economic growth. The unemployment rate is the percentage of people in the labor force who are actively looking for work but are unable to find it. Inflation is a sustained increase in the average price level of all goods and services. It is often measured by the consumer price index. Economic growth is measured by the rate of increase in real gross national product. (The term *real* is used to refer to economic quantities that have been adjusted for inflation. Quantities that have not been adjusted for inflation are known as *nominal* quantities.)

5. A theory is an explanation of how facts are related. In economics, a mathematical rendition of a theory is called a model. Often a theory simplifies economic reality, but if the theory is well conceived, this does not detract from its usefulness.

6. The part of economics that is limited to conditional forecasts and statements of fact is known as positive economics. The part that is devoted to making judgments about whether economic policies or events are good or bad is called normative economics. Making a judgment about the value of an economic policy requires both a positive analysis of the policy's likely effects and a normative judgment of the desirability of those effects.

Questions for Review

1. Define the following terms:
   scarcity
   economics
   microeconomics
   factors of production
   labor
   capital
   natural resources
   markets
   macroeconomics

unemployment rate
inflation
gross national product (GNP)
nominal
real
business cycle
recession
recovery
theory
model
forecast
positive economics
normative economics

2. How are the terms *scarcity* and *economics* related? Can you think of any resources that are not scarce? Do people need to make economic decisions regarding those resources?

3. Which of the following are microeconomic issues? Which are macroeconomic issues?
   a. How will an increase in the tax on cigarettes affect smoking habits?
   b. What caused the rate of inflation to fall so fast between 1980 and 1984?

   c. Does a high federal budget deficit tend to slow the rate of real economic growth?
   d. How would quotas on steel imports affect profits and jobs in industries that use steel as an input, such as automobiles and construction?

4. What is a market? What three tasks do markets perform? Describe the arrangements through which people buy and sell houses, football tickets, and haircuts. Are all of these markets?

5. Compare the 1960s with the 1970s in terms of inflation, unemployment, and growth in the U.S. economy. So far, how do the 1980s look by comparison?

6. What is an economic theory? An economic model? Why do economists use theories and models instead of limiting themselves to verbal descriptions of economic events?

7. What are the major sources of disagreement among economists? Why is it important to distinguish between positive and normative economics?

Problems and Topics for Discussion

1. Suppose you won a million dollars in a lottery. Would this remove all problems of scarcity and choice from your life? Would time still be scarce for you? What other things might still be scarce? Can you imagine any person who would not face economic problems of any kind?

2. What kind of household do you belong to? How large is the group of people with whom you pool income and share decision making? Are you a member of a one-person household for some purposes and of a larger household for others? How are economic decisions made in your household?

3. After a boom in the early 1980s, the video game industry ran into trouble. Consumer interest in these games leveled off, and competition forced prices and profit margins down. Some firms left the industry; others gave serious thought to doing so. How does this illustrate the three functions of markets?

4. As a student, you are a buyer in the market for

education. What price signals affected your decision to go to college? What market incentives, if any, caused you to decide as you did? How do you think your education will affect your future position in the distribution of income?

5. Boxes 1.3, 1.4, and 1.5 give data on unemployment, inflation, and economic growth through the end of 1984. Extend the charts using the most recent available data. For annual data, a good source is the *Economic Report of the President*, published each year in January or February. For current-year data, check business news sources such as the *Wall Street Journal* or *Business Week*. Two government publications, the *Survey of Current Business* and the *Federal Reserve Bulletin*, are also useful sources of data. The government releases information on the unemployment rate and the consumer price index each month, and information on the growth of real GNP each three months.

6. Professor Alverez began teaching economics

at State University in 1967. In that year she earned a salary of $9,500. Sixteen years later her salary had risen to $26,000. Meanwhile the consumer price index had risen 100 to 298. How much did her real income grow or shrink?

7. **Case for Discussion**

Whether or not the government should require cars to be equipped with airbags has been a matter of debate for years. The following editorial on the subject appeared in *Business Week*:

Transportation secretary Elizabeth H. Dole will issue by July 11 a final ruling as to whether or not auto manufacturers must start including airbags as required equipment in cars. This issue is hotly controversial, and Secretary Dole will rule on it in a climate of renewed concern over drunk driving. She will probably issue mandatory accident-safety standards that can be met either by airbags or automatic seat belts. If so, this shows a commendable degree of flexibility. What the Secretary should not do is flatly order airbags in all automobiles.

Airbag enthusiasts say the device will save lives. But the safety issue is not airbags vs. nothing at all—in that case, the airbag would win hands down—but airbags vs. the shoulder-lap harness, which is cheaper and less risky. Estimates are that the airbag will add anywhere from $300 to $500 to the cost of a car.

Regular seat belts add about $60 to a car's cost, automatic seat belts about twice that. As to the far more important issue of reliability, the airbag is an electronic device subject to failure. The chances that it might not inflate when needed or inflate at the wrong time are small but real, and in either case could produce injury or death. Neither problem arises with seat belts, which are highly effective when used.

The catch, of course, is that only 10 percent to 15 percent of drivers use belts. A state law requiring their use will probably make many people buckle up. Automatic belts are a good idea. Auto makers, insurance companies, and safety organizations should work harder to promote seat belt use. Over time, though, it is likely that the new attack on drunk driving by raising the national drinking age to 21 will save more lives than making airbags mandatory in everybody's car.[2]

Analyze this editorial in terms of the three steps of policy analysis. What statements of positive economics are used to support the argument? What normative judgments are made or implied? What role does the standard of efficiency play in the argument? What view of fairness underlies the argument, or is there any way to tell?

[2]"Airbags: A Matter of Choice," *Business Week*, July 16, 1984, p. 160. Reprinted from the July 16, 1984 issue of *Business Week* by special permission, © 1984 by McGraw-Hill, Inc.

Chapter 2
The Economic Problem

After reading this chapter, you should be able to

1. Define the central choices faced by all economies.
2. Use the *production possibility frontier* and the concept of *opportunity cost* to discuss the constraints on what an economy can produce.
3. Give examples of ways in which factors of production can be substituted for one another.
4. Explain *comparative advantage* and how it applies to the question of deciding who does the producing.
5. Show how positive and normative economics bear on the question of for whom goods should be produced.
6. Define *efficiency* as applied to production and to the mix and distribution of outputs.
7. Explain the role of *entrepreneurship* in economic decision making.
8. Discuss differences among economic systems in terms of *capitalist* and *socialist* forms of ownership and in terms of *markets, regulation,* and *economic planning* as methods of decision making.

Ideas for Review

Here are some terms and concepts that you should review before you read this chapter:

Factors of production
Labor
Capital
Natural resources
Markets
Positive economics
Normative economics

Moscow, USSR.: Gastronom No. 1 isn't your ordinary grocery store. Its mirrored walls, stained-glass windows, 60-foot-high ceilings, and chandeliers give it a distinctly prerevolutionary appearance. It's a place for the determined buyer, not for casual browsing. Anyone who stands still tends to get battered like a stalled bumper car at a county fair.

Vasily, an engineer from Siberia, has come to Gastronom to buy five bottles of Armenian brandy. The brandy, like everything else in the store, is neatly stacked on a shelf behind a counter tended by a clerk.

Vasily visits Gastronom twice a year, so he knows the rules. First he looks to see if his brandy is in stock. It is. The price isn't marked on the bottle, so he stands in line to find out how much he will have to pay. Next he moves to the cashier's line. When he reaches the head of the line, he pays his money. In return he gets not the bottle of brandy but a receipt showing that he has paid for it. This prepares him for the third and longest line, where he finally trades the receipt for his five bottles.

"People know of this place all over the country," Vasily tells an American visitor. Does he think spending 45 minutes standing in three lines is unreasonable? Why, no—why would anyone think that? After all, the brandy can't be found anywhere else in the country.[1]

The story of Vasily's shopping trip brings us back to the central problem of economics—dealing with scarcity. In this chapter we will take a closer look at that problem. We will begin by focusing on four choices that any economy must face in dealing with scarcity:

1. *What* should be produced, given limited supplies of labor, capital, and natural resources? How much brandy? How much bread? How many tanks?
2. *How* should goods and services be produced? Should brandy be made in old-fashioned pot stills or in modern industrial stills? Should it be brought to market by truck, rail, or air? Should the stores that sell it have many clerks using adding machines, or only a few clerks using computers?
3. *Who* should produce which goods? Why should brandy be made by workers in Armenia instead of workers in Leningrad? Why should Vasily be an engineer instead of a steelworker?
4. *For whom* should the goods and services be produced? For the few people who travel to Moscow regularly? For export? For ordinary people shopping in ordinary stores?

As we look at each of these questions in detail, we will learn more about the economic problem and more about the tools economists use to understand it.

This chapter has another purpose as well. Vasily's shopping trip opens the chapter partly because it highlights the questions of what, how, who, and for whom. But it also shows that different societies deal with the

---

[1]Based on Frederick Kempe, "You Can't Get Caviar at Gastronom No. 1, but Goodies Abound," *Wall Street Journal*, September 12, 1984, p. 1. Reprinted by permission of The Wall Street Journal, © Dow Jones & Company, Inc. 1984. All rights reserved.

problem of scarcity in different ways. The economic system of the Soviet Union answers the questions of what, how, who, and for whom quite differently than the economic system of the United States. And these are only two of the world's many economic systems. Although this book will look more closely at the U.S. economy than at the economies of other countries, we do not want to lose sight of the fact that the basic problems of economics are universal.

THE ECONOMIC PROBLEM

"Let our desires match our means!" says an ironic toast from the mountains of the Caucasus. If our desires and our means truly matched, there would be no scarcity, no choices to make, nothing we wanted that we couldn't have, and no economic problem. But few people ever reach such a state. Always, there seems to be a gap between our limited resources, on the one hand, and our wants and needs, on the other. Those who try to bridge the gap by amassing wealth often find their desires scampering ahead of them, always just out of reach. Those who try to bridge the gap by limiting their desire for material things still face the problem of lack of time. Even saints have been known to pray for a longer life in which to prepare for eternity.

But economists do not spend much time worrying about the gap between means and desires. They take the gap for granted and spend their time studying the choices people make in dealing with it. Let's look at some of those choices.

What to Produce?

Later in the chapter we will return to Vasily and his brandy, but here we will use a simpler example, that of the Robinson Crusoe. Crusoe, hero of Daniel Defoe's eighteenth-century novel, is stranded alone on a barren island when his ship is wrecked. The morning after the wreck, he wakes up and wants something to eat. He has two ways to get food: fishing and hunting. He can hunt all day and eat roast pheasant, fish all day and dine on broiled rockfish, or divide his day between hunting and fishing and have some variety in his diet.

Box 2.1 shows the choices open to Crusoe. Look first at the table. It shows that if Crusoe spends 12 hours fishing and does not hunt at all, he can catch 11 fish. If he spends 12 hours hunting and does not fish at all, he can shoot 14 birds. If he spends some time doing each, he can choose among the various combinations of fish and birds shown in the table.

The production possibility frontier   Box 2.1 also shows Crusoe's production possibilities in the form of a graph.[2] Point A in the graph represents all fishing and no hunting. Point G represents all hunting and no fishing. The other points represent other combinations shown in the table.

---

[2]If you need to review the use of graphs, turn to the appendix to this chapter before reading further.

**Box 2.1
Crusoe's Production
Possibility Frontier**

Crusoe has 12 hours each day to devote to hunting or fishing. The table shows the number of fish and birds that he can obtain by dividing his time in various ways. The same information is also displayed in the form of a graph called a production possibility frontier. Points on the frontier correspond to the lines of the table. Points like H, which require less than 12 hours total, are also possible. But Crusoe cannot reach any point outside the frontier within the limits of a 12-hour day.

Point on Graph	Hours Spent Fishing	Hours Spent Hunting	Number of Fish Caught	Number of Birds Shot
A	12	0	11	0
B	10	2	10	4
C	8	4	9	7
D	6	6	8	9
E	4	8	6	11
F	2	10	3	13
G	0	12	0	14

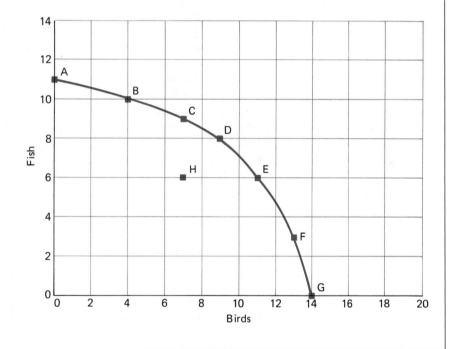

Production possibility frontier

A graph showing the possible combinations of goods that can be produced by an economy, given available resources and technology.

A graph like the one in Box 2.1 is called a **production possibility frontier**. It defines the choices open to Crusoe in deciding what to produce. His time is a scarce resource. He has to spend some time sleeping and some doing chores around his camp. That leaves him at most 12 hours for hunting and fishing. There is no way he can get any combination of birds and fish outside the frontier. If he spends a full 12 hours seeking food, he can have his choice of points on the frontier. If he wants to spend less than 12 hours hunting and fishing, he will have to be content with a combination of birds and fish like the one represented by point H, which lies inside the frontier.

The position and shape of the frontier depend on the resources available to Crusoe, the technology he uses, and his skill as a hunter. A change in any of these conditions would change the frontier. For example, a better gun would allow him to shoot more birds per hour. This would stretch the frontier outward toward the right.

Opportunity cost   At any point along the production possibility frontier, taking the time to catch more fish means giving up a chance to shoot some birds. Suppose we begin at point G (all hunting and no fishing) and then switch two hours to fishing. This will net us three fish at the cost of just one bird. The cost of a good measured in terms of lost opportunity to do something else with the same time and resources is known as the **opportunity cost** of that good. In the range between point G and point F on the chart, the opportunity cost of each fish is one third of a bird.

Notice that as Crusoe moves upward and to the left along the production possibility frontier, the trade-off between birds and fish changes. This reflects the fact that the number of birds (or fish) obtained from each added hour of hunting (or fishing) tends to fall as more hours are devoted to that activity. For example, Crusoe can catch three fish in his first two hours of effort each day. However, the longer he spends fishing, the more stirred up the water becomes, and the harder it is to catch more fish. Much the same applies to hunting. For this reason, Crusoe's production possibility frontier is curved.

Our own economy is much like Crusoe's island: Getting more of something we want requires paying an opportunity cost in terms of something else. For a person living on a limited budget, buying a car may mean giving up a chance to move to a better apartment. Getting a college education may mean giving up several years of work and income. (See Box 2.2.) Working full-time while going to college may mean giving up sleep, vacations, and maybe good grades.

As we will see at many points in this book, the concept of opportunity cost applies to national economic policy as well as to individual decisions. The opportunity cost of an arms buildup may take the form of less public housing. The opportunity cost of a clean environment may be higher prices and smaller amounts of electricity, steel, and chemicals. Opportunity cost is a basic fact of economic life that must be faced whenever one is deciding what to produce.

How to Produce?

A second major part of the economic problem is how to produce the mix of goods and services that has been chosen. There is more than one way to produce almost anything. Take Crusoe's fishing, for example. The simplest way to catch fish is to stand on the shore and use a hook and line. Crusoe could catch enough fish to live on that way. However, he could also use another method. He could stop fishing for a few days and use the time to weave a net and build a boat. Then, using the boat and net, he could catch many more fish per hour spent fishing.

Switching from a hook and line to a boat and net shows how one

Opportunity cost
The cost of a good measured in terms of lost opportunity to pursue the best alternative activity with the same time and resources.

Box 2.2
The Opportunity Cost of
a College Education

How much does it cost you to go to college? If you are a resident student at a typical four-year private college in the United States, you could answer this question by making up a budget like the one shown in Table A. This can be called a budget of *out-of-pocket costs* because it includes all the items, and only those items, that you or your parents actually have to pay for in a year.

Your own out-of-pocket costs may be much higher or lower than these average figures. Chances are, though, that these are the items that come to mind when you think about the costs of college. As you begin to think like an economist, you may find it useful to recast yor college budget in terms of *opportunity costs*. Which of the items in Table A represent opportunities that you have foregone in order to go to college? Are any foregone opportunities missing from the table? To answer these questions, compare Table A with Table B—a budget of opportunity costs.

The first three items in the out-of-pocket budget show up again in the opportunity cost budget. In order to spend $4,000 on tuition and fees and $325 on books and supplies, you have to give up the opportunity to buy other goods and services—say, to buy a car or rent a ski condo. In order to spend $350 getting to and from college, you have to pass up the opportunity to travel somewhere else or to spend the money on something other than travel. But the last two items in the out-of-pocket budget are not opportunity costs. By spending $3,200 a year on room, board, and personal expenses during the year, you're not really giving up the opportunity to do something else. Whether you had gone to college or not, you would have to eat, to live somewhere, and to buy clothes. Because these are expenses that you would have in any case, they do not count as opportunity costs of going to college.

Thinking about what you would have done if you had not gone to college suggests a major item that needs to be added to the opportunity cost budget—one that does not show up at all in the out-of-pocket budget. If you had not gone to college, you probably would have taken a job and started earning money soon after leaving high school. The average earnings for a high school graduate would be about $7,500 during the nine months of the school year. (You can work in the summer even if you do go to college.) This potential income is something that you have to forgo for college, so it is a true opportunity cost.

Which budget you use depends on the kind of decision you are making. If you have already decided to go to college and are doing your financial planning, the out-of-pocket budget will tell you how much you will have to raise from savings, parents' contributions, and scholarships in order to make ends meet. But suppose you are making the more basic decision of whether to go to college or take up some career that does not require college. Then the opportunity cost of college is what counts.

a. Budget of Out-of-Pocket Costs

Tuition and fees	$ 4,000
Books and supplies	325
Transportation to and from home	350
Room and board	2,500
Personal expenses	700
Total out-of-pocket costs	$ 7,875

b. Budget of Opportunity Costs

Tuition and fees	$ 4,000
Books and supplies	325
Transportation to and from home	350
Foregone income	7,500
Total opportunity costs	$12,175

factor of production can be substituted for another. In this case capital is substituted for labor. The boat and net are capital because they are durable means of production made by people. The act of building them is an investment by Crusoe, just as building a new continuous-casting mill would be an investment by a steel company. Once the investment has been made, fewer hours of labor are needed to produce each unit of output.

Substitution of factors is possible in every line of production. In the United States, crops are grown on large farms with relatively little labor. In Indonesia, large amounts of labor are used to grow crops on small fields. Electricity can be generated by burning coal, a process that uses large quantities of natural resources. Or it can be generated with solar collectors, which use fewer resources but require large capital investments. Coal can be strip-mined, using huge machines and relatively little labor, or it can be mined underground, using relatively more labor. The choices are endless.

As these examples suggest, there is no one way of producing a good that is right at all times and places. Which method is best depends on the relative scarcity of the various factors of production. In a country like China, which is poor but has a large population, it makes sense to build roads with huge pick-and-shovel gangs. It makes just as much sense to build roads with bulldozers and small work crews in Australia, where capital is abundant and labor less so. But making the right choices is important. If the wrong choices are made and scarce factors of production are wasted, the total amount of goods and services produced will be less than it could be.

Who Does the Producing?

In discussing the question of how things are to be produced, we spoke of substituting labor for capital and vice versa as if "labor" were a homogeneous substance like fertilizer. Of course this is not the case. No two people's skills and talents are exactly the same. This means that some people are best suited to one kind of job and others to other kinds of jobs.

Let's go back to Crusoe's island for one more example. One day Crusoe finds that he is not alone. He sees a group of natives fishing from a canoe. Their canoe is faster than Crusoe's boat, and their net is much better designed. Each native can catch ten fish an hour, compared with five an hour at best for Crusoe.

Crusoe follows the natives at a distance. Later in the day he watches them hunt. They are very skilled at creeping up close to a flock of birds and shooting them with their arrows. But here their advantage is not as great. They can kill five birds an hour, but Crusoe, with his gun, can kill four.

"Ah," says Crusoe, "here is a chance to cooperate. I'll spend more time hunting and trade some of the extra birds for the natives' fish. If I take an hour away from fishing, I'll bag four extra birds at an opportunity cost of five fish. I'll give the natives the four extra birds. Then they can take four-fifths of an hour off from hunting, in which time they can catch eight fish. They can give me seven of those fish, and we'll both end up with just as many birds as before and more fish!" Carried away by the brilliance of his idea, Crusoe runs up to the natives and draws a diagram in the sand to explain it. (The diagram is shown in Box 2.3.) The natives quickly agree, and they all become the best of friends.

**Box 2.3
Division of Labor Based
on Comparative
Advantage**

One day Crusoe meets some natives. He observes that they are better at both fishing and hunting than he is, but that their advantage is greater in fishing. In economic terms, the opportunity cost of fish is lower for the natives and the opportunity cost of birds is lower for Crusoe. Crusoe suggests a division of labor based on comparative advantage: He will spend an extra hour hunting, shooting 4 birds and giving up the chance to catch 5 fish. He will give the 4 birds to the natives. They, in exchange, will give up 48 minutes of hunting, at a cost of 4 birds, in order to catch 8 extra fish. Crusoe will get 7 of the fish and the natives will keep 1. Both parties will end up with just as many birds as before and with more fish!

	Crusoe	Natives
Initial situation:		
Birds per hour	4	5
Fish per hour	5	10
Opportunity cost of birds (in terms of fish)	1-1/4	2
Opportunity cost of fish (in terms of birds)	4/5	1/2
Details of proposed trade: Change in hunting time	+1 hour	−48 minutes
Change in birds shot	+4	−4
Change in fishing time	−1 hour	+48 minutes
Change in fish caught	−5	+8
Birds given to natives	4	
Fish given to Crusoe		7
Change in total birds consumed	no change	no change
Change in total fish consumed	+2	+1

Comparative advantage
The ability to produce a good or service at a lower opportunity cost than someone else.

Comparative advantage   The immense productivity of a modern economy is a result of a vast division of labor that is based on the same principle that Crusoe and the natives used in deciding what to produce. This is the principle of **comparative advantage**. A person is said to have a comparative advantage in producing some good or service if he or she can produce it at a lower opportunity cost than someone else. In our example, Crusoe has a comparative advantage in hunting: for him, each bird has an opportunity cost of one and one quarter fish, compared to an opportunity cost of two fish per bird for the natives. The natives have a comparative advantage in fishing: each fish costs them half a bird, compared to Crusoe's opportunity cost of four-fifths of a bird per fish.

The principle that everyone gains from a division of labor based on comparative advantage can be applied very widely. It guides students' career choices. Leroy gets A's in math and A–'s in English. He could excel as either an engineer or an editor, but he majors in engineering because that's where his comparative advantage lies. Larry gets C+'s in English and C-'s in math. He won't make much of a show in either engineering or editing. Still, he majors in English because doing so will make it comparatively easier for him to find a job.

On a larger scale, comparative advantage guides the division of labor among nations. The Japanese are very good at making cars. They also have many skilled farmers. But raising food is more costly in Japan compared with other countries, so Japan exports cars and imports food. We will return to the principle of comparative advantage in international trade in Chapter 34.

The comforting thing about comparative advantage is that everyone has a comparative advantage in something. Crusoe is less skilled than the natives in both hunting and fishing. Yet comparative advantage gives him a place in island society as a hunter. Larry is poorer at both math and English than Leroy. Yet his comparative advantage in English will permit him to get a job at which he can at least make a living.

For Whom Should Goods Be Produced?

The last part of the economic problem is the question of for whom goods should be produced. This is a touchy question, since it raises complex normative issues. Family fights, lawsuits, and even wars have turned on different views of what constitutes a fair distribution of the goods produced by an economy. However, some basic principles of positive economics apply here too.

The positive economics of "for whom" can be seen most clearly when production has already occurred and there is a fixed supply of goods. Suppose 30 students get on a bus to go to a football game. Bag lunches are handed out. Half the bags contain a ham sandwich and a root beer. The other half contain a tuna sandwich and a cola. What happens when the bags are opened? People don't just eat whatever they find—they start trading. Some people swap sandwiches; others swap drinks. Maybe there isn't enough of everything to give each person his or her first choice. Still, the trading makes at least some people better off than they were when they started. And no one ends up worse off, because if they don't want to trade, they can always eat what was given them in the first place.

This example points to a principle that is somewhat like comparative advantage: Once the total amount of goods that each person gets has been set, the specific mix of goods should be adjusted through trades until it fits people's preferences. The federal food stamp program illustrates this principle in action. How many food stamps, if any, a family should get is a subject of debate. But once that question has been settled, it is agreed that each family should be allowed to choose the mix of foods it prefers.

Positive economics can be useful in thinking about distribution even when the total amount of goods is not fixed in advance. The reason is that the rules for distribution are likely to affect the amount of goods produced. If goods are distributed in a way that rewards hard work and careful use of resources, there will be more goods to be distributed. If they are distributed in a way that is unrelated to people's efforts and choices, less will be produced. Still less will be produced if the distribution system rewards people for wasting scarce resources.

This is not to say that incentives are the only thing that count in deciding for whom goods and services should be produced. Almost everyone would agree that fairness should be kept in mind too (although not everyone will agree about what fairness means). We will return to the issues of distribution, incentives, and fairness at many points in this book.

EFFICIENCY AND ENTREPRENEURSHIP

Efficiency

In Chapter 1 we mentioned efficiency and promised a more detailed discussion in this chapter. The usual definition of efficiency is acting with a minimum of expense, waste, and effort. Economists have refined that definition in a way that our earlier discussion of what, how, who, and for whom can help us understand.

Efficiency of technique   In our discussion of how goods should be produced, we stressed that production techniques must be fitted to the situation. Techniques should be chosen that use scarce factors of production sparingly and more abundant ones more generously. The labor, capital, and natural resources used for a given task should be applied with the best available degree of skill and knowledge.

If mistakes are made, the economy will not reach its production possibility frontier. Box 2.4 gives an example. It shows the possible choices between clean air and other goods. Suppose that we are at point A. Making the air a little cleaner will require that we forgo some other goods—that is easy to understand. But there is more than one way to clean up the air. For example, electric power plants can be made cleaner either by switching to low-sulfur coal or by installing stack scrubbers that clean the gases given off by high-sulfur coal. Which choice is best depends on where the plant is located relative to coal sources, how old the plant is, and so on.

If the right choice of technique is made, the economy will slide down the production possibility frontier from A to, say, B. If the wrong choice is made, more other goods will have to be given up to attain the same level of clean air. That will leave the economy at a point like C, inside the production possibility frontier.

Economists say that a situation like that represented by point C is *inefficient*. This is so because starting from that situation, the economy could produce more other goods without producing less clean air. Points A and B, although they represent different choices regarding clean air versus other goods, are both *efficient*. Starting from either of those points, there is no way to have more of one thing without having less of the other.

This is what efficiency of technique means: choosing the methods of production that, given available resources, leave no opportunity to produce more of one thing without producing less of another.

**Box 2.4
Efficiency in Cleaning
Up the Air**

This production possibility frontier shows the trade-off between clean air and other goods. Suppose that we are at point A. Starting from this point, the air cannot be made cleaner without some sacrifice of other goods. If efficient pollution control techniques are chosen, the economy can slide down the frontier to another efficient point such as B. If inefficient techniques are chosen, the economy may end up at a point like C. Moving from A to C sacrifices more than the necessary amount of other goods to achieve a given increase in clean air.

Efficiency in the division of labor   Efficiency also requires a division of labor that is based on comparative advantage. In the example of Crusoe and the natives we saw how trading fish for birds improved the division of labor in such a way that everyone ended up with more fish and the same number of birds. The division of labor cannot be said to be efficient until all the opportunities for exchange and specialization have been carried out.

In the domestic, or national, economy, efficiency in the division of labor means fitting people to the jobs for which they are best suited. At one time, for example, black students were not allowed to attend good engineering schools in many states. That meant that some of the best would-be engineers ended up in other jobs for which they were less well suited. As a result, power plants, coal mines, and factories were not quite as well designed and run as they could have been. As a result, the economy was pushed off the production possibility frontier to a point inside the frontier.

In the world economy, efficient division of labor means trade based on comparative advantage. If goods are produced where their opportunity costs are lowest, total worldwide output will be greater. International trade thus has the potential to bring citizens of every country more, and more varied, goods and services without the need to work any harder or use any more resources.

In short, on either a worldwide or a national scale, getting to the production possibility frontier requires both efficient choices of technique and efficient division of labor.

Efficiency in the mix and distribution of output   We have applied the concept of efficiency to the questions of how and who; now we turn to the questions of what and for whom. Suppose we are on the production possibility frontier. Are some points on the frontier more efficient than others?

From the point of view of production, they are not. As long as no more of one good can be produced without having to produce less of another, production is efficient. But from the point of view of consumer welfare, some points are better than others. For example, a cafeteria that made nothing but tuna sandwiches could be producing efficiently. It could be sitting squarely on its tuna sandwich–ham sandwich production possibility frontier, right at the point where it met the tuna sandwich axis. (See point A in Box 2.5.) But customers would be better off if the cafeteria slid along the frontier to a point like B, where the mix of sandwiches would fit differences in taste and the desire for variety.

**Box 2.5
Efficiency in Selecting
and Distributing the
Output Mix**

All points on the production possibility frontier are equally efficient from the point of view of production. However, some may be more efficient than others from the point of view of consumers. This figure shows a production possibility frontier for tuna and ham sandwiches. At first only tuna sandwiches are made (point A). Moving to point B would satisfy consumers' taste for variety. It would therefore be more efficient.

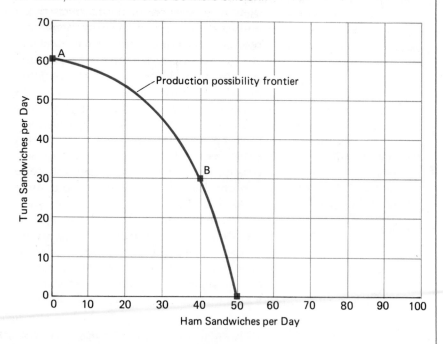

Much the same reasoning can be applied to efficiency in the distribution of output. Even if the economy is producing efficiently and is turning out the right mix of output, it is not fully efficient if the distribution of output does not take preferences into account. What if all the tuna sandwiches went to the ham lovers and all the ham sandwiches to the tuna lovers? That would be inefficient, since a redistribution could make everyone better off.

Efficiency
A state of affairs in which, given available knowledge and resources, no change can be made that will make one person better off without making another worse off.

Summary   We have discussed the concept of efficiency in terms of choice of technique, division of labor, mix of outputs, and distribution of the output mix. Can these four strands be tied together in a single definition? They can. **Efficiency**, we can say, is a state of affairs in which, given available knowledge and resources, no change can be made that will make one person better off without making another worse off. Producing more of one good without producing less of another would result in at least one person being better off without anyone else being worse off; therefore, an efficient economy must produce efficiently. It must also produce the right mix of outputs and distribute that mix on the basis of people's preferences.[3]

Entrepreneurship

Efficiency, as we have defined it, applies to an economy in which certain amounts of knowledge and factors of production are given. Such an economy has a production possibility frontier beyond which it cannot go any more than Crusoe could make a microwave oven with sticks and shells picked up on the beach. But in the real world, knowledge and factors of production don't stay given for long. Knowledge is always increasing. Population growth expands the amount of labor available, and education improves its quality. The supply of capital grows as people set aside part of their income as savings and invest what they save in new machinery, buildings, and so on. And in many cases, though not all, new natural resources become available faster than old ones are used up.

Entrepreneurship
The process of looking for new possibilities: making use of new ways of doing things, being alert to new opportunities, and overcoming old limits.

As these things happen, the production possibility frontier expands, as shown in Box 2.6. The economy breaks through old limits. New production techniques are developed. New consumption opportunities are opened up. If productive efficiency means getting to a fixed production possibility frontier, what do we call the force that allows the economy to keep up with the frontier as it expands over time? Economists call it **entrepreneurship**. Entrepreneurship is the process of looking for new possibilities: making use of new ways of doing things, being alert to new opportunities, and overcoming old limits. It is a dynamic process that breaks out of the static constraints set by efficiency.

In the world of business, entrepreneurship is often linked with the founding of new firms. When a Henry Ford sets out to start a whole new industry, there are few givens to deal with. New production processes have to be invented. The constraints of existing sources of supply have to be overcome. Consumers are encouraged to satisfy wants and needs to which they gave little thought before because there were no products that

---

[3]Efficiency, in this sense, is often called *Pareto optimality* after the Italian economist Vilfredo Pareto, who proposed this definition.

**Box 2.6
Expansion of the
Production Possibility
Frontier**

Production possibility frontiers assume given supplies of factors of production and a given state of knowledge. As new factors of production become available and as scientific discoveries are made, entrepreneurs become aware of new opportunities, and break through old constraints. The production possibility frontier then expands. Points that used to be unattainable come within reach.

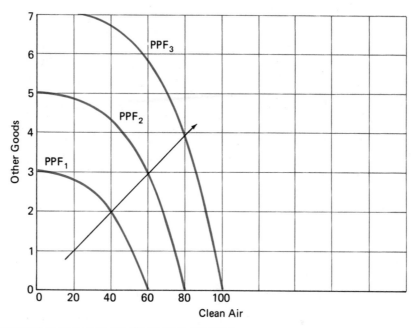

could satisfy them. This kind of exploring and experimenting is the essence of entrepreneurship.

But entrepreneurship is not limited to founding new firms. The manager of a Ford plant may be less of an entrepreneur than the founder, but the manager's work is not entirely routine. Unexpected problems arise that must be solved somehow—often by figuring out a new way of doing things.

Consumers can be entrepreneurs, too. They do not simply repeat the same patterns of work and leisure every day. They seek variety—new jobs, new foods, new places to visit. Each time you try something new, you are taking a step into the unknown. In a small way, you are playing the role of entrepreneur.

ECONOMIC SYSTEMS

As we have stressed in this chapter, the questions of what, how, who, and for whom are all parts of the economic problem. They apply to the economy of the United States, that of the Soviet Union, that of Crusoe's island, and all other economies, real or fictional. But although all economies are alike in the problems they face, they are not all alike in the way they make decisions.

Ownership: Who Makes Decisions

To *own* something means to have the right to use it and to prevent others from using it. If you own something, that makes you an economic decision maker. You decide who uses it, how it is used, and so on. Because owners are decision makers, ownership of business firms is a key trait of any economic system, since it governs who makes decisions about production.

In the United States most firms are owned by the people who put up the capital to start them—their proprietors, partners, or stockholders. (Chapter 4 will discuss these three forms of ownership in detail.) A system in which ownership and control of business firms rests with the suppliers of capital is called **capitalism**.

Capitalism
An economic system in which ownership and control of business firms rests with the suppliers of capital.

Even in the United States, however, not all firms are owned and controlled by suppliers of capital. First, there are mutually or cooperatively owned firms. They are owned by the people who work in them or use their services. Examples include mutual insurance companies and savings banks, agricultural and consumer cooperatives, private colleges and universities, and not-for-profit publishers like Consumer Reports. Second, some firms are owned by the government. Examples include Conrail (which, at this writing, the government is trying to sell), the Tennessee Valley Authority, and the U.S. Postal Service. Mutual, cooperative, and government ownership are all forms of *social* ownership. A system in which social ownership prevails is called **socialism**.

Socialism
An economic system in which business firms are owned and controlled by the people who work in them, or by the government, acting in the name of the workers.

There are no purely capitalist or socialist systems in the real world. All existing systems are mixtures of the two forms. In the United States, Canada, Western Europe, Japan, and some less developed countries, capitalism prevails. Mutual, cooperative, and government-owned firms are common in these economies, however—more common in most of them than in the United States. In the Soviet Union, Eastern Europe, China, and many other less developed countries, social ownership prevails. The theories on which these economies are based can be traced to the writings of the nineteenth-century economist Karl Marx. (See Box 2.7.) Following Marx's precepts, almost all industry is government owned, but some private ownership can be found in farming, retail trade, and services. One country, Yugoslavia, has its own home-grown brand of cooperative ownership and control.

But our purpose here is not to list the world's economic systems. Instead, it is to show that different forms of ownership imply different answers to the question of who decides. Under capitalism, the owners of capital are the managers and entrepreneurs. Under mutual and cooperative ownership, managers are chosen by workers, consumers, or some other group. Under forms of socialism that feature government ownership, managers are public employees.

How Decisions Are Made

No less important than differences in who makes production decisions are differences in how those decisions are made. Broadly speaking, there are three styles of decision making: market decision making, regulation, and planning.

**Box 2.7
Karl Marx, Economist
and Socialist**

Karl Marx
(1818–1883)

Karl Marx—German philosopher, revolutionary, and patron saint of socialism—was also a well-known economist. From the age of 31, he lived and worked in London. His thinking was strongly influenced by the British classical school of economics, and especially by the writings of David Ricardo, a follower of Adam Smith. But whereas economists of the classical school were, for the most part, sympathetic to the capitalist system, Marx took the tools of classical economics and turned them against capitalism.

The keystone of classical economics was the labor theory of value—the doctrine that the values and relative prices of various goods are determined mainly by the number of labor hours that go into their production. For Marx, the labor theory of value was more than just a description of how prices are determined. He went on to argue that if labor is the source of all value, workers ought to receive the whole product of their labor. He viewed it as unjust that under capitalism a large part of the product was paid to owners of land and capital in the form of rent, interest payments, and profit—"surplus value," to use Marx's term.

In his massive work *Capital*, Marx tried to show that capitalism was headed for collapse and that it would be followed by a socialist revolution. All his life he worked with revolutionary groups to prepare for that day. Following the revolution, he envisioned an economy based on collective ownership and economic planning. He gave the name *communism* to the highest form of socialism, toward which the revolution would strive. Today the term communism is used to describe the economic systems of the Soviet Union, Eastern Europe, and other countries that follow Marxist principles.

Marx was not the first socialist, and not all socialists today are followers of Marx. Still, he must be regarded as the most influential thinker in the history of socialism and one of the most influential economists of all time.

Markets   Chapter 1 discussed the role of markets in decision making. Markets perform three tasks: They transmit information about the values of resources to firms and households. They set incentives for workers, traders, and entrepreneurs. And in the process of doing these things they determine the distribution of income. Much of the rest of this book, beginning with Chapter 3, will be devoted to the ways in which markets do all this.

Although the role of markets in decision making is greatest in capitalist systems, most socialist economies also use markets. Take Vasily and his brandy as a case in point. The brandy was produced by a government-owned firm and sold in a government-owned store: Even so, Vasily's choice of what to buy—brandy, sausage, shoes, or whatever—is a market decision, one that is governed at least partly by the prices of available goods. What's more, the Soviet Union depends to a large extent on market incentives to steer people into certain jobs. Vasily chose to become an engineer partly because that occupation is well paid. And it is quite possible that he chose to work in Siberia because the pay for all kinds of jobs is higher there.

Other socialist countries use markets much more extensively. In Poland, the bulk of the farm sector relies on markets. China has tried using market incentives in light industry, with some success. Hungary and Yugoslavia use market incentives throughout their economies. In fact, systems like Hungary's and Yugoslavia's are often called *market socialism*.

Regulation
Government intervention in the market for the purpose of influencing the production and distribution of particular goods and services.

Regulation   No economic system leaves all decisions to the market, however. Even in the most strongly capitalist systems, the government plays a major role in the decisions of what, how, who, and for whom. Its activities in this area are known as **regulation**. Here are some examples: The U.S. Food and Drug Administration's regulation of prescription drugs affects *what* is produced by pharmaceutical firms. The Environmental Protection Agency's rules on air and water pollution affect *how* firms produce their outputs. The Equal Employment Opportunity Commission sets rules for hiring that affect *who* is hired for many jobs. And laws like the federal minimum wage and the Davis-Bacon Act determine levels of pay for many workers. This affects *for whom* goods and services are produced. We will discuss many kinds of regulation in later chapters.

Economic planning
Systematic intervention in the economy by government with the goal of improving coordination, efficiency, and growth.

Planning   The governments of many countries go beyond regulation and engage in **economic planning**. This can be defined as systematic intervention in the economy with the goal of improving coordination, efficiency, and growth.

Because planning and regulation differ mainly in degree, the distinction between them is not a sharp one. The most comprehensive planning is found in socialist economies like that of the Soviet Union. There each firm, be it a steel mill or a distillery, is supposed to follow a plan that governs its level of output, its methods of production, its sources of supply, and much else. We will look at Soviet-style planning in Chapter 37.

Other socialist countries engage in more limited planning. They try to coordinate the work of the largest firms and to set a framework for economic growth, but they leave more detailed decisions to the managers of each firm. Some countries in which capitalist ownership prevails have tried this style of planning too. France is a leading example.

Industrial policy
A policy under which the government sets an overall framework to promote the growth of new industries and ease the problems of declining ones.

The United States probably has less national economic planning than any other country in the world. Proposals that would change this are often made, however. Recent proposals for a national **industrial policy** are an example. They call for the federal government to set an overall framework to promote the growth of high-tech industries, ease the pains of declining industries, control imports and exports, coordinate basic research, and so on. The economic policies of the Japanese government are often pointed to as a model.

Industrial policy falls somewhere between planning and regulation. It could be viewed either as a weak form of planning or as a coordinated set of regulations.

Looking Ahead

This is not a book on comparative economics. Except for Chapters 36 and 37, most examples are based on the U.S. economic system. Still, it is worthwhile to keep the variety of economic systems in mind. The basic problems of what, how, who, and for whom are universal ones that have many possible solutions. And even within the U.S. economy, a great many forms of ownership and ways of making decisions coexist and compete.

Summary

1. The central economic problem is how to deal with scarcity. Deciding what should be produced, how it should be produced, who should produce it, and for whom it should be produced are all parts of this problem. These questions must be faced by every economy.

2. A range of production choices can be presented in graphic form as a *production possibility frontier*. The frontier is the boundary between the mixes of goods that can be produced with available resources and know-how, and mixes that lie outside the frontier—that is, cannot possibly be produced. Movement along the frontier represents a trade-off of one good for another. The *opportunity cost* of a good is its cost in terms of lost opportunity to do something else with the same time and resources.

3. There are many different ways to produce any good or service. Differences in production techniques often reflect substitutions of one factor of production for another. Techniques should be chosen that use scarce factors carefully and less scarce ones more generously.

4. No two people are alike in terms of skills and abilities. Output and satisfaction can be increased by means of a division of labor based on *comparative advantage*. According to this principle, each person should specialize in the goods or services that he or she can produce at the least opportunity cost. Comparative advantage applies to the division of labor among countries as well.

5. Getting the most satisfaction from a set amount of goods requires that they be distributed according to people's preferences. Incentives should also be taken into account. The normative issue of fairness also plays a major role in determining for whom goods and services should be produced.

6. *Efficiency*, as economists use the term, means a state of affairs in which, with available knowledge and resources, no change can be made that will make one person better off without making someone else worse off. Producing more of one good without producing less of another would make it possible for at least one person to be better off; therefore, an efficient economy must produce efficiently. It must also produce the right mix of output and distribute that output according to people's preferences.

7. *Entrepreneurship* is the process of finding new alternatives, thinking of new ways of doing things, being alert to new opportunities, and overcoming constraints. It is a dynamic process that can be thought of as constantly bringing new knowledge and factors of production to bear as the economy's production possibility frontier expands.

8. Although all societies face the same economic problem, they do not solve it in the same way. Ownership of the means of production is a major factor in determining who makes production decisions. Under *capitalism*, business firms are controlled by the owners of capital. Under *socialism*, mutual, cooperative, and government ownership prevail. Economic systems also differ in their methods of decision making. Some rely on markets to decide what, how, who, and for whom. Others use *regulation* to intervene in the economy in order to get specific results. Still others engage in *economic planning*—a policy of systematic intervention in the economy with the goal of improving coordination, efficiency, and growth.

Questions for Review

1. Define the following terms:
   production possibility frontier
   opportunity cost
   comparative advantage
   efficiency
   entrepreneurship
   capitalism
   socialism
   regulation
   economic planning
   industrial policy
2. What is the opportunity cost to you of studying more in order to improve your grade in economics? Is there a cost in terms of money? In terms of other activities?
3. Give examples of ways in which methods of farming and construction have changed over time. Do these changes include the substitution of some factors of production for others?

Do you think they were caused, in part, by changes in the relative scarcities of those factors of production?
4. Why can it be said that everyone has a comparative advantage in something, even if there is nothing they can do that someone else can't do better?
5. Give examples of the concept of efficiency as applied to the questions of what, how, who, and for whom.
6. How can a production possibility frontier be used to compare the notions of efficiency and entrepreneurship?
7. Give examples of social forms of ownership in the United States and capitalist forms of ownership in the Soviet Union and Eastern Europe. Also give examples of markets, regulation, and economic planning as methods of decision making in various countries.

Problems and Topics for Discussion

1. A farmer has four fields spread out over a hillside. He can grow either wheat or potatoes in any of the fields, but the low fields are better for potatoes and the high ones are better for wheat. Here are some combinations of wheat and potatoes that he can produce:

Number of Fields Used for Potatoes	Tons of Potatoes	Tons of Wheat
4	1,000	0
3	900	400
2	600	700
1	300	900
0	0	1,000

Use these data to draw a production possibility frontier for wheat and potatoes. What is the opportunity cost of wheat, stated in terms of potatoes, when the farmer switches the highest field into wheat production? What happens to the opportunity cost of wheat as more and more fields are switched to wheat?

2. Suppose that you learned that Vladimir Horowitz, the great pianist, was also an amazingly good typist. Knowing this, would it surprise you to discover that he hired a secretary to type his correspondence, even though he could do the job more quickly himself? What does this have to do with comparative advantage?
3. In the United States, a tractor can be produced with 100 labor hours, while shoes require 2 labor hours per pair. In China, it takes 500 labor hours to build a tractor and 2.5 labor hours to make a pair of shoes. Which country has a comparative advantage in shoes? In tractors? How can they gain from trade, even though both tractors and shoes can be produced with less labor in the United States?
4. As mentioned in the chapter, the federal food stamp program leaves low-income families free to choose a mix of foods that they prefer. This is in line with the principle of efficiency. Would it be more efficient still if low-income

families were allowed to trade their food stamps for cash? (Such trading does happen, but it is restricted by law.) Or perhaps low-income families should be given cash in the first place and allowed to spend it on whatever they want. Discuss this issue, taking both positive and normative economics into account.

5. **Case for Discussion**

Wu Xiangtin, a farmer in Wenjiang County, is growing rich—at least by Chinese standards—off the so-called responsibility system. This is a program in which plots of land have been turned over to farmers for up to 15 years to use in producing goods for consumer markets. Wu earns about $15 a day by selling the eggs produced by his 200 chickens. Last year, he claims, his total income was about 10,000 yuan, or roughly $4,800.

The newly affluent Wu has purchased a new house, a new chicken coop, and a TV set. His next project is to begin raising rabbits, ducks, and geese. He notes that duck and goose eggs command higher prices than chicken eggs.

Wu's projects are typical of the entrepreneurial energy that was bottled up by Mao's policies. In 1966, at the start of the Cultural Revolution (a campaign to shape Chinese society along more purely socialist lines), he was working as a veterinarian at a nearby commune. The turmoil made it impossible for him to remain at that job, so he began raising pigs. Local socialist activists, known as Red Guards, denounced him as an "exploiter" and warned, "You will be taking the capitalist road if you raise ducks or chickens."

Wu becomes indignant at the suggestion that the Communist party might someday take away his chickens. "It's the policy of the party," he says. "The party will never take away my 10,000 yuan."

Maybe not. For the time being, local party officials—far from denouncing Wu—are showing him off to foreign visitors as a success story of the new China. Moreover, they say that because of the responsibility system, the average income of the 1,300 people in Wu's production brigade has more than doubled since 1978.

But there are problems that could hinder further change. The most obvious of these is inequality of income, which could trigger a backlash. Take Wu's neighbor, Li Xiaochuan, who lives in a cramped and dirty house. Li has only four pigs, six chickens, and an income about one tenth of Wu's. At some point he and other poor peasants may become resentful of their "rich" neighbor and seek a return to what they see as more egalitarian policies.[4]

Questions:

a. In what ways does Wu fit the definition of an entrepreneur?

b. How does this story illustrate the three functions of markets? How does it illustrate the use of markets in a socialist society?

c. What examples are given in this story of the what, how, who, and for whom decisions that every economy faces?

d. Discuss the tension between the Maoist belief that pure socialism should strive for equality above all and the desire of China's current leaders to make the economy more efficient and productive.

---

[4]Adapted from David Ignatius, "China's Capitalistic Road Is Uphill from Here," *Wall Street Journal*, May 4, 1984, p. 30. Reprinted by permission of the Wall Street Journal, © Dow Jones & Company, Inc. 1984. All rights reserved.

Suggestions for Further Reading

Defoe, Daniel. *The Adventures of Robinson Crusoe.* London, 1719.

The examples used in this chapter are only fancifully related to this classic novel. But try reading the novel with an eye to understanding the economic problems faced by Crusoe and, later, by Crusoe and Friday together.

Goodman, John C., and Edwin G. Dolan. *The Economics of Public Policy,* 3rd ed. St. Paul: West, 1985.

Chapter 2 uses the issue of the military draft versus the volunteer army to illustrate the concepts of opportunity cost and the production possibility frontier. Chapter 3 compares the U.S. and British methods of deciding who receives medical treatment.

Wiles, P. J. D. *Economic Institutions Compared.* New York: Wiley, 1977.

This book compares the methods used by different economic systems to solve the problems they all face. Chapter 6, which deals with cooperatives, communities, and communes, is of particular interest.

Appendix to Chapter 2

Working with Graphs

How Economists Use Graphs

At a well-known college the students have their own names for all the courses. They call the astronomy course "Stars," the geology course "Rocks," and the biology course "Frogs." Their name for the economics course is "Graphs and Laughs." This choice of names shows two things. First, it shows that the students think the professor has a sense of humor. Second, it shows that in the minds of students, economics is a matter of learning about graphs in the same way that astronomy is a matter of learning about stars and geology is a matter of learning about rocks.

Economics is not about graphs; it is about people. It is about the way people make choices, use resources, and cooperate in efforts to overcome the universal problem of scarcity. But if economics is not about graphs, why are there so many of them in this book? The answer is that economists use graphs to illustrate their theories about people's economic behavior. They do so in order to make those theories more vivid and easier to remember. Everything that can be said in the form of a graph can also be said in words, but saying something in two different ways is a well-known aid to learning. The purpose of this appendix is to show how to make the best use of this learning aid.

Pairs of Numbers and Points

The first thing to learn is how to use points on a graph to represent pairs of numbers. Look at Box 2A.1. The small table presents five pairs of numbers. The two columns are labeled x and y. The first number in each pair is called the x *value* and the second is called the y *value*. Each pair of numbers is labeled with a capital letter. Pair A has an x value of 2 and a y value of 3; pair B has an x value of 4 and a y value of 4; and so on.

Next to the table is a diagram. The two lines that meet at the lower lefthand corner are called *coordinate axes*. The horizontal axis is marked off into units for measuring the x value and the vertical axis into units for measuring the y value. In the space between these axes, each pair of numbers from the table can be shown as a point. For example, point A is found by going two units to the right along the horizontal axis and then three units straight up, parallel to the vertical axis. This represents the x value of 2 and the y value of 3. The other points are located in the same way.

Usually, the visual effect of a graph can be improved by connecting the points with a line or curve. When this is done, it can be seen at a glance that as the x value increases, the y value also increases.

Common Economic Graphs

Box 2A.2 shows three typical economic graphs. Each type of graph will appear many times in this book. Part a of Box 2A.2 shows the relationship

**Box 2A.1
Pairs of Numbers and
Points**

Each lettered pair of numbers in the table corresponds to a lettered point on the graph. The *x* value of each point corresponds to the horizontal distance of the point from the vertical axis, and the *y* value corresponds to the vertical distance from the horizontal axis.

	x	*y*
A	2	3
B	4	4
C	6	5
D	8	6
E	10	7

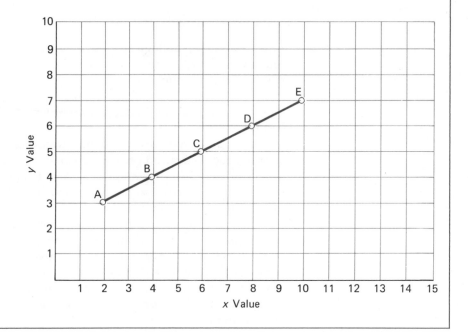

between the price of a subway token and the number of people who ride the subway each day at any given price. The table shows that as the price of tokens goes up, fewer people ride the subway. The graph shows the same thing. In economics, whenever a graph involves both money values and quantities, the vertical axis is used to measure the money values (here, the price of tokens) and the horizontal axis is used to measure the quantities (here, the number of riders per day).

Part b of Box 2A.2 uses quantities on both axes. Here the purpose is to show the various combinations of milkshakes and hamburgers that can be bought at the local carry-out when milkshakes cost 50 cents each, hamburgers cost 50 cents each, and the buyer has exactly $2.50 to spend. The table shows that the possibilities are five burgers and no shakes, four burgers and one shake, three burgers and two shakes, and so on. The graph gives a visual picture of this "menu." The points are drawn in and labeled, and a diagonal line is used to connect the points. If the purchase of parts of hamburgers or milkshakes is allowed, the buyer can choose among all the points along this line (for example, 2.5 burgers and 2.5 shakes). A buyer who wanted to have some money left over could buy a lunch shown by a point within the shaded area, such as point G (which stands for two burgers and one shake and costs just $1.50). But unless the buyer gets more money, points outside the shaded area cannot be chosen.

Part c of Box 2A.2 shows a third kind of graph that is often used in economics—one that indicates how a magnitude varies over time. This example shows what happened to the unemployment rate of nonwhite teenage males over the years 1969–1978. The horizontal axis represents the

Box 2A.2
Three Typical Economic Graphs

This exhibit shows three graphs typical of those used in economics. Part a shows the relationship between the price of tokens and the number of riders per day on a certain city subway system. When a graph shows the relationship between a price and a quantity, it is conventional to put the price on the vertical axis. Part b shows the possible choices open to a person who has $2.50 to spend on lunch and can buy hamburgers at $.50 each or milkshakes at $.50 each. Part c shows how a graph can be used to represent change over time.

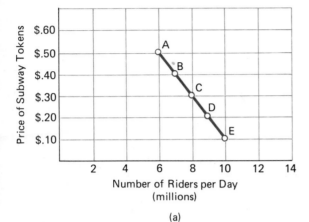

(a)

	Price of Subway Tokens	Number of Riders per Day (millions)
A	$.50	6
B	$.40	7
C	$.30	8
D	$.20	9
E	$.10	10

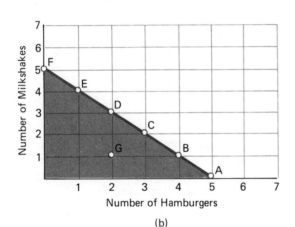

(b)

	Number of Hamburgers	Number of Milkshakes
A	5	0
B	4	1
C	3	2
D	2	3
E	1	4
F	0	5

(c)

Year	Unemployment Rate (nonwhite males, 16–19 years old)
1969	21.4%
1970	25.0
1971	28.9
1972	29.7
1973	26.9
1974	31.6
1975	35.4
1976	35.4
1977	37.0
1978	34.4

Source: Part c is from President's Council of Economic Advisers, *Economic Report of the President* (Washington, D.C.: Government Printing Office, 1979), Table B-30.

Box 2A.3
Slopes of Lines

The slope of a straight line drawn between two points is defined as the ratio of the change in the *y* value to the change in the *x* value between the two points. For example, the line drawn between Points A and B in this exhibit has a slope of +2, whereas the line drawn between Points C and D has a slope of −1/2.

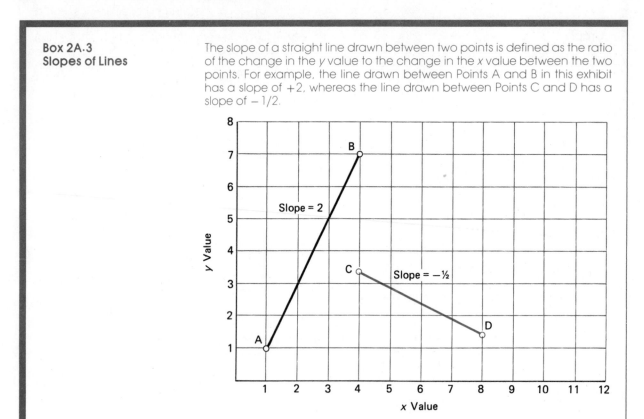

passage time and the vertical axis shows the percentage of nonwhite teenage males who were unemployed. Graphs like this one are good for showing trends. Although teenage unemployment has had its ups and downs, the trend in the 1970s was clearly upward.

Slopes

When we talk about graphs, it is convenient to describe lines or curves in terms of their slopes. The *slope* of a straight line between two points is defined as the ratio of the change in the *y* value to the change in the *x* value between the two points. In Box 2A.3, for example, the slope of the line between points A and B is 2. The *y* value changes by six units between these two points, whereas the *x* value changes by only three units. The slope is the ratio 6/3 = 2.

When a line slants downward like the line between points C and D in Box 2A.3, the *x* and *y* values change in opposite directions. Going from point C to point D, the *y* value changes by −2 (that is, it decreases by two units) and the *x* value changes by +4 (that is, it increases by four units). The slope of this line is the ratio −2/4 = −1/2. A downward-sloping line like this one is said to have a negative slope.

The slope of a curved line, unlike that of a straight one, varies from one point to the next. The slope of a curve at any given point is defined as the slope of a straight line drawn tangent to the curve at that point. (A tangent line is one that just touches the curve without crossing it.) Look at

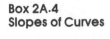
**Box 2A·4
Slopes of Curves**

The slope of a curve at any given point is defined as the slope of a straight line drawn tangent to the curve at that point. A tangent line is one that just touches the curve without crossing it. In this exhibit the slope of the curve at Point A is 1, and the slope of the curve at Point B is −2.

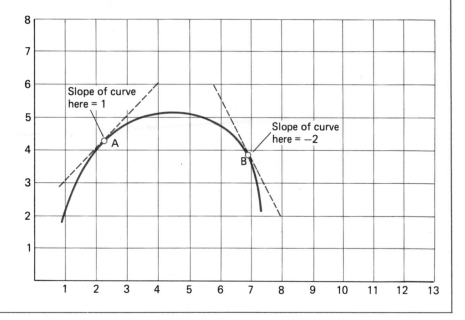

the curve in Box 2A.4. The slope of this line at point A is 1, and the slope at point B is −2.

Abstract Graphs

In all the examples given so far, there have been specific numbers for the x and y values. But sometimes we know only the general nature of the relationship between two magnitudes. For example, we might know that when incomes rise, people tend to increase their meat consumption. The increase is rapid at first, but at very high incomes meat consumption levels off. If we want to show a relationship like this without worrying about the exact numbers involved, we can draw a graph like the one in Box 2A.5. The vertical axis is the quantity of meat consumed per month, without any specific units. The horizontal axis is income, again without specific units. The curve, which rises rapidly at first and then levels off, shows the general nature of the relationship between income and meat consumption: When income goes up, meat consumption rises, but not in proportion to the change in income. We will use abstract graphs quite often in this book. They express general principles, in contrast to graphs with numbers on the axes, which present specific information.

Study Hints

When you come to a chapter that is full of graphs, how should you study it? The first and most important rule is not to try to memorize graphs. I have never taught economics without having at least one student come to me after failing an exam and say, "But I learned every one of those graphs!

Box 2A.5
An Abstract Graph

When we know the general form of an economic relationship but do not know the exact numbers involved, we can draw an abstract graph. Here we know that as people's incomes rise, their consumption of meat increases rapidly at first, then levels off. Because we do not know the exact numbers for meat consumption or income, we have not marked any units on the axes.

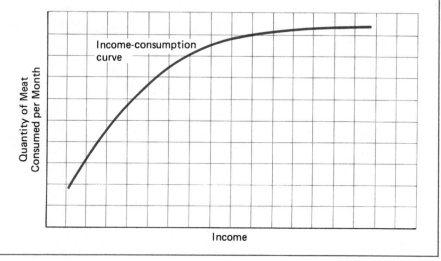

What happened?" I always tell them that they should have learned economics instead of memorizing graphs.

Here are some hints for working with graphs: After reading through a chapter that uses several graphs, go back through the graphs one at a time. Cover the note beside each graph and try to put what the graph says into words. If you cannot say as much about the graph as the note does, read the text again.

If you do all right going from graphs to words, half the battle is won. Next, cover each graph and use the note as a guide. Try to sketch the graph on a piece of scratch paper. If you understand what the words mean and can go back and forth between the words and the graphs, you will find that the two together are much easier to remember than either would be separately.

Making Your Own Graphs

For some students, the hardest kind of test question to answer is the kind that requires an original graph as part of an essay. Here are some hints for making your own graphs:

1. Write down the answer to the question in words. If you cannot do that, you might as well skip to the next question. Underline the most important quantities in what you have written. The result might be something like "The larger the *number of students* who attend a college, the lower the *cost per student* of providing them with an education."
2. Decide how you want to label the axes of your graph. In our example (Box 2A.6) we label the vertical axis "cost per student" and the horizontal axis "number of students."

Box 2A·6
Constructing a graph

To construct a graph, first put down in words what you want to say: "The larger the *number of students* at a university, the lower the *cost per student* of providing them with an education." Next label the coordinate axes. Then, if you have exact numbers to work with, construct a table. Here we have no exact numbers, so we draw an abstract graph that slopes downward to show that cost goes down as numbers of students go up. For graphs with more than one curve, repeat these steps.

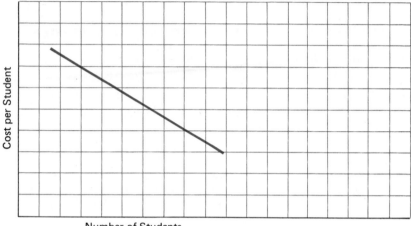

Cost per Student

Number of Students

3. Do you have exact numbers to work with? If so, the next step is to make up a table showing what you know and use it to sketch your graph. If you do not have numbers, you will draw an abstract graph. In this case, all you know is that the cost per student goes down when the number of students goes up. Sketch in a downward-sloping line like the one in Box 2A.6.

4. If your graph involves more than one relationship between quantities, repeat steps 1–3 for each relationship you want to show. When making up a graph with more than one curve, pay special attention to points where you think two curves ought to intersect. (This happens whenever the x and y values of the two relationships are equal.) Also pay attention to points where you think two curves ought to be tangent (which will happen whenever the slopes of two curves are equal at the point where they touch).

5. When your graph is finished, try to translate it back into words. Does it really say what you want it to say?

A Reminder

As you read this book and are introduced to various kinds of graphs, turn back to this appendix now and then. Do not memorize graphs as meaningless pictures; if you do, you are lost. If you can go back and forth between graphs and words, the underlying point that both are trying to make will be clearer than if you rely on either graphs or words alone. Remember that economics is about people and the ways they deal with the challenge of scarcity; it is not about graphs.

Chapter 3

Supply and Demand

After reading this chapter, you should be able to

1. State the *law of demand*, and explain the condition "other things being equal."
2. Draw a *demand curve*, given data on the relationship between price and quantity demanded.
3. Illustrate movements along a demand curve and shifts in a demand curve, and explain the causes of each.
4. Draw a *supply curve*, given data on the relationship between price and quantity supplied, and explain why supply curves usually slope up.
5. Illustrate movements along a supply curve and shifts in a supply curve, and explain the causes of each.
6. Explain how supply and demand interact to produce an *equilibrium* in each market.
7. Apply supply-and-demand analysis to situations in which economic conditions are changing. Also apply it to price floors and ceilings.

Ideas for Review

Here are some terms and concepts that you should review before you read this chapter:

Markets and their functions (Chapter 1)
Real and nominal values (Chapter 1)
Opportunity cost (Chapter 2)

"People who don't have the real thing pretend their fakes are real, and people like me pretend the real is fake."

Marylou Whitney—Mrs. Cornelius Vanderbilt Whitney—is well aware that there are a lot of fake diamonds around these days. She wears them much of the time.

"I'm delighted with fake jewelry," says Whitney, who can certainly afford the real thing. She explains: "I would like to wear real, but it isn't safe." And when she does wear real, she says, she passes it off as fake, saying that she is amused "that people who don't have the real thing pretend their fakes are real, and people like me pretend the real is fake."

Marylou Whitney's fakes and many others are CZs, made from a substance called cubic zirconia. CZs have about the same refractive index (brilliance) as diamonds and more light-dispersion (fire) than the real thing. They can be very convincing. In 1983 reporter John Stossel of the TV show "20/20" embarrassed the jewelry industry by taking a CZ and a $50,000 diamond to New York's jewelers' row. Half the jewelers he visited thought the CZ was a diamond.

But there is one big difference between diamonds and CZs: price. CZs sell for $15 to $150 a carat, compared to $2,000 to $20,000 a carat for diamonds. Why? Supply and demand, of course. About 200 million carats of CZs are made every year, compared to about 9 million carats of jewelry-quality diamonds. And although CZs are pretty, there is no demand for them for nonjewelry uses. CZs are too soft to make cutting tools, and they are no help in laser technology. So if you want to sparkle like a Whitney, CZs could be your best friend.[1]

Prices and markets, we have seen, play a key role in deciding what gets produced, how it is produced, who produces it, and who consumes it. In this chapter we look more closely at the way markets work—at how supply and demand affect the prices of wheat, milk, dental services, air travel, diamonds, CZs, and just about everything else.

The concepts of supply and demand are nothing new. For as long as there have been markets, sellers have known that one way to get people to buy more of a product is to offer it at a lower price. At the same time, buyers have long known that one way to get more of the things they want is to offer more for them. Only in the past hundred years, though, have economists used these concepts in a systematic way. In the English-speaking world, much of the credit for showing how useful they can be goes to Alfred Marshall. (See Box 3.1.) This chapter builds on Marshall's work.

DEMAND

Law of demand
The principle that, other things being equal, the quantity of a good demanded by buyers tends to rise as the price of the good falls, and to fall as the price of the good rises.

We can begin with a formal statement of the **law of demand**: In any market, other things being equal, the quantity of a good demanded by buyers tends to rise as the price of the good falls, and to fall as the price rises.

---

[1]Joan Kron, "If Diamonds Can Be a Girl's Best Friend, CZs Are Good Pals," *Wall Street Journal*, June 15, 1984, p. 1. Reprinted by permission of The Wall Street Journal, © Dow Jones & Company, Inc. 1984. All rights reserved.

**Box 3.1
Alfred Marshall on
Supply and Demand**

**Alfred Marshall
(1842–1924)**

The work of Alfred Marshall is a watershed between the classical economics of Adam Smith and the modern or neoclassical school that dominates the field today. Unlike Smith, who came to economics from philosophy, Marshall came from mathematics. Although historians sometimes refer to the "Marshallian revolution" in economic thought, Marshall did not see himself as a revolutionary. Instead, he viewed his work as strengthening classical economics through the use of mathematics.

Marshall is best known for his emphasis on supply and demand. In the second edition of his *Principles of Economics,* he wrote:

> *In spite of a great variety in detail, nearly all the chief problems of economics agree in that they have a kernel of the same kind. This kernel is an inquiry as to the balancing of two opposed classes of motives, the one consisting of desires to acquire certain new goods, and thus satisfy wants; while the other consists of desires to avoid certain efforts or retain certain immediate enjoyment. . . . In other words, it is an inquiry into the balancing of the forces of supply and demand.*

We expect this to happen for two reasons. First, if the price of one good falls while the prices of other goods stay the same, people are likely to substitute the cheaper good for goods that they would have bought instead. (When chicken is on sale and beef is not, people have chicken for dinner more often.) Second, when the price of one good falls while incomes and other prices stay the same, people feel a little richer. They use their added buying power to buy a little more of many things, including a little more of the good whose price went down. In many cases, as we will see, these two factors act together to boost the sales of goods whose prices fall and to cut sales of goods whose prices rise.

Behind the Law of Demand

The main difference between the commonsense version of the law of demand and the economist's version is the care with which it is stated. Three points that lie behind the economist's version are worth noting.

Quantity demanded   First, it is important to understand what is meant by *quantity demanded.* This is the quantity that buyers plan to buy and are able to buy over a given period, such as month or a year. Quantity demanded is not the same thing as want or need. I might *want* a Porsche, but the sticker price, last time I checked, was over $40,000. At that price I do not plan to buy one. The quantity I demand at the going price is zero. I might *need* dental surgery to avoid losing my teeth, but suppose I am poor. If I cannot pay for the surgery, and if no one is willing to pay in my place, I am out of luck. The quantity of dental surgery I demand is zero, however great my need.

Other things being equal   Second, why is the phrase *other things being equal* part of the law of demand? The reason is that a change in the price of a product is only one of a number of things that affect the quantity people plan to buy. If real incomes go up, people are likely to buy more of many goods even though their prices do not go down. If tastes change, people will buy more of some goods and less of others, even if prices do not change. Other factors can affect demand even when prices remain fixed. We will look at several of these.

Relative prices   Above all, "other things being equal" means that the prices of other goods are assumed to remain the same as buyers respond to a change in the price of a good. As economists put it, *relative prices* are what count.

It is important to distinguish between changes in relative prices and changes in nominal prices—the number of dollars actually paid per unit—during periods of inflation. If the price of eggs goes up 10 percent at the same time that consumers' nominal incomes and the prices of all other goods also go up 10 percent, we should not expect any change in the quantity of eggs demanded. The law of supply and demand does not apply to this situation because other things are not equal as the price of eggs climbs.

In fact, during a period of inflation the relative price of a good may fall even though its nominal price is going up. Box 3.2 gives a striking example. From 1974 to 1978, the nominal price of gasoline rose, but not as fast as the rate of inflation. People responded to the lower relative price of gasoline by buying more. In 1979 and 1980, the nominal price of gasoline went up faster than the prices of other goods. People responded to the increase in the relative price by buying less.

The Demand Curve

The law of demand states a relationship between the quantity of a good that people intend to buy, other things being equal, and the price of that good. This one-to-one relationship can be shown in a table or a graph, as is done in Box 3.3. Look first at the table. The first line of the table shows that when the price of wheat is $6.40 a bushel, the quantity demanded per year is 1.4 billion bushels. Reading down the table, we see that as the price falls, the quantity demanded rises. At $6 per bushel, buyers plan to purchase 1.5 billion bushels per year; at $5.60, they plan to buy 1.6 billion bushels; and so on.

Demand curve
A graphic representation of the relationship between the price of a good and the quantity of it demanded by buyers.

Box 3.3 also presents the same information in graphic form. The graph is called a **demand curve** for wheat. Suppose we want to use the demand curve to find out what quantity of wheat will be demanded when the price is $4 per bushel. Starting at $4 on the vertical axis, we move across, as shown by the arrow, until we reach the demand curve at point A. We then drop down to the horizontal axis, again following the arrow. Reading from the scale on that axis, we see that the quantity demanded at a price of $4 per bushel is 2 billion bushels per year. This is the quantity demanded in line A of the table.

Movements Along the Demand Curve

The effect of a change in the price of wheat, other things being equal, can be shown as a movement along the demand curve for wheat. Suppose the price drops from $4 per bushel to $2 per bushel. As the price falls, the quantity that buyers plan to buy rises. This moves the quantity demanded along the demand curve to point B, which corresponds to line B in the table.

Box 3.2
Demand and the Price of Motor Fuel

The law of demand assumes that the prices of other goods remain unchanged. During a period of inflation, when prices are rising, it is important to distinguish between changes in nominal prices (the number of dollars actually paid for the good) and changes in relative prices (the price of the good compared to other prices). As this chart shows, from 1974 to 1978 the nominal price of motor fuel rose, but not as fast as the average of all prices. This produced a fall in the relative price of motor fuel. Consumers reacted by buying more motor fuel. In 1979 and 1980 the nominal price rose faster than the prices of other goods, resulting in an increase in the relative price. In these years sales of motor fuel fell.

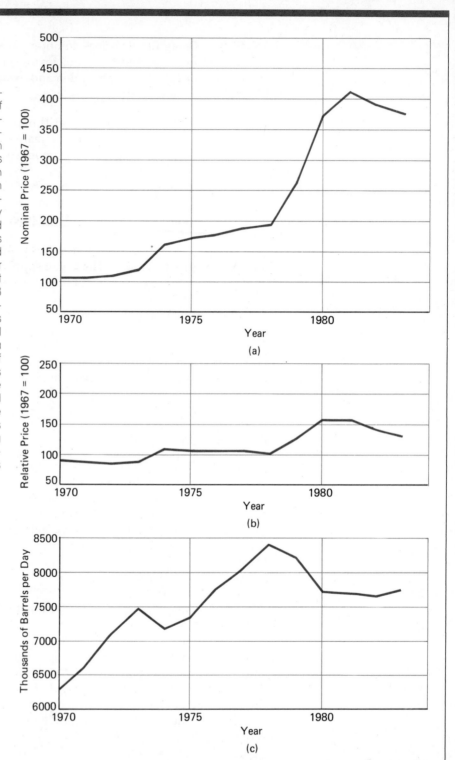

Source: For prices, *Economic Report of the President* (Washington, D.C.: Government Printing Office, 1984), Tables B–53, B–54; for motor fuel use, U.S. Department of Energy, Energy Information Agency, *Annual Energy Review*, (Washington, D.C.: Government Printing Office, 1984), Table 49. The nominal price is given as an index, with 1967 equal to 100. The relative price is the ratio of the motor fuel price index to the index of all consumer prices less energy; again, 1967 is equal to 100.

Box 3.3
A Demand Curve for
Wheat

Both the table and the chart show the quantity of wheat demanded at various prices. For example, at a price of $4 per bushel buyers are willing and able to purchase 2 billion bushels of wheat per year. This price-quantity combination is shown by line A of the table and point A of the graph.

(a)

Price of Wheat (dollars per bushel)	Quantity of Wheat Demanded (billions of bushels per year)
$6.40	1.4
6.00	1.5
5.60	1.6
5.20	1.7
4.80	1.8
4.40	1.9
A 4.00	2.0
3.60	2.1
3.20	2.2
2.80	2.3
2.40	2.4
B 2.00	2.5
1.60	2.6

(b)

Change in quantity demanded
A change in the quantity buyers are willing and able to purchase that results from a change in the price of the good, other things being equal; a movement along a demand curve.

Economists speak of a movement along a demand curve as a **change in quantity demanded**. This refers to the effect of a change in the price of the good in question, other things being equal.

Shifts in the Demand Curve

Demand curves like the one in Box 3.3 are always drawn on an "other things being equal" basis. They assume that as the price of wheat changes, other factors, such as the incomes of consumers, consumer tastes, and the prices of other goods, do not change. If any of these other factors changes, we have to draw a new demand curve. The new curve, like the old one, will slope downward, following the law of demand, but it will be shifted to the right or the left.

Change in demand
A change in the quantity buyers are willing and able to purchase that results from a change in some factor other than the price of the good; a shift in the demand curve.

Economists speak of a shift in the demand curve that is produced by a change in an economic factor other than price of that good as a **change in demand**. Several sources of changes in demand are worth looking at.

Changes in consumer income   One of the key factors affecting the demand for a good is consumer income. If income rises, people tend to buy larger quantities of many goods, assuming that their prices do not change.

Box 3.4 shows the effect of a rise in consumer income on the demand for wheat. Demand curve D_1 in this figure is the same as that shown in Box 3.3. According to this curve, the quantity demanded at a price of $4 is 2

**Box 3.4
Effect of an Increase in
Consumer Income on
the Demand for Wheat**

Demand curve D_1 in this graph is the same as the demand curve shown in Box 3.3. It assumes some given level of consumer income. If their income changes, other things being equal, consumers will want to buy more wheat-based foods at any given price. This will shift the demand curve to the right, to, say, D_2. At $4 per bushel, the quantity demanded will be 3 billion bushels (B) rather than 2 billion (A); at $2 per bushel, the quantity demanded will be 3.5 billion bushels (D) instead of 2.5 billion (C); and so on.

billion bushels and the quantity demanded at $2 is 2.5 billion bushels. Consumer income was one of the items covered by the "other things being equal" clause when this demand curve was drawn.

Suppose, however, that consumer income throughout the world rises. With higher income, people will want to buy more wheat-based foods than before at any given price. The greater demand for wheat-based foods will mean greater demand for wheat in the form of grain. Suppose that buyers of wheat are now willing to buy 3 billion bushels of wheat instead of 2 billion at a price of $4. This change is shown as a move from point A to point B in Box 3.4. Given the new, higher income, even more wheat would be bought if the price were $2. Instead of 2.5 billion bushels, as shown by D_1, buyers might now plan to purchase 3.5 billion bushels. This corresponds to a move from point C to point D.

In both cases the effects of a change in consumer income, at a given price, are shown by a movement off the original demand curve, D_1. Points B and D are on a new demand curve, D_2. We say that the increase in income has *shifted* the demand curve for wheat to the right. What if the price of wheat changes while income remains at the higher level? If this happens, the effects are shown as movements along the new demand curve.

In sum, there is a demand curve for each possible income level. Each of these demand curves represents a one-to-one relationship between price and quantity demanded, *given* the assumed level of income.

Normal and inferior goods   In the example just given, we assumed that an increase in income would cause an increase in the demand for wheat. Experience shows that this is what normally happens. Economists therefore call wheat a **normal good,** which means that when consumer incomes rise, other things being equal, people will buy more of it.

There are some goods, however, that people will buy less of if their incomes rise, other things being equal. When their incomes rise, people tend to buy less flour; they buy more baked goods instead. They tend to buy fewer shoe-repair services; instead, they buy new shoes. And they tend to ride intercity buses less, since they would rather fly or drive. Goods like flour, shoe-repair services, and intercity bus travel are called **inferior goods.** When consumer incomes rise, the demand curve for an inferior good shifts to the left instead of to the right.

Changes in the Prices of Other Goods

The demand for a good may be affected by changes in the prices of related goods as well as by changes in incomes. Look at Box 3.5, which shows

Normal good
A good for which an increase in consumer income results in an increase in demand.

Inferior good
A good for which an increase in consumer income results in a decrease in demand.

**Box 3.5
Effects of an Increase in the Price of Lettuce on the Demand for Cabbage**

An increase in the price of lettuce from 69 cents to 99 cents per pound, other things being equal, results in an upward movement along the lettuce demand curve from point A to point B. This is called a decrease in the quantity of lettuce demanded. With the price of cabbage unchanged at 49 cents per pound, consumers will substitute cabbage for lettuce. This will cause an increase in the demand for cabbage, which is shown as a shift in the cabbage demand curve from D_1 to D_2.

(a)

(b)

demand curves for lettuce and cabbage. Either can be used to make salad. People's decisions about whether to eat tossed salad or cole slaw depend on many things, including the prices of lettuce and cabbage.

Suppose that the price of lettuce starts out at 69 cents a pound and then rises to 99 cents a pound. The effect of this change is shown in the lefthand figure as a movement along the lettuce demand curve from point A to point B. With the price of lettuce higher than before, consumers will tend to buy more cabbage than they otherwise would have. Suppose the price of cabbage is 49 cents a pound. Before the price of lettuce went up, consumers would have bought 20 million pounds of cabbage a week (point A' on the cabbage demand curve D_1). After the price of lettuce has gone up, they will buy 26 million pounds of cabbage a week at the same price (point B' on the cabbage demand curve D_2).

In sum, an increase in the price of lettuce causes a *movement along* the lettuce demand curve and, at the same time, a *shift* in the cabbage demand curve.

Substitute goods
A pair of goods for which an increase in the price of one causes an increase in demand for the other.

Substitutes and complements   People tend to buy more cabbage when the price of lettuce goes up because they use it to replace lettuce in their salads. Economists say that such pairs of goods are **substitutes** because an increase in the price of one causes an increase in the demand for the other—a rightward shift in the demand curve. Consumers react differently to price changes when two goods tend to be used together. Tires and gasoline are an example. When the price of gasoline goes up, people drive less, so they buy fewer tires even if there is no change in the price of tires. An increase in the price of gasoline thus causes a movement along the gasoline demand curve; at the same time, it causes a leftward shift in the demand curve for tires. Pairs of goods that are related in this way are known as **complements**.

Complementary goods
A pair of goods for which an increase in the price of one results in a decrease in demand for the other.

Changes in expectations   Changes in buyers' expectations are a third factor that can shift demand curves. If people expect the price of a good to rise relative to the prices of other goods, they are likely to increase their purchases right away, before the price actually goes up. In late 1979, for example, news reports of a peanut crop failure caused people to expect an increase in the price of peanut butter. Many people reacted by stocking up on peanut butter before the price rose.

The graph in Box 3.6 portrays these events. D_1 is the normal demand curve for peanut butter. At a price of 99 cents a jar, consumer demand is assumed to be 20 million jars per week (point A). When they hear the news of the crop failure, consumers step up their purchases to 30 million jars per week. This is shown as a move off demand curve D_1 to point B on a new, temporary demand curve, D_2. Later the price of peanut butter does in fact rise to $2.99. If the price stays at the higher level, people will become used to it. The temporary demand curve will no longer apply, and they will end up at point C on their normal demand curve.

Changes in tastes   Changes in tastes are a fourth source of changes in demand. Sometimes these happen fast; this is the case, for example, in such areas as popular music, clothing styles, or nightclubs. The demand curves for these goods and services shift often. In other cases, changes in tastes

**Box 3.6
Effects of an Expected
Price Increase on the
Demand for Peanut
Butter**

In this graph D_1 shows the normal demand for peanut butter. Starting from a price of 99 cents per jar, consumers are told to expect a price increase. In order to beat the increase, they increase their consumption of peanut butter from point A to point B. This causes a shift in the demand curve to D_2. If the price increases to $2.99 and is expected to remain there, consumers will return to the original demand curve, but they will choose point C on that curve rather than point A.

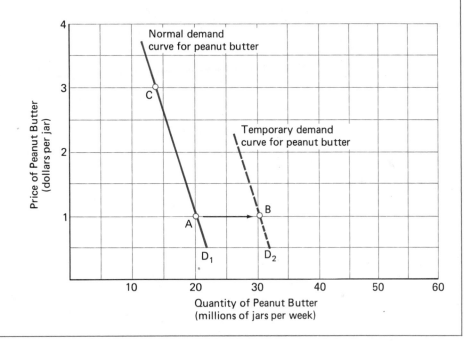

take longer to occur but are more permanent. For example, for many years consumers have been more health conscious than they tended to be in the past; as a result, they have reduced their demand for high-cholesterol foods like butter, eggs, and whole milk. This trend away from dairy products is shown in Box 3.7 as a leftward shift in the demand curve.

SUPPLY

Supply curve
A graphic representation of the relationship between the price of a good and the quantity of it supplied.

We turn now from the demand side of the market to the supply side. As in the case of demand, we can construct a one-to-one relationship between the price of a good and the quantity of it that sellers intend to offer for sale, given the market conditions they expect.

Box 3.8 shows a **supply curve** for wheat. Like demand curves, supply curves are based on an "other things being equal" condition. The supply curve for wheat shows how sellers change their plans in response to a change in the price of wheat, assuming that there are no changes in the prices of other goods, in production techniques, in the prices of inputs, or in any other relevant factors.

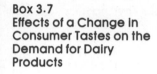

Box 3.7
Effects of a Change in
Consumer Tastes on the
Demand for Dairy
Products

A change in consumer tastes can cause a shift in the demand curve for a good. For example, during the 1970s consumers became wary of high levels of cholesterol in their diets. As a result, they decreased their demand for dairy products. In this graph the decrease in demand is shown as a shift in the demand curve from D_1 to D_2.

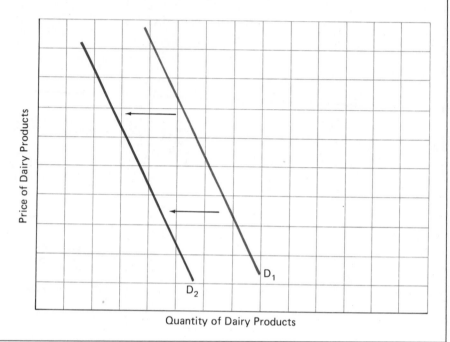

The Slope of the Supply Curve

Why does the supply curve have an upward slope? Why, that is, do sellers, other things being equal, plan to supply more wheat to the market at higher prices than at lower prices? In your study of microeconomics, you will look at the reasoning behind the upward-sloping supply curve in detail, but we can give a commonsense explanation here.

Incentives for increased production   Part of the reason for the upward slope of the supply curve has to do with incentives for producing more. When the price of wheat goes up, other things being equal, farmers have an incentive to put more time and energy into growing wheat. They may decide to substitute wheat for other crops. They may also decide to put more labor, capital, and natural resources into growing wheat. It is possible that some farmers will enter the wheat market for the first time. In short, just as we saw in Chapter 1, the higher price of wheat not only provides farmers with a key piece of information but also gives them an incentive to act on it.

Limits to increased production   Incentives explain why a higher price tends to call forth an increased supply, but what limits the increase? The answer is cost. In Chapter 2 we used the production possibility frontier to explain the concept of opportunity cost. As long as a production possibility

**Box 3.8
A Supply Curve for
Wheat**

Both the table and the graph in this box show the quantity of wheat supplied at various prices. As the price rises, other things being equal, the quantity supplied increases. The higher price gives farmers an incentive to grow more wheat, but the rising cost of growing additional wheat limits the supply produced in response to any given increase in price.

(a)

Price of Wheat (dollars per bushel)	Quantity of Wheat Supplied (billions of bushels per year)
$6.40	2.6
6.00	2.5
5.60	2.4
5.20	2.3
4.80	2.2
4.40	2.1
A 4.00	2.0
3.60	1.9
3.20	1.8
2.80	1.7
2.40	1.6
B 2.00	1.5
1.60	1.4

(b)

frontier is curved outward, as is normally the case, the opportunity cost of producing any good tends to increase as more of the good is produced. (Recall the example of Crusoe's fishing and hunting, set out in Box 2.1, p. 25.) The same is true of wheat: the more wheat produced, the greater the opportunity cost of producing more.

It is not hard to see why the opportunity cost of producing an added bushel of wheat should rise as the quantity supplied rises. Suppose first that farmers try to grow more wheat without using any more land. By using more machinery, labor, and fertilizer, they can increase yields per acre somewhat. Soon, however, a point of "diminishing returns" is reached. Beyond this point each added unit of input yields a smaller and smaller addition to total output. And what if the amount of land available for growing wheat is not fixed? We still expect the opportunity cost of wheat to rise as output expands. The reason is that farmers tend to plant each crop on the type of land that is best suited to it. New land brought into wheat production is likely to be less suitable for wheat, compared to other crops, than land that is already being used for wheat. This means that the cost of production on the new land will be higher.

Given higher costs, farmers will increase their wheat output in response to higher wheat prices only up to the point at which the cost of producing another bushel catches up with the price at which it can be sold. Beyond some point, then, cost puts a limit on increases in supply. The result is an upward-sloping supply curve.

Change in quantity supplied
A change in the quantity producers are willing and able to sell that results from a change in the price of the good, other things being equal; a movement along a supply curve.

Change in supply
A change in the quantity producers are willing and able to sell that results from a change in some factor other than the price of the good; a shift in the supply curve.

Shifts in the Supply Curve

As in the case of demand, the effects of a change in the price of wheat, other things being equal, can be shown as a movement along the supply curve for wheat. This is called a **change in quantity supplied**. A change in some factor other than the price of wheat can be shown as a shift in the supply curve. This is referred to as a **change in supply**. Four sources of change in supply are worth noting.

Technological change   A supply curve is drawn on the basis of a particular production technique. If a technological change reduces costs, producers will plan to sell more of the good than before at any given price. Box 3.9 shows how such an event would affect the wheat supply curve. Supply curve S_1 is the same as the one shown in Box 3.8. According to S_1, farmers will plan to supply 2 billion bushels per year at a price of $4 per bushel (point A).

Now suppose that new farming techniques reduce the cost of growing wheat. Using the new techniques, farmers will be willing to supply more wheat than before at any given price. They may, for example, be willing to supply 2.6 billion bushels of wheat at $4 per bushel (point B). The move from A to B is part of a shift in the whole supply curve from S_1 to S_2. Once

**Box 3.9
Shifts in the Supply
Curve for Wheat**

Several kinds of changes can cause the supply of wheat to increase or decrease. For example, a new production method that lowers costs will shift the curve to the right, from S_1 to S_2. An increase in the price of inputs, other things being equal, will shift the curve to the left, from S_1 to S_3. Changes in sellers' expectations or in the prices of competing goods can also cause the supply curve to shift.

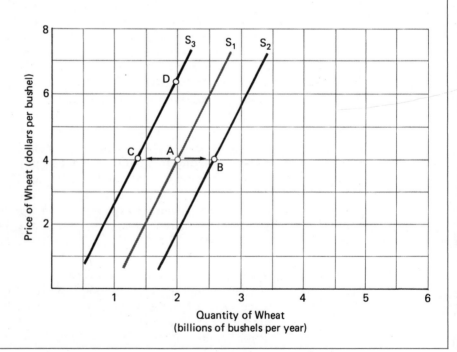

the new techniques are established, an increase or decrease in the price of wheat, other things being equal, will result in a movement along the new supply curve.

Changes in input prices   Changes in input prices are a second factor that can cause supply curves to shift. An increase in input prices, other things being equal, tends to reduce the quantity of a good that producers plan to supply at a given price. Refer again to Box 3.9. Suppose that, starting from point A on supply curve S_1, the price of tractor fuel increases. No other changes occur to offset this increase in costs. Now, instead of supplying 2 billion bushels of wheat at $4 per bushel, farmers will supply, say, just 1.4 billion bushels at that price (point C). The move from A to C is part of a leftward shift in the supply curve, from S_1 to S_3.

If the price of fuel remains at the new level, changes in the price of wheat will cause movements along the new supply curve. For example, farmers could be induced to supply the original quantity of wheat—2 billion bushels—if the price rose enough to cover the increased cost of fuel. As you can see in Box 3.9, that would require the price to rise to $6.40 per bushel (point D).

Changes in prices of other goods   Changes in the prices of other crops can also produce a shift in the wheat supply curve. Suppose that the price of corn rises while the price of wheat stays at $4. The change in the price of corn gives farmers an incentive to shift some of their land from wheat to corn. The effect of the increase in the price of corn is to raise the opportunity cost of growing wheat; each bushel of wheat grown means a certain quantity of corn not grown, but the corn is now worth more. The effect of an increase in the price of corn can thus be shown as a leftward shift in the wheat supply curve.

Changes in expectations   Changes in expectations can cause supply curves to shift, much as they cause demand curves to shift. Again we can use farming as an example. At planting time a farmer's selection of crops is influenced not so much by current prices as by the prices expected at harvest time. Long-term expectations also affect supply. Each crop requires special equipment and know-how. We have just seen that an increase in the price of corn gives farmers an incentive to shift from wheat to corn. The incentive will be stronger if the increase in the price of corn is expected to be long lasting. If it is, farmers are more likely to buy the special equipment needed for growing corn.

THE INTERACTION OF SUPPLY AND DEMAND

As we have seen, markets transmit information, in the form of prices, to people who buy and sell goods. Taking these prices into account, along with other knowledge they might have, the buyers and sellers make their plans. As shown by the demand and supply curves, buyers and sellers plan to buy or sell certain quantities at any given price.

In each market, many buyers and sellers make different plans. When they meet to trade, some of them may be unable to carry out their plans.

Perhaps the total quantity that buyers plan to purchase is greater than the total quantity that suppliers are willing to sell at the given price. In that case some of the would-be buyers must change their plans. Or perhaps planned sales exceed planned purchases. In that case some would-be sellers will be unable to carry out their plans.

Sometimes no one is disappointed. The total quantity that buyers plan to purchase exactly matches the total quantity that producers plan to sell. When the plans of buyers and sellers exactly match when they meet in the marketplace, no one needs to change plans. Under these conditions the market is said to be in **equilibrium**.

Equilibrium
A condition in which the plans of buyers and sellers exactly match in the marketplace, so that the quantity supplied exactly equals the quantity demanded at a given price.

Market Equilibrium

Supply and demand curves, which reflect the plans of sellers and buyers, can be used to give a graphic picture of market equilibrium. Box 3.10 uses the same supply and demand curves that we have seen before, but this time they are both drawn on the same diagram. If the quantity of planned sales at each price is compared with the quantity of planned purchases at that price—either the table or the graph can be used to make the comparison—it can be seen that there is only one price at which the two sets of plans match. This price—$4 per bushel—is the equilibrium price. If all buyers and sellers make their plans in the expectation of a price of $4, no one will be disappointed and no plans will have to be changed.

Shortages

But what will happen if, for some reason, buyers and sellers expect the price of wheat to be something other than $4 a bushel? Suppose, for example, that they base their plans on an expected price of $2. Box 3.10 shows that at a price of $2, buyers will plan to purchase wheat at a rate of 2.5 billion bushels per year. Farmers, however, will plan to supply only 1.5 billion bushels. When the quantity demanded exceeds the quantity supplied, as in this example, the difference is an **excess quantity demanded** or, more simply, a **shortage**. In Box 3.10 the shortage is 1 billion bushels of wheat per year when the price is $2 per bushel.

Excess quantity demanded (shortage)
A condition in which the quantity of a good demanded at a given price exceeds the quantity supplied.

Inventory
Stocks of a finished good awaiting sale or use.

Shortages and inventories   In most markets, the first sign of a shortage is a drop in **inventories**, that is, in stocks of the good that have been produced and are waiting to be sold or used. Sellers plan to hold a certain quantity of goods in inventory to allow for minor changes in demand. When they see inventories dropping below the planned level, they change their plans. Some may try to rebuild their inventories by increasing their output. Some may take advantage of the strong demand for their product to raise its price. Many sellers will do a little of both. If sellers do not take the initiative, buyers will do so—they will offer to pay more if the seller will supply more. Whatever the details, the result will be an upward movement along the supply curve as price and quantity increase.

As the shortage puts upward pressure on price, buyers will change their plans too. Moving up and to the left along their demand curve, they will cut back on their planned purchases. As both buyers and sellers move in the direction of the arrows shown in Box 3.10, the market moves toward

**Box 3.10
Equilibrium in the
Wheat Market**

The graph and table in this box show the same supply and demand curves for wheat that have been shown several times before. The demand curve shows how much buyers plan to purchase at a given price. The supply curve shows how much producers plan to sell at a given price. At only one price, $4 per bushel, do the plans of buyers and sellers exactly match. That price is the equilibrium price. A higher price causes a surplus of wheat and puts downward pressure on price. A lower price causes a shortage and puts upward pressure on price.

(a)

(b)

Price per Bushel (1)	Quantity Supplied (billions of bushels) (2)	Quantity Demanded (billions of bushels) (3)	Shortage (billions of bushels) (4)	Surplus (billions of bushels) (5)	Direction of Pressure on Price (6)
$6.40	2.6	1.4	—	1.2	Downward
6.00	2.5	1.5	—	1.0	Downward
5.60	2.4	1.6	—	0.8	Downward
5.20	2.3	1.7	—	0.6	Downward
4.80	2.2	1.8	—	0.4	Downward
4.40	2.1	1.9	—	0.2	Downward
4.00	2.0	2.0	—	—	Equilibrium
3.60	1.9	2.1	0.2	—	Upward
3.20	1.8	2.2	0.4	—	Upward
2.80	1.7	2.3	0.6	—	Upward
2.40	1.6	2.4	0.8	—	Upward
2.00	1.5	2.5	1.0	—	Upward
1.60	1.4	2.6	1.2	—	Upward

equilibrium. When the price reaches $4 per bushel, both the shortage and the pressure to change plans will disappear.

Shortages and queues   In the markets for most goods, sellers have inventories of goods ready to be sold. There are exceptions, however. Inventories are not possible in markets for services—haircuts, tax preparation, lawn care, and the like. Also, some custom-made products, such as houses and specialized machine tools, are not held in inventories. Sellers in these markets do not begin production until they have a contract with a buyer.

In markets where there are no inventories, the sign of a shortage is a "queue" of buyers. The queue may take the form of a line of people waiting to be served or a list of names in an order book. The queue is a sign that buyers would like to purchase the good at a faster rate than producers have planned to supply it. Some plans cannot be carried out, at least not right away. Buyers are served on a first-come, first-served basis.

The formation of a queue of buyers has much the same effect on the market as a fall in inventories. Sellers react by increasing their rate of output or raising their prices or both. Buyers react to the rising price by reducing the quantity they plan to purchase. The result is a movement up and to the right along the supply curve, and at the same time up and to the left along the demand curve, until equilibrium is reached.

Surpluses

Suppose instead that for some reason buyers and sellers expect the price of wheat to be higher than the equilibrium price—say, $6 per bushel. Box 3.10 shows that farmers will plan to supply 2.5 billion bushels of wheat per year at $6, but their customers will plan to buy only 1.5 billion bushels. When the quantity supplied exceeds the quantity demanded, there is an **excess quantity supplied,** or a **surplus.** As Box 3.10 shows, the surplus of wheat at a price of $6 per bushel is 1 billion bushels per year.

Excess quantity supplied (surplus)
A condition in which the quantity of a good supplied at a given price exceeds the quantity demanded.

Surpluses and inventories   When there is a surplus of a product, sellers will be disappointed. They will not be able to sell all that they had hoped to sell at the planned price. As a result, their inventories will begin to grow beyond the level they had planned to hold in preparation for normal changes in demand.

Sellers will react to the inventory buildup by changing their plans. Some of them will cut back their output. Others will cut their prices in order to reduce their extra stock. Many will do a little of both. The result of these changes in plans will be a movement down and to the left along the supply curve, following the arrow in Box 3.10.

As unplanned inventory buildup puts downward pressure on the price, buyers change their plans too. Finding that wheat costs less than they expected, they buy more of it. This is shown as a movement down and to the right along the demand curve. As this happens, the market is brought back into equilibrium.

Surpluses and queues   In markets where there are no inventories, surpluses lead to the formation of queues of sellers looking for customers.

Taxi queues at airports are a case in point. At least at some times of the day, the fare for taxi service from the airport to downtown is more than enough to attract a number of taxis equal to the demand. In some cities drivers who are far back in the queue try to attract riders with offers of cut-rate fares. More often, though, there are rules against fare-cutting. The queue then grows until a surge of business shortens it again.

APPLICATIONS OF SUPPLY AND DEMAND

As we move through this book, we will add to the outline of supply-and-demand theory that has just been given. But even this brief version of that theory can be applied in many ways.

Many applications concern situations in which changing economic conditions produce shifts in supply and demand curves, and these shifts, in turn, affect equilibrium prices and quantities. Beginning from equilibrium, a rightward shift in the demand curve, other things being equal, moves the market to a new equilibrium at a higher price and quantity. A leftward shift in the demand curve moves the market to a new equilibrium where both the price and quantity are lower. If, instead, the supply curve shifts, the effects are different. A rightward shift in the supply curve results in a new equilibrium where the price is lower and the quantity is higher. A leftward shift in the supply curve reduces quantity and raises the price. Let's look at three examples illustrating these effects.

Changing Market Conditions: The Case of Dentists[2]

There are a lot of dentists in the United States—52 for every 100,000 people. Many of them were drawn into the profession by the dream of a BMW in the driveway and a summer house by the shore.

But dentistry is not the passport to an upper-middle-class life-style that it once was. Dentists' incomes have been rising slower than the rate of inflation for more than a decade. Since 1972 the average real income of dentists—that is, their income adjusted for inflation—has fallen about 10 percent. Many dentists in private practice say that their waiting rooms are half full. Others have given up private practice for the security, but lower pay, of jobs in dental clinics.

This sounds like a classic case of excess quantity supplied, and it is. Box 3.11 takes us back to the mid-1960s for a look at the origins of the problem. Part a of Box 3.11 shows the market for dental services in equilibrium. (The numbers and shapes of the curves in the diagram are approximate.) There were 40 dentists per 100,000 people, and there was enough demand for their services to keep them all busy. The average real income of dentists, stated in 1967 dollars, was $40,000 per year.

Then two things happened. First, the federal government decided that people were not getting adequate dental care. It therefore provided funds for the expansion of existing dental schools and the founding of new ones. This policy is portrayed in part b of the box as a rightward shift in the supply curve, from S_1 to S_2.

---

[2]This section is based on Richard Greene, "What's Good for America Isn't Necessarily Good for the Dentists," *Fortune*, August 13, 1984, pp. 79–84.

**Box 3.11
Supply and Demand for
Dental Services**

The graph in part a of this box shows the dental-services market in equilibrium. There are 40 dentists per 100,000 people, and they are earning the equivalent of $40,000 per year in 1967 dollars. Starting from this position, market conditions change. The government supports expansion of dental schools, which shifts the supply curve to S_2, as shown in part b. At the same time, better dental health reduces the demand for dental services. This is shown as a shift of the demand curve to D_2. The result is a surplus of dentists, along with downward pressure on dentists' incomes. In the long run the number of people entering the dental profession will decline, and the market will return to equilibrium.

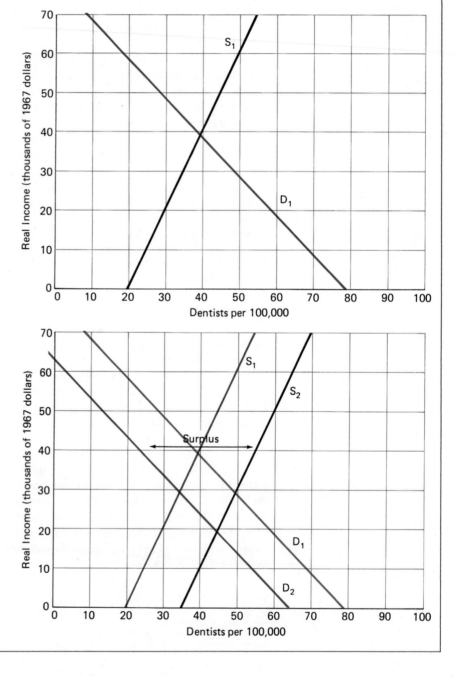

Students who are choosing a career tend to be influenced by the current earnings of people in the professions they are interested in. Expecting incomes of about $40,000 a year, enough people enrolled in dental school to raise the number of dentists per 100,000 population from 40 to 55.

The shift in supply by itself would have been enough to begin moving the market toward an equilibrium at a lower real income. But while eager dental students were planning to supply more services, things were happening on the demand side of the market too. Better dental education, better preventive dentistry, and the fluoridation of drinking water were having a dramatic impact on dental health. Between the mid-1960s and the mid-1980s, tooth decay dropped by almost 50 percent. Filling cavities had long been the bread and butter of the dental profession. Improved dental health resulted in a strong leftward shift in the demand curve for dental services, from D_1 to D_2.

By the end of the 1970s, then, a large gap had developed between the supply of dental services and the demand for them. Slowly the market began to adjust. Many dentists saw fewer patients. They hesitated to raise their fees to keep pace with inflation, so their real incomes began to fall. Some of them filled their waiting rooms with patients from prepaid dental-care plans, who pay lower fees. Others moved their offices to shopping malls. Critics called them "doc-in-a-box" dentists, but they brought convenient, inexpensive service to some patients who had not gone to dentists often before. The shopping center clinics were costly to run, however. This put further downward pressure on real incomes.

As dentists' incomes fell, students became more likely to choose other careers. Dental school enrollment peaked in 1978. Applications fell sharply. By 1985 only one dental school applicant out of five was rejected, compared with one rejection for every acceptance for medical schools. But being a dentist is a lifetime commitment for most people. A market like the one for wheat moves quickly from one equilibrium to another, but the dental-service market will take years to adjust. Meanwhile the BMWs in dentists' driveways are being replaced by Fords, and weekends in a tent are taking the place of houses by the shore.

Price Restrictions: The Dairy Industry[3]

Like the market for dental services, the market for milk has faced a surplus in recent years. This surplus can be explained in part by changes in supply and demand. Changing tastes have caused consumers to drink less milk: between 1960 and 1982, annual milk consumption per person dropped from 302 to 242 pounds. At the same time, high rates of production put upward pressure on supply. Over the 22-year period, milk output per cow rose from 6,000 pounds to 12,000 pounds per year.

According to the law of supply and demand, these events should have resulted in lower prices for consumers. But they did not. Federal price

---

[3]This section is based in part on Brooks Jackson, "Dairy Lobby Obtains U.S. Subsidies with Help from Urban Legislators," *Wall Street Journal*, November 18, 1983, p. 33, and Albert R. Karr, "Government Program to Cut Milk Surplus Isn't Meeting Goal," *Wall Street Journal*, 16, 1984, p. 1.

supports for milk kept the wholesale price, adjusted for inflation, almost unchanged. The result is shown in Box 3.12. If the market had been in equilibrium at the point where the demand curve meets the supply curve S_1, the price of milk would have been $10 per hundred pounds. Instead, federal price supports kept the price at about $13 per hundred pounds, thereby creating a surplus of some 20 billion pounds of milk per year. The surplus milk was bought by the government, converted into cheese and other products with a long shelf life, and stored. In 1983 this program cost the government $2.5 billion.

In its first years the Reagan administration tried to form a coalition of milk-using industries and consumer groups to force Congress to reduce the support price. These efforts met with only partial success. In 1983 the administration changed its tactics and decided to pay farmers not to produce milk. They encouraged farmers to sell their dairy cows for beef, offering them $10 for each hundred pounds by which they cut back their milk output. The aim was to shift the supply curve to the left. If it could be shifted all the way to S_2, the surplus would be eliminated.

The program failed. Although many farmers signed up, others made

**Box 3.12
The Effect of Price
Supports for Milk**

In recent years the demand for milk has fallen while the supply has increased. The result has been a surplus of milk. This should have caused the market to move to a new equilibrium at a price of about $10. However, a government price support program has kept the price of milk at about $13. In 1983, in an attempt to cut the cost of buying and storing the surplus milk, the government introduced a plan under which it paid dairy farmers to cut back their output of milk. It was hoped that this program would shift the supply curve to the left, to S_2. The 1983 program was only partly successful, however.

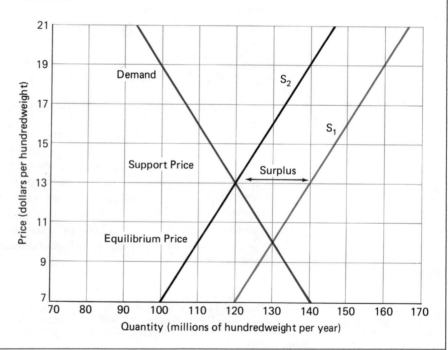

up the difference by producing even more milk than before. Output fell by less than 2 percent instead of the hoped-for 10 percent. Senator Robert Dole commented that the program was such a flop that "even the cows were laughing."

The administration and consumer groups vowed to renew the fight for cuts in the support price in 1985. But any cut faced strong opposition in a Congress where each member who voted for a high support price in 1983 received an average campaign contribution of $5,549 from dairy industry lobbyists.

Market vs. Nonmarket Rationing: Airport Congestion

After looking at two markets that have had to deal with surpluses, we turn to one that faces a shortage. This is the market for landing rights at congested airports.

Box 3.13 sets the stage. The graph represents an airport that has 40 takeoff and landing "slots" per hour. The supply curve for slots in a given hour is vertical because, at least in the short run, there is no safe way to let more planes land or take off. (In the long run, runway expansion or improved air traffic control could increase the number of slots.)

Box 3.13
The Market for Takeoff and Landing Slots

Safety factors limit traffic at major airports during peak periods. In this graph the supply of takeoff and landing slots is assumed to be limited to 40 per hour. If no price is charged, the demand for slots falls short of the supply during off-peak hours (D_1), but it exceeds the supply during peak hours (D_2). The result is congestion and delayed flights at peak hours. Some airlines favor a system in which the government would auction peak-period slots. In this graph, the equilibrium price for a peak-period slot would be $400.

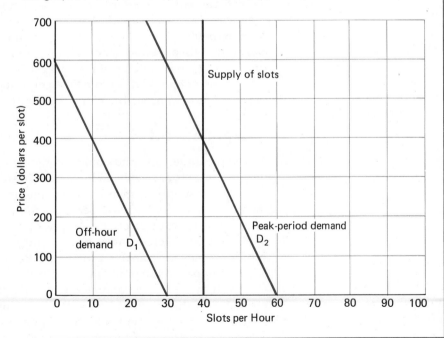

The number of slots that airlines would like to use—that is, the number of takeoffs and landings they would like to schedule per hour—depends both on the time of day and on the cost of slots. Demand curve D_1 shows the demand at a slack hour, lunchtime. Even if airlines didn't have to pay anything for the slots, they would not use the airport fully. D_2, on the other hand, shows demand at a peak hour, the end of the business day. At a zero price, airlines will schedule 60 flights per hour—more flights for that hour than the airport can handle.

Under current Federal Aviation Administration (FAA) rules, airlines do not have to pay for slots. They pay a fee to land, but the fee is the same at all times. Scheduling a flight for a peak hour does not cost anything extra.

As a booming economy boosted air travel in 1984, this policy caused an increase in delays at major airports. Travelers and airlines complained. Something needed to be done—but what? The agency held a meeting at which major airlines were pressured into dividing up the available peak-period slots. Any other flights must be scheduled for less convenient hours. But some airlines cried foul. Aggressive, low-fare airlines like PEOPLExpress saw this as a scheme to cut them out of major new markets. The meeting was so harmful to competition, in fact, that it could not even be held until the Civil Aeronautics Board, another federal agency, gave the airlines a special exemption from the antitrust laws.

What alternative did the low-fare airlines propose? They suggested that market rationing should replace nonmarket rationing. Let the FAA hold an auction of landing slots in each hour. At off-peak hours (D_1), there would not be enough demand to raise the price above zero. At peak hours (D_2), the price of slots would be bid up until the quantity demanded was equal to the supply. As Box 3.13 shows, this would happen at a price of $400 per slot.

Under this scheme, people who wanted to fly at peak hours would have to pay more in order to cover the airline's cost of buying a slot. But they would probably see a $4 surcharge for a ticket on a plane with 100 seats as better than waiting in line on the runway or flying at a less convenient time. People who did not care as much about their departure time could take advantage of lower fares for off-peak hours. To top things off, the airlines pointed out, the FAA could spend the money it collected at the auctions to improve the nation's air traffic control system.

Looking Ahead

As you continue your study of economics, you will find a great many uses for the concepts of supply and demand. In studying macroeconomics, you will see that supply, demand, and changes in inventories play key roles in the business cycle. You will see how the demand for money and other assets and the control of the supply of money by the Federal Reserve System affect interest rates, prices, and incomes. You will also apply supply-and-demand analysis to the market for labor services in order to better understand the problem of unemployment.

In studying microeconomics, you will add many details to the theory presented in this chapter. You will take a closer look at what lies behind demand curves. You will see how supply curves can be constructed for competitive markets. And you will apply supply-and-demand analysis to problems of regulation, agricultural policy, labor unions, poverty, and environmental policy. In each of these cases you will be building on the concepts discussed in this chapter.

Summary

1. According to the *law of demand*, in any market, other things being equal, the quantity of a good demanded by buyers tends to rise as the price falls, and to fall as the price rises. For any given market, the law of demand sets up a one-to-one relationship between price and quantity demanded, other things being equal. This relationship can be shown by a downward-sloping *demand curve*.

2. A movement along the demand curve, which is caused by a change in the price of the good, other things being equal, is known as a *change in quantity demanded*. A shift in the demand curve, which is caused by a change in income, the prices of other goods, tastes, or expectations, is known as a *change in demand*.

3. If an increase in income causes the demand for a good to increase, it is a *normal good*. If an increase in income causes the demand for a good to decrease, it is an *inferior good*. If an increase in the price of one good causes the demand for another good to increase, the two goods are *substitutes*. If an increase in the price of one good causes the demand for another good to decrease, the two goods are *complements*.

4. In most markets, an increase in the price of a good will increase the quantity that producers are willing to supply. This relationship can be shown as an upward-sloping supply curve. The higher price gives producers an incentive to supply more, but rising opportunity costs set a limit on the amount they will supply at any given price.

5. A movement along the supply curve, which is caused by a change in the price of the good, other things being equal, is known as a *change in quantity supplied*. A shift in the supply curve is known as a *change in supply*. Factors that can cause a shift in the supply curve include changes in production techniques, changes in the cost of inputs, changes in the price of other goods, and changes in expectations.

6. In a market with an upward-sloping supply curve and a downward-sloping demand curve, there is only one price at which the quantity that producers plan to supply will exactly match the quantity that buyers plan to purchase. This is known as the equilibrium price. If the price rises above the equilibrium, an increase in inventories or the formation of a queue of sellers will put downward pressure on the price until equilibrium is restored. If the price falls below the equilibrium, depletion of inventories or the formation of a queue of buyers will put upward pressure on the price until equilibrium is restored.

7. When economic conditions change, supply curves and demand curves can shift. Normally the price moves smoothly to a new equilibrium. However, price floors may lead to persistent surpluses and price ceilings may lead to persistent shortages.

Questions for Review

1. Define the following terms:
   law of demand
   demand curve
   change in quantity demanded
   change in demand
   normal good
   inferior good
   substitutes
   complements
   supply curve
   change in quantity supplied
   change in supply
   equilibrium
   excess quantity demanded (shortage)
   excess quantity supplied (surplus)
   inventory
2. How does the concept of demand differ from the concepts of want and need?
3. What conditions are covered by the "other things being equal" clause in the law of demand? What effect does a change in any of these conditions have on the plans of buyers?
4. What is the difference between a change in quantity demanded and a change in demand? Why is it important to distinguish between them? Does the same distinction also apply in the case of supply?
5. Give examples, other than those used in the text, of the following: normal goods, inferior goods, complements, and substitutes.
6. Using an example from agriculture or industry, explain why we normally expect the supply curve for a good to slope upward.
7. Give examples, other than those used in the text, of events that can cause a supply curve to shift.
8. How do inventories put upward or downward pressure on prices when markets are not in equilibrium? How is equilibrium restored in markets in which there are no inventories of finished goods?

Problems and Topics for Discussion

1. A vending machine company has studied the demand for soft drinks sold in cans from machines. In the firm's territory, consumers will buy about 2,000 cans of soda at a price of 50 cents on a 70-degree day. For each 5 cents by which the price is raised, the quantity sold falls by 200 cans per day. For each 5-degree rise in the temperature, the quantity sold rises by 150 cans per day. The same relationships hold for decreases in price or temperature.

   Using this information, draw a set of curves showing the demand for soft drinks on days when the temperature is 60, 70, and 85 degrees.
2. Make a sketch of the markets for CZs and diamonds. You know the approximate equilibrium price and quantity, but you must guess at the slopes of the demand and supply curves. Do you think the demand curves for these goods slope downward in the usual way? Why or why not? Do you think the supply curves slope upward? Why or why not?

   Suppose that there is a breakthrough in mining technology that lowers the cost of producing natural diamonds. Use your diagram to show what will happen in the diamond market. Will the supply curve shift? Will the demand curve shift? Will the new equilibrium price be higher or lower than the original price? What about the new equilibrium quantity? What will happen in the CZ market? Will the supply curve shift? The demand curve? Both? In which direction will the equilibrium price and quantity of CZs move?
3. Box 3.2 shows the relative price of motor fuel and the quantities sold in various years. In 1979 and 1980, the relative price of motor fuel rose sharply and, as we would expect, the quantity sold decreased. In 1981 and 1982, the

relative price leveled off and then began to fall, but the quantity sold did not increase. Instead, it continued to fall. Which one or more of the following hypotheses do you think best explains the behavior of motor fuel sales in 1981 and 1982? Illustrate each hypothesis with supply and demand curves.

a. In the 1970s the demand curve had the usual downward slope. However, in 1981 and 1982 the demand curve shifted to an unusual upward-sloping position.

b. The demand curve sloped downward throughout the period. However, the recession of 1981 and 1982 reduced consumers' real incomes and shifted the demand curve.

c. The demand curve has a downward slope at all times, but the slope depends in part on how long consumers have to adjust to a change in prices. Over a short period, the demand curve is fairly steep because few adjustments can be made. Over the long term, it has a somewhat flatter slope because further adjustments, such as buying more fuel-efficient cars or moving closer to work, can be made. Thus, the decreases in fuel sales in 1981 and 1982 were delayed reactions to the 1979 and 1980 price increases—movements along a flatter, long-run demand curve.

4. In 1974 and again in 1979, shortages in the world oil market caused long lines of motorists to form at gas stations in the United States but not in European countries. Do you think this had anything to do with the fact that the United States had price controls on gasoline but European countries did not? Back up your reasoning with supply and demand curves.

5. Turn to Box 3.11, which shows supply and demand for dental services before and after shifts in the demand and supply curves. Use the graph to answer these questions: If the supply curve remained at S_1 while the demand curve shifted to D_2, what would the new equilibrium price and quantity be? If the demand curve remained at D_1 while the supply curve shifted to S_2, what would the new equilibrium price and quantity be? In each case, describe the sequence of events leading to the new equilibrium.

6. You are a member of the Metropolitan Taxi Commission, which sets taxi fares for your city. You have been told that long lines of taxis form at the airport during off-peak hours. At rush hours, on the other hand, few taxis are available and there are long lines of passengers waiting for cabs. It is proposed that taxi fares from the airport to downtown be cut by 10 percent during off-peak hours and raised by 10 percent during rush hours. How do you think these changes would affect the queuing patterns of taxis and passengers? Do you think the proposal is a good one from the point of view of passengers? From the point of view of cabbies? From the point of view of efficiency? Discuss.

Suggestions for Further Reading

Breit, William, and Roger L. Ransom. *The Academic Scribblers*, 2nd ed. New York: Holt, Rinehart and Winston, 1982.

Chapter 3 is an essay on Alfred Marshall, the founder of supply-and-demand analysis in its modern form. Chapters 1 and 2 provide useful background.

Campbell, Colin D., ed. *Wage and Price Controls in World War II: United States and Germany.* Washington, D.C.: American Enterprise Institute, 1971.

Vivid descriptions and insightful analysis of what happens when governments overrule the law of supply and demand.

Marshall, Alfred. *Principles of Economics*, **various** editions.

First published in 1891, this book remains remarkably accessible to browsing even by beginning students.

Chapter 4

The Role of Private Business

After reading this chapter, you should be able to

1. Explain why the *sole proprietorship* is a common form of organization for small firms.
2. Discuss the advantages and disadvantages of the *partnership*.
3. Explain why most large firms are organized as *corporations*.
4. Explain the role of business firms in coordinating economic activity, and distinguish between *market* and *managerial coordination*.
5. Interpret a *balance sheet* and explain the relationships among *assets*, *liabilities*, and *networth*.
6. Show how *financial markets* link borrowers and lenders, and distinguish between *direct* and *indirect* financing.
7. Distinguish between *primary* and *secondary* financial markets, and explain how changes in interest rates affect the prices of *bonds* traded in secondary markets.
8. Discuss the issue of ownership versus control of a corporation.

Ideas for Review

Here are some terms and concepts that you should review before you read this chapter:

Markets and their functions (Chapter 1)
Entrepreneurship (Chapter 2)
Supply and demand (Chapter 3)

"I just couldn't work inside any longer."

After Tony Bullard finished high school, he went to night school and took courses in management, engineering, and machine design. Then he found a job as a management trainee at a large machine tool company. It was a good job, but it wasn't quite what he wanted. "I just couldn't work inside any longer," he says.

For a while he maintained heavy equipment for construction companies. That got him outside, but it still wasn't quite right. Finally he realized that what he really wanted was a business of his own. Zoning laws would not allow him to set up a business at his home in Connecticut, so he moved to the small mountain village of Chelsea, Vermont. Ten years later, Bullard Welding has become a fixture in central Vermont. Besides doing routine work like diesel engine repair, Bullard has solved some challenging problems. He has made special adaptations for fire truck bodies, a custom-designed machine to cut styrofoam sheets, and a unique automatic furnace that heats his shop.[1]

Tony Bullard's welding shop is a private business, part of a system that supplies some 85 percent of the total output of the U.S. economy. Private business includes huge firms like Exxon, General Motors, and IBM. But small firms like Bullard's are important too. About one person in three works for a firm with fewer than 100 employees. And small firms account for more than half of all new jobs.

Whenever we look at markets we find businesses. They appear on the supply side as producers and sellers of goods and services. On the demand side they appear as buyers of raw materials, labor, and capital goods. Clearly, then, in studying economics we need to understand how firms are organized, what they do, and who controls them.

FORMS OF BUSINESS ORGANIZATION

Business firms vary widely in terms of their size and the scope of their operations. They also differ in terms of their form of organization. In this section we will discuss the three most common types of firms—sole proprietorships, partnerships, and corporations. We will also look briefly at a few less common types.

The Sole Proprietorship

Sole proprietorship
A firm that is owned and usually operated by one person, who receives all the profits and is responsible for all of the firm's liabilities.

A **sole proprietorship** is a firm that is owned and operated by a single person, who receives all the profits from the firm and is personally responsible for all its liabilities. Sole proprietorships are very common. As Box 4.1 shows, more than three-quarters of the firms in the United States take this form. They are usually small, however. All proprietorships together account for less than 10 percent of total business receipts. Proprietorships are common in farming, construction, and wholesale and retail trade. In other sectors of the economy they are much less common.

---

[1]Based on Sandy Vondrasek, "Tony Bullard's Welding Business Just Grew Naturally," *White River Valley Herald*, March 15, 1984, p. B-1.

**Box 4.1
Forms of Business
Organization**

These charts show the distribution of firms in the United States according to form of ownership. Proprietorships are by far the most numerous. They are the main form of ownership in agriculture and are also common in retail trade and construction. However, most proprietorships are small. In terms of total receipts, they are overshadowed by corporations. The corporate sector, in turn, is dominated by the small number of firms (some 418,000 in 1980) that reported receipts of $1 million or more.

(a) Share of firms

(b) Share of sales

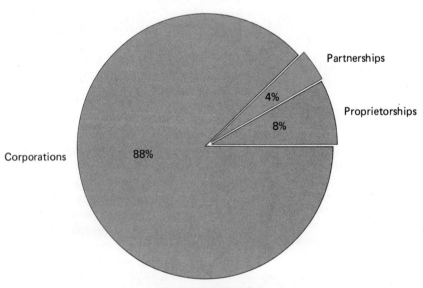

Source: U.S. Department of Commerce, *Statistical Abstract of the United States*, 104th ed. (Washington, D.C.: Government Printing Office, 1984), Tables 887, 888.

Advantages of proprietorships

Proprietorships have a number of advantages that make them well suited to small firms. Perhaps the biggest one is that they are easy to form. Starting a proprietorship requires little more than registering the firm's name. Proprietorships are also easy to dissolve. The owner simply stops doing business, and the firm ceases to exist.

A second advantage of the proprietorship is the fact that its owner receives all the profits (if any) directly. Income from a proprietorship is subject only to the personal income tax. Finally, proprietors have the advantage of working for themselves, without being accountable to employers or other owners. Many people value this independence so highly that they are willing to run their own business in return for a lower income than they could earn working for someone else.

Disadvantages of proprietorships

Proprietorships have some drawbacks that limit their usefulness for large ventures. One of these is the unlimited liability of the owner. Just as the owner receives all the profits, he or she must bear any losses. Any liabilities that the firm incurs— business debts, lawsuits, damages for breach of contract, or whatever—are borne by the proprietor. Thus, bankruptcy for a proprietorship also means bankruptcy for its owner.

The fact that a proprietorship cannot be separated from its owner has other drawbacks as well. If the growth of the firm requires more capital than the owner can supply, it is not easy for a proprietorship to tap outside sources of funds. Also, the life of a proprietorship is limited. The death of the proprietor ends the legal life of the firm.

The Partnership

Partnership
An association of two or more people who operate a business as co-owners by voluntary legal agreement.

A **partnership** is an association of two or more people who operate a business as co-owners. Partnerships are the least common of the three major forms of business organization. They account for only about 7 percent of all firms in the United States and for less than 4 percent of all business receipts. Partnerships are most often found in professions like law, medicine, and accounting. In these fields, state laws restrict the use of the corporation by groups of professionals. Some of these laws have been relaxed in recent years, however, and professional corporations are becoming more common.

Advantages of partnerships

Forming a partnership is one way for a proprietorship to grow. Two or more partners can pool their skills and capital to make a firm that is larger and stronger than any one of them could support alone. In certain situations, partnerships have tax advantages over corporations.

Disadvantages of partnerships

Offsetting these advantages are some serious drawbacks. One is the unlimited liability of the partners. In terms of liability, a partner is worse off than a proprietor because each partner bears the liabilities of the entire firm. If the firm fails, a partner can lose far more than he or she has put into the firm. In professional partnerships a partner may even be held liable for damages awarded in suits against other members of the firm.

Continuity is another serious problem for partnerships, since the death of any partner ends the legal life of the firm. Withdrawal by a partner can also create problems. If a partner wants to leave the firm, someone—either a new partner or the existing ones—must be willing to buy his or her interest in the firm. Until a buyer is found, the partner's investment may be "frozen;" it cannot be withdrawn as cash or invested in another business.

Limited partnerships   For some purposes, such as real estate ventures, a special kind of partnership called a *limited partnership* is used in order to avoid the problem of unlimited liability. A limited partnership includes one or more general partners, who are in charge of running the firm and have much the same status as the co-owners of an ordinary partnership. It also includes one or more limited partners, who put in capital and share profits but whose liability can never exceed the amount they have invested. A limited partnership has many of the advantages of a corporation as a means of raising capital. At the same time, it retains the tax advantages of a partnership.

The Corporation

Corporation
A firm that takes the form of an independent legal entity with ownership divided into equal shares and each owner's liability limited to his or her investment in the firm.

The **corporation** is the third major form of business organization. A corporation is a business that is organized as an independent legal entity, with ownership divided into shares. The corporation is the dominant form of organization for large firms. Only about 16 percent of all firms in the United States are corporations, but they account for more than 85 percent of all business receipts. Box 4.2, which lists the 25 largest industrial corporations in the United States, contains many familiar names. Small corporations are also common, however. A quarter of all corporations report receipts of less than $25,000 a year.

Advantages of corporations   The usefulness of the corporate form for large businesses stems from two facts: (1) the corporation is a legal entity apart from its owners, and (2) the owners have limited liability.

The legal independence of the corporation makes it stable and long-lived. Stockholders can enter or leave the firm at will. Creditors and customers have only one legal entity to deal with, rather than a number of partners. And the firm can own property and enter into contracts in its own name, not just in the names of its owners.

Limited liability means that stockholders cannot suffer a loss greater than the sum they have invested in the business. This is the stockholder's most important protection. A person can own shares in dozens of corporations without ever facing the risks that are faced by a partner or a proprietor.

Together, these two features of the corporation make it ideal for raising large sums from many small investors. We will discuss some of the ways in which this is done later in the chapter.

Disadvantages of corporations   Corporations also have some disadvantages. If they didn't, every firm would be a corporation.

One disadvantage is the relative cost and difficulty of forming or

**Box 4.2
The 25 Largest U.S.
Industrial Corporations**

Each year *Fortune* magazine publishes a list of the 500 largest industrial corporations in the United States, ranked by sales. This list of the top 25 contains many familiar names.

Rank	Company	Sales ($ millions)	Net Income ($ millions)
1	Exxon	88,561	4,977
2	General Motors	74,581	3,730
3	Mobil	54,607	1,503
4	Ford Motor	44,454	1,866
5	International Business Machines	40,180	5,485
6	Texaco	40,068	1,233
7	E. I. du Pont de Nemours	35,378	1,127
8	Standard Oil (Indiana)	27,635	1,868
9	Standard Oil of California	27,342	1,590
10	General Electric	26,797	2,024
11	Gulf Oil	26,581	978
12	Atlantic Richfield	25,147	1,547
13	Shell Oil	19,678	1,633
14	Occidental Petroleum	19,115	566
15	U.S. Steel	16,869	−1,161
16	Phillips Petroleum	15,249	721
17	Sun	14,669	453
18	United Technologies	14,669	509
19	Tenneco	14,353	716
20	ITT	14,155	674
21	Chrysler	13,240	700
22	Procter & Gamble	12,452	866
23	R. J. Reynolds Industries	11,957	881
24	Getty Oil	11,600	494
25	Standard Oil (Ohio)	11,599	355

Source: *Fortune*, April 30, 1984, p. 276. Reprinted by permission from the FORTUNE DIRECTORY; ©1984 Time Inc. All rights reserved.

dissolving a corporation. Although each state has its own laws in this area, forming a corporation usually requires the services of a lawyer and the payment of fees. These costs make the corporation poorly suited to most small or temporary business ventures.

Corporations also have a major tax disadvantage in that corporate income is taxed twice. When it is earned, it is subject to corporate income taxes; when it is paid out to stockholders as dividends, it is subject to the personal income tax.

This double taxation can be very costly. If state and federal taxes take half of a firm's profit when it is earned and personal income taxes take half of the remainder when it is paid out as dividends, the firm's owners receive only 25 cents of each dollar earned. Box 4.3 takes a look at the long-running debate over double taxation of corporate income.

**Box 4.3
Should Corporate
Income Be Taxed?**

In recent years the corporate income tax has fallen in importance as a source of revenue (see chart). Some see this as a sign of growing unfairness—a shifting of the tax burden from corporate fat cats to working people. But many economists approve of this trend and would like to see the corporate income tax scuttled entirely.

The first point critics make about this tax is that corporations, being nothing but legal abstractions, cannot really pay taxes at all. Corporations write the checks that are sent to the Treasury, but the economic burden of the tax must fall on people—customers, workers, and stockholders.

No one is quite sure how the burden of the tax is shared among these three groups. However, it is doubtful that the corporate income tax is an effective tax on the rich. The employees and customers of corporations are no richer than anyone else. And while individual owners of corporate stock are richer than average, by no means all stock is owned by individuals. Vast amounts of it are owned by pension funds, universities, charitable foundations, and other institutions that provide benefits to the public at large.

The corporate tax is suspect not only on grounds of fairness but also on grounds of efficiency. Corporate income that is paid out as dividends is taxed twice: once at the corporate rate when it is earned and once at the stockholder's individual rate when it is paid out. But corporate income that is held for reinvestment is taxed only once, at the corporate rate. Corporate managers thus have a strong incentive to hold earnings for reinvestment.

Is this bad? Some economists think so. If corporations paid more dividends, they say, the stockholders (whether individuals or institutions) would probably reinvest most of the money. But they would not always invest it in the same corporations that earned the profits. They would choose the ventures that seemed to them to be the best managed, most dynamic, and most promising. The corporate tax, the critics say, subsidizes the growth of big established corporations at the expense of smaller newcomers.

Could the Treasury afford the loss of revenue that would result from doing away with the corporate tax? Or would some other tax, just as unfair and inefficient, have to be raised instead? To hold down the tax loss for the Treasury, many critics of the corporate tax recommend one further change. After the corporate income tax is abolished, stockholders should have to start paying personal income tax on profits of the corporations they own.

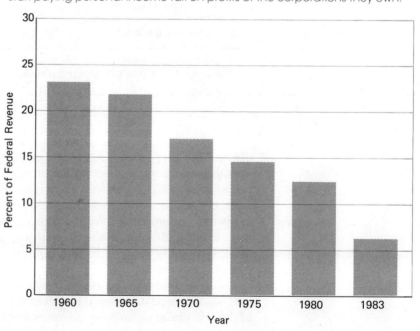

Not-for-Profit Firms

In addition to profit-seeking proprietorships, partnerships, and corporations, the private sector contains many not-for-profit firms. These include churches, colleges, charities, labor unions, country clubs, and the like. These organizations, like profit-seeking firms, take part in markets, produce goods and services, and provide jobs.

Most not-for-profit firms are corporations. Unlike profit-seeking corporations, however, they have no stockholders. They are run by independent boards of trustees whose members are chosen under rules set forth in the organization's bylaws. In a typical private college, for example, the trustees are elected by alumni, faculty, and sometimes students.

Some not-for-profit firms depend on donations for their income. Many also receive income from fees and from sales of goods and services. Not-for-profit hospitals, publishers, and theater groups are examples. If a not-for-profit firm takes in more in donations and sales revenues than it spends, it is required by law to plow the surplus back into the business.

Cooperatives are closely related to not-for-profit firms. They are formed by consumers, farmers, and sometimes factory workers to run a business for their mutual benefit. Unlike not-for-profit firms, cooperatives may distribute any surplus they earn to their members. For example, the surplus of a co-op supermarket might be distributed to members at the end of the year on the basis of each member's total purchases during the year. Unlike ordinary corporations, however, cooperatives do not always have profits as their main goal. Other benefits of forming a cooperative include the chance for consumers to pool their purchasing power and buy at wholesale prices and the chance for farmers to control the marketing of their crops.

THE FIRM AS COORDINATOR

Whatever their form of organization, all business firms have one thing in common: They coordinate economic activity. They are responsible, in large part, for deciding what goods are made, who makes them, and how they are made. They do this by means of two types of coordination, which we will call *market coordination* and *managerial coordination*.

Coordinating the work of many people requires a system of incentives. It also requires a means by which people can communicate with one another. **Market coordination** uses the price system both as a means of communication and as a source of incentives. As prices change in response to supply and demand, buyers are led to substitute lower-priced goods and services for higher-priced ones. At the same time, changing prices create new profit opportunities for entrepreneurs who expand their output of goods whose prices have been bid up by strong consumer demand. All of this is done in a decentralized fashion. No central authority makes decisions or issues commands.

There are large areas of economic activity in which market coordination is not used, however. Take, for example, the coordination of work in a television factory. Workers do not decide on their own, in response to price changes, that they will spend the day making portables rather than cabinet models. Instead, they make portables because their boss tells them to. This

Market coordination
A means of coordinating economic activity that uses the price system to transmit information and provide incentives.

Managerial coordination
A means of coordinating economic activity that uses directives from managers to subordinates.

is an example of **managerial coordination**, which is based on directives from managers to subordinates. The subordinates follow the directives because they have agreed to do so as a condition of employment.

Coordination Within the Firm

In a well-known essay on the nature of the firm, Ronald Coase posed a question about these two ways of coordinating economic activity.[2] If the market works as well as economists say it does, Coase asked, why is managerial coordination used at all? Why do the workers in a television factory have to be employees taking orders from a boss? If market coordination were used everywhere, TV cabinets and picture tubes would all be built by independent firms working on contract. Changes in the relative prices of various components would keep the right number of workers on each job and at the same time keep the right amounts of goods flowing to consumers.

Coase found an answer to his question. He said that market coordination is not used in every case where coordination is needed because it entails **transaction costs**. These costs include the costs of gathering information about market conditions. They include the costs of negotiating contracts, writing invoices, and making payments. They also include the costs of straightening things out when contracts are not carried through.

Transaction costs
The costs of gathering information, making decisions, carrying out trades, writing contracts, making payments, and other tasks involved in coordinating economic activity.

Transaction costs put a limit on the use of the market as a means of coordination. Imagine that you had to negotiate with each person who helped build a TV set that you wanted—the person who built the cabinet, the one who put the finish on, the one who installed the picture tube, and so on. The transaction costs of all these dealings would make buying a TV set very expensive. To avoid these costs, you might have a local shop build a set from scratch. But then the benefits of large-scale production would be lost, and the set would still cost a lot. When a firm like Magnavox acts as an intermediary between you and all the people who build the set, thousands of transactions are avoided. You can buy your TV set in a store, and the job of building them is coordinated within the firm through the giving of directives that workers carry out.

Coase realized, though, that in answering one question he had raised another. If managerial coordination works so well, why use the market at all? Why not run the entire economy as one big firm, with all people acting as employees and a single, central manager running the whole show? Then coordination would be a matter not only of giving TV or auto workers orders about what to do that day but also of giving high school graduates orders about whether to become technicians or welders. Not only would the question of how many portables and how many cabinet model TVs be answered by managerial coordination, but so would such questions as how many firms should be in each industry and where they should be located.

But managerial coordination has transaction costs of its own. Under managerial coordination, the person who actually does a job does not need to know all the reasons for doing it, and that is a saving. Offsetting this is the fact that managers have to know a great deal about all the jobs they

---

[2]Ronald H. Coase, "The Nature of the Firm," *Economica*, November 1937, pp. 386-405.

coordinate, and that is a cost. Sometimes the costs of giving information to a central decision maker are greater than the costs of giving information to people close to the job. When that is the case, managerial coordination loses its advantage over market coordination.

The Limits of the Firm

Coase saw that the two coordinating mechanisms that we have discussed are the key to understanding the nature of the firm and its role in the economy. A firm, he said, uses managerial coordination for its internal activities. It uses the market to coordinate its activities with those of people on the outside. Each firm finds it worthwhile to expand its operations only to the point at which the costs of organizing one more task within the firm are equal to the costs of organizing the same task outside the firm through the market.

In some cases this principle leads to very large firms. Magnavox, for example, is a large firm in itself. It is also part of the Philips organization, the twenty-eighth-largest firm in the world. Such a firm coordinates a vast number of activities. It builds hundreds of different products, makes parts in one plant for products that will be assembled in another halfway around the world, and so on. But even a firm like Philips does not do everything for itself. If it wants to ship goods by rail, it does not build a railroad. Some jobs are so big that even the largest firms find it more efficient to use outside specialists.

In other cases, Coase's principle leads to firms that are very small. Take Bullard's Welding, for example. Bullard does a few things for himself that most firms of that size would not do. Building the furnace that heats his shop is an example. But Bullard does not make the parts for the diesel engines he repairs or set up a rolling mill to make the sheet steel he needs or hire a lawyer as an employee of his firm. Instead, he finds it more efficient to buy those goods and services on the market.

In Bullard's case as in that of Philips, allowing each firm to expand to its optimal size while leaving coordination among firms to the market keeps total transaction costs down. The concept of the firm as a means of making economic coordination more efficient should be kept in mind throughout the study of economics.

FINANCING PRIVATE BUSINESS

Balance sheet
A financial statement showing a firm's or households assets, liabilities, and net worth.

Assets
All the things to which a firm or household holds legal claim.

The Balance Sheet

Whether large or small and whatever their legal form, all private firms need capital. One way to understand how a firm obtains and uses capital is to look at its **balance sheet**—a financial statement that shows what the firm owns and what it owes. Box 4.4 shows a balance sheet for an imaginary firm, Great Falls Manufacturing Inc. (GFMI).

The lefthand column of the balance sheet lists the firm's **assets**. These are all the things to which the firm holds a legal claim. GFMI's assets include $10 million in cash and accounts receivable; $15 million in inventory; and $100 million in real estate, plant, and equipment. Its assets thus total $125 million.

**Box 4.4
Balance Sheet of Great
Falls Manufacturing Inc.**

A firm's balance sheet gives a snapshot of its financial position. The lefthand side lists the firm's assets—all the things to which it holds legal claim. The righthand side lists the firm's liabilities—claims against it by nonowners—and its net worth, or owners' equity. According to the accounting equation, assets always equal liabilities plus net worth.

Assets (millions)		Liabilities and Net Worth (millions)	
Cash and accounts receivable	$ 10	Accounts payable	$ 5
Inventory	15	Short-term debt	15
Property, plant, and equipment	100	Long-term debt	55
		Total liabilities	$ 75
		Net worth	50
		Total liabilities plus	
Total assets	$125	net worth	$125

Liabilities
All the legal claims against a firm by nonowners or against a household by nonmembers.

Net worth (owners' equity)
A firm's or household's assets minus its liabilities.

The righthand column of the balance sheet lists the firm's liabilities and net worth. A firm's **liabilities** are all the legal claims that outsiders hold against it. For GFMI, these include $5 million in accounts payable, $15 million in short-term loans from banks, and $55 million in long-term debts such as mortgages on the firm's property.

The final item on the righthand side of the balance sheet is the firm's **net worth**, also known as **owners' equity**. This is the difference between total assets and total liabilities. The firm's net worth represents its owners' claims against its assets. The fact that GFMI's net worth is $50 million means that if its owners closed it down, sold all its assets at the values listed on the balance sheet, and paid off all its liabilities, they would have $50 million left over.

The balance sheet gets its name from the fact that the totals of the two columns always balance. This follows from the definition of net worth. Because net worth is defined as assets minus liabilities, liabilities plus net worth must equal assets. In equation form, this basic rule of accounting reads as follows:

Assets = liabilities + net worth

As a firm grows, the entries on its balance sheet also grow. The growing firm will need more plant and equipment and a larger inventory. It will also need more cash, and its accounts receivable will increase as it does business with more workers, customers, and suppliers.

According to the accounting equation, the firm's liabilities or net worth, or both, must grow as its assets grow. If the firm is profitable, it can obtain funds for growth by plowing profits back into the business. If it does this, its assets will grow without a matching increase in its liabilities. Therefore, by definition, its net worth will grow. Thus, by plowing profits back into the business, owners increase their stake in the firm. If the firm does not make enough profits to finance its own growth, it must turn to outside sources of funds.

Broadly speaking, there are two ways to raise capital from outside the firm. One is to bring in more owners—new partners for a partnership, new stockholders for a corporation, or new members for a cooperative. The capital raised from these new owners is listed on the firm's balance sheet as additions to its net worth. The firm can also borrow from individuals, banks, or other lenders. If it does this, its liabilities increase.

The markets in which a firm obtains funds are known as **financial markets**. It is worthwhile to take a careful look at these markets, since they play key roles in both macro- and microeconomics.

Financial markets
Markets through which borrowers obtain funds from savers.

Financial Markets

Box 4.5 gives an overview of financial markets. Such markets serve as a link between economic units that are net savers (those that spend less than they earn) and units that are net borrowers (spend more than they earn). Firms and households can be either net savers or net borrowers. However, total saving by households exceeds their total borrowing, so the household sector is shown in Box 4.5 as a source of funds for financial markets. And total borrowing by business firms exceeds their total saving, so the business sector is shown as a user of funds provided through financial markets.

**Box 4.5
Financial Markets**

This chart shows how financial markets channel investment funds from households (which are net savers) to businesses (which are net borrowers). Two types of financing are shown. Direct financing is the sale of claims against firms (such as stocks or bonds) directly to households. Indirect financing channels the funds through financial intermediaries—firms that gather funds from households and use them as a basis for making loans to other firms. The chart shows flows of funds as solid arrows and flows of financial claims issued in exchange for funds as dotted arrows.

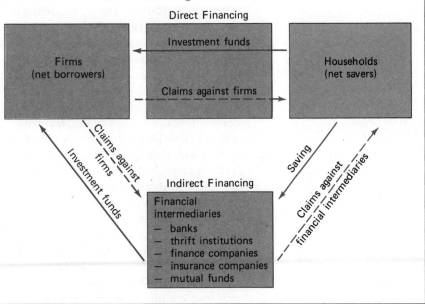

Direct financing
The process of raising investment funds directly from savers.

Bond
A promise, given in return for a loan, to make a fixed annual or semiannual payment over a set number of years plus a larger final payment equal to the amount borrowed.

Common stock
A certificate of part ownership in a corporation that gives the owner a vote in the selection of the firm's directors and the right to a share of dividends, if any.

Financial intermediaries
Financial firms, including banks, savings and loan associations, insurance companies, pension funds, and mutual funds, that gather funds from net savers and make loans to net borrowers.

Indirect financing
The process of raising investment funds via financial intermediaries.

Direct financing   One way for a firm to raise funds is to approach households directly. This process is called **direct financing**. In exchange for the funds they invest, households receive claims against the firm. These claims take several forms, of which the most common are bonds and stocks.

A **bond** is a promise, given in return for a loan, to make interest payments at an agreed-upon rate over a set period, plus a final payment equal to the amount borrowed. Most bonds are issued in denominations of $1,000 for periods of 10 to 30 years. Suppose that GFMI wanted to raise $1 million to buy some new injection molding equipment. It could sell a thousand bonds with a face value of $1,000 each, promising to pay the lenders, say, $150 a year for 30 years, and to repay the $1,000 at the end of that period.

Instead of selling bonds, GFMI could raise the $1 million by selling stock. A share of **common stock** is a certificate of part ownership in the firm. In return for their funds, the new stockholders become co-owners with all other stockholders.

Unlike bondholders, holders of common stock are not promised a fixed return on their investment. Instead, they expect to be rewarded for their investment through dividends or capital gains. Dividends are payments to stockholders that are made out of profits. Capital gains are sums that are realized when and if stockholders are able to sell their shares at a higher price than they paid for them.

Besides selling bonds and stock, corporations can issue other kinds of financial obligations. These include commercial paper (similar to bonds, but scheduled for repayment in a year or less); preferred stock (stock with guaranteed dividends but without voting rights); convertible bonds (bonds that can be exchanged for stock at a set price); and many others. These securities are often mentioned in the business press, but a detailed discussion of them is beyond the scope of this book.

Indirect financing   Direct financing is by no means the only source of funds for a firm like GFMI. Instead of approaching households directly, a firm can turn to **financial intermediaries** such as banks, savings and loan associations, insurance companies, mutual funds, and pension funds. These firms gather funds from net savers and pass them along to net borrowers, either by making loans, or by buying stocks, bonds, or other securities from them. The process of raising funds through financial intermediaries is known as **indirect financing**. Indirect financing accounts for about two-thirds of all funds raised in U.S. financial markets.

Suppose that GFMI needs $100,000 to build a new warehouse. Instead of selling stocks or bonds to the public, it applies to the Great Falls National Bank for a mortgage loan. In return for the funds, GFMI gives the bank a mortgage note, promising to repay the $100,000, with interest, over a period of 15 years. If it fails to make the payments, the bank can take possession of the warehouse.

Where does the bank get the funds it needs to make the loans? It gets them by accepting checking and savings deposits from the citizens of Great Falls. As Box 4.5 shows, indirect financing involves a double exchange of funds and claims. Households give their funds to the bank in return for claims against the bank, and the bank passes the funds along to GFMI in return for a claim against the new warehouse.

Indirect financing has a number of advantages over direct financing. First, it is more flexible. A bank could, for example, lend a retail store a few thousand dollars for 90 days to finance a buildup of inventory for the Christmas season. Selling stocks or bonds for this purpose would not be practical. Second, indirect financing can be used by small firms, including proprietorships and partnerships. Because these firms are not widely known and do not always have high credit ratings, they may not find it easy to sell stocks or bonds. Finally, financial intermediaries perform a useful service by matching the needs of borrowers and lenders. For example, the Great Falls National Bank would be able to give GFMI a 15-year mortgage loan for $100,000 even though none of its depositors may have that much in savings or want the savings tied up for so long a time.

Not all indirect financing takes the form of loans. Sales of stocks and bonds to financial intermediaries also count as indirect financing. Pension funds, mutual funds, and insurance companies have large holdings of corporate stocks and bonds.

Secondary Financial Markets

The financial markets shown in Box 4.5 are called **primary financial markets** because they are markets in which newly issued claims against firms are exchanged for new investment funds. There are also many **secondary financial markets** in which households and firms buy and sell previously issued stocks, bonds, and other securities. The best-known of these secondary markets is the New York Stock Exchange. There are similar exchanges in New York, Philadelphia, Chicago, and elsewhere. Stocks and bonds are also traded in so-called *over-the-counter* markets, which are networks of dealers who do business by telephone or computer hookup.

Secondary financial markets give holders of stocks and bonds a great deal of flexibility. Firms sell stocks and bonds to raise long-term capital funds, but the people who buy those securities do not have to hold them for long terms. They can turn to the secondary markets to find buyers who are willing to pay cash for their securities. Thus, secondary financial markets, like financial intermediaries, play a major role in matching the requirements of lenders and borrowers. Active secondary markets also make it easy for savers to reduce their risks by diversifying their holdings. Instead of putting all its eggs in one basket, a household can own the stocks or bonds of several companies. If one firm runs into trouble, the household's losses are limited.

Although secondary markets make it possible for stockholders and bondholders to find buyers for their securities, there is no guarantee that those securities can be sold at a particular price. Stock and bond prices vary from hour to hour and from day to day as supply and demand vary. Let's take a brief look at the factors that affect stock and bond prices.

Factors that affect stock prices   Stock prices are listed daily in the financial pages of major newspapers. In addition, stock price averages, such as the Dow Jones Average of the prices of 30 major industrial stocks, are widely published.

Primary financial markets
Markets in which newly issued stocks, bonds, and other securities are sold to investors.

Secondary financial markets
Markets in which previously issued bonds, stocks, and other securities are traded among investors.

What determines the price of a stock on a given day? The simplest answer is that the price reflects the expectations of investors about the firm's future profits. Anything that is viewed as likely to raise the firm's profits will mean more dividends or capital gains for stockholders. As a result, the price of the stock will be bid up. Anything that is likely to lead to lower profits will cause the price to be bid down. Union Carbide's poison gas disaster at Bhopal, India, described in Box 4.6, is a dramatic example of the way unforeseen events can affect a company's fortunes and its stock price. Fortunately, disasters on such a scale are rare, but little items of good or bad news cause stock prices to move up or down a bit every day. Stock prices are affected by developments that affect the economy as a whole as well as by those that affect particular firms. Usually stock prices tend to fall during a recession, when corporate profits are low, and rise during a recovery.

The Effects of Speculation   Although long-run trends in stock prices are affected mainly by general economic conditions and prospects for particular firms, day-to-day changes in prices are strongly influenced by **speculation**. Speculation is the activity of buying low in the hope of selling high and realizing a capital gain.

One way to succeed as a speculator would be to have above-average foresight about trends that will affect the profits of particular companies. Large brokerage firms employ thousands of analysts who study annual reports and economic forecasts, trying to be the first to spot a trend. Another way to be a successful speculator is to have superior foresight about what other speculators are going to do. If you think speculators are going to bid up the price of AMF tomorrow, you can make money by buying that stock today. Wall Street speculators have employed everyone from psychologists to astrologers in their efforts to guess what other speculators will do next.

The ups and downs of stock prices are a fascinating field of study, but

Speculation
The activity of buying goods or securities in the hope of selling them later at a higher price.

**Box 4.6
Disaster in India Jolts
Union Carbide**

The worst industrial accident in history took place on December 3, 1984, in Bhopal, India. A cloud of poisonous methyl isocyanate gas leaked from a pesticide plant into a neighborhood of 200,000 people. Two thousand of them died. As many as 100,000 needed medical treatment. And an unknown number of the survivors will suffer blindness or lung and liver damage.

The plant was 51 percent owned by Union Carbide Corp., an American firm. Although the plant operated as an independent unit under Indian management, the parent firm was hit by massive lawsuits. Based on awards in similar cases in the past, it seemed possible that total awards in the Bhopal case might exceed $5 billion—more than Union Carbide's net worth.

Union Carbide Chairman Warren Anderson called it a "shattering experience." Employees at U.S. plants wept at the news. The reaction on Wall Street was shattering too, in its own way. The price of Union Carbide's stock quickly fell more than 25 percent—a total loss of almost $1 billion in value.

Box 4.7
How to Win in the Stock Market: Throw Darts at the Financial Page

The efficient-market hypothesis says that new knowledge that affects a corporation's profit potential becomes reflected in its stock price so quickly that no one analyst or investor can beat the market. Rather than pay big fees to analysts to pick your stocks for you, say the fans of this approach, you might just as well pick them by throwing darts at the financial page.

In 1967 the editors of *Forbes* magazine set out to test this hypothesis. They taped a copy of the financial page of a newspaper to the wall and threw real darts at it. They hit 28 companies, in each of which they invested $1,000.

By 1984 the original $28,000 investment had grown to $132,000, not counting dividends. This 370 percent gain was ten times better than the performance of the Dow Jones Industrial Average.

A big part of *Forbes'* winnings came from one lucky hit, Texas Oil & Gas. The $1,000 invested in that one firm in 1967 grew to $72,755.15 by 1984. But even without Texas Oil & Gas, the dartboard portfolio still gained 118 percent, four times better than the Dow Jones average.

Looking back from 1984 on the dartboard fund's performance, *Forbes'* editors had just one regret: they had used real darts to pick the stocks, but they hadn't invested real money. Why, oh why, they wrote, couldn't we have taken the whole game more seriously!

Source: Steve Kichen, "Smart Darts and Other Games," *Forbes*, July 30, 1984, pp. 95–99.

to economists this is only a sideline. Economists study the stock market not in the hope of earning a personal fortune, but because of the market's importance as a means of transmitting information. Each time analysts or speculators learn a new fact or get a new hunch about the future of a company, they use it as a basis for purchases or sales. Those purchases and sales push stock prices up or down. The result is that changes in stock prices transmit the findings of analysts and speculators to the outside world. The only way traders could keep their findings secret would be by not using them as a basis for trades.

Many economists believe that the stock market transmits information so fast and so well that nearly all knowledge about the profit prospects of a firm is reflected in the price of its stock as soon as it becomes known to anyone. This view is known as the *efficient-market hypothesis*. (See Box 4.7.) According to this hypothesis, the efforts of analysts and speculators to be the first to learn some relevant fact and to act on it continue until the returns to any further effort are pushed down nearly to zero.

But if everything that can be known about future profits is already reflected in stock prices by the time they are printed in the newspapers, why should the average investor bother with research at all? Why not just pick stocks at random by throwing darts at a chart on the wall? The idea that an investor who picks stocks at random can do as well as one who studies published information stems from the idea that only *new* information affects stock prices in any systematic way. Yet, although this idea implies that no one can consistently beat the market without inside information, it does not imply that all traders who are not the first to learn a piece of news are wasting their time. In fact, they are performing a useful service. Through their attempts to beat the market, new information is transmitted to the public and capital is pulled out of industries where prospects are weak and into those where prospects are strong.

Factors that affect bond prices   As we saw earlier, a firm that issues bonds makes regular payments of a set amount until the bond matures. The payments made during the life of the bond are determined by the prevailing rate of interest at the time that the bond is issued. Suppose, for example, that the prevailing interest rate is 15 percent per year when the bond is issued. In that case, each $1,000 bond will pay the person who buys it $150 per year. (Actually, in most cases there would be two semiannual payments of $75 each.)

The annual payment is agreed to at the time that the bond is issued and is known as the **coupon rate** for the bond. (The term comes from the fact that bond owners used to have to turn in paper coupons that were attached to the bond certificate in order to claim their interest payments. Today, computers keep track of who gets the interest payments.) The coupon rate remains fixed for the life of the bond. The coupon rate is expressed as a percentage of the bond's $1,000 face value. Thus a bond that pays $150 a year has a 15 percent coupon rate.

But what happens if market conditions change after the bond is issued? For example, what if interest rates on bonds, mortgages, and long-term loans fall to 12 percent? In this case, sellers of newly issued bonds will only have to offer a coupon rate of 12 percent in order to attract buyers. What then happens to the price of the old bond with the 15 percent coupon?

Put yourself in the position of an investor who has a choice between a bond that will pay $1,000 at maturity and $150 per year in the meantime, and one that will pay $1,000 on maturity (at about the same time) but only $120 per year in the meantime. Clearly, you would pay more for the first bond—the one with the $150 annual payment. To be more precise, if $1,000 will buy a bond that pays $120 per year, you would be willing to pay up to $1,250 for a bond that pays $150 per year, assuming the maturity date to be the same. At those prices, the **yield**—that is, the interest income from the bond expressed as a percentage of its purchase price—would be equal for the two bonds. This reasoning leads to two principles about bond prices:

Coupon rate
The annual interest payment of a bond, expressed as a percentage of the bond's face value.

Yield (of a bond)
The income received from a bond expressed as a percentage of its current market price.

1.   When market interest rates fall, firms reduce the *coupon rate* promised on newly issued bonds. The prices of previously issued bonds then rise by enough to make their *yield* equal to that of the newly issued bonds.
2.   When market interest rates rise, firms increase the *coupon rate* promised on newly issued bonds. The prices of previously issued bonds then fall by enough to make their *yield* equal to that of newly issued bonds.

The appendix to this chapter presents a fuller explanation of the connection between bond prices and interest rates. For most purposes, however, it is enough to remember that when interest rates go up, bond prices fall, and when interest rates go down, bond prices rise.

OWNERSHIP AND CONTROL OF THE CORPORATION

Sole proprietorships are owned and controlled by their proprietors, and partnerships are owned and controlled by the partners. Corporations are legally owned by their stockholders, but the matter of control is much less clear-cut than it is for other types of firms. Because corporations account for such a large part of business activity in the United States, no survey of the role of the firm in the economy would be complete without some mention of the debate over who actually controls a corporation.

Stockholder Rights

One of the advantages of the corporation is that it can raise capital from many thousands of people, each of whom need not invest much in any one firm. Legally, the stockholders have the power to control the corporation. Their main channel of control is the right to elect the firm's board of directors, who set its broad policies and appoint its top managers.

However, most stockholders do not make active use of their ownership rights. Small stockholders are not in a position to know what goes on in the corporation and why decisions are made the way they are. They tend to accept the policies set by the firm's managers without question. If they disapprove of those policies, it is easier to sell their stock and buy shares in a better-managed company than to try to throw their weight around at annual stockholder meetings. The result is a degree of separation of ownership and control that is not found in proprietorships or partnerships.

Stockholders vs. Managers

Why is the separation of ownership and control an important issue? The answer is that the interests of stockholders and managers may differ. Most stockholders have only one interest in the firm whose stock they own—they want it to earn the highest possible profit for them. Managers do not always put this goal above all others.

For one thing, managers are concerned about their jobs. They know that they must earn at least some profit or the stockholders will throw them out. But when it comes to decisions that involve trade-offs between risk and profit, their interests and those of the stockholders may differ widely. Stockholders do not normally tie up all their assets in a single firm. They hold some shares in each of many firms. If by taking prudent risks they can earn higher average returns, the failure of a single firm is not a disaster. But since a manager's career is tied to the fate of a single firm, or even a single product of the firm, managers may tend to be more cautious than stockholders would like them to be.

Corporate growth is another area in which the interests of managers and stockholders may conflict. Stockholders favor growth to the extent that it means more profits per share, but managers may favor growth for its own sake. The power and prestige of managers, the number of people they have working under them, and even their salaries tend to be enhanced by growth, whether or not it increases the firm's profits.

Finally, it is claimed that managers who identify with their firms may be more willing than stockholders to spend money to improve the firm's image. Lavish headquarters, donations to charities, corporate jets, and the like may attract customers and swell profits. But because they also swell managerial pride, managers may be tempted to carry such spending too far.

In short, the picture offered by some observers is one of contrast between the traditional firm, which pursues profits and nothing else, and the modern management-controlled corporation, for which profits are only one of many goals—and not always the one that is ranked highest.

Constraints on Managers

How much truth is there in this picture? There is some, but the picture is not complete. There are strong reasons to believe that managers cannot really act as independently of stockholders as the preceding arguments might suggest.

Stock options   For one thing, many firms allow their managers to share directly in their profits. One of the most common types of profit-sharing plans is the stock option, which gives a manager the right to buy a certain number of shares of the firm's stock at a set price before a certain date.

Suppose that in July of 1985 a manager is given the option to buy a thousand shares of the firm's stock at any time until 1990 at the 1985 price of $25. If the manager does a good job of running the firm, the price of the stock is likely to rise. If it rises to, say, $45 by 1990, the option to buy a thousand shares at $25 is worth $20,000. This is a nice reward for a job well done. But if the company is poorly managed and the stock's price falls below $25, the option will be worthless.

Takeovers   A second major constraint on managers is the threat of a takeover. It is true that when stockholders do not like a firm's policies they are likely to sell their shares and buy shares in another firm. But what if so many stockholders decide to sell that the price of the stock is driven down to a low level? In that case, the firm may be subject to a *takeover* bid.

A takeover bid may be made by an individual, a group, or, most often, another corporation. One tactic is to make a *tender offer*—an offer to buy a controlling interest in the firm's stock at a stated price, usually well above the stock's current market price. Another tactic is to ask stockholders for *proxies*, that is, promises to vote for a new board of directors at the next stockholder meeting. In either case, if the takeover succeeds, the new management will do its best to raise profits. When investors see this, the price of the firm's stock will be bid up and the takeover group will reap handsome gains.

Economists have long argued that the threat of takeover, together with stock options and other profit-sharing devices, act as carrots and sticks to keep managers from straying too far from their duty of earning profits for their stockholders. However, this view is not shared by all observers of the business scene. Box 4.8 explores the controversy.

**Box 4.8
Are Takeovers Good for
the Economy?**

In all of U.S. business history through 1980, there were only four mergers in which the acquired firm was worth $1 billion or more. In the next four years there were 40, topped by Chevron's $13.2-billion purchase of Gulf Oil. Corporate managers began to live in terror of losing their jobs. Congressional committees held hearings. "Takeovers are bad for the economy," screamed the critics. "Do something!"

Meanwhile corporate raiders like T. Boone Pickens Jr. portrayed themselves as champions of the stockholder. Fat-cat managers, they claimed, had forgotten their duty to earn profits. Small stockholders could do nothing but sell out in despair, lowering the market price of corporate stocks. The raiders could pick up the pieces and make everyone rich. Pickens claims that raids on four oil companies netted $13 billion for 750,000 stockholders. "Takeovers are good," said the raiders. "We're heroes!"

On the sidelines, observers of the business scene debated the takeover question. The debate revolved around three main issues:

Debt. To persuade stockholders to sell out, raiders offer to buy a company's shares at a price substantially higher than its current market value. They finance the purchases with borrowed money. As a result, after the takeover the company has more debt in relation to its net worth than before. The critics say all that debt makes the firm financially weak. Not to worry, say the raiders. The debt can be repaid with higher earnings once the old management is replaced by a sharper bunch. Also, some of the debt can be paid off by selling real estate, subsidiaries, and other assets that the old management was not using efficiently.

Defensive strategies. The critics say fear of takeovers prompts managers to adopt defensive strategies that hurt the company. They may sell off the firm's "crown jewels." They themselves may load up the firm with debt so that it will be less attractive. They may design "poison pills"—complex financial traps that they hope would-be raiders will choke on. They pay "greenmail"—huge ransoms to raiders who agree to go away—leaving their firms impoverished. The raiders reply that these tactics simply reveal the managers' contempt for stockholders. They will ruin their firms in order to entrench themselves in the executive suite. Such managers deserve to be gobbled up.

Short-run bias. The threat of takeovers, the critics say, forces managers to stress the short run over the long run. Managers do everything they can to keep short-term profits up, hoping that these actions will boost their stock prices and keep them from becoming shark bait. In doing so, they slight research and development and pass over risky but potentially profitable long-term projects. "Nonsense," say the raiders. Since when were U.S. managers famous for their long-term point of view? They have been paying themselves bonuses based on short-term performance for years. In fact, past shortsightedness of managers is often what knocks down the value of the firm's stock price in the first place. The things that managers need to do to resist a takeover—restructure, sell assets they can't manage well, and so on—will strengthen their firms in the long run, not weaken them.

Who is right? It may take a decade or more to know whether firms taken over in the early 1980s end up being managed better or worse than before. Meanwhile, the debate is sure to go on.

Looking Ahead

As you continue your study of economics, you will need to draw on the material of this chapter at many points. In both macroeconomics and microeconomics, frequent reference will be made to financial markets.

Interest rates and credit availability are crucial to the performance of individual firms, and to the growth of the economy as a whole. The balance sheet concepts of assets, liabilities, and net worth will be needed to understand the operation of the banking system (a part of macroeconomics) and of individual firms (a part of microeconomics). Sometimes you will be dealing with simplified models, in which firms are treated as identical, interchangeable units. But you should keep in mind that behind those models lies a world of business marked by diversity, change, and often drama.

Summary

1. A *sole proprietorship* is a firm that is owned and operated by a single person, who receives all the profits and is responsible for its liabilities. This form of organization has advantages that make it suited to small firms. Proprietorships are easy to form and give the proprietor complete control. However, unlimited liability, limited life of the firm, and limited ability to raise capital are disadvantages.

2. A *partnership* is an association of two or more people who operate a business as co-owners. Forming a partnership can add to the financial and management resources of a proprietorship. However, partnerships, like proprietorships, suffer from unlimited liability and limited life of the firm.

3. A *corporation* is a business that is organized as an independent legal entity, with ownership divided into shares. It is the dominant form of organization for large firms. Its advantages include limited liability for stockholders and unlimited life of the firm. Disadvantages include a somewhat higher cost of formation and, in many cases, higher taxes.

4. Business firms play a major role in solving the economic problems of what, how, who, and for whom. They do so by means of both market and managerial coordination. *Market coordination* uses the price system as a means of communication and a source of incentives. *Managerial coordination* relies on directives from managers to subordinates. Each form of coordination entails certain *transaction costs* that limit its usefulness. Firms tend to expand their operations to the point at which the transaction costs of organizing one more task within the firm are equal to the transaction costs of organizing the same task through the market.

5. A firm's *balance sheet* is a financial statement that shows what it owns and what it owes. The firm's *assets*—all the things to which it holds a legal claim—are listed on the lefthand side of the balance sheet. The firm's *liabilities*—all the claims that outsiders hold against it—are listed on the righthand side. The righthand side of the balance sheet also lists *net worth* (*owners' equity*), which is the difference between total assets and total liabilities. Owners' equity represents owners' claims against the firm. According to a relationship known as the accounting equation, assets = liabilities + net worth.

6. *Financial markets* are the markets in which firms obtain funds for operations and investment. They serve as a link between savers and borrowers. In *direct financing*, firms borrow directly from or sell securities directly to households. In *indirect financing*, they deal with households via *financial intermediaries* such as banks, insurance companies, and pension funds.

7. Markets in which newly issued securities are sold are called *primary financial markets*. Those in which previously issued securities are traded are called *secondary financial markets*. The prices of stocks traded in secondary markets vary with changes in investors' expectations about the future profits of the firms that

issued them. Bond prices in secondary markets tend to rise when interest rates fall and to fall when interest rates rise.

8. Stockholders have the legal power to control the corporations they own. Their main channel of control is the right to elect the firm's board of directors. However, in practice managers have a good deal of independence from stockholders.

Questions for Review

1. Explain the following terms and concepts:
   sole proprietorship
   partnership
   corporation
   market coordination
   managerial coordination
   transaction costs
   balance sheet
   assets
   liabilities
   net worth
   owners' equity
   financial markets
   direct financing
   bond
   common stock
   financial intermediaries
   indirect financing
   primary financial markets
   secondary financial markets
   speculation
   coupon rate
   yield
2. List the main advantages and disadvantages of the sole proprietorship, the partnership, and the corporation.
3. What are the advantages of market coordination? Give an example of a situation in which transaction costs limit the use of market coordination. In what way do the costs of managerial coordination limit the size of a firm?
4. What kinds of things would be listed as assets of a typical manufacturing firm? What kinds of things would be listed as its liabilities? What is the relationship among the firm's assets, liabilities, and net worth?
5. Distinguish between direct and indirect financing. List some common types of financial intermediaries, and explain the role they play in financial markets.
6. Distinguish between primary and secondary securities markets. What are bonds and common stocks, and what factors affect the prices of bonds and stocks that are traded in secondary markets?
7. What is the main channel through which stockholders exercise control of corporations? Why is their control often less than complete?

Problems and Topics for Discussion

1. Look around your community for businesses organized as proprietorships, partnerships, corporations, and not-for-profit firms. Do you think each of those firms has chosen the most appropriate form of organization? Why or why not?
2. Obtain a copy of a corporation's annual report. (You may find one in your library. If not, you can get one by writing or telephoning the corporation, or you can borrow a report from a friend or relative who is a stockholder of a corporation.) In the back of the report you will find a balance sheet for the firm. Compare this balance sheet with the one given in Box 4.4.

What similarities do you see? What differences?

3. Howard Winters is a graduate student in economics at Catatonic State University. He owns a '74 Chevrolet worth about $800; a $1,000 stereo system; and about $500 worth of other personal possessions. He has $420 in his checking account and no other financial resources. Over the past seven years he has borrowed $8,700 under a student loan program, which he plans to pay back after he has received his degree and landed a job. He also owes $125 on a credit card account.

   Draw up a personal balance sheet for Winters. What items go on the righthand side? On the lefthand side? What is his net worth? What "assets" does he have (not listed on his balance sheet) that have made it possible for him to borrow so much money?

4. Each day for a week, look at the stock and bond market reports in a newspaper with a good financial section. (The *Wall Street Journal* has the most complete reports, but any big-city paper will do.) Also look for stories that discuss increases or decreases in the prices of stocks and bonds traded in secondary financial markets. What reasons are given for the price changes?

5. Scan recent issues of business magazines, such as *Business Week*, *Fortune*, or *Forbes*, to find a story about a merger that has taken place recently or is being considered. What reasons are given for the merger? Do you think the merger makes sense in terms of Coase's theory of the firm? Is this a "friendly" merger, in which the management of the acquired company is cooperating? Or is it a "hostile" merger, which the management of the acquired company is trying to resist? What controlling role, if any, are the acquired firm's stockholders expected to play in the merger?

6. Case for Discussion

In 1981 Ashland Oil Inc.'s annual report described the year's two big acquisitions— United States Filter Corp. and Integron Corp. The petroleum refiner boasted that these acquisitions had "dramatically" advanced its diversification strategy.

But Ashland's diversification soon looked less dramatic than tragic. Two weeks ago, the company said it will take a $270 million charge as it gets rid of Integron and most of U.S. Filter. "We were trying to do too many different things," says John R. Hall, Ashland's chairman and chief executive officer.

Similar management mea culpas are growing increasingly common as many conglomerates that aggressively diversified in the late 1960s and 1970s are rushing to shed the businesses they bought.

The same day Ashland announced its divestments, R. J. Reynolds Industries Inc. said it agreed to sell its Aminoil Inc. energy unit, acquired in 1970. A few months earlier it spun off its big shipping company, Sea-Land Industries Investments Inc., acquired in 1969. Reynolds and Ashland joined companies such as Atlantic Richfield Co., which recently said it will take a $785 million charge, mostly on the sale of the money-losing metals business it acquired when it bought Anaconda Co. in 1976. And for months, Armco Inc. has been trying to find a buyer for its financial-services business after shedding both its coal properties and its oil and gas exploration business.[3]

Questions:
a. Discuss these diversifications and divestments in terms of Coase's theory of the firm.
b. Comment on these mergers and divestitures in terms of the controversy over the effects of takeovers on the economy.

---

[3]Geraldine Brooks, "Some Concerns Find that the Push to Diversify Was a Costly Mistake," *Wall Street Journal*, October 2, 1984, p. 33. Reprinted by permission of The Wall Street Journal, © Dow Jones & Company, Inc. 1984. All rights reserved.

Suggestions for Further Reading

Galbraith, John Kenneth. *The New Industrial State.* Boston: Houghton Mifflin, 1967.

In this unorthodox book Galbraith suggests that the market plays little or no role in coordinating the U.S. economy and that corporations are not run by their stockholders but by something called the technostructure.

Gordon, Scott. "The Close of the Galbraithian System." *Journal of Political Economy* 76 (July–August 1968): 635–644.

A critique of Galbraith's view of the economy and the corporation.

Keating, Barry P., and Maryann O. Keating. *Not for Profit.* Glen Ridge, N.J.: Thomas Horton and Daughters, 1980.

An analysis of the not-for-profit sector of the U.S. economy. Government as well as private not-for-profit firms are covered.

Malkiel, Burton G. *A Random Walk Down Wall Street.* New York: Norton, 1975.

A readable and informative introduction to the stock market.

Appendix to Chapter 4

Discounting and the Time Element in Business Decision Making

Planning for the future is a central part of business decision making, especially where financial decisions are concerned. The purpose of this appendix is to introduce briefly certain principles for dealing with the time element in financial decisions.

The first principle is that of compound interest. If a firm puts funds to work earning interest, by placing them in a bank account, making a loan, or buying a bond, the original sum it invests will grow year by year. At 10 percent per year interest, $100 invested today will be worth $110 a year from now. After two years, it will be worth $121. (The $11 gain in the second year reflects interest of $10 on the original principal, and $1 interest on the $10 interest that was earned in the first year. The payment of interest on previously earned interest gives the process the name of *compound* interest.) After three years, the investment would be worth $133.10, and so on.

In a world where funds can be invested at compound interest, it is always an advantage to receive a payment earlier rather than later. The opportunity cost of receiving a sum later rather than sooner is the interest that could otherwise have been earned. Consider, for example, the cost of receiving a sum of $100 a year from now rather than today, assuming the same interest rate of 10 percent per year. Delaying receipt of the sum would mean forgoing a year's interest. Rather than give up the year's interest, a firm would be just as well off to receive a smaller sum now than the $100 a year from now. To be precise, it would be just as good to get $91 now as $100 a year from now, because the $91 invested for a year at 10 percent would grow to $100 (give or take the odd dime). Similarly, $100 payable two years from now is equivalent to about $83 today, assuming 10 percent interest; $100 three years from now is worth about $75; and so on.

This kind of example can be generalized to any time period and any rate of interest. Let V_p be the sum of money that, if invested today at r percent per year interest, will grow to the sum V_t after t years. V_p is known as the *present value* of the sum V_t payable t years from now, discounted at r percent per year. *Discounting* is the name for the procedure by which the present value is calculated. The formula for calculating the present value of any future sum is:

$$V_p = \frac{V_t}{(1 + r)^t}$$

This discounting formula can be used to calculate the fair market price of a bond. The calculation is based on the principle that when market interest rates on other long-term assets change, the price of a previously issued bond will rise or fall until its *yield* is equal to the prevailing interest rate. Box 4A.1 gives a numerical example. The example is based on a bond

**Box 4A.1
Calculating the Market
Price of a Bond**

This box shows how to calculate the market price of a bond, given its coupon rate, the maturity date of the bond, and the current market interest rate on other long-term investments. The calculations take into account the principle that when market interest rates change, the prices of previously issued bonds rise or fall until their yield, calculated as a percentage of their market price, is equal to the market interest rate. This example deals with a bond that has a face value of $1,000, a maturity date seven years in the future, and a coupon rate of 8 percent. Column 2 gives the payments the bondholder will receive each year. Column 3 gives a discount factor, based on the present value formula given in the text. Column 4 is the product of columns 2 and 3. The sum of the discounted payments in column 4 gives the fair market price of the bond.

Year (1)	Payments (2)	Discount Factor (3)	Discounted Payments (4)
a. Price of Bond at 12 Percent Interest			
1	$ 80	0.89	$ 71.20
2	80	0.80	64.00
3	80	0.71	56.80
4	80	0.64	51.20
5	80	0.57	45.60
6	80	0.51	40.80
7	1,080	0.45	486.00
		Fair market price of bond	$815.60
b. Price of Bond at 18 Percent Interest			
1	$ 80	0.85	$ 68.00
2	80	0.72	57.60
3	80	0.61	48.80
4	80	0.52	41.60
5	80	0.44	35.20
6	80	0.37	29.60
7	1,080	0.31	334.80
		Fair market price of bond	$615.60

with a face value of $1,000 and a coupon rate of 8 percent, maturing seven years from the present. Such a bond will pay its holder $80 a year for six years plus a final payment of $1,080 on maturity. In this example, we assume all payments are made at the end of each year.

Part a of the box calculates the value of the bond assuming that market interest rates on similar long-term loans rise to 12 percent. Column 2 of the table shows the payment from the bond each year—$80 in each of the first six years and $1,080 in the seventh year. Column 3 gives the discount factor for each year, derived from the present value formula. Column 4 gives the discounted payment from the bond (column 2 times column 3). Adding up the figures in column 4, we see that the bond produces a total discounted payment of $815.60. That is its present value discounted at 12 percent. A buyer who paid $815.60 for this bond would earn a yield of 12 percent on the investment—the same yield as a percentage of the sum invested that would be earned if $1,000 were paid for a newly issued bond with a 12 percent coupon rate.

Part b of the box shows what happens to the present value of the bond if market interest rates rise to 18 percent. The calculations are as before, except that the discount factor for each year is adjusted to take into account the higher interest rate. At 18 percent, the present value of the bond is only $615.60. An investor who bought the bond when the market interest rate was 12 percent and sold it after the interest rate had risen to 18 percent would suffer a capital loss of some $200.

The principle of discounting applied to bond prices thus confirms the point that was established in the chapter: When market interest rates fall, bond prices in secondary markets rise, and when interest rates rise, bond prices fall.

Chapter 5

The Role of Government

After reading this chapter, you should be able to

1. Discuss the growth of government in the United States in terms of *government purchases* and *transfer payments*.
2. List five economic functions of government.
3. Describe the main features of the federal budgets in terms of spending programs and sources of funds.
4. Compare the budgets of state and local governments to that of the federal government.
5. Use supply-and-demand analysis to show the *incidence* of a sales tax.
6. Distinguish between *progressive* and *regressive* taxes, and discuss the U.S. tax system in terms of these concepts.
7. Explain government decision making in terms of *public choice theory*.

Ideas for Review

Here are some terms and concepts that you should review before you read this chapter:

Gross national product (Chapter 1)
Opportunity cost (Chapter 2)
Supply-and-demand analysis (Chapter 3)

After four of its delivery trucks were hijacked in as many weeks, Sanders Langsam Tobacco Company of New York City hired off-duty detectives to ride shotgun. The Sanders hijackings were part of a national trend. Cigarette hijacking fell for a time after 1978, when Congress made it a federal crime to transport cigarettes across state lines to evade taxes. But now, as some cities and states raise cigarette taxes while others hold the line, there is greater incentive to find ways of evading the tax.

In 1984 a pack of cigarettes that cost 78 cents in North Carolina, where they were made, cost $1.10 in New York City. Most of the difference was due to taxes. North Carolina, Virginia, and Kentucky keep their cigarette taxes low to please tobacco growers. New York city and state taxes total 29 cents a pack. That's enough of a profit to make many criminals less reluctant to tangle with the Feds.

But not all the people who haul cigarettes around to evade taxes are criminals. Many are consumers who duck across state lines to save a few cents a pack. For example, tiny New Hampshire leads the nation in cigarette sales. Does this mean that all those farmers and woodsmen are nicotine addicts? Guess again. Most of the extra cigarettes end up in neighboring Massachusetts, where the tax is 9 cents a pack higher.

Federal policies come into play in the cigarette story too. Washington lets military bases and Indian reservations sell cigarettes free of state and local taxes. This has resulted in widespread illegal selling of cigarettes to outsiders. Base and reservation sales cost state governments an estimated $179 million in 1983—not a small piece of change at a time when many state governments are scratching for pennies.[1]

Compared to the great debates on war and peace or taxes and deficits, cigarette bootlegging seems like a small footnote to the role of government in the economy. The dollar amounts are small compared to the costs of social security or an MX missile. But cigarette bootlegging, both criminal and casual, is a prime example of how government policies affect the economy. It shows how policies of federal, state, and local governments interact with one another. It shows how taxes, imposed to pay for government spending, have indirect effects. And it shows how economic policies are influenced by interest groups like tobacco growers and military personnel. These are all themes that we will take up in this chapter and return to throughout the book.

WHAT DOES GOVERNMENT DO?

Governments at various levels do many things. They run military bases and prisons, pay benefits to rich farmers and poor city dwellers, build dams, print money, and buy schoolbooks. There are many debates over whether governments do too much or too little or the wrong mix of things. But whether people agree or not on what government should do, they can agree that the economic role of government has grown.

[1]Based on Eugene Carlson, "Cigarette Bootlegging Threat Rising Due to Tax Disparities," *Wall Street Journal*, October 2, 1984, p. 33. Reprinted by permission of The Wall Street Journal, © Dow Jones & Company, Inc. 1984. All rights reserved.

The Growth of Government

Government purchases of goods and services (government purchases) Purchases of finished goods by government plus the cost of hiring the services of government employees and contractors.

Transfer payments Payments by government to individuals that are not made in return for goods and services currently supplied.

Box 5.1 shows how government in the United States has grown over the past 25 years. Two different measures are used to show how federal, state, and local governments have grown in relation to the economy as a whole.

The first measure is **government purchases of goods and services**, or **government purchases**, for short. It includes all the finished goods bought by governments (everything from submarines to typewriter ribbons) plus the cost of hiring the services of government employees and contractors (everyone from the president to the courthouse janitor).

As the chart shows, purchases by federal, state, and local governments have remained roughly constant at about 20 percent of GNP over the past 25 years. **Transfer payments**, on the other hand, have grown a great deal. They include all payments by governments to individuals that are not made in return for current services, such as social security benefits, unemployment compensation, and welfare outlays. Until 1967 transfer payments by all levels of government were about 5 percent of GNP. Since then they have grown to almost 12 percent.

Which is a better measure of the growth of government—government purchases or total expenditures, including transfers? The answer depends

**Box 5.1
Growth of Government in the United States, 1958–1984**

This chart shows the growth of the federal, state, and local governments combined, using two measures. In terms of government purchases of goods and services, the government sector has stayed roughly steady at about 20 percent of GNP. When transfer payments are taken into account, however, the government sector has grown from about one quarter to about one third of GNP.

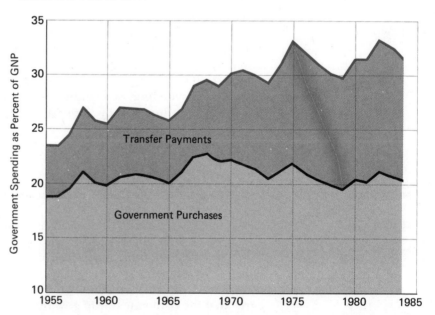

Source: *Economic Report of the President* (Washington, D.C.: Government Printing Office, 1985), Table B–75.

**Box 5.2
Size of Government in
Selected Countries**

Government spending as a percentage of GNP has grown in all of the advanced industrial countries for which data are given here. It remains far smaller in the United States than in these countries, however. The data cover all levels of government and include transfer payments as well as government purchases.

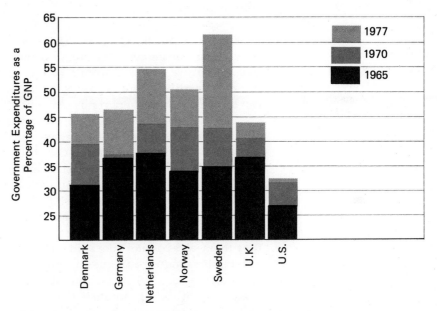

Source: Theodore Geiger, assisted by Frances M. Geiger, *Welfare and Efficiency: Their Interactions in Western Europe and Implications for International Economic Relations* (Washington, D.C.: National Planning Association, 1977), Table 1–1. Reprinted with permission.

on what you are trying to measure. Government purchases measure the percentage of GNP that is "used up" by government. They represent real resources that are shifted from satisfying private wants to satisfying public wants. By this measure, government has grown little, if at all, in the past 25 years. Transfer payments, in contrast, are funds that flow through the government without being used up. After they have been collected (through taxation or borrowing) and paid back out, they are still available to satisfy private wants.

Even so, total expenditures, including transfers, are in some ways a better measure of the growth of government than government purchases alone. For although transfer payments do not use up resources, the transfer process does determine who uses them and how they are used. Total government spending thus measures the share of the economy for which government decision making replaces market decision making. By this measure, government has continued to grow.

Even though the economic role of government in the United States is growing, however, it is still modest by world standards. Box 5.2 presents some comparisons. The data show that spending by all levels of government, as a percentage of GNP, is lower in the United States than in other advanced industrial countries.

The Functions of Government

Federal, state, and local governments use the portion of GNP that passes through their hands to perform a wide variety of functions. These can be classified under five main headings: provision of public goods, transfer of income, stabilization of the economy, regulation of private business, and administration of justice.

Public good

A good or service that (1) cannot be provided to one person without also being provided to others and (2) once provided to one person can be provided to others at zero added cost.

Provision of public goods   The first function of government is to provide **public goods**. In economics, public goods are goods and services that cannot be provided to one person without being provided to that person's neighbors, and that once they have been provided to one person, can be provided to others at no extra cost.

Perhaps the closest thing to a pure public good is national defense. One person cannot be protected against nuclear attack without having the protection extend to everyone. Also, it costs no more to protect a single resident of an area than to protect an entire city or region. Police and fire protection are also public goods in part. (Police and fire departments also provide many individual services.) Some people think the space program and even national parks are public goods, too. The idea is that people everywhere get satisfaction from reading or hearing about them even if they themselves do not take a ride in orbit or a hike in the mountains.

Public goods are frequently provided by government. It is difficult (although, as Box 5.3 shows, not always impossible) for private firms to make a profit selling products that, as soon as they are provided to one customer, become available to others at no additional cost. Imagine what would happen if someone tried to set up a private missile defense system, to be paid for by selling subscriptions to people who wanted protection from a nuclear attack. If my neighbors subscribed and got their houses protected, I would not need to subscribe too. Instead, knowing that if their houses could not be hit mine would be safe too, I would be tempted to be a "free rider."

The only problem is that my neighbors might reason the same way. They might not subscribe, hoping that I would. Then they could be the free riders. True, some people might be willing to pay their fair share. But that would not be enough to cover the whole cost. Those few public-spirited people would have to pay far more than their fair share to keep the service from going bankrupt. In short, it is unlikely that a private missile defense firm would ever get off the ground.

Transfers of income   The second function of government consists of transferring income from one household to another. As we saw in Box 5.1, transfer payments account for about one third of government expenditures in the United States.

Transfer payments include cash transfers, such as social security benefits and unemployment compensation, and in-kind transfers, such as Medicaid and food stamps. Besides these, the government provides certain services to all citizens in the belief that everyone deserves a certain share as a matter of right, regardless of ability to pay. Public education is a prime example. Education does not share the two properties of a true public good. It is possible to provide it to some people without providing it to their

Box 5.3
Private Marketing and the Public Goods Problem: The Case of Computer Software

To a substantial degree, computer software has the properties of a public good. Once a program for a game, a word processing system, or a spreadsheet system has been provided to one user, others are likely to make copies for their own use. And the cost of copying many kinds of software is near zero. Yet, despite these traits, writing and selling of computer software is a booming, multimillion-dollar private business. How is it done?

One technique is to "copy protect" software before it is sold. A program that cannot be copied no longer resembles a public good. Lotus Development Corp., creator of the popular 1-2-3 spreadsheet program for personal computers, uses this strategy. Copy protection has its drawbacks, however. For one thing, the codes used to protect the software can be broken, and the means of breaking them spread quickly along the grapevine of computer users. Also, copy-protected software is somewhat less convenient to use, a fact that gives competitors an advantage.

For these reasons, other major software suppliers sell their programs in a form that can be easily copied. Buyers are required as part of their purchase contract to pledge that they will not copy the program except to make extra copies for their own convenience. However, there is no barrier to copying by dishonest users. SoftWord Systems, designer of the MultiMate word processing program, is an example of a firm that restricts copying only by contract. The fact that thousands of users pay several hundred dollars for SoftWord's programs rather than using pirated copies attests to the fact that most people are honest.

A third approach to the free-rider problem relies even more directly on honesty. This is the Freeware® approach developed by the Headlands Press of Tiburon, California. This firm does not sell its popular program PC-Talk through computer stores or other retail channels. Instead, users are encouraged to make copies of the program and pass them around to their friends. A message encoded in the program invites new users to send a moderate contribution to The Headlands Press, and then to pass copies of the program along to their friends in turn. This unusual business strategy has earned tens of thousands of dollars (he won't say exactly how much) for computer author Andrew Fluegelman, Freeware's inventor. This example shows that the free-rider problem is not an absolute barrier to the private marketing of products that have the properties of a public good.

neighbors, and the cost of educating an additional student is not zero. Because public education is available even to people who pay few taxes, and because the costs are shared by taxpayers who do not use public schools, spending on education counts as a transfer of income.

Many details of federal, state, and local tax systems are also designed to transfer income. An example is the policy of excusing military personnel and residents of Indian reservations from payment of cigarette taxes. Other examples are tax deductions for charitable contributions, interest payments on home mortgages, and employer-paid health benefits.

Economic stabilization   The government's role in stabilizing the economy includes all policies aimed at promoting price stability, full employment, and economic growth. The major tools of stabilization policy are taxation, government spending, and monetary policy.

Regulation of private business   Regulation of private business is a fourth major function of government. Numerous agencies carry out regulation within a framework of laws passed by Congress and state legislatures. As Chapter 2 explained, government regulation affects the whole range of what, how, who, and for whom decisions made by households and firms. Many types of regulation are included in the subject matter of both macroeconomics and microeconomics.

Administration of justice   The fifth economic function of government is the administration of justice. Although courts and police are not always thought of in economic terms, they have a major effect on what, how, who, and for whom.

Think what happens, for example, when a judge makes a decision in a case involving an unsafe product, a breach of contract, or an auto accident. The decision has an immediate economic effect, in that one party must compensate the other. But the indirect economic effects of the decision are much wider. Other people see the outcome of the case and may change the way they do things. If the courts say that buyers can collect damages from the makers of unsafe products, firms may change their product designs. If certain standards are set for liability in auto accidents, automakers, road builders, and insurance companies will take notice.

Public Expenditures by Type of Program

The description of government activities that we have just given helps us understand the role of government in the economy, but it does not match the breakdown of government activities by program or agency.

Many government programs perform more than one function. For example, the main business of the Defense Department is to provide a public good, national defense, but the department does other things as well. It affects the distribution of income through its recruitment policies, especially in choosing whether to use a draft or voluntary enlistment as a means of gaining recruits. Its huge budget for the purchase of goods and services serves as a means of stabilizing the economy. The Defense Department regulates the activities of defense contractors, and it has its own system of military justice.

To get a full picture of the role of government in the economy, then, it is useful to break government activities down not only by function but also by program. This is done in Box 5.4.

Part a shows the pattern of federal government expenditures. The biggest category is income security. This includes the social security program, unemployment compensation, public assistance (welfare), and federal employee retirement and disability benefits. Income security has become the largest category of federal expenditures only since 1974. Before that, national defense, now in second place, took a larger share of the budget. As recently as 1968, national defense accounted for 40 percent of federal spending; now it has fallen to less than 30 percent. Because of large federal government deficits in recent years, interest payments on the national debt are growing rapidly.

Part b of Box 5.4 shows the pattern of state and local goverment spending. State governments accounted for about two fifths of this. By far the largest item in state and local government budgets is education.

**Box 5.4
Government
Expenditures, by
Program**

These charts compare federal government expenditures with those of state and local governments by program. Income security, which includes social security, unemployment benefits, public welfare, and so on, is the largest item for the federal government, followed by national defense. Because of high interest rates and extensive borrowing by the federal government, interest on the national debt is growing fast. Education is the largest item for state and local governments, followed by public welfare, highways, health and hospitals, and police and fire protection.

(a) Federal

(b) State and local

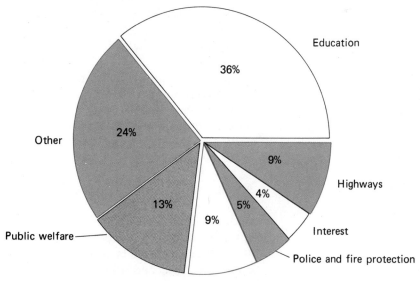

Sources: *Economic Report of the President* (Washington, D.C.: Government Printing Office, 1985), Table B-72; U.S. Department of Commerce, *Statistical Abstract of the United States: 1984*, 104th ed. (Washington, D.C.: Government Printing Office, 1983), Table 459.

Highways, welfare, police and fire protection, and hospitals and health programs are other major items.

FINANCING THE PUBLIC SECTOR

The other side of government budgets concerns sources of funds. These are shown in Box 5.5. Part a shows the sources of funds for the federal government for the 1984 budget year. Personal income taxes were the largest source of revenue, followed closely by social security taxes paid by employers and employees. Corporate income taxes, excise taxes, and other items such as customs receipts covered another 16 percent of federal spending. The remaining 22 percent of funds spent were raised by borrowing.

Part b of Box 5.5 gives similar information for state and local governments for 1981. For state governments, sales taxes were the largest source of revenue, and property taxes were the largest source for local government. Personal and corporate income taxes, and other sources such as fees and charges for services, were also important. The federal government contributed 21 percent of state and local funds through a variety of programs, including highway and sewage treatment grants, Medicaid, income security programs, and general revenue sharing. The data on which the graph is based do not reflect the operations of liquor stores, utilities, and pension trust funds of state and local governments. Some state and local units relied on borrowed funds in 1981, but the state and local government sector as a whole showed a small budget surplus for that year.

The Problem of Tax Incidence

Box 5.5 shows the kinds of taxes that support spending by various levels of government, but it does not show who really pays them. Economists refer to the question of who actually bears a tax burden as the problem of **tax incidence**.

Tax incidence
The question of who bears the actual burden of a tax, as opposed to who has the legal obligation to pay the tax.

It is not enough just to look up the tax records of federal, state, and local governments to determine the incidence of a tax. That would reveal only who had handed over the tax money, not who bore the economic burden. What makes tax incidence a difficult problem is the fact that the party who by law must pay the tax can often shift the economic burden to someone else.

An illustration of tax incidence   The cigarette tax mentioned at the beginning of this chapter will serve as an illustration. As Box 5.6 shows, finding out the incidence of a tax on cigarettes is a straightforward application of supply-and-demand analysis.

If there were no tax, the equilibrium price of cigarettes would be 80 cents per pack, and 100 million packs would be sold each day. Now suppose that cigarette makers are not allowed to sell cigarettes until a stamp has been attached to each pack showing that a tax of 40 cents has been paid. This tax upsets the equilibrium. Paying 40 cents for the tax stamp adds to the producers' costs of doing business, and the supply curve is shifted upward by 40 cents.

**Box 5.5
Sources of Government
Funds**

These charts show the sources of funds for federal, state, and local governments. The personal income tax is the largest item for the federal government, followed by employer and employee Social Security contributions. In 1984, 22 percent of federal spending was financed by borrowing. Individual and corporate income taxes are less important at the state and local levels. Sales taxes are the largest source of revenue for state governments, and property taxes are the largest source for local governments. The federal government provided 21 percent of state and local funds through revenue sharing and other programs. In 1981 state and local governments had a modest budget surplus, so borrowing does not appear as a source of funds.

(a) Federal

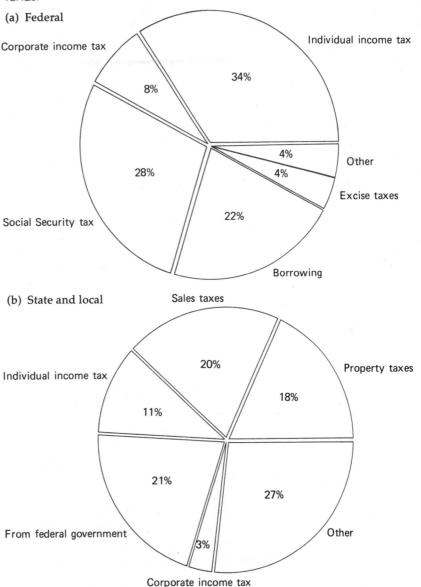

(b) State and local

Sources: *Economic Report of the President* (Washington, D.C.: Government Printing Office, 1985), Table B-72; U.S. Department of Commerce, *Statistical Abstract of the United States: 1984*, 104th ed. (Washington, D.C.: Government Printing Office, 1983), Table 459. The data for state and local governments do not reflect the activities of state utilities and liquor stores, or those of state and local trust funds and pension funds.

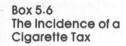

Box 5.6
The Incidence of a
Cigarette Tax

This graph shows how supply-and-demand analysis can be used to determine the incidence of a 40-cent tax on cigarettes. The tax shifts the supply curve upward by 40 cents. In the new equilibrium, buyers pay 20 cents per pack more than before the tax was imposed, and sellers get 20 cents per pack less. There is also an excess burden of the tax, in that output drops by 20 percent after the tax is imposed.

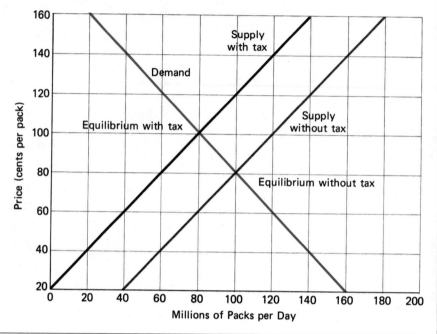

What will the new equilibrium price and quantity be? According to the new supply curve, if the price rose to $1.20 per pack, producers would be willing to supply the same 100 million packs a day as before. However, smokers would not buy 100 million packs a year at that price. An attempt by sellers to pass the entire 40-cents-a-pack tax on to consumers would result in a surplus of 40 million packs a day. This surplus would force the price back down. Sellers would then move down along their supply curve to the point where it intersects the demand curve at $1.00 per pack. That is the new equilibrium.

When we compare the old and new equilibriums, we see who bears the economic burden of the tax. Producers have shifted half of the tax to smokers, who now pay 20 cents a pack more than before. The other half of the tax is paid by producers, who receive 20 cents less, after paying the tax, than before.

In this example the tax burden is divided equally between buyers and sellers, but the division need not take this form. If the demand curve had happened to be steeper and the supply curve flatter, a larger share of the burden would have fallen on buyers. If the supply curve had been steeper than the demand curve, sellers would have borne a bigger share.

In practice, deciding who bears the burden of a tax can be difficult.

One reason is that it is hard to measure the slopes of the supply and demand curves. A second reason is that more than two parties may share the burden. For example, as mentioned in Chapter 4, the burden of the corporate income tax is shared partly by consumers, partly by stockholders, and partly by employees of corporations. Finally, many kinds of taxes interact in complex ways. For example, a complete analysis of the incidence of a cigarette tax might have to take into account the corporate income tax, general sales taxes added to the price of cigarettes at the point of sale, individual income taxes on tobacco company stockholders, and payroll taxes paid by corporate employees.

The excess burden of taxes   The cigarette tax described in the preceding example brings in $32 million a day on sales of 80 million packs. The burden of that $32 million is divided equally between consumers and producers. However, consumers and producers bear another burden as a result of the tax—a burden that is not reflected in any revenue for the government. This burden, which takes the form of lost opportunities for production and consumption, is called the **excess burden** of the tax.

Excess burden
An economic burden of a tax, besides the direct burden, that takes the form of lost opportunities for production and consumption.

The excess burden of the cigarette tax arises from the fact that consumers and producers, if left to themselves, would willingly make and buy another 20 million packs a day. The reduction of output from 100 million to 80 million units per day as a result of the tax is just as much a loss to them as if it had been caused by an explosion in a cigarette factory or a plague of locusts that ate up one fifth of the tobacco crop. Resources that formerly were used in this industry are shifted by the tax to other uses that are less preferred by consumers.

Now, in the case of cigarettes it can be argued that a drop in consumption is not all bad. Maybe smokers and tobacco growers would have been better off, in their own judgment, if output had remained at 100 million packs a day. But nonsmokers benefit from cleaner air and fewer cigarette burns on their furniture. This line of argument is a narrow one, however, that applies only to "goods" like cigarettes that happen also to be "bads" for people who are exposed to them unwillingly.

In the more general case, the excess burden of taxation is a true burden that is not offset by other factors. Taxes on income make people less willing to work, and thus cut output and employment. Taxes on profits, interest income, and capital gains make people less willing to save and invest, and thus cut economic growth and technological progress. Taxes on food and clothing make people less well fed and well dressed, and so on for other taxes. Economists often urge government decision makers to keep excess burdens in mind when they make taxing and spending decisions. Every dollar of tax revenue that the government raises imposes direct plus excess burdens on the economy that total more than a dollar.

Progressive and Regressive Taxes

Progressive tax
A tax that takes a larger percentage of income as income increases.

Regressive tax
A tax that takes a smaller percentage of income as income increases.

Up to this point, taxes have been discussed in terms of burdens on certain categories of people—consumers, producers, workers, and the like. Economists also ask how the burden of a tax is divided among taxpayers on the basis of their incomes. A **progressive tax** is one that takes an increasing percentage of income as income rises. A **regressive tax** takes a smaller

Proportional tax

A tax that takes an equal percentage of income at all levels.

Marginal tax rate

The percentage of each added dollar of income that is paid in taxes.

percentage of income as income rises. The intermediate case, in which a tax takes a constant percentage of income at all levels, is known as a **proportional tax**.

Box 5.7 presents data for two taxes, one regressive, the other progressive. Column 1 of the table shows six levels of household income, ranging from $5,000 to $100,000. Column 2 shows the amount of gasoline tax paid by families at each income level. The gasoline tax rate is 10 cents per gallon, so the amount paid depends on how much gasoline the family uses. Even poor families own cars and do some driving. Driving increases somewhat as income rises, up to an income of $15,000. Beyond that, gasoline consumption does not vary with further increases in income. Column 3 shows the gasoline tax paid as a percentage of income. The tax is regressive, since it takes a smaller percentage of income as income rises.

Column 4 of the table shows the income tax paid by households at each level of income. The income tax paid on each dollar of added income—that is, the **marginal tax rate**—increases as income increases, as shown in Column 5. The marginal tax rate is zero for the first $5,000 of income. Ten percent of the next $5,000 goes to taxes, as does 15 percent of income between $10,001 and $15,000, 20 percent of income between $15,001 and $20,000, and so on. This makes the income tax *progressive*, in that the amount paid increases as a percentage of income as income increases.

Columns 6 and 7 in Box 5.7 show the combined effects of the income and gasoline taxes both in absolute terms and as a percentage of income. In this hypothetical example, the effects of the progressive income tax more than outweigh the effects of the regressive gasoline tax, making the tax system as a whole progressive. This also appears to be the case for the tax system of the United States. State and local sales taxes, federal excise taxes

---

Box 5.7
Progressive and
Regressive Taxes

This box shows tax schedules for a gasoline tax and an income tax. The amount of gasoline tax paid increases somewhat with income at lower levels; but above a certain maximum, added income does not result in more miles driven or more tax paid. The gasoline tax is regressive because it takes a smaller share of income as income rises. The income tax, on the other hand, takes a larger share of income as income rises. This makes it a progressive tax. The combined effect of the two taxes is progressive, since the income tax outweighs the gasoline tax.

Income (1)	Gasoline Tax Paid (2)	Gasoline Tax as Percent of Income (3)	Income Tax Paid (4)	Marginal Tax Rate (5)	Total Taxes Paid (6)	Total Taxes as Percent of Income (7)
$ 5,000	$ 50	1.00	$ 0	0	$ 50	1.00
10,000	75	0.75	500	10	575	5.75
15,000	100	0.66	1,250	15	1,350	9.00
20,000	100	0.50	2,250	20	2,350	11.75
25,000	100	0.40	3,500	25	3,600	14.40
100,000	100	0.10	33,500	40	33,600	33.60

**Box 5.8
Distribution of the
Federal Income Tax
Burden**

The federal income tax is a progressive tax because it takes a higher percentage of income as income rises. This chart shows the distribution of the income tax in 1982. In that year, people in the upper half of the income distribution paid 92.8 percent of all federal income taxes, leaving just 7.2 percent of the federal tax burden to be paid by people in the lower half of the income distribution. As income increased, the percentage of taxes paid rose faster than the percentage of income received. At the very top, the 1 percent of taxpayers with the highest incomes paid almost 20 percent of all taxes but received only 9 percent of all income.

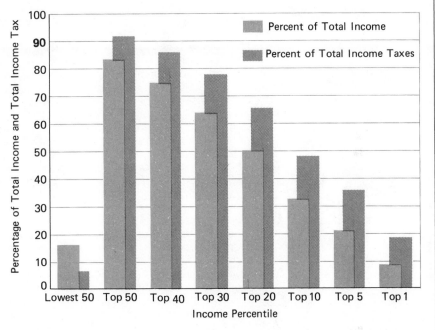

Source: Institute for Research on the Economics of Taxation, *Economic Policy Bulletin* 17 (Washington, D.C., n.d.), p. 5.

like the gasoline and cigarette taxes, and the social security payroll taxes are all regressive. However, the federal income tax is steeply progressive. (Box 5.8 gives some data.) Almost all studies of the matter have concluded that the tax system as a whole is progressive, although there is some disagreement as to just how progressive it is.

In recent years, many people have become concerned that the U.S. income tax has some serious flaws. In terms of marginal tax rates, say the critics, it is too progressive. The top tax rate of 50 percent provides too little incentive to save and invest. But at the same time, "loopholes" in the system allow many high-income households to avoid paying taxes. For these households the tax system is not progressive enough. As Box 5.9 relates, the critics would prefer a move to a more nearly proportional tax—a so-called *flat tax* that would have lower marginal rates and fewer loopholes.

Box 5.9
The Flat Tax—An Idea Whose Time Has Come?

The current U.S. federal income tax has many critics. It is too complex, say some. Too many people need professional help to fill out their tax forms. This complexity invites cheating. The tax is not fair, say other critics. Households with equal incomes do not pay equal taxes. Single people are taxed more heavily than married couples. Income from capital gains is less heavily taxed than wage and salary income. Homeowners are taxed less heavily than renters. Investors in tax shelters pay less than their fair share, leaving others to make up the difference. The tax system encourages inefficiency, say still others. Marginal tax rates of up to 50 percent discourage saving and investment. Firms in high-tech and service industries pay more tax than those in mining and smokestack industries, distorting the pattern of investment. The chorus of criticism goes on and on.

Is there a better way to meet the government's need for revenue? Yes, say advocates of a *flat tax*. A pure flat tax would be a proportional tax on all income from all sources. If all deductions, exclusions, and loopholes were eliminated, a single marginal tax rate of 20 percent or even less would bring in the same amount of revenue as today's income tax.

But not everyone loves the flat tax. Homeowners and homebuilders don't like the idea of giving up the tax deduction for home mortgage payments. Union members don't like the idea of giving up exclusions for employer-paid health insurance, life insurance, and pension programs. Colleges, churches, and charities don't like the idea of giving up the deduction for charitable contributions. And low-income households, which now pay little or no income tax, would find their tax rates rising under a pure flat-tax system. So the flat tax has its natural enemies as well as its natural friends.

Is a compromise possible? Maybe. As of 1985, at least three major proposals for "modified flat taxes" were before Congress. Typically, these plans would exempt low-income households from the income tax and would retain at least some of the most popular deductions, such as those for charitable contributions and mortgage interest payments. But compared to the present system, they would broaden the definition of taxable income, simplify the tax code, and lower tax rates for most households. The top marginal tax rates under the leading modified flat-tax plans range from 25 to 35 percent, compared to a top marginal rate of 50 percent under the present system.

So would you like to make the tax system fairer and more efficient and cut your own tax rate at the same time? If so, the flat-taxers are waiting to welcome you aboard their bandwagon.

THE ECONOMICS OF PUBLIC CHOICE[2]

We now have an idea of how much governments spend, what they spend it on, and how their spending is financed. In this section we turn to the question of why governments spend the amounts they do. This area of economics is known as *public choice theory*.

How Much Should Be Spent?

We begin with the question of how much government ought to spend on any particular program, once it is decided that the matter will not be left to

---

[2]This section can be omitted in an abbreviated course without loss of continuity.

the private sector. The usual approach is that of *benefit-cost analysis*. The object of such an analysis is to find out whether the benefits the public receives from a government program are great enough to justify its costs.

Box 5.10 gives an example of a benefit-cost analysis for the project of providing streetlighting in a community of three people, whom we will call Smith, Jones, and Brown. All three people would get some benefit from streetlights. However, they would not all benefit equally, because some of them go out at night more often than others. For the sake of the example, we will assume that Smith gets half of the total benefit of the streetlights, Jones gets 30 percent, and Brown 20 percent.

The more lights are provided, the greater the total benefits. However, the benefits are greatest for the first few lights. As more and more lights are added, each additional light adds less to the total benefit. Box 5.10 shows the marginal benefit at various levels of lighting, that is, the increase in benefits produced by adding one more light in the form of a downward-sloping line. Box 5.10 also shows the per-unit cost of the lighting program, assuming that lights cost $300 per unit. The cost per unit is shown as a horizontal line.

The information given in Box 5.10 is all we need for a benefit-cost

Box 5.10
Benefit-Cost Analysis of Streetlighting

This box shows the costs and benefits of streetlighting in a small community inhabited by three people: Smith, Jones, and Brown. Because they do not all go out at night equally often, the benefits are not distributed equally. Smith is assumed to get 50 percent of the total benefits, Jones 30 percent, and Brown 20 percent. Streetlights are assumed to cost $300 each. The efficient number of streetlights for this town is seven. Beyond that point, the added benefits of another light are less than the added cost.

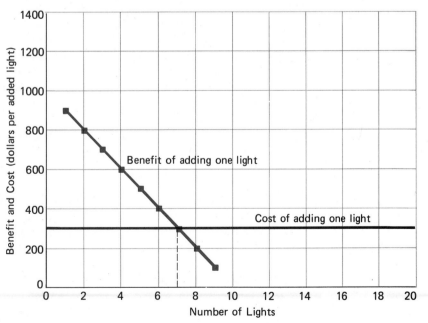

analysis of the streetlight program. The rule for efficient streetlighting is to add lights up to the point where the benefits of the last light just equal its costs. That means putting in seven lights. Smith gets $150 in benefits from the last light added; Jones gets $90 in benefits; and Brown gets $60 in benefits, for a total of $300. That is enough to justify the $300 cost of the last light. An eighth light would give them only $200 more in benefits—not enough to justify the cost.

How Much Will Be Spent: Direct Democracy

Now that we know how much should be spent, using the benefit-cost standard, we move on the question of how much will be spent. A basic principle of public choice theory is that the amount that will be spent depends on the community's political structure. In particular, we need to know the rules for decision making and the rules for sharing the costs of the program among members of the community.

We begin with the case of direct democracy, in which all citizens vote on each issue. This is the procedure followed in the New England town meeting. Within the framework of direct democracy, we will look at three ways of sharing costs among members of the community.

Costs shared in proportion to benefits received   First let's look at the case in which costs are shared in proportion to the benefits received. This means, in our example, that for each dollar of taxes raised, Smith pays 50 cents, Jones 30 cents, and Brown 20 cents.

Under these conditions the town meeting will be a model of harmony. "Should we put up, say, five lights?" says Smith. Smith calculates that the fifth light will give him $250 in benefits (half of the total benefit of $500) and will cost him $150 (half of the $300 cost of an extra light). Jones and Brown also see that the fifth light will give them more in benefits than their share of the cost. The vote for five lights is unanimous.

"Let's vote a sixth light," says Jones. He figures that the sixth light will bring him $120 in benefits (30 percent of the total benefit) and will cost him just $90 (30 percent of the total cost). Smith and Brown make their calculations, and again the vote is unanimous.

"Why not a seventh light?" says Brown. His share of the $300 benefit will be $60, exactly the same as his share of the $300 cost. Indeed, why not? Smith and Jones agree.

Then the meeting falls silent. No one wants to vote another light. Each sees that his share of the eighth light's benefits would be smaller than his share of its costs. They all go home, having hit the benefit-cost nail on the head.

Conclusion: In a direct democracy where taxes are shared in exact proportion to the benefits of public programs, the most efficient amount of spending, no more and no less, will take place, provided that everyone votes according to his or her own self-interest.

Costs shared equally   The next case we will look at is that of a direct democracy in which costs are shared equally but benefits are not. To continue our example, this would mean that Smith, Jones, and Brown would each pay $100 of the $300 cost of each light.

Given this distribution of benefits, the town meeting would go a bit differently. The proposal for a fifth light would still be passed by a unanimous vote, but just barely. Smith would be looking at $250 in benefits to offset his $100 in costs; Jones would see $150 in benefits and $100 in costs; and Brown $100 in benefits and $100 in costs. The proposal for a sixth light would pass by a vote of 2 to 1. This time Brown would be looking at $80 in benefits and $100 in costs. If he voted in his own self-interest (as public choice theorists assume), he would vote no. And the proposal for a seventh light would lose by a 1-to-2 vote. Smith would see $150 in benefits and $100 in costs; Jones, $90 in benefits and $100 in costs; and Brown, $60 in benefits and $100 in costs.

Conclusion: In a direct democracy, when the costs of a program are distributed evenly but the benefits are not, there will be a tendency to spend less than the efficient amount on each government program.

Benefits equal, costs shared unequally   Our third case assumes that the benefits of the streetlights are distributed equally but the costs are shared unequally: Smith now pays 60 percent of total taxes while Jones and Brown pay 20 percent each.

By now the reasoning is familiar, although the results are different. Smith drops out on the vote for the fifth light, since his share of the benefits ($166) now falls short of his share of the costs ($180). Lights six and seven also pass by 2-to-1 votes. Then the eighth light comes up for a vote. The total benefits of the eighth light are just $200—less than the cost. But Jones and Brown's share of the benefit is $66—more than their $60 share of the cost. So eight lights, one more than the efficient number, are approved.

Conclusion: In a direct democracy, when the benefits of a program are spread evenly but the costs are shared unequally, there will be a tendency to spend more than the efficient amount on each government program.

How Much Will Be Spent: Representative Democracy

It is possible to come up with real-world examples that fit each of the three cases we have just reviewed. Highway construction can be compared with the example in which costs and benefits fall equally on each citizen, in that much of the cost of highway construction is paid for by gasoline taxes and other road use taxes. For an example in which costs are spread equally but benefits are not, think of a town in which there are many retired people but only a few young families. Such a town is likely to be stingy with its school budget. And for an example in which benefits are spread equally but costs are shared unequally, think of a proposal to fight a war using an army of draftees. All citizens benefit from national defense, whereas the burden of the draft falls only on young men.

However, there are many government programs that do not fit any of the three patterns we have discussed. In a direct democracy one would never see programs that benefit a small group of people at the expense of taxpayers in general. One also would never see votes for tax loopholes that excuse a small group of citizens from bearing their fair share of the costs of programs that benefit all citizens equally. Yet such programs are the meat and potatoes of Congress, state legislatures, and city councils. How do such programs make it through the democratic process?

Public choice theorists think the answer lies in the ways in which the representative democracy of most of the United States differs from the direct democracy of a town meeting. In this section we will look at three features of representative democracy that tend to favor programs that would not stand up to a vote by the whole population.

Costs of information and political expression   In a representative democracy the population as a whole elects representatives, and they in turn vote on each issue that comes up. This means that citizens who want to influence government decisions must follow a two-step process. First, they must become informed about the issues and decide what decisions they would like to see made. And second, they must convince their representatives to favor their views.

Both steps in this process have opportunity costs. Becoming informed takes time, at the very least. Expressing oneself through letters, telegrams, newspaper ads, and lobbying in Washington or the state capital costs both time and money. Few voters feel that they have enough at stake in any one issue to repay the effort of even writing a letter.

But groups of people with shared interests are in a different situation. They can share the costs both of keeping informed and of making their views known to their representatives. They can hire full-time lobbyists. As a result, their influence may be greater than would be possible if each member acted alone.

The case of airport congestion, discussed in Chapter 3, provides an example. One way to relieve airport congestion would be to charge higher fees for "general aviation"—the small private planes that account for 16 percent of all flights at the nation's busiest airports. As of now, fees paid by general aviation account for only about 6 percent of the FAA's fund for airport improvements, far less than the share of the benefits enjoyed by general aviation. But general aviation has a strong lobby, the 270,000-member Aircraft Owners and Pilots Association. Although the AOPA has a membership that is only a fraction of the number of people who suffer delays on commercial flights each year, its president, John L. Baker, says its members will "make a hell of a nuisance of ourselves" if the government threatens to raise their fees. One airline executive rates the AOPA lobby as "100-to-1" more effective than that of commercial airlines and their passengers.[3]

Vote trading   Representative democracy differs from direct democracy in another key way. Voters do not vote often, and few of them meet for political purposes between elections. Representatives, on the other hand, vote on hundreds of issues every session, and they meet daily. As a result, they routinely engage in vote trading—or *logrolling*, as the practice is often called.

The idea of logrolling is very simple. Each representative selects a few issues that are important to the voters in his or her home state or district. In exchange for yes votes on those issues, he or she promises to vote for issues that are important to other representatives. Trading away a vote on an issue that affects people far away in order to gain a vote on an issue that affects

---

[3]See John Paul Newport, Jr., "The Big Role of Little Planes," *Fortune*, October 1, 1984, p. 38.

the folks at home is a good deal for both the representative and the voters back home.

Logrolling leads to the passage of certain kinds of programs that would never be approved by a direct democracy. These are programs that have great benefits for a few people and costs that are spread widely among all taxpayers. A recent Senate vote on the Hoover Dam is a case in point. Since 1937, the Hoover Dam has been generating electricity that, by federal law, is sold to consumers in California, Nevada, and Arizona at rates that are one fourth to one fourteenth of commercial electric rates. The law was scheduled to expire in 1987, at which time rates would have gone up to normal market levels. But just before the 1984 elections a bill was brought up in the Senate to extend the law for another 30 years.

The bill would directly benefit the citizens of only three states. Taxpayers in the rest of the country would have to make up for the federal revenue lost through cut-rate electricity sales from the Hoover Dam. Yet the bill passed the Senate by a vote of 64 to 34. Every senator from a state west of Missouri voted to continue the subsidy. In return for supporting their colleagues from Arizona, Nevada, and California on this issue, they could expect their colleagues' votes for subsidized water or power projects in their own states.[4]

The self-interest of representatives   A third major difference between representative and direct democracies lies in the fact that representatives have interests of their own that do not always match those of the voters who elect them. One of these is the interest in being reelected. Whether representatives want to promote the interests of voters, want to fight for a cause, want power and prestige, or simply want to have a job, getting reelected is a must.

Getting reelected costs money, though, so the representative must become an entrepreneur. Sources of campaign contributions must be found. Lobbyists for special-interest groups are one of the richest sources of contributions to political candidates.

As a case in point, consider the dairy lobby, mentioned in Chapter 3. When the Reagan administration started talking about cutting dairy subsidies, the lobby got out its checkbook. In the next 23 months it gave $1,343,868 to 293 members of the House of Representatives. Included in this number were 117 representatives from urban districts—those with farm populations of less than 1 percent. Of those, 72 voted with the dairy lobby and against the milk drinkers in their own districts.[5]

Members of Congress are very sensitive about charges of vote selling. It is doubtful that many of them would sell a vote outright. But campaign contributions do buy time on representatives' crowded schedules. And often the side that gets the time to present its views most fully is the side that wins.

---

[4]See George F. Will, "Conservative Cowboys Head 'em Off at the Hoover Dam," *Washington Post*, August 9, 1984, p. A–23.

---

[5]See Brooks Jackson and Jeffrey Birnbaum, "Dairy Lobby Obtains U.S. Subsidies with Help from Urban Legislators," *Wall Street Journal*, November 18, 1983, p. 33.

Strengths and Weaknesses of Democracy

It should not be thought that lobbying and logrolling are all bad. The economic problems of government would not be solved by running the country as one huge town meeting. It is quite possible for programs that give great benefits to a minority in return for small costs for the majority to pass strict benefit-cost tests. Lobbying and logrolling are used to fund national parks, pass civil rights laws, send people to the moon, ratify arms control treaties, and promote other causes that many people think are noble. Representative government simply would not work without these practices.

Public choice theorists do not seek to praise or condemn the economic workings of government so much as simply to explain them. They believe that when the costs and benefits of programs are shared in certain ways, the government tends to fund them at an efficient level. When the costs and benefits are shared in other ways, programs are funded that cannot stand up to benefit-cost analysis. Representative democracy, they conclude, is neither all good nor all bad. It simply lacks an economic rudder to make sure that the political equilibrium matches the economic optimum.

Summary

1. The size of government can be measured in two ways. *Government purchases of goods and services* include all the goods bought by government and the cost of hiring the services of all government employees and contractors. By this measure, the size of the federal, state, and local governments combined has held steady at about 20 percent of GNP for the last 25 years. *Transfer payments*, on the other hand, have increased from about 5 percent of GNP to almost 12 percent over the same period.

2. Five key functions of government are provision of *public goods*, transfer of income, stabilization of the economy, regulation of private business, and administration of justice.

3. Income security (transfer payments) is the largest item on the spending side of the federal budget, followed by defense and interest on the national debt. The personal income tax and social security taxes are the largest sources of tax revenue for the federal government. In some recent years, the federal government has raised more than one fifth of the funds it needs by borrowing.

4. Education is by far the largest item on the spending side of the budgets of state and local governments, followed by public welfare, highways, health and hospitals, and police and fire services. Property taxes are the largest source of revenue for local governments, and sales taxes are the largest source for state governments. Many state and local governments also use an income tax. In recent years the federal government has provided about one fifth of the funds spent by state and local governments.

5. Economists refer to the question of who bears the burden of taxes as the problem of *tax incidence*. In simple cases like that of cigarette taxes, supply-and-demand analysis can show how the burden of the tax is shared by producers and consumers. In more complex cases, like that of corporate income taxes, it is less easy to determine the incidence of the tax. All taxes, however, produce an *excess burden*. This takes the form of lost opportunities for production and consumption that result from decisions people make in response to taxes.

6. A *progressive* tax is one that takes a greater percentage of income as income rises. A *regres-*

sive tax takes a smaller percentage of income as income rises. A *proportional* tax takes a constant percentage of income at all levels. The amount of each added dollar of income that is taken by an income tax is known as the *marginal tax rate*. The social security tax, state and local sales taxes, and property taxes tend to be regressive. The federal income tax is steeply progressive, however. The 50 percent of taxpayers with the highest incomes pay 93 percent of all income taxes. As a result, the U.S. tax system as a whole is progressive.

7. The area of economics that studies decision making in government, including the question of why governments choose the programs they do and spend the amounts they do, is known as *public choice theory*. Public choice theory holds that these decisions depend on a community's political structure and its rules for sharing the costs of government programs. In some cases, voting rules and cost-sharing rules favor efficient levels of government spending; in others, they favor over- or underspending on certain kinds of programs.

Questions for Review

1. Explain the following terms and concepts:
   government purchases of goods and services (government purchases)
   transfer payments
   public goods
   tax incidence
   excess burden
   progressive tax
   regressive tax
   proportional tax
   marginal tax rate
2. How can the size of the government sector of the U.S. economy be measured? By what measures, if any, has it grown in the past 25 years? Is government in the United States large or small compared with government in other advanced industrial countries?
3. List five key functions of government and give examples of each.
4. What are the main categories of spending by federal, state, and local governments in the United States? What are their main sources of funds?
5. Who really bears the economic burden of a sales tax? What is meant by the "excess burden" of such a tax? Why is it hard to determine the incidence of many taxes?
6. Define and give examples of progressive and regressive taxes. Is the U.S. tax system as a whole progressive or regressive?
7. What is public choice theory? According to that theory, under what conditions will a government tend to over- or underspend on a program? Under what conditions will it tend to spend just the right amount?

Problems and Topics for Discussion

1. Look for data to use in updating Boxes 5.1, 5.4, 5.5, and if possible, 5.2. The source notes in the boxes will tell you where to start looking.
2. "When a police department patrols the streets to deter muggings, it is producing a public good. When it investigates a specific burglary or works to solve a specific murder, on the other hand, it is performing a service that is not a public good in the technical sense." Do you agree or disagree with this statement? Discuss.
3. Turn to Box 3.11a (p. 68), which shows the market for dental services in equilibrium. Change the title of the horizontal axis to read

"Millions of Fillings per Year." Change the title of the vertical axis to read "Dollars per Filling." Leave the numbers on the axes the same. What is the equilibrium price and quantity for fillings?

Suppose that the government imposes a tax on fillings. Each time a dentist fills a tooth, he or she must pay a $15 fee to the Bureau of Dental Revenue. How much revenue will this tax raise? How will the burden be split between dentists and their patients? Does the tax have an excess burden? What is the nature of the excess burden?

4. The text suggests that the excess burden of a tax on cigarettes is offset by the benefit to nonsmokers in the form of cleaner air. Could this suggestion be applied to taxes on "bads" of all kinds? What about a tax on car ownership based on the amount of pollution the car emits? A tax on electric power stations of so much per ton of sulfur dioxide they let escape from their smokestacks? Discuss.

5. A city of 10,000 citizens is divided into 100 wards, each containing 100 voters. Each ward elects one member of the city council by majority vote. The council makes its decisions by majority vote. There is no logrolling, lobbying, or vote buying in the council. Of the 10,000 citizens, 2,601 are smokers and 7,399 are nonsmokers. The nonsmokers favor a law that would ban all smoking in public places. Smokers oppose the law. Can you distribute the smokers among the wards in such a way that they will be able to block passage of the antismoking law? Does this example suggest another technique for passing special-interest legislation, or blocking legislation that is favored by a majority, in a representative democracy? Can you think of any real-world examples of this phenomenon?

6. **Case for Discussion**
Bethel, Vermont: By a close vote of 198 to 179, Bethel voters last Wednesday rejected a plan to build a sewage treatment plant for the village at a local cost of $950,000.

As a result, Bethel will continue to be the only municipal polluter of the White River.

The total project cost was to be $4.4 million, with the federal and state governments picking up the balance of the tab. . . .

Over 100 more people voted last Wednesday than had voted in early August, when a slightly more expensive plan was turned down, also by a narrow margin. Some observers guessed that the extra 100 voters were those from outside the Village area, taxpayers who would have to help support the new system but would receive no direct benefit from it.[6]

Note: In Vermont, a "village" is a built-up area of houses and streets. A "town" is a political unit that includes both a village and the surrounding rural areas. All issues—those that affect only village residents and those that affect the whole town—are decided by a majority vote of town residents.

Questions:
a. Compare the Bethel vote to the Smith-Jones-Brown examples in the text. What pattern does the Bethel case fit?

b. Do you think the federal policy of paying all or most of the costs of local sewage plants would, other things being equal, encourage spending of just the right amount, too much, or too little on the construction of such plants? In answering, consider the fact that much of the benefit of the Bethel sewage plant would go to people downstream in other towns and states along the White River and the Connecticut River.

c. If you were a Bethel selectman (selectmen prepare proposals to be presented at the town meeting) how would you change the sewage plant proposal to increase its chances of passing?

---

[6]*White River Valley Herald* (Randolph, VT), October 4, 1984, p. 1.

Suggestions for Further Reading

Buchanan, James, and Gordon Tullock. *The Calculus of Consent*. Ann Arbor: University of Michigan Press, 1962.

A classic treatment of the economics of public goods and public choice.

Gifford, Adam, Jr., and Gary J. Santoni. *Public Economics*. Hinsdale, Ill.: Dryden Press, 1979.

A treatment of the economics of government that focuses on public goods and public choice theory.

Musgrave, Richard A., and Peggy B. Musgrave. *Public Finance in Theory and Practice*, 4th ed. New York: McGraw-Hill, 1984.

Public finance theory is the field of economics that studies government. This is one of the most widely used texts.

Posner, Richard A. *Economic Analysis of Law*. Boston: Little, Brown, 1973.

A good introduction to the economic analysis of the administration of justice. Recommended for anyone who is thinking about a career in law.

John Maynard Keynes, a noted economist and prominent society figure of the 1920s and 1930s.

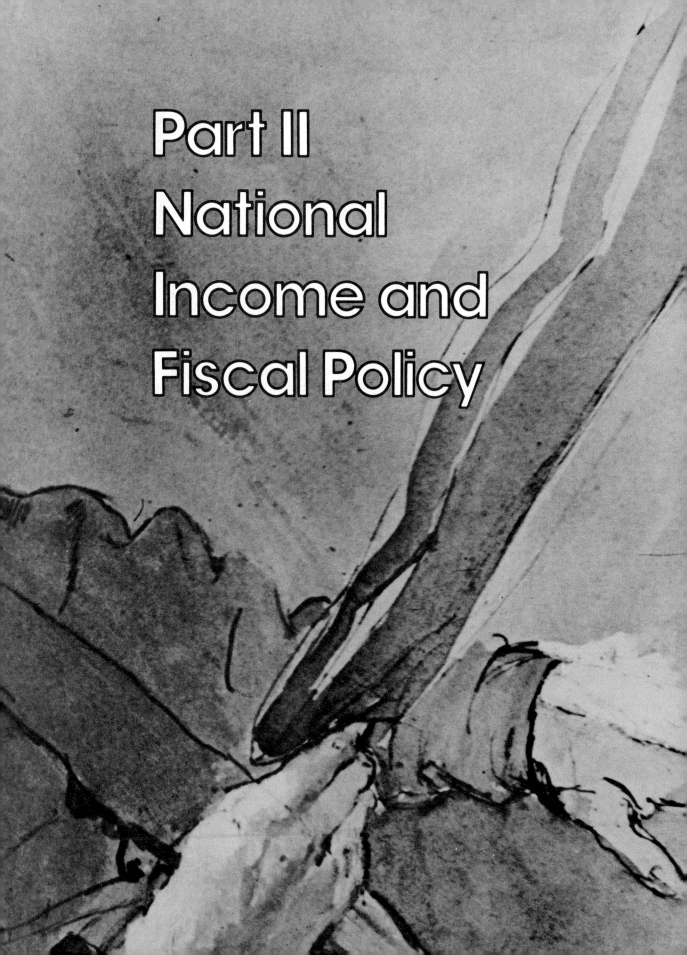

Part II
National
Income and
Fiscal Policy

Chapter 6

The Circular Flow of Income and Product

After reading this chapter, you should be able to

1. Outline the *circular flow of income and product* in an economy made up of households and firms.
2. Distinguish between *stocks* and *flows* in the economy.
3. Define *national income* and *national product* and explain how they are related.
4. Show how *saving* and *investment* fit into the circular flow of income and product.
5. Explain what is meant by *aggregate nominal supply* and *aggregate nominal demand*.
6. Apply the concept of equilibrium to the circular flow of income and product.
7. Show how the government sector fits into the circular flow.
8. Show how imports and exports fit into the circular flow.
9. Explain the concepts of *leakages* and *injections* and the relationship between them.

Ideas for Review

Here are some terms and concepts that you should review before you read this chapter:

Macroeconomics (Chapter 1)
Factors of production (Chapter 1)
Gross national product (Chapter 1)
Real and nominal values (Chapter 1)
Supply and demand (Chapter 3)
Equilibrium (Chapter 3)
Inventories (Chapter 3)
Financial markets (Chapter 4)
Balance sheet, asset, and liability (Chapter 4)
Government purchases of goods and services (Chapter 5)
Transfer payments (Chapter 5)

"Summer doldrums"

Summer doldrums beset the largest sector of the economy in 1984 as consumers retrenched sharply. After a 6 percent annual rate of increase in real terms during the first 18 months of the recovery from the 1981–1982 recession, personal consumption expenditures fell back in July and August to a level barely above the second-quarter average. A 5 percent decline in third-quarter auto sales contributed to the weakness, no doubt partly due to shortages of popular models. But consumers stayed away from lots of other goods.

Business outlays for capital goods also slowed dramatically during the third quarter, judging by monthly data available for shipments of machinery and equipment as well as for business construction. After rising at a 20 percent annual rate in real terms for a year, the pace probably slowed to around 10 percent. But although increases are likely to be smaller in the months ahead, construction contracts and orders for new equipment indicate continued expansion.

The most worrisome signal about third-quarter activity is from a sector that speeded up—inventory accumulation. Business replenishing empty shelves and showrooms added a powerful push to the economy right from the start of the recovery. Now a few hints are appearing that they have enough stocks on hand. *Fortune* estimates that the ratio of inventory to final sales increased 2 percent in the third quarter, bringing it above what business wants for the first time since early 1983. To the extent that the third-quarter bulge in inventory was unplanned and unwanted, the effect will be felt quickly. Industrial production, which hardly grew in August, could level off for a few more months.[1]

The summer doldrums of 1984 proved to be only a brief pause in the economy's expansion. But year in and year out, the news brings us stories like this one. The stories focus on the way each part of the economy— consumer spending, business outlays for capital goods, inventory levels or whatever—influence the economy as a whole. The picture is one of an economy in which millions of separate firms and households, each making decisions independently, interact to produce recessions, recoveries, slowdowns, and booms. This chapter gives an overview of the way the various parts of the economy fit together. In doing so, it lays the foundation for all of the macroeconomic theories that follow.

THE BASIC CIRCULAR FLOW

Circular flow of income and product
The flow of goods and services between households and firms, balanced by the flow of payments made in exchange for the goods and services.

The concept around which this chapter is built is the **circular flow of income and product**—that is, the flow of goods and services between households and firms, which is balanced by the flow of money payments made in exchange for the goods and services.

To see the circular flow in its simplest form, imagine an economy in which there is no government, no financial markets, and no imports or exports. To make things even simpler, imagine that the households in this

[1]"Growth Will Slow—But Not Too Much," *Fortune*, October 15, 1984, pp.48–49. Reprinted by permission of FORTUNE Magazine.

economy live entirely from hand to mouth, spending all their income on consumer goods as soon as that income is received, and that firms sell all their output directly to consumers as soon as it is produced.

Box 6.1 shows the circular flow of income and product for this ultrasimple economy. Real goods and services are shown flowing clockwise. Two sets of markets link households and firms. Product markets, which appear at the top of the diagram, are those in which households buy goods and services produced by firms. Factor markets, which appear at the bottom, are those in which firms obtain the labor services, capital, and natural resources they need from households.

The clockwise flows of goods and services through these markets are balanced by counterclockwise flows of money payments. Households make payments for the things they buy in product markets. Firms make factor payments—wages, interest payments, rents, royalties, and so on—in exchange for the factor services they buy. These money flows are measured

**Box 6.1
The Basic Circular Flow**

In this simple economy, households spend all their income on consumer goods as soon as they receive it, and firms sell all their output to households as soon as they produce it. Goods and services flow clockwise and the corresponding payments flow counterclockwise.

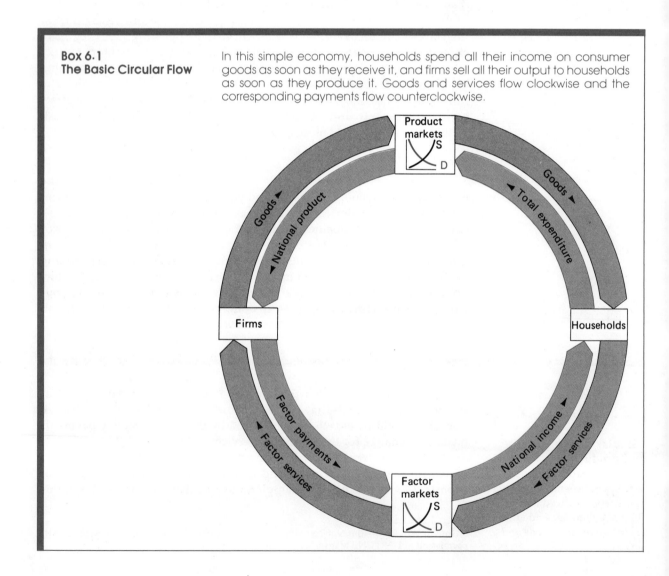

in nominal terms, that is, in terms of the dollar prices at which goods and services are bought and sold.

By convention, when firms use labor, capital, or natural resources that they themselves own, they are counted as "buying" those factors from the households that are the ultimate owners of the firms. All costs of production therefore can be viewed as factor payments. If a firm has something left over after it meets all its costs, it earns a profit. Profits too are counted as flowing directly to the households that own the firms, even though some profit may be retained by a firm to increase owners' equity rather than being paid out as dividends. For purposes of the circular flow, then, profit is lumped together with payments for labor, capital, and natural resources to make up total factor payments.

Flows
Processes that occur continuously through time, measured in units per time period.

We refer to all the amounts shown as arrows in Box 6.1 as **flows** because they are processes that occur continuously. Flows are measured in units per time period—in dollars per year, gallons per minute, or tons per month. Measurements of flows are measurements of rates at which things are happening.

Stocks
Quantities that exist at a point in time, measured in terms of units only.

It is important to distinguish flows from stocks. **Stocks** are quantities that exist at a point in time. (The word *stock* in this sense has nothing to do with the common stocks that represent shares of ownership in a corporation.) Stocks are measured in terms of dollars, gallons, tons, and so on at a given point in time.

To illustrate the difference between stocks and flows, we can think of a bathtub filling. When we talk about how fast the water is running into the tub, we are talking about a *flow*, measured in gallons per minute. When we talk about how much water is in the tub at any given moment, we are talking about a stock, measured in gallons. To take an example that is more closely related to economics, we might talk about the rate of housing construction in Buffalo, New York, in terms of new units built per month (a flow). This would be distinct from the total number of houses standing in Buffalo on January 1, 1985 (a stock).

National Income and Product

National income
The total income received by households, including wages, rents, interest payments, and profits.

Two of the flows in Box 6.1 deserve special attention. The first is **national income**—the total value, measured in nominal terms, of all wages, rents, interest payments, and profits received by households. The second is **national product**—the total nominal value of all goods and services produced. National product is the dollar flow to firms that balances the flow of goods and services from firms to product markets. National income and national product are, by definition, equal in this simple economy.[2] This can be verified in two ways.

National product
The total value of all goods and services produced in the economy.

First, consider expenditures by households as a link between national income and national product. Households are assumed to spend all their

---

[2]As we will see in Chapter 8, establishing the equality of national income and product as measured in the official national income accounts requires a bit more detail than is shown here. Among other things, we will have to distinguish between *gross* and *net* national product, which are two ways of measuring this part of the circular flow. These details of national income accounting are not very important for the discussion of macroeconomic theory in this and later chapters, however.

income on consumer goods as soon as they receive it, and firms are assumed to sell all their output directly to households. The payments made by buyers must be equal to the payments received by sellers, so national product must be equal to national income, viewed from this side of the circular flow.

Now consider factor payments as a link between national income and national product. When firms receive money for the goods and services they sell, they use part of it to pay workers, resource owners, and suppliers of capital. Anything left over is profit. Factor payments, including profits, thus account for all the money received by households, and total factor payments therefore are equal to national income. It follows that national income and national product are equal when viewed from this side of the circular flow too.

Saving and Investment

The circular flow shown in Box 6.1 is only a first step in representing all the linkages between households and firms. The next step is to add a second set of linkages to the circular flow—linkages that involve saving, investment, and financial markets.

Chapter 4 introduced the idea of financial markets as links between firms, which on the average spend more for new investment than they take in, and households, which on the average take in more than they spend. Box 6.2 shows households as lenders that supply the funds flowing into financial markets and firms as borrowers that use those funds. To simplify this and the following circular-flow diagrams, the clockwise flows of real goods and services have been left out and only the nominal flows of funds are shown. Also, no distinction is made between direct financing (sales of stocks and bonds directly to households) and indirect financing (borrowing from financial intermediaries such as banks, thrift institutions, and insurance companies).

Saving   The part of household income that is not used to buy goods and services or pay taxes.

Saving   The flow of funds from households to financial markets is labeled "Saving" in Box 6.2. **Saving** is the part of household income that is not used to buy goods and services or to pay taxes. (There are no taxes in this economy yet, but they will soon be added.) The most familiar form of saving is the use of a part of a household's income to make deposits in bank accounts, to buy stocks or bonds, and so on rather than to buy goods and services. Economists, however, have a broader view of saving. They also consider households to be saving when they repay debts. Debt repayments are a form of saving because they too are income that is not devoted to consumption or taxes. Like other saving, debt repayment is a source of funds for financial markets. For example, if a bank receives a $100 payment on an auto loan, it can use that $100 to make new loans much as it could use a $100 deposit in a savings account.

Fixed investment   Purchases by firms of newly produced capital goods, such as production machinery, newly built structures, and office equipment.

Inventory investment   Changes in the stocks of finished products and raw materials that firms keep on hand; this figure is positive if such stocks are increasing and negative if they are decreasing.

Investment   Firms use the funds they obtain from financial markets to make two kinds of investments. The first is **fixed investment**—the purchase of newly produced capital goods, including production machinery, newly built structures, and office equipment. The second is **inventory**

**Box 6.2
The Circular Flow with
Saving and Investment**

When saving and investment are added to the circular flow, there are two paths by which funds can travel on their way from households to product markets. One path is direct, via consumption expenditures. The other is indirect, via saving, financial markets, and investment. The clockwise flows of goods and services have been left out of this diagram. Only flows of funds are shown.

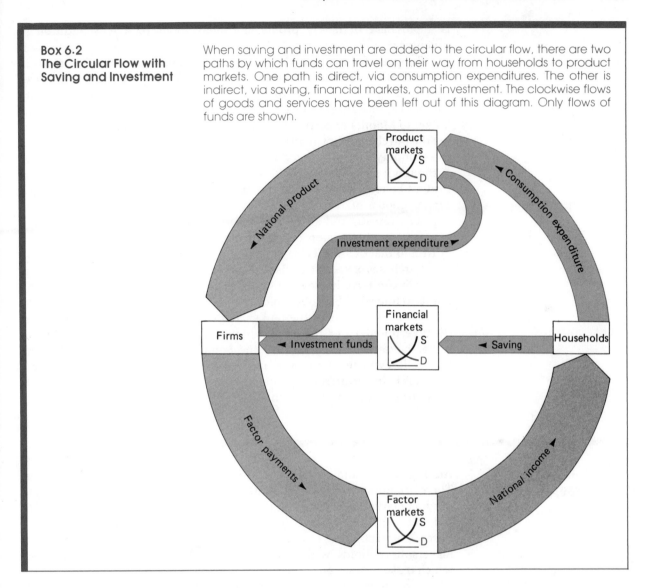

Investment
The sum of fixed investment and inventory investment.

investment—the accumulation of stocks of raw materials prior to use or of finished products prior to sale. (Inventory investment can be less than zero in periods when firms are reducing their stocks of raw materials and finished products.) When the term **investment** is used by itself in this book, it means total investment—the sum of fixed investment and inventory investment.

Note that *investment* is defined somewhat more narrowly in economics than in everyday usage. In everyday usage the purchase of almost any kind of asset is called an investment. Thus, a person or firm might be said to "invest" in stocks, real estate, or secondhand oil tankers. None of these purchases is an investment in the economic sense, however, because none is a purchase of newly produced capital goods or a new addition to inventory.

Suppose, for example, that Exxon buys a brand new oil tanker, made to order. That would be an investment, part of the flow of goods and services produced by the economy in the year it is built. The tanker goes onto Exxon's balance sheet as an asset. A few years later Exxon decides to sell the tanker to Mobil. For carrying oil, a used tanker is just as good as a new one; yet the purchase is not an investment in the economic sense. It is not part of the economy's output of goods and services in the year it changes hands. Although it shows up on Mobil's balance sheet as a new asset, it passes off Exxon's balance sheet at the same time. Likewise, purchases of other used capital goods, of real estate (other than new structures), or of mineral deposits, forests, and so on are not investments in the economic sense. They are simply transfers of assets from the balance sheet of one household or firm to that of another.

Purchases of securities also are not investments in the economic sense. When Exxon buys its new tanker, it may finance the purchase by selling bonds to households. Households use part of their saving to buy the bonds, but it is the purchase of the tanker, not the purchase of the bonds, that is the investment. Later, the holders of the bonds may decide that they would rather have cash. They can sell the bonds to other households, but the transaction will again not be an investment in the economic sense. No new tanker is being built; instead, households are adjusting their balance sheets by trading one kind of asset (the bonds) for another (money).

AGGREGATE NOMINAL SUPPLY AND DEMAND

Adding saving and investment to the circular flow raises a new issue. There are now two pathways along which funds flow from households to product markets: a direct path, through consumption expenditures, and an indirect path, through saving and financial markets to investment expenditures. Corresponding to these two paths are two separate sets of decision makers: households, which make consumption decisions, and businesses, which make investment decisions. When the two types of expenditures are added together, how can we be sure they will match the amount of goods and services available? How, that is, can we be sure that national income will still be equal to national product?

These questions can be answered using the familiar concepts of supply and demand. First we define **aggregate nominal supply** as the total dollar value of all goods and services produced in the economy. We already have another term for the same thing: *national product*. Aggregate nominal supply and national product, also measured in nominal terms, are two different names for the same quantity. Next we define **aggregate nominal demand** as the total dollar value of all the purchases of newly produced goods and services that buyers plan to make. Aggregate nominal supply and aggregate nominal demand can be compared to see whether, for the economy as a whole, the plans of buyers mesh with the plans of sellers, much as supply and demand in a single market can be compared to see whether the plans of buyers and sellers mesh.

Aggregate nominal supply
The total value of all goods and services produced in the economy, measured in terms of the prices at which they are sold.

Aggregate nominal demand
The total dollar value of all planned expenditures.

Equilibrium in the Circular Flow

An example will show how aggregate supply can be compared with aggregate demand. Imagine an economy in which only three goods are produced: apples, milling machines, and radios. The firms in this economy plan to produce apples at a rate of $30,000 per year, radios at a rate of $30,000 per year, and milling machines at a rate of $40,000 per year. As they carry out their plans, output flows at a rate of $100,000 units per year. This flow, which can be called either nominal national product or **aggregate nominal supply**, is shown in lines 1–4 of Box 6.3.

While producers are busy carrying out their plans, buyers make plans too. Consumers plan to buy apples at a rate of $30,000 per year and radios at a rate of $30,000 per year. The firms that make radios plan to buy milling machines at a rate of $40,000 per year in order to increase their radio-producing capacity. No one plans either to increase or decrease the stocks of finished products held in inventory, so planned inventory investment is zero. All of these buying plans are expressed in lines 5–11 of Box 6.3. The total dollar value of all planned expenditures (consumption plus fixed investment plus planned inventory investment) is listed in line 11 as **aggregate nominal demand**.

Comparing line 1 with line 11, we see that the plans of buyers and sellers match perfectly. Aggregate supply and aggregate demand are equal. When the plans of buyers and sellers mesh like this, we say that the

---

**Box 6.3
An Example of a Simple
Economy in Equilibrium**

This box shows a simple economy in which aggregate nominal supply is exactly equal to aggregate nominal demand. The plans of buyers and sellers match when they are tested in the marketplace, and no unplanned inventory changes take place. National product and total planned expenditures are equal.

Output Resulting from Producers' Plans		
1 Total national product (aggregate nominal supply)		$100,000
2 Apples	$30,000	
3 Radios	30,000	
4 Milling machines	40,000	

Expenditures Resulting from Buyers' Plans		
5 Total consumption expenditures		$60,000
6 Apples	$30,000	
7 Radios	30,000	
8 Total planned investment		40,000
9 Fixed investment (milling machines)	40,000	
10 Planned inventory investment	0	
11 Total planned expenditure (aggregate nominal demand)		$100,000

circular flow as a whole is in *equilibrium,* just as we say that a market is in equilibrium when the plans of its buyers and sellers mesh.

Disequilibrium

In practice, the plans of buyers and sellers almost never fit together as neatly as they do in Box 6.3. It would be surprising if they did. After all, buyers and sellers do not always consult one another before production takes place. Each firm bases its production plans on the information available to it. Buyers base their plans on market prices and expectations about the future. Often, production plans are set before buyers' plans are formed, so there is no way to be sure they will mesh.

As an example of what happens when buyers' and sellers' plans do not mesh, look at Box 6.4. The situation is the same as in Box 6.3 except that now consumers plan to buy only $25,000 worth of apples and firms plan to buy only $35,000 worth of investment goods (milling machines). Thus, aggregate nominal demand (line 11) is only $90,000 even though aggregate nominal supply (line 1) is $100,000, as before.

Now when buyers' and sellers' plans are tested in the marketplace there will be some disappointments. All the radios will be sold, but $5,000 worth of apples and $5,000 worth of milling machines will be left over. What will happen to these unsold goods? Once produced, they cannot vanish into thin air. Instead, they will pile up as inventories in the warehouses of apple farmers and machine tool companies. Those producers did not *plan* to make any inventory investments, but they find themselves doing so despite their plans. The $5,000 of unsold apples and the $5,000 of unsold milling machines are therefore listed in lines 12–14 of Box 6.4 as *unplanned* inventory investments. Because the plans of buyers and sellers do not mesh, the circular flow is said to be in disequilibrium.

Reactions to Disequilibrium

In Box 6.4 aggregate nominal supply exceeded aggregate nominal demand. Because buyers' and sellers' plans failed to mesh, there was an unplanned buildup of inventories. Firms would not want this inventory buildup to go on and on. In order to limit or reverse it, they would reduce their rates of output or lower their prices in order to stimulate sales, or they would do a little of both. Whether they cut output or cut prices, the volume of the circular flow, measured in nominal terms (that is, in terms of dollars' worth of goods and services at current prices), would shrink.

At another time aggregate nominal demand might exceed aggregate nominal supply. Suppose, for example, that instead of the planned expenditures shown in Box 6.4, consumers plan to buy $35,000 worth of apples and firms plan to buy $45,000 worth of milling machines. Now when plans are tested in the marketplace, sales will exceed current output. The result is unplanned depletion of inventories as stocks of apples and milling machines are used to meet the strong demand. Firms will react in a way opposite to their reaction to an unplanned inventory buildup. They will try to stop the inventory depletion by increasing output or raising prices or doing a little of both. Whichever they do, the volume of the circular flow, measured in nominal terms, will rise.

Box 6.4
An Example of a Simple
Economy in
Disequilibrium

In this example planned purchases of apples and milling machines fall short of the amounts of those goods produced. When plans are tested in the marketplace, producers of apples and milling machines experience an unplanned increase in inventories. Total planned expenditure (aggregate nominal demand) falls short of national product (aggregate nominal supply). However, total expenditures, including both planned expenditures and unplanned inventory investment, are equal to national product.

Output Resulting from Producers' Plans

1	Total national product (aggregate nominal supply)		$100,000
2	Apples	$30,000	
3	Radios	30,000	
4	Milling machines	40,000	

Expenditures Resulting from Buyers' Plans

5	Total consumption expenditures		$55,000	
6	Apples	$25,000		
7	Radios	30,000		
8	Total planned investment		35,000	
9	Fixed investment (milling machines)	35,000		
10	Planned inventory investment	0		
11	Total planned expenditure (aggregate nominal demand)			$ 90,000

Other Expenditures

12	Total unplanned inventory investment		10,000
13	Unsold apples	5,000	
14	Unsold milling machines	5,000	

Summary

15	Total national product		$100,000
16	Total national expenditure		100,000
17	Planned	$90,000	
18	Unplanned	10,000	

The Equality of National Income and Product

As Boxes 6.3 and 6.4 show, national product (aggregate nominal supply) is equal to planned expenditure (aggregate nominal demand) only when the economy is in equilibrium. However, whether the economy is in equilibrium or not, national product is always equal to *total* expenditure, taking both planned and unplanned expenditures into account. This is true because unplanned inventory investment acts as a balancing item. When planned expenditure falls short of aggregate nominal supply, inventories pile up. In that case, adding unplanned inventory investment to planned expenditure makes the total equal to aggregate nominal supply. On the other hand, if planned expenditure exceeds aggregate nominal supply, inventories are run down. In that case, adding the negative unplanned inventory investment to planned consumption and investment makes the total equal to aggregate nominal supply. In equation form:

$$\begin{array}{c} \text{National} \\ \text{product} \end{array} = \begin{array}{c} \text{total} \\ \text{planned} \\ \text{expenditure} \end{array} + \begin{array}{c} \text{unplanned} \\ \text{inventory} \\ \text{investment} \end{array} = \begin{array}{c} \text{total} \\ \text{expenditure} \end{array}$$

Another way to write the same thing:

$$\begin{array}{c} \text{Aggregate} \\ \text{nominal} \\ \text{supply} \end{array} = \begin{array}{c} \text{aggregate} \\ \text{nominal} \\ \text{demand} \end{array} + \begin{array}{c} \text{unplanned} \\ \text{inventory} \\ \text{investment} \end{array}$$

Having shown that national product is equal to total expenditure in this economy, we can also show that national product is equal to national income. As in the ultrasimple economy of Box 6.1, the equality of national income and product can be shown in either of two ways.

First, we can make use of the link that factor payments provide between national income and national product. In Boxes 6.3 and 6.4 firms are shown to produce $100,000 worth of goods each year, all of which is either sold to investors and consumers or added to inventory. In the course of producing this $100,000 worth of goods, firms incur factor costs, which go into the national-income stream as wages, interest payments, rents, and so on. Anything left over after all costs are paid is profit for the firms—and this too is counted as going into the national-income stream. Total factor payments, including profits, thus account for the whole $100,000 of national product (sales to final users plus inventory change).

Second, the equality of national income and product can be shown using expenditures as a link. In Box 6.3 households plan to spend $60,000 on consumer goods (radios and apples). The other $40,000 leaves the circular flow as saving. Firms plan to invest $40,000 in milling machines; the missing $40,000 is injected back into the economy as investment spending. Total expenditures (consumption plus investment) thus equal national income (saving plus consumption). And total expenditures, as shown earlier, are equal to national product.

In Box 6.4 the plans of households and firms do not mesh so neatly, but total expenditures still provide a link between national income and national product. Households plan to spend just $55,000 and to save $45,000. Firms plan to invest only $35,000. Saving thus exceeds planned investment by $10,000. However, as we saw before, the $10,000 of goods that firms produce and no one plans to buy cannot vanish into thin air. Instead, they pile up in inventory, where they are counted as unplanned inventory investment. When this is taken into account, total investment ($35,000 planned plus $10,000 unplanned) is equal to saving. Again, then, national income (saving plus consumption) is equal to total expenditure (consumption plus planned investment plus unplanned investment). And, as always, total expenditure is equal to national product.

ADDING GOVERNMENT TO THE CIRCULAR FLOW

The next step in our analysis of the circular flow is to add the public sector. As we know from Chapter 5, government is linked to the rest of the economy in three ways: through taxes, expenditures, and government borrowing. These three links are added to the circular flow in Box 6.5.

First consider taxes. For purposes of macroeconomic theory we need to measure the flow of dollars withdrawn from the household sector by government. Clearly, taxes—income taxes, payroll taxes, property taxes, and all the rest—are withdrawals. But this flow of funds out of the

**Box 6.5
The Circular Flow with
Government Included**

This circular-flow diagram shows three links between government and the rest of the economy. The first is net taxes (taxes minus transfer payments), which flow from households to government. The second is government purchases, which flow from government to product markets. If government purchases exceed net taxes (a budget deficit), the government must borrow from financial markets. The deficit case is shown here. If net taxes exceed government purchases, government repayments of past loans will exceed new borrowing by government, so there will be a net flow of funds from government to financial markets. This case is not shown here.

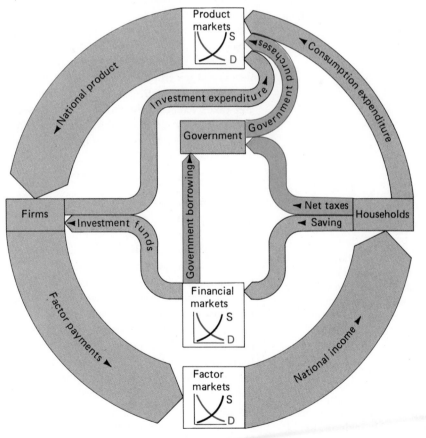

household sector is partly offset by a flow of funds returned to households in the form of transfer payments. For a proper measure of the net flow of funds from households to government, then, we must subtract transfer payments from total taxes. The difference between taxes and transfers is called **net taxes**, and the arrow linking households and government in Box 6.5 is given that label.

Next consider the link between government and product markets. We have already accounted for transfers in calculating net taxes. The rest of government spending consists of purchases of goods and services. These include the goods and services that government buys from private firms and the wages and salaries of government employees. For purposes of the circular flow, the wages and salaries of government employees can be treated as if they passed through product markets on their way to households.

Finally, consider the link between government and financial markets. As we saw in Chapter 5, governments do not always balance their budgets. Taking federal, state, and local governments together, the public sector tends to spend more than it takes in as taxes. (The federal government almost always runs a deficit. State and local governments often have surpluses but, at least in recent years, these have not been large enough to offset the federal government's deficit.)

The government deficit must be financed by borrowing. Usually this takes the form of sales of short- or long-term securities to the public or to financial intermediaries. An arrow is drawn from financial markets to government in Box 6.5 to represent government borrowing. Over the years, repeated borrowing by government adds to the national debt. The *debt* is a stock that corresponds to the annual *deficit*, which is a flow.

When the public sector as a whole runs a budget surplus (that is, when net taxes exceed government purchases), the arrow is reversed. Governments pay off old loans at a faster rate than they take out new ones, thereby creating a net flow of funds into financial markets.

Leakages and Injections

Take a moment to compare the circular flow shown in Box 6.5 with the ultrasimple flow shown in Box 6.1. In Box 6.1, all of national income flowed directly from households to product markets in the form of consumption spending. Nothing was withdrawn from the stream of consumption spending, and nothing was added to it. In Box 6.5, there has been a major change: The circular flow is no longer closed.

First, there are two uses for income that do not result directly in purchases of goods or services. These are net taxes, which flow to government rather than to product markets, and saving, which flows to financial markets rather than to product markets. These two uses are **leakages** from the circular flow. Because saving is defined as whatever income is left over after households buy goods and services and pay net taxes, consumption plus the two leakages always add up to national income.

Second, there are two kinds of expenditures that do not come directly from households. These are government purchases of goods and services, and investment. They are **injections** into the circular flow. Because

Net taxes
Taxes paid to government minus transfer payments made by government.

Leakages
The parts of national income that are not used by households to buy domestic consumer goods; included are saving, net taxes, and purchases of imports.

Injections
Flows of funds into domestic product markets that do not begin with consumption expenditures of domestic households; included are investment, government purchases, and exports.

investment includes unplanned inventory investment, total expenditures—consumption plus injections—always equal national product.

The Equality of National Income and Product

Adding more leakages and injections to the circular flow does not disturb the equality of national income and national product. Box 6.6 shows an economy in equilibrium with the government sector added. Line 1 shows that nominal national product is $100,000. Lines 2–6 show the spending plans of households, firms, and government. Households plan to buy $70,000 worth of consumer goods and services; firms plan to buy $15,000 worth of investment goods; and the government plans to buy $15,000 worth of goods and services. Total planned expenditures come to exactly $100,000, and there are no unplanned inventory changes. When planned expenditures (aggregate nominal demand) are just equal to national product (aggregate nominal supply), we know that the economy is in equilibrium.

Production of $100,000 worth of goods and services generates a national income, consisting of wages, interest, profits, and so on, of $100,000 (line 8). Lines 9–11 show how this national income is used: $70,000 goes for consumption (as we saw before); $20,000 is saved; and

---

Box 6.6
An Example of the Circular Flow with Government Included

This example shows the equality of national income and product for an economy with government purchases and taxes included. Note that the total of consumption plus investment plus government purchases equals the total of consumption plus saving plus net taxes. As shown here, the economy is in equilibrium; there is no unplanned inventory investment. However, the equality would hold even if total investment included some unplanned inventory investment.

1	National product		$100,000
Expenditures			
2	Consumption		$ 70,000
3	Investment		15,000
4	Planned	$15,000	
5	Unplanned	0	
6	Government purchases		15,000
7	Total expenditures		$100,000
8	National income		$100,000
Uses of National Income			
9	Consumption		$ 70,000
10	Saving		20,000
11	Net taxes		10,000
12	Total uses		$100,000

$10,000 is taken in taxes. These three uses account for the entire national income of $100,000.

The relationships shown in Box 6.6 can be summarized in the following equation:

National product
= consumption + investment + government purchases
= consumption + saving + net taxes
= national income

These equations hold even if the economy is not in equilibrium. In that case, investment includes some unplanned inventory investment along with planned investment. But national product, including planned plus unplanned investment, is equal to national income whether the economy is in equilibrium or not.

Government Influence over the Circular Flow—A Preview

A close look at Box 6.5 shows that the government is able to regulate the size of the circular flow of income and product through its control over some of the injections and leakages. Much of the discussion in the next 11 chapters will be devoted to describing this power and how it is used, but we can give a preview here.

One way in which government can affect the circular flow is through its purchases of goods and services. A reduction in government purchases, starting from a state of equilibrium, would lead to unplanned inventory buildup by firms that made the products government decided not to buy. As unwanted inventories piled up, firms would react by cutting output or reducing prices, or by doing some of both. As they did so, the volume of the circular flow, measured in nominal terms, would fall. If instead the government increased its purchases of goods and services, again starting from equilibrium, there would be unplanned inventory depletion. Firms would react by increasing output or raising prices, or by doing some of both. This would cause the volume of the circular flow, measured in nominal terms, to rise. We see, then, that by adding to aggregate demand through increased purchases or reducing aggregate demand through reduced purchases, government can cause the level of nominal national product to rise or fall.

Taxes give the government a second means of controlling the circular flow. If taxes are raised, households will have less after-tax income to spend on consumer goods. This will reduce aggregate demand and cause unplanned inventory buildup. In response, firms will cut output or prices, or both, thereby reducing the volume of the circular flow. If taxes are cut, the process will work in reverse. With more after-tax income, consumer spending will increase. The added aggregate demand will cause unplanned inventory depletion, to which firms will react by raising output or prices, or by doing some of both. In this case the volume of the circular flow and national product, measured in nominal terms, will rise. Changes in taxes and government purchases, which together are known as *fiscal policy*, will be discussed in Chapter 10.

The government also has a third, indirect means of regulating the volume of the circular flow: its influence on financial markets. The Federal Reserve System, an agency of the federal government, can take actions that affect the levels of money, credit, and interest rates. By restricting the availability of money and credit and raising interest rates, the Federal Reserve can discourage private firms from making new investments. Such a policy will restrain aggregate demand and the level of nominal national product. On the other hand, by making money and credit more freely available and lowering interest rates, the Federal Reserve can encourage firms to borrow and increase their rate of investment. Such a policy will add to aggregate demand and will cause the volume of the circular flow to increase. These actions, known as monetary policy, will be discussed in Chapters 11–13.

ADDING THE FOREIGN SECTOR TO THE CIRCULAR FLOW[3]

The final step in putting together the circular flow is to add the foreign sector. This is done in Box 6.7. The foreign sector, like the government, is linked to the rest of the economy in three ways.

Imports of goods and services provide the first link. Remember that all the parts of the circular flow represent nominal flows of funds, not flows of goods. Payments for imports are shown by an arrow leading away from the economy to the rest of the world. Like saving and net taxes, payments for imports are counted as a leakage from the circular flow. Households, firms, and government all buy some imported goods and services. To keep the diagram manageable, however, only imports by consumers, which form a part of total consumption expenditure, are shown in Box 6.7.

Exports provide the second link between the domestic economy and the rest of the world. Funds received in payment for goods and services sold abroad flow into product markets, where they join funds received from sales of goods and services to domestic households, government, and firms. Receipts from the sale of exports are shown as an arrow into product markets. Like investment and government purchases, payments received for exports are treated as an injection into the circular flow.

The third link between the domestic economy and the rest of the world consists of international borrowing and lending. This link exists because a country's imports do not always exactly equal its exports. If, say, the United States imports more goods and services than it exports, it is said to run a balance-of-payments deficit. In that case it cannot pay for all of its imports with earnings from exports. To pay for the rest, it borrows from other countries. These borrowings are shown as a flow of funds into domestic financial markets.

On the other hand, the United States sometimes exports more than it imports, in which case it is said to run a balance-of-payments surplus. In this case foreign buyers of U.S. exports need to borrow in order to pay for them. In the case of a U.S. balance-of-payments surplus, Box 6.7 would have to be redrawn with the arrow running from U.S. financial markets to foreign economies.

---

[3]This section may be omitted in an abbreviated course.

**Box 6·7
The Circular Flow with
the Foreign Sector
Included**

This circular-flow diagram shows three links between the domestic economy and the rest of the world. Imports are the first link. Payments for imports are shown as an arrow from households to foreign economies. Exports are the second link. Payments by foreign buyers of exports are shown as an arrow pointing to domestic product markets. If not enough goods and services are exported to pay for all the imports, some imports must be bought on credit. Borrowing from foreign lenders is shown as a flow into domestic financial markets. Exports might also exceed imports, in which case the arrow would be reversed to show borrowing by foreigners to pay for exports from the domestic economy.

The Equality of National Income and Product with the Foreign Sector

Adding the foreign sector to the circular flow still leaves all of the basic equalities intact, as a final example will show. Look at Box 6.8, in which the economy is once again shown with a national product of $100,000 (line 1). Lines 2–12 of the table list expenditures. Line 2 shows that households plan to spend $70,000 on consumer goods during the year. Of this, they will spend $10,000 on imports, which means that only $60,000 of their total spending flows into domestic product markets. An adjustment is made for this fact farther down in the table, as we will see in a moment.

Lines 5–7 show that firms plan to invest $10,000, and line 8 shows planned government purchases of $15,000. Next, lines 9 and 11 show the contribution of the foreign sector. Foreign buyers plan to purchase $15,000 of domestically produced goods and services (line 10). These purchases represent a flow of expenditures into domestic product markets. However, $10,000 of this flow of expenditures into the economy is offset by the planned purchases of imported goods by domestic consumers. This item, first shown in line 3, is repeated in line 11. The net contribution of foreign trade to expenditures on domestic goods and services thus is $15,000 minus $10,000, or $5,000. The difference between exports and imports, called **net exports**, is shown in line 9. Adding total consumption (consumption of domestic goods plus consumption of imports), planned investment, government purchases, and net exports gives total expenditures on domestic goods and services of $100,000 (line 12).

Lines 13–16 of Box 6.8 show the uses of national income. Consumption expenditures account for $70,000 (of which $10,000 is consumption of imports). Another $10,000 goes to the government as net taxes. The remaining $20,000 is saving. These uses of funds thus account for the entire $100,000 of national income, which in turn is equal to total expenditures on domestic goods and to national product.

Net exports
Exports minus imports.

**Box 6.8
Equality of Leakages and Injections in the Complete Circular Flow**

This example shows the equality of national income and product and of leakages and injections for the complete circular flow. Only the totals of leakages and injections need be equal. The various pairs of leakages and injections need not match.

1	National product		$100,000	
	Expenditures on Domestic Goods and Services			
2	Consumption (including imports)		$ 70,000	
3	Imports	$10,000		
4	Consumption of domestic goods	60,000		
5	Investment		10,000	
6	Planned	10,000		Total
7	Unplanned	0		injections:
8	Government purchases		15,000	$40,000
9	Net exports		5,000	
10	Exports	15,000		
11	Imports	10,000		
12	Total expenditures on domestic goods		$100,000	
	Uses of National Income			Total
13	Consumption		$ 70,000	leakages:
14	Saving		20,000	$40,000
15	Net taxes		10,000	
16	Total uses of national income		$100,000	

In Box 6.8 the plans of buyers and sellers mesh, putting the circular flow in equilibrium. If they did not, national income and product would still be equal. Suppose, for example, that firms planned to invest a little less, or foreign buyers planned to purchase fewer exports, or government planned to spend less on goods and services, or consumers planned to spend more on imports. If any or all of these things happened, total planned expenditures on domestic goods would fall short of national product. Some sellers would be disappointed and would find themselves holding inventories of unsold goods. These would be entered in the table as unplanned investment, just making up the shortfall in planned expenditures. Total expenditures, including planned and unplanned expenditures, would, as always, be equal to national product and, in turn, equal to national income.

Instead, the combined spending plans of households, firms, government, and foreign buyers might add up to more than national product. If this were the case, producers would find themselves selling goods faster than they were producing them. As a result, their inventories would fall below planned levels. The inventory change would show up as a negative number on the unplanned-investment line, just balancing the excess aggregate demand. The basic equality of national income and product would, as always, hold.

As before, these rules can be expressed in the form of a four-part equation, as follows:

National product
  = consumption + investment + government purchases
    + exports − imports
  = consumption + saving + net taxes
  = national income

The Equality of Leakages and Injections

Notice that consumption appears twice in this four-part set of equalities. First, it appears as one of the categories of expenditures on national product, and then it appears again as one of the uses of national income. If we subtract consumption from both of these and shift imports to the lefthand side, we get another useful equation:

Investment + government purchases + exports
  = saving + net taxes + imports

This equation says that total injections equal total leakages. Note that it is only the totals of leakages and injections that need to add up. Their components do not have to match; saving need not equal investment, net taxes need not equal government purchases, and imports need not equal exports. The example in Box 6.8 is a case in point. Total injections are $40,000, exactly equal to total leakages. However, exports ($15,000) exceed imports ($10,000), meaning that the country has a balance-of-payments surplus of $5,000. The sum of saving ($20,000) and net taxes ($10,000) exceeds the sum of investment ($10,000) plus government purchases ($15,000) by an amount just equal to the balance-of-payments surplus.

Looking Ahead

The circular-flow model presented in this chapter gives a good overview of the macroeconomy, but it leaves many questions unanswered. In the circular-flow diagram, we represented product markets, factor markets, and financial markets with supply-and-demand diagrams. What exactly are the prices and quantities determined in these markets? We will address this question in the next chapter. Another question is how national product, national income, and so on can actually be measured. This matter will be dealt with in Chapter 8. Other unanswered questions have to do with the government's control over the volume of the circular flow via spending, taxes, and monetary policy. Just how are these policy tools used, how large are the effects of a given policy tool, and how do the various tools interact? These questions will be answered in Chapters 9–13.

Still another set of questions have to do with the connections between changes in nominal national product, changes in real national product, and changes in the average level of prices. We have said many times that when aggregate nominal demand rises, firms respond by increasing real output or raising prices, or by doing some of both. Under what conditions will they do one rather than the other? The answer is crucial for the macroeconomic goals of full employment, price stability, and real economic growth. This set of questions will be given a preview in the next chapter and will be dealt with more fully in Chapters 14–18.

Summary

1. The *circular flow of income and product* is the flow of goods and services between households and firms, balanced by the flow of money payments made in exchange for those goods and services. In the simplest case, households spend all their money on consumer goods produced by firms, and firms use all the proceeds of the sales to pay wages, rent, interest, and profits to households.

2. In economics, the term *flow* refers to any process that occurs continuously through time. For example, the rate at which the automobile industry produces cars, measured in units per year, is a flow. A *stock* is the total amount of something that exists at a point in time. For example, the total number of cars registered in the United States as of a certain date is a stock.

3. *National product* is the total value of all goods and services produced in the economy. *National income* is the total income received by households, including wages, rents, interest payments, and profits. The two are always

equal because for every dollar that firms receive from the sale of their products they pay out one dollar in factor payments and profits.

4. *Saving* is the part of income that households do not spend on consumer goods or use to pay taxes. *Investment* refers to purchases of newly produced capital goods or the building up of inventories by firms. Saving passes from households to financial markets; firms borrow funds through financial markets to finance investment.

5. *Aggregate nominal supply* is the total value of goods and services produced in the economy, measured in terms of the prices at which they are sold. It means the same thing as nominal national product. *Aggregate nominal demand* is the total dollar value of all planned expenditures in the economy.

6. The circular flow is said to be in equilibrium when aggregate nominal supply and aggregate nominal demand are equal. In this case

there are no unplanned changes in inventories. If aggregate nominal demand exceeds aggregate nominal supply, there will be unplanned decreases in inventory (negative inventory investment). Firms will tend to react by raising output, raising prices, or doing some of both. The circular flow will then expand. If aggregate nominal supply exceeds aggregate nominal demand, there will be unplanned increases in inventories. The reactions of firms will cause the circular flow to shrink.

7. The government sector is connected to the circular flow in three ways. First, households pay *net taxes* (taxes minus transfer payments) to the government. Second, the government buys goods and services in product markets. And third, the government borrows from financial markets to finance a deficit, or supplies funds to financial markets when it runs a surplus.

8. The foreign sector is also connected to the circular flow in three ways. First, households pay foreign sellers for imported goods. Second, foreign buyers make payments to domestic firms for exported goods. And third, foreign lenders supply funds to domestic financial markets if the country has a balance-of-payments deficit, or foreigners borrow from domestic financial markets if the country has a balance-of-payments surplus.

9. Saving, net taxes, and imports are known as *leakages* from the circular flow. Investment, government purchases, and exports are known as *injections*. When both planned and unplanned investments are included, leakages must equal injections. In an economy of households, firms, and government, this means that saving + net taxes = investment + government purchases. In an economy that is connected to the rest of the world, it means that saving + net taxes + imports = investment + government purchases + exports. The various pairs of leakages and injections need not balance; only the totals have to be equal.

Questions for Review

1. Define the following terms:
    circular flow of income and product
    flow
    stock
    national income
    national product
    saving
    fixed investment
    inventory investment
    investment
    aggregate nominal supply
    aggregate nominal demand
    net taxes
    leakage
    injection
    net exports

2. Sketch the circular flow of income and product for an economy made up only of households and firms. Show both flows of payments and flows of goods and services. Give examples of payments that flow from households to firms and of payments that flow from firms to households.

3. Give several examples, other than those used in the chapter, of flows and related stocks.

4. Explain why national income and product are equal. Why, when profits are included, do the payments made by firms to households exactly equal the value of the products that firms produce?

5. Sketch a circular flow for an economy in which there are households, firms, and financial markets. Include the pathways along which saving and investment travel.

6. What is the link between aggregate nominal supply and national product? Between aggregate nominal demand and national product?

7. What does it mean to say that the circular flow of income and product is in equilibrium? What does inventory investment have to do with equilibrium and disequilibrium in the circular flow?

8. Sketch a circular flow for an economy in which there are households, firms, financial markets, and government. Show the three connections between the government sector and the rest of the economy.

9. Sketch a circular flow for an economy in which the foreign sector is added. How is the foreign sector linked to households, product markets, and financial markets?

10. Give examples of leakages and injections. Why are leakages always equal to injections when both planned and unplanned investment are taken into account?

Problems and Topics for Discussion

1. Turn to the balance sheet for Great Falls Manufacturing Company that was given in Box 4.4 (p. 86). Are the firm's assets, liabilities, and net worth stocks or flows? Are its receipts from sales and its payments to workers, suppliers, and owners stocks or flows? How are these receipts and payments related to the balance sheet items?

2. Not all changes in inventories are unplanned. Why would a firm plan to increase or decrease its inventories? How would you plan your inventories over the course of the year if you were a seller of children's toys? Of air conditioners? How would you plan your inventories of parts if you were an automobile repair shop in a town with a growing population? In one with a shrinking population?

3. Rework the table in Box 6.4 for the case of excess aggregate demand. (Let consumption of apples be $35,000, consumption of radios $30,000, and planned investment in milling machines $40,000. How would producers tend to adjust to these changes? Now assume that radio dealers plan to add $5,000 to their inventories. What does this do to total aggregate demand? Will they be able to carry out their plans?

4. The circular-flow diagrams in this chapter show arrows passing in to and out of the box labeled "financial markets." Using what you learned about financial intermediaries in Chapter 4, give some examples of these flows. Give examples of direct and indirect financing, the role of financial intermediaries, and the role of primary and secondary financial markets.

5. Starting from a state of equilibrium, trace the effects of each of the following through the circular flow. What happens to inventories? How do firms tend to react? What happens to the size of the circular flow, measured in nominal terms?

   a. Business managers suddenly decide to increase investment in order to expand their firms' productive capacity.

   b. The federal government cuts income taxes.

   c. Good crops throughout the world reduce the demand for exports of U.S. farm products.

6. Rework Box 6.8 for the following cases. In each case, be sure to adjust all of the entries you need to in order to keep total injections equal to total leakages.

   a. Planned investment exceeds saving by $5,000 and the government runs a $10,000 budget deficit.

   b. Imports exceed exports by $6,000 and the government budget is exactly balanced.

   c. Saving exceeds investment and net taxes exceed government purchases.

   Bonus question: Can you work out an example in which saving exceeds investment, the government runs a budget surplus, and there is a foreign trade deficit? If not, why not?

Chapter 7

Supply and Demand in the Macroeconomy

WHAT YOU WILL LEARN IN THIS CHAPTER

After reading this chapter, you should be able to

1. Use the *price level* to adjust nominal wages for the effects of inflation.
2. Discuss the role of labor markets as a source of income, a source of jobs, and an element of costs.
3. Draw supply and demand curves for financial markets, and explain why the interest rate is the "price" of credit.
4. Distinguish between *real* and *nominal interest rates*.
5. Sketch an *aggregate real demand curve* for the economy, given a level of aggregate nominal demand.
6. Explain the effects of a shift in the aggregate real demand curve, and sketch the economy's *aggregate real supply curve*.

Ideas for Review

Here are some terms and concepts that you should review before you read this chapter:

Real and nominal values (Chapter 1)
Supply and demand (Chapter 3)
Relative prices (Chapter 3)
Financial markets (Chapters 4 and 6)
Aggregate nominal demand and supply (Chapter 6)

"Education is just darned expensive to produce."

Hard-pressed parents and struggling students are in for a disappointment if they expect college costs to level off anytime soon. Early estimates put tuition increases next fall at 7 to 9 percent.

That's better than the double-digit increases of a few years ago, but hardly what some might expect when annual inflation is running at less than 4 percent.

College officials say they have no choice. Many are still trying to overcome problems caused by spiraling inflation in the late 1970s and the more recent strains of declining enrollment. At the same time, computers and new areas of study require big investments. Colleges are also spending more on student aid, largely because government funding hasn't kept pace.

"Most universities aren't spendthrifts," says William D. Johnson, provost of George Washington University. "Education is just darned expensive to produce."

The need to raise faculty salaries is by far the largest factor pushing costs higher. The American Association of University Professors estimates that professors' salaries, which averaged $29,130 last year, fell 21 percent in real purchasing power between 1970 and 1980. Pay in real terms began to gain slowly in 1982, but there is a long way to go. The need is particularly serious in such areas as engineering, computer sciences, and biochemistry. Industry jobs at far higher pay have drawn professors from these areas while student demand is rising.[1]

The case of rising college tuitions shows supply and demand at work. In Chapter 3 we focused on supply and demand in individual markets—an issue in microeconomics. But, as this case shows, supply and demand are an issue in macroeconomics, too. Macroeconomic concerns, ranging from inflation to government policies to the real purchasing power of wages and salaries, affect the pricing and production decisions of individual firms, including not-for-profit firms like colleges. And the price and production decisions of individual firms, in turn, add up to changes in aggregate supply and demand within the circular flow of income and product.

This chapter will act as a bridge between the micro view of supply and demand, introduced in Chapter 3, and the macro view, introduced in Chapter 6. In it we will look at the three sets of markets that are highlighted in Box 7.1: factor markets, financial markets, and product markets. These key markets tie the circular flow together.[2] We will return to each of them many times as our study of macroeconomics progresses.

---

[1]Anne Mackay-Smith, "College Officials Say Costs Push Tuitions Higher," *Wall Street Journal*, March 8, 1985, p. 33. Reprinted by permission of The Wall Street Journal, © Dow Jones & Company, Inc. 1984. All rights reserved.

---

[2]The complete circular flow also contains a fourth set of markets that is not shown in Box 7.1. These are the international markets for imports and exports of goods and services, international borrowing and lending, and exchange of currency. We will discuss these markets in Chapters 34 and 35.

**Box 7.1
Markets in the Circular
Flow**

The elements of the circular flow are tied together by markets. Three key sets of markets are shown here. Factor markets link households and firms via the exchange of factor services for income. Financial markets link households, which serve as sources of loanable funds, with firms and units of government, which tend to be users of borrowed funds. Product markets link firms with households, units of government, and firms via the exchange of goods and services for monetary payments.

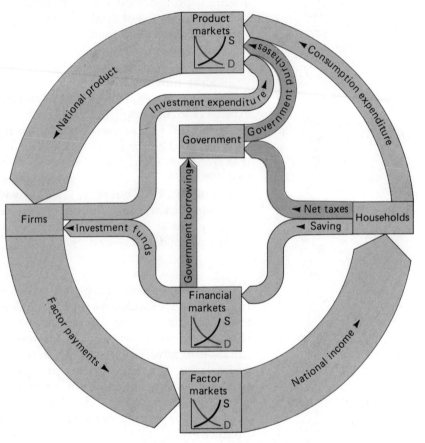

FACTOR MARKETS

Factor markets link households and firms through the supply and demand for labor, capital, and natural resources. The detailed study of factor markets is part of microeconomics, but factor markets, especially labor markets, also enter into macroeconomics. Let's look briefly at labor markets from a macroeconomic point of view, as a source of income, as a source of jobs, and as an element of costs.

Real Wages and the Price Level

Income from wages and salaries accounts for about three fourths of all income in the United States. Total wage and salary income is the product of wages and salaries per employed worker and total employment. The level of wages is the price in labor markets while the level of employment is the quantity. The level of wages and salaries serves as a key indicator of the health of the economy as a whole. As Box 7.2 shows, however, care must be taken to distinguish between the *real wage* and the *nominal wage*. The nominal wage is measured in terms of *current dollars*—that is, in terms of the number of dollars actually paid to the wage earner. The real wage is stated in terms of *constant dollars*—that is, in terms of dollar values that have been adjusted for changes in the average prices of goods and services.

Price level
The ratio of the average price of goods and services in the current year to the average price of goods and services in a chosen base year.

To convert data on nominal wages into real terms, we divide the nominal wage by the **price level**, which is the ratio of the average prices of goods and services in the current year to the average prices of goods and services in some **base year** used for comparison. In Box 7.2, for example, 1977 is used as the base year for calculating real wages. The price level for the base year is, by definition, 1.0. Thus, real and nominal wages are equal for the base year.

Base year
The year chosen as a basis for comparison in calculating the price level.

The year 1977 was part of an extended period of inflation. By 1984 the average level of prices was 1.7 times as high as it had been in 1977. The 1984 real wage of $173.48 per week thus is equal to the 1984 nominal wage

**Box 7.2
Real and Nominal
Weekly Earnings in the
U.S. Economy,
1947–1984**

This chart shows real and nominal weekly earnings in the nonfarm U.S. economy since 1947. Real earnings are calculated using 1977 as a base year. In years before 1977, the price level is less than 1.0, so real earnings are higher than nominal earnings. In years after 1977, real earnings are less than nominal earnings because the price level is higher than 1.0.

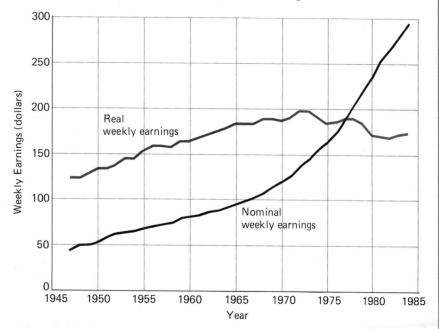

Source: President's Council of Economic Advisers, *Economic Report of the President* (Washington, D.C.: Government Printing Office, 1985), Table B–39.

of $294.05 per week divided by the 1984 price level of 1.7. In years before 1977, prices were lower on the average, so the price level had a value of less than 1.0. For example, in 1964 workers were paid a nominal wage of only $91.33 per week. The price level in that year was just 0.51, however— barely more than half the 1977 price level. In terms of the 1977 base year, then, the 1964 real wage was $178.38 per week.

Box 7.2 shows that average real weekly earnings rose steadily from the end of World War II to the early 1970s and then declined, reaching a low point in 1982. Neither the rise nor the fall was uniform for all occupations. At the same time that the average level of wages changes, the relative wages of various jobs also change. For example, college professors, whose real wages fell faster than the average in the 1970s, had gained ground in the previous decade. Focusing on average earnings makes the trends stand out more clearly, however. The increase in the first 25 years of the post–World War II period reflected strong growth of the economy and rising output per worker. But in the next ten years inflation and rising prices of imported oil disrupted the economy, and output per worker stagnated. This episode will be examined in detail in Chapter 15. The prospects for continued growth of real earnings in the later 1980s appear reasonably good at this time.

Labor Markets and Jobs

Labor markets are not just a source of income; they are also a source of jobs. In fact, jobs are more important than income in the public's perception of the health of the economy. For example, some people look back at the decade of the 1950s, when the unemployment rate averaged just 4.5 percent, as a golden age of prosperity compared to the 1980s, in which unemployment rates have ranged from 7 to 11 percent. (Turn back to Box 1.3, p. 8, for details.) Do they forget that real weekly earnings were as much as 20 percent lower in the 1950s? Or is it that having a job is more important than what the job pays?

But even if jobs, rather than real earnings, are taken as a measure of performance, the economy of the 1980s does not compare as badly with the past as the unemployment figures indicate. Instead of looking at the unemployment rate, which is the percentage of the labor force looking for jobs and unable to find them, many economists prefer to focus on the **employment rate**. This is the percentage of all working-age people who do have jobs.

Employment rate
The percentage of the working-age population that is employed.

Between 1950 and 1984 the total number of jobs in the economy nearly doubled, from 59 million to 105 million. In the same period the employment rate rose from 56 percent of the adult population to 59 percent. The employment rate for women rose from 31 percent to 50 percent. As Box 7.3 explains, this ability of the U.S. economy to create jobs for a growing population is viewed as nothing short of remarkable compared with the record of other countries.

But if the economy is so good at creating jobs, why are unemployment rates so much higher today than they were in the 1950s and 1960s? In part, the answer has to do with the changing age and sex composition of the labor force. In part, too, it has to do with the recessions of 1980 and 1981–1982, from which, at this writing, the economy has not yet recovered

Box 7.3
Job Creation: The
United States vs. Europe

Americans have grown used to gloomy news about employment. The average unemployment rate drifted upward from 4.5 percent of the labor force in the decade 1965–1974 to 7.6 percent in the decade 1975–1984. Over the same period, the percentage of manufacturing jobs fell from 25 percent of all jobs to 20 percent. The latter figures are sometimes taken to indicate that the United States is becoming a nation of hairdressers and fast-food stands, no longer able to compete with the manufacturing might of Europe and Japan. But looking at the U.S. economy from the outside, another set of statistics tells a much brighter story.

First, there has been a remarkable growth in the number of jobs in the United States. Between 1973 and 1983 the U.S. economy created 15 million new jobs. Over the same period, total employment in Britain actually fell by 2 million jobs, and in West Germany total employment fell by a million jobs. It is the huge increase in total jobs that caused manufacturing jobs in the U.S. to fall in percentage terms. In absolute terms, the number of manufacturing jobs actually grew by 343,000 over this period; in many other countries it fell. Manufacturing jobs were down by 457,000 in France, 1,234,000 in West Germany, and 2,089,000 in Britain. Even Japan has lost 70,000 manufacturing jobs in the last decade.

These trends are mirrored in the changing relationship between U.S. and European unemployment statistics. In 1975, the jobless rate in Western Europe as a whole was a low 5 percent, compared to 8.3 percent in the United States. By 1984, the U.S. rate had edged down to 7.8 percent while the rate in Western Europe had soared to 10.8 percent. If the European jobless figures were adjusted for differences in measurement techniques, they would appear even higher. The greater ability of the U.S. economy to create jobs is matched by the greater willingness of Americans to work. In the United States 59 percent of the working-age population is employed, versus 51 percent in West Germany, 53 percent in France, 56 percent in Britain, and 46 percent in Italy. Only Japan has a higher figure, with 61 percent of the working-age population on the job. Notably, this figure has been rising in the United States while it has been falling elsewhere. Labor force participation by women is especially high in the United States at 53 percent, compared with 47 percent in Japan, 43 percent in France, 39 percent in West Germany, and just 30 percent in Italy.

A number of factors are blamed for lower labor market participation rates and higher unemployment in Europe. Workers are said to be less willing to move in order to take new jobs. Europe is said to lack a dynamic small-business sector, the source of more than half of all new jobs in the United States. Restrictions on layoffs are thought to discourage European firms from taking on new workers even when business picks up, for fear that they won't be able to cut their payrolls when business turns down again. And generous jobless benefits in Europe are said to give unemployed workers little incentive to look for jobs that pay less than those they held before.

Sources: Alfred L. Malabre Jr., "U.S. Economy Excels at Generating Jobs," *Wall Street Journal*, April 9, 1984, p. 1, and Lawrence Ingrassia, "Persistent Joblessness Still Troubles Europe," *Wall Street Journal*, November 13, 1984, p. 1.

fully. And in part it has to do with the changing structure of the economy. The number of jobs in smokestack industries such as steel and automobiles is shrinking, while the number of jobs in high-tech and service industries is growing. But the skills of the workers who have been laid off don't always match those required by the newly created jobs. We will return to these questions in Chapter 17.

The Labor Market and Costs

In looking at the labor market as a source of incomes and jobs, we take the point of view of the employee. In our study of macroeconomics, we will sometimes also take the point of view of the employer and look at wages as an element of costs of production.

As we will see shortly, the expectations of firms regarding wages and other input prices that they pay are a major factor in how they respond to changes in demand. If they expect input prices to rise, they tend to react to increases in demand by raising their prices; if they expect the prices of the inputs they use in production to stay the same, they tend to react by increasing their output. Because wages and salaries are the biggest cost item for most firms, it is not surprising that changes in the average level of labor costs per unit of output are closely related to changes in the price level, as Box 7.4 shows.

Although changes in labor costs are closely linked to changes in prices, it would be wrong to think that there is a simple cause-and-effect relationship between them. True, other things being equal, rising labor

Box 7.4
Labor Costs and Prices
in the U.S. Economy

Labor costs are the largest set of costs for most firms. Not surprisingly, then, the rate of change in labor costs per unit of output is closely linked to the rate of inflation. Labor costs per unit of output shown in this chart take into account both changes in wage rates per hour and changes in output per worker hour.

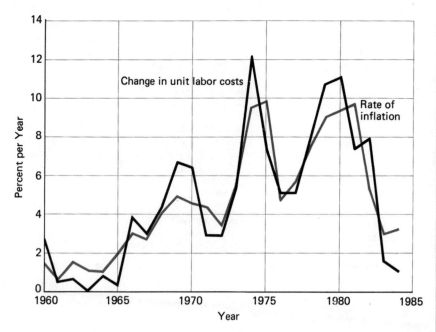

Source: President's Council of Economic Advisers, *Economic Report of the President* (Washington, D.C.: Government Printing Office, 1985), Table B–41.

costs tend to push the price level up. But it is equally true that a rising price level tends to push up labor costs. Some workers may allow their real wages to be eroded for a time as the price level rises faster than their nominal wages. College professors were in this position in the 1970s. But sooner or later depressed real wages are likely to result in shortages—today's shortage of engineering professors is a case in point. Then nominal wages must catch up with inflation.

Sometimes the link between the price level and real wages is more than a matter of falling behind and then catching up. Workers may demand higher nominal wages to protect themselves against inflation that they expect to occur in the future. If the inflation takes place as expected, this will keep their real wages from falling. If inflation unexpectedly slows down, their real wages will rise. Sometimes they will rise enough to produce a surplus in the labor market. Then workers may have to choose between layoffs and concessions aimed at bringing real wages back into line with supply and demand. In Chapters 14 to 18 we will often refer to the complex interactions among wages, other input prices, and the level of output prices.

Other Factor Markets

Other factor markets—those for capital and natural resources—are less important as a source of income. Far fewer people make their living from these markets compared with the number who depend on wage and salary income. As an element of cost, however, these markets can play a major role in macroeconomic events.

An impressive example was the effect of the huge increases in the prices of imported oil that took place in 1974 and again in 1979–1980. Because every sector of the economy depends directly or indirectly on energy derived from oil, the costs of all firms increased as a result. Chapter 14 will discuss this effect in detail.

The cost of capital is also a major factor affecting the economy. Increases in capital per worker are a major source of increases in output per worker. Investment in new capital thus raises the economy's real output, and, other things being equal, lowers production costs per unit of output. In recent years many economists have expressed concern that high interest rates will prevent firms from investing in new equipment. If this is true, it would slow the economy's rate of growth. We will return to the interactions among interest rates, investment, and growth in later chapters too.

FINANCIAL MARKETS

In Chapters 4 and 6 we looked at financial markets as links between households, whose saving provides a source of funds, and firms, whose need to borrow in order to invest provides a use of funds. Financial intermediaries, including banks, pension funds, and so on, stand in the middle. Now we want to look briefly at financial markets in terms of supply and demand.

Interest Rates as Prices in Financial Markets

Box 7.1 shows a sketch of supply and demand curves in the square labeled "financial markets," but it does not make clear what the prices and quantities in those markets are. Box 7.5 adds these details. The horizontal axis measures the quantity of *loanable funds*, that is, credit flows that households, directly and through financial intermediaries, make available to potential borrowers. The vertical axis measures the *interest rate*, which can be thought of as playing the role of the price of credit in financial markets. The interest rate, stated in percentage terms, is the number of dollars per year that the borrower must pay to the lender for each $100 borrowed. It is a price in that, like the price of shoes or jelly beans, it represents the opportunity cost to the buyer (the borrower, in this case) and the receipts of the seller (the lender, in this case).

Changes in supply and demand conditions in financial markets cause the interest rate to change, just as prices in other markets change in response to shifts in supply and demand. Suppose, for example, that firms expect the demand for their products to increase. They will want to invest in new production capacity in order to meet the higher demand. The change in their plans appears in financial markets as a rightward shift in the demand curve for loanable funds. The immediate result is an excess

Box 7.5
Supply and Demand in Financial Markets

This graph applies the concepts of supply and demand to financial markets. The supply curve represents the willingness of savers to supply loanable funds at various interest rates. The demand curve represents the willingness of borrowers to take out loans at various interest rates. The interest rate is the "price" of credit—the opportunity cost to the borrower and the gain to the lender.

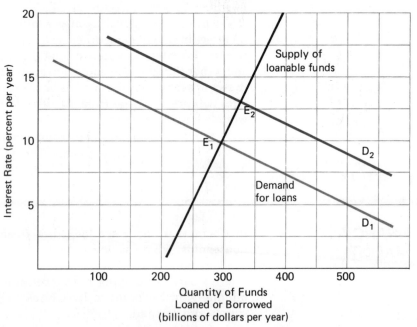

demand for loanable funds. Competition among firms for the limited supply of credit pushes up the interest rate. The rising interest rate, in turn, causes some firms to cut back on their investment plans (a movement along the new demand curve). As Box 7.5 shows, it also causes households to make more funds available to be loaned (a movement upward along the supply curve). As a result of the shift in demand, the economy moves from an equilibrium at E_1 to a new equilibrium at E_2, where the interest rate is somewhat higher than before and the quantity of loanable funds (or credit flows) is also larger.

The Family of Interest Rates

Box 7.5 is a highly simplified picture of financial markets. In practice, there is no such thing as "the" financial market or "the" interest rate. Just as "the" market for shoes ignores the fact that there are many sizes and styles of shoes, each with its own price, "the" financial market ignores the fact that there is more than one way to move funds from lenders to borrowers.

A full picture of financial markets, then, would show a whole family of markets and a whole family of interest rates. Part a of Box 7.6 shows the levels of several kinds of interest rates for 1984. The vertical axis of this graph gives the rate, and the horizontal axis gives the *term* of the loan—that is, the length of time until the loan must be repaid.

The various members of the interest rate family are not scattered at random over the graph. There are some logical relationships among the interest rates on various kinds of loans.

One of those relationships links the interest rate to the term of the loan. Usually, long-term loans bear higher interest rates than short-term loans. The line connecting points A, B, C, D, and E shows this tendency. These five points stand for 3-month, 6-month, 3-year, and 10-year loans to the government and 25-year loans to private firms with top credit ratings. The longer the term of the loan, the higher the interest rate.

Interest rates are also related to the riskiness of the loan. For a given term, interest rates rise with degree of risk. For example, compare points E and F. Point E is the interest rate on long-term bonds issued by Aaa-rated corporations—the best credit risks. It is lower than F, the interest rate on bonds issued by Baa-rated corporations, which are viewed as not quite so creditworthy. Likewise, points H and I, which represent short-term loans to firms, lie above similar short-term loans to the government. The reason is that the government is considered to be more certain to repay its debts than the private firms to whom these loans are made.

Given this diverse set of interest rates, does it make any sense to speak of "the" interest rate? The answer is yes, if we use changes in "the" interest rate to stand for an upward or downward shift in the whole family of interest rates. Part b of Box 7.6 illustrates this point by comparing interest rates in two years, 1981 and 1984. Given the fact that all members of the interest rate family shifted downward between 1981 and 1984, it is not unreasonable to talk about a fall in "the" interest rate, or in interest rates in general. Note, however, that not all rates changed by exactly the same amount. Short-term rates fell by more than long-term rates. In later chapters we will often use one particular rate, such as the rate on 3-month Treasury bills, to represent movements in the whole family of rates, but it

**Box 7.6
The Family of Interest
Rates**

There is no such thing as "the" interest rate. Instead, there is a family of interest rates on loans with varying terms and degrees of risk. Part a shows the interest rates on various kinds of loans. Note that long-term interest rates tend to be higher than short-term rates. Also, interest rates on loans to the government, which are viewed as very safe, are lower than interest rates for comparable terms on loans to firms. As supply and demand conditions in financial markets change, the whole family of interest rates tends to shift. Part b illustrates such a shift by comparing the family of interest rates for 1981 with that for 1984. When economists speak of a change in "the" interest rate, they are really talking about a shift in the whole family of interest rates.

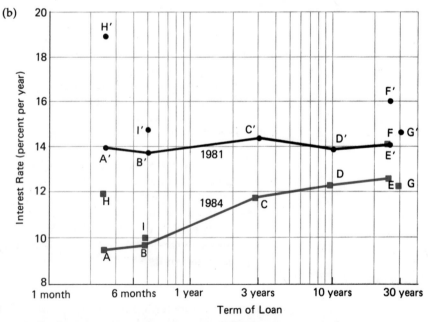

Key:
A 3-month Treasury bills
B 6-month Treasury bills
C 3-year Treasury notes
D 10-year Treasury bonds
E 25-year corporate bonds rated Aaa
F 25-year corporate bonds rated Baa
G 30-year home mortgages
H Prime rate charged by banks on short-term commercial loans
I 6-month commercial paper

Source: President's Council of Economic Advisers, *Economic Report of the President* (Washington, D.C.: Government Printing Office, 1985), Table B-66.

should be kept in mind that no one rate shows exactly what is going on in all financial markets.

Real vs. Nominal Interest Rates

A key detail is still needed to complete our picture of supply and demand in financial markets. This detail is the distinction between *real* and *nominal* interest rates—which is just as important as the distinction between real and nominal wages.

Nominal interest rate
The interest rate stated in the usual way, in terms of current-dollar interest payments per dollar of principal.

Real interest rate
The nominal interest rate minus the rate of inflation.

The **nominal interest rate** on a loan is the rate stated in the usual way, in terms of current-dollar interest payments per dollar of principal. All of the interest rates given in Box 7.1 are nominal interest rates. But interest rates, like other quantities, need to be adjusted to take inflation into account in order to get a picture of the real costs of borrowing and lending. The adjusted rate, known as the **real interest rate**, is equal to the nominal interest rate minus the rate of inflation.

An example will show why the rate of inflation needs to be subtracted from the nominal rate to get the real cost to the borrower and the real gain to the lender. Suppose that in a year of 10 percent inflation I borrow $100 from you, promising to pay you back $115 a year from now. The nominal interest rate on this loan is 15 percent. However, we both know that $10 of the interest I promise to pay is needed just to make up for inflation. The reason is that each dollar I pay you next year will be worth 10 percent less, in terms of real purchasing power, than the dollars I borrow today. Thus, the real interest cost of the loan to me, and the real gain to you, is just $5 after the $10 allowance for inflation is subtracted from the $15 nominal interest payment.

Following this reasoning, lenders ask (and borrowers are willing to pay) higher nominal rates during periods of inflation than during periods of price stability, as Box 7.7 shows. The adjustment for inflation is not exact, however, largely because borrowers and lenders do not always correctly predict the rate of inflation that will prevail over the life of the loan. In some recent years of high inflation, nominal interest rates have not risen by enough to compensate lenders fully for the effects of inflation. In those years, real interest rates have actually fallen below zero. These rates were a windfall for borrowers and an unwanted burden for lenders.

We will return to financial markets at many points in our discussion of macroeconomics. As we do so, we will take care to make clear whether we are talking about real or nominal interest rates.

PRODUCT MARKETS

Product markets are the third set of markets that tie the circular flow together. These include all markets in which finished goods and services are sold to consumers, firms, units of government, and foreign buyers.

Chapter 3 gave us a grounding in the microeconomics of product markets. That chapter focused on the way in which supply and demand determine *relative* prices—the price of wheat relative to that of corn; that of cabbage relative to that of lettuce; that of dental services relative to doctors' services; and so on. In this section we will focus instead on the *price level*—the average price of all goods and services relative to the average

Box 7.7
Real and Nominal
Interest Rates in the U.S.
Economy, 1970–1984

The real interest rate is the nominal interest rate minus the rate of inflation. This chart shows interest rates on 3-month Treasury bills, the rate of inflation measured as the year-to-year change in the consumer price index, and the real interest rate measured as the difference between the two. Lenders demand, and borrowers are willing to pay, higher interest rates when the rate of inflation is high than when it is low. However, in some years the increase in the nominal interest rate was not enough to protect lenders fully against inflation. In those years the real interest rate fell below zero.

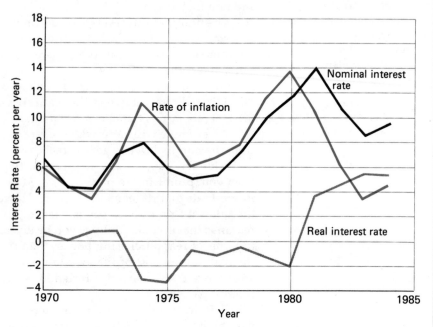

Source: President's Council of Economic Advisers, *Economic Report of the President* (Washington, D.C.: Government Printing Office, 1985), Tables B–55 and B–66.

price prevailing in a chosen base year. In doing this, we will build on the concepts of aggregate nominal supply and demand discussed in Chapter 6.

In Chapter 6 we pointed out several times that when aggregate nominal demand rises, inventories will fall and firms will react by raising their output, raising their prices, or doing some of both. Likewise, when aggregate nominal demand falls, inventories will build up and firms will react by lowering prices, lowering output, or doing some of both.

The matter of how a given change in nominal national product is divided between a change in the price level and a change in real output is crucial. If the volume of the circular flow increases by 10 percent in nominal terms and this represents an increase in real output, everyone will be pleased. People's standard of living will rise; there will be more jobs; and there will be no inflation. On the other hand, the entire 10 percent growth of nominal output might take the form of higher prices. In that case firms do not raise their output at all. There will be no more goods and services than before and no more jobs than before. There will, however, be inflation, and this will make very few people happy. The key to which of these outcomes or what mix of them occurs lies in **aggregate real supply and demand**. Let's turn to these concepts now.

Aggregate Real Demand

Aggregate real demand
The total planned purchases of all spending units, expressed in constant dollars.

Aggregate nominal demand is the total planned purchases of all spending units measured in terms of current dollars per year. **Aggregate real demand**, in contrast, is total planned purchases adjusted for inflation. To convert one to the other, we divide aggregate nominal demand by the price level (relative to a chosen base year) to get aggregate real demand, or we multiply aggregate real demand by the price level to get aggregate nominal demand.

Box 7.8 gives examples of these calculations for the case in which aggregate nominal demand is $1,200 billion. In this table the base year price level is assigned the value of 1.0. At that price level, real and nominal aggregate demand are equal. If the price level doubles while aggregate nominal demand stays the same, people will be able to buy only half the real quantity of goods that they were able to buy before. This means that aggregate real demand will fall to $600 billion. If the price level were to fall to 0.5 while aggregate nominal demand stayed the same, aggregate real demand would rise to $2,400 billion, and so on.

Aggregate real demand curve
A graph showing the real quantity of goods and services that people plan to purchase at each price level, assuming a given level of aggregate nominal demand.

The Aggregate Real Demand Curve   The data on aggregate real demand given in Box 7.8 are plotted as a graph in Box 7.9. This graph can be thought of as an **aggregate real demand curve**—a graph showing the real quantity of goods and services that people plan to buy at each price level, assuming a given level of aggregate nominal demand.

Like all demand curves, this one makes an other-things-being-equal assumption. It assumes that the level of aggregate nominal demand stays the same. Maintaining a constant level of aggregate nominal demand is likely to require action by the government. In Chapter 6 we gave a preview of the ways in which the government can use taxes, government spending,

Box 7.8
The Relationship of Aggregate Real Demand to Aggregate Nominal Demand

Aggregate real demand is equal to aggregate nominal demand divided by the price level. The price level for the base year is 1.0. In this table aggregate nominal demand is assumed to be $1,200 billion. Values of aggregate real demand are given for various price levels.

Aggregate Nominal Demand (billions of dollars)	Price Level	Aggregate Real Demand (billions of dollars)
$1,200	0.25	$4,800
1,200	0.5	2,400
1,200	1.0	1,200
1,200	2.0	600
1,200	3.0	400
1,200	4.0	300
1,200	10.0	120

**Box 7.9
The Aggregate Real
Demand Curve**

The aggregate real demand curve shows total planned expenditures, in real terms, at various price levels. This graph assumes a constant $1,200 billion aggregate nominal demand at all price levels. If the price level in the current year is the same as that in the chosen base year (a price level of 1.0), aggregate real demand and aggregate nominal demand are equal at $1,200. This corresponds to point C. If the price level doubles while aggregate nominal demand remains at $1,200 billion, aggregate real demand falls to $600 billion (point B). If the price level falls to half the base year level (a price level of 0.5), aggregate real demand doubles to $2,400 billion (point D).

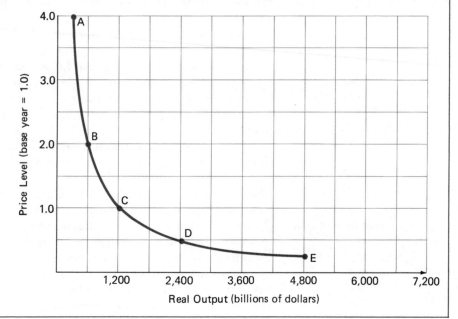

and monetary policy to adjust aggregate nominal demand. We will see how these policies work in the next few chapters. Here it will be enough to assume that they do work, and that the government uses them to keep aggregate *nominal* demand steady as the economy moves along the aggregate *real* demand curve.

Shifts in the Aggregate Real Demand Curve   The aggregate real demand curve in Box 7.9 assumes $1,200 billion of aggregate nominal demand. It follows that if aggregate nominal demand changes, the aggregate real demand curve will shift. Such a shift is shown in Box 7.10. There the curve ARD$_1$ assumes an aggregate nominal demand of $1,200 billion, as before. Now suppose that the government takes some action—an increase in government purchases, a tax cut, an expansionary monetary policy— that causes aggregate nominal demand to double. The aggregate real demand curve will shift to the position ARD$_2$. If aggregate nominal demand is twice as high as before, the real quantity of goods and services that people plan to buy at any given price level will be twice as high as before.

Aggregate Real Supply

Aggregate real supply
The planned level of production of goods and services, expressed in constant dollars, at a given price level.

Now we come to the supply side of our aggregate real supply and demand theory. We can define **aggregate real supply** as the planned level of production of goods and services, measured in real terms, that will take place at a given price level.

At the beginning of this section we asked, When the volume of the circular flow expands in nominal terms, do firms react by increasing their output, by raising their prices, or by doing some of both? Now this question can be restated in terms of aggregate real supply and demand: When aggregate real demand increases, does the quantity of aggregate real supply increase, does the price level increase, or is there some increase in both? The answer depends on how firms adjust their production plans when demand increases.

Put yourself in the position of the manager of a typical firm in a typical market like those discussed in Chapter 3. Suppose that aggregate demand stays the same, but that demand shifts among goods in such a way that demand for the good you are selling increases by 10 percent. The demand curve in your market shifts to the right by that amount, and the price of the good you sell begins to rise. How will you react?.

Box 7.10
A Shift in the Aggregate Real Demand Curve

If the level of aggregate nominal demand changes, the aggregate real demand curve will shift. Here the curve ARD₁ assumes an aggregate nominal demand of $1,200 billion. If an expansionary policy, such as an increase in government purchases or a tax cut, causes aggregate nominal demand to rise to $2,400 billion, the aggregate real demand curve shifts to the position ARD₂. Whatever the price level, people will plan to buy twice the volume of goods and services as before.

In part, your reactions will depend on what you expect to happen to wages and the prices of other inputs you use. Suppose that recently the wages and other input prices you pay have been stable, in line with a stable average price level for all goods and services. Assuming that your industry is small in relation to the economy as a whole, you have no reason to think that wages will rise if you or your competitors hire more workers. You also do not expect the prices of other inputs you use to rise.

Under these conditions, as the price in your market is bid up, you will find it profitable to increase your output. The increase in output represents a movement upward along the supply curve in your market. As this takes place, the increase in the quantity supplied by your industry will keep the price from rising by a full 10 percent even though the demand curve for your product has shifted to the right by 10 percent. Thus, in the new equilibrium both your price and your output will increase somewhat.

Now suppose that demand in all markets increases—that is, that the economy's *aggregate* real demand curve shifts to the right. Again suppose that the economy is starting from a position of wage and price stability, in which firms have become accustomed to a constant average level of wages and other input prices. The increased aggregate demand will be reflected in your market in the form of greater demand for your product and upward pressure on its price. But now, although you are not aware of it at first, the same thing is happening in all markets. All firms would now respond as you were just assumed to have done, by raising output as the price of their products rise. This appears to be the normal short-term response to an increase in aggregate demand.

The result is shown in Box 7.11. The circular flow starts out in equilibrium at a price level of 1.0 and a level of aggregate nominal demand of $1,200 billion. This corresponds to point A. Then aggregate nominal demand rises to $2,400 billion, shifting the aggregate real demand curve to the position ARD_2. Firms respond by raising their prices somewhat and by increasing real output somewhat. The economy ends up at point B, where the price level is 1.5, real output is $1,600 billion, and nominal national product is $2,400 billion ($2,400 = 1.5 × $1,600).

The upward-sloping line in Box 7.11 shows the path along which the economy travels from A to B. This path is the economy's short-run **aggregate real supply curve**. It traces the relationship between the price level and real quantity supplied for the economy as a whole, much as the supply curve for, say, wheat traces the relationship between price and quantity supplied for a single market.

In Chapter 3, we saw that the position of the supply curve for an individual product, such as wheat, depends, among other things, on the prices of inputs used in its production. In much the same way, the position of the economy's aggregate real supply curve depends, in the short run, on the average level of input prices that all firms expect. In the case shown in Box 7.11, they expected input prices not to change. In later chapters we will see that over time these expectations are subject to change. In particular, in the case of an economy-wide shift in the aggregate real demand curve, increases in output prices will sooner or later affect the expected level of input prices. This happens partly because some firms' outputs are the inputs of other firms. It also happens in part because changes in consumer goods prices affect the cost of living, and hence affect wages. As this

Aggregate real supply curve
A graph that shows the connection between the price level and the planned level of production of goods and services, measured in real terms.

Box 7.11
The Aggregate Real
Supply Curve

The aggregate real supply curve traces the connection between price and real quantity supplied. Here a shift in the aggregate real demand curve causes firms to raise both their prices and their level of output, thus moving from A to B along the short-run aggregate real supply curve. This is the normal short-run response. It reflects the fact that firms initially expect the prices of their inputs to remain unchanged. This being the case, they initially react to a change in aggregate real demand as if it were a change in demand for their product alone.

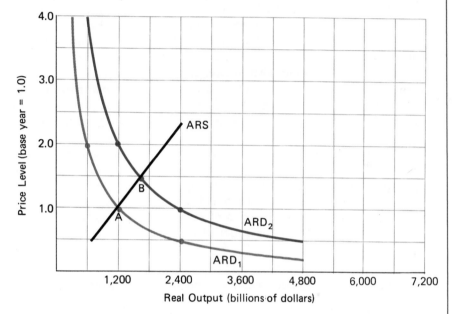

happens, the economy's aggregate real supply curve will shift up. The point B in Box 7.11 turns out to be only a temporary equilibrium.

We will save the details of shifts in the aggregate real supply curve and of the path to a new long-run equilibrium for later chapters. In the meantime we need a better understanding of what determines the volume of the circular flow in nominal terms, and of the fiscal and monetary policies that the government can use to influence aggregate nominal demand. That will be our job in Chapters 8–13.

Summary

1. The *price level* is the ratio of the average price of goods and services in the current year to the average price of goods and services in a chosen *base year*. The price level for the base year is, by definition, 1.0. To convert the nominal wage to the real wage, divide the nominal wage rate by the price level.

2. Labor markets account for three quarters of all payments for factor services. Labor markets are important as a source of income, a source of

jobs, and an element of costs. Changes in labor costs per unit of output are closely linked with inflation rates. Changes in the prices of capital and raw materials also affect costs of production and, hence, the rate of inflation.

3. Financial markets can be described in terms of supply and demand curves for loanable funds. The supply curve represents the willingness of savers to extend credit at various interest rates, and the demand curve represents the willingness of borrowers to take out loans. The interest rate serves as the price in these markets. It is the opportunity cost to the borrower and the gain to the lender. In practice, there is a family of interest rates on different kinds of loans. When we speak of a change in "the" interest rate, we are really talking about an upward or downward shift in the whole family of interest rates.

4. Interest rates can be stated in either nominal or real terms. The *nominal interest rate* is the rate stated in the usual way, in terms of current-dollar interest payments per dollar of princi-pal. The *real interest rate* is the nominal interest rate minus the rate of inflation.

5. The *aggregate real demand curve* is a graph that shows the real quantity of goods and services that people plan to buy at each price level, assuming a given level of aggregate nominal demand. Movements along the aggregate real demand curve assume that the level of aggregate nominal demand stays the same. A change in the level of aggregate nominal demand causes a shift in the aggregate real demand curve.

6. The *aggregate real supply curve* shows the planned level of production of goods and services at each given price level. An increase in aggregate nominal demand shifts the aggregate real demand curve to the right. As a result, the economy moves upward and to the right along its aggregate real supply curve to a new short-run equilibrium in which both the price level and the quantity of real output are greater.

Questions for Review

1. Define the following terms:
   price level
   base year
   employment rate
   nominal interest rate
   real interest rate
   aggregate real demand
   aggregate real demand curve
   aggregate real supply
   aggregate real supply curve

2. If the nominal salary of college professors was $29,130 in 1984 and the 1984 price level, using 1968 as a base year, was 3.11, what was the real salary of college professors in 1984, stated in constant 1968 dollars?

3. What has happened to each of the following in recent years: real weekly earnings, nominal weekly earnings, the employment rate?

4. In what sense is the interest rate the "price" of credit?

5. If the nominal interest rate on 3-month Treasury bills is 9.8 percent and the rate of inflation is 4 percent, what is the real interest rate on these securities?

6. What is the "other things being equal" assumption that underlies the aggregate real demand curve?

7. Why does the economy's aggregate real supply curve have a positive slope? Explain in terms of a typical firm's reactions to a shift in the aggregate real demand curve.

Problems and Topics for Discussion

1. Using the *Economic Report of the President* or another source, update the charts in Boxes 7.2, 7.4, 7.6, and 7.7. Interpret the most recent data in the light of what you have learned in this chapter.

2. Use the *Economic Report of the President* or another source to find the most recent value for the consumer price index for this year and for last year. Also find the current level of tuition at your college, and the level last year. Has the real level of tuition at your college gone up or down? (*Hint*: To find this year's real tuition, using last year as a base year, divide this year's nominal tuition by the ratio of this year's consumer price index to last year's consumer price index.)

3. In 1984 the employment rate for the U.S. economy was higher than in 1972, but real weekly earnings were lower. In your opinion, do these data, taken together, show that the economy was performing better or worse in 1984 than in 1972? What is the correct standard of performance? Discuss.

4. Your college offers to lend you $1,000 to pay your tuition this year. The interest rate will be 8 percent per year, and you will not have to start repaying the loan until after you graduate. Why is the loan more attractive to you if you expect inflation to average 10 percent per year over the next few years than if you expect inflation to average only 3 percent? How does inflation affect the number of hours per year that you expect to have to work in order to earn money to make the loan payments, assuming that salaries in your chosen field rise in step with the overall price level?

5. Rework Boxes 7.8 and 7.9 for the case in which aggregate nominal demand is $1,800 billion. What is the relationship between your new aggregate real demand curve and the one shown in Box 7.9?

6. Rework Box 7.11 for the case of a decline in aggregate nominal demand. What happens to the aggregate real demand curve? Tell the story of a movement downward and to the left along the aggregate real supply curve in terms of the reactions of a typical firm.

Chapter 8

Measuring National Income and Product

WHAT YOU WILL LEARN IN THIS CHAPTER

After reading this chapter, you should be able to

1. Define *gross* and *net* national product and explain how they are measured.
2. Distinguish between *national product* and *national income* in terms of both concept and method of measurement.
3. Define *personal income* and *disposable personal income*.
4. Use the *GNP deflator* as a measure of the changing level of average prices.
5. Compare the GNP deflator to other *price indexes*.
6. Discuss the accuracy and completeness of the U.S. national income accounts.

Ideas for Review

Here are some terms and concepts that you should review before you read this chapter:

Real and nominal values (Chapter 1)
Government purchases and transfer payments (Chapter 5)
National income and product (Chapter 6)
Investment (Chapter 6)
Price level (Chapter 7)

"We appear to be passing through a transitional slowdown and heading for sustained prosperity."

December 20, 1984: The nation's economy appeared to pick up to a 2.8 percent annual growth rate in the fourth quarter from the summer's 1.6 percent rate, raising hopes that the worst of the slowdown is past.

The Commerce Department reported the improvement in its initial "flash" estimate of the economy's performance for October through December. If that figure is not revised, growth for the year will be 6.7 percent, below the administration's forecast of 7.2 percent real growth over 1983 but still the best gain in output since 1955. Last year, real gross national product increased 3.7 percent.

The Commerce Department also reported an improvement in inflation in the current quarter. Inflation, using a measure of changes in prices and type of output, proceeded at a 2.9 percent rate, compared with 3.9 percent in the third quarter; for the year, the rate is the same as last year's 3.8 percent, according to yesterday's estimate.

White House spokesman Larry Speakes said, "We appear to be passing through a transitional slowdown and heading for sustained prosperity." He called the report on gross national product and inflation "quite encouraging" and said other recent economic statistics had been "on the positive side."

For the year, real gross national product is expected to increase $103.2 billion to $1.6 trillion, up from $1.534 trillion in 1983. Nominal gross national product, without adjustment for inflation, is expected to be $3.659 trillion for the year, up from $3.304 trillion last year.[1]

By now national product and income are familiar as concepts—but how are they actually measured? What is the Commerce Department's "flash" estimate of GNP? What method is used to convert nominal data into real data in calculating real GNP? Why do White House policymakers cheer or lament every decimal point of upturn or downturn in these numbers? Are the numbers accurate enough to serve as a guide to policymakers? This chapter will address these questions and others.

MEASURING NOMINAL INCOME AND PRODUCT

Gross national product
The dollar value at current market prices of all final goods and services produced by a nation's factors of production in a given year.

Final goods and services
Goods and services that are sold to or are ready for sale

Gross National Product

National income accounting begins with the measure of total production known as **gross national product (GNP)**, a concept that we have mentioned before but have not defined precisely. GNP is the dollar value at current market prices (that is, the nominal value) of all final goods and services produced annually by a nation's factors of production.

Why final goods?   The term **final goods and services** is a key part of the definition of gross national product. GNP attempts to measure the sum of

---

[1]Jane Seaberry, "U.S. Economic Growth Picks Up," *Washington Post*, December 20, 1984, p. A1. © The Washington Post.

to parties that will use them for consumption, investment, government purchases, or export.

the economic contributions of each firm and industry, without missing anything and without counting anything twice. To do this, care must be taken to count only goods sold to *final users*—parties that will use them for domestic consumption, government purchases, investment, or export. *Intermediate goods*—those that are purchased to be used as inputs in producing other goods or services—are excluded.

Box 8.1 shows why counting both final and intermediate goods would overstate total production. The example traces the process of producing a loaf of bread that sells for $1 at retail. The final stage of bread production is baking, but the baker does not do a dollar's worth of work. Instead, the baker takes 60 cents' worth of flour, turns it into a loaf of bread, and gets 40 cents in exchange for the labor, capital, and other factors of production used in the process of baking. The 60 cents' worth of flour is an intermediate good; the 40-cent contribution made by the baker is the **value added** to the product at its final stage. (Of course, in practice other intermediate goods, such as yeast, fuel for the oven, and so on, are used in baking. It is only to simplify the example that we assume that bread is made solely from flour plus the effort of the baker.)

The next section of Box 8.1 shows the next-to-last stage of production: milling the flour. The miller buys 35 cents' worth of wheat, produces flour that sells for 60 cents, and gets 25 cents in exchange for the work of milling. The value added at the milling stage is 25 cents.

Going still further back, we come to the stage at which the wheat was

Value added
The dollar value of an industry's sales less the value of intermediate goods purchased to be used in production.

Box 8.1
Value Added and the Use of Final Products in GNP

This table shows why GNP must include only the value of final goods and services if it is to measure total production without double counting. The value of sales at each stage of production can be divided into the value added at that stage and the value of purchased inputs. The selling price of the final product (a $1 loaf of bread, in this case) is equal to the sum of the values added at all stages of production.

Final stage: baking		
Value of one loaf of bread	$1.00	
Less value of flour	−.60	
Equals value added in baking	$ .40	→ $ .40
Next to final stage: milling		
Value of flour	$ .60	
Less value of wheat	−.35	
Equals value added in milling	$ .25	→ $ .25
Second from final stage: farming		
Value of wheat	$ .35	
Less value of fuel, fertilizer, and so on	−.20	
Equals value added in farming	$ .15	→ $ .15
All previous stages		
Value added in fuel and fertilizer industries, plus value added in suppliers to those industries, and so on	$ .20	→ $ .20
Total value added		$1.00

grown. To grow 35 cents' worth of wheat, some farmer bought 20 cents' worth of fuel, fertilizer, and so on and kept 15 cents in exchange for the effort of growing the wheat. That makes 15 cents more of value added.

Clearly, the process of making bread could be traced back endlessly. The last section of the box sums up the value added at all stages of production prior to farming—the fuel and fertilizer suppliers, the suppliers of those suppliers, and so on. If production were traced back far enough, every penny could be attributed to the value added somewhere in the chain of production.

Now compare the first and last lines of the box. Lo and behold, the value of the final good, bread, turns out to be an exact measure of the sum of the values added at each stage of production. That is why only final goods are counted in GNP. Adding together the dollar's worth of bread plus the 60 cents' worth of flour plus the 35 cents' worth of wheat and so on would far overstate the true rate of productive activity (the true total value added) in the economy.

The expenditure approach to measuring GNP   In principle, GNP could be measured by adding together the value of each final good or service sold, or by adding up the value added at each stage of production, as shown in Box 8.1. To simplify the process, however, national income accountants make use of the equality of national product and total expenditure. It is easier to gather data on the total expenditures of households, investors, governments, and buyers of exports on final goods produced in the domestic economy than it is to stand at factory gates and count goods as they roll off assembly lines. This way of measuring GNP is known as the *expenditure approach*. Box 8.2 shows how it works, using 1984 data for the U.S. economy.

Consumption   The first line of Box 8.2 gives total household consumption of both domestically produced and imported goods and services. The national income accounts divide consumption into three categories: durable goods, nondurable goods, and services. In principle, goods that do not wear out in one year—such as cars, furniture, and appliances—are durable; goods that are used up in less than a year—such as soap, food, and gasoline—are nondurable. In practice, however, these categories are somewhat arbitrary. For example, all clothing is considered nondurable, whether it is a pair of stockings that may last only a few weeks or a woolen coat that may last ten years. The remaining item, services, includes everything that is not in the form of a physical object when it is sold, such as haircuts, legal advice, and education.

Both the goods and the services components of consumption contain some items that do not pass through the marketplace on their way to consumers. One such item is an estimate of food produced and consumed on farms. Another is an estimate of the rental value of owner-occupied homes. As we will see later in this chapter, however, by no means all nonmarket goods and services are captured in the national income accounts.

Investment   The item called *gross private domestic investment* is the sum of all purchases of newly produced capital goods (fixed investment) plus

**Box 8.2
Nominal Gross National
Product, by Type of
Expenditure, 1984 (in
billions)**

Gross national product is estimated using the expenditure approach. This involves adding together the values of expenditures on newly produced goods and services made by all economic units to get a measure of aggregate economic activity. Net national product is derived from gross national product by excluding the value of expenditures to replace worn-out or obsolete capital equipment.

Personal consumption expenditure		$2,342.3
Durable goods	$ 318.4	
Nondurable goods	858.3	
Services	1,165.7	
Plus gross private domestic investment		637.3
Fixed investment	580.4	
Change in business inventories	56.8	
Plus government purchases of goods and services		748.0
Federal	295.5	
State and local	452.4	
Plus net exports of goods and services		−66.3
Exports	363.7	
Less imports	−429.9	
Equals gross national product (GNP)		$3,661.3
Less capital consumption allowance		−402.9
Equals net national product (NNP)		$3,258.4

Source: President's Council of Economic Advisers, *Economic Report of the President* (Washington, D.C.: Government Printing Office, 1985), Tables B-1, B-19.

changes in business inventories. Fixed investment includes all new equipment and structures bought by firms, plus new residential housing. In the national income accounts, then, a home-owning household is treated as if it were a small firm. When the house is bought, it is counted as an investment. Then, as we saw earlier, the "product" of the firm, the rental value of its shelter services, is considered to be part of consumption each year.

Government purchases   The contribution that government makes to GNP at the federal, state, and local levels is treated much like consumption. The goods and factor services bought by government are considered to be "used up" as soon as they are purchased. Government purchases are valued at cost in the national income accounts. No attempt is made to measure the value added by government because most outputs of government—education, defense services, and police protection, to name a few—are provided free rather than sold to the public. Transfer payments are not included in the expenditure approach to GNP because they do not represent purchases of newly produced final goods and services.

Net exports   The last item in the GNP account is *net exports*—exports minus imports. Imports must be subtracted from exports in calculating

GNP in order to avoid double counting. Some of the goods bought by consumers, investors, and government and included in their expenditures are not produced in the domestic economy. The figures for consumption, investment, and government purchases therefore overstate final use of domestically produced goods and services to the extent that some of those goods and services were produced abroad. To correct for the overstatement in earlier lines of the table, imports are subtracted from exports at the bottom. Total consumption plus total investment plus total government purchases plus exports less imports gives the same sum as would be obtained by adding consumption of domestically produced goods plus purchases of domestically produced capital goods plus government purchases of domestically produced goods plus total exports.

Gross vs. Net National Product

What makes gross national product "gross"? It is the fact that gross private domestic investment measures total additions to the nation's capital stock without adjusting for losses through wear and tear or obsolescence. Gross private domestic investment minus an allowance for depreciation and obsolescence gives *net private domestic investment*, a measure of the actual net addition to the nation's capital stock each year. Although it is hard to measure depreciation and obsolescence accurately, national income accountants use an approximate measure called the *capital consumption allowance*. Gross national product minus the capital consumption allowance is called **net national product (NNP)**.

Net national product
Gross national product minus an allowance (called the capital consumption allowance) that represents the value of capital equipment used up in the process of production.

National Income

In Chapter 6 we learned that it is possible to cut into the circular flow of income and product at several different points. The official national income accounts cut into the circular flow at two points, one where they measure GNP by the expenditure approach and the other where they measure national income by the income approach. As the name implies, the *income approach* measures economic activity by adding together all the different kinds of income earned by households.

In Chapter 6 national income was divided into wages, rents, interest, and profits according to the theoretical classification of factors of production. The version of the income approach used in the national income accounts breaks total income down into a set of categories that is only loosely related to the theoretical breakdown of factor payments. These categories are shown in Box 8.3.

Compensation of employees includes wages and salaries plus certain supplements. The first is employer contributions to social insurance (social security). As the social security tax law is written, employees are legally required to pay only half of the tax; employers must pay the other half. Because both halves contribute to the employee's retirement benefits, however, both are counted as part of the compensation of employees.[2] The

---

[2]Also, studies of the incidence of social security taxes show that employees bear most of the economic burden of both the employer and employee contributions.

**Box 8.3
Nominal National
Income, 1984 (in
billions)**

National income is measured using the income approach. This involves adding together the values of all forms of income earned by households. Some items of income, such as the portion of corporate profits that goes to pay corporate profits taxes, are counted as "earned" by households even though households never receive the income.

Compensation of employees		$2,172.7
Wages and salaries	$1,803.7	
Supplements	369.0	
Plus rental income of persons		62.5
Plus net interest		285.0
Plus corporate profits		284.5
Dividends	80.5	
Corporate profits taxes	88.4	
Undistributed corporate profits	65.3	
Inventory and capital consumption adjustments	50.2	
Plus proprietors' income		154.7
Equals national income		$2,959.4

Source: President's Council of Economic Advisers, *Economic Report of the President* (Washington, D.C.: Government Printing Office, 1985), Table B–21.

supplements line of the national income accounts also includes fringe benefits other than social insurance that are paid for by employers, such as health insurance and private pension plans.

Rental income of persons includes all income in the form of rent and royalties received by owners of property. It does not correspond exactly to the theoretical concept of payments for natural resources as a factor of production. For example, some rental income of persons is received as rent on housing and other structures, which in theory count as capital rather than as natural resources. *Net interest* includes interest income received by households less consumer interest payments.

Corporate profits include all income earned by the stockholders of corporations, whether or not they actually receive that income. Dividends are the part of corporate income that stockholders actually receive. Another part of corporate profits goes to pay corporate profits taxes. A third part, undistributed corporate profits, is kept by corporations to use in making investments. In measuring national income, corporate profits must be adjusted for changes in inventory values and for capital consumption (depreciation). Again, the national income profit category does not correspond exactly to the theoretical concept of profit. For example, much of the "profit" of oil companies constitutes rental payments for the natural resources they own, rather than true economic profit.

The final component of national income, *proprietors' income*, lumps together all forms of income earned by self-employed professionals and owners of unincorporated businesses. No attempt is made to divide this income among labor, capital, and natural resources.

Reconciling the Income and Expenditure Approaches

In the simplified circular flows of Chapter 6, national income and national product were always equal. In the official national income accounts the two sums do not fit together so neatly. Some adjustments must be made in order to match GNP, measured by the expenditure approach, with national income, measured by the income approach. Box 8.4 shows these adjustments.

First, the capital consumption allowance must be subtracted from gross national product to give net national product. In a sense, gross national product overstates the volume of the circular flow because it includes investments that are made solely to replace worn-out or obsolete equipment. Such expenditures are counted as costs by the firms that make them, so they do not show up as income of proprietors or stockholders.

Next, an adjustment must be made for the fact that part of the revenue firms receive for their products never reaches the suppliers of factor services or the owners of the firm. Instead, it is taken by government in the form of so-called *indirect business taxes*, which include sales taxes, excise taxes, and business property taxes. These taxes are treated differently than the corporate profits tax, which is viewed as being earned by owners and then taken from them by the tax collector. Indirect taxes are included in the prices at which goods and services are sold; therefore, they are part of national product but they are not counted as earned in national income.

In principle, subtracting the capital consumption allowance and indirect business taxes from GNP should yield national income, but in practice there is a further problem. GNP is measured by the expenditure approach, using one set of data, and national income is measured by the income approach, using a different set of data. No matter how carefully the

Box 8.4
National Income
Related to Gross
National Product, 1984
(in billions)

In economic theory, national income and national product are equal by definition. In the official accounts, however, some adjustments must be made to get the two to fit because they are measured in different ways. First the capital consumption allowance is subtracted from GNP to get net national product. Then indirect business taxes and the statistical discrepancy are subtracted from NNP to get national income.

Gross national product	$3,661.3
Less capital consumption allowance	−402.9
Equals net national product	3,258.4
Less indirect business taxes[a]	−307.2
Less statistical discrepancy	8.2
Equals national income	$2,959.4

[a]Includes minor adjustments for business transfer payments and subsidies to government enterprises.

President's Council of Economic Advisers, *Economic Report of the President* (Washington, D.C.: Government Printing Office, 1985), Table B–19.

work is done, there are some errors and omissions, and therefore the two sets of figures do not quite fit. The difference between NNP minus indirect business taxes on the one hand and national income on the other is called the *statistical discrepancy*. Most of the time this error is well below 1 percent of GNP.

Personal Income

National income, as we have said a number of times, is a measure of income earned by households, whether or not those households ever actually get their hands on it. For some purposes it is more useful to measure what households actually receive than what they earn. The total income received by households is called **personal income**.

Box 8.5 shows the steps required to go from national income to personal income. First, three items that are earned by households but not received by them are subtracted. These are contributions for social insurance (both employer and employee), corporate profits taxes, and undistributed corporate profits. Next, transfer payments—payments that are received by households but not earned by them—are added. The result is personal income.

One further income measure is shown at the bottom of Box 8.5: **disposable personal income**, or **disposable income** for short. This is the personal income that is left over after households have paid personal taxes (especially income taxes) to federal, state, and local governments.

This completes our discussion of the nominal side of national income accounting. The next section turns to the problem of adjusting nominal income and product measures for changing price levels.

Personal income
The total income received by households, including both earned income and transfer payments.

Disposable personal income (disposable income)
Personal income less personal taxes (especially income taxes).

**Box 8.5
National Income and
Personal Income, 1984
(in billions)**

National income is a measure of all income earned by households; personal income is a measure of the income that households actually receive. To go from national income to personal income, subtract payroll taxes, corporate profits taxes, and undistributed corporate profits; then add transfer payments. If personal taxes are subtracted from this figure, the result is disposable personal income.

National income	$2,959.4
Less contributions for social insurance	−305.9
Less corporate profits taxes and undistributed profits	−206.8
Plus transfer payments[a]	566.5
Equals personal income	$3,013.2
Less personal taxes	−435.1
Equals disposable personal income	2,578.1

[a]Includes business and personal transfer payments, plus adjustments for interest payments.

President's Council of Economic Advisers, *Economic Report of the President* (Washington, D.C.: Government Printing Office, 1985), Tables B–20, B–23.

MEASURING REAL INCOME AND THE PRICE LEVEL

Real Gross National Product and the Deflator

Between 1972 and 1984 the U.S. gross national product, measured in nominal terms, rose from $1,186 billion to $3,661 billion. To anyone living through those years, however, it is clear that even though nominal GNP more than tripled, the real output of goods and services did not triple. Some of the increase in the dollar value of GNP reflected an increase in the prices at which goods and services were sold. To know what really happened to output in those years, then, we need to adjust the growth of nominal GNP to take inflation into account.

As Chapter 7 explained, we need a measure of the price level in order to make this adjustment—a measure of the change in the average prices of all goods and services. The most broad-based measure of the price level for the U.S. economy is the one known as the **GNP deflator**. The appendix to this chapter explains how the GNP deflator is calculated, but for now it is enough to say that it is a weighted average of prices of all the final goods and services that go to make up GNP.

GNP deflator
A price index that covers all final goods and services produced in the economy.

In discussions of economic theory, the price level is stated in relation to a base year value of 1.0. Official government statistics, however, commonly use a base year value of 100. Multiplying the price level by 100 gives a measure known as a **price index**. The GNP deflator is one example of a price index. In 1972, which is the base year used in calculating the GNP deflator, its value was 100. By 1984 it had reached 223. This can be interpreted as meaning that the 1984 "market basket" of goods—so many gallons of gasoline, so many loaves of bread, so many trips to the hairdressers—cost 2.23 times as much in 1984 as it would have if sold at the prices of 1972.

Price index
A weighted average of the prices of goods and services expressed in relation to a base year value of 100.

If we divide 1984 nominal GNP by the ratio of the 1984 GNP deflator to the 1972 GNP deflator, we get a value of $1,639 billion for 1984 real GNP. This figure can also be referred to as the value of 1984 GNP measured in constant 1972 dollars. By comparing the 1984 real GNP of $1,639 billion with the 1972 real GNP of $1,186 billion, we can see that the real output of goods and services rose by only about 38 percent over the period. The remaining part of the more than tripling of nominal GNP was pure inflation.

Using the GNP deflator   Box 8.6 shows nominal GNP, real GNP, and the GNP deflator for the United States in each year since 1960. To convert nominal GNP for any year to real GNP stated in constant 1972 dollars, we simply divide nominal GNP by the ratio of the deflator for that year to the base year deflator. For convenience, we can refer to the year for which we are making the adjustment as the *current year*. In equation form, then, the rule for adjustment can be stated as follows:

$$\text{Current year real GNP} = \frac{\text{current year nominal GNP}}{\text{current year deflator/base year deflator}}$$

As Box 8.6 shows, applying this formula to current years after 1972 gives values for real GNP that are less than current year nominal GNP. Applying

Box 8.6
Nominal GNP, Real
GNP, and the GNP
Deflator, 1960–1984

This table shows nominal and real GNP (in billions of dollars) and the GNP deflator for the U.S. economy for the years 1960–1984. The base year for the GNP deflator is 1972. To calculate real GNP in constant 1972 dollars for any current year, divide current year nominal GNP by the ratio of the current year GNP deflator to the base year GNP deflator.

Year	Nominal GNP	GNP Deflator	Real GNP
1960	$ 506.5	68.7	$ 737.2
1961	524.6	69.3	756.6
1962	565.0	70.6	800.3
1963	596.7	71.6	832.5
1964	637.7	72.7	876.4
1965	691.1	74.4	929.3
1966	756.0	76.8	984.8
1967	799.6	79.0	1,011.4
1968	873.4	82.5	1,058.1
1969	944.0	86.8	1,087.6
1970	992.7	91.5	1,085.6
1971	1,077.6	96.0	1,122.4
1972	1,185.9	100.0	1,185.9
1973	1,326.4	105.7	1,254.3
1974	1,434.2	115.8	1,246.3
1975	1,549.2	125.8	1,231.6
1976	1,718.0	132.3	1,298.2
1977	1,918.3	140.5	1,369.7
1978	2,163.9	150.4	1,438.6
1979	2,417.8	163.4	1,479.4
1980	2,631.7	178.4	1,475.0
1981	2,957.8	195.6	1,512.2
1982	3,069.3	207.4	1,480.0
1983	3,304.8	215.3	1,534.7
1984	3,661.3	223.4	1,639.0

Source: President's Council of Economic Advisers, *Economic Report of the President* (Washington, D.C.: Government Printing Office, 1985), Tables B-1, B-2, B-3.

the formula to current years before 1972, when the GNP deflator had values that were less than 100, gives values for real GNP in 1972 dollars that exceed nominal GNP for those years.

The shrinking dollar   As long as we speak in nominal terms, a dollar is a dollar. When we begin to speak in real terms, as we have just been doing, a 1972 dollar is no longer the same as a 1967 dollar or a 1984 dollar. The reason is that inflation shrinks the purchasing power of the dollar each year. The GNP deflator (or any of the other price indexes to be discussed) can be used to measure the shrinking value of the dollar, beginning from any year we choose. Box 8.7 shows how the value of the dollar has shrunk since 1960. The purchasing power of the dollar in each year is calculated by dividing $1 by the ratio of the current year GNP deflator to the 1960 GNP deflator. For example, to calculate the purchasing power of the 1975 dollar relative to that of the 1960 dollar, we first find the ratio of the 1975 GNP deflator to the 1960 GNP deflator. That ratio is 125.8/68.7 = 1.83. Dividing $1 by 1.83 gives 55 cents. In 1975 the dollar was worth only 55 cents compared with its value in 1960. The choice of 1960 as a year from which to measure the shrinking value of the dollar is arbitrary; any other year could be used instead.

The Consumer Price Index

Consumer price index (CPI)

A price index based on the market basket of goods and services purchased by a typical urban household.

Although the GNP deflator is the broadest-based price index for the U.S. economy, it is not the best-known one. That honor belongs to the **consumer price index (CPI)**. Rather than taking into account the prices of all final goods and services, as the GNP deflator does, the consumer price index considers only the goods and services that make up the **market basket purchased by a typical urban household**.

**Box 8.7
Inflation and the
Shrinking Value of the
Dollar**

The GNP deflator (or any other price index) can be used to calculate the decreasing purchasing power of the dollar, starting from any chosen year. This chart shows the GNP deflator for the years 1960–1984 and shows the shrinking value of the dollar, relative to 1960, at five-year intervals. To find the value of the dollar for any current year relative to 1960, simply divide $1 by the ratio of the current year GNP deflator to the 1960 GNP deflator.

Value of dollar relative to 1960

Source: President's Council of Economic Advisers, *Economic Report of the President* (Washington, D.C.: Government Printing Office, 1985), Table B–3.

Indexing
Adjusting a value or payment automatically in proportion to changes in a specific price index.

Box 8.8 gives values for the CPI from 1960 to the present. Note that the CPI uses 1967, rather than 1972, as its base year. The appendix to this chapter explains how the CPI is calculated.

The CPI plays a key role in economic policy partly because it is widely used to "index" wages, government transfers, and many other payments. To **index** a payment means to adjust it automatically, on a regular schedule, for changes in whatever price index is involved. Take, for example, the indexing of social security payments. From 1983 to 1984 the CPI rose from 298.4 to 311.1, an increase of 4.2 percent. As a result, social security payments were automatically increased by the same percentage. Millions of workers whose contracts include *cost of living adjustment (COLA)* clauses also have their wages raised as a result of increases in the CPI.

Producer Price Indexes

Producer price index
A price index based on a sample of goods and services bought by business firms.

Another widely publicized set of price indexes consists of **producer price indexes.** These are price averages for three classes of goods traded among business firms. Box 8.8 shows the producer price index for finished goods—investment goods plus other goods ready for final use but not yet sold to consumers. Other producer price indexes cover intermediate goods and crude materials ready for further processing. Because producer price indexes measure prices at early stages in the production process, they are often studied for hints of trends in consumer prices. The indexes also are often used to index payments that firms agree to make to one another.

**Box 8.8
Consumer and
Producer Price Indexes,
1960–1984**

This table shows two commonly used price indexes that are more narrowly based than the GNP deflator. The first is the consumer price index, which is based on a market basket of goods purchased by a typical urban household. The second is the producer price index for finished goods, which is based on a sample of finished goods traded among business firms.

Year	CPI	PPI	Year	CPI	PPI
1960	88.7	93.7	1973	133.1	127.9
1961	89.6	93.7	1974	147.7	147.5
1962	90.6	94.0	1975	161.2	163.4
1963	91.7	93.7	1976	170.5	170.6
1964	92.9	94.1	1977	181.5	181.7
1965	94.5	95.7	1978	195.4	195.9
1966	97.2	98.8	1979	217.4	217.7
1967	100.0	100.0	1980	246.8	247.0
1968	104.2	102.8	1981	272.4	269.8
1969	109.8	106.6	1982	289.1	280.7
1970	116.3	110.3	1983	298.4	285.2
1971	121.3	113.7	1984	311.1	291.2
1972	125.3	117.2			

Source: President's Council of Economic Advisers, *Economic Report of the President* (Washington, D.C.: Government Printing Office, 1985), Tables B-52, B-57.

HOW GOOD ARE THE NATIONAL INCOME ACCOUNTS?

This chapter began by stressing the importance of the national income accounts to economics and warning that they are less than perfect. Now that we have surveyed the main parts of the nominal and real national income accounts, it is time to try to answer the question of how good those accounts are. We will focus on four possible problem areas: the timeliness of the data, the unobserved sector of the economy, price index biases, and the nonmaterial aspects of the standard of living.

Timeliness

As can be seen from the news story at the beginning of this chapter, government decision makers pay close attention to national income accounting data. At the end of 1984, for example, the Reagan administration was making a number of crucial decisions on economic policy. What would the federal deficit be? Should taxes be raised? Should expenditures be cut? If the economy was growing at a strong pace, a different set of policies would be called for than if growth was slowing.

The "flash" estimate of real GNP for the fourth quarter of 1984—announced in mid-December, before the quarter had even ended—gave the administration a first indication that growth had speeded up again after having slowed down in the third quarter of 1984. Many important budget decisions had to be made before more nearly complete GNP data for the quarter were available, that is, mid-January of 1985.

But although the earliest estimates of GNP and inflation clearly have an effect on policy decisions, there is a trade-off between timeliness and accuracy. The flash estimate and the estimate released 15 days after the end of the quarter are subject to a series of revisions 45 days and 75 days after the close of each quarter, as well as in July of each year. The revisions are often large. For example, the flash estimate for the third quarter of 1984, released in mid-September, showed third-quarter GNP growth to be running at a rate of 2.9 percent. In mid-October this was revised downward to 1.9 percent, and in December it was revised downward again to 1.6 percent. On the average, the quarterly estimates made 15 days after the quarter's end have been revised up or down by about a percentage point, and the flash estimates by more than a percentage point, in recent years.

We will see in later chapters that lags in the availability of accurate data on GNP, inflation, and other economic quantities have major implications for the ability of policymakers to fine-tune economic policy to fit events as they unfold.

The Unobserved Sector

The economic activity that is measured in the national income accounts constitutes the observed sector of the economy. But a vast amount of production, consumption, and investment is never officially measured. This unobserved sector of the economy includes everything from teenage baby-sitting to multimillion-dollar drug and gambling rings to the multibillion-dollar value of cooking, cleaning, and child care performed in the home. The national income accounts make an effort to observe the unobserved sector when they include estimates of the rental value of owner-occupied housing and the value of food produced and consumed on farms. Those items are only the tip of the iceberg, however. The bulk of the unobserved sector is missing from the official accounts. Although no one knows exactly how big this sector is, some parts of it are enormous.

Organized crime alone has been estimated to produce some $150 billion a year in illegal goods and services in the form of drugs, gambling, pornography, and so on. If this estimate is correct, it would make organized crime the second-largest industry in the United States, after the oil industry. However, organized crime is probably not the largest sector of the so-called *underground economy*. Unreported income of businesses and self-employed people probably adds another $250 billion. This includes cash income that goes unreported for tax purposes (a plumber fixing leaky faucets for cash on her day off) and barter transactions that involve no cash at all (the plumber gets her teeth straightened in exchange for installing a new bathroom in the orthodontist's home).

But even if the underground economy in the United States adds up to more than 10 percent of officially measured GNP, that is moderate by world standards. The French underground economy is thought to equal a third of that country's GNP. In Italy, the figure may be 40 percent. And as Box 8.9 suggests, even more extreme cases exist.

Price Index Biases

A third problem with the official national income accounts is that of price index biases. The accuracy with which price level changes are measured became a matter of growing concern as inflation increased in the late 1970s and as indexing and automatic cost-of-living adjustments became more widespread. If the official price indexes are found to understate inflation, we may want to make a greater effort than we now do to restore price stability. On the other hand, if price indexes overstate inflation, we may be too generous to those who receive automatic adjustments in their incomes.

The problem of price index biases has been closely studied, and the results are far from reassuring. The consumer price index is criticized for two built-in biases that have led it to overstate inflation in recent years.

The substitution bias   The first reason that the consumer price index tends to overstate the true rate of increase in the cost of living is the so-called *substitution bias*. As the appendix to this chapter explains, the CPI is a weighted average of the prices of goods that are typically purchased by urban consumers. At present the weights assigned to various goods are based on the consumption patterns of 1972–1973. Over time, however, patterns of consumption have changed, and therefore the 1972–1973 patterns are no longer typical.

If changes in buying patterns were random, an obsolete set of weights would cause only random errors in the CPI, not an upward bias. The bias results from the fact that consumer demand is influenced by changes in relative prices. As time passes, consumers tend to buy less of goods whose prices have risen most and more of those whose prices have lagged behind the average or have actually fallen. Today's CPI tends to overstate the increase in the cost of living because it assigns unrealistically large weights to products such as heating oil and gasoline, whose prices have soared but

**Box 8.9
Peru's Underground
Economy**

Lima, Peru: The biggest asset of Hugo Contreras' rubber-parts business is that it is almost impossible to find. After winding through a maze of streets and alleys, a visitor must open a pair of steel doors, cross a parking lot, open a gate, walk through a garden, and enter a house. A well-trained rooster crows an alarm.

Inside is a tiny, dirt-floor factory where a work force of four is making miniature tires that a U.S. rubber company will distribute as promotional ash trays. "We are well camouflaged here," says the 36-year-old proprietor, whose real name isn't Contreras.

A low profile is part of life in the "informal sector," Peru's euphemism for the mélange of companies that don't pay taxes, that ignore the labor law, and whose production doesn't show up in the official statistics.

Thanks mostly to Peru's quagmire of business regulations, the informal sector has grown into what proportionately may be the world's largest underground economy. According to a study by Peru's Institute for Liberty and Democracy, it is bigger than the formal sector, accounting for 60 percent of GNP and for two of every three jobs.

In addition to Contreras' rubber-parts firm, the underground economy includes an informal bus service that provides 85 percent of Lima's public transportation; firms that make bus bodies to fit truck chassis supplied by customers; street vendors that sell consumer goods; building contractors; and building supplies manufacturers. There are even individuals who, on their own initiative, fill potholes in the city's streets and then flag down motorists for tips.

The official attitude toward the underground economy is ambivalent. The official private business sector, heavily subsidized by the government, opposes the underground firms. To them, "free enterprise doesn't mean freedom to enter the market," says Hernando de Soto of the Institute for Liberty and Democracy. "It means freedom to keep others out." But some government officials praise the informal sector as a source of native entrepreneurial talent that could be nurtured to provide fuller economic development.

Source: Condensed from Everett G. Martin, "In Lima, Even Buses and Clothes Are Part of 'Informal' Economy," *Wall Street Journal*, August 15, 1984, p. 1, and Claudia Rosett, "How Peru Got a Free Market Without Really Trying," *Wall Street Journal*, January 27, 1984, p. 31. Reprinted by permission of The Wall Street Journal, © Dow Jones & Company, Inc. 1984. All rights reserved.

which are now consumed in relatively smaller amounts than in the early 1970s.

While working for the U.S. Bureau of Labor Statistics, economist Steven D. Braithwait estimated the size of the substitution bias for the CPI.[3] According to Braithwait, the bias added about 1.5 percentage points to the CPI over the period 1958–1973. This is a rather large error when it is remembered that inflation averaged only about 3 percent per year in the period Braithwait studied. In the late 1970s and early 1980s, when the rate of inflation was over 10 percent, the bias was probably greater.

The quality bias   A second source of bias in the consumer price index is the failure to adjust product prices for changes in quality. It would be

---

[3]Steven D. Braithwait, "The Substitution Bias of the Laspeyres Price Index: An Analysis Using Estimated Cost of Living Indexes," *American Economic Review*, 70 (March 1980): 64–77.

highly misleading, for example, to say that a 1985 model car cost three times as much as a 1965 model car without taking into account the fact that the 1985 model got better gas mileage, went farther between tune-ups, and was much safer than the 1965 model. In terms of dollars per unit of transportation service, the new car would clearly be less than three times as expensive.

For automobiles and a few other major goods, the Bureau of Labor Statistics does try to make quality adjustments. This effort is haphazard, however, and fails to adjust many items at all. Robert J. Gordon of Northwestern University, who has studied this problem, cites the case of calculators. As recently as the late 1960s, it cost over $1,000 to buy a desk-sized electromechanical calculator that would add, subtract, multiply, and divide. Today, $5 will buy a calculator that will add, subtract, multiply, divide, take square roots, remember things, and perhaps even play a Mozart sonata. Yet because of the way the prices of the new electronic calculators were "linked" to those of the old electromechanical calculators, the true decrease in price was understated in official price indexes by at least a factor of ten.[4]

Nonmaterial Sources of Welfare

The final problem with gross national product is that it measures only material sources of welfare (which, after all, is all it tries to do). But when one is comparing living standards over time and between countries, nonmaterial sources of welfare are important too.

One key nonmaterial component of the standard of living is the quality of the environment. This not only varies widely from place to place but also has changed greatly over time. Today's problems of acid rain, toxic wastes, and nuclear radiation are "bads" that in principle should be subtracted from GNP just as "goods" are added to it. Yet the direction of environmental change over the years has not been entirely for the worse. A dramatic example can be found in Colonial Williamsburg, a restored eighteenth-century town in rural Virginia. This is surely one of the most pleasant towns in the country, with its carefully restored houses, hidden telephone wires, and cars banned from the streets during daylight hours. But as the official Williamsburg guidebook notes,

> The paved streets, brick sidewalks, streetlights, and fire hydrants would look strange to 18th century eyes. . . . The whole town would seem tidier than the former inhabitants remembered. . . . They would miss the dozens of saddle and draft horses. . . ; the cows, chickens, sheep, and other livestock in every part of town; the streets and paths mired with mud or deep in dust; and the clouds of flies and mosquitoes in summer. Perhaps most of all they would miss the pungent smells of animal manure, rooting hogs, backyard privies, and unwashed humanity.[5]

A second nonmaterial source of welfare is the state of human health.

---

[4]This example is used by Gordon in his *Macroeconomics*, 2nd ed. (Boston: Little, Brown, 1981), p. xii.

---

[5]*Colonial Williamsburg Official Guidebook* (Williamsburg, Va.: Colonial Williamsburg Foundation, 1979), p. v.

By broad measures, especially life expectancy, standards of health in the United States appear to be improving. Since World War II, for example, the life expectancy of a typical 45-year-old in the United States has increased from 72 to 77 years. A 65-year-old in the United States can now expect to live to be 81. This increase clearly improves human welfare, even in the case of people who add nothing to measured GNP after they retire from their jobs.

The list of nonmaterial sources of welfare is endless. How important are satisfying work, friendship, social justice, economic equality, freedom? Everyone knows of people who have been willing to give up income and wealth in pursuit of these things; yet they must remain unmeasured.

For all these reasons, then, GNP cannot be used as a measure of the true level of human welfare, and it can be used only with the greatest caution even for comparisons over time and place.

Summary

1. Two national product concepts are featured in the official accounts of the United States. *Gross national product* is defined as the dollar value at current market prices of all final goods and services produced by the nation's factors of production in a given year. Including only final goods in the total avoids double counting of goods that are used to produce other goods and used goods that are resold. Imports are subtracted from exports in order to allow for the fact that some consumption, investment, and government expenditures are used to purchase imported goods. *Net national product* is derived from GNP by subtracting a capital consumption allowance that accounts for the fact that capital goods wear out or become obsolete.

2. National product is measured by adding together the total of consumption, investment, government purchases, and net exports. National income is measured by adding together the total of wages and supplements, rental income of persons, corporate profits, and proprietors' income. Gross national product and national income differ by the amount of the capital consumption allowance, indirect business taxes, and the statistical discrepancy.

3. Personal income is the total income that households receive, as opposed to national income, which is the total that they earn. Personal income includes transfer payments, which households receive but do not earn, and excludes contributions to social insurance, corporate profits taxes, and undistributed corporate profits, which they earn but do not receive. Personal income less personal taxes equals disposable personal income.

4. The *GNP deflator* is the most broad-based measure of the price level. It can be thought of as an average of the prices of all final goods and services that go into GNP. The GNP deflator can be used to calculate real GNP for any year, stated in terms of constant dollars of the base year. To find current year real GNP in terms of a chosen base year, divide current year nominal GNP by the ratio of the current year deflator to the base year deflator.

5. The GNP deflator takes the prices of all final goods and services into account. The consumer price index (CPI) includes only the market basket of goods purchased by a typical household. A third price index, the producer price index, is based on goods that are typically bought and sold by business firms.

6. The national income statistics of the United States are considered to be among the best in the world. However, they have some limitations. Potential problem areas include timeliness of the data, the unobserved sector of the economy, price index biases, and nonmaterial aspects of the standard of living.

Questions for Review

1. Define the following terms:
   gross national product
   final goods and services
   value added
   net national product
   personal income
   disposable personal income
   GNP deflator
   price index
   consumer price index
   producer price index
   indexing
2. What is the difference between *gross* and *net* national product?

3. What three items are subtracted from gross national product to arrive at national income?
4. How does personal income differ from national income? How does disposable personal income differ from personal income?
5. How can the GNP deflator be used to calculate real income for a given current year in terms of the prices of a chosen base year?
6. What are the differences among the GNP deflator, the consumer price index, and the producer price index?
7. What are four potential problem areas related to the accuracy and completeness of the U.S. national income accounts?

Problems and Topics for Discussion

1. Using the *Survey of Current Business*, the *Economic Report of the President*, or another suitable data source, update the national income and product accounts in this chapter to the most recent quarter. Notice that in some ways the official accounts are more detailed than the ones given in the text.
2. In 1967, the base year for the consumer price index, the average earnings of construction workers were $154.95 per week. By 1984, earnings in construction had reached $454.73 per week, but the consumer price index had risen to 311.1. What were the real earnings of construction workers in 1984, stated in 1967 dollars?
3. A firm sells $10,000 worth of shoes that it has held in inventory for several years. What happens to GNP as a result? Which of its components are affected, and how?
4. The government raises the employer share of the social security payroll tax from 6 percent to 10 percent of wages. What happens to GNP, national income, and personal income?

5. Using a library source, find the most recent data for GNP and the GNP deflator for the fourth quarter of 1984. Compare these to the "flash" estimates reported in the news item that opens this chapter. How much revision, if any, was needed? Were the policy decisions based on the flash estimates valid?
6. Try to find a Sears catalog that is at least ten years old and a new catalog. (A pair of catalogs for different years from another store could be used instead.) Compare the ads for such items as (a) a basic work shirt, (b) a set of top-quality automobile tires, (c) a can of tennis balls, and (d) a stereo or record player. How much has the price of each item gone up? What changes in quality have there been? Assuming that you could buy at list price from either the new or the old catalog, which items would you buy from the old one and which from the new one?

Suggestions for Further Reading

Porter, Richard D., and Amanda S. Bayer. "A Monetary Perspective on Underground Economic Activity in the United States," *Federal Reserve Bulletin* 70 (March 1984) pp. 178–190.

This article reviews evidence from monetary statistics as they bear on the question of the size and growth of the underground sector of the U.S. economy.

President's Council of Economic Advisers. *Economic Report of the President.* Washington, D.C.: Government Printing Office, published annually.

A readily available source for national income data and much other useful data.

U.S. Department of Commerce. *Survey of Current Business.* Washington, D.C.: Government Printing Office, published monthly.

The most recent data on national income may be found in this publication.

U.S. Department of Commerce. *The National Income and Product Accounts for the United States, 1929–74.* Washington, D.C.: Government Printing Office, 1976.

Provides historical data on all items in the national accounts.

U.S. General Accounting Office. *A Primer on Gross National Product Concepts and Issues.* Washington, D.C.: U.S. General Accounting Office, 1981.

Gives detailed definitions of national income accounting concepts.

Appendix to Chapter 8

Computation of
Price Indexes

This appendix provides further details about the GNP deflator and the consumer price index. Knowing these details will make it easier to see the differences between the two and to understand the source of the substitution bias, which affects the two indexes differently.

The GNP Deflator for a Simple Economy

A much simpler economy than that of the United States will serve to illustrate the computation of price indexes. Box 8A.1 shows price and quantity data for two years for an economy in which only three goods are produced: movies, apples, and shirts. The box shows that nominal GNP grew from $400 in 1972 to $1,000 in 1985. But what do these figures mean? Do they mean that people really had more of the things they wanted in 1985 than in 1972? More precisely, do they mean that people had 2.5 times as much? These questions cannot be answered easily by looking at the box as it stands.

A line-by-line comparison of the two years shows that the figures on nominal product do not tell the whole story. Clearly, prices went up sharply between 1972 and 1985. Movies cost twice what they used to, apples three times as much, and shirts half again as much. We notice also

---

**Box 8A.1
Nominal GNP for a
Simple Economy**

In this simple economy, in which only three goods are produced, nominal national product grew from $400 in 1972 to $1,000 in 1985. Prices also went up in that time, though, so people did not really have 2.5 times as many goods in 1985 as they did in 1972.

1972	Quantity	Price	Value
Movies	50	$ 2.00	$ 100
Apples	1,000	.20	200
Shirts	10	10.00	100
1972 nominal GNP			$ 400

1985	Quantity	Price	Value
Movies	100	$ 4.00	$ 400
Apples	500	.60	300
Shirts	20	15.00	300
1985 nominal GNP			$1,000

**Box 8A.2
Nominal and Real GNP
for a Simple Economy**

This table shows how the figures from Box 8A.1 can be adjusted to take changing prices into account. The 1985 quantities are multiplied by 1972 prices to get the value of 1985 GNP as it would have been if prices had not changed. The total of 1985 quantities valued at 1972 prices is a measure of real GNP for 1985, stated in constant 1972 dollars. The implicit GNP deflator for 1985, calculated as the ratio of 1985 nominal GNP to 1985 real GNP multiplied by 100, has a value of 200.

	1985 Quantity	1985 Price	Value at 1985 Price	1972 Price	Value of 1985 Output at 1972 Price
Movies	100	$ 4.00	$ 400	$ 2.00	$200
Apples	500	.60	300	.20	100
Shirts	20	15.00	300	10.00	200
Totals		1985 nominal GNP = $1,000		1985 real GNP = $500	

that the amounts of goods produced have changed. Twice as many movies and shirts were produced in 1985 as in 1972, but only half as many apples.

If we want to know how much better off people were in 1985 than in 1972, we need a way to separate the quantity changes that have taken place from the price changes. One way to do this is to ask how much the total value of output would have changed from 1972 to 1985 if prices had not changed. This approach gives the results shown in Box 8A.2. There we see that the 1985 output of 100 movies, 500 apples, and 20 shirts, which had a value of $1,000 in terms of the prices at which the goods were actually sold, would have had a value of only $500 in terms of the prices that prevailed in 1972. The $500 thus is a measure of real GNP for 1985. It is this measure that should be compared to the 1972 GNP of $400 if we want to know what really happened to output between the two years. Instead of having 150 percent more output in 1985 than in 1972, as indicated by the change in nominal GNP from $400 to $1,000, the people in this simple economy really had only about 25 percent more, as indicated by the change in real GNP from $400 to $500.

We have now seen how to compute real and nominal GNP for 1985 directly from price and quantity data, without using a price index to convert nominal values into real values. But although we have not explicitly used a price index, we have created one implicitly. This implicit index, or implicit GNP deflator, is the ratio of current-year nominal GNP to current-year real GNP times 100, as expressed by the following formula:

$$\text{GNP deflator} = \frac{\text{current year output valued at current year prices}}{\text{current year output valued at base year prices}} \times 100$$

Applying the formula to the data in Boxes 8A.1 and 8A.2 gives a value of 200 for the deflator.

The Consumer Price Index for a Simple Economy

The consumer price index differs from the GNP deflator in two ways. First, as mentioned in the body of the chapter, it takes into account only the prices of goods and services consumed by a typical urban household. Second, it is calculated according to a formula that uses base year quantities rather than current year quantities. The first difference does not matter for this simple economy, in which all goods are consumer goods, but the second difference does matter, as Box 8A.3 shows.

To calculate the CPI for this economy, instead of asking how much current year output would have cost at base year prices, we begin by asking how much base year output would have cost at current year prices. The index is then calculated as the ratio of the two different valuations of base year quantities:

$$\text{Consumer price index} = \frac{\text{base year market basket valued at current year prices}}{\text{base year market basket valued at base year prices}} \times 100$$

The CPI is calculated using base year quantities partly because current price data are easier to collect than current output data. This index therefore can be announced each month with little delay.

Comparing the CPI and the GNP Deflator

As Box 8A.3 shows, the CPI for 1985 in our simple economy had a value of 237.5, whereas the GNP deflator for 1985 was only 200. Both indexes were

---

Box 8A.3
A Consumer Price Index for a Simple Economy

The consumer price index can be calculated as the base year market basket of goods valued at current year prices divided by the base year market basket valued at base year prices, multiplied by 100. This table shows how such an index can be calculated for a simple economy. The 1972 output cost $400 at the prices at which it was actually sold. If it had been sold at 1985 prices, it would have cost $950. The CPI for 1985 thus is 237.5.

Good	1972 Quantity	1972 Price	Value of 1972 Quantity at 1972 Price	1985 Price	Value of 1972 Quantity at 1985 Price
Movies	50	$ 2.00	$100	$ 4.00	$200
Apples	1,000	.20	200	.60	600
Shirts	10	10.00	100	15.00	150
Totals			$400		$950

$$\text{CPI} = \frac{\$950}{\$400} \times 100 = 237.5$$

calculated using the same data, and both used 1972 as a base year. Which, if either, is the true measure of the change in prices between the two years?

The answer is that neither the CPI nor the GNP deflator is the only correct measure of change in the price level. Instead, each is the answer to a different question. The GNP deflator is the answer to the question: How much more did the 1985 output cost at the prices at which it was actually sold than it would have cost if it had been sold at 1972 prices? The CPI, in contrast, is the answer to the question: How much more would the 1972 output have cost if it had been sold at 1985 prices instead of 1972 prices?

A close look at the data shows why the answers to the two questions are not the same. In 1972 lots of apples and not very many shirts were produced compared to 1985. Yet between the two years the price of apples increased 200 percent while the price of shirts increased only 50 percent. Because the CPI uses base year quantities, it gives a heavy weight to apples, which showed the greatest relative price increase, and not much weight to shirts, which showed only a modest price increase. In contrast, the GNP deflator uses current year quantities, thereby decreasing the importance of apples and increasing that of shirts.

We see now why it is that the CPI tends to have an upward substitution bias relative to the GNP deflator. But that does not make the GNP deflator a true measure of change in the cost of living. It could just as well be said that the GNP deflator has a downward substitution bias relative to the CPI or that each has an opposite bias from some "true" price index. No foolproof way has yet been found to calculate the true cost-of-living index, although some interesting attempts have been made. (See, for example, the method used by Braithwait in his study of the substitution bias, cited in the body of the chapter.) A discussion of these more complex types of price indexes would take us far beyond the scope of this book. However, the basic types of price indexes covered here are the ones most commonly used for policy purposes.

Chapter 9

The Equilibrium Level of National Income

Ideas for Review

Here are some terms and concepts that you should review before you read this chapter:

Recession (Chapter 1)
Progressive, regressive, and proportional taxes (Chapter 5)
Marginal tax rate (Chapter 5)
Aggregate nominal demand and supply (Chapter 6)
Leakages and injections (Chapter 6)
Aggregate real supply and demand (Chapter 7)
GNP, NNP, and disposable income (Chapter 8)

It is late 1982. The economy is near the low point of its most severe recession since World War II. Consumers are deeply pessimistic.

Jack Lenburg could easily afford the things he desperately wants: a car, an apartment, and furniture. The 35-year-old divorced job placement officer earns $24,000 a year and has only $500 of debt.

But he is postponing his spending plans. He worries about the high cost of credit and says he will wait until late next year, when he will have saved enough to pay cash for his purchases.

That means living at his mother's house for the third year in a row. It means scrimping on clothing and entertainment. And it means avoiding impulse purchases the way a reformed addict avoids drugs.

"If I see a store where I might be even tempted to buy something, I'll walk right past," Lenburg says. "If I can show some degree of self-sacrifice, I'll be a happier person."[1]

The Jack Lenburgs of the world—the consumers—have enormous power over the economy. As we saw in the last chapter, consumers control some two thirds of the spending flows that pour into national product. In this chapter we will focus on the factors that determine how much consumers spend and on those that may cause them to change their spending plans. We will see how consumer pessimism can make a bad recession worse, and how a return to optimism—as occurred at the beginning of 1983—can fuel a recovery.

KEYNES AND THE GREAT DEPRESSION

Changes in consumer spending are one reason why nominal national income does not expand at a constant rate over the years but, instead, moves in fits and starts. Box 9.1 shows the course of nominal GNP for the U.S. economy since the turn of the century. During the two world wars, both real output and prices grew rapidly, producing large jumps in nominal GNP. During the inflationary 1970s, real output grew sluggishly, but rapid price increases boosted nominal GNP. The most traumatic economic episode of the century stands out sharply: the Great Depression of the 1930s, when, in a few years, nominal GNP dropped by half, with real output and the price level falling together.

The 1930s were traumatic not only for the economy but for the economics profession as well. Economic theory seemed powerless to explain what was happening, let alone find a cure. The profession was looking for a new approach. It found that new approach in the work of the British economist John Maynard Keynes. (See Box 9.2.)

Say's Law and the Paradox of Insufficient Demand

The Great Depression posed a paradox: The economy clearly could produce far more, but firms could not find buyers for their output. The problem was

---

[1]John Curley, "Penny Pinchers: Fearing Loss of Jobs, Many Consumers Cut Purchases, Save More," *Wall Street Journal*, November 24, 1982, p. 1. Reprinted by permission of The Wall Street Journal, © Dow Jones & Company, Inc. 1982. All rights reserved.

**Box 9.1
Nominal GNP in the U.S.
Economy, 1900–1984**

This box shows the course of nominal GNP in the U.S. economy during the twentieth century. During the two world wars, both real output and prices surged, and nominal GNP grew rapidly. During the 1970s, real output stagnated but inflation caused a noticeable upturn in the trend of nominal GNP growth. The most dramatic economic event of the century was the Great Depression of the 1930s, when real output and prices fell together, cutting nominal GNP by half between 1929 and 1932.

Source: Survey of Current Business.

Say's law
The proposition that producing a given level of national product will automatically generate an equal level of aggregate demand.

not, strictly speaking, that people could not afford to buy all that the firms could make. It had long been known that the process of production automatically yields a national income equal to the value of national product. **Say's law**—named after the French economist Jean-Baptiste Say—had transformed the equality of national income and product within the circular flow into the idea that supply creates its own demand. The households that received wages, rents, interest, and profits from firms would tend to use all that purchasing power to buy the goods they had produced. Keynes corrected Say's law by observing that although the process of production did generate a stream of income great enough to support an aggregate demand equal to aggregate supply, there was no guarantee that people's plans would always call for spending all that income.[2]

---

[2] In an effort to stress the originality of his own ideas, Keynes probably overstated the extent to which earlier theorists had relied on Say's law. For example, even his teacher Alfred Marshall had written that "though men have the power to purchase they may choose not to use it." Clearly, then, the concept that aggregate demand might fall short of aggregate supply did not originate with Keynes. For a discussion of pre-Keynesian macroeconomics, see Mark Blaug, *Economic Theory in Retrospect* (Homewood, Ill.: Irwin, 1968), chap. 5.

Keynes was impressed by the fact that aggregate demand is a result of the spending decisions of individual firms and households that do not coordinate their plans in advance. Consumers plan to spend only part of their incomes on domestically produced goods and services. The rest goes into the various leakages from the circular flow: saving, net taxes, and imports. As we saw in Chapter 6, if firms, governments, and buyers of

**Box 9.2
John Maynard Keynes
and the *General Theory***

**John Maynard Keynes
(1883–1946)**

John Maynard Keynes was born into economics. His father, John Neville Keynes, was a lecturer in economics and logic at Cambridge University. John Maynard began his own studies at Cambridge in mathematics and philosophy. However, his ability so impressed Alfred Marshall that the distinguished teacher urged him to concentrate on economics. In 1908, after Keynes had finished his studies and done a brief stint in the civil service, Marshall offered him a lectureship in economics at Cambridge, which he accepted.

Keynes is remembered above all for his *General Theory of Employment, Interest, and Money*, published in 1936, although that was by no means his first major work. Keynes' reputation as the outstanding economist of his generation rests on this book, in which he departed from classical and neoclassical theory. Its major features are a bold theory based on broad macroeconomic aggregates and a strong argument for activist and interventionist policies.

Keynes was no "narrow" economist. He was an honored member not only of the British academic upper class but also of Britain's highest financial, political, diplomatic, administrative, and even artistic circles. He had close ties to the colorful "Bloomsbury set" of London's literary world. He was a friend of Virginia Woolf, E. M. Forster, and Lytton Strachey; and in 1925 he married the ballerina Lydia Lopokovia. He was a dazzling success at whatever he turned his hand to, from mountain climbing to financial speculation. As a speculator he made a huge fortune for himself, and as bursar of Kings College he turned an endowment of £30,000 into one of £380,000.

Keynes wrote in the *General Theory*, that

the ideas of economists and political philosophers, both when they are right and when they are wrong, are more powerful than is commonly understood. Indeed the world is ruled by little else. Practical men, who believe themselves to be quite exempt from any intellectual influences, are usually the slaves of some defunct economist. Madmen in authority, who hear voices in the air, are distilling their frenzy from some academic scribbler of a few years back. . . . There are not many who are influenced by new theories after they are twenty-five or thirty years of age, so that the ideas which civil servants and politicians and even agitators apply to current events are not likely to be the newest.

Was Keynes issuing a warning here? Whether or not he had any such thing in mind, his words are ironic, in that he himself has become one of the economists of the past whose ideas remain influential, even though they are not the most up-to-date.

exports do not plan to inject enough spending back into the circular flow to balance those leakages, aggregate nominal demand will fall short of aggregate supply. The volume of the circular flow will tend to shrink as firms cut back output, reduce prices, or both, as they did during the Great Depression.

Today this reasoning seems straightforward enough. To readers of Keynes' *General Theory of Employment, Interest, and Money*, however, it provided the new theoretical framework they needed to understand the Great Depression. As we study the determinants of the equilibrium level of output in this and later chapters, we will in a sense retrace the steps taken by Keynes and his followers.

Some Simplifications

To keep things simple, in this chapter and throughout the macroeconomics section of the book we will make three assumptions that eliminate certain differences between the circular-flow models of Chapter 6 and the official national income accounts of Chapter 8. First, we will drop the distinction between gross and net national product by assuming the capital consumption allowance to be zero. Second, we will eliminate the difference between net national income, as measured by the income approach, and national product, as measured by the expenditure approach, by assuming that indirect business taxes and the statistical discrepancy are zero. Finally, we will assume undistributed corporate profits to be zero so that disposable personal income will be equal to national income minus net taxes. These assumptions can be expressed in equation form as follows:

Disposable income + net taxes = national income = national product

---

THE DETERMINANTS OF CONSUMPTION EXPENDITURE

Consumption schedule (consumption function)
A graphic or numerical schedule that shows how consumption expenditure varies as disposable income varies, other things being equal.

The Consumption Schedule

Keynes saw clearly that households' choices between consumption and saving play a key role in regulating the circular flow. Each year consumers spend most, but not all, of their disposable income on consumption. As Box 9.3 shows, this connection between disposable income and consumption is as clear for the post-World War II U.S. economy as it was in Keynes's day.

Starting from this observation, Keynes proposed a relationship between disposable income and consumption that resembled the one shown in Box 9.4. This box shows how consumption changes in response to short-run changes in disposable income—not for the actual U.S. economy but for a simple economy in which households consume exactly 75 cents out of each dollar of added disposable income. The relationship shown in Box 9.4 is known as the **consumption schedule** or **consumption function.**

Autonomous consumption   Notice that the consumption schedule in Box 9.4 does not pass through the origin. Instead, it intersects the vertical axis somewhat above zero. This indicates that even when disposable income is zero, consumption does not drop to zero. The amount of

**Box 9.3
Disposable Income
and Personal
Consumption
Expenditures in the U.S.
Economy, 1950–1984**

Each year U.S. consumers spend most, but not all, of their disposable personal income on personal consumption. The percentage of income devoted to consumption (that is, the average propensity to consume) has remained roughly constant over the period, although it has risen a bit since 1970.

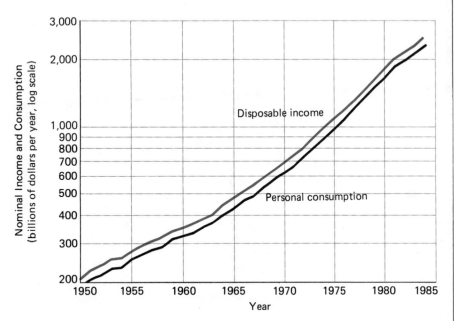

Source: President's Council of Economic Advisers, *Economic Report of the President* (Washington, D.C.: Government Printing Office, 1985), Tables B–14, B–20.

Autonomous consumption

The part of total consumption expenditure that is independent of the level of disposable income; for any given consumption schedule, autonomous consumption is equal to the level of consumption associated with zero disposable income.

Marginal propensity to consume

The fraction of each dollar of added disposable income that goes to consumption.

consumption associated with a zero level of disposable income (equal to the height at which the consumption schedule intersects the vertical axis) is called **autonomous consumption.**

Taken at face value, the $100 billion level of autonomous consumption shows that aggregate consumption expenditures are $100 billion even if aggregate disposable income is zero. In practice, of course, disposable income never falls to zero for the economy as a whole. Individual households, however, sometimes have zero income, and when they do, they do not cut consumption to zero. Instead, they draw on past savings or borrow against future income to maintain some minimal level of consumption. In this sense the concept of autonomous consumption is rooted in actual consumer behavior.

The marginal propensity to consume   Turn now to columns 1–4 of Box 9.4. They show that whenever disposable income rises, some of the additional income is spent on consumption above and beyond autonomous consumption. The fraction of each added dollar of disposable income that goes to added consumption is called the **marginal propensity to consume (MPC).** (The term *marginal* here, as elsewhere, refers to the effects of a small

**Box 9.4
The Consumption
Schedule**

The table and graph both offer a simple example of the connection between disposable income and consumption. The level of autonomous consumption is shown on the graph by the height of the intersection of the consumption schedule with the vertical axis. The slope of the consumption schedule is equal to the marginal propensity to consume.

(a)

Disposable Income (1)	Consumption Expenditure (2)	Change in Income (3)	Change in Consumption (4)	Marginal Propensity to Consume (5)	Average Propensity to Consume (6)
$ 0	$ 100				—
100	175	$100	$75	0.75	1.75
200	250	100	75	0.75	1.25
300	325	100	75	0.75	1.08
400	400	100	75	0.75	1.00
500	475	100	75	0.75	0.95
600	550	100	75	0.75	0.91
700	625	100	75	0.75	0.89
800	700	100	75	0.75	0.88
900	775	100	75	0.75	0.86
1,000	850	100	75	0.75	0.85
1,100	925	100	75	0.75	0.84
1,200	1,000	100	75	0.75	0.83

Note: All amounts are in billions of dollars per year.

(b)

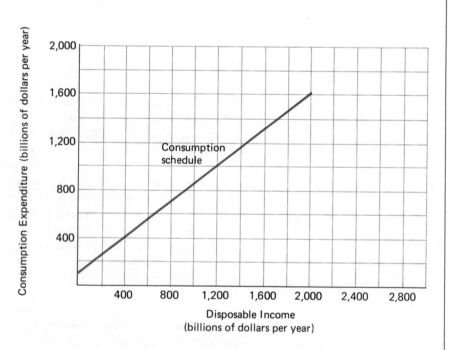

increase or decrease in some economic variable—in this case, disposable income. A *propensity* is simply a tendency.)

The box shows, for example, that a $100 billion increase in disposable income, from $500 billion to $600 billion, raises consumption by $75 billion, from $475 billion to $550 billion. Likewise, a $100 billion decrease in disposable income, from $500 billion to $400 billion, causes consumption to fall by $75 billion, from $475 billion to $400 billion. The value of the marginal propensity to consume for this example thus is 0.75 ($75 divided by $100).

In geometric terms, the marginal propensity to consume is equal to the slope of the consumption schedule. In part b of Box 9.4 a horizontal movement of $100 billion in disposable income corresponds to a vertical movement of $75 billion in planned consumption. The slope of the consumption schedule thus is $75 divided by $100, or 0.75, the same as the marginal propensity to consume.

Marginal vs. average propensity to consume   It is helpful to contrast the marginal propensity to consume with the average propensity to consume. The **average propensity to consume (APC)** for any level of income is equal to total consumption divided by income. It is shown in column 6 of Box 9.4. For levels of income below $400 billion, consumption exceeds disposable income, so that the average propensity to consume is greater than 1. As disposable income increases, the average propensity to consume falls. However, because total consumption always includes a constant level of autonomous consumption, at least in the short run, the average propensity to consume is always greater than the marginal propensity to consume.[3]

Average propensity to consume

Total consumption for any level of income divided by total disposable income.

Short run vs. long run   The actual values of both the average and the marginal propensity to consume depend in practice on the time horizon. In the United States, consumption spending has tended to rise over long periods by about 90 cents for each dollar increase in disposable income, which implies a long-run marginal propensity to consume of about 0.9. (Since 1970, however, the implied long-run marginal propensity to consume has been somewhat higher than the historical average.) Also, the long-run level of autonomous consumption, as implied by historical data, approaches zero. As a result, the average and marginal propensities to consume are equal in the long run.

In the short run (a year or less), people tend to change their consumption by less than 90 cents for each dollar change in income. Also, autonomous consumption is positive in the short run, so the marginal propensity to consume is less than the average propensity to consume.

---

[3]The relationship between average and marginal propensity to consume can also be expressed in algebraic terms. Let C represent consumption, Y_d disposable income, a autonomous consumption, and b the marginal propensity to consume. The consumption schedule can then be written as $C = a + bY_d$, and the average propensity to consume can be expressed as $C/Y_d = (a + bY_d)/Y_d = a/Y_d + b$. The last expression shows clearly that the average propensity to consume exceeds the marginal propensity to consume as long as autonomous consumption is greater than zero.

One reason for this is that year-to-year changes in disposable income are not always permanent. People tend to make smaller changes in their spending in response to temporary changes in income than they do in response to permanent ones. For example, a household that is used to a $20,000 annual income would no doubt cut back somewhat on its spending in a year when its income temporarily dropped to $18,000, but as long as it expected good times to return, it would probably reduce its spending by less than if it expected the lower income level to be permanent. So long as the drop in income was seen as temporary, it would be offset to some degree by dipping into past savings or by borrowing.

Even permanent changes in income are not always perceived as permanent in the short run. Thus, a household that experiences a permanent increase in income of $2,000 per year might at first tend to treat part of the added income as temporary and spend less of it than it otherwise would. Over a longer period, as it became clear that the increase in income was permanent, more of the increase would tend to be consumed.

Because this book focuses mainly on short-run economic stabilization policy, the examples in this and later chapters will use a marginal propensity to consume of 0.75, somewhat lower than the observed long-run marginal propensity to consume for the United States. There is nothing sacred about the value of 0.75, however. Under different short-run conditions a higher or lower value might be appropriate. Box 9.5, for example, shows what the consumption schedule looks like for marginal

Box 9.5
Consumption Schedules for Various Marginal Propensities to Consume

The slope of the consumption schedule is equal to the marginal propensity to consume. Here, consumption schedules are shown for marginal propensities to consume of 0.9, 0.66, and 0.5. Autonomous consumption of $100 billion is assumed for all the curves.

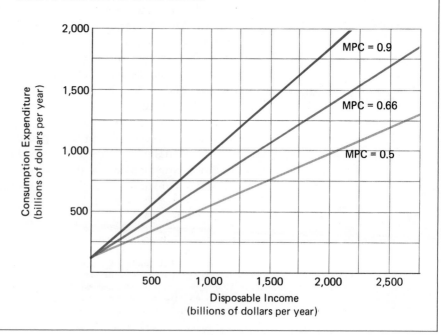

propensities to consume of 0.9, 0.66, and 0.5. A $100 billion level of autonomous consumption is assumed for each of these schedules, so they differ only in their slope. The higher the marginal propensity to consume, the steeper the consumption schedule.

The Saving Schedule

Saving schedule
A graphic or numerical schedule that shows how saving varies as disposable income varies, other things being equal.

Once we know the level of consumption that corresponds to each level of disposable income, we can easily calculate the level of saving. The relationship between saving and disposable income, called the **saving schedule**, is given in numerical form in part a of Box 9.6 and in graphic form in part b. The numbers for saving at each level of disposable income are found by simply subtracting consumption from disposable income.

For comparison, part c of Box 9.6 shows the consumption schedule. Saving at each level of disposable income is equal to the vertical distance between the consumption schedule and the 45-degree reference line of part c.

Dissaving
Negative saving, which occurs when consumption exceeds disposable income.

In this example, **dissaving**—negative saving—of $100 billion occurs when disposable income is zero. Saving at zero disposable income is the negative of autonomous consumption. There is a break-even point at $400 billion of disposable income, where neither saving nor dissaving occurs. Below that point consumption exceeds income, and above it income exceeds consumption.

Marginal propensity to save
The fraction of each dollar of added income that goes to saving.

The fraction of each added dollar of disposable income that is saved is called the **marginal propensity to save (MPS)**. Because all disposable income is, by definition, either saved or consumed, it follows that the marginal propensity to save (MPS) is equal to 1 minus the marginal propensity to consume (MPC). In equation form,

$$MPS = 1 - MPC$$

In geometric terms, the marginal propensity to save is equal to the slope of the saving schedule, which is 0.25 in part b of Box 9.6.

SHIFTS IN THE CONSUMPTION SCHEDULE

The consumption schedules that we have drawn show the link between nominal disposable income and consumption spending in nominal terms. A movement along the consumpton schedule shows how nominal consumption spending changes as nominal disposable income changes, other things being equal. In this section we will see what is covered by the other-things-being-equal clause in this case. This will give us a list of factors that can shift the consumption schedule.

Wealth

One factor that is assumed to remain constant as we move along the consumption schedule is *wealth*. Wealth is another term for a household's net worth—its assets minus its liabilities. Of two households that have equal income, we expect the one with greater wealth to spend more freely

Box 9.6
The Saving Curve

The saving curve shows the connection between saving and income. In the table (part a), saving is found by subtracting consumption from disposable income. In part b, the saving curve is given in graphic form. The level of saving shown by the saving curve in part b is equal to the gap between the consumption schedule and the 45-degree reference line shown in part c.

(a)

Disposable Income (1)	Consumption (2)	Saving (3)
$ 0	$ 100	−$100
100	175	−75
200	250	−50
300	325	−25
400	400	0
500	475	25
600	550	50
700	625	75
800	700	100
900	775	125
1,000	850	150
1,100	925	175
1,200	1,000	200
1,300	1,075	225
1,400	1,150	250
1,500	1,225	275
1,600	1,300	300
1,700	1,375	325
1,800	1,450	350
1,900	1,525	375
2,000	1,600	400

Note: All amounts are in billions of dollars per year.

(that is, to have a higher average propensity to consume) than the one with less wealth.

Because greater wealth leads to greater consumption out of a given income, anything that happens to increase the total nominal wealth of all households will cause an upward shift in the consumption schedule. For example, many people hold some of their wealth in the form of corporate stocks. A rise in the average price of all corporate stocks thus could produce an upward shift in the consumption schedule.

Expectations

People's spending decisions depend not only on their current income and wealth but also on their expected future income and wealth. Any change in their expectations can cause a shift in the consumption schedule. This chapter opened with an example of a person who was holding down his level of spending because he was pessimistic about the state of the economy. When all consumers become pessimistic, as they tend to do during a recession, the consumption schedule can shift downward. When they become more optimistic, it can shift upward again.

Box 9.6
Continued

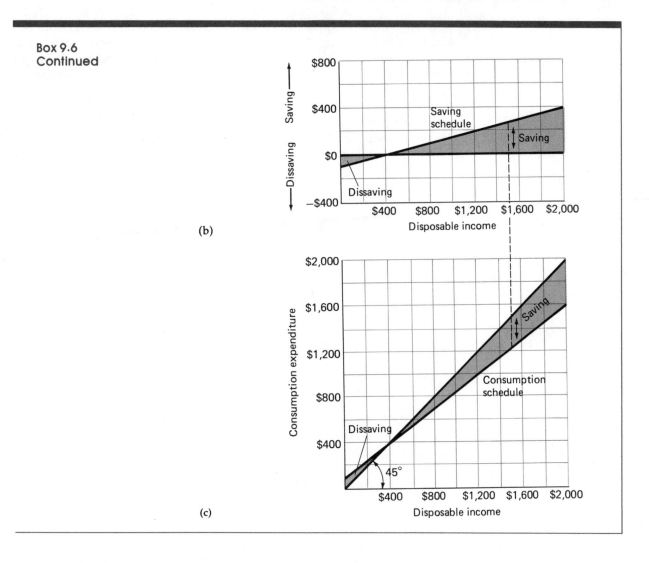

(b)

(c)

Changes in the Price Level

For a given level of real disposable income, an increase in the price level increases nominal disposable income. This effect of a change in the price level is built into the consumption schedule as we have drawn it. It is represented by a movement along the consumption schedule. However, it is worth noting that a change in the price level may have secondary effects on consumption apart from its effects on the level of nominal disposable income. These secondary effects of a change in the price level, if present, would be represented by a shift in the consumption schedule.

These secondary effects on consumption of a change in the price level stem largely from the impact on households' wealth. Some forms of wealth have fixed nominal values, for example, bank deposits and currency. When the price level goes up, the real value of these forms of wealth goes down. This tends to reduce real consumption and, by itself, would tend to shift the consumption schedule downward. Other forms of wealth, such as real estate and corporate stocks, do not have fixed nominal values. During a period of inflation these forms of wealth can retain their real value or even increase in real value. This tends to work against a downward shift in the consumption schedule. Finally, a change in the price level may cause an increase in the nominal level of autonomous consumption in order to maintain a constant real value of autonomous consumption.

Exactly what secondary effect if any a change in the price level will have on the nominal consumption schedule depends on the balance between these conflicting upward and downward shifts. To keep matters simple, we will ignore these secondary effects of changes in the price level in this book.

Taxes

Up to this point, we have drawn the consumption schedule using disposable income on the horizontal axis of the graph. For many purposes, however, it is more useful to draw it using national income on the horizontal axis. In a world with no taxes, making this change would not affect the consumption schedule at all, because without taxes, national income and disposable income would be equal. Once we introduce taxes, however, the level of disposable income on which consumption decisions depend will differ from the level of national income. As a result, changes in taxes become another source of shifts in the consumption schedule. Let's see why this is true, first taking the case of so-called lump sum taxes, and then the case of income taxes.[4]

Lump sum taxes

Taxes that do not vary with the level of nominal national income (for example, property taxes).

Lump sum taxes   Taxes that do not vary as the taxpayer's income varies are called **lump sum taxes**. Personal property taxes are a major example on the revenue side of the net tax picture. On the transfer side of net taxes, many items, from interest on the national debt to government pensions, are not directly linked to income changes.

Box 9.7 shows how the consumption schedule is affected by introducing a lump sum tax of $100 billion into an economy that had no taxes before. The first two columns, which are the same as those in Box 9.4, show national income and the level of consumption from national income that would take place if there were no taxes. The consumption schedule assumes autonomous consumption of $100 million and a marginal propensity to consume of 0.75. Columns 3 and 4 of the table show that the $100 billion lump sum tax reduces disposable income to a level $100 billion below that of national income. As column 5 shows, this $100 billion reduction of personal income cuts $75 billion from consumption at each income level, in accordance with the 0.75 marginal propensity to consume. The remaining $25 billion of the tax is accounted for by a reduction in saving. As before, consumption is at the autonomous level of $100 billion when disposable income is zero. However, zero disposable income now corresponds to $100 billion of national income, as line 2 of the table shows. At a national income of zero, consumption is $25.

---

[4]We continue to assume that there are no indirect business taxes or corporate profits taxes. Only personal taxes, such as personal income taxes and personal property taxes, are taken into account. Thus it continues to be true that national income minus net taxes equals disposable income.

**Box 9.7
National Income and
Consumption with
Lump Sum Taxes**

Lump sum taxes do not change when the level of nominal national income changes. This box shows how introducing a lump sum net tax of $100 billion shifts the consumption schedule downward, when the schedule is drawn with national income on the horizontal axis. The amount of the shift is equal to the level of lump sum taxes times the marginal propensity to consume.

(a)

National Income (1)	Consumption with No Tax (2)	Lump Sum Tax (3)	Disposable Income (4)	Consumption with Tax (5)
$ 0	$ 100	$100	$−100	$ 25
100	175	100	0	100
200	250	100	100	175
300	325	100	200	250
400	400	100	300	325
500	475	100	400	400
600	550	100	500	475
700	625	100	600	550
800	700	100	700	625
900	775	100	800	700
1,000	850	100	900	775
1,100	925	100	1,000	850
1,200	1,000	100	1,100	925

Note: All amounts are in billions of dollars per year.

(b)

Part b of Box 9.7 shows the effect of the new lump sum tax in graphical terms. Introducing the tax produces a downward shift in the consumption schedule, when the schedule is drawn, as it is here, with nominal national income on the horizontal axis. The new schedule is parallel to the old one, but is shifted downward by an amount equal to the marginal propensity to consume times the level of lump sum taxes. In this case, the shift is $75 billion dollars. The vertical intercept of the new schedule is equal to autonomous consumption minus the marginal propensity to consume times the level of lump sum net taxes, or $25 in this case.

Income taxes   Lump sum taxes are an important source of revenue for state and local governments, and lump sum transfers are an important item on the expenditure side of the federal budget. The largest sources of federal revenue, however, are the social security payroll tax and the personal income tax. These income-linked taxes have a somewhat different effect on the consumption schedule, as Box 9.8 shows.

The table in part a of Box 9.8 assumes a 20 percent proportional income tax on income from all sources, but lump sum net taxes of zero. As columns 3 and 4 of the table show, this tax takes 20 cents of each dollar of national income. Disposable income thus comes to 80 cents for each dollar of national income. As columns 4 and 5 show, the marginal propensity to consume of 0.75 applies to this 80 cents of personal income. All told, then, of each dollar of national income 20 cents goes for taxes, and 60 cents of the remaining 80 cents goes for consumption.

Part b of Box 9.8 shows the effect of introducing the income tax in graphic terms. Instead of a downward shift that leaves the new schedule parallel to the old one, the income tax reduces the slope of the consumption schedule. With no income tax in effect, the slope of the schedule is equal to the marginal propensity to consume (0.75 in this case). With a 20 percent proportional income tax in effect, the slope is reduced to 0.6. The formula for the slope of the consumption schedule with an income tax in effect is:

$$\text{Slope of consumption schedule} = \text{MPC} \times (1 - t)$$

where t stands for the marginal tax rate.

AGGREGATE NOMINAL DEMAND AND SUPPLY

In Chapter 6 we saw that the circular flow could be in equilibrium only when aggregate nominal demand was equal to aggregate nominal supply, that is, only when total planned expenditures were equal to total national product. If planned expenditures exceeded national product, buyers' attempts to purchase more than was being produced would lead to unplanned decreases in business inventories. Firms would react to those decreases by increasing their output or by raising their prices, thereby causing the level of the circular flow, measured in nominal terms, to rise. If planned expenditures fell short of national product, business inventories would build up faster than planned, and firms would react by cutting their production or lowering their prices so that the nominal level of the circular flow would drop.

Box 9.8
The Consumption
Schedule and an
Income Tax

When the consumption schedule is drawn with nominal national income on the horizontal axis, introducing a proportional income tax reduces the slope of the schedule. This example assumes a marginal propensity to consume of 0.75 and a marginal tax rate of 0.20. The slope of the consumption schedule with the income tax in effect is equal to MPC(1 − t), where t is the marginal tax rate.

(a)

National Income (1)	Consumption with No Tax (2)	20% Income Tax (3)	Disposable Income (4)	Consumption with Tax (5)
$ 0	$ 100	$ 0	$ 0	$100
100	175	20	80	160
200	250	40	160	220
300	325	60	240	280
400	400	80	320	340
500	475	100	400	400
600	550	120	480	460
700	625	140	560	520
800	700	160	640	580
900	775	180	720	640
1,000	850	200	800	700
1,100	925	220	880	760
1,200	1,000	240	960	820

Note: All amounts are in billions of dollars per year.

(b)

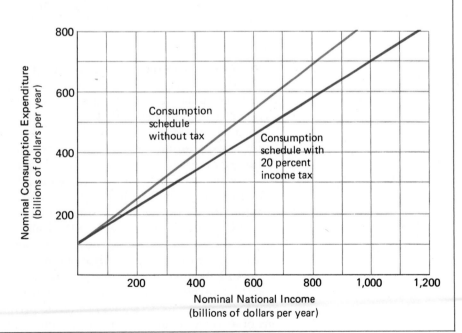

Consumption schedule without tax

Consumption schedule with 20 percent income tax

Nominal Consumption Expenditure (billions of dollars per year)

Nominal National Income (billions of dollars per year)

These are the ideas on which Keynes based his theory. The next step in developing the theory will be to make these ideas more precise by developing the relationship between aggregate nominal demand, aggregate nominal supply, and nominal national income in graphic form.

The Aggregate Nominal Demand Curve

Aggregate nominal demand curve

A graph showing the level of total planned expenditure associated with each level of nominal national income.

The first step is to construct an **aggregate nominal demand curve** for the economy. This is a graph that shows total planned purchases of goods and services corresponding to each level of nominal national income. Note that this curve differs in two ways from the aggregate *real* demand curve introduced in Chapter 7: First, it deals with aggregate demand measured in nominal terms (that is, in current dollars) rather than in real terms (that is, in constant dollars). And second, it relates the level of aggregate demand to the level of nominal national income, rather than to the price level. As we will see in coming chapters, both the nominal and the real aggregate demand curves are needed to give a complete picture of the economy.

Aggregate nominal demand is made up of consumption, planned investment, government purchases, and net exports. In constructing the aggregate nominal demand schedule, we will deal with each of these components in turn.

Consumption   We have already discussed the relationship between nominal consumption and nominal national income. The consumption schedule forms the foundation of the aggregate nominal demand curve. The vertical intercept of the consumption schedule is equal to the level of autonomous consumption, adjusted, if need be, for lump sum taxes. The slope of the consumption schedule is equal to the marginal propensity to consume, adjusted, if need be, for the marginal income tax rate. In this, our initial effort to construct an aggregate nominal demand schedule, we will assume there is no income tax, and that lump sum taxes are fixed by law at $100 billion.

Investment   The second component of aggregate nominal demand is planned investment. As explained in Chapter 6, this includes fixed investment plus planned changes in inventories. Unplanned changes in inventories are not included.

The level of planned investment depends on interest rates and business expectations. Interest rates represent the costs of obtaining funds for investment. These costs are weighed against the expected returns from the investments. Other things being equal, the lower interest rates are, the more investment will be planned; likewise, the more optimistic business expectations are, the more investment will be planned.

In Chapter 13 we will explore the links among interest rates, expectations, national income, and investment planning in some detail. For the time being, however, we will treat planned investment as a given. But even in treating planned investment as a given for any single year, we will not want to pass over the fact that investment tends to vary greatly from one year to the next. Box 9.9 shows how gross private domestic investment and one of its components, inventory investment, have varied over time in the U.S. economy. Keynes himself believed that the most important source of variations in national income and product was changes in private invest-

**Box 9.9
Investment
Expenditures in the U.S.
Economy, 1929–1984**

As part a of this chart shows, investment expenditure in the U.S. economy has often changed sharply from year to year. The inventory component is especially unstable, as part b shows. Inventory investment is shown as a share of GNP. The data on inventory investment shown here lump together planned and unplanned inventory expenditure.

(a)

(b)

ment. The collapse of investment in the early stages of the Great Depression (1929–1932) gave strong support to this belief.

Once the level of planned investment for a given year is known, it can be added to planned spending for consumption as a second component of aggregate demand, as shown in Box 9.10. The $C + I$ schedule in part b of the box is the sum of the consumption and planned investment shown in columns 2 and 3 of part a.

Government purchases   The third component of aggregate nominal demand is government purchases. Under the federal government's current budget procedures, the president proposes a level of expenditures for each year as part of the administration's budget message. Congress takes the proposed budget into account, together with the views of its own members, in setting a spending limit for the coming year. The congressional budget resolution is supposed to serve as a nominal ceiling on expenditures for the year, including both government purchases and transfer payments. Similar budget procedures are used at the state and local levels. (Box 10.1 in the next chapter gives details of federal budget procedures.)

In practice, political and economic conditions often disrupt these budget procedures. Then adjustments have to be made in the course of the year. For purposes of this chapter, however, we will proceed as if government purchases for each year really were fixed by law in nominal terms. In later chapters we will introduce greater realism into our discussions of government budget procedures.

Box 9.10 shows how government purchases can be added to consumption and planned investment as a third component of aggregate nominal demand. The $C + I + G$ schedule in part b of the box corresponds to the sum of columns 2–4 of the table in part a. Regardless of the level of nominal national income, government purchases are assumed to be limited to $150 billion.

Net exports   The final component of aggregate nominal demand is net exports. In constructing Box 9.10, exports are assumed to exceed imports by a constant $25 billion, regardless of the level of nominal national income. This last component of aggregate nominal demand is added to the others to give the complete $C + I + G + X - M$ schedule.

The assumption of a constant level of net exports simplifies the task of drawing the aggregate nominal demand schedule, but it is not altogether realistic. In practice, the level of imports tends to rise as the economy expands. The reason is that for each dollar of consumption, planned investment, and government purchases, about 10 cents tends to go for imported goods. Unless aggregate demand in the economies of the country's trading partners expands at an equal rate, imports will grow faster than exports, and therefore net exports will fall.

For example, in 1982, when the U.S. economy was deep in recession, net exports were $19 billion dollars. As the economy recovered from recession in 1983 and 1984, imports soared while exports rose only slightly. By 1984, imports greatly exceeded exports, causing net exports to swing from plus $19 billion to minus $66 billion in nominal terms.

We treat imports and exports in detail in Chapters 34 and 35. Meanwhile, however, we will stick with the simplifying assumption that net exports are not affected by the level of nominal national income.

**Box 9.10
Construction of the
Aggregate Nominal
Demand Curve**

Aggregate nominal demand is the nominal value of all planned expenditures. This box shows how an aggregate nominal demand curve can be built up from consumption, planned investment, government purchases, and net exports. In the simple case represented here, consumption is the only element that varies directly with nominal national income. The slope of the aggregate nominal demand curve thus is equal to the marginal propensity to consume of 0.75.

(a)

Nominal National Income (1)	Nominal Consumption Expenditure (2)	Nominal Planned Investment (3)	Nominal Government Purchases (4)	Nominal Net Exports (5)	Total Nominal Planned Expenditure (aggregate demand) (6)
$ 0	$ 25	$100	$150	$25	$ 300
100	100	100	150	25	375
200	175	100	150	25	450
300	250	100	150	25	525
400	325	100	150	25	600
500	400	100	150	25	675
600	475	100	150	25	750
700	550	100	150	25	825
800	625	100	150	25	900
900	700	100	150	25	975
1,000	775	100	150	25	1,050
1,100	850	100	150	25	1,125
1,200	925	100	150	25	1,200
1,300	1,000	100	150	25	1,275
1,400	1,075	100	150	25	1,350
1,500	1,150	100	150	25	1,425
1,600	1,225	100	150	25	1,500

Note: All amounts are in billions of dollars per year.

(b)

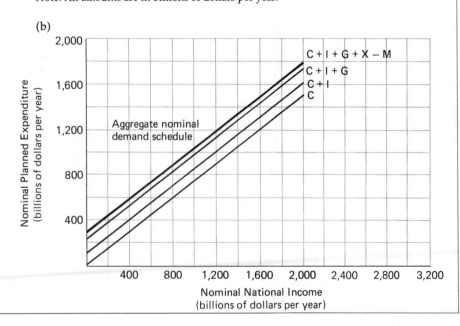

Adding net exports to consumption, planned investment, and government purchases completes construction of the aggregate nominal demand schedule. Now we turn to its companion, the aggregate nominal supply schedule.

The Aggregate Nominal Supply Curve

Aggregate nominal supply curve
A graph showing the level of aggregate nominal supply (nominal national product) associated with each level of nominal national income.

The aggregate nominal demand curve, which we have just constructed by adding together consumption, planned investment, government purchases, and net exports, shows the level of planned nominal expenditures that corresponds to each possible level of nominal national income. To go with this aggregate nominal demand curve we need an **aggregate nominal supply curve**. This curve shows the level of nominal national product that corresponds to each level of nominal national income. It differs from the aggregate *real* supply curve introduced in Chapter 7 in the same two ways that the aggregate nominal demand curve differs from the aggregate real demand curve: First, it refers to national product measured in nominal, rather than in real, terms; second, it shows the relationship between nominal national product and nominal national income, rather than the relationship between real national product and the price level.

For the simple economy in our example, in which there is no capital consumption allowance, indirect business taxation, or statistical discrep-

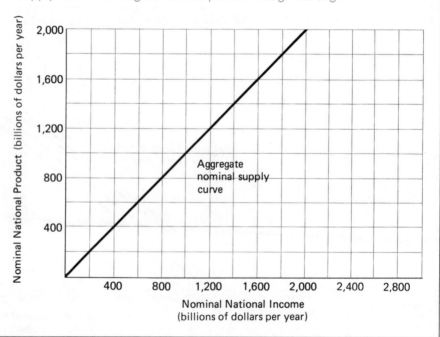

Box 9.11
The Aggregate Nominal Supply Curve

Aggregate nominal supply is another name for nominal national product. The structure of the circular flow is such that the act of producing each dollar of national product automatically generates a dollar of national income. Aggregate nominal supply and nominal national income therefore are equal for all levels of income. This makes the aggregate nominal supply curve a 45-degree line that passes through the origin.

ancy, constructing an aggregate nominal supply curve is simple. From our analysis of the circular flow, we know that each dollar of nominal national product generates a dollar of nominal national income. Every dollar of every firm's revenue either goes to pay costs of production (thus generating income for wage earners, owners of natural resources, and suppliers of capital) or, if not needed to cover costs, becomes profit, which is income for the owners of the firm. Nominal national product (also called **aggregate nominal supply**) and nominal national income are thus equal because the act of production automatically generates an equal stream of income.

To construct a graphic aggregate nominal supply curve we first draw a vertical axis labeled nominal national product and a horizontal axis labeled nominal national income. Then we draw a line through all the points for which nominal national income and nominal national product are equal. As shown in Box 9.11, this aggregate nominal supply curve is a straight line that passes through the origin at a 45-degree angle.

THE MULTIPLIER THEORY OF NATIONAL INCOME DETERMINATION

Keynesian cross
A diagram, consisting of aggregate nominal supply and demand curves, that shows how the equilibrium level of nominal national income is determined.

Drawing the aggregate nominal demand and supply curves together, as we have in Box 9.12, makes it possible to determine the equilibrium level of nominal national income. We call this type of graph a **Keynesian cross** because early followers of Keynes used a diagram much like it to show how equilibrium is determined.

The Equilibrium Level of Nominal National Income

From the discussion in Chapter 6 we know that the circular flow can be in equilibrium only when total planned expenditure (aggregate nominal demand) is equal to national product (aggregate nominal supply). The Keynesian cross shows exactly what level of national income permits aggregate supply and demand to be equal, with all quantities measured in nominal terms. The two curves in Box 9.12 intersect at a level of nominal national income of $1,200 billion. That is the equilibrium point, given the consumption schedule and the assumed levels of planned investment, government purchases, and net exports that underlie the aggregate nominal demand curve.

It is easy to show that no other level of nominal national income can represent equilibrium in the circular flow. If nominal national income was lower than the equilibrium level, say $1,000 billion, planned expenditure (aggregate nominal demand) would exceed nominal national product (aggregate nominal supply). There would be an unplanned drop in business inventories equal to the vertical distance between the aggregate nominal demand and supply curves. Firms would try to restore inventories to their planned levels by increasing output or prices or both. In doing so, they would cause nominal national income and product to rise until equilibrium was restored.

If, on the other hand, nominal national income was higher than the equilibrium level, say $1,500 billion, planned expenditures would fall short of output. The unsold goods would become unplanned inventory investment equal in current dollars to the gap between the aggregate

Box 9.12
Using the Keynesian
Cross to Determine the
Equilibrium Level of
Nominal National
Income

The aggregate nominal supply and demand curves form a figure known as the Keynesian cross. This figure provides a simple way to determine the equilibrium level of nominal national income, given the underlying conditions that determine the position of the aggregate nominal demand curve. Any national income higher than the equilibrium level will cause excess aggregate nominal supply, unplanned inventory buildup, and downward pressure on prices, real output, or both. Any level of national income below equilibrium will cause excess aggregate nominal demand, unplanned inventory depletion, and upward pressure on prices, real output, or both.

(a)

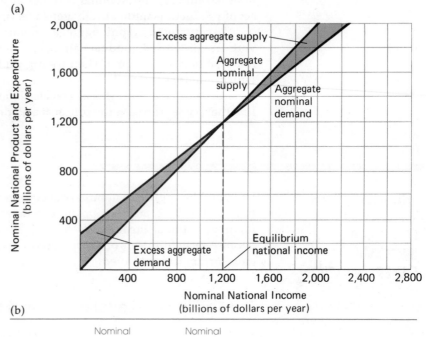

(b)

Nominal National Income (1)	Nominal Planned Expenditure (aggregate demand) (2)	Nominal National Product (aggregate supply) (3)	Unplanned Inventory Change (4)	Tendency of Change in National Income (5)
$ 0	$ 300	$ 0	−$300	Increase
100	375	100	−275	Increase
200	450	200	−250	Increase
300	525	300	−225	Increase
400	600	400	−200	Increase
500	675	500	−175	Increase
600	750	600	−150	Increase
700	825	700	−125	Increase
800	900	800	−100	Increase
900	975	900	−75	Increase
1,000	1,050	1,000	−50	Increase
1,100	1,125	1,100	−25	Increase
1,200	1,200	1,200	0	No change
1,300	1,275	1,300	25	Decrease
1,400	1,350	1,400	50	Decrease
1,500	1,425	1,500	75	Decrease
1,600	1,500	1,600	100	Decrease

Note: All amounts are in billions of dollars per year.

nominal demand and supply curves at the $1,500 billion income level. Firms would react to the unplanned inventory buildup by cutting production or prices or both. Their actions would cause national income and product, measured in nominal terms, to fall to the equilibrium level.

In Box 9.12 the same story is told twice, graphically in part a and numerically in part b. Both approaches confirm that $1,200 billion is the only possible equilibrium level for aggregate nominal income, given the underlying assumptions on which the demand and supply curves are based.

The Leakage-Injection Approach to Nominal Income Determination[5]

The concepts of leakages and injections, introduced in Chapter 6, provide another means of determining the equilibrium level of nominal national income. As Box 9.13 shows, the leakage-injection approach uses the saving curve rather than the consumption curve as its starting point. Columns 2–5 of the table show how nominal national income is divided into consumption, saving, net taxes, and imports. Saving, net taxes, and imports are all leakages from the circular flow. Their total appears in column 6. In part b of Box 9.13 a sloping line is drawn to show how total leakages vary as nominal national income varies. This line, which is labeled $S + T + M$ on the graph, can be called a nominal leakage curve and has a slope equal to the marginal propensity to save.

Columns 7–9 of the table show the components of planned injections: planned investment, government purchases, and exports. The total of injections is shown in column 10. Under the assumptions made in this chapter, none of these components varies as nominal national income varies. The planned injection curve (labeled $I + G + X$ in Box 9.13) therefore is horizontal.

Leakages are the part of nominal national income that households do not spend on domestically produced consumer goods. Planned injections are sources of demand for domestically produced goods and services that do not arise directly from the household sector. At the point where the planned injection and leakage curves intersect, then, the portion of output that consumers do not take from the market is absorbed by other users of final goods and services. At that point, and only at that point, the separate spending plans of households, businesses, units of government, and foreign buyers of exports exactly mesh with the production activities of domestic firms. There is neither unplanned inventory buildup nor unplanned inventory depletion. The circular flow is in equilibrium.

A comparison of Boxes 9.12 and 9.13 shows that the equilibrium level of nominal national income is the same using both approaches. For nonequilibrium levels of nominal national income, the vertical gap between the aggregate nominal supply and demand curves is always the same as the vertical gap between the leakage and planned injection curves. For both approaches, this gap is equal to the rate of unplanned inventory change (plus or minus) when the plans of buyers and sellers do not mesh.

---

[5]In an abbreviated course this section may be skipped without loss of continuity.

Box 9.13
The Leakage-Injection Approach to National Income Determination

This box shows how the equilibrium level of nominal national income can be determined by finding the point where planned injections to the circular flow (planned investment plus government purchases plus exports) are equal to total leakages (saving plus net taxes plus imports). The level of equilibrium nominal national income arrived at using this approach is the same as the level arrived at using the Keynesian cross in Box 9.12.

(a)

Nominal National Income (1)	Consumption (2)	Saving (3)	Net Taxes (4)	Imports (5)	Total Leakages (6)	Planned Investment (7)	Government Purchases (8)	Exports (9)	Total Planned Injections (10)
$ 0	$ 25	−$125	$100	$25	$ 0	$100	$150	$50	$300
100	100	−100	100	25	25	100	150	50	300
200	175	−75	100	25	50	100	150	50	300
300	250	−50	100	25	75	100	150	50	300
400	325	−25	100	25	100	100	150	50	300
500	400	0	100	25	125	100	150	50	300
600	475	25	100	25	150	100	150	50	300
700	550	50	100	25	175	100	150	50	300
800	625	75	100	25	200	100	150	50	300
900	700	100	100	25	225	100	150	50	300
1,000	775	125	100	25	250	100	150	50	300
1,100	850	150	100	25	275	100	150	50	300
1,200	925	175	100	25	300	100	150	50	300
1,300	1,000	200	100	25	325	100	150	50	300
1,400	1,075	225	100	25	350	100	150	50	300
1,500	1,150	250	100	25	375	100	150	50	300

Note: All amounts are in billions of dollars per year.

(b)

Effects of a Change in Expenditures

The level of nominal planned expenditure for the economy depends on many things. First and foremost, nominal planned spending varies as nominal national income varies. These variations, which can take the form of changes in real national income, changes in the price level, or a mix of the two, are shown in the graphs used in this chapter as movements upward or downward along the aggregate nominal demand curve. Other factors that affect planned nominal expenditure—changes in expectations, consumer wealth, interest rates, taxes, government purchases, or foreign markets—cause upward or downward shifts in the aggregate nominal demand curve. In the last section we saw how, under given conditions, the level of nominal national income tends to move upward or downward along the aggregate nominal demand curve to the point of equilibrium. Now we turn to the effects of shifts in the aggregate nominal demand curve on the equilibrium level of nominal national income.

Look at Box 9.14, for example. It shows the effects of a $100 billion per year increase in planned expenditures at each possible level of nominal national income. For the moment, it does not matter whether the shift begins in the household, investment, government, or foreign sector. The effect in any case is to shift the aggregate nominal demand curve upward by $100 billion, from the position AND_1 to the position AND_2.

The Multiplier Effect

What happens to the equilibrium level of nominal national income when the planned expenditure curve shifts upward by $100 billion? The immediate effect is that nominal planned expenditure exceeds nominal national product, so inventories start to be depleted at a rate of $100 per year. Firms

Box 9.14
The Multiplier Effect of a Shift in the Aggregate Nominal Demand Curve

A given vertical shift in the aggregate nominal demand curve produces a greater increase in the equilibrium level of nominal national income. This is known as the multiplier effect. Here a $100 billion upward shift in the aggregate nominal demand curve causes a $400 billion increase in equilibrium nominal national income. The ratio of the change in equilibrium income to the initial shift in demand, known as the expenditure multiplier, has a value of 4 in this example.

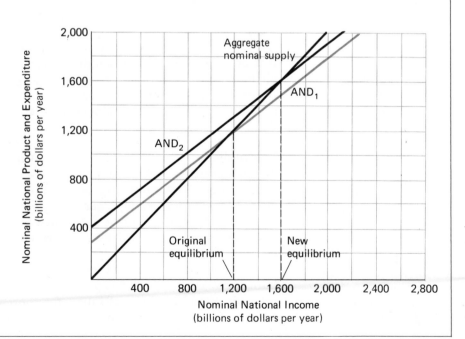

react to this unplanned inventory depletion by increasing output, prices, or both. As a result, the volume of the circular flow, measured in nominal terms, begins to increase. It continues to rise until the gap between aggregate nominal supply and aggregate nominal demand disappears. This occurs at an income level of $1,600 billion.

Notice what has happened: A $100 billion upward shift in the aggregate demand curve has caused a $400 billion increase in equilibrium nominal national income. This ability of a given vertical shift in aggregate nominal demand to cause a greater increase in the equilibrium level of nominal national income is known as the *multiplier effect*.

The multiplier effect, round by round   One way to gain further insight into the multiplier effect is to imagine the effects of the initial upward shift in aggregate demand moving through the economy "round by round." Suppose, for example, that the original shift is caused by a $100-billion-per-year increase in the rate of autonomous consumption expenditure, which in turn was caused by increased consumer optimism. This increase in demand depletes business inventories, and firms respond by raising output or prices or both by enough to cause a $100 billion increase in nominal national product. The $100 billion increase in turn generates $100 billion in additional income in the form of wages, rents, interest, or profits. This part of the reaction to the shift in aggregate demand, which can be called the first round of the multiplier effect, is represented by line 1 of Box 9.15.

The second round consists of tracing the effects of the $100 billion in new income that was generated in the first round. Given the assumed marginal propensity to consume of 0.75, the people who receive this income will spend $75 billion of it on consumer goods and services. Their spending will again deplete inventories and cause firms to raise prices, output, or both. Another $75 billion of national income will be generated, as shown in line 2 of Box 9.15.

In the third round, three quarters of the $75 billion is spent, generating $56,250 million of additional product, factor payments, and income. In the fourth round, $42,190 million is added; in the fifth round, $31,640 million, and so on until the additions become too small to measure. When all the additions to income caused by the original $100 billion upward shift in the aggregate nominal demand curve are added together, the total is $400 billion. The entire process is summarized in the remaining lines of Box 9.15.

The multiplier   As Box 9.14 shows, each dollar increase in nominal national income generates an increase of a fraction of a dollar in planned expenditure. The vertical gap between aggregate nominal demand and aggregate nominal supply caused by the initial upward shift in the planned expenditure curve is eliminated as the economy expands. In the new equilibrium, planned expenditure and national income are again equal.

The ratio of the induced increase in nominal national income to the initial increase in planned expenditure is called the **expenditure multiplier**, or often just **the multiplier**, for short. Its value depends on the fraction of each added dollar of income that goes to added planned

Expenditure multiplier
The ratio of an induced change in the equilibrium level of nominal national income to an initial shift in the aggregate nominal demand curve.

Box 9.15
The Multiplier Effect,
Round by Round

This box shows the multiplier effects of an initial $100 billion upward shift in the aggregate nominal demand curve. Each increase in aggregate nominal demand initially causes an equal increase in nominal national income. Each dollar increase in nominal national income then causes 75 cents' worth of new consumer demand, given a marginal propensity to consume of 0.75. In total, the endless series of increases of ever smaller and smaller size amounts to a $400 billion increase in aggregate nominal demand and nominal national income.

Round	Change in Aggregate Demand (billions of dollars per year)	Change in National Income (billions of dollars per year)
1 (initial change)	$100.00	$100.00
2	75.00	75.00
3	56.25	56.25
4	42.19	42.19
5	31.64	31.64
6	23.73	23.73
7	17.79	17.79
8	13.35	13.35
9	10.00	10.00
10	7.50	7.50
All later rounds	$ 22.56	$ 22.56
Totals	$400.00	$400.00

expenditure. The value of the expenditure multiplier is given by the following formula:

$$\text{Expenditure multiplier} = \frac{1}{1 - \text{MPC}}$$

where MCP stands for the marginal propensity to consume.[6]

Because the marginal propensity to save is equal to 1 minus the marginal propensity to consume, the formula for the multiplier can also be written as

$$\text{Expenditure multiplier} = \frac{1}{\text{MPS}}$$

where MPS stands for the marginal propensity to save. Whichever way the formula is written, the larger the marginal propensity to consume, the larger the multiplier; and the larger the marginal propensity to save, the smaller the multiplier. The values of the multiplier that correspond to

---

[6]The algebraic derivation of the multiplier is given in the appendix at the end of this chapter.

Box 9.16
Expenditure Multipliers
for Various Values of
the Marginal Propensity
to Consume

The multiplier can be calculated from either the marginal propensity to consume (MPC) or the marginal propensity to save (MPS), using the formulas given in this box. The marginal propensity to consume plus the marginal propensity to save must, by definition, always equal 1. The higher the marginal propensity to consume, the larger the multiplier.

Formulas for calculating the multiplier:

$$\text{Expenditure Multiplier} = \frac{1}{1 - \text{MPC}}$$

or

$$\text{Expenditure Multiplier} = \frac{1}{\text{MPS}} .$$

MPC	MPS	Expenditure Multiplier
0.95	0.05	20.0
0.90	0.10	10.0
0.80	0.20	5.0
0.75	0.25	4.0
0.60	0.40	2.5
0.50	0.50	2.0

various values of the marginal propensities to consume and save are shown in Box 9.16.

Income taxes and the multiplier   The multiplier formulas given above are valid only for an economy that has no income tax. It is not difficult to modify the formula to take the income tax into account, however. First, we recognize that for an economy with no income tax, the term $1 - \text{MPC}$ in the denominator of the multiplier formula is equal to one minus the slope of the aggregate nominal demand schedule. The formula can thus also be written as:

$$\frac{\text{Expenditure}}{\text{multiplier}} = \frac{1}{1 - \text{slope of aggregate nominal demand schedule}}$$

Next we recall that an income tax changes the slope of the aggregate nominal demand schedule from MPC to $\text{MPC}(1 - t)$, where t is the marginal tax rate. The formula for the multiplier in an economy with a proportional income tax imposed at a marginal tax rate of t is thus

$$\text{Expenditure multiplier with an income tax} = \frac{1}{1 - \text{MPC}(1 - t)}$$

Looking Ahead

The multiplier effect plays a central role in Keynesian economic theory and policy analysis. It implies that even small changes in planned spending will have magnified effects on the national economy. Early Keynesian economists saw the instability of private planned spending, magnified by the multiplier effect, as the main reason for the boom-and-bust cycle that had plagued market economies since at least the nineteenth century. They also saw the multiplier effect as the key to economic stabilization policy. This part of their analysis is the subject of the next chapter.

Later, in Chapter 16, we will return to the issue of sources of instability in the economy. There, we will compare the Keynesian view that instability arises in the private economy with an alternative view that mistakes in government policy are the source of most instability. This issue is central to the modern debate over strategies for economic stabilization.

Summary

1. *Say's law* states that the process of producing a given level of national product will automatically generate an equal level of aggregate demand. This belief was challenged by the Great Depression of the 1930s, in which the economy was clearly able to produce more but firms could not find enough customers to buy their output. This situation was the background for the work of John Maynard Keynes, who observed that although the process of production does generate enough income to buy all of the output, there is no guarantee that people's plans will call for spending all of the income.

2. Keynes observed that as consumers' incomes increase, their spending also increases, but by less than one dollar for each dollar added to disposable income. This relationship can be shown in the form of a *consumption schedule* that intersects the vertical axis at a level equal to *autonomous consumption* and has a slope equal to the *marginal propensity to consume*.

3. Saving is the portion of disposable income that is not spent on consumption. When disposable income is zero, there is negative saving, or *dissaving*, equal to autonomous consumption. For each added dollar of disposable income, saving increases by a fraction of a dollar—the *marginal propensity to save*. The marginal pro-

pensity to save is equal to 1 minus the marginal propensity to consume.

4. To construct the *aggregate nominal demand curve* begin with the consumption schedule, drawn using nominal national income on the horizontal axis. If there are *lump sum taxes*, the consumption schedule needs to be shifted downward to take these into account. The second component of aggregate nominal demand is planned investment, which we assume does not vary as the level of national income varies. The third component of aggregate nominal demand is government purchases, and the fourth is net exports. Under these assumptions, the slope of the complete aggregate nominal demand curve is equal to the marginal propensity to consume.

5. The *aggregate nominal supply curve* shows the level of nominal national product that corresponds to each level of nominal national income. With certain simplifying assumptions national income and national product are always equal. The aggregate nominal supply curve therefore is a straight 45-degree line that passes through the origin.

6. The equilibrium level of nominal national income is found at the point where the aggregate nominal demand curve intersects the aggregate nominal supply curve on the

Keynesian cross diagram. At any higher level of nominal national income, aggregate nominal supply exceeds aggregate nominal demand. There will be unplanned inventory buildup, and the level of nominal national income will tend to fall toward the equilibrium level. At any lower level of nominal national income, aggregate nominal demand exceeds aggregate nominal supply and there will be unplanned inventory depletion. In this case nominal national income will tend to rise toward the equilibrium level.

7. The leakage-injection approach is another method of finding the equilibrium level of nominal national income. The total planned injections curve is a horizontal line at a height equal to the sum of planned investment, government purchases, and exports. The leakages

curve shows the sum of saving, net taxes, and imports. It has a slope equal to the marginal propensity to save. The equilibrium level of nominal national income is found at the point where the two curves intersect. This is the same equilibrium level of nominal national income given by the Keynesian cross.

8. When the aggregate nominal demand curve shifts upward by $100 billion, the equilibrium level of nominal national income increases by more than $100 billion. This is known as the multiplier effect. The ratio of the increase in nominal national income to the increase in aggregate nominal demand is called the expenditure multiplier. It is given by the formula $1/(1 - \text{MPC})$. In an economy with a proportional income tax, the formula is $1/[1 - \text{MPC}(1 - t)]$.

Questions for Review

1. Define the following terms:
   Say's law
   consumption schedule (consumption function)
   autonomous consumption
   marginal propensity to consume
   average propensity to consume
   saving schedule
   dissaving
   marginal propensity to save
   lump sum taxes
   aggregate nominal demand curve
   aggregate nominal supply curve
   Keynesian cross
   expenditure multiplier

2. Under what economic conditions did Keynes write *The General Theory of Employment, Interest, and Money*? What was Keynes's view of Say's law?

3. What happens to consumption spending as the level of disposable income rises? What is the meaning of the slope of the consumption schedule? What is the meaning of the height at which the consumption schedule intersects the vertical axis?

4. Explain how a saving curve can be constructed from the information given by the consumption schedule.

5. List the steps in constructing the aggregate nominal demand curve, given the consumption schedule, net taxes, government purchases, planned investment, and net exports. What is the slope of the aggregate nominal demand curve?

6. What does the aggregate nominal supply curve show? Why is it always a 45-degree line that passes through the origin?

7. Use a Keynesian cross to show the direction of unplanned inventory change at levels of nominal national income above and below the equilibrium level.

8. What items are included in the planned injections curve? In the leakages curve? What is the slope of each curve? What is shown by the intersection of the two curves?

9. What is the value of the expenditure multiplier when the marginal propensity to consume is 0.9? 0.8? 0.75? 0.5?

Problems and Topics for Discussion

1. Suppose you won $1,000 in a lottery. How much of the money would you spend and how much would you save? (Remember that debt repayment counts as saving.) Would you save more or less of this $1,000 windfall than of the first $1,000 of a yearly pay increase that you expected to be permanent? Would it surprise you to learn that some surveys have found that the marginal propensity to consume from windfall income is smaller than the marginal propensity to consume from permanent income changes? Explain.

2. On a piece of graph paper, draw consumption schedules for the following values of autonomous consumption (a) and the marginal propensity to consume (MPC): $a = 1,000$, MPC = 0.5; $a = 1,200$, MPC = 0.6; $a = 500$, MPC = 0.9. Next draw saving curves for each set of assumptions.

3. On a sheet of graph paper draw a consumption schedule assuming autonomous consumption of $100 billion and a marginal propensity to consume of 0.8. Label the horizontal axis "nominal national income." Now modify this schedule for the following tax assumptions:
   a. Lump sum net taxes of $50 billion.
   b. A proportional income tax with a marginal tax rate of 25 percent.
   c. Both of the above taxes at the same time. Bonus question: Calculate the value of the expenditure multiplier for each of these three cases.

4. On another sheet of paper draw the consumption schedule using the same assumptions as before. Now sketch the effect on the consumption schedule of a progressive income tax, a regressive income tax, and a proportional tax. For this question, you are concerned only with the general shape of the curve, not exact values.

5. Although we have assumed that net exports do not vary as income varies, this assumption is not strictly true. Assume instead that exports are constant but that households spend 10 cents of each dollar of disposable income on imported goods and services, and that imports and exports are equal at a nominal national income of $1,000 billion. Can you sketch an aggregate nominal demand curve that includes these assumptions? What would the slope of this aggregate nominal demand curve be? Bonus question: Develop a formula for the value of the expenditure multiplier assuming a "marginal propensity to import" of 0.10. Consider both the case without an income tax and the case with an income tax at a marginal rate t.

6. Rework the example given in Box 9.15 assuming the same levels of autonomous consumption, planned investment, government purchases, and net exports, but using a marginal propensity to consume first of 0.9 and then of 0.5. What happens to the multiplier effect in each case?

7. **Case for Discussion**

   June 1984: Capital spending is where the beef is. It leaped last quarter at a 14 percent annual rate, about equal to 1983's exceptionally rapid pace. Now it's slowing—but not much. Expect confident business managers to spend at a 9 percent rate for the rest of the year before reining in again.

   One reason is that manufacturing capacity utilization, which powerfully shapes the need for new plant and equipment, has grown faster than in previous recoveries. Over the last few years, business has not been adding much new capacity. By year-end the capacity utilization rate should approach 84 percent, the average for the late 1970s. Since business spending on plant and equipment usually accelerates when utilization reaches that area, the pressure to expand facilities should keep growing.

   Source: "Investment Marches On," *Fortune*, June 11, 1984, p. 27. Reprinted by permission of FORTUNE Magazine.

   Questions:
   a. How does an increase in capital spending by businesses affect the economy? First explain in terms of the circular-flow model discussed in Chapter 6. Then explain in terms of the Keynesian cross. Compare the two explanations.

b. At the end of the second quarter of 1984, total capital spending in the U.S. economy was about $400 billion. Assuming that the aggregate nominal demand curve has a slope of 0.75, how much would the equilibrium level of nominal national income increase as a result of a 9 percent increase in capital spending, other things being equal?

c. In this chapter we have assumed that the level of planned investment is not affected by the level of nominal national income. However, this article suggests that growth of the economy pushes up the capacity utilization rate, which, in turn, triggers investment. How would the assumption that investment increases when nominal national income increases affect the slope of the planned injections curve? The slope of the aggregate nominal demand curve? Would this assumption affect the value of the multiplier? Why or why not?

Suggestions for Further Reading

Blaug, Mark. *Economic Theory in Retrospect*, rev. ed. Homewood, Ill.: Irwin, 1968.

Chapters 5, 14, and 15 discuss Keynesian and pre-Keynesian macroeconomics, including Say's law.

Breit, William, and Roger L. Ransom. *The Academic Scribblers*, revised ed. Hinsdale, Ill.: The Dryden Press, 1982.

Chapter 7 is on Keynes; Chapter 8 is on Alvin Hansen, an early follower of Keynes; and Chapter 9 is on Paul Samuelson, who played a key role in refining and extending Keynes' ideas.

Keynes, John Maynard. *The General Theory of Employment, Interest, and Money.* New York: Harcourt, Brace Jovanovich, 1936.

Not all of this classic will be understood by the beginning student, but it provides a taste of the problems that concerned economists during the Great Depression.

Appendix to Chapter 9

An Algebraic Approach to
Income Determination
and the Multiplier

All the theoretical propositions that have been illustrated with graphs and numerical examples in this chapter can also be expressed in algebraic terms. We will begin with the consumption schedule. Using a for the constant term in the schedule (autonomous consumption), b for the marginal propensity to consume, C for nominal consumption expenditure, T for nominal net taxes, and Y for nominal national income, we can write the consumption schedule as follows:

$$C = a + b(Y - T) \tag{9A.1}$$

The expression $(Y - T)$ on the righthand side of this expression represents nominal disposable income.

With the consumption schedule as a basis, the aggregate nominal demand (AND) schedule is put together by adding planned investment (I), government purchases (G), and exports (X) and subtracting imports (M). This gives

$$AND = C + I + G + X - M \tag{9A.2}$$

Substituting in equation 9A.1, we get

$$AND = a + b(Y - T) + I + G + X - M \tag{9A.3}$$

It is convenient to rewrite this equation by grouping the constant terms so that it becomes

$$AND = (a - bT + I + G + X - M) + bY \tag{9A.4}$$

The term in parentheses in equation 9A.4 represents the constant term, or vertical intercept, of the aggregate nominal demand schedule; b, the marginal propensity to consume, represents its slope.

This equation can now be used to determine the equilibrium level of nominal national income. The theory set forth in this chapter showed that for the economy to be in equilibrium, national income must be equal to planned expenditure so that there is no unplanned inventory buildup or depletion. This equilibrium condition can be written as follows:

$$Y = AND \tag{9A.5}$$

Substituting equation 9A.4 into equation 9A.5, we find that the equilibrium condition becomes

$$Y = (a - bT + I + G + X - M) + bY \tag{9A.6}$$

Solving equation 9A.6 for Y gives the following formula for the equilibrium value of nominal national income:

$$Y^* = \frac{1}{1 - b}(a - bT + I + G + X - M) \tag{9A.7}$$

The asterisk after the Y in this formula is a reminder that the equation holds only for the equilibrium value of nominal national income.

Equation 9A.7 can now be used to solve a number of problems.

Problem 1   Use equation 9A.7 to derive the formula for the multiplier.

Solution   In Chapter 8 the multiplier was defined as the ratio of an induced change in the equilibrium level of nominal national income to an initial shift in the aggregate nominal demand schedule. In algebraic terms, a shift in the aggregate nominal demand schedule means an increase or decrease in the intercept term $(a - bT + I + G + X - M)$. For ease in notation, let A represent this intercept term:

$$A = a - bT + I + G + X - M \tag{9A.8}$$

Equation 9A.7 then becomes

$$Y^* = \left(\frac{1}{1 - b}\right) A \tag{9A.9}$$

Suppose now that this constant term changes from an initial value of A_0 to a new value, A_1, thereby causing a shift in the aggregate nominal demand schedule of $A_1 - A_0$. This increases the equilibrium value of nominal national income from

$$Y^*_0 = \left(\frac{1}{1 - b}\right) A_0$$

to a new value of

$$Y^*_1 = \left(\frac{1}{1 - b}\right) A_1$$

The multiplier, as the ratio of the change in equilibrium income to the shift in the aggregate nominal demand schedule, can now be calculated as follows:

$$\text{Multiplier} = \frac{Y^*_1 - Y^*_0}{A_1 - A_0} = \frac{(A_1 - A_0)/(1 - b)}{A_1 - A_0} = \frac{1}{1 - b}$$

This is exactly the result given in the chapter, except that b is used in place of MPC to represent the marginal propensity to consume.

Problem 2   Suppose that $a = 100$, $b = 0.75$, $T = 100$, $I = 100$, $G = 150$, $X = 50$, and $M = 25$. What is the equilibrium value of aggregate nominal demand?

Solution   Simply substitute the values into equation 9A.7. This gives

$$Y^* = \left(\frac{1}{1 - 0.75}\right)[100 - 0.75(100) + 100 + 150 + 50 - 25]$$

$$= 4\ (\$300) = \$1{,}200$$

Problem 3   Derive the multiplier for an economy in which there is a proportional income tax with a marginal rate of t but lump sum net taxes of zero.

Solution   With a proportional income tax, total taxes are equal to income times the marginal tax rate. Substituting $T = tY$ into Equation 9A.1 gives this restatement of the consumption function:

$$C = a + b(Y - tY) = a + b(1 - t)Y \qquad (9A.10)$$

The aggregate nominal demand curve then becomes

$$AND = a + b(1 - t)Y + I + G + X - M \qquad (9A.11)$$

Regrouping terms, this can be written as

$$AND = (a + I + G + X - M) + b(1 - t)Y \qquad (9A.12)$$

From this form of the equation, we see that the vertical intercept of the aggregate nominal demand curve is now equal to the sum of autonomous consumption, planned investment, government purchases, and net exports. The slope of the aggregate nominal demand curve, as explained in the chapter, is equal to the marginal propensity to consume times one minus the marginal tax rate.

The final step is to substitute equation 9A.12 into the equilibrium condition, $AND = Y$, and solve for Y. This gives

$$Y^* = \frac{1}{1 - b(1 - t)}(a + I + G + X - M) \qquad (9A.13)$$

The first term in this equation is the value of the multiplier for an economy with a proportional income tax.

Chapter 10

Fiscal Policy

After reading this chapter, you should be able to

1. Discuss the use of projections and targets for national income in making fiscal policy.
2. Explain how a change in government purchases can be used to control the equilibrium level of nominal national income.
3. Discuss the effectiveness of tax changes and changes in government purchases as means of controlling aggregate nominal demand.
4. Explain how the federal budget deficit is affected by changes in fiscal policy and by changes in unemployment, inflation, and interest rates.
5. Discuss the debate over the danger of a large budget deficit and a growing national debt.

Ideas for Review

Here are some terms and concepts that you should review before you read this chapter:

Receipts and expenditures of government (Chapter 5)
Excess burden of taxation (Chapter 5)
Marginal tax rate (Chapter 5)
Aggregate real supply and demand curves (Chapter 7)
Aggregate nominal supply and demand curves (Chapter 9)
The expenditure multiplier (Chapter 9)

*"We must get control of
the budget monster."*

"We must get control of the budget monster, get control of our economy and, I assure you, get control of our lives and destinies." So said Ronald Reagan in March of 1981, shortly after he was inaugurated president of the United States. But Reagan did not manage to gain control over the budget. By the 1984 election the federal deficit was approaching $200 billion and economic policy had become a major election issue.

Reagan's 1984 opponent, Walter Mondale, stated his position on the budget issue early in the campaign. Reagan had cut taxes too far and spent too much, especially on the military. If elected, Mondale pledged to raise taxes, restrain the growth of military spending, and restore some of Reagan's cuts in social programs.

Candidate Reagan remained coy about his economic policy plans for a second term. Would he raise taxes? Only as a last resort—maybe not even then. Would he cut spending? Of course—but at the same time military spending and social security, the largest budget items, were placed off limits for cuts.

In the end, Reagan won reelection easily. The day after the election the deficit was still there and the debate over taxes and spending went on much as before. The budget monster was still on the loose.

Fiscal policy
Management of aggregate demand through changes in net taxes and government purchases.

The growth of the budget deficit has brought **fiscal policy**—the management of aggregate demand through changes in net taxes and government purchases—to center stage as a topic of national debate. This chapter uses the Keynesian multiplier model to explore the economics of fiscal policy. (As Box 10.1 points out, fiscal policy decisions are as much a matter of politics as of economics, but we will not be able to give that side of the issue much attention here.) After looking at fiscal policy in this chapter, we will turn to monetary policy in Chapters 11 and 12. Then in Chapter 13 we will return to fiscal policy, seeing how it interacts with monetary policy to determine interest rates as well as the level of national income.

In this chapter, as in the last one, the discussion continues primarily in nominal terms. It is important to keep in mind, however, that control of nominal national income is not the ultimate goal of macroeconomic policy. It is an intermediate goal behind which lie the goals of full employment, price stability, and real economic growth.

The changes in nominal national income that result from fiscal policy actions can, as we have seen, reflect either changes in real output (accompanied by changes in employment), changes in the price level, or some mix of the two. Naturally, when policymakers use tax cuts or spending increases to stimulate aggregate demand and drive up the level of nominal national income, they hope all or most of the expansion will take the form of job-creating increases in real output. Likewise, when fiscal policy is used to restrain aggregate demand and slow the growth of nominal national income, policymakers hope that most of the slowdown will take the form of a reduction in the rate of inflation. Some of it, however, may also take the form of a slowdown in real economic growth, accompanied by a rise in unemployment. As Arthur Okun, a long-time practitioner and critic of stabilization policy, once put it, "The evidence of recent years suggests that

Box 10.1
The Budget Process and Its Limits

Economists define fiscal policy as the management of aggregate demand through changes in net taxes and government purchases. But the federal budget process is more complex than this definition suggests. For one thing, no single agency is responsible for fiscal policy. Budget authority is divided between the president and Congress. Also, budget policy must serve many goals, ranging from national security and social equity to simple political ambition, besides the macroeconomic goals we focus on in a textbook discussion.

A brief look at the federal budget process will give an idea of where the formal authority for fiscal policy lies. The U.S. government operates on a fiscal year that runs from October through September. (For example, fiscal 1987 runs from October 1, 1986, through September 30, 1987.) About 18 months before a fiscal year starts, the executive branch begins preparing the budget. The Office of Management and Budget (OMB) takes the lead in this process. It receives advice from the Council of Economic Advisers (CEA) and the Treasury Department. After an outline of the budget has been drawn up, it is sent to the various departments and agencies. A period of bargaining ensues in which the Pentagon argues for more arms spending, the Transportation Department for more highway spending, and so on. During this process the OMB is supposed to act as a restraining force and to keep macroeconomic goals in mind.

By January, nine months before the fiscal year starts, the president must submit the budget to Congress. After that Congress takes the lead in the budget process. Its committees and subcommittees look at the president's proposals for the programs and agencies under their jurisdiction. The Congresssional Budget Office (CBO) maintains a staff of professionals who advise the committees on economic matters, somewhat as the OMB and the CEA advise the president. In May the House and Senate are supposed to pass a first budget resolution that sets overall spending targets and revenue goals.

Bargaining among committees, between the House and Senate, and between Congress and the executive branch continues throughout the summer. Committees prepare specific spending and tax laws during this period; these are supposed to be guided by the May resolution. Finally, in September, Congress is supposed to pass a second budget resolution that sets binding limits on spending and taxes for the fiscal year begin-

through its fiscal and monetary policies the federal government can control—within a reasonable margin—the total growth of GNP measured in dollars. But it cannot control the division of that growth between increases in output and increases in the price level."[1]

In this chapter we will touch only briefly on the question of how changes in nominal income are divided between real growth and inflation. We will see that Okun's observation, restated in terms of the theory introduced in Chapter 7, amounts to saying that fiscal and monetary policy can control the position of the aggregate real demand curve, but not that of the aggregate real supply curve. But details of changes in real output, the price level, and employment will have to wait until Chapters 14–18.

---

[1]"An Efficient Strategy to Combat Inflation," *Brookings Bulletin*, 15, Spring 1979, p. 4.

ning October 1. If any bills passed earlier do not fit within the limits of the resolution, they are supposed to be changed to fit it.

In practice, many things can and do go wrong with this process.

The first and most basic problem is that macroeconomic goals—full employment, price stability, and economic growth—do not carry much weight in the budgetary process. The real tax and spending decisions are made in dozens of subcommittees, where they are dominated by interest group pressures, vote trading, and the desire of each member of Congress to help the folks at home.

A second problem is that Congress has not proved willing to follow its own rules. The required budget resolutions often do not get passed on time. If they are passed, they are not treated as binding. Often the fiscal year starts without a budget. Then agencies must operate on the basis of "continuing resolutions," meaning that they can go on doing whatever they were doing the year before. In some cases even the continuing resolutions have not been passed on time, and federal workers have had to be sent home until there was money to pay them.

Finally, there is the problem of so-called "un-controllable" costs. These are the costs of programs that arise under long-term laws that are not subject to an annual budget review. Social security, military retirement pay, and medicare are examples. Today well over half of the federal budget is in the "uncontrollable" category. Of course, Congress could control these costs by passing a new law to replace the old one, but doing so is not part of the normal budget process.

"The basic fact is," writes Herbert Stein, a former chairman of the Council of Economic Advisers, "that we have no long-run budget policy—no policy for the size of deficits and for the rate of growth of the public debt over a period of years." Each year the president and Congress make short-term budget decisions that are wholly inconsistent with their declared long-run goals, hoping "that something will happen or be done before the long-run arrives, but not yet."

Where does all this leave fiscal policy? Yes, the government does have a fiscal policy, in the sense that decisions do get made that affect taxes and spending. But in the sense of using the budget as a tool to control aggregate demand, there is room for doubt.

Source of Stein quote: Herbert Stein, "After the Ball," *AEI Economist*, December 1984, p. 2.

FISCAL POLICY AND THE MULTIPLIER THEORY

Forecasts and Targets

Although policymakers cannot directly control the way a change in nominal national income will be divided between real output and price changes, they can make forecasts. These forecasts, in the form "If A, then B, other things being equal," provide the starting point for fiscal policy decisions. Two kinds of forecasts are especially useful in policy making: those that consist of projections of current trends and those that are used to translate normative policy goals into positive policy targets. We will begin our discussion of fiscal policy by looking at each of these types of predictions.

Current-services budget
A version of the federal budget that assumes no changes in laws governing taxes, transfer payments, or government purchases.

Forecasting trends in nominal income   Put yourself in the place of a policymaker looking ahead to the 1987 fiscal year at the beginning of January 1986. The first thing you want to know is where the economy is headed, assuming that government retains its current tax laws and its current programs for government services. To put it more precisely, you want a forecast based on the **current-services budget**—a version of the federal budget that assumes that no changes are made in the tax laws, in the formulas by which transfer payments are distributed, or in the programs determining the level of government purchases. You will not be surprised if your economic advisers, as well as forecasters outside government, disagree on this question. There will be disagreements about the likely equilibrium level of nominal national income for the coming year and about the levels of employment, prices, and real output. However, the range of forecasts will at least give you a working basis for decision making.

Setting a nominal income target   Next, you must decide whether you like what you see in the forecast based on the current-services budget. At this point you will want to draw on advice based on an aggregate real supply-and-demand model—a more elaborate version of the model presented in Chapter 7. Such a model can indicate how the projected paths of aggregate nominal demand and nominal national income will affect real output, the price level, and unemployment.

When you have received forecasts for nominal national income, real output, the price level, and unemployment, you will have to evaluate them. Do the projections based on the current-services budget indicate that the level of aggregate nominal demand will be too low, so that real output will stagnate and unemployment will rise? In this case you may want to set a **nominal income target** that is higher than the current-services projection. Does the projection indicate too high a level of nominal national income, in which case inflation will be the main threat? If so, you may want to set a target that is lower than the current-services projection of nominal national income. In either case, your nominal income target will reflect your judgments about normative economics and political realities as well as the technical advice of your staff economists.

Nominal income target
A level of nominal national income judged to be most compatible with progress toward the goals of full employment, price stability, and real economic growth.

Comparing the projection and the target   Box 10.2 presents two possibilities. Part a shows the situation in which a target has been set that is higher than the current-services projection for nominal national income. With no policy change, equilibrium would occur at $800 billion. At the target level of nominal national income, $1,200 billion in this case, aggregate nominal demand is projected to fall short of aggregate nominal supply by $100 billion.

In contrast, part b of Box 10.2 shows what happens when there is too much aggregate nominal demand under the current-services projection. At the target level of nominal national income, aggregate nominal demand will exceed aggregate nominal supply by $100 billion. Without some policy action, nominal national income and product are projected to expand far beyond the $1,200 billion target level, to an equilibrium at $1,600 billion.

**Box 10·2
Comparing the
Projected Equilibrium
Level of Nominal
National Income with
the Nominal Income
Target**

Part a of this box shows a situation in which aggregate nominal demand is too low. At the target level of nominal national income, aggregate nominal demand falls short of aggregate nominal supply by $100 billion. The level of equilibrium nominal national income projected on the basis of the current services budget is only $800 billion, compared with a target of $1,200 billion. Part b shows a situation in which aggregate nominal demand is projected to be too high. Aggregate nominal demand exceeds aggregate nominal supply by $100 billion at the nominal income target.

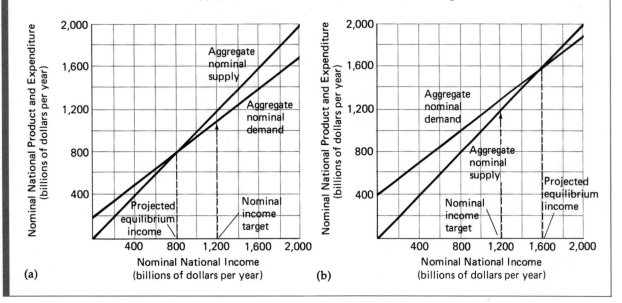

(a)   (b)

Using a Change in Government Purchases to Control Aggregate Nominal Demand

If the projected equilibrium level of nominal national income for the coming year does not match the nominal income target, something will have to be done. The fiscal policy tools available for this purpose are changes in government purchases and changes in net taxes. We will look at each of them, starting with government purchases.

Box 10.3 shows how an increase in government purchases above the levels of the current-services budget can be used to boost aggregate nominal demand. In part a the projected aggregate demand schedule, assuming no policy change, is shown by AND_1. The consumption schedule on which this curve is based assumes a marginal propensity to consume of 0.75, autonomous consumption of $100 billion, lump sum net taxes of $100 billion, and no income tax. To this schedule are added projected planned investment of $100 billion, government purchases of $50 billion, and net exports of $25 billion.

The shortfall in aggregate demand can be overcome by authorizing an extra $100 billion of government purchases. To be specific, suppose the decision is made to spend $100 billion on a highway project in the coming year. To keep the tax and spending sides of fiscal policy distinct, assume

Box 10.3
Using an Increase in Government Purchases to Control Aggregate Nominal Demand

Part a shows a situation in which the aggregate nominal demand curve AND_1 is $100 billion too low to achieve equilibrium at the nominal income target. A $100 billion increase in government purchases shifts the curve upward to the position AND_2, correcting the shortfall. Part b shows the effect of the increase in government purchases from the point of view of aggregate real supply and demand. The increase in government purchases boosts aggregate nominal demand, which in turn shifts the aggregate real demand curve to the right, from ARD_1 to ARD_2. As the economy moves along the aggregate real supply curve from E_1 to E_2, real output increases, the price level rises, and unemployment falls.

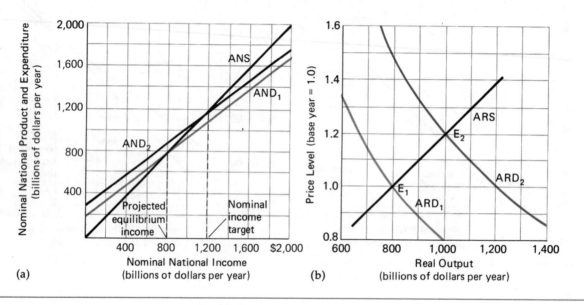

(a)

(b)

that the extra $100 billion of government purchases is financed by borrowing rather than by raising taxes. Suppose also that this borrowing does not affect the assumed $100 billion of private planned investment. Given these assumptions, let's look at the effects of the increase in government purchases.

The multiplier effect   Let's begin by tracing the multiplier effect of the increased government purchases as it works its way through the economy. Spending $100 billion on the highway project creates $100 billion in new income for construction workers, thereby initially raising nominal national income from $800 billion to $900 billion. Given a marginal propensity to consume of 0.75, the workers save one quarter of their added income and spend the rest on, say, clothing. This expenditure generates $75 billion in new income for workers and retailers in the clothing industry, which raises nominal national income to $975 billion. In the third round, clothing workers and retailers spend three quarters of their added income on something else, thereby adding $56,250 million more to the stream of income and expenditure. In later rounds the $1,200 billion target level of nominal national income is approached more and more closely.

Government purchases and the Keynesian cross   Part a of Box 10.3 uses a Keynesian cross diagram to show the effects of the increase in government purchases. The decision to spend $100 billion on the highway project shifts the aggregate nominal demand schedule upward by $100 billion, to the position AND_2. At the initial $800 billion level of national income, planned expenditures now exceed national product by $100 billion. This added demand causes an unplanned drop in business inventories. In response, firms either step up output or raise prices or both, sending the level of nominal national income and product upward. As the circular flow expands, planned expenditures rise less quickly than output, since part of each added dollar of output is saved. By the time nominal national income reaches its $1,200-billion target level, the excess aggregate demand has been eliminated and equilibrium has been restored.

Effects on real output, the price level, and unemployment   Part b of Box 10.3 uses aggregate real supply and demand curves to show the effects of the policy change on real output and the price level in the coming year. The projected $800 billion equilibrium level of aggregate nominal demand puts the aggregate real demand curve in the position ARD_1. This would result in an equilibrium at E_1, with a price level of 1.0 and real output of $800 billion per year. The increase in government purchases, as shown in part a of Box 10.3, raises the equilibrium level of aggregate nominal demand to $1,200. This shifts the aggregate real demand curve to the position ARD_2. As explained in Chapter 7, this shift in demand moves the economy up along the aggregate real supply curve to a new equilibrium at E_2. As this takes place, real output increases from $800 billion to $1,000 billion, and the price level rises from 1.0 to 1.2. At E_2, the new price level times the new level of real output equals the new equilibrium level of nominal national income ($1.2 \times \$1,000$ billion = $1,200 billion). The increased number of workers required to produce the higher level of real output will cause unemployment to fall.

Summary of the effects   We can summarize the effects of an increase in government purchases as follows: When government purchases are increased while taxes, planned investment, net exports, and the consumption schedule remain unchanged, equilibrium nominal national income changes by an amount equal to the change in government purchases times the expenditure multiplier. In this case, in which the change in government purchases is $100 billion and the multiplier is 4, the change in equilibrium nominal national income, in billions of dollars, is $4 \times 100 = 400$.

The increase in aggregate nominal demand shifts the aggregate real demand curve to the right. Assuming no shift in the aggregate real supply curve, the result will be an increase both in real output and in the price level. As real output rises, unemployment will fall.

Restraining excess aggregate nominal demand   The same reasoning applies in reverse when aggregate nominal demand is too great. Such a situation was presented in part b of Box 10.2, where aggregate nominal demand was projected to be $100 billion too high at the target level of nominal national income. The excess could be eliminated by cutting $100 billion from the level of government purchases in the current-services budget. If this reduction were carried out in a way that did not disturb the level of net taxes or private investment, it would shift the aggregate nominal demand schedule down just enough to bring the projected equilibrium in line with the nominal income target. The multiplier effect would operate in reverse. People whose incomes were directly affected by the reduction in government purchases would cut back their spending, although not by the full amount of the loss in income. This first-round reduction in spending would cause a second-round reduction in income to producers of consumer goods, who in turn would cut back their spending, and so on. With a marginal propensity to consume of 0.75, a $100 billion cut in government purchases would reduce equilibrium nominal national income by $400 billion.

The reduced level of aggregate nominal demand would shift the economy's aggregate real demand curve to the left. As this happened, the economy would move downward and to the left along its aggregate real supply curve. Real output would fall, the price level would fall, and unemployment would rise.

Using a Lump Sum Tax Change to Control Aggregate Nominal Demand

Instead of stimulating or restraining aggregate nominal demand with a change in government purchases, fiscal policymakers could accomplish the same thing with a change in net taxes. The change could take the form of a lump sum increase or decrease in net taxes or a change in income tax rates. We will discuss the lump sum case first.

A lump sum change in net taxes acts on aggregate nominal demand via the consumption schedule. Each dollar increase in transfer payments or dollar decrease in taxes collected adds a dollar to disposable income. Part of the increase is saved; the rest is spent, shifting the consumption schedule and the whole aggregate nominal demand curve upward.

In reverse, if transfer payments are cut by a dollar or tax payments are increased by a dollar, disposable income falls by the same amount. Households adjust to the dollar loss of disposable income partly by reducing saving and partly by cutting back consumption. A lump sum increase in net taxes thus shifts the consumption schedule downward.

Box 10.3, which showed the effects of an increase in government purchases, can also be used to show the effects of a cut in lump sum taxes. At first aggregate nominal demand is assumed to fall $100 billion short of aggregate nominal supply at the target level of nominal national income. This situation is shown by the demand curve AND_1, which intersects the aggregate nominal supply curve at $800 billion. To restore equilibrium the curve must be shifted to the position AND_2, which is $100 billion higher.

More than a $100 billion cut in taxes will be needed to shift the aggregate nominal demand curve upward by $100 billion, because not all the increase in disposable income will be spent. If households are assumed to treat added disposable income from the tax cut just like added disposable income from any other source, saving 25 cents and spending 75 cents of each dollar, the amount of the tax cut must be $133 billion. This will shift the aggregate nominal demand schedule up to the position AND$_2$ and bring the equilibrium level of nominal national income up to the target level.

The only difference between the case of a lump sum tax cut and that of an increase in government purchases is the origin of the shift in the aggregate nominal demand curve. The effects on real output, the price level, and unemployment would be exactly the same.

Using an Income Tax Change to Control Aggregate Nominal Demand

Lump sum tax changes have sometimes been used as tools of fiscal policy. In 1975, for example, when the economy was deep in recession, Congress passed a $31.2 billion one-time lump sum tax rebate. In recent years, however, more attention has been given to changes in income tax rates. As Chapter 9 explained, a change in the income tax works by changing the slope of the aggregate nominal demand curve instead of producing a parallel shift in the curve, as a change in lump sum taxes does.

Box 10.4 shows how a change in the income tax rate can be used as a tool of fiscal policy. In this case the target level of nominal national income is $1,000 billion. The initial aggregate nominal demand curve, AND$_1$,

Box 10.4
Using a Change in the Income Tax Rate to Control Aggregate Nominal Demand

In this box the initial aggregate nominal demand curve, AND$_1$, which assumes a 33 percent income tax, is too low to achieve the nominal income target. A cut in the tax rate to 20 percent will shift the aggregate nominal demand curve to the position AND$_2$ and raise the equilibrium level of nominal national income from $800 billion to $1,000 billion, thereby meeting the target.

assumes marginal propensity to consume of 0.75, a 33 percent marginal tax rate, and no lump sum net taxes. This puts the projected equilibrium nominal national income at $800 billion. At the target level of nominal national income, aggregate nominal demand will fall $100 billion short of aggregate nominal supply, according to AND_1. An increase in government purchases or a lump sum tax cut can be used to boost income to the target level, but as the box shows, a cut in the income tax rate from 33 percent to 20 percent will also do the job. By raising the share of each dollar of national income left to households, the tax cut increases consumption and eliminates the shortfall of aggregate nominal demand.

The Effectiveness of Tax Cuts

The analysis of fiscal policy to this points suggests that either changes in government purchases or changes in net taxes can be used to shift the aggregate nominal demand curve. But dollar for dollar, an increase in government purchases produces a larger shift in demand than a tax cut because people save part of the increased disposable income that the tax cut gives them. For example, a $100 billion increase in government purchases injects $100 billion of planned spending directly into the circular flow. By comparison, a $100 billion lump sum tax cut adds $100 billion to disposable income, but, assuming a marginal propensity to consume of 0.75, it adds only $75 billion of new planned expenditures to the circular flow.

The net tax multiplier   Because the change in planned expenditure is less for a tax cut, the multiplier effect of the tax cut is reduced in proportion to the marginal propensity to consume. In Chapter 9 we showed that the multiplier for a change in government purchases (the expenditure multiplier) is equal to $1/(1 - MPC)$. To calculate the effect of a lump sum tax cut we multiply the expenditure multiplier by the marginal propensity to consume. The result, which is sometimes called the **net tax multiplier**, can be written as follows:

Net tax multiplier
The change in the equilibrium level of nominal national income that results from a $1 change in lump sum net taxes.

$$\text{Net tax multiplier} = \frac{MPC}{1 - MPC}$$

For a marginal propensity to consume of 0.75, the net tax multiplier is 3, compared to an expenditure multiplier of 4. Thus, as explained earlier, it takes a $133 billion cut in lump sum taxes to equal a $100 billion increase in government purchases. This formula applies only to an economy in which all taxes are of the lump sum form.

Evidence on the effectiveness of tax cuts   Recent U.S. experience suggests, however, that tax cuts have less of an effect on nominal national income than this formula for the net tax multiplier implies. The formula gives the correct results only if people treat a dollar of added income received through a tax cut in the same way as a dollar of income received from any other source, dividing it between saving and consumption in proportion to the marginal propensity to consume. But evidence suggests

**Box 10.5
Personal Taxes and
Personal Saving in the
U.S. Economy,
1960–1984**

This chart shows personal taxes and personal saving as a percent of personal income for the U.S. economy from 1960 to 1984. It is clear from the chart that changes in taxes have often been offset, at least in part, by opposite changes in saving. For example, the tax surcharge of 1968 led to a jump in tax payments and a drop in saving. The effects of the tax rebate of 1975 are even more dramatic, producing a sharp downward spike on the tax line and a matching upward spike on the saving line.

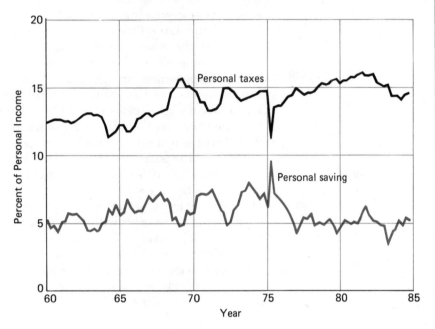

Source: Federal Reserve Board of Governors.

that in practice, saving is more strongly affected by tax changes than by other changes in disposable income.

Consider Box 10.5, for example. This box charts personal saving and personal tax payments as a percent of personal income since 1960. Tax cuts, such as the tax rebate of 1975, appear to produce an offsetting jump in saving. As a result, they add little to consumption. Likewise, tax increases, such as the tax surcharge of 1968, produce a jump in tax payments but an offsetting drop in saving. The implication of this behavior is that the numerator of the net tax multiplier formula should be a much smaller number than the normal marginal propensity to consume. In the extreme case, in which a tax change is fully offset by a change in saving, the numerator would be zero. Then a net tax change would have no multiplier effect at all.

Explanations of the seeming ineffectiveness of tax cuts   Economists differ in their explanations of the seeming ineffectiveness of tax cuts. One far-reaching hypothesis has been put forward by Robert J. Barro of the

University of Rochester. Barro points out that a tax cut today has implications for fiscal policy tomorrow. If the government cuts taxes today and does not cut spending, it will have to increase its borrowing to cover the resulting deficit. In the future, then, taxes will have to be raised to repay this borrowing, or at least to pay interest on it. If households think ahead, Barro says, they will react to a tax cut today by increasing their saving. Income from assets they buy with the added saving will make it possible for them to afford the higher future taxes needed to cover today's government borrowing. In order to fully protect themselves against the higher future taxes, they must save 100 percent of today's tax cut.[2]

Other economists doubt that consumers are so farsighted as to adjust their saving to offset in full the future effects of today's tax cuts. They see a simpler explanation of the seeming ineffectiveness of tax cuts. Their explanation is based on the tendency, discussed in Chapter 9, for consumers to save a higher percentage of temporary changes in income than of permanent changes in income. Some recent tax changes have been explicitly labeled as temporary. This was the case with the income tax surcharge of 1968 and the tax rebate of 1975. As Box 10.5 indicates, these tax changes were almost fully offset by changes in saving, at least in the short run. Even tax changes that are said to be permanent may at first be treated as if they were temporary. Only after enough time has passed for consumers to adjust to the tax changes will these changes affect consumption in proportion to the full marginal propensity to consume.

Whichever explanation is accepted, it does appear that the net tax multiplier overstates the short-term—and possibly also the long-term—impact of tax cuts. As we will see in the next section, this fact is important for the ongoing debate over the effects of the federal deficit.

FISCAL POLICY AND THE FEDERAL BUDGET

Up to this point we have discussed fiscal policy without saying much about the federal budget. As we saw in Chapter 5, government receipts do not match expenditures on a year-to-year basis. When the government spends more than it takes in, thereby running a budget deficit, it must borrow in financial markets. When it takes in more than it spends, it runs a budget surplus; by paying off old debt, it becomes a net supplier of funds to financial markets.

As Box 10.6 shows, federal budget deficits have been much more common than surpluses in the post-World War II period. Between 1950 and 1981 the cumulative deficit was some $388 billion, against a cumulative surplus of only about $17 billion. In the early 1980s the deficit, measured as a percentage of GNP, rose still higher. Looking ahead from 1985, current-services budget projections showed deficits of $200 billion or more.

This situation gave rise to a widespread debate over fiscal policy. Since the debate is likely to be a long-running one, it will be worth looking at some economic principles that shed some light on changes in the deficit.

---

[2]Barro traces this reasoning to the nineteenth-century economist David Ricardo and calls it the "Ricardian equivalence theorem." See Robert J. Barro, *Macroeconomics* (New York: Wiley, 1984), pp. 380–383. The Ricardian equivalence theorem is an example of the thinking of the rational expectations school of economics, which we will discuss more fully in Chapter 14.

Box 10.6
Federal Receipts,
Expenditures, and
Deficits as a
Percentage of GNP

The chart shows federal receipts and expenditures as a percentage of GNP from 1950 to 1984. The federal deficit is shown as the difference between the two. As the chart shows, deficits have been much more common than surpluses over this period.

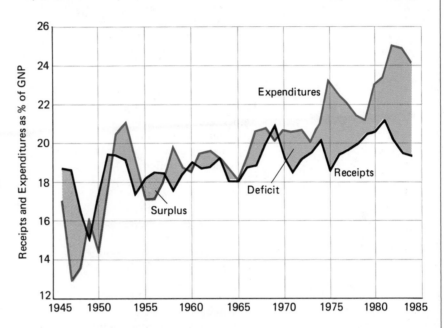

Source: Federal Reserve Board of Governors. The data for receipts and expenditures are for calendar years on a national income accounts basis.

The Structural vs. the Cyclical Deficit

The first distinction that needs to be made concerns the origins of the federal deficit. In part, the deficit is a result of policy decisions made by the administration and Congress. But policymakers do not decide exact levels of government receipts and expenditures. Instead, they pass general laws setting tax rates, benefit formulas for transfer payments, and programs for purchases of goods and services. Given these laws, the actual levels of receipts and expenditures are strongly affected by the stage of the business cycle in which the economy finds itself. In a recession, tax collections tend to fall and payments for unemployment compensation tend to rise, adding to the deficit. During a recovery, tax collections rise and transfer payments fall, reducing the deficit. Changes in interest rates and the rate of inflation also affect the levels of receipts and expenditures. Box 10.7 gives the estimated impact of changes in real output, unemployment, interest rates, and inflation on the federal budget.

The structural deficit   It is possible, at least approximately, to sort out the effects of policy changes from the effects of the business cycle by calculating what the federal surplus or deficit would be given a standard level of unemployment. An unemployment rate of 6 percent is commonly

**Box 10.7
Effects of Changes in
Economic Conditions
on the Federal Budget**

This box shows the estimated impact of changes in economic conditions on federal receipts, expenditures, and deficits. The changes refer to the 1985 and 1986 fiscal years, assuming that the changes in economic conditions take place in January 1985. Comparing the data for the two fiscal years shows that the longer the change in economic conditions remains in effect, the greater will be the impact on the budget. A plus (+) indicates an increase in receipts, expenditures, and the deficit, respectively.

	Fiscal Year 1985	Fiscal Year 1986
Effect of a one percentage point higher rate of growth of real output:		
Change in receipts	+$5 billion	+$16 billion
Change in expenditures	−1	−3
Change in deficit	−5	−19
Effect of a one percentage point lower unemployment rate:		
Change in receipts	+20	+32
Change in expenditures	−4	−7
Change in deficit	−24	−40
Effect of a one percentage point higher nominal interest rate:		
Change in receipts	—	+1
Change in expenditures	+3	+10
Change in deficit	+3	+9
Effect of a one percentage point higher rate of inflation:[a]		
Change in receipts	+5	+13
Change in expenditures	+3	+12
Change in deficit	−2	−1

[a]Assumes a one percentage point higher nominal interest rate.

Source: Congress of the United States, Congressional Budget Office, *The Economic and Budget Outlook: Fiscal Years 1986–1990* (Washington, D.C.: Government Printing Office, 1985), p. 75. The data refer to changes in revenues and outlays on a unified budget basis.

Structural deficit
The federal budget deficit that would prevail if the economy operated at a constant benchmark rate of unemployment.

Discretionary fiscal policy
Changes in laws or policies governing taxes, transfer payments, and government purchases.

used as a benchmark. This is lower than the rate reached at the trough of a recession but higher than the rate reached at the peak of many past recoveries.

The budget surplus or deficit that the federal government would run given the 6 percent benchmark rate of unemployment is called the **structural deficit**. Changes in the structural deficit are interpreted as representing changes in policies regarding taxes, transfer payments, and government purchases. These policy changes are known as **discretionary fiscal policy**. During recessions the actual deficit is greater than the structural deficit.

The cyclical deficit   The difference between the actual and structural deficits is called the **cyclical budget deficit**. When unemployment rises above the 6 percent benchmark level, the cyclical deficit becomes positive

Cyclical deficit
The difference between the actual federal deficit in any year and the structural deficit for that year.

Automatic fiscal policy
Changes in taxes, transfer payments, or government purchases that occur automatically as a result of changes in economic conditions without a change in laws or policies.

since the actual deficit exceeds the structural deficit. When unemployment falls below the 6 percent benchmark, the actual deficit is less than the structural deficit. At such times the cyclical deficit is negative. Changes in the cyclical deficit reflect changes in receipts and expenditures that occur automatically as real output and unemployment change. These changes in the deficit are known as **automatic fiscal policy**.

Box 10.8 shows actual and structural federal budget deficits for the U.S. economy in recent years in relation to GNP. The cyclical deficit appears on the chart as the difference between the two.

Automatic stabilizers   It is significant that the cyclical deficit rises during recession and falls during recovery, rather than the other way around. This behavior of the cyclical deficit means that automatic fiscal policy works to moderate the business cycle. Even without changes in the current-services budget, automatic fiscal policy "leans against the wind" to

**Box 10.8
Cyclical and Structural
Federal Deficits**

This chart separates the effects of changes in discretionary fiscal policy from those of automatic fiscal policy by showing the structural and cyclical deficits for the federal budget in recent years as a percentage of GNP. The structural deficit shows what the deficit would be if the economy operated at a benchmark rate of unemployment, with a corresponding level of real output. A benchmark unemployment rate of 6 percent for 1984 is assumed in this chart. When unemployment is above the benchmark, the actual deficit is greater than the structural deficit, and when unemployment is below the benchmark, the actual deficit is less than the structural deficit. The difference between the actual and structural deficits is called the cyclical deficit.

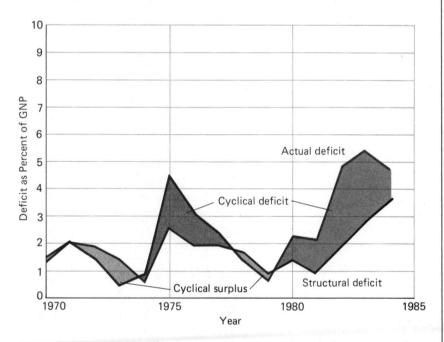

Source: U.S. Department of Commerce, Bureau of Economic Analysis.

boost aggregate demand during downturns and damp it during booms. Because they moderate the business cycle, income taxes, unemployment compensation programs, and other elements of automatic fiscal policy are known as **automatic stabilizers**.

Automatic stabilizers
Programs, such as income taxes and unemployment compensation, that tend to push the federal budget toward surplus as nominal income rises and toward deficit as nominal income falls.

Many economists blame the severity of the Great Depression of the 1930s on the weakness of automatic stabilizers at that time. In 1929, total expenditures of all levels of government were only 10 percent of GNP. Today they are over 30 percent. The most powerful of the automatic stabilizers—the federal income tax and unemployment compensation—were insignificant in the 1930s. The strength of these automatic stabilizers today, it is thought, has prevented any repeat of the Great Depression in the post-World War II period.

Problems of the Deficit and the National Debt

As far back as the 1930s, when the Keynesian idea of using discretionary fiscal policy for economic stabilization was first gaining popularity, fiscal conservatives became worried about the asymmetry of fiscal policy. They issued a warning: If the government allows larger and more frequent deficits than surpluses, it will run up an endlessly growing national debt that could lead to financial ruin. They also raised some important questions: Can the government go on spending beyond its means forever? Should the government be required to balance its budget each year, financing all programs on a pay-as-you-go basis, in order to avoid bankruptcy? Even if debts are paid on time, does financing today's spending programs with borrowed money create distortions in the economy of today and place an unfair burden on future generations?

Almost half a century after Keynes, these questions are still being asked. They have been given new prominence by the growing size of the deficit. The federal deficit has approached $200 billion in nominal terms in recent years, and has at times exceeded 5 percent of gross national product—a post-World War II record (see Box 10.6). In addition, the size of the national debt—the accumulated result of past deficits—has begun to grow as a percent of GNP, after reaching a post-World War II low in 1974 (see Box 10.9). The larger debt plus interest rates that remain high in comparison with past years have combined to increase the percentage of federal expenditures required to pay interest on the debt. Interest payments accounted for more than 13 percent of all federal expenditures in 1984, up from less than 7 percent in 1974.

Many economists and noneconomists as well regard the ballooning deficit and the growing debt with foreboding. We will look at their reasons for worrying shortly. But before turning to the worries, we should look briefly at the thinking of a minority of economists who think the current level of the federal deficit is nothing to be concerned about.

Reasons Not to Worry About the Deficit

Economists who argue that the federal deficit is nothing to worry about begin by making a series of numerical adjustments. These adjustments, they say, show that the federal deficit is not really as large as it seems to be, either in absolute terms or by comparison with past years. We will look at four of these adjustments here.

Box 10.9
Federal Debt Held by Private Investors as a Percentage of Gross National Product, 1945–1984

As this chart shows, the federal debt reached a record high of 108 percent of GNP at the end of World War II. From that time through 1974, the debt grew less rapidly than GNP. Since 1974 this trend has been reversed. The debt is now growing in relation to GNP.

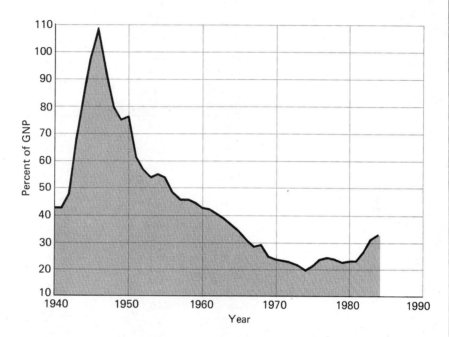

Source: Office of Management and Budget. Data exclude the portion of the federal debt held by federal agencies and the Federal Reserve.

Adjusting for the state and local surplus   The first adjustment is based on the notion that it is not the federal deficit that matters, but the combined deficit or surplus of federal, state, and local governments. While the federal government ran record-breaking deficits of $179 billion in 1983 and $176 billion in 1984, state and local governments ran record-breaking surpluses of $44 billion and $52 billion in those two years.[3] When these are taken into account, the consolidated government deficit falls to around $125 billion. This is a smaller share of GNP than in 1975, when the federal deficit was $69 billion but the state and local surplus was a paltry $5.5 billion.

Adjusting for the cyclical component   In assessing the impact of fiscal policy on the economy, the federal deficit should also be adjusted to remove its cyclical component. When the economy is in recession, it is argued, a deficit is a useful aid to recovery. For 1983, when the unemploy-

---

[3]The deficit figures used in this section refer to calendar years and are given on a national income accounts basis. Sometimes deficits are reported for fiscal years on the basis of the so-called unified budget. By this measure, the federal deficits were $208 billion in 1983 and $185 billion in 1984.

ment rate averaged 9.6 percent, this adjustment would take some $88 billion off the deficit. Even in 1984, when the unemployment rate averaged 7.5 percent, the cyclical component accounted for about $46 billion of the federal deficit.

Adjusting for capital expenditures   Households and private firms routinely make a distinction between borrowing for purposes of capital investment and borrowing to cover current expenses. Suppose, for example, that you borrow $1,000 to take a vacation. You enjoy the vacation, but you acquire nothing tangible to offset the burden of paying off the loan in the months ahead. On the other hand, suppose you borrow $60,000 to buy a town house. Doing so allows you to move out of your rented apartment. In this case you acquire a tangible asset to offset the debt, and your saving in rent offsets your monthly mortgage payments.

The federal government makes no such distinction between capital and current expenses in figuring its surplus or deficit, but many economists think such an adjustment should be made. After all, suppose the government builds a new office building to replace rented office space. The funds borrowed to finance the construction are no burden on taxpayers because interest payments on the borrowing will be offset by reduced payments of rent. Adjusting the federal budget for capital spending would reduce the deficit by an estimated $21 billion in 1983 and $23 billion in 1984.[4]

Adjusting for inflation   A final adjustment is needed to take the effects of inflation into account. Each year inflation erodes the real value of federal debt held by the public. In order to maintain the real value of federal securities they hold, private investors have to reinvest a portion of the federal interest payments they receive. For example, in 1984 the nominal value of federal debt in the hands of private investors was about $1 trillion and the rate of inflation was about 4 percent. Thus, private investors would be willing to absorb $40 billion in new nominal debt just to keep the real value of the total debt constant. To the extent this is the case this part of the deficit puts no burden on the rest of the economy. Some economists argue that the deficit should be adjusted for the expected rate of inflation, rather than for the actual rate. In 1983 and 1984 the expected rate of inflation was estimated to be 5 to 6 percent, which would increase the adjustment to the deficit to between $50 and $60 billion.

Box 10.10 summarizes these four adjustments to the federal deficit. When allowances are made for state and local surpluses, the cyclical component of the deficit, capital spending by government, and inflation, the awesome deficits of 1983 and 1984 don't look so bad. The $176 billion 1984 deficit dwindles to $15 billion, and the $179 billion 1983 deficit actually turns into a $14 billion surplus.

Another reason not to worry about the deficit   Some economists offer another, rather different reason not to worry about the deficit. This is

---

[4]These figures are based on an estimate given by Robert Eisner, "Which Budget Deficit," *American Economic Review*, 74, May 1984, pp. 138–143. Eisner's estimate of $20 billion for 1982 is projected to 1983 and 1984 by assuming that federal capital purchases grew in proportion to overall federal purchases.

Box 10.10
Adjustments to the
Federal Deficit, 1983
and 1984

The federal deficit, in nominal terms, rose to record levels of more than $175 billion in 1983 and 1984. Many people found these numbers alarming, but some economists think they overstate the impact of the deficit on the economy. To assess the true impact, they say, the deficit should be adjusted to take into account state and local government surpluses, the cyclical component of the federal deficit, capital spending by the federal government, and the effects of inflation. As this table shows, these adjustments turn the $179 billion federal deficit for 1983 into a $14 billion surplus, and reduce the $176 billion federal deficit for 1984 to $15 billion. These data are for calendar years on a national income accounts basis.

	1983	1984
Actual federal deficit	$179 billion	$176 billion
Less:		
State and local surplus	−44	−52
Cyclical component of federal deficit	−88	−46
Capital spending by federal government	−21	−23
Inflation adjustment	−40	−40
Equals: Adjusted deficit	−$14	15

based on Robert Barro's argument, discussed earlier, that changes in taxes tend to be fully offset by changes in private saving. If true, this means that the burden that the federal budget puts on the rest of the economy depends only on the level of government purchases, not on how they are financed. In Barro's world, the public would respond to a tax cut by increasing saving by just the amount needed to buy the extra securities the Treasury would have to sell to finance the added deficit. Likewise, a tax increase made to reduce the deficit would reduce saving by the same amount, and thus no added resources would be available to finance private investment.

To be sure, most economists doubt that changes in taxes are fully offset by changes in saving. But even if there is only a partial adjustment of saving, the burden of the deficit is eased and the case for raising taxes to cut the deficit is weakened.

Reasons to Worry About the Deficit After All

Despite the arguments just given, many economists—probably a majority of them—still think current and projected federal deficits are a problem. Let's look at some of their concerns.

Effects on interest rates   In Chapter 7 we showed how interest rates are determined in financial markets by the supply and demand for loanable funds. According to conventional economic theory, when the Treasury borrows to finance a deficit, it adds to the total demand for loanable funds, thus pushing up interest rates. Private borrowers are then "crowded out" of financial markets. The reduction in private investment is a burden on the economy that slows economic growth and reduces living standards of future generations. Even if increases in the deficit are partly offset by increased private saving, there is still some upward pressure on interest rates.

Borrowing from abroad   In defense of deficits, it is sometimes said that the national debt is something "we owe to ourselves." By this it is meant that taxes collected to repay the debt come out of the pockets of some U.S. citizens but go back into the pockets of other U.S. citizens, leaving the country as a whole no poorer. However, suppose federal budget deficits push up real interest rates in the United States relative to those in the rest of the world. In this case loanable funds will be attracted to U.S. financial markets from abroad. In later years, repaying the part of the debt owed to foreign investors will place a real burden on the U.S. economy. The argument that we owe it to ourselves does not apply in this case.

The high budget deficits of the mid-1980s have in fact been accompanied by large inflows of funds into U.S. financial markets from abroad. We will explore the consequences of these inflows, including their effects on the international value of the dollar, in Chapter 35.

The growing structural deficit.   It is widely agreed that the cyclical component of the federal deficit is less of a problem than the structural component. What worries many economists is the way the structural component has grown even as the cyclical component has fallen. For example, the cyclical component of the deficit fell by $44 billion between 1982 and 1984. Yet the actual federal deficit rose by $27 billion. A $71 billion increase in the structural deficit more than wiped out the budgetary benefits of the strong 1983–1984 economic recovery. What is more, budget deficits in the neighborhood of $175 billion to $200 billion were being projected for 1985 and beyond, even with continued economic growth. Critics see this as evidence of a dangerous breakdown of the federal budgetary process.

Some critics make an adjustment of their own to the federal deficit that cuts the opposite way from the adjustments given in Box 10.10. They point out that in addition to the stated national debt, which consists of securities held by the public, the government has another set of liabilities. These are the sums it has promised to future recipients of social security benefits and other federal retirement benefits. Each year these liabilities grow. If the deficit were adjusted to take these liabilities into account, it might appear to be more than $100 billion higher than currently reported.

The danger of an exploding deficit   The growth of the structural deficit calls attention to another worry: the growth of the part of the deficit associated with interest payments on the debt. As mentioned earlier, this part of the deficit has already doubled, as a percentage of expenditures, since 1974. Some economists think that interest payments are poised for "explosive" growth.

In the explosive-growth scenario, the amount of borrowing needed just to make interest payments on the debt is so great that the debt grows faster than national income even if the rest of the budget deficit does not grow faster than national income. As the government borrows more and more each year to make interest payments, it adds to the demand for loanable funds in credit markets. This pushes nominal interest rates higher, making it necessary to borrow even more to make the interest payments. The deficit begins to "explode" and threatens eventually to swallow the entire national income.[5]

As explosive growth begins, the government is left with only one way out. It begins to "monetize" the deficit, which, in effect, means that it finances the deficit by creating new money rather than by borrowing. But financing the deficit with newly created money is the classic formula for inflation—too much money chasing too few goods. Thus, monetization of the deficit converts an explosive deficit into explosive inflation.

Is this scenario too farfetched to be a real threat? Not at all. Creating new money to cover the government deficit is the source of the runaway inflation, at rates of hundreds or even thousands of percent per year, that has devastated countries such as Bolivia, Argentina, Brazil, and Israel in recent years. In the next three chapters we will look at the mechanisms used to create and control money in the U.S. economy. Then in Chapter 16 we will return to the topic of runaway inflation.

Today inflation is not running out of control in the United States. It has in fact slowed from the double-digit rates of a few years ago. Nonetheless, many economists think that the large federal deficits of the mid-1980s are a time bomb just waiting to explode. Perhaps President Reagan was right after all—perhaps we *do* need to get control of the budget monster.

Summary

1. The planning of fiscal policy is a forward-looking process. The first step is to project what the equilibrium level of nominal national income is likely to be under the *current-services budget*, that is, if no changes are made in tax or spending laws. Next a *target level of nominal national income* is chosen, taking effects on real output, the price level, and unemployment into account. Finally, a set of tax and spending policies is chosen that will bring the projected level of nominal national income in line with the nominal income target.

2. An increase in government purchases causes an upward shift in the aggregate nominal demand schedule. This leads to excess aggregate nominal demand, which causes the circular flow, measured in nominal terms, to expand. The new equilibrium level of nominal national income is higher by an amount equal to the increase in government purchases times the expenditure multiplier. The expansion of aggregate nominal demand shifts the economy's aggregate real demand curve to the right. The economy then moves upward and to the right along its aggregate real supply curve. As this happens, real output rises, the price level rises, and the unemployment rate falls. In the

---

[5]The issue of the exploding deficit was raised by Thomas J. Sargent and Neil Wallace in "Some Unpleasant Monetarist Arithmetic," *Federal Reserve Bank of Minneapolis Quarterly Review*, Fall 1981, pp. 1–17. In "Some Pleasant Monetarist Arithmetic" in the Spring 1984 issue of the same journal, Michael R. Darby refines the argument. Darby shows that the deficit will explode if the real rate of interest, adjusted for the average tax rate on federal interest payments, exceeds the long-term rate of growth of real GNP.

case of a decrease in government purchases, the whole process is reversed.

3. A cut in lump sum net taxes or a reduction in the marginal income tax rate also has an expansionary effect on the economy. Each dollar of tax reduction increases disposable income by a dollar. This, in turn, adds a fraction of a dollar to consumption expenditure, shifting the aggregate nominal demand curve upward (or, in the case of an income tax cut, increasing its slope). Evidence from recent tax cuts in the United States suggests that the fraction consumed of each added dollar of disposable income received as a result of a tax cut is less than the marginal propensity to consume that applies to other income. Some economists think that changes in taxes may be fully offset by changes in saving.

4. Federal receipts and expenditures are affected both by discretionary changes in policy and by changes in real output, unemployment, interest rates, and inflation. In an attempt to separate the two kinds of effects, economists define the *structural* deficit as the deficit that would prevail under given policies if unemployment were at a benchmark rate of 6 percent. When the economy is in recession, receipts fall and expenditures for unemployment compensation and other transfer programs rise. As a result, the actual deficit is greater than the structural deficit. The difference between the actual deficit and the structural deficit is known as the *cyclical* deficit.

5. The federal government has run large budget deficits in recent years, and the national debt has grown as a percentage of GNP. Some economists think that deficits and the national debt are not matters of great concern. They point out that the deficit is not as large as it appears to be if it is adjusted for the surpluses of state and local governments, the cyclical component of the federal deficit, federal capital expenditures, and the effects of inflation on the debt. Others worry that the growing structural deficit will place upward pressure on interest rates. This will increase borrowing from abroad, and in the long run could lead to renewed inflation.

Questions for Review

1. Define the following terms:
   fiscal policy
   current-services budget
   nominal income target
   net tax multipliers
   structural deficit
   cyclical deficit
   discretionary fiscal policy
   automatic fiscal policy
   automatic stabilizers

2. As a policymaker, what factors would you take into account in deciding whether the projected level of nominal national income for the coming year was too high, too low, or just right?

3. If the projected level of nominal national income is below the target level for the coming year, what kind of change in government purchases would be called for?

4. Why is a $1 change in government purchases thought to have a greater impact on aggregate nominal demand than a $1 change in net taxes?

5. How are federal receipts and expenditures affected by changes in real output, unemployment, inflation, and interest rates? How is the federal budget deficit affected by an increase in nominal national income?

6. What has been the trend over the last ten years in the size of the federal budget deficit, expressed as a percentage of gross national product? What has been the trend in the size of the national debt relative to GNP?

Problems and Topics for Discussion

1. As the federal budget deficit rose toward the $200 billion mark in the mid-1980s, a majority of policymakers (but not all of them) agreed that efforts should be made to reduce the deficit. However, there was much disagreement as to whether this should be done by raising taxes or by cutting government spending. Outline a debate between two people, one of whom favors a tax increase and the other a cut in spending. What normative as well as positive economic arguments might each use?

2. It has been proposed from time to time that a law or constitutional amendment should be passed that would force the federal government to balance its budget every year. Do you think it would be possible to keep the actual budget deficit at zero each year? Or should an amendment aim only to keep the structural deficit at zero? Discuss.

3. Rework the graphs in Box 10.3 to show the effects of a cut in government purchases or an increase in lump sum taxes.

4. Find the most recent edition of the *Economic Report of the President* in your library. Does the the report discuss trends in the deficit and current policies toward the deficit? If so, what policies have been undertaken or are recommended?

5. **Case for Discussion**

   In February of 1982, when the U.S. economy was deep in recession, the Chicago Tribune *published the following item discussing the tax and spending problems of the Illinois state government:*

   Warning that state revenues are lagging behind expectations, Governor James R. Thompson announced Tuesday that he has halted most new state construction work for the next six months.

   Referring to "disturbing news on the economic front" the governor also announced that:

   - He is reworking his proposed state budget to include additional spending cuts.
   - He has ordered state agencies under his control to cut $30 million from their budgets.
   - He repeated his call for a new state liquor tax to raise an additional $50 million a year.

   To save an extimated $20 million in interest payments, the amount of money to be raised by State of Illinois bond issues during the next five months will be cut almost in half, from $380 million to $200 million.

   "Interest rates are too high," the governor told a press conference in the Westin Hotel here.

   Later, in a speech to the Illinois Board of Higher Education, Thompson said that in January state income tax revenues were $10 million lower than projected while sales tax revenues were $25 million less than projected.

   "Right now, we don't know if it's an aberration or a trend. I suspect it's a trend," Thompson said.

   He warned that if the revenue shortfalls continue for a full year, the loss in state revenue could total $420 million.

   Thompson also had other bad news for the educators.

   Speaking of the financial problems facing the state, he said, "There will be some pain for higher education and for elementary and secondary education."

   He described the upcoming budget as "the tightest of the six budgets I have presented to the General Assembly."[6]

   Questions:

   a. Do Governor Thompson's policy actions count as fiscal policy, even though they take place at the state level? Assuming a simple multiplier of 2.5 for the economy as a whole, what would his $30 million in spending cuts do to the

---

[6] Casey Banas, "Thompson Cuts State Construction," *Chicago Tribune*, February 3, 1982, sec. 1, pp. 1, 8. Reprinted by courtesy of the Chicago Tribune.

equilibrium nominal national income of the United States?

b. Why do you think income tax revenues were $10 million lower than had been projected and sales tax revenues $25 million lower?

c. Suppose all state governors follow Thompson's lead and try to cut spending and raise taxes when state budget deficits rise during a recession. Does it make it easier or harder for the economy to recover from a recession? What would happen if the federal government followed policies similar to Thompson's when the economy entered a recession?

Suggestions for Further Reading

Gordon, Robert A. *Macroeconomics*, 3rd ed. Boston: Little, Brown, 1984.

Chapter 17 of this text provides further detail on fiscal policy and its limits.

Heilbroner, Robert L., and Peter L. Bernstein. *A Primer on Government Spending*, 2nd. ed. New York: Random House, 1970.

A view of fiscal policy as it looked before the inflationary 1970s.

President's Council of Economic Advisers. *Economic Report of the President*. Washington, D.C.: Government Printing Office, annually.

Discusses current issues of fiscal policy each year. The 1982 issue contains a discussion of adjustments to the deficit. Use the table of contents to find the relevant sections.

U.S. House of Representatives, Committee on the Budget. *Economic Stabilization Policies: The Historical Record, 1962–1976*. Washington, D.C.: Government Printing Office, 1978.

Contains studies of the effectiveness of fiscal policy, with comments by leading economists.

Money can take many forms. On the South Pacific island of Yap, huge stone wheels serve as money.

Part III
Money and
Banking

Chapter 11

Money and the Banking System

After reading this chapter, you should be able to

1. Define *money* in terms of the functions it serves.
2. Explain how the quantity of money is measured.
3. List the main assets and liabilities of a *commercial bank*.
4. Discuss sources of stability and instability in the banking system.
5. Describe the functions of the federal agencies that regulate banking.
6. Explain how the Federal Reserve System can increase or decrease the quantity of bank reserves.
7. Show how banks create money through the expansion of deposits.

Ideas for Review

Here are some terms and concepts that you should review before you read this chapter:

Assets, liabilities, and net worth (Chapter 4)
Financial intermediaries (Chapter 4)
Financial markets (Chapters 4 and 7)
The circular flow (Chapter 6)
Stocks and flows (Chapter 6)

"Life is easy and the currency is hard."

On the tiny South Pacific island of Yap, life is easy and the currency is hard.

Elsewhere, the world's troubled monetary system creaks along; floating exchange rates wreak havoc in currency markets, and devaluations are commonplace. But on Yap the currency is as solid as a rock. In fact, it is rock. Limestone, to be precise.

For nearly 2,000 years the Yapese have used large stone wheels to pay for major purchases, such as land, canoes, and permission to marry. Yap is a U.S. trust territory, and the dollar is used in grocery stores and gas stations. But reliance on stone money, like the island's ancient caste system and the traditional dress of loincloths and grass skirts, continues.

Stone wheels don't make good pocket money, so for small transactions, Yapese use other forms of currency, such as beer. Beer is proffered as payment for all sorts of odd jobs, including construction. Besides stone wheels and beer, the Yapese sometimes spend "gaw," consisting of necklaces of stone beads strung together around a whale's tooth. They also can buy things with "yar," a currency made from large seashells. But these are small change.

The people of Yap have been using stone money ever since a Yapese warrior named Anagumang first brought the huge stones over from limestone caverns on neighboring Palau, some 1,500 to 2,000 years ago. Inspired by the moon, he fashioned the stone into large circles. The rest is history.

By custom, the stones are worthless when broken. Rather than risk a broken stone—or back—Yapese tend to leave the larger stones where they are and make a mental accounting that the ownership has been transferred—much as gold bars used in international transactions change hands without leaving the vault of the New York Federal Reserve Bank.

Just three decades ago, Yap was little changed from the way it had been for centuries. But now things are changing. To help preserve the tradition of stone money, Andrew Ken, a Yapese monetary thinker, is trying to persuade the Yap government to start a stone money exchange. This would allow the Yapese to trade their boulders for dollars, or buy them back, whenever they wish. "We're losing because we can't liquidate," Ken complains.[1]

As the case of Yap shows, money can take many different forms. We have mentioned money many times in this book. In this chapter and the next two, money will take center stage. We will begin with a formal definition of money and a brief discussion of the not-so-simple matter of measuring how much of it there is in the economy. Next we will describe the banking system. In Chapter 12 we will look at the ways in which the Federal Reserve, a government agency, can control the stock of money. From there we will turn to a discussion of the demand for money and how that demand interacts with supply in financial markets.

Having covered all these topics, we will, in Chapter 13, come to the

---

[1]Excerpted from Art Pine, "Fixed Assets, or: Why a Loan in Yap Is Hard to Roll Over," *Wall Street Journal*, March 29, 1984. Reprinted by permission of The Wall Street Journal, © Dow Jones & Company, Inc. 1984. All rights reserved.

central question of why money matters. We will see that changes in the stock of money can have a strong impact on the decisions of households, firms, and units of government. This fact makes monetary policy a very powerful weapon in the fight for price stability, full employment, and economic growth. Without further introduction, then, let's begin our study of monetary economics.

MONEY: WHAT IT IS AND WHAT IT DOES

Money
An asset that serves as a means of payment, a store of purchasing power, and a unit of account.

Money is best defined in terms of what it does: It serves as a means of payment, a store of purchasing power, and a unit of account. Money serves these functions regardless of its name or form—U.S. dollars, Japanese yen, or Yapese stones.

The Functions of Money

As a means of payment, money reduces the costs of making transactions. Using money avoids the drawbacks of barter. In a money economy we don't have to find out what the dentist wants for dinner before we go to get our teeth fixed. Instead of taking a steak or a basket of potatoes with us, we take money; the dentist then visits the supermarket on the way home and picks out whatever looks good. Not all countries have money that works as well as a means of payment as the U.S. dollar. Yapese stones, for example, are used for some large transactions, but because they are hard to carry around, beer, beads, shells, or U.S. dollars are used for smaller purchases. Israel is an example of another kind of problem. Israelis use U.S. dollars for many transactions because a 1,000 percent per year rate of inflation has made their money, the shekel, almost useless.

As a store of purchasing power, money makes it possible to arrange economic activities in a convenient manner over time. Income-producing activities and spending decisions do not have to occur at the same time. Instead, we can accept payment in money for our productive efforts and keep the money handy until we decide how to spend it. The U.S. dollar is a fairly good store of purchasing power, although, as we saw in Chapter 7, its purchasing power has been hurt by inflation in recent decades. By this standard, Yapese stone money does a better job than the dollar. It has maintained its value for some 2,000 years. The Israeli shekel, on the other hand, is a very poor store of purchasing power. At the 1,000 percent annual inflation rate of the mid-1980s, people were forced to spend shekels almost as fast as they got them, or else they wouldn't be able to buy much with them at all.

Finally, as a unit of account, money makes it possible to measure and record economic stocks and flows. A household's needs for food, shelter, and clothing can be expressed in dollar terms in planning a household budget. The nation's output of movies, apples, and warplanes can be added together in dollar terms to provide a basis for planning economic policy. Without money as a unit of account, private and public economic planning would be impossible. The Yapese stone money serves as a unit of account even though some of the stones are too heavy to move. All that is necessary is to keep track of who owns each stone. The battered Israeli shekel, on the other hand, is a poor unit of account because its value changes from day to day. Many Israeli businesses keep their accounts in dollars, even though they still use the shekel to pay their bills.

Money, the Liquid Asset

Any asset that a household, firm, or unit of government owns is a store of purchasing power in that it can be sold and the proceeds used to buy something else. Money, however, has two important traits that no other asset has, or at least not to the same extent. One is that money itself can be used as a means of payment, without first having to be exchanged for something else. A house, a bond, or a blast furnace may have great value, but it can rarely be traded without first being exchanged for an equivalent amount of money. The other trait is that because money serves as a unit of account, it can, by definition, neither gain nor lose in nominal value. A house, bond, or blast furnace may be worth more or fewer dollars next year than this year, but the nominal value of a dollar is always a dollar, no more and no less.

An asset that can be used directly as a means of payment and that is protected against gain or loss in nominal value is said to have **liquidity.** No other asset is as liquid as money. In fact, a comparison of the definition of money (an asset that can be used as a means of payment and serves as a unit of account) and the definition of liquidity (usefulness as a means of payment plus unchanging value relative to the nominal unit of account) suggests that any perfectly liquid asset is, by definition, a form of money.

Liquidity
An asset is said to possess liquidity if it can be used directly as a means of payment and if it does not vary in nominal value.

Measuring the Stock of Money

For purposes of economic policy, it is important not only to know what money is but also to be able to measure how much of it there is. In all modern economies the amount of money is controlled by government. As we will see, if government fails to supply enough money, real output and employment will decrease. Indeed, some economists believe that the Great Depression was caused, or at least made much worse, by such a failure. On the other hand, flooding the economy with too much money can be highly inflationary. Many economists blame the wild inflation in countries like Israel and Argentina on excessive growth of the money stock. And the slowing of inflation in the United States in the mid-1980s is often credited to more restrained growth of the money stock.

Although the post–World War II U.S. economy has been free from major depressions and extreme rates of inflation, the record in recent years has not been as good as we might like. If the economy is to perform better in the future, better monetary policy will be needed. And because the money supply cannot be controlled if it cannot be measured, the problem of measurement is more important now than ever before.

Currency and Transactions Deposits

Currency
Coins and paper money.

Transactions deposits
Deposits from which funds can be withdrawn by check in order to make payments to third parties.

Traditionally, the nation's money stock has been defined as consisting of two highly liquid types of assets—currency and transaction deposits. **Currency** is coins and paper money. **Transactions deposits**—also known as checking accounts—are deposits from which money can be withdrawn by check, without advance notice, for the purpose of making payments to third parties. (*Third parties*, in this sense, are parties other than the depositor or the institution where the account is kept.)

In the United States, currency consists of the familiar Federal Reserve notes, which are issued in denominations of $1, $2, $5, $10, $50, and $100, and of coins issued by the Treasury. Coins and paper money were once backed by precious metals. Until 1934 the U.S. government issued both gold coins and paper currency that could be exchanged for gold on demand. Silver coins and silver-backed paper money survived until the mid-1960s. Today, coins and paper money are in effect tokens whose value is based on the public's faith in their usefulness as means of payment for goods and services. Box 11.1 shows that the currency in circulation in the United States as of December 1984 totaled $166 billion. A small quantity of traveler's checks is included in this total.

Transactions deposits are available in a number of forms from several kinds of institutions. One major type of transactions deposit is the **demand deposit**. These are issued predominantly by **commercial banks**. These are financial intermediaries offering a broad range of services, including making business and consumer loans and accepting business and consumer deposits. By law, demand deposits cannot pay interest, but banks do provide their demand-deposit customers various services below cost. Until the mid-1970s, demand deposits were the only kind of transactions deposits available in the United States. They have since been joined by interest-bearing checkable deposits such as NOW accounts and super-NOW accounts. These deposits are available not only at commercial banks but also at savings and loan associations, mutual savings banks, and credit unions—a group of financial intermediaries that are known as **thrift institutions** or **thrifts**. As Box 11.1 shows, at the end of 1984 demand

Demand deposits
Non-interest-bearing transactions deposits at commercial banks.

Commercial banks
Financial intermediaries that provide a broad range of banking services, including accepting demand deposits and making commercial loans.

Thrift institutions (thrifts)
A group of financial intermediaries that operate much like commercial banks, including savings and loan associations, mutual savings banks, and credit unions.

**Box 11.1
Components of the U.S. Money Stock, December 1984 (billions of dollars)**

This table breaks down the U.S. money supply into its components as of December 1984. Two of the most commonly used money supply measures are given. M1 is the total of currency and transactions deposits. M2 includes M1 plus other highly liquid assets.

Currency		$165.8
Plus transactions deposits		404.6
Demand deposits	$257.4	
Other checkable deposits	147.2	
Equals M1		570.4
Plus money market mutual fund shares		168.1
Plus money market deposit accounts		415.2
Plus savings deposits		286.2
Plus small-denomination time deposits		886.4
Plus overnight repurchase agreements		45.2
Plus selected other liquid assets		5.1
Equals M2		$2,376.6

Source: Federal Reserve H-6 Statistical Release, March 7, 1985.

deposits made up a little less than two thirds of total transactions deposits, and all other checkable deposits made up a little more than one third.

Currency plus transactions deposits of all kinds totaled $570 billion as of December 1984. The sum of currency and transactions deposits, known as **M1**, is a widely used measure of the nation's money stock.

The Broadly Defined Money Supply

M1 is not the only measure of the money stock. There are a number of other very liquid assets that are such close substitutes for currency or transactions deposits that they too may in effect function as money.

Take shares in money market mutual funds, for example. A **money market mutual fund** is a financial intermediary that sells shares to the public. The proceeds of these sales are used to buy short-term fixed-interest securities, such as Treasury bills. Almost all the interest earned on the securities bought by the fund is passed along to shareholders. The fund charges only a small fee for its services. Shareholders can redeem their shares in a number of ways—by writing checks on the fund (usually with a minimum amount of $500 per check), by telephone transfer, or by transfer to another fund.

These characteristics of money market mutual funds make their shares almost as liquid as balances in ordinary transactions accounts. However, until 1983 money market mutual funds were able to pay higher interest rates than banks could pay on their transaction accounts. In some years the return on the funds was as high as 15 percent, while banks were limited to paying 5-1/4 percent on NOW accounts. Until 1981, even NOW accounts were not available nationwide. As a result, money market funds grew quickly. They added $100 billion in assets in 1981 alone.

Beginning in late 1982, banks and thrifts were given a chance to compete directly with money market mutual funds by offering so-called *money market deposit accounts* (MMDAs). Banks and thrifts can pay as high an interest rate as they want on these accounts, and they can offer some checking privileges. MMDAs therefore are fairly liquid. The volume of MMDAs grew very rapidly after their introduction. Many of the funds deposited in these accounts were drawn from money market mutual funds. By 1984, as Box 11.1 shows, MMDAs had reached a total of $415 billion.

Banks and thrifts also offer the public a number of other liquid accounts. **Savings deposits** are a familiar example. Although checks cannot be written on these deposits, they are fully protected against loss in nominal value, and they can be redeemed at any time. Beginning in 1986, savings accounts are subject to no interest rate ceiling. Banks and thrifts also offer **time deposits**. Funds in time deposits must be left for a fixed period, ranging from less than a month to many years, to earn the full rate of interest. They are not subject to an interest ceiling, and usually pay higher interest rates than savings accounts and MMDAs. Because they are protected against loss of nominal value, and because depositors who are willing to pay a penalty can withdraw funds from time deposits before maturity, they too are fairly liquid.

One additional liquid asset that deserves mention is the **repurchase agreement**. A repurchase agreement is an arrangement in which firms

---

M1
A measure of the money supply that includes currency and transactions deposits.

Money market mutual fund
A financial intermediary that sells shares to the public, using the proceeds to buy short-term securities and passing the interest income (less a small service charge) along to shareholders.

Savings deposits
Deposits at banks and thrift institutions from which funds can be withdrawn at any time without payment of a penalty.

Time deposits
Deposits at banks and thrift institutions from which funds can be withdrawn without payment of a penalty only at the end of an agreed-upon period.

Repurchase agreement
A short-term liquid asset that consists of an agreement by a firm or person to buy securities from a financial institution for resale at an agreed-upon price at a later date, often the next business day.

(and, less often, consumers) buy securities from a financial institution subject to an agreement to sell them back, often the next business day, at a slightly higher price. The difference between the buying and selling prices amounts to an interest payment for the institution's use of the funds. Repurchase agreements are popular because they allow firms to put large sums of cash to work earning interest for short periods. They are even more attractive because firms are not allowed to use interest-bearing transactions deposits such as NOW accounts. As Box 11.1 shows, overnight repurchase agreements totaled $45 billion at the end of 1984.

Money market mutual fund shares, MMDAs, savings deposits, small time deposits, and overnight repurchase agreements, along with small amounts of other liquid assets, are added to M1 to get a measure of the money supply known as **M2**. As Box 11.1 shows, M2 amounted to $2,377 billion in December 1984.

Nearly all economists now agree that M1 is a better measure of "money" than the broader M2 because of its focus on transactions balances. However, both measures are really arbitrary cutoff points along a range of assets of varying degrees of liquidity, from currency at one end to time deposits at the other. Also, changes in M2 sometimes seem to signal changes in monetary conditions more accurately than do changes in M1. As a result, money watchers tend to keep their eyes on both M1 and M2, and both are widely publicized.

Much more could be said about money and how it is measured. For example, we have not yet said anything about the place of credit cards and debit cards in the monetary system. These are discussed in Box 11.2. We

M2
A measure of the money supply that includes M1 plus money market mutual fund shares, repurchase agreements, savings deposits, small time deposits, and certain other liquid assets.

**Box 11.2
"Plastic Money"**

What about "plastic money"—the MasterCards, Visa cards, and other bank cards that so many people carry these days? Where do they fit into the M's?

Credit cards, the most common form of plastic money, are not really a form of money at all. What sets credit cards apart from currency, bank deposits, and other forms of money is the fact that they are not a store of value. Instead, they are documents that make it easy for their holders to obtain a loan.

When you go into a store, present your credit card, and walk out with a can of tennis balls, you have not yet paid for your purchase. What you have done, instead, is to borrow money from the bank that issued the card. At the same time, you have instructed the bank to turn over the proceeds of the loan to the store. Later the bank will send money to the store (either in the form of a check or by crediting the amount to the store's bank account). This will pay for the tennis balls. Still later, you will send money to the bank to pay off the balance on your credit card account.

A less common form of plastic money—but one that is spreading fast—is the *debit card*. A debit card looks just like a credit card, but it doesn't work the same way. When you present your credit card to a merchant, you instruct your bank to transfer money directly from your bank account to the store's account. If the store is linked to the bank by a special computer hookup, the transfer may be made instantly. If you don't have any money in your account, you can't use your debit card. Whether you write a check or present your debit card when making a purchase, the balance in your transactions account is part of M1.

also have not discussed certain other liquid assets that are included in still broader measures of the money supply. But the brief outline we have given is enough for the purposes of this book.

THE BANKING SYSTEM

In Chapter 4 we introduced banks and thrift institutions as financial intermediaries. In that role they help match the needs of borrowers with those of lenders. In this chapter we have seen them in another role, as a source of money. In fact, of the nearly $2.4 trillion total of M2 listed in Box 11.1, all but $166 billion in currency and travelers checks, plus $168 billion in money market mutual fund shares, are liabilities of banks and thrifts.

The Banking Balance Sheet

A good way to understand the connection between the role of banks as financial intermediaries and their role as suppliers of money is to look at a balance sheet. Box 11.3 shows a total balance sheet for U.S. commercial banks as of December 26, 1984. Items on the balance sheets for thrift institutions would differ in size, but the concepts involved would be the same.

Assets   On the assets side of the balance sheet, the first line lists the noninterest-bearing deposits that banks maintain with the Federal Reserve System (about which we will have more to say shortly). The next line, vault cash, consists of currency that banks keep in their own vaults. Deposits at the Federal Reserve plus vault cash constitute a bank's **reserves**. In the past, the reason banks held reserves of cash or deposits that could quickly be converted into cash was that at any moment some depositors might want to

Reserves
Cash in bank vaults and non-interest-bearing deposits of banks with the Federal Reserve System.

Box 11.3
Total Balance Sheet for U.S. Commercial Banks, December 26, 1984 (billions of dollars)

This table shows the total balance sheet for U.S. commercial banks as of December 26, 1984. Assets of banks include noninterest-bearing reserves and interest-bearing loans and securities. Liabilities include deposits of all kinds and other borrowings. Net worth is equal to assets minus liabilities. The balance sheets of thrift institutions would show the same basic categories but would differ in details.

Assets		Liabilities and Net Worth	
Reserve deposits with		Transactions deposits	$ 490.5
Federal Reserve banks	$ 20.5	MMDAs and savings deposits	386.0
Cash in vaults	23.2	Time deposits	753.5
Other cash assets	158.1	Borrowings	301.7
Loans	1,460.6	Miscellaneous liabilities	196.2
Securities	400.5	Total liabilities	$2,128.0
Miscellaneous assets	210.6	Net worth	145.8
		Total liabilities and	
Total assets	$2,273.8	net worth	$2,273.8

withdraw their funds from the bank. This could be done either by writing a check to someone who would deposit it in another bank or by walking up to the teller's window and asking for currency. Today the level of reserves is not left to the judgment of banks. Instead, minimum reserves are set by federal regulation. As we will see shortly, these regulations make the Federal Reserve's power to control the level of reserves in the banking system a major tool of monetary policy. Other cash assets, shown in line three of the balance sheet, provide banks with liquidity to meet unexpected needs.

The next two items on the assets side of the balance sheet show the bank's main income-earning assets. The largest item is loans made to businesses and consumers. These amounted to $1.5 trillion in December 1984. In addition, commercial banks held $400 billion worth of government and private securities.

The final item on the assets side of the balance sheet includes some smaller income-earning items plus the value of the banks' buildings and equipment. Altogether, banks' assets came to $2.3 trillion.

Liabilities   The first three items on the liabilities side of the bank balance sheet are various kinds of deposits. These are liabilities of banks, since they represent funds to which depositors hold legal claim.

Funds that have been borrowed by banks also appear as liabilities on the balance sheet. A small part of these are borrowed from the Federal Reserve, and the rest from private sources. Because banks' total liabilities are less than their assets, they have a positive net worth. This sum, about $150 billion in December 1984, represented the claim of the banks' owners against the banks' assets.

The Federal Reserve System

We have already mentioned the Federal Reserve System—the Fed, as it is known in financial circles. The Fed is the central banking system of the United States. It operates the payments system and provides other banking services to private banks and thrifts as well as to the federal government. It is one of the major regulators and supervisors of the banking system. Its responsibility for monetary policy makes it a major partner in overall macroeconomic policy making, together with Congress and the executive branch of the federal government.

The Fed was established in 1913 as an independent agency of the federal government, not under the direction of the executive branch. It is subordinate to Congress, but Congress does not intervene in its day-to-day decision making. The reason for making the Fed independent was to prevent the Treasury Department from using monetary policy for political purposes. In practice, however, the monetary actions of the Fed are coordinated with the fiscal actions of the Treasury. The chairman of the Fed's Board of Governors is in frequent contact with the secretary of the Treasury, the chairman of the president's Council of Economic Advisers, and the director of the Office of Management and Budget. The Fed also reports to Congress twice a year. Its reports cover its monetary policy objectives and explain how these are related to economic conditions and the economic goals set by the administration and Congress.

The Federal Reserve Banks   The structure of the Federal Reserve System is shown in Box 11.4. At the heart of the system are the 12 Federal Reserve Banks. These district banks have 25 branches. The district boundaries and the locations of the district banks are also shown in Box 11.4.

Each of the Federal Reserve Banks is a separate unit chartered by the federal government. Its stockholders are commercial banks that are members of the Federal Reserve System. Although Federal Reserve Banks issue stock to their members, they are not typical private firms in that they are not operated for profit, and are not ultimately controlled by their stockholders. The Federal Reserve Banks earn income from their holdings of federal securities and, since 1981, from charges for services they provide to banks and thrift institutions. Each year the Reserve Banks return all their income, minus operating costs, to the Treasury.

Each of the banks is managed by a nine-member board. Six of those members are selected by the member banks, while the other three are appointed by the Fed's Board of Governors. Each board sets the policies of its own bank, under supervision of the Board of Governors. The Board of Governors also approves appointments of each Reserve Bank's top officers.

The Federal Reserve Banks perform a number of key functions in the banking system. These include clearing checks, handling reserve deposits, making loans to depository institutions, and providing currency to the banking system. They also issue paper currency in the form of Federal Reserve notes. In addition, they provide banking services to the Treasury.

The Board of Governors   The highest policy-making body of the Federal Reserve System is its Board of Governors. The board, which supervises the 12 Federal Reserve Banks, has seven members who are appointed by the President and confirmed by the Senate. Each governor serves a single 14-year term, with one term expiring every other year. The president appoints one of the board members to serve as chairman for a four-year term. The Board of Governors has the power to approve changes in the interest rate on loans to banks and thrifts made by the Reserve Banks. It also sets, within limits determined by law, the minimum level of reserves that banks and thrifts are required to hold. The board supervises and regulates many types of banking institutions, including some state-chartered banks, bank holding companies, and U.S. offices of foreign banks. It also approves bank mergers and implements consumer credit regulations.

The Federal Open Market Committee   Authority over purchases and sales of securities held by the Fed—its most important monetary policy tool—rests with the Federal Open Market Committee. It is made up of the seven members of the Board of Governors plus five district bank presidents. The president of the Federal Reserve Bank of New York is a permanent member; the remaining four seats rotate among the other 11 district banks. The committee meets about eight times a year, and confers by telephone more often, to set a general strategy for monetary policy. Decisions of the committee regarding changes in the Fed's holdings of securities are carried out through the open-market trading desk of the Federal Reserve Bank of New York.

Box 11.4
The Structure of the
Federal Reserve System

Part a of this box shows the structure of the Federal Reserve System. The highest policy-making body of the Fed is the Board of Governors. The map in part b gives the locations of the 12 Federal Reserve banks.

(a)

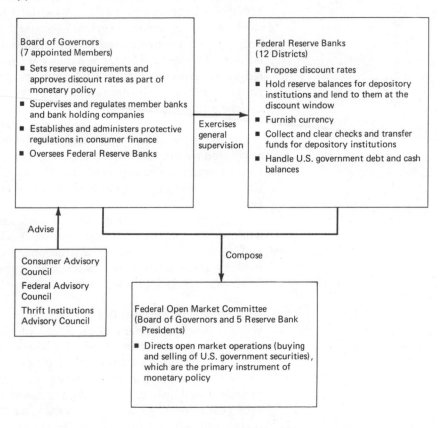

Source: Board of Governors, Federal Reserve System, *The Federal Reserve System: Purposes and Functions,* 7th ed. (Washington, D.C.: Federal Reserve System, 1984), pp. 5 and 8.

Member and nonmember banks   About 5,700 of the country's approximately 15,000 commercial banks, including most large banks, are members of the Federal Reserve System. National banks—those that are chartered by the federal government—are required to be members; state-chartered banks may or may not be members. Until 1980 member banks enjoyed certain privileges and free services from the Fed, but in return they were subject to generally stricter regulation than nonmember banks, especially with regard to the minimum levels of reserves they were required to hold. The reserve requirements were felt to be burdensome, and as a result, many banks were leaving the Federal Reserve System. This made it more difficult to conduct monetary policy.

In 1980, hoping to improve the Fed's ability to conduct monetary policy, Congress passed the Depository Institutions Deregulation and Monetary Control Act. This act did away with many of the distinctions between member and nonmember banks and between commercial banks

(b)

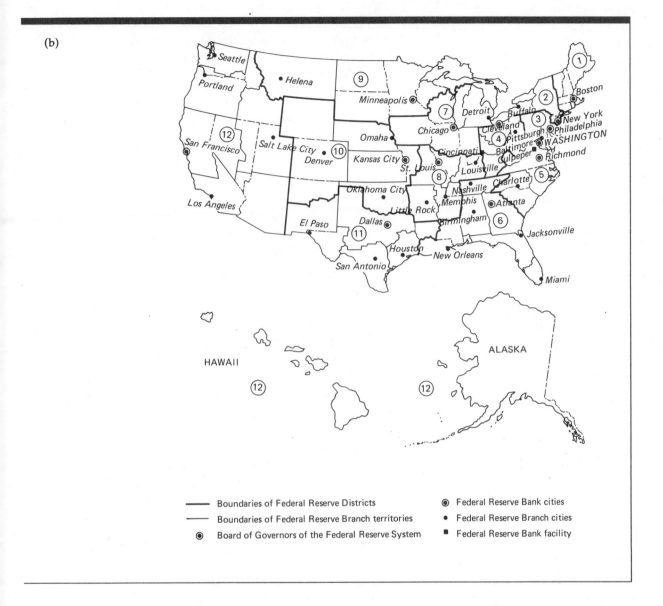

———— Boundaries of Federal Reserve Districts

——— Boundaries of Federal Reserve Branch territories

◉   Board of Governors of the Federal Reserve System

◉   Federal Reserve Bank cities

•   Federal Reserve Branch cities

■   Federal Reserve Bank facility

and thrift institutions. Since 1980, as a result, member banks, nonmember commercial banks, savings and loans, mutual savings banks, and credit unions have all been subject to more uniform federal reserve requirements. In return, thrift institutions won the right to compete more directly with commercial banks in making certain types of loans and offering transactions accounts, and nonmember institutions were given access to such services of the Fed as check clearing, wire transfers, and loans on the same terms as member banks. (In 1982, small depository institutions were exempted from reserve requirements.)

As a result of the Monetary Control Act, the distinction between banks, on the one hand, and thrift institutions, on the other, has become less important. Except where the remaining distinctions between banks and thrifts are crucial, then, we will use the term "bank" to refer to both types of institutions.

The Fed's balance sheet   Box 11.5 shows a balance sheet for the Federal Reserve System as of December 31, 1984. Government securities are by far the largest asset. As we will see shortly, these security holdings play a key role in the Fed's control of the money stock. Loans to banks and thrifts are small by comparison to other assets, but they are listed separately because they are important for policy purposes. Normally, these loans are made on a short-term basis to depository institutions to enable them to meet reserve requirements. However, in special circumstances loans are made for longer terms to banks experiencing financial difficulties.

Federal Reserve notes, which account for almost all of the nation's stock of currency, are the largest liability of the Federal Reserve System. The next-largest liability consists of the reserves deposited with the Fed by banks and thrifts. Other liabilities include deposits of the Treasury and of foreign central banks. Since the Fed's assets exceed its liabilities, it has a positive net worth.

Some Risks of Banking

Banks are able to earn a profit only because they lend out or invest most of the deposits they accept at an interest rate higher than the rate they pay to depositors. They keep only a fraction of their total deposits, as required by the Fed, in the form of noninterest-bearing reserves. Banks have been doing business much this way for hundreds of years, but it entails some well-known risks.

One is the risk of loan losses. What happens if a bank makes a loan to a customer who is unable to repay the loan? When a loan goes bad, the loss is at first absorbed by the net worth of the bank's owners. (In balance sheet terms, the bad loan is a reduction in assets. Liabilities, that is, deposits and borrowings, do not change. Thus, net worth, which is equal to assets minus liabilities, must fall.) If loan losses are too great, however, the bank's net worth may be used up. At that point the bank no longer has enough assets to pay off its depositors and other creditors, and it is in real trouble. Technically, a bank whose liabilities exceed its assets is said to be *insolvent*.

**Box 11.5
Consolidated Balance
Sheet of the Federal
Reserve Banks,
December 26, 1984
(billions of dollars)**

The Federal Reserve banks have liabilities to the general public in the form of Federal Reserve notes and to banks and thrifts in the form of reserve deposits. The Fed's main assets are government securities. Loans to banks to meet reserve requirements are small, but they are a key aspect of monetary policy.

Assets		Liabilities and Net Worth	
Securities	$169.9	Federal reserve notes	$168.3
Loans to banks and thrifts	2.4	Reserves on deposit	22.1
Other assets	34.5	Other liabilities and net worth	16.4
Total	$206.8	Total	$206.8

Source: *Federal Reserve Bulletin*, March 1985, Table A–10.

A second risk that banks face is the loss of deposits. When a depositor withdraws funds, the bank must dip into its reserves or other cash assets. This is not a problem under normal conditions, when new deposits more or less offset withdrawals. If there is a wave of withdrawals, however, the bank may have to convert some of its earning assets into cash to pay off depositors. Some assets, such as short-term government securities, are easy to convert into cash, but others, such as long-term business or mortgage loans, may be more of a problem. At that point the bank is in a different kind of trouble—it is *illiquid*.

Whether the bank's troubles begin with loan losses or deposit losses, there is a danger that they may trigger a *run* on the bank. A run means a situation in which depositors begin to withdraw their funds from a bank because they fear it may not be able to honor all of its liabilities. Fearing that the bank may be able to pay only the first depositors in line, they all compete to be first in line. Their fears become self-fulfilling, and the bank fails.

In the worst possible case, not just one bank but the whole banking system can get into trouble. When many banks face loan losses or runs at the same time, they cannot help each other out through temporary loans of reserves. If large banks fail, smaller banks, which keep deposits in the large ones or make other loans to them, may be brought down too. If many banks at the same time try to meet deposit outflows by selling their holdings of securities, the market price of the securities may fall, adding to their losses. A general bank *panic* can ensue in which the stability of the whole system is threatened.

Ensuring the Safety and Soundness of the Banking System

During the nineteenth century there were a number of bank panics touched off by recessions. In 1907 an especially severe panic took place; it led to the establishment of the Federal Reserve System in 1913. The Fed was supposed to help maintain a safe and sound banking system in two ways. First, it was to act as a lender of last resort, loaning reserves to troubled banks to allow them to pay off their depositors. Second, the Fed was supposed to inspect and regulate banks to make sure they did not take excessive risks. (Today it shares this function with other federal and state agencies.)

Despite its powers, the Fed failed to prevent a major bank panic in 1933, during the Great Depression. In response to the collapse of the banking system, Congress established the Federal Deposit Insurance Corporation (FDIC) in 1934. Today the FDIC insures all deposits up to $100,000 per customer per bank—in special cases, even more. The idea of deposit insurance is to short-circuit runs on banks. If deposits are insured, depositors don't need to run to the bank to withdraw their funds. Even if a bank fails, the government will pay them their money. And if runs can be avoided, the problems of one or a few banks will not touch off a panic that threatens the whole system. Banks bear the cost of deposit insurance through a small premium charged by the FDIC for its services.

Since 1933 there has not been a widespread bank panic in the United States. Individual banks have failed, including some large ones. In fact, more banks failed in the mid-1980s than at any time since the 1930s.

Several factors have combined to cause bank failures. Many of the failures have been caused by loans that have gone bad. In the 1970s, when oil prices seemed headed ever higher, banks loaned vast sums to energy-related industries. When oil prices fell in the 1980s, many of these loans could not be repaid. Banks also made large loans in the 1970s to third-world countries, partly to help them pay for oil imports. Not all of these loans have been paid on time. Finally, banks made a large volume of loans to farmers, based on the rising value of farmland. When the prices of crops and farmland turned down in the 1980s, some of these loans too went sour. The problems of Continental Illinois, the largest bank to get in trouble in recent years, stemmed largely from bad loans. (See Box 11.6.)

Not all the problems were caused by bad loans. The thrift industry faced a different problem. During the 1960s and early 1970s, savings and loans and mutual savings banks had made billions of dollars in home

**Box 11.6
Continental Illinois
Rattles Some Windows**

The stability of the U.S. banking system is maintained by means of bank inspections, deposit insurance, and loans to troubled banks. For more than 50 years these precautions have prevented banking panics. However, there have been some close calls. The collapse of Continental Illinois Bank & Trust Co. of Chicago in 1984 did not bring down the banking system, but it certainly rattled some windows.

In the late 1970s Continental soared to a leadership position among midwestern banks. Parts of its growth strategy were risky, however. It made many loans in the energy field, including $1 billion that it took over from Penn Square Bank of Oklahoma City. To obtain the funds it needed to make these loans, Continental relied heavily on short-term borrowing from other banks and large 30-day certificates of deposit—"hot money," in banking jargon. At least one officer of Continental saw danger signs and wrote a warning memo to her superiors, but the memo went unheeded. Although the Comptroller of the Currency inspected Continental on a regular basis, it failed to see how serious its problems were getting to be.

Penn Square Bank was closed by regulators in July 1982. When energy prices began to slip, most of the $1 billion in loans that Continental had taken over from the smaller bank turned out to be bad. Other loans to troubled companies like Chrysler, International Harvester, and Braniff looked questionable. Seeing these problems, owners of "hot money" began to pull their funds out of Continental.

By the spring of 1984 a run on Continental had begun. In May the bank had to borrow $3.5 billion from the Fed to replace deposits that it had lost. But this was not enough. To try to stem the outflow of deposits from Continental, the FDIC agreed to guarantee not just the first $100,000 of each depositor's money but all of it. Still the run went on.

Federal regulators tried hard to find a sound bank that could take over Continental—a common way of rescuing failing banks. But Continental was just too big for anyone to buy. By July all hope of a private-sector rescue was gone. Regulators faced a stark choice: Let Continental fail, or take it over themselves.

Letting the bank fail seemed too risky. It was estimated that more than 100 other banks had placed enough funds in Continental to put them at risk if Continental failed. So on a rainy Thursday at the end of July the FDIC in effect nationalized Continental Illinois at a cost of $4.5 billion. This kept the bank's doors open and prevented a chain reaction. However, in all but a technical sense Continental had become the biggest bank failure in U.S. history.

mortgage loans at rates around 6 or 7 percent per year. These loans were profitable at a time when they were paying interest of only 3-1/2 percent on savings deposits. By the early 1980s, the combined effects of inflation and the removal of interest rate ceilings on certain deposits had pushed the thrifts' cost of funds above the interest rates earned on outstanding loans. The resulting losses caused many savings and loan associations to fail. In Ohio and Maryland, where deposits in some savings and loans were not covered by federal insurance, serious runs on privately insured thrifts took place.

The problems of the banking system in the mid-1980s have caused economists to wonder whether some of the government's efforts to ensure the soundness of the banking system may have backfired. In particular, it may be that deposit insurance and the Fed's function as a lender of last resort have encouraged banks to take undue risks. The government's safety net has, in effect, put banks in a position in which the government ends up bearing the risks of bad loans, while banks get the profits if enough of the risky loans by luck are repaid. To counter this problem, the FDIC has been considering reforms in its system of deposit insurance. The goal would be to make banks bear the costs of risk taking by charging higher insurance premiums to the banks that take heavier risks.

Whatever reforms may be made in the future, the fact remains that the three main tools for ensuring the safety and soundness of the banking system—bank inspections, loans of reserves to troubled banks, and deposit insurance—have up to now kept the banking system intact.

CREATION OF MONEY BY BANKS

As we have seen, the major part of the U.S. money supply consists of the liabilities of banks and thrift institutions. We turn now to a discussion of the way these institutions create money on the basis of reserves supplied by the Federal Reserve System.

A Simplified Banking System

With as many kinds of financial institutions and forms of money as there are in the U.S. economy, we cannot cover all details. To keep things manageable, we will limit our discussion to the following simplified banking system:

1. The system consists of ten banks, all of which are identical.
2. The banks' only assets are reserve deposits at the Fed and loans.
3. The banks' only liabilities are demand deposits; net worth is zero.
4. Demand deposits are the only form of money in the banking system.
5. The system is regulated by a simplified Federal Reserve System that has the power to set uniform reserve requirements on all deposits.
6. The Fed's only assets are government securities, and its only liabilities are the reserve deposits of member banks. Banks do not borrow reserves from the Fed in this system.

Simplified though it is, this ten-bank system can tell us a great deal about the mechanics of money creation in the U.S. banking system.

Required reserves
The minimum percentage of certain deposits that depository institutions are required to hold as reserves.

Required-reserve ratio
Required reserves stated as a percentage of deposits.

Excess reserves
Total reserves minus required reserves.

Reserves: Required and Excess

As we have seen, the Federal Reserve System regulates bank reserves. It does so by setting a minimum percentage of certain deposits that each bank must hold in the form of reserve deposits with the Fed or vault cash. These are called **required reserves**. The ratio of required reserves to deposits is the **required-reserve ratio**. If the bank holds more than the minimum required reserves, the balance is known as **excess reserves**. In equation form, the relationships among required reserves, excess reserves, and the required-reserve ratio can be stated as follows:

$$\text{Required reserves} = \text{deposits} \times \text{required-reserve ratio}$$

and

$$\text{Excess reserves} = \text{total reserves} - \text{required reserves}$$

For our simplified banking system we will assume a required-reserve ratio of 10 percent on all deposits. This is somewhat above the average required-reserve ratio for transactions deposits in the U.S. banking system.[2]

Balance sheet equilibrium   If a bank's reserves fall below its required-reserve level, it must make up the difference. It can do this either by selling assets or by borrowing. Legally, a bank can hold more than the required level of reserves, but there is a strong incentive not to do so since reserves earn no interest. As profit-seeking firms, banks want to earn all the interest they can, so they normally use up almost all excess reserves by making loans or buying securities. In recent years excess reserves of U.S. banks have tended to be less than 2 percent of total reserves.

The situation in which total reserves equal required reserves can be thought of as a state of equilibrium. Excess reserves may exceed their equilibrium level for a while, but in our simplified banking system we will assume that banks soon reduce them to zero.

Creation of Money in the Simplified Banking System

We come now to the central topic of this short course in money mechanics: creation of money by the banking system. As an example will show, money creation is governed by the required-reserve ratio, the amount of reserves supplied, and the efforts of banks to maximize their profits.

Initial balance sheets   To begin with, we will assume that each of the banks in the system starts out with a balance sheet that looks like this:

---

[2]In the actual U.S. banking system, reserve requirements vary according to the volume and type of deposit and type of institution. Under the Monetary Control Act of 1980, the structure of reserve requirements is undergoing a process of simplification that will not be complete until late 1987. We will return to this matter in Chapter 12.

Initial Balance Sheet of a Representative Bank

Assets			Liabilities	
Reserves		$10,000	Demand deposits	$100,000
Required	$10,000			
Excess	0			
Loans		90,000		
Total assets		$100,000	Total liabilities	$100,000

We will assume that the initial balance sheet for the simplified Federal Reserve System looks like this:

Assets		Liabilities	
U.S. government securities	$100,000	Reserve deposits	$100,000

The Fed's liabilities consist of $10,000 in reserve deposits by each of the ten banks in the system.

Injecting new reserves   We want to look now at the effects of an injection of new reserves into the banking system. Any bank in the system receives new reserves each time a customer deposits funds that were withdrawn from another bank, but this does not increase the reserves in the banking system as a whole. In order to increase total reserves, new reserves must come from outside the system. The chief source of new reserves is the Fed.

Suppose the Fed decides to increase the amount of reserves available to the banking system. The usual way it does this is to add to its holdings of government securities by buying from the public or directly from banks. Such an action is called an **open-market operation** (an open-market purchase, in this case) because the Fed, acting through the New York Federal Reserve Bank, goes to the securities market and bids against other buyers to purchase the securities.

Let's assume that the Fed buys the securities it needs from a member of the public and pays for them by writing a check. The check is drawn on the Fed itself, not on a private bank. The seller of the securities deposits this check in a local bank account. To keep track of things, we will call that bank the Albany National Bank. The Albany bank, in turn, sends the check to the Fed, which credits Albany's reserve account with $10,000.

At that point the Fed's initial goal of injecting $10,000 of new reserves into the system has been achieved. The balance sheets of the Fed and of the Albany National Bank now look like the following ones. (In this and subsequent balance sheets, changes from the previous balance sheet are shown in parentheses.)

Open-market operation
A purchase (or sale) by the Fed of government securities from (or to) the public.

The Fed

Assets		Liabilities	
U.S. government securities	$110,000	Reserve deposits	$110,000
	(+10,000)		(+10,000)

Albany National Bank

Assets			Liabilities	
Reserves		$20,000	Demand deposits	$110,000
		(+10,000)		(+10,000)
Required	$11,000			
	(+1,000)			
Excess	9,000			
	(+9,000)			
Loans		90,000		
Total assets		$110,000	Total liabilities	$110,000
		(+10,000)		(+10,000)

Loaning out the excess reserves   Notice how the $10,000 in new reserves at the Albany National Bank is divided between required and excess reserves. Deposits have gone up by $10,000, which means that the bank must hold $1,000 more in required reserves. The other $9,000 in new reserves need not be held against deposits, so it is listed as excess reserves. The Albany National Bank is no longer in equilibrium; it can increase its profits by loaning out the excess reserves.

To make a loan the bank must, of course, find a borrower. Suppose that on the very morning that Albany gets its new reserves, James Anderson walks in and applies for a $9,000 auto loan. If Anderson wanted to, he could have the bank count out $9,000 in cash for him to take to the auto dealer, but instead he arranges for the bank to credit $9,000 to his checking account balance. Then he can pay for the car by check, without carrying all that cash around.[3] At the moment that the loan is completed, but before Anderson pays for the car, the balance sheet of the Albany National Bank looks like this:

Albany National Bank

Assets			Liabilities	
Reserves		$20,000	Demand deposits	$119,000
Required	$11,900			(+9,000)
	(+900)			
Excess	8,100			
	(−900)			
Loans		99,000		
		(+9,000)		
Total assets		$119,000	Total liabilities	$119,000
		(+9,000)		(+9,000)

---

[3]If Anderson did not have an account at the Albany National Bank, the bank might give him a check for the proceeds of the loan instead of crediting his account. In that case the intermediate steps in the process would be slightly different, but once the bank's check had cleared, the result would be the same.

Checking away the proceeds of the loan   In crediting Anderson's account with $9,000, the Albany National Bank has created a new $9,000 asset (the loan) matched by a new $9,000 liability (the deposit). Because of the new deposit, its required reserves have risen by $900. At this point Albany still has $8,100 in excess reserves. Why doesn't it use those reserves to make yet another loan?

The reason the bank cannot safely make new loans greater than the original addition to its excess reserves is that it knows Anderson will not leave the $9,000 sitting in his account. Instead, he is going to write a check to pay for his new car. Let's see what happens when he does that.

Again, using some names will help us keep track of things. We will call the dealer who sells the car Joyce Barnard, and we will suppose that she keeps her checking account at the Bethel National Bank. When Barnard deposits Anderson's Albany National Bank check in her Bethel account, the Bethel National Bank sends it to the Fed to be cleared. *Clearing the check* means simply that the Fed credits $9,000 to Bethel's reserve account and subtracts $9,000 from Albany's reserve account. The Fed then puts the check itself (the actual piece of paper) in the mail so that the Albany National Bank can forward it to Anderson for his records. When all these transactions have taken place, the balance sheets of the two banks look like this:

Albany National Bank

Assets			Liabilities	
Reserves		$11,000	Demand deposits	$110,000
		(−9,000)		(−9,000)
Required	$11,000			
	(−900)			
Excess	0			
	(−8,100)			
Loans		99,000		
Total assets		$110,000	Total liabilities	$110,000
		(−9,000)		(−9,000)

Bethel National Bank

Assets			Liabilities	
Reserves		$19,000	Demand deposits	$109,000
		(+9,000)		(+9,000)
Required	$10,900			
	(+900)			
Excess	$8,100			
	(+8,100)			
Loans		90,000		
Total assets		$109,000	Total liabilities	$109,000
		(+9,000)		(+9,000)

A careful look at these balance sheets reveals two important things. First, we see clearly why the Albany National Bank could not safely loan out more than its initial $9,000 of excess reserves. The bank knew that the $9,000 deposit it created by writing the loan to Anderson would not stay on its books for long. As soon as the check cleared, $9,000 of deposits and reserves would be lost (unless the seller of the car also kept an account at Albany). The loss of $9,000 in deposits lowered its required reserves by only $900 (10 percent of the change in deposits), so that the $8,100 of excess reserves was needed to make up the difference.

Second, we see that Albany's loss is Bethel's gain. Albany lost $9,000 in reserves ($900 required and $8,100 excess) when the check was written and cleared, and Bethel gained exactly the same amounts. The process of clearing the check thus leaves the total reserves of the banking system unchanged.

Keeping the expansion going with another loan   The clearing of Anderson's check put the Albany National Bank back in equilibrium, with $10,000 more in total assets and $10,000 more in liabilities than it started with. But now Bethel is out of equilibrium, with $8,100 in excess reserves. The logical thing for Bethel to do is to make a loan of its own, using its excess reserves. We know now that the proceeds of this loan will be checked away quickly, so we will skip the intermediate balance sheet. After Bethel's borrower has written a check for $8,100, which is deposited in, say, the Cooperstown National Bank, Bethel's and Cooperstown's balance sheets will look like this:

Bethel National Bank

Assets			Liabilities	
Reserves		$10,900 (−8,100)	Demand deposits	$109,000
Required	$10,900 (unchanged)			
Excess	0 (−8,100)			
Loans		98,100 (+8,100)		
Total assets		$109,000 (+8,100)	Total liabilities	$109,000 (+8,100)

Cooperstown National Bank

Assets			Liabilities	
Reserves		$18,000 (+8,100)	Demand deposits	$108,100 (+8,100)
Required	$10,810 (+810)			
Excess	$7,290 (+7,290)			
Loans		90,000		
Total assets		$108,100 (+8,100)	Total liabilities	$108,100 (+8,100)

Further rounds in the expansion of deposits   We do not need to go through all the rounds of the expansion process in detail, since a clear pattern has emerged. The initial open-market purchase of securities by the Fed injected $10,000 of new reserves into the system. The first bank to receive the funds kept $1,000 (10 percent) as required reserves and loaned out the remaining $9,000. When the loan proceeds were checked away, they became $9,000 in new deposits and reserves for a second bank, which kept $900 (10 percent) and loaned out the remaining $8,100. This bank in turn would be able to loan out $7,290, the next bank $6,561, and so on round after round. New deposits are created at each round by the loans, so the money supply, made up entirely of deposits, expands by $10,000 + $9,000 + $8,100 + $7,290 + $6,561, and so on. The whole process, which is summarized in Box 11.7, creates $100,000 in new deposits.

If we compare the initial and final balance sheets for the ten banks (shown in the last column of the box), we see that the expansion of the money supply continues until excess reserves are reduced to zero for the banking system as a whole. With a 10 percent required-reserve ratio, this means that deposits must expand by a total of $100,000.

Contraction of the Money Supply

When the Fed withdraws reserves from the banking system, the whole process works in reverse. Assume, for example, that all the banks are back in the position from which they started in the last example and that the Fed decides to withdraw, say, $1,000 in reserves. It can do this by making an open-market sale of $1,000 of securities from its portfolio. Suppose that the securities are bought by Victor Dymowski, who pays for them with a check drawn on the Denver National Bank. When the Fed gets Dymowski's check, it clears it by deducting $1,000 from Denver's reserve account. At that point Denver's balance sheet looks like this:

Denver National Bank

Assets			Liabilities	
Reserves		$9,000	Demand deposits	$99,000
		(−1,000)		(−1,000)
Required	$9,900			
	(−100)			
Excess	−900			
	(−900)			
Loans		90,000		
Total assets		$99,000	Total liabilities	$99,000
		(−1,000)		(−1,000)

The loss of $1,000 in deposits when Dymowski wrote his check reduced required reserves by only $100, whereas Denver's total reserves fell by $1,000 when the Fed cleared the check. This leaves the bank with negative excess reserves, that is, a $900 reserve deficiency. It must act to correct the deficiency.

In the simplified banking system of this example, Denver must make up the deficiency by reducing its loans. It therefore takes the next $900 it

**Box 11.7
Expansion of Deposits
After an Injection of
Reserves**

This table shows, in summary form, the effects of an injection of $10,000 of new reserves into a simplified banking system. The first three sets of balance sheets show the process from the point of view of the first three banks in the deposit expansion chain. The final set of balance sheets shows the starting and ending positions of the ten-bank system as a whole.

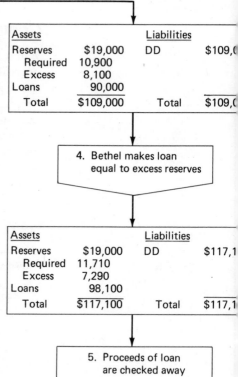

Albany National Bank

Initial Balance Sheet

Assets		Liabilities	
Reserves	$10,000	DD	$100,000
Required	10,000		
Excess	0		
Loans	90,000		
Total	$100,000	Total	$100,000

Bethel National Bank

Assets		Liabilities	
Reserves	$10,000	DD	$100,0
Required	10,000		
Excess	0		
Loans	90,000		
Total	$100,000	Total	$100,0

1. Fed injects $10,000 via open market purchase

After deposit, before loan

Assets		Liabilities	
Reserves	$20,000	DD	$110,000
Required	11,000		
Excess	9,000		
Loans	90,000		
Total	$110,000	Total	$110,000

Assets		Liabilities	
Reserves	$19,000	DD	$109,0
Required	10,900		
Excess	8,100		
Loans	90,000		
Total	$109,000	Total	$109,0

2. Albany makes loan equal to excess reserves

4. Bethel makes loan equal to excess reserves

After loan, before checking away

Assets		Liabilities	
Reserves	$20,000	DD	$119,000
Required	11,900		
Excess	8,100		
Loans	99,000		
Total	$119,000	Total	$119,000

Assets		Liabilities	
Reserves	$19,000	DD	$117,1
Required	11,710		
Excess	7,290		
Loans	98,100		
Total	$117,100	Total	$117,1

3. Proceeds of loan are checked away

5. Proceeds of loan are checked away

Final balance sheet

Assets		Liabilities	
Reserves	$11,000	DD	$110,000
Required	11,000		
Excess	0		
Loans	99,000		
Total	$110,000	Total	$110,000

Assets		Liabilities	
Reserves	$10,900	DD	$109,0
Required	10,900		
Excess	0		
Loans	98,100		
Total	$109,000	Total ·	$109,0

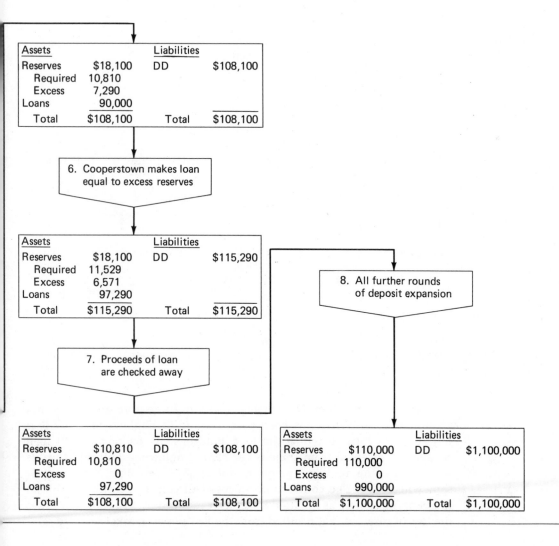

Cooperstown National Bank

Assets		Liabilities	
Reserves	$10,000	DD	$100,000
Required	10,000		
Excess	0		
Loans	90,000		
Total	$100,000	Total	$100,000

Consolidated balance sheet of
entire banking system (10 banks)

Assets		Liabilities	
Reserves	$100,000	DD	$1,000,000
Required	100,000		
Excess	0		
Loans	900,000		
Total	$1,000,000	Total	$1,000,000

Assets		Liabilities	
Reserves	$18,100	DD	$108,100
Required	10,810		
Excess	7,290		
Loans	90,000		
Total	$108,100	Total	$108,100

6. Cooperstown makes loan
equal to excess reserves

Assets		Liabilities	
Reserves	$18,100	DD	$115,290
Required	11,529		
Excess	6,571		
Loans	97,290		
Total	$115,290	Total	$115,290

8. All further rounds
of deposit expansion

7. Proceeds of loan
are checked away

Assets		Liabilities	
Reserves	$10,810	DD	$108,100
Required	10,810		
Excess	0		
Loans	97,290		
Total	$108,100	Total	$108,100

Assets		Liabilities	
Reserves	$110,000	DD	$1,100,000
Required	110,000		
Excess	0		
Loans	990,000		
Total	$1,100,000	Total	$1,100,000

receives in loan payments and deposits the funds in its reserve account. (We assume that if the bank did not have the reserve deficiency, it would make new loans as old ones were paid off, keeping its total loan holdings steady.)

In the real world, a bank with a reserve deficiency has a number of other options. One is to sell other assets, such as government securities. Another is to borrow from a bank that has excess reserves. Still another option is to borrow from the Fed itself. We will return to these options in the next chapter.

When the Denver bank reduces its loan holdings to make up its reserve deficiency, it drains reserves from some other bank in the system. Suppose, for example, that Maria Espinosa writes a check on the Englewood National Bank to pay off $900 that she borrowed from the Denver National Bank. At the moment that the transaction was complete and the check had cleared, the balance sheets of the Denver and Englewood banks would look like this:

Denver National Bank

Assets			Liabilities	
Reserves		$9,900 (+900)	Demand deposits	$99,000
Required	$9,900 (unchanged)			
Excess	0 (+900)			
Loans		89,100 (−900)		
Total assets		$99,000	Total liabilities	$99,000

Englewood National Bank

Assets			Liabilities	
Reserves		$9,100 (−900)	Demand deposits	$99,100 (−900)
Required	$9,910 (−90)			
Excess	−810 (−810)			
Loans		90,000		
Total assets		$99,100 (−900)	Total liabilities	$99,100 (−900)

At this point, then, Denver has made up its reserve deficiency, but $810 of the deficiency has been passed along to Englewood. Now it is Englewood's turn to reduce its loan holdings. By using an $810 loan repayment received from some other bank, Englewood will build up its reserves by the required amount, but a $729 deficiency will appear somewhere else. The contraction process will continue until deposits in the banking system as a whole have been reduced by $10,000—ten times the loss of reserves that resulted from the Fed's open-market security sale.

The Money Multiplier for the Simplified Banking System

As these examples have shown, the total amount of demand deposits that can be held by the banking system depends on the total amount of reserves supplied by the Fed and on the required-reserve ratio. In equation form, with rr standing for the required-reserve ratio, the relationship is as follows:

$$\text{Total demand deposits} = \frac{1}{\text{rr}} \times \text{total reserves}$$

Thus, when total reserves were $100,000, the total money supply (consisting entirely of demand deposits in our example) was $1 million. When the Fed injected $10,000 of new reserves, bringing total reserves to $110,000, the money stock rose by $100,000, to $1.1 million. And when the Fed withdrew $1,000 of reserves through an open-market sale, reducing total reserves to $99,000, the money stock fell by $10,000, to $990,000.

Money multiplier
The ratio of the equilibrium money supply to the total reserves of a banking system.

The term 1/rr in the equation is called the **money multiplier**. It is the ratio of the equilibrium money supply to total reserves. In our simplified banking system, where the required-reserve ratio was 10 percent, the value of the money multiplier was 10. Each injection or withdrawal of reserves by the Fed thus increases or decreases the money supply by ten times the change in reserves.

The next chapter will flesh out this bare outline of the money creation process and the money multiplier. Although a number of details will be added, the basic principles discussed here will still apply.

Summary

1. *Money* is an asset that serves as a means of payment, a store of purchasing power, and a unit of account. Because it can be used directly as a means of payment, and because it has a fixed nominal value, it is said to have *liquidity*.

2. In practice, many kinds of assets have some or all of the features of money. The two assets that fit the definition of money most closely are *currency* (coins and paper money) and *transactions deposits* (checking accounts). Together, these make up the measure of the money supply known as *M1*. *Shares* in *money market mutual funds, repurchase agreements, savings and time deposits,* and certain other assets are nearly as liquid as currency and transactions deposits. When these are added to M1, the result is the measure of the money supply known as *M2*.

3. *Commercial banks* and *thrift institutions* earn a profit by accepting deposits from the public and using the funds to make loans and buy securities. The most important assets of a bank are its *reserves,* which do not earn interest, and its loans and securities, which do earn interest. The liabilities of banks include deposits and other kinds of borrowing.

4. A *fractional-reserve* banking system faces a potential problem in that it uses short-term liabilities, such as deposits, as a basis for longer-term, less liquid assets, such as commercial and mortgage loans. If depositors suddenly decide to withdraw their funds from a bank, it may fail. A bank can also fail because of loan losses or operating losses.

5. A number of government agencies regulate the banking system. These include the Federal

Reserve System and the Federal Deposit Insurance Corporation. Through loans to troubled banks, deposit insurance, and bank inspections, they reduce the risk of bank failures and increase the stability of the banking system.

6. The Fed can inject new reserves into the banking system by buying government securities. It can withdraw reserves from the system by selling government securities. These actions are called open-market operations. They are the chief means of controlling the amount of reserves in the banking system.

7. Transactions deposits are an important part of the money supply. The total amount of transactions deposits in the economy is limited by the amount of reserves available to banks and by the percentage of such deposits that banks are required to hold as reserves. An increase in reserves leads to a multiple expansion of deposits by the banking system. The ratio of the equilibrium money supply to a given amount of total reserves is known as the *money multiplier*.

QUESTIONS FOR REVIEW

1. Define the following terms:
   money
   liquidity
   currency
   transactions deposits
   demand deposits
   commercial banks
   thrift institutions (thrifts)
   M1
   money market mutual fund
   repurchase agreement
   savings deposits
   time deposits
   M2
   reserves
   required reserves
   required-reserve ratio
   excess reserves
   open-market operation
   money multiplier

2. Give examples from your own experience of each of the three functions of money.

3. What forms of money do you own? Do you own any that are part of M1? Any that are part of M2?

4. What are the main items on the assets side of a commercial bank's balance sheet? What are the main items on the liabilities side?

5. How can loan or deposit losses cause a bank to fail? What is meant by a "run" on a bank? What is meant by a "banking panic"?

6. What are the three main policies used to stabilize the U.S. banking system? How well have they worked?

7. How do open-market operations affect the amount of reserves in the banking system? Which type of operation increases bank reserves—an open-market purchase or an open-market sale? Which type decreases bank reserves?

8. Outline the process by which an increase in the total reserves of a simple banking system sets off a multiple expansion of the money supply.

Problems and Topics for Discussion

1. Money serves three functions: It is a means of payment, a store of purchasing power, and a unit of account. How does inflation undermine each of these functions?

2. Look in your library for news articles or other accounts of a country that has experienced very rapid inflation—what is sometimes called *hyperinflation*. Argentina, Brazil, Bolivia, and Israel are recent examples; Germany in the 1920s is a historical example. How did this

experience affect the functions performed by money in that country?

3. For most purposes, money lowers the cost of making transactions compared with barter—the direct exchange of one good or service for another. However, barter has not disappeared, even in an advanced economy like that of the United States. Can you give an example of the use of barter in the U.S. economy today? Why is barter used instead of money in this case?

4. Do you use any credit cards? Does the use of credit cards reduce the amount of money you need? What forms of money do you need less of because you have a credit card?

5. Go to a commercial bank or thrift institution in your area and ask for a copy of a summary balance sheet. (At most banks they are readily available.) How does this balance sheet compare to the balance sheet of all commercial banks given in Box 11.3? Bonus question: Obtain the balance sheets of both a bank and a thrift and compare them.

6. Rework the deposit expansion examples in this chapter on the basis of the following assumptions:
   a. Injection of $5,000 of reserves via an open-market purchase.
   b. Injection of $10,000 of reserves, with a 20 percent instead of a 10 percent required-reserve ratio.
   c. Withdrawal of $500 of reserves via an open-market sale.

7. Every Thursday the Federal Reserve reports certain key data on money and the banking system. These are published in the Friday edition of the *Wall Street Journal* and other major financial newspapers. Find the Federal Reserve report from the *Wall Street Journal* for the most recent Friday, and use it to answer the following questions:
   a. What items are included in M2 that are not included in M1? What was the total of such items in the most recent month for which data are reported? M3 is a money supply measure that includes large-denomination certificates of deposit and long-term repurchase agreements. What is the total of these items? Which of these

money measures grew most quickly in the most recent month for which data are reported?
   b. The tables report key assets and liabilities of the 10 leading New York banks. Demand deposits and other transactions deposits at these banks account for about what percentage of M1?
   c. A rough estimate of the money multiplier for the U.S. banking system as a whole can be obtained by dividing the most recent figure for M1 (not seasonally adjusted) by the most recent figure for the total reserves of the banking system. What is this multiplier?
   d. Given this multiplier, how much could M1 be expanded if banks were to convert all of their excess reserves into earning assets?

8. **Case for Discussion**
   March 1985. Ohio Governor Richard F. Celeste, fearing a run on deposits, Friday declared a three-day "bank holiday" at all state-chartered savings and loan institutions, which are insured by a privately held fund.

   It was the most far-reaching such action since President Franklin D. Roosevelt shut down all the nation's banks during the Great Depression, officials said.

   The run on deposits was precipitated by the closing last week of the Cincinnati-based Home State Savings Association. It closed its doors after suffering severe losses in the collapse of a Florida investment firm, ESM Government Securities Inc.

   Home State's deposits were insured by the Ohio Deposit Guarantee Fund, a privately held, state-regulated firm. The failure of Home State is expected to deplete the entire $130 million fund, leaving other state-chartered savings and loan institutions unprotected.[4]

Questions:
   a. Explain why, if you were a depositor in a privately-insured Ohio savings and loan in March 1985, you might want to withdraw your funds from the institution.
   b. What similarities do you see between the Ohio

---

[4]Bill Peterson, "Ohio Governor's Talks with Bankers Fail to Produce S&L Rescue Plan," *Washington Post*, March 17, 1985, p. A–21. © The Washington Post.

crisis and what might have happened if federal officials had allowed Continental Illinois to fail outright?

c. In the light of this article, comment on the adequacy of federal deposit insurance as a method of ensuring the safety and stability of the banking system.

Suggestions for Further Reading

Board of Governors, Federal Reserve System. *The Federal Reserve System: Purposes and Functions*, 7th ed. Washington, D.C.: Federal Reserve System, 1984.

This useful booklet provides many details on topics covered in this and the following chapters. A copy can be obtained free from Publications Services, Division of Support Services, Board of Governors of the Federal Reserve System, Washington, D.C., 20551.

Campbell, Colin, and Rosemary Campbell. *An Introduction to Money and Banking*, 4th ed. Hinsdale, Ill.: Dryden Press, 1984.

Chapters 1–11 parallel the discussion in this chapter, but in much more detail.

Federal Reserve Bank of New York.
   The Story of Money
   The Story of Checks and Electronic Payments
   The Story of Consumer Credit
   The Story of Banks
   The Story of Inflation

These comic-book-style publications of the Federal Reserve Bank of New York look almost silly—but they pack in a lot of information that textbooks leave out. They are available from the bank's Public Information Department, 33 Liberty Street, New York, NY 10045.

Federal Reserve Bulletin. Monthly.

Each issue contains the most recent monetary data, which can be used to update the boxes in this chapter.

Chapter 12
The Supply and Demand for Money

WHAT YOU WILL LEARN IN THIS CHAPTER

After reading this chapter, you should be able to

1. Explain the equation of exchange and the concept of *velocity*.
2. Show how interest rates and nominal national income affect the demand for money, using the *portfolio balance* theory.
3. Draw a money demand curve and explain the causes of shifts in the curve.
4. List the Fed's three main tools of monetary control and show how each works.
5. Use money supply and demand curves to explain the reaction of the money market to a change in the money supply.
6. Use money supply and demand curves to explain the reaction of the money market to a change in nominal national income.
7. Show how changes in the Fed's monetary control strategy affect the shape of the money supply curve.
8. Trace the response of the money stock and interest rates to changes in money demand under different monetary control strategies.
9. Describe the evolution of the Fed's monetary control strategy.

Ideas for Review

Here are some terms and concepts that you should review before you read this chapter:

Opportunity cost (Chapter 2)
Bond prices, yields, and interest rates (Chapter 4)
Stocks and flows (Chapter 6)
The price level (Chapter 7)
Real and nominal interest rates (Chapter 7)
The Federal Reserve System (Chapter 11)
Creation of money by banks (Chapter 11)

"The money supply soared. . . . Bond prices tumbled. . . . Interest rates rose sharply."

New York, February 1, 1985. Bond prices slumped yesterday amid speculation that the Federal Reserve System is tightening its credit hold in an attempt to stem the recent sharp growth of the money supply.

Fears about Fed policy intensified after the central bank reported that the basic money supply, known as M1, soared $4.7 billion in the week ended January 21. The rise was nearly twice as much as most analysts had expected and left the money measure far above the Fed's target.

Prices of some actively traded U.S. government long-term bonds tumbled about ⅝ point, or about $6.25 for each $1,000 face amount. Interest rates on short-term Treasury bills rose sharply.

Some analysts pointed to a recent climb in the interest rate on federal funds as an indication that the Fed has become less generous in its monetary policy. The funds rate, which is the fee banks charge on loans of reserves to one another, rose to 9 percent at one point yesterday. In the week ended Wednesday, the rate averaged 8.45 percent, up from 8.19 percent the previous week.

"It looks like the Fed may be in the process of tightening its credit policy," said Rudolf Thunberg, an economist at Ried, Thunberg, & Co., a New Canaan, Connecticut, investment advisory firm.[1]

Every Thursday the Fed announces the latest data on changes in the money supply, and every Friday the financial papers are full of stories like this one. Some of the concepts in the story are familiar from the preceding chapter. For example, we know what M1 is and how it is measured. But clearly there is more to learn.

For one thing, we need to look into the connection between monetary policy and interest rates. The *Wall Street Journal* story makes it clear that there is a connection—one that bond traders and business planners pay attention to. In this chapter we will use the tools of supply and demand to analyze the link between monetary policy and interest rates. This will set the stage for the next chapter, in which we will take up the broader relationships among monetary policy and inflation, unemployment, and economic growth.

THE DEMAND FOR MONEY

We begin with the demand for money. In talking about demand for most goods and services, such as watches, radios, or movies, we deal in terms of *flows*—so many watches sold per year, so many radios sold per month, so many movies viewed per week. The case of money is different. Here we are concerned with the demand for a *stock*. The amount of money demanded is the stock of money that people want to possess at a given point in time under given conditions.

---

[1]Edward P. Foldessy and Tom Herman, "Surging Money Supply Sparks Fears of Tighter Credit, Cutting Bond Prices," *Wall Street Journal*, February 1, 1985, p. 31. Reprinted by permission of The Wall Street Journal, © Dow Jones & Company, Inc. 1985. All rights reserved.

Early Views of the Demand for Money

Equation of exchange
An equation that shows the relationships among the money stock (M), the velocity of money (V), the price level (P), and the level of real income (y), written $MV = Py$.

Velocity
The ratio of nominal national income to the money stock; a measure of the average number of times each dollar of the money stock is used each year for income-producing purposes.

One early view of the demand for money arose from the so-called **equation of exchange**. This equation can be written in the form

$$MV = Py$$

where M stands for the quantity of money, V for the **velocity** of money (that is, the average number of times each dollar of the money stock is spent each year for income-producing purposes), P for the price level, and y for real national income. This equation must always hold, given the way the term *velocity* is defined. Suppose, for example, that real national income is $1,000 billion in constant dollars and that the price level is 2. Nominal national income thus will be $2 \times $1,000 billion, or $2,000 billion per year. If each dollar is spent for income-producing purposes an average of five times a year, a money stock of $400 billion will be required to sustain the $2,000-billion-per-year nominal national income. Sustaining that income with a smaller money stock would require each dollar to be used more than five times a year. If the money stock is larger, the same level of nominal national income can be sustained with a velocity of less than five. In short, the stock of money times the velocity of money must always, because of the way *velocity* is defined, equal nominal income (real income times the price level).

The equation of exchange itself is not a theory; it simply shows the relationships among money, velocity, real income, and the price level. An early step toward a theory of the demand for money, however, was to assume that velocity is a constant. This constant number of times that each dollar could be spent each year was thought to be determined by custom and certain other factors, such as how often workers were paid and how fast banks could clear checks. With velocity constant, the amount of money required to sustain any given level of nominal national income could be found by dividing nominal national income by velocity. In equation form, using MD to stand for money demand, Py to stand for nominal income, and V to stand for velocity, this theory of money demand could be written as follows:

$$MD = \frac{Py}{V}$$

Keynes on the Demand for Money

When John Maynard Keynes began work on his *General Theory of Employment, Interest, and Money*, he was not content with the simple view that the demand for money would be proportional to nominal income because equilibrium velocity was constant. Instead, he developed a more complex theory based on three motives for holding money.

Keynes called the need to hold money as a means of payment the *transactions motive*. Besides holding money for day-to-day purchases, people may also hold some extra money to deal with unexpected events. Keynes called this the *precautionary motive* for holding money. He believed that both the transactions and the precautionary motives were roughly proportional to nominal income, as in the equation of exchange.

Keynes also believed that people had a third motive for holding money, one that was somewhat different from the other two. People may want to hold part of their wealth in the form of money, Keynes said, if they think other forms of wealth are temporarily too risky. Suppose, for example, that interest rates are unusually low. As we saw in Chapter 4, an unusually low level of interest rates implies unusually high prices for bonds. Under these conditions people may hesitate to hold bonds for fear that their prices will fall. Thus, when bond prices are unusually high, Keynes suggested, people may prefer to hold much of their wealth in the form of money, hoping to exchange the money for bonds after interest rates rise and the price of bonds falls. Keynes call this the *speculative motive* for holding money.

In sum, Keynes thought that the demand for money depends both on the level of nominal income and on nominal interest rates. As nominal income rises, other things being equal, the demand for money will increase because of the transactions and precautionary motives. But given the level of nominal national income, the speculative motive will tend to make the quantity of money demanded increase as nominal interest rates fall and to make it decrease as nominal interest rates rise.

The Portfolio Balance Theory of Money Demand

Portfolio
A person or firm's collection of assets.

Today most economists accept the notion that the demand for money responds to changes in both nominal national income and interest rates. Keynes' three-way classification of motives for holding money is widely viewed as too rigid, however, and his concept of the link between interest and money demand is seen as too narrow. Today the demand for money is often explained in terms of the importance of liquidity to holders of a balanced *portfolio* of assets. (Economists use the word **portfolio**—meaning a case for carrying papers—as a shorthand term for all of a person's assets, including money, stocks, bonds, real estate, and so on.)

An asset is said to be liquid, we recall, if it can be used directly as a means of exchange and if it has a fixed nominal value. There are thus two potential advantages to holding a liquid asset such as money instead of less liquid assets such as stocks, bonds, or real estate. The first advantage is that liquidity reduces transactions costs. One doesn't want to have to make a trip to a bank or a broker each week in order to exchange stocks or bonds for money to buy groceries. The second advantage of holding liquid assets is that one can avoid the risk of loss of nominal value that is associated with less liquid assets.

The opportunity cost of liquidity   The advantage of liquidity is offset by a major disadvantage: More liquid assets tend to pay less interest. Currency and demand deposits pay no interest at all. NOW accounts and other interest-bearing transactions deposits included in M1 pay some interest, but not as much as less liquid assets. Some of the assets included in M2, such as money market mutual funds and overnight repurchase agreements, pay higher interest than transactions deposits and are almost as liquid. But even these assets tend to pay a smaller return than some others, such as stocks or long-term bonds, when yields are averaged over a long period. Thus, loss of the higher interest rates available on other assets is an opportunity cost of holding money, to be weighed against money's liquidity value.

Nominal and real interest rates   To be precise, we should say that it is the higher *nominal* rates of interest that measure the opportunity cost of holding non-interest-bearing forms of money. The nominal interest rate, it will be recalled, is the rate stated in the usual way, in terms of current-dollar interest payments per dollar of principal, whereas the real interest rate is the nominal rate minus the rate of inflation.

A simple example will show why the nominal interest rate is the correct measure of the opportunity cost of holding money. Suppose that the nominal interest rate on, say, long-term bonds is 10 percent and the inflation rate is zero. Under these conditions a person who holds currency or some other non-interest-bearing form of money maintains a constant level of purchasing power but earns zero real return. A person who holds a bond earns a real rate of return equal to the assumed 10 percent nominal rate of interest. On the other hand, suppose that when the nominal rate of interest is 10 percent the inflation rate is 6 percent. Under these conditions the bondholder earns only a 4 percent real rate of return, but the person holding currency loses real purchasing power at the rate of 6 percent per year. The difference between the real return on bonds and the real return on money is 10 percent in either case. Thus, regardless of the rate of inflation, the nominal interest rate correctly measures the opportunity cost of holding non-interest-bearing money. For interest-bearing forms of money such as NOW accounts, the opportunity cost is the difference between the nominal rate of interest paid on a representative nonmonetary asset (say, a government bond) and the nominal rate earned on the interest-bearing form of money.

A Money Demand Schedule

In the portfolio balance theory of money demand, the amount of money that people want to hold depends on both their nominal income and the family of nominal interest rates on nonmonetary assets. Other things being equal, an increase in nominal national income increases the demand for money. This is because with higher incomes people will make more transactions, and they will need more money if they are to do so conveniently. At the same time, other things being equal, an increase in the nominal interest rate will decrease the amount of money demanded. The reason is that an increase in the nominal interest rate increases the opportunity cost of holding money.[2]

The relationship of the amount of money demanded to the interest rate and the level of nominal national income for a simple economy is shown in Box 12.1. The entries in the table give the amount of money

---

[2]This statement needs some modification in the case of interest-bearing forms of money. In order for an increase in nominal interest rates on nonmonetary assets to increase the opportunity cost of holding interest-bearing forms of money, such as NOW accounts, their rates must rise by less than market rates. This happens partly because until 1986 some interest-bearing forms of money were subject to legal ceilings on interest that can be paid, and partly because even when banks are free to vary the interest rates on these deposits, they tend to raise them by only a fraction of the increase in market rates.

**Box 12·1
A Money Demand
Schedule for a Simple
Economy**

The table and graph show how the amount of money demanded varies in a simple economy as the nominal interest rate on a representative nonmonetary asset and the level of nominal national income vary. The entries in the body of the table show the amount of money demanded at the nominal interest rate that corresponds to the row and at the nominal national income that corresponds to the column. Each column in the table can be graphed to get a money demand curve for a given level of nominal national income. MD_1 corresponds to the fourth column, and MD_2 to the last column. All dollar figures are in billions.

(a)

Nominal Interest Rate (percent)	Level of Nominal National Income					
	$200	$400	$600	$800	$1,000	$1,200
2	$120	$240	$360	$480	$600	$720
4	60	120	180	240	300	360
6	40	80	120	160	200	240
8	30	60	90	120	150	180
10	24	48	72	96	120	144
12	20	40	60	80	100	120
14	17	34	51	68	85	102
16	15	30	45	60	75	90

(b)

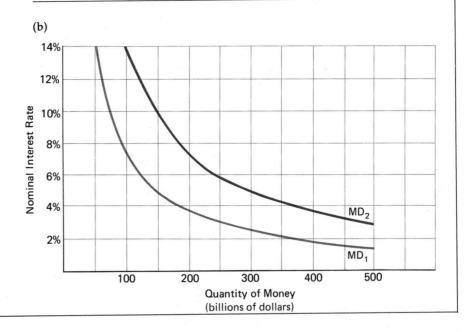

demanded when the interest rate is as shown at the left-hand border of the table and the level of nominal national income is as shown at the top of the table. For example, when the interest rate is 10 percent per year and the level of nominal national income is $600 billion, the amount of money demanded is $72 billion.

Box 12.1 also presents the money demand schedule in graphic form. At any given level of income, the relationship between the amount of money demanded and the interest rate takes the form of a downward-sloping curve that looks much like any other demand curve. For example, the curve labeled MD_1 shows the way money demand varies as the interest rate varies when nominal national income is $600 billion. This curve is based on the data in the $600 billion column of the table. A change in the level of income will produce a shift in the money demand curve. For example, if income increases to $1,200 billion, the money demand curve will shift to the position labeled MD_2. The data given in the last column of the table show that when income doubles, the amount of money demanded at any given interest rate also doubles.

The Stability of Money Demand

The money demand curve in Box 12.1 shifts when the level of nominal national income changes, but other factors can also cause it to shift. In order to focus on the other factors that affect money demand, the curve is sometimes redrawn as shown in Box 12.2, where the horizontal axis shows the ratio of money to nominal national income. A change in nominal national income (equivalent to moving across a row of the table in Box 12.1) does not cause this income-adjusted money demand curve to shift. Other things might do so, however. Changes in the payment practices of businesses are one thing that could shift the curve. The curve can also be shifted by the introduction of new types of bank deposits. For example, the

Box 12.2
An Income-Adjusted
Money Demand Curve

The money demand curve is sometimes drawn in an income-adjusted form, as shown here. The horizontal axis in this graph shows the quantity of money demanded per dollar of nominal national income. A change in nominal national income will not cause this curve to shift, but shifts may be caused by changes in payments practices of businesses or by changes in banking regulations, such as the introduction of new types of accounts or the removal of interest ceilings on existing types of accounts.

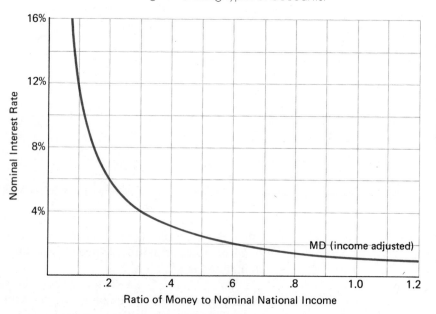

introduction of super-NOW accounts, paying higher interest rates than ordinary NOW accounts, attracted funds into M1 from other liquid assets. On the other hand, the introduction of money market deposit accounts (MMDAs), which have attractive interest rates and limited checking privileges, had an opposite effect. Because MMDAs are counted as part of M2, funds shifted to them from transactions deposits reduced the demand for M1. In general, anything that reduces people's desired ratio of money to income at a given interest rate will cause the income-adjusted money demand curve to shift to the left. Anything that increases this ratio will cause the curve to shift to the right.[3]

Box 12.3 presents data for the U.S. economy that show that the income-adjusted M1 demand curve has shifted to the left over the past two decades. Three patterns of connected points, for 1961–1970, 1971–1974, and 1975–1984, show that for given interest rates, less money is needed per dollar of nominal GNP now than in the past.

**Box 12.3
Shifts in Money
Demand, 1961–1984**

This box shows the link between income-adjusted money demand (M1 divided by nominal national income) and the nominal interest rate (the rate on three-month Treasury bills) from 1961 to 1984. The three groups of points for 1961–1970, 1971–1974, and 1975–1984 show a leftward shift in the money demand curve over time. This indicates that households and firms have found ways to conduct their business using less money for a given nominal volume of transactions.

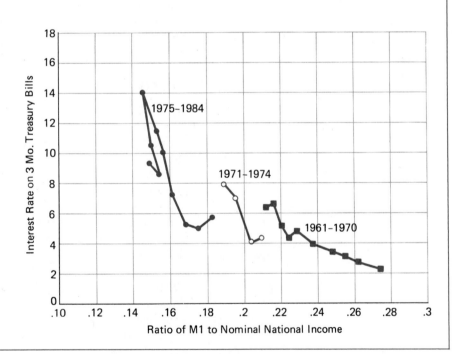

---

[3]Instead of speaking in terms of the desired ratio of money to income, we could speak in terms of velocity, which is the ratio of income to money. We would then say that anything that increases velocity (for a given interest rate) shifts the income-adjusted money demand curve to the left, and anything that reduces velocity shifts the demand curve to the right.

Several factors have been suggested to explain this pattern. First, it has probably been caused in part by the growing popularity of highly liquid M1 substitutes, such as money market mutual funds, MMDAs, and repurchase agreements. Second, the shifts may also have reflected changes in cash management practices. During the mid-1970s and again in the early 1980s, interest rates rose to new highs. As this happened, firms found new ways to invest their liquid funds for short periods, thus avoiding the opportunity cost of holding large demand deposit balances. Finally, the shifts have been brought about in part through wider use of computerized financial information systems, which allow firms to keep closer track of their funds.

Besides the long-term shifts shown, there have been shorter-term shifts to the right or left in money demand as well. Such short-term shifts in money demand can be hard to predict and are not always easy to explain.

THE SUPPLY OF MONEY

We turn now from the demand for money to the supply of money. The supply of money is subject to control by the Federal Reserve System. Twice a year the Fed announces target ranges for the growth of various money measures for the coming year. Its chief monetary policy-making body, the Federal Open Market Committee (FOMC), meets about eight times a year to set shorter-term goals for the money stock that are consistent with the targets. In this section we will look at the policy tools that the Fed uses to achieve the goals it sets for the money supply and at some of the problems it may encounter in meeting its goals.

Tools of Monetary Policy

As we saw in Chapter 11, the bulk of the money stock (in the narrow sense of M1) consists of transactions deposits at banks and thrift institutions. The Fed is able to control the volume of transactions deposits by means of three policy tools: open-market operations, changes in required-reserve ratios, and changes in the interest rate that it charges when lending reserves to banks. Let's look briefly at each of these.

Open-market operations   Open-market operations were described in Chapter 10. If the Fed wants to expand the money supply, it instructs the open-market trading desk at the Federal Reserve Bank of New York to buy government securities. This is known as an open-market purchase. The Fed pays for the securities with a check that it writes on its own account. When the person or firm selling the securities deposits the check in a bank, those funds are added to the reserves of the banking system. And each dollar of reserves added to the banking system permits the volume of transactions deposits to expand by several dollars. The ratio of the money stock to total reserves is known as the money multiplier.

If the Fed wants to decrease the money supply, it reverses this process. It instructs the trading desk to carry out an open-market sale of securities. If a member of the public buys securities from the Fed and pays for them with a check written on a commercial bank or thrift institution, reserves are drained from the banking system. The money supply contracts by an amount equal to the money multiplier times the size of the open-market sale.

Changes in the discount rate   Open-market operations are the main source of new reserves for the banking system, but they are not the only one. Banks also have the right to borrow reserves from the Fed through the so-called **discount window** (which, needless to say, is a department of the Fed, not an actual window).

Banks borrow reserves from the Fed in two kinds of situations. Most often they borrow reserves when unexpected withdrawals have left them with less than the required quantity of reserves. Banks are discouraged from borrowing too often or too much, however. To balance their reserves and reserve requirements on a day-to-day basis, banks that have a temporary shortage of reserves can borrow from banks that have a temporary surplus of reserves. The market in which banks borrow and lend reserves among themselves is known as the **federal funds market**, and the rate of interest that prevails in this market is known as the **federal funds rate**.

In addition to short-term loans from the discount window, the Fed sometimes makes larger, longer-term loans to troubled banks to give them time to get their affairs in order. Its huge loan to Continental Illinois Bank and Trust in the spring of 1984 (see Box 11.6, p. 274) is a case in point.

The interest rate that the Fed charges on loans made through the discount window—known as the **discount rate**—is a second policy tool that can be used to control the money supply. If the Fed wants to encourage banks to borrow reserves through the discount window, it lowers the discount rate relative to the federal funds rate. With funds at the discount window relatively cheap, total borrowed reserves tend to expand. If the Fed wants to discourage borrowing from the discount window, it raises the discount rate relative to the federal funds rate. This makes the discount window less attractive as a source of funds, so total borrowed reserves fall.

Changes in required-reserve ratios   Changes in required-reserve ratios are a third policy tool that the Fed has sometimes used to control the money supply. In Chapter 11 we showed that the total volume of transactions deposits in a simplified banking system was determined by the formula

$$\text{Total transactions deposits} = \frac{1}{\text{rr}} \times \text{total reserves}$$

where rr stands for the required-reserve ratio. It follows that any reduction in the required-reserve ratio will increase the money supply that can be supported by a given quantity of reserves. Likewise, an increase in the required-reserve ratio will decrease the money supply for a given quantity of reserves.

In the past, although changes in required-reserve ratios were never used for day-to-day control over the money supply, the Fed sometimes

Discount window
The department through which the Federal Reserve lends reserves to banks.

Federal funds market
A market in which banks lend reserves to one another for periods as short as 24 hours.

Federal funds rate
The interest rate charged by banks for overnight loans of reserves to one another.

Discount rate
The interest rate charged by the Fed on loans of reserves to banks.

changed the ratios when it wanted to make a strong move toward expansion or contraction of the money supply. For example, during the severe recession of 1974-1975 the Fed lowered reserve requirements three times.

The Monetary Control Act of 1980 broadened the coverage of the Fed's required-reserve ratios. Before the act was passed, the Fed could set such ratios only for member commercial banks. Once the reserve provisions of the act are fully phased in, in late 1987, the Fed will be able to set reserve requirements on transactions deposits at all but the smallest depository institutions. By law the Fed can adjust the required reserve ratio within a range of 8 to 14 percent for institutions with transactions deposits over a certain amount. It can also impose supplemental reserve requirements on transactions deposits under some conditions. The Fed can also impose a required reserve ratio of no more than 3 percent on nonpersonal time deposits at institutions above a minimum size.

In practice, however, certain technicalities of the eight-year phase-in of the new reserve requirements have dissuaded the Fed from changing the ratios as a policy tool, at least for the time being. Whether the Fed will return to active use of this tool after 1987 is not known at this time.

Limits on the Fed's Control of the Money Supply

In the simplified banking system described in Chapter 11, the Fed's control over the money supply was direct and complete. In the real world things are not quite so simple. For a number of reasons, the Fed does not have complete control over the money supply.

Some of the limits on the Fed's ability to control the money supply stem from unpredictable variations in the money multiplier. In the simplified banking system, the money multiplier was equal to one divided by the required-reserve ratio. In the real world, however, the money multiplier can vary from month to month even if no changes are made in required-reserve ratios, as Box 12.4 shows.

One source of variation in the money multiplier is the fact that required-reserve ratios vary from one type of deposit to another, and from one kind of bank to another. As a result, when funds are withdrawn from one bank and deposited in another, moving reserves move from one bank to another, the average required-reserve ratio for the system changes. This, in turn, changes the money multiplier. Full phase-in of the Monetary Control Act of 1980 will make this source of variation smaller than in the past.

Another source of variation in the money multiplier is changes in the way the public divides its holdings of M1 between currency and transactions deposits. As Chapter 10 showed, currency accounts for nearly 30 percent of M1. If people decide to increase their holdings of currency, the ratio of M1 to total reserves will rise even if the ratio of transactions deposits to total reserves remains constant. Finally, changes in the level of excess reserves held by banks can affect the ratio of deposits to total reserves, and hence affect the money multiplier.

The level of total reserves, like the money multiplier, is subject to disturbances that cannot be predicted exactly. This adds another factor

**Box 12.4
Variations in the Money
Multiplier**

As this chart shows, the money multiplier, here measured as the ratio of M1 to total reserves, is subject to variations from month to month. Some, but not all, of the variations in the money multiplier can be predicted. The Fed can neutralize the effects of predictable variations in the money multiplier by making offsetting changes in the level of total reserves. However, unpredicted changes in the multiplier will cause the money stock to depart from its desired level.

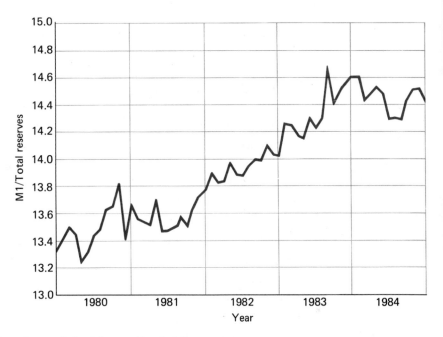

Source: Federal Reserve Board of Governors.

limiting the Fed's ability to control the money supply precisely. For one thing, changes in the public's holdings of currency relative to transactions deposits can affect the level of total reserves at the same time that they affect the money multiplier. In addition, total reserves can be affected by receipts and expenditures of the U.S. Treasury and financial operations of foreign governments.

INTEREST RATES AND THE MONEY MARKET

The last two sections have discussed the demand and supply of money separately. In this section and the next one we will put supply and demand together. The result is a graph like that shown in Box 12.5. The horizontal axis shows the stock of money, measured in dollars. The vertical axis shows the nominal interest rate as a percent per year. The nominal interest rate is the "price" of holding money—or, as explained earlier, the opportunity cost of holding part of a portfolio of assets in the form of non-interest-bearing money rather than in the form of a representative nonmonetary interest-bearing asset.

**Box 12.5
Equilibrium in the
Money Market**

The money demand curve shown here is based on the data given in Box 12.1, assuming a nominal national income of $1,200 billion. The money supply curve assumes that the Fed sets a money supply target of $180 billion and adjusts total reserves to maintain this quantity of money regardless of what happens to interest rates. Under these conditions, the equilibrium interest rate is 8 percent.

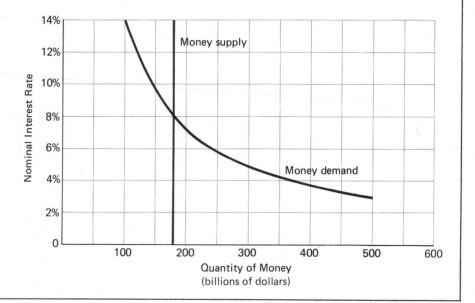

The money demand curve in Box 12.5 shows the amount of money that people want to hold at each given interest rate. An increase in nominal national income will shift the money demand curve to the right; a decrease in nominal national income will shift it to the left. Other factors, such as changes in payments practices, can also cause the demand curve to shift, as we have seen.

The shape of the money supply curve depends on the policy of the Federal Reserve. The supply curve in Box 12.5 assumes that the Fed sets a target for the money stock ($180 billion in this case) and adjusts reserves to hold the money stock on target regardless of what happens to the nominal interest rate. This assumption results in a vertical money supply curve. (In the last section of this chapter we will discuss other kinds of money supply curves.)

We will refer to the supply-and-demand situation shown in Box 12.5 as the "money market," but it should be understood that this is not a market in quite the usual sense. We usually think of a market as a place where people buy and sell things, that is, exchange things for money. They do not "buy" and "sell" money in this sense. Also, the vertical axis in this market does not show the price of money relative to the price of something else. Instead, it shows the opportunity cost of holding money as measured by the nominal interest rate. Despite these unusual features, supply and demand do interact in the so-called money market to produce an equilibrium much as they do in markets of the more familiar kind.

Equilibrium in the Money Market

The supply and demand curves in Box 12.5 intersect at an interest rate of 8 percent. At that interest rate, the amount of money supplied by the banking system (which is determined, in turn, by the amount of reserves supplied by the Fed to the banking system) is just equal to the amount that people want to hold in their portfolios. There is neither upward nor downward pressure on interest rates.

No other interest rate would permit such an equilibrium. Suppose, for example, that the interest rate were just 4 percent. With the opportunity cost of money so low, people would want to hold more of it. Any one person or firm can add money to a portfolio by selling something else—stocks, bonds, Treasury bills, or real goods. Take bonds as an example. If many people try to sell bonds for money at the same time, the price of bonds will tend to fall. As Chapter 4 explained, a fall in the price of bonds means an increase in the yield on bonds. If people were trying to sell other kinds of assets to get money, yields on those assets would rise too. In time, the whole family of interest rates would rise to the level corresponding to 8 percent on the vertical axis of Box 12.5. Then the money market would be back in equilibrium.

Note that as Box 12.5 is drawn, a rising interest rate brings the market back into equilibrium by reducing the amount of money demanded, not by increasing the amount of money supplied. As long as the Fed does not provide more reserves to the banking system, banks cannot supply any more money. Even though any one person can add money to his or her portfolio by selling some other asset, this does not affect the amount of money in the banking system as a whole. It just moves reserves from the buyer's bank to the seller's bank.

Exactly the same story can be told in reverse for the case in which the interest rate is higher than its equilibrium value. In that case people will want to hold less money. They will try to get rid of money by buying other assets. This will drive up the price of those assets and will drive interest rates down. But as long as the Fed keeps the total reserves of the banking system constant, this buying and selling only moves money from one bank to another. It does not change the money stock as a whole.

The process of reaching an equilibrium in the money market is closely connected to the process of reaching an equilibrium in other financial markets. In those markets, as explained in Chapter 7, funds flow from savers to borrowers in the form of loans and in exchange for securities. Purchases of newly issued securities by savers and purchases of existing securities by people who want to adjust their portfolios of assets by exchanging money for securities take place at the same prices. Thus the family of interest rates that establishes an equilibrium in the financial markets discussed in Chapter 7 also establishes equilibrium in the money market.

Effects of a Change in the Money Supply

The description we have given of the money market is useful for a number of purposes. Let's begin by using it to analyze the effects of changes in the money supply.

Box 12.6 shows the money market in equilibrium at E_1 with a money supply of $180 billion and an interest rate of 8 percent. Starting from this point, the Fed decides to increase the money supply to $360 billion. Assuming a money multiplier of 10, it can do this by injecting $18 billion of new reserves into the banking system by means of open-market purchases.

The immediate impact of the open-market operation is to boost banks' excess reserves. In order to restore their balance sheets to equilibrium, banks set out to convert the excess reserves into earning assets. In part, this means buying securities. The increased demand for securities pushes up their price and pushes down their yield. The banks also convert their excess reserves into earning assets by making new loans. Competition among banks in making loans tends to push down interest rates on loans.

As banks work off their excess reserves, the money supply expands, as explained in Chapter 11. In Box 12.6 this is shown as a shift in the money supply curve from MS_1 to MS_2. At E_1 people were content to hold the old quantity of money, $180 billion, in their portfolios. Now falling interest rates reduce the opportunity cost of holding money and make people willing to absorb the increased quantity that banks supply. Thus, as the injection of reserves shifts the money supply curve to the right, falling interest rates cause people to move downward and to the right along their money demand curve. In time a new equilibrium is reached at E_2, where the stock of money is greater and the interest rate is lower than before.

**Box 12.6
Effects of an Increase in
the Money Supply**

The money supply starts out at $180 billion, putting the money supply curve in the position MS_1. An open-market purchase by the Fed injects new reserves into the banking system. Efforts by banks to put the new reserves to work by buying securities and making loans drive the interest rate down as the money supply expands. At the new equilibrium, E_2, the interest rate has fallen by enough to make people willing to hold the larger quantity of money.

If the Fed withdraws reserves from the banking system through an open-market sale, the same process happens in reverse. Banks find themselves with less than the required quantity of reserves. They respond by selling securities or reducing their volume of loans—actions that tend to raise the interest rate. As the money supply curve shifts to the left, rising interest rates make people content to hold only the reduced quantity of money in their portfolios. A new equilibrium is reached in which the money supply is smaller and the interest rate higher than before.

Effects of an Increase in Income

In discussing the effects of a change in the money supply, we assumed that the level of nominal national income stayed constant. Let's reverse that assumption and see what happens to the money market when nominal national income changes while the money supply remains constant.

Box 12.7 sets the stage. It shows the market in equilibrium at E_1 with an interest rate of 8 percent and a money supply of $180 billion. Nominal national income is assumed to be $600 billion, which puts the money demand curve in the position MD_1.

Assume now that nominal national income rises to a level of $1,200 billion. As we saw earlier in the chapter, an increase in nominal national income, other things being equal, shifts the money demand curve to the right. The new position of the money demand curve is MD_2.

Box 12.7
Effects of an Increase in Nominal National Income

A nominal national income of $600 billion puts the money demand curve at MD_1. The equilibrium nominal interest rate is 4 percent, given this income and the money supply of $180 billion. If an increase in nominal income to $1,200 billion shifts the money demand curve to MD_2, there will be an excess demand for money at the initial interest rate. People will try to increase the quantity of money in their portfolios by selling other assets. In the process, the prices of those assets are bid down and interest rates rise.

At the new, higher income level, people will be making a greater volume of transactions than before. Other things being equal, they would want more money to carry out the extra transactions—but the supply of money is limited to $180 billion by Federal Reserve policy. Because banks are not supplying more money to support the higher income, people try to get the extra money by selling other assets. This does not increase the money supply as a whole, but it does drive up interest rates. The higher interest rates make people willing to get along with the limited money supply that is available, despite the fact that their incomes are now higher. Thus, the economy moves to a new equilibrium at E_2. There, nominal national income and the nominal interest rate are higher than before and the money supply has not changed.

If nominal national income falls, the same process occurs in reverse. With lower incomes, people do not need as much money. They buy other assets to replace money in their portfolios. Doing this tends to push interest rates down. When interest rates fall enough to make people content to hold the existing stock of money even at a lower level of nominal national income, the money market will be back in equilibrium. The interest rate will be lower than before; nominal national income will be lower; and the money supply will be unchanged.

MONETARY CONTROL STRATEGIES AND INTEREST RATES[4]

Our analysis of the money market suggests that traders in the bond and stock market—and anyone who is interested in interest rates—need to pay attention to what the Fed is doing. In this section, we shift our point of view from that of private individuals and firms to that of the Fed.

Exactly what role interest rates should play in planning and carrying out monetary policy is a matter of considerable debate. Some economists believe that the Fed's job is to keep the money supply under control; having done that, it should let interest rates go wherever the market sends them. Other economists, along with many businesspeople, think that part of the Fed's job should be to prevent sharp ups and downs in interest rates. Large swings in interest rates, they say, can disrupt business planning, thus hurting employment and productivity. In this section we will explore three different strategies of monetary control and their relationship to interest rates.

Three Monetary Control Strategies

Box 12.8 shows three possible monetary control strategies, each represented by a different money supply curve. The first strategy is one of strict money supply targeting. This is the strategy that was assumed in the last section: the Fed selects a target for the money supply and adjusts the level of bank reserves to maintain the money supply at that level regardless of what happens to interest rates. This strategy is represented by the vertical money supply curve, MS_1. With the money demand curve in the position MD, a money supply of $200 billion would, as shown, result in an equilibrium interest rate of 8 percent.

---

[4]This section can be omitted in an abbreviated course.

**Box 12.8
Three Monetary Control
Strategies**

The slope of the money supply curve depends on the Fed's monetary control strategy. The Fed can set a target for the money supply and stick to it regardless of what happens to interest rates. In this case the money supply curve will be vertical (MS_1). Instead, the Fed can set a target for the interest rate and use open-market operations to stabilize the rate (at least in the short run) regardless of what happens to the money stock. In this case the money supply curve is horizontal (MS_2). Finally, the Fed can allow the money supply to expand as the interest rate rises. This results in an upward-sloping money supply curve (MS_3).

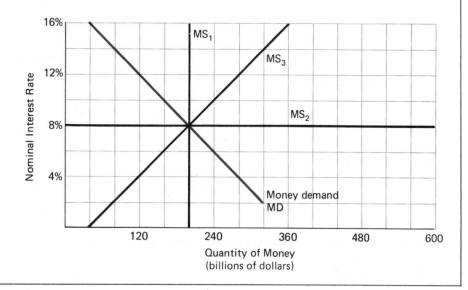

The second strategy is one of interest rate targeting. In this strategy the Fed begins by deciding what it would like the nominal interest rate to be. It then uses open-market operations to adjust the money supply so that the equilibrium interest rate will be at the target level. This strategy is represented by a horizontal money supply curve. If the interest rate target is 8 percent, the money supply curve will be in the position MS_2. Given the money demand curve MD, the Fed would have to allow the money stock to settle at $200 billion to hit the 8 percent target. If the money demand curve were to shift to the right or left, the Fed would use open-market purchases or sales to adjust the money stock along the path MS_2.

The third strategy is the one represented by MS_3. In this case the Fed does not target either the money supply or the interest rate. Instead, it allows the money supply to expand whenever the interest rate rises, but not to expand enough to offset the rise in the interest rate completely.

Responses to Changes in Money Demand

The economy's money demand curve, as we have seen, is subject to shifts from time to time. Changes in nominal income are one major source of such shifts. Institutional changes, such as the introduction of new types of transactions deposits, are another source. Short-term shifts that are hard to predict or explain also take place. The response of the money market to shifts in money demand under each of the three monetary control strategies is shown in Box 12.9.

The first case—that of a strict money supply target—has already been discussed. When the money demand curve shifts from MD_1 to MD_2, there is an excess demand for money at the initial interest rate of 8 percent. People try to obtain more money by selling other assets. This pushes down the price of those assets and pushes up interest rates, but as long as the Fed does not supply more reserves to the banking system, the money supply as a whole cannot increase. A new equilibrium is reached at E_1, with an interest rate of 12 percent. This response is similar to the one shown in Box 12.7.

Next consider the effects of a shift in the money demand curve when the Fed is following a strategy of interest rate targeting. This strategy corresponds to the money supply curve MS_2. Again assume that the money demand curve shifts from MD_1 to MD_2. As before, the initial effect is an excess demand for money, which puts upward pressure on interest rates. Now, however, the Fed's reaction is different. The traders at the Fed's open-market desk in New York have been instructed to keep an eye on interest rates. Above all, they watch the federal funds rate. This, the rate that banks charge each other for overnight loans of reserves, is the first to respond to changes in money supply and demand.

As soon as the excess demand for money starts to push up the federal

Box 12.9
Response of the Money Market to Demand Shifts Under Different Control Strategies

This box shows the effects of shifts in the demand for money under different monetary control strategies. With a strict money supply target (MS_1), an increase in the demand for money moves the market from E_0 to E_1. The interest rate rises, but the money stock does not. With an interest rate target (MS_2), the shift in demand moves the market from E_0 to E_2. In this case the money stock increases but the interest rate does not. Finally, in the intermediate case (MS_3) the economy moves from E_0 to E_3. In this case the increased demand for money causes both the money stock and the interest rate to rise.

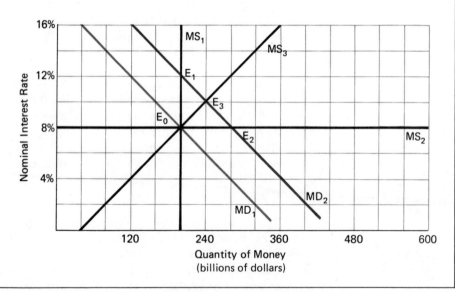

funds rate, the Fed's traders begin buying securities in the open market. As explained in Chapter 11, this increases the total reserves of the banking system. The increase in reserves relieves the upward pressure on interest rates. And as banks expand deposits on the basis of the new reserves, the money supply grows. The result of this whole process is a movement rightward along the money supply curve MS_2 to a new equilibrium at E_2. In the new equilibrium, the money supply has increased to $280 billion and the interest rate is unchanged at 8 percent.

Finally, consider the third strategy, represented by the money supply curve M_3. In this case, as in the previous one, the Fed reacts to an upward movement in the federal funds rate by injecting new reserves into the banking system. Enough reserves are supplied either through open-market operations or through discount window loans to let the money supply expand some, but the amount supplied is not enough to keep the interest rate from rising. The result is a new equilibrium at E_3. The interest rate rises less than with a strict money supply target but more than with an interest rate target. And the money supply expands more than with a strict money supply target but less than with an interest rate target.

The Evolution of the Fed's Monetary Control Strategy

Over the years the Fed's strategy for the conduct of monetary policy has changed. At one time or another it has included elements of each of the three approaches just described.

Interest rate targeting and its problems   During World War II the Fed set strict interest rate targets. Those targets were very low by today's standards: 2 1/2 percent on government bonds with maturities longer than 10 years, 7/8 percent on one-year government securities, and just 3/8 percent on 90-day Treasury bills. The purpose of these low ceilings was to reduce the interest cost to the Treasury of financing the huge federal budget deficit caused by the war. Also, because the interest rate ceilings would stabilize bond prices, they would prevent wartime speculation in government bonds.

The interest rate ceilings were kept in force for several years after the war. They were abandoned in 1951, but interest rates remained the chief focus of the Fed's policy. Interest rates were allowed to rise and fall to some extent, but there was still a strong tendency for the Fed to respond to increases in money demand by supplying new reserves.

As inflation began to accelerate in the late 1960s and early 1970s, economists became critical of the Fed's emphasis on stabilizing interest rates. The problem, the critics said, was that targeting interest rates gave monetary policy an inflationary bias. They saw monetary policy as part of a feedback process that worked like this:

- Expansion of nominal national income increases money demand.
- The Fed responds by increasing bank reserves.
- Increased reserves lead to an expansion of the money supply and to more borrowing and spending by firms and households.
- More borrowing and spending causes nominal national income to rise further.

Growth of nominal national income is a good thing—up to a point. But if nominal national income grows faster than the economy's capacity to produce real goods and services, the result is inflation—too much money chasing too few goods. According to the critics, as long as the Fed keeps supplying new money to feed the growth of nominal income, there is nothing to stop inflation from getting out of hand.

The mid-1970s   By the mid-1970s the Fed was paying attention to these critics. It continued to use a federal funds rate target as its guide for day-to-day open-market operations, but it also set targets for the growth rate of M1 and M2. Those targets were set at a level that the Fed believed would keep inflation in check. If the money supply grew faster than the targets over a period of weeks or months, and if inflation seemed to be speeding up, the Fed took this as a sign that its federal funds rate target was too low. To slow the rate of growth of the money supply, it would set a new, higher federal funds rate target to guide its day-to-day operations.

Unfortunately, this strategy did not work very well. It appears that the Fed's reactions to faster-than-intended money growth and the resulting inflation tended to be too little and too late. The rate of inflation and interest rates continued to drift upward. By 1979 both the inflation rate and short-term interest rates were in the teens, and there was a feeling that something had to be done.

1979–1982   In October of 1979 the Fed announced a dramatic shift in its strategy of monetary control. It would cease to use the federal funds rate as a guide to day-to-day policy. Instead, it would focus on bank reserves. At each meeting of the Federal Open Market Committee a target would be set for *nonborrowed* reserves of the banking system. By nonborrowed reserves, it meant all bank reserves except those that the Fed loans to banks through its discount window. By maintaining tight control over nonborrowed reserves, the Fed would restrain excess money supply growth and inflation.

This strategy did not amount to strict targeting of the money supply. Total reserves and the total money supply could still vary to the extent that banks' borrowings from the discount window varied. In practice, the nonborrowed-reserves strategy produced an upward-sloping money supply curve. Banks could respond to increased demand for money by borrowing more reserves from the Fed. But because the Fed does not allow unlimited or continual borrowing from its discount window, increased money demand still put upward pressure on interest rates.

The Fed stuck to this strategy for three turbulent years, from October 1979 to October 1982. The results were dramatic. On the plus side, the chain reaction from money growth to inflation to more money growth and more inflation was broken. On the negative side, however, interest rates as well as real output went on a roller-coaster ride, as Box 12.10 shows. There were two sharp recessions in this period, along with record levels of unemployment. There were also many business failures, aggravated by high interest rates.

The volatile behavior of interest rates during the 1979–1982 period fit well with our model of the money market. During the preceding period, the Fed's interest rate targeting strategy had limited short-term ups and downs in interest rates but had failed to control the growth of the money supply. Between 1979 and 1982, the Fed tilted its money supply curve to an upward-sloping position. During the same period demand for money became unstable, partly because of the two recessions and partly because of changes in the banking system.

An unstable money demand curve moving back and forth along an upward-sloping money supply curve produced just the results that economic theory predicts. As Box 12.10 shows, both interest rates and the money stock were subject to sharp variations. In periods when money demand strengthened, the money stock was pulled above its target level, and interest rates rose. When the demand for money moderated, the money stock fell below its target range and interest rates declined.

The current period   In October 1982 the Fed changed its strategy again. It was pleased with the progress that had been made in fighting inflation, but it was concerned about possible adverse effects of continuing its policy. For one thing, experience had shown that the policy of nonborrowed-reserves targeting could produce huge swings in interest rates in periods when money demand was unstable. The Fed wanted to avoid another extreme peak of interest rates. It felt that another such episode would be very damaging to a depressed U.S. economy, and also to the economies of third-world countries that owed billions of dollars to U.S. banks. In addition, the Fed was unsure of the impact of certain changes in banking regulations that were under way. These included the relaxing of interest rate ceilings on certain kinds of deposits, and the introduction of super-NOW accounts and MMDAs, scheduled around year-end 1982. Finally, the Fed had doubts about the wisdom of continuing to focus so closely on M1. The growth of highly liquid assets that are not included in M1—money market mutual funds, MMDAs, repurchase agreements, and others—was viewed as a sign that the links between M1 and economic activity might be less predictable than in the past. At the same time, the popularity of NOW accounts meant that more savings-type balances had entered M1.

In the face of all these concerns and doubts, the Fed decided that its monetary policy should not be guided by hard-and-fast rules for the time being. Instead, the Fed would take a broad range of factors—interest rates, the growth of broader measures of money and credit as well as M1, the growth of real national income, changes in the price level—into account in guiding open-market operations and changes in the discount rate. This shift toward a more discretionary policy was followed by a smoother path of money growth and more moderate fluctuations in interest rates during 1983 and 1984, compared with the previous three years.

It is difficult to present the Fed's current policy in graphic form. It is safe to say, though, that that policy lies somewhere between the extremes of strict money supply targeting and strict interest rate targeting. The Fed seems willing to allow shifts in money demand to affect both interest rates and the money supply. In this sense, the Fed seems to be operating along an upward-sloping money supply curve.

The *Wall Street Journal* story with which this chapter opens supports the notion of an upward-sloping supply curve for money. The story described a situation in which an unexpectedly large increase in the money stock was associated with a fall in bond prices and a jump in interest rates. Such an association occurs when an unexpectedly strong rightward shift in

**Box 12·10
Interest Rates and the
Money Stock,
1979–1982**

During the period from October 1979 to October 1982, the Fed pursued a strategy of holding nonborrowed reserves at a chosen target level. Given the level of nonborrowed reserves, total reserves were allowed to vary as banks increased or decreased the quantity of reserves they borrowed from the discount window. The result was an upward-sloping supply curve for money. Two recessions plus changes in banking institutions caused the demand for money to be unstable during this period. With the upward-sloping supply curve, increases in money demand tended to pull M1 above its target level and increase interest rates. (The family of interest rates is represented here by the federal funds rate.) In periods of weak money demand, M1 tended to fall below its target level and interest rates tended to fall.

(a)

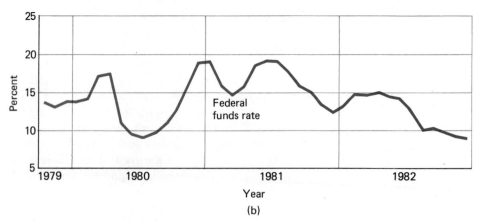

(b)

Source: Federal Reserve Board of Governors.

the money demand curve moves the money market up and to the right along the supply curve. In contrast, an increase in the money stock caused by a rightward shift in the money supply curve while the demand curve remained in place would be associated with a rise in bond prices and a drop in interest rates.

This episode also calls attention to the discretionary nature of the Fed's current policy. Although its short-term operating procedures result in an upward-sloping money supply curve, it retains the option of shifting the supply curve when necessary. In this case, strong money demand appears to have carried the money market too far to the right along the supply curve. As a result, the money stock grew faster than the Fed's target growth range allowed. Analysts expected the Fed to "tighten its credit policy"—Wall Street jargon for shifting the money supply curve upward and to the left. That expectation, combined with the strong demand for money, pushed bond prices even lower and interest rates even higher.

Looking Ahead

This chapter has filled out our picture of the banking system and the money market. It has shown how the Fed controls the money supply and how its actions affect interest rates. And it has described the evolution of the Fed's monetary policies.

Before we move on to the next set of policy controversies, we need to do some more theory building. Our job in the first part of the next chapter will be to explore the interaction between monetary and fiscal policy. Once we have done that, we will return to monetary policy issues.

Summary

1. Using M for the quantity of money, V for the velocity of money, P for the price level, and y for real national income, the equation of exchange can be written $MV = Py$. The term *velocity* means the average number of times each year that each dollar of the money stock is used for income-producing purposes.

2. According to the modern theory of money demand, people hold part of their portfolios—that is, their assets—in the form of money in order to gain the benefits of liquidity. Since most forms of money pay no interest, or a lower interest rate than less liquid assets, the nominal interest rate can be thought of as the opportunity cost of holding money. Other things being equal, a decrease in the nominal interest rate tends to increase the amount of money demanded. Also, other things being

equal, an increase in nominal national income tends to increase the demand for money.

3. The demand for money can be represented by a downward-sloping curve on a graph where the horizontal axis measures the quantity of money and the vertical axis measures the nominal interest rate. An increase in nominal national income shifts the money demand curve to the right; a decrease in nominal national income shifts it to the left. Other factors, including changes in payments practices, can also cause shifts in the money demand curve.

4. Open-market operations are the Fed's most often used tool of monetary control. An open-market purchase injects new reserves into the banking system, causing the money supply to expand; an open-market sale drains reserves

from the banking system, causing the money supply to contract. An increase in the *discount rate* charged by the Fed for borrowed reserves tends to cause the money supply to contract; a decrease in the discount rate tends to cause it to expand. Finally, the Fed has sometimes, but not in recent years, used changes in reserve requirements as a tool of monetary control.

5. The money market can be represented by a vertical money supply curve and a downward-sloping money demand curve. If the quantity of money is increased while nominal national income remains constant, the market will move to a new equilibrium in which the interest rate is lower than before. The lower interest rate is needed to induce people to hold the greater quantity of money.

6. If nominal national income rises while the quantity of money remains constant, there will be an excess demand for money. This will cause people to try to adjust their portfolios, selling other assets in order to obtain money. In the process of doing so, they will push up interest rates and move the money market to a new equilibrium. A decrease in nominal national income will cause an excess supply of money, leading to a fall in interest rates.

7. The slope of the money supply curve is determined by the Fed's money control strategy. If the Fed chooses a target for the money supply and sticks to it regardless of what happens to interest rates, the money supply curve will be vertical. If it sets an interest rate target, the money supply curve will be horizontal. In cases in which the interest rate is allowed to vary but an increase in the interest rate is partly offset by an increase in the money stock, the money supply curve is upward sloping.

8. With a vertical money supply curve, shifts in the money demand curve show up as changes in the interest rate. With a horizontal money supply curve, shifts in the demand for money change the stock of money without affecting the interest rate. With an upward-sloping money supply curve, shifts in the demand for money cause the money stock and interest rates both to change in the same direction.

9. During and after World War II, the Fed set targets for interest rates on government securities. Later, interest rates were allowed to move somewhat, but they remained the focal point of the Fed's policies. During the 1970s, the Fed began to place more emphasis on the money supply. From 1979 to 1982, it pursued a strategy of targeting nonborrowed reserves. This resulted in a much steeper, though not vertical, money supply curve. Since 1982, monetary policy has depended more on the judgment of FOMC members and less on any formal rule.

Questions for Review

1. Define the following terms:
   equation of exchange
   velocity
   portfolio
   discount window
   discount rate
   federal funds market
   federal funds rate

2. If the quantity of money is $100 billion and nominal national income is $500 billion, what is velocity? If the money supply and real national income remain constant while velocity increases to 10, what will happen to the price level?

3. According to the portfolio balance theory, how does a change in the nominal interest rate affect the demand for money? How does a change in nominal national income affect the demand for money?

4. Are the effects of an increase in nominal national income best shown by a movement along the money demand curve or by a shift in the curve? In which way are the effects of a change in the nominal interest rate best shown?

5. What are the Fed's three main tools of monetary control? Which of them is most often used? Which is least often used at present?

6. Are the effects of an open-market purchase by the Federal Reserve best shown by a rightward shift in the money supply curve, a leftward shift in the curve, or a movement along the curve? How does the interest rate change in response to an open-market purchase, other things being equal?

7. Are the effects of an increase in nominal national income, with no change in the money supply, best shown by a rightward shift in the money demand curve, a leftward shift in the curve, or a movement along the curve? What happens to interest rates as a result of an increase in nominal national income?

8. What is the shape of the money supply curve when the Fed pursues a strategy of setting a strict target for the money supply? A strategy of setting an interest rate target? An intermediate strategy?

9. If the demand for money increases, what happens to the amount of money supplied and the interest rate, assuming that the Fed follows a strategy of setting a strict target for the money supply? What happens if the Fed follows a strategy of setting an interest rate target? What happens if it follows an intermediate strategy?

10. How has the Fed's monetary control strategy changed over time? How can the evolution of its strategy be represented in terms of the money supply curve?

Problems and Topics for Discussion

1. Using the *Economic Report of the President*, the *Federal Reserve Bulletin*, or another source, find the most recent values for the money supply (both M1 and M2), the price level (use the GNP deflator), and real national income. Use the equation of exchange to determine the velocities of M1 and M2. Which velocity is greater?

2. Some economists draw a different sort of money demand curve than the one used in this book. They begin with a diagram that shows the quantity of money demanded on the horizontal axis and the price level on the vertical axis. Sketch these axes on a sheet of graph paper. Number the vertical axis from 0 to 10 and the horizontal axis from 0 to 500 billion. Assume a constant real national income of $200 billion and a constant nominal interest rate of 4 percent. Now, using the table in Box 12.1 as a guide, draw a curve showing how the quantity of money demanded varies as the price level varies. (*Hint*: Remember that nominal national income equals real national income divided by the price level.) How does this version of the money demand curve shift if the interest rate rises from 4 percent to 6 percent?

3. The appendix to Chapter 4 shows how to calculate the market value of a bond, given its annual coupon payment and its maturity date. If you have not already worked through that appendix, do so now. Using the method explained there, calculate the market value of a bond with a $1,000 face value, a $100 annual coupon payment, and a maturity date 5 years from the present. First evaluate the bond at a market interest rate of 8 percent and then at a market interest rate of 12 percent. Is an increase in the market interest rate associated with an increase or a decrease in the price of the bond?

4. Find the most recent available data on nominal national income and M1. Plot them on the chart in Box 12.3. Do the data indicate a continued leftward drift in the income-adjusted money demand curve? Discuss.

5. Review the multiple expansion of deposits as explained in Chapter 10. Assume an initial equilibrium in which each of the ten banks in the system has deposits of $100,000, total reserves of $10,000, and required reserves of $10,000. Now assume that the Fed cuts the required-reserve ratio from 10 percent to 8 percent. Use the balance sheet of the Albany National Bank to show the impact of this change on a typical bank's excess reserves. What will the bank do to move toward balance sheet equilibrium? Sketch the expansion of the

money supply for the system as a whole as all banks react to the change in the reserve requirement. What will the final quantity of money be when the entire banking system is back in equilibrium? What will the balance sheet of a typical bank look like when the entire system is back in equilibrium?

6. Rework the example given in Box 12.6 for the case of a decrease in the money supply from $180 billion to $120 billion.

7. Rework the example given in Box 12.7 for the case of a decrease in nominal national income from $600 billion to $400 billion. (Use the table in Box 12.1 to draw the demand curve for nominal national income of $400 billion.)

8. Discussions of monetary policy often refer to "tight" or "easy" policy. If the Fed pursues a strategy of strict money supply targeting, the meaning of these terms is simple: Tightening policy means shifting the money supply curve to the left, while easing policy means shifting it to the right. If the Fed is using a strategy of interest rate targeting, tightening policy means raising the interest rate target and easing policy means lowering the interest rate target. Sketch a graph that shows the effects of tightening and easing policy, using a horizontal money supply curve and assuming no shift in the money demand curve. If the Fed is pursuing an intermediate policy, tightening means a shift upward and to the left in the sloping money supply schedule and easing means a shift downward and to the right in the sloping money supply schedule. Sketch these cases as well.

9. Box 12.10 shows the relationship between interest rates and the money supply from 1979 to 1982. In that period the interest rate tended to rise during periods when the money stock was moving above its target growth range and to fall when the money stock was moving below its target range. Use a supply-and-demand diagram to explain why this pattern is best explained by a stable, upward-sloping money supply curve and a shifting demand curve. What would the relationship between money and interest rates have been if the money demand curve had remained fixed while the money supply curve shifted? Illustrate this case by sketching the pattern of interest rates and money supply over time, using a pair of diagrams similar to Box 12.10.

Suggestions for Further Reading

Campbell, Colin D., and Rosemary G. Campbell. *An Introduction to Money and Banking*, 5th ed. Hinsdale, Ill.: Dryden Press, 1984.

Chapter 13 discusses the Fed's tools for monetary control; Chapter 14 covers the evolution of the Fed's monetary control strategy.

Gordon, Robert J. *Macroeconomics*, 3rd ed. Boston: Little, Brown, 1984.

Reviews the Keynesian and portfolio balance theories of money demand.

Simpson, Thomas D. "Changes in the Financial System: Implications for Monetary Policy," *Brookings Papers on Economic Activity* 1 (1984), pp. 249–272.

This article discusses the impact of recent changes in banking and financial institutions on the demand for money and on the ability of the Fed to affect the economy through its control over the money supply.

Chapter 13

The Interaction of Monetary and Fiscal Policy

"If Congress could come up with at least $50 billion in deficit reductions, interest rates would come down."

Washington, D.C., January 16, 1985: Chairman Paul Volcker of the Federal Reserve Board told Senate Republicans yesterday that a $50 billion reduction in the deficit was a minimum target for fiscal 1986. "$50 billion in a convincing way is what you need," the Fed chairman told reporters after a freewheeling breakfast meeting with Republican leaders.

Volcker indicated that if Congress could come up with at least $50 billion in deficit reductions for 1986 plus some convincing follow-through in later years, interest rates would come down. The chairman did not offer a prediction, only indicating that interest rates would be lower than they otherwise would be.

Volcker is known to prefer that the deficit reductions take the form of reduced spending. However, if sufficient cuts can't be found, he would "look elsewhere" to higher taxes. Volcker emphasized the need to pin down savings in future years if the budget package is to be effective in lowering interest rates. And this argument was made by corporate executives representing the Business Roundtable, who also met with the Republican leaders yesterday.

Separately, President Reagan met with business leaders and promised an all-out assault on domestic spending. The business leaders also urged cuts in Social Security and defense spending.[1]

We have discussed taxes, spending, and the deficit in a chapter on fiscal policy, and we have looked at the Federal Reserve and interest rates in a chapter on monetary policy. Here, in this news story, they are all mixed together. Why is the Fed's chairman talking to congressional leaders about fiscal policy? Why are the president's budget plans crucial to interest rates? These are questions that we want to ask as we break down the barriers that have separated monetary and fiscal policy in our discussion up to this point.

In this chapter we will look at how monetary and fiscal policy interact. We will then be prepared to take up in more detail how changes in the level of nominal national income become translated into changes in real output and the price level.

In exploring the interaction of fiscal and monetary policy, we will begin with a theoretical framework based on the work of Keynes and his followers. Recent experience has cast doubt on the usefulness of many of their specific policy suggestions. Still, the theoretical framework set forth by Keynes in *The General Theory of Employment, Interest, and Money* remains alive and well. It is the language in which Keynesians, neo-Keynesians, anti-Keynesians, and post-Keynesians conduct their debates.

THE KEYNESIAN THEORY OF INCOME DETERMINATION

In discussing fiscal and monetary policy, we have looked at different sectors of the economy without explaining how they interact. One sector is that of the circular flow of nominal income and product and the Keynesian cross. Here we deal with markets for goods and services. Another is the monetary sector, which is concerned with the supply and demand for

[1]Adapted from David Rogers, "Volcker Says Deficit Must Be Reduced by at Least $50 Billion in Fiscal 1986," and "Incentive System" (editorial), *Wall Street Journal*, January 16, 1985.

assets such as money, bonds, and other securities. Finally, we have looked at financial markets, in which the supply of saving and the demand for loanable funds interact.

We know in a general way that financial markets and the circular flow are linked, because we know that investment funds flow through financial markets on their way from households to firms. We have also seen that financial markets are linked to the money market through the family of interest rates. Now it is time to look more closely at how events in the monetary sector affect the circular flow of income and product and how these sectors interact to produce an equilibrium level of nominal national income.

Our starting point in linking these sectors will be a simple theory of investment. At first we will limit our discussion to an economy in which there is no inflation. All changes in nominal income will take the form of changes in real income. The real and nominal rates of interest will be equal. These assumptions are justified not because they are realistic but simply because it is easier to take things one at a time.

A Simple Theory of Investment

Business firms must constantly invest. They must acquire new plant and equipment to replace what wears out each year. They must invest in more plant and equipment in order to grow and to adapt to changing conditions, such as foreign competition and higher energy costs. They must invest in inventory to smooth out variations in the timing of input purchases, rates of production, and sales of final products. To do all this, they must somehow acquire the needed funds. Many firms are fortunate enough to have steady flows of profits, some of which can be used for investment before the rest is paid out to owners. Other firms obtain funds by borrowing, either directly from the public or through financial intermediaries. Still others bring in new partners or stockholders as a means of raising funds for investment.

The opportunity cost of capital   Whatever the source of a firm's investment funds, acquiring new fixed capital or inventories always involves an opportunity cost. The opportunity cost of capital is the interest rate that must be paid for funds that are obtained from outside the firm or that could be earned by investing the firm's own funds elsewhere. There is no free capital. A firm that spends its own profits on new office equipment could have earned interest on those funds by depositing them in a bank, buying government securities, or lending them to another firm. A firm that borrows to buy its capital goods must pay the interest rate charged by lenders. And a firm that obtains investment funds by drawing in new partners or stockholders must offer those new owners a rate of return on the capital they bring with them that is at least equal to what they could have obtained by putting their funds to work elsewhere.

In the real world, of course, the opportunity cost of capital may vary according to the source of funds. The job of the firm's financial managers is to choose carefully among the sources of funds so as to keep the firm's total cost of capital to a minimum. Because this is not a course on managerial finance, however, we will ignore such details; as far as we are concerned, the firm will face the same opportunity cost or interest rate regardless of the source of funds.

How much to invest?   At any given time, dozens or hundreds of investment opportunities may present themselves to a firm. A regional sales office may be built in a distant city. Production equipment may be modernized. Larger supplies of raw materials may be kept on hand to guard against supply disruptions. Somehow the firm's managers must decide which projects to undertake and how far to carry each one. In doing so, it must balance the potential benefits, in terms of increased profits, against the opportunity cost of obtaining the investment funds.

A simple example will illustrate the main elements of investment decision making. A small firm, Great Falls Manufacturing, Inc. (GFMI), is concerned about high energy costs. It hires a consultant to see what can be done. The consultant reports that the heat loss through the roof of its warehouse is costing the firm $2,000 per year. The problem could be greatly reduced by putting in insulation. But how much should be put in?

To help GFMI's managers reach a decision, the consultant presents the table shown in Box 13.1. This table gives the heat losses and costs associated with various amounts of insulation. If the firm does nothing, it will continue to waste $12,000 worth of energy costs each year. For $10,000 the firm can put in 6 inches of insulation. This will cut the heat loss in half, to $6,000 a year. For another $10,000 the firm can put in 12 inches of insulation. The consultant's calculations show that this will reduce the heat loss by another $2,000 a year, to $4,000. For another $10,000 the insulation can be brought up to 18 inches, cutting the heat loss to $3,000 a year, for a further $1,000 annual saving. Once the insulation has been installed, it will never have to be replaced, so the saving will continue in later years.

To decide how much insulation to put in, GFMI must compare the potential cost saving with the opportunity cost of capital. To make the comparison easier, both quantities can be expressed in percentage terms. Column 5 of Box 13.1 gives the cost saving as a percentage rate of return.

**Box 13.1
Evaluation of Returns
from an Insulation
Project**

This table shows the returns that a certain firm would receive as a result of investing in various amounts of insulation for the roof of its warehouse. Each 6 inches of added insulation costs $10,000. Each time the amount of insulation is increased, the rate of heat loss falls. Thus, as column 5 shows, the annual saving in fuel costs as a percentage of the added investment decreases as the amount of insulation increases.

Inches of Insulation Added (1)	Heat Loss (dollars per year) (2)	Change in Heat Loss (dollars per year) (3)	Cost of Added Insulation (4)	Saving as Percent of Investment (5)
0	$12,000	—	—	—
6	6,000	$6,000	$10,000	60
12	4,000	2,000	10,000	20
18	3,000	1,000	10,000	10

The first 6 inches of insulation saves $6,000 per year, an annual return equal to 60 percent of the initial $10,000 investment. The second 6 inches yields a saving of $2,000 a year on the second $10,000 investment, for a rate of return of 20 percent. The third 6 inches costs another $10,000 but saves only $1,000 more per year, a rate of return of just 10 percent. Each added 6 inches of insulation thus results in a smaller saving.

A local bank is willing to supply the funds for the project, secured by a mortgage on the warehouse, at an interest rate of 18 percent per year. We take this representative interest rate as the firm's opportunity cost of capital. The 60 percent rate of return on the first 6 inches of insulation far exceeds the 18 percent cost of capital. (Annual interest payments on the first $10,000 borrowed would be $1,800, compared with the $6,000 annual saving.) The second 6 inches is also worthwhile, since its 20 percent rate of return still is greater than the opportunity cost of capital. The third 6 inches, however, would not pay for itself. The rate of return of 10 percent obtained by going from 12 to 18 inches of insulation falls far short of the 18 percent cost of funds. It would be worth borrowing $10,000 to install the final 6 inches of insulation only if the interest rate were 10 percent or less.[2]

Marginal efficiency of investment

The expected rate of return on an additional dollar of planned investment.

Planned-investment schedule

A downward-sloping schedule that shows the connection between planned investment and the interest rate, other things being equal.

The planned-investment schedule   Simple though it is, this example illustrates two basic principles that underlie all theories of investment. First, as a firm's investment outlays increase, the expected rate of return on the last dollar invested tends to fall. In the language of economics, the **marginal efficiency of investment** is said to decrease as the annual flow of investment increases. Second, it is profitable for a firm to expand its investment outlays up to, but not beyond, the point at which the marginal efficiency of investment drops below the opportunity cost of capital, as measured by a representative rate of interest.

Putting these two principles together makes it possible to draw a **planned-investment schedule** for a firm and, by extension, for the economy as a whole. Such a schedule shows the amount of planned investment associated with each interest rate; the height of the schedule at each point is equal to the marginal efficiency of investment. Part a of Box 13.2 shows the planned-investment schedule for GFMI, using the data in Box 13.1. At an interest rate of 60 percent or more, it would not be worthwhile to do any insulating. As soon as the interest rate drops below 60 percent, the first $10,000 of insulation is worthwhile. The second 6 inches of insulation begins to pay for itself when the interest rate falls below 20 percent, and the third when the interest rate drops below 10 percent. Given the 18 percent rate shown in the diagram, investment is cut off at $20,000.

Part b of the box shows an investment schedule for the economy as a whole. With tens of thousands of firms and millions of potential investment projects, the stair steps of the single-firm, single-project investment schedule are smoothed out. As this schedule is drawn, a 20 percent interest

---

[2]Appendix A to this chapter explains how investment projects can be evaluated when returns are not equal in each year or do not continue in later years. In a world where inflation must be taken into account, the distinction between real and nominal interest rates must be kept in mind when evaluating investment projects. If a real-interest-rate standard is used, future returns from the investment must be stated in constant dollars. If a nominal-interest-rate standard is used, future returns must be stated in current dollars, allowing for estimated inflation. The two methods give the same results.

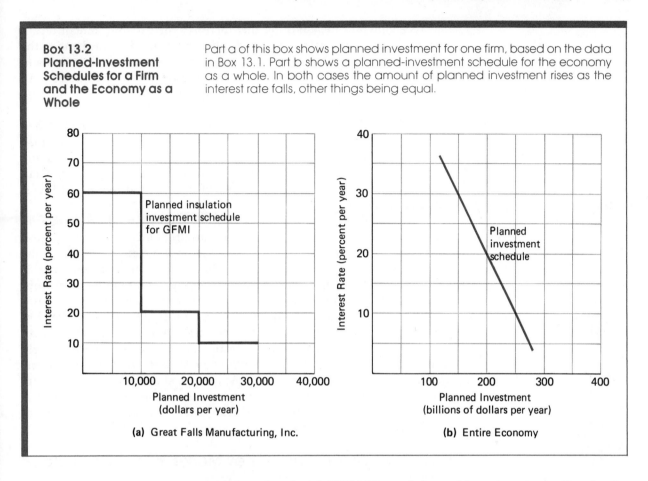

Box 13.2
Planned-Investment Schedules for a Firm and the Economy as a Whole

Part a of this box shows planned investment for one firm, based on the data in Box 13.1. Part b shows a planned-investment schedule for the economy as a whole. In both cases the amount of planned investment rises as the interest rate falls, other things being equal.

Planned insulation investment schedule for GFMI

(a) Great Falls Manufacturing, Inc.

Planned investment schedule

(b) Entire Economy

rate is associated with $200 billion of planned investment spending for the economy as a whole.

Any change in the interest rate, other things being equal, will produce a movement along the planned-investment schedule. In part b of Box 13.2, for example, a decrease in the interest rate to 10 percent will increase planned investment to $250 billion. Likewise, an increase in the interest rate to 25 percent will reduce total planned investment to $175 billion.

Shifts in the planned-investment schedule   Any change in one of the conditions covered by the "other things being equal" clause will shift the planned-investment schedule. A complete analysis would have to consider two kinds of changes: changes in the price level and changes in the expected return on investment. In this section, however, we are dealing with an economy in which there is no inflation, so the price level never changes. Later in the chapter we will consider how the simple Keynesian theory can be modified to take inflation into account, but for the moment we will discuss only changes in the expected nominal rate of return.[3]

---

[3]When the planned-investment schedule is drawn with the nominal interest rate on the vertical axis and nominal planned investment on the horizontal axis, a once-and-for-all increase in the price level with no change in the expected rate of inflation will shift the planned-investment schedule to the right. A change in the expected rate of inflation, other things being equal, will shift the planned-investment schedule upward by a distance equal to the expected change in the inflation rate.

As a general rule, anything that increases the expected rate of return on investment will shift the planned-investment curve upward and to the right, and anything that decreases the expected return will shift it downward and to the left. Take GFMI's warehouse insulation project. An increase in the cost of heating fuel, other things being equal, will increase the expected rate of return from any given amount of insulation.[4]

For example, if the cost of fuel doubles, the saving from each added layer of insulation will be twice as great as was shown in Box 13.1. Increasing the amount of insulation from 12 to 18 inches will yield a saving of $2,000 rather than just $1,000. At any interest rate up to 20 percent, it will be worthwhile to put in a full 18 inches of insulation if the cost of fuel is expected to double.

Many investments are made in order to increase productive capacity rather than to reduce costs per unit of output. Sometimes technological advances can spur investment in a major sector of the economy, as was the case with railroads in the nineteenth century and automobiles early in this century. Today investment in "high-tech" equipment, ranging from word processors to welding robots, is booming. More broadly, expectations about long-term growth trends and population trends affect the level of planned investment. In the short run, forecasts of business conditions can strongly affect the timing of fixed investments and can even more strongly influence the level of planned inventory investment. Whatever the source, an increase in confidence regarding the long- or short-run economic future will tend to shift the planned-investment schedule upward and to the right. A decrease in confidence will tend to shift the planned-investment schedule downward and to the left.

Linkages Between the Money Market and the Circular Flow

Transmission mechanism
The mechanism through which monetary policy affects the equilibrium level of nominal national income.

In the Keynesian theory of income determination, the planned-investment schedule serves as the linkage, or **transmission mechanism**, through which monetary policy acts on the circular flow of income and product. In turn, changes in the level of income within the circular flow have a feedback effect on the money market. In Box 13.3 these effects are represented by arrows.

The interest rate-investment transmission mechanism   First look at the arrow running from the money market to the planned-investment schedule to the aggregate nominal demand curve. The intersection of the money supply and demand curves determines the equilibrium interest rate—8 percent in the box. Given the position of the planned-investment schedule, the interest rate determines the volume of planned investment spending—$100 a year in this case. This $100 of planned investment then becomes the I component of $C + I + G + X - M$—that is, of aggregate nominal demand. Finally, the intersection of the aggregate nominal demand curve with the aggregate nominal supply curve determines the equilibrium level of nominal national income within the circular flow.

---

[4]In this case the price of heating fuel is assumed to increase with no change in the general price level.

**Box 13.3
The Interaction of
Money and National
Income**

The money market and the circular flow can be in equilibrium at the same time only if a certain pair of values for nominal national income and the interest rate prevail. The large arrows in this diagram show how the interest rate and nominal national income interact. The equilibrium interest rate determines the equilibrium level of planned investment, thereby determining the position of the aggregate nominal demand curve. The intersection of the aggregate nominal demand and supply curves determines the equilibrium level of nominal national income, which in turn determines the position of the money demand curve.

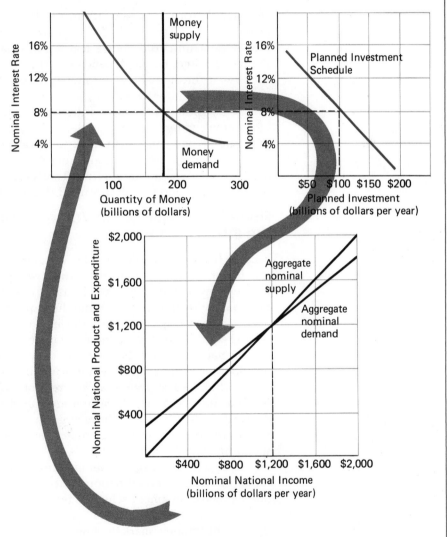

Any change in the interest rate will transmit itself along this channel. For example, an increase in the interest rate, other things being equal, will cause a movement upward and to the left along the planned-investment schedule. This will reduce the level of planned investment. As the *I* component of aggregate nominal demand falls, the entire aggregate nominal demand curve will shift downward. The equilibrium level of nominal national income thus will be reduced.

A decrease in the interest rate, other things being equal, will produce a movement downward and to the right along the planned-investment schedule. This will increase the investment component of aggregate nominal demand and shift the aggregate nominal demand curve upward. The point at which the aggregate nominal supply and demand curves intersect will move to the right, indicating an increase in the equilibrium level of nominal national income.

Feedback from national income to the money market   The second arrow in Box 13.3 shows the feedback from nominal national income to the money demand curve. As we learned in Chapter 12, the position of the money demand curve depends on the level of nominal income. An increase in income shifts the money demand curve to the right, and a decrease shifts it to the left.

The position of the money demand curve, as determined by the level of nominal national income, determines the point at which it intersects with the money supply curve. A rightward shift in the money demand curve (caused by an increase in nominal national income) will raise the equilibrium interest rate; a leftward shift (caused by a decrease in nominal income) will lower the equilibrium interest rate.

Finding the Equilibrium Values of Nominal Income and the Interest Rate

Because the money market and the circular flow are so closely linked, they can be in equilibrium together only when certain values of nominal national income and the interest rate prevail. Let the required level of nominal national income be Y and the required interest rate be r. The value of r must be just right to induce the level of planned investment needed to put the equilibrium level of nominal national income exactly at the level Y, and the value of Y must be just right to put the money demand curve in the position needed to keep the equilibrium interest rate at r.

As Box 13.3 is drawn, an interest rate of 8 percent and a nominal national income of $1,200 billion are called for. The aggregate nominal demand curve is based on the assumptions that autonomous consumption is $145 billion, the marginal propensity to consume is 0.75, government spending is $75 billion, net exports are $25 billion, and lump sum net taxes are $60 billion. Planned investment must therefore be $100 billion in order for equilibrium nominal national income to be $1,200 billion. A check of the planned-investment schedule reveals that an interest rate of 8 percent is needed to encourage just that amount of investment.

In the money market, where a money supply of $180 billion is assumed, the money demand curve must be in exactly the position shown in Box 13.3 for the equilibrium rate of interest to be 8 percent. This position corresponds to a nominal national income of $1,200 billion. Thus, $r = 8$ percent and $Y = \$1,200$ are an equilibrium pair of values for the interest rate and nominal national income. Any higher level of nominal national income would put the money demand curve too far to the right, giving too high an interest rate, and any lower level would put it too far to the left, giving too low an interest rate.

MONETARY AND FISCAL POLICY IN THE KEYNESIAN MODEL

In previous chapters we have discussed fiscal and monetary policy under assumptions that left out interactions between the money market and the circular flow. In Chapter 10, for example, when we looked at the effects of changes in taxes and government purchases, we assumed that these policy changes would leave private planned investment unchanged. In Chapter 12, we looked at the effects of changes in the money supply while assuming that the money demand curve did not move. Now we will relax these assumptions to take into account the economic interactions shown in Box 13.3. The result will be a modification of our earlier conclusions regarding both fiscal and monetary policy.

A Revised Look at the Effects of Fiscal Policy

Effects of a change in government purchases   In Chapter 10 we concluded that when government purchases increase while net taxes, planned investment, net exports, and the consumption schedule stay the same, equilibrium nominal national income will change by an amount equal to the change in government purchases times the expenditure multiplier. If interactions between the level of nominal national income and the level of planned investment are taken into account, however, this conclusion must be revised.

Suppose that the economy starts out in equilibrium with interest rate r and nominal national income Y. Fiscal policymakers then decide to increase government purchases by $100, with no change in net taxes.[5] What are the effects of this fiscal policy as they work their way through the economy?

The first effect of the increase in government purchases is to shift the aggregate nominal demand schedule upward by $100 billion. Planned expenditure now exceeds national product at the initial income level. This causes unplanned depletion of inventories, to which firms respond by increasing output and prices. The level of nominal national income begins to rise.

Money market effects   As nominal national income rises, the change in fiscal policy begins to affect the money market. The increase in nominal national income causes the money demand curve to shift rightward. In Box 13.4 this is shown as a shift of the money demand curve from its initial position, MD_1, to a new position, MD_2. The money demand curve shifts to the right because when incomes rise, people tend to want more money in their portfolios. Because the money supply does not increase, people's attempts to get more money by selling securities simply drives down their prices, thereby driving up interest rates. In sum, then, the effect on the money market of the increase in government purchases is to push up the interest rate.

The crowding-out effect   Turn now to the planned-investment schedule, also shown in Box 13.4. Increased demand for money has driven up the

---

[5]Throughout this discussion all taxes are assumed to be lump sum taxes.

Box 13.4
The Crowding-Out
Effect

An increase in government purchases causes nominal national income to rise via the multiplier effect. The increase in income shifts the money demand curve from its initial position, MD_1, to a new position, MD_2. The equilibrium interest rate rises from r_1 to r_2. An amount of private investment equal to ΔI is crowded out.

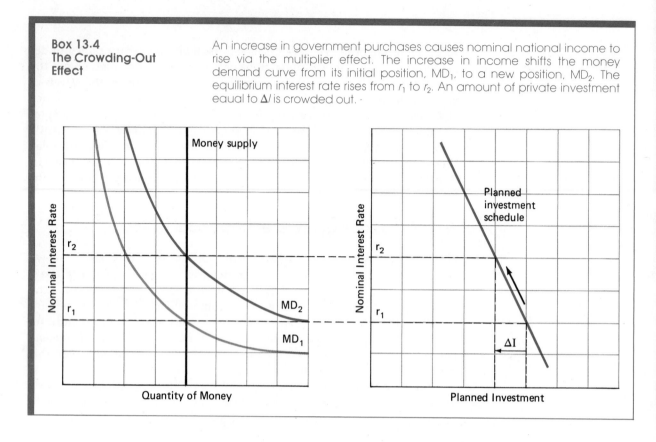

interest rate. As a result, firms find it more costly to undertake fixed investment projects and to increase their inventories of raw materials or finished goods. They therefore reduce their planned investment spending. This is shown by a movement upward and to the left along the planned-investment schedule. This decrease in planned investment as a result of an increase in government purchases is called the **crowding-out effect**. The amount of investment crowded out is labeled ΔI in the box.

The change in planned investment that results from crowding out has an effect, in turn, on aggregate nominal demand. This is shown in Box 13.5, where the original position of the aggregate nominal demand curve is shown as AND_1. Taken by itself, the increase in government purchases would have pushed the schedule all the way up to the position AND_2. That position is never reached, however. When the crowding-out effect is taken into account, it is clear that the upward shift in aggregate nominal demand is less than the amount of the increase in government purchases. If ΔG stands for the increase in government purchases and ΔI for the amount of investment that is crowded out, the upward shift is reduced to $\Delta G - \Delta I$. This puts the highest and final position reached by the aggregate nominal demand curve at AND_3 rather than AND_2.

If we look at Boxes 13.4 and 13.5 together, we can see that both income and the interest rate have changed as a result of the increase in government purchases. The new equilibrium interest rate, r_2, and the new equilibrium nominal income, Y_2, are both higher than they were to begin with, but private planned investment is lower.

Crowding-out effect

The tendency of an increase in government purchases to increase the interest rate and thereby decrease the level of planned investment.

**Box 13.5
The Crowding-Out
Effect and the
Keynesian Cross**

Here the crowding-out effect is shown from the standpoint of aggregate nominal demand and supply. Taken by itself, the increase in government purchases (ΔG) would push the aggregate nominal demand curve from AND_1 to AND_2. The crowding-out effect chops ΔI off planned investment, however, so the actual shift is only from AND_1 to AND_3, a distance equal to $\Delta G - \Delta I$.

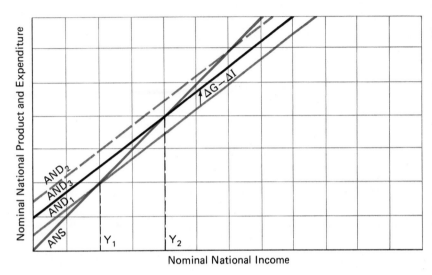

Crowding out and the multiplier   Because an increase in government purchases crowds out some private investment, nominal national income does not increase by the full amount of the expenditure multiplier times the increase in government purchases. This fact does not directly contradict the conclusion reached in Chapter 10, however. That conclusion was based on the assumption that planned investment would not change when the level of nominal national income changed. However, as we have now seen, that assumption must be revised when the interactions between the money market and the level of nominal national income are taken into account. This means that we have to modify the way the multiplier theory is applied to the analysis of fiscal policy. The multiplier must now be applied not just to the change in government purchases but to the change in government purchases minus the induced change in private planned investment.

The new way of applying the multiplier theory can be put in the form of a simple equation. Using ΔY to represent the change in nominal national income resulting from a change in government purchases (ΔG) and using $1/(1 - \text{MPC})$ to stand for the multiplier, we find that

$$\Delta Y = \frac{1}{1 - \text{MPC}} \times (\Delta G - \Delta I)$$

Estimates of the crowding-out effect   Statistical estimates have been made of the multiplier effect of a change in government purchases for the U.S. economy both with and without crowding out. These estimates,

Box 13.6
Estimates of the
Crowding-Out Effect for
the U.S. Economy

This table presents estimates of the multiplier effect of a dollar increase in government purchases for the U.S. economy. The estimates are based on four large-scale computer models. Results are given for one- and two-year time horizons for each model. The estimates in part a assume no crowding out. Part b uses the same four models to estimate the multiplier effect with crowding out. For each model and time horizon, the size of the crowding-out effect appears as the difference between the estimated multiplier effect without crowding out and the effect with crowding out.

Time Horizon	Multiplier as Estimated by:			
	Bureau of Economic Analysis	Data Resources Incorporated	MIT-Penn-SSRC	Wharton School
a. *Without Crowding Out*				
1 year	2.3	2.3	2.6	2.0
2 years	2.3	2.7	3.9	2.6
b. *With Crowding Out*				
1 year	1.9	2.3	2.5	1.8
2 years	1.9	2.5	3.0	2.2

Source: Gary Fromm and Lawrence R. Klein, "The NBER/NSF Model Comparisons Seminar: An Analysis of Results," *Annals of Economic and Social Measurement* 5 (Winter 1976): Tables 6 and 7, pp. 22–23. Reprinted by permission.

derived from four large-scale computer models, are shown in Box 13.6. In part a it is assumed that planned investment does not change when government purchases change—that is, that there is no crowding out. The estimates in part a thus correspond to the assumptions we made in Chapter 10. Part b gives results based on the same four models when crowding out is taken into account, that is, when planned investment is allowed to vary. The size of the crowding-out effect can be determined by comparing the estimates of the expenditure multiplier in part a with those in part b.

For example, in the Bureau of Economic Analysis estimate, a $1 increase in government purchases would cause a $2.30 increase in equilibrium nominal national income after two years if crowding out were not taken into account. With crowding out, the increase in equilibrium nominal national income after two years would be only $1.90. According to this estimate, then, crowding out reduces the multiplier effect of an increase in government purchases by more than 25 percent. Various other estimates of the crowding-out effect are higher or lower, but in all but one case some crowding out is estimated to take place. The crowding-out effect works in reverse when government purchases are cut back with the level of taxes unchanged. The effect of the spending cut is diminished somewhat because the interest rate falls as nominal national income falls. The decline in the interest rate, in turn, causes a movement downward and to the right along the planned-investment schedule. The added planned investment partly offsets the decrease in government purchases.

Crowding out and tax policy   There can also be a crowding-out effect when taxes are changed. As we saw in Chapter 10, a tax cut, with government purchases unchanged, tends to shift the consumption component of the aggregate nominal demand schedule upward. As aggregate nominal demand expands, the money demand curve is shifted to the right, just as it was when the expansion began with increased government purchases. The resulting rise in the interest rate and decline in planned investment partly offset the expansionary impact of the tax cut. In the Keynesian theory, then, a tax cut, like an increase in government purchases, will cause both the equilibrium level of nominal national income and the interest rate to rise.

However, it should be pointed out that the size of the crowding-out effect of a tax cut depends on the size of the net tax multiplier. Chapter 10 pointed out that the multiplier effect of a tax cut may be less than the Keynesian model indicates, because, at least in the short run, it may be offset by an increase in saving. Likewise, a tax increase may be offset by a decrease in saving. Most economists believe the offset is only partial and applies only in the short run, although a minority think that tax changes are wholly offset by changes in saving.

The size of the crowding-out effect of a tax cut was a key issue in the debate over the Reagan administration's 1981 tax cuts. Critics of the cuts pointed out that they added to an already large federal deficit. To finance the deficit, the Treasury would have to sell huge amounts of securities, thus driving up interest rates and crowding out private investment. Treasury officials replied that there was no clear relationship between deficits and interest rates. If the tax cut increased saving, additional securities could be sold without driving interest rates up. These officials maintained that the high level of government purchases, not the tax cut, was the real threat to investment. A cut in government purchases, they said, would be a much more effective way than a tax increase to reduce interest rates and stimulate investment.

A Revised Look at the Effects of Monetary Policy

Chapter 12 described the effects of a change in the money supply, given the assumption that the money demand curve would remain fixed when the money supply curve shifted. In this section we will look at the effect of a money supply change within the framework of the Keynesian theory, taking interactions between the money market and the level of national income into account.

An open-market purchase   To be precise, suppose that the Federal Reserve begins an expansion of the money supply by means of an open-market purchase of securities. (Expanding the money supply by cutting the discount rate or reserve requirements would have the same effect.)

The initial effect of the open-market purchase is to create an increase in bank reserves. Banks set to work to convert their excess reserves into earning assets by buying securities and making loans. In the process, as explained in Chapter 12, the money supply expands and interest rates fall. This is shown in Box 13.7 by the shift in the money supply curve from the position MS_1 to the position MS_2. The decrease in interest rates causes people to move downward along money demand curve MD_1 toward its intersection with the new money supply curve, MS_2.

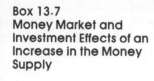

Box 13.7
Money Market and
Investment Effects of an
Increase in the Money
Supply

An increase in the money supply shifts the money supply curve from MS_1 to MS_2. The immediate effect of this shift is a movement downward along money demand curve MD_1 toward its intersection with the new money supply curve. The interest rate falls, and planned investment increases. This pushes up nominal national income via the multiplier effect. The rise in income, in turn, shifts the money demand curve to a new position, MD_2, cutting short the drop in the interest rate. A new equilibrium is reached with the interest rate at r_2.

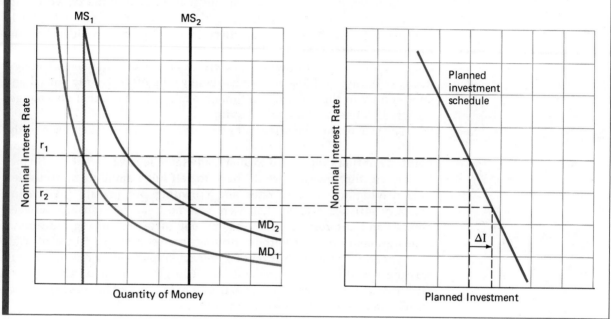

Effects on income and investment   As the interest rate begins to fall, firms increase their planned investment. This is shown by a movement downward and to the right along the planned-investment schedule. The increase in investment shifts the aggregate nominal demand schedule upward, as shown in Box 13.8. Planned expenditure now exceeds nominal national income and, by the multiplier process, nominal national income begins to increase.

As nominal income increases, the money market is affected again. Now the money demand curve begins to shift to the right, moving toward the position marked MD_2 in Box 13.7. This shift cuts off the fall in the interest rate, and a new equilibrium interest rate is reached where MD_2 and MS_2 intersect. The new money demand curve is higher than the old one, but it is not high enough to prevent the interest rate from falling at least somewhat.

Once interest rate r_2 is reached, planned investment stops expanding. The aggregate nominal demand schedule comes to rest at a new equilibrium position, AND_2, as shown in Box 13.8. This means that the new equilibrium interest rate will be lower than before and the new equilibrium nominal national income will be higher.

**Box 13.8
The Effects of an
Increase in the Money
Supply on Nominal
National Income**

An increase in planned investment caused by an increase in the money supply shifts the aggregate demand curve upward. The amount of the shift is equal to the change in investment, ΔI. A new equilibrium is reached, with nominal national income rising from Y_1 to Y_2.

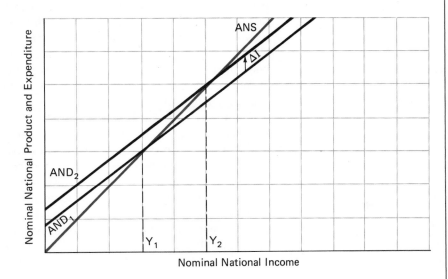

Inflationary Expectations, Interest Rates, and Monetary Policy

The Keynesian theory was developed at a time when inflation was not a major concern. As inflation worsened in the 1970s and 1980s, it became more and more apparent that some conclusions of the Keynesian theory did not apply well to a world in which the price level was variable rather than constant. One of the most striking examples has to do with the connection between monetary policy and interest rates. In the Keynesian theory, as just presented, expansionary monetary policy leads to lower interest rates. Yet throughout the 1970s and into the 1980s, as the average rate of monetary expansion increased, interest rates rose to record highs instead of falling.

To be sure, Chapter 12 showed that a fixed, upward-sloping money supply curve can cause the money stock and interest rates to rise together when the money demand curve shifts to the right. However, this is primarily a short-run phenomenon. The increase in interest rates during the 1970s took place at a time when expansionary monetary policy was shifting the money supply curve to the right, and doing so at an increasing rate.

The key to understanding the relationship between monetary policy and interest rates during the 1970s and 1980s is the distinction between real and nominal interest rates. This distinction was ignored earlier in the chapter, where we assumed zero inflation. It is time now to drop this assumption and look at the effects of monetary policy on interest rates in a world where the price level is variable. In such a world the long-run effect of increasing the rate of money supply growth, at least beyond some point, will be higher, rather than lower, nominal interest rates. The reasoning behind this statement is as follows.

First, although there is no practical limit to the rate at which monetary policy can cause nominal national income to expand, there is a limit to how fast real national income can expand. This limit is established by trends in technology, capital accumulation, and the labor force. As we first saw in Chapter 1, the trend rate of growth of real GNP in the United States has been in the neighborhood of 3 percent per year. In the long run, then, if expansionary monetary policy forces the rate of growth of nominal GNP above 3 percent, the excess growth must take the form of inflation.

The next step in the reasoning has to do with the reaction of asset holders to inflation. In deciding how to balance their portfolios, potential buyers of fixed-interest securities, especially long-term bonds, will look closely at the real rate of interest they expect to earn, that is, at the nominal rate of interest minus the expected rate of inflation. For any given nominal rate of interest, an increase in the expected rate of inflation will drive the expected real rate of interest down, making bonds less attractive. Investors will try to reduce their holdings of bonds, thereby driving down bond prices and driving up their nominal yields. For the same reason, potential buyers of newly issued long-term bonds will demand an "inflation premium" in the form of a higher nominal coupon rate if they are to buy the new bonds at face value. Much the same thing will happen in financial markets other than the bond market. Thus an increase in the expected rate of inflation will push up the whole family of nominal interest rates.

Coordination of Monetary and Fiscal Policy

Although we have looked at monetary and fiscal policy separately up to this point, in practice both kinds of policy are carried on at once. In some periods they have been closely coordinated. In others, the Fed has openly defied the Treasury and conducted monetary policies that were counter to the trend of fiscal policy.

The 1950s and 1960s   During World War II, as we mentioned at the end of Chapter 12, the Fed cooperated closely with the Treasury. While the Treasury was selling large numbers of bonds to finance the war, the Fed supported bond prices through open-market purchases. The aim was to stabilize interest rates at a low level, making the deficit less expensive to finance. This policy of cooperation continued until 1951.

The so-called Treasury-Federal Reserve accord of 1951 ended bond price supports and left the Fed free to pursue its own policies. Throughout most of the next three decades, a spirit of cooperation prevailed. There were some notable exceptions, however. In the late 1960s, during the Vietnam War, President Johnson was reluctant to raise taxes even though military spending was rising fast. In the second half of 1966 the Fed became worried that the economy was overheating. It cut the rate of growth of M1 from 6.4 percent per year to zero. Johnson, who wanted continued economic expansion at home to offset criticism of the unpopular war abroad, was angered by the Fed's move. He called William McChesney Martin, then chairman of the Federal Reserve Board, to his Texas ranch for consultation. Martin flew to Texas but remained unconvinced. Supporters of the Fed's independence from political control dubbed this episode "the Fed's finest hour." The Fed's restraint did slow economic growth.

Monetary policy and deficits in the 1980s   In the 1980s, federal budget deficits of record size have put a new focus on the interaction between monetary and fiscal policy. The results of the large deficits were much as Keynesian theory would lead us to expect: The economy recovered briskly from the 1981–1982 recession. Nominal interest rates fell, but not as rapidly as the rate of inflation fell. As a result, real interest rates rose. High real interest rates were a source of worry to many people. They were afraid the high rates would discourage business investment and consumer spending on housing, cars, and other durable goods. Some people urged the Fed to ease its monetary policy, hoping that this would bring interest rates down.

But the Fed was reluctant to ease monetary policy as much as some of its critics wanted. If monetary policy were eased while fiscal policy remained expansionary, it warned, growth of aggregate nominal demand would further outrun growth of real productive capacity. The result would be higher inflation. This would push nominal interest rates higher without necessarily reducing real interest rates.

Instead, as indicated in the news item that began this chapter, the Fed urged that the deficit be reduced by cuts in government purchases and transfer payments. If fiscal policy were tightened in this way, according to the Keynesian model, interest rates would tend to fall. To prevent the tighter fiscal policy from slowing the growth of nominal GNP, the Fed could then put monetary policy on a more expansionary path. Such a shift in the monetary-fiscal policy mix would give room for both nominal and real interest rates to fall substantially.

This analysis calls attention to a broader conclusion that can be drawn from the Keynesian model: For any given nominal national income target there is a trade-off between monetary and fiscal policy. The desired growth of nominal national income can be achieved by an expansionary fiscal policy together with a tight monetary policy; by an expansionary monetary policy combined with a tight fiscal policy; or by a balanced program somewhere between these two extremes. According to the Keynesian model, the main difference between the two strategies would be in the level of interest rates and investment. With an easy money/tight fiscal policy approach, both real and nominal interest rates would be relatively low and investment would be relatively high as a share of GNP. With a tight money/easy fiscal policy approach, both nominal and real interest rates would be higher, while consumption and government purchases would be larger in relation to GNP.

International effects   An expansionary fiscal policy combined with a tight monetary policy, as we have seen, implies high real interest rates. High real interest rates, in turn, can cause a crowding out of private investment. Yet during the recovery from the 1981–1982 recession, both business fixed investment and consumer investment in housing and durable goods were strong, despite high real interest rates. Where did the funds come from to finance both strong investment and the large federal deficit?

The answer is that a large part of the needed funds came from abroad. High real interest rates in the United States made dollar-denominated investments attractive to foreign investors. These foreign investors increased their purchases of securities issued by the U.S. government and private U.S. firms. They also increased their direct investments by expanding U.S.-based subsidiaries and by buying U.S. companies.

These inflows of funds from abroad supplemented domestic saving (that is, saving by U.S. households and firms), making it possible for both private investment and the federal deficit to grow. Box 13.9 gives some details. The chart shows that total demands on saving—private investment plus the federal budget deficit—grew from 7.2 percent of GNP in 1981 to 11.4 percent of GNP in 1984. Of this increase, about one third was financed by an increase in domestic saving and the remaining two thirds by an inflow of saving from abroad.

Box 13.9
Demands on Saving and Sources of Saving, 1975–1984

Part a shows demands on net saving in the U.S. economy by private investment (business fixed investment, inventory change, and housing investment) and by the federal budget deficit. Part b shows sources of net saving. Domestic sources include personal saving by U.S. households, plus business saving in the form of undistributed corporate profits and the surpluses of state and local governments. Foreign sources of saving represent flows of funds into the U.S. economy above the flows needed to pay for exports from the United States. (In years when U.S. exports exceed imports, this item is negative.) Chart a shows a sharp increase in demands on saving over the period since 1981. This growing demand was largely the result of the rising federal budget deficit. Chart b shows that increased foreign saving flows supplied about two thirds of the funds needed to finance the greater demand.

Source: Statement of Paul A. Volcker, chairman, Board of Governors of the Federal Reserve System, before the Joint Economic Committee of the U.S. Congress, February 5, 1985.

This inflow of funds from abroad meant that interest rates rose less during the recovery of 1983–1984 than they otherwise would have. This allowed investment to grow despite the growing federal deficit. Nonetheless, with a smaller deficit, investment might have grown still more.

Moreover as the Fed many times pointed out, the inflow of funds was not an unmixed blessing. The most dramatic impact was on the international value of the dollar. Increased demand for dollar-denominated assets caused the value of the dollar relative to foreign currencies to rise by about 70 percent between 1980 and early 1985.[6] A high value for the dollar made goods produced abroad cheap for U.S. buyers, and U.S. goods expensive for foreign buyers. U.S. producers of export goods—farm products, aircraft, pharmaceuticals—found it difficult to sell their wares in world markets. U.S. producers of import-competing goods—automobiles, steel, consumer electronics—faced stiff price competition and reduced profit margins. In a sense, many economists argue, production of exports and import-competing goods were "crowded out" by the federal deficit even though private investment continued to grow.

In addition, the Fed has cautioned, too much dependence on foreign saving to finance the federal budget deficit has long-run costs. As noted in Chapter 10, the argument that "we owe it to ourselves" does not apply to securities that the Treasury sells to foreign buyers. Sooner or later this part of the debt will have to be repaid, and the cost of doing so will squeeze U.S. living standards.

BEYOND KEYNES'S GENERAL THEORY

Keynes's general theory of employment, interest, and money was intended to be "general" in the sense that it would take into account both monetary and fiscal factors. However, in the first years after Keynes's work appeared, it was not the general theory as a whole that dominated the thinking of economists. Instead, some economists stressed planned expenditure and downplayed the role of money. Early followers of Keynes saw the events of the Great Depression as justifying the view that "money doesn't matter." The fact that monetary policy failed to prevent both the 46 percent decline in nominal national income and the increase in unemployment to 25 percent of the labor force between 1929 and 1933 was due, in their opinion, not to poor conduct of monetary policy but to the ineffectiveness of such policies. The fact that the depression did not end until World War II brought on a massive increase in government spending seemed to support their view.

After the war, many of the early Keynesians forecast a new depression and economic stagnation. They thought that private investment would dry up with the end of wartime spending. They were wrong. The postwar recovery of the United States and Western Europe was rapid. Central banks in most of the major economies pursued easy monetary policies during

---

[6]The factors determining the international value of the dollar will be examined in detail in Chapter 35.

those years, and inflation was more widespread than depression. The countries that were able to control inflation did so only by using standard monetary policies. Economists started to wonder whether money mattered after all and began to look again at the general Keynesian theory as a whole.

The Monetarists

The reaction against the one-sided theories of the early Keynesians received major support during the 1950s and 1960s from a group of economists led by Milton Friedman. (See Box 13.10.) Friedman's research led him to think that movements in the money supply had a much greater effect on economic events than the early Keynesians had been willing to admit. It seemed to be possible to explain even the Great Depression in terms of faulty monetary policy—especially the 25 percent decrease in the narrowly defined money supply that the Fed allowed between 1929 and 1933. Because of the emphasis they gave to monetary policy, Friedman and his followers came to be known as **monetarists**.

Monetarism
A school of economic thought that stresses changes in the money supply as a determinant of prices, income, and employment.

The economics profession did not immediately convert to monetarism. In fact, in some ways the 1960s were the heyday of Keynesian policy. Many leading Keynesians left their university posts to join the Council of Economic Advisers under Presidents Kennedy and Johnson. Even so, the ideas of the monetarists proved influential in persuading the Keynesians to return to the concept of a general theory in which monetary and fiscal policy played equal roles. And the work of the monetarists in the 1950s and 1960s paved the way for extensions of economic theory in the 1970s and 1980s. These have blurred the distinction between the two schools of thought.

Here we will focus on just one of the issues in the Keynesian-monetarist debate. (Other aspects of the debate will be discussed in Chapter 16.) This issue concerns the nature of the transmission mechanism.

The Debate Over the Transmission Mechanism

The Keynesian view   In the Keynesian theory the transmission mechanism through which monetary policy affects the rest of the economy is narrow and indirect. As we have told the story, it begins when an increase in the money supply cause households and firms to readjust their portfolios of assets. In the process of adjusting to the larger money stock, they drive up the prices of bonds and other securities and drive down nominal interest rates. This, in turn, is supposed to encourage planned investment, which, finally, stimulates aggregate demand.

There are two weak links in the transmission mechanism for monetary policy. First, it might not take much of a change in the interest rate to make people content to hold the money injected into the system. As an extreme case, early Keynesians were worried that, during a depression, people would be willing to absorb endless amounts of money without any reduction in the interest rates. The money demand curve, in effect, would be horizontal. In this situation, called a "liquidity trap," trying to stimulate the economy with monetary policy would be like "pushing on a string."

**Box 13.10
Milton Friedman,
Monetarist**

Milton Friedman
(1912–   )

In October 1976 Milton Friedman received the Nobel Memorial Prize in economics, becoming the sixth American to win or share that prize. Few people were surprised. The main surprise was that he had had to wait in line so long. The reason is that Friedman has built his career outside the economics establishment—built it, in fact, by challenging almost every major doctrine of that establishment.

Friedman was born in New York in 1912, the son of immigrant garment workers. His hardworking parents sent him to Rutgers University in New Jersey, where he came under the influence of Arthur Burns, then a young assistant professor and later to become Chairman of the Federal Reserve. From Burns, Friedman learned the importance of empirical work in economics. Statistical testing of all theory and policy prescriptions became a key feature of Friedman's later work. From Rutgers, Friedman went to the University of Chicago for an M.A. and then east again to Columbia University, where he got his Ph.D. in 1946. With his degree in hand, he returned to Chicago to teach. There he became the leading member of the Chicago school of economists, who posed a major challenge to the economists of the eastern establishment.

If one were to single out a theme that runs through all of Friedman's work, it would be his belief that the market economy works—and that it works best when it is left alone. This can be seen in his best-known work, *A Monetary History of the United States*. Written with Anna Schwartz, this book attacks two major tenets of Keynesian economics: (1) that the market economy is unstable without the guiding hand of government and (2) that monetary policy was tried and found useless as a cure for the Great Depression. Friedman and Schwartz found both beliefs to be far from the truth. "The Great Depression," Friedman later wrote, "far from being a sign of the inherent instability of the private enterprise system, is a testament to how much harm can be done by mistakes on the part of a few men when they wield vast power over the monetary system of the country."

Friedman strongly favors a hands-off policy by government in almost every area, not just in monetary matters. The trouble, in his view, is not that government is evil by nature but, rather, that so many policies end up having the opposite of their intended effect. "The social reformers who seek through politics to do nothing but serve the public interest invariably end up serving some private interest that was no part of their intention to serve. They are led by an invisible hand to serve a private interest." Transport regulation, public education, agricultural subsidies, and housing programs are among the many policy areas in which Friedman believes the government has done more harm than good and a free competitive market would do better.

Today Friedman continues to take on new challenges. He promotes his ideas before congressional committees, in professional journals, in the press, and in face-to-face debates with his colleagues. Economics has never had a more respected heretic.

The second weak link in the Keynesian transmission mechanism lies in the planned-investment schedule. Even if monetary policy were to affect interest rates, planned investment might not respond. The planned-investment schedule might be so steep that only a massive dose of monetary policy would have much effect. If this were the case, fiscal policy would be a much more effective way of stimulating aggregate nominal demand than monetary policy.

The monetarist view   Monetarists—as well as many post-Keynesian economists—see the Keynesian transmission mechanism as only one of many ways that money affects aggregate nominal demand. If, under special conditions, weak spots appear in the money-interest-investment linkage, other transmission mechanisms take over. In the extensive literature on the transmission mechanism, at least three major extensions of the Keynesian viewpoint appear.

Other portfolio effects   The Keynesian transmission mechanism begins when people adjust their portfolios in response to an increase in the money supply. Keynesians tend to stress the trade-off between money and fixed-interest securities like bonds. In the real world the choices are much broader. Besides bonds and money, people own common stocks, real estate, commodities, consumer durables, and even stocks of consumer nondurables. In the monetarist view, an excess supply of money is likely to spill over into spending on these other goods and securities.

As it does so, aggregate nominal demand is thought to be stimulated in many ways. An increase in stock prices can stimulate new investment by making it easier for corporations to issue new shares. Increases in the demand for real estate can stimulate new construction. Increases in commodity prices—prices of wheat, gold, rubber, or whatever—can stimulate production of those goods. Even consumption spending can respond directly to a change in the money supply.

In this view, then, the effect of an injection of money spreads through the whole economy. People become content to hold the newly issued money not just as a result of a change in interest rates but as a result of a broader change in the composition of their portfolios.

Wealth effects   A second extension of the Keynesian transmission mechanism involves so-called wealth effects. As we first suggested in Chapter 9, consumption spending—and hence aggregate nominal demand—may depend on people's stock of wealth as well as on their flow of income. According to economists who stress the wealth effect, money creation involves a net increase in private wealth. Partly this is because the new money itself may be viewed as a form of wealth. And partly it is because changes in portfolios increase the prices of securities, which are also forms of wealth. Feeling wealthier, people spend more on both consumer goods and investment goods. This spending stimulates aggregate demand.

Credit rationing effects   Finally, some economists believe that a complete understanding of the transmission mechanism must take into account imperfections in financial markets. Many interest rates do not vary smoothly in response to supply and demand. To the extent this is the case, "tight" money may make itself felt not so much in the form of high interest rates as in the form of credit rationing. Interest rates on home or auto loans, for example, may rise somewhat, but at the same time lenders may stop lending to any but their most creditworthy customers. When the Fed drains reserves from the banking system, then marginal borrowers may find that they cannot get loans at any price. They are forced to cut back on spending. Likewise, when the Fed injects new reserves into the system, interest rates on such loans may not fall much, but some people may find that they qualify for loans that they couldn't get before. In this way aggregate demand is stimulated. It should be noted, however, that deregulation of interest-rate ceilings on bank deposits since the late 1970s has muted these credit rationing effects.

The debate over the details and importance of these non-Keynesian transmission mechanisms is still going on. However, most economists have been convinced that money matters more than some early Keynesians were willing to admit.

Looking Ahead

This completes our discussion of monetary and fiscal policy. We now have a fairly clear picture of the ways in which these policy tools can be used together to control the level of aggregate nominal demand and, thus, the equilibrium level of nominal national income. However, as we have pointed out many times, control over nominal income is not the final goal of macroeconomic policy. It is time now to focus directly on the linkages between changes in aggregate nominal demand and nominal income, on the one hand, and inflation, unemployment, and real economic growth, on the other. That will be the job of the next five chapters.

Summary

1. The opportunity cost of capital for a firm is the interest rate that must be paid for funds obtained from outside the firm or the rate that could be earned by investing the firm's own funds elsewhere. A firm should invest up to the point at which the expected rate of return obtained from the last dollar of investment (the *marginal efficiency of investment*) falls below the opportunity cost of capital.

2. The economy's *planned-investment schedule* is a downward-sloping curve that shows total planned investment for each interest rate. A change in the interest rate, other things being equal, causes a movement along the schedule. An increase in the expected rate of return on investment shifts the schedule upward and to the right. A decrease in the expected rate of return shifts it downward and to the left.

3. The money market is linked to the circular flow of income and product in two ways. First, a change in interest rates brought about by a shift in money supply or demand will affect planned investment and, hence, the position of the aggregate nominal demand curve. Second, a change in the level of nominal national income will affect the position of the money demand curve and, hence, the equilibrium interest rate.

4. Keynesian theory takes the linkages between the circular flow and the money market into account. According to this theory, any given set of conditions results in a unique equilib-

rium pair of values for nominal national income and the interest rate.

5. In the Keynesian theory, an expansionary fiscal policy shifts the aggregate nominal demand curve upward and raises the equilibrium value of nominal national income. Rising nominal national income shifts the money demand curve to the right, raising the interest rate. The rise in the interest rate causes a drop in planned investment. This partly offsets the upward shift in aggregate nominal demand— a phenomenon known as the *crowding-out effect*. The final result of an expansionary fiscal policy is a higher level of nominal national income and a higher interest rate.

6. In the Keynesian theory, an increase in the money supply shifts the money supply curve to the right and drives down the interest rate. This stimulates planned investment. The rise in investment pushes up the aggregate nominal demand curve, thus raising the equilibrium value of nominal national income. The increase in nominal national income shifts the money demand curve to the right, thus partly offsetting the drop in the interest rate. The end result is a higher level of nominal national income and a lower interest rate. However, when inflation is taken into account, this result must be modified. In the long run, a rate of money growth so high that it causes inflation will cause the nominal interest rate to rise, not fall.

7. Monetary and fiscal policy both affect nominal national income and interest rates. This means that a variety of policy mixes can be used to achieve any given nominal national income target: a tight fiscal policy combined with an easy monetary policy; a tight monetary policy combined with an easy fiscal policy; or moderate use of both types of policies. According to the Keynesian theory, a mix that combines tight fiscal policy and easy monetary policy will, other things being equal, result in lower nominal and real interest rates than the opposite mix.

8. The term *monetarism* refers to a school of thought that places more emphasis on monetary policy than Keynesian economists do. The two schools differ in their views of the transmission mechanism of monetary policy. Keynesians stress the linkage from interest rates to planned investment to aggregate nominal demand. Monetarists also call attention to other portfolio effects, wealth effects, and credit rationing effects.

Questions for Review

1. Define the following terms:
   marginal efficiency of investment
   planned-investment schedule
   transmission mechanism
   crowding-out effect
   monetarism

2. Why does the interest rate represent the opportunity cost of capital for a firm that finances a project with funds retained from its own earnings?

3. Explain whether each of the following would be shown better by a shift in the planned-investment schedule or by a movement along the schedule: (a) a change in the nominal interest rate, given no change in the rate of inflation; (b) an increase in the expected rate of return on investment.

4. In the Keynesian theory, why does a shift in the position of the aggregate nominal demand curve cause a shift in the position of the money demand curve? Why does a change in the interest rate cause a shift in the aggregate nominal demand curve?

5. In the Keynesian model, how does an expansionary fiscal policy affect nominal national income and the interest rate? How does a contractionary fiscal policy affect them?

6. In the Keynesian model, how does an expansionary monetary policy affect nominal national income and the interest rate? How does a contractionary monetary policy affect them? How is the relationship between monetary policy and interest rates affected when inflation is taken into account?

7. If the Fed wants to maintain low interest rates, is its job made easier or harder by an expansionary fiscal policy? What are the international implications of a policy that combines expansionary fiscal policy with tight monetary policy?

8. What lessons about monetary policy did Keynesians tend to draw from the events of the Great Depression? What lessons did monetarists tend to draw from the same events?

Problems and Topics for Discussion

1. Your college football stadium is sold out for ten games each year. Tickets cost $20 each. The school is thinking of adding a new section to the stands that would hold 1,000 more people. Building the section would cost $1 million. The school can borrow the money at an interest rate of 14 percent. Should it do so? If it keeps adding seats, at some point it will not be possible to fill them all for every game. What does this imply about the marginal efficiency of investment in stadium seats?

2. Rework the graphs in Boxes 13.4 and 13.5 for the case of a tax increase. Trace the sequence of events step by step. Will the interest rate be higher or lower in the new equilibrium? Will nominal national income be higher or lower? Assume that the full marginal propensity to consume applies to changes in disposable income that result from changes in taxes.

3. Make two more sets of graphs like the ones in Boxes 13.4 and 13.5. In one of them, make the money demand schedule steeper than MD_1 and the planned-investment schedule flatter. In the other, make the money demand schedule flatter and the planned-investment schedule steeper. Now trace the effects of an increase in government spending through both sets of graphs. In which case is the crowding-out effect greater? Why?

4. Make yet another set of graphs like the ones in Boxes 13.4 and 13.5. This time, assume that the Fed follows a policy of holding interest rates constant by allowing the money supply to expand each time money demand increases. (You can represent this policy with a horizontal money supply curve drawn at the interest rate r_1.) Now trace the effects of an increase in government spending. Is there a crowding-out effect? Why or why not?

5. Rework the graphs in Boxes 13.7 and 13.8 for the case of a decrease in the money supply. What will this do to interest rates? To nominal national income? To the position of the money demand curve?

6. As in question 3, prepare two sets of graphs with different slopes for the money demand curve and the planned-investment schedule. Using the graphs, trace the effects of an increase in the money supply. In which case do the results match monetarist predictions more closely? In which case are they closer to Keynesian predictions? Why is there a difference?

7. **Case for Discussion**
   The 1984 presidential election campaign was marked by sharp economic policy differences between Ronald Reagan, the Republican candidate, and Walter Mondale, his Democratic opponent. Mondale promised that if he was elected he would raise taxes, cut arms spending, and restore only a few of the cuts that Reagan had made in domestic spending during his first term. This, he said, would result in a reduction of the bloated federal deficit—a problem that polls showed to be a major concern of voters. Reagan, in contrast, pledged to hold down taxes and maintain arms spending. He held out hope for further cuts in domestic spending, but it was clear that his fiscal policy would be more expansionary than Mondale's. The president's economists attacked Mondale's economic program as too contractionary, saying that it would end the 1983-1984 expansion and bring on a new recession.

Questions:
a. Is there any basis in Keynesian theory for Reagan's charge that Mondale's program could have brought on a recession? Explain.
b. You are the chairman of the Federal Reserve.

Mondale has been elected and has persuaded Congress to adopt his economic program. You were happy with the rate at which nominal national income was growing under the Reagan program and would like to maintain that rate of growth. What would you do?

c. Because high interest rates are unpopular, both Reagan and Mondale promised to take steps to bring interest rates down. On the basis of the Keynesian theory, which candidate's program would have had a better chance of bringing interest rates down? Why?

d. You are the head of a large steel company that has been suffering from import competition brought on by the strong U.S. dollar. Which program would you prefer, Reagan's or Mondale's? Why?

Suggestions for Further Reading

Friedman, Milton, and Walter J. Heller. *Monetary vs. Fiscal Policy.* New York: Norton, 1969.

A classic debate between a leading monetarist and a leading Keynesian.

Gordon, Robert J. *Macroeconomics*, 3rd ed. Boston: Little, Brown, 1984.

Chapters 4 and 5 cover the subject of this chapter at a more advanced level. Readers who work through Appendix B to this chapter may want to go on and try the IS-LM diagrams in Gordon.

Tobin, James. "The Monetarist Counter-Revolution Today—An Appraisal." *Economic Journal* 91 (March 1981), pp. 29–42.

An appraisal of monetarism by a leading Keynesian thinker. The article by David Laidler in the same issue is also of interest.

Appendix A to Chapter 13

Discounting and Investment Decision Making

The GFMI insulation example given in the chapter illustrates investment decision making for the simple case in which the benefits of an investment are equal in every year and continue in later years. This appendix applies the concept of discounting, first discussed in the appendix to Chapter 4, to investment decision making for cases in which the benefits of an investment continue for a fixed length of time and may not be equal in each year.

The Discounted Net Cash Flow Approach

Suppose, for example, that GFMI is thinking of buying a stamping machine to make certain small metal parts that it formerly bought from a subcontractor at a cost of $40,000 a year. Two firms submit bids to supply the machine. Supplier A offers its machine for $100,000. The machine will cost $15,000 a year to operate and will last five years. At the end of the fifth year it will have a salvage value of $5,000. Supplier B offers its machine for $95,000. This machine will also last five years and have a salvage value of $5,000, but it will cost $20,000 a year to operate. In an effort to offset the higher operating costs, supplier B offers to pay the entire $20,000 operating cost during the first year. Which machine is a better buy?

Box 13A.1 presents the data needed to make a decision. Column 2 shows GFMI's annual net cash flow (plus for dollars flowing in, minus for dollars flowing out) for each machine. The initial cost of the machine is listed as a negative net cash flow at year zero. Each year's net cash flow after that is equal to the $40,000 that GFMI will save by not buying parts, minus the operating expenses of the machine, plus operating subsidies from the supplier (if any), plus salvage value in the last year.

It is not clear from the net cash flow figures alone which machine is a better buy or even whether either is worth buying. Supplier A's machine gives a larger net cash flow in every year except year 1; however, it costs more to buy. Supplier B's machine is cheaper and gives a larger net cash flow in year 1 because of the operating subsidy. In the long run both machines yield total savings $30,000 greater than their purchase prices, but the time pattern of the savings is different.

To evaluate the two bids, GFMI must apply the discounting formula to each year's net cash flow. First it must figure out the interest rate to use in the formula. The correct interest rate is the opportunity cost of capital to GFMI. If GFMI plans to borrow the funds needed for the project, the opportunity cost of capital is the rate of interest charged on the loan. If GFMI plans to finance the project with retained earnings, the opportunity cost is measured by the rate of interest that the firm could have earned if it had used the funds to buy bank certificates of deposit, bonds of another firm, or some other interest-bearing asset. Suppose the opportunity cost of capital for this project is 10 percent per year. Column 3 of Box 13A.1 shows

Box 13A.1
The Net Present Value
Approach

This box shows how GFMI can evaluate the bids of two suppliers of stamping machines. Supplier A's machine costs $100,000, shown by the negative net cash flow at year 0. Because of lower operating costs, it yields a greater net cash flow than B's $95,000 machine in years 2–5. To offset this, B offers an operating subsidy in year 1. Column 3 gives the discount factor for each year. This factor is the present value of $1 payable in the given year, using the present-value formula given in the appendix to Chapter 4. Column 4 is the product of columns 2 and 3. Comparing the bottom lines of column 4 for the two suppliers, we see that B's machine gives the higher net present value.

Year (1)	Net Cash Flow (2)	Discount Factor (10 percent discount rate) (3)	Discounted Net Cash Flow (4)
Supplier A			
0	−$100,000	1.00	−$100,000
1	25,000	0.91	23,750
2	25,000	0.83	20,750
3	25,000	0.75	18,750
4	25,000	0.68	17,000
5	30,000	0.62	18,600
		Total discounted net cash flow	−$ 2,150
Supplier B			
0	−$95,000	1.00	−$95,000
1	40,000	0.91	36,400
2	20,000	0.83	16,600
3	20,000	0.75	15,000
4	20,000	0.68	13,600
5	25,000	0.62	15,500
		Total discounted net cash flow	$ 2,100

the discount factor that needs to be applied in each year. That factor is the present value of one dollar payable in each year, discounted at 10 percent, using the present-value formula given in the appendix to Chapter 4.

Column 4 of the box gives the discounted net cash flow for each year (column 2 times column 3). Adding the figures in column 4, we get the total discounted net cash flow, or present value, for each option. For supplier A's machine the discounted net cash flow is negative, which means that the present value of the cost savings from this machine is less than its purchase price. If A's machine were the only choice, GFMI would do better to go on buying its parts from the subcontractor. Supplier B's machine produces a total discounted net cash flow of $2,100. This machine is worth buying. By the time it wears out, in year 5, it will have returned savings whose present value exceeds the purchase price by $2,100.

The Internal Rate of Return Approach

Another approach to investment decision making asks which discount rate would make the discounted net cash flow for a given investment just equal to zero. This discount rate, called the project's *internal rate of return*, is the break-even point for the project. If the opportunity cost of capital is below the internal rate of return, the project is worthwhile; if it is above the internal rate of return, the project is not worthwhile.

If two forms of the same investment are under consideration, as in the GFMI example, the one with the higher internal rate of return should be chosen. Financial analysis textbooks provide ways of calculating the exact internal rate of return for any project, but for the simple examples given here a trial-and-error method can be used. By this means we can verify that the internal rate of return for supplier A's bid is about 8 percent, whereas the internal rate of return for supplier B's bid is about 12.5 percent.

The higher internal rate of return indicates that supplier B's bid is superior to supplier A's. Given the assumed opportunity cost of capital of 10 percent, supplier B's stamping machine should be purchased. If the opportunity cost of capital rose above 12.5 percent, however, neither project would be worthwhile.

For most purposes the net present value and internal rate of return approaches to investment decision making are equivalent. Of the two, however, the internal rate of return approach comes closer to the reasoning behind the planned-investment schedule discussed in Chapter 13. The internal rate of return for a given project can be viewed as the marginal efficiency of investment for that project. One way to view the downward slope of the planned-investment schedule is to note that as the interest rate falls, it becomes worthwhile for firms to undertake investment projects with lower internal rates of return.

Appendix B to Chapter 13

The Elementary Algebra of Money and Income Determination

This appendix is a continuation of the appendix to Chapter 9, which presented a simple algebraic version of the multiplier theory. It adds no new theory to what has been discussed in Chapter 13. However, readers who feel comfortable with elementary algebra may find that the approach given here can help them better understand the model Keynesian theory. Throughout this appendix the inflation rate is assumed to be zero, as in the first part of Chapter 13.

Aggregate Demand

The basic equation for aggregate nominal demand or planned expenditure is

$$\text{AND} = C + I + G + X - M \tag{13A.1}$$

In the appendix to Chapter 9 the C in this equation was replaced with a consumption schedule, which was written as

$$C = a + b(Y - T) \tag{13A.2}$$

where a and b were constants representing autonomous consumption and the marginal propensity to consume and $Y - T$ stood for nominal disposable income. Now the I in equation 13A.1 will be replaced with a simple planned-investment schedule:

$$I = c + dr \tag{13A.3}$$

where I stands for planned investment and r for the interest rate, and c and d are constants. The constant d, which is the reciprocal of the slope of the planned-investment schedule, will have a negative value because planned investment increases as the interest rate falls.

Putting together equations 13A.1, 13A.2, and 13A.3, we arrive at the following general expression for the aggregate-demand schedule:

$$\text{AND} = a + c + b(Y - T) + dr + G + X - M \tag{13A.4}$$

Money Demand

The Keynesian model also requires a money demand schedule. The one used in Chapter 12 gave a money demand curve in the shape of a rectangular hyperbola. (Box 12.1, for example, is based on the formula MD $= 1.2Y/r$.) To retain this kind of money demand schedule would involve the use of quadratic equations and greatly complicate the arithmetic, so it is replaced with a linearized money demand schedule written as

$$MD = e + fY + gr \qquad (13A.5)$$

where MD stands for the quantity of money demanded, r for the interest rate, and Y for income, and e, f, and g are constants. The constant g is the reciprocal of the slope of the money demand schedule. It is negative because the amount of money demanded decreases when the interest rate rises.

This linear formulation of the money demand function has certain drawbacks, however. One is that, except for a certain central range of the variables, algebraic solution of the equilibrium equations (to be presented shortly) may produce negative values for income or the interest rate. Such values have no economic meaning. We will be careful to keep within the safe range of values in the examples given here.

Numerical Values

The constants in these equations can be replaced with numerical values to show how the algebraic formulations of planned expenditures and money demand can be put to work. Using $a = 100$, $b = 0.75$, $c = 200$, $d = -500$, $e = 80$, $f = 0.2$, and $g = -400$, equations 13A.4 and 13A.5 can be rewritten as

$$AND = 300 + 0.75(Y - T) - 500r + G + X - M \qquad (13A.6)$$

and

$$MD = 80 + 0.2Y - 400r \qquad (13A.7)$$

Equilibrium Conditions

As shown in Chapter 13, the economy as a whole can be in equilibrium only when both the money market and the circular flow are in equilibrium. Money market equilibrium requires that the money supply equal the demand for money, and equilibrium in the circular flow requires that national product be equal to planned expenditure. These equilibrium conditions can be written as

$$MS = MD \qquad (13A.8)$$

for the money market, where MS stands for the money supply, and as

$$Y = AND \qquad (13A.9)$$

for the circular flow.

Substituting equations 13A.6 and 13A.7 into equations 13A.8 and 13A.9, we find that

$$MS = 80 + 0.2Y - 400r \qquad (13A.10)$$

and

$$Y = 300 + 0.75(Y - T) - 500r + G + X - M \qquad (13A.11)$$

which simplifies to

$$Y = 1{,}200 - 3T + 4(G + X - M) - 2{,}000r \qquad (13A.12)$$

Equilibrium in the economy is possible only for pairs of values for r and Y that satisfy both equation 13A.10 and equation 13A.12.

Policy Variables

Besides r and Y, there are five variables in equations 13A.10 and 13A.12 for which numerical values have not yet been specified. Two of these values are X (exports) and M (imports). The problems that follow will be simplified by the assumption that imports equal exports, so that the two cancel out and can be ignored. The remaining three variables are G (government purchases), T (lump sum net taxes), and MS (the money supply). These are referred to as *policy variables* because they stand for the aspects of the economy that are under the direct control of the government. The following problems show how these variables can be manipulated by policymakers in attempting to hit certain economic targets.

Problem 1   Policymakers set their policy variables at the values $G = 150$, $T = 100$, and MS $= 300$. Use equations 13A.10 and 13A.12 to determine the equilibrium values of r and Y.

Solution   Equation 13A.10 becomes

$$300 = 80 + 0.2Y - 400r$$

and equation 13A.12 becomes

$$Y = 1{,}200 - 300 + 600 - 2{,}000r$$

Simplifying and setting the equations equal to zero, we find that

$$220 - 0.2Y + 400r = 0$$
$$1{,}500 - Y - 2{,}000r = 0$$

The usual methods for solving simultaneous equations give the pairs of values $r = 0.10$ and $Y = 1{,}300$ as the equilibrium levels for interest rate and nominal national income.

Problem 2   Using the solution to problem 1 as a starting point, assume that policymakers want to raise the equilibrium level of nominal national income to a target level of $1,400 using monetary policy alone. How much will the money supply have to be increased to meet this goal?

Solution   Substitute $Y = 1{,}400$, $G = 150$, and $T = 100$ into equation 13A.12 in order to find the required equilibrium value for r. The substitution gives

$$1,400 = 1,200 - 300 + 600 - 2,000r$$

which simplifies to

$$100 - 2,000r = 0$$

The solution to the last equation is $r = 0.05$.

Next, substitute the equilibrium values $Y = 1,400$ and $r = 0.05$ into equation 13A.10 in order to determine the money supply required to give a 0.05 interest rate when nominal national income is $1,400. This substitution gives

$$MS = 80 + 0.2(1,400) - 400(0.05) = 340$$

The solution to the problem, then, is that the money supply must be increased by $40—from $300 to $340—in order to raise nominal national income to $1,400.

Problem 3   Using the solution to problem 1 as a starting point, show that an increase of $50 in government purchases will be more effective in raising the equilibrium level of nominal national income if the Fed holds the interest rate to a target level of 10 percent than if it pursues a policy of holding the money supply constant at $300.

Solution   To maintain the interest rate target, the Fed must expand the money supply enough to keep the interest rate unchanged. Substitute the values $T = 100$, $G = 200$, and $r = 0.10$ into equation 13A.12 to get the new value that equilibrium nominal national income will reach if the needed monetary policy is pursued. Without going into details, we can say that the new equilibrium, Y, with the needed monetary policy is $1,500. (Further substitution of $Y = 1,500$ and $r = 0.10$ into equation 13A.10 will show that the money supply would have to be increased to $340 to achieve this result.)

Without this accommodating monetary policy, the new values of Y and r are found by going through the steps outlined in the solution to problem 1, using $G = 200$. Again without going into details, we can say that the solution is $Y = 1,400$ and $r = 0.15$. Substitution of the new, higher value of the interest rate into the investment schedule ($I = 200 - 500r$) shows that $25 of the original $150 in private planned investment is crowded out by the $50 increase in government purchases. This accounts for the lower equilibrium value of Y when accommodating monetary policy is not used.

DPT AMOUNT

45,000

ALARM % (—) VO ST TL CG SHORT

TABLA DE LA NUEVA MONEDA

‹desde el 1° de Junio de 1983›

PESO ACTUAL	PESO ley 18.188	PESO 'VIEJO'
	10.000	1.000.000
1	100.000	10.000.000
10	1.000.000	100.000.000
100	100	10.000
1 Centavo	500	50.000
5 Centavos	1.000	100.000
10 Centavos	5.000	500.000
50 Centavos		O.C.V.

In some countries inflation is so rapid that cash registers can't keep up with all the added zeros. This picture shows a shop scene in Argentina.

DGI

Part IV
Inflation, Unemployment, and Economic Growth

Chapter 14

Changes in Prices, Real Output, and Employment

After reading this chapter, you should be able to

1. Explain what is meant by the economy's *natural level of real output,* and show how this is related to the *natural rate of unemployment.*
2. Distinguish between movements along the economy's aggregate real supply curve and shifts in the curve.
3. Use aggregate real supply and demand curves to show how a drop in aggregate demand causes a recession and two ways in which the economy can recover from a recession.
4. Define *demand-pull inflation* and explain how it affects real output.
5. Define *cost-push inflation* and show how it can lead to an *inflationary recession.*
6. Distinguish between the *adaptive-expectations hypothesis* and the *rational-expectations hypothesis.*
7. Explain the implications of the rational-expectations hypothesis for economic policy.
8. Discuss the factors that give the economy's short-run aggregate real supply curve an upward slope.

Ideas for Review

Here are some terms and concepts that you should review before you read this chapter:

The business cycle (Chapter 1)
The production possibility frontier (Chapter 2)
Aggregate real supply and demand (Chapter 7)
Fiscal policy (Chapter 10)
Target level of nominal national income (Chapter 10)
Monetary policy (Chapters 12 and 13)

"We weren't talking revolution; we were talking jobs."

Ed Paulsen's family was from South Dakota. He finished high school in 1930, as the country was sliding toward the depths of the Great Depression. He went west to pick apples in Washington State and then worked on road gangs. In 1931 he ended up in San Francisco.

I tried to get a job on the docks. I was a big husky athlete, but there just wasn't any work. Already by that time, if you were looking for a job at a Standard Oil Service Station, you had to have a college degree. It was that kind of market. . . . I'd get up at five in the morning and head for the waterfront. Outside the Spreckles Sugar Refinery, outside the gates, there would be a thousand men. You know dang well there's only three or four jobs. The guy would come out with two little Pinkerton cops: "I need two guys for the bull gang. Two guys to go into the hole." A thousand men would fight like a pack of Alaskan dogs to get through there. Only four of us would get through. I was too young a punk. . . . These were fathers, eighty percent of them. They had held jobs and didn't want to kick society to pieces. They just wanted to go to work and they just couldn't understand. There was a mysterious thing. You watched the papers, you listened to rumors, you'd get word somebody's going to build a building. So the next morning you get up at five o'clock and you dash over there. You got a big tip. There's three thousand men there, carpenters, cement men, guys who knew machinery and everything else. These fellas always had faith that the job was going to mature somehow. More and more men were after fewer and fewer jobs. . . . We weren't greatly agitated in terms of society. Ours was a bewilderment, not an anger. Not a sense of being particularly put upon. We weren't talking revolution; we were talking jobs.[1]

The last five chapters have spent a lot of time discussing the factors that determine national income and product in nominal terms. The real goals of economic policy—prosperity, jobs, and price stability—have appeared on the stage only occasionally. Controlling nominal national income through changes in net taxes, government purchases, and the money supply can help achieve these goals, but it is not the whole story. A drop in nominal national income that throws millions of people out of work can be a national disaster. But an increase in nominal national income is no blessing if it only takes the form of higher prices.

In this chapter we shift the focus back to a set of tools that were introduced in Chapter 7—the analysis of aggregate real supply and demand. This chapter will develop these tools further and use them to explain events like the Great Depression of the 1930s and the inflation of the 1970s. The next chapter will apply the tools to the problems of long-run economic growth and productivity. Then Chapters 16–18 will examine further issues relating to inflation and unemployment in more detail.

---

[1]From Studs Terkel, *Hard Times: An Oral History of the Great Depression*, (New York: Pantheon Books, 1970), pp. 29–31. Reprinted by courtesy of Pantheon Books, a Division of Random House, Inc.

AGGREGATE REAL SUPPLY AND DEMAND IN THE SHORT AND THE LONG RUN

The Short Run: A Review

In Chapter 7 we introduced aggregate real supply and demand curves in short-run contexts. Box 14.1 reviews the short-run case. The economy is initially in equilibrium at point E_1. The equilibrium value of aggregate nominal demand is $1,000 billion, which puts the aggregate real demand curve in the position ARD_1. The price level is 1.0 and real output is $1,000 billion.

Beginning from that point, aggregate nominal demand increases to $1,100 billion. As we now know, this could be caused by any of a number of factors: a shift in the consumption schedule caused by increased consumer confidence; a shift in the planned investment schedule; an increase in exports; an increase in government purchases or a cut in net taxes; and finally, a shift toward expansionary policy by the Federal Reserve. Whatever the origin of the increase, the result will be a rightward shift of the aggregate real demand curve to ARD_2.

Box 14.1
The Short-Run Reaction to a Shift in Aggregate Real Demand

In this box the economy starts out in equilibrium at E_1 with real output of $1,000 billion and a price level of 1.0. An increase in the level of aggregate nominal demand from $1,000 billion to $1,100 billion shifts the aggregate real demand curve to the right, from ARD_1 to ARD_2. Expecting no change in the level of input prices, each firm reacts to the increase in aggregate demand as if it were an increase in demand for the product of its industry alone. As firms in each industry move up along their industry supply curves, the economy as a whole moves up and to the right along the aggregate real supply curve ARS. At point E_2 both real output and the price level have increased.

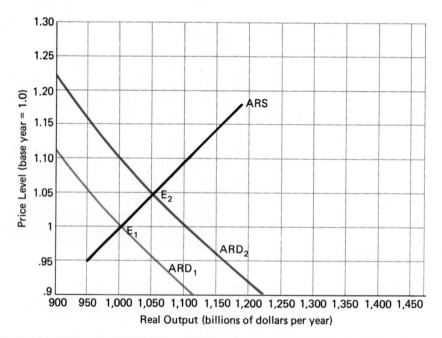

As we saw in Chapter 7, the way that firms react to this shift in aggregate real demand depends on their expectations regarding the average price level and the prices of the inputs they use in production—wages, the prices of raw materials, and so on. If the economy has previously experienced stability in the average price level, firms will have no particular reason to expect input prices to increase. In this case, each firm will respond to the increase in aggregate real demand as if it were an isolated shift in the demand curve just for the product it sells. As firms in each industry move up and to the right along the industry's supply curve, both prices and real output will increase. As a result, the economy as a whole moves up and to the right along its aggregate real supply curve from E_1 to E_2.

The Natural Level of Real Output

Natural level of real output (natural real output)
The level of output at which long-run equilibrium with stable prices is possible.

Although it is perfectly possible for the economy to move from one level of real output to another in the short run, it is not possible, in the long run, to choose just any level of real output as a point of equilibrium. Instead, at any time, every economy has just one level of real output, called the **natural level of real output** or **natural real output**, at which a long-run equilibrium with stable prices is possible. This level is determined by the economy's capital stock, its natural resources, and the size and productivity of its labor force.

The natural level of real output is not an absolute limit to what the economy can produce. Output can rise above the natural level for a brief period if more people than usual go to work, if firms add overtime work, and if standby plant capacity is brought into use. (As we will show shortly, however, the price level tends to rise during such periods.) On the other hand, in a period of recession when resources lie idle, real output falls below the natural level. (In such periods the rate of inflation and sometimes the price level itself tends to fall.)

The natural level of real output is closely related to the concept of the economy's production possibility frontier, introduced in Chapter 2. Points on the frontier represent different possible mixes of output within the natural level of overall output. If resources are not used fully, the economy will fall inside its production possibility frontier, that is, below its natural level of real output. Output above the natural level corresponds to a point outside the production possibility frontier. Such a point can be reached temporarily through overtime work, the use of standby capacity, and so on. But a permanently higher level of real output requires an expansion of the frontier as the result of investment, technological advance, or the like.

Natural rate of unemployment
The unemployment rate associated with the natural level of real output.

There is also a **natural rate of unemployment** linked with the natural level of real output. In the United States in the mid-1980s, the natural rate of unemployment is thought to be in the area of 6 to 6.5 percent of the labor force.

This natural rate reflects normal turnover within labor markets. (At all times there are some people who are entering the labor force, changing jobs, or leaving the labor force.) During periods when real output rises above its natural level, unemployment tends to fall below the natural rate. And in recessions, when output is below its natural level, unemployment moves above its natural rate. We will look more closely at the natural rate of unemployment and its connection with the natural rate of real output in Chapter 17.

Shifts in the Aggregate Real Supply Curve

The natural level of real output serves as an important benchmark as we move from the economy's short-run response to a shift in aggregate real demand to an analysis of its long-run response. Box 14.2 picks up the story where Box 14.1 left off. In this box, we have drawn a vertical line to indicate that our original starting point, a real output of $1,000 billion, is this economy's natural level of real output.

In explaining how firms react in the short run to an increase in aggregate demand, we stressed the importance of their expectations about input prices. The aggregate real supply curve ARS_1 is drawn on the assumption that firms expect input prices to remain at levels correspond-

**Box 14.2
Aggregate Real Supply
In the Long Run**

The upward-sloping aggregate real supply curve applies only in the short run because sooner or later each firm's increases in output prices become increases in other firms' input prices. As this happens, firms revise their plans to take their higher costs into account. The increase in the expected level of input prices shifts the aggregate real supply curve upward. Assuming that the aggregate real demand curve remains fixed, the economy will move upward along ARD_2 as the aggregate real supply shifts upward. In time the economy will reach a new long-run equilibrium at E_3. At that point the price level will have risen fully in proportion to the increase in demand. Real output will then have returned to its natural level of $1,000 billion, shown by the vertical line. Expected input prices will have risen to a level consistent with the new average level of output prices, 1.1.

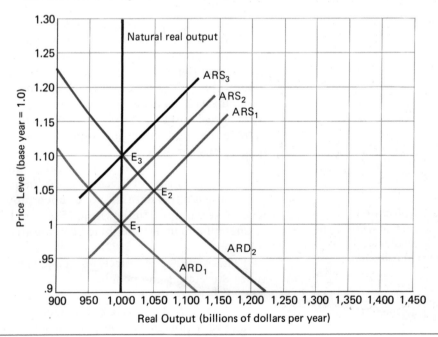

ing to an average price level for all goods of 1.0. Given this expected level of input prices, they move from E_1 to E_2 along the aggregate real supply curve.

But E_2 is not a point of long-run equilibrium. The reason is that the rise in the general price level (from 1.0 to 1.05, as Box 14.2 is drawn) will inevitably cause firms to revise their initial expectations about input prices. This happens because the prices of each firm's output affect the prices of other firms' inputs.

In the case of firms that make intermediate goods, the relationship between input prices and output prices is simple and direct: If steel mills raise the prices of their sheet steel and beams, automakers and construction firms will face an increase in their input prices. But there is also a pass-through from output prices to input prices in the case of firms that make consumer goods. In this case, the linkage runs from consumer goods prices to the cost of living to the level of wages. If firms that make shirts and radios and potato chips raise their prices, workers will face an increase in the cost of living. To maintain their standard of living, they will seek higher wages. Sooner or later these higher wages will affect the costs of all firms.

At E_2, then, the price level has risen to 1.05. The aggregate real supply curve ARS_1 assumed a level of input prices corresponding to an average level of output prices of 1.0. As the prices of each firm's outputs begin to be passed through to increases in the input prices of other firms, the expected level of input prices will rise. In Chapter 3 we saw how an increase in the prices of inputs used in producing one good—say, the fuel, fertilizer, and machinery used to produce wheat—would cause an upward shift in the supply curve for that good. In much the same way, an increase in the expected average price of all inputs causes the economy's aggregate real supply curve to shift up.

In this case, the price level has increased to 1.05. If firms now expect a level of input prices corresponding to this new average level for output prices, the aggregate real supply curve will shift up to the position ARS_2. This new aggregate real supply curve has shifted up by exactly the amount that the expected price level has risen. Thus, it passes through the natural level of real output at a height corresponding to a price level of 1.05. In fact, we can make the following generalization about the relationship between the natural level of real output and the aggregate real supply curve: The aggregate real supply curve will intersect the natural level of real output at a point corresponding to the average level of output prices on which firms base their expectations regarding input prices. For the moment, we assume that firms base their expectations regarding input prices on the average level of output prices that prevailed in the previous year.

Applying this rule will make it easy to keep track of what is going on as aggregate supply and demand conditions change. On the one hand, suppose the aggregate real demand curve shifts, other things being equal. "Other things being equal" in this case includes no change in the expected level of input prices. The result, in the short run, is a *movement along* the aggregate real supply curve. On the other hand, suppose there is a change in the expected level of input prices, other things being equal. In this case, the result is a *shift* in the aggregate real supply curve.

Moving to a New Long-Run Equilibrium

Still using Box 14.2, we can now trace the economy's path to a new long-run equilibrium. In doing so, we assume that the aggregate real demand curve remains in the position ARD_2. As the aggregate real supply curve shifts to ARS_2, reflecting a higher expected level of input prices, firms do not find it profitable to expand their output as much as they initially did. As the quantity supplied in each market is reduced, prices rise further. This is represented by a move up and to the left along the aggregate real demand curve ARD_2.

As this happens, the price level moves higher than the level of 1.05 that had been reached at E_2. As ongoing increases in output prices continue to affect the input prices of other firms, the aggregate real supply curve shifts still higher. In the long run, if there is no further change in demand, the economy will reach the point E_3, where the aggregate real supply curve has shifted all the way to ARS_3. At that point the price level has risen to 1.1 and real output is back at its natural level of $1,000 billion.

At E_3, the entire increase in demand has been converted into price increases. There is no reason for firms to expect input prices to rise more unless something new happens to demand. At this point the expected level of input prices has finally been brought back into line with the average level of output prices. Only such a point, where the intersection of the aggregate real supply and demand curves occurs at the natural level of real output, can be a point of long-run equilibrium.

APPLICATIONS OF AGGREGATE REAL SUPPLY AND DEMAND: INFLATION AND RECESSION

Aggregate real supply and demand curves make it possible to deal with a number of policy issues. They allow us to go beyond the effects of monetary and fiscal policy on nominal variables. With the help of our new tools, we can see directly the effects these policies have on real output and the price level. In this section we will begin by looking at the economy in a period of recession. After that we will look at two kinds of inflation. Throughout the discussion we will be careful to distinguish between the short-run and long-run effects of economic policy.

The Economy in Recession

A classic recession is brought about by a drop in aggregate demand. Box 14.3 illustrates the process. The story begins with the economy in equilibrium at E_1. This corresponds to the assumed natural level of real output of $1,000 billion and a price level of 1.0. Suppose now that something causes aggregate nominal demand to fall to $900 billion. Whatever the cause, falling aggregate nominal demand shifts the aggregate real demand curve from ARD_1 to ARD_2.

The first effect of the drop in demand will be unplanned inventory buildup as sales fall short of output rates. As in the case of an increase in aggregate demand, we will assume that firms at first expect no change in input prices. This being the case, they will react just as they would if their industry were the only one affected by the decline in demand. As firms in each industry move down and to the left along their own industry supply

**Box 14.3
The Economy in
Recession**

This graph shows a recession brought on by a decrease in aggregate nominal demand from $1,000 billion to $900 billion. As the aggregate real demand curve shifts from ARD₁ to ARD₂, the economy moves downward and to the left along aggregate real supply curve ARS₁. As it does so, real output falls below its natural level, and unemployment rises above its natural rate. At E_2 the economy reaches the trough of the recession. It can recover from the recession through a return of aggregate demand to its initial level. If aggregate demand remains depressed, the aggregate real supply curve will shift downward to ARS₂ and the economy will return to the natural level of real output at a lower price level. This process could be very slow, however.

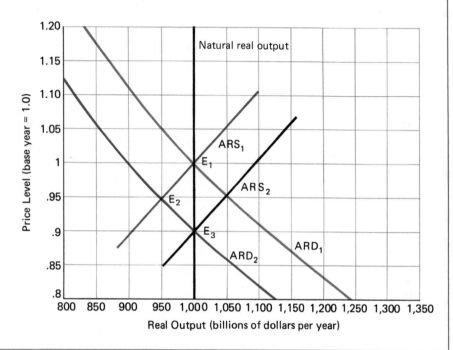

curves, the economy as a whole will move downward and to the left along the aggregate real supply curve ARS₁.

As this happens, real output and the price level both fall. Firms reduce their output or shut down. Workers are laid off and have trouble finding new jobs. The unemployment rate rises, and the economy approaches the low point of a recession.

Two paths to recovery   From E_2 there are two paths that the economy can take to return to the natural level of real output. The first possibility is that aggregate nominal demand remains at its new level of $900 billion. If this happens, the economy will not remain at E_2. Price cuts that some firms made as the economy fell into recession will increasingly come to represent cuts in other firms' input prices. As this happens, the expected level of input prices will fall, and the aggregate real supply curve will shift downward. As it does so, the economy will slowly work its way down along aggregate real demand curve ARD₂ toward a new long-run equilibrium at E_3. There, real output will return to its natural level of $1,000 billion. The price level will have fallen from 1.0 to 0.9, in proportion to the drop in aggregate nominal demand. And the expected level of input prices will be brought into line with this new lower average level of all prices.

The other path by which the economy can return to the natural level of real output is by way of a rebound of aggregate nominal demand. If

Box 14.4
A Supply-and-Demand Analysis of the Great Depression

During the 1930s the United States went through its longest and most severe economic contraction, which has become known as the Great Depression. The worst recession since World War II lasted less than two years and brought a peak unemployment rate of less than 11 percent. By comparison, the Great Depression lasted a decade and brought an unemployment rate of 24 percent in its worst year. Even half a century later, it is not fully understood why the depression was so long and so severe. But the concepts of aggregate real supply and demand can help us understand what happened, even if we are not sure why it happened.

The diagram in this box describes the Great Depression in terms of real output and the price level. The numbered points, connected by line segments, show the course of the depression from 1929, the peak of pre-depression prosperity, to 1940, when the economy began to gear up for war production.

The first phase of the Great Depression, from 1929 to 1933, was marked by a collapse of aggregate demand. Aggregate nominal demand can be found for any point on the diagram by multiplying real output by the price level. Aggregate real demand curves have been drawn through the points for 1929 and 1933. In this four-year period, nominal GNP fell from $103.5 billion to $55.8 billion—almost a 50 percent drop.

What caused the collapse? A look at the components of aggregate demand shows that demand returns to its initial level, the aggregate real demand curve will shift back to the position ARD₁. If the original shift in aggregate demand was caused by a temporary drop in consumption, investment, or net exports, the rebound in demand may take place without government action. If it does not, an expansionary fiscal or monetary policy can be used

the greatest change was in investment. Gross private domestic investment fell from a 1929 level of $58.1 billion (in 1972 dollars) to just $8.6 billion in 1933. But this does not mean that investors caused the Great Depression. Government policy was far from blameless. Economists today think that one of the biggest policy mistakes was President Hoover's decision to raise income taxes in an attempt to keep the federal deficit from rising as incomes collapsed. Hoover thought that reducing the deficit would restore business confidence. Instead, the tax increase just hastened the decline of demand. Government spending rose by only $2 billion between 1929 and 1933, far from enough to offset the $50 billion drop in investment.

Monetary policy made things worse still. The Fed failed to supply enough reserves to prevent a contraction of the money supply. Instead of boosting the money supply to stimulate aggregate demand, it allowed the money supply to fall in step with the falling price level. M1 fell by about one quarter from 1929 to 1933, while M2 fell by one third.

In theory, the economy can recover from a recession either by moving quickly back up along its short-run aggregate real supply curve or by waiting for the aggregate real supply curve and the price level to fall. Our diagram suggests that the recovery from the Great Depression followed a middle course. Prices did not continue to fall after output began to rise, as they would have if the economy had moved downward along a fixed aggregate real demand curve. However, the recovery did not move back up along its 1929–1933 path either. Except for 1934, all the points for the recovery years lie below the 1929–1933 path. This suggests that the economy's aggregate real supply curve shifted downward. By mid-1940, when the economy finally made it back up to

the 1929 level of nominal GNP, it crossed the old aggregate nominal demand curve at a point well below and to the right of the starting point.

Almost everyone agrees that the economy could have recovered faster from the Great Depression if demand had been stimulated more vigorously. However, modern economic theory also suggests that real output would have recovered more rapidly if the aggregate real supply curve had fallen faster than it did.

Was the supply side of economic policy in the 1930s as inept as the demand side? It appears in retrospect that it was. At the time, falling prices were thought to be as much a cause as a consequence of the depression. Each firm thought that if only it could charge more for its goods, it could afford to hire more workers and get production back in gear. Policymakers thought that if only nominal wages could be raised, workers could afford to buy more goods, pulling the economy up by its own bootstraps.

Following this line of thought, many policies aimed at propping up prices and wages. President Roosevelt's National Recovery Act (eventually declared unconstitutional) was designed to allow price-fixing agreements among firms. A number of farm programs were started to boost crop prices. Transportation and communications were brought under an umbrella of regulation that protected firms from competition and price cutting. And major labor legislation strengthened the hand of labor unions in bargaining for wage increases. These actions seem to have had just the effect intended: They made downward price adjustment more difficult. But, if the theory of aggregate real supply and demand is to be believed, they also made the depression longer and more painful than it need have been.

to speed the recovery. In either case, a quick recovery by aggregate demand will allow the economy to move back up along the aggregate real supply curve to E_1 before the supply curve has time to begin shifting downward.

Which path out of a recession is better? Many economists favor a policy of restoring aggregate demand, using active fiscal or monetary policy if necessary. They think that recovery through falling prices would take too long. For a number of reasons—some psychological, some having to do with long-term contracts—firms tend to raise prices more readily than they cut them. And workers seem to accept cuts in nominal wages much less willingly than they accept wage increases.

Recent recessions in the United States have not lasted long enough to bring about reductions in the general price level. (Wages and prices in hard-hit sectors such as lumber, steel, or copper often fall during recessions, but in recent recessions these have been offset by price increases in other sectors, such as services.) During the Great Depression, however, both prices and real output fell dramatically. It took a whole decade for the economy to recover. Since that time, policymakers have tried to deal with recessions by restoring aggregate demand as quickly as possible. Box 14.4 reviews the experience of the Great Depression in terms of aggregate real supply and demand.

Demand-Pull Inflation

Demand-pull inflation
An increase in the price level caused by an increase of aggregate demand relative to natural real output.

The opposite of recession is **demand-pull inflation**. This means an increase in the price level caused by an expansion of aggregate demand relative to the economy's natural level of real output. Box 14.2 gave us a first look at demand-pull inflation, although we did not use the term there. Now Box 14.5 continues the story.

The onset of demand-pull inflation
The economy starts out in equilibrium at E_0, where the price level is 1.0 and real output is equal to its natural level. Then an increase in planned expenditures shifts the aggregate real demand curve to ARD_1. The surge in demand results in unplanned inventory depletion. Expecting to be able to restock their inventories at an unchanged level of input prices, firms in each industry move up along their industry supply curves. As this happens, the economy moves up along the aggregate real supply curve ARS_1 toward a new short-term equilibrium at E_1.

This is the first stage of demand-pull inflation. The increase in demand has pulled prices up, although not fully in proportion to the increase in demand. As we stressed earlier, however, E_1 is not a point of long-run equilibrium. Soon the output price increases that have taken place on the way to E_1 will become increases in other firms' input prices. Then firms will revise their expectations of input prices and the aggregate real supply curve will begin to shift upward.

Ongoing demand-pull inflation
There are two ways in which events can unfold from this point. One was shown in Box 14.2, where aggregate nominal demand was assumed to remain fixed at its new level. In that case the aggregate real demand curve stays in the position ARD_1, and the

Box 14.5
Demand-Pull Inflation

Demand-pull inflation occurs when aggregate nominal demand increases relative to natural real output. In this graph the economy starts out at E_0, where real output is at its natural level. An increase in demand shifts the aggregate real demand curve to ARD_1. Both prices and real output rise as the economy moves upward along ARS_1. This is the first phase of demand-pull inflation. If aggregate nominal demand did not increase further, the economy would return to the natural level of real output at E_{2a} as the aggregate real supply curve shifted upward. However, a continued expansionary policy may allow the aggregate real demand curve to keep pace with the rising aggregate real supply curve. In that case the economy moves upward along the path shown by the arrow. Real output remains above its natural level, but the economy continues to experience demand-pull inflation.

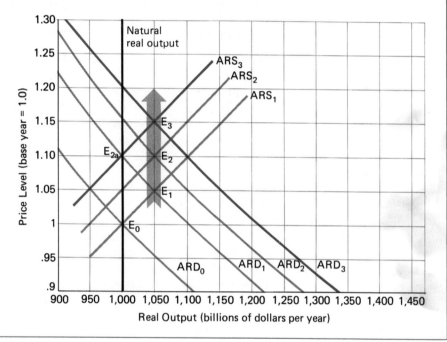

economy would drift up along the aggregate real demand curve toward E_{2a}. As it does so, the increase in real output that took place during the initial phase of demand-pull inflation would be reversed.

Instead, expansionary fiscal or monetary policy may allow aggregate nominal demand to keep on growing. In this case, as the aggregate real supply curve is driven upward by firms' expectations of rising input prices, the aggregate real demand curve keeps up with it. Real output does not fall back toward its natural level. Instead, the whole increase in aggregate nominal demand is being reflected in higher prices.

This is the second phase of demand-pull inflation, in which rising aggregate demand and expectations of a rising price level keep pace with each other. The aggregate real demand and supply curves both shift upward, and the economy follows a path from E_1 to E_2 to E_3 and so on, as shown by the arrow in Box 14.5.

Policy implications   Box 14.5 has major implications for economic policy. It says that in the short run, starting from a state of equilibrium, an expansionary fiscal or monetary policy is an effective way to stimulate real economic growth and lower unemployment. In the short run, the cost of such a policy is a small amount of inflation. However, the theory says, the benefits of demand-pull inflation are not permanent.

After the first benefits of the expansion have been enjoyed, policy-makers face a dilemma. One choice is to stop the stimulus. If they do this, inflation will slow again, but output will fall and unemployment will rise. The other choice is to continue the expansionary fiscal or monetary policy. In this case, the theory says, real output can be held above its natural level for some time, and unemployment can be kept below its natural rate. Choosing this path, however, means ongoing inflation.[2]

Cost-Push Inflation

Demand-pull inflation occurs when the aggregate real demand curve shifts upward while the aggregate real supply curve remains fixed or shifts upward at an equal rate. But inflation is also possible when the aggregate real supply curve shifts upward while the aggregate real demand curve stays in place or shifts upward at a slower rate. This type of inflation is known as **cost-push inflation** because upward shifts in the aggregate real supply curve are linked with increases in firms' costs of production.

Supply shocks   Box 14.6 shows the economy beginning in long-run equilibrium at E_1. The price level is 1.0 and real output is at its natural level of $1,000 billion. At this point something happens that raises input prices for all or most firms, and also raises workers' costs of living. The sudden increases in the cost of imported oil that hit the U.S. economy in 1974 and 1979–1980 are examples of such an event. A major crop failure or natural disaster would be another example. Such an upward push to the price level from an outside source is known as a **supply shock**.

The effect of a supply shock is to raise the level of input prices above the level that firms had expected. As firms see what has happened and adjust their expectations accordingly, the aggregate real supply curve shifts upward from ARS_1 to ARS_2. With the higher expected level of input prices but with no matching increase in demand, firms must revise their plans. They find it is no longer profitable to produce as much as before. As they cut back their output, each industry moves up and to the left along its industry demand curve. As this happens, the economy as a whole moves upward and to the left along aggregate real demand curve ARD_1 to E_2.

At E_2, real output is below its natural level and unemployment is above its natural rate. The economy cannot remain in this position, but what happens next depends on what is done with aggregate nominal demand.

Cost-push inflation
Inflation that is caused by an upward shift in the aggregate real supply curve while the aggregate real demand curve remains fixed or shifts upward more slowly.

Supply shock
An event, such as an increase in the price of imported oil, a crop failure, or a natural disaster, that raises input prices for all or most firms and pushes up workers' cost of living.

[2]As Box 14.5 is drawn, the rate of inflation is steady from year to year as the economy moves up along the path from E_1 to E_2 to E_3. In Chapter 18, which will present a more complete theory of the process of inflation, we will show that the policy implications of demand-pull inflation are even more discouraging than is suggested here. We will show that a steady rate of inflation is not enough to keep real output above its natural level for a prolonged period. Instead, a steadily accelerating rate of inflation is required.

**Box 14.6
Effects of a Supply
Shock**

A supply shock is an event, such as an increase in the price of imported oil, that drives up input prices. In this graph the economy starts out in equilibrium at E_1. Then a supply shock pushes the aggregate real supply curve upward from ARS_1 to ARS_2. As a result the economy moves from E_1 to E_2. E_2 is not a point of long-run equilibrium, since real output is below its natural rate. If the aggregate real demand curve stays in the position ARD_1, the economy will return to E_1 as the relative prices of nonenergy products fall. This will bring the average price level back to 1.0. The economy can recover from the supply shock faster if aggregate nominal demand is increased, shifting the aggregate real demand curve to ARD_2. This will move the economy to E_3. However, the result of responding to a supply shock with an increase in demand is a higher price level.

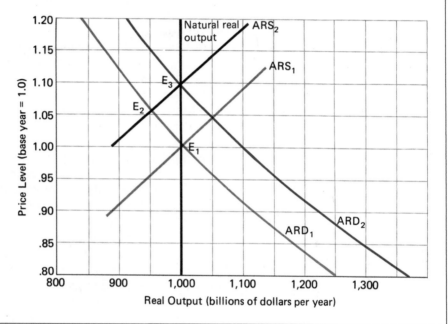

If aggregate nominal demand remains at $1,000 billion, the aggregate real demand curve will stay at ARD_1. In this case the excess capacity of firms and excess unemployment will tend to put downward pressure on wages and prices. Some unemployed workers will accept jobs at lower wages than they had hoped for. Firms will find that although energy prices remain high, the average level of input prices is not as high as they initially expected it to be. This will give them a little room to cut their prices in order to boost sales. In time the economy will move back down along ARD_1 from E_2 to E_1. The price level will fall back to where it was before oil prices rose, and output will return to its natural level.

This path to recovery from a supply shock is likely to be quite slow, however. To follow this path, average prices—output prices as well as the expected prices of inputs—must fall while energy prices, the assumed source of the supply shock, remain high. This means that there must be a major adjustment in relative prices. Real wages and the prices of goods and services other than energy must fall more than the average to bring the average down. This is likely to be a painful process for everyone.

And until it is complete, unemployment will remain above its natural rate and output below its natural level.

There is, however, another way to recover from a supply shock. This is through expansion of aggregate nominal demand. If aggregate nominal demand is raised from $1,000 to $1,100, the aggregate real demand demand curve in Box 14.6 will shift upward from ARD_1 to ARD_2. The economy can then move to an equilibrium at E_3, where output will be back at its natural level. In fact, if the expansion of aggregate nominal demand follows the supply shock quickly enough, the economy may be able to avoid any major loss of real output. Instead of moving to E_2, it will move straight up along the natural level of real output from E_1 to E_3.

Recovery from a supply shock through expansion of demand is likely to be faster than recovery through adjustment of relative prices. Also, the cost of recovery in terms of lost real output is likely to be less. But the cost in terms of inflation is greater. If policymakers respond to the supply shock by raising aggregate nominal demand, the price level will end up permanently higher. If they keep the lid on aggregate nominal demand, the impact of the supply shock on the average price level will be only temporary. After the adjustment is complete, declines in the prices of goods and services other than energy will be great enough to offset rises in energy prices, so that there is no lasting increase in the price level.

There is no general agreement on the best way to react to supply shocks. The reaction depends in part on the extent of one's dislike for inflation on the one hand and unemployment on the other. Some economists have suggested that temporary supply shocks, such as crop failures or natural disasters, should not be met by raising aggregate nominal demand. The reasoning is that the aggregate real supply curve will soon shift back down as the damage is repaired. But, they suggest, a long-lasting supply shock like the oil price increases of the 1970s might best be at least partially accommodated by raising aggregate nominal demand. It may be worth suffering the resulting permanent increase in the price level in order to avoid a prolonged transition period of low real output and high unemployment.

Inflationary expectations   Supply shocks are not the only source of cost-push inflation. Cost-push inflation can also be caused by inflationary expectations, fueled by the experience of demand-pull inflation in the past. To get this result, we need to modify our assumptions about the way firms form their expectations about the level of input prices. Up to this point we have assumed that firms expect input prices in the current year to be at a level consistent with the level of output prices in the previous year. However, this assumption is probably unrealistic in an economy that has experienced inflation for several years in a row. Under conditions of ongoing inflation, it is likely that firms will expect the level of input prices to increase this year by a percentage equal to last year's rate of inflation. To put it another way, it is likely that when firms have seen inflation in the past, they will expect more inflation in the future, and will make their plans accordingly.

Box 14.7 shows what happens when inflationary expectations become established in the economy. We begin from a situation of ongoing

Box 14.7
Inflationary Recession

In this graph the economy has been experiencing demand-pull inflation, moving along the arrow from E_1 to E_2. At that point a shift in fiscal and monetary policy stops the growth of aggregate nominal demand. The aggregate real demand curve becomes fixed in the position ARD_2. Firms and workers expect inflation to continue, pushing up input prices and the cost of living. As a result, the aggregate real supply curve continues to shift upward. As the aggregate real supply curve shifts from ARS_3 to ARS_4, the economy goes through an inflationary recession, in which prices continue to rise while real output drops below its natural level and unemployment rises above its natural rate.

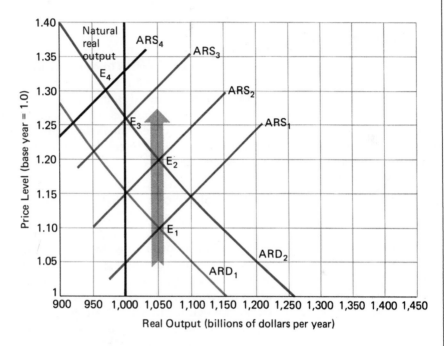

demand-pull inflation. An expansionary fiscal or monetary policy has held output above its natural level for some time. The economy is moving upward along the arrow through E_1 and E_2. After several years of inflation, firms and workers expect more inflation in the future. They have adjusted their plans to cope with it as best they can. Their plans are reflected in a series of upward-shifting aggregate real supply curves that keep pace with the upward-shifting aggregate real demand curve.

What happens now if the government decides to stop inflation by stopping the growth of aggregate nominal demand? We are not talking about reducing the level of aggregate nominal demand—only about stopping its growth. In terms of the graph, the effect would be to stop the upward shift of the aggregate real demand curve, leaving it in the position ARD_2.

Stopping the growth of aggregate demand would not stop inflation in its tracks. We have assumed that firms and workers have grown used to inflation and expect it to continue. Workers expect their cost of living to rise and have made contracts with their employers that give them offsetting wage increases each year. Firms expect their input prices to rise and have become used to passing the increases along to their customers. As long as firms expect their input prices to rise and set their prices and output plans on that basis, the aggregate real supply curve will continue to drift upward.

Inflationary recession   With the aggregate real supply curve moving upward while the aggregate real demand curve stays put, real output will start to fall and unemployment will start to rise. Meanwhile, the price level will keep going up. Soon the economy will reach E_3, where real output has returned to its natural level and unemployment is back at its natural rate. This is not the end of the story, however. Inflation is still going on, and there is no reason for firms or workers to expect it to stop. Because firms and workers expect prices to continue to rise, they continue to make their plans on this basis and the aggregate real supply curve keeps on drifting upward, as shown by ARS_4 in Box 14.7.

As the economy moves along the aggregate real demand curve toward E_4, the economy enters an **inflationary recession**. This is an episode in which inflation, high unemployment, and depressed real output all occur at the same time.

Inflationary recession
An episode in which real output falls below its natural level and unemployment rises above its natural rate while rapid inflation continues.

Policy implications   What can be done to bring the economy out of an inflationary recession? A "cold turkey" approach would be to sit tight and keep the lid on aggregate nominal demand. Rising unemployment, slowing sales, and an unplanned inventory buildup would, in time, cause firms and workers to revise their inflationary expectations. Prices of raw materials would begin to fall. Workers would accept lower wages. Slowly the economy would slip back down along the the aggregate real demand curve toward an equilibrium at E_3. But the experience would be a painful one.

A more moderate approach would be to slow the growth of aggregate demand gradually rather than stopping it cold. With luck, this could bring the economy to a "soft landing" at the natural level of real output. It might take longer to slow inflation this way, but a severe inflationary recession might, with luck, be avoided.

In practice, though, there is a danger that policymakers will overreact to an inflationary recession. Instead of easing the growth of demand gradually and bringing the economy to a soft landing, they may step on the accelerator with a burst of expansionary fiscal and monetary policy. Such a policy of "reflation" may restore economic growth, but only at the expense of ongoing price increases.

The truth of the matter is that no one knows a quick, painless way to stop inflation once it has become part of public expectations. As we will see, many economists think the best hope is not to let inflation get started in the first place. This is a theme that we will come back to in the next chapter and again in Chapter 18, where we will present a more complete analysis of inflationary recession. But even this preliminary look at the problem has drawn attention to the importance of the assumptions we make regarding the way in which firms and workers form their expectations of inflation. To conclude this chapter, let's look in more detail at the issue of how expectations are formed.

RATIONAL EXPECTATIONS AND ECONOMIC POLICY

The theory given in this chapter is built on the idea of an upward-sloping aggregate real supply curve along which the economy moves, in the short run, when aggregate demand rises or falls. We explained the aggregate real supply curve by saying that when demand rises firms do not, at least at first, expect the prices of their inputs to rise. As a result, each firm behaves as if the increase in aggregate demand was affecting its industry alone. Firms move up along their industry supply curves, and real output rises along with the price level.

Is it reasonable for firms to behave this way? Is this the way they do behave? These questions are a matter of debate in economics today—a debate that hinges on how people form their expectations.

The Adaptive-Expectations Hypothesis

Adaptive-expectations hypothesis
The hypothesis that people form their expectations about future economic events mainly on the basis of past economic events.

The simplest view about expectations is that people expect the future to be like the past, and adapt their plans accordingly. The theory presented in this chapter is based on this view, which has come to be known as the **adaptive-expectations hypothesis**. In the early part of the chapter we assumed that firms expected the level of input prices each year to be consistent with the level of output prices the previous year. In our discussion of inflationary recession we modified the hypothesis by assuming that firms expected not the level of prices each year, but rather the rate of inflation to be the same as the previous year. More complex economic models often assume that expectations are based on a weighted average of rates of inflation over several years in the past. But these assumptions are all variations on the theme that people form their expectations of the future primarily on the basis of past experience.

There is a good deal of common sense in this view. If it simply means that people learn from experience and adjust their plans on that basis, it would be hard to disagree with it. What is more, the experience of the U.S. economy in the 1970s seems to bear this hypothesis out, at least in general terms. When inflation first began to get serious in the early 1970s, people were caught off guard. They didn't know how to react. As inflation continued, however, people began to expect more inflation. They changed their plans and their ways of doing business. When inflation slowed in the mid-1980s, they did not go right back to the old ways of doing business. The memory of high rates of inflation influenced their plans for a time even after inflation slowed.

The adaptive-expectations hypothesis is also useful because it produces the kind of aggregate real supply curve that we want—one that slopes upward in the short run and shifts upward in the long run. Adaptive expectations thus provide a basis for a plausible theory of recession and inflation. Even so, many economists are not happy with the adaptive-expectations hypothesis.

The Rational-Expectations Hypothesis

The main challenge to the adaptive-expectations hypothesis has come from a group of economists who see past experience as only one of a number of

Rational-expectations hypothesis

The hypothesis that people form their expectations about future economic events not only on the basis of past events but also on the basis of their expectations about economic policies and their likely effects.

factors that affect people's expectations. In forming their expectations about the future, they say, rational people should look forward as well as backward. In particular, they should look at what government policymakers are saying and doing, and take into account the likely effects of current policy on future economic events. This view, promoted by economists such as Robert Lucas, Thomas Sargent, and Robert Barro, has come to be known as the **rational-expectations hypothesis.** Suppose, for example, that the economy has experienced an inflation rate of 10 percent for the last year or two, and that political pressure has built up for policymakers to do something about it. The president responds with a hard-hitting television speech saying that the government is going to whip inflation now. What will people expect to happen?

The adaptive-expectations hypothesis assumes that people will expect inflation to continue in the future just as it has in the past, regardless of what the president says. The rational-expectations hypothesis takes a different view. It assumes that people are not simpleminded. They will listen to the president, and then they try to find out what policies are being undertaken to back up the president's statements.

Suppose they conclude that the president has no influence on Congress and will not be able to control government spending. They also see that the Fed is not concerned about inflation and is continuing to pump up the money supply at ever-faster rates. In this case it is unlikely that they will expect inflation to slow. In fact, they will expect inflation to speed up. Firms therefore will base their plans on the expectation of a higher rate of inflation. Unions will negotiate contracts that protect their members against future inflation. Households will take inflation into account when buying houses or cars. It would be irrational for people not to act this way.

On the other hand, say backers of the rational-expectations hypothesis, people might listen to the president's speech and conclude that it will be followed up by strong action. Suppose Congressional leaders cheer the president's statements and promise to restrain government spending. Suppose the Fed joins the anti-inflation campaign by slowing the growth of the money supply. In this case, according to the rational-expectations theory, firms, workers, and households will modify their plans to prepare for a slowdown in inflation.

Policy Implications of Rational Expectations

The rational-expectations hypothesis has strong implications for economic policy. It suggests that the effects of policy moves that are expected by the public will be quite different from the effects of policy moves that are unexpected. Look at Box 14.8, for example. This box, which is much like Box 14.2, deals with the effects of an increase in aggregate demand. Under the adaptive-expectations hypothesis, firms would at first respond to the shift in the aggregate real demand curve by moving upward from E_1 along ARS_1 to E_2. As this happens, the price level will rise. As firms adapt their plans to the higher price level, the aggregate real supply curve will shift upward, and in time the economy will move to a long-run equilibrium at E_3. Meanwhile, however, the economy has gained something in return for the experience of inflation. From the time of the initial increase in demand

**Box 14.8
Policy Implications of
Rational Expectations**

According to the rational-expectations hypothesis, the economy will respond differently to increases in demand that are expected than it will to those that come as a surprise. Suppose that the aggregate real demand curve shifts from ARD_1 to ARD_2. If the shift is unexpected, the economy will, in the short run, move upward along ARS_1 to E_2. Real output will rise and unemployment will fall. Only later, as input price expectations adapt to the inflation that has taken place, will the aggregate real supply curve shift to ARS_2. Then the economy will move to a long-run equilibrium at E_3. However, if the shift in aggregate nominal demand is fully expected, the result will be different. Firms and workers will expect costs to go up and will change their plans right away. The aggregate real supply curve will shift directly to ARS_2, and the economy will move straight up from E_1 to E_3. There will be no change in real output or unemployment, only a change in the price level.

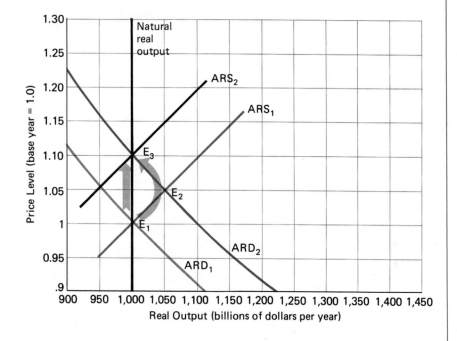

until the economy finally reaches E_3, real output has been above its natural level and unemployment below its natural rate.

Supporters of the rational-expectations hypothesis say that this sequence of events will take place only if the cause of the increase in aggregate demand is unexpected—say, an unexpected surge in consumer spending or investment. But if the increase in demand is caused by a shift in fiscal or monetary policy that is expected by firms and households, the outcome will be different. This might be the case, for example, if the Fed announced an increase in its target for the money supply or aggregate nominal demand for the coming year.

An expected change in policy, according to the rational-expectations hypothesis, will affect the plans that firms make for dealing with the increase in demand. They will know that an expansionary policy will soon cause a rise in prices, including the prices of their inputs. Workers will expect the cost of living to increase and will demand higher wages. If firms learn about the policy in advancē and expect it to raise input prices, they will no longer each react as if their industry is the only one affected by the increase in demand. They know the whole economy is going to be affected, and knowing this, they modify their plans accordingly. As a result the aggregate real supply curve will shift upward to ARS_2 the moment the policy goes into effect. Instead of moving from E_1 to E_2, the economy will move directly from E_1 to E_3. The expansionary policy will have little or no effect on real output. Instead, it will only push prices up, and it will do so very soon.

In sum, say supporters of the rational-expectations hypothesis, the economy will follow an upward-sloping aggregate real supply curve only when shifts in aggregate demand come as a surprise. If they are expected, the upward-sloping aggregate real supply curve does not apply. Instead, the shift in demand will affect only prices while real output remains at its natural level and unemployment at its natural rate. In effect, under the rational-expectations hypothesis, the economy's aggregate real supply curve in the case of anticipated policy changes is a vertical line that coincides with the natural level of real output. Thus expected changes in macroeconomic policy have no effect on real output or employment.

Doubts About Rational Expectations

The rational-expectations hypothesis has had a big impact on macroeconomic thinking in a fairly short time. However, many economists have doubts about this hypothesis, or at least about its policy implications. Some think it expects too much of firms, workers, and consumers. Do people really pay that much attention to what fiscal and monetary policymakers are doing? Do they understand what policy shifts imply for prices, interest rates, and so on? Can ordinary people form rational expectations about the future course of the economy when even professional forecasters so often disagree?

Supporters of the rational-expectations hypothesis say that they don't require every farmer and shopkeeper to have a Ph.D. in economics. They just say that people don't ignore what they read in the papers and see on the TV news. This information has an impact on their economic decisions—more of an impact than the adaptive-expectations hypothesis takes into account. And many key economic decision makers—big corporations, stock market traders, banks, union leaders, and so on—do act on the basis of professional economic advice.

A more telling criticism focuses on the policy implications of rational-expectations theory rather than on the way in which expectations themselves are formed. In practice, the critics point out, shifts in economic policy seem to affect more than just the price level. On the average, according to one estimate, a one-percentage-point change in the growth rate of aggregate nominal demand has a first-year effect on prices of only 0.44 percent. The remaining 0.56 percent takes the form of a movement in real output.[3] In part, this estimate may reflect the result of averaging episodes of expected demand shifts with episodes of unexpected demand

[3]Robert J. Gordon, "Output Fluctuations and Gradual Price Adjustment," *Journal of Economic Literature* 19, June 1981, pp. 493–530.

shifts. But economists who are not hard-line rational expectationists think there are reasons why even expected shifts in nominal demand have major effects on real output and unemployment, at least in the short run.

First, they point out, prices do not respond immediately to every change in demand because it is often costly to adjust prices. True, there are some markets, such as the commodity exchanges where grain and metals are traded, in which prices respond to demand minute by minute. But in other markets price responses are more sluggish. For example, it tends to be more costly to change prices in markets for goods that have many styles and sizes, such as clothing and auto parts. Catalogs and price tags for such goods are changed only every now and then. In other markets sellers are reluctant to change prices too often for fear of offending steady customers. In still other markets—unionized labor markets being a case in point— prices are subject to long-term contracts. They are rarely changed before the contracts expire.

A second reason for gradual price changes is that inventories slow the rate at which demand shifts are transmitted from one sector of the economy to another. Any increase in aggregate demand tends to be felt first by sellers of final goods. For example, a shoe store may quickly see the effect of a tax cut in the form of a surge of customers. But instead of raising its prices right away, the store will probably be glad to sell more shoes, thereby running down its inventory. When the shoe store puts in an order to restock, the manufacturer will feel the increase in demand. But it probably will not raise its prices right away either. Instead, it will make more shoes to fill the retailer's order. Sooner or later its inventories of leather will be depleted, and it too will have to put in an order to restock. Only then will raw-materials markets feel the increase in demand.

At that point prices may begin to move. When the shoe manufacturers' buyers go out to get more leather, they will find only a limited supply of hides on the market. The market for hides is one in which prices respond quickly to changes in demand. So the buyers will go back to the factory and say, "We'll have to raise our shoe prices because the price of leather has gone up." The next time the retailer puts in an order, the price increase will be passed along. Then the customer will be told, "We have to raise our shoe prices because the wholesale price has gone up." But the whole process takes time because of the cushioning effect of inventories at each stage.

Finally, there is the fact that firms get information about demand for their own products faster than they get information about changes in aggregate demand for the economy as a whole. When a shoe store sees its inventories drop, it does not know at first whether this is an isolated piece of luck or whether demand is booming throughout the economy. If the firm thinks the demand increase is something local, it is less likely to think the increase in demand will push its input prices up. It responds at first by increasing output. Only later, when the price increases of other firms are passed through to affect input prices does the firm revise its plans.

This kind of reasoning leads to a middle ground between the rational-expectations and adaptive-expectations hypotheses. In this view, the rational-expectations hypothesis is seen as right in stressing that people take available information into account when they make their economic plans. They are right in saying that the response to expected changes in policy may not be the same as the response to unexpected changes. Even so, there are many frictions and adjustment lags in the economy. Because of these, people do not respond right away to every bit of news that comes their way. In practice, then, an economy with rational expectations but also with many frictions and lags does not work much differently than one in which expectations are formed adaptively. In both cases, the economy will follow an upward-sloping aggregate real supply curve in the short run.

Looking Ahead

Throughout this chapter we have focused mainly on the short run. In the short run, unexpected shifts in aggregate demand cause prices to rise somewhat, but they also cause real output to rise above its natural level and unemployment to fall below its natural rate. Many economists think that even expected shifts in demand can have these effects. However, few economists today think that real output can be raised permanently above its natural level by expansionary monetary or fiscal policy alone—at least not without causing severe inflation.

There are many applications of aggregate real supply and demand theory that we have not yet touched upon, however. These concern long-run situations in which natural real output itself can change. Population growth, investment, new technology, changed work incentives—these and many other things cause natural real output to grow over time. In the next chapter we turn our attention to policies for managing the long-run growth of the economy.

Summary

1. The *natural level of real output* is the level at which long-run equilibrium with stable prices is possible. This level of output is determined by the economy's capital stock, its natural resources, and the size and productivity of its labor force. Linked with natural real output is a *natural rate of unemployment* that corresponds to a normal rate of turnover as people enter and leave jobs. During periods of expansion, the output can rise above its natural level and unemployment can fall below its natural rate. During recessions, real output falls below its natural level and unemployment rises above its natural rate.

2. The position of the economy's aggregate real demand curve depends on firms' expectations regarding input prices. In long-run equilibrium, the expected level of input prices is consistent with the actual average price level for all goods and services. This point is marked by the intersection of the aggregate real supply curve with the natural level of real output. Beginning from such a point, a rightward shift in the aggregate real demand curve, assuming no change in the expected level of input prices, produces a *movement along* the aggregate real supply curve. As the general price level increases, the output prices of some firms are passed through to become increases in the input prices of other firms. When firms revise their expectations to take into account this rise in input prices, there is an upward *shift* in the aggregate real supply curve.

3. A recession can be caused by a drop in aggregate nominal demand. As the aggregate real demand curve shifts to the left, the economy moves downward along its aggregate real supply curve. Real output and the price level fall, while unemployment rises. In theory the economy could recover from the recession even if aggregate nominal demand stayed at its new, lower level. This might take a long

time, however. Recovery from the recession will be faster if aggregate nominal demand rises again.

4. *Demand-pull inflation* means a rise in the price level caused by an expansion of aggregate demand relative to the economy's natural level of real output. In the first phase of demand-pull inflation, the aggregate real demand curve shifts to the right and the economy moves upward along the aggregate real supply curve. If aggregate demand remains fixed, the economy will return to the natural level of real output as expectations of higher input prices push the aggregate real supply curve upward. If the aggregate real demand curve shifts upward to keep pace with the rising aggregate real supply curve, real output can be held above its natural level for an extended period. However, such a policy will result in ongoing inflation.

5. *Cost-push inflation* is said to occur when the aggregate real supply curve shifts upward while the aggregate real demand curve remains fixed. This can happen as the result of a *supply shock* such as an increase in the price of imported oil. It can also happen after a prolonged period of inflation when the expectation of more inflation pushes the aggregate real supply curve upward. As the economy moves upward and to the left along the aggregate real demand curve, real output may drop below its natural level while prices are still going up. This is known as an *inflationary recession*.

6. According to the *adaptive-expectations hypothesis*, people form their expectations about the economic future mainly on the basis of their past economic experience. In contrast, according to the *rational-expectations hypothesis*, people form their expectations not solely on the basis of what has happened in the past, but also on the basis of judgments of the likely course of economic policy and its effects.

7. According to the rational-expectations hypothesis, changes in aggregate demand will affect real output and unemployment only to the extent that they are not fully expected. The upward-sloping short-run aggregate real supply curve, in this view, does not apply to expected changes in aggregate nominal demand caused by fiscal or monetary policy. Such policies affect only the price level and cause the economy to move upward or downward along a vertical line that coincides with natural real output.

8. Many economists continue to think that the economy follows an upward-sloping aggregate real supply curve in the short run. They think that the costs of adjusting prices, the cushioning effect of inventories, and incomplete information cause even well-publicized fiscal and monetary policy actions to affect real output and unemployment as well as the price level, at least in the short run.

Questions for Review

1. Define the following terms:
   natural level of real output
   natural rate of unemployment
   demand-pull inflation
   cost-push inflation
   inflationary recession
   adaptive-expectations hypothesis
   rational-expectations hypothesis

2. What determines the economy's natural level of real output? Is this an absolute limit on output? When can output rise above or fall below the natural level?

3. What determines the point at which the aggregate real supply curve intersects the natural level of real output? Under what circumstances does the economy move along its aggregate real supply curve? Under what circumstances does the aggregate real supply curve shift?

4. When the level of aggregate nominal demand falls, what happens to real output, unemployment, and the price level in the short run? What happens to them in the long run?

5. What causes demand-pull inflation? What

happens to the aggregate real supply curve during the first phase of demand-pull inflation? During the second phase?

6. What causes cost-push inflation? How can cost-push inflation lead to an inflationary recession?

7. How does the rational-expectations hypothesis differ from the adaptive-expectations hypothesis?

8. What distinction do supporters of the rational-expectations hypothesis make between the effect of expected changes in economic policy and the effects of unexpected changes?

9. What factors tend to cause prices to adjust only slowly to changes in demand, thus giving the aggregate real supply curve an upward slope?

Problems and Topics for Discussion

1. Review Chapter 7. On a piece of graph paper, plot aggregate real demand curves corresponding to levels of aggregate nominal demand of $600 billion, $1,200 billion, and $1,800 billion.

2. Review Chapter 13, in which the effects of monetary and fiscal policy are discussed in terms of the supply and demand for money and the Keynesian cross. On a single page, draw diagrams showing the money market, planned investment, the Keynesian cross, and aggregate real supply and demand. Use these diagrams to outline the short-run effects on the nominal interest rate, nominal GNP, real GNP, and the price level of

   a. a tax cut.
   b. a decrease in the money supply.
   c. a decrease in government purchases.

3. We have seen that the intersection of the aggregate real supply curve with the natural level of real output takes place at the average price level corresponding to the expected level of input prices. We have also seen that in the short run, the actual average level of all prices is determined by the intersection of the aggregate real demand curve with the aggregate real supply curve. Use aggregate real supply and demand diagrams to show that real output can be above its natural level only when the expected level of input prices is lower than the level consistent with the actual average level of all prices. Also show that real output can be below its natural level only when the expected level of input prices is higher than the level corresponding to the actual average level of all

prices. Why can a level of real output above or below the natural level not be a situation of long-run equilibrium?

4. In 1974–1975, real output fell by almost 2 percent, the unemployment rate rose from 4.9 to 8.5 percent, and inflation averaged over 10 percent per year. In 1980, real output fell by 0.3 percent, unemployment rose from 5.8 to 7.1 percent, and inflation reached 13.5 percent. In each case, previous inflation had fueled inflationary expectations. Slowing the growth of aggregate nominal demand thus resulted in an inflationary recession. At the same time, the economy was hit by supply shocks in the form of oil price increases. It could therefore be said that two sources of cost-push inflation were operating at once. Is there anything that policymakers could have done to prevent real output from falling below its natural level and unemployment from rising above its natural rate? If so, what, and what would have been the effect on inflation?

5. Assume that the economy has been going through a long period of demand-pull inflation. The government decides to try to stop the inflation by means of restrictive monetary and fiscal policies. Should it make the required policy changes quietly, with as little fanfare as possible? Or should it publicize them widely? Will it make any difference? Why or why not?

6. What do you expect the rate of inflation to be next year? Do you know what it was last year? Last month? What sources do you rely on for information about past and present inflation and for forming your expectations about the

future? Do you think this course will affect your ability to forecast future inflation? Discuss.

7. **Case for Discussion**

The following table gives data for real output (billions of dollars) and the price level (GNP deflator, 1972 = 1.0) for the U.S. economy for the years 1961–1969. Plot these data points on a graph. (Label the vertical axis from 0.5 to 1.0 and the horizontal axis from $500 billion to $1,500 billion), and connect the points with arrows as in Box 14.4.

Year	Real GNP	Price Level
1961	756	0.69
1962	800	0.71
1963	833	0.72
1964	876	0.73
1965	929	0.74
1966	985	0.77
1967	1,011	0.79
1968	1,058	0.83
1969	1,088	0.87

Questions:

a. Do you think the points you have plotted are best viewed as a series of points lying along a single upward-sloping aggregate real supply curve or as the intersections of a series of upward-shifting aggregate real supply curves with an aggregate real demand curve that is also shifting upward? Why?

b. Do you think these years were a period of demand-pull inflation or one of cost-push inflation? Why?

c. During the period for which data are given, the unemployment rate fell from 6.7 percent of the labor force to 3.5 percent. At that time the natural rate of unemployment was about 5 percent. Natural real output can be assumed to have grown during the period because of investment, population growth, and other factors. Do you think that the actual level of real output grew faster or slower than the natural level? On what do you base your conclusion?

Suggestions for Further Reading

Barro, Robert J. *Macroeconomics*. New York: Wiley, 1984.

An intermediate-level macroeconomics text by a leading member of the rational-expectations school.

Gordon, Robert J. *Macroeconomics*, 3rd ed. Boston: Little, Brown, 1984.

Chapters 6–9 of this intermediate text parallel the discussion in this chapter.

McCallum, Bennett T. "The Significance of Rational Expectations Theory." *Challenge*, January/February 1980, pp. 37–43.

A nontechnical discussion of rational-expectations theory.

Terkel, Studs. *Hard Times: An Oral History of the Great Depression*. New York: Pantheon, 1970.

The source of the story that opens this chapter. If you want to get an idea of what the Great Depression was really like (not just curves on a graph), read this book.

Chapter 15

Economic Growth and Productivity

WHAT YOU WILL LEARN IN THIS CHAPTER

After reading this chapter, you should be able to

1. Use aggregate real supply and demand curves to show economic growth with price stability.
2. Explain how insufficient growth of aggregate nominal demand can cause a *growth recession*.
3. Show how a rate of growth of aggregate nominal demand that exceeds the rate of growth of natural real output can cause inflation.
4. Discuss the productivity slowdown that occurred in the United States in the 1970s.
5. Explain the traditional Keynesian strategy for promoting economic growth.
6. Discuss *supply side* economic policies and their basis in economic theory.

Ideas for Review

Here are some terms and concepts that you should review before you read this chapter:

Marginal tax rate (Chapter 5)
Real and nominal interest rates (Chapter 7)
The Keynesian model (Chapter 13)
Aggregate real supply and demand (Chapter 14)

"From a war zone, the plant has been transformed into a showcase."

Ford Motor Company's Louisville plant used be like a war zone. In one form or another, it had just about every problem of the U.S. auto industry—low productivity, high absenteeism, and poor quality. In the cluttered plant, workers sometimes had to sit on crates of parts to eat lunch. This practice was not only uncomfortable, but led to damaged components that found their way into the cars on the assembly line. A consultant found an atmosphere of "deep distrust and alienation" and a "top-down, blame-oriented" management style.

Then Don Baker, a new plant manager, and Ron Gettelfinger, a new local union head, got together and decided that there must be a better way of doing business. They started with small things, such as cleaning up the filthy plant and putting in picnic tables on which workers could eat their lunches. In the improved atmosphere, workers and managers began talking to each other and solving problems. By 1980 the plant was getting high marks from Ford headquarters.

The Louisville plant looked so good, in fact, that Ford chose it as the place to build its new Ranger and Bronco II vehicles. The plant was gutted and an all-new automated assembly line was installed. But before the new machines went in, Ford did something it would never have done in the past: It displayed drawings and mockups of the Ranger and Bronco II in the plant where workers could comment on them and make suggestions about how they should be built. The workers made 749 proposals, of which 542 were adopted. In this way the workers became involved in the success of the new product.

Today the Ranger and Bronco II rate among the best-quality products of the U.S. auto industry. Productivity at the Louisville plant has soared. From a war zone, the plant has been transformed into a showcase.[1]

The rebirth of Ford's Louisville plant meant profits for Ford and better working conditions for its employees—but it has meaning for the economy as a whole, too. In the long run higher productivity—more output per worker—is the main source of increases in living standards. The Ford case is typical in that some of the increased productivity came from new equipment and a lot of it from people finding better ways to work together to get things done. The example is being repeated, with variations, in thousands of plants around the country. As this happens, and as other changes take place, productivity in the U.S. economy is beginning to speed up after a slump from the mid-1970s to the early 1980s.

In this chapter we will look at the past productivity slowdown and current prospects for growth using the same aggregate real supply and demand tools that were applied in the last chapter. We will begin by discussing the policies required for long-run economic growth without inflation. Next we will look at the record of productivity growth in the U.S. economy and the likely trends for the future. In the final section of the chapter, we will discuss policies for promoting economic growth—both traditional Keynesian policies and the newer policies known as supply side economics.

---

[1]Based on Jeremy Main, "Ford's Drive for Quality," *Fortune,* April 18, 1983, pp. 62–70. Based on material which originally appeared in FORTUNE magazine.

ECONOMIC GROWTH AND PRICE STABILITY

Chapter 13 showed that real output can, in the short run, rise above its natural level in response to an increase in aggregate demand or fall below its natural level during a recession. Long-run growth, on the other hand, has to do not with these short-run ups and downs but, rather, with growth in natural real output itself.

The sources of growth in the natural level of real output are increases in the size of the labor force and in output per worker. Output per worker depends, in turn, on a number of factors. One of these is the amount of capital and natural resources available per worker. The investments that Ford made in its Louisville plant are an example. Improvements in technology are another source of gains in productivity. The use of robot welding machines on Ford's assembly line is an example. Finally, human factors such as motivation, organization, and quality of management have an impact on productivity. Making use of workers' ideas for improving Ford's auto assembly methods is a case in point.

Edward F. Denison of the Brookings Institution has estimated the importance of various sources of economic growth in the United States. In the period 1948–1973 real output grew at the healthy rate of 3.6 percent per year. Of this, increases in the size and quality of the labor force accounted for about 1 percentage point and increases in the capital stock for about 0.6 percentage point. The remaining 2 percentage points of annual growth reflected increases in output per unit of input, including improvements in technology, organization, and quality of management.[2]

Effects of Economic Growth

Box 15.1 shows the effects of economic growth in terms of aggregate real supply and demand. The economy starts out in equilibrium at E_1, with natural real output of N_1. Then, over time, the labor force grows, capital investments are made, and productivity is increased. The result is a rightward shift in natural real output to N_2.

As natural real output grows, the economy does not move upward along its aggregate real supply curve, as it does when aggregate real demand shifts. Instead, the aggregate real supply curve shifts to the right along with natural real output. The reason is that the factors causing the growth of real output—more workers, more capital, better technology, better management, and so on—make it possible for output to grow without an increase in costs per unit of output, and thus without an increase in the average price level. At first the economy was able to produce $1,000 billion worth of goods and services at a price level of 1.0. The shift in natural real output means that it can now produce $1,150 billion worth of goods and services at the same price level. As we will see shortly, movements of real output above or below the new natural level would be linked with changes in the price level. These would be shown as movements upward or downward along the new aggregate real supply

---

[2]Edward F. Denison, *Accounting for Slower Economic Growth* (Washington, D.C.: Brookings Institution, 1979), Table 8-1.

**Box 15.1
Growth with Stable
Prices**

Over time, growth of the labor force and of output per worker causes natural real output to rise. As natural real output shifts from N_1 to N_2, the aggregate real supply curve also shifts to the right. If aggregate nominal demand is allowed to grow at the same rate, the economy will move smoothly from its initial equilibrium at E_1 to a new equilibrium at E_2. Prices will be stable and unemployment will remain at its natural rate.

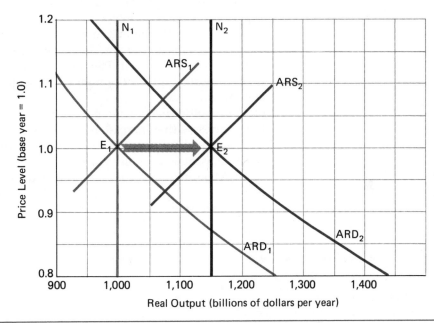

curve, ARS_2. But a movement of the economy from one natural level of real output to another does not require a change in the price level.

Finally, Box 15.1 shows the aggregate real demand curve also shifting to the right, by the same amount as natural real output. Without such an increase in demand, firms would not be able to sell all the output produced at the new natural level without cutting their prices. If the demand curve does shift as shown, the economy will move smoothly from E_1 to E_2. At E_1 and E_2, as well as all points in between, the economy remains in equilibrium. Prices are stable; input prices remain at the level expected by business managers; real output keeps up with its growing natural level; and unemployment is steady at its natural rate.

Managing the Growth of Demand

Box 15.1 shows the ideal condition of steady economic growth without inflation or excessive unemployment. However, the economy does not always run smoothly. A number of things can go wrong. Fiscal and monetary policy may not be managed in such a way as to offset swings in aggregate demand originating in consumption, investment, or net exports. Or fiscal and monetary policy may be mismanaged in a way that disturbs the smooth growth of the economy. In this section we will look at what happens when demand grows too fast or too slowly.

Growth recession   Box 15.2 shows what happens when aggregate nominal demand doesn't keep up with natural real output. As before, the economy starts from an equilibrium at E_1. Natural real output then rises from $1,000 billion to $1,150 billion, as shown by the shift from N_1 to N_2. This time, however, tight monetary and fiscal policy keeps the lid on aggregate nominal demand. With the aggregate real demand curve stuck at ARD_1, the economy cannot reach the intersection of the new aggregate real supply curve ARS_2 with N_2.

So what will happen? At E_1 the economy is in long-run equilibrium. This means that firms are producing at their normal capacity; their standby capacity is not fully used. The unemployment rate is about 6 percent. This is about normal, given the number of people who change jobs each year and the time it takes new workers to find their first job. The spending plans of households, firms, and government add up to just enough so that inventories neither increase nor decrease.

The economy cannot stand still in this position, however. New equipment, new technology, and improved skills of workers and managers increase output per worker. As this happens, the rate of real output increases, but macroeconomic policy is holding aggregate nominal demand constant.

**Box 15.2
A Growth Recession**

In the case shown here, natural real output grows while aggregate nominal demand remains fixed. Thus, as natural real output and the aggregate real supply curve shift to the right, the aggregate real demand curve does not move. The economy will move downward and to the right along the aggregate real demand curve, and at the same time it will move downward and to the left along the new aggregate real supply curve as it shifts to the right. The economy will end up at E_2, where unemployment is higher than its natural rate even though real output has grown. This is called a growth recession.

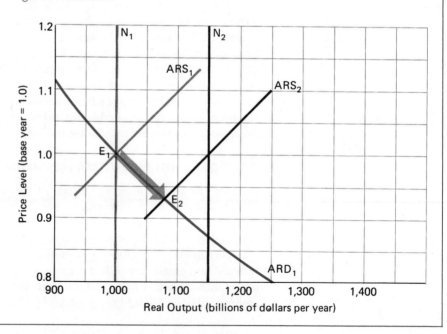

The initial result is unplanned inventory buildup. The firms' managers are disappointed; they are producing more at the same average cost as before, but they can't sell all their output. To keep stocks of unsold goods from building up, firms cut their prices, hoping to boost sales. At the same time, they cut back their production plans. They increase output somewhat, but not by as much as they otherwise would have, given the growth of capacity and productivity.

In terms of the box, what happens is this: Growth of productivity and the labor force have shifted natural real output from N_1 to N_2, and they have also shifted the aggregate real supply curve from ARS_1 to ARS_2. But at the same time that the aggregate real supply curve is shifting to the right, firms' price cuts and cuts in output are moving them downward and to the left along the curve. Throughout this process, aggregate nominal demand is assumed to be unchanged at $1,000 billion. The economy can reach a new equilibrium only when aggregate nominal supply (real output times the price level) is also at that level. In Box 15.2 this happens at E_2. There, real output has risen from $1,000 billion to $1,075 billion, but the price level has fallen from 1.0 to about 0.93. This makes aggregate nominal supply equal to the $1,000 billion level of aggregate nominal demand.

Now look at what happens to employment as the economy moves from E_1 to E_2. Firms have increased their output, but not by as much as natural real output has grown. Given the new investment that has been made and other gains in productivity, the economy could produce $1,150 billion in real output, but at E_2 output is just $1,075 billion. Some firms may need a few new workers, while others may lay off a few. Total employment may rise a little or fall a little. But the feeble growth of real output means that not enough jobs will be created to absorb all the new workers entering the labor force. Thus, the unemployment rate will rise.

Growth recession

A situation in which real output grows, but not fast enough to keep unemployment from rising.

A situation in which real output grows, but not by enough to keep unemployment from rising above its natural rate, is called a **growth recession**. In the U.S. economy real output has to grow by about 3 percent per year just to keep the unemployment rate from rising. If growth is slower, the unemployment rate tends to rise. Because real output is growing, the real incomes of employed workers continue to rise during a growth recession. However, they do not rise by as much as they would if demand kept up with the growth of natural real output.[3]

Growth with inflation   A growth recession is a result of economic policy that is too cautious. The economy has the capacity to grow, but policymakers, perhaps fearing inflation, do not give it the room it needs. This has happened from time to time in the United States, but more often policymakers have made the opposite mistake. They have pushed the economy

---

[3]Box 15.2 is an extreme case in that aggregate nominal demand does not grow at all and the price level actually falls. A milder form of growth recession can occur when aggregate real demand does grow, but not as fast as natural real output. In still other cases a growth recession can be combined with cost-push inflation. For example, expected inflation, based on past experience, may push the aggregate real supply curve upward at the same time that productivity growth is raising natural real output. When that happens, the economy can go through a period in which real output, the price level, and the unemployment rate are all rising at the same time. If we wanted to give this a name, we could call it an "inflationary growth recession."

beyond the capacity of natural real output to grow. The result has been growth with inflation.

The situation of growth with inflation is very much like that of demand-pull inflation discussed in Chapter 13. The difference, as Box 15.3 shows, is that natural real output shifts to the right. As it does so, the aggregate real supply curve shifts with it. But while natural real output grows from $1,000 billion to $1,100 billion, an expansionary policy boosts the level of aggregate nominal demand to $1,200 billion. The new aggregate real demand curve, ARD_2, intersects the new aggregate real supply curve ARS_2 at E_2. The actual level of real output grows by more than its natural level. As it does so, firms begin using their standby capacity and unemployment falls below its natural rate.

In moving from E_1 to E_2, the economy experiences demand-pull inflation. This inflation will affect the expectations of both firms and workers. In the following period, an increase in the expected level of input prices will push the aggregate real supply curve upward at the same time that growth in natural real output carries it farther to the right. This will put it in the position E_3. To keep real output above its natural level, the aggregate real demand curve will have to shift to ARD_3. In moving from E_2 to E_3, output stays just the same distance above its potential level, so unemployment does not fall further. And prices rise by more than they did during the move from E_1 to E_2.

**Box 15.3
Growth with Inflation**

In this example aggregate nominal demand is allowed to grow faster than natural real output. As the economy grows, it also experiences demand-pull inflation. As the economy moves from E_1 to E_2, the unemployment rate falls and there is only mild inflation. In later years the rate of inflation must increase just to keep unemployment from rising again. As a result, the inflation/unemployment trade-off worsens.

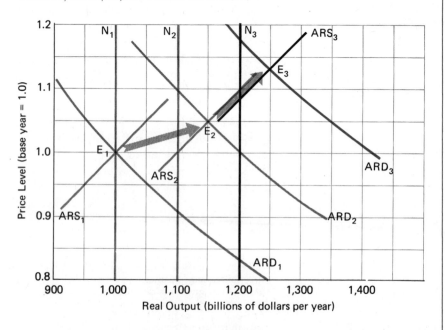

The policy implications of growth with inflation can be summarized as follows: In the short run, pushing the growth of aggregate nominal demand to a rate faster than the growth of natural real output can speed the growth of real output and cut unemployment. The price of doing so is a moderate amount of demand-pull inflation. After this initial gain, however, the trade-off between output and inflation becomes less favorable as firms and workers come to expect higher prices. Then aggregate nominal demand has to grow faster and faster just to keep real output from falling back to its natural level and to keep unemployment from rising back to its natural rate. The growth rate of real output slows, and the rate of inflation speeds up.

RECENT TRENDS IN U.S. ECONOMIC GROWTH

Up to this point we have treated the rate of growth of natural real output as a given. Until the 1970s this seemed like a reasonable assumption for the U.S. economy. To be sure, fiscal and monetary policy did not prevent a number of recessions during this period. There were also some years of low unemployment and rising inflation. But on the average, real output increased by 3.6 percent per year from 1948 to 1973.

Then problems developed. In the period 1973–1981 the average rate of growth of real output fell to 1.8 percent. More troubling still was the fact that this happened despite an increase in the rate of growth of the labor force. Growth of output per worker came to a virtual halt. This section looks at the productivity slowdown of the 1970s. Then the next section looks at policies designed to promote the growth of natural real output.

The Productivity Slowdown of the 1970s

Box 15.4 gives some data on the productivity slowdown of the 1970s. The data are based on another study by Denison. The first line of the table shows that the rate of growth of real output fell by about half from the 1948–1973 period to the 1973–1981 period. At the same time, the rate of growth of the labor inputs to production rose from 1.03 percent per year to 1.67 percent per year. The data on labor inputs are adjusted to reflect changes in hours worked, education, and the age and sex composition of the labor force. The speedup in the growth of labor inputs reflected, in part, the entry into the job market of the post-World War II "baby boom" generation. In part also, it reflected an increase in the percent of women in the labor force, from 43 percent in the early 1970s to 53 percent a decade later.

The remaining growth of real output is explained by increases in productivity. The rate of productivity growth fell from 2.56 percent per year in the earlier period to just 0.13 percent in 1973–1981. The slowdown is even more dramatic if we subtract the part of productivity growth that results from the increase in the quantity of capital available to each worker. The contribution of added capital to productivity growth slowed only a little, from 0.57 percentage point to 0.46 percentage point. The part of productivity growth due to factors other than more capital per worker (better organization, better technology, and so on), which had contributed almost 2 percentage points to annual economic growth in 1948–1973, actually turned negative in 1973–1981.

Box 15.4
The Productivity
Slowdown of the 1970s

During the 1970s the rate of growth of productivity slowed. As a result, the rate of growth of real output slowed even though new workers entered the labor market at an increased rate. These data, based on a study by Edward F. Denison, show changes in the factors contributing to growth between 1948–1973 and 1973–1981.

Growth Rates of Output and Inputs (percent per year)

	1948–1973	1973–1981
Growth of real output	3.59	1.80
Growth of labor input[a]	1.03	1.67
Growth of output per worker	2.56	0.13
Of which:		
Attributed to more capital per worker	0.57	0.46
Attributed to all other factors	1.99	−0.33

[a]Adjusted for changes in education, hours worked, and age and sex composition of the labor force.

Source: Based on data from Edward F. Denison, *Accounting for Slower Economic Growth* (Washington, D.C.: Brookings, 1979), Table 8-1, and "The Interruption of Economic Growth in the United States," *Economic Journal* 93, March 1983, Table 2, p. 60.

Sources of the Slowdown

What went wrong? In the last ten years economists have spent a lot of time trying to answer this question. The blame has been placed on many different factors. The following are among those mentioned most often.

Changes in the labor force   Many accounts of the productivity slowdown point to the entry of millions of women and young people into the labor force during the 1970s. These new workers were on the whole skilled and motivated, but they tended to have less experience than those who already held jobs. At the same time, by their sheer numbers the new workers pulled down the ratio of capital to labor.

Denison's study found that the shift in the age and sex mix of the labor force could explain only a small part of the productivity slowdown, however. For one thing, the age and sex mix of the labor force was already shifting against productivity before 1973. And in addition, it was more than offset after 1973 by improvements in education.

Supply shocks   Chapter 13 explained how supply shocks, such as the oil price increases of 1974 and 1979–1980, can push real output below its natural level. Some economists believe that the oil price shocks of the 1970s also reduced natural real output. This is thought to have happened because higher oil prices made a large part of the economy's capital stock obsolete. Many older trucks, planes, furnaces, generators, and so on had to be retired or placed on standby because high oil prices made them too costly to operate. The effect was almost the same as if the equipment had been destroyed by fire or flood.

Inflation   Many economists have noted that the productivity slowdown of the 1970s occurred at the same time as the speedup of inflation. In part, the productivity slowdown can be seen as a factor contributing to the inflation; for a given rate of growth of aggregate demand, any slowdown in the growth of aggregate real supply will cause prices to rise faster. But some economists think cause and effect worked both ways. Inflation disrupted business planning and labor-management relations. Inflation also distorted the impact of taxes on business and investment income. This not only reduced total investment but also tended to channel investment toward uses that enhanced productivity less, such as housing and tax shelters, and away from more productive projects.

Research and development   A number of economists have noted that research and development (R&D) spending lagged during the 1970s. From a high of 3 percent of GNP in the mid-1960s, it fell to a low of 2.2 percent of GNP in 1977. This may have slowed the development of new cost-cutting ideas. However, others have pointed out that much of the slowdown was in military R&D, which would not affect the growth of productivity in the rest of the economy.

Regulation   The 1970s saw an upsurge in government regulation of business. Regulations dealing with health, safety, the environment, and discrimination in hiring and promotion are just a few examples. Firms had to spend vast sums to comply with these regulations. Although the regulations produced some welcome benefits, such as cleaner air and safer highways, they did not contribute to the growth of real output. As a result, they pulled down the growth of productivity. Denison's data suggest that regulation and related factors cut about two tenths of a percentage point from real growth in 1973–1981. The effect is hard to measure, however, and might have been greater.

Death by a thousand cuts   Lester Thurow of MIT has compared the productivity slowdown to a "death by a thousand cuts." In this view, no single factor was decisive. A number of causes, such as inflation, regulation, oil shocks, and so on, each played a role. In addition, special factors affected many industries. These ranged from management errors to labor problems to depletion of natural resources. If this view is correct, it is not surprising that studies like Denison's have not been able to pinpoint the cause of the productivity slowdown.

Prospects for the Future

Whatever its cause, there is reason to hope that the slowdown of the 1970s may be behind us. Prospects for the next decade or so look bright by comparison.

Many of the likely causes of the slowdown are now operating in reverse. For one thing, the age and sex makeup of the labor force is changing in favor of higher productivity as the new workers of the 1970s gain experience. Second, oil price shocks are less likely to be a problem in coming years. Recently, world oil prices have actually been falling. And even if they rise again, the economy is now equipped to use energy much more efficiently than in the past. Third, inflation has slowed, so managers can focus on improving production rather than simply fighting for financial survival. Finally, the regulatory picture has changed. Most health and environmental regulations remain in place, but more efficient ways of meeting their goals are being found. Meanwhile, regulatory reform and increased competition have benefited such industries as transportation, communications, and financial services.

New factors are at work as well. The last few years have seen an upsurge of investment in computers and other high-tech equipment. This investment boosts productivity in industries like automobiles and steel. But perhaps more important, computers are raising productivity in the fast-growing service industries that now account for more than half of U.S. GNP.

Finally, labor-management relations are changing in ways that tend to raise productivity. The story of Ford's Louisville plant is being repeated in thousands of other companies. Although technology helps, American managers have begun to realize that people are the real key to productivity. If given responsibility and challenges, they can do more than has been asked of them in the past. The new attitude has affected unions as well as management. Cooperating with management in efforts to raise productivity is less often seen as a sellout. Instead, it is seen as a way to create jobs and raise living standards by making employers more competitive in the world economy.

POLICIES FOR PROMOTING ECONOMIC GROWTH

For the near term, then, the prospects for economic growth look favorable. But whether the potential for growth is realized depends on economic policy. For one thing, as we saw in the first section of this chapter, policymakers must allow a rate of growth of aggregate nominal demand that matches the rate of growth of natural real output. If demand is allowed to grow too fast, higher rates of inflation will return. And rapid inflation, as we have seen, was one of the villains of the productivity slowdown of the 1970s. On the other hand, if demand grows too slowly, the economy may slip into a growth recession or worse. We will return to the topic of matching growth of demand with growth of natural real output in the next chapter.

To complete this chapter, we will turn to policies that are intended to promote the growth of natural real output itself. First we will look at traditional Keynesian policies. Then we will return to the so-called supply side economics that came into fashion in some circles during the early 1980s.

Keynesian Growth Policies

Today's economists are not the first to be concerned with promoting economic growth. Growth was also a top priority of the Keynesian economists who served under Presidents Kennedy and Johnson in the 1960s. We can begin by looking at their ideas, many of which are still very much alive.

Fine-tuning for growth   In part, these economists believed that their job was to fine-tune the economy so as to avoid recessions. They noted that during a recession investment tends to fall more than in proportion to output. A recession thus represents a pause in the growth of the economy's capital stock. Even after the economy recovers from the recession, it is left with less capital per worker than would have been the case if the recession had not occurred. Today some economists are skeptical of Keynesian techniques of fine-tuning. But almost all would agree that smooth growth is better than bumpy growth.

Shifting the policy mix   Second, Keynesian economics teaches that the mix of fiscal and monetary policies is important to long-run economic growth. This follows from the theory presented in Chapter 13. There, we showed that there is more than one way to achieve any given nominal income target. A target can be reached through an expansionary fiscal policy combined with a tight monetary policy. Or it can be reached through a tight fiscal policy and an expansionary monetary policy. But the two policy mixes have different effects on real interest rates. An easy monetary/tight fiscal policy mix, in the Keynesian theory, leads to lower real interest rates than a tight monetary/easy fiscal policy mix.

Because the easy monetary/tight fiscal policy mix yields lower real interest rates, it also results in more investment. With real interest rates lower, firms move farther down and to the right along their planned-investment schedules. While low real interest rates encourage investment, tax and spending policies are used to keep the consumption and government spending portions of aggregate nominal demand from growing too fast.

Keynesian economists of the 1960s saw no problem with federal budget deficits as a means of pulling the economy out of a recession, should one occur. But they firmly believed that the deficit should disappear as the economy approached its natural level of real output. A high budget deficit when the economy was operating near capacity would, as explained in Chapter 13, crowd out private investment. In doing so, it would tend over time to crowd out economic growth.

These ideas from the policy debates of the 1960s are by no means dead today. The Reagan administration is just as much pledged to economic growth as the Democratic administrations of the 1960s. But in the Keynesian view it is pursuing the wrong mix of policies. The Reagan program has used tight monetary policy to fight inflation. Meanwhile, its fiscal policy is set on a course that would produce a large budget deficit even with the economy operating at its natural level. In his unsuccessful bid for the presidency in 1984, Walter Mondale made a shift in the policy mix through higher taxes and easier monetary policy a major theme of his campaign.

Supply Side Economics

Supply side economics
A school of economics that focuses on efforts to increase the growth of natural real output, especially through the incentive of tax cuts.

A spirited defense of the Reagan administration's fiscal policy initiative is offered by economists of the so-called supply side school. **Supply side economics** focuses on efforts to raise the growth of natural real output, especially through the incentive of tax cuts. Supply-siders criticize Keynesians for looking only at the effects of tax policy on aggregate demand and ignoring its effects on saving, investment, and work effort.

The supply side tax cut program   The supply side defense of the Reagan administration's fiscal policy runs something like this: During the 1970s productivity stagnated. A major reason for the slowdown, in the supply-siders' view, was the U.S. tax system, which was biased against saving, investment, and work effort. Inflation made the problem worse. Taxes on interest and capital gains pushed the inflation-adjusted after-tax rate of return on investment below zero in many cases. Depreciation allowances that were based on historical costs of business equipment, instead of on costs adjusted for inflation, drained companies of funds needed to replace worn-out equipment. While taxes discouraged investment in productive plant and equipment, tax loopholes encouraged wasteful investment in tax shelters ranging from luxury condominiums to racehorse breeding partnerships. And it was not just corporations and the wealthy who were hit by high taxes. Inflation, the progressive income tax, and the rising social security payroll tax combined to push ordinary wage earners into ever-higher tax brackets. Marginal tax rates of 30 or even 40 percent on the incomes of clerks and factory workers discouraged them from improving their skills, working overtime, or even showing up regularly at their jobs.

The centerpiece of the supply side program was a carefully designed set of tax cuts. First, these would improve work incentives by lowering marginal tax rates on earned incomes. Second, they would remove the bias against saving and investment by reforming capital gains taxes and depreciation allowances. Finally, they would index the tax system so that tax rates would not be pushed back up again if inflation returned. In 1981 Congress passed a set of tax cuts that included many of the items on the supply-siders' wish list. Some supply siders also called for large cuts in government spending, but Congress was less willing to go along with that part of the program.

Tax cuts and deficits   Keynesians warned that the Reagan tax cuts would push up deficits. The deficits, in turn, would raise interest rates. High interest rates, they said, would crowd out investment, thereby canceling out the incentive effects of the supply side tax cuts. But supply side economists had an answer to this argument.

In the supply-siders' view, cuts in marginal tax rates would not have the kind of crowding-out effects their critics said they would. For one thing, the supply-siders believed that tax cuts would boost saving. As we saw in Chapter 13, this would in itself tend to mitigate the crowding-out effect. In addition, the supply-siders said that their critics failed to take the incentive effects of tax cuts into account. The supply-siders counted on incentive effects to work in two ways. First, they designed cuts in business taxes in a way that would boost the after-tax return on investment. This would cause an upward shift in the economy's planned investment schedule, and as a result, in their view, would cause investment to increase rather than to be crowded out. Second, they believed that the incentive effects of individual income tax cuts would prevent total tax revenues from falling even when marginal tax rates were reduced. This last point deserves fuller explanation.

To forecast the effects of a tax cut on total revenue, one must forecast what will happen to the *tax base*. For an income tax, the tax base means total reported income; for a sales tax, it means total sales; and so on. If the tax base is assumed to stay the same when tax rates are changed, then tax revenue will be proportional to the tax rate. This is shown by the straight line in Box 15.5. A revenue forecast that assumes no change in the tax base is often known as a *static forecast*.

If the tax base does not remain constant, a static forecast of revenues will be wrong. Supply-siders stress that the tax base tends to shrink as the tax rate rises. This happens because people have a greater incentive than before to avoid the activity that is being taxed or avoid reporting taxable income. In the case of an income tax, this may mean reducing work in favor of leisure or shifting work to the underground economy. In the case of taxes on investment income, it may mean investing less and consuming more, or it may mean investing only in tax-sheltered projects. If the tax base shrinks as the tax rate rises, the revenue that a tax raises will fall short of the static forecast. This is shown by the curved line in Box 15.5. Such a graph is sometimes known as a **Laffer curve** after Arthur Laffer, a strong advocate of supply side tax cuts.

Laffer curve
A graph that shows the connection between the marginal rate at which a tax is imposed and the revenues raised by the tax.

**Box 15.5
Tax Rates and
Revenues**

The horizontal axis of this graph shows the marginal rate at which a tax is assessed, and the vertical axis shows the amount of revenue the tax raises. A static estimate of the effect of the tax rate on revenue raised assumes that the tax base (total reported income for an income tax) remains fixed as the rate changes. In this case, tax revenue will be proportional to the tax rate, as shown by the straight 45-degree line. In practice, however, higher tax rates have an adverse affect on incentives to earn and report income. As a result, revenue at any given tax rate tends to be lower than the static estimate. The Laffer curve takes these effects into account. It shows that beyond some point, increases in the marginal tax rate will actually reduce tax revenue. The point at which the Laffer curve reaches a peak need not be exactly a 50 percent marginal tax rate as it is here.

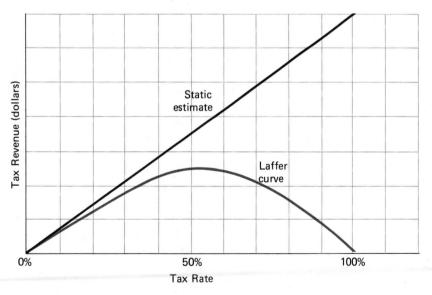

The Laffer curve lies below the straight line of the static forecast at all points. This indicates that the static forecast will always overestimate the revenue gain from a tax increase and the revenue loss from a tax cut. Also, the Laffer curve reaches a peak at a tax rate of less than 100 percent and then begins to turn downward. Beyond a point, then, the gain in tax revenue from a higher tax rate is more than offset by shrinkage in the tax base. In the extreme case of a 100 percent income tax, no one would have any incentive to earn or report income, so tax revenue would drop to zero.

Using their own assumptions about the incentive effects of tax cuts, the supply-siders projected large gains in the tax base and small, if any, revenue losses. In some cases, they said, the lower tax rates would raise more revenue rather than less. Thus, there was no reason to fear an ever-growing federal deficit.

Box 15.6 presents evidence from three major tax cuts in this century. The data show that it is possible for revenue to rise as tax rates fall, at least in the highest income groups, which are subject to the highest marginal tax rates to begin with. In the case of lower income groups, for which marginal tax rates are lower, a tax cut reduces revenue.

The box shows the percentage change in tax revenues by income group for three tax cuts. The first, which was phased in from 1922 to 1925, lowered marginal tax rates from a range of 4–73 percent to a range of 1.5–25 percent. The second, which took effect in 1964, cut marginal rates from a range of 20–90 percent to a range of 14–70 percent. The third set of data refer to the effects of the first two years of the Reagan tax cuts, which took effect in 1982. (The results of the full Reagan tax cut, which was phased in over three years, were not available when this was being written.)

These data support a surprising conclusion about the effect of across-the-board tax cuts: Even when the biggest cuts in marginal rates go to the highest income groups, the effect of the cuts is to *increase* the share of the total tax burden borne by upper-income taxpayers, and to *decrease* the share of the total burden borne by lower-income taxpayers.

Other aspects of the supply side program   Tax cuts are the most publicized part of the supply side program, but they are not all there is to it. Other measures were also planned to boost the growth rate of natural real output. Regulatory reform in transportation, communications, and financial services was supposed to spur competition and productivity. Environmental regulations that were viewed as burdensome were to be eased. The welfare system was to be reformed in ways that increased work incentives for the poor. In short, wherever the productivity slowdown of the 1970s could be blamed on public policies, those policies were to be changed.

Meanwhile, the Fed was urged to support the expected speedup of the growth of natural real output. Supply-siders did not, any more than anyone else, want to let growth of aggregate nominal demand outrun the growth of real output. However, they expected natural real output to grow by as much as 5 percent per year over an extended period, in contrast to more conventional estimates of 3 percent or so, even with productivity

Box 15.6
Revenue Response to
Three Major Tax Cuts

These charts show the effects on revenue of three major tax rate cuts. At least for upper income groups, lower tax rates led to increased revenue. This result is consistent with the Laffer curve.

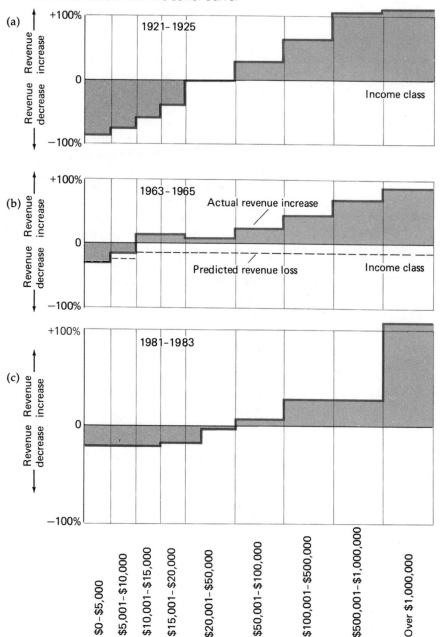

Sources: John Mueller, "Lessons of the Tax Cuts of Yesteryear," *Wall Street Journal*, March 5, 1981, p. 24, and "Soaking the Rich Through Tax Cuts," *Wall Street Journal*, March 21, 1985, p. 30.

gains. Expecting more real growth, the supply-siders urged the Fed to adopt a somewhat easier monetary policy.

Has supply side policy worked?   The tax cuts proposed by the supply-siders began to take effect in the depths of the 1982 recession. Then, from the end of 1982 through the end of 1984, the U.S. economy experienced its most vigorous recovery in the post-World War II period. From a high of 10.7 percent, the unemployment rate fell to less than 7.5 percent. Real output grew by 3.7 percent in 1983 and by 6.7 percent in 1984, while productivity increased rapidly. Investment, as we noted in Chapter 13, was not crowded out, but instead grew strongly. And inflation, which had fallen to a rate of about 4 percent per year during the 1982 recession, remained low. Not surprisingly, the supply side team was ready and willing to take its share of the credit for the solid performance of the U.S. economy during these years.

However, not everyone became a convert to supply side economics. Some critics pointed out that despite the economy's rapid growth, the federal budget deficit remained very high. Although there were signs that the Laffer curve was working to raise revenues in some high tax brackets, total revenues did not keep up with government spending. Also, although the rate of inflation fell, nominal interest rates did not fall in proportion to the decrease in inflation. As a result, real interest rates rose to historic highs. High real interest rates, in turn, drew in funds from abroad and made the U.S. economy heavily dependent on foreign sources of saving. Critics of the supply siders were as quick to blame the economy's remaining problems on the Reagan tax cuts as supply siders were to credit the cuts for everything good that happened.

In fairness to the supply-siders, it should be said that not all aspects of their program were enacted. The tax cuts voted by Congress in 1981 were seen by some as only a step toward a true flat-rate tax system that would reduce everyone's marginal tax rates to a minimum. The spending cuts that were supposed to go with the tax cuts were never made. Regulatory reform, welfare reform, and other aspects of the supply side program were carried out only in part. Finally, the Federal Reserve maintained a somewhat tighter monetary policy than many supply-siders would have liked.

In sum, if the economy performs well for the rest of the 1980s, supply-siders will be there to take the credit. If it falters, they will be able to say that the program as a whole was not given a fair trial. Whatever the outcome, though, supply side economics will have had a lasting impact on debates about macroeconomic policy. There will be no return to the one-sided emphasis on the demand side of macroeconomic policy that was typical of Keynesian economics from the Great Depression through the 1960s.

Summary

1. Over time, natural real output grows as a result of increases in the size and productivity of the labor force. As natural real output shifts to the right, the aggregate real supply curve shifts with it. If aggregate nominal demand is allowed to grow at the same rate as natural real output, the aggregate real demand curve will also shift along with the others. Under these conditions output will grow smoothly, the price level will be stable, and unemployment will remain at its natural rate.

2. If aggregate nominal demand does not keep up with the growth of natural real output, firms will not be able to sell all the output they are able to produce at an unchanged price level. Unplanned inventory buildup will put downward pressure on prices and cause the actual level of real output to grow more slowly than the natural level. The economy will move downward and to the left along the aggregate real supply curve at the same time that the curve is shifting to the right. This is called a *growth recession*. During such a recession real output grows but the rate of unemployment rises.

3. If aggregate nominal demand grows faster than natural real output, the result will be demand-pull inflation. In the short run, pushing the growth of aggregate nominal demand to a rate faster than the growth of natural real output will speed the growth of real output and cut unemployment at the cost of only moderate inflation. After the initial gain, however, the trade-off between inflation and unemployment worsens. The rate of inflation must speed up just to keep the unemployment rate from rising.

4. During the 1970s the rate of growth of productivity fell from over 2.5 percent per year almost to zero. Explanations of this slowdown include changes in the age and sex composition of the labor force, supply shocks caused by oil price increases, inflation, a slowdown in research and development spending, and an increase in regulation. No one of these factors seems to explain the slowdown fully. However, many of them are now working in reverse, and the prospects for productivity growth in the coming decade look brighter.

5. Keynesian economists have long been concerned with promoting economic growth. In part, their program calls for fine-tuning the economy so as to avoid recession and inflation. They also call for a mix of macroeconomic policies that includes a balanced budget as the economy approaches the natural level of real output, and a monetary policy that will permit relatively low interest rates. Keynesians have criticized the Reagan administration's policy mix for budget deficits that are too large and a monetary policy that is too tight.

6. *Supply side economics* focuses on efforts to increase the growth of natural real output, especially through the incentive provided by cuts in marginal tax rates. The Reagan administration's tax cuts were inspired by supply side theory. According to this theory, well-designed tax cuts will result in little or no revenue loss for the government. If the incentive effect of the tax cuts speeds the rate of growth of natural real output, monetary policy can be eased without the danger of inflation.

Questions for Review

1. Define the following terms:
   growth recession
   supply side economics
   Laffer curve

2. If natural real output is growing, what must happen to aggregate nominal demand for prices to remain stable?

3. Under what conditions can the unemploy-

ment rate rise and the price level fall while real output is growing?

4. What are the short-run effects on inflation and unemployment if aggregate nominal demand grows faster than natural real output? What are the long-run effects?

5. What factors contributed to the slowdown of productivity growth in the United States in 1973–1981?

6. What are the main elements of the Keynesian strategy for promoting economic growth?

7. What are the main elements of the supply side strategy for promoting economic growth?

Problems and Topics for Discussion

1. Using the *Economic Report of the President* or another source, find data on real GNP, the price level, and the unemployment rate for 1983–1985, and for later years if possible. Assume that the natural rate of unemployment is 6.5 percent. Sketch a series of aggregate real supply and demand curves (including vertical lines to show the approximate level of natural real output) and discuss the movement of the economy.

2. Footnote 3 (p. 385) describes what could be called an "inflationary growth recession." Draw a set of aggregate real supply and demand curves to illustrate this situation.

3. Box 15.3 illustrates growth with inflation. What would happen to the economy if, starting from the situation represented by point E_3, policymakers were to stop the growth of aggregate nominal demand while natural real output continued to grow? Use aggregate real supply and demand curves to illustrate your answer.

4. **Case for Discussion**
   The following are excerpts from an editorial that appeared in the Wall Street Journal *in November 1984.*

   A debate—which ultimately will influence every issue of public policy in the second Reagan administration—has been clearly drawn between the "Three Percenters" and the supply-siders.

   The former are those who insist the economy must be held to a 3 percent growth rate or else inflation will accelerate. The latter argue that growth can and must be at a higher rate for several years and that monetary and fiscal

policies should be aimed at achieving that growth.

Three percent growth is a level barely sufficient to accommodate new entrants into the work force and a subdued pace of technological advance. It is clearly not sufficient to lower the unemployment rate below its 7 percent-plus level. It isn't enough to reduce the federal budget deficits. And it isn't enough for the economy to absorb imports from the developing world at a level that will enable these countries to service their debts to American banks.

Where did this 3 percent idea come from? The 1981 Report of President Carter's Council of Economic Advisers originated the idea that long-term potential economic growth had slowed from nearly 4 percent a year in 1960–1973 to 3.4 percent in 1973–1983. That "sustainable pace" was mainly the sum of rapid 2.5 percent labor force growth and a pathetic 0.9 percent annual productivity increase.

We dispute this idea and observe that in the first six quarters of this recovery the sum of labor-force and productivity growth was 5.1 percent, which means potential was growing almost as fast as real GNP—even as the Three Percenters were worried about "running out of capacity."

A faster growth path is attainable. Five percent for a decade is not unrealistic. But even the more conservative 3.4 percent track cannot be reached if the Three Percenters dominate policy making and are able to force the economy to that pace by restrictive monetary and fiscal policies.[4]

---

[4]Jude Wanniski, "Grip of the Three Percenters," *Wall Street Journal*, November 8, 1984. Reprinted by permission of the Wall Street Journal, © Dow Jones & Company, Inc. 1984. All rights reserved.

Questions:

a. Suppose the supply-siders are right and potential real output (another term for natural real output) grows at 5 percent per year, but the "Three Percenters" hold the growth of aggregate nominal demand to 3 percent per year. What will happen? Explain, and illustrate with a diagram.

b. Suppose the supply-siders are wrong and potential real output grows by only 3 percent per year. However, they persuade fiscal and monetary policymakers to allow aggregate nominal demand to grow by 5 percent per year. What will happen? Explain, and illustrate with a diagram.

c. Suppose you are a policymaker and are not sure how fast natural real output is growing. Which risk would you rather take— the risk of letting aggregate nominal demand grow too fast or that of letting it grow too slowly? Why?

Suggestions for Further Reading

Fink, Richard H., ed. *Supply Side Economics: A Critical Appraisal.* Frederick, Md.: University Publications of America, 1983.

This volume contains papers on all aspects of supply side economics by authors with a wide range of views.

Gordon, Robert J. *Macroeconomics,* 3rd ed. Boston: Little, Brown, 1984.

Chapter 18 discusses economic growth and the productivity slowdown.

Reich, Robert B. *The Next American Frontier.* New York: Times Books, 1983.

A liberal lawyer at Harvard's Kennedy School of Government makes a case for promoting economic growth and suggests ways of doing so.

Chapter 16

Strategies for Economic Stabilization

| WHAT YOU WILL LEARN IN THIS CHAPTER | After reading this chapter, you should be able to |

WHAT YOU WILL LEARN IN THIS CHAPTER

After reading this chapter, you should be able to

1. Outline the debate between Keynesians and monetarists over policy activism versus policy rules.
2. Discuss the assumptions that underlie the case for policy activism.
3. Explain why lags in decision making and in the effects of fiscal and monetary policies pose a problem for economic stabilization.
4. Discuss political problems of economic stabilization.
5. Compare different rules for the conduct of monetary policy.
6. Compare different alternatives of a balanced-budget rule for fiscal policy.
7. Outline the U.S. experience with wage and price controls and discuss problems with controls.
8. Explain the conditions under which indexing can help or harm efforts to reduce inflation.
9. Discuss a change of policy regime as a means of stopping inflation.

Ideas for Review

Here are some terms and concepts that you should review before you read this chapter:

The business cycle (Chapter 1)
The multiplier effect (Chapter 9)
The federal budget process (Chapter 10)
Cyclical and structural deficits (Chapter 10)
Velocity and money demand (Chapter 12)
Targets of monetary policy (Chapter 12)
Aggregate real supply and demand (Chapters 7 and 14)
Rational expectations (Chapter 14)
Growth and inflation (Chapter 15)

"The 1,000 peso bill costs more to print than it purchases. It buys one bag of tea."

La Paz, Bolivia: A courier stumbles into Banco Boliviano Americano, struggling under the weight of a huge bag of money he is carrying on his back. He announces that the sack contains 32 million pesos, and the teller slaps on a notation to that effect. The courier pitches the bag into a corner.

"We don't bother counting the money any more," explains Max Loew Stahl, a loan officer standing nearby. "We take the client's word for what's in the bag." Pointing to the courier's load, he says, "That's a small deposit."

At that moment the 32 million pesos—enough bills to stuff a mail sack—were worth only $500. Two weeks later, they were worth $180 less.

In January 1984, prices in Bolivia rose at an annual rate of 116,000 percent. At that rate, prices go up by the day, the hour, or the customer. Julia Blanco Sirba, a vendor on the capital city's main street, sells a bar of chocolate for 35,000 pesos. Five minutes later, the next bar goes for 50,000 pesos. The two-inch stack of money needed to buy it far outweighs the chocolate.

Tons of paper money are printed to keep the country of 5.9 million inhabitants going. Planeloads of money arrive twice a week from printers in West Germany and Britain. Purchases of money cost Bolivia more than $20 million in 1983, making it the third-largest import, after wheat and mining equipment.

The 1,000 peso bill, the most commonly used, costs more to print than it purchases. It buys one bag of tea. The inflation makes use of credit cards impossible, and merchants generally don't take checks either. Jorge Von Bergen, an executive of a paper products company, says his wife has to take the maid along to the market to help carry the bales of cash needed for her shopping. But all that money buys so little that Mrs. Von Bergen easily carries her purchases back home on her own.[1]

Hyperinflation
Very rapid inflation.

How do countries get into a situation like Bolivia's **hyperinflation**, as such an extreme inflation is called? How do they get out of it? What policies are needed to avoid the fate of Bolivia, Israel, Argentina, and other countries that have fallen victim to massive economic instability? It's not enough just to know how the tools of economic policy work—changes in government spending, tax cuts, open-market operations, and all of the rest. There must also be a *strategy* for using them. This means a consistent long-term set of economic goals and the proper means for reaching them.

We will begin this chapter by looking at one of the most important debates over stabilization strategy—that between advocates of policy activism and their critics who advocate long-term rules for the conduct of economic policy. Next, we will discuss the various kinds of rules that could be followed as an alternative to policy activism. Rules for both monetary and fiscal policy will be covered. Finally, we will look at strategies for fighting inflation when, as in Bolivia, it gets out of hand.

---

[1]Sonia L. Nazario, "When Inflation Rate Is 116,000 Percent, Prices Change by the Hour," *Wall Street Journal*, February 7, 1985, p. 1. Reprinted by permission of the Wall Street Journal, © Dow Jones & Company, Inc. 1985. All rights reserved.

Box 16.1
Business Cycles in the
United States

As this chart shows, a pattern of alternating booms and recessions has been observed in the United States for almost 200 years. Economists differ in their explanations of the business cycle. Some think it shows that the private economy is unstable and that the government must take action to moder-

POLICY ACTIVISM AND ITS CRITICS

In Chapter 1 we first called attention to the fact that the economy does not grow steadily year after year but, instead, tends to go through a business cycle. Growth is halted from time to time by recessions. When the economy recovers from a recession, it often overshoots its natural level of output. The boom periods that result are followed by new recessions. This pattern has been observed as far back as the 1790s. (See Box 16.1.)

Nobody really likes the business cycle. It is disruptive and wasteful in both dollar terms and human terms. Almost all economists agree that the right policy could moderate the swings in the business cycle. But behind this general agreement lies one of the major debates in economics today: Just what kind of policy is right for dealing with the business cycle?

Keynesians and Monetarists

On the one hand, there are the *policy activists*. They see the business cycle as a flaw in the capitalist system that the government must try to correct. They see the source of the problem as unpredicted ups and downs in consumer confidence, investment plans, the foreign trade balance, and the demand for money and credit. These cause shifts in aggregate nominal demand, which are amplified by the multiplier effect.

To moderate the business cycle, government should use monetary and fiscal policy actively to offset disturbances arising in the private sector. Whether the business cycle is on an upward or a downward swing, government should lean against the wind in order to shorten recessions and restrain booms. This view can be traced to the ideas of John Maynard Keynes for dealing with the Great Depression. Most Keynesians today favor an activist approach.

ate the extremes of the cycle. Others believe that the economy is only moderately unstable. They see mistakes in government policy as causing the larger cycles of inflation and depression.

On the other hand, there are those who see mistakes in government policy behind all but the mildest swings of the business cycle. To be sure, they say, there are unpredicted ups and downs in the spending plans of consumers and businesses. But the private economy has built-in stabilizers that prevent serious depressions, prolonged unemployment, and persistent inflation. The really bad episodes—the Great Depression, the double-digit inflation of the 1970s—can be traced to policy errors. Things got out of hand in these cases because attempts to fine-tune the economy only made things worse. The way to control the business cycle, then, is to prevent the government from making mistakes by tying it to stable, long-term *policy rules*. This is the view taken by most monetarists and also by most supporters of the rational-expectations hypothesis.

Over the years, the issue of policy activism versus policy rules has come to dominate macroeconomic policy debates. The issues of the power of fiscal and monetary policy and the nature of the transmission mechanism have taken a back seat; in fact, the gap between Keynesians and monetarists on these issues has narrowed greatly. They now agree that both fiscal and monetary policies matter. (For some of Keynes own views, see Box 16.2.) However, Keynesians tend to argue that fiscal and monetary policies should both be used actively, whereas monetarists and rational expectationists argue that both should be guided by fixed policy rules.

The Case for Policy Activism

The case for policy activism rests on four assumptions:

1. The government can directly control aggregate nominal demand by means of fiscal and monetary policy, and can indirectly control real output, employment, and the price level with these policy tools.

Box 16.1
(cont.)

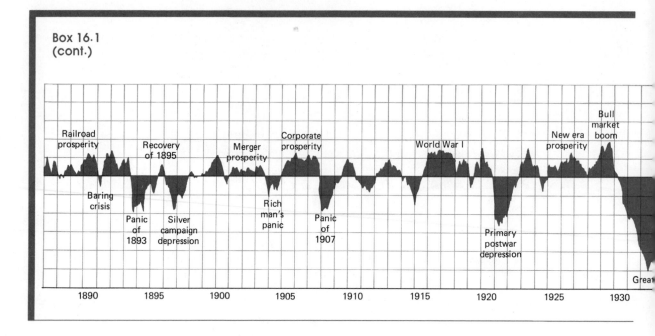

2. Changes in policy have reasonably predictable effects on the economy.
3. Economists can forecast well enough to tell policymakers what actions will be needed in time for those actions to be taken.
4. Policymakers will follow the advice of economists.

To picture the job of the policymaker under these assumptions, think of yourself as the captain of an ocean liner. Your tools for controlling the ship are the engine telegraph, which controls the ship's engine speed, and the wheel, which controls the ship's rudder. You can predict the effects of any movement of the controls. For example, calling for full speed ahead will cause the ship to reach its maximum speed of 30 knots; turning the wheel to the right will swing the rudder and cause the ship to turn; and so on. Your ship is not a sports car—it takes a long (but predictable) time to stop the ship or make a turn. Because of the time it takes the controls to act, you must look ahead and plan ahead. Fortunately, you have charts that show reefs and currents, satellite reports that predict changes in wind speed, and radar to tell you the course and location of other ships in your area. You and your crew agree on where you are headed and when you want to get there. Thus, although you are responsible for the ship, you are happy to follow the technical advice of your navigator, engineer, and harbor pilot.

So it is, in the world of the policy activists, if you are the president or the chairman of the Federal Reserve Board. You have levers and wheels at your command that are labeled "net taxes," "government purchases," and "money supply." You have computer models of the economy that predict what will happen to real output, employment, the price level, and interest rates when you pull any of these levers or turn the wheels. Your staff economists give you weekly printouts warning you of trends in invest-

Source: AmeriTrust Corp. The vertical scale shows, in percentage terms, how high the level of business activity in a given year rose above the long-term trend, or how far it fell below the trend.

Box 16.2
Was Keynes a Monetarist at Heart?

Popular accounts of economic controversies often portray "monetarists" as hard-liners on inflation, regardless of the cost in terms of jobs, and "Keynesians" as go-go expansionists who care nothing about inflation. Stated in these terms, the distinction is far overdrawn. If the offending journalists took the time to read some of Keynes's own writings, they would be surprised at certain passages dealing with inflation and the money supply.

For example, in his book *The Economic Consequences of Peace*, Keynes wrote that "[Russian revolutionary leader Vladimir] Lenin is said to have declared that the best way to destroy the capitalist system was to debauch the currency [through inflation]. . . . Lenin was certainly right. There is no subtler, no surer means of overturning the existing basis of society."[a]

When Keynes was consulted on how to deal with the inflation that affected Britain after World War I, he rejected a gradual approach, and instead advocated a shock-treatment in the form of "dear money," that is, contractionary monetary policy. When asked how severe the shock should be, he replied that he would "go for a financial crisis. . . . Go to whatever [interest] rate is necessary . . . and keep it at that for three years."[b]

Finally, in *A Tract on Monetary Reform*, Keynes wrote that "Inflation is unjust and deflation is inexpedient. . . . Both are evils to be shunned. The individualistic capitalism of today, precisely because it entrusts saving to the individual investor and production to the individual employer, presumes a stable measuring rod of value, and cannot be efficient—perhaps cannot survive—without one."[c]

Yes, John Maynard Keynes said that, not Milton Friedman.

Sources: [a]*Collected Writings*, Vol II. (London: Macmillan, 1971), pp. 148–149. [b]Quoted in Susan Howson, "A 'Dear Money Man'?": Keynes on Monetary Policy, 1920," *Economic Journal* (June 1973), p. 458. [c]*Collected Writings*, Vol. IV, p. 36. Thanks to Joe Meskey of East Carolina University for supplying these quotations.

ment, money demand, and other factors that you may have to offset with policy actions. You agree with other policymakers and leaders of Congress that prices should be kept stable, that real output should be kept at its natural level, and that unemployment should be kept at its natural rate. And since your economic advisers speak with one voice on the policy actions needed to reach these goals, you are willing to follow their technical advice.

To be sure, there is more uncertainty in running the economy than in steering an ocean liner. Even the most ardent policy activists admit that mistakes will be made. These will cause the economy to drift off course now and then; the business cycle will be moderated but not eliminated. Even so, they believe the best way to stay on course is to adjust the controls quickly when there is any sign of trouble.

Challenging the Assumptions

Critics find fault with all the activists' assumptions. They do not think the tools and forecasts available to policymakers are good enough to do the job, even with the best of intentions. They also doubt the ability of the U.S. political system to focus on consistent long-run economic goals. Let's look at the case against policy activism, beginning with the question of whether policymakers have adequate tools for the job.

Are the tools adequate?   The activists assume that the government has a set of tools that can directly affect aggregate nominal demand and indirectly affect real output, employment, and the price level. Their critics wonder how adequate the tools really are. They agree that monetary and fiscal policy affect aggregate nominal demand, but they argue that changes in aggregate nominal demand have only short-term effects at best on real output and employment. In the long run, they say, the economy always returns to the natural level of real output and the natural rate of unemployment. On this point economists who favor the rational-expectations hypothesis are even more skeptical than the old-style monetarists. They doubt the ability of expected changes in monetary and fiscal policy to affect real output and employment even in the short run.

Are the effects of a policy predictable?   Unless the effects of monetary and fiscal policies can be predicted, policy activists will not know how hard to pull their levers and twist their dials. They depend extensively on large-scale computer models to predict the effects of any given policy. These models, although they are very elaborate, have the same basic structure as the general Keynesian model we discussed in Chapter 13. They will make accurate predictions only if the correct values are used for the marginal propensity to consume, the various multipliers, the crowding-out effect, and so on. But different computer models give widely different values for these constants. For example, as Box 13.6 (p. 330) showed, four of the most widely used models give estimates of the expenditure multiplier over a two-year time horizon that range from 2.0 to 3.9. Their estimates of the size of the crowding-out effect range nearly as widely. How can policy activists fine-tune the economy, ask the critics, if they cannot agree on how much of a policy change is needed to produce a desired effect?

Are forecasts reliable?   Policy activists must rely on the same computer models to forecast where the economy is headed in order to decide what corrections are needed. As Box 1.6 (p. 11) showed, the record of forecasting in the past decade has been mixed at best. During tranquil periods the forecasting models have not done badly. However, they missed crucial turning points in 1973–1975, 1979–1980, and 1981–1982. The average of the various forecasts is often wrong, and typically the forecasts also encompass a wide range of outcomes.

The Problem of Lags

In addition to challenging the assumptions on which the case for fine-tuning is based, the critics make much of the problem of delays or *lags* in the policy process. Two kinds of lags deserve attention. The delay between the time when a policy change is needed and the time when a decision is made is called the **inside lag**. The delay between the time when a decision is made and the time when it has its main effect on the economy is known as the **outside lag**.

Inside lag
The delay between the time when a policy change is needed and the time when a decision is made.

Outside lag
The delay between the time when a policy decision is made and the time when the policy change affects the economy.

Lags in monetary policy   For monetary policy, the inside lag is fairly short. Data on inflation and unemployment are available to the Federal Reserve within a month. Data on changes in real output are available in estimated form within about two months, and in fairly accurate form in three months. Once the Fed has data on changes in the economy, it can decide quickly to make whatever policy changes are needed. The Federal Open Market Committee—its chief monetary policy-making body—meets at least eight times a year. If a change in plans is needed between meetings, the committee holds telephone conferences.

The outside lag for monetary policy is a good deal longer than the inside lag, and it also varies. Monetarist studies indicate that slowing the rate of growth of the money stock in recent years has slowed the rate of growth of real output some 3 to 12 months later. The effect on the price level takes even longer—2 to 3 years—to make itself felt. An increase in the rate of growth of the money stock appears to act with similar lags.

Lags in fiscal policy   Overall lags for fiscal policy seem longer but harder to measure. The long inside lag for fiscal policy is a result of the budget process, in which the administration must first decide on the need for a policy action and then submit a proposal to Congress. (See Box 10.1, pp. 230.) Consider some examples:

- President Kennedy's advisers began urging him to ask for a tax cut soon after he took office early in 1961, but a proposal was not submitted to Congress until 1962. Congress did not pass the tax cut until 1964, some three years after the need for it was clear.
- For about two years in the late 1960s, during the Vietnam War, President Johnson resisted his economists' advice that taxes be raised. In that case, Congress acted quickly on the call for a tax surcharge once it was submitted.
- During the 1974–1975 recession President Ford called for tax cuts, including a one-time tax rebate. In this case Congress again acted swiftly. Even so, the rebate was not paid out until the month in which

unemployment hit its peak. The rebate thus came in time to help speed the recovery, but not in time to shorten the recession.

- Congress also acted fairly promptly (within nine months) on President Reagan's call for tax cuts in 1981. However, the cuts were phased in over three years. Only the first phase of the tax cuts came while the economy was still in recession. The rest went into effect after the recovery was already under way.

On the basis of these examples, the inside lag for fiscal policy appears to range from about six months to more than three years. Also, there is a fairly long outside lag for fiscal policy. This is the length of time it takes the multiplier effect to work itself out once a change has been made in taxes or government spending. Some effect on aggregate nominal demand is felt very quickly, but various computer models differ widely in their estimates of how long it takes for the bulk of the effect to be felt. Some models show the peak effect coming only six months after policy action is taken. Others indicate that the peak effect is not felt for two years. All the models agree that a fiscal policy action continues to affect the economy to some degree even three years later.

The total lag for fiscal policy is the sum of the inside and outside lags. At best, the total lag is not less than a year. This allows only six months for the president to make a proposal and Congress to act on it, and six more months for the multiplier effect to be played out. However, a total lag of several years is quite possible.

The interaction of lags and forecasting errors Lags mean that policymakers cannot wait until a problem develops before taking action. If they did, the measures they took to boost the economy during a recession would not take effect until the recovery was already under way. The effect would be to turn a normal recovery into an inflationary boom. Actions intended to restrain the inflation might take effect only after the economy was already plunging into the next recession.

To avoid this problem, policymakers must act on the basis of forecasts. If they knew that a recession would begin in a year or two, they could take action now. If they knew when inflation would begin to develop, they could adjust money growth or taxes in time to prevent it. But what if the forecasts are wrong, as they often are? A policy of stimulus or restraint based on a faulty forecast is as likely to make things worse as it is to make them better.

Political Problems of Fine-Tuning

Many activists would agree that lags and forecasting errors are good reasons to proceed with caution. However, they claim that following their advice, even if it is not perfect, is better than doing nothing and letting the business cycle run its course. At this point their critics bring up the fourth assumption on which the case for policy activism is based. The problem, they say, is that even when economists are able to offer valid advice, policymakers may not follow it. They see two main reasons for this.

First, when things go wrong with the economy, there is great political pressure to "do something." For example, as the economy slides into a recession there is pressure to create jobs. However, because of policy lags, that pressure may reach a peak only after the time for action has passed. A spending program or tax cut that is undertaken at the trough of a recession, when unemployment is at its highest, will not create jobs when they are needed most. Instead, it will add to inflationary pressures six months to two years later, after a recovery is already under way.

Second, there is the tendency of politics to stress the short run. This is a problem because the short-run effects of economic policies often differ from their long-run effects. Take, for example, the effects of an expansionary fiscal or monetary policy, which we discussed in Chapters 13 and 14. If an expansionary policy is applied when real output is at its natural rate, the short-run effects are an increase in real output and a reduction in unemployment as the economy moves upward along its aggregate real supply curve. At first only a moderate amount of inflation will result. However, the long-run effects of an expansionary policy are less positive. To keep real output high and unemployment low, policymakers must be willing to accept ongoing inflation, probably at an ever-increasing rate. Reversing the expansionary policy in order to get rid of the inflation is likely to cause an inflationary recession.

In the U.S. political system, the next congressional or presidential election is never more than two years away—not a long time when compared to the lags in macroeconomic policy. As a result, critics of policy activism say, fiscal policymakers who will soon be running for reelection are under pressure to produce short-term results. They will want to look as if they are doing something to help the economy as the election approaches. If the policy has negative long-term effects, well, those will not be felt until after the election.

As the critics see it, the problem is not one of bad intentions on the part of politicians. Instead, it is a matter of the way in which intelligent, well-intentioned people react to the pressures of the system in which they operate. In their view, the case for fine-tuning, already weakened by lags and forecasting errors, should be thrown out of court because of these political problems.

What about Federal Reserve officials? Members of the Fed's Board of Governors are appointed to terms of 14 years and cannot be reappointed after serving a full term, specifically to shield them from the kind of short-term pressures that elected fiscal policymakers face. Nonetheless, critics of policy activism believe that monetary policymakers too face a problem of inconsistency between their long-term and short-term goals.

To see the problem, suppose that the Fed announces a long-term intention not to allow the money stock (and hence, aggregate nominal demand) to grow faster than natural real output. This policy, if carried out, would eliminate inflation in the long run. If firms and workers believe the Fed's announcement, they will base their plans on the expectation of zero inflation, and the economy will grow smoothly.

Once this happy state of affairs is established, however, the Fed will face a temptation. Why not speed up money growth for a time, causing the aggregate real demand curve to shift rightward faster than natural real output? If this is done at a time when people still expect long-term price stability, there will be only a little inflation, and a relatively big gain in real output. Then, before expectations fully adjust to the faster money growth, the Fed will issue another reassuring policy announcement, claiming that its goal is still long-term price stability.

The trouble with this policy, say the critics, is that repeated departures from announced long-term goals to achieve desirable short-term results will cause both the expected and the actual rates of inflation to drift upward over time. Economists of the rational-expectations school think the public would see through the policymakers' temptation from the beginning, and would, as a result, expect a higher rate of inflation all along. In this case, the surprise element in the policy change, and its ability to boost economic growth, would be lost. All in all, the long-term results of yielding to temptation are not desirable, even though each short-term departure from the long-term goals is made with the best of intentions.

THE SEARCH FOR POLICY RULES

To avoid the problems of policy activism, the critics propose that fiscal and monetary policy be guided by long-term policy rules. If we again think of the economy as an ocean liner, the advocates of policy rules want to put it on automatic pilot. In view of lags and forecasting errors, they say, it is better to follow rules that are correct on the average than to follow an activist policy that is just as likely to do harm as good. As an added benefit, strict policy rules will prevent decision makers from bowing to short-run political pressures regardless of the long-term effects.

The argument that policy rules are safer than fine-tuning is only half of the case, however. To complete their case, critics of policy activism need to spell out in detail the rules they would like policymakers to follow. On this point there is not full agreement even among those who favor policy rules in principle. Let's look first at rules for monetary policy and then at fiscal policy rules.

Rules for Monetary Policy

A monetary growth rule   The best-known proposal is the one put forward by Milton Friedman. Friedman asks that the Fed follow a rule of 3 percent per year growth of the money supply. If the growth of the money supply rises above this target rate, the Fed should slow it down with open-market sales of securities; if the money supply grows too slowly, the Fed should speed it up with open-market purchases. For many years, such a rule has been regarded as the centerpiece of monetarist macroeconomic policy.

Friedman's target of 3 percent is equal to the long-run average rate of growth of natural real output. As the growth of natural real output shifts the economy's aggregate real supply curve to the right, Friedman's rule is supposed to let the aggregate real demand curve shift just enough to keep up on the average. As Box 15.1 (p. 383) showed, such a policy would permit steady growth of real output without inflation.

The money growth rule avoids problems of lags and forecasts. The Fed receives data on changes in the money supply within a week, and it can adjust open-market operations within a few hours. However, it has a potential flaw: Stabilizing money supply growth at such a rate will result in growth without inflation only if velocity is constant. (Velocity, we recall, is the ratio of nominal national income to the quantity of money.) If velocity rises, aggregate nominal demand will grow at a rate greater than 3 percent even if money is held to its 3 percent target. Assuming constant growth of natural real output, a sustained rise in velocity would cause inflation. Likewise, if velocity falls, aggregate nominal demand will grow by less than 3 percent even with the money supply on target. This could result in a recession, or at least a growth recession.

As Box 16.3 shows, velocity of M1 has risen since the early 1950s at an annual trend of about 3 percent per year. Moreover, the rate of change of velocity has varied from year to year and quarter to quarter. This evidence has led some economists to call Friedman's proposed rule into question. With such a pattern of velocity, they say, a 3 percent money growth rule would avoid neither inflation nor short-term variations in aggregate demand. Friedman responds that the trend in velocity is largely the result of rising inflation and the consequent rise in nominal interest rates during the 1960s and 1970s. Given a stable monetary policy, both the upward trend in M1 velocity and at least some of the short-term variability of velocity would disappear. But short-term variations in velocity would not disappear entirely.

Box 16.3
The Income Velocity of Money in the United States

As this chart shows, the income velocity of M1 has risen over time, but not always at a steady rate from one quarter to the next. In part, the variations reflect the tendency of velocity to rise when interest rates rise and to fall when interest rates fall. Changes in business practices and financial institutions also affect the income velocity of money.

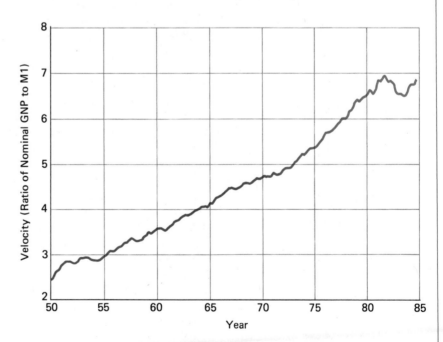

Source: Federal Reserve Board of Governors.

A nominal national income rule   To avoid inflations and recessions caused by variation in velocity, a number of economists, including some former monetarists, have concluded that the Fed should use nominal national income instead of the money supply as a policy target. This, they say, would do a better job of holding the economy to a course of inflation-free economic growth.

But a nominal national income target has its problems too. One problem is that data on national income are not available as fast as data on the money supply. A second is that a variety of factors other than monetary policy—fiscal policy being one—also affect nominal national income. And a third problem is that the Fed cannot control nominal national income directly. It can do so only indirectly, by adjusting the money supply. But changes in the money supply act on aggregate nominal demand only with a lag. In order to stabilize the growth of nominal national income, therefore, the Fed would have to rely on forecasts of velocity. Thus, the problems of lags and forecasting errors creep in through the window after having been thrown out through the door.

There is still another problem. A fixed rate of growth for nominal national income will not work well unless natural real output grows at the same fixed rate. During a productivity slowdown like the one that occurred in the 1970s, a nominal national income rule would produce inflation. During a period of faster-than-expected productivity growth, such a rule could lead to a growth recession.

A price level rule   These problems have led some other economists to propose yet another rule for monetary policy—one that sets its sights on a stable price level. Under such a rule the Fed would drain reserves from the banking system if the price level rose, and would inject new reserves into the system if it fell. This rule would keep aggregate nominal demand synchronized with natural real output even if the rate of growth of natural real output varied from year to year.

Unfortunately, a price level rule raises the same problems of lags and forecasting errors as a nominal national income rule. Also, a price level rule works poorly when a supply shock shifts the aggregate real supply curve upward. To keep the price level from rising in the face of a supply shock, the Fed would have to reduce the money supply, shifting the aggregate real demand curve to the left. This would cause a substantial loss of real output and a sharp rise in unemployment. But as we pointed out in Chapter 14, many economists think it's better to respond to the supply shock with an increase in aggregate nominal demand, at least if the shock is likely to be long-lasting. This would allow the price level to rise, but a supply shock is going to hurt the economy in some way no matter what is done. The pain of a little inflation, in this case, may be less than the pain of a major recession.

The Fed's position   To date, the Fed has not adopted any of the proposed policy rules. The Fed agrees that a stable monetary policy is needed. As required by law, it announces target ranges for growth of the money stock each year, although these targets are not binding. It agrees that lags and forecasting errors make fine-tuning a dangerous game. But it also insists that there is no one policy rule that is best under all conditions. An inflexible money growth rule would not let the Fed respond to unexpected changes in velocity, such as the drop in velocity that took place in 1982. A nominal national income rule would not let the Fed respond to changes in productivity, such as the slowdown in the 1970s and the recovery in the 1980s. And a price level rule would not let the Fed respond flexibly to supply shocks, such as the oil price rises of 1974 and 1979–1980. For these reasons, the Fed reserves the right to depart from its announced guidelines for money growth when necessary.

Rules for Fiscal Policy

Fiscal policy rules raise a different set of issues than monetary policy rules. The reason is that, as we have noted, there is no single set of policymakers in charge of fiscal policy. Instead, policies regarding taxes, government spending, and the deficit are the outcome of many separate decisions. In making these decisions, macroeconomic goals are often overshadowed by issues of social policy, defense policy, and vote trading. Even when tax cuts or job programs focus on macroeconomic issues, political factors such as elections are likely to affect their timing.

Under these conditions, most proposed policy rules do not call for use of fiscal policy as a tool of economic stabilization. Instead, they have the more modest aim of making fiscal policy less likely to be a source of instability. The greatest need, in the view of many economists, is to set up a firm link between spending and taxes—in other words, a balanced budget.

An annually balanced budget   The most drastic proposal is for a constitutional amendment that would require the federal government to balance its budget each year. Any shortfall of revenue would have to be made up right away, either by raising taxes or by spending less.

Proposals for an annually balanced federal budget score high in public opinion polls. Many people think that the government should be forced to live within its means just as they themselves are. But an annually balanced budget is not favored by many economists. The reason is that, as explained in Chapter 10, tax revenues tend to fall during a recession while transfer payments tend to rise. To maintain an annually balanced budget, then, taxes would have to be raised or spending cut during a recession. But these actions would tend to make the recession worse. Thus, an annually balanced budget might well make the economy not more but less stable than it is now.

A cyclically balanced budget   To overcome this problem, economists suggest that the budget should be balanced only over the business cycle. During recessions a cyclical deficit would be permitted. As the economy moves strongly into expansion, the budget would be required to show a cyclical surplus. At all times the structural deficit would be held at zero.

A cyclically balanced budget would strengthen the economy's automatic stabilizers. However, it is not clear how the proposal could be put into practice. It does not lend itself to a simple constitutional amendment. In making spending decisions, the president and Congress would have to be guided by forecasts of tax revenues for the coming fiscal year. What would keep them from relying on forecasts that are too optimistic, as they do now? Who would be punished, and how, if the forecasts turned out to be wrong? Answers to these questions are far from obvious. They lead many economists to doubt that any form of balanced-budget rule would be truly effective.

STRATEGIES FOR ENDING INFLATION

Up to this point, we have looked at strategies for stabilizing the economy. There is also a debate over what to do when stabilization fails. In Keynes' time, half a century ago, the debate focused on how to get the economy out of a depression. In recent years, by contrast, inflation has been the biggest problem. The late 1970s and early 1980s saw the worst peacetime inflation ever in the United States. The rate of inflation has fallen since then, but policy activists and those who favor policy rules are still arguing about what to do about it. Both have ideas about what can be done to control inflation when it gets out of hand.

Conventional Policies

All economists agree that inflation can be slowed by conventional demand management policy. The costs of doing so are likely to be high, however. As Chapter 14 explained, inflation can gain momentum as expectations of more inflation push the aggregate real supply curve higher and higher. Stopping inflation by slowing the growth of aggregate nominal demand will then cause an inflationary recession. The momentum of the inflation will be broken, but only at the cost of a period of high unemployment and low real output.

Just how great is the cost of stopping inflation by demand management policy alone? A well-known article by Arthur Okun examined six studies of this cost.[2] These studies show that reducing the rate of inflation by just one percentage point would require real output to drop 10 percent below its natural level for a full year. Such a decline in real output would mean an unemployment rate of almost 10 percent, compared to a natural unemployment rate that today is estimated to be in the range of 6 to 6.5 percent.

The cost of stopping the double-digit rate of inflation of the late 1970s was not quite as great as Okun's estimate suggests, but it was not small. Inflation had reached an annual rate of about 13 percent in late 1979. At that time the rate of unemployment was 6.3 percent, or about its natural rate. Restrictive monetary policy then slowed the growth of aggregate nominal demand. The economy went through back-to-back recessions in 1980 and 1981–1982, with only a brief recovery in between. Unemployment rose to 10.6 percent by the end of 1982. Real output hardly grew at all, so that by the end of 1982 it was at least 10 percent below its natural level. The reward for this pain was a drop in the inflation rate to a little under 4 percent by 1983—a welcome reduction, but still a rate that would have been seen as far too high only a few years earlier.

Small wonder, then, that economists have looked for a less costly strategy for stopping inflation. Let's look at some ideas.

---

[2]Arthur Okun, "Efficient Disinflationary Policies," *American Economic Review* 68, May 1978, pp. 348–352.

Wage and Price Controls

Wage and price controls are an idea that was popular among policy activists in the 1970s. These may range from mild guidelines to mandatory wage and price ceilings. The United States has tried using such controls a number of times, and they are a permanent feature in many European countries. Let's look at how these policies work and why they are controversial.

The case for controls   The case for wage and price controls is strongest when they are used as a temporary measure to fight an inflationary recession. When policymakers apply the brakes after a period of rapid inflation, firms and workers do not expect inflation to stop right away. Their inflationary expectations push the aggregate real supply curve upward, causing cost-push inflation. In effect, the expectation of more inflation becomes a self-fulfilling prophecy. The result is an inflationary recession.

Suppose now that just as the growth of aggregate nominal demand is slowed, the government imposes a program of strict wage and price controls. This is done with great fanfare and a show of firm resolve to lick inflation once and for all. What is hoped is that workers and firms will believe that the controls are really going to stop inflation. If they do, they will revise their inflationary expectations much sooner than they would if they had to learn from experience.

This reduction in expected inflation, if it happens, will remove the cost-push element from the inflationary recession. Workers will know that they do not have to push for high wages to beat inflation, so they will accept controls. Firms will know that their input prices will not be rising, so they will keep the prices of their output in line. A larger part of the slowdown in the growth of nominal GNP will take the form of a slowdown in price increases than would otherwise be the case. The drop in real output and the rise in unemployment will be less than otherwise. As a result, the transition to price stability will be faster and less painful than it would have been without controls.

Problems with controls   So much for theory. The problem is that often wage and price controls are used not as a supplement to demand management policy but as a substitute for it. Either the government tries to use wage and price controls to fight inflation without also slowing the growth of aggregate demand, or it leaves controls in force after the transition is over and a new boom is under way. If this is done, either price and wage controls will be ineffective or they will lead to shortages, rationing, and black markets.

The U.S. experience   As noted earlier, there have been several experiments with wage and price controls in the United States. One was during World War II. The high level of wartime government spending made it hard to control aggregate demand. Strict price controls were used to suppress inflation. The results were predictable: Rationing was introduced for gasoline, tires, sugar, and many other goods, and widespread black markets emerged.

**Box 16.4
Nixon's Wage and Price Controls**

On August 15, 1971, President Nixon announced a dramatic new economic policy. The part of the program that drew the most attention was a strict 90-day freeze on all wages and prices. The freeze later became known as Phase I of what proved to be a long-drawn-out experiment with wage and price controls. Phase I was followed by Phase II, in which firms could raise their prices to cover higher costs but not to increase their profit margins. Wage increases were limited to 5.5 percent except under special conditions.

Phases I and II of the Nixon controls came at the time when controls could be expected to work best. As the chart shows, inflation was already slowing down. Phase I caused the rate of inflation to fall more quickly. Some of this gain was lost in a price bulge when the strict controls of Phase I were lifted, but after that, inflation continued to fall through mid-1972.

According to a study by Alan S. Blinder and William J. Newton, the combined effect of Phases I and II was to hold the price level 1.22 percent below the level it would have reached in the absence of controls. This modest but measurable reduction in inflation was achieved at the cost of only a few shortages, mainly in lumber. No widespread disruptions of the economy were felt.

Believing that Phases I and II had done their job, Nixon began to put controls back on the shelf. In January of 1973 Phase II was replaced by Phase III. This phase imposed slightly looser standards and stressed self-enforcement by firms and unions. By the time Phase III came into effect, a strong recovery of aggregate demand was under way, and the rate of inflation turned upward. According to Blinder and Newton, during Phase III prices rose only slightly faster than they would have if controls had never been imposed. This indicates that there was some "catch-up" effect during that phase.

As the rate of inflation increased, political pressure built up to "get tough." Nixon responded in August 1973 with a renewed freeze on wages and prices that came to be called Phase III 1/2. During this phase inflation was temporarily slowed, but this time, with demand booming, there were serious shortages. Firms began to hoard raw materials in fear of more shortages to come.

It was judged that these distortions were too high a price to pay for keeping the rate of inflation down. The freeze was soon dropped in favor of Phase IV, which was a phaseout. In April of 1974 Congress let the controls expire. According to Blinder and Newton, catch-up inflation then began in earnest. By August of 1974 prices had reached the level they would have reached if controls had never been in force. Even after that, catch-up inflation continued for many months. By 1975 the price level was about 1 percent higher than it would have been if controls had never been tried.

Another experiment with wage and price controls took place from 1971 to 1974, during the Nixon administration. As indicated in Box 16.4, the Nixon controls were a mixed success at best. The controls were first introduced when inflation was falling anyway, and they may have helped a little to speed the decline. But they were left in place after prices began to rise again in mid-1972. At that point they proved useless or worse.

Despite the scant success of Nixon's controls, President Carter continued to experiment with controls throughout his four years in office. Carter's guidelines, as he called them, were voluntary, but they were backed by the threat that government contracts would not be awarded to

^aAnnual rate of change from level of consumer price index 12 months previously.

Source: Alan S. Blinder and William J. Newton, "The 1971–1974 Controls Program and the Price Level: An Econometric Postmortem," *National Bureau of Economic Research Working Paper No. 279*, September 1978. The chart is based·on data from President's Council of Economic Advisers, *Economic Report of the President* (Washington, D.C.: Government Printing Office, various issues).

firms that refused to follow them. Because aggregate demand continued to grow strongly, the controls did nothing to prevent a doubling of the rate of inflation during Carter's four years in office.

Because of their failure in the 1970s, controls have lost favor even among policy activists. One of President Reagan's first acts upon taking office in 1981 was to end the Carter controls. If rapid inflation returns to the United States, however, controls may be revived. They allow politicians to make a show of getting tough with big business and big labor, which the public often sees as the villains of inflation. And in matters of policy, appearances are sometimes more important than effects.

Indexing

Indexing is sometimes suggested as a means of dealing with inflation. As explained in Chapter 7, indexing means making wages, taxes, debts, interest rates, and a host of other things inflation-proof by adjusting nominal payments in response to changes in the price level.

Indexing is sometimes used just to make it easier to live with inflation. That is how it has been used in countries like Brazil and Israel, which have lived with double- and even triple-digit inflation for years. However, some economists, including Milton Friedman, have suggested that indexing can be used to control inflation as well as to ease its pain.

The argument is that indexing can help squeeze the cost-push elements out of inflationary recessions. During a period of inflation all long-term contracts—union wage contracts, contracts for industrial supplies, loan contracts, and so on—must provide protection against price increases. If they do this simply by setting higher nominal wage rates, prices, and interest rates, these contracts will continue to push up costs even after inflation slows elsewhere in the economy. However, if wages, prices, and interest rates in long-term contracts are tied to the rate of inflation, they will slow down in step with the general price level. Thus, if indexing is widespread, an inflation may respond more quickly to a slowdown in the growth of aggregate demand.

However, it has become clear that indexing can make matters worse when inflation is caused by a supply shock rather than by excess demand. As Chapter 14 explained, adjusting to a supply shock—say, an increase in the price of imported oil—requires a change in relative prices. The price of oil has to rise faster than the rate of inflation while other prices rise more slowly. Indexing tends to lock all prices and wages to the average, making the adjustment more difficult. The highly indexed Israeli economy is often cited as a case in point. The oil shocks of the 1970s touched off a spiral of inflation in Israel that approached a rate of 1,000 percent per year by the mid-1980s. In the U.S. economy, where indexing is much less widespread, the oil price shocks added only a few percentage points to the rate of inflation.

Changing the Policy Regime

At best, indexing and controls only ease the task of taming inflation. When inflation really gets out of control, something more basic is needed. Monetarists and, even more so, rational-expectationists like to say that what is needed is a change in *policy regime*. By this they mean a change in the basic rules that underlie the conduct of economic policy.

Thomas Sargent, a leader of the rational-expectations school, has developed this line of thought in detail. In Sargent's view, the policy regime of the post–World War II U.S. economy has been one of stop and go, with an inflationary bias. The government, that is to say, has alternately fought unemployment (with expansionary policies) and inflation (with contractionary policies). On the average, however, the expansionary periods have been longer and stronger than the contractionary ones.

Sargent points out that Okun's high estimate of the cost of stopping inflation is based on the record of this policy regime. It should be no surprise, says Sargent, that prices respond slowly to a contractionary policy in such a regime. After all, people know that the contractionary policy won't last long. They therefore resist price and wage cuts in order to position themselves for the inflation that they know will return.

But, says Sargent, think what would happen if, during a period of rapid inflation, there were a credible change in policy regime. What if the government convinced everyone that it would never again, no matter what, allow aggregate nominal demand to grow faster than natural real output? Believing this, firms and workers would expect the rate of inflation to fall to zero. Their changed expectations would alter their short-run response to a contractionary policy. The aggregate real supply curve would promptly stop drifting upward. As it came to rest, the economy could make a quick, painless transition to price stability.

This sounds too good to be true, but Sargent claims there is evidence that it can work. The evidence comes from cases in which hyperinflation has been brought under control. The story of the German hyperinflation of the 1920s is one of the most dramatic examples. (See Box 16.5.)

THE STATE OF THE DEBATE

Sargent's call for a change of policy regime brings us back to the debate over policy activism versus policy rules. We will end the chapter with some comments on the state of that debate. Over the years the two sides have come closer together on many points. Both agree that stopping inflation is not easy; it is better to have a strategy that will keep inflation from getting out of hand in the first place. Policy activists recognize that forecasting errors and lags are serious problems. And those who favor policy rules admit that there may be no one rule that works perfectly all the time. What differences remain?

Technical differences   The technical differences that remain revolve around how best to deal with lags and forecasting errors and how to choose a policy rule. On these issues, some economists see a middle ground: If activists are not willing to see human policymakers replaced with rigid rules, why not at least develop a somewhat looser set of rules to guide the policymakers' actions? To use the ocean liner example once again, this approach would not put the ship on automatic pilot, but neither would it leave the course entirely up to the captain's moods. Instead, the captain would be required to announce the chosen course in advance and to react to unforeseen events according to the guidelines contained in a manual of seamanship.

The Fed has already moved in this direction, in that it now announces target growth ranges for money and credit for the coming year. The next step, say those who favor this middle ground, would be to announce a set of rules for adjusting money growth within those ranges and for adjusting the ranges themselves when macroeconomic conditions develop in a different way than was expected. For example, the target growth range for money might be adjusted upward or downward each quarter according to whether nominal national income was running above or below some target value.

The rules need not work perfectly. The important thing would be that

**Box 16.5
The End of
Hyperinflation in
Germany**

The political system that the allied powers imposed on Germany after World War I was a prescription for irresponsible fiscal policy. A weak socialist government was caught between demands for spending by its supporters and resistance to taxes by business. In addition, the Allies were demanding reparation payments that went far beyond Germany's ability to pay. In the face of these troubles, the government did the only thing it could: it ran huge deficits and printed endless amounts of currency.

The result was an inflation like no other either before or since. From a level of 245 in December 1918, the German price index rose to an incredible 126,160,000,000,000,000 in December 1923. In 1923 alone, prices increased almost a billionfold. In the single month of September 1923, prices went up by some 35,000 percent. People had to haul their money to the store in a wheelbarrow to get a day's groceries.

But perhaps the most astonishing thing about the German hyperinflation was its end. The chart shows the course of the German price level from 1919 through 1924. After becoming almost vertical in 1923, the price level line turns a sharp corner, with inflation stopping almost overnight.

According to Thomas Sargent, the hyperinflation was ended by a complete change in policy regime. The change consisted of three parts. First, it became possible to convert German marks into U.S. dollars (which at that time were convertible into gold.) Second, a strict limit was placed on increases in the money supply. And third, the budget was swung from deficit to surplus by a combination of permanent tax increases and spending cuts. Two further measures helped out. One was the issue of a new unit of currency whose value was set equal to one trillion of the old marks. The other was a rescheduling of reparation payments by the allied powers.

It appears that inflationary expectations and economic behavior adjusted to the change in policy regime right away. There seems to have been no adverse effect on real output or unemployment; both measures showed improvement in 1924 compared with their 1923 levels.

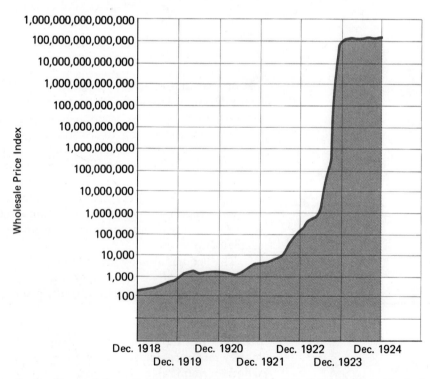

Source: Thomas J. Sargent, "The Ends of Four Big Inflations," *Federal Reserve Bank of Minneapolis Working Paper No. 158*, May 1981.

firms, workers, stock market traders, and everyone else would know the rules. In that case the rules would become a stable framework for expectations. The rules would build in some room for policy activism, but they would reduce the scope for discretionary changes in policy compared with the present situation. They would, in effect, discourage policymakers from turning the ship's rudder violently from one side to the other, but at the same time they would allow them to react effectively to supply shocks, changes in financial institutions, and other unforeseen events.

Political differences   While a middle ground might well be found on technical issues, various schools of thought remain farther apart on political questions. To put it bluntly, monetarists simply do not trust policymakers to use their power in a responsible manner. It is no help that policymakers are, for the most part, honest and well intentioned. The system tempts them to stress the short run at the expense of the long run, to mask their true intentions from the public, and to make frequent changes of course. In the monetarist view, even an imperfect set of rules would be better than leaving economic policy to the politicians.

Policy activists are not so pessimistic. They admit that policymakers have made mistakes in the past, but not that they always do more harm than good. In a complex real world, they believe that no set of rules fixed in advance could cover all possible contingencies. Thus, any reasonable policy regime needs to allow some scope for human judgment. The activists do think policymakers and the public can be taught to take a longer-term view of things. They think that the big forecasting failures of the last decade will become a thing of the past. Above all, they look forward to a world in which professional economists have a bigger say in making policy. And so the debate goes on.

Summary

1. Economists have long disagreed over the best strategy for economic stabilization. Keynesians have favored the active use of fiscal and monetary policies to fine-tune the economy, keeping it on a path of steady growth without inflation. Monetarists and rational expectationists have tended to see mistakes in policy as a major source of instability in the economy. They favor fixed, long-term policy rules as the best way to moderate the extremes of the business cycle.

2. The case for policy activism rests on four assumptions: (1) that fiscal and monetary policy allow the government to affect real output, employment, and the price level; (2) that changes in policy have predictable effects on the economy; (3) that economists can forecast

well enough to guide policy decisions; and (4) that policymakers will follow the advice of economists. Critics of activism challenge all of these assumptions as either untrue or only partly true.

3. Opponents of policy activism draw attention to lags in the policy process. The *inside lag* is the delay between the time when policy change is needed and the time when a decision is made. The *outside lag* is the delay between the time when a decision is made and the time when it affects the economy. Lags in fiscal and monetary policy range from as short as three months to several years. Because of lags, policymakers must act on the basis of forecasts. However, if the forecasts turn out to be wrong, their decisions may make things

worse rather than better by the time they take effect.

4. Even when economists offer valid advice, policymakers may not follow it. One reason for this is that there is great political pressure to "do something" when things go wrong with the economy. However, because of policy lags, it may be too late to do anything useful by the time this pressure reaches its peak. Also, some types of policy have favorable effects in the short run but unfavorable effects in the long run. Politicians who want to be reelected may place undue stress on the short-run effects. Monetary authorities too may be tempted to seek short-term advantages by departing from announced long-term policies. Critics of policy activism see these political factors as a major problem.

5. A number of rules have been proposed for monetary policy. One is to let the money supply grow at a steady rate equal to the long-term rate of growth of natural real output. A second is to let nominal national income grow at a steady rate equal to the long-term growth of natural real output. A third is to use a stable price level as a policy target. None of these policy rules works perfectly all the time.

6. The most often proposed rule for fiscal policy is to require the federal government to balance its budget. An annually balanced budget would require the government to raise taxes or cut spending during a recession. This might lead to less, rather than more, stability. Many economists favor a budget that would be balanced on a structural basis, but which would allow cyclical deficits and surpluses over the course of the business cycle.

7. The United States has imposed wage and price controls a number of times. Mandatory controls were used during World War II and in 1971–1974. Voluntary guidelines were tried at other times. If used in conjunction with a contractionary monetary or fiscal policy, guidelines can, in theory, help slow inflation by making the anti-inflationary policy more credible. If they are used while demand continues to grow rapidly, controls either will be ineffective or will lead to shortages, rationing, and black markets.

8. Indexing means making wages, prices, interest rates and so on inflation-proof by linking them to a price index. Indexing can help moderate an inflationary recession caused by a slowdown in the rate of growth of aggregate demand. However, it can make matters worse when the cause of the inflation is a supply shock.

9. Some supporters of the rational-expectations hypothesis think that inflation can be stopped fairly quickly and painlessly by a change in policy regime, by which they mean a change in the rules that policymakers follow. As an example, they cite the end of the German hyperinflation of the 1920s.

Questions for Review

1. Explain the following terms and concepts:
   hyperinflation
   inside lag
   outside lag
2. What is the main cause of the business cycle, according to economists who favor a strategy of policy activism? According to those who favor policy rules?
3. What four assumptions underlie the case for policy activism?
4. What are the sources of the inside and outside lags for monetary policy? for fiscal policy?
5. According to critics of policy activism, what features of the U.S. political system interfere with attempts to stabilize the economy?
6. Describe three possible rules for the conduct of monetary policy.
7. Which is more likely to contribute to economic stability, a federal budget that is balanced every year or one that is balanced, on the average, over the course of the business cycle? Why?
8. When have wage and price controls been used in the United States? What were the effects of the controls?
9. Under what conditions is indexing likely to

help control inflation? Under what conditions can it make inflation worse?

10. What do rational-expectationists mean by a change in policy regime? Give an example.

Problems and Topics for Discussion

1. Here is a game that will give you a feeling for the effects of policy lags and forecasting errors: In your classroom or another large room, arrange a dozen chairs to form a "slalom course." The course should consist of pairs of chairs placed about three feet apart to form "gates." The gates should be laid out to form a path of S-shaped turns. The goal is to walk through the gates without bumping into them or wandering off the path. When your slalom course is set up, form teams of three and compete to see who can finish the course fastest. Whoever hits a gate is disqualified:

   a. For practice, select one member from the team to walk through the course. Make a note of the time it takes to complete it.

   b. Next, blindfold team member A, who walks the course. Team member B watches and tells A when to turn to the right or left.

   c. Team member A, the walker, is still blindfolded. Team member B watches A and writes directions to turn left or right on a memo pad. The directions are passed to team member C, who reads them aloud so that A can hear them. Team member C must sit facing away from the course so that he or she cannot see B's progress.

   d. Conditions are the same as for part c, except that this time team member B also sits facing away from the course. B is allowed to view the course only by looking over his or her shoulder using a hand-held mirror. B thus must check on A's progress using the mirror and then write instructions for C, who reads them to A.

   What does this game teach you about strategies for steering the economy through the "gates" of the business cycle? Discuss.

2. At a certain university, a professor always tells his class at the start of the semester that grades will be based on a final exam. The reason for the exam is to give students an incentive to study hard and learn all they can about economics. One semester, as exam time approaches, the professor thinks to himself, "My students have studied hard and learned everything they should. My job is done. Why go to the trouble of giving the exam?" He gives everyone an A and cancels the exam. The next semester he again announces that he will grade on the basis of the exam, and again he cancels it at the last minute. But by the end of the third semester, he notices something amiss. Even though he had announced a final exam at the start of the semester, no one has studied at all. They didn't believe him. Now he thinks to himself, "Too bad. But what is the point of giving the exam now? They don't know a thing. It would just be a lot of work for me to grade the things." Again he cancels the exam.

   One day during vacation there is a knock on our professor-hero's office door. There stands the head of his department. "What are you going to do about this?" she says. "Your students aren't learning a thing any more!"

   "I know it's a problem," he replies, "but I don't know what to do. If I announce the exam and everyone believes me, then at the end of the semester the optimal strategy is not to give the exam. But if I announce the exam and no one believes me, then at the end of the semester it is still the optimal strategy to cancel the exam. You can't really blame me for what has happened. After all, every semester I'm doing what is best under the circumstances I'm faced with."

   The department head walks out without saying a word. The next morning there is a big notice on the department bulletin board, where both faculty and students can see it: BY ORDER OF THE DEPARTMENT HEAD, ALL PROFESSORS MUST GIVE FINAL EXAMS OR THEY WILL BE FIRED. Our friend reads this notice and breathes a sigh of relief. Now he can start giving exams again and be certain that his students will study for them.

How does this fable bear on the issue of policy activism versus policy rules? (Thanks to Gary Gorton for suggesting the story.)

3. Draw an aggregate real supply and demand diagram to illustrate the use of a policy rule calling for a fixed rate of money growth equal to the rate of growth of natural real output. Show what will happen to real output and the price level when velocity rises or falls unexpectedly while the rate of growth of natural real output stays the same.

4. Draw an aggregate real supply and demand diagram to illustrate the use of a monetary policy rule calling for a fixed rate of growth of nominal national income equal to the rate of growth of natural real output. Show what will happen to real output and the price level if the growth of natural real output unexpectedly slows down or speeds up.

5. Use an aggregate real supply and demand diagram to compare the effects of a supply shock when the Fed (a) follows a rule calling for a fixed price level; (b) follows a rule calling for a fixed level of nominal national income; and (c) accommodates the supply shock in order to keep real output equal to its natural level. What are the advantages and disadvantages of each policy?

6. Policy activists have long been aware that the process of getting the approval of Congress adds a long and uncertain period to the inside lag for fiscal policy. As a solution to this problem, it has often been proposed that the federal government "stockpile" a number of projects, such as highway improvements, bridges, post office buildings, and so on. All planning and design work for the projects would be completed and the projects would be kept "on the shelf" until needed. When the economy enters a recession, the president could order that the projects be started. Work on them could begin in a matter of weeks.

Do you think this strategy would reduce the inside lag for fiscal policy? What problems of lags and forecasting would remain? How would the proposal affect the political problems of fine-tuning?

Suggestions for Further Reading

Blinder, Alan S., and William J. Newton. "The 1971–1974 Controls Program and the Price Level: An Econometric Postmortem," *National Bureau of Economic Research Working Paper No. 279*, September 1978.

This paper is the basis for Box 16.4.

Gordon, Robert J. *Macroeconomics*, 3rd ed. Boston: Little, Brown, 1984.

Chapter 12 covers the debate over fine-tuning versus policy rules.

President's Council of Economic Advisers. *Economic Report of the President.* Washington, D.C.: Government Printing Office, 1985.

The 1985 edition of the report leans toward monetarism in its discussion of economic policy for the late 1980s.

Rivlin, Alice M., ed. *Economic Choices 1984.* Washington, D.C.: Brookings Institution, 1984.

This volume discusses economic policy for the late 1980s from a nonmonetarist point of view.

Chapter 17

A Closer Look at Unemployment

WHAT YOU WILL LEARN IN THIS CHAPTER

After reading this chapter, you should be able to

1. Show how people are classified by job market status as a basis for calculating the unemployment rate.
2. Contrast the official definition of unemployment with the common-sense notions of "not working" and "can't find a job."
3. Discuss the link between real output and unemployment that is known as *Okun's law*.
4. Distinguish among *frictional, structural,* and *cyclical* unemployment.
5. Discuss the connection between unemployment rates and the job search process.
6. Explain the link between inflation and unemployment that is known as the *Phillips curve*.

Ideas for Review

Here are some terms and concepts that you should review before you read this chapter:

The business cycle (Chapter 1)
Transaction costs (Chapter 4)
Stocks and flows (Chapter 6)
Aggregate real supply and demand (Chapters 7 and 14)
The natural rate of unemployment (Chapter 14)

"Retraining blue-collar workers is going to become as commonplace as sending white-collar workers to get their MBAs."

Wyandotte, Michigan: Robert Schnau still has privileges at the club run by the firm he used to work for, and he occasionally nurses a beer at the bar that overlooks the bowling alley. But his old job is long gone. Even the building where he worked for 28 years has been demolished.

He hasn't had regular work for a year. "My resumes are out around the country," says Schnau, who is 50 years old. Meanwhile, he earns pocket money running bingo games for the club.

A lot of people in this town and its neighbors just south of Detroit thought they had jobs for life in the factories making cars and chemicals and steel. Instead, they find themselves tossed out by faltering industries and rebuffed by a changing labor market.

Here, at least, they have a place to turn. Since August 1980, a consortium of 16 towns called the Downriver Community Conference has tried to retrain the nearly 2,400 workers who have shown up at its door, often emotionally and financially exhausted. Despite some disappointments, more than half have gotten back to work, which some experts consider a sign of the program's success.

Downriver, a pioneer in the field, is being emulated elsewhere. Eventually, "training blue-collar workers is going to become as commonplace as sending white-collar workers to get their MBAs," says Albert Angrisani, assistant secretary of the U.S. Labor Department.

Without emphasis on retraining, says another economist, "you're going to force a large segment of the work force off the edge into the permanently unemployed."[1]

Unemployment has many faces. Robert Schnau, a skilled worker who has been displaced from a job in a shrinking smokestack industry, is one of them. A high school dropout with no skills or job experience is another. A Yale Law School graduate taking the summer off before starting a fast-track career with a big New York firm is part of the unemployment picture too. It is time to take a closer look at what unemployment is all about.

MEASURING UNEMPLOYMENT

Classifying People by Labor Status

The official measure of unemployment is based on a breakdown of the U.S. population into a number of groups and subgroups, as shown in Box 17.1. The box on the left represents all people under 16 years of age plus people in the armed services and those in prisons and other institutions. For statistical purposes, these people are not considered to be even potential members of the labor force, although some of them do work. Movements into and out of this part of the population are a result of noneconomic factors such as aging and institutionalization.

All people who are not in the group just described belong to what is called the *noninstitutional adult civilian population*. This group is divided

---

[1]Richard Koenig, "Detroit-Area Retraining Program Being Emulated as Funding Grows," *Wall Street Journal*, March 30, 1983, p. 29. Reprinted by permission of the Wall Street Journal, © Dow Jones & Company, Inc. 1983. All rights reserved.

**Box 17.1
Breakdown of the
Population by
Employment Status**

This box shows how the U.S. population is broken down into groups and subgroups based on employment status. People under 16, in the armed forces, in prisons, or in other institutions are viewed as not even potential participants in the labor market. Of the noninstitutional adult civilian population, only people who are working or looking for work are considered to be part of the labor force. The unemployment rate is the ratio of the number of unemployed people to the total labor force.

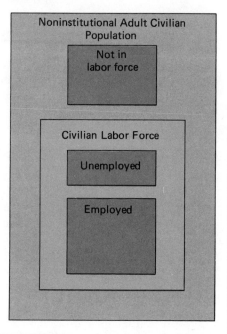

into three subgroups, as shown on the right-hand side of Box 17.1. The first subgroup consists of all people who are *employed*. The Bureau of Labor Statistics counts as employed all people who work at least one hour a week for pay or at least 15 hours a week as unpaid workers in a family business. People who have jobs from which they are absent because of bad weather, labor disputes, or vacations are also counted as employed.

The second subgroup is made up of the officially unemployed. To be counted as *unemployed* a person must be without a job but must be actively looking for work. There are two exceptions to this rule. One is that people who have found a job that they expect to start within 30 days are counted as unemployed even if they are not actively looking for work to fill the time until the job begins. The other is that people who have been laid off from a job to which they expect to be recalled need not actively look for other work in order to be counted as unemployed.

Taken together, the employed and the unemployed make up the *civilian labor force*. The remaining subgroup in Box 17.1 thus consists of all noninstitutionalized people age 16 and over who are not in the labor force—that is, who are neither working nor looking for work. Even though these people are not employed, they are not officially counted as unemployed. This division of the population into groups and subgroups is the basis of the official *unemployment rate,* which is simply the percentage of the civilian labor force that is not employed.

A Critique of the Unemployment Rate

The Bureau of Labor Statistics, in conjunction with the Bureau of the Census, gets the data needed to calculate unemployment from a monthly sample of about 50,000 randomly selected households. Field agents go to those households and ask a series of questions about the job status of each member of the household. The questions include such things as: Did anyone work last week? Did anyone look for work? How long has the person been looking for work? How did the person go about looking? The result is one headline-making percentage and a wide range of other data.

Clearly, there are a lot of gray areas in the measurement of unemployment. The official unemployment rate can be criticized for both understating and overstating the "true" number of the unemployed. One way to understand these gray areas better is to compare the official definition of unemployment with two commonsense definitions—namely, "not working" and "can't find a job."

Unemployment vs. "not working"   The official definitions of employment and unemployment are clearly far different from the simple definitions of "working" and "not working."

On the one hand, there are many people who work but are not officially employed. By far the largest such group consists of people who work full time at housekeeping and child care. These occupations are counted as employment if they are done for pay, but the bulk of such work is not done for pay. There are also a certain number of children under 16 who work for pay, although they are not counted as employed. Children under 16 working without pay for a family farm or business also are not counted as employed, although they are counted as employed for doing the same work once they reach their sixteenth birthday.

On the other hand, not everyone who doesn't work is counted as unemployed. There are, of course, millions of people who are not looking for work and who therefore are not counted in the labor force. There are also those who are absent from their jobs because of illness, bad weather, or labor disputes; they are counted as employed even though they are not working. Finally, there are those who are working part time and are counted as employed but are actively seeking full-time employment. People in this situation are sometimes referred to as "underemployed."

Unemployment vs. "can't find a job"   The second commonsense definition of unemployment, "can't find a job," also fits the official definition of unemployment only loosely.

In some ways the official definition overstates the number of people who can't find jobs. As just mentioned, some people who are counted as unemployed actually have jobs to which they expect to be recalled or jobs that they expect to start within 30 days. Other people who are counted as unemployed could easily find a job of some kind but prefer to take their time and find just the kind of job they want. (People who are not the only income earners in their households, for example, may be able to afford to look longer and be more selective than those in households with no other income.) Still other people register as unemployed in order to meet the requirements of certain income transfer programs even though they may not be qualified for any available work and may only go through the motions of looking for a job. Finally, there is some doubt as to whether the description "can't find a job" fits people who could have stayed on at their last job but instead quit to look for another one.

In other ways, however, the official definition of unemployment understates the number of people who can't find a job. The most important group of people who can't find jobs but are not counted as unemployed are the so-called **discouraged workers.** These are people who are not looking for work because they believe no suitable jobs are available. Officially, the Bureau of Labor Statistics considers anyone who has looked for work within the last six months but is no longer actively looking for a job to be a discouraged worker. The description "can't find a job" also fits many workers who have part-time jobs but would take full-time jobs if they could find them. Robert Schnau is an example. If he works even an hour a week running bingo games for his club, he is officially counted as employed. But most people would think of him as unemployed because he can't find a "real" job.

Discouraged worker
A person who is available for work and has looked for work within the last six months, but is no longer actively looking.

Employment Stocks and Flows

Up to this point we have viewed unemployment only in terms of stocks of workers in various groups and subgroups of the population. In order to understand the sources of change in employment and unemployment rates, however, we also must look at the flows that connect the various stocks. These flows are shown in Box 17.2. (To keep things simple, flows into and out of the noninstitutional adult population are ignored.) First consider flows into and out of the labor force. Flows into the labor force, called *entries,* can be either successful or unsuccessful. A successful entrant finds a job right away; an unsuccessful entrant actively looks for a job but does not find one right away, thereby entering the ranks of the unemployed.

Two kinds of flows out of the labor force are also shown in the box. First, people can quit or lose their jobs and not look for others. Second, people who have been officially unemployed can give up looking for a job without ever having found one. If they remain available for work, they officially become discouraged workers.

Next are the flows into and out of employment. A person can become employed either by being hired for a new job or by being recalled to a former job. Hires plus recalls are shown in the diagram as *total accessions.* There are also a number of ways of leaving employment. They include being fired, being laid off, quitting, and retiring. The sum of all these ways of leaving employment is shown as *total separations.*

Finally, we come to the flows into and out of unemployment. Additions to the stock of unemployed people occur whenever people enter the labor force unsuccessfully or are separated from jobs and start looking for new ones right away. Subtractions from the stock of unemployed people occur when unemployed workers find jobs or when they stop looking and leave the labor force. The number of unemployed people grows if

**Box 17.2
Unemployment Stocks
and Flows**

This box shows the relationship between major stocks and flows within the noninstitutional adult population. When new jobs are created, they can be filled either by workers who are unemployed or by new entrants into the labor force. Sometimes new workers enter the labor force without finding work. Workers who quit or lose their jobs may either become unemployed or leave the labor force.

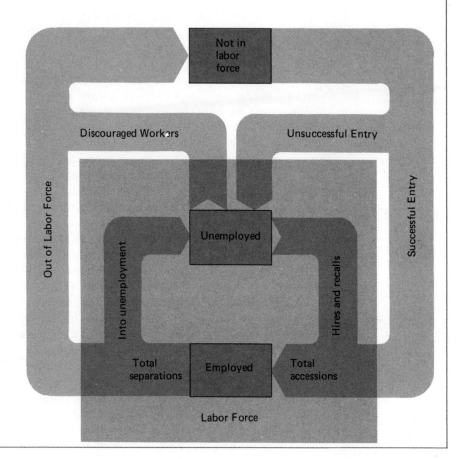

additions to the total exceed subtractions from it; it falls if subtractions exceed additions.

UNEMPLOYMENT, GROWTH, AND THE BUSINESS CYCLE

Now that we have a better idea of what unemployment is and how it is measured, we will pick up a theme that has been mentioned several times in earlier chapters: the links among unemployment, economic growth, and the business cycle. We already know that during a recession the unemployment rate tends to rise above its natural level. During a recovery, the unemployment rate falls again. At the peak of the business cycle, it may fall below the natural level. Now we can take a closer look at the causes of these variations in the level of unemployment.

Okun's Law

Okun's law

A rule of thumb according to which each 3 percent by which real output rises above (or falls below) its natural level results in an unemployment rate one percentage point below (or above) the natural rate.

The swings of unemployment above and below its natural rate can be related to the swings in real output below and above its natural rate by means of a rule of thumb known as **Okun's law**. The law is named after Arthur Okun, who was a member of President John Kennedy's Council of Economic Advisers at the time that he discovered it. According to Okun's law, for each 3 percent by which real output rises above its natural level, the unemployment rate tends to fall below its natural rate by one percentage point. Likewise, for each 3 percent by which real output falls below its natural level, the unemployment rate tends to rise by one percentage point above its natural rate.

Suppose, for example, that the natural level of real output is $1,000 billion and the natural rate of unemployment is 6.5 percent. In that case, a 6 percent decrease in real output to $940 billion would tend to raise the unemployment rate to 8.5 percent. Likewise, a 3 percent increase in real output from its natural level of $1,000 billion to $1,030 billion would push unemployment one percentage point below its natural rate, to 5.5 percent.

Why the three-to-one ratio between changes in real output relative to its natural level and changes in unemployment relative to its natural rate? Why doesn't adding one percent to real output cut unemployment by a full percentage point? There seem to be two basic reasons.

First, hires and layoffs in labor markets, like exchanges in any other market, involve transaction costs. Firms that hire new workers must bear the costs of advertising for applicants and screening them when they arrive. And new workers may not be fully productive until they have gone through a period of on-the-job training. Firms that lay off workers also bear some transaction costs. Some contracts call for severance payments. Some skilled workers may get other jobs after being laid off and thus may not be available for recall. And employers that have made many layoffs may be required by law to make higher payments to state and federal unemployment insurance funds. Because of these transaction costs, firms tend to "hoard" labor during business downturns by cutting their workers' hours or finding make-work projects for them instead of laying them off. And during upturns they may find it cheaper to put workers on overtime, even at time-and-a-half wages, rather than go to the trouble of finding new workers.

But labor hoarding does not fully explain the three-to-one ratio of Okun's law. A second reason for the ratio lies in the way the unemployment rate itself is calculated. The unemployment rate is the ratio of unemployed workers to the total labor force. During a business upturn, when firms are creating new jobs at a rapid rate, some previously unemployed workers find jobs. But at the same time the improved job market draws into the labor force workers who previously had not even looked for work. Not all the new entrants find work right away; some instead join the ranks of the unemployed. The upshot is that when output expands, the number of employed people, the number of unemployed people, and the size of the total labor force all grow. As a result, a 1 percent increase in the number of jobs tends to be linked with less than a one percentage point drop in the unemployment rate.

Types of Unemployment

A rise in the unemployment rate, as we now know, reflects a change in the flows into and out of the pool of unemployed workers. Given a constant size for the labor force as a whole, the unemployment rate rises when the rate of flow into the pool of the unemployed exceeds the rate of outflow. It falls when the rate of flow out of the pool exceeds the rate of inflow. The difference between the rate of inflow and the rate of outflow determines how long the average person remains in the pool of unemployed workers. During the past 20 years the average duration of unemployment has ranged from a low of 7.8 weeks in 1969 to a high of 20.0 weeks in 1983.

The duration of unemployment not only varies from year to year; it also varies from one unemployed worker to another. As Box 17.3 shows, depending on the state of the business cycle, between one third and one half of all unemployed people are out of work for less than five weeks. At the other end of the scale, 10 to 20 percent of unemployed people are out of work for six months or more. Variations in the duration of unemployment serve as a basis for distinguishing among *frictional*, *structural*, and *cyclical* unemployment.

**Box 17.3
Duration of
Unemployment,
1965–1984**

As this box shows, there is a considerable variation in the length of time people are unemployed. Depending on the state of the economy, about a third to a half of all unemployed workers spend less than five weeks out of work. On the other hand, 10 to 20 percent are out of work for six months or more.

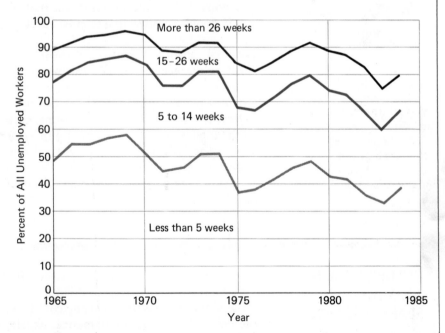

Source: President's Council of Economic Advisers, *Economic Report of the President* (Washington, D.C.: Government Printing Office, 1985), Table B–31.

Frictional unemployment
Short periods of unemployment needed to match jobs with job seekers within the mainstream of the economy.

Frictional unemployment   The term **frictional unemployment** refers to the short periods of unemployment needed to match jobs and job seekers within the mainstream of the economy. Much of this short-term unemployment is voluntary. It represents people who have quit old jobs to look for new ones, people taking a week or so to move or go on vacation before starting a newly found job, and people who have entered occupations, such as construction work, in which temporary layoffs are a part of life but earnings are good on a year-round basis. Economists view a certain level of frictional unemployment as necessary to match workers with jobs in a labor market where information is incomplete and transaction costs are often high.

Structural unemployment
The part of unemployment that is accounted for by people who are out of work for long periods because their skills do not match those required by available jobs.

Structural unemployment   The term **structural unemployment,** on the other hand, refers to people who are spending long periods out of work, often with little prospect of ever finding an adequate job. In part, these workers face prolonged joblessness because the shifting structure of the economy has made their skills obsolete. Robert Schnau and other unemployed workers in the Downriver area of Michigan are examples of this kind of structural unemployment. The structurally unemployed also include people with few skills and little work experience. Teenagers and some minority groups are especially affected by this type of unemployment. For these people, structural unemployment is not merely a problem of lack of jobs. Certain types of jobs—hospital orderly jobs, fast food work, and car washing, for example—are almost always available and require few specific skills. But structurally unemployed workers either avoid these kinds of jobs or work at them only for short periods before quitting. Working for short periods at dead-end jobs tends to build up a pattern of poor work habits and absenteeism that makes many structurally unemployed people unattractive to most employers.

Cyclical unemployment   Frictional plus structural unemployment make up the economy's natural rate of unemployment. The unemployment rate is not always at its natural level, however. Year-to-year variations in the unemployment rate from the natural level are referred to as **cyclical unemployment**. In recessions, cyclical unemployment rises, pulling the total unemployment rate up in accordance with Okun's law. At the peak of the business cycle, when real output is above its natural level, cyclical unemployment is negative. Then the total of frictional, structural, and cyclical unemployment is less than the natural rate of unemployment.

Cyclical unemployment
The part of unemployment that can be attributed to the difference between the actual level of real output and the natural level of real output.

UNEMPLOYMENT AND THE JOB SEARCH PROCESS

It is hard to draw a precise line between frictional and cyclical unemployment. In a sense, recessions could be said to increase the "friction" in labor markets, and periods of expansion could be said to reduce that friction. But whereas frictional unemployment is usually thought to reflect the voluntary job search activities of workers, cyclical unemployment is not voluntary in this sense. Lack of information about the job market and rigidities in wage rates make it hard for some unemployed workers to find jobs even when they would "voluntarily" accept reduced pay in order to keep on working. To understand the nature of cyclical unemployment more fully, we need more than a description of three types of unemployment; we need a theory. In this section we will present a theory of unemployment based on the fact that unemployed people are, by definition, looking for work.

The Balance of Labor Market Flows

The balance of flows into and out of the stock of unemployed workers is a close one. Flows into and out of unemployment are quite large in relation to the number of workers who are unemployed at any time. Depending on the time of year, some 4 to 6 percent of all workers undergo a change in employment status each month. Given the large volume of these flows, anything that changes even slightly the average length of time that a worker is unemployed can have a big impact on the measured unemployment rate. The result, shown in Box 17.4, is that the unemployment rate and the average duration of unemployment move closely together over time.

**Box 17.4
The Unemployment
Rate and the Average
Duration of
Unemployment,
1965–1984**

The unemployment rate and the average duration of unemployment tend to move closely together over time. In 1969, when the unemployment rate was at the very low level of 3.5 percent, the average duration of unemployment was under eight weeks. The average duration reached a peak of 20.0 weeks in 1983, one year after the unemployment rate reached its peak of 9.7 percent. The lag is explained by the fact that the recovery of 1983 benefited the short-term unemployed more quickly than the long-term unemployed.

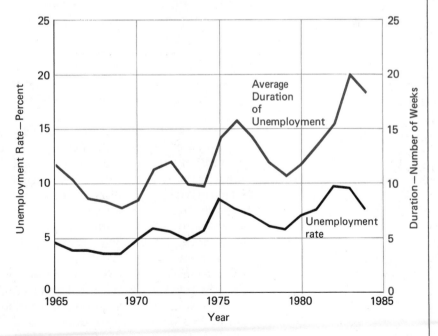

Source: President's Council of Economic Advisers, *Economic Report of the President* (Washington, D.C.: Government Printing Office, 1985), Tables B–31, B–33.

For this reason, much recent work on the theory of unemployment has focused on the job search process as the key to the average duration of unemployment and, hence, the unemployment rate itself. There are many variations of the job search approach to unemployment. Certain basic assumptions, however, are shared by almost all economists working in this field. We will emphasize these assumptions in our discussion and not pay too much attention to differences in detail.

Information and the wage offer curve   One basic assumption underlies all job search theories: the notion that workers looking for jobs and employers looking for workers do not have complete information about one another's needs and about current and future macroeconomic trends. In the case of jobs, as elsewhere in the economy, the market acts as a mechanism for distributing information.

Consider an unemployed worker who is looking for a new job. At the start of the job search, the worker knows that somewhere a number of employers are looking for workers. The first task is to find out who and where those employers are and what the jobs are like.

The jobs will not all be equally good. Some will pay better wages than others. Some will offer pleasant surroundings and some will not; some will be near and others far; and some will be interesting and others dull. To keep things simple, this discussion will deal only with wage differences among jobs, but the job seekers themselves will, of course, also take other factors into consideration.

The worker, then, sets out to find out what kinds of jobs are available. Common sense tells us that people will not always take the first job they are offered. To play it safe, even after learning about one job they will often check on a few others to see whether something better will turn up. The longer the worker searches, the more job opportunities will be found.

The job opportunities that are found by a single worker can be recorded in graphic form as shown in parts a and b of Box 17.5. In those graphs, each job opportunity found by the worker is represented by a dot. The height of the dot represents the wage offered by the job (adjusted for nonwage factors, as noted earlier), and the horizontal position of the dot represents the day of the search process on which the job opportunity was found.

Alice, the worker in part a, is a lucky job seeker in that she turns up a $12-an-hour job at the end of her first week of looking. On subsequent days she finds jobs that would pay hourly rates of $10, $11, $8, and so on, as shown by the additional dots. The line in part a shows the wage level of the best job offer Alice has received to date as of each day of her search. Because on the first day of her search she finds an opening as good as any she will ever find, this line has a single large step.

In contrast, Bill, the worker in part b of Box 17.5, is not quite so lucky. He is sampling from the same pool of jobs as Alice, but he doesn't find the good ones so soon. The first job he finds pays only $4 an hour, the second $3.50, the third $6, and so on. Not until the end of the eighth week of his search does he find a $12-an-hour job. Thus, the line recording his best offer to date has many small steps.

Alice was unusually lucky in her job search, and Bill was unusually unlucky. Other workers would be spread out in the range between them. On the average, the best offer received to date tends to rise as the search

**Box 17.5
Wage Offer Curves**

Parts a and b of this box show wage offers received by two unemployed workers, Alice and Bill. Both search randomly for jobs from the same pool. Alice is somewhat luckier than Bill; she gets a good offer sooner. The dots record various job offers; the lines represent the best offer each worker has received to date. Averaged over all workers, the line recording the best offer received to date, or the wage offer curve, slopes upward smoothly, as shown in part c.

(a) Alice

(b) Bill

(c) Average for All Workers

Wage offer curve
A graph that shows the relationship between duration of job search and the best job offer (in terms of wage rate) received to date.

period is extended. When the experience of all workers is considered, the stair steps and right angles tend to average out. Thus, a line showing the best offer to date for an average of all job seekers would have the smoothly curved shape shown in part c of Box 17.5. We will call this graph the **wage offer curve** for the economy.

Reservation wage

The lowest wage that a job seeker will accept.

The reservation wage   There is a limit to how long people will look for a job when jobs are available. If a worker searches longer, there is always a chance that something better will turn up, but searching has its costs too. The costs come partly from the search itself—traveling to interviews, writing letters, making phone calls, and so on. But the biggest cost of extending the job search is the opportunity cost of the wages that could have been earned if the best job found earlier in the search had been accepted. Given the fact that a job search is costly, each seeker has some notion of a wage offer that is good enough to accept without looking further. The lowest wage that a job seeker will accept at any point in the search process is called that person's **reservation wage.**

People's reservation wages tend to decrease as their job search continues. There are at least three reasons for this. First, people may be very optimistic at first, overestimating their worth in the eyes of potential employers, and may become more realistic as the hoped-for offers do not turn up. Second, even if unemployment insurance is available, long periods without work tend to cut into people's savings and the financial pressure to get back to work increases. And third, unemployment benefits are subject to a time limit. Statistical studies have confirmed the idea that the reservation wage tends to fall as the job search lengthens.

In graphic terms, the reservation wage can be shown by a downward-sloping curve, as in Box 17.6. The job search ends when the worker receives the first job offer equal to or better than his or her reservation wage. In the box this event is shown by the intersection of the wage offer curve and the reservation wage curve. If these curves are taken to indicate averages for all unemployed workers, the average duration of unemployment is ten weeks under the conditions represented in the box.

**Box 17.6
Factors That Determine
the Average Duration
of Unemployment**

In this box the average duration of unemployment is determined by the intersection of a wage offer curve and a reservation wage curve. The latter records the lowest wage offer a worker is willing to accept at any point during the job search. The first wage offer that meets this minimum is accepted, ending the period of unemployment after an average of ten weeks.

Causes of Changes in the Unemployment Rate

Unemployment and demand-pull inflation   The reservation wage and wage offer curves just discussed can be combined with the aggregate real supply and demand curves of Chapter 14 to show what happens to the unemployment rate as conditions change. Let's look first at the case of demand-pull inflation, shown in Box 17.7.

Box 17.7
Unemployment and
Demand-Pull Inflation

This box uses both the job search diagram (part a) and aggregate real supply and demand curves (part b) to show how unemployment behaves in a period of demand-pull inflation. Rising aggregate demand first affects the wage offer curve, shifting it toward W_2. The average duration of unemployment falls as real output rises. After workers adjust their reservation wages to R_2, a level that corresponds to the new price level, the economy returns to a new long-run equilibrium in which unemployment is back at its natural rate and real output is back at its natural level.

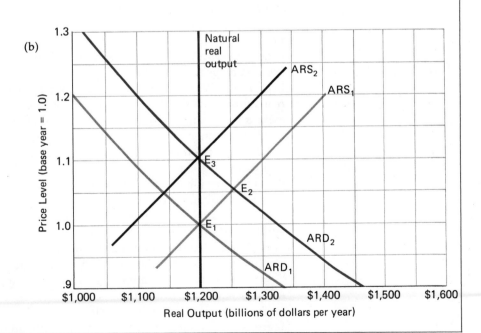

To start with, we will suppose that the reservation wage curve R_1 and the wage offer curve W_1 apply, giving an average duration of unemployment of ten weeks (point e_1 in part a of Box 17.7). Real output is at its natural level and unemployment is at its natural rate. The economy is in equilibrium with aggregate real demand curve ARD_1 and aggregate real supply curve ARS_1 (point E_1 in part b of Box 17.7).

Now suppose that an expansionary policy shifts the aggregate real demand curve rightward to the position ARD_2. Firms in each industry respond by moving along their industry supply curves, and the economy as a whole moves upward and to the right along the aggregate real supply curve. Some of the increase in output may come from putting existing workers on overtime, but the number of new workers hired will rise too. As the number and quality of job openings increase, the wage offer curve shifts from W_1 toward W_2. The wage offer curve can begin to shift in a direction favorable to job seekers even if each employer offers the same nominal wage as before for each type of job. The reason is that the greater number of job openings permit the average worker to find a job of a given quality with less search time.

How will workers react to this change in the job market? To understand their initial reaction, we have to keep in mind that workers do not have complete information. Because the wage offer curve has shifted, they will, on the average, find a job at any given wage level after a shorter search than before. But at least at first, job seekers are likely to view such finds as isolated pieces of good luck rather than as a general improvement in the job market. Given their reservation wages, as represented by R_1 in part a of Box 17.7, they will pounce on the new jobs after an average of only six weeks of searching. In the short run, then, the job market will move from point e_1 to point e_2. The average duration of unemployment will fall, and measured unemployment will drop below its natural rate. In part b of the box the falling unemployment rate corresponds to rising output as the economy moves from E_1 to E_2.

Neither e_2 in part a nor E_2 in part b can be a permanent equilibrium, however. After a while workers will become aware that job market conditions as a whole have improved. They will then take another look at their wage prospects. At the same time, they will find out that prices have begun to rise as a result of the economy's move upward along its aggregate real supply curve, as shown in part b of Box 17.7. That will cause them to make a new estimate of the level of nominal wages they need to maintain their accustomed standard of living. The realization that average nominal wages have risen combined with the expectation of a higher price level will push up the reservation wages of job seekers. They will not snap up the abundant job offers quite so fast. The duration of unemployment and the unemployment rate will begin to rise.

As workers become more selective in their choice of jobs, employers will begin to compete more vigorously with one another. They find they have to offer higher nominal wages to get the workers they want. As employers revise their expectations about the wage component of their input prices, the economy's aggregate real supply curve shifts up from ARS_1 to ARS_2. As this happens, the economy moves upward along the aggregate real demand curve. More and more of the original increase in aggregate nominal demand is converted into an increase in the price level. If there were no further changes in demand, the economy could reach a new equilibrium at point E_3. This would correspond to the intersection of wage offer curve W_2 with the new reservation wage curve, R_2, in part a of Box 17.8. Unemployment would return to its natural rate.

To summarize: In the short run, starting from an overall equilibrium, an increase in aggregate demand raises real output, increases the quantity and quality of job offers, and reduces the average duration of unemployment and the unemployment rate. In the long run, assuming no further changes in demand, real output returns to its initial rate at a higher price level; reservation wages adjust fully to the new conditions. The average duration of unemployment returns to where it started, and unemployment returns to its natural rate.

The Phillips Curve

Phillips curve
A graph that shows the connection between the rate of inflation and the unemployment rate, other things being equal.

Box 17.7 gives added insight into the well-known tendency of higher rates of inflation to be linked with lower levels of unemployment, at least in the short run. This trade-off between inflation and unemployment is often shown by means of a graph called a **Phillips curve**, named after the British economist A. W. H. Phillips, who first described it in a 1958 paper.[2] (See Box 17.8.)

**Box 17.8
A. W. H. Phillips and the Phillips Curve**

**A. W. H. Phillips
(1914–1975)**

A. W. H. Phillips was an economist whose reputation was based largely on a single paper on the right topic published at the right time. In the late 1950s the connection between inflation and unemployment ranked as the major unsolved problem of macroeconomic theory. The curves that Phillips drew in his famous article in *Economica* suggested a simple, stable relationship between inflation and unemployment. Phillips' paper did not present a theory to explain the relationship, but his curves became the peg on which all further discussion of the problem was hung. Every subsequent article on inflation and unemployment discussed the shape of the Phillips curve, the point on the Phillips curve that was best as a policy target, how the Phillips curve could be shifted, and so on. Today the term is so familiar that Phillips' name enjoys a sort of immortality even though his own interpretation of the famous curve has fallen into disfavor.

Phillips was born in New Zealand, but he made London his base for most of his academic career. He taught at the London School of Economics during the 1950s and 1960s, moving to the Australian National University in 1967. Phillips was trained in electrical engineering, and this training seems to have influenced his approach to economic problems, which has been described as "scientistic." In the mid-1950s he was suggesting the use of an "electric analog machine or simulator" as an aid to the study of economic dynamics. This idea seems to foreshadow the widespread use of electronic computers in modern economic research.

---

[2]A. W. H. Phillips, "The Relationship Between Unemployment and the Rate of Change of Money Wage Rates in the United Kingdom, 1861–1957," *Economica*, new series, 25, November 1958, pp. 283–299.

The Phillips curve as a policy menu   A sample Phillips curve is drawn in Box 17.9. During the 1960s, when the Phillips curve first attracted the attention of economists, it was viewed as a menu of policy choices. Liberals argued that we should choose a point such as L on the Phillips curve; this point would "buy" full employment and prosperity at the price of a modest rate of inflation. Conservatives expressed horror at the thought of inflation and argued for a point such as C, which would achieve price stability at the expense of some jobs.

But the problem with viewing the Phillips curve as a policy menu was that it would not stand still while the diners enjoyed their meal. As the 1960s progressed, economists began to notice that inflation-unemployment points for recent years did not fit the curves they had plotted using data from the 1950s. It became common to speak of an upward drift of the Phillips curve; a given level of inflation would "buy" less and less of a reduction in unemployment.

The menu was getting less attractive as time went by. Still, if the upward drift of the Phillips curve had been caused by factors outside their control, policymakers could still have chosen the point they preferred from a new, higher Phillips curve. With the advent of the 1970s, however, the way economists viewed the Phillips curve began to change. It began to appear that shifts in the Phillips curve were caused by the very policies that had sought to move the economy along the curve.

The Phillips curve and the natural rate of unemployment   The distinction between the long-run and short-run effects of aggregate demand on prices, output, and unemployment provides the key to this new view of the Phillips curve. As Chapter 14 and Box 17.7 have shown, a once-and-for-all rise in the level of aggregate nominal demand leads to only a temporary reduction in unemployment. The reason is that the levels

**Box 17.9
The Phillips Curve as a
Policy Menu**

When A. W. H. Phillips first drew attention to the inverse relationship between inflation and unemployment, his "Phillips curve" was treated as a policy menu. Liberals argued that a point such as L should be chosen; this would "buy" a permanent reduction in unemployment at the expense of a little inflation. Conservatives seemed to favor a point like C, which would offer stable prices at the cost of more joblessness.

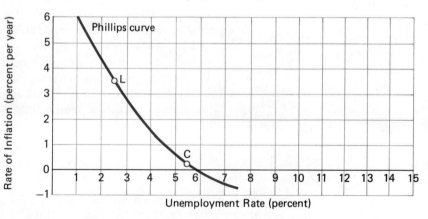

Box 17.10
Short-Run and Long-Run
Phillips Curves

In the modern view, there is an inverse relationship between unemployment and inflation only in the short run. Unexpected inflation lowers the unemployment rate, but only until people's expectations adjust to the new inflation rate. Any change in the expected rate of inflation shifts the short-run Phillips curve. The long-run Phillips curve is a vertical line drawn at the natural rate of unemployment. The long- and short-run curves intersect at the expected rate of inflation for which the short-run curve is drawn.

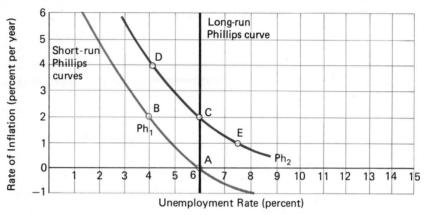

of input prices and wages expected by firms and workers adjust to actual changes in the price and wage levels, thereby pushing up the short-run aggregate real supply curve. Thus, real output can rise above its natural level only as long as the aggregate real supply curve does not completely catch up with the shifting aggregate real demand curve.

In Chapter 14 we used the term *natural rate of unemployment* to refer to the unemployment rate that would prevail when real output was at its natural level. We now see that the natural rate of unemployment can also be described as the rate that prevails when the expected rate of inflation is equal to the actual rate of inflation. This rate can be achieved when the economy is in static equilibrium, with real output at its natural level and the expected and actual rates of inflation both equal to zero. But unemployment can also be at its natural rate when the economy is in a moving equilibrium, with a constant rate of inflation that everyone has become used to.

This modern view of the Phillips curve is illustrated in Box 17.10. Two short-run Phillips curves are shown there, each corresponding to a different expected rate of inflation. If no inflation is expected, the Phillips curve takes the position Ph_1. The intersection of this Phillips curve with the horizontal axis indicates the natural rate of unemployment, here taken to be 6 percent. If the actual rate of inflation unexpectedly goes up to 2 percent per year, the economy will initially move upward and to the left along this Phillips curve, from point A to point B. This will correspond to a movement upward and to the right along the economy's short-run aggregate real supply curve; real output and the price level will rise as inflation gets under way and the unemployment rate falls. In terms of the job search diagram, the move from A to B on the Phillips curve corresponds to an upward movement of the wage offer curve that is not accompanied by an equal upward shift of the reservation wage curve; thus, the average duration of unemployment falls as the unemployment rate falls.

If the rate of inflation remains at 2 percent per year, people will sooner or later adjust their expectations accordingly. The aggregate real supply curve will catch up with the aggregate real demand curve, and both will from then on move upward at the same rate. As this happens, real output will return to its natural rate. Reservation wages will be continuously adjusted to match the upward drift of the wage offer curve, and the duration of the job search will return to where it started. Unemployment will return to its natural rate at point C in Box 17.10. The move from B to C represents a shift in the short-run Phillips curve from Ph_1 to Ph_2.

From point C the economy can move upward or downward along the new short-run Phillips curve, depending on what happens to the actual inflation rate. If inflation increases to 4 percent while people expect it to remain at 2 percent, the economy will initially move to point D. If inflation slows to 1 percent while people expect it to remain at 2 percent, the economy will initially move from point C to point E. But these movements along the short-run Phillips curve will not represent new long-run equilibrium points. As soon as people get used to the changed rate of inflation, the short-run Phillips curve will shift again.

The long-run Phillips curve   A final implication of the new view of the Phillips curve is that it must be vertical in the long run. This follows from the conclusion that unemployment attains its natural rate whenever the actual and expected rates of inflation are equal, and from the notion that any given steady rate of inflation will be expected to continue. Such a long-run Phillips curve is shown in Box 17.10 as a vertical line drawn at the natural rate of unemployment. Each short-run Phillips curve intersects the long-run Phillips curve at the expected rate of inflation for which the short-run curve is drawn. Thus unemployment will be at its natural rate only when the actual and expected rates of inflation are equal.

Looking Ahead

In this chapter and the preceding ones we have looked at a number of interactions among macroeconomic policy goals: the connection between real output and the price level embodied in the aggregate real demand curve, the link between unemployment and real output embodied in Okun's law, and the relationship between inflation and unemployment embodied in the Phillips curve. The next chapter will show how these three relationships can be put together to analyze the dynamics of inflation in the U.S. economy. That analysis will give us greater insight into the transition from the low inflation and low unemployment of the 1950s and 1960s to the high inflation and high unemployment of the 1970s and early 1980s, and then back again to the moderate inflation and unemployment of the mid-1980s.

Summary

1. The official measure of unemployment is based on a breakdown of the total population into various groups. The noninstitutional adult civilian population consists of people 16 years of age or older who are not in the armed forces, prisons, or other institutions. Of these, people who work at least one hour a week for pay or at least 15 hours per week as unpaid workers in a family business are counted as *employed*. People who are not working but are looking for work are counted as *unemployed*. The sum of the employed and the unemployed is known as the *civilian labor force*. The *unemployment rate* is the percentage of the civilian labor force that is unemployed.

2. The official concept of unemployment differs from the commonsense notions of "not working" and "can't find a job." People who work full-time without pay at housekeeping and child care are not counted as employed. On the other hand, people who are absent from work because of illness, bad weather, or labor disputes are counted as employed even though they are not working. Some people are counted as unemployed even though they have found a job. Examples are people who are waiting to start a job and people who expect to be recalled to a job from which they have been laid off. Some people who can't find a job aren't counted as unemployed because they have stopped looking for a job. These are known as *discouraged workers*.

3. According to *Okun's law*, for each 3 percent by which real output rises above its natural rate, the unemployment rate tends to fall below its natural rate by one percentage point, and for each 3 percent by which real output falls below its natural level, unemployment tends to rise above its natural rate by one percentage point. The ratio between changes in real out-

put and changes in the rate of unemployment is determined by labor hoarding on the part of employers and by the fact that rising employment tends to draw more workers into the labor force.

4. The term *frictional unemployment* refers to short periods of unemployment needed to match jobs and job seekers in the mainstream of the economy. *Structural unemployment* refers to people who are out of work for long periods, often with little chance of finding an adequate job, because they have few skills or their skills are obsolete. The natural rate of unemployment is the sum of frictional and structural unemployment. When the economy is below its natural level of real output, unemployment is above its natural rate. The excess unemployment is known as *cyclical* unemployment. When the economy is above its natural level of real output, cyclical unemployment is negative.

5. Unemployed workers, by definition, are looking for jobs. The unemployment rate is closely related to the average duration of the job search. Anything that lengthens the average duration of the job search, such as an increase in workers' *reservation wages*, tends to raise the unemployment rate. Anything that shortens the duration of the job search, such as higher wage offers, tends to lower the unemployment rate.

6. The *Phillips curve* is a downward-sloping curve that shows that, for a given expected rate of inflation, lower rates of inflation tend to be linked with higher rates of unemployment. An increase in the expected rate of inflation tends to shift the Phillips curve upward. Unemployment will be at its natural rate only when the actual rate of inflation is equal to the expected rate of inflation.

Questions for Review

1. Explain the following terms and concepts:
   discouraged workers
   Okun's law
   frictional unemployment
   structural unemployment
   cyclical unemployment
   wage offer curve
   reservation wage
   Phillips curve

2. How are people assigned to the following groups and subgroups of the population: the noninstitutional adult population; the civilian labor force; employed; unemployed?

3. Using the commonsense notions of "not working" and "can't find a job," give examples of ways in which the official measure of unemployment overstates and understates the problem of unemployment.

4. Which kinds of unemployment are considered to be part of the natural rate of unemployment? What kind of unemployment accounts for differences between the actual and natural rates of unemployment?

5. Why does it take more than a 1 percent change in real output to change the unemployment rate by one percentage point?

6. Other things being equal, how do upward and downward shifts in the wage offer curve affect the average duration of unemployment and the unemployment rate? How do upward and downward shifts in the reservation wage curve affect the average duration of unemployment and the unemployment rate?

7. Why does the Phillips curve have a negative slope? Why can the Phillips curve not be viewed as a policy menu?

Problems and Topics for Discussion

1. What is your current labor force status? Are you a member of the noninstitutional adult civilian population? Of the labor force? Are you employed? Unemployed? Explain the basis for your answers. When was the last time your labor force status changed? Do you expect to make a change soon? Give details.

2. It is sometimes suggested that the government should try to keep involuntary unemployment to a minimum but that voluntary unemployment is not a problem. Do you agree? How would you distinguish between voluntary and involuntary unemployment?

3. It has been suggested that the unemployment rate should be replaced by an "employment hardship index" that tries to measure the percentage of people who suffer hardship because of their labor force status. What kinds of people who are not now counted as unemployed might go into the hardship category? What kinds of people who are now counted as unemployed do not suffer hardship as a result? Discuss.

4. The Labor Department announces unemployment data for each month early in the next month. Watch the newspapers or business magazines such as *Business Week* for discussions of the most recent unemployment data. What changes have there been? What is happening to the employment rate? Are the employment rate and the unemployment rate moving in the same or opposite directions?

5. Rework the graphs in Box 17.7 for the case of a recession caused by a leftward shift of the aggregate real demand curve. What happens to the wage offer curve and the reservation wage curve during the recession? Why does unemployment tend to rise during the recession?

6. Rework the graphs in Box 17.7 for the case of cost-push inflation caused by workers' expectations of a rising price level. The first step is an upward shift of the reservation wage curve (workers won't settle for a job that doesn't pay enough to make up for the expected increase in the cost of living). As workers become more

selective in taking jobs, employers compete with one another for workers, and the wage component of their input prices goes up. This causes an upward shift in the aggregate real supply curve. Complete the story from this point, keeping track of what happens to real output, the price level, and unemployment.

7. **Case for Discussion**

Washington, D.C.: January's unemployment figures, which showed a rise in joblessness of 0.2 percentage points, suggest the economy grew at a modest pace during the month.

The nation's civilian unemployment rate increased to a seasonally adjusted 7.4 percent of the work force last month from 7.2 percent in December, the Labor Department said. But that rise came amid a number of contradictory signals. It was largely the result of an unusual surge in job seekers, after adjustment for predictable seasonal variations.

Total employment clearly rose last month, but how much it increased isn't clear from the department's report. The department's survey of households showed a modest gain of 118,000 jobs in the month. But its survey of business payrolls indicated 348,000 jobs were created, a surprisingly large increase. Adding further confusion, the increase in employment was partly offset by a decline in the hours worked weekly by the average employee to 35.2 hours in January from 35.3 hours in December.

Nonetheless, the numbers, which are the government's first statistical hint of the economy's performance in January, suggest that the economy continued to grow during the month, although not at December's sturdy pace.

By a separate measure, which counts the military among the employed, unemployment in January rose to 7.3 percent from 7.1 percent the previous month.[3]

Questions:

a. Why were the January figures thought to indicate growth of the economy even though the unemployment rate rose? Discuss.

b. Unemployment figures are published with a shorter lag than any other major macroeconomic data. As such, they would be especially useful to policymakers pursuing a strategy of policy activism. (See Chapter 16.) If you were a policy activist, how would you react to the data presented in this article? What support, if any, does the article give to the case against policy activism?

c. The *civilian unemployment rate*—the unemployment rate as defined in this chapter and the rate that is most widely reported—does not count military personnel as part of the labor force. The so-called *total unemployment rate* counts them both as part of the labor force and as employed. Explain why the total unemployment rate is always lower than the civilian unemployment rate. Which do you think gives a more realistic picture of the nation's job market?

Suggestions for Further Reading

Feldstein, Martin S. "The Economics of the New Unemployment." *Public Interest*, Fall 1973, pp. 369–402.

A nontechnical statement of the job search theory of unemployment.

Friedman, Milton. *Unemployment versus Inflation? An Evaluation of the Phillips Curve.* London: Institute for Economic Affairs, 1975.

An early and influential statement of the job search theory of inflation and the reasons for shifts in the Phillips curve.

Phelps, Edmund S., et al. *Microeconomic Foundations of Employment and Inflation Theory.* New York: Norton, 1970.

A collection of important papers on the job search theory of unemployment.

---

[3]Excerpted from Alan Murray, "Jobless Rate Climbed to 7.4 Percent During January," *Wall Street Journal*, February 4, 1985, p. 2. Reprinted by permission of the Wall Street Journal, © Dow Jones & Company, Inc. 1985. All rights reserved.

Chapter 18

The Dynamics of Inflation

After reading this chapter, you should be able to

1. List the building blocks of the *accelerationist theory of inflation*.
2. Explain the behavior of inflation and unemployment during a period of accelerating inflation.
3. Analyze inflationary recession in terms of the accelerationist theory.
4. Outline the stop-go policy cycle and discuss post–World War II economic data in terms of this cycle.
5. Discuss differing views of the behavior of inflation and unemployment in the United States since 1980.

Ideas for Review

Here are some terms and concepts that you should review before reading this chapter:

Inflationary recession (Chapter 14)
Adaptive and rational expectations (Chapter 14)
Supply shocks (Chapter 14)
Supply side economics (Chapter 15)
Strategies for fighting inflation (Chapter 16)
Okun's law (Chapter 17)
The Phillips curve (Chapter 17)

"We bent all of our efforts to correct these problems, not by unsustainable short-run measures, but by measures that would increase long-term growth without renewed inflation."

In 1981, when I first assumed the duties of the Presidency, our Nation was suffering from declining productivity and the highest inflation of the postwar period—the legacy of years of government overspending, over-taxing, and overregulation.

We bent all of our efforts to correct these problems, not by unsustainable short-run measures, but by measures that would increase long-term growth without renewed inflation. We removed unnecessary regulations, cut taxes, and slowed the growth of Federal spending, freeing the private sector to develop markets, create jobs, and increase productivity. With conviction in our principles, with patience and hard work, we restored the economy to a condition of healthy growth without substantial inflation.

Although employment is now rising, business opportunities are expanding, and interest rates and inflation are under control, we cannot relax our economic vigilance. A return to the policies of excessive government spending and control that led to the economic "malaise" of the late seventies would quickly draw us back into that same disastrous pattern of inflation and recession. Now is the time to recommit ourselves to the policies that broke that awful pattern: policies of reduced Federal spending, lower tax rates, and less regulation to free the creative energy of our people and lead us to an even better economic future thorough strong and sustained economic growth.[1]

Brave words, these words in Ronald Reagan's economic report to Congress, delivered a few days after the start of his second term. Will they prove to be so much hot air, like his 1981 pledge to "slay the budget monster"? Or did the years of the first Reagan administration really represent a break with the "awful pattern" of inflation and recession that marked the earlier post–World War II period? Given the fact that Democratic and Republican presidents alike had sworn to break the cycle and then pursued policies that continued it, there is room for doubt. Yet, as we will see, early in 1985 there were signs that the postwar pattern had been broken, at least in some respects.

By the time you read this book, you will know more about where the economy is headed in the second half of the 1980s. This chapter will not attempt to forecast the future. But it will give you some useful tools for judging the economy's performance. The chapter will look in detail at the dynamics of inflation and at the postwar inflationary spiral. It will discuss the political as well as the economic causes of this pattern. And it will describe a theoretical cure for the spiral—a cure that according to some is already working.

THE EFFECTS OF ACCELERATING INFLATION

Inflation has entered our discussion at many points in this book, but we have not yet developed a theory to explain the *rate* of inflation. In Chapter 14 we used aggregate real supply and demand curves to show how the economy moves from one price *level* to another. But a true theory of

---

[1]Ronald Reagan, *Economic Report of the President* (Washington, D.C.: Government Printing Office, 1985), p. 3.

inflationary dynamics must show not only how the price level changes but also how fast it changes. After all, no one would think twice these days about a doubling of the price level that took 25 years to occur, as was the case in the United States from 1948 to 1973. But a doubling of the price level in less than a month, as recently occurred in Bolivia, is another matter entirely.

Foundations of the Accelerationist Theory of Inflation

The modern theory of inflationary dynamics is based on the idea that the economy behaves differently in periods in which the inflation rate is accelerating or slowing down than it does in periods when the rate stays the same. Because of its emphasis on changes in the inflation rate, this theory is known as the **accelerationist theory of inflation**. Four building blocks discussed in earlier chapters will serve as a foundation for the theory.

Accelerationist theory of inflation

A theory according to which changes in the inflation rate affect unemployment and real output.

Management of aggregate nominal demand   The first building block of the accelerationist theory is the notion that policymakers, using the fiscal and monetary policy tools, can, at least to some extent, control the volume of aggregate demand, national income, and national product measured in nominal terms. We looked at fiscal and monetary policy in Chapters 10–13. In Chapter 14 we saw that control over the nominal level of national income and product is equivalent to control over the position of the economy's aggregate real demand curve. And we saw that although economists disagree about some details of the effects of demand shifts on real variables, they all agree that nominal variables will be affected.

Inflation and the growth of real output   The second building block is the rule that the growth rate of nominal national product must be equal to the growth rate of real output plus the rate of inflation. Given this rule and the ability of government to control the rate of change of nominal GNP, the job of a theory of inflation becomes simply one of determining how a given rate of change of nominal national product will be split between the rate of change in real output and the rate of change in prices. Will a 10 percent increase in nominal GNP come out as a 3 percent gain in real output and 7 percent inflation? As no inflation and a 10 percent gain in real output? As 12 percent inflation and a 2 percent drop in real output? The outcome must fall somewhere along the continuum of inflation and unemployment rates that total 10 percent.

Okun's law   The third building block is the rule of thumb known as Okun's law. In Chapter 17 we stated Okun's law in terms of the connection between the level of real output and the level of unemployment. Here it is more useful to restate that law in terms of the rate of change in real output and unemployment: The unemployment rate will remain unchanged in any year in which actual real output grows at the same rate as natural real output. The growth rate of natural real output is thought to be about 3 percent per year. For each three percentage points by which growth of real output exceeds growth of natural output in a given year, the unemployment rate tends to fall by about one percentage point. For each three percentage points by which the growth rate of real output lags behind the growth of its natural level, the unemployment rate tends to rise by one percentage point.

The Phillips curve   The fourth building block of the accelerationist theory is the Phillips curve. This was discussed in Chapter 16 in terms of the job search theory of unemployment. The Phillips curve provides both a short-run and a long-run relationship between the inflation rate and the unemployment rate. In the short run, for a given expected inflation rate, an increase in the actual inflation rate is linked with a decrease in the unemployment rate, and a decrease in the actual inflation rate is linked with an increase in the unemployment rate. In the long run, given time for expectations to adjust fully to a steady rate of inflation, unemployment tends toward its natural rate. Hence, the long-run Phillips curve is vertical.

Some Simplifications

In putting these building blocks to work, we will make two simplifying assumptions. These assumptions will allow us to get a good look at the basics of the accelerationist theory. In the last section of the chapter we will deal with the implications of dropping these assumptions.

First, we will assume that the growth rate of natural real GNP is zero. From the mid-1970s to the early 1980s, the rate did in fact slow down, although not to zero. It has since returned to its trend of 3 percent or so. But this assumption is not a reference to the productivity slowdown of the 1970s. It is just an effort to simplify the application of Okun's law. That law relates changes in unemployment to the difference between the rates of growth of actual and natural real GNP. With the growth rate of natural real GNP assumed to be zero, Okun's law in its simplified form can be written as follows:

$$\Delta U = -\frac{\dot{y}}{3}$$

in which ΔU stands for the percentage point change in the unemployment rate over a year's time, and $\dot{y}$ stands for the growth rate of real output over the year. The minus sign indicates that an *increase* in the rate of growth of real output is associated with a *decrease* in the unemployment rate, and vice versa.

Second, we will make a simple assumption about inflationary expectations. We will assume that the expected inflation rate in any year is equal to the actual inflation rate in the previous year. You will recognize this as a form of the adaptive-expectations hypothesis that we discussed in Chapter 14. Later in this chapter we will relax this assumption in order to consider other hypotheses about the formation of expectations.

With these four building blocks and two assumptions in hand, we turn now to the effects of accelerating inflation. Because our simplifying assumptions do not exactly fit the U.S. economy, we will base our discussion on a hypothetical country. Like the United States, this country is a democracy dominated by two political parties, which we will call the Blues and the Grays.

Expansionary Policy from a Standing Start

Our analysis begins in year 0 with the economy in a "standing start" position. By this we mean that both the actual and the expected rates of inflation are zero; the growth rate of actual real GNP is equal to the growth rate of natural real GNP, which in this case is also zero; and unemployment is at its natural rate, here assumed to be 6 percent. In year 0 an election is held. The Blues base their campaign on a promise to "get the country moving." They convince the voters that 6 percent is too high an unemployment rate and that a little economic growth would be a good thing. Upon taking over the machinery of government, they reset the dials of fiscal and monetary policy so as to raise the growth rate of nominal GNP from zero to, say, 8 percent per year. What will happen next?

Box 18.1 shows how the economy will react to this dose of expansionary policy. The box shows a vertical long-run Phillips curve drawn at the natural rate of unemployment and a negatively sloped short-run Phillips curve labeled Ph_1. In year 0 the economy is at point A. As the expansionary policy takes hold, a familiar chain of events unfolds. Increased aggregate demand causes inventories to fall throughout the economy. Some firms react by raising their output, others by raising their prices, and still others by doing some of both. In terms of the diagrams in Chapter 14, the economy is moving upward along its aggregate real supply curve at this point.

**Box 18.1
The Effects of an
Expansionary Policy
from a Standing Start**

This box shows the effects of an increase in the growth rate of nominal GNP to 8 percent from a standing start. As the economy moves from A to B, the unemployment rate drops by two percentage points. Following Okun's law, this means a 6 percent rate of growth of real output. The remaining 2 percent of the 8 percent growth of nominal GNP is accounted for by 2 percent inflation. The 8 percent growth rate of nominal output is more than enough to reach point B' and less than enough to reach point B". No inflation-unemployment combination other than B is possible under these conditions.

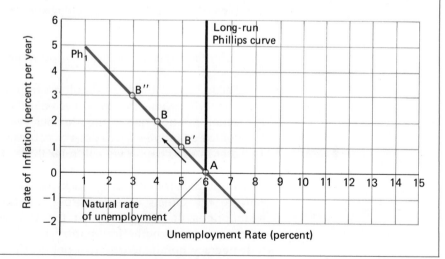

Effects on the labor market   Soon the effects of the expansionary policy will be felt by the labor market. The firms that are stepping up their output will be recruiting new workers. Some will offer higher wages, knowing that improved demand conditions will allow them to pass along the higher labor costs, at least in part, to their customers. In terms of the job search diagrams in Chapter 17, the wage offer curve will be shifting upward at this point. Job seekers will find both the quantity and the quality of job opportunities better than before. Acting without full knowledge of current and future economic trends, however, they will not adjust their reservation wages right away. Instead, each job seeker will be likely to view the improved labor market conditions as mere good luck. The newly offered jobs will be quickly snapped up. The average duration of unemployment will fall, and the unemployment rate will fall with it.

Moving up the Phillips curve   At this point the economy is moving up and to the left along the Phillips curve, with the unemployment rate falling and the inflation rate rising. How far up the Phillips curve will it go? The answer can be found by combining two of the building blocks described earlier. First, the economy must move to a point where the inflation rate plus the growth rate of real output equals the 8 percent growth rate of nominal GNP. Second, according to Okun's law, the rate of increase of real output must be equal to three times the drop in the unemployment rate. (This is the simplified form of Okun's law, using zero growth of natural real output.) Putting the two together, we conclude that the economy will move to a point on the Phillips curve where the inflation rate plus three times the drop in the unemployment rate equals the rate of increase of nominal GNP. This occurs at point B in Box 18.1. The inflation rate at B is 2 percent, and the two-percentage-point drop in the unemployment rate (from 6 to 4 percent) produces a 6 percent increase in real output, for a total of 8 percent.[2] No other point on the Phillips curve satisfies the required condition. Consider point B', for example. There the inflation rate is 1 percent and the unemployment rate has fallen by 1 percent, giving a 3 percent real growth rate. The 1 percent inflation plus 3 percent real growth sum to only 4 percent, well short of the assumed 8 percent growth rate of nominal GNP. Or consider point B''. There the inflation rate is 3 percent and unemployment has fallen by three percentage points, giving a 9 percent rate of real growth. Adding the rate of inflation to the rate of real growth tells us that point B'' could be reached only if nominal GNP grew at 12 percent rather than at the assumed rate of 8 percent.

In short, once the growth rate of nominal output, the initial unemployment rate, the slope of the short-run Phillips curve, and the expected inflation rate are given, only one combination of inflation and unemployment rates is possible.

The Effects of Repeated Expansionary Policy

The Blues have every reason to be proud of the economic record of their first year in office. From the stagnation of the standing-start position, a

---

[2]See the appendix to this chapter for an algebraic/graphic model that provides further detail on the determination of the inflation rate.

little dose of expansionary demand management in year 1 has cut unemployment by a third and jumped the growth rate of real output to 6 percent at the cost of only a 2 percent inflation rate. These results are so encouraging that the Blues repeat exactly the same policy and maintain the 8 percent growth rate of nominal GNP in year 2. Box 18.2 shows what will happen.

The most noticeable difference between Box 18.2 and Box 18.1 is the shift in the short-run Phillips curve to the position Ph₂. The Phillips curve shifts because, after experiencing 2 percent inflation in year 1, firms and workers expect 2 percent inflation in year 2. In terms of the type of diagram used in Chapter 14, this is represented by an upward shift in the aggregate real supply curve. In terms of the job search diagrams of Chapter 17, it is represented by an upward shift of the reservation wage curve. And in terms of the present diagram, it means an upward shift of the short-run Phillips curve to a point where it intersects the long-run Phillips curve at the new expected inflation rate of 2 percent.

Having concluded that in year 2 the economy will move to some point on the new Phillips curve Ph₂, we next need to determine which point it will move to. The same reasoning can be used as before: In year 2 the economy must move to a point where the rate of inflation plus the rate of increase in real output equals the rate of growth of nominal GNP.

As before, the growth rate of real output can be calculated using Okun's law, but now the starting point is the 4 percent unemployment rate reached in year 1 rather than the 6 percent natural rate. Real output will grow in year 2 only to the extent that the unemployment rate falls further. If it stays at 4 percent, no real growth will occur. A little trial and error quickly shows, then, that the economy must end year 2 at point C. There, a

Box 18.2
Effects of a Second
Year of Expansionary
Policy

If an 8 percent rate of growth of nominal GNP is maintained for a second year, the trade-off between inflation and unemployment will become less favorable. As a result of the 2 percent inflation experienced in year 1, the short-run Phillips curve for year 2 shifts to the position Ph₂. The economy moves from B to C. The one-percentage-point drop in unemployment causes a 3 percent rate of increase in real output. The remaining 5 percent of nominal-GNP growth is accounted for by inflation.

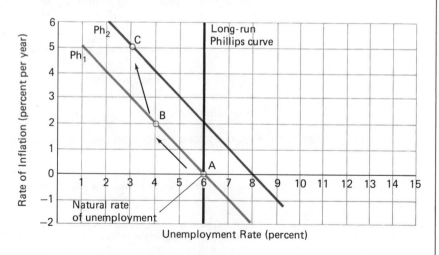

further one-percentage-point drop in the unemployment rate, from 4 to 3 percent, will yield a 3 percent rate of growth of real output. That plus a 5 percent inflation rate equals the assumed 8 percent growth rate of nominal GNP.

The Effects of Continued Acceleration

Clearly, the Blues' record is not quite as good in year 2 as in year 1. The growth rate of real output has slowed to 3 percent, and the inflation rate has risen to 5 percent. On the plus side, though, unemployment has dropped to just 3 percent. All in all, the campaign promise to get things moving has been kept. So let's suppose that the growth rate of nominal GNP is held at 8 percent for a third year.

As Box 18.3 shows, in year 3 the economy will be operating on a new short-run Phillips curve, Ph_3. The upward shift of this curve reflects the fact that firms and workers expect the inflation rate in year 3 to be the same 5 percent that was actually experienced in year 2. (Thus, Ph_3 intersects the long-run Phillips curve at a 5 percent inflation rate.) To find the point on Ph_3 where the inflation rate plus the growth rate of real output equals 8 percent, we must now move straight up from point C to point D. There is no room for any further decrease in unemployment or any growth of real output. The entire 8 percent growth rate of nominal GNP is absorbed in an 8 percent inflation rate.

Box 18.3
The Effects of Continued Expansionary Policy

A third year of 8 percent growth of nominal GNP will result in no further reduction in unemployment. The short-run Phillips curve shifts to Ph_3, and 8 percent inflation is required merely to keep unemployment from rising (point D). To keep unemployment at 3 percent for a fourth year, the growth rate of nominal GNP must increase to 11 percent (point E).

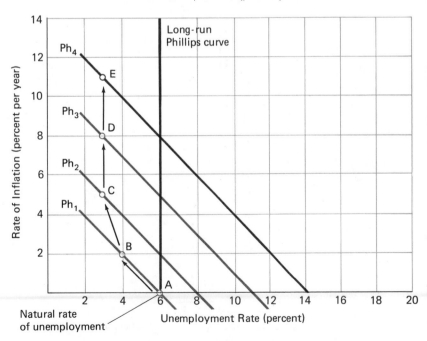

This result leaves the Blues little to brag about except a continued low unemployment rate. Clinging to this one remaining achievement, the Blue policymakers decide that in year 4 they will maintain the 3 percent unemployment rate at all costs. Turning again to Box 18.3, it is easy to see what is needed. In year 4 the short-run Phillips curve will shift upward to Ph_4 as a result of the 8 percent inflation rate of year 3. To keep unemployment at 3 percent in year 4, then, the economy must move straight up from point D on Ph_3 to point E on Ph_4. Point E corresponds to an 11 percent inflation rate and zero real growth, so keeping the growth rate of nominal GNP at 8 percent, as in previous years, will not be enough. Instead, an even more expansionary monetary and fiscal policy will have to be used to raise the growth rate of nominal GNP to 11 percent per year. The cost of

Box 18.4
Acceleration in the
Kennedy-Johnson Era

John Kennedy came to the presidency in 1960 with the stated intent of getting the country moving again after two recessions late in the Eisenhower years. Lyndon Johnson, who succeeded him, was equally determined to pursue an expansionary policy. Economists are still debating the relative impact of the Kennedy tax cut, heavy defense spending, and accelerating monetary growth. But there is no doubt that this combination of policies was as expansionary as anyone could have wished. The result was a sustained period of growth and low unemployment. This diagram shows the unemployment-inflation record for the economy during the Kennedy-Johnson era. (Inflation is measured as the annual rate of increase of the Consumer Price Index.) The pattern is just what the accelerationist theory would lead us to expect. At first the expansionary policy produced major gains in employment with little added inflation. But starting in 1964, the year of the tax cut, each successive drop in unemployment was accompanied by a bigger jump in prices. By the end of Johnson's term in office, inflation was rising higher and higher each year just to keep unemployment from growing.

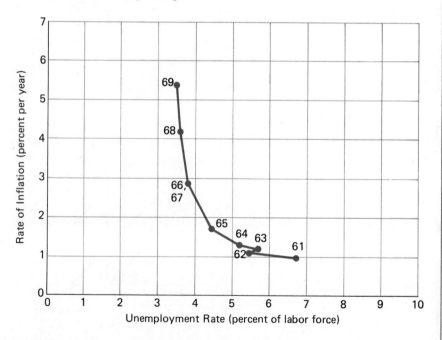

maintaining the low rate of unemployment, then, is accelerating inflation.

Some Generalizations

Let's leave the world of the Blues and Grays for a moment and draw some generalizations from our example. The first is that, starting from the natural rate of unemployment and zero inflation, expansionary policy initially produces falling unemployment and rapid real growth, with only moderate inflation. The second is that as people begin to adjust their expectations to the inflationary effects of the expansionary policy, the trade-off between inflation and unemployment becomes less and less favorable. And the third generalization is that the unemployment rate can be kept below the natural rate for a prolonged period only at the expense of a constantly accelerating inflation rate, which keeps the actual inflation rate always above the expected rate.

This last conclusion lies at the heart of the accelerationist theory of inflation. Indeed, it is the conclusion that gives the theory its name. The early treatment of the Phillips curve as a policy menu suggested that a low unemployment rate could be bought at the cost of only a moderate rate of inflation. More than anything else, what led to the demise of this view was the U.S. macroeconomic experience in the 1960s, as discussed in Box 18.4.

INFLATIONARY RECESSION AND THE STOP-GO CYCLE

Given our assumption of adaptive expectations, there is no limit to the number of years that unemployment can be held below its natural rate by accelerating inflation. In practice, though, political pressure builds up to a point at which something has to be done about inflation. Let's suppose that this happens in the land of the Blues and the Grays. In year 4 another election is held. The Blues have a record of 11 percent inflation and stagnant real output. They point proudly to the low unemployment rate they have achieved, but the Grays' promise to do something about inflation wins the day. True to their promise, once in office the Grays put on the monetary and fiscal brakes.

The Effects of Deceleration

Let's assume that the growth rate of nominal GNP is cut from 11 percent in year 4 to just 6 percent in year 5. Box 18.5 shows what happens as a result. First, in year 5 the Phillips curve is still shifting upward as people adjust to the inflationary experience of year 4. In year 5, then, the economy must end up somewhere on the short-run Phillips curve Ph_5, which intersects the long-run Phillips curve at an 11 percent rate of inflation. To keep unemployment from rising, inflation would have to accelerate to 14 percent in year 5, but this is impossible given the Grays' restrictive monetary and fiscal policy. Unemployment therefore rises. Each one-percentage-point rise in the unemployment rate, according to Okun's law, will produce a negative 3 percent growth (a 3 percent decline, that is) in real output. As real output falls and unemployment rises, the economy will move toward a point where the rate of inflation plus the rate of real growth

**Box 18.5
An Inflationary
Recession**

If the growth rate of nominal GNP is cut back from 11 percent in year 4 to, say, 6 percent in year 5, the result will be an inflationary recession. The Phillips curve continues to shift upward from Ph_4 to Ph_5, catching up with the actual rate of inflation in year 4. Unemployment rises by 2 percentage points, resulting in a minus 6 percent rate of real growth. With such a large negative real growth rate, the rate of inflation must increase to 12 percent to account for the entire 6 percent nominal growth rate.

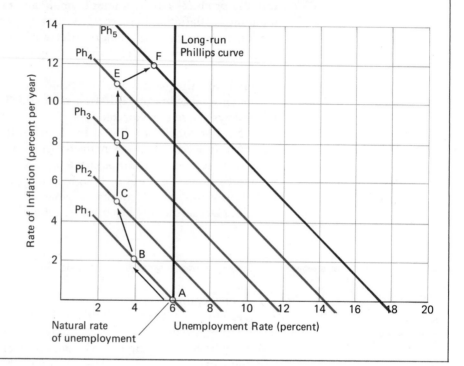

(which is now negative) is equal to the assumed 6 percent growth rate of nominal GNP. This happens at point F on Ph_5. There the economy experiences a 6 percent drop in real output as a result of the two-percentage-point rise in unemployment, and a 12 percent inflation rate. The sum of 12 percent inflation and minus 6 percent real growth is the 6 percent growth rate of nominal output, as required.

We already have a name for the events of year 5: inflationary recession. Every possible bad thing is happening at once. Real output is falling. Unemployment is rising. And inflation, instead of slowing down, is still being carried upward by inflationary expectations. Economists used to think that such a combination of events just couldn't happen. President Eisenhower's chief economic adviser supposedly promised to eat his hat if rising inflation and rising unemployment ever struck in the same year. Luckily for him, hats had gone out of style by the 1970s, so he probably didn't have one left to eat.

To make sure that we clearly understand the mechanics of inflationary recession, we can relate the events of Box 18.5 to the graphic frameworks used in Chapters 14 and 17. In terms of Chapter 14's diagrams, an inflationary recession is caused when inflationary expectations push the short-run aggregate real supply curve up while the aggregate real demand curve remains fixed or (as in this case) rises less rapidly. As the aggregate real supply curve shifts upward, firms become worried about rising input prices and raise the prices of their outputs. But with aggregate nominal demand rising only slowly, there is not enough real purchasing power to absorb a constant rate of real output at a higher price level. Inventories pile up, and firms react by cutting back their output. The economy moves upward and to the left along its aggregate real demand curve.

The events of the inflationary recession can also be explained in terms of the kind of job search diagram used in Chapter 17. Because workers are expecting ever-higher prices, they raise their reservation wages. But the new demand management policy means that the wage offer curve is no longer being pushed up as fast as reservation wages are rising. Workers find it harder and harder to find the jobs they want. However, since they lack complete information, they attribute their problems to bad luck. They go on looking for work, stretching out the average duration of unemployment. The unemployment rate therefore rises.

Turning the Corner

Although the events of year 5 win no praise for the Grays, let's suppose that they remain committed to their policies. In year 6 they decide to cut the inflation rate back to 10 percent no matter what the cost in terms of jobs and output. What nominal GNP target should they set to achieve this goal?

As Box 18.6 shows, in year 6 policymakers are still fighting against the momentum of inflationary expectations, which are pushing the short-run Phillips curve upward. Under our assumption of adaptive expectations, because the actual inflation rate in year 5 was 12 percent, people will expect 12 percent inflation to continue in year 6. That will put the Phillips curve in the position Ph_6. In the short run, then, policymakers must pick some point along that curve. The point on Ph_6 that meets the 10 percent inflation goal is point G.

To get to point G, the unemployment rate must rise by three percentage points, from 5 percent at F to 8 percent at G. According to Okun's law, a three-percentage-point rise in the unemployment rate (with no growth of natural GNP) will produce a 9 percent drop in real output. As always, the rate of change of real output plus the inflation rate must equal the rate of growth of nominal GNP. Inflation of 10 percent plus real growth of negative 9 percent gives 1 percent as the required target for nominal-income growth in year 6. Thus, the Grays must lean even harder on the fiscal and monetary brakes in year 6 than in year 5.

After year 6 things get a little bit easier because the momentum of inflationary expectations has finally been broken. As Box 18.7 shows, the short-run Phillips curve begins to drift slowly downward. For year 7 the expected inflation rate drops to the 10 percent rate experienced in year 6, putting the Phillips curve at Ph_7. Inflation can be cut by two more percentage points if the economy moves straight down from point G to point H. (This move calls for an 8 percent growth rate for nominal GNP—a moderate easing of demand management policy.) In year 8 a further two

Box 18.6
Turning the Corner on Inflation

In order to cut the inflation rate to 10 percent in year 6, the growth rate of nominal GNP must be slowed further. Because the actual inflation rate in year 5 was 12 percent, the Phillips curve will shift upward again in year 6, to Ph_6. To reach point G on Ph_6, where the inflation rate is 10 percent, unemployment must rise by three percentage points. That in turn will produce a minus 9 percent rate of real growth. Thus, if inflation is to be limited to 10 percent in year 6, nominal GNP can be allowed to increase by only 1 percent.

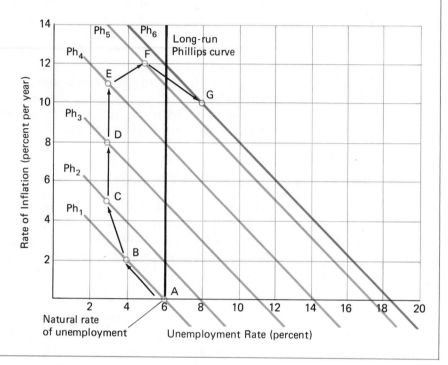

percentage points can be trimmed if the economy moves to point I, and so on.

In short, the deflationary policy of the Grays is the mirror image of the policy of accelerating inflation pursued by the Blues. The Blues used accelerating inflation to hold the unemployment rate below its natural level. At first the trade-off between unemployment and inflation was very favorable, but it became less so over time as expectations adjusted. The Grays, on the other hand, have held the unemployment rate above its natural level in order to bring inflation down. At first the trade-off between unemployment and inflation was terrible, but over time it became more favorable as expectations adjusted. Thus, the accelerationist theory of inflation works both ways: Unemployment below the natural level is linked with a rising inflation rate, and unemployment above the natural level is linked with a falling inflation rate.

Reflation

After year 8 the Grays' game plan calls for three more years of continued high unemployment and falling inflation; then the economy can be eased to a "soft landing" back at point A, with zero inflation and unemployment

**Box 18.7
Continued
Deceleration**

In a mirror image of the initial acceleration, inflation can be slowed steadily year by year by holding the unemployment rate above its natural level. Each year the short-run Phillips curve shifts downward as the expected rate of inflation falls. In principle, the deceleration could be continued until a "soft landing" is reached back at point A.

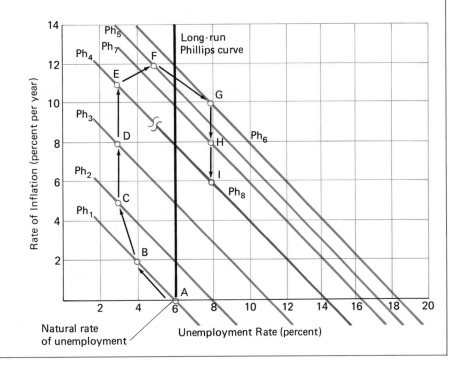

back down to its natural level. But year 8 is an election year. What kind of record do the Grays have? In year 4 they took over an economy with 11 percent inflation. By year 8 they have cut that figure almost in half, to 6 percent. But the reduced inflation rate has been won only at the cost of a major recession. The unemployment rate is five percentage points higher than it was four years before, and real output is a full 15 percent lower. By this time voters are likely to remember the Blue era more as one of prosperity than as one of excessive inflation.

Besides, the Grays' program offers the Blues a tempting opportunity. If the Blues win, for the first year after the election they can pursue an expansionary policy while still taking advantage of the downward momentum of inflationary expectations. Box 18.8 shows how such a **reflation** program can work.

Reflation
An episode in which policy becomes more expansionary while the expected rate of inflation is still falling.

By year 8 the economy will have reached point I, with 6 percent inflation and 8 percent unemployment. In year 9 the short-run Phillips curve will shift to the position Ph₉, reflecting the inflation of the previous year. Consider what will happen if, at this point, the growth of nominal GNP is allowed to jump upward from 6 percent per year in year 8 to, say, 16 percent. Because firms will still be expecting increases in input prices to remain moderate, they will react to the renewed burst of demand almost entirely by increasing their real output. Prices will be pushed up only a

**Box 18.8
Reflation**

If the growth rate of nominal GNP is again increased after a period of deceleration, the result will be falling unemployment with a minimal increase in inflation. For example, increasing the nominal growth rate from 6 percent in year 8 to 16 percent in year 9 will move the economy from point I to point J. The initial expansion will take advantage of the continued downward drift of the Phillips curve, from Ph_8 to Ph_9.

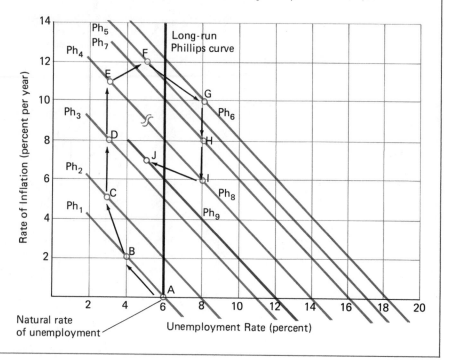

little faster than in the previous year. Because workers are expecting a relatively moderate rate of increase in the cost of living, they will snap up the newly created job opportunities without much of an increase in nominal wages. As a result, the economy will move almost horizontally to the left, from point I to point J. Real output will grow by 9 percent, and unemployment will fall by three percentage points, at the cost of only one added percentage point of inflation.

The Stop-Go Cycle

Compared with the prospect of continued belt-tightening under a reelected Gray government, the Blues' promise of prosperity is likely to win them the election. But the reflation trick works only for one year. After that, the inflationary price that must be paid for keeping unemployment below its natural rate will rise each year. The economy will enter a new upswing until political pressure to do something about inflation leads to another reversal of policy.

Alternating periods of expansionary and contractionary demand management policy produce what can be called a *stop-go policy cycle*. If the political system is, on the average, more sensitive to the evils of unemployment than it is to those of inflation, an inflationary bias is added to the stop-go cycle, with each upswing lasting longer than each downswing. Without pursuing the matter in detail, we can say that the result is an upward spiral of the economy, as shown in Box 18.9.

Of course, the assumptions that produce the stop-go policy cycle in the world of the Blues and Grays are highly restrictive. The actual economy of the United States is far more complex, as is the political system that goes with it. Even so, as Box 18.10 shows, the path followed by the U.S. economy from the early 1950s through 1980 is very similar to the spiral pattern of Box 18.9.

THE U.S. EXPERIENCE SINCE 1980

The chapter began with a quotation from President Reagan's 1985 economic report to Congress, in which Reagan stressed the need to break the "disastrous pattern of inflation and recession" of the post–World War II period. We have looked in some detail at this stop-go pattern and its causes. What are the chances that it will really be broken? As this is written, the question is a subject of heated debate. Let's take a look at this debate.

Box 18.9
The Stop-Go Cycle with an Inflationary Bias

The so-called stop-go cycle means the alternation of acceleration, inflationary recession, deceleration, and reflation as political pressure builds up first to do something about inflation and then to do something about unemployment. If the pressures to reduce unemployment are, on the average, stronger than the pressures to control inflation, the stop-go cycle will become an upward spiral, as shown in this box.

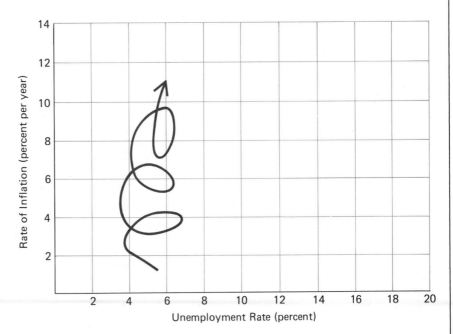

Box 18.10
The U.S. Experience with Unemployment and Inflation, 1954–1980

This box presents data on inflation and unemployment in the U.S. economy from 1954 to 1980. One part of this record—the Kennedy-Johnson expansion—has already been discussed. Now some other features will be explored.

The overall impression one gets from the figure is that of a series of clockwise loops. The lengths and strengths of successive expansions and contractions are irregular, but it does not take much imagination to see an upward spiral in them.

Although the rate of inflation has drifted upward over the years, it has not done so over every single cycle. Consider the period following the recession of 1957. The recovery from this recession was very weak. The vertical line between the points for 1959 and 1960, which forms the upward portion of the next loop, is shorter and farther to the right than most. This weak recovery seems to have happened because President Eisenhower had been frightened by the inflation of 1956 and 1957 and did not want to repeat the experience. Restrictive policies cut the recovery off before the previous peak of inflation was reached.

During the 1970s, in contrast, the loops in the stop-go cycle resumed their upward drift and became more stretched out. The acceleration of inflation from the 1972 rate to the high 1974 rate was especially abrupt and was followed by the sharp recession of 1974–1975. Beginning in 1976 and continuing throughout the Carter administration, inflation took off again, reaching a 30-year high in 1980.

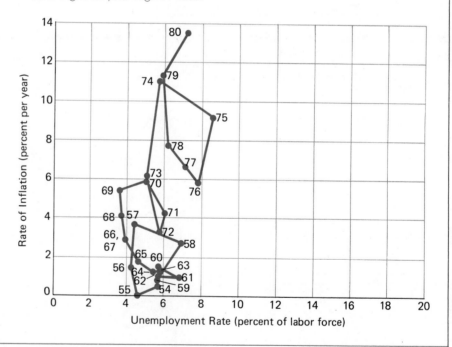

The Slowdown of Inflation

Box 18.11 adds the record for the years 1981–1984 to the inflation-unemployment chart. These years include the back-to-back recessions of 1980 and 1981–1982 and the strong recovery of 1983–1984. On the face of it, they indicate a break with the past pattern in several respects:

- In each of five previous inflation-recession cycles, the low point of inflation (1955, 1959, 1961, 1972, and 1976) was higher than the low point of the previous cycle. In contrast, the inflation rate reached in 1983 was the lowest in 16 years.
- The deceleration phase of the cycle was longer than it had been in any previous case.
- The upturn in inflation during 1984, the second year of the recovery, was smaller in relation to the drop in unemployment than at any time since the period 1961–1964.

What do these differences mean? Not surprisingly, explanations differ.

Claiming Credit

Supporters of the Reagan administration claim that the stop-go cycle has finally been broken and that their policies, aided by the Fed, deserve the credit. They like to compare the record for the period from 1980 to 1983 with earlier estimates of the cost of stopping inflation. For example, they cite Arthur Okun's 1978 estimate that an unemployment rate three percentage points above the natural rate would trim only one percentage point a year from the inflation rate. (See Chapter 16, pp. 414.) Box 18.12 presents Okun's estimate in graphic form. Between 1980 (point A) and 1983

**Box 18.11
The Deceleration of
Inflation, 1980–1984**

Between 1980 and 1983 the economy experienced back-to-back recessions. Unemployment reached a post-World War II high, and inflation fell by nearly ten percentage points. In 1983, for the first time in 30 years, the low point reached by inflation dropped below the low point of the previous cycle.

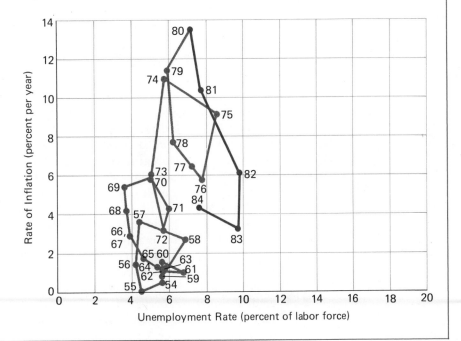

**Box 18.12
Was the Cost of the
1980–1983
Deceleration Less than
Expected?**

Backers of the Reagan administration's policies were quick to claim that the ten-percentage-point drop in the inflation rate was bigger than had been predicted. They cite estimates from the 1970s that implied that six years of unemployment rates of 11 percent or more would be needed to slow inflation that much. The pessimistic estimate is represented by the broken line from A to B. The actual path of the economy is shown by the solid line. Reagan supporters say that the economy's good performance was a result of supply side policies and the credibility of the administration's anti-inflation campaign. However, skeptics attribute much of the slowdown to favorable supply shocks. The performance of the economy in this period is reasonably consistent with earlier predictions when falling oil prices and the rising international value of the dollar are taken into account, they say.

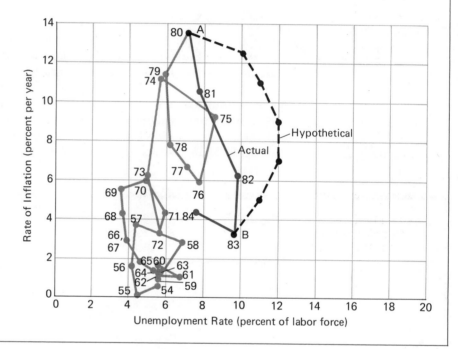

(point B), the rate of inflation fell by ten percentage points. In this period the unemployment rate averaged 9 percent—2.5 to 3 percentage points above its natural level. In contrast, Okun's estimate implies that six years of unemployment averaging five percentage points above the natural rate—that is, 11 to 11.5 percent—would be needed to get from point A to point B. This implied path is shown as a broken line in Box 18.12.

What aspects of policy deserve the credit for this seemingly remarkable achievement? Administration supporters usually cite two factors.

The first factor is the *credibility* of the administration's and the Fed's anti-inflation campaign. To understand the role of credibility, we need to replace our adaptive-expectations assumption with a rational-expectations hypothesis. Under previous administrations, the argument goes, people could rationally expect each recession to be followed by renewed inflation. After all, that is what had always happened in the past. Their expectations of renewed inflation limited the downward shift of the short-run Phillips curve even during periods when the actual rate of inflation was falling.

Okun's pessimistic estimate of the cost of stopping inflation makes good sense under such conditions.

In contrast, the team of Ronald Reagan in the White House and Paul Volcker at the Fed convinced people that the government was serious about fighting inflation. With people expecting the inflation rate to fall, the short-run Phillips curve shifted downward faster than adaptive expectations alone would predict. Hence, the cost of slowing inflation from 1980 to 1983 was lower than had been predicted.

Supply side economists who support the Reagan administration cite a second factor in the slowdown of inflation. They point out that, for any given rate of growth of nominal GNP, the higher the rate of growth of real output the lower the rate of inflation. There are two sources of growth of real output: cyclical growth that, according to Okun's law, is linked with changes in unemployment, and long-run growth of natural real output. The second of these is not captured in our simplified accelerationist model, which assumes no growth of natural real output. However, say the supply-siders, faster growth of natural real output after 1980 helped the anti-inflation effort. They credit the improved growth to supply side tax cuts and other policies.

In sum, supporters of the Reagan administration claim that there has been a change of policy regime. The policies of the administration's first four years deserve the credit, and if they are continued, the stop-go cycle will not be renewed.

The Skeptics

Not everyone buys the argument that the early 1980s represent a complete break with the past. The skeptics include not only political opponents of the Reagan administration but many economists who claim that the recent progress in the battle against inflation isn't all that remarkable. Let's look at their arguments.

To begin with, say the skeptics, an analysis of inflation in the 1980–1984 period must take into account the role played by supply shocks. Two major supply shocks were at work in the period, one having to do with oil prices and the other having to do with the international value of the dollar.

The first supply shock involved energy prices. In one year, from 1979 to 1980, the producer price index for energy products rose by a stunning 40 percent. This pushed costs and prices up in every sector of the economy. Then energy prices not only stopped rising—they started to fall. From 1982 to 1984 producer prices for energy dropped by 5 percent. This downward supply shock depressed costs and prices in other sectors of the economy.

The second supply shock concerns the international value of the dollar. In 1980, the dollar was at a low point. It would buy just 4.2 French francs, 1.8 West German marks, or 227 Japanese yen. By early 1985, the dollar had rebounded to historic highs. It would buy more than 10 francs, more than 3 marks, and more than 250 yen. A low value for the dollar, as in 1980, makes imports expensive. High prices for imported finished goods and raw materials push up prices directly. A low value for the dollar also promotes inflation indirectly by shielding domestic firms from import competition and giving them more room to raise their own prices. In contrast, a high value for the dollar makes imports cheap. And low-priced imports mean stiff competition for domestic firms, which find it hard to raise their own prices.

Describing the rise of the dollar and the fall in oil prices as supply shocks is in one sense misleading. The term "shock" seems to imply something that affects the economy from the outside, independently of any policy actions that are taken. This is not entirely true of the favorable supply side developments under discussion here. Both the rise in the international value of the dollar and the fall in oil prices were intensified by the earlier movement to monetary restraint and the high level of real interest rates in the United States. Nonetheless, in evaluating the claims made by supporters of the Reagan administration for success of its policies, it seems fair to treat these developments as if they were true supply shocks. Although they were related to U.S. economic policies, they were not brought on specifically by the credibility effect or by the incentive effect of tax cuts.

Whether we choose to call them supply shocks or something else, the changes in world oil prices and the international value of the dollar account for a large part of the slowdown in the rate of inflation. High oil prices and a depressed dollar pushed the inflation rate to a peak of 13 percent in 1980. Without these developments, the rate for that year would probably have been no higher than 10 percent. And falling oil prices and a soaring dollar pushed inflation down in 1983 and 1984. Without these factors, the inflation rate would very likely have been 5 percent or so in those years.

In short, favorable developments in the world economy not connected with the credibility effect or supply side elements of Reagan administration policy appear to account for about half of the ten-percentage-point drop in the inflation rate in the early 1980s. Of the remaining five percentage points, most can be explained by high unemployment. Even under Okun's assumptions, unemployment was high enough in the 1981–1984 period to cut 3.5 percentage points from the inflation rate. That leaves the Reagan administration with only a 1.5-percentage-point gain to credit to credibility and the supply side effects of tax cuts.

What is more, some economists now claim that Okun's estimate was too pessimistic in the first place. The studies Okun looked at in 1978 assumed that the Phillips curve became flatter as the economy moved farther to the right along it. Such a shape for the Phillips curve would reduce the impact of high unemployment rates on inflation. However, experience since that time suggests that the short-run Phillips curve has a fairly constant slope, as in the diagrams of this chapter. If Okun's estimate of the effects of high unemployment on inflation is recalculated assuming a straight-line Phillips curve, all of the slowdown in inflation since 1980 can be accounted for without appealing to the credibility effect or to the incentive effects of tax cuts.

Looking Ahead

It is too soon to be sure whether the stop-go cycle has been broken and, if so, who deserves the credit. Events of the next few years may settle the issue, however. What should you watch for?

One possibility is that the cycle of inflation and recession will continue much as before. If the cycle runs true to form, each successive year of the recovery from the double recession of 1980–1982 will bring higher inflation with less of a drop in unemployment. Sooner or later the economy will fall back into a recession and the pattern will repeat itself.

But more favorable developments are also possible. Moderate monetary policy and continued good luck with international economic developments may be able to contain inflation as the recovery continues. A real-output growth rate of 3 to 4 percent may allow further reductions in unemployment. If this happens, the economy could move horizontally to the left on the inflation-unemployment chart to a "soft landing" at about 4 percent inflation and about 6 percent unemployment. It could even move down and to the left to a soft landing at a still lower inflation rate. From there, productivity growth could continue to boost natural real output and living standards without renewed inflation. It would be unrealistic to expect the business cycle to disappear entirely. But the wild spiral of the 1960s and 1970s might be replaced with a more gentle looping motion around a point of long-run equilibrium.

Play the role of macroeconomist yourself. Read and watch the story of the economy as it unfolds.

Summary

1. According to the *accelerationist theory* of inflation, the economy behaves differently in periods when the inflation rate is accelerating or slowing down than in periods when the rate of inflation stays the same. The accelerationist theory rests on four building blocks. The first is the control of aggregate nominal demand through monetary and fiscal policy. The second is the rule that the growth rate of real output plus the rate of inflation must equal the rate of growth of nominal output. The third is Okun's law, which relates changes in real output to changes in the unemployment rate. And the fourth is the Phillips curve, which relates the unemployment rate to the actual and expected rates of inflation.

2. If an expansionary policy is pursued from a standing start, it will at first cut unemployment below its natural rate with only a moderate increase in inflation. As time goes by, however, the trade-off between inflation and unemployment becomes less favorable. Inflation must accelerate at a faster rate each year just to keep unemployment from rising back toward its natural rate.

3. Slowing the growth of aggregate nominal demand after a period of accelerating inflation will cause an inflationary recession. Until the momentum of inflationary expectations is broken, the inflation rate and the unemployment rate may both rise while real output falls. After the expected rate of inflation begins to fall, the actual rate of inflation can continue to decelerate as long as unemployment remains above its natural rate. The deceleration may continue until the economy reaches a "soft landing" at zero inflation and the natural rate of unemployment, or it may be interrupted by a renewal of expansionary policy, or *reflation.*

4. Alternating expansionary and contractionary demand management policies creates a stop-go policy cycle. On the inflation-unemployment chart, the economy moves in clockwise loops around the vertical long-run Phillips curve. If the political system is, on the average, more sensitive to the problem of unemployment than it is to that of inflation, the loops may become an upward spiral. The post–World War II macroeconomic experience of the United States fits such a spiral pattern.

5. From 1980 to 1983, the economy went through severe back-to-back recessions during which the rate of inflation dropped about ten percentage points. Backers of the Reagan adminis-

tration's policies claim that this represents a complete break with the earlier stop-go policy cycle. Other economists attribute much of the slowdown to favorable supply shocks. They take a wait-and-see attitude on the question of whether the stop-go cycle has really been broken.

Questions for Review

1. Define the following terms:
   accelerationist theory of inflation
   reflation
2. What are the four building blocks of the accelerationist theory of inflation?
3. Use an inflation-unemployment chart to trace the response of the economy to accelerating inflation over a period of years. Has this pattern ever been observed in the U.S. economy?
4. Use an inflation-unemployment chart to trace an inflationary recession. Why is it possible for the rate of inflation and the unemployment rate both to rise in the same year?
5. Under what conditions will the stop-go policy cycle turn into an upward spiral?
6. What explanations have been given for the rapid slowdown of inflation in the United States between 1980 and 1983?

Problems and Topics for Discussion

1. Using the *Economic Report of the President* or another source, obtain inflation and unemployment data for 1985, and for later periods if available. Also find the most recent monthly data on inflation and unemployment in business magazines or newspapers. Use the data to update the inflation-unemployment chart of Box 18.11. How would you interpret the most recent developments?
2. Turn to Box 16.1. What rate of growth of nominal GNP would be needed to reach point B'? Point B"?
3. Turn to Box 16.2. If the Blues want only to keep the unemployment rate at 4 percent in year 2, what target rate of growth should they set for nominal GNP? If they want to keep the inflation rate at 2 percent, what rate of growth of nominal GNP will be needed?
4. Turn to Box 18.3. If the rate of growth of nominal GNP slows to 7 percent in the fourth year instead of accelerating to 11 percent, what will happen to unemployment? To inflation? To real output?
5. Turn to Box 18.5. What rate of growth of nominal GNP would be needed to keep the rate of inflation at 11 percent in year 5? What would happen to the unemployment rate in that case?
6. Turn to Box 18.7. Suppose the Grays decided to aim for a "soft landing" at a 6 percent rate of inflation and 6 percent unemployment, instead of at zero inflation and 6 percent unemployment. What policy for nominal GNP would they need to do this, beginning from point I? Could they keep the economy at 6 percent inflation and 6 percent unemployment forever? If so, what policy would be required?

Suggestions for Further Reading

Friedman, Milton. "The Role of Monetary Policy," *American Economic Review* 58, May 1968, pp. 1–17.

Friedman's presidential address to the American Economics Association, thought to be the first statement of the accelerationist theory discussed in this chapter.

Gordon, Robert J. *Macroeconomics*, 3rd ed. Boston: Little, Brown, 1984.

Chapter 8 provides a more advanced treatment of the accelerationist theory.

Phelps, Edmund S. *Inflation Policy and Unemployment Theory*. New York: Norton, 1972.

A readable statement of the accelerationist theory by one of its pioneers. The theory is sometimes known as the Friedman-Phelps theory of inflation.

Appendix to Chapter 18

A Simple Algebraic Model
of the Dynamics of Inflation

This appendix shows how the theory of the dynamics of inflation presented in this chapter can be expressed in terms of a simple set of algebraic equations and how these equations, in turn, can be used as the basis for a somewhat more complete graphic presentation of the theory. Either the equations or the graphs can be used to calculate the way any given rate of growth of nominal national product will be split up between inflation and real growth under specified initial assumptions.

Building Blocks

The algebraic model is based on the four building blocks given in the chapter. The first of those blocks is the theory of nominal national income determination that was developed in Chapters 9 through 13. An algebraic version of this theory was presented in the appendix to Chapter 13, but that part of the analysis will not be repeated here. Instead, we will assume that the growth rate of nominal national product in any year is a fixed quantity, determined by monetary and fiscal policy decisions. The growth rate of nominal output in year t will be represented as $\dot{Y}_t$, with the dot meaning that the quantity in question is a growth rate expressed in percent per year and with the subscript referring to the year in question.

The Phillips Curve

The second building block to be used here is the short-run Phillips curve. This curve expresses a relationship between the inflation rate and the unemployment rate, given the expected rate of inflation. The Phillips curve equation can be written as

$$\dot{P} = \dot{P}_e + h(U - U_n) \tag{18A.1}$$

in which $\dot{P}$ is the actual rate of inflation, $\dot{P}_e$ is the expected rate of inflation, U is the actual rate of unemployment, U_n is the natural rate of unemployment, and h is a negative constant equal to the slope of the Phillips curve.

As in the chapter, a one-year adaptive-expectations rule will be used so that the expected rate of inflation in each year is equal to the actual rate of inflation in the previous year. To keep track of the years, subscripts are added, with t standing for the current year, $t-1$ for the previous year, and so on. Finally, a value of -1 is assumed for the constant h. The natural rate of unemployment is assumed to be 5 percent. When we have made all these changes, equation 18A.1 becomes

$$\dot{P}_t = \dot{P}_{t-1} - (U_t - 5) \qquad (18A.2)$$

Box 18A.1 shows how this equation can be used to draw the short-run Phillips curve for any given situation. It is clear from the equation that when the unemployment rate in the current year (U_t) is equal to the natural rate of unemployment (here assumed to be 5 percent), then the actual rate of inflation ($\dot{P}_t$) will be equal to the expected rate of inflation (which we assume to be the previous year's inflation rate, $\dot{P}_{t-1}$). The short-run Phillips curve for any year thus must pass through the point that corresponds to the natural rate of unemployment and the expected rate of inflation. If the expected rate of inflation is 0, then the short-run Phillips curve will be in the position Ph$_1$ in Box 18A.1. If, instead, the expected rate of inflation is 4

Box 18A.1
Graphing the Short-Run Phillips Curve

The Phillips curve is a straight line with a slope of -1. A reference point for sketching the short-run Phillips curve for any given year is provided by the following rule: When the actual and expected rates of inflation are equal, the actual unemployment rate must be equal to the natural rate of unemployment. The Phillips curve is further simplified by a one-year adaptive-expectations assumption under which the current year's expected rate of inflation is equal to the previous year's actual rate of inflation. For example, Phillips curve Ph$_1$, shown here, reflects zero expected inflation (zero actual inflation in the previous year), and curve Ph$_2$ reflects 4 percent expected inflation (4 percent actual inflation in the previous year). The natural rate of unemployment is assumed to be 5 percent.

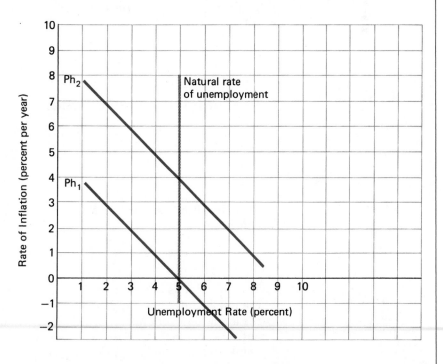

percent per year, the short-run Phillips curve will be in the position Ph_2, and so on. Thus, each one-percentage-point increase in the expected rate of inflation shifts the Phillips curve upward by one percentage point.

Okun's Law

The next building block to be added to the model is Okun's law. This law provides a link between the rate of real economic growth and changes in the unemployment rate: The rate of real economic growth in any year will be equal to the growth rate of natural real output minus three percentage points for each percentage point by which the unemployment rate rises from its rate for the previous year. In this appendix we will assume the growth rate of natural real output to be 3 percent per year (rather than zero, as in the body of the chapter). Given this assumption, Okun's law can be put in the form of the following equation:

$$\dot{y}_t = 3 - 3(U_t - U_{t-1}) \tag{18A.3}$$

where $\dot{y}$ stands for the rate of growth of real output and the subscripts t and $t-1$ stand for the current year and the previous year, as before.

The final building block needed for the simple algebraic model is the rule that the growth rate of nominal output in any year is equal to the growth rate of real output plus the rate of inflation. In equation form, this can be written as follows:

$$\dot{Y}_t = \dot{y}_t + \dot{P}_t \tag{18A.4}$$

Another way to state the same relationship is to say that the growth rate of real output is equal to the growth rate of nominal output minus the rate of inflation; that is,

$$\dot{y}_t = \dot{Y}_t - \dot{P}_t \tag{18A.5}$$

The Demand Pressure Equation

The system of equations given here can be simplified by substituting equation 18A.5 into Okun's law, as stated in equation 18A.3, to give

$$\dot{Y}_t - \dot{P}_t = 3 - 3(U_t - U_{t-1}) \tag{18A.6}$$

This, in turn, can be rewritten in the form of the following useful equation:

$$\dot{P}_t = \dot{Y}_t - 3 + 3(U_t - U_{t-1}) \tag{18A.7}$$

This equation is a version of Okun's law restated as a relationship among the rate of inflation, the rate of nominal GNP growth, and the change in the unemployment rate. In words, it says that the inflation rate in any year will be equal to the growth rate of nominal output minus three percentage points to allow for the growth of natural real GNP plus three percentage points for each percentage point by which the unemployment rate increases over its level for the previous year. Equation 18A.7 will be referred to as the *demand pressure equation* because it shows how much upward pressure is put on the inflation rate by the growth of aggregate nominal demand ($\dot{Y}_t$), given the change in the unemployment rate.

The demand pressure equation, like the equation for the Phillips curve, can be presented in graphic form. Box 18A.2 shows how. A convenient reference point is provided by the case in which the unemployment rate does not change from one year to the next. A look at equation 18A.7 shows that if the current year's unemployment rate (U_t) is

---

**Box 18A.2
Graphing the Demand
Pressure Curve**

The demand pressure curve can be graphed on the set of axes used for the Phillips curve, with unemployment on the horizontal axis and inflation on the vertical axis. The demand pressure curve has a slope of 3 because, according to Okun's law, each one-percentage-point drop in the unemployment rate tends to be linked with a three-percentage-point increase in the growth rate of real output and, hence, with a three-percentage-point drop in the inflation rate associated with a given growth rate of nominal GNP. A reference point for drawing the demand pressure curve is provided by the fact that if the unemployment rate in the current year does not change from that in the previous year, the inflation rate will be equal to the current year's growth rate of nominal GNP minus three percentage points to allow for the trend growth of real output. For example, the curve DP_1 applies to a year in which the growth rate of nominal GNP is 7 percent and the previous year's unemployment rate was 5 percent. It therefore passes through point A (5, 4). The demand pressure curve could be shifted to the position DP_2 in year 2 either by a decline in the year 1 unemployment rate to 4 percent while nominal growth stayed at 7 percent (point B), or by an increase in the nominal growth rate to 10 percent in year 2 with the unemployment rate in year 1 still assumed to be 5 percent (point C).

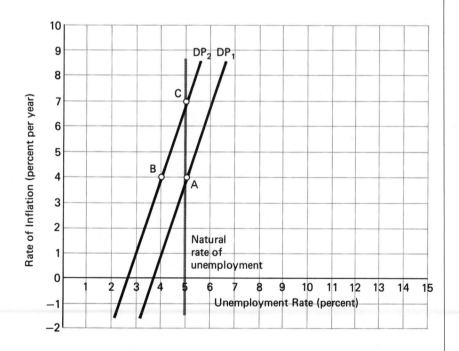

equal to the previous year's unemployment rate (U_{t-1}), then the inflation rate in the current year must be equal to the growth rate of nominal national income ($\dot{Y}_t$) minus three percentage points to allow for the growth of natural real GNP. For example, the demand pressure curve DP$_1$ in Box 18A.2 is based on the assumption that the unemployment rate for the previous year was 5 percent and the growth rate of nominal GNP in the current year is 7 percent. If unemployment does not change in the current year, the inflation rate must be 4 percent ($7-3$). DP$_1$ accordingly passes through point A, where the unemployment rate is 5 percent and the inflation rate is 4 percent. Moving downward and to the left along DP$_1$, then, we find that the inflation rate decreases by three percentage points for each one-percentage-point drop in the unemployment rate, given the growth of nominal output.

A change in either the current year's nominal-GNP growth rate ($\dot{Y}_t$) or the previous year's unemployment rate (U_{t-1}) can shift the demand pressure curve. For example, if the unemployment rate falls to 4 percent in year 1 while the growth rate of nominal GNP remains at 7 percent, the demand pressure curve for year 2 will shift to the position DP$_2$. This curve passes through point B, which corresponds to 4 percent unemployment and 4 percent ($7-3$) inflation. Thus, each one-percentage-point decrease in the previous year's unemployment rate shifts the demand pressure curve to the left by one percentage point. On the other hand, if unemployment remains at 5 percent in year 1, the demand pressure curve can still be shifted to the position DP$_2$ if the growth rate of nominal GNP in the current year (year 2) rises to 10 percent. This is shown by the fact that DP$_2$ also passes through point C, where the unemployment rate is 5 percent and the rate of inflation is 7 percent ($10-3$). Thus, each one-percentage-point increase in nominal output growth shifts the demand pressure curve upward by one percentage point. In short, the demand pressure curve for any year (t) can always be constructed by locating the point (U_{t-1}, $\dot{Y}_t-3$) and drawing a line with a slope of 3 through that point.

Determining the Inflation Rate and the Unemployment Rate

Equation 18A.2 (the Phillips curve) and equation 18A.7 (the demand pressure curve) can be solved simultaneously for the inflation rate and the unemployment rate in the current year, given the growth rate of nominal output as determined by monetary and fiscal policy, the unemployment rate in the previous year, the inflation rate in the previous year (which is assumed to be the expected rate of inflation in the current year), and the natural rate of unemployment (which is assumed to be 5 percent). The following problem shows how these equations can be put to work.

Problem 1   Assume that in year 0 the economy is in a standing-start position, with $U_0 = U_n = 5$ and $\dot{P}_0 = \dot{P}_{-1} = 0$. The growth rate of real and nominal output is 3 percent per year. In year 1, fiscal and monetary policy is used to increase the growth rate of nominal output from 3 percent to 7 percent per year. What will the inflation rate and the unemployment rate be for that year?

Solution   Putting the values given here into equation 18A.2 gives the following short-run Phillips curve for year 1:

$$\dot{P}_1 = 0 + 5 - U_1 = 5 - U_1 \tag{18A.8}$$

Putting the given values into the demand pressure equation (equation 18A.7) provides a second relationship between the inflation rate and the unemployment rate:

$$\dot{P}_1 = 7 - 3 + 3(U_1 - 5) = -11 + 3U_1 \tag{18A.9}$$

Solving equations 18A.8 and 18A.9 using the usual methods for solving simultaneous equations gives the values $U_1 = 4$ and $\dot{P}_1 = 1$. The result of the policy of accelerating the growth rate of nominal GNP to 7 percent in year 1, then, is to pull the unemployment rate 1 percent below the natural rate, to 4 percent, and to produce an inflation rate of 1 percent. Real output grows by 6 percent—7 percent nominal growth minus 1 percent inflation—up from 3 percent in year 0.

This problem can also be solved graphically as shown in Box 18A.3. First we graph the short-run Phillips curve, defined by equation 18A.8, for year 1. This gives the curve labeled Ph_1 in Box 18A.3. The curve passes through the reference point (5, 0), which corresponds to the 5 percent

**Box 18A.3
Graphic Solutions to
Problems 1 and 2**

The short-run Phillips curve Ph_1 and the demand pressure curve DP_1 give the solution to problem 1. Beginning from a standing start (point 0), an increase in the growth rate of nominal GNP to 7 percent in year 1 results in an inflation rate of 1 percent and a drop in the unemployment rate to 4 percent (point 1). In the first part of problem 2, the growth rate of nominal GNP is held at 7 percent for year 2. The curves Ph_2 and DP_2 show that this policy results in 2.5 percent inflation and 3.5 percent unemployment in year 2 (point 2). In year 3 the growth rate of nominal GNP is cut back to 3 percent, producing a rise in unemployment, while the inflation rate continues to accelerate (point 3).

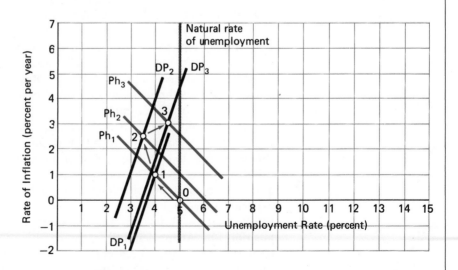

natural rate of unemployment and the expected year 1 inflation rate of 0 percent. Next we graph the demand pressure curve, given by equation 18A.9, for year 1. This gives the demand pressure curve labeled DP_1 in Box 17A.3. The demand pressure curve passes through the reference point (5, 4), which corresponds to the previous year's (year 0) unemployment rate of 5 percent and the 7 percent year 1 growth rate of nominal GNP, reduced by three percentage points to allow for natural real GNP growth. The intersection of these two curves occurs at the point (4, 1)—that is, at the same 4 percent unemployment rate and 1 percent inflation rate given by the algebraic solution for year 1.

Problem 2   Beginning from the same standing-start position assumed in problem 1, suppose that policymakers accelerate the growth rate of nominal output from 3 percent in year 0 to 7 percent in year 1, keep it at 7 percent in year 2, and then cut it back to 3 percent again in year 3. Use the graphs of equations 18A.2 and 18A.7 to trace the path taken by the economy in terms of inflation and unemployment.

Solution   Under the adaptive-expectations assumption, the expected rate of inflation in year 2 has risen to 1 percent. This increase causes the short-run Phillips curve to shift upward by one unit, to the position Ph_2 in Box 18A.3. In accordance with the Phillips curve rule of thumb, it passes through the point (5, 1). At the same time, the decline in the unemployment rate that occurred during year 1 shifts the demand pressure curve to the left. With the growth rate of nominal output still assumed to be 7 percent, holding the unemployment rate to 4 percent in year 2 will not be enough to keep inflation down to the 1 percent level of year 1. Instead, a further 1 percent decline in the unemployment rate will be required. The new position of the demand pressure curve thus is DP_2, and it passes through the point (4, 4) as required by the demand pressure curve rule of thumb.

The intersection of Ph_2 and DP_2 shows that in year 2 the inflation rate will be 2.5 percent and the unemployment rate will be 3.5 percent. Keeping the growth rate of nominal output at 7 percent for a second year thus results in a less attractive trade-off between inflation and unemployment than in the first year. In year 1, unemployment fell by a full percentage point and the inflation rate increased by only one percentage point. In year 2, unemployment falls only half a percentage point and the inflation rate rises by a point and a half. Real output growth in year 2 is 4.5 percent—the difference between the 7 percent nominal growth rate and the 2.5 percent inflation rate.

In year 3 policymakers will cut the growth rate of nominal output back to 3 percent, the same rate as in year 0. Doing so does not, however, return the economy to its standing-start position. Instead, it brings on an inflationary recession, as can be discovered by drawing the Phillips curve and the demand pressure curve for year 3. Because the inflation rate expected in year 3 rises to the rate that was experienced in year 2, the Phillips curve shifts upward by another one-and-a-half units, to the position Ph_3. At the same time, the combined effect of the decline in the unemployment rate to 3.5 percent during year 2 and the decline in the growth rate of nominal output to 3 percent in year 3 shifts the demand pressure curve to the position DP_3.

Substituting $\dot{Y}_3 = 3$ and $U_2 = 3.5$ into equation 18A.7, we can confirm that this is the correct position for the demand pressure curve. Or we can apply the rule of thumb given earlier, which says that DP_3 must pass through the point $(U_{t-1}, \dot{Y}_t - 3)$ or, in this case, the point $(3.5, 0)$. The intersection of Ph_3 and DP_3 gives an unemployment rate of 4.5 percent and an inflation rate of 3 percent for year 3. The inflation and unemployment rates have both risen, and the rate of real growth has fallen to zero.

Problem 3   Beginning from the position of the economy for year 3 in the previous problem, outline a four-year program for growth of nominal output that will bring the economy to a soft landing at zero inflation and 5 percent unemployment in year 7.

Solution   The solution is left to the reader. (*Hint*: Use a graphic trial-and-error method. The solution is not unique.)

In the computer industry small companies can grow quickly, but they face fierce competition. This picture shows an assembly line at Altos Computer Systems of San Jose, California.

Part V
The Theory of
Prices and
Markets

Chapter 19

Supply and Demand: Building on the Basics

After reading this chapter, you should be able to

1. Explain how the forces of supply and demand determine the equilibrium price and quantity for each market.
2. Show how markets respond to changes in supply and demand.
3. Define *elasticity* and distinguish among *elastic, inelastic,* and *unit elastic* demand curves.
4. Compute elasticity of demand, given data on changes in price and quantity demanded.
5. Show how revenue changes in response to a change in price under various conditions of elasticity.
6. Discuss the factors that determine the elasticity of demand.
7. Define and compute *income elasticity of demand, cross elasticity of demand,* and *price elasticity of supply.*

Ideas for Review

Here are some terms and concepts that you should review before you read this chapter:

Demand and supply curves (Chapter 3)
Changes in demand versus changes in quantity demanded (Chapter 3)
Equilibrium (Chapter 3)

"Even when fares rise again the public transit habit, they hope, will remain."

Big-city transit systems have raised their prices by an average of 65 percent over the past five years. Often the price increases have sent riders back to their cars, clogging streets at rush hour and making city air dirtier than ever. But on February 1, 1984, riders on the Chicago Regional Transit Authority's commuter rail lines got a break: Fares were cut 10 percent across the board.

At first the results were disappointing. In February, ridership on the system rose just 2.6 percent compared to the figure for February 1983, and March saw an increase of only 2.2 percent. Then things began to pick up. The system carried 5.5 percent more passengers in April 1984 than it had in April of 1983. In May, the increase was 7.1 percent. The law of demand seemed to be taking hold.

Was the fare cut a success? It depends on how you judge the results. Judged strictly in dollar terms, the results were not enough to make the money-losing system profitable. But RTA officials decided to keep the fares where they were. They took a long-run view of the matter. Their goal was not to earn a quick profit but to cause a long-run change in commuting habits. The fare cut got a lot of people's attention. It let them know that public transportation was still there. Even when fares rise again, the public transit habit, they hope, will remain.[1]

We have now seen many examples of supply and demand in action. In this chapter we review the basics of supply and demand and then build on them. In doing so, we shift our focus somewhat. Instead of looking only at the *direction* of changes that result from changing supply and demand conditions, we will stress the *size* of the changes.

As the case of the RTA fare cuts shows, the size of the response to a change in price is crucial. The law of demand tells us that, except in rare cases, a price cut will increase the quantity demanded. But will the greater quantity be enough to offset the loss in revenue per unit so that the total revenue received by the seller will increase? By the end of this chapter we will have an answer to this question.

A REVIEW OF THE BASICS

The Supply and Demand Curves

Box 19.1 uses the market for wheat to set the stage for a review of supply and demand. The demand curve for wheat has a negative slope, showing that as the price of wheat falls, other things being equal, the quantity demanded rises. The supply curve has a positive slope: Other things being equal, farmers are willing to increase the quantity of wheat they will supply if they are given the incentive of a higher price.

Both the supply and demand curves are drawn on the basis of other things being equal. This is done in order to keep the effects of changes in the price of wheat separate from those of other changes that can influence the decisions of buyers and sellers. The demand curve for wheat is based

---

[1]Based on a telephone interview with John Camper, Chicago Regional Transit Authority.

Box 19.1
Equilibrium in the
Market for Wheat

The equilibrium price occurs at the point where the downward-sloping demand curve and the upward-sloping supply curve intersect. That is the only point where the plans of buyers exactly match those of sellers, so there is neither a surplus nor a shortage.

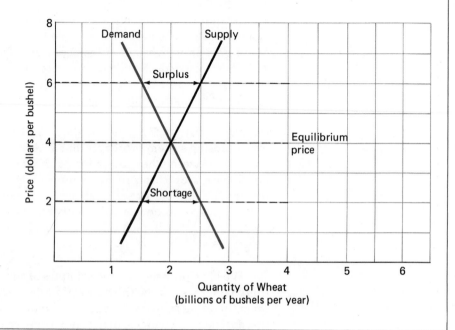

on the assumption that tastes, incomes, the prices of other goods, and expectations about future prices remain unchanged as the price of wheat changes. The supply curve for wheat is based on the assumption that production technology, the prices of inputs, the prices of other goods, and expectations about future prices remain unchanged as the price of wheat changes.

Equilibrium

The price of $4 per bushel, where the supply and demand curves intersect, is the *equilibrium price*. This is the price at which the plans of buyers and sellers exactly match when tested in the marketplace.

Consider any price higher than $4. At a price of, say, $6 the quantity supplied will be 2.5 billion bushels and the quantity demanded will be only 1.5 billion bushels. There will be a surplus (excess quantity supplied) of 1 billion bushels a year. Farmers will not be able to sell all the wheat that they are willing to offer at that price. As inventories of unsold wheat build up, farmers will become willing to sell it at a lower price. As the price falls, the quantity demanded will increase and the quantity supplied will decrease. The surplus will gradually be sold, and equlibrium will be restored.

In much the same way, there will be price changes if the price of wheat falls below $4. In Box 19.1, for example, at a price of $2 buyers will plan to purchase 2.5 billion bushels of wheat per year, but producers will plan to supply only 1.5 billion bushels. Not all buyers will be able to get as much wheat as they want. Unsatisfied buyers will offer higher prices. Farmers will accept these offers, and as the price rises toward equilibrium, more wheat will be offered for sale. Gradually the shortage will disappear.

Changes in Equilibrium

As economic conditions change, the equilibrium price and quantity change also. Box 19.2 shows that in analyzing changes in equilibrium, it is important to distinguish between shifts in supply or demand curves and movements along those curves.

The effect of a change in the price of a good, other things being equal, is shown as a movement along the demand curve for that good. We call such a movement a *change in quantity demanded.* In contrast, when the plans of buyers are affected by a change in something other than the price of the good, the result is shown as a shift in the demand curve. This is called a *change in demand.* All the things covered by the other-things-being-equal clause in the law of demand can cause shifts in the demand curve. Changes in the demand for a good can be caused by changes in tastes, incomes, expectations, or the prices of other goods.

The same distinction between movements along a curve and shifts in the curve itself applies to the supply curve. The effect of a change in the price of a good, other things being equal, is shown as a movement along

**Box 19.2
Changes in Price
Caused by Changes in
Demand and Supply**

Part a shows the effects of a change in the demand for wheat caused by an increase in consumer incomes. The demand curve shifts to the right, from D_1 to D_2, creating a shortage at the original price of $4 per bushel. The market moves up along the supply curve, as shown by the arrow, until a new equilibrium is reached, at E_2, with a price of $6 per bushel. Part b shows the effects of a change in supply caused by an increase in labor costs. The supply curve shifts upward from S_1 to S_2, creating a shortage at the original price. The market moves along the demand curve to the new equilibrium, E_3.

(a)

(b)

the supply curve. This is called a *change in quantity supplied*. A change in one of the things covered by the other-things-being-equal clause—technology, input prices, prices of other goods, or expectations—causes a shift in the supply curve. Such a shift is called a *change in supply*.

These points about shifts in curves and movements along curves are illustrated in Box 19.2. In part a of the box, an increase in consumer income shifts the demand curve for wheat to the right, from D_1 to D_2. This causes a shortage of wheat, which in turn drives up the price. As the price rises, the market moves along the supply curve from the original equilibrium, E_1, to the new equilibrium, E_2. In part b, a price rise is touched off by a decrease in supply. An increase in labor costs shifts the supply curve upward, from S_1 to S_2. This causes a shortage of wheat at the original price, which again pushes the price upward. As the price rises, the market moves along the demand curve from the original equilibrium point, E_1, to the new equilibrium point, E_2.

ELASTICITY

Elasticity
The responsiveness of quantity demanded or supplied to changes in the price of the good or changes in other economic conditions.

Supply-and-demand analysis stresses that the plans of buyers and sellers change as prices or other conditions change. It is often useful to know how responsive such plans are to changes in economic conditions. The responsiveness of a quantity demanded or supplied is known as the **elasticity** of demand or supply for the good or service in question.

One of the key uses of the concept of elasticity concerns the responsiveness of quantity demanded to a change in price. This is known as the

**Box 19.3
Elastic, Inelastic, and
Unit Elastic Demand**

These graphs show the relationship between changes in price and changes in revenue for three demand curves. As the price of good A decreases from $5 to $3, revenue increases from $15 to $18; the demand for good A is elastic. As the price of good B decreases over the same range, revenue falls from $15 to $12; the demand for good B is inelastic. As the price of good C decreases, revenue remains unchanged; the demand for good C is unit elastic.

(a)

(b)

(c)

Price elasticity of demand
The ratio of the percentage change in the quantity of a good demanded to a given percentage change in its price, other things being equal.

Elastic demand
A situation in which quantity changes by a larger percentage than price, and therefore total revenue increases as price decreases.

Inelastic demand
A situation in which quantity changes by a smaller percentage than price, and therefore total revenue decreases as price decreases.

Unit elastic demand
A situation in which price and quantity change by the same percentage, and therefore total revenue remains unchanged as price changes.

price elasticity of demand; it is the ratio of the percentage change in the quantity of a good demanded to a given percentage change in its price. Box 19.3 presents three demand curves showing different degrees of price elasticity of demand. In part a the quantity demanded is highly responsive to a change in price. In this case a decrease in price from $5 to $3 causes the quantity demanded to increase from three units to six. Because the percentage change in quantity is greater than the percentage change in price, the drop in price causes total revenue from sales of the good to increase. (This increase can be seen by looking at the shaded rectangles before and after the price change.) When a price decrease causes total revenue to increase, demand is said to be **elastic**.

Part b of Box 19.3 shows a case in which the quantity demanded is much less responsive to a change in price. Here a $2 decrease in price, from $5 to $3 per unit, causes the quantity demanded to increase by just one unit, from three units to four. This time the percentage change in quantity is less than the percentage change in price. As a result, the decrease in price causes total revenue to fall. (Again, look at the shaded rectangles.) Demand is said to be **inelastic** in such a case.

A third case is shown in part c, in which a change in price causes an exactly proportional change in quantity demanded, so that total revenue does not change. When the percentage change in quantity demanded is equal to the percentage change in price, demand is said to be **unit elastic**.

Besides the cases of elastic, inelastic, and unit elastic demand shown in Box 19.3, there are two limiting cases, which are shown in Box 19.4. Part a shows a demand curve that is perfectly vertical. No matter what the price, the quantity demanded is five units—no more, no less. Such a demand

---

**Box 19.4
Perfectly Elastic and
Perfectly Inelastic
Demand**

Part a of this box shows a demand curve that is a vertical line. No matter what the price, the quantity demanded is five units. Such a demand curve is described as perfectly inelastic. Part b shows a perfectly elastic demand curve, which is a horizontal line. Above the price of $5, no units of the good can be sold. At the price of $5, suppliers can sell as much of the good as they want, without further reductions in price.

(a) Perfectly Inelastic Demand

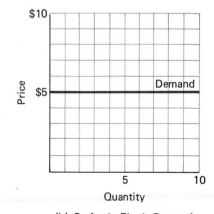

(b) Perfectly Elastic Demand

Perfectly inelastic demand

A situation in which the demand curve is a vertical line.

Perfectly elastic demand

A situation in which the demand curve is a horizontal line.

curve is said to be **perfectly inelastic**. Part b shows a demand curve that is perfectly horizontal. Above the price of $5, no units of the good can be sold. But as soon as the price drops to $5, producers can sell as much of the good as they care to produce, without cutting the price any more. A horizontal demand curve like this one is described as **perfectly elastic**.

Measuring Elasticity of Demand

It is often useful to attach numerical values to elasticity of demand. The basis for such values is the definition of elasticity of demand as the ratio of the percentage change in quantity demanded to the percentage change in price.

Percentage changes   To apply this definition to the measurement of elasticity, we need a way to measure percentage changes. Everyday ways of doing this are not very useful. Suppose, for example, that we are dealing with a 25-cent increase in the price of strawberries, from 75 cents a pint to $1 a pint. Ordinarily we use the initial price as the denominator in calculating a percentage change, so we would call this a 33 percent increase (0.25/0.75 = 0.33). However, suppose the initial price were $1 a pint and we were considering a 25-cent decrease in price to 75 cents a pint. In this case, we would use $1 in the denominator, and we would call it a 25 percent decrease (0.25/1 = 0.25).

In measuring elasticity, it is awkward to have to state whether we are dealing with a price increase or a price decrease before we can calculate the percentage change. We can get around this problem by using the midpoint of the price range as the denominator in calculating the percentage change for both increases and decreases in price. To find the midpoint, we take the sum of the initial price and the final price and divide by two. In this case the midpoint is (0.75 + 1)/2 = 0.875. Using the midpoint value of 0.875 as the denominator, the percentage change in price becomes 0.25/0.875 = 0.285 (approximately)—a 28.5 percent change, the same for an increase as for a decrease over the specified price range.

With P_1 representing the price before the change and P_2 the price after the change, the midpoint formula for calculating the percentage change in price can be written as

$$\text{Percent change in price} = \frac{P_2 - P_1}{(P_1 + P_2)/2}$$

The same approach can be used in defining the percentage change in the quantity demanded that results from a given change in price. Suppose that when the price of strawberries falls from $1 to 75 cents, the quantity demanded rises from 100 pints a day to 150 pints a day. We use the midpoint of the quantity range as the denominator in calculating the percentage change in quantity. If Q_1 and Q_2 are the quantities before and after a change in price, the midpoint formula for the percentage change can be written as:

$$\text{Percent change in quantity} = \frac{Q_2 - Q_1}{(Q_1 + Q_2)/2}$$

Applying this formula to the example just given, we say that either an increase in quantity from 100 to 150 or a decrease in quantity from 150 to 100 represents a 40 percent change in quantity:

$$\text{Percent change in quantity} = \frac{150 - 100}{(150 + 100)/2} = 0.40$$

An elasticity formula   Defining percentage changes in this way allows us to write a useful formula for calculating elasticities. The formula can be applied to the elasticity of either supply or demand. With P_1 and Q_1 representing price and quantity before a change and P_2 and Q_2 representing price and quantity after the change, the midpoint formula for elasticity is

$$\begin{array}{c} \text{Price} \\ \text{elasticity} \\ \text{of demand} \end{array} = \frac{(Q_2 - Q_1)/(Q_1 + Q_2)}{(P_2 - P_1)/(P_1 + P_2)}$$

The following problem illustrates the use of this formula.

Problem   A change in the price of strawberries from $1 a pint to 75 cents a pint causes the quantity demanded to increase from 100 pints per day to 150 pints per day. What is the price elasticity of demand for strawberries over the range of price and quantity given?

Solution
P_1 = price before change = $1
P_2 = price after change = 75 cents
Q_1 = quantity before change = 100
Q_2 = quantity after change = 150

$$\text{Elasticity} = \frac{(150 - 100)/(100 + 150)}{(\$0.75 - \$1.00)/(\$1.00 + \$0.75)}$$

$$= \frac{50/250}{-\$0.25/\$1.75}$$

$$= \frac{0.2}{-\$0.1428} = -1.4$$

Because the demand curves slope downward, this formula yields a negative value for elasticity. The reason is that the quantity changes in the direction opposite to the change in price. When the price decreases, the term $(P_2 - P_1)$, which appears in the denominator of the formula, is negative, whereas $(Q_2 - Q_1)$, which appears in the numerator, is positive. When the price increases, the numerator is negative and the denominator is positive. However, in this book we follow the widely used practice of dropping the minus sign when discussing price elasticity of demand. Thus, the elasticity of demand for a good will be given as, say, 2 or 0.5 rather than as −2 or −0.5. Applying this convention to the preceding problem, the elasticity of demand for strawberries would be stated as 1.4 over the range of price and quantity shown.

Elasticity Values and Changes in Revenue

Earlier in the chapter we defined *elastic, inelastic, unit elastic, perfectly elastic,* and *perfectly inelastic demand.* They were defined in terms of the relationship between change in price and change in total revenue. Each of these terms corresponds to a numerical value or range of values of elasticity as calculated using the elasticity formula. A perfectly inelastic demand curve has a numerical value of 0, since any change in price produces no change in quantity demanded. The term *inelastic* (but not perfectly inelastic) *demand* applies to numerical values from 0 up to, but not including, 1. *Unit elasticity,* as the name implies, means a numerical value of exactly 1. *Elastic demand* means any value for elasticity that is greater than 1. *Perfectly elastic demand,* represented by a horizontal demand curve, is not defined numerically; as the demand curve approaches horizontal, the denominator of the elasticity formula approaches 0, so that the numerical value of elasticity approaches infinity.

Varying and Constant-Elasticity Demand Curves

The midpoint formula for calculating the elasticity of demand shows the elasticity of demand over a certain range of prices and quantities. Measured over some other range, the elasticity of demand for the same good may or may not be different. Whether the elasticity of demand for a good changes along the demand curve depends on the exact shape of the curve. This can be seen in Boxes 19.5 and 19.6.

A linear demand curve   First look at Box 19.5, which shows a demand curve that, like most of those in this book, is a straight line. The elasticity of demand is not constant for all ranges of price and quantity along this curve. Measured over the price range $8–$9 , for example, the elasticity of demand is 5.66. Measured over the range $2–$3, it is 0.33. (The calculations are shown in the box.)

This illustrates the general rule that elasticity declines as one moves downward along a straight-line demand curve. It is easy to see why. With a straight-line demand curve, a $1 reduction in price always causes the same absolute increase in quantity demanded. At the upper end of the demand curve, though, a $1 change in price is a small percentage change, but the change in quantity is a large percentage of the quantity demanded at that price. At the lower end of the curve, the situation is reversed. A $1 change is now a large percentage of the price, but the change in quantity is smaller in relation to the larger quantity demanded. Because it is percentages, not absolute amounts, that count in elasticity calculations, the demand curve is less elastic near the bottom than near the top. Because elasticity changes along a straight-line demand curve, it makes sense to apply the formula only to small changes.

Part b of Box 19.5 shows the relationship between elasticity of demand and total revenue for a good with a straight-line demand curve. In the elastic range of the demand curve, total revenue rises as price falls. Total revenue reaches a peak at the point of unit elasticity and declines again in the range of inelastic demand.

**Box 19.5
Variation in Elasticity
Along a Straight-Line
Demand Curve**

These graphs show how elasticity varies along a straight-line demand curve. At low quantities, demand is elastic. For example, in the range from 10 to 20 units, the elasticity of demand is 5.66. At 50 units of output (halfway down the curve) a point of unit elasticity is reached. From there to 100 units of output, demand is inelastic; in the range from 70 to 80 units, for example, elasticity is 0.33. Part b shows that total revenue increases as the quantity increases over the elastic portion of the demand curve, and decreases as the quantity increases over the inelastic portion. Total revenue reaches a maximum at the point of unit elasticity.

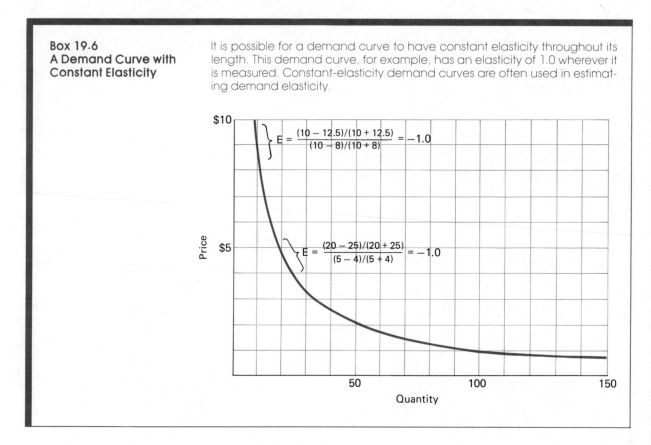

**Box 19.6
A Demand Curve with
Constant Elasticity**

It is possible for a demand curve to have constant elasticity throughout its length. This demand curve, for example, has an elasticity of 1.0 wherever it is measured. Constant-elasticity demand curves are often used in estimating demand elasticity.

$$E = \frac{(10 - 12.5)/(10 + 12.5)}{(10 - 8)/(10 + 8)} = -1.0$$

$$E = \frac{(20 - 25)/(20 + 25)}{(5 - 4)/(5 + 4)} = -1.0$$

A constant-elasticity demand curve If the demand curve is not a straight line, these results need not always apply. There is an important special case in which the demand curve has just the amount of curvature needed to keep elasticity constant throughout its length. Such a curve is shown in Box 19.6. As you can see from the calculations in the box, elasticity is 1.0 at every point on this curve. It is possible to construct demand curves with constant elasticities of any value. Such curves are often used in statistical studies of demand elasticity.

Determinants of Elasticity of Demand

Why is the price elasticity of demand high for some goods and low for others? The most important factor in the elasticity of demand for a good is the availability of substitutes or complements. If a good has close substitutes, demand for it tends to be elastic, since when its price rises, people can switch to the substitutes. For example, the demand for olive oil is more elastic than it would be if other salad oils could not be substituted for it. Likewise, the demand for cars is less elastic than it would be if public transportation were available everywhere, since cars and public transportation can be substituted for each other. On the other hand, if something is a minor complement to an important good, its demand tends to be inelastic. For example, the demand for motor oil tends to be inelastic because it is a complement to a more important good—gasoline. The price of gasoline has more of an effect on the amount of driving a person does than the price of motor oil.

Elasticity is also influenced by the portion of a person's budget spent on a good. Matches, for example, are not a necessity, and there are good substitutes for them. Yet the demand for matches is very inelastic because people spend so little on them that they hardly notice a price change. In contrast, the demand for things like housing and transportation is not perfectly inelastic, even though these things are necessities. Since they account for a large part of people's budgets, changes in their prices cannot be ignored.

Finally, elasticity of demand is influenced by time. Demand often is less elastic in the short run than in the long run. Consider the demand for home heating fuel. In the short run, people find it hard to cut back the amount they use when the price goes up. They are accustomed to keeping their homes at a certain temperature and dressing a certain way. Given time, though, they may find ways to cut back. They can put better insulation in their homes, dress more warmly, or even move to a warmer climate.

The commuter fare cut described at the beginning of this chapter illustrates the role of time in elasticity of demand. In the first month of the fare cut, there was only a modest increase in ridership. After the fare cut had been in effect a few months, the increase in ridership was greater. RTA officials hoped that if it became necessary to raise the fare again, the delayed response would work to their advantage. At least for a while, they hoped, riders would continue to use the system even after the fare was raised.

Other Elasticities

So far we have applied the concept of elasticity only to the price elasticity of demand for a good. This concept has other applications as well. All of them are based on the the ratio of the percentage change in one variable to the percentage change in another.

Income elasticity of demand   As shown in Chapter 3 and again earlier in this chapter, changes in income can cause changes in the demand for a good. The **income elasticity of demand** for a good is defined as the ratio of the percentage change in demand for the good to the percentage change in income. In measuring the income elasticity of demand for a good, it is assumed that the good's price does not change. Using Q_1 and Q_2 to represent quantities before and after the income change and y_1 and y_2 to represent income before and after the change, the formula for income elasticity of demand can be written as

Income elasticity of demand

The ratio of the percentage change in the demand for a good to a given percentage change in consumer income, other things being equal.

$$\frac{\text{Income}}{\text{elasticity}} = \frac{(Q_2 - Q_1)/(Q_1 + Q_2)}{(y_2 - y_1)/(y_1 + y_2)} = \frac{\text{Percent change in quantity}}{\text{Percent change in income}}$$

The income elasticity of demand for a good is closely linked to the concepts of *normal* and *inferior* goods. For a normal good, an increase in income causes demand to increase. Because income and demand change in the same direction, the income elasticity of demand for a normal good is positive. For an inferior good, an increase in income causes demand to decrease. Because income and demand change in opposite directions, the income elasticity of demand for an inferior good is negative.

Cross-elasticity of demand

The ratio of the percentage change in the demand for a good to a given percentage change in the price of some other good, other things being equal.

Cross-elasticity of demand   Another factor that can cause a change in the demand for a good is a change in the price of some other good. The demand for lettuce is affected by changes in the price of cabbage; the demand for motor oil is affected by changes in the price of gasoline; and so on. The concept of elasticity can be applied here also: The **cross-elasticity of demand** for a good is defined as the percentage change in demand for the good divided by the percentage change in the price of another good.

Box 19.7
Demand for Amtrak Passenger Service

The National Railroad Passenger Corporation (Amtrak) was formed by Congress in 1970 to take over the fast-disappearing passenger services of private railroads. At the time that Amtrak came into being, total passenger miles traveled by train had been declining for half a century, and railroads had been losing money on passenger services for more than 30 years. Amtrak too has found it hard to make a profit on passenger service. In most years its revenues have covered less than half of its costs.

Much of the difficulty Amtrak has in turning a profit is caused by the demand conditions it faces. The price elasticity, cross-elasticity, and income elasticity of demand for rail passenger service have all been studied in the hope of finding a segment of the intercity passenger market that Amtrak can serve successfully.

In most markets the price elasticity of demand is quite high—about 2.2 on the average, according to a study by Amtrak. This means that Amtrak cannot raise fares without losing large amounts of revenue. A fare cut would bring in many more passengers, but when fares are already below cost, more passengers just mean greater losses. The Northeast corridor—Washington, D.C., to Boston—is an exception. The price elasticity of demand there is estimated at 0.67. This low elasticity is believed to be linked with the high percentage of business-related trips in the Northeast. In the rest of the nation, most intercity trips are taken for pleasure.

High price elasticity of demand is typical of goods and services that have close substitutes. Estimates of cross-elasticity give an idea of what the substitutes are. In 1977 a study found a cross-elasticity of 0.6 with air travel and 1.29 with bus travel, indicating that intercity bus service was Amtrak's closest competitor. Since then discount airlines like PeoplExpress, Continental, and Midway have forced buses to keep their fares low. This has not improved Amtrak's situation.

In the past, intercity rail service has been viewed as an inferior good. Estimates of income elasticities of demand made in the 1950s found a value of −0.6 for rail, compared to values of +1.2 for automobile and +2.5 for air. Because incomes have grown steadily and will continue to do so, these numbers would make Amtrak's job almost hopeless if it tried to compete head-on with automobile and airline travel. However, Amtrak believes that the demand for recreational and vacation travel by rail has a positive income elasticity. In effect, there may be a market for Amtrak as something like a land-bound cruise ship. Cruise ships have prospered while transatlantic ocean travel has all but disappeared. The wave of the future in rail passenger travel may be scenic cruises in luxurious railcars with champagne, caviar, and linen tablecloths.

Source: George W. Hilton, *Amtrak: The National Railroad Passenger Corporation* (Washington, D.C.: American Enterprise Institute, 1980).

The formula for cross-elasticity of demand is the same as the one for price elasticity of demand, except that the numerator shows the percentage change in the quantity of one good while the denominator shows the percentage change in the price of some other good.

Cross-elasticity of demand is related to the concepts of *substitutes* and *complements*. Because lettuce and cabbage are substitutes, an increase in the price of cabbage causes an increase in the quantity of lettuce demanded. The cross-elasticity of demand is positive. Because motor oil and gasoline are complements, an increase in the price of gasoline causes a decrease in the quantity of motor oil demanded. The cross-elasticity of demand is negative. Box 19.7 shows how the concepts of price elasticity, cross-elasticity, and income elasticity of demand can be applied in an actual situation—that of the demand for intercity rail passenger service.

Price elasticity of supply
The ratio of the percentage change in quantity supplied to a given percentage change in the price of a good, other things being equal.

Price elasticity of supply   The definition of the **price elasticity of supply** for a good closely resembles that of the price elasticity of demand: It is the percentage change in the quantity of the good supplied divided by the percentage change in the price of the good. The formula for calculating price elasticity of supply is the same as that for determining price elasticity of demand. Because price and quantity change in the same direction along a positively sloped supply curve, the formula gives a positive value for the elasticity of supply. Box 19.8 applies the elasticity formula to two supply curves, one of which has constant elasticity and the other variable elasticity.

**Box 19.8
Calculating Price
Elasticity of Supply**

This box uses four examples to show how price elasticity of supply is calculated. Price elasticity of supply is shown for two ranges on each of the two supply curves. The supply curve S_1, which is a straight line passing through the origin, has a constant elasticity of 1.0. The supply curve S_2, which is curved, is elastic for small quantities and inelastic for larger quantities.

Looking Ahead

This chapter has set the stage for a discussion of a number of questions. First, what really lies behind the supply and demand curves? The text has given some broad explanations of why these curves have the shapes they do, but now it must show how they can be explained in terms of people's efforts to deal with the problems of scarcity and choice. This explanation will take up several chapters.

Next, do the principles of supply and demand apply to all markets or to only certain types of markets? This chapter mainly limited its examples to markets, like those for wheat and milk, in which there are many buyers and sellers who are all relatively small. But we also need to know how to apply these principles to markets that are dominated by one or a few large sellers.

Finally, how can we use the principles of supply and demand to help us understand the role of government in the economy? In many markets, government regulations have a strong impact on the prices and quantities of goods that consumers can buy and producers can sell.

In answering all these questions, future chapters will build on the basics reviewed in this chapter.

Summary

1. The higher the price of a good like wheat, the smaller the quantity demanded by buyers and the larger the quantity supplied by producers. These responses can be represented by a downward-sloping demand curve and an upward-sloping supply curve. The intersection of the two curves marks the equilibrium price—the price at which the plans of buyers and sellers exactly match when tested in the marketplace.

2. The effects of changes in the price of a good, other things being equal, are shown as movements along supply and demand curves. Changes in demand or supply that are caused by changes in the prices of other goods, incomes, costs, and so on are shown as shifts in demand or supply curves. If either the demand curve or the supply curve shifts, the market will move to a new equilibrium price and quantity.

3. *Elasticity* is the responsiveness of quantity demanded or supplied to changes in the price of the good or to changes in other factors. If quantity demanded changes by a larger percentage than price, demand is said to be *elastic*.

If quantity changes by a smaller percentage than price, demand is said to be inelastic. And if quantity and price change by the same percentage, demand is said to be *unit elastic*.

4. The price elasticity of demand between two points on a demand curve is computed as the percentage change in quantity divided by the percentage change in price. The formula for price elasticity of demand is

$$\frac{(Q_2 - Q_1)/(Q_2 + Q_1)}{(P_2 - P_1)/(P_2 + P_1)}.$$

5. If the demand for a good is elastic, a decrease in price will increase total revenue. If it is inelastic, an increase in price will increase total revenue. A straight-line demand curve is elastic at the upper end, reaches a point of unit elasticity in the middle, and becomes inelastic at the lower end.

6. A number of factors can affect the elasticity of demand for a good. Demand for goods that have ready substitutes tends to be elastic. Demand for goods that are minor complements to more important goods tends to be

inelastic. Goods that account for a small portion of a person's budget tend to have inelastic demand. And demand tends to be more elastic the more time people are given to adjust to a change in price.

7. The concept of elasticity can be applied to many situations besides movements along demand curves. The income elasticity of demand for a good is the percentage change in the demand for a good divided by the percentage change in income. The cross-elasticity of demand between goods A and B is the percentage change in the demand for good A divided by the percentage change in the price of good B. And the price elasticity of supply is the percentage change in the quantity of a good supplied divided by the percentage change in its price.

Questions for Review

1. Explain the following terms and concepts:
   elasticity
   price elasticity of demand
   elastic demand
   inelastic demand
   unit elastic demand
   perfectly inelastic demand
   perfectly elastic demand
   income elasticity of demand
   cross-elasticity of demand
   price elasticity of supply
2. Explain market equilibrium in terms of the plans made by buyers and sellers of a good or service.
3. Sketch an example of a market in equilibrium. Then show how equilibrium changes when the demand curve shifts to the left or right with the supply curve not changing, and when the supply curve shifts to the left or right with the demand curve not changing. Explain how inventories or queues of buyers and sellers play a role in movements from one equilibrium to another.
4. Sketch examples of demand curves that are elastic, inelastic, unit elastic, perfectly inelastic, and perfectly elastic. Can a demand curve have different elasticities at different points? If so, give an example.
5. Write the formula for price elasticity of demand. Sketch two or three demand curves on a piece of graph paper. Calculate the price elasticity of demand at two or three points on each demand curve.
6. How does revenue change in response to changes in price under conditions of elastic, inelastic, and unit elastic demand? Sketch a straight-line demand curve and a second curve showing total revenue for each point along the demand curve.
7. What factors affect the elasticity of demand? What role is played by substitutes and complements? What is the effect of the amount of time consumers are given to adjust to a change in the price of a good?
8. Show how the concept of elasticity can be extended to income elasticity of demand, cross-elasticity of demand, and price elasticity of supply.

Problems and Topics for Discussion

1. Review the account of Chicago rail fares at the beginning of this chapter. From February 1983 to February 1984, a 10 percent fare cut produced a 2.6 percent increase in ridership. From May 1983 to May 1984, ridership rose by 7.1 percent. What is the elasticity of demand for each of the two time periods? Does it surprise you to find that elasticity was greater after the fare cut had been in effect for four months than it was at first? Discuss.
2. Measurements of elasticity like those you made in question 1 carry an "other things

being equal" condition. To be exact, they are accurate only if it is assumed that the demand curve did not shift between the two periods. How would the measurement for February be distorted if the weather was worse in February of 1983 than in the same month of 1984, and you knew that more people ride the train when there is snow or ice on the roads? Use a diagram to show the nature of the distortion. How would the measurement for June be distorted if the total number of jobs in Chicago rose between June 1983 and June 1984, and you knew that more jobs mean more commuters? Again, illustrate your answer with a diagram.

3. You are an officer of your campus film club. You are at a meeting in which ticket prices are being discussed. One member says, "What I hate to see most of all is empty seats in the theater. We sell out every weekend showing, but there are always empty seats on Wednesdays. If we cut our Wednesday night prices by enough to fill up the theater, we'd bring in more money." Would this tactic really bring in more money? What would you need to know to be sure? Draw diagrams to illustrate some of the possibilities.

4. Between 1979 and 1981 the price of heating oil rose by 104 percent while the price of LP gas, also used for home heating, rose by just 56 percent. Over the period, use of fuel oil fell slightly while use of LP gas rose. What does this suggest about the cross-elasticity of demand for LP gas with respect to the price of fuel oil? Draw a pair of diagrams to illustrate these events. (Suggestion: Draw upward-sloping supply curves for both fuels. Then assume that the heating oil supply curve shifts upward while the LP gas supply curve stays the same.)

5. **Case for Discussion**
    The early 1980s saw repeated fare wars in the airline industry. Low-cost newcomers such as PeoplExpress slashed fares, and the established carriers followed suit in order to avoid losing passengers. At one point in 1983, 88 percent of all passengers flew on discount fares. The industry as a whole lost money.

    In 1984 a new fare war broke out, but this one was different. In 1983 United, American, and other major airlines had cut fares across the board. In 1984 they were more selective. They cut fares on routes where they competed with the discount airlines, but they raised fares on other routes. They sold few discount tickets on midweek flights favored by business travelers, but many on weekend flights favored by vacationers. And travelers were forced to buy their tickets up to a few weeks in advance if they wanted to qualify for the lower fares. With this selective price cutting, the major carriers hoped to fight the competition without the painful loss of revenue that had occurred in 1983.[2]

Questions:

a. What assumptions do the major airlines seem to be making about the elasticity of demand for their services on routes where they face competition, compared with routes where they face no competition?

b. What assumptions are the major airlines making about the cross-elasticity of demand between their own flights and those of the low-cost airlines? Are they making different assumptions for business and vacation travelers? Discuss.

[2]Source: Kenneth Labich, "Fare Wars: Have the Big Airlines Learned to Win?" *Fortune*, October 29, 1984, pp. 24–28.

Suggestions for Further Reading

Nicholson, Walter. *Intermediate Microeconomics and Its Application*, 3rd ed. Hinsdale, Ill.: Dryden Press, 1983, chap. 5.

This or any other intermediate microeconomics text will give further details on the definition of elasticity and practical problems of measuring elasticity of demand.

Chapter 20

The Logic of Consumer Choice

WHAT YOU WILL LEARN IN THIS CHAPTER

After reading this chapter, you should be able to

1. Explain what economists mean by *utility* and *diminishing marginal utility*.
2. State the conditions for *consumer equilibrium*.
3. Show how the effects of a price change on quantity demanded can be separated into an *income effect* and a *substitution effect*.
4. Apply the concepts of income and substitution effects to the cases of normal and inferior goods.

Ideas for Review

Here are some terms and concepts that you should review before you read this chapter:

Real and nominal quantities (Chapter 1)
The law of demand (Chapter 3)
Normal and inferior goods (Chapter 3)

"Federal government mandates safety caps on aspirin bottles. Danger, children!"

Federal government mandates air bag or seat belt use on cars. Watch out bicyclists and pedestrians!

Federal government mandates safety caps on aspirin bottles. Danger children!

Do these warnings sound strange? Can air bags, seat belts, and safety caps really hurt people? Some economists think so. Economist Sam Peltzman started the controversy with a study that found that when people felt their cars to be safer, they reacted by driving faster and less carefully. The number of pedestrians and bicyclists they mowed down rose as much as the number of drivers and passengers that were killed fell. Other studies have challenged the finding that there was no net gain in safety from seat belts and air bags, but these studies too found that safer cars result in at least a little more danger to people on the street.

Other studies suggest similar effects of safety caps on aspirin bottles. A study by W. Kip Viscusi found that the safety-cap regulation did not reduce the rate of aspirin poisoning among children. In fact, safety-capped aspirin bottles account for a greater proportion of poisonings than of aspirin sales. The reason may be that the caps are so hard for even adults to use that they are left off the bottles.

Are these findings evidence of human stupidity? Of evil intent? Economists think not. They are just an outcome of the logic of consumer choice—a logic that government regulators do not always take into account.[1]

A chapter with a title like "The Logic of Consumer Choice" may conjure up an image of people filling their shopping carts in a supermarket. To be sure, the economic theory of consumer choice does apply to the supermarket. But its uses extend much further. In fact, it applies to any situation in which consumers are faced with the need to get the most satisfaction they can, given the prices and opportunity costs that they face and the limited budgets they have at their disposal. The examples of seat belts and aspirin bottle caps suggest one direction in which the theory of consumer choice can be extended, namely, to choices involving goods that are not bought in a store. In the following chapters we will see other directions as well. For example, although households are buyers in many markets, they are sellers in some markets, especially labor markets. Chapter 30 will show how the logic that underlies consumer buying applies to the choices people make in job markets. In other chapters consumers will play starring roles in the discussion of price discrimination, antitrust law, farm policy, the economics of poverty, the theory of international trade, and so on. But before we can deal with all of these topics, we need to understand the basics of consumer choice. That is the job of this chapter.

---

[1]See Sam Peltzman, "The Effects of Automobile Safety Regulation," *Journal of Political Economy* 83, August 1975, pp. 677–725; Robert W. Crandall and John D. Graham, "Automobile Safety Regulation and Offsetting Behavior: Some New Empirical Estimates," *American Economic Review* 74, May 1984, pp. 328–331; and W. Kip Viscusi, "The Lulling Effect: The Impact of Child-Resistant Packaging on Aspirin and Analgesic Ingestions," *American Economic Review* 74, May 1984, pp. 324–327.

CONSUMPTION AND UTILITY

Utility
The pleasure, satisfaction, or need fulfillment that people get from the consumption of goods and services.

Marginal utility
The amount of added utility gained from a one-unit increase in consumption of a good, with the quantities of other goods consumed remaining constant.

Principle of diminishing marginal utility
The principle that the greater the rate of consumption of some good, the smaller the increase in utility from a one-unit increase in consumption of that good.

When it comes to consumer choice, the most basic question we can ask is why people consume goods and services at all. The answer seems to be that they get pleasure and satisfaction from doing so. A loaf of bread to eat, a warm bed to sleep in, or a book to read—each serves some need or desire. Economists have their own term for this sort of thing. They say that the use or consumption of goods and services gives people **utility**.

The relative utilities of various goods—that is, the intensity of people's wants for some goods relative to the intensity of their wants for others—determines how much of those goods they will demand in the marketplace. The concept of utility thus is linked to the law of demand.

Diminishing marginal utility   In the late nineteenth century economists took a major step forward in their understanding of the relationship between utility and economic behavior when they came up with the principle of diminishing marginal utility. (See Box 20.1.) The **marginal utility** of a good to a consumer is the amount of added utility the consumer gains from the consumption of one additional unit of the good, assuming that constant quantities of other goods are consumed. The **principle of diminishing marginal utility** says that the greater the quantity of any good consumed, the less the marginal utility from a further increase in consumption.

For a simple but vivid example of this principle, imagine yourself in a blackberry patch, eating berries by the handful. As you eat more and more berries, you get more and more satisfaction; but at the same time, the satisfaction from each additional handful is less. If you eat enough, you may even get to a point where more berries give you no additional utility at all. Then you stop eating berries, at least until the next day.

Utility, to be sure, is a subjective concept. No one has yet invented a "utility meter" that can be hooked up to a person to read utility the way blood pressure is read. But suppose that there were such a meter. If you allowed yourself to be hooked up to it during your spree in the blackberry patch, the results could be recorded as shown in Box 20.2, using the "util" as an imaginary unit for measuring utility.

Both the table and the graphs show that as the quantity of berries consumed per day increases, total utility increases—but at a decreasing rate. Marginal utility—the added utility gained from each additional handful of berries—falls as the rate of consumption rises. For example, the third handful of berries increases utility by two units, from 5.5 to 7.5, whereas the fourth handful gives only 1.5 units more.

The consumer as economizer   For better or worse, the world is not one big blackberry patch where people can eat as much as they want without making choices. To put the principle of diminishing marginal utility to work, one must look at a world more like the one that really exists. This is a world in which

1. There are many different desirable goods.
2. Consumers must pay for the goods they want.
3. Consumers have limited budgets.

Box 20.1
William Stanley Jevons and Marginal Utility Theory

William Stanley Jevons
(1835–1882)

The English economist William Stanley Jevons is credited with the first systematic statement of the theory of marginal utility. Jevons was trained in mathematics and chemistry. With this background, it is not surprising that when his interest turned to economics he tried to restate economic theories in mathematical terms. It was this effort that led him to the theory of marginal utility.

In his *Theory of Political Economy*, published in 1871, Jevons set forth the principle of diminishing marginal utility in these words:

Let us imagine the whole quantity of food which a person consumes on an average during twenty-four hours to be divided into ten equal parts. If his food be reduced by the last part, he will suffer but little; if a second tenth part be deficient, he will feel the want distinctly; the subtraction of the third part will be decidedly injurious; with every subsequent subtraction of a tenth part his sufferings will be more and more serious until at length he will be upon the verge of starvation. Now, if we call each of the tenth parts an increment, the meaning of these facts is, that each increment of food is less necessary, or possesses less utility, than the previous one.

Jevons was the first economist to put the new theory into print, but he shares credit for the "marginal revolution" with at least three others who were working along the same lines at the same time. The Austrian economist Karl Menger published his version of marginal utility theory in 1871 also. Three years later the Swiss economist Leon Walras, who did not know of either Jevons' or Menger's work, came out with still another version. Finally, Alfred Marshall worked out the basics of marginal utility theory at about the same time in his lectures at Cambridge, although he did not publish them until 1890.

In such a world, consumers who want to get the greatest satisfaction, given their limited budgets, have to economize—they have to make choices, each of which involves an opportunity cost. If people spend more on one good, they have less to spend on something else. What can be said about how consumers economize?

Solving the consumer problem   Begin with the consumer you know best—yourself. Suppose you are deciding how to divide your monthly spending between, say, food and clothing. If you spend an extra dollar a month on food, you get some added utility from doing so. At the same time, though, you must bear an opportunity cost equal to the utility you would have gotten by spending the dollar on clothing instead of food. Whether or not you really think in such terms, then, your choice will depend on which utility is greater—that of the extra dollar's worth of food or that of the extra dollar's worth of clothing.

Which is greater depends, in turn, on how much of each good you consume. If you have a lot of clothing and not much food, the marginal utility of clothing will tend to be low and that of food will tend to be high. By shifting a dollar from clothing to food, you can give up a small utility and gain a large one. Doing so will increase your total utility.

**Box 20.2
Diminishing Marginal
Utility**

As the rate at which a person consumes a good increases, the utility gained from one additional unit decreases. The table and graphs in this box show that as the rate of consumption of berries increases, total utility also increases—but at a decreasing rate.

(a)

Quantity of Berries (handfuls per day)	Total Utility (utils)	Marginal Utility (utils per handful)
0	0	
1	3.0	3.0
2	5.5	2.5
3	7.5	2.0
4	9.0	1.5
5	10.0	1.0
6	10.5	0.5

(b)

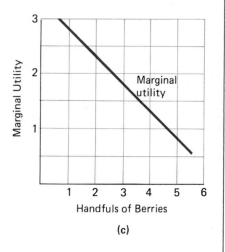

(c)

If, instead, you have a lot of food and not much clothing, the marginal utilities may be reversed. You will gain a lot of utility from spending an extra dollar on clothing and only a little from spending an extra dollar on food. Again, you can increase total utility by shifting your pattern of expenditure without an increase in total spending.

Consumer equilibrium   It is clear, then, that if the marginal utility of a dollar's worth of clothing is different from that of a dollar's worth of food, you can increase your satisfaction by changing your pattern of consumption. The only situation in which you cannot make yourself better off by changing your pattern of spending on food and clothing will be that in which the marginal utility per dollar's worth of the two goods is exactly the same.

Generalizing from this example, we can say that consumers tend to shift their spending from one kind of good to another as long as they can increase their satisfaction by doing so. When spending is divided in such a way that for each consumer the marginal utility of a dollar's worth of each good consumed is equal to the marginal utility of a dollar's worth of each other good consumed, no further increase in utility is possible within the given budget. A state of **consumer equilibrium** is said to prevail.

Consumer equilibrium
A state of affairs in which a consumer cannot increase the total utility gained from a given budget by spending less on one good and more on another.

An alternative   There is another way to state the conditions for consumer equilibrium. Suppose that a person is consuming just the right quantities of chicken and beef to make the marginal utility of a dollar's worth of chicken equal to that of a dollar's worth of beef. It must be true, then, that the marginal utility of a pound of chicken divided by the price of chicken per pound is equal to the marginal utility per pound of beef divided by the price of beef per pound. In equation form, this comes out as:

$$\frac{\text{Marginal utility of chicken per pound}}{\text{Price of chicken per pound}} = \frac{\text{marginal utility of beef per pound}}{\text{price of beef per pound}}$$

Assume that chicken costs $1 per pound and beef $3. If the equation holds, an extra pound of beef will give the consumer three times as much utility as an extra pound of chicken. As in the earlier statement of the conditions for consumer equilibrium, this means that the marginal utility of a dollar's worth (one pound) of chicken is equal to the marginal utility of a dollar's worth (one third of a pound) of beef.

The equation can be extended to a world with any number of goods and services. MU_A, MU_B, and so on stand for the marginal utilities of goods A, B, and so on. Likewise, P_A, P_B, and so on stand for the prices of those goods. The general equation for consumer equilibrium then becomes:

$$\frac{MU_A}{P_A} = \frac{MU_B}{P_B} = \frac{MU_C}{P_C} = \cdots$$

From consumer equilibrium to the law of demand   The concepts of consumer equilibrium and diminishing marginal utility can be combined to give an explanation of the law of demand that is useful even though it is not entirely precise. The explanation goes like this: Suppose that you have adjusted your pattern of consumption until you have reached an equilibrium in which, among other things,

$$\frac{\text{MU of chicken}}{\$1} = \frac{\text{MU of beef}}{\$3}$$

As long as this equality holds, it will not benefit you to increase your consumption of beef; doing so would, according to the principle of diminishing marginal utility, soon push down the marginal utility of beef. The marginal utility per dollar's worth of beef would drop below the marginal utility per dollar's worth of chicken, and you would be better off if you switched back toward more chicken.

But what if the price of beef were to drop to, say, $2.50 per pound, upsetting the equality just given? To make the two ratios equal again, given the new price of beef, either the marginal utility of chicken would have to rise or the marginal utility of beef would have to fall. According to the principle of diminishing marginal utility, one way to get the marginal utility of beef to fall is to consume more beef, and one way to get the marginal utility of chicken to rise is to consume less chicken. Because chicken and beef are substitutes, you would probably do a little of both—that is, cut back a little on chicken and consume a little more beef. In doing so, you would be acting just as the law of demand predicts: A fall in the price of beef would have caused you to buy more beef.

SUBSTITUTION AND INCOME EFFECTS AND THE LAW OF DEMAND

We have linked diminishing marginal utility to the law of demand in an intuitively appealing way, but this approach does not suit all economists. Is there a way to make the connection without relying on the slippery, unmeasurable concept of utility? There is. An alternative approach is to break down the effects of a price change into two components, known as the substitution and income effects.

The Substitution Effect

We can use the same example as before. Let's return to the point where you had reached an equilibrium, given a price of $3 per pound for beef and a price of $1 per pound for chicken. As before, suppose that the price of beef drops to $2.50 per pound. At that price you will tend to substitute beef for chicken. You may substitute beef for other things, too. Since a steak dinner is cheaper than before, you may substitute an evening in a restaurant for an evening at the movies. This effect of a change in price is known as the substitution effect. The **substitution effect** of the change in the price of a good is the part of the change in the quantity demanded that is due to the tendency of consumers to substitute relatively cheap goods for relatively costly ones.

Substitution effect
The part of the increase in quantity demanded of a good whose price has fallen that is caused by substitution of the good that is now relatively cheaper for others that are now relatively more costly.

The Income Effect

The substitution effect is not the only reason that a drop in the price of beef is likely to increase your consumption of beef. Suppose that when the price of beef is $3 a pound you buy ten pounds per month. You will welcome the decline in price to $2.50 a pound not just because it will allow you to substitute beef for chicken but for another reason as well: It will increase the purchasing power of your budget. With beef at $2.50 a pound, you can buy the same quantities of all goods, including beef, and have $5 left over at the end of the month to spend any way you like. In short, a fall in the price of any good, other things being equal, results in an increase in real income.

With your increased real income, you will tend to buy more of all normal goods and less of all inferior goods. For most people, beef is a normal good. Some of your newfound $5 in real income, then, will probably go to the purchase of more beef. This effect of the change in the price of beef is known as the income effect. In general terms, the **income effect** of a change in the price of a good is the part of the change in quantity demanded that is due to the change in real income resulting from the change in price.

Income effect
The part of the change in quantity demanded of a good whose price has fallen that is caused by the increase in real income that results from the price change.

Substitution and Income Effects and the Law of Demand

The concepts of substitution and income effects can help us understand the law of demand itself and why the law of demand might, in rare cases, have exceptions. Let us consider the cases of normal and inferior goods.

For a normal good, the law of demand must hold. This is so because the substitution and income effects work together to cause an increase in quantity demanded when the price of a good falls. The example just given illustrates this. When the price of beef drops, you buy more beef partly because you substitute beef for chicken and other goods. Also, you buy still more beef because you spend part of your higher real income on beef—a normal good. Taking the two effects together, there is no doubt that a drop in the price of beef increases the quantity of beef you demand.

In the case of an inferior good, things are not as simple. Suppose that we focus on a change in the price of hamburger, with the prices of other cuts of beef held constant. Suppose also that you view hamburger as an inferior good—one that you tend to phase out of your diet as your real income rises.

As before, a drop in the price of hamburger will tend to make you substitute hamburger for other foods. By itself, this will increase the quantity demanded. However, a drop in the price of hamburger will also result in a slight increase in your real income; and that, taken by itself, will tend to make you buy less hamburger. For an inferior good, then, the substitution and income effects operate in opposite directions.

It follows that the law of demand holds for an inferior good only if the substitution effect is greater than the income effect. In practice, this is always the case. No one has ever reported a convincing real-world case in which a rise in the price of a good, other things being equal, caused people to buy more of it, or in which a drop in price, other things being equal, caused people to buy less.

Applications of the Income and Substitution Effects

The law of demand and the concepts of income and substitution effects can be applied to many situations besides the ones we have discussed so far. They apply, in fact, to every situation of consumer choice. This is true even when the choices are not between goods for sale in a store, and even when the opportunity costs of the choices are not stated in terms of money.

Substitution and safety   The studies of safety regulations cited at the beginning of this chapter illustrate this point. First take the case of automobile safety equipment. When you get in a car to go somewhere, you face a trade-off between travel time and safety. A quick trip is good, but a safe one is good too. Making the trip safer by driving more slowly, stopping for yellow lights, and so on has an opportunity cost in terms of time. Cutting travel time by driving faster and going through yellow lights has an opportunity cost in terms of safety.

If the opportunity costs change, the choices drivers make also tend to change. For example, suppose that there is snow on the road. That makes the road less safe and raises the opportunity cost of speed. When it snows, then, drivers shift their choices away from speed and toward safety, just as the substitution effect would predict.

A change in the design of cars to make them safer also changes the opportunity cost of speed relative to that of safety. Cutting travel time by speeding up and running yellow lights entails giving up less safety in a car with airbags than in one without them. Logically, the substitution effect would cause people to drive faster and less carefully in safer cars. A side effect of this choice would be more deaths of pedestrians and bicyclists. This is the result found by the studies cited earlier. The studies disagree on the size of the effect, but not on its direction.

Some of the studies have found an income effect on driving behavior as well as a substitution effect. The studies by Graham and Crandall indicate that safety is an inferior good. It seems that as people's incomes go up, they begin to feel that their time is too valuable to be spent in a car. They speed up so they can get to their high-paying jobs or fancy parties faster. If they decide to run a greater risk of killing themselves and others along the way—well, that's part of the logic of consumer choice.

The aspirin bottle case can also be explained in terms of the logic of consumer choice. Putting the cap back on the aspirin bottle has a benefit: It decreases the chance that young children will poison themselves. If the cap is a safety cap, the benefit is greater still, since it is even less likely that a young child will open the bottle. However, putting the cap back on the bottle also has an opportunity cost: It will be less easy to grab an aspirin the next time you have a headache. If the cap is a safety cap, the opportunity cost is greater, since safety caps are often hard even for adults to get off. Thus, fitting aspirin bottles with safety caps raises both the benefit in terms of safety and the cost in terms of convenience. If the increase in cost is greater than the increase in benefit, putting a safety cap on the bottle raises the opportunity cost of safety. Following the logic of the substitution effect, people shift their behavior away from safety and toward convenience. The result, Viscusi found, is that 73 percent of all aspirin poisonings involve bottles with safety caps, even though only half of all aspirin bottles sold have such caps. And half of all the poisonings involve bottles that were left open.

Are animals logical consumers, too?   Studies like the ones we have described can be interpreted as illustrations of income and substitution effects and the law of demand. There are problems with these interpretations, however. In the real world, it is never possible to observe how people's behavior changes, "other things being equal," because other things are changing too. Thus, studies of responses to changes in automobile safety have been clouded by changes in speed limits, the average age of drivers, the quality of roads, and other factors. And studies of aspirin bottle safety caps have been clouded by changes in total aspirin use, the marketing of new painkillers, and so on.

Because the real world is such a messy place, economists have often envied the controlled laboratory environments of their colleagues in the sciences. At least one set of economic researchers has actually done an experiment in a laboratory. Box 20.3 reports the results of an experiment on the consumer behavior of white rats. The rats, it seems, are subject to the substitution effect just as you and I are. Think about that the next time you are threading your way through the aisles in your local supermarket.

**Box 20.3
Testing Consumer
Demand Theory with
White Rats**

Two white male rats were placed in standard laboratory cages, with food and water freely available. At one end of each case were two levers that activated dipper cups. One dipper cup provided a measured quantity of root beer when its lever was depressed; the other provided a measured quantity of nonalcoholic Collins mix. Previous experimentation had shown that rats prefer these beverages to water.

Within this setup, each rat could be given a fixed "income" of so many pushes on the levers per day. The pushes could be distributed in any way between the two levers. Experimenters could also control the "price" of root beer and Collins mix by determining the number of pushes the rat had to "spend" to obtain one milliliter of liquid.

In an initial experimental run lasting two weeks, the rats were given an income of three hundred pushes per day, and both beverages were priced at twenty pushes per milliliter. Under these conditions, Rat 1 settled down to a pattern of drinking about eleven milliliters of root beer per day and about four milliliters of Collins mix. Rat 2 preferred a diet of almost all root beer, averaging less than one milliliter of Collins mix per day.

Next came the crucial test. By manipulating incomes and prices, could the rats be induced to shift their consumption patterns in the way economic theory predicts? To see if they could, the experimenters proceeded as follows. First, the price of root beer was doubled, and the price of Collins mix was cut in half. At the same time, each subject's total income of pushes was adjusted to make it possible for each to afford to continue the previous consumption pattern if it should be chosen. (This adjustment in total income was made in order to eliminate any possible income effect of the price change and to concentrate solely on the substitution effect.) Economic theory predicts that under the new conditions the rats would choose to consume more Collins mix and less root beer than before, even though they would have the opportunity not to change their behavior.

The rats' behavior exactly fitted these predictions. In two weeks of living under the new conditions, Rat 1 settled down to a new consumption pattern of about eight milliliters of root beer and seventeen milliliters of Collins mix per day. Rat 2, which had chosen root beer almost exclusively before, switched over to about nine milliliters of root beer and twenty-five milliliters of Collins mix.

Source: Adapted by permission from John H. Kagel and Raymond C. Battalio, "Experimental Studies of Consumer Demand Behavior," *Economic Inquiry* 8 (March 1975): 22–38, Journal of the Western Economic Association.

Looking Ahead

Food and clothing, speed and safety, root beer and Collins mix—these are just a sampling of the many choices that consumers make. As we move through the following chapters we will encounter many more examples. In Chapters 22–25 we will look at the way firms react when they face demand curves of various kinds, and a knowledge of the logic of consumer choice will give a better understanding of what lies behind the demand curves. In Chapter 25 we will discuss the effects of advertising on consumer choice. Chapters 30 and 31 will apply the theory of consumer choice to the decisions that people make as suppliers of labor. And the later chapters on poverty, pollution, and energy will provide still more applications of the theories set forth in this chapter.

Summary

1. *Utility* refers to the pleasure and satisfaction that people get from goods and services. The added utility obtained from a one-unit increase in consumption of a good or service is its *marginal utility*. The greater the rate of consumption of a good, the smaller the increase in utility from an additional unit consumed.

2. Typically, a consumer must choose among many goods, given a fixed budget. A consumer is said to be in equilibrium when the total utility obtained from a given budget cannot be increased by shifting spending from one good to another. In equilibrium, the marginal utility of a dollar's worth of one good must be equal to the marginal utility of a dollar's worth of any other good.

3. The change in quantity demanded that results from a change in the price of a good, other things being equal, can be separated into two parts. The part that comes from the tendency to substitute cheaper goods for more costly ones is the *substitution effect*. The part that comes from the increase in real income that results when the price of a good falls, other things being equal, is the *income effect*.

4. For a normal good, the substitution and income effects work in the same direction. The demand curves for normal goods therefore slope downward. For inferior goods, the income effect of a price change works in the opposite direction from the substitution effect. For inferior goods, therefore, the demand curve will slope downward only if the substitution effect outweighs the income effect. In practice, this is always the case.

Questions for Review

1. Explain the following terms and concepts:
   a. From the chapter:
      utility
      marginal utility
      principle of diminishing marginal
         utility
      consumer equilibrium
      substitution effect
      income effect
   b. From the appendix (optional):
      indifference set
      indifference curve
      marginal rate of substitution
      indifference map
      transitivity
      budget line

2. Do all goods give consumers utility? What form does the utility gained from a hamburger take? From a house? From a novel? Do you think these different kinds of utility have enough in common that we can speak of trade-offs between them?

3. Assume that soft drinks cost 50 cents a cup and popcorn costs 75 cents a box. Under what conditions would a consumer be in equilibrium in the consumption of soft drinks and popcorn, assuming that at least some of each good is bought?

4. Packaged chocolate chip cookies are a normal good. Flour for baking cookies is an inferior good. Explain how the quantity demanded of each of these goods is affected by an increase in its price, taking into account both the substitution and income effects.

5. What role do the income and substitution effects play in determining the slope of the demand curve for a normal good? For an inferior good?

Problems and Topics for Discussion

1. Is it true for all goods that more is always better than less, or are there some for which marginal utility could start out positive but then become negative?

2. Suppose that it would take eight rolls of wallpaper to decorate your kitchen. If someone gave you seven rolls of wallpaper, you would get only limited utility from them. An eighth roll, however, would bring great utility. Do you think this is a valid exception to the principle of diminishing marginal utility?

3. Martha Smith consumes two pounds of pork and five pounds of beef per month. She pays $1.50 a pound for the pork and $2 per pound for the beef. What can you say about the ratio of the marginal utility of pork to the marginal utility of beef, assuming that this pattern represents a state of consumer equilibrium for Smith? Is the ratio 3/4, 4/3, 5/2, 2/5, or none of these?

4. Imagine a very poor country in which people spend most of their income on food. They eat bread when they can afford it, but they cannot afford to eat bread very often. More than half of their diet is made up of cheaper, but less tasty, oatmeal. One year the price of oatmeal rises while the price of bread does not change, but oatmeal remains a bit cheaper than bread. Observing the local market after the price change, you notice that the quantity of oatmeal that people are buying has increased. Can you explain this in terms of the income and substitution effects? What is implied about the slope of the demand curve for oatmeal? Is this a valid exception to the law of demand?

5. **Case for Discussion**
   In 1983, more than 15 percent of the U.S. population was living in poverty, up from about 11 percent in 1973. Conservatives like David Stockman, director of the federal Office of Management and Budget, argue that these figures are misleading. The official figures, they note, include only cash income earned and cash benefits received. They fail to take into account the fact that poor people receive many "in-kind" benefits from the government, such as medical care, food stamps, and subsidized housing.

   Stockman suggests that these benefits should be counted at their market value. For example, suppose a family of four had $4,000 in earned income and $4,000 in cash benefits. Officially, it would be below the $10,178 poverty line for 1984. But suppose it also received enough food stamps to buy $1,500 worth of food; a rent reduction worth $1,000 a year; and medical coverage that would cost $1,000 if it were bought from a private firm. Stockman would say that such a family is just as well off as one that had $11,500 in earned income. It should be considered to be above the poverty line.

   Stockman's method, applied to the whole population, would reduce the official poverty rate to 9.6 percent for 1983. But the socialist Michael Harrington, in his book *The New American Poverty* (Holt, Rinehart and Winston, 1984), argues that the Stockman method is not valid. Although in-kind aid is a great help to the poor family, he says, it cannot be compared to cash income because it cannot always be used efficiently. The poor family might have more free medical coverage than it needs, but fewer food stamps. Yet it has no way to convert the unwanted medical coverage into more food.[2] Who is right? Comment on Stockman's and Harrington's reasoning in the light of what you have learned about the logic of consumer choice.

---

[2]Daniel Seligman, "Why Are People Poor?" *Fortune*, October 1, 1984, pp. 189–192.)

Suggestions for Further Reading

Blaug, Mark. *Economic Theory in Retrospect*, 3rd ed. Cambridge, England: Cambridge University Press, 1978.

> Chapter 8 discusses the origins of utility theory and the work of William Stanley Jevons. Chapter 9 discusses Alfred Marshall's refinements of utility theory and the modern restatement of the theory in terms of preference and indifference.

Nicholson, Walter. *Intermediate Microeconomics and Its Application*, 3rd ed. Hinsdale, Ill.: Dryden Press, 1983.

> Chapters 3 and 4 of this book (or the comparable chapters of any other intermediate microeconomics text) discuss the logic of consumer choice in detail.

Appendix to Chapter 20

Indifference Curves

This chapter has described two versions of the theory of consumer choice—one based on marginal utility, the other on income and substitution effects. This appendix gives a third version that uses what are known as indifference curves. Indifference curves are not featured in this book, but they are often used in intermediate- and advanced-level economic writing. Many students and instructors find it worthwhile to study them, even if briefly, as part of an introductory course. This appendix will serve their needs.

Constructing an Indifference Curve

Begin by supposing that I am an experimenter and you are my subject. I want to find out how you feel about consuming various quantities of meat and cheese. It would be convenient if I had a utility meter, but I do not. Therefore, to find out your attitudes toward the consumption of these goods I offer you a number of baskets (two at a time) containing varying amounts of meat and cheese.

As I offer each pair of baskets, I ask: Would you prefer the one on the left to the one on the right? The one on the right to the one on the left? Or are you indifferent between the two? In this way I hope to get a meaningful answer from you. I know I have a better chance of getting such an answer by this means than I would if I asked you how many utils you would get from each basket.

At some point in the experiment, I offer you a basket (A) that contains eight pounds of meat and three pounds of cheese, and another (B) that contains six pounds of meat and four pounds of cheese. I ask you the usual questions, and you answer that you are indifferent between the two baskets. The extra pound of cheese in basket B, you feel, just makes up for the fact that it has two pounds less meat than basket A. This gives me a useful bit of information: It tells me that, for you, basket A and basket B belong to an **indifference set**—a set of consumption choices each of which yields the same amount of satisfaction, so that no member of the set is preferred to any other. Exploring the matter further, I find that two other baskets (C and D) also belong to the same indifference set, which now has the following four members:

Indifference set
A set of consumption choices each of which yields the same utility, so that no member of the set is preferred to any other.

513

Basket	Meat (pounds)	Cheese (pounds)
A	8	3
B	6	4
C	5	5
D	4	7

I thank you for taking part in my experiment and get out a piece of graph paper. First I draw a pair of axes, as in Box 20A.1. Pounds of meat are measured on the horizontal axis and pounds of cheese on the vertical axis. Each basket of goods can be shown as a point in the area between the two axes. The points representing baskets A–D are shown in their proper places on the graph. These points and all the points between them that lie on the smooth curve joining them are members of the same indifference set. The curve itself is an **indifference curve**—a curve composed of points that are all members of the same indifference set.

Indifference curve
A graphic representation of an indifference set.

Some Traits of Indifference Curves

Indifference curves have traits that reflect certain regularities in patterns of consumer preferences. Five of these traits are of interest to us.

**Box 20A.1
An Indifference Curve**

Each point in this diagram stands for a basket of meat and cheese. A, B, C, and D are all baskets among which a certain consumer is indifferent. All give equal utility. Those points and all the others on a smooth curve connecting them form an indifference set. An indifference curve is a graphic representation of an indifference set.

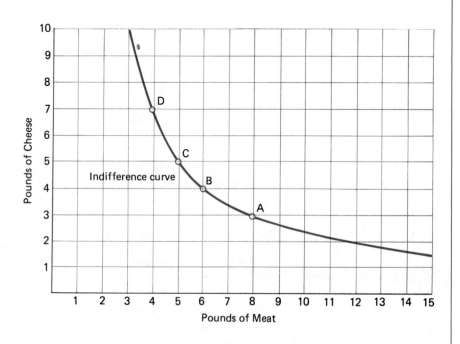

1. *Indifference curves normally have negative slopes.* For example, the curve in Box 20A.2 is not possible if both meat and cheese are desired goods—that is, if the consumer prefers more to less, other things being equal. The basket shown by point A contains more of both goods than the one shown by point B. This implies that if greater amounts of meat and cheese give greater satisfaction, A must be *preferred* to B. It cannot be a member of the same indifference set as B.

2. *The absolute value of the slope of an indifference curve at any point is the ratio of the marginal utility of the good on the horizontal axis to the marginal utility of the good on the vertical axis.* For an example, look at Box 20A.1. Between D and C, the slope of the curve is approximately –2 (or simply 2 when the minus sign is removed to give the absolute value). This shows that the marginal utility of meat is approximately twice the marginal utility of cheese—when the amounts consumed are in the region of baskets C and D. Because the marginal utility of meat is twice that of cheese in this region, the consumer will feel neither a gain nor a loss in total utility in trading basket D for basket C, that is, in giving up two pounds of cheese for one extra pound of meat. Because it shows the rate at which meat can be substituted for cheese without a gain or loss in satisfaction, the slope of the indifference curve is called the **marginal rate of substitution** of meat for cheese.

3. *Indifference curves are convex; their slope decreases as one moves downward*

Marginal rate of substitution
The rate at which one good can be substituted for another without any gain or loss in satisfaction.

Box 20A.2
Indifference Curves Slope Downward

Indifference curves normally have negative slopes. The upward-sloping portion of the indifference curve shown here is impossible if both goods give increased satisfaction with increased quantity. A has more of both goods than B. Therefore, point A should be preferred to point B, and hence it could not lie on the same indifference curve.

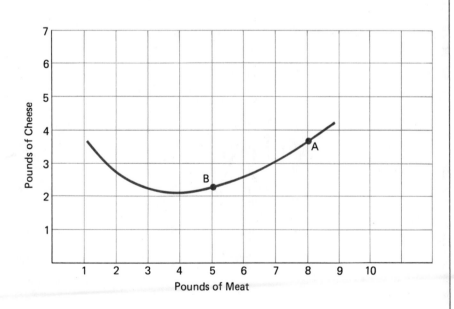

and to the right along them. This implies that the ratio of the marginal utility of meat to the marginal utility of cheese (also known as the marginal rate of substitution of meat for cheese) decreases as one moves downward and to the right along the curve. Look once more at Box 20A.1. In the region betwen D and C, the slope of the curve is approximately –2, showing that the ratio of the marginal utility of meat to that of cheese is approximately 2:1. By comparison, in the region between B and A the slope is only about –1/2. The ratio of the marginal utility of meat to the marginal utility of cheese is now approximately 1:2.

4. *An indifference curve can be drawn through the point that represents any basket of goods whatsoever.* Look at Box 20A.3. It shows the same indifference curve as in Box 20A.1, but the curve is labeled I_1. Point E, which represents a basket that contains seven pounds of meat and five pounds of cheese, is not a member of the indifference set represented by this curve. Because it lies above and to the right of point B and has more of both products than B, it must be preferred to B. There are other points, such as F and G, that have more cheese and less meat than E and, on balance, give the same satisfaction as E. The consumer is indifferent among E, F, G, and all other points on the curve I_2, and prefers all of these points to any of the points on I_1.

Box 20A.3
Multiple Indifference Curves

An indifference curve can be drawn through any point. Here the curve I_1 represents an indifference set that contains points A, B, C, and D, while I_2 represents a set that contains points E, F, and G. All points on I_2 are preferred to all points on I_1. A representative set of indifference curves like the one shown here can be called an indifference map.

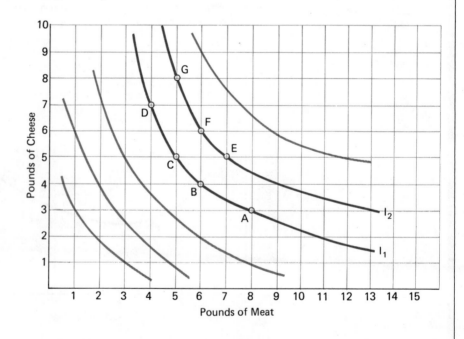

Any point taken at random, along with the other points that happen to give the same amount of satisfaction, can form an indifference curve. Several other curves, unlabeled, are sketched in Box 20A.3. If all possible curves were drawn in, they would be so close together that the ink of the lines would run into a solid sheet that completely filled the space between the axes. A selection of indifference curves, showing their general pattern but leaving enough space to make the graph easy to read, is called an **indifference map**.

Indifference map

A selection of indifference curves for a single consumer and pair of goods.

Transitivity

The principle that if A is preferred to B and B is preferred to C, then A must be preferred to C.

5. *Indifference curves do not cross.* Consumer preferences are **transitive**. This means that if you prefer A to B and B to C, you will prefer A to C. Looking at Box 20A.4, you can see that crossed indifference curves are not possible. Consider points A, B, and C. A and B lie on the same indifference curve, I_1. Hence, the consumer is indifferent between them. A and C both lie on I_2. Hence, the consumer is indifferent between them also. Since consumer preferences are transitive, if B is as good as A and A is as good as C, C is as good as B. But C lies above and to the right of B. It represents a mix of goods that contains more of both meat and cheese. If more is better, the consumer must prefer C to B. Since crossed indifference curves imply a contradictory set of preferences, we conclude that they cannot cross.

**Box 20A.4
Indifference Curves
Cannot Cross**

Because consumer preferences are transitive, indifference curves cannot cross. The impossible curves shown here represent contradictory preferences. A and B are both on I_1, so the consumer must be indifferent between them. A and C are both on I_2, so the consumer must be indifferent between them as well. Transitivity implies that the consumer is indifferent between B and C, but this is impossible because C contains more of both goods than B does.

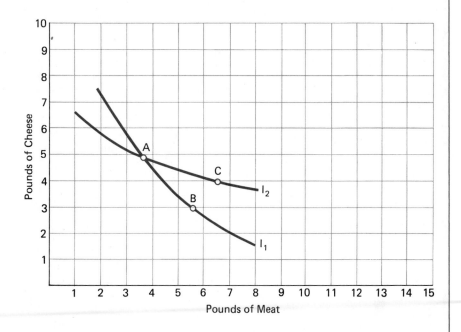

The Budget Line

The range of choices open to a consumer with a given budget and with given prices can be shown on the same kind of graph that has been used for indifference curves. Box 20A.5 shows how this can be done. Suppose that you have a food budget of $10 per week, that the price of meat is $2 a pound, and that the price of cheese is $1 a pound. If you spend all your money on meat, you can have up to five pounds of meat. If you spend all your money on cheese, you can have up to ten pounds of cheese. Combinations such as two pounds of meat and six of cheese or four pounds of meat and two of cheese are also possible. Taking into account the possibility of buying a fraction of a pound of meat or cheese, these choices can be shown on the graph as a diagonal line running from 10 on the cheese axis to 5 on the meat axis. This line is called the **budget line**.

Using m to stand for amount of meat and c to stand for amount of cheese, the equation for the budget line can be written as $2m + 1c = 10$. This equation simply says that the number of pounds of meat bought times the price of meat plus the number of pounds of cheese bought times the price of cheese must add up to the total budget if no money is left unspent. In more general terms, the equation for a budget line for goods x and y—with P_x the price of x, P_y the price of y, and B the consumer's total budget—is $P_x x + P_y y = B$. The slope of such a budget line is $-P_x/P_y$. In the case shown in Box 20A.5, where the price of meat is $2 a pound and the price of cheese is $1 a pound, the slope of the budget line is –2.

Budget line
A line showing the various combinations of goods and services that can be purchased at given prices within a given budget.

**Box 20A.5
The Budget Line**

Suppose that you have a food budget of $10 per week. You can spend your money on meat at $2 a pound, on cheese at $1 a pound, or on some mix of the two goods. The consumption opportunity line (budget line) shows all the possible combinations, given these prices and your budget.

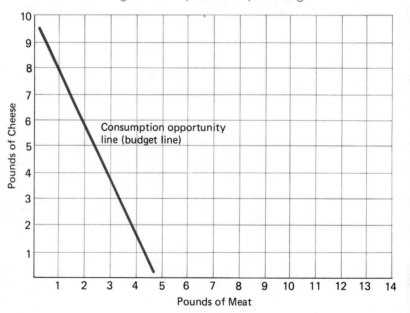

Consumption opportunity line (budget line)

Pounds of Cheese

Pounds of Meat

A Graphic Representation of Consumer Equilibrium

Indifference curves and the budget line can be used to give a graphic representation of consumer equilibrium. Box 20A.6 shows the budget line from Box 20A.5 superimposed on an indifference map like the one shown in Box 20A.3. In this way consumer preferences and consumption choices can be compared easily. For example, point B is preferred to point A because it lies on a "higher" indifference curve (one that at some point, like C, passes above and to the right of A). By similar reasoning, point B is preferred to point D. Of all the points on or below the budget line, it is clear that point E, which represents 2.5 pounds of meat and 5 pounds of cheese, is the most preferred, since all the other points on the budget line lie on lower indifference curves. Every point that, like F, is better lies outside the range of consumption choices.

Because E is the point that gives the greatest possible satisfaction, it is the point of consumer equilibrium. At E the relevant indifference curve is just tangent to the budget line; this means that the slope of the curve and the budget line are the same at this point. The slope of the indifference curve, as shown earlier, is equal to the ratio of the marginal utility of meat to the marginal utility of cheese. The slope of the budget line is equal to the ratio of the price of meat to the price of cheese. It follows that in consumer equilibrium,

$$\frac{\text{Marginal utility of meat}}{\text{Marginal utility of cheese}} = \frac{\text{price of meat}}{\text{price of cheese}}$$

**Box 20A.6
Consumer Equilibrium**

E is the point of consumer equilibrium, given the indifference curves and budget line shown. All points that are better than E (such as F) lie outside the budget line. All other points for goods that the consumer can afford to buy (such as A and D) lie on lower indifference curves than E and thus are preferred.

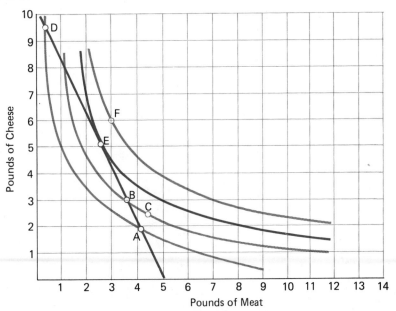

This is the condition for consumer equilibrium given in Chapter 20.

Derivation of the Demand Curve

This appendix concludes with Box 20A.7, which shows how a demand curve for meat can be derived from a set of indifference curves. Along with the curves, Box 20A.7 shows a set of budget lines. Each line is based on the assumption that the price of cheese is $1 a pound and that the consumer's budget is $10, as before. Now, though, each budget line assumes a different price, P, of meat. The budget line running from 10 on the vertical axis to 2.5 on the horizontal axis assumes that $P = \$4$. The budget line running from 10 on the vertical axis to 5 on the horizontal axis assumes that $P = \$2$. (This is the same budget line as the one in Boxes 20A.5 and 20A.6.) The other two budget lines assume that $P = \$1.50$ and $P = \$1$, respectively.

The equilibrium pattern of consumption will be different for each price of meat, other things being equal. When $P = \$4$, point A, which represents six pounds of cheese and one pound of meat, is the best the consumer can do; when $P = \$2$, B is the most preferred point.

Given this information, it is a simple matter to draw the consumer's demand curve for meat. Part b of Box 20A.7 shows a new set of axes, with the quantity of meat on the horizontal axis as before, but with the price of meat now on the vertical axis. From part a of Box 20A.7, when $P = \$4$ the consumer chooses combination A, which includes one pound of meat. In part b, therefore, point a is marked as the quantity of meat demanded at a price of $4. Then point b (which corresponds to point B in part a) is added, and so on. Drawing a smooth line through points a, b, c, and d gives the consumer's demand curve for meat. As expected, it has the downward slope predicted by the law of demand.

**Box 20A·7
Derivation of a
Demand Curve**

Part a of this box shows a consumer's indifference map for meat and cheese and a set of budget lines. Each budget line corresponds to a different price, *P*, of meat, as shown. All four budget lines assume the price of cheese to be $1 and the total budget to be $10. Points A, B, C, and D in part a show the choices the consumer makes at meat prices of $4, $2, $1.50, and $1. In part b the data on consumption of meat at the various prices is plotted on a new set of axes. The smooth line connecting points a, b, c, and d is the consumer's demand curve for meat.

(a)

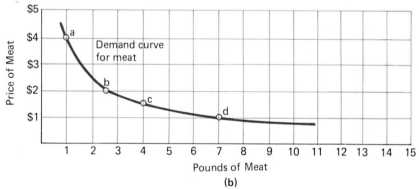

(b)

Chapter 21

The Theory of Cost

WHAT YOU WILL
LEARN IN THIS
CHAPTER

After reading this chapter, you should be able to

1. Distinguish between *implicit* and *explicit* costs, and between *pure economic profit* and *accounting profit*.
2. Explain the concepts of *short run* and *long run* in terms of *fixed* and *variable inputs*.
3. Show how output increases as the amount of a variable input is increased for a typical production process.
4. State and illustrate the *law of diminishing returns*.
5. Construct a family of short-run cost curves for a typical firm, given data on the firm's fixed and variable costs.
6. Explain how average costs vary in the long run as output varies for a typical firm.
7. Discuss the concept of *economies of scale* in terms of long-run cost curves.

Ideas for Review

Here are some terms and concepts that you should review before you read this chapter:

Opportunity cost (Chapter 2)
Entrepreneurship (Chapter 2)
The nature of the firm (Chapter 4)

Andrea and Ralph Martin shared a dream with millions of Americans: having a business of their own. For some, that dream means a hamburger franchise, a dry cleaning shop, or a couple of hundred acres of soybeans. The Martins were more ambitious: they dreamed of having their own computer company.

The Martins had no illusions about the life of the entrepreneur. They knew that starting their own firm would take hard work and sacrifice. Both were engineers with high-paying jobs at large corporations. On their combined income of $80,000 a year, they could have lived the good life—a house in the suburbs, a Mercedes in the driveway, and a condominium in the Virgin Islands. Instead, they lived in a small apartment and saved every dollar they could to build a nest egg with which to start their firm.

The Martins knew they couldn't take on IBM in hand-to-hand combat. They needed to find a small corner of the computer market where they could start small and offer customers something new. Ralph's job with an oil company gave him an idea. On his visits to refineries and drilling sites, he often carried a notebook-sized computer with which to record data and make on-the-spot computations. But all the small computers available were designed for use in offices. Out in the heat and dust of the field, they often broke down. Ralph was sure there would be a market for a more ruggedly built computer for use under field conditions. Andrea was sure she could design one.

The design for the new machine took shape on paper. The company, Fieldcom Inc., took shape on paper too. Then one day it was time to take the plunge. The Martins quit their jobs, hired two technicians and an office manager, and went into production. Their factory was an abandoned service station available at a rock-bottom price. Within a month the first of their new products, the Fieldcom I, rolled off the assembly line.

In this chapter and the next one, we will use Fieldcom Inc. as a case study around which to build a theory of supply in competitive markets. Along with the theory of consumer choice that underlies the demand curve, this theory will give us a better understanding of the factors that affect equilibrium prices and quantities in a market economy. The first step, which we will take in this chapter, will be to develop a theory of cost. In the next chapter we will show how costs interact with demand conditions to determine the amount of output that the firm supplies.

THE NATURE OF COSTS

One of the most basic ideas in economics is that all costs arise from the need to choose among possible uses of scarce resources. All costs, in other words, are opportunity costs. The true measure of the cost of doing something is the value of the best alternative use of the same resources.

Implicit and Explicit Costs

The opportunity costs that a firm like Fieldcom faces include the payments it must make to suppliers of parts, materials, and services, plus the incomes

Explicit costs
Opportunity costs that take the form of payments to outside suppliers, workers, and others who do not share in the ownership of the firm.

Implicit costs
Opportunity costs of using resources owned by the firm or contributed by its owners.

it must provide to workers, investors, and owners of resources in order to attract factors of production away from alternative uses. These costs are of two kinds—explicit and implicit.

Explicit costs are opportunity costs that take the form of payments to outside suppliers, workers, and others who do not share in the ownership of the firm. These include payments for the labor and raw materials used in production, the services of hired managers and salespeople, insurance, legal advice, transportation, and a great many other things.

Implicit costs are the opportunity costs of using resources owned by the firm or contributed by its owners. Like explicit costs, they represent real sacrifices by the firm. Unlike explicit costs, however, they do not take the form of explicit payments to outsiders. When a firm uses a building that it owns, it doesn't have to make a payment to anyone, but it gives up the opportunity to receive payments from someone else to whom it could rent the building. To take another example, if the proprietor of a small firm works along with the firm's hired employees, he or she gives up the opportunity to earn a salary by working for someone else. Firms do not normally record implicit costs in their accounts, but that does not make them any less real.

Costs and Profits

Pure economic profit
The sum that is left when both explicit and implicit costs are subtracted from total revenue.

Accounting profit
Total revenue minus explicit costs.

The distinction between explicit and implicit costs is important for understanding the concept of profit. As economists use the term, profit means the difference between a firm's total revenues and its total costs, including both explicit and implicit costs. This concept is often called **pure economic profit**. In this book the term *profit* always means pure economic profit.

Special care must be taken to keep the economic concept of profit in mind because the language of business and accounting uses the term in a quite different sense. There, profit means revenue minus explicit costs only. Economists call this concept **accounting profit** to distinguish it from the pure economic profit just defined. Putting the two definitions together gives us the following relationship:

$$\text{Pure economic profit} = \text{accounting profit} - \text{implicit costs.}$$

An example   Box 21.1 uses Fieldcom Inc. to illustrate the difference between pure economic profit and accounting profit. The box shows Fieldcom earning total revenues of $500,000 in all of 1984. Explicit costs—materials purchased and salaries paid to employees—come to $350,000. This leaves an accounting profit of $150,000.

These explicit costs do not include all of the firm's opportunity costs, however. Both Andrea and Ralph Martin gave up high-paying jobs to start the firm. Their combined former income of $80,000 is listed in Box 21.1 as an implicit cost of production. Also listed as an implicit cost is $20,000 of interest income foregone. This is the amount of interest the Martins could have earned on their savings if they had left them in a high-yield bank account rather than investing them in Fieldcom's plant and equipment.

When both implicit and explicit costs are subtracted from revenue, the firm is left with a pure economic profit of $50,000. This sum is profit, not

Box 21.1
Accounts of Fieldcom,
Inc.

Total revenue	$500,000
Less explicit costs	
Wages and salaries	300,000
Materials and other	50,000
Equals accounting profit	$150,000
Less implicit costs	
Foregone salary, Andrea Martin	40,000
Foregone salary, Ralph Martin	40,000
Interest foregone on invested savings	20,000
Equals pure economic profit	$ 50,000

cost, because it is what the Martins earned from their new company over and above the $100,000 needed to attract their labor and capital away from the best alternative uses. It is their reward for acting as entrepreneurs—that is, for recognizing and entering a profitable niche in the computer market that no other entrepreneur had yet entered.

PRODUCTION AND COSTS IN THE SHORT RUN

Having pinned down the economic meaning of cost, our next step is to build a theory of cost. The job of this theory is to explain how costs vary as the amount of output produced by a firm varies and, in doing so, to provide a basis for the firm's supply curve. Our discussion of the theory of cost will be divided into two parts, corresponding to two time ranges—the short run and the long run. We will explain this distinction before presenting the theory of cost itself.

The Long Run and the Short Run

A firm uses many kinds of inputs to produce its output. The amounts of inputs it uses vary as the amount of output varies. The amount of some inputs used can be adjusted quickly, but others are not as easy to adjust.

The inputs that cannot be adjusted quickly as the level of output changes can be thought of as those that define the size of the firm's plant. The physical size of structures and the production capacity of machinery are examples. These are known as **fixed inputs**. In some cases the services of employees—those who cannot be replaced easily—can also be viewed as fixed inputs.

In addition to fixed inputs, the firm uses **variable inputs** that can be adjusted quickly and easily within a plant of a given size as output changes.

Fixed inputs
Inputs that cannot easily be increased or decreased in a short time.

Variable inputs
Inputs that can easily be varied within a short time in order to increase or decrease output.

Short run

A time range within which output can be adjusted only by changing the amounts of variable inputs used while fixed inputs remain unchanged.

Long run

A time range that is long enough to permit changes in all inputs, both fixed and variable.

Raw materials, energy, and hourly labor are variable inputs for most firms. It should be kept in mind that which inputs are fixed and which are variable depends on the situation. As Box 21.2 shows, inputs that are variable for some firms may be fixed for others.

The distinction between fixed and variable inputs is the basis for the distinction between the short run and the long run in cost theory. The **short run** is a time range that is too short to change the size of a firm's plant, so variations in output can come only from changes in the amounts of variable inputs used. The **long run**, in contrast, is a time range that is long enough to permit changes in the amounts of fixed inputs and the size of the firm's plant.

Production with One Variable Input

Most firms have many inputs that can be varied. A change in any one of them will have some effect on output, other things being equal. Let's turn once again to Fieldcom for an example.

One of the many variable inputs that Fieldcom uses in making small computers is fuel oil. The oil is used to heat the building in which the Martins have set up shop. Box 21.3 shows what happens to the rate of production on a cold winter day as the rate of fuel consumption is varied over the range of zero to ten gallons per day.

If no fuel is burned, no production can take place. The plant will be so cold that the technicians will refuse to come to work. Burning just one

---

Box 21.2
Labor Costs—Fixed or Variable?

Hourly labor is considered to be a variable cost of production. When demand for a firm's product declines, layoffs of hourly workers are often one of the first steps taken to adjust to a lower rate of output. However, some firms' contracts with their unions make hourly labor a fixed rather than a variable cost, at least in part.

The big steel firms' contract with the United Steel Workers are a case in point. This contract calls for pensions, health and life insurance, unemployment benefits, and severance pay when a plant is closed. The benefits can cost up to $70,000 for each employee.

If labor costs remain fixed even when a plant is closed, it may make sense to keep a plant running even though it is losing money. For example, in 1980 Kaiser Steel's directors voted to keep 11,000 workers on the job because shutting down would have cost the company more than $350 million in benefits.

In another case, the need to treat labor costs as fixed prompted a firm to adopt an unusual strategy to get rid of a money-losing operation. In 1981 National Steel decided that it could no longer afford to invest in its Weirton, West Virginia, steel division. Closing the plant would have cost the firm about $320 million in benefits for former employees. To escape this burden, National sold the Weirton operation to its 10,000 employees. They have kept the plant open and are hoping that wage cuts and increases in productivity will make it profitable again.

Source: Thomas F. O'Boyle, "High Cost of Liquidation Keeping Some Money-Losing Plants Open," *Wall Street Journal*, November 29, 1982, p. 29.

**Box 21.3
Response of Output to
Changes in One
Variable Input**

This chart and table show how the output of computers at Fieldcom Inc. responds to changes in one variable input, fuel oil. All other inputs remain constant while the amount of oil burned to heat the plant varies. If too little oil is burned, the building is too cold for employees to work. Output improves as the building approaches the preferred temperature. If more than seven gallons of oil per day are burned, people open the windows to keep the building from overheating, so there is no further gain in output. Column 3 of the table shows the amount of added output that results from each added gallon of oil used. This is known as the marginal physical product of the variable input.

Input (gallons of oil)	Output (units per day)	Marginal Physical Product (units)
0	0	0
1	0	1
2	1	2
3	3	4
4	7	3
5	10	2
6	12	1
7	13	0
8	13	0
9	13	0
10	13	

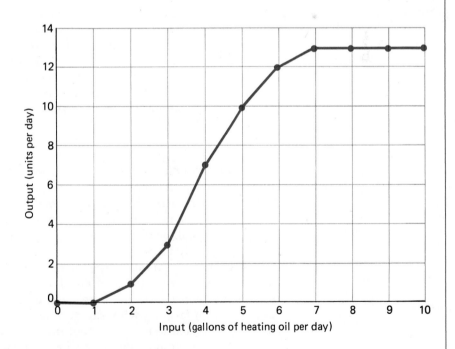

gallon of fuel won't help. When the rate of fuel consumption rises to two gallons per day, the workers will show up, but they will spend most of the day running next door for coffee and hot chocolate. Only one computer will be built. Increasing the fuel input to three and then four gallons per day has a dramatic impact on output. Even though people still have to wear sweaters, they can at least keep their minds on their jobs. The fifth and sixth gallons of fuel help still more. Fingers loosen up, sweaters come off, and morale rises. Burning a seventh gallon of oil each day raises the temperature in the work room to the point that the technicians find just right. At that point their output reaches 13 computers a day.

What happens if still more oil is burned? Nothing much. When the room starts to get hot, the workers open the windows. The extra fuel is wasted, but it does no harm either. Output remains at 13 computers a day. Of course, it could be raised further by varying *other* inputs—by giving the workers better equipment, stocking more parts, hiring more help, and so on. But for the moment we are looking at the effects on output of varying just one input, other things being equal.

Marginal physical product

The amount of output, expressed in physical units, produced by each added unit of one variable input, other things being equal.

Marginal physical product   The chart in Box 21.3 and columns 1 and 2 of the table show the relationship between rate of fuel use and rate of output. In the range of one to seven gallons, output increases as fuel input increases, but not at a constant rate. Column 3 of the table shows how much output is added by each additional gallon of fuel burned. This is called the **marginal physical product** of the variable input. As oil use is increased from one gallon per day to two gallons, the marginal physical product is one unit of output. As oil use is stepped up from two gallons per day to three, marginal physical product rises to two units; and so on. The step from three gallons to four gives the greatest boost to ouput. After that, output increases at a diminishing rate with each added gallon of fuel burned. Finally, after fuel consumption reaches seven gallons per day, the marginal physical product drops to zero.

Law of diminishing returns

The principle that as one variable input is increased, with all others remaining fixed, a point will be reached beyond which the marginal physical product of the variable input begins to decrease.

The law of diminishing returns   The example of fuel oil use at Fieldcom illustrates one of the most useful principles in all of economics, the **law of diminishing returns**. According to this principle, as the amount of one variable input is increased, with the amounts of all other inputs remaining fixed, a point will be reached beyond which the marginal physical product of the input will decrease.

The law of diminishing returns applies to all known production processes and to all variable inputs. It applies in manufacturing, as can be seen in the Fieldcom case. But the law could be illustrated just as well by an example from farming with, say, fertilizer as the variable input: As more fertilizer is added to a field, output increases, but beyond some point the gain in output brought about by an additional ton of fertilizer tapers off. (Too much fertilizer might even poison the plants, in which case marginal physical product would become negative.) Oil refineries, power plants, barbershops, government bureaus—in fact, any production process whatsoever could be used to illustrate the law of diminishing returns.

From Marginal Physical Product to Marginal Costs

Marginal cost
The increase in cost required to increase the output of some good or service by one unit.

Our next step is to move from the marginal physical product of an input to the **marginal cost** of output. Marginal cost means the increase in cost required to increase the output of a good or service by one unit. As before, we will use Fieldcom as an example.

Some conclusions about marginal cost can be drawn from the example of fuel oil consumption. Box 21.3 showed how output increased as oil consumption increased. Box 21.4 shows how the same data can be read in reverse to show the cost, in terms of oil, of making one more computer over various output ranges. Two gallons have to be burned before the first unit of output can be produced. The next gallon of oil adds two units to output—a marginal cost of one-half gallon per unit. Over the next range, adding a unit of output costs only a quarter of a gallon of oil.

Beyond four gallons of oil and seven units of output, the marginal physical product of oil begins to fall. At this same point, the marginal cost of added computers, measured in terms of oil, begins to rise. Over the output range of seven to ten computers a day, each added computer costs a third of a gallon of oil. From 10 to 12 computers, the marginal cost rises to a half gallon per unit of output. The thirteenth unit of output costs another whole gallon. The result is a marginal-cost curve that is roughly U-shaped.

More Than One Variable Input

It is time to drop the assumption that only one input can be varied at a time. In practice, short-run increases or decreases in Fieldcom's output would require changes in many inputs, although not in all of them. For example, if the firm wanted to raise its output from 13 to 26 units a day, it might burn more fuel to keep the shop heated longer each day, hire an extra technician, and double the rate at which it orders parts. At the same time, its costs for an office manager and the opportunity costs of plant and equipment would remain fixed.

The appendix to this chapter outlines a way of analyzing changes in two or more variable inputs. Without going into details, we can say that taking more variable inputs into account, and allowing them to be varied in smaller steps, tends to smooth out the steps in the crude cost curve shown in Box 21.4. Box 21.5 shows how total and marginal costs respond to changes in output when all variable inputs are taken into account. The result is a total-variable-cost curve with a smooth reverse-S shape and a smooth U-shaped marginal-cost curve.

A Set of Short-Run Cost Curves

The marginal-cost and total-variable-cost curves shown in Box 21.5 are only two of a set of short-run cost curves that can be constructed for

**Box 21.4
Marginal Cost and
Output with One
Variable Input**

This box shows how the cost of production at Fieldcom Inc. changes as output changes. The table and graph are based on the same data that were used for Box 21.3, but here they are recast to stress marginal cost—the added cost of making each added unit of output. The cost is stated in terms of gallons of oil per unit of added output. For example, increasing the amount of fuel oil burned from three to four gallons raises output from three computers per day to seven computers. Over this range, then, the cost of each added computer is one quarter of a gallon of oil. The graph shows a marginal-cost curve for the firm that is roughly U-shaped.

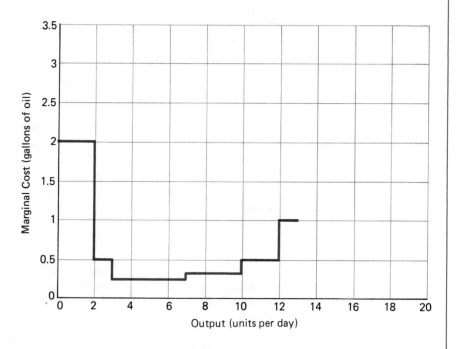

Output (computers per day)	Total Oil Used (gallons per day)	Marginal Cost (gallons of oil per added unit of output)
0	0	
1	2	2.0
3	3	0.5
7	4	0.25
10	5	0.33
12	6	0.5
13	7	1.0

**Box 21.5
Marginal-Cost and
Total-Variable-Cost
Curves**

This box shows the relationship between cost and output for Fieldcom Inc. under less restrictive assumptions than those used in Box 21.4. Now several inputs (labor, materials, and so on, as well as fuel oil) are allowed to vary, although some others (office staff, test equipment, rent) remain fixed. This added flexibility tends to smooth out the steps in the firm's marginal-cost curve, producing a smooth U. The corresponding total-variable-cost curve has a reverse-S shape. The slope of the total-variable-cost curve is equal to the height of the marginal-cost curve. The minimum point on the marginal-cost curve corresponds to the inflection point of the total-variable-cost curve, that is, the point at which it stops becoming flatter and begins to become steeper.

Fieldcom. The complete set is shown in Box 21.6. This box also contains some often-used formulas and abbreviations that pertain to cost curves.

Total variable cost, from Box 21.5, appears in column 2 of part c of Box 21.6. Not all costs are variable in the short run. Fixed costs (office manager, test equipment, and so on) are assumed to be $2,000 per day, as shown in column 3. Adding fixed cost to variable cost gives short-run total cost, which is shown in column 4.

The three total-cost curves—total variable, total fixed, and total cost—are shown graphically in part a of Box 21.6. Because fixed cost by definition does not vary as output varies, the total-fixed-cost curve is a horizontal line $2,000 above the horizontal axis. Adding fixed cost to variable cost gives total cost. The total-cost curve parallels the total-variable-cost curve at a higher level. The distance between the total-cost and total-variable-cost curves is equal to total fixed cost.

The next column in part c of Box 21.6 is marginal cost, again taken from Box 21.5. These data appear on lines between the total-cost entries in order to stress the fact that marginal cost shows how total cost changes as the level of output changes. The marginal-cost curve drawn in part b of Box 21.6 is the same as the one in Box 21.5.

The last three columns in part c of Box 21.6 are all average-cost concepts: average variable cost, average fixed cost, and average total cost. Average variable cost is equal to total variable cost divided by quantity of output; average fixed cost is equal to total fixed cost divided by output; and average total cost is equal to total cost divided by output. The three average-cost curves are also drawn in part b of Box 21.6.

Some Geometric Relationships

If we examine parts a and b of Box 21.6, we will find some important geometric relationships among the cost curves. First, compare the marginal-cost curve with the total-variable-cost curve drawn above it. The bottom of the U-shaped marginal-cost curve lies at exactly the level of output at which the slope of the reverse-S-shaped total-variable-cost curve stops getting flatter and starts getting steeper. This occurs because the slope of the total-variable-cost curve is the *rate* at which that curve is rising, just as marginal cost measures the *rate* at which total variable cost is rising. In graphic terms, then, the *height* of the marginal-cost-curve is always equal to the *slope* of the total-cost curve.

A second feature of the cost curves in Box 21.6 deserves comment. The marginal-cost curve intersects both the average-variable-cost and average-total-cost curves at their lowest points. This is not a coincidence. It is a result of a relationship that can be called the **marginal-average rule**. This rule can be explained as follows: Beginning at any given point, ask what the cost of making one more unit will be. The answer is given by marginal cost. Then ask whether this cost is more or less than the average cost of all units produced up to that point. If the added cost of the next unit made is less than the average cost of previous units, then making that unit will have the effect of pulling down the average. If the next unit costs more, its production will pull the average up. It follows that whenever marginal cost is below average variable cost, the average-variable-cost curve must be

Marginal-average rule
The rule that marginal cost must be equal to average cost when average cost is at its minimum.

falling (that is, negatively sloped); and whenever marginal cost is above average variable cost, the average-variable-cost curve must be rising (that is, positively sloped). This in turn implies that the marginal cost curve cuts the average variable cost curve at its lowest point. All this is equally true of the relationship between marginal cost and average total cost.

The marginal-average rule is not unique to economics; it can be seen in many everyday situations. Consider, for example, the effect of your grade in this course on your grade point average. You could call your grade in this course your "marginal grade," because it represents the grade points earned by taking one more course. If your grade in this course (that is, your marginal grade) is higher than your average grade in other courses, the effect of taking this course wil be to pull your average up. Your grade point average must be rising if your marginal grade exceeds your average grade. If you do worse than average in this course, your grade point average will fall. When your marginal grade falls short of your average grade, your grade point average must be falling. This is the same as the relationship between marginal cost and average cost. If the cost of making one more unit is less than the average cost of making previous units, the average is pulled down; if it is more, the average is pulled up.

Some people find it easier to remember the relationships between the various cost concepts if they are presented as formulas. If you are such a person, you may find the formulas in Box 21.6 useful. The box also gives some common abbreviations. These are not used in this text, but you may want to use them in your note taking, and your instructor will probably use them on the blackboard.

LONG-RUN COSTS AND ECONOMIES OF SCALE

It is sometimes said that firms operate in the short run and plan in the long run. This slogan reflects the distinction between variable and fixed costs: In the short run, a firm varies its output within a plant of fixed size; in the long run, it plans (and carries out) expansions or contractions of the plant itself.

The previous section, then, can be thought of as an analysis of the cost factors that affect operating decisions. Many key aspects of economics turn on the operating decisions that firms make within plants of given sizes. How will farmers change the quantities of the crops they grow? During a recession, how much will a firm reduce its output, and how many workers will it lay off? Should a moving and storage company charge higher rates during its peak moving season? Any change in prices or quantities supplied that does not involve a change in plant size will be affected by the shape and position of the short-run cost curves of the firms involved.

In many other cases, however, we need to know something about the factors that affect firms' plans for expansion or contraction of their plant. We might want to know, for example, how the price of milk would be affected by a reduction in federal dairy subsidies, once farmers had eliminated their surplus production capacity. We might want to know how coal output would respond to increases in oil prices once time had been

**Box 21.6
A Set of Short-Run Cost
Curves**

A whole set of short-run cost curves can be derived from data on fixed and variable costs, as this box shows. The data are presented in the form of a table and a pair of graphs. The box also lists a number of useful abbreviations and formulas.

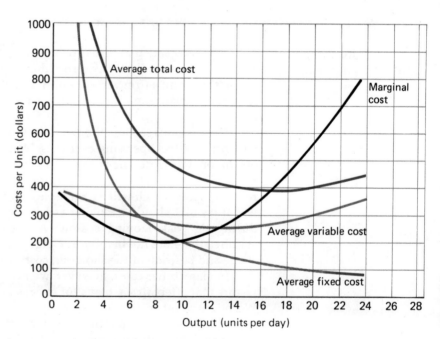

Common abbreviations:

Q   Quantity of output
TC   Total cost
TFC   Total fixed cost
TVC   Total variable cost
MC   Marginal cost
AVC   Average variable cost
AFC   Average fixed cost
ATC   Average total cost

Useful formulas:

$$TC = TFC + TVC.$$

$$MC = \frac{\text{Change in TC}}{\text{Change in Q}} = \frac{\text{Change in TVC}}{\text{Change in Q}}.$$

$$AVC = \frac{TVC}{Q}.$$

$$AFC = \frac{TFC}{Q}.$$

$$ATC = \frac{TC}{Q}.$$

Quantity of Output (units) (1)	Total Variable Cost (2)	Total Fixed Cost (3)	Total Cost (4)	Marginal Cost (dollars per unit) (5)	Average Variable Cost (dollars per unit) (6)	Average Fixed Cost (dollars per unit) (7)	Average Total Cost (dollars per unit) (8)
0	$ 0	$2,000	$ 2,000		—	—	—
1	380	2,000	2,380	$380	$380	$2,000	$2,380
2	720	2,000	2,720	340	360	1,000	1,360
3	1,025	2,000	3,025	305	342	667	1,009
4	1,300	2,000	3,300	275	325	500	825
5	1,550	2,000	3,550	250	310	400	710
6	1,780	2,000	3,780	230	296	333	629
7	1,995	2,000	3,995	215	285	286	571
8	2,200	2,000	4,200	205	275	250	525
9	2,400	2,000	4,400	200	266	222	488
10	2,605	2,000	4,605	205	260	200	460
11	2,820	2,000	4,820	215	256	181	437
12	3,050	2,000	5,050	230	254	169	421
13	3,300	2,000	5,300	250	254	154	408
14	3,575	2,000	5,575	275	255	143	398
15	3,880	2,000	5,880	305	259	133	392
16	4,220	2,000	6,220	340	264	125	389
17	4,600	2,000	6,600	380	271	118	389
18	5,025	2,000	7,025	425	279	111	390
19	5,500	2,000	7,500	475	289	105	394
20	6,030	2,000	8,030	530	302	100	402
21	6,620	2,000	8,620	590	315	95	410
22	7,275	2,000	9,275	655	331	91	422
23	8,000	2,000	10,000	725	348	87	435
24	8,800	2,000	10,800	800	367	83	450

allowed for new mines to be opened and new equipment installed. Such questions require an analysis of long-run costs, to which we now turn.

Planning for expansion   Put yourself in the position of an entrepreneur about to set up a small firm like Fieldcom. You think it will be wise to start with a small plant, but you want to do some long-range planning too. After consulting with specialists in the field, you sketch some average-cost curves for various plant sizes. Five such curves are drawn in Box 21.7. The first one shows short-run average costs for the range of output that is possible with a very small plant; the second one corresponds to a slightly larger plant; and so on. As you build up the market for your product, you hope to expand your plant and move from one of these curves to the next.

Of course, the five short-run cost curves in the box represent only a sample of plant sizes. Other positions are also possible. The size of the plant you choose to build will depend, in the long run, on the amount of output you expect to produce. For any given level of output, you will choose the size that will permit that output to be produced at the lowest possible average total cost.

The long-run average-cost curve   As your firm expands, then, you will move along a *long-run average-cost curve* like the one shown in Box 21.8. This curve is the "envelope" of all the possible short-run average-cost curves; that is, it fits around the group of short-run curves, touching each of them without crossing any of them. The size of plant chosen in the long run for each output will be the one that corresponds to a short-run average-total-cost curve that is just tangent to the long-run average-total-cost curve at that point.

Boxes 21.7 and 21.8 make it clear that there is one best plant size for any given level of output that the firm plans to produce in the long run. Typically, a plant designed for one level of output can be run at a higher or lower level of output only at a penalty in terms of cost. As a young firm expands, it must build more or larger plants as it moves along the downward-sloping portion of the long-run average-total-cost curve. Likewise, a firm that is planning to reduce its output will eliminate some plant rather than keep production facilities operating at lower levels of output than they were designed for.

Economies of Scale

Economies of scale
A situation in which long-run average cost decreases as output increases.

Diseconomies of scale
A situation in which long-run average cost increases as output increases.

Constant returns to scale
A situation in which there are neither economies nor diseconomies of scale.

Economists have developed some special terms to describe what happens to long-run average costs as output increases. In any range of output where long-run average cost *decreases* as output increases, the firm is said to experience **economies of scale**. In any range of output where long-run average cost *increases*, the firm is said to experience **diseconomies of scale**. Finally, if there is any range of output for which long-run average cost does not change as output changes, the firm is said to experience **constant returns to scale** in that range.

The long-run average-cost curve in Box 21.8 is smoothly U-shaped, but that is not the only possible shape for such a curve. In fact, statistical studies suggest that L-shaped long-run average-cost curves are the rule, at least in many manufacturing industries. Such a curve appears in Box 21.9, which shows a range of economies of scale followed by a range of roughly

**Box 21.7
Alternative Short-Run
Average-Total-Cost
Curves**

The position of the short-run average-total-cost curve for a firm depends on the size of the plant. In the long run, the firm has a choice of operating with any size of plant it chooses. Each plant size can be represented by a U-shaped short-run average-total-cost curve. Five such curves are shown in this graph. A new firm might begin with a plant that could be represented by a curve like the first one shown here. Then, as demand for its product expanded, it might move to one of those farther to the right.

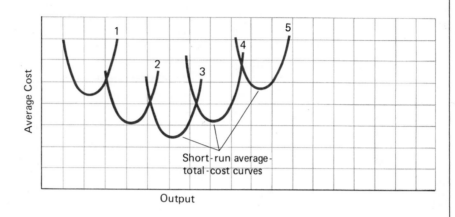

**Box 21.8
Derivation of a
Long-Run Average-Cost
Curve**

A firm can build a plant of any size, and each possible plant size implies a different short-run average-total-cost curve. This box shows a number of short-run average total-cost curves. As the firm expands in the long run, it moves from one curve to another, always choosing the plant size that minimizes the average total cost for the output the firm plans to produce at any given time. The path along which a firm will expand—the firm's long-run average-cost curve—is the "envelope" of all the possible short-run average-total-cost curves.

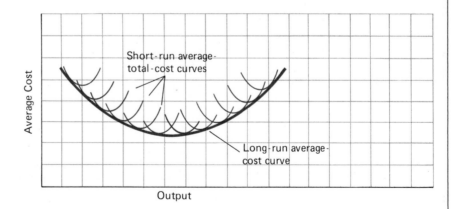

constant returns to scale. The curve could turn out to be a flat-bottomed U if it were followed out far enough (as the broken extension of the curve in Box 21.9 shows). In a given industry, however, there may be no firms that are large enough to show diseconomies of scale. If there are none, the upward-sloping portion of the curve will not be represented in the statistical sample.

Statistical studies of long-run average cost often try to measure the level of output where economies of scale end and constant returns to scale begin. This level is called the **minimum efficient scale** for the firm. As shown in Box 21.9, it corresponds to the point where the L-shaped long-run average-cost curve stops falling and begins to level out. If the cost curve does not have a sharp kink at this point—and there is no reason to think it must—the minimum efficient scale can be identified only approximately. This is not a major problem, however, since statistical studies of cost must deal in approximations in any case.

Minimum efficient scale
The level of output at which economies of scale stop.

Sources of economies of scale

Where do economies of scale come from? Why is it ever true that a large firm can produce at a lower unit cost than a smaller firm? Economists who have studied these questions have found that there is no single source of economies of scale for all firms. Rather, there are a number of sources, some of which are important in certain industries and others in other industries.

When most people think of economies of scale, they probably have in mind an automobile assembly plant or a steel mill. Costs per unit tend to fall with the rate of output per plant in industries like autos and steel, for a number of reasons. One is that a metal-forming machine or steel furnace designed to produce twice as much as another is likely to cost less than twice as much to build. Another is that larger plants can take advantage of

**Box 21.9
An L-Shaped
Average-Cost Curve**

Statistical studies have found that long-run average-cost curves are often L-shaped, as shown here. The point at which economies of scale end and the curve begins to flatten out is called the minimum efficient scale for the firm. If a firm continued to expand without limit, long-run average costs would probably begin to rise. However, in many industries there are no firms operating in the range of diseconomies of scale.

more specialized divisions of labor. The automobile assembly line, on which each worker performs a single operation on each car as it moves by, is the classic example of this.

But not all economies of scale are linked with increases in the rate of output of a single plant. Sometimes they originate in the total amount of a product or model that is produced rather than in the rate at which it is produced. With a long production run, the costs of product design, equipment setup, and training can be spread over a large number of units. A comparison of General Motors with Volkswagen will show the difference between economies of scale linked with rate of production and those linked with volume of production. General Motors achieves major economies of scale through a high rate of production, but it changes models often. Volkswagen, by contrast, makes fewer cars per year but keeps each model in production longer. Its famous "beetle" was produced, with variations, for over four decades.

In addition to the rate and volume of production at a single plant, multiplant operation can yield economies of scale. The McDonald's hamburger chain provides a good example. The minimum efficient scale for a single plant (a single restaurant) is very small in the fast-food industry. Yet McDonald's gains some important economies by running a large number of restaurants as a system. Some of these economies are production economies. Individual food items and ingredients can be made in central kitchens; workers can be trained at "Hamburger University"; and so on. A multiplant firm like McDonald's also realizes economies of scale in such areas as finance, advertising, and marketing.

Looking Ahead

This chapter has only scratched the surface of the theory of cost. The appendix to this chapter and the books listed in the suggestions for further reading extend the theory in many ways. Still, the treatment of cost theory given here will be enough to serve as a basis for analyzing supply decisions in the next few chapters.

Chapter 22 will show how short- and long-run cost curves can be used to derive supply curves for an industry in which there are a large number of competing firms. Chapter 23 will use cost curves to analyze markets in which a single firm has a monopoly. Chapters 24 and 25 will look at intermediate cases, and still other chapters will apply cost theory to problems of public policy.

Summary

1. *Explicit costs* of production take the form of payments to workers, suppliers, and other nonowners of the firm. *Implicit costs* are opportunity costs of using resources owned by the firm or contributed by its owners. Profit is often calculated by subtracting only explicit costs from revenue. This concept is called *accounting profit*. Economists use the term *profit* to mean revenue minus all costs, both implicit and explicit. This concept is called *pure economic profit*.

2. *Fixed inputs* are those that cannot be easily increased or decreased in a short time. They are linked with the size of the firm's plant.

Variable inputs can be quickly and easily varied in order to increase or decrease output. Hourly labor, energy, and raw materials are variable inputs. The *short run* is a period within which only variable outputs can be adjusted. In the *long run* changes can be made in fixed inputs, including plant size.

3. As the amount of one input to a production process is increased while the amounts of all other inputs remain fixed, output will increase, at least over some range. The amount of output added by each one-unit increase in the variable input is known as the *marginal physical product* of that input.

4. According to the law of diminishing returns, as the amount of one variable input used in a production process is increased (with the amounts of all other inputs remaining fixed), a point will be reached beyond which the amount of output added per unit of added variable input (that is, the marginal physical product of the variable input) will begin to decrease. This principle applies to all production processes.

5. A whole set of cost curves can be constructed for a firm, given data on its fixed and variable costs. The most commonly used cost curves are total cost, total fixed cost, total variable cost, average fixed cost, average variable cost, average total cost, and marginal cost. Following the *marginal-average rule*, the marginal-cost curve cuts the average-variable-cost and average-total-cost curves at their lowest points.

6. In the long run a firm can adjust the amounts of fixed inputs that it uses by expanding or reducing its plant. Each possible plant size has a U-shaped short-run average-total-cost curve. The firm's long-run average-cost curve is a shallower U-shaped curve based on a set of short-run curves.

7. When long-run average cost decreases as output increases, the firm is said to experience *economies of scale*. When long-run average cost increases as output increases, the firm is said to experience *diseconomies of scale*. If there are neither economies nor diseconomies of scale, the firm is said to experience *constant returns to scale*.

Questions for Review

1. Explain the following terms and concepts:
   explicit costs
   implicit costs
   pure economic profit
   accounting profit
   fixed inputs
   variable inputs
   short run
   long run
   marginal physical product
   law of diminishing returns
   marginal cost
   marginal-average rule
   economies of scale
   diseconomies of scale
   constant returns to scale
   minimum efficient scale

2. Why are implicit and explicit costs both opportunity costs? Give examples of some implicit and explicit costs for a typical firm.

3. How are the concepts of short run and long run related to the concepts of fixed and variable inputs?

4. What happens to the output of a typical firm as one variable input is increased while all other inputs remain fixed?

5. Illustrate the law of diminishing returns for a vegetable garden in which the area of soil and the amounts of seeds and fertilizer are fixed, while the amount of labor used varies.

6. Write a formula for each of the following:
   a. The relationship between total cost, on the one hand, and total fixed and total variable costs, on the other.
   b. The relationship between marginal cost and changes in total cost or total variable cost.
   c. The relationship between average variable cost and total variable cost, and the similar relationships for average fixed cost and average total cost.

7. How do average costs vary in the long run as

the size of a firm's plant is increased? Draw a sketch to show the relationship between short-run and long-run average-cost curves.

8. What is the difference between diminishing returns and diseconomies of scale? Draw sketches to illustrate the concepts of economies of scale, diseconomies of scale, and constant returns to scale.

Problems and Topics for Discussion

1. List the basic costs of owning and operating an automobile. Which are explicit costs? Which are implicit costs? Does driving an automobile create any opportunity costs for the economy as a whole that do not show up on your list as either implicit or explicit costs? If so, what are they?

2. Divide the costs of owning and operating an automobile into fixed and variable costs. Suppose you were deciding whether to drive to a nearby college's football game or to take the bus instead. Would you take both fixed and variable costs into account? Suppose you were deciding whether to buy a house in a neighborhood where you could walk to work or a house in one where you would have to buy a second car to drive to work every day. Would you then take both fixed and variable costs into account? Explain the difference between the two situations.

3. Do you think the business of running a college is subject to economies or diseconomies of scale? Which parts of the college's operation (e.g., library, dormitories, faculty salaries, moving students between classes, and so on) are subject to economies of scale, diseconomies of scale, or constant returns to scale?

4. Take a piece of graph paper and draw a set of coordinate axes. Label the x axis "quantity of output" (0 to 20 units) and the y axis "cost" (0 to 20 units). Plot the following (x, y) points on your graph: (0, 4); (2, 6); (4, 7); (7, 8); (9, 9); (11, 11); (13, 14). Connect these points with a smooth curve and label it "total cost." Working from this curve, construct a total-fixed-cost curve and a total-variable-cost curve for the same firm.

5. On another piece of graph paper draw a second set of coordinate axes. Label the horizontal axis "quantity" (0 to 20 units) and the vertical axis "cost per unit" (0 to 2 units, in tenths of a unit). Using the total-cost, total-variable-cost, and total-fixed-cost curves you drew for question 4 as a basis, construct the following curves on your new graph: marginal cost, average total cost, average variable cost, and average fixed cost.

6. Turn to Box 21.8. Copy the diagram onto a sheet of graph paper, drawing the long-run average-total-cost curve and one of the short-run average-total-cost curves. Use the curves you have drawn to construct the matching long-run and short-run total-cost curves. The total-cost curves should both be reverse-S shaped, and they should be tangent to one another at the same level of output for which the average-total-cost curves are tangent.

7. Suppose you look into the relationship between the amount of coal burned per week in a certain power plant and the amount of electricity generated per week. You find the following: For tiny amounts of coal, not enough even to bring the boiler up to the temperature needed to make steam, no electricity could be produced. After a certain minimum amount of coal is burned, the plant begins to operate. From that point on, the added amount of electricity generated per added ton of coal burned is constant over a wide range. Then a ceiling is reached beyond which burning more coal produces no more electricity at all. Sketch the total-physical-product curve for this plant, and draw a graph showing how marginal physical product varies as output varies. Does this production process obey the law of diminishing returns?

8. It has been said that if it were not for the law of diminishing returns, all the food that the world needs could be grown in a flowerpot. Discuss this statement. (Suggestion: Think of land as the only fixed factor and fertilizer as the only variable factor. How much food could

be grown in the flowerpot if the marginal physical product of fertilizer were constant regardless of the amount of fertilizer used per unit of land?)

9. **Case for Discussion**

The early 1980s were hard times for the tractor industry. Farm incomes were low and farmers were burdened with debt, making it hard for them to buy new equipment. By 1984 output had fallen to a third of the peak level reached in 1979.

   The tractor market was expected to improve somewhat in the later 1980s, but most observers thought the 1979 sales peak would not be reached again any time soon. Working on the basis of this forecast, the leading tractor makers scrambled to cut their losses. Plant closings were a major factor in the strategies of most firms. Massey-Ferguson had built $700 million worth of new plant. After 1980, half of the firm's total plant was scrapped or sold.

Ford closed its European headquarters and began assembling tractors at fewer locations. Even John Deere, the strongest firm in the market, was forced to close a combine plant. J. I. Case, the fifth-largest tractor maker, was reported to be thinking of leaving the industry altogether.[1]

Questions:

a. Faced with the prospect of a permanent drop in sales, why would a tractor firm shut down some plants rather than keep all of its plants running at reduced levels of output? Would the firm react the same way to a temporary drop in sales? Why or why not?

b. The tractor slump is forcing all firms to cut back their level of operations. Why might this situation force Case, the smallest of the major tractor makers, out of the business entirely? Suggest an explanation that makes use of cost theory.

Suggestions for Further Reading

Alchian, Armen A. "Costs and Outputs." In *The Allocation of Economic Resources*, ed. Moses Abramovitz et al. Stanford, Calif.: Stanford University Press, 1959. Also reprinted in William Breit and Harold M. Hochman, eds., *Readings in Microeconomics*, 2nd ed. New York: Holt, Rinehart and Winston, 1968.

An attempt to clarify certain aspects of the theory of costs. Alchian emphasizes that cost varies in response to variations in total expected volume of output as well as variations in the rate of output.

Blaug, Mark. *Economic Theory in Retrospect*, 3rd ed. Cambridge, England: Cambridge University Press, 1978.

Chapter 10 discusses Alfred Marshall's contributions to cost theory.

Peters, Thomas J., and Robert H. Waterman. *In Search of Excellence*. New York: Harper & Row, 1982, chap. 8.

The authors of this best-selling book on management point out that there is more to keeping average costs low than building as big a plant as possible. In fact, bigness may be the enemy of productivity.

---

[1]Faye Rice, "Cruel Days in Tractorville," *Fortune*, October 29, 1984, pp. 30–36.

Appendix to Chapter 21

Cost and Output

with Two Variable

Inputs

In this chapter we looked at the relationship between cost and output when just one input is varied, with all other inputs remaining constant. In this appendix we will extend the theory of cost to the case in which more than one input is varied.

Substitution of Inputs

The main new feature of situations in which more than one input is varied is the possibility of substituting one input for another. Consider the case of Henry Hathaway, a farmer who makes his living growing corn. Hathaway spends all his time working on his farm and does not hire anyone to help him. The amount of labor used in growing corn is, for him, a fixed input. In addition to fixed amounts of labor and machinery, he uses two variable inputs: land, which he rents, and fertilizer, which he buys.

Hathaway can grow any given quantity of corn—say, 200 bushels—in many different ways. Some of the possibilities are shown in Box 21A.1. One way to grow 200 bushels of corn is to use 2.5 tons of fertilizer and 10 acres of land. This is represented by point P on the graph. If Hathaway wants to grow the same amount of corn on less land, he can substitute fertilizer for land. For example, at point Q he can grow 200 bushels of corn on 5 acres by using 5 tons of fertilizer. By substituting still more fertilizer for land, he can move to point R, where the 200 bushels are grown on just 2.5 acres, using 10 tons of fertilizer.

Diminishing Returns in Substitution

In the chapter we defined the law of diminishing returns as it applies to a situation in which one input is varied while all others remain constant. In that situation, after a certain point the amount of the variable input needed to make an extra unit of output increases. (This is another way of saying that the marginal physical product of the variable input decreases.) A similar principle applies when one input is substituted for another in such a way as to keep output at a constant level: as the amount of input x is increased, the amount of x needed to replace one unit of y increases.

The example in Box 21A.1 illustrates this principle. In moving from point P to point Q, 2.5 tons of fertilizer replace 5 acres of land, while output stays constant at 200 bushels. But in moving from point Q to point R, 5 more tons of fertilizer are needed to replace just 2.5 acres of land.

543

**Box 21A.1
An Isoquantity Line**

This graph shows an isoquantity line, or isoquant, for the production of 200 bushels of corn. The variable inputs are land and fertilizer. The other inputs, labor and machinery, are assumed to be fixed. Points P, Q, and R represent various ways of growing the given quantity of corn. A movement downward along the isoquant represents the substitution of fertilizer for land while output is maintained at 200 bushels per year. As more and more fertilizer is substituted for land, the isoquant becomes flatter because of diminishing returns.

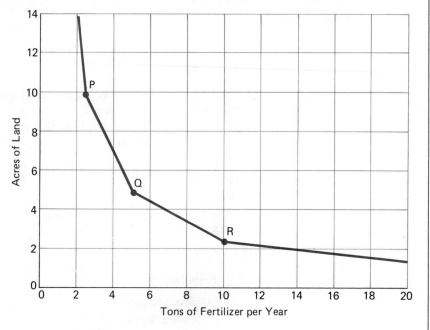

As a result of the law of diminishing returns in substituting one input for another, a line connecting points P, Q, and R becomes flatter as one moves downward and to the right along it. This reflects the decreasing ratio of the marginal physical product of fertilizer to the marginal physical product of land as more fertilizer is substituted for land.

Choosing the Least-Cost Method of Production

Isoquantity line (isoquant)

A line showing the various combinations of variable inputs that can be used to produce a given amount of output.

The line connecting points P, Q, and R in Box 21A.1 is called an **isoquantity line** or **isoquant** because it shows the combinations of inputs that can be used to produce a given amount of output. (The prefix *iso* comes from a Greek word meaning "equal.") But while all the points on the isoquant are equal in terms of output, they are not equal in terms of cost. To see how a producer can choose the least-cost method of producing a given level of output, we need to know the prices of the inputs.

In the appendix to Chapter 20 we used budget lines to give a graphic picture of the prices of consumer goods. As Box 21A.2 shows, the same technique can be used to represent the prices of inputs. The graph assumes a cost of $50 a ton for fertilizer and a rental price of $50 per year for land. The sum of $400 can buy 8 tons of fertilizer and no land, 8 acres of land with no fertilizer, or any of the other points on line A. The sum of $500

**Box 21A.2
Finding the Least-Cost
Method of Production**

This graph shows how the least-cost method of production can be found from among the points on an isoquant, given the prices of the variable inputs. Here, the price of fertilizer is assumed to be $50 a ton and the rental price of land $50 per year. A set of budget lines is drawn to represent various levels of spending on inputs. Line A, which corresponds to a total variable cost of $400, does not provide enough inputs to produce 200 bushels of corn. Line C, which corresponds to a total variable cost of $625, provides enough inputs to grow 200 bushels of corn using methods P or R. Line B, which corresponds to a total variable cost of $500, permits the 200 bushels to be grown using method Q, which is the least-cost method given these input prices.

will buy 10 tons of fertilizer, 10 acres of land, or any of the other points on line B; and so on.

When the isoquant for 200 bushels of corn is drawn on top of a set of budget lines for the inputs, it is easy to see the least-cost method of producing that level of output. It is the method that uses 5 tons of fertilizer and 5 acres of land. This corresponds to point Q on the graph, where the isoquant just touches budget line B. Points P and S are possible ways of growing 200 bushels of corn, but they lie on budget line C, which corresponds to a cost of $625. And a budget of less than $500 (say, $400, as shown by budget line A) is not enough to reach the 200-bushel isoquant no matter how it is split between fertilizer and land.

The Response to Changes in Input Prices

If input prices change, the least-cost combination of inputs is also likely to change. Suppose that the suburbs begin to expand in the direction of our friend Hathaway's farm, driving up the price of land. Now land that used to rent for $50 per acre per year rents for $200 per acre. The price of fertilizer remains unchanged at $50 a ton.

The results of the increase in the price of land are shown in Box 21A.3. Now $500 will not be enough to buy the combinations of inputs that fall along budget line B. Even if all of the money were spent on land, only 2.5 acres could be rented. The new $500 budget line is C, which does not reach the 200-bushel isoquant at any point.

To grow 200 bushels, Hathaway must now spend more than $500. As he increases his budget for land and fertilizer, the budget line shifts upward but stays parallel to C. When the budget line reaches D, which corresponds to spending $1,000 on inputs, it just touches the isoquant at R. We see, then, that $1,000 is the lowest cost at which 200 bushels of corn can be grown, given a price of $50 a ton for fertilizer and $200 an acre for land. With those prices, R is the least-cost combination of inputs.

The effect of an increase in the price of an input in this case is typical. Less of the input whose price has gone up is used, and the other input, which has become relatively less costly, is substituted for it. We will return to this topic in Chapters 30 and 31, where we will discuss the markets for the factors of production.

Box 21A.3
Effects of a Change in
Input Prices

If the rental price of land increases from $50 to $200 per year while the price of fertilizer remains fixed at $50 a ton, 200 bushels of corn can no longer be produced for $500. The $500 budget line shifts from position B to position C, and it now falls short of the 200-bushel isoquant. Increasing the amount spent on variable inputs to $1,000 shifts the budget line up to position D, where it just touches the isoquant at point R. The increase in the price of land thus not only raises the total variable cost of growing 200 bushels of corn but also causes fertilizer to be substituted for land, which is now relatively more costly.

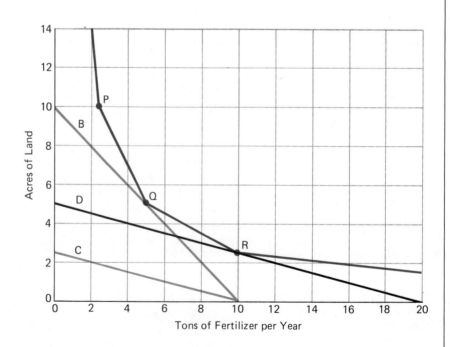

Box 21A.4
Expansion of Output and Total Variable Costs

Part a of this box shows three isoquants for the production of corn, corresponding to outputs of 100, 200, and 300 bushels. Assuming input prices of $50 an acre for land and $50 a ton for fertilizer, budget lines can be drawn to show the minimum total variable cost for each level of output. As output expands, the firm will move from T to Q and then to W along the expansion path. Part b of the box plots the amount of output and the total variable cost for each of these points. The result is a reverse-S-shaped total-variable-cost curve that shows the effects of diminishing returns for levels of output above 200 bushels per year.

(a)

(b)

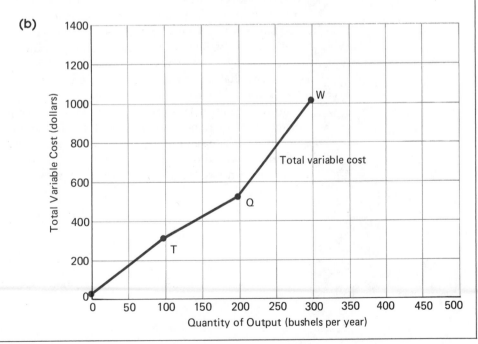

Varying Output

The isoquant technique can also be used to analyze variations in output with two variable inputs. Turn to Box 21A.4. Part a of that diagram shows an isoquant "map" on which three sets of points have been drawn that correspond to three levels of output. As before, P, Q, and R represent three ways of growing 200 bushels of corn. Points S, T, and U represent three ways of growing 100 bushels. And Points V, W, and X are three ways of growing 300 bushels. An isoquant has been drawn through each of these sets of points.

In this box we return to the assumption that land costs $50 an acre and fertilizer $50 a ton. Using these prices, a set of budget lines has been drawn, each of which corresponds to a different total variable cost. Budget line A corresponds to a total variable cost of $300, B to a cost of $500, and C to a cost of $1,000.

As the graph clearly shows, there is a least-cost method for producing each level of output, given these prices. Point T is the best way of producing 100 bushels; Q is best for 200 bushels; and W is best for 300 bushels. Other levels of output would also be possible. These would lie along the line drawn from the origin through points T, Q, and W. This is called the firm's *expansion path*. As the firm moves along its expansion path, more of both the variable inputs, land and fertilizer, is used. Meanwhile, the fixed inputs—labor and machinery, in Hathaway's case—remain constant.

Deriving a Cost Curve from the Isoquant Map

Once the expansion path has been identified, it is easy to construct a total-variable-cost curve. All we need to do is construct a graph that links each of the points on the expansion path with the variable-cost level of the corresponding budget line. This is done in part b of Box 21A.4. At the origin, output is zero and total variable cost is zero. At point T, output is 100 bushels and total variable cost is $300. At Q, we have 200 bushels and $500; and at W, 300 bushels and $1,000. Plotting these points and connecting them gives the firm's total-variable-cost curve.

Note that this curve has the same reverse-S shape as the cost curve of Fieldcom Inc., discussed in the chapter. This shape is a result of the law of diminishing returns, applied to the case in which two inputs vary while all others remain fixed. Beyond point Q, the amounts of inputs needed to produce each added unit of output begin to rise, just as they did when only one input was allowed to vary. Only if all inputs are allowed to vary and none remain fixed can a firm escape the effects of the law of diminishing returns.

Chapter 22

Supply Under Perfect Competition

WHAT YOU WILL LEARN IN THIS CHAPTER

After reading this chapter, you should be able to

1. Describe the *market structure* of *perfect competition*.
2. Show how the profit-maximizing output for a perfectly competitive firm is determined in the short run.
3. Explain the conditions under which a perfectly competitive firm will stay open or shut down in order to cut its losses.
4. Draw a supply curve for a perfectly competitive firm, given its cost curves.
5. List the conditions for long-run equilibrium for a perfectly competitive firm.
6. Show how a perfectly competitive industry adjusts to long-run changes in demand.
7. Explain what is "perfect" about perfect competition.

Ideas for Review

Here are some terms and concepts that you should review before you read this chapter:

The supply curve (Chapters 3 and 19)
Cost theory (Chapter 21)
Long run and short run (Chapter 21)

"They thought they had the world by the tail."

When Ralph and Andrea Martin started Fieldcom Inc., they thought they had the world by the tail. Their rugged portable computer, the first one that was designed for use under hot and dusty field conditions, would be a sure source of profits, they figured. With only a small investment, they quickly got their firm off the ground and their computer into production.

Then came the competition. What the Martins didn't realize was that the very factors that made the portable-computer market easy for them to enter would make it easy for everyone else to enter too. As soon as their machine proved that there was a market for rugged portable computers, copies sprang up on all sides. Makers of office-type portable computers beefed up their carrying cases and shock-mounted their components. Other start-up firms brought out machines that, from the user's point of view, were just as good as Fieldcom's. Equipment supply dealers contracted with little-known electronics firms in the Far East to produce rugged portable computers to be sold under the dealers' own brand names.

Within a year there were many similar products available, no one of which was able to capture a dominant share of the growing market. The pressure to trim prices was relentless. At the end of two years in business, the Martins were working hard and earning almost no profit, if the full opportunity costs of their firm were taken into account.

In Chapter 21 we looked at Fieldcom by itself, but firms like the Martins' do not operate alone in the real world. They face competition. Competition may take the form of giants like General Motors and Toyota struggling to dominate a market. Or it may take the form of advertising campaigns by rivals trying to woo fickle consumers. Sometimes it takes the form of rapid increases in the number of brands and styles, as often happens in the markets for breakfast cereal or clothing.

In the next few chapters we will look at all of these kinds of competition, but here we will deal with a simpler case. This is the type of competition faced by Fieldcom, in which many small firms with similar products share a market that is easy to enter and easy to leave. This is the case that economists call *perfect competition*.

THE STRUCTURE OF PERFECT COMPETITION

Market structure
The key traits of a market, including the number of firms in each industry, the extent to which the products of different firms are different or similar, and the ease of entry into and exit from the market.

Let's begin with a more formal definition of perfect competition. Economists classify types of competition by the structure of the markets in which firms operate. **Market structure** in this sense means such factors as the number of firms in each industry, the extent to which the products of those firms differ, and the ease or difficulty of getting into and out of the market.

As a market structure, **perfect competition**, the subject of this chapter, has four defining features:

1. There are many buyers and sellers, each of whom buys or sells only a small fraction of all that is bought and sold in the market.
2. The product traded in the market is *homogeneous*; that is, the product sold by one firm is just like the product sold by any other.

Perfect competition
A market structure that is characterized by a large number of small firms, a homogeneous product, access to information by all buyers and sellers, and freedom of entry and exit.

Price taker
A firm that sells its outputs at prices that are determined by forces beyond its control.

3. All of the participants in the market, buyers and sellers alike, are informed about prices, sources of supply and so on.
4. Entry into and exit from the market are easy.

The Perfectly Competitive Firm as a Price Taker

Taken together, these features of perfect competition ensure that all firms in the market will be **price takers**—firms that sell their outputs at fixed prices determined by forces beyond their control. When a firm like Fieldcom supplies only a small fraction of total output, its decisions have little effect on supply and demand in the market as a whole. Because the product is homogeneous, buyers are just as happy to buy from one firm as from another. Thus, a firm that raised its price even a fraction above what its competitors were charging would soon lose all its customers. And because all buyers and sellers are well informed, no one would be willing to pay or be able to get a higher price than the prevailing one.[1]

Under perfect competition, then, the decisions facing individual firms are simple. The firm does not have to decide at what price to sell its product, since price is beyond its control. Product design, advertising, and other marketing activities are not a major focus of decision making because the products of all firms are very much alike in the eyes of consumers. In effect, when the conditions of perfect competition are met, the only decision left to the firm is that of how much output to produce.

Perfect Competition and Business Rivalry

Before going on, it is important to mention a paradox associated with perfect competition. The paradox is that perfect competition is in many ways the opposite of competition as many people think of it in everyday business life.

When we think of business competition, we ordinarily think of rivalry and struggle—head-to-head contests of design, quality, service, discounting, advertising, and personal selling. Under perfect competition we find none of these things. In a perfectly competitive market, there is no reason to battle for market shares because there is plenty of room for each small firm to sell as much as it wants at the going price. There is no advertising in such a market because buyers are assumed already to be well informed and goods are perfectly homogeneous—not only in fact but in the eyes of consumers as well. The market environment is still competitive in the sense that any firms that fail to operate as efficiently as their rivals will fail to earn profits and will be forced out of the market. Firms are not sheltered from the possibility of loss by licenses, patents, or other special privileges. Nonetheless, many more colorful or personalized aspects of competition are absent. Much more will be said about the relationship of "perfect" competition to real-world competition in the next few chapters.

---

[1]The fourth feature of perfect competition—easy entry and exit—is not necessary, in the short run, to make firms price takers. But, as will be explained later, it is important in the long run.

PERFECT COMPETITION AND SUPPLY IN THE SHORT RUN

Having defined perfect competition, we turn now to the main topic of this chapter: showing how the profit-maximizing decisions of individual firms affect the shapes of supply curves in perfectly competitive markets. We will proceed step by step. First we will look at the individual firm and its supply curve in the short run. Next we will show how the market supply curve is derived from the supply curves of all the firms in the market. Then we will look at profit maximization for the firm, and at the industry's supply curve in the long run.

Short-Run Profit Maximization for a Single Firm

We begin with an example showing how a perfectly competitive firm sets the amount of output it supplies at a level that results in the greatest possible profit. Part a of Box 22.1 shows short-run cost data for Fieldcom, as first given in Chapter 21. It also shows the revenue earned by Fieldcom from the sale of each quantity of output, assuming a constant price of $500 per unit. The price per unit is the same at all levels of output because Fieldcom is assumed to be a price taker.

Subtracting total cost in column 3 from total revenue in column 2 gives the total profit the firm earns at each level of output. The maximum is reached at 19 units per day, where a profit of $2,000 per day is earned. This profit-maximizing level of output is shown graphically in part b of Box 22.1. There, the firm's total profit is indicated by the distance between the total revenue and total cost curves. That distance is greatest at 19 units of output.

A marginal approach   Instead of comparing total cost and total revenue, we can use a marginal approach to find the profit-maximizing level of output. Turn first to columns 5 and 6 of the table in Box 22.1. Column 5 gives data on marginal cost. (As in Chapter 21, these data are printed on lines between the entries in the first four columns to show that marginal cost is the change in cost as output moves from one level to another.) Column 6 presents a new concept—marginal revenue. **Marginal revenue** is the amount by which total revenue increases when output increases by one unit. For a firm that is a price taker, as this one is, marginal revenue is equal to the price of the product. Each computer that Fieldcom sells adds $500 to its total revenue.

As the table shows, both total cost and total revenue increase as output increases. If the increase in revenue exceeds the increase in cost (that is, if marginal revenue is greater than marginal cost), increasing output by one unit increases total profit. If the increase in cost exceeds the increase in revenue (that is, if marginal cost is greater than marginal revenue), increasing output by one unit reduces total profit. It follows that in order to maximize profit, a firm should expand its output as long as marginal revenue exceeds marginal cost. It should stop as soon as marginal cost begins to exceed marginal revenue. A comparison of columns 5 and 6 of Box 22.1 shows that for Fieldcom this means producing 19 units of output per day—the same number that we arrive at when we compare total cost and total revenue.

Marginal revenue
The amount by which total revenue increases as a result of a one-unit increase in quantity sold.

Box 22.1
Short-Run Profit
Maximization Under
Perfect Competition

This box shows the profit-maximizing level of output chosen by a perfectly competitive firm, Fieldcom Inc., given a market price of $500 per unit. The output can be found by comparing total cost and total revenue, as shown in the table and the upper graph. It can also be found by comparing marginal cost and marginal revenue. (Because the firm is a price taker, marginal revenue is equal to price.) Profit increases up to the point where marginal cost begins to exceed marginal revenue, after that point it declines. Whichever approach is used, the profit-maximizing output is 19 units per day and the maximum profit per day is $2,000.

(a)

Quantity of Output (1)	Total Revenue (2)	Total Cost (3)	Total Profit (2) − (3) (4)	Marginal Cost (5)	Marginal Revenue (6)
0	$ 0	$ 2,000	−$2,000	$380	$500
1	500	2,380	−1,880	340	500
2	1,000	2,720	−1,720	305	500
3	1,500	3,025	−1,525	275	500
4	2,000	3,300	−1,300	250	500
5	2,500	3,550	−1,000	230	500
6	3,000	3,780	−780	215	500
7	3,500	3,995	−495	205	500
8	4,000	4,200	−200	200	500
9	4,500	4,400	100	205	500
10	5,000	4,605	395	215	500
11	5,500	4,820	680	230	500
12	6,000	5,050	950	250	500
13	6,500	5,300	1,200	275	500
14	7,000	5,575	1,425	305	500
15	7,500	5,880	1,620	340	500
16	8,000	6,220	1,780	380	500
17	8,500	6,600	1,900	425	500
18	9,000	7,025	1,975	475	500
19	9,500	7,500	2,000	530	500
20	10,000	8,030	1,970	590	500
21	10,500	8,620	1,880	655	500
22	11,000	9,275	1,725	725	500
23	11,500	10,000	1,500	800	500
24	12,000	10,800	1,200		

The marginal approach to short-run profit maximization is shown graphically in part c of Box 22.1. At up to 19 units of output, the marginal-cost curve lies below the marginal-revenue curve, so that each added unit of output increases profit. Beyond 19 units, the marginal-cost curve is above the marginal-revenue curve, so that each added unit of output reduces profit. The point of profit maximization, where the marginal-cost and marginal-revenue curves intersect, matches the point in part b at which the spread between total revenue and total cost is greatest.

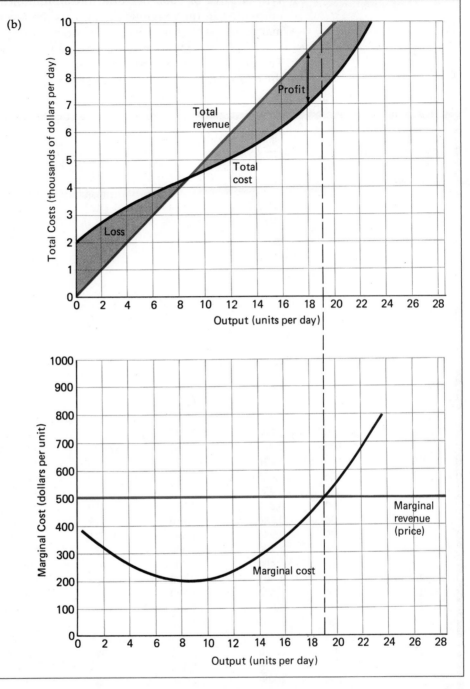

Minimizing short-run losses   In the example just given, Fieldcom was able to make a profit at a price of $500. But market conditions are not always so favorable. Suppose, for example, that the market price drops to $300. The firm, being a price taker, can do nothing about the price and will have to adjust its output as best it can to meet the new situation. The adjustments required are shown in Box 22.2.

There is no level of output at which the firm can earn a profit. Unable to earn a profit, the firm must focus on keeping its losses to a minimum.

With a price of $300 per unit, the minimum loss occurs at 14 units of output. As in the previous case, this is the level of output beyond which marginal cost begins to exceed the price of the product.

The two graphs in Box 22.2 give two views of Fieldcom's situation. The upper graph presents the total-cost–total-revenue approach. Because the total-cost curve is higher than the total-revenue curve at all points, the

Box 22.2
Minimizing Short-Run
Losses Under Perfect
Competition

If the market price of the product is too low for the firm to earn a profit, it must try to keep its losses to a minimum. The two approaches shown in Box 22.1 can be used to find the point of minimum loss, which is 14 units of output per day at a price of $300. Note that the marginal-cost curve intersects the marginal-revenue curve at a point higher than average variable cost but lower than average total cost. Each unit of output sold earns more than its share of variable cost, but not enough to pay for its share of total cost when its share of fixed cost is included.

(a)

Quantity of Output (1)	Total Revenue (2)	Total Cost (3)	Total Profit or Loss (4)	Average Total Cost (5)	Average Variable Cost (6)	Marginal Cost (7)	Marginal Revenue (8)
0	$ 0	$2,000	−$2,000	—	—		
1	300	2,380	−2,080	$2,380	$380	$380	$300
2	600	2,720	−2,120	1,360	360	340	300
3	900	3,025	−2,125	1,009	342	305	300
4	1,200	3,300	−2,100	825	325	275	300
5	1,500	3,550	−2,050	710	310	250	300
6	1,800	3,780	−1,980	629	296	230	300
7	2,100	3,995	−1,895	571	285	215	300
8	2,400	4,200	−1,800	525	275	205	300
9	2,700	4,400	−1,700	488	266	200	300
10	3,000	4,605	−1,605	460	260	205	300
11	3,300	4,820	−1,520	437	256	215	300
12	3,600	5,050	−1,450	421	254	230	300
13	3,900	5,300	−1,400	408	254	250	300
14	4,200	5,575	−1,375	398	255	275	300
15	4,500	5,880	−1,380	392	259	305	300
16	4,800	6,220	−1,420	389	264	340	300
17	5,100	6,600	−1,500	389	271	380	300

firm cannot make a profit. Total revenues come closest to meeting total costs at 14 units of output.

The lower graph shows why it is worthwhile to produce 14 units of output even though no profit is earned by doing so. It shows the complete set of short-run cost curves for the firm. The point where marginal cost is equal to price lies between the two average-cost curves. The vertical

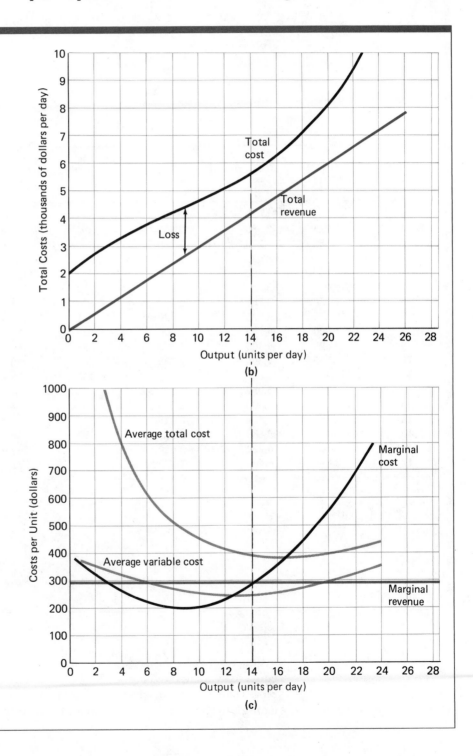

(b)

(c)

Box 22.3
Shutting Down to
Minimize Short-Run Loss

Sometimes the price of a firm's output may drop so low that the firm must shut down in order to keep short-run losses to a minimum. This is illustrated here at a price of $225 per unit. Eleven units of output yield a smaller loss ($2,345) than any other level of output. However, the loss can be reduced to just $2,000 a day if the firm shuts down. Notice that the marginal-cost curve in this case intersects the marginal-revenue curve at a point below the minimum average variable cost. That is the signal to shut down.

(a)

Quantity of Output (1)	Total Revenue (2)	Total Cost (3)	Total Profit or Loss (4)	Average Total Cost (5)	Average Variable Cost (6)	Marginal Cost (7)	Marginal Revenue (8)
0	$ 0	$2,000	−$2,000	—	—		
						$380	$225
1	225	2,380	−2,155	$2,380	$380		225
						340	
2	450	2,720	−2,270	1,360	360		225
						305	
3	675	3,025	−2,305	1,009	342		225
						275	
4	900	3,300	−2,400	825	325		225
						250	
5	1,125	3,550	−2,425	710	310		225
						230	
6	1,350	3,780	−2,430	629	296		225
						215	
7	1,575	3,995	−2,420	571	285		225
						205	
8	1,800	4,200	−2,400	525	275		225
						200	
9	2,025	4,400	−2,375	488	266		225
						205	
10	2,250	4,605	−2,355	460	260		225
						215	
11	2,475	4,820	−2,345	437	256		225
						230	
12	2,700	5,050	−2,350	421	254		225
						250	
13	2,925	5,300	−2,375	408	254		225
						275	
14	3,150	5,575	−2,425	398	255		225
						305	
15	3,375	5,880	−2,505	392	259		225
						340	
16	3,600	6,220	−2,620	389	264		225
						380	
17	3,825	6,600	−2,775	389	271		225

distance between the average-variable-cost and average-total-cost curves is equal to average fixed costs. Thus, at 14 units of output the price of $300 is more than enough to cover each unit's share of variable costs but not quite enough to cover each unit's share of fixed costs too.

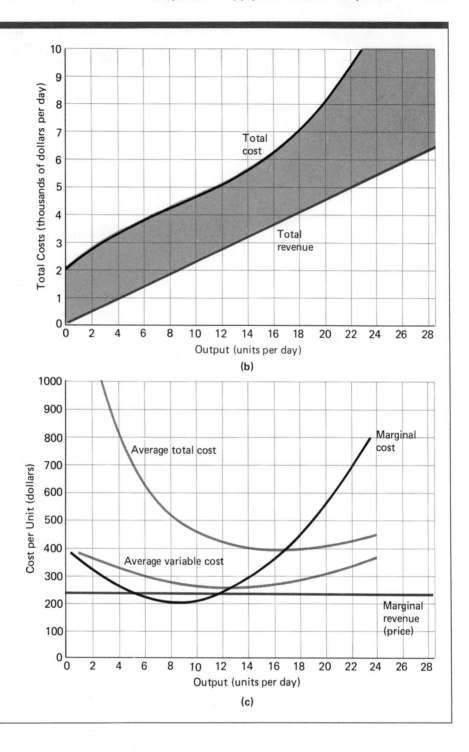

(b)

(c)

Shutting down to cut short-run losses   What would happen if the price of portable computers dropped even lower than $300? Would it always be worthwhile for the firm to keep making computers, even though it was losing money? The answer, as shown in Box 22.3, is no.

This box assumes a price of $225 per unit. The table shows that with the price so low, the firm cannot make a profit at any level of output. But this time the best thing for the firm to do in the short run is to shut down. If things get better and the price rises again, the firm can start making computers again. If things never get better, the firm will have to wind up its affairs and go out of business.

In this case it can be misleading to look only at the marginal-revenue and marginal-cost columns. After 7 units of output, marginal cost drops below the price of $225 and stays there until an output of 11 units is reached. If the firm were to stay in production, 11 units of output would give it a lower loss than any other level of output. But in this case the firm takes an even smaller loss by not producing at all.

As in the previous examples, the graphs tell the same story as the table. The upper graph shows once again that the total-revenue curve never reaches the total-cost curve. It comes fairly close at 11 units of output, but not as close as it comes at zero output.

The lower graph shows that marginal cost and price are equal at 11 units of output. However, even at 11 units the price does not cover average variable cost. Losses are minimized by shutting down.

The Firm's Short-Run Supply Curve

The examples just given provide all the information needed to draw a short-run supply curve for Fieldcom, our perfectly competitive firm. Turn to Box 22.4 and work through it, starting with a price of $500. As we saw earlier, Fieldcom will turn out 19 computers a day at this price. Point E_1 of the firm's short-run marginal-cost curve is a point on the firm's supply curve.

Suppose now that the demand for portable computers slackens and the price begins to fall. As it does, the point where price equals marginal cost moves downward along the firm's marginal-cost curve. Soon point E_2 is reached—the point where marginal cost and average total cost are equal. This happens at an output of about 17 units and a price of about $385. At that price, the best the firm can do is break even. Either a greater or a smaller output will result in a loss.

If the price falls still lower, the firm's problem becomes one of keeping loss to a minimum rather than making the maximum profit. At a price of $300, for example, the firm minimizes its loss by making 14 units, at point E_3. In the range of prices between minimum average total cost and minimum average variable cost, the supply curve continues to follow the marginal-cost curve.

Below a price of about $254, a change occurs. Now the price is lower than the lowest point on the average-variable-cost curve. This means that the firm minimizes its losses by shutting down. For a price of $254, then, point E_4 on the vertical axis is the preferred point of operation. This point must then be a point on the firm's short-run supply curve. As the graph shows, for this and all lower prices, the supply curve coincides with the vertical axis.

All that has been learned so far about the firm's short-run supply decision can be summed up in the following statement: *The short-run supply*

**Box 22.4
Derivation of the
Short-Run Supply Curve**

This graph shows how a short-run supply curve for Fieldcom Inc. can be derived from its cost curves. When the price is $500, the firm will produce at point E_1. As the price falls, the firm moves downward along its short-run marginal-cost curve, as shown by points E_2 and E_3. The firm will continue to produce at the point where price equals marginal cost until marginal cost falls below average variable cost. At that price the firm will do just as well to shut down—that is, to produce at point E_4. The part of the vertical axis below E_4 thus can be viewed as part of the firm's short-run supply curve.

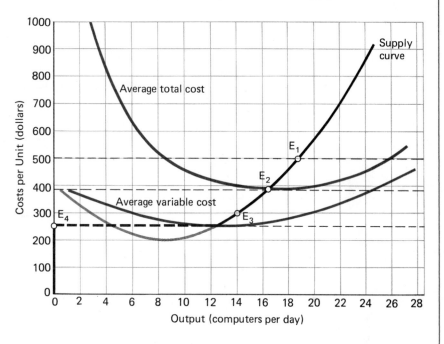

curve of a profit-maximizing firm operating in a perfectly competitive market coincides with the upward-sloping part of the marginal-cost curve lying above its intersection with the average-variable-cost curve.

The Industry's Short-Run Supply Curve

The supply curve of a whole industry can now be constructed on the basis of the supply curves of the firms in the industry. Box 22.5 shows the supply curves for three firms. To get the total supply of this three-firm industry at each price, the quantities supplied by each of the firms are added together. In the graph, this means adding the supply curves horizontally. For an industry with many firms, it would simply be necessary to add the supply curves of more and more firms in the same way.

It should be noted that in adding the firms' supply curves together we assumed that input prices did not change as output expands. For a small firm in a perfectly competitive industry, this is a realistic assumption. However, if all firms in an industry try to grow at the same time, the

**Box 22·5
Derivation of a
Short-Run Industry
Supply Curve**

A short-run industry supply curve can be obtained by summing the supply curves of individual firms. Here this method is shown for an industry with only three firms. If the prices of inputs vary as industry output varies, it will be necessary to adjust the industry supply curve.

(a)

| Price | Quantity Supplied | | | |
	Firm X	Firm Y	Firm Z	Total
$ .40	1,500			1,500
.80	5,500	3,000	3,333	11,833
1.20	9,500	7,000	10,000	26,500
1.50	12,500	10,000	15,000	37,500

(b)

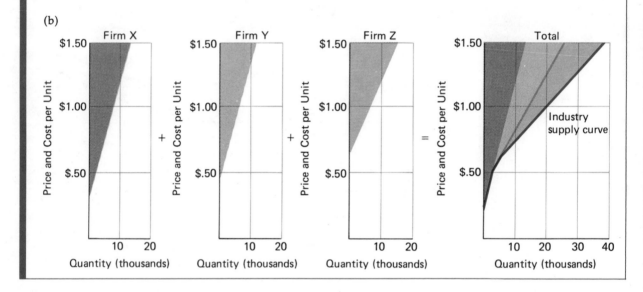

assumption may not hold. In fact, input prices will rise unless the supply curve of the input is perfectly elastic. If input prices rise as the industry's total output grows, the cost curves of each firm will shift upward as the output of all firms increases. This will make the short-run industry supply curve somewhat steeper than the sum of the individual supply curves.

LONG-RUN EQUILIBRIUM UNDER PERFECT COMPETITION

In Chapter 21 we distinguished between the long run and the short run. In the short run, not all inputs can be varied. In the long run, firms can increase or decrease any of their inputs, even durable ones such as land, structures, and major pieces of equipment.

This ability to vary all inputs in the long run means that firms can enter a market for the first time, starting with a new plant and work force.

It also means they can leave a market for good, releasing all their employees and selling their plant and equipment. (Sometimes firms leave peacefully, with the owners selling the firm's assets and dividing up the proceeds. Other times they go with a crash, leaving their creditors to collect only pennies for each dollar of mortgages, bonds, and other debts they hold.) Typically, as an industry expands and contracts, many firms enter and leave it.

Free entry and exit of firms is one of the basic traits of a perfectly competitive market. Free entry, in this case, does not mean that firms can enter at no cost. They may have to pay a great deal to set up shop, hire employees, gain useful contacts, and so on. Free entry simply means that if they are willing to invest the needed capital, new firms are free to compete with existing ones on a level playing field. They are not kept out by patents or licensing requirements. They are not kept out by trade secrets, or by collusion on the part of firms already in the industry, or by the lack of a location or raw materials. Likewise, free exit means that firms face no legal barriers to shutting down or moving out of town if they find that they cannot make a profit.

Free entry and exit did not play a direct role in our discussion of a firm's short-run supply decision. However, as we will now see, it is crucial to explaining how a competitive market works in the long run.

Long-Run Equilibrium for a Competitive Firm

At a number of points we have used the term *equilibrium* to refer to a state of affairs in which buyers and sellers are satisfied with the outcome of their economic plans. For a perfectly competitive firm, short-run equilibrium means being satisfied with the current level of output. As we have seen, this is the case when marginal cost is equal to marginal revenue, that is, to the price of the product.

In the long run, equilibrium under perfect competition requires two other things: Each firm must be content with the size of its current plant (that is, with the amount of fixed inputs it uses). And firms that are not already in the market must be content to stay out while firms in the market are content to stay in.

Box 22.6 shows how these three requirements are met in the long-run equilibrium for a perfectly competitive firm. First, marginal cost is equal to price at the chosen level of output. There is no reason in the short run for the firm to either increase or decrease its output. Second, the firm has a plant that is just the right size to make short-run average total cost equal to the lowest possible long-run average cost at the chosen level of output. No change in the amount of fixed inputs can cut average cost. And third, average total cost (both long-run and short-run) is equal to price at the equilibrium level of output. As always, average total cost includes implicit as well as explicit costs. When average total cost is equal to price, then, there is no incentive for firms either to enter or leave the industry. Outsiders are not attracted by profits higher than the opportunity cost of capital, and firms in the industry do not need to leave in order to avoid a loss.

These three conditions for long-run equilibrium can be expressed in the following equation:

$$\text{Price} = \frac{\text{marginal}}{\text{cost}} = \frac{\text{short-run average}}{\text{total cost}} = \frac{\text{long-run}}{\text{average cost}}$$

If any part of this equation does not hold, firms will have a reason to change their plans. Either they will want to change the level of output given the size of their plants, or they will want to change the size of the plants they are using to produce their current output, or they will want to enter or leave the industry. Unless all parts of the equation hold, then, the market is not in long-run equilibrium.

Industry Adjustment to Falling Demand

A state of long-run equilibrium like that shown in Box 22.6 exists only as long as outside conditions do not change. Suppose, though, that those conditions do change—for example, that there is a long-run decrease in the demand for its product. Box 22.7 shows what will happen.

Part a of Box 22.7 shows a set of cost curves for a typical firm. Part b is a supply-and-demand diagram for the market as a whole. The short-run industry supply curves shown are built up from those of the individual firms in the market. (See Box 22.5.) The demand curves are short-run market demand curves of the usual kind.

**Box 22.6
A Perfectly Competitive
Firm in Long-Run
Equilibrium**

Long-run equilibrium in a perfectly competitive industry requires that the typical firm (1) have no short-run incentive to change the level of its output; (2) have no long-run incentive to change the size of the plant used to produce its output; and (3) have no long-run incentive to enter or leave the industry. This requires that price, short-run marginal cost, short-run average total cost, and long-run average cost all have the same value in equilibrium, as shown.

Suppose that, to begin with, the short-run supply and demand curves are in the positions S_1 and D_1. The equilibrium price is $5. Each firm takes this price as given and adjusts its output on that basis, producing 25 units of output. At that price and output, a typical firm would just break even. (Remember, though, that breaking even in the economic sense means earning enough to cover all costs, including the opportunity cost of capital.)

Now something happens—say, a change in consumer tastes or incomes—that shifts the demand curve to a new position, D_2. The short-run result is a drop in the market price to $4. Each firm, being a price taker, will view the decline in price as beyond its control and will adjust to it as best it can. As shown in part a of the box, this means cutting back output a little in order to keep losses to a minimum, but not shutting down completely. The movement of each firm back along its marginal-cost curve is what causes the movement of the market as a whole downward and to the left along the short-run supply curve S_1.

However, this new situation cannot be a long-run equilibrium. The reason is that each firm is operating at a loss. Owners are not earning

Box 22.7
Long-Run Adjustment to Declining Demand

The left-hand graph in this pair represents a typical firm in a perfectly competitive industry and the right-hand graph represents the industry as a whole. At first both the firm and the industry are in long-run equilibrium at a price of $5. Then something happens to shift the demand curve leftward, from D_1 to D_2. In the short run the price falls to $4, at the intersection of D_2 and S_1. The firm's short-run response is to move downward along its marginal-cost curve. After a while some firms (not the one shown) get tired of taking losses and leave the industry. This causes the supply curve to shift toward S_2 and the market price to recover. The typical firm returns to the break-even point. The market has traced out part of its long-run supply curve, as shown by the large arrow.

(a) A Typical Firm

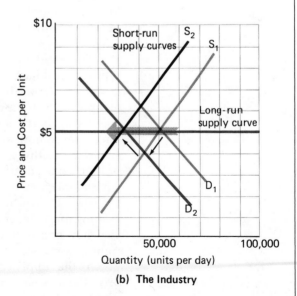

(b) The Industry

enough to cover the opportunity costs of keeping their capital invested in the industry. If the demand curve does not show any hope of shifting back to the right, some owners will pull their capital out of the industry. Some may go bankrupt; others will sell their plant and equipment and get out while they can. Still others will keep their firms running but change over to making goods for other, more profitable markets.

There is no way to tell which firms will be the first to go; but let us assume that the typical firm shown in the box is not one of the first. Look what happens to it as some of the others leave. As some firms withdraw, the market loses their output. The market supply curve, which is now made up of fewer individual supply curves, shifts to the left, toward S_2. As it does so, the market price begins to move upward along demand curve D_2. When the price gets all the way back to $5, the firms that are still left in the industry will no longer be losing money. Firms will stop leaving the industry, and the market will have reached a new long-run equilibrium. In the new equilibrium, price, marginal cost, short-run average total cost, and long-run average cost will once again be equal.

This sequence of events has traced out a portion of the industry's *long-run supply curve*, as shown by the arrow. A long-run supply curve for an industry shows the path along which equilibrium price and quantity move when there is a lasting change in demand. Movement along the long-run industry supply curve requires time both for firms to adjust the sizes of their plants and for firms to enter the market or leave it.

The long-run supply curve shown in Box 22.7 is perfectly elastic. In the long run, the leftward shift of the demand curve causes no change in price, only a decrease in quantity supplied.

Industry Adjustment to Rising Demand

When there is a long-run increase in demand, freedom of entry plays the same role that freedom of exit plays when demand falls. This case is shown in Box 22.8. The starting position in this box is the same as that in Box 22.7. Short-run supply curve S_1 and demand curve D_1 give an equilibrium price of $5. The individual firm breaks even at an output of 25 units. Now watch what happens as the demand curve shifts to D_2, to the right of D_1.

The short-run result is an increase in the market price to $6. The typical firm adjusts to the new price by moving upward along its marginal-cost curve. As all firms do this, the market moves upward and to the right along short-run supply curve S_1.

But again this short-run adjustment is not the new long-run equilibrium, because now all firms are making a profit. Entrepreneurs will soon spot this healthy, growing market as a good one in which to invest. Some of them may start new firms in this market. Others may shift plant and equipment from making something else to to making goods for this industry. It does not matter whether the entry is by new firms or by existing ones that are producing for this market for the first time. In either case, new entries into the market will cause the supply curve to shift to the right, toward S_2.

As the supply curve shifts, the price falls. It does not fall far enough to drive the new entrants back out, but it does fall enough to drive everyone's profits back to the normal level. Entry of firms into the industry will stop,

Box 22.8
Long-Run Adjustment to
an Increase in Demand

In this box, both the firm and the industry start out in equilibrium at a price of $5. Then something happens to shift the demand curve rightward, to D_2. In the short run the price rises to $6, at the intersection of D_2 and S_1. The firm's short-run response is to move upward along its marginal-cost curve, earning better-than-normal profits. After a while these high profits attract new firms into the industry. As new firms enter, the supply curve shifts toward S_2. Profits for the typical firm return to normal, and new firms stop entering the industry. Again the market has traced out part of its long-run supply curve, as shown by the large arrow.

(a) A Typical Firm

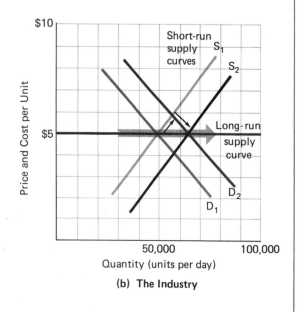

(b) The Industry

and the market will be in a new long-run equilibrium at the intersection of S_2 and D_2.

Once again, a portion of the long-run supply curve for the industry has been traced out, as shown by the large arrow. And once again this long-run supply curve is perfectly elastic. A rightward shift in the demand curve has, in the long run, produced an increase in quantity supplied but no increase in price.

Other Long-Run Supply Curves

The long-run industry supply curve need not always be perfectly elastic as in the examples just given. Box 22.9 shows some other possibilities—supply curves that are upward-sloping, downward-sloping, and U-shaped.

Which shape the long-run industry supply curve takes depends mainly on what happens to the industry's input prices in the long run as output expands. If the long-run supply curve for all inputs is perfectly elastic, the price of those inputs will not change as the quantity of them demanded by the industry increases. It may also be that the industry uses

**Box 22.9
Long-Run Supply
Curves for a
Competitive Industry**

The shape of an industry's long-run supply curve depends largely on what happens to the prices of inputs as demand and output expand in the long run. If input prices do not change much, the long-run industry supply curve will be horizontal, as shown in part a. If input prices rise, the long-run supply curve will slope upward, as shown in part b. Falling input prices will cause a downward-sloping long-run industry supply curve, as shown in part c. Finally, mixed cases, in which the long-run supply curve first falls and then rises, are possible, as shown in part d.

such a small part of the total supply of each input that whatever change in input prices does occur will be slight. Industry output can therefore expand without affecting the costs of the individual firms, and the supply curve will be perfectly elastic. This was the case in Boxes 22.7 and 22.8, and it is also the case in part a of Box 22.9. There a set of short-run supply and demand curves are shown lying along a horizontal long-run supply curve. Each pair of short-run curves represents one stage in the industry's long-run expansion.

Suppose, though, that the industry uses some special input of which the supply cannot easily be increased. Perhaps some skilled labor is needed, and more workers can be induced to acquire the needed skill only at a higher wage rate. The rising price of this key input will cause an upward shift in the cost curves of all the firms in the industry as new firms enter the industry and output expands. In this case the industry's long-run supply curve will slope upward, as shown in part b of Box 22.9.

It is also possible that the price of an input can decrease as the total output of the industry increases. For example, as sales of electronic equipment expand, the firms that make the components that go into that equipment may be able to use cheaper production methods. If this occurs, the cost curves for all firms will drift downward as new firms enter the industry. The long-run supply curve will then be downward-sloping, as shown in part c of Box 22.9.

Finally, it is possible for a combination of forces to be at work. In the industry shown in part d of Box 22.9, long-run supply is at first influenced by the falling price of one special input; but beyond a certain point some other special input becomes a limiting factor that causes the long-run supply curve to bend upward. Many variants are possible. Only through direct observation of the industry in question can we tell which possibility applies.

WHAT IS PERFECT ABOUT PERFECT COMPETITION?

Our discussion of perfect competition is nearly complete. We have a fairly good picture of how perfectly competitive markets work. One question still remains, however: What is so perfect about perfect competition?

As suggested early in the chapter, the answer is not that such a market is the perfect place to observe all forms of business rivalry. Far from it. Many forms of rivalry are absent from perfectly competitive markets. Under perfect competition, managers do not care very much what other firms do. After all, no one of those firms is big enough to have an impact on market prices. They cannot, by definition, be getting ready to introduce a new version of the industry's product. And they cannot, by definition, have any secrets.

They are instead perfect in another sense. Think for a moment about just what a market really is. Very simply, it is a means of getting buyers and sellers together to carry out transactions from which both can benefit. It makes sense, then, to say that *a perfect market is one in which all potential mutually beneficial transactions are in fact carried out—a market in which none is missed*. That is the sense in which perfectly competitive markets are perfect.

To see why, look at Box 22.10. This is a supply-and-demand diagram (long-run variety) just like many that have been shown before. But now we will look at it in a slightly different way.

Start with the demand curve. Usually one thinks of a demand curve as showing the quantity that consumers are willing and able to buy at any given price. But the demand curve can also be thought of as showing the maximum amount that consumers are willing to pay for a marginal unit of the good, given the quantity already available. Our demand curve, for example, has a height of $12 at 100 units of output. This means that someone is willing to pay barely $12 for the marginal 100th unit and someone is willing to pay almost, but not quite, that much for the 101st unit of output.

The supply curve can be thought of in much the same way. Usually one thinks of it as showing how much producers are willing to supply at a given price. But it also shows the lowest price that will induce producers to supply the marginal unit. The supply curve in this box, for example, has a height of $6 at an output of 100 units. That means that someone is barely willing to supply the 100th unit for $6, and no one will supply a 101st unit unless a slightly higher price is offered.

Suppose now that producers are supplying goods to this market at a rate of only 100 units per period. At that level of output, the demand curve is above the supply curve. Some consumer is willing to pay nearly $12 for the 101st unit. And some producer is willing to supply it for just over $6. If production stops at 100 units, then, buyers and sellers will be passing up a chance for a mutually beneficial transaction. The market will not be perfect.

The same will be true, although somewhat less so, if output stops at 101, 110, or 149 units. Even the production and sale of the 150th unit would be a mutually beneficial exchange, although only barely so. It can be said, then, that the whole shaded area in the diagram gives a measure of the amount of mutual benefit that will be wasted if production stops at 100 units.

Now we can see the sense in which perfectly competitive markets, when they are in equilibrium, are perfect. In such markets production is

**Box 22·10
Why Perfectly
Competitive Markets
Are Perfect**

Think of the demand curve in this graph as showing how much people are willing to pay for additional units of output. Think of the supply curve as showing how much producers will have to be paid to supply them. If production is limited to a rate of 100 units per period, opportunities for mutually beneficial exchange will be passed up. Consumers will be willing to pay nearly $12 for the 101st unit, whereas producers will have to be given barely more than $6 to make it. All mutually beneficial exchange will not take place until output reaches 150 units. The shaded area gives a rough measure of the opportunities for mutual benefit that will be wasted if production is limited to 100 units. But a competitive market will carry output all the way to 150 units.

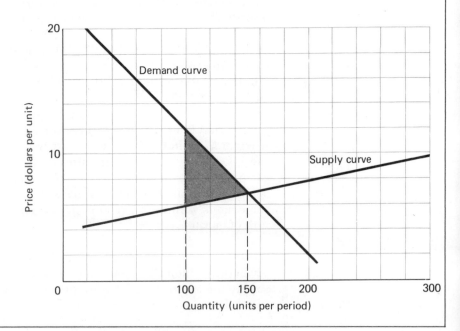

carried out up to, but not beyond, the point where the long-run supply and demand curves intersect. All possible mutually beneficial transactions between consumers and producers are carried out. And, as shown earlier in the chapter, each firm in long-run perfectly competitive equilibrium produces at the minimum average total cost. This means that no further gains are possible on the production side, at least within the limits of current technology. With no improvements possible through changes in either the amount of output traded or the way that output is produced, the market does as well as it can in satisfying the needs of consumers. In that sense, it is a perfect market.

Some Qualifications

It would be tempting to draw some broad conclusions from the preceding section. Would an economy in which all markets were perfectly competitive be the best of all possible worlds? Although prefectly competitive markets work well in some cases, a few qualifications should be noted.

One qualification is that technology does not cooperate. In many industries economies of scale make it impractical to spread production among a large number of small firms. In such markets, a perfectly competitive structure is not efficient.

A second qualification is that consumers are not always indifferent between the products of different firms. For many goods—cars, clothing, restaurants—consumers want to have a choice. Forcing all firms to make an identical product in the name of perfect competition would cost more in terms of consumer satisfaction than it would gain in terms of efficiency.

A third qualification is the fact that perfect competition leaves little or no room for entrepreneurship. It does not allow for innovation or changing tastes. It assumes that all buyers and sellers are informed, even though in the real world information is one of the scarcest and most valuable goods. Do markets with large numbers of small firms guarantee efficient decision making in a world of change and uncertainty? Are such markets most likely to produce new and better ways to satisfy human wants? The theory of perfect competition says nothing one way or the other in answer to these questions. Later chapters will return to them.

When all is said and done, perfect competition must be understood for what it is—a powerful economic model, but nothing more. It yields many useful insights. It allows us to think more clearly about what lies behind the law of supply and demand. It provides some insights into economic efficiency that can be of value in comparing economic policies. And for some markets, it is not so far from reality in a descriptive sense. Even so, perfect competition is not the whole story by any means.

Summary

1. A perfectly competitive market has the following traits: (a) There are many buyers and sellers, each of whom is small compared to the market as a whole; (b) the product is homogeneous; (c) all buyers and sellers have access to complete information; and (d) entry into and exit from the market are easy.

2. In the short run, the relationship between

marginal cost and marginal revenue (price) determines the profit-maximizing level of output for a perfectly competitive firm. The firm should expand output to the point where marginal cost rises to the level of marginal revenue, provided that marginal revenue is at least equal to average variable cost at that point.

3.   If marginal revenue is below average total cost at the point where marginal cost and marginal revenue are equal, the firm cannot earn a profit. It will keep its loss to a minimum in the short run by staying open if marginal revenue is above average variable cost. If marginal revenue is below average variable cost at the point where marginal cost and marginal revenue are equal, the firm will minimize loss by shutting down.

4.   The short-run supply curve for a perfectly competitive firm is the upward-sloping part of the marginal-cost curve lying above its intersection with the average-variable-cost curve.

5.   Long-run equilibrium for a perfectly competitive firm requires that price, marginal cost, short-run average total cost, and long-run average cost all be equal.

6.   A perfectly competitive industry adjusts to long-run changes in demand through exit of firms (in the case of a drop in demand) or entry of new firms (in the case of a rise in demand). If input prices do not change as the industry's output changes, the industry's long-run supply curve will be flat. If input prices rise, the long-run supply curve will have a positive slope; if they fall, it will have a negative slope.

7.   A perfectly competitive market is "perfect" in the sense that it allows all mutually beneficial transactions to be carried out. Perfect competition is not the best structure for all markets, however.

Questions for Review

1.   Explain the following terms and concepts:
     market structure
     perfect competition
     price taker
     marginal revenue

2.   Name four traits that define the market structure of perfect competition.

3.   What is the relationship between the total-cost and total-revenue curves at the point of short-run profit maximization for a perfectly competitive firm? What is the relationship between the marginal-cost and marginal-revenue curves at the same point?

4.   Under what conditions will a perfectly competitive firm find it worthwhile to operate even though, in the short run, it operates at a loss?

5.   What part of the perfectly competitive firm's supply curve coincides with its marginal-cost curve in the short run? What part of the supply curve does not coincide with the marginal-cost curve?

6.   List four quantities that must be equal for a perfectly competitive firm to be in long-run equilibrium.

7.   Under what conditions will the long-run supply curve for a perfectly competitive industry be perfectly elastic? Under what conditions will it slope upward or downward?

8.   Explain what is "perfect" about perfect competition.

Problems and Topics for Discussion

1.   The concept of being a price taker can apply to buyers as well as sellers. A price-taking buyer is one who cannot influence prices by changing the amount purchased. Are you are price taker for the goods you buy? Can you give an example of a firm that might not be a price

taker in the market where it buys one or more of its inputs?

2. Make a list of half a dozen products that you buy often. Do you buy any of these things from firms that are perfect competitors? If the firms that you buy from are not perfect competitors, which of the four market structure traits given in this chapter do not apply to them?

3. Fieldcom buys some automated equipment in order to speed up production of its computers. The equipment adds $500 per day to the firm's fixed costs, but it saves $50 per unit in variable costs. Rework the graph in Box 22.4 to show how the new equipment affects Fieldcom's supply curve. (You may want to rework the table in Box 22.1 as a basis for the new supply curve.) What is the minimum price the firm now needs to charge in order to continue to operate in the short run? What is the lowest price at which it can break even?

4. Box 22.8 shows the long-run adjustment of a competitive industry to an increase in demand in the case in which input prices do not change as output changes. Assume instead that input prices rise as output rises. Draw a new set of diagrams to show how a typical firm and the industry as a whole respond to an increase in demand. When demand first increases, the industry will move upward along its short-run supply curve as before. When that happens, what will happen to the typical firm's cost curves? How will the typical firm's new equilibrium point compare to its starting point?

5. The restaurant industry has many firms, each of which is small. Entry into and exit from the industry are easy. However, the industry is not perfectly competitive because the product is not homogeneous—there are Italian restaurants, French restaurants, hamburger huts, and so on. Suppose the Federal Restaurant Commission decides to enforce perfect competition in the industry by requiring all restaurants to have the same menu. Do you think this action will increase consumer satisfaction? Why or why not? (We will return to this question at the end of Chapter 25.)

6. **Case for Discussion**

The next time you are out on the highway, take a look at the trucks that are passing you. You will see many that belong to large firms, such as PIE and Yellow Freight, that haul large numbers of small shipments all over the country on regular schedules. You will also see trucks that bear the names of companies like Sears or Sun Oil, for which transportation is a sideline.

If you look closely, though, you will see that about one truck in four looks a little different. The tractors, many of which are brightly painted and highly chromed, often have sleepers attached to them. The trailers, often refrigerated, are likely to be filled with farm produce moving to market. These are the trucks of independent owner-operators, who move much of the nation's output of farm goods and some manufactured goods.

Most firms in this market consists of a man or woman who owns and drives just one truck. There are many such firms—as many as 35,000 by some estimates.

From the shipper's point of view, one refrigerated truck is about as good as another, as long as it is headed in the right direction. And most independent truckers will go wherever their loads take them.

A widespread information network helps independent truckers find loads. Some parts of the network are informal—based, for example, on gossip exchanged at truck stops. Other parts are more systematic. A key figure in the network is the truck broker—a specialist who matches the needs of farmers for trucks with the needs of owner-operators for loads in return for a 5 or 10 percent commission. A call to a broker can give a trucker a tip that load rates have shifted slightly and the time has come to switch from hauling Florida citrus to hauling California lettuce.

Entry and exit are easy. Some people go into business with a used truck and as little as $5,000. Most operators buy their trucks on credit. Exit is also easy—too easy, some say. Many independent truckers go broke every year, and the number of firms rises and falls with the state of the economy.

People who run the giant trucking companies that haul manufactured goods often look down their noses at the independent truckers with their loads of apples and potatoes. They call them "gypsies" or worse. But this system succeeds in putting fresh produce on the dinner table in every town every day.

Questions:

a. In what ways does the independent trucking industry meet the requirements of perfect competition? Are there any ways in which it does not?

b. On the average, the firms in a perfectly competitive industry earn no pure economic profits. However, average conditions do not always apply. What would you expect to happen to the profits of independent truckers when the economy enters a recession? When it enters a period of prosperity? What would you expect to happen to the number of firms in the industry at such times?

c. Turn back to Box 3.2 (p. 54). As this box shows, the relative price of motor fuel, a major input for independent truckers, has varied a lot over the last decade. What would you expect to happen to the profits of independent truckers and the number of firms in the industry as the price of motor fuel rises and falls? Outline the sequence of events in each case. Drawing a graph may help.

Suggestions for Further Reading

Nicholson, Walter. *Intermediate Microeconomics and Its Application*, 3rd ed. Hinsdale, Ill.: Dryden Press, 1983.

Chapters 11 and 12 parallel this chapter. Chapter 10 contains a useful discussion of the profit maximization assumption and some alternatives.

Robinson, Joan. "What Is Perfect Competition?" *Quarterly Journal of Economics* 49 (November 1934): 104–120.

This classic paper attempts to pin down some of the fine points of the concept of perfect competition. Not all of the issues raised in it have yet been laid to rest.

Chapter 23

The Theory of Monopoly

After reading this chapter, you should be able to

1. Define the terms *monopoly* and *cartel*.
2. Show how marginal revenue is related to price for a monopoly, and construct a monopolist's marginal-revenue curve given a straight-line demand curve.
3. Demonstrate the process of profit maximization for a monopolist.
4. Explain why monopoly is viewed as an imperfect market structure.
5. List the conditions required for a monopoly to practice price discrimination, and discuss the effects of price discrimination on consumers.
6. Explain why cartels encounter problems of cheating and instability.

Ideas for Review

Here are some terms and concepts that you should review before you read this chapter:

Efficiency (Chapter 2)
Price elasticity of demand (Chapter 19)
Theory of cost (Chapter 21)
Perfect competition (Chapter 22)

"He saw himself as a man of peace."

Cecil Rhodes was one of the great imperialists of the nineteenth century. He brought most of southern Africa under British control. Although he did all he could to expand the empire, he saw himself as a man of peace and took pride in his ability to bring warring factions together. As a member of the Cape Assembly, the local governing body in South Africa, he put his energy into getting the Dutch and British factions to work together. He once settled a dispute between the British government and a rebellious tribal army by riding alone and unarmed into enemy territory to listen to the grievances of local chiefs.

The British Empire is gone now, and the country once called Rhodesia, now Zimbabwe, no longer bears Rhodes's name. One of Rhodes's creations lives on, however, and stands as a memorial to his ability to get diverse interests to work together. This is De Beers Consolidated Mines, Ltd., a diamond mining concern that Rhodes founded in 1881. Today De Beers controls the marketing of more than 80 percent of the world's uncut diamonds. Diamond producers are an odd assortment—black-ruled Zaire, the Soviet Union, Australia with its democratic socialist government, and conservative South Africa. Yet under De Beers' leadership they work together toward the shared goal of keeping diamond prices high. And for over a hundred years, through good times and bad, De Beers has never had to cut its listed price for diamonds.

When we brought up the subject of diamonds in Chapter 19, we ascribed their high price compared to CZs to supply and demand. Supply and demand do account for much of the difference between the price of CZs and that of diamonds, but as we will see in this chapter, there is more to the story. CZs can be produced in large quantities, while diamonds are in short supply. But as almost the sole seller of uncut diamonds, De Beers can make diamonds even scarcer by keeping them off the market when it chooses to do so. By agreeing to sell only through De Beers, the producing countries can increase their profits.

Monopoly
A market that is dominated by a single seller.

Pure monopoly
A market structure in which a single firm makes and sells 100 percent of the output of a product.

Cartel
An organization through which several producers cooperate to control the sale of all or most of the output of a product.

Any market that is dominated by a single seller is known as a **monopoly**. A single firm that makes and sells 100 percent of the output of a product is a **pure monopoly**. There is no distinction between the firm and the industry in this case; the firm is the industry. An organization like De Beers, through which producers cooperate to control the sale of all or most of the output of a product, is known as a **cartel**. We discuss pure monopolies and cartels together in this chapter because the rules for profit maximization are the same for both. Toward the end of the chapter, however, we will see that cartels face problems of organization that do not affect pure monopolies.

PROFIT MAXIMIZATION FOR THE PURE MONOPOLIST

As a market structure, pure monopoly is the opposite of perfect competition. In a perfectly competitive market, each firm has so many small rivals that no one of them, acting alone, can affect the market price. A pure monopolist, by contrast, has no competitors at all.

What is more, the pure monopolist is shielded against the entry of competitors. Sometimes the barriers to entry take the form of control of a unique natural resource, or a production method that gives the monopolist an unbeatable cost advantage. In this case, the firm is said to be a *natural monopoly*. In other cases, the monopolist may be protected by law, as in the case of monopolies based on patents, licenses, and permits. As Chapters 26, 27, and 28 will show, the government sometimes fights monopoly and sometimes promotes it.

Whatever their origin, monopolies differ from perfectly competitive firms in an important way: they are not price takers. The fact that a monopolist's choice of a level of output directly affects the product's price is the starting point of the theory of monopoly.

Output, Price, and Marginal Revenue Under Monopoly

For an example of the relationships among output, price, and revenue under monopoly, look at Box 23.1. Columns 1 and 2 of the table give data on the demand for the product of a pure monopolist. The data are also presented as a demand curve. As both the table and the graph make clear, the greater the output, the lower the price at which buyers will be willing to purchase the entire amount produced.

As the monopolist raises or lowers output, changes in both price and quantity affect the firm's total revenue. For any output, total revenue is equal to price times quantity. Starting from zero, the box shows that as output increases, total revenue first rises, then reaches a maximum at about 17 units of output, and then falls.

Notice the similarity between this box and Box 19.5 (p. 491), which was used to illustrate price elasticity of demand. Box 19.5 showed that when demand is *elastic*, a drop in price causes total revenue to rise. (The reason is that, in percentage terms, the quantity sold rises by more than the price falls, so the product of the two increases.) In contrast, when demand is *inelastic*, revenue falls when the price goes down. (This is because, with inelastic demand, the percentage increase in quantity is less than the percentage decrease in price.) With a straight-line demand curve like the one in Box 23.1, the upper half is elastic and the lower half inelastic. That accounts for the shape of the "revenue hill" drawn as a separate graph below the demand curve.

The relationship between output and revenue for a pure monopolist can also be viewed in marginal terms. Chapter 22 defined *marginal revenue* as the change in total revenue that results from a one-unit increase in a firm's output. Column 4 of the table in Box 23.1 gives data on marginal revenue for the firm in this example. The figures in the column are the differences between the entries in column 3. Part b of the box shows the firm's marginal-revenue curve. The marginal-revenue curve is above the horizontal axis when total revenue is increasing (elastic demand) and below it when total revenue is decreasing (inelastic demand). It intersects the horizontal axis at the point of maximum total revenue.[1]

---

[1]Here is an easy rule that will help in sketching the marginal-revenue curve that corresponds to any straight-line demand curve: *The marginal-revenue curve for a straight-line demand curve always cuts the horizontal distance from the demand curve to the vertical axis exactly in half.* This rule does not work for curved demand curves, but the examples in this book will be kept simple.

Notice that the marginal-revenue curve is always below the demand curve. This means that the increase in total revenue that the monopolist gets from the sale of one additional unit is less than the price at which that unit is sold. The reason is that the monopolist must cut the price on all units sold, not just on the last unit sold, in order to increase total sales volume. The price cut on earlier units thus partly or wholly offsets the revenue gain from increasing the amount sold.

Profit Maximization

The relationship between output and revenue for a pure monopolist forms the basis for an analysis of short-run profit maximization. The best way to present such an analysis is through the use of a numerical example like the one we used in discussing perfect competition.

Box 23.2 takes the demand and revenue data from Box 23.1 and adds data on the firm's total and marginal costs. One way to determine the profit-maximizing level of output for the firm is to compare total cost and total revenue. Subtracting total cost (column 6) from total revenue (column 2) gives total profit (column 7). A glance at column 7 shows the profit-maximizing level of output to be 13 units. The total-revenue, total-cost approach to profit maximization is shown in a graph in part b of Box 23.2. Total profit is shown as the vertical gap between the total-cost and total-revenue curves. It reaches a maximum at 13 units of output, where the two curves are farthest apart.

Note that maximizing profit is not the same thing as maximizing revenue. Between 13 and 17 units of output, total revenue continues to rise. But total cost rises even faster, so profit falls.

The profit-maximizing level of output for the pure monopolist can also be found by comparing marginal cost and marginal revenue, as shown in columns 4 and 5 of the table in Box 23.2. Marginal revenue is the amount by which total revenue increases when output is increased by one unit, and marginal cost is the amount by which total cost increases. It follows that as long as marginal revenue exceeds marginal cost, adding one more unit of output will add more to total revenue than to total cost and hence will add to total profit. Beyond 13 units of output, marginal revenue falls below marginal cost, so any further expansion of output reduces total profit.

Part c of Box 23.2 compares marginal revenue and marginal cost in graphic terms. The profit-maximizing quantity is found where the marginal-cost and marginal-revenue curves intersect. It matches the point of maximum profit, which is shown in part b of Box 23.2 as the point where the gap between the total-revenue and total-cost curves is greatest.

The intersection of the marginal-cost and marginal-revenue curves in Box 23.2 gives the profit-maximizing level of output for the firm; the profit-maximizing price is given by the height of the demand curve for that level. For a pure monopolist, this price is always above marginal cost. For the firm in the example, marginal cost at 13 units of output is $2.60 per unit, but according to the demand curve, consumers are willing to buy 13 units for as much as $6.40. Therefore, $6.40 is what the monopolist will charge for the 13 units of output in order to earn the maximum profit.

**Box 23·1
Demand, Total
Revenue, and Marginal
Revenue for a
Monopolist**

This box shows how demand, total revenue, and marginal revenue are related for a typical monopolist. Total revenue is found by multiplying price by quantity at each point on the demand curve. Marginal revenue is the increase in total revenue that results from a one-unit increase in output.

(a)

Quantity (1)	Price (2)	Total Revenue (3)	Marginal Revenue (4)
1	$10.00	$10.00	$9.40
2	9.70	19.40	8.80
3	9.40	28.20	8.20
4	9.10	36.40	7.60
5	8.80	44.00	7.00
6	8.50	51.00	6.40
7	8.20	57.40	5.80
8	7.90	63.20	5.20
9	7.60	68.40	4.60
10	7.30	73.00	4.00
11	7.00	77.00	3.40
12	6.70	80.40	2.80
13	6.40	83.20	2.20
14	6.10	85.40	1.60
15	5.80	87.00	1.00
16	5.50	88.00	.40
17	5.20	88.40	−.20
18	4.90	88.20	−.80
19	4.60	87.40	−1.40
20	4.30	86.00	−2.00
21	4.00	84.00	−2.60
22	3.70	81.40	−3.20
23	3.40	78.20	−3.80
24	3.10	74.40	−4.40
25	2.80	70.00	−5.00
26	2.50	65.00	−5.60
27	2.20	59.40	−6.20
28	1.90	53.20	−6.80
29	1.60	46.40	−7.40
30	1.30	39.00	−8.00
31	1.00	31.00	−8.60
32	.70	22.40	−9.20
33	.40	13.20	−9.80
34	.10	3.40	−3.40
35	.00	.00	

When demand is elastic, marginal revenue is more than zero and total revenue is increasing. When demand is inelastic, marginal revenue is less than zero and total revenue is decreasing. Marginal revenue is less than price at all levels of output.

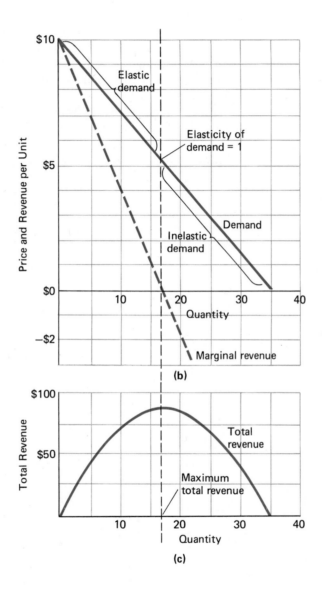

(b)

(c)

Profit Maximization or Loss Minimization?

If market conditions are unfavorable, a monopolist, like a perfectly competitive firm, may not be able to earn a profit in the short run. If that is the case, it will try to keep losses to a minimum. Whether a profit is possible depends on the position of the demand curve relative to the monopolist's average-cost curves.

One possibility is shown in Box 23.3. Here, demand is strong enough for the monopolist to make a pure economic profit above and beyond the opportunity cost of capital that is built into the definition of average total cost. As in Box 23.2, the profit-maximizing quantity, at the intersection of the marginal-cost and marginal-revenue curves, is roughly 13 units of output. The demand curve shows that the profit-maximizing price for that level of output is about $6.40 per unit.

At 13 units of output, average total cost is about $4.08 per unit. That

---

Box 23.2
Profit Maximization for a Monopolist

A monopolist maximizes profits by producing the amount of output for which marginal cost is equal to marginal revenue. The price charged for the product is determined by the height of the demand curve (not the height of the marginal-revenue curve) at the profit-maximizing quantity. Note that maximizing profit is not the same as maximizing revenue. Beyond 13 units of output (the profit-maximizing level in this case), total revenue continues to rise for a while, but profit falls because total cost rises even faster.

(a)

Output (1)	Price (2)	Total Revenue (3)	Marginal Revenue (4)	Marginal Cost (5)	Total Cost (6)	Total Profit (7)
1	$10.00	$10.00			$23.80	−$13.80
			$9.40	$3.40		
2	9.70	19.40			27.20	−7.80
			8.80	3.05		
3	9.40	28.20			30.25	2.05
			8.20	2.75		
4	9.10	36.40			33.00	3.40
			7.60	2.50		
5	8.80	44.00			35.50	8.50
			7.00	2.30		
6	8.50	51.00			37.80	13.20
			6.40	2.15		
7	8.20	57.40			39.95	17.45
			5.80	2.05		
8	7.90	63.20			42.00	21.20
			5.20	2.00		
9	7.60	68.40			44.00	24.40
			4.60	2.05		
10	7.30	73.00			46.05	26.95
			4.00	2.15		
11	7.00	77.00			48.20	28.80
			3.40	2.30		
12	6.70	80.40			50.50	29.90
			2.80	2.50		
13	6.40	83.20			53.00	30.20
			2.20	2.75		
14	6.10	85.40			55.75	29.65
			1.60	3.05		
15	5.80	87.00			58.80	28.20
			1.00	3.40		
16	5.50	88.00			62.20	25.80
			.40	3.80		
17	5.20	88.40			66.00	22.40

means that the monopolist earns a pure economic profit of just over $2.32 per unit above and beyond all costs, including the opportunity cost of capital. At 13 units of output, total profit is $30.20. This is shown in Box 23.3 as a shaded rectangle. The base of the rectangle is equal to the level of output (13 units). Its height is equal to the difference between the price of $6.40 per unit and the average total cost of $4.08 per unit—that is, to the $2.32 average profit the firm earns.

Under less favorable conditions, however, the same firm may be able only to keep losses to a minimum. This possibility is shown in Box 23.4. The demand curve lies below the average-cost curve at all points. This might be the case, for example, during a recession, when incomes fall. Following the usual rule, the profit-maximizing (here, loss-minimizing) level of output is found where the marginal-cost and marginal-revenue curves intersect—at about ten units. According to the demand curve, that much output cannot be sold for more than $4 per unit, but average total

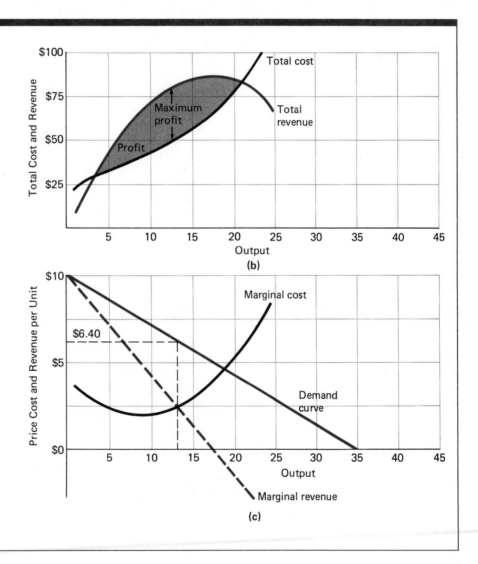

cost at ten units of output is $4.60. At a price of $4 per unit, then, the monopolist will lose 60 cents on each unit sold. This total loss is shown by the shaded rectangle.

Although the monopolist suffers a loss at ten units of output, no other level of output will yield a smaller loss. As Box 23.4 is drawn, $4 per unit is more than enough to cover average variable costs. The monopolist, like the perfectly competitive firm, is better off staying in business in the short run, even at a loss, as long as the price at which the output can be sold is greater than the average variable cost. If the demand curve shifts so far to the left that it falls below the average-variable-cost curve at all points, a pure monopolist, like a perfectly competitive firm, will minimize short-run losses by shutting down.

In the long run, if demand conditions do not improve, the firm is in trouble despite its monopoly. If it must depend entirely on private sources of capital, it will go out of business because potential investors will invest elsewhere. However, as Box 23.5 shows, if the monopoly provides an essential public service, it may be kept in business by means of a government subsidy.

Box 23.3
A Monopolist Earning a
Pure Economic Profit

Whether or not a monopolist earns a profit depends on the relationship of price to average total cost. In this example the monopolist's demand curve is high enough to allow it to earn a pure economic profit. Total profit is shown by the shaded rectangle, which has a height equal to the difference between price and average total cost, and a width equal to the profit-maximizing level of output.

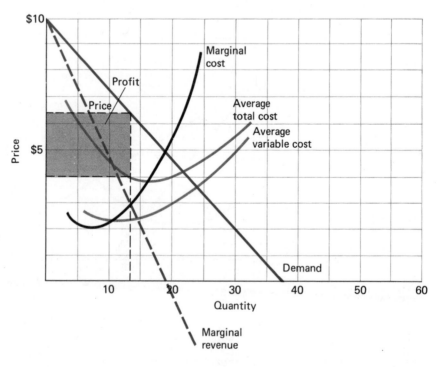

Long-Run Profit Maximization

One of the basic conclusions reached in Chapter 22 was that, in the long run, pure economic profits are impossible under perfect competition. The reason is that when an increase in demand for the product raises the market price above average total cost, new firms are drawn into the industry. As the new firms enter, the total quantity supplied to the market increases, driving the price back to the level of average total cost.

Under pure monopoly, in contrast, pure economic profits can continue as long as demand conditions are favorable. The reason is that a monopolist is protected against competition. Even if short-run demand conditions permit a rate of return higher than the opportunity cost of capital, as in Box 23.3, no other firm can enter the market. If nothing happens to disturb the favorable position of its cost and demand curves, a pure monopolist can earn pure economic profits above and beyond the normal rate of return even in the long run.

**Box 23.4
A Monopolist Earning a
Short-Run Loss**

Sometimes demand may not be high enough to allow a monopolist to earn a profit. In this graph, for example, the demand curve lies below the average-total-cost curve at all points. The best the monopolist can do, in the short run, is to cut losses by producing at the point where marginal cost equals marginal revenue. If the demand curve were to shift downward even farther, so that the firm could not obtain a price that would cover average variable cost, the short-run loss-minimizing strategy would be to shut down.

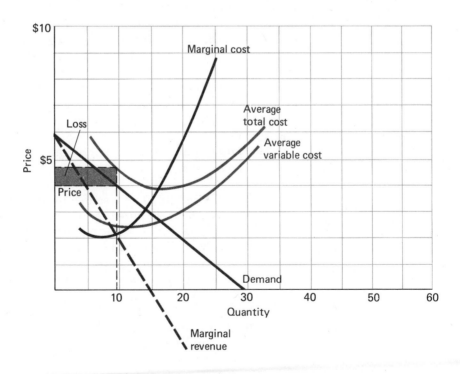

**Box 23.5
Subsidized Monopoly:
The Case of Mass
Transit**

If demand conditions turn against a private monopoly to the point at which it cannot expect, in the long run, to charge a price at least equal to average total cost, it will have to go out of business. However, if the monopoly provides a service that is essential to the public, it may continue to operate under a government subsidy. The mass transit systems of many cities are in this position. At one time they were able to make a profit as private monopolies. Over time, however, rising costs and falling demand cut into their earnings. At that point many transit systems were taken over by local government.

Public mass transit systems face a dilemma in their pricing decisions. On the one hand, the interests of taxpayers, many of whom are not regular users of mass transit, call for a pricing policy that would equate marginal cost and marginal revenue in order to keep the subsidy to a minimum. On the other hand, the interests of riders call for as low a fare and as large a subsidy as possible.

In practice, almost all mass transit systems do not attempt to minimize the subsidy. To do so would require raising the price until the system was operating on the elastic part of its demand curve—the part of the demand curve on which further fare increases would reduce total revenue. However, fare increases on most systems result in higher revenues, showing that they are on the inelastic portion of the demand curve. The rule seems to be to keep the price low and the subsidy high until the taxpayers scream, and then to raise fares a little, but not all the way to the point at which the subsidy could be kept to a minimum.

Indirect Competition and Long-Run Profits

Although protection from direct competition makes it possible for pure monopolists to earn pure economic profits in the long run, there are other cases in which long-run profits are reduced by indirect competition. In one such case, a monopolist faced with indirect competition might find itself in the position pictured in Box 23.6. There the demand curve just touches the average-total-cost curve at the level of output for which marginal revenue equals marginal cost, so that the best the firm can do is break even. It takes in enough revenue to cover all its costs, including the opportunity cost of capital, but no more.

Two kinds of indirect competition can push a monopolist toward this long-run break-even position. One is competition in the process of gaining a monopoly in the first place. A firm may have to bid against others for a key patent or access to a key resource in order to establish a monopoly. Perhaps it will have to hire lawyers and consultants to convince a government agency that it, and not some other firm, should get a key license or permit. If entrepreneurs compete actively for a monopoly, it may very well turn out that the winner never does more than break even. Its efforts, though successful, may cost so much that it ends up in the position shown in Box 23.5.

Competition from substitute products can also force a monopolist to the break-even point. A firm with a monopoly in steel production, for example, may find that, over time, entrepreneurs in the aluminum or plastics industries are stealing more and more of its customers. This competition may erode the demand for steel so much that the demand curve will fall all the way to a position that is tangent with the average-cost-curve.

Box 23.6
The Breakeven Position
for a Pure Monopolist

This graph shows a monopolist that is just breaking even. The firm earns enough revenue to cover all costs, including the opportunity cost of capital, but not enough to permit a pure economic profit. This situation could be due to the high cost of obtaining or defending the firm's monopoly position, or to the erosion of demand by indirect competition from makers of substitute products.

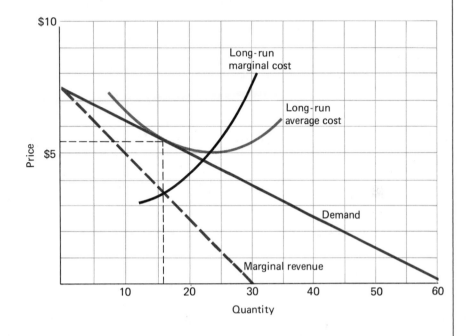

The likelihood of actually reaching the point of zero profits depends on the closeness of the substitutes offered by other firms. For example, a firm whose monopoly consists of owning the only Italian restaurant in town will clearly feel more competitive pressure than a firm that owns the only restaurant of any kind. In fact, when a firm's "monopoly" is so narrow that many competing firms offer products that are close substitutes, economists no longer classify the firm as a pure monopolist. We will return to market structures of this type in Chapter 25.

Monopoly as an Imperfect Market Structure

Chapter 22 showed that production is carried out in a perfectly competitive market up to the point at which price is equal to marginal cost. This, it was argued, makes perfect competition a "perfect" market form in the sense that no opportunities for mutually beneficial exchange are passed up. Under monopoly, however, production stops short of the amount needed to bring market price down to the level of marginal cost. Monopoly is, in this sense, an imperfect market structure.

Look at Box 23.7, for example. There the monopolist makes the maximum profit by producing 2,000 units of output per month and selling each unit for $3. At a rate of output of 2,000 units per month, marginal cost is only $1 per unit. There is a $2 gap between marginal cost and the market price. This gap represents an imperfection in the market. It is not efficient, since a further increase in production would increase consumer satisfaction by more than it would raise the monopolist's costs.

The height of the demand curve at 2,000 units of output in Box 23.7 shows that consumers are willing to pay $3 for the 2,000th unit of output. The height of the marginal-cost curve at that point shows what the monopolist has to pay for the various inputs needed to produce the 2,000th unit. Clearly, if consumers value the 2,000th unit at $3 and it costs only $1, it is efficient to produce that unit.

The same can be said for a 2,001st unit of output. Consumers will value the 2,001st unit at just under $3, and the inputs will cost only a little more than $1. If the 2,001st unit could be sold at a price of, say, $2, both the firm and its customers would be better off. But under monopoly conditions there's a catch: Although a price of $2 looks like a good deal for all concerned when the 2,001st unit is viewed by itself, it is not a good deal for the monopolist if we remember that the firm is assumed to sell all units at the same price. Unless the monopolist can discriminate among customers, selling some of the output at a higher price and some at a lower price, it will be necessary to cut the price on the first 2,000 units in order to sell the

**Box 23.7
Why Monopoly Is an
Imperfect Market
Structure**

A perfect market is one in which all goods are produced on which buyers place a value higher than marginal cost. Monopoly is, in this sense, an imperfect market structure. In the case shown here, a pure monopolist will maximize profits at an output of 2,000 units per month and a price of $3 per unit. But at that price and quantity, there is a gap between the demand curve and the marginal-cost curve. The shaded triangular area represents the value of potential gains in efficiency that are foregone as a result of the monopoly.

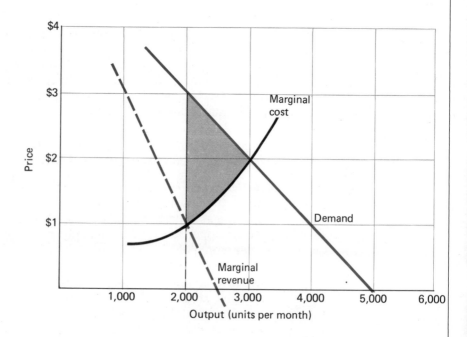

2,001st. To put it another way, even though the 2,001st unit can be sold at a *price* higher than its marginal cost, the *marginal revenue* earned from the sale of the 2,001st unit will be less than the marginal cost. And it is not profitable for the monopolist to increase its output beyond the point at which marginal revenue falls below marginal cost.

What is true of the 2,001st unit is also true of the 2,002nd, the 2,003rd, and all units up to and including the 3,000th. Consumers place a value greater than marginal cost on each of those units. But the monopolist will not produce those units. So long as all units must be sold at the same price, the extra units cannot be sold unless the price of all units is reduced. And in this case, the loss of revenue from cutting the price of previous units more than offsets the gain from selling one more unit. So production stops short of the point at which marginal cost and marginal revenue are equal. The shaded triangle between the marginal-cost and demand curves in Box 23.7 represents the opportunities for efficient production that are lost under monopoly conditions.

PRICE DISCRIMINATION

In our discussion of the imperfection of monopoly, we have assumed that the monopolist sells all units of output at the same price. Such a policy is forced on the monopolist whenever resale by buyers is possible. For example, it is unlikely that your campus bookstore (a monopoly on many campuses) could get away with selling economics texts at list price to seniors and at a 25 percent discount to everyone else. If it tried to do so, some clever sophomore would soon go into business buying books for resale to seniors at a split-the-difference price. The bookstore's list-price sales would soon fall to zero.

Some firms, however, do not sell their product to all customers at the same price. Such sellers are said to practice **price discrimination**. Two things are required for price discrimination to be possible. First, resale of the product by consumers must be impossible, or at least inconvenient. And second, the seller must be able to classify consumers into groups based on the elasticity of their demand for the good. Those with highly inelastic demand can then be charged high prices, and those with more elastic demand will be charged lower prices.

The conditions for price discrimination are not found in every market, but they are not rare. Box 23.8 gives one example of price discrimination in action. Others may be found at theaters that offer lower prices for children than for adults; stores that give senior-citizen discounts; airlines that find ways to charge business travelers more than vacation travelers; and so on.

Price discrimination is widely viewed as unfair, especially by those who pay a high price while others pay less. Attempts have been made to outlaw price discrimination in some markets. (We will look at these in Chapter 26.) However, the example of price discrimination in the form of college scholarships suggests that this practice may have benefits as well as drawbacks.

A key question to ask about any price discrimination scheme is whether it moves the market closer to or farther from an efficient level of production. When price discrimination allows some people to buy the good who would otherwise be excluded from the market, but still ensures

Price discrimination
The practice of charging different prices for different units of a single product, when the price differences are not justified by differences in cost.

**Box 23·8
Price Discrimination in
Higher Education**

Colleges and universities practice price discrimination in selling their main product—education. Usually it works like this. First the business office sets tuition at some high level. Then the admissions office gives its approval to a certain number of qualified applicants. After this is done, the financial aid office works out a price discrimination strategy. The strategy consists of giving price rebates, called scholarships, to students who it thinks will be unwilling or unable to attend if they are charged full tuition.

A college or university is in an ideal position to practice price discrimination. For one thing, the product cannot be transferred. If you are admitted to both Harvard and Dartmouth, you can't sell your Dartmouth admission to someone who didn't get into either place. Also, the college collects a lot of information that allows it to classify students by their willingness and ability to pay. For example, most colleges require you to submit a family financial statement when you apply for financial aid. Each college then calculates the "family contribution" toward your education (in plain terms, the price that it will charge).

If the price discrimination strategy is successful, everyone may benefit. Students who could not attend college at all without financial aid benefit most. Students who pay full tuition find their college life enriched by the presence of students with a wider range of backgrounds and abilities than would have been possible without a scholarship program. Meanwhile, the college benefits by keeping its classrooms full with the help of scholarship students, and its budget balanced with the help of tuition and fees collected from those without scholarships.

that everyone pays a price at least equal to marginal cost, it is likely to have some value. After all, price discrimination makes it possible for some students to attend colleges that they otherwise could not afford. It allows parents to take young children to the movies. And it makes it possible for standby passengers, who could not afford the full fares that business travelers pay, to fill airplane seats that would otherwise be empty.

On the other hand, price discrimination can be carried too far. The lowest price should always be at least as high as marginal cost. When some buyers pay less than marginal cost, another kind of market imperfection occurs. Output becomes too large, rather than too small, compared with the case in a perfectly competitive market. Too many, rather than too few, resources are attracted to the industry in question.

Does this ever happen? In some regulated markets, it does. Public utility commissions in some states encourage electric utilities to discriminate against industrial users and in favor of residential users. Often this practice is carried so far that some power for residential use is sold below long-run marginal cost. Many economists believe that this has led to wasteful use of electricity by homeowners and caused utilities to overexpand their capacity for producing electricity.

CARTELS

A monopoly position in a market, as we have seen, offers a firm a chance, although not a guarantee, of earning pure economic profits in the long run. Most firms, of course, do not expect to be able to get rid of their competitors. However, there is another route to monopoly profits—the formation of a cartel, in which competitors cooperate to restrict output and raise prices.

How Cartels Work

A simple example will show just how cartels work. Imagine an industry made up of 100 small firms. Assume that the marginal cost of production for all firms in the industry is $1 per unit, regardless of the amount produced. Because marginal cost is the same for all units of output, the marginal-cost curve also serves as the long-run average-cost curve and the long-run supply curve for the industry. This perfectly elastic long-run supply curve is shown, along with a demand curve for the industry, in Box 9.9.

The equilibrium price and level of output of the industry depend on how the market is organized. Suppose, to begin with, that all firms act like perfect competitors. Under the theory set forth in Chapter 8, this will result in an equilibrium in which the market price is $1 per unit (equal to long-run average cost and long-run marginal cost) and in which 400,000 units of output are produced each month. In this equilibrium, firms earn no pure economic profit.

Now suppose that one day the heads of the 100 firms meet to form a cartel. They hope that by replacing competition with cooperation they can all benefit. They elect a cartel manager, who is asked to work out a production and marketing plan that will result in the maximum total profits for the industry and divide these profits fairly among its members.

The profit-maximizing problem faced by the cartel manager is exactly the same as that faced by a pure monopolist. Industry profits are highest at the output where marginal revenue equals marginal cost. That output is 200,000 units per month. If output is restricted to that quantity, the price

**Box 23.9
The Effects of a Cartel**

This graph shows an industry made up of 100 firms, each producing at a constant long-run average and marginal cost. If the firms act like perfect competitors, the industry will be in equilibrium at the point where the demand and marginal-cost curves intersect. If the firms form a cartel, however, they can jointly earn profits by restricting output to the point where marginal cost is equal to marginal revenue and raising the price from $1 to $2.

can be raised to $2 per unit, which yields $200,000 per month of pure economic profit.

To divide this profit among all the members of the cartel, the manager will give each firm an output quota of 2,000 units a month, half as much as each was producing before the cartel was formed. In this way the member firms will reap the benefits of pure monopoly despite their small size and large number.

The Stability Problem of Cartels

Although cartels are good for their members, they are not so good for consumers. For them, cartels mean a smaller supply of goods and higher prices. Fortunately for consumers, though, cartels have some built-in problems that make them hard to form and unstable.

The first problem from which cartels suffer is control over entry. As

---

Box 23.10
The Decline of the OPEC Cartel

At the end of 1982 the Organization of Petroleum Exporting Countries (OPEC) faced a crisis of overproduction and falling prices. The following passages are taken from an article that appeared in the Wall Street Journal *at that time.*

When they meet in December, the members of OPEC will decide whether they can hold their cartel together for another year, or whether their attempt to keep both prices high and all production going has failed. The OPEC countries currently produce only about 60 percent of the oil they pumped before the quadrupling of prices in 1973, and now even prices are under pressure. Indeed, a strong case can be made that OPEC is declining just the way cartels have always declined.

To understand what is happening to OPEC, it is helpful to review the rules of cartel theory, first formulated in 1905 by a young German economist, Robert Liefmann, in his book *Die Kartelle*—and validated by all subsequent experience.

The first of these rules is that a cartel is always the product of weakness. Growing industries don't form cartels; only declining ones do.

At first, it was assumed that this rule did not apply to OPEC. It was assumed that OPEC could raise prices so astronomically because oil consumption had been growing exponentially and was slated to grow even faster.

But study after study since the price explosion of 1973 shows that the developed countries had

previously been growing *less* dependent on petroleum. From 1950 to 1973, the energy required to produce an additional unit of manufactured output in developed countries declined by 1.5 percent per year; since then the decline has been much more rapid.

According to the second rule of cartel theory, if a cartel succeeds in raising the price of a commodity, it will depress the prices for all other commodities of the same general class. When OPEC raised oil prices in 1973, it was generally believed that the prices of all other primary commodities—agricultural products, metals, and minerals—would rise in parallel with the petroleum price. But a year later, the prices of all other primary products began to go down. They have been going down ever since.

A cartel, according to the third rule, will begin to unravel as soon as its strongest member—the largest and lowest-cost producer—must cut production by 40 percent to support the smaller and weaker members. Even a very strong producer will not and usually cannot cut further. The weaker members will then be forced to maintain their production by undercutting the cartel price. In the end, the cartel will collapse into a free-for-all. Or the strongest member will use its cost advantage to drive the weaker and smaller members out of the market.

we saw in Chapter 22, any industry that has prices above the level of long-run average cost tends to attract new firms. Since the whole point of a cartel is to raise prices above the competitive level, a cartel acts as a magnet for entrepreneurs. But the entry of new firms does not increase the total amount that the cartel can sell at the profit-maximizing price. More firms only mean that the profits must be divided into smaller shares. Any cartel, then, needs to find a way to control entry into its market if it is to serve the interests of its founding members.

The second, even more serious, built-in problem of cartels is enforcing output quotas. In a cartel, each member has an incentive to cheat by producing extra output beyond its quota. Take the cartel in Box 23.9. The quota for each of the 100 members is 2,000 units per month, just half of what each firm would produce under perfect competition.

What would happen if one firm cheated on its quota by stepping up its output while the others went on playing by the rules? The answer is

OPEC has been singularly lucky. Its second strongest member, Iran, has been forced to cut output by more than 50 percent as a result of revolution and war. Even so, the largest producer, Saudi Arabia, has had to cut its output by more than 40 percent to prevent the collapse of the cartel price. The other, weaker members, as predicted by the theory, have begun to sell petroleum at substantial discounts of as much as 15 percent below the posted price.

In the meantime, as the fourth of the cartel rules predicts, OPEC has lost its dominance of the oil market. "Any cartel undermines the market shares of its members within 10 years or so," Liefmann concluded in 1905. In 1973, the OPEC countries accounted for almost 60 percent of the oil supply of the industrialized countries. Their share nine years later has fallen to about 45 percent. As predicted by cartel theory, OPEC is losing market position to newcomers outside it such as Mexico, the North Sea, and Gabon.

The final rule is that the end of a cartel permanently impairs the position of its product, unless it cuts prices steadily and systematically—as did the only long-lived monopolists on record, the explosives cartel before World War I and the Bell Telephone System from 1910 through 1970. However, the experience of most past cartels, for example the European steel cartel between the wars, suggests that for a long time to come, petroleum will lose markets fast when it becomes more expensive and will not regain markets by becoming cheaper.

One cannot yet rule out what all the energy specialists predict: that the oil market is different, and OPEC will behave differently than other cartels. The test will come with the first sustained economic upturn in the developed countries. We will then know whether petroleum consumption will go up as fast as the economy, or whether, as cartel theory predicts, it will rise much more slowly or perhaps not at all.

Three years later, by 1985, the economic upturn had occurred. OPEC was still in crisis. Oil prices had fallen; Saudi Arabia's production fell to as low as 25 percent of capacity in some months; and many small OPEC members were selling below the agreed-upon price.

Source: Peter F. Drucker, "The Decline of the OPEC Cartel," *Wall Street Journal*, November 26, 1982, p. 12. Reprinted by permission of The Wall Street Journal, © Dow Jones & Company, Inc. 1982. All rights reserved.

simple. An extra 2,000 units per month would have only a small effect on the market price, since it would represent only a 1 percent increase in industry output. By producing 4,000 units a month, the cheater would double its monthly profit—as long as others did not cheat too.

But what if the others did cheat? What if all the other 99 firms stepped up their output to 4,000 units while only one firm stuck to its quota? With industry output at 398,000 units, the price would be forced down to the competitive level of $1. The firm that played fair would gain nothing for doing so.

The conclusion to which this leads is that each member of a cartel will have an incentive to cheat if it expects other members to play fair—and to cheat if it expects others to cheat too.

No cartel is free from the problems of entry by new firms and cheating on quotas. Box 23.10 describes the problems faced by OPEC, one of the world's best-known cartels. Even De Beers, a much older cartel, has not been free of these problems. In 1979 De Beers faced the threat of a major new entrant, the gigantic Argyle mine newly discovered in Australia. Two years later it faced another crisis when Zaire tried to make a quick killing by selling more diamonds than its quota allowed. De Beers managed to bring both Zaire and Australia into line, but only at great cost. To keep the cartel intact, it had to accept a lower quota for its own South African mines, and it agreed to give Australia more freedom of action within the cartel than had ever been allowed before. In the end the De Beers cartel was able to hang together only because the Soviet Union strongly backed the South Africans.

Some Qualifications

It would be tempting to wrap up this chapter with a sweeping comparison of monopoly and competition: Competition is perfect; monopoly is flawed. But not so fast. The conclusions that can safely be drawn from a comparison of the two market structures are more limited than they may appear. And a lot more groundwork must be laid before even those limited conclusions can be drawn.

For one thing, our analysis of perfect competition and pure monopoly has taken such factors as technology, product quality, and consumer tastes as given. Before we reach any conclusions on the merits of various market structures we need a more complete picture of these other aspects of competition. These topics are taken up in Chapters 24 and 25.

Second, up to this point we have compared two different markets—one competitive and the other monopolistic. That is not the same as figuring out how any one market would perform under two different market structures. In practice, it is rarely, if ever, possible to change the structure of a market without making other changes in it as well.

Any change in market structure that involves increasing or decreasing the number of firms is likely to affect costs and product quality as well. If competition reduces costs and improves the product, its advantage over monopoly may be much greater than the little triangle in Box 23.7 shows. On the other hand, if dividing production among many firms raises costs or reduces quality, those effects may more than outweigh the benefits of competition.

Finally, it would be premature to make any comparisons between perfect competition and monopoly until we have studied many other market structures. That job will take up most of the next four chapters.

Summary

1. Any market that is dominated by a single seller is a *monopoly*. A single firm that makes and sells 100 percent of the output of a product is a *pure monopoly*. An organization of producers that act together to control the sale of most or all of a product is a *cartel*.

2. A monopolist is not a price taker. As output is increased or decreased, both price and quantity change, causing changes in total revenue. For a firm with a straight-line downward-sloping demand curve, marginal revenue is always below price. In such a case the marginal-revenue curve cuts the horizontal distance from the demand curve to the vertical axis in half.

3. A monopolist makes the maximum profit by producing the level of output that makes marginal cost equal to marginal revenue. The price is determined by the height of the demand curve at the profit-maximizing level. If a monopoly cannot earn a profit in the short run, it will try to keep its loss to a minimum. If the loss-minimizing price is above average variable cost, the firm will continue to operate in the short run. If the loss-minimizing price is below average variable cost, it will shut down.

4. A monopoly is said to be an imperfect market structure because the amount of output it produces is less than the amount that would make marginal cost equal to marginal revenue. This means that some consumers who would be willing to pay a price greater than marginal cost are not able to buy from a monopolist.

5. A monopolist can practice price discrimination if its product cannot be resold by buyers, and if it has some way of classifying buyers by elasticity of demand. Although price discrimination is resented by buyers that have to pay higher prices, it may increase efficiency by allowing some customers to buy the product who would otherwise have been shut out of the market.

6. In theory, a cartel can restrict the output of its members and raise prices to levels that benefit all. In practice, cartels face two disruptive forces. One is the threat of new firms coming into the cartel. The other is the threat of cheating by existing members. Because of these problems, few cartels are successful in the long run.

Questions for Review

1. Explain the following terms and concepts:
   monopoly
   pure monopoly
   cartel
   price discrimination

2. What is the difference between a pure monopolist and a cartel? Is there any difference in the profit-maximizing price and quantity for the two market structures, under given cost conditions?

3. Why is marginal revenue always less than price for a monopolist? Under what elasticity conditions will marginal revenue be positive, negative, or zero?

4. Given data on cost and demand, how is the profit-maximizing level of output for a monopolist determined? Given the profit-maximizing output, how is the price determined?

5. Why is monopoly thought to be an imperfect,

or inefficient, market structure?

6. Under what conditions can a monopolist practice price discrimination? Who gains and who loses from price discrimination? Is price discrimination always inefficient?

7. What two problems threaten the stability of all cartels?

Problems and Topics for Discussion

1. "A monopolist can always make a profit because, with no competition, it can charge any price it wants to." Do you agree? Why or why not?

2. The form of price discrimination discussed in the text involves charging different prices to different customers when the price difference is not justified by differences in cost. Can you think of any examples in which different prices are justified by differences in cost? Discuss.

3. In what ways do labor unions resemble cartels? In what ways do they differ? Do you think labor unions ever suffer from the instability that plagues product market cartels? (We will return to the subject of labor unions in Chapter 31.)

4. **Case for Discussion**

   The U.S. Post Office was organized in 1789 and started losing money right away. One of the reasons that it lost money was competition. The Post Office charged the same price to deliver a letter anywhere in the country, but its costs were not the same in every case. For letters mailed between points in the East, the post office charged more than cost. For letters mailed to points in the West, it charged less than cost.

   Competitors flocked to the routes where costs were low. For example, in the 1840s Henry Wells, who later founded the famous Wells-Fargo Company, set up a mail service between Philadelphia and New York. He charged 6 cents for a first-class letter, compared to the Post Office's rate of 25 cents. By the early 1840s private firms were carrying at least a third of all mail in the United States.

   To fight off the competition, the Post Office turned to Congress. In 1845 Congress strengthened the restrictions on private first-class mail service. This saved the Post Office from extinction and allowed it to continue its policy of uniform rates regardless of cost of service. This policy remains in force for first-class mail to this day. The cost of mailing a letter to any address in the United States is the same, whatever the distance. However, the cost of delivering the letter clearly is not the same for all addresses. Deliveries to post office boxes are least expensive; deliveries to homes in suburban neighborhoods are a bit more expensive; and rural free delivery service is much more expensive.

   Questions:

   a. Do you think the practice of charging the same price when costs differ from one customer to another should be viewed as price discrimination? Do you think it has any benefits? Why or why not?

   b. Although the U.S. Postal Service (as it is now called) has retained its monopoly of ordinary first-class mail, it allows competition from firms like United Parcel Service and Federal Express in carrying overnight mail and third-class mail (parcels). In these cases both the USPS and its private competitors charge different prices according to weight and distance, and according to whether pickup and delivery service are provided. Why does a policy of one price regardless of cost not work in a market in which there is competition?

   (Source: Based in part on John C. Goodman and Edwin G. Dolan, *Economics of Public Policy*, 2nd ed. (St. Paul: West, 1982, chap. 11.)

Suggestions for Further Reading

Bork, Robert H. *The Antitrust Paradox: A Policy at War With Itself*. New York: Basic Books, 1978.

Chapter 4 presents an excellent summary of the economic theory of monopoly, stressing its implications for efficiency.

McGee, John S. "Ocean Freight Rate Conferences and the American Merchant Marine," *University of Chicago Law Review* 27, Winter 1960, pp. 191–314.

This book-length article discusses cartels and their problems (with many useful references) and applies the general analysis to the problem of ocean-shipping cartels.

Nicholson, Walter. *Intermediate Microeconomics and Its Application*, 3rd ed. Hinsdale, Ill.: Dryden Press, 1983.

Chapter 13 discusses monopoly and includes a graphic treatment of price discrimination.

Chapter 24

Oligopoly: Competition Among the Few

WHAT YOU WILL LEARN IN THIS CHAPTER

After reading this chapter, you should be able to

1. Distinguish *oligopoly* from other market structures.
2. Explain how market concentration is measured, and discuss the factors that cause it.
3. Illustrate the concept of *oligopolistic interdependence*.
4. List some of the factors that affect the performance of oligopolistic markets.
5. Discuss the debate over the link between market concentration and performance.

Ideas for Review

Here are some terms and concepts that you should review before you read this chapter:

Efficiency (Chapter 2)
Perfect competition (Chapter 22)
Monopoly (Chapter 23)
Cartels (Chapter 23)

"The daily pricing meeting at Delta Airlines would make a good setting for an aspirin commercial."

Judging from a recent session, the daily pricing meeting at Delta Airlines would make a good setting for an aspirin commercial.

Seated around an L-shaped desk, a group of Delta tariff experts hash out possible countermoves to the fare changes that were just announced by the competition. "What are the yields on those new Braniff fares again?" asks Robert Coggin, assistant vice-president for marketing development. He wants to know how much revenue the fares will bring in per passenger per mile.

"It's bad," replies a colleague. "They start at 4.7 cents." Delta figures it needs an average yield of 15 cents to break even.

Slumping in his chair, Coggin looks pained. "Damn, I hate to match that," he moans. "Its like a rerun of a horror movie."

"It's like a nonstop poker game," Coggin says later. His job of deciding whether or not to match competitors' fare changes is "easily the toughest job I've had. Some days you just think all hell has broken loose."

Coggin's day begins at 7 A.M., when a Delta computer begins spitting out a list, sometimes several hundred pages long, showing the new fares filed the prior day with Air Tariff Publishing Co. Once Delta learns of a competitor's pricing move, it can put a matching fare into its own reservation system within two hours.

The day may come, Coggins says, when airlines will, in effect, "auction" off seats, charging prices that change with supply and demand, the same way stock prices move. "For a long time I prayed the industry would go back to the good old days of simple pricing," he says. "Now I realize it could get a heck of a lot worse."[1]

The term *competition* has two meanings in economics. In the phrase "perfect competition," it refers to market structure. A market is perfectly competitive if it has large numbers of small firms, a homogeneous product, well-informed buyers and sellers, and easy entry and exit of firms. In contrast, when used as the verb "to compete," competition refers to business rivalry. In this sense it is a matter of behavior rather than of market structure. Two firms are said to compete if they treat each other as rivals in their efforts to do the best they can in the marketplace.

As we pointed out in Chapter 22, there is no rivalry in perfectly competitive markets because each firm sees every other firm as too small to have much of an impact on market conditions. Rivalry is absent from pure monopoly because there is only one firm in the market. And as long as members obey the rules they agree to, rivalry is absent in a cartel.

In most markets, however, rivalry plays too big a role to be pushed into the background. Most markets have more than a single firm but fewer than the number required for perfect competition. Most also lack formal agreements among competing firms to refrain from business rivalry. Such markets are known as **oligopolies**.

Oligopoly
A market structure in which there are two or more firms, at least one of which has a large share of total sales.

[1]John Koten, "Fare Game: In Airlines' Rate War, Small Daily Skirmishes Often Decide Winners," *Wall Street Journal*, August 24, 1984, p. 1. Reprinted by permission of The Wall Street Journal, © Dow Jones & Company, Inc. 1984. All rights reserved.

In an oligopoly—the airline industry is a case in point—it matters very much to each firm what its rivals do, and not just in relation to price. In many markets an oligopolist must be prepared to respond to moves that its competitors make in terms of style changes, product innovations, customer service, and advertising as well.

The need to focus on the interaction of many firms rather than on the behavior of each firm by itself makes it hard to come up with a complete theory of oligopoly. So instead of building this chapter around a formal theory as we did in the case of perfect competition and monopoly, we will build it around a major question: *Is perfect competition required for satisfactory market performance, or is competition among a few large rival firms enough?* Some economists give one answer, and some another. Some believe that even without formal agreements, oligopolists can restrict output and raise prices almost as easily as cartels. Others reject this idea. They argue instead that competition among the few serves consumer needs most efficiently. Still others hedge their bets by saying that some oligopolies seem to perform better than others for reasons that are not fully understood. While we cannot settle this controversy here, we can at least provide a map of the territory.

MARKET CONCENTRATION

Before getting to the main topics of this chapter, we need to ask two questions: How many markets are really dominated by just a few firms (and how many is "a few")? And what determines the number of firms in a market and the size of each firm's market share?

Measuring Market Concentration

Concentration ratio
The percentage of all sales that is accounted for by the four or eight largest firms in a market.

Concentration ratios give a rough-and-ready measure of the extent to which markets are dominated by a few firms. The most common of these ratios are the four-firm concentration ratio (which measures the percentage of sales accounted for by the top four firms in a given market) and the eight-firm concentration ratio (which measures the share of the top eight firms).

Box 24.1 gives concentration ratios for a number of industries. At the top of the chart are tight oligopolies; a handful of firms control almost the whole market. In other industries, shown in the middle of the chart, the top four firms account for less than half of total sales, although these firms are clearly too large to fit the definition of perfect competition. Of the industries listed, only in the case of commercial lithographic printing is it safe to say that there are "many" firms, each of which is "small" relative to the size of the market. All in all, somewhere between a third and a half of all manufacturing output in the United States comes from markets in which the top four firms control half the market or more.

Causes of Market Concentration

Box 24.1 gives a rough idea of the extent of market concentration. The next question is: Why are some markets more concentrated than others? The concept of economies of scale provides a logical place to start answering this question.

**Box 24.1
Concentration Ratios
for Selected Industries**

Concentration ratios measure the percentage of an industry's sales that is accounted for by the largest firms. This list of thirty-one U.S. industries shows a wide range of ratios. The figures given here do not take into account foreign competition or the fact that some industries produce mainly for local markets.

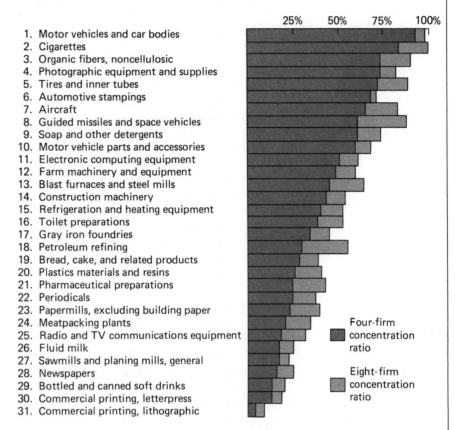

1. Motor vehicles and car bodies
2. Cigarettes
3. Organic fibers, noncellulosic
4. Photographic equipment and supplies
5. Tires and inner tubes
6. Automotive stampings
7. Aircraft
8. Guided missiles and space vehicles
9. Soap and other detergents
10. Motor vehicle parts and accessories
11. Electronic computing equipment
12. Farm machinery and equipment
13. Blast furnaces and steel mills
14. Construction machinery
15. Refrigeration and heating equipment
16. Toilet preparations
17. Gray iron foundries
18. Petroleum refining
19. Bread, cake, and related products
20. Plastics materials and resins
21. Pharmaceutical preparations
22. Periodicals
23. Papermills, excluding building paper
24. Meatpacking plants
25. Radio and TV communications equipment
26. Fluid milk
27. Sawmills and planing mills, general
28. Newspapers
29. Bottled and canned soft drinks
30. Commercial printing, letterpress
31. Commercial printing, lithographic

Four-firm concentration ratio

Eight-firm concentration ratio

Source: U.S. Department of Commerce, Bureau of the Census, *Statistical Abstract of the United States*, 98th ed. (Washington, D.C.: Government Printing Office, 1977), pp. 808–809.

Economies of scale   Chapter 21 discussed the concept of economies of scale. A firm is said to experience economies of scale if its long-run average costs decline as its output increases. The shapes of long-run average-cost curves vary from one industry to another, but studies have found that many industries have L-shaped long-run average-cost curves. Such a curve shows initial economies of scale followed by a range of constant returns to scale.

The point at which the average-total-cost curve stops falling and begins to flatten out, known as the minimum efficient scale for the firm, is thought to affect market concentration. Box 24.2 gives estimates of the minimum efficient scale for a single plant in several industries, stated as a percentage of U.S. consumption of the product. The second column of the table shows the theoretical minimum four-firm concentration ratio implied by the minimum efficient plant size. The industry could not be any less concentrated than this without forcing some firms to use plants that are too small. The third column in the table shows the actual four-firm concentration ratio for each industry. In every case this ratio is much larger than the theoretical minimum. It is clear that, with the possible exception of refrigerators, economies of scale *at the plant level* are not enough to explain the observed degree of market concentration.

Some caution should be used in interpreting the data in Box 24.2. The study from which they are taken defined *economies of scale* quite narrowly, so that the numbers given should be viewed as lower bounds for the minimum efficient scale even at the plant level. Also, as stressed in Chapter 21, there are many sources of economies of scale above the plant level. Operating more than one plant may result in savings in scheduling, transportation, research and development, finance, marketing, and administration costs. To the extent that cost savings in producing a given product or model depend on "learning by doing," a plant with a large market share builds up experience more quickly than a plant with a small market share. These kinds of economies of scale may lie beyond the ability of economists and accountants to measure accurately.[2]

Even after all such qualifications are taken into account, and even if the minimum economic scales shown in Box 24.2 are increased several times, it appears that economies of scale alone do not fully account for the degree of concentration found in U.S. industry. It is therefore worth looking at other factors.

Barriers to entry   One reason that an industry may be more concentrated than economies of scale would indicate is that there may be barriers to entry by new firms. For our purposes here, a **barrier to entry** may be defined as any factor that prevents a new firm from competing on an equal footing with existing firms. In a market that does not have either large economies of scale or high barriers to entry, growth may come about mainly through the entry of new firms, leading to a decrease in concentration over time. With barriers to entry, the first firms in the industry may be able to maintain their market shares as the industry grows, even without the help of economies of scale.

Barrier to entry
Any factor that prevents a new firm from competing on an equal footing with existing ones.

Sometimes barriers to entry into oligopolistic industries are created on purpose by federal, state, or local governments. In such cases the government stops short of creating a pure monopoly but still limits the number of firms to a number below that which would exist under conditions of free entry. For example, the Federal Communications Commission controls the number of radio and TV stations allowed in each community. In most places the number of stations allowed is smaller than the number that would be technically possible. At the state level, entry into many professions—law, medicine, plumbing, hairdressing, and dozens of others—is limited by licensing boards. In many areas, entry into rental housing or retailing is limited by local zoning regulations. The list of such barriers goes on and on.

A second kind of barrier to entry is ownership of a nonreproducible resource. For example, entry into the ski resort industry is limited by the

[2]See John S. McGee, "Efficiency and Economies of Size," in Harvey J. Goldschmid, H. Michael Mann, and J. Fred Weston, eds., *Industrial Concentration: The New Learning* (Boston: Little, Brown, 1974), pp. 55–96.

Box 24.2
Plant-Level Economies of Scale and Market Concentration

Column 1 of this table gives estimates of the minimum efficient scale for a single plant in 12 industries. Multiplying these estimates by 4 gives column 2, the theoretical minimum four-firm concentration ratio for each industry. Comparing columns 2 and 3 tells us that all the industries shown are much more concentrated than plant-level economies of scale alone can explain.

Industry	Minimum Efficient Plant Size as Percent of U.S. Consumption	Theoretical Minimum Four-Firm Concentration Ratio	Actual 1967 Four-Firm Concentration Ratio
Ball and roller bearings	1.4	5.6	54
Beer brewing	3.4	13.6	40
Cement	1.7	6.8	29
Cigarettes	6.6	26.4	81
Cotton and synthetic fabrics	0.2	0.8	36
Glass containers	1.5	6.0	60
Paints	1.4	5.6	22
Petroleum refining	1.9	7.6	33
Refrigerators	14.1	56.4	73
Shoes	0.2	0.8	26
Storage batteries	1.9	7.6	61
Wide strip steel works	2.6	10.4	48

Source: F. M. Scherer, Alan Beckenstein, Erich Kaufer, and R. D. Murphey, *The Economics of Multi-Plant Operation: An International Comparisons Study* (Cambridge, Mass.: Harvard University Press, 1975). Table 3.11, p. 80. © 1975 by the President and Fellows of Harvard College; all rights reserved. Reprinted by permission.

number of suitable mountains. Entry into extractive industries is limited, at least in some cases, by the fact that existing firms already own the best available natural resources. In other markets the nonreproducible resources are human. Entry into the movie industry may be difficult, for example, if the top stars are all under contract to existing firms. Whatever the reason, ownership of a nonreproducible resource gives existing firms an advantage over new ones and in this way acts as a barrier to entry.

Patents and copyrights, another class of barriers to entry, are important in both oligopoly and monopoly. A patent or copyright can be treated as a restrictive regulation, or it can be treated just like ownership of any other nonreproducible resource. In either case, patents and copyrights clearly can make entry difficult and contribute to market concentration.

As the term is used here, a *barrier to entry* is something that keeps new firms from duplicating the performance of existing ones in terms of cost or quality of product. It does not mean that every effort or expense that a firm must undertake to enter a market should be thought of as a barrier. To start a new firm, an entrepreneur must take risks, find investors, recruit workers, attract customers, and so on. All these things are hard work— hard enough to discourage some people from making the effort. But the need for hard work is not a barrier to entry in the economic sense. When entrepreneurs are freely able to buy the building blocks for their new firms on the same terms as existing firms, barriers to entry are not a factor in market structure.

Random influences   Finally, even in a market with no great economies of scale and no barriers to entry, random influences may lead to concentration over time. Suppose a large number of firms start out with equal opportunities in an industry that grows at an average rate of, say, 6 percent per year. By chance, in any given year some firms will grow faster and some will grow slower than average. A few firms can be expected to be lucky and to grow faster than average several years in a row. Once they lead the pack, it will be hard for the others to catch up. The leaders will maintain a large market share even if their performance becomes merely average. Computer studies suggest that random factors alone can explain a large part of the concentration of U.S. industry quite aside from economies of scale or barriers to entry.[3]

INTERDEPENDENCE AND COORDINATION

It is much more difficult to state a theory of oligopoly than it is to state a theory of pure competition or monopoly. The theories of competition and monopoly presented in Chapters 22 and 23 focus on decision making by a single firm under given conditions. Those conditions, which include technology, input prices, and the demand curve for the product, are assumed not to be affected by the decisions the firm itself makes. Under pure competition it is possible to isolate the firm's actions because the firm is so small; under monopoly the firm to be studied is assumed to be isolated from rivals. The ability to isolate the decisions of a pure competitor or a monopolist greatly simplifies the task of theory building.

Oligopolistic interdependence
The need, in an oligopolistic market, to pay close attention to the actions of one's rivals when making price or production decisions.

Industries that are dominated by a few large firms, in contrast, raise the problem of **oligopolistic interdependence**. This refers to the need for each firm to take the likely reactions of its rivals into account when planning its market strategy. Even with given cost and demand conditions, there is no "best" price and quantity decision for the oligopolist. Instead, there are a number of possible strategies, each of which is more or less suitable, depending on what the firm's rivals do.

The case of airline pricing is a good example of oligopolistic interdependence. In that market, the prices each firm sets depend on the prices its rivals set, and vice versa. In such a market any changes made by one firm are likely to touch off a long series of moves and countermoves. Each airline tries to work out some general rules to guide its actions. For example, Delta Airlines almost always matches price reductions by its rivals, but it rarely makes cuts of its own. Other airlines are more aggressive, trying to be the first to move when demand conditions change. But applying the pricing rules to any given case always requires judgment. No simple theory can say when a given price move should be made, or predict the outcome of a series of moves by a firm and its rivals.

---

[3]Such an experiment is described in F. M. Scherer, *Industrial Market Structure and Economic Performance*, 2nd ed. (Chicago: Rand McNally, 1980), pp. 145–150.

Oligopoly and Shared Monopoly

Although the simple theories of monopoly and perfect competition do not fit the complex world of oligopolistic interdependence, they do provide a framework within which we can discuss the theory of oligopoly. Such a framework is given in Box 24.3. A similar diagram was used in Chapter 23 to show the effects of a cartel, but now we assume that a formal cartel does not exist.

We will also assume that the industry we are looking at is dominated by a few large firms, with perhaps some small ones on the fringe. Profits are maximized for these firms by a price of $2 and an output of 200,000 units per month, which corresponds to a point directly above the intersection of the marginal-cost and marginal-revenue curves. At this point the firms can be said to enjoy a **shared monopoly**. Such a monopoly is, in effect, a cartel without formal agreement or enforcement mechanisms.

The opposite extreme is *cutthroat competition*—price competition so complete that pure economic profit is impossible. This extreme is shown in Box 24.3 by the intersection of the demand and marginal-cost curves. Cutthroat competition among oligopolists could duplicate the price-output

Shared monopoly
A situation in which the firms in an oligopoly coordinate their activities in such a way as to earn maximum profits for the industry as a whole.

Box 24.3
Range of Possible Prices and Output Levels for an Oligopoly

The cost and demand curves given here are those of an oligopolistic industry. If the firms cooperate they can, at one extreme, achieve a *shared monopoly*. At the other extreme they can compete so fiercely that pure economic profit is impossible and the price is driven down to the level of cost. This extreme is labeled "cutthroat competition." In practice, cooperation becomes more risky as the industry moves upward along the demand curve toward the shared-monopoly position. The likely outcome is a price somewhere between the $1 and $2 limits shown on the graph.

performance of perfect competition. In the long run, no lower price could be sustained without driving firms and resources out of the industry.

The range of price-output combinations that an oligopoly can achieve, then, includes the extremes of shared monopoly and cutthroat competition and the segment of the demand curve between the two extremes. Where along this range will any given oligopoly end up? The answer clearly depends on the balance struck between the risks and benefits of the cooperation needed to achieve shared monopoly.

The risks are of three kinds. First, there is a risk that the rivals with whom one seeks to cooperate will not respond in kind. Second, there is a risk that even if a firm does achieve a degree of cooperation with its present rivals, the fruits of the effort will have to be shared with new firms attracted by the resulting higher profits. And third, there is a risk that if cooperation is pursued too openly, the firms will be found in violation of the antitrust laws. (These laws will be discussed in detail in Chapter 26.) The benefits of shared monopoly are clear enough to keep cutthroat competition at bay at least some of the time, but the risks increase as rival firms edge their way upward and to the left along the demand curve. As a result, it seems likely that most oligopolies operate somewhere between the two extremes shown in Box 24.3.

Formal and Informal Theories of Oligopoly

In the light of the discussion so far, the job of a theory of oligopoly can be viewed as that of finding the point on the demand curve that any given industry will reach. There have been many attempts to construct formal theories that would solve this problem. Some of these attempts are discussed in an appendix to this chapter. But none of these theories is really satisfactory. They either raise as many questions as they answer or apply only to narrow cases.

As a result, much writing on oligopoly deals with informal theories that, while they are less elegant than formal ones, are more realistic. These theories consist of conjectures about the conditions that tend to make cooperation by oligopolists easier or more difficult. Some of the most common themes in those theories are the following.

Number and size of firms   There is little doubt that the number and size of the firms in a market make a lot of difference. Cooperation is easier in a market with only two or three big firms of roughly equal size than in a market where a dozen firms of equal size have half the market and the rest is made up of smaller firms. A major reason is that the larger the number of firms, the more likely it is that any one firm can cut prices under the table.

Price leadership
In an oligopoly, a situation in which increases or decreases in price by one dominant firm, known as the price leader, are matched by all or most other firms in the market.

The relative size of the various firms in the market is also important. Many observers have suggested that tacit coordination of prices is easier in an industry where there is one dominant firm. That firm may be able to act as a price leader. Under the strongest form of **price leadership**, firms are no longer uncertain about how their rivals will react to price changes. The leader knows that the others will follow it both up and down. The others know that if they follow the leader, others will too; but if they raise or lower prices on their own, others will not follow. When it works, this arrangement results in a shared monopoly.

However, tacit coordination cannot always be inferred from the timing of price changes. In any industry someone has to be the first to change prices if market conditions change. Even if one firm is usually the first to make a move, its role may be no more than that of a barometer. It tells the others that the pressure of demand or cost has made a price change necessary.

Nature of the product   The nature of the product also affects the ease or difficulty of coordination. A homogeneous product with a smooth flow of orders tends to make coordination easier. A variable product with an irregular flow of orders tends to make it more difficult. With a variable product, there are simply too many things to coordinate. It is not enough that all firms tacitly agree to sell at the same price. They also have to agree on a set of price variations for changes in quality, fast or slow delivery, size of order, and so on. Under these conditions, an agreement to raise the price above the competitive level, even if it can be sustained, is unlikely to lead to higher profits. It is more likely to lead to an outbreak of competition in terms of quality, scheduling, volume discounts, and so on. These things will add to the cost of doing business until excess profits disappear.

Information   Coordination under oligopoly, if possible at all, is likely only in a market where firms have fairly good information about what their rivals are doing. Clearly, there can be no tacit understanding that all firms will charge the same price or follow a price leader if prices are kept secret. So there is little doubt that secrecy is an enemy of coordination under oligopoly.

There is a danger in trying to reverse this formula, however. If secrecy is the enemy of coordination, does that make secrecy the friend of competition? From there it is only a short step to the idea that bad information is the friend of good market performance. But this last statement is clearly nonsense. The primary function of the market system, after all, is to facilitate the flow of information among buyers and sellers. Perfect markets require perfect information, not perfect secrecy.

Growth and innovation   The rates of growth and innovation in a market are a final factor that is likely to affect the ease or difficulty of coordination among rival oligopolists. In a market where product features, production techniques, and the personalities of buyers and sellers do not change from year to year, an agreement among firms, whether tacit or overt, will never have to be revised. In a market where things change quickly, any agreement will soon be made obsolete by changing conditions or disrupted when new buyers or sellers enter the market. Given the uncertainties of tacit agreements and the fact that overt ones are illegal, one would expect that the faster the pace of growth and change, the less successful rival firms will be at coordinating their activities.

MEASURING MARKET PERFORMANCE UNDER OLIGOPOLY

Neither the formal theories discussed in the appendix to this chapter nor the informal theories just explained give conclusive answers to the question asked at the beginning of the chapter—whether rivalry among a few firms in a concentrated market is enough to secure good market performance. In this context, good market performance means performance like that of a perfectly competitive market, with prices equal or close to marginal cost. Poor performance means performance like that of a monopoly or cartel, in which prices remain higher than marginal cost.

Not being able to answer questions about market performance by means of pure theory, economists turn to statistical methods. Because it is hard to measure directly whether a gap exists between a firm's output prices and its marginal costs, the most common approach is an indirect one. If firms in concentrated industries can be shown, on the average, to earn higher than normal rates of return on capital, one can infer that they are behaving more like monopolists than like perfect competitors. If, on the other hand, firms in concentrated industries earn rates of return no higher, on the average, than firms in less concentrated industries, it can be inferred that oligopolies perform about as well as more competitive industries.

Early Empirical Studies

The first person to try this approach in a systematic way was University of California professor Joe Bain. In 1951 he published the results of a study of 42 selected industries for the years 1936–1940. According to Bain's analysis of the data, industries with concentration ratios over 70 earned higher profits than less concentrated industries. The link between profits and concentration was neither perfect nor strong, but it did exist.

During the 1950s and 1960s many of Bain's students and followers repeated his studies for other industries and other years. Most of them got the same results—a weak but persistent link between profits and concentration. It became one of the general beliefs of economists that the more highly concentrated an industry, the more it would tend to perform like a cartel or monopoly. This would be true even if there were no agreement among rivals to raise prices and divide markets.

More Recent Results

As faith in this idea grew, economists tried as hard as they could to prove it, using the more advanced statistical techniques and better data that became available each year. But the harder they tried, the more elusive the connection became. Some studies showed that if the data were adjusted for the size of firms in different markets, the link between concentration and profits tended to disappear. Other studies showed that if the data were adjusted for differences in advertising expenditures, the connection would disappear. Still others seemed to show that results like Bain's held only in periods of recession and disappeared with the return of prosperity.

What is more, as the link between concentration and profits was becoming less certain, economists were also becoming less certain about how such a link should be interpreted even if it could be confirmed. New reasons were found for why firms in more concentrated industries might appear to earn higher profits than firms in less concentrated industries. These reasons had nothing to do with monopoly pricing or tacit coordination. For example, a concentrated industry that was growing fast might need to earn high profits to attract more capital. Or the high profits of the largest firms in each concentrated industry might simply reflect the fact that those firms were more efficient than smaller firms in the same industry. Finally, the higher profits that some concentrated industries appeared to earn might not be profits at all in the economic sense. They might merely reflect the fact that the categories used by accountants to record business transactions are different from those used by economic theorists.

One major problem that prevented a final resolution of the dispute lay in the nature of the available data. Until quite recently, most data on profits and concentration were gathered at the company level, whereas the theories being tested were stated in terms of markets. In one market after another, the firms with big market shares were highly diversified in terms of either the product markets or the geographic markets in which they participated. Thus, relationships that might be present at the market level simply did not show up clearly enough in data collected at the company level. Recent information on market-by-market concentration ratios and market shares indicates that larger firms are indeed more profitable. However, the source of profits seems to be lower costs rather than higher prices.[4]

Conclusions

This chapter began with the question of whether rivalry among a few firms is enough to produce satisfactory market performance. After reviewing the causes of market concentration, some formal and informal theories of oligopoly, and the available evidence on the link between concentration and profits, the answer seems to be maybe yes, maybe no—it all depends.

Perhaps, though, economists are looking in the wrong place for an answer. The search for a theory of oligopoly is a search for a theory like the theories of perfect competition and monopoly but somewhere between them. However, in some ways all of these theories are too limited. They deal with only one aspect of business decision making—the search for maximum profits under given conditions of demand, technology, and resource availability. Perhaps economists would do better in their efforts to understand competition among the few if they took into account more of the entrepreneurial elements in business decision making.

There have already been some hints that this is where they should look. The subjects of advertising and nonprice competition have come up more than once. These forms of competition involve entrepreneurial decision making. The question of barriers to entry has been raised. Whether a new firm will enter an industry is an entrepreneurial decision. And such variables as product homogeneity, growth, and innovation have a major effect on how firms behave in concentrated markets. The next chapter will look into some of these things.

---

[4]See Bradley T. Gale and Ben Branch, "Concentration and Market Share: Which Determines Performance and Why Does It Matter?" *Antitrust Bulletin* 27, Spring 1982.

Summary

1. An *oligopoly* is a market in which there are two or more firms, at least one of which has a large share of total sales. In an oligopoly, deciding how to react to the actions of rival firms with regard to price, output, and product features is a major aspect of decision making.

2. *Concentration ratios* are a common measure of the degree to which a market is dominated by a few firms. The most commonly used ratios measure the share of total sales in the market accounted for by the top four or eight firms in the market. Somewhere between a third and a half of all manufacturing output in the United States comes from industries in which the top four firms control half or more of the market.

3. *Oligopolistic interdependence* refers to the need for each firm in an oligopoly to pay close attention to the actions of its rivals. For example, in the airline industry fares on many routes are changed each day. Whenever one airline changes a fare, its rivals must decide whether to stand pat, match the new fare, undercut it, or take some other action.

4. A major question in oligopoly theory is how well oligopolies perform—that is, how closely they approach the outcome of perfect competition, in which equilibrium prices equal market cost. Among the factors that are thought to affect market performance are the number and size of firms, the presence or absence of price leadership, the nature of the product (homogeneous or varied), access to information, and the pace of growth and innovation.

5. Early studies suggested that firms in industries with high concentration ratios earned higher profits than those in less concentrated industries. This was taken as a sign that firms in concentrated industries engaged in tacit coordination and earned joint monopoly profits. More recent research suggests that the connection is not so simple, and that at least part of the higher profits in more concentrated industries is accounted for by the fact that firms with dominant market shares tend to have lower production costs than smaller firms.

Questions for Review

1. Explain the following terms and concepts:
   oligopoly
   concentration ratio
   barrier to entry
   oligopolistic interdependence
   shared monopoly
   price leadership

2. What key traits distinguish an oligopoly from a perfectly competitive market? From a monopoly? From a cartel?

3. What is the common method for measuring the degree to which a market is concentrated in the hands of a few firms? How much of U.S. manufacturing output is produced by oligopolistic industries?

4. Provide one or more illustrations, other than those used in the text, of oligopolistic interdependence.

5. How is the performance of an oligopoly affected by the number and size of the firms in the industry? By the nature of the product? By access to information? By the pace of growth and innovation?

6. What evidence suggests that concentrated industries do not perform as efficiently as perfectly competitive ones? In what ways has this idea been challenged?

Problems and Topics for Discussion

1. Look around your community for a case in which a firm is carrying out a special sale or promotion of its product. To what extent, if any, is the firm's action a response to something its rivals have done? To what extent, if any, have its rivals reacted with sales or promotions of their own?

2. The data on market concentration in Box 24.1 relate only to manufacturing, the sector of the economy that has received the most attention in oligopoly studies. To what extent do you think these other sectors of the economy—agriculture, transportation, services, retail trade, and communications—are concentrated? What do you think accounts for the degree of concentration or lack of it in each of these sectors?

3. "Barriers to entry are lower in the restaurant industry than in the airline industry because a restaurant requires only a few workers and a few thousand dollars in capital, whereas even a small airline requires many workers and millions of dollars in capital." Do you agree? Why or why not?

4. Is the market for college education an oligopoly? What factors do you think affect the structure of the college education industry? How important are economies of scale? Barriers to entry? Chance factors?

5. **Case for Discussion**
   Star Supermarkets' profits fell 10 percent last year and were flat in the first quarter of this year, victims of the practice of "bonus" couponing—paying consumers double or even triple the face value of coupons that appear in newspapers and magazines and sometimes in the mailbox. But Theodore Levinson, president of the upstate New York chain, isn't about to halt the self-defeating promotions.

"I'm not ready to give them up until my competitors do," he says. "I will protect my market share." Levinson isn't alone. In Cleveland, it took 34 Stop-N-Shop supermarkets six months to recoup profits lost during four days of triple couponing in 1980. During the first two months of this year, the chain was at it again with double coupons.

And in Connecticut, store managers for Mott's Super Markets keep "double coupon" signs in their offices to post as soon as competitors announce similar deals. Bonus couponing has reached record proportions: It can be found in about three dozen major cities and, says Zal Venet, president of a New York ad agency with several supermarket clients, "has become a basic, though expensive, marketing tool."

The supermarket manager's dilemma: Bonus couponing usually is started by one of a region's smaller chains to steal market share. If the leaders ignore the challenger, they stand to lose sales. If they reciprocate, they stimulate a coupon war.

Questions:
a. Is bonus couponing an example of oligopolistic interdependence? Why or why not?
b. How do incentives for small and large chains differ in deciding whether to start bonus coupon campaigns? Whether to follow campaigns begun by others?
c. The title of the article suggests that coupon wars produce "only victims." What about consumers? Do they suffer from coupon wars?

(Source: Excerpted from Jeffrey H. Birnbaum, "Bonus Coupon Wars Produce Only Victims, Analysts Warn," *Wall Street Journal*, June 4, 1981, p. 29. Reprinted by permission of The Wall Street Journal, © Dow Jones & Company, Inc. 1981. All rights reserved.)

Suggestions for Further Reading

Brozen, Yale, ed. *The Competitive Economy.* Morristown, N.J.: General Learning Press, 1975.

Many of the articles reprinted in this book are relevant to this chapter. Brozen is skeptical of the view that concentration implies poor market performance, and many of the readings reflect this point of view.

Goldschmid, Harvey J., H. Michael Mann, and Fred J. Weston. *Industrial Concentration: The New Learning.* Boston: Little, Brown, 1974.

This book takes the form of a series of debates between representatives of contrasting views on many of the problems discussed in this chapter.

Especially relevant are Chapter 2 (a debate between F. M. Scherer and John S. McGee on economies of scale as a cause of concentration) and Chapter 4 (which matches Harold Demsetz against Leonard Weiss on the concentration-profits issue).

Scherer, F. M. *Industrial Market Structure and Economic Performance,* 2nd ed. Chicago: Rand McNally, 1980.

This is the definitive text on all facets of industrial organization theory.

Appendix to Chapter 24

Formal Theories of Oligopoly

Over the years, many economists have tried to state a formal theory of oligopoly. The goal of such a theory would be to determine the equilibrium price and level of output for an oligopolistic firm and its industry, given such aspects of market structure as number of firms, concentration ratio, cost and technology, and demand curve. No general theory has been developed, but some useful partial theories and clever analyses of special cases exist. These provide some insight into the broader problem of oligopoly. The three theories discussed in this appendix are a sample from the literature on formal theories of oligopoly.

The Cournot Theory and Its Variations

The oldest attempt at a theory of oligopoly began with a work published by Augustin Cournot in 1838. Cournot recognized the problem of oligopolistic interdependence—the need for each firm to take its rivals' behavior into account when deciding on its own market strategy. The way to understand the behavior of rival firms, Cournot thought, was to make a simple assumption about the way each firm would react to the moves of its rivals.

In his initial statement of the problem, Cournot assumed that each firm would act as if it did not expect its rivals to change their levels of output even if it changed its own output level. Later theorists who expanded Cournot's theory, however, usually made price rather than quantity the crucial variable. In the price-based version of the Cournot theory, each firm is assumed to set its price as if it expected other firms in the industry to leave their prices unchanged.

Box 24A.1 shows how the price-based Cournot theory might work for an industry with just two firms. Each firm has a definite price that will yield maximum profits for each possible price that its rival may charge. These prices are shown in the form of the firms' *reaction curves*. For example, firm 1's reaction curve indicates that it will charge $60 if its rival charges $50 (point S). If firm 2 charges $150, firm 1 will charge $130 (point T). In the limiting case, firm 2 may charge so much that it will price itself out of the market, leaving firm 1 with a pure monopoly. In that case, firm 1 will maximize its profits by charging $150, as shown by the broken line labeled "Firm 1's monopoly price." Firm 2's monopoly price is shown in the same way. The two reaction curves can be derived from the cost and demand curves of the two firms. The derivation is not given here, but it can be found in many advanced texts.

Given these reaction curves, the oligopoly story, according to Cournot, can be told somewhat as follows: Imagine that at first firm 1 is the only producer of the good in question. Since it has a pure monopoly, it maximizes profits by setting a price of $150. Then firm 2 enters the market. Under the Cournot theory, firm 2 will set its price as if it expected firm 1 to go on charging $150 forever. Given this assumption, firm 2 sets its price at $125, as shown by point A on firm 2's reaction curve.

At this point firm 1 begins to notice its rival. Seeing that firm 2 has taken away many of its customers with its much lower price, it moves to point B on its reaction curve, cutting its own price to $115.

Firm 2, which entered the market on the assumption that firm 1 would maintain its price at $150, must react next. Given firm 1's $115 price, firm 2 cuts its price to $108 (point C). That sparks a price cut by firm 1, which goes to $107 (point D). After a series of ever-smaller moves and countermoves, the prices of the two firms converge at an equilibrium of $100 at point E.

Two things are appealing about the Cournot theory. First, it gives a stable equilibrium. At prices above the intersection of the two reaction curves, each firm has an incentive to undercut its rival's price. At prices below the intersection, each firm has an incentive to charge more than its rival. Thus, given the assumptions, there is only one price that the market can reach.

A second appealing feature of the Cournot theory is that as it is expanded to allow three-, four-, and multifirm oligopolies, it can be shown that the equilibrium price moves steadily away from the monopoly price

Box 24A·1
The Cournot Theory of Oligopoly

The Cournot theory assumes that each firm will set its price as if it expects its rival's price to remain fixed. The reaction curves show the best price for each firm, given the other's price. For example, point S on firm 1's reaction curve indicates that firm 1 should charge $60 if firm 2 charges $50. If firm 1 has a monopoly, it will set a price of $150. If firm 2 then enters the market, it will touch off a price war, moving the industry step by step to points A, B, C, D, and finally E. Point E is a stable equilibrium.

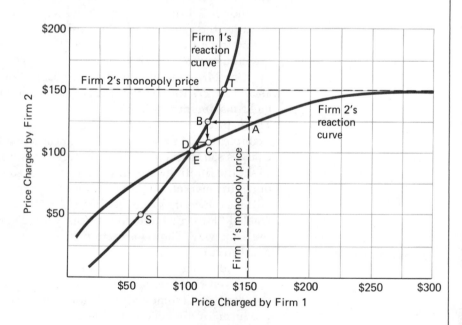

and toward a price equal to marginal cost. Thus, the Cournot equilibrium for an industry with one firm is equal to the monopoly price; the Cournot equilibrium for an industry with an infinite number of firms is equal to the competitive price; and the Cournot equilibriums for oligopolies of various sizes are ranged along a continuum between these two extremes.

Still, there is one feature of the Cournot story that has always bothered economists. The structure of the theory depends on each firm's assuming that its rival will not react to its price changes. Yet daily life in the Cournot world proves that assumption to be wrong. In our example, firm 2 enters on the assumption that firm 1 will pay no attention to the fact that it comes in and takes away a large chunk of its sales. But firm 1 does react, as does firm 2. Instead of this mindless price war, wouldn't each firm have second thoughts about its price cutting, fearing its rival's reaction? The Cournot theory refuses to face up to this possibility.

The Kinked Demand Curve Theory

A century after Cournot, in 1939, another major theory of oligopoly came along. This was the so-called kinked demand curve theory, which was proposed at about the same time by the British economists R. L. Hall and C. J. Hitch and the American economist Paul M. Sweezy. Like the Cournot theory, the kinked demand curve theory begins from a simple assumption about how oligopolists will react to price changes made by their rivals. Each firm is supposed to assume that if it cuts its price, its rivals will match the cuts, but if it raises its price, no other firms will follow. Box 24A.2

**Box 24A.2
The Kinked Demand
Curve Theory of
Oligopoly**

An oligopolist will have a kinked demand curve if its rivals will follow any price decrease it makes but not any increase. There is a sharp step in the marginal-revenue curve that corresponds to the kink in the demand curve. Here the marginal-cost curve crosses the marginal-revenue curve just at the step. This makes the equilibrium very stable.

shows how the market looks to an oligopolist who makes these two assumptions. Let P be the price ($1.70 in this case) that happens to prevail in the market. If the firm cuts its price below P, other firms will also lower their prices. Sales in the industry as a whole will expand. The firm in question will keep about the same share of the market and will move down the lower slope of the demand curve. In contrast, if the firm raises its price, the others will not follow suit. Instead of keeping its share of the market, our firm will lose customers to its rivals. As a result, the part of the firm's demand curve above price P is much more elastic than the part below P.

Now bring marginal cost and marginal revenue into the picture. Give the firm a short-run marginal-cost curve with the usual upward slope. The marginal-revenue curve has a step in it that corresponds to the kink in the demand curve. To the left of the step, marginal revenue is very high, showing that revenue will be lost quickly if the firm moves up the very elastic part of the demand curve. To the right of the step, marginal revenue is much lower, showing that little extra revenue can be obtained by moving down the less elastic part of the demand curve. As it is drawn, the marginal-cost curve cuts the marginal-revenue curve right at the step. The prevailing price is an equilibrium price for the firm, since it will be unprofitable to move in either direction.

The kinked demand curve equilibrium for an oligopolist is a very stable kind of equilibrium. Unlike a pure monopolist, the oligopolist with a kinked demand curve will not change its price or output in response to small- or medium-sized changes in cost. The level of marginal cost shown in Box 24A.2 can move by as much as 30 cents in either direction, and the firm will not change its price or output. The marginal-cost curve will still cross the marginal-revenue curve at the step. Only if marginal cost changes by more than 30 cents per unit will the firm break with the prevailing price.

Like the Cournot theory, the kinked demand curve theory is simple and elegant. Its assumptions about the way each oligopolist views its rivals' actions are clearly more plausible than Cournot's. But the kinked demand curve theory has a major flaw of its own. Although it explains why an oligopolist might be reluctant to change its price once the price was set, it fails to explain how the price comes to be set at any particular level in the first place. The theory thus provides an answer to a question that is not central to the analysis of oligopoly.

Game Theory and Oligopoly Behavior

Oligopoly, it has often been remarked, is really a game of sorts—one in which, as in chess or poker, each player must try to guess the opponent's moves, bluffs, countermoves, and counterbluffs as many moves ahead as possible. Hence, economists who specialize in oligopoly theory were very excited by the appearance in 1944 of a thick, highly mathematical book entitled *The Theory of Games and Economic Behavior*.[1] Could it be that the authors, John von Neumann and Oskar Morgenstern, had at last solved the oligopoly puzzle?

Clearly, Neumann and Morgenstern had taken a major step. Instead of

---

[1]John von Neumann and Oskar Morgenstern, *The Theory of Games and Economic Behavior* (Princeton, N. J.: Princeton University Press, 1944).

using as their starting point an assumption about how one firm would react to the other's moves, they decided to ask, in effect, what *optimal assumption* each firm should make about its rivals' behavior.

A simple example of an oligopoly game will convey the spirit of the Neumann-Morgenstern approach. Imagine a market in which there are only two firms—Alpha Company and Zed Enterprises. Their product costs $1 a unit to make. If both firms set their price at $5 a unit, each will sell 100 units per month at a profit of $4 a unit, for a total monthly profit of $400. If both firms set their price at $4 a unit, each will sell 120 units at a profit of $3 a unit, for a total profit of $360. Which price will the firms actually set? Clearly, $5 is the price that will maximize their joint profits, but under oligopoly this price may not be a stable equilibrium.

Box 24A.3 shows why. It presents the pricing strategies available to Alpha Company. Besides the two already mentioned, Alpha must consider two more. One is to cut its price to $4 while Zed holds at $5. That will allow Alpha to take away a lot of Zed's customers and to sell 150 units, for a profit of $450. The other new possibility is for Alpha to hold its price at $5 while Zed cuts its price to $4. Then Zed will take away a lot of Alpha's customers and leave Alpha selling only 60 units, for a total profit of $240.

So what will happen? One way to seek an answer is to look at the effects of different assumptions that each firm might make about the

**Box 24A.3
Profits for Alpha
Company Under
Various Pricing
Strategies**

This table shows the profits that Alpha Company would earn under various pricing strategies for Alpha and its rival, Zed Enterprises. If both firms set their price at $5, each earns $400. If both cut their price to $4, they continue to split the market and each earns $360. If Alpha cuts its price while Zed does not, Alpha steals many of Zed's customers and earns $450. If Zed cuts its price while Alpha's remains at $5, Zed steals many of Alpha's customers, leaving Alpha with only $240 in profits.

Zed's Price Strategy

	$5	$4
$5	$400	$240
$4	$450	$360

Alpha's Price Strategy

other's behavior. If Alpha assumes that Zed will charge $5, then Alpha will be best off charging $4. If Alpha assumes that Zed will charge $4, then Alpha will again be best off charging $4. It looks as if Alpha will be best off charging $4 regardless of what Zed does. Alpha will also be aware that Zed's view of the game is the mirror image of its own. After thinking about the likely effects of the different assumptions, each firm will see that it is rational to assume the worst. Unless the two firms can agree to keep the price at $5 (and such agreements are assumed to be against the rules of the game as it is played here), it seems that $4 is the equilibrium price.

Despite the high hopes of oligopoly theorists, however, it turned out that game theory could not be used to solve the general problem of oligopoly. Some games had a structure that made it impossible to come up with the kind of determinate solution of our example. And efforts to expand the game to three or more players quickly bogged down in a swamp of mathematical complications. Alas, game theory has remained little more than a brilliant solution to an extremely small set of special cases.

Chapter 25

Entrepreneurship and Competition

Ideas for Review

Here are some terms and concepts that you should review before you read this chapter:

"What Darwinian forces could have caused the toothpaste pump to replace the tube—the dominant life form in the bathroom cabinet for over 100 years?"

The 1980s will long be remembered as a time of innovation and entrepreneurship. Just think of the triumphs of technology—the personal computer, the space shuttle, genetic engineering, the toothpaste pump. . . .

Yes, the toothpaste pump. What will future archaeologists think when they dig these little gizmos out of late-twentieth-century landfills? In a stratum that will be shown by carbon-14 dating techniques to belong to the year 1984, they will note the appearance of Colgate-Palmolive's Colgate brand, Procter & Gamble's Crest brand, and Lever Brothers' Aim brand. They will find that the pumps have two kinds of innards—one works by vacuum and the other by direct mechanical pressure.

Dates, brands, mechanics—these are facts for the archaeologists to note in their journals. But what will they make of the subjective aspects of the toothpaste pump? What Darwinian forces could have caused the toothpaste pump, at this moment in history, to begin to displace the toothpaste tube—the dominant life form in the bathroom cabinet for over 100 years? Why indeed, when the tube is so much simpler, so much cheaper, and (if squeezed from the bottom) so much less wasteful?

If future linguists are still able to translate the ancient language of the *Wall Street Journal*, they will find a simple explanation: The pump introduces an element of gadgetry, and fun, to the humdrum process of brushing one's teeth. And who could resist the chance to pay 20 percent more for toothpaste if by doing so they could brighten one of the dullest moments of the day?[1]

The example of the toothpaste pump reminds us that our account of competition is not yet complete. In three chapters on the topic of competition, we have focused on just two aspects of competitive decision making—price and quantity. Decisions on these matters are important, to be sure, but they are only two of the many factors that make up a firm's competitive strategy—its *marketing* strategy, to use the more common term. In this chapter we will try to broaden our view of competition. We will begin with a survey of the many aspects of marketing. Next we will look at a market structure known as *monopolistic competition*, in which competition takes place largely through product quality, innovation, location, and advertising. In the last section of the chapter, we will discuss efficiency and innovation, and how they are related to market structure.

THE ECONOMICS OF MARKETING

Marketing
Finding out what customers want and channeling a flow of goods and services to meet those wants.

Marketing means the process of finding out what customers want and channeling a flow of goods and services to meet those wants. Marketing consists of four activities: creating a *product* that will meet consumer needs; getting it to a *place* where consumers can conveniently buy it; *promoting* the product through advertising, personal selling, and other means; and

---

[1]Stephen MacDonald, "Competing Designs of Toothpaste Pumps Are Vying for Supremacy in Marketplace," *Wall Street Journal*, November 13, 1984, p. 35.

**Box 25.1
Marketing Costs and
Consumer Spending**

As this chart shows, marketing costs account for about half of all consumer spending. The costs and profits of wholesale and retail trade are the largest single item, followed by freight transportation. Advertising, although it is the most visible of marketing activities, accounts for only about 3 percent of the cost of consumer goods and services. All aspects of marketing are important to the process of competition.

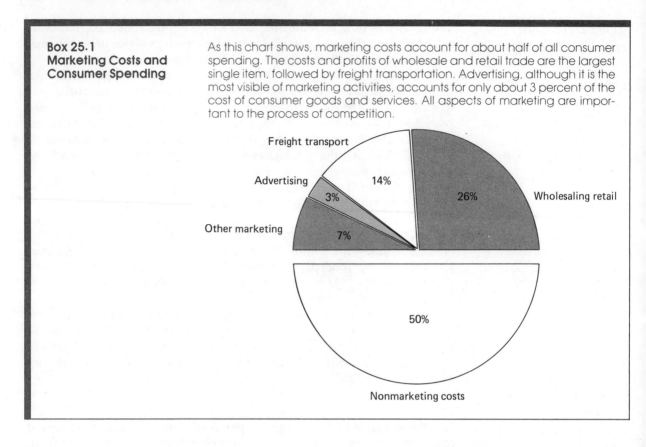

putting the right *price* on the product. These four activities are often called the "four P's" of marketing. As Box 25.1 shows, the costs of the four P's account for about half of all consumer spending in the United States. Let's look at the role that each of these activities plays in a competitive economy.

Competition and the Product

In a perfectly competitive market the product—wheat, trucking services, or whatever—is thought of as given. Some oligopolies also have products that change little from year to year—the aluminum and cement industries are examples. But there are a great many markets in which shaping the product to fit consumer needs is a key part of competition.

Innovation is one major aspect of product competition. Consider the case of stereo equipment. It is clear what customers want—they want music in their living rooms that sounds like a live performance. That is an ideal that is never quite reached, but long-playing records, metal-oxide cassette tapes, Dolby noise suppression systems, and compact disks each represent a step closer to the ideal. The first competitor to take each step has at least a temporary advantage.

Diversity is another aspect of product competition. Consumers have different needs and tastes. Economists talk about "the market" for cars, but this market is really composed of many segments: the markets for economy cars, vans, sports cars, and so on. Competition ensures that products will be made that will meet the needs of consumers in each segment; a neglected segment would soon attract a firm in search of profits.

Quality is still another aspect of product competition—one that has been getting more attention in recent years. The quality of many goods made in the United States has been improving for years. Tires last longer; fabrics wash more easily; contact lenses give better vision. However, the demand for quality seems to have risen even faster than the supply. Foreign firms—especially Japanese firms—have gained a competitive advantage in many markets by being the first to respond to this demand for quality. As U.S. firms scramble to catch up, consumers are the winners.

Competition in Distribution

The second of the four P's of marketing—place—refers to all the activities needed to get a product to consumers. It includes transportation and other aspects of physical distribution and, even more important, the services of wholesale and retail firms.

Innovation and diversity affect distribution systems as much as they affect products themselves. Tried-and-true methods of retailing such as supermarkets and department stores (which were innovations earlier in the century) are under pressure. On the one hand, specialized boutique-type retailers and direct-mail companies are winning a bigger share of the wealthiest consumers. On the other hand, discount stores, off-price retailers, and warehouse-type food stores are making inroads among budget-conscious consumers. Often the prize in competition among manufacturing firms goes to those that have the best distribution networks.

Competition in Promotion

Promotion—which includes advertising, personal selling, store displays, and public relations—is the most visible aspect of competition in many markets. Promotion is the communication link between producers and their customers.

A major part of promotion is spreading information. The theory of consumer choice and perfect competition assumes that consumers are well informed about the choices available to them, but in the real world information is a scarce resource. Advertising, personal selling, and other promotional activities lower the cost to consumer of learning about prices, product features, and where to buy desired goods and services.

However, it is well known that advertising does more than just inform consumers. It also shapes their tastes and, as Box 25.2 shows, even their perceptions. The power of advertising to shape tastes and perceptions has made this aspect of marketing a subject of controversy. Economists like John Kenneth Galbraith argue that a distinction should be made between true wants and those that are created by advertising. In the view of such critics, advertising that goes beyond a simple statement of the facts about a product is at best a waste and at worst harmful to consumer welfare.

But others doubt that there are such things as true or natural wants other than the very basic needs for food, security, affection, self-esteem,

**Box 25.2
The Effect of Advertising on Consumer Perceptions**

In an experiment to determine the effect of a well-known brand name on consumer preferences, 150 subjects from Detroit were presented with two plates, on each of which was a slice of turkey meat. Although the two slices were actually from the same turkey, they had different labels. One bore a brand name that was heavily advertised and well known in Detroit, and the other bore a name that was much less familiar. Of the 150 subjects, only 10 percent thought the two samples tasted alike; 56 percent expressed a strong preference for the known brand, and 34 percent preferred the unknown brand.

In another part of the experiment, 61 subjects were presented with two plates. On one was a slice of tender turkey meat and on the other a slice of tough turkey meat. When no brand names were used, 49 of the subjects preferred the tender meat, 4 preferred the tough meat, and 8 could not tell the difference. After they had said which slice they preferred, they were asked to say which brand they thought the slices belonged to—the advertised brand or the unknown brand. Thirty-four of the subjects said that the turkey they preferred must have been the known brand; 18 thought the slice they liked was probably the unknown brand.

The experimenter concluded that advertising affected the consumers' perceptions even when the samples were identical, and that when the samples were not identical advertising created an expectation that the better sample would be the advertised one.

Source: James C. Makens, "Effect of Brand Preferences upon Consumers' Perceived Taste of Turkey Meat," *Journal of Applied Psychology* 49 (November 4, 1965): 261–263.

and so on. Advertising may affect which goods people choose to satisfy these needs. It may cause them to choose round-toed boots rather than square-toed boots to keep their feet dry, but that does no harm. Economists who take this point of view believe that efforts to limit consumer choice in the name of giving people what they "truly" want are a greater threat to consumer welfare than advertising is.

Price as a Marketing Tool

This brings us to price, the last of the four P's of marketing. Marketers agree with economists that good pricing decisions are vital to a firm's success. But in the real world, they say, the right price can't be found by picking a point on a graph. Instead, pricing decisions have to be coordinated with other marketing decisions in order best to serve consumers.

Take quality and variety, for example. Some consumers are willing to pay top price for top quality, while others would prefer less than the top quality at a lower price. Some are willing to pay high prices to satisfy unusual tastes, while others will accept cheaper, mass-produced goods. Pricing is a key factor in distribution, too. Often the same goods are available at different prices in swanky boutiques and barnlike off-price outlets. Some consumers prefer one, some the other. Finally, price and promotion interact. While some consumers will pay extra for advertised brands, others prefer low-priced generic goods that don't even have a brand name.

In sum, when all aspects of marketing are taken into account, competition begins to look like a much more complex process than it appears to be on a graph, where only price and quantity appear as variables. But although some areas of economic theory seem to ignore these aspects of real-world competition, not all of them do. In the rest of this chapter we will look at three areas of economic theory where all facets of marketing play a role.

THE THEORY OF MONOPOLISTIC COMPETITION

Monopolistic competition
A market structure in which many small firms offer differing products.

In earlier chapters we looked at industries in which many small firms produce a homogeneous product, and at others in which a few large firms make products that need not all be alike. These cases leave out a very large class of markets in which there are many small firms, each of which makes a product that is a little different from those of its competitors. This market structure is known as **monopolistic competition**. Examples include restaurants, service stations, bakeries, some kinds of book publishing, and countless others.

Equilibrium for the Firm Under Monopolistic Competition

The theory of monopolistic competition blends monopolistic and competitive aspects. The theory can be understood with the help of Box 25.3, which shows short- and long-run equilibrium positions for a typical firm under monopolistic competition.

The demand curve for a firm under monopolistic competition, like that for a pure monopolist, slopes downward. Each firm's product is a little different from those of its competitors. Each firm therefore can raise its price at least a little without losing all its customers, because some customers attach more importance than others to the special style or location or other marketing advantage the firm offers. Given this downward-sloping demand curve, the short-run profit-maximizing position shown in the box is found in the same way as that for a pure monopolist: The level of output is determined by the intersection of the marginal-cost and marginal-revenue curves, and the price charged is determined by the height of the demand curve at that point.

But this short-run equilibrium cannot also be a long-run equilibrium under monopolistic competition. The reason is freedom of entry. In the short-run position shown in part a of Box 25.3, the firm is earning a pure economic profit. This is shown by the fact that price exceeds average total cost. But high profits attract new firms. As new firms enter the market, the demand curves of firms that are already there will shift downward. The reason is that although the new firms' products are not the same, they are to some extent substitutes for those of the original firms. If the original firms improve their products or market them more aggressively, those efforts will raise their average total costs. The downward shift in the demand curve of the original firms or the upward shift in their cost curves, or both, will continue until there are no more profits to attract new firms. The result will be the long-run equilibrium position that is shown in part b of Box 25.3.

This long-run equilibrium position is sometimes said to be a sign of poor performance. For one thing, as under pure monopoly, each firm turns out too little of its product. The gap between price and marginal cost

**Box 25.3
Short-Run and Long-Run
Equilibrium Under
Monopolistic
Competition**

Under monopolistic competition, each firm has a downward-sloping demand curve, but there are no barriers to entry by new firms. In the short run, a firm that produces at the point where marginal cost is equal to marginal revenue can earn pure economic profits, as shown in part a. In the long run, however, new firms are attracted to the market. This diverts part of the demand from the firms that are already in the market, thus lowering the demand curve of each. Also, those firms may fight to keep their share of the market, using means that increase their costs. Entry by new firms will continue until a long-run equilibrium is reached in which profits are eliminated, as shown in part b.

(a) The Short Run

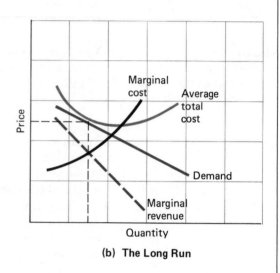

(b) The Long Run

indicates potential added production that would increase economic efficiency. In addition, under monopolistic competition a firm does not operate at the lowest point on its long-run average-cost curve. If there were fewer firms, each producing a greater amount of output, the same quantity of goods could be provided at a lower total cost. The hallmark of monopolistic competition, then, is too many gas stations, supermarkets, and restaurants, each operating at a fraction of capacity and each charging inefficiently high prices. Yet, despite the high prices, each earns the minimum return needed to stay in business.

Are Perfect Competition and Monopolistic Competition Different?

Not all economists accept the criticisms of monopolistic competition just noted. Many articles have been written on the subject, and many variations on the theory have been suggested. Setting aside differences in detail, most of what is said in favor of monopolistic competition comes down to the idea that monopolistic competition and perfect competition are not really very different.

One argument is that the belief that there is a difference comes from a mistaken idea about the nature of the product being sold. Take restaurants, for example. The restaurants in any town sell meals that are highly varied according to location, cuisine, atmosphere, service, and many other features. But perhaps meals are not really the product. Instead, think of all restaurants as selling a homogeneous good called dining pleasure. The differences among restaurants should be thought of not as differences in product but as differences in the methods used to produce dining pleasure, as well as differences in the packages of dining pleasure being sold. Likewise, different farmers grow potatoes in assorted sizes and use a variety of farming methods, but the potato market is still thought to be close to perfectly competitive. The dining pleasure market, by this line of reasoning, is just like the potato market.

A variation on this argument admits that there are differences among products but points out that such differences are valuable in themselves. Suppose it were true, as the theory of monopolistic competition suggests, that prices would be a little lower if there were fewer barbershops, each one not quite as conveniently located; or fewer supermarkets, each one a little more crowded; or fewer flavors of ice cream. Would a move in that direction benefit consumers? Not if consumers are willing to pay something for variety. Imagine that there were some way to split the market for, say, ice cream into two markets—one for the good called ice cream and the other for the good called variety. If that were possible, then each good could have its own price, and each market could be perfectly competitive. But this isn't possible. In the real world a single market for both goods, with the structure known as monopolistic competition, is as close as one can come to the ideal.

ADVERTISING AND MARKET PERFORMANCE

In this chapter and the last one, we have seen that both oligopoly and monopolistic competition have been criticized for poor performance. What is more, advertising is said to make things worse because it overstates the differences between the products of various firms (or even creates differences where there are none). This, in turn, makes each firm's demand curve less elastic than it otherwise would be, and increases the gap, in equilibrium, between price and marginal cost.

Advertising as a Barrier to Entry

In the case of oligopoly, advertising is seen as a barrier to entry by new firms. As such, it is said to lead to high levels of market concentration. And concentration, in the view of some economists, is linked with poor market performance.

The way in which advertising acts as a barrier to entry is by creating brand loyalties. Consumers who might otherwise treat all cola drinks as close substitutes are divided into opposing camps, some fiercely loyal to Pepsi, others to Coke. Each firm can raise its price with little fear that doing so will cause its customers to go elsewhere. And each firm does not have to worry about the resulting high profits attracting new firms to the market, since the new firms not only have to spend money to build plants and hire workers but also have to mount expensive advertising campaigns.

In 1967 this view of the effects of advertising got a major boost from the economists W. S. Comanor and T. A. Wilson. They looked at the statistical link between advertising spending and profits in 41 industries and reached the following conclusion:

> It is evident that . . . advertising is a highly profitable activity. Industries with high advertising outlays earn, on the average, at a profit rate which exceeds that of other industries by nearly four percentage points. This differential represents a 50 percent increase in profit rates. It is likely, moreover, that much of this profit rate differential is accounted for by the entry barriers created by advertising expenditures and by the resulting achievement of market power.[2]

Not all economists have accepted the idea that advertising is a barrier to entry. Yale Brozen, for one, sees the connection between advertising and competition in a different light.[3]

According to Brozen, the theory that advertising is a barrier to entry ignores reality. Advertising is not a barrier to competition; it is a means of competition. Existing firms have no advantage over new ones in buying advertising. Advertising agencies will sell their services to anyone who will pay their fees. In fact, advertising is even more important for new firms than for existing ones. In Brozen's view, firms aim their advertising not so much at building up loyalty in their own customers as at getting their rivals' customers to try their product. The real way to create a barrier to entry and protect existing firms, in this view, would be to ban advertising. Then it would be far harder for a new firm to enter a market.

What about the Comanor and Wilson study, though? Brozen thinks it is flawed by a confusion between accounting categories and categories of economic theory. Partly because of the way tax laws are written, accountants treat advertising as a current expense, like wages or purchases of supplies. In fact, however, advertising is an investment that has long-term effects. A brand image takes years to develop, and after that it is a long-lasting asset for the company that created it. If advertising is viewed as an investment, firms that advertise heavily no longer appear to be more profitable than average.

Advertising and Market Performance

In the case of both oligopoly and monopolistic competition, the debate over the benefits of advertising and other marketing techniques seems to turn on two opposing views of the world. Is the real world one in which consumers treat all sources of supply as alike and move freely among them in response to small changes in price? Or is it one in which lack of incentive and information causes consumers to cling to familiar sources of supply, giving each firm a monopoly with regard to its own customers? And advertising—does it set up barriers between firms, thereby adding to their monopoly power, or does it break down barriers, thereby destroying

---

[2]W. S. Comanor and T. A. Wilson, "Advertising, Market Structure, and Performance," *Review of Economics and Statistics* 49, November 1967, p. 437.

[3]For a representative exposition of Brozen's views, see Yale Brozen, "Entry Barriers: Advertising and Product Differentiation," in Harvey J. Goldschmid, H. Michael Mann, and J. Fred Weston, eds., *Industrial Concentration: The New Learning* (Boston: Little, Brown, 1974), pp. 115–137.

**Box 25.4
The Effects of
Advertising on the
Market for Legal
Services**

Until 1977 there was no advertising in the market for legal services. Lawyers who were so daring as to advertise their fees or even, in some states, the nature of their legal specialties could be thrown out of the profession by bar association ethics committees. Then along came John Bates and Van O'Steen, partners in a legal clinic in Phoenix, Arizona. Bates and O'Steen were not willing to live with the advertising ban. They ran an ad in the local paper in which they described their clinic and listed standard fees for certain services, such as filing for uncontested divorces. The state bar association pounced, but Bates and O'Steen fought their case all the way to the United States Supreme Court—and they finally won. The ban on advertising, said the Court, violated their constitutional right of free speech.

Following the Bates decision, advertisements for legal services became commonplace. The results were striking.

For one thing, prices dropped sharply. In Phoenix the fee for an uncontested divorce dropped from about $350 to a range of $150 to $200. In New York City a legal name change, which once cost $150 to $200, fell to about $75. Similar price decreases took effect for the preparation of wills, title searches, and other routine services.

A second effect of the Supreme Court decision was the growth of lawyer referral services. These firms offer no legal services themselves but simply act as go-betweens, helping people with legal problems find the right attorney to handle their problems for a price they can afford.

Perhaps even more important in the long run, the increased competition has spurred the growth of many new kinds of legal services. John Bates, for example, left the legal clinic to design and sell self-help packages for consumers with routine legal problems. At one time, for only $16.95 he sold a do-it-yourself divorce kit complete with all the needed instructions and forms. In another city, an outfit called The Law Store offered its customers a telephone consultation for $9.95; for another $10, it would follow up with a letter or phone call.

In this instance at least, advertising has clearly led to improved market performance.

monopoly power? A number of kinds of evidence might help answer these questions.

One kind of evidence comes from studies of consumer behavior like the one described in Box 25.2. There it was shown that advertising affected the perceived taste of different samples of meat that all came from the same turkey. This shows that advertising can increase brand loyalty. But other studies, such as the one given at the end of this chapter as a case for discussion, suggest that brand loyalty can arise even in the absence of advertising.

Another kind of evidence comes from studies of how advertising is used by firms. For example, it has been shown that new products are advertised more heavily than old products. This may indicate that makers of old products tend to depend on consumer loyalty and that advertising is a way of breaking down that loyalty. It has also been shown that consumers in markets where advertising is heavy are less loyal to one brand than consumers in markets where advertising is light. This too might indicate that advertising helps make consumers more willing to try substitute products.[4]

---

[4]The article by Brozen cited in footnote 3 contains discussions of these and similar studies.

Perhaps most interesting of all, real-life experiments have been done in which advertising has been introduced into a market where it was not permitted before. The market for legal services, discussed in Box 25.4, is one such case. There, the introduction of advertising seems to have improved market performance. Another study compared the prices of eyeglasses in states where advertising was restricted with prices in states where glasses could be advertised freely. It found the prices in states that restricted advertising of eyeglasses to be more than twice as high.[5] And so the debate goes on.

MARKET DYNAMICS AND COMPETITION

The issue of the relative efficiency of perfect competition, oligopoly, and monopolistic competition is not fully resolved and may never be. But before we leave the topic, there is one more aspect of competition and efficiency that we need to consider.

Static vs. Dynamic Efficiency

Static efficiency
The ability of an economy to get the greatest degree of consumer satisfaction from given resources and technology.

Dynamic efficiency
The ability of an economy to increase consumer satisfaction through growth and innovation.

Up to this point our discussion of market structure and economic performance has focused on the problem of **static efficiency**—the ability of an economy to get the greatest amount of consumer satisfaction with given resources and technology. Static efficiency is a measure of how close an economy comes to its production possibility frontier. But market structure may also have an impact on the economy's **dynamic efficiency**—its success in increasing the rate of output per unit of resources. Dynamic efficiency, thus, is a measure of the rate at which the production possibility frontier shifts outward over time.

Of the two kinds of efficiency, dynamic efficiency is much more important in the long run. In the past, the most important single factor in U.S. economic growth was gains in knowledge, that is, innovation and technological change. Economic growth from this source alone has been estimated at 1.5 percent per year.[6] The remaining economic growth is due to capital accumulation, population growth, increased education, and other factors. The contribution of innovation and technological change is very large compared to the loss in static efficiency caused by monopolistic and oligopolistic market structures. The highest estimate of that loss ever made is about 2.5 percent of gross national product. Innovation and technological change add more than that to GNP every two years.

The Schumpeter Hypothesis

If every policy that promotes static efficiency also contributed to dynamic efficiency, the distinction would not matter much. However, there is a widely shared belief that the greatest dynamic efficiency is found in the concentrated markets that are thought to be sources of static inefficiency. This will be referred to as the Schumpeter hypothesis, after the economist

---

[5]Lee Benham, "The Effect of Advertising on the Price of Eyeglasses," *Journal of Law and Economics* 15, October 1972, pp. 337–352.
[6]See Edward F. Denison, *Accounting for U.S. Economic Growth, 1929–1969* (Washington, D.C.: Brookings Institution, 1974), especially pp. 124–150.

Joseph Schumpeter, who first brought it to widespread attention. (See Box 25.5.)

According to Schumpeter, the source of innovation and growth is competition—but not the kind of competition found in markets that are perfectly competitive. He saw two ways in which less than perfect competition could promote dynamic efficiency.

First, the hope of achieving monopoly power is often the chief incentive for competition. The first firm to obtain new knowledge and put it to use is able to make pure economic profits because its new discovery gives it a temporary monopoly. If each new product had to be brought out at a price that just covered cost, or if each cost-reducing innovation had to be followed by a matching reduction in price, there would be little reason to innovate at all. If the first firm to adjust to changing conditions were unable to increase the gap between costs and revenues by doing so, there would be no incentive to be first. Competition among entrepreneurs is competition for monopoly power, at least in the short run. In this sense, monopoly is not the opposite of competition but a normal result of it.

Second, monopoly power acts as a spur to competition. This is true in the sense that an industry where monopoly profits are being made tends to attract new firms. It also applies to competition among industries and

---

**Box 25.5
Joseph Schumpeter on
Competition and
Entrepreneurship**

Joseph Schumpeter
(1883–1950)

Joseph Schumpeter was born in Austria in 1883. He studied law at the University of Vienna and attended lectures by the leading economists of the day. He served briefly as minister of finance after World War I. In 1932 he left Austria for Harvard University, where he wrote most of the works for which he is known today.

Schumpeter had little use for the kind of economics that reduces everything to graphs and equations. He thought economic theories paid too little attention to the role of the entrepreneur. He saw competition among entrepreneurs, not the abstract notion of perfect competition, as the source of economic progress. As he wrote in *Capitalism, Socialism, and Democracy,*

> *The competition that counts is the competition from the new commodity, the new technology, the new source of supply, the new type of organization (the largest scale unit of control, for instance)—competition which commands a decisive cost or quality advantage and which strikes not at the margins of the profits and the outputs of the existing firms, but at their foundations and their very lives. This kind of competition is as much more effective than the other as a bombardment is in comparison with forcing a door, and so much more important that it becomes a matter of comparative indifference whether competition in the ordinary sense functions more or less promptly; the powerful lever that in the long run expands output and brings down prices is in any case made of other stuff.*

"In this respect," he added in another place, "perfect competition is not only impossible but inferior, and has no title to being set up as a model of ideal efficiency."

Source: Joseph Schumpeter, *Capitalism, Socialism and Democracy* (New York: Harper & Row, 1942), pp. 84–85, 106.

product groups for the consumer's dollar. For example, OPEC's attempts to exploit its monopoly power in the 1970s led to a speedup in the rate of innovation in energy production and conservation techniques. In this sense, monopoly is not the opposite of competition but a spur to it.

Can the Schumpeter Hypothesis Be Tested?

The Schumpeter hypothesis poses a sweeping challenge to economic theory and policy. Not surprisingly, many attempts have been made to verify or refute it by studying the data on economic growth, market concentration, and innovation. The results to date, however, have been inconclusive.[7]

The main problem in testing the Schumpeter hypothesis lies in measuring innovation. Schumpeter had in mind a fairly broad view of innovation. Inventing new products or techniques, figuring out how to apply new inventions, working out new forms of business organization, finding new ways of financing investment, and creating new methods of marketing and distribution were, to Schumpeter, all major sources of dynamic efficiency. But clearly, most of them can be measured only indirectly, and some not at all. As a result, attempts to test the Schumpeter hypothesis have had to make do with rather crude substitutes for some of its central concepts.

One indirect test has used research and development (R&D) spending to indicate the innovative efforts of firms. The answer to the simple question, "Do large firms in concentrated industries account for more than their share of all R&D spending?" seems to be yes. The 400 to 500 largest firms, with 5000 or more employees each, account for 80 to 90 percent of all R&D spending and only 25 to 30 percent of all output. This alone is enough to suggest that the Schumpeter hypothesis cannot be dismissed out of hand.

However, a number of qualifications must be added. For example, using patented investments rather than R&D spending as a measure of innovative activity appears to weaken the link between concentration and innovation. Also, such factors as the nature of the industry's product or the scientific environment in which the industry operates seem to have a major effect on innovative activity. Finally, some studies have suggested that size of firms and degree of market concentration affect innovation only up to a certain threshold, with giant firms having no advantage over firms that are merely large.

Perhaps the safest conclusion is that innovation—in Schumpeter's sense—is simply too complex to be subjected to rigorous analysis. Looking at all the studies in perspective, we find that under favorable conditions firms of all sizes in markets with all degrees of concentration are able to contribute to the dynamic efficiency of the economy as a whole. This implies that neither a policy of breaking up large firms into smaller ones nor one of welding small firms into larger ones can be counted on to speed the pace of innovation. The ability of large corporations to assign R&D teams to solve tough technical problems is important, but so is the flash of insight that may come to a lone inventor. In short, for all we know, the

---

[7]For a survey of these efforts, see Jesse W. Markham, "Concentration: A Stimulus or Retardant to Innovation?" in Harvey J. Goldschmid, H. Michael Mann, and J. Fred Weston, eds., *Industrial Concentration: The New Learning* (Boston: Little, Brown, 1974), pp. 247–272.

present mix of large and small firms may be just about right from the point of view of dynamic efficiency.

Looking Ahead

The past four chapters have looked at the connection between market structure and performance. Before we go on to the next three chapters, which look at public policies that deal with competition and market structure, it will be useful to summarize two key controversies that economic theory has not resolved.

The first has to do with the extent to which perfect competition, or something close to it, can be viewed as the natural state of the economy. If a great deal of concentration is needed in most markets for firms to take advantage of economies of scale, perfect competition will be very rare. If, in industries that are not highly concentrated, a large amount of product variety is needed to meet consumer demand, there will be even less room for perfect competition. However, if both market concentration and product variety are "unnatural," caused by such factors as advertising, barriers to entry, and government regulation, there will be room to expand the area of perfect competition.

The second controversy concerns the question of whether perfect competition, or something close to it, is a necessary or even a sufficient condition for good market performance. If, in concentrated markets, shared monopoly is rare and active competition is the rule, perfect competition may not be necessary. And if, at least in some markets, concentration is needed for dynamic efficiency, perfect competition may not be even a sufficient condition for good market performance.

As we will see in the following chapters, these controversies underlie many debates on matters of public policy.

Summary

1. *Marketing* means finding out what customers want and channeling a flow of goods and services to meet those wants. It consists of four activities: creating a *product* that will meet consumer needs; getting it to a *place* where consumers can conveniently buy it; *promoting* it through advertising, personal selling, and other means; and putting the right *price* on it. All aspects of marketing are important to competition.

2. A market structure in which many small firms each make a product that is a little different from those of its competitors is known as *monopolistic competition*. In long-run equilibrium, each firm in such a market produces at a point where its demand curve is tangent to its long-run average-total-cost curve.

3. Monopolistic competition is said to be ineffi-

cient in that price exceeds marginal cost in long-run equilibrium. This means that fewer firms, each producing more output, could supply the market at a lower average total cost. However, consumers would have to give up some variety, so they would not necessarily be better off.

4. Some economists view advertising as a barrier to entry of a market by new firms and a source of monopoly profits. Others dispute these claims, contending that advertising is used more by new firms entering a market than by firms that are already in that market. They also suggest that if more realistic accounting concepts are used, firms that advertise heavily are not more profitable, on the average, than other firms.

5. *Static efficiency* means the ability of an econ-

omy to get the greatest amount of consumer satisfaction from given resources and technology. *Dynamic efficiency* means achieving growth in the rate of output per unit of resources.

6. Joseph Schumpeter believed that perfectly competitive markets are less dynamically efficient than more concentrated ones. In his view, the hope of achieving at least a temporary monopoly is a spur to innovation. Modern research suggests that this is probably true in at least some markets, but not in all.

Questions for Review

1. Explain the following terms and concepts:
   marketing
   monopolistic competition
   static efficiency
   dynamic efficiency
2. What are the "four P's" of marketing?
3. Give examples of monopolistic competition. In each case, explain why the market does not fit the definition of perfect competition or that of oligopoly.

4. Why is monopolistic competition said to be inefficient? What would consumers give up if average costs were lowered by reducing the number of firms in such a market?
5. Use a production possibility frontier to show the difference between static and dynamic efficiency.
6. How did Schumpeter think market structure was related to dynamic efficiency? What have tests of his hypothesis shown?

Problems and Topics for Discussion

1. What aspects of competition can be seen in the example of the toothpaste pump? What real benefits do consumers derive from an innovation like this one? If your answer is none, why do you think such products are successful?
2. In downtown Moscow there are far fewer restaurants than in similar U.S. cities. These restaurants are, on the average, much larger and much busier than those in American cities. The quality of the food served is high, though the service leaves something to be desired by U.S. standards. Do these facts suggest to you that the central planners who control Moscow's restaurants have designed their system to perform better than the restaurant market in most U.S. cities? Using what you have learned in this chapter, argue both sides of this question.
3. Total motor fuel consumption in the United States rose slightly between 1974 and 1984, but the number of service stations fell sharply. One explanation runs as follows: Before the 1973–1974 oil price shock, buyers of gasoline tended to be strongly brand loyal. The shortages of the 1970s forced consumers to shop around and buy gasoline wherever they could find it. In doing so, they found that their cars ran just about the same on any gas. They therefore ceased to be loyal to any brand.

   Assume that reduced brand loyalty means a flatter demand curve for any given gas station. Using what you know about monopolistic competition, why would this lead to a new equilibrium with a reduced number of service stations even if conditions did not change in other ways?

4. **Case for Discussion**
   In a study of brand loyalty, a random sample of 60 beer drinkers was drawn from Stanford University students living in married-student housing. The subjects were told that they were taking part in a marketing test of three types of beer produced by a local brewer.

   Once a week the subjects were presented, in their homes, with a chance to choose from among three bottles labeled "M," "L," and "P." They were told that Brand M was a high-priced beer, Brand L a medium-priced beer, and Brand P a bargain-priced beer. The subjects did not have to pay for their beer; but to make the price difference more realistic, the medium-priced beer had a 2-cent "refund" taped to the bottle while the low-priced beer had a 5-cent "refund." The subjects could keep the refunds.

In point of fact, the three brands of beer were all drawn from the same production run at the brewery. Only the labels differed. However, this did not prevent the development of fierce brand loyalty by many of the subjects. (Subjects were considered to be brand loyal if they chose the same brand four times in a row.) Although at first the subjects experimented with the three brands, by the end of 24 trials 57 of the 60 had developed brand loyalty. Of those 57, 26 chose Brand M, 12 Brand L, and 19 Brand P.

Since the beer was all the same, it is surprising how firmly set in their opinions some of the subjects became. One subject reported, "M is a good strong malty beer, but I like L because it is lighter. Mmm!!! P would poison me—make me ill." Another subject, who developed a strong taste for P, once tried a bottle of M and reported, "Worst I've ever had; you couldn't give it away."[8]

Questions:

a. Critics of advertising blame it for creating brand loyalty. This in turn is said to create barriers to entry in oligopolistic industries, and to make the demand curves of firms in monopolistic competition less elastic than they otherwise would be. In both cases, advertising is thought to contribute to poor market performance. What does this case suggest about the connection between advertising and brand loyalty? Does it support a policy of setting limits on advertising as a means of improving market performance in the beer industry?

b. Economies of scale have led to a high degree of concentration in the brewing industry. That industry is now an oligopoly dominated by a few major brewers. Yet those brewers still produce a great many brands of beer. If one looked only at the number of brand names displayed in a typical store, one would think brewing was an example of monopolistic competition. What does brand loyalty have to do with this market structure? Do you think market performance would be improved by limiting each large firm to just one brand? By returning to a situation in which each brand was made by a different firm? Discuss.

Suggestions for Further Reading

Galbraith, John Kenneth. *The Affluent Society*. Boston: Houghton Mifflin, 1958.

Contains an attack on advertising as a violation of consumer sovereignty.

Goldschmid, Harvey J., H. Michael Mann, and Fred J. Weston. *Industrial Concentration: The New Learning*. Boston: Little, Brown, 1974.

Chapter 3 is a debate between Yale Brozen and H. Michael Mann on advertising as a barrier to competition. In Chapter 5 Jesse W. Markham discusses market concentration and innovation, citing several attempts to test the Schumpeter hypothesis.

Hayek, Friedrich A. von. "The Non Sequitur of the Dependence Effect." *Southern Economic Journal* 27 (April 1961).

In this article Hayek challenges Galbraith's critiques of advertising.

Schumpeter, Joseph. *Capitalism, Socialism, and Democracy*. New York: Harper & Row, 1942.

Part 2 of this book contains Schumpeter's discussion of the link between market concentration and dynamic efficiency.

---

[8]Source: J. Douglass McConnell, "The Development of Brand Loyalty: An Experimental Study," *Journal of Marketing Research* 5, February 1968, pp. 13–19.

Government involvement with business is nothing new, as this nineteenth-century cartoon shows.

Part VI
Government
and Business

Chapter 26

Antitrust Policy

WHAT YOU WILL LEARN IN THIS CHAPTER

After reading this chapter, you should be able to

1. Discuss the social, political, and economic goals of *antitrust laws*.
2. List the major antitrust laws and their main provisions.
3. Define *price fixing* and explain how it is treated under antitrust law.
4. Distinguish among *horizontal*, *vertical*, and *conglomerate mergers*, and explain how mergers are treated under antitrust law.
5. Discuss competing views of antitrust law.

Ideas for Review

Here are some terms and concepts that you should review before you read this chapter:

Monopoly (Chapter 23)
Price discrimination (Chapter 23)
Barriers to entry (Chapter 24)
Oligopoly (Chapter 24)
Shared monopoly (Chapter 24)

"The river symbolizes the barriers that LTV still needs to bridge."

James V. Stack supervises two LTV Steel Co. plants in Cleveland, Ohio. The plants are only 40 yards apart. Yet Stack often spends an hour a day getting from one to the other. One of the plants, formerly owned by Republic Steel, is on the east bank of the Cuyahoga River. The other, formerly owned by Jones & Laughlin Steel, is on the west bank. The two steel makers were merged in 1984 to create LTV Steel, but no bridge has yet been built to link the two plants.

The river symbolizes the barriers that LTV still needs to bridge in order to become an efficient, unified firm. Differences in computer systems, personnel practices, and management styles must also be worked out. But before LTV Steel could come into being at all, it had to bridge a major legal barrier posed by the nation's antitrust laws.

The antitrust laws, which date from the turn of the century, give the U.S. Department of Justice the authority to block mergers that might tend to create a monopoly. The Justice Department therefore gave the merger of Republic with Jones & Laughlin a close look. Before the merger, Republic had 7.1 percent of the steel market in the United States while Jones & Laughlin had 8.6 percent. Although the two firms together would be far from a true monopoly, their merger would clearly make the steel market more of an oligopoly than it already was.

Those in favor of the merger argued that joining the two firms would do more good than harm. The steel industry as a whole faced falling demand and growing competition from imports. The merger, they said, would make one strong company out of two sick ones. Besides, they claimed, international competition would keep steel prices in line even if the U.S. steel industry became more concentrated. The Justice Department at first announced that it would block the merger, but later, after the merger agreement was modified, it reversed its decision. Now it is up to the firm's managers to meet their goal of making LTV a strong firm that will help bring the steel industry back to health.[1]

Antitrust laws
A set of laws, including the Sherman Act and the Clayton Act, that seek to control market structure and the competitive behavior of firms.

The **antitrust laws** that were brought to bear on the LTV Steel case, and on many other cases that have to do with market structure and performance, are the subject of this chapter. There is a connection between the antitrust laws and economists' concern with market structure and performance, but the connection is not as close as one might think. The antitrust laws are not a simple translation into law of the economic theories discussed in earlier chapters. The foundations of these laws were laid in the last century, before the modern theories of monopoly and oligopoly had seen the light of day. Today, as then, antitrust policy reflects broad social concerns rather than economic theory.

In the United States of the nineteenth century, people were hostile toward "trusts," as they called the large firms of their day, not because they were inefficient but because they were rich and powerful. If they were

---

[1]Based in part on Thomas F. O'Boyle and Mark Russell, "Troubled Marriage: Steel Giants' Merger Brings Big Headaches, J&L and Republic Find," Wall Street Journal, November 30, 1984, p. 1.

efficient as well, that made them richer and more powerful still. Consider the point of view reflected in this passage from an 1897 Supreme Court decision:

> [Large firms] may even temporarily, or perhaps permanently, reduce the price of the article traded in or manufactured, by reducing the expense inseparable from the running of many different companies for the same purpose. Trade or commerce under those circumstances may nevertheless be badly and unfortunately restrained by driving out of business the small dealers and worthy men whose lives have been spent therein and who might be unable to readjust themselves to their altered surroundings. Mere reduction in the price of the commodity dealt in might be dearly paid for by the ruin of such a class.[2]

The concerns of a judge who would dismiss the benefits of "mere" price reductions in favor of the interests of "small dealers and worthy men" are very different from the concerns of economists today. The theories of market structure and economic performance discussed in the last few chapters all stress the need to promote efficiency and consumer welfare. The main reason for antitrust laws, in this view, is to keep prices low through active competition. As long as competition makes consumers better off, economists tend not to care whether some firms—no matter how "worthy" the men or women who run them—don't survive the contest.

The connection between the social and political goals of the antitrust laws on the one hand and their economic purposes on the other will be a major theme of this chapter. The chapter will try to explore just how much of an overlap there is between the kind of antitrust policy that actually exists and the kind that economic theory suggests ought to exist. Of course, there are different opinions as to how large the overlap is, but what follows will deal as much with areas of broad agreement among economists as with areas of disagreement.

ANTITRUST LAWS AND POLICIES

The Sherman Antitrust Act

The logical starting point for a description of antitrust laws is the Sherman Antitrust Act of 1890. This act is at the heart of antitrust policy in the United States. It outlaws "every contract, combination in the form of a trust or otherwise, or conspiracy in restraint of commerce among the several states, or with foreign nations." It also declares that "every person who shall monopolize, or attempt to monopolize, or combine or conspire with any other person or persons, to monopolize any part of the trade or commerce among the several States, or with foreign nations, shall be deemed guilty of a misdemeanor." (In 1974 the act was amended so that violations of its provisions are counted as felonies.)

Under the Sherman Act the government can sue firms that violate its provisions and ask for any of several types of penalties. It can ask for fines or jail sentences. (The latter, once rare in antitrust cases, have become much

---

[2]*United States* v. *Trans-Missouri Freight Ass'n.*, 166 U.S. 323 (1897).

more common now that violations are felonies.) It can also obtain an *injunction* (a court order that bars the offending firm from continuing the action that it is in violation of the act). In extreme cases it can even ask the court to order the offending firm to be broken up into smaller units that would compete with each other.

In addition, private parties who claim to be injured by violations of the Sherman Act can bring suits of their own. If they win, they can obtain damages equal to three times the value of any loss they can prove to have suffered. Private antitrust suits are quite common.

The Clayton Act and the Federal Trade Commission Act

Antitrust officials of the federal government won some notable early victories under the Sherman Act, of which the most dramatic were the breakups of Standard Oil and American Tobacco in 1911. Still, many people felt that the Sherman Act was not enough. For one thing, the act was unclear about the status of monopolies that were achieved through merger. Also, people felt that the law should state more clearly the kinds of business practices that were likely to have anticompetitive effects. The outcome of these concerns was the Clayton Act of 1914, which has four major provisions:

1. It outlaws price discrimination among purchasers of goods, except when such discrimination is based on the grade, quality, or quantity of the product sold or on clear differences in selling costs. Any other form of price discrimination is illegal if the effect is to reduce competition greatly or to tend to create a monopoly.
2. It forbids sellers from making *tying contracts*—contracts for the sale of a firm's products that include an agreement that the purchaser will not use or deal in a competitor's products—when the effect of such contracts is to reduce competition.
3. An antimerger section of the act forbids any firm that is engaged in commerce to acquire the shares of a competing firm or to purchase the stocks of two or more competing firms. Again, the ban is not total; it applies only when the effect is to reduce competition greatly.
4. The act outlaws *interlocking directorates*—situations in which the same person is on the boards of directors of two or more firms: (a) if the firms are competitors; (b) if they are of a certain size or larger; and (c) where reduction of competition will violate the antitrust laws. Such situations are illegal whether or not proof of a reduction of competition can be found.

In the same year that it passed the Clayton Act, Congress passed the Federal Trade Commission Act, which supplements it. This act declares broadly that "unfair methods of competition in commerce are illegal." It leaves the question of what constitutes an unfair method to the Federal Trade Commission, which was formed by the act as an independent agency whose purpose is to attack unfair practices. (The FTC also has some regulatory functions; it protects the public against false and misleading advertisements for foods, drugs, cosmetics, and therapeutic devices.) The importance of the Federal Trade Commission Act lies not so much in broadening the definition of illegal business behavior as in setting up an independent antitrust agency with the power to bring court cases.

Since 1914 the Clayton Act has received two major amendments. One is the Robinson-Patman Act of 1936, which strengthened the law against price discrimination. The other is the Celler-Kefauver Antimerger Act of 1950, which, as the name implies, strengthened the law against mergers. These key acts will be discussed in the next section.

Antitrust Policy

In practice, U.S. antitrust policy is not determined by the antitrust laws alone. The laws are broadly written. What is an "attempt to monopolize"? A "substantial lessening of competition"? An "unfair method of competition"? Congress left these questions to be answered by the courts. The government's two major antitrust agencies—the Federal Trade Commission and the antitrust division of the Department of Justice—also have a great deal of discretion in setting the course of antitrust policy. Within the framework of the laws and prior court decisions, it is their job to decide just what kinds of business conduct should be viewed as anticompetitive.

This section attempts to outline the growth of antitrust policy over the years. It is organized under the headings of price fixing, mergers, vertical restraints, and price discrimination.

Price fixing

Any action by two or more firms to cooperate in setting prices.

Price fixing   Whatever else the Sherman Act may do, no one denies that it outlaws **price fixing**. Competing firms must make their pricing decisions on their own; they cannot cooperate to set prices more to their liking than those that result from independent action. The recent tendency of the courts and antitrust officials has been to treat price fixing as a *per se* violation of the law—which means that only the fact of a price-fixing agreement need be proved in order to win a conviction. It is not necessary to prove that the price-fixing attempt was successful or that the prices set were unreasonable. It also means that accused price fixers cannot defend themselves on the ground that their action might have had beneficial effects.

Besides making price fixing illegal, the law has been interpreted as applying to other forms of cooperative conduct that might affect prices indirectly. For example, certain practices engaged in by cartels, such as agreeing to restrict output or divide markets, have been treated just as severely as agreements on prices. Generally, though, the law has not made much headway against tacit coordination of prices. Enforcement agencies have often argued that such things as price leadership or the exchange of price information among competitors also amount to price fixing, but the courts have not always ruled against these practices.

Mergers   Not long after the passage of the Sherman Act, the question of what to do about monopolies created by mergers arose. There seemed to be a danger that competing firms could get around the law against cartels by merging into one big firm. That would make price-fixing and output restrictions matters of company policy and, thus, beyond the reach of the law.

In an early case that involved the merger of two railroads, the Supreme Court ruled that a merger by direct competitors was a combination in restraint of trade and, hence, a violation of the antitrust laws. This precedent was not always followed in later decisions, however. Nor did the antimerger section of the Clayton Act prove very effective. Not until the Clayton Act was amended by the Celler-Kefauver Act in 1950 did control of mergers become a major part of antitrust law enforcement.

After the passage of the Celler-Kefauver Act, the courts and antitrust agencies moved in a direction that brought almost any merger under scrutiny. Not only were mergers by giants like Republic Steel and Jones & Laughlin challenged, but so were mergers of rather small firms.

Besides opposing **horizontal mergers**—mergers of firms that compete in the same market—the government often opposed **vertical mergers**— mergers of firms with a supplier-customer relationship. (An automaker buying a spark plug manufacturer would be an example.) **Conglomerate mergers**—mergers of firms in unrelated markets—may also be opposed by the government. (An oil company buying a retail chain would be an example of such a merger.)

Horizontal merger
A merger between firms that compete in the same market.

Vertical merger
A merger between firms with a supplier-purchaser relationship.

Conglomerate merger
A merger between firms in unrelated markets.

Current policy on mergers   In the mid-1980s, merger and takeover activity in the U.S. economy reached a new peak. Faced with the rash of mergers, many involving billion-dollar firms, antitrust officials worked to develop new standards. While antitrust officials still look closely at large horizontal mergers, the new standards on mergers tend to be less strict than was once the case. The Von's Grocery case, given as a case for discussion at the end of this chapter, shows how strict merger policy was some years ago. Today, approval of even much larger mergers, like the one that formed LTV Steel, is not uncommon.

In part, the more relaxed policy on mergers stems from trends in economic theory. Economists are less sure that increased market concentration leads to poor performance than they were a few years ago. Also, it is recognized that mergers can add to efficiency if they cause weak management to be replaced by stronger management. (The hope that a firm's stock price will rise after its management is replaced is often the main motive for a merger.) Finally—and this was a factor in the LTV Steel case—in markets where international competition is strong, concentration in the U.S. market is seen as less of a threat to consumer interests.

The trend toward a somewhat less strict merger policy was confirmed in 1982 when the Justice Department published a new set of merger guidelines. The new guidelines allow some mergers that the old ones (which had not been revised since 1968) would have challenged. Under the new guidelines, vertical and conglomerate mergers are challenged only when it is likely that they would result in harm to consumers.

Herfindahl index
An index of market concentration that is arrived at by squaring the percentage market shares of all firms in an industry and summing the squares.

Current merger guidelines use the so-called **Herfindahl index** to measure market concentration, rather than the four-firm concentration ratio. As Box 26.1 explains, the Herfindahl index is arrived at by squaring the percentage market share of each firm and then adding those squares. In cases in which the index is below 1,000 after the merger, the Department of Justice normally would not challenge a merger. It would be acceptable, for example, for mergers to result in an industry in which ten firms of equal size share the market. In more concentrated markets, mergers that would result in an increase of 100 points or more in the index are likely to be challenged unless other factors indicate that the merger would have no harmful effects on consumers.

In borderline cases, the merger guidelines indicate that attention will be given to a number of factors that are likely to affect market performance. Several of these were mentioned in Chapter 24. They include the following:

- Mergers are more likely to be challenged in industries with homogeneous products.
- Mergers are less likely to be challenged in industries that face competition from products that are fairly close substitutes.

Box 26.1
The Herfindahl Index

The Herfindahl index of market concentration is calculated by squaring the percentage market shares of all the firms in the market and summing the squares. For an industry with n competing firms, the formula is

$$H = S_1^2 + S_2^2 + S_3^2 + \cdots + S_n^2$$

As the examples in the table show, the index rises as a market becomes more concentrated, reaching a maximum of 10,000 under pure monopoly. The U.S. Department of Justice considers a market with an index of less than 1,000 to be "unconcentrated." A market with an index between 1,000 and 1,800 is "moderately concentrated," and one with an index of 1,800 or more is "highly concentrated."

The chief difference between the Herfindahl index and the four-firm concentration ratio is the added weight that the Herfindahl index gives to large firms. For example, a market that contains eight firms of equal size has a four-firm concentration ratio of 50 and a Herfindahl index of 1,250. A market that contains one firm with a 35 percent market share and 13 others with 5 percent each has the same four-firm concentration ratio, but it has a Herfindahl index of 1,550—much higher than in the case of equal market shares.

To calculate the Herfindahl index for a market, one needs to know the market shares of all firms in the industry. In the case of a merger, however, one needs to know only the market shares of the firms involved to calculate the *increase* in concentration that would result from the merger. For example, the merger of Republic Steel (7.1 percent) with Jones & Laughlin (8.6 percent) to make LTV Steel (14.2 percent) increased the Herfindahl index for the steel market by about 122. The formula for calculating the outcome of a merger of firms A and B to create a new firm, C, is

$$S_C^2 - (S_A^2 + S_B^2)$$

Herfindahl Concentration Indexes for Various Industries

Industry Structure	Index
100 equal-sized firms	100
10 equal-sized firms	1,000
8 equal-sized firms	1,250
1 firm with 30 percent market share plus 7 with 10 percent each	1,600
5 equal-sized firms	2,000
A pure monopoly	10,000

- Mergers are less likely to be challenged in industries where orders are large and infrequent than in industries where orders are small and frequent.
- Mergers are less likely to be challenged in industries where technological change is rapid, or where the merger would increase efficiency.
- Mergers are more likely to be challenged in industries where there has been collusion among firms in the past.

In most cases vertical and conglomerate mergers are less likely to be challenged than horizontal mergers by firms of equal size. However, several factors could cause the Justice Department to object to such mergers. These factors include

- the elimination of potential entrants into a market.
- the creation of barriers to entry into a market.
- a tendency to make collusion among competitors easier.
- the elimination of a firm that has not "played along" with tacit cooperative arrangements among firms in a market.

Vertical restraints   Like vertical mergers, vertical restraints on trade involve agreements between a supplier and a customer. They are distinguished from horizontal restraints, which involve agreements between competing suppliers. Many kinds of vertical restraints have been attacked under the antitrust laws, not always successfully. Among the kinds that have been challenged most often are resale price maintenance, territorial restrictions, tying agreements, and exclusive dealing.

Under resale price maintenance agreements, retailers agree not to sell a good below a price set by the manufacturer. Such agreements have been held to be unlawful restraints on trade. The reason is that they limit price competition among the retailers that carry a manufacturer's product. In practice, the restriction on resale price maintenance has never been watertight; agreements that indirectly achieve the same thing have sometimes survived court tests.

Manufacturer-imposed limits on the area in which a retailer can sell also reduce competition at the retail level. Antitrust officials have viewed such limits with suspicion; but as in the case of resale price maintenance, the restriction has not been watertight.

The Clayton Act outlaws tying agreements when their effect is to limit competition greatly. The Supreme Court has found that "tying arrangements serve hardly any purpose beyond the suppression of competition."[3] Among the tying agreements that have been declared illegal by the Court was one in which IBM required buyers of its business machines also to buy IBM-brand punchcards.

In an exclusive dealing agreement, a manufacturer obtains from a retailer a promise that the latter will not deal in products supplied by the manufacturer's competitors. Many exclusive dealing agreements have been overturned by the courts, although the practice of exclusive dealing survives in some industries.

---

[3]*Standard Oil Co. of California and Standard Stations Inc.* v. *U.S.*, 337 U.S. 293, 305 (1949).

Price discrimination   In the original Clayton Act, price discrimination was listed as an illegal practice, but this section was not widely or successfully enforced for some time. Things changed in 1936, when the Clayton Act was amended by the Robinson-Patman Act, which greatly strengthened the law against price discrimination. Although the act is complex, its basic purpose is to prevent sellers from offering different discounts to different buyers unless it can be shown that those discounts reflect cost savings or are efforts to meet competition.

Both the Federal Trade Commission and the Department of Justice could bring suits under the Robinson-Patman Act, although for practical reasons the FTC has done most of the enforcement work. Private suits for triple damages can also be brought in price discrimination cases.

The Robinson-Patman Act has been criticized by economists more than any other aspect of antitrust law. The reason is the ease with which this act can be turned from a tool for promoting competition into a means of allowing a firm to shield itself from competition by its rivals.

Box 26.2 summarizes a case that shows what can go wrong under the Robinson-Patman Act. Utah Pie had a virtual monopoly over its local market in 1958. Then Pet, Carnation, and Continental tried to move in. Their efforts resulted in lower prices and more pies for consumers, although prices stayed high enough to give all four companies a profit. True, the three national companies did engage in price discrimination— they sold their pies more cheaply in Salt Lake City than elsewhere. But if that was a sign that something was wrong, critics say, the solution surely should have been to encourage more competition in the other markets, not less competition in Salt Lake City.

Box 26.2
The Utah Pie Case

In 1958 Utah Pie Company, a local bakery in Salt Lake City, built a new frozen-pie plant. The frozen-pie market in that city was growing fast. It more than quadrupled in size between 1958 and 1961. Through an aggressive campaign stressing low prices, Utah Pie was able to capture fully two-thirds of this market soon after building its plant.

Utah Pie's main competitors were three national food product companies—Pet Milk Company, Carnation Milk Company, and Continental Bakery Company. Nowhere else had these firms faced the kind of competition that Utah Pie was giving them. But rather than pulling out of the Salt Lake City market, they decided to fight back. By cutting prices on their own pies and making special deals with supermarkets to sell their pies under house brands, they succeeded in cutting Utah Pie's slice of the market back to 45 percent by 1961. (In absolute terms, Utah Pie's sales grew steadily throughout the period.)

Angered by the actions of the three outside companies, Utah Pie sued them under the Robinson-Patman Act. Its lawyers claimed that Pet, Carnation, and Continental were engaging in illegal price discrimination by selling pies at lower prices in Salt Lake City than elsewhere. When the case reached the Supreme Court, it was decided in favor of Utah Pie. In the words of the Court, Pet, Carnation, and Continental "contributed to what proved to be a deteriorating price structure over the period covered by this suit," thus harming the local firm. And that, said the Court, was just the sort of action the Robinson-Patman Act was designed to prevent.

Source: Information from Ward S. Bowman, "Restraint of Trade by the Supreme Court: The Utah Pie Case," *Yale Law Journal* 77 (1967): 70–85; *Utah Pie* v. *Continental Baking Co.,* 386 U.S. 685 (1967).

Partly because of the tendency of the Robinson-Patman Act to produce bizarre results like the Utah Pie case, the government has sharply cut back its enforcement efforts. In 1976 the Department of Justice issued a report that favored repeal of the act, but efforts in this direction have not made much headway. Private suits are still brought under the act, however. Many small firms see Robinson-Patman as a weapon with which to defend themselves against competition by larger and more efficient rivals.

ANTITRUST POLICY TODAY

As our discussion so far has shown, the growth of antitrust law over the past nine decades has been gradual. The limits of each major act were tested in cases and shaped by court decisions. From time to time, as the limits were approached, Congress passed new legislation, setting off another round of cases.

The Traditional View

Some people believe the scope of antitrust law should continue to expand. They are critical of the tendency of antitrust officials to focus only on the economic effects of competition and on the interests of consumers. Robert Katzman of the Brookings Institution writes that "antitrust was intended also to further a social and moral vision of America. At the core of that vision was a conviction that the past greatness, and future potential, of the country depended on the kind of character—resourceful, practical, and determined—that only competitive individualism would foster."[4] A former assistant attorney general for antitrust, John H. Shenefield, spoke of "the rich blend of American themes—diversity, opportunity, local ownership, economic liberty—that play eloquently through the legislative history of the antitrust laws." And former FTC Chairman Michael Pertschuk sees the proper focus of antitrust policy as a "Jeffersonian preference for dispersed power."

Current Trends

The traditional view of antitrust policy has been challenged in recent years. For some time, the criticism was largely confined to scholarly journals and university campuses. The agencies that brought antitrust cases, the lawyers who argued them, and the judges who decided them were not affected. Now, however, things seem to be changing.

For one thing, a number of academic critics of the traditional view of antitrust have left their universities for posts in government. They include William Baxter, who headed the antitrust division of the Department of Justice during the first term of the Reagan administration, and James C. Miller III, who heads the Federal Trade Commission. Perhaps more important, several academic critics of the traditional view, including Robert Bork, Richard Posner, and Ralph Winter, have been appointed to federal judgeships.

Trends in legal education have also had an effect on the thinking of antitrust lawyers. Legal education has long stressed learning from past

[4]Robert A. Katzman, "The Attenuation of Antitrust," *Brookings Review*, Summer 1984, p. 24.

cases and judicial opinions. In the antitrust area, as we have pointed out, these reflect a broad range of social and political as well as economic views. Today, however, it is common for this aspect of legal training to be supplemented by formal training in economics. As a result, students of antitrust law are encouraged to focus more closely on the questions of efficiency and consumer welfare raised by the cases they deal with.

The new generation of lawyers, judges, and antitrust officials bring to their jobs the idea that antitrust policy should be guided by economic rather than social or political values. Their views can be summarized as follows:

1. Antitrust policy should be clearly focused on the welfare of consumers. The idea that antitrust laws are there to protect firms against competition and change should be set aside.
2. In judging consumer welfare, the benefits that any action might have in terms of efficiency of production or distribution should be weighed against possible anticompetitive effects.
3. The main enforcement targets should be conspiracies to fix prices or divide markets, horizontal mergers that would create very large market shares, and predatory actions aimed at harming competitors (with predation carefully distinguished from active competition).
4. Enforcement actions should not be greatly concerned with vertical restraints that do not have much effect on the efficiency of economic activity; nor should they be concerned with small horizontal mergers or with any vertical or conglomerate merger, or with price discrimination.

In setting forth a similar program for antitrust policy a few years ago, Robert Bork wrote that these are "not prescriptions for the nonenforcement of the antitrust laws, but rather for their enforcement in a way that advances, rather than retards, competition and consumer welfare."[5]

Summary

1. The *antitrust laws* seek to control market structure and the competitive behavior of firms. They are shaped by a mix of social, political, and economic factors. To a great extent they are hostile toward large, powerful firms, whether efficient or not, and sympathetic to small, local firms. The economic concerns of antitrust law—promoting efficiency and consumer welfare—sometimes clash with social and political goals.
2. The oldest of the antitrust laws is the Sherman Act of 1890. It outlaws combinations and conspiracies in restraint of trade and makes any attempt to monopolize a market illegal. The Clayton and Federal Trade Commission Acts of 1914 seek to control unfair trade practices. The Robinson-Patman Act of 1936 focuses on price discrimination, and the Celler-Kefauver Act of 1950 controls mergers.
3. Price fixing means any attempt by competing firms to cooperate in setting prices. Actions that might affect prices indirectly—such as dividing markets or restricting output—are treated as forms of price fixing. Price fixing is a felony and often results in jail sentences.
4. *Horizontal mergers* involve firms that compete

---

[5]See Robert H. Bork, *The Antitrust Paradox* (New York: Basic Books, 1978), pp. 405–406.

in the same market. *Vertical mergers* involve firms with a customer-supplier relationship. *Conglomerate mergers* involve firms in unrelated markets. Under current antitrust guidelines, horizontal mergers are more likely to be challenged than vertical or conglomerate mergers.

5. The traditional view of antitrust law has favored expansion of the law to new areas and

has stressed social and political goals as well as economic ones. At present this view is on the defensive. The dominant view today puts more emphasis on efficiency and consumer welfare. It takes a harsh view of price fixing and horizontal mergers, and is less likely to challenge vertical restrictions, nonhorizontal mergers, and price discrimination.

Questions for Review

1. Define the following terms:
   antitrust laws
   price fixing
   horizontal merger
   vertical merger
   conglomerate merger
   Herfindahl index
2. What are the social and political goals of antitrust laws? In what cases do they conflict with their economic goals?

3. List four major antitrust laws and their main provisions.
4. What kinds of actions are viewed as forms of price fixing? What are the penalties for price fixing?
5. Give examples of horizontal, vertical, and conglomerate mergers. Which kinds of mergers can be challenged under the antitrust laws?
6. Describe recent trends in antitrust law.

Problems and Topics for Discussion

1. What do you think the main focus of antitrust law should be? Should the law seek solely to promote efficiency and consumer welfare? Or are other social and political goals also important? If so, what are those goals?
2. It has been said that the best antitrust law would be one that led to completely free trade between nations. In what ways would such a law promote competition?
3. "Everyone should have the unrestricted right both to sell goods and services in any market and also to withhold goods and services from sale." Are the antitrust laws consistent with this statement? Why or why not?
4. **Case for Discussion**
   On March 28, 1960, Von's Grocery Company of Los Angeles, a large supermarket chain, merged with a direct competitor, Shopping Bag Food Stores. The government had opposed the merger before it took place, and in 1966 the case went to the Supreme Court. The Court

ruled that the merger was a violation of the Clayton Act.

In terms of market concentration, the facts of the case are not impressive. Von's was the third-largest supermarket chain in Los Angeles; but even so it accounted for only 4.7 percent of sales. Shopping Bag was even smaller. Together the merged firms controlled only 7.5 percent of the market, slightly less than the leader, Safeway. At the time of the merger, besides the various competing chains, there were also some 3,800 single-store supermarkets in Los Angeles.

What impressed the Court, however, was not the large number of competitors in the market but the fact that the number of single-store supermarkets seemed to be falling. In his decision Justice Black noted that in 1950 there had been 5,365 such stores. Not persuaded by the argument that even 3,000 stores was enough to ensure active competition, he instead cited the Court's nineteenth-century concern with the fate of "small dealers and worthy men." "The basic purpose of the 1950 Celler-Kefauver Act," he wrote, "was to prevent economic concentration in the American economy by keeping a large number of small competitors in business. . . . Thus where concentration is gaining momentum in a market, we must be alert to carry out Congress' intent."

Questions:

a. How much did the Herfindahl index for the Los Angeles retail food market rise as a result of this merger? Would the merger have been challenged under the Justice Department's 1982 guidelines?

b. Discuss the balance struck in this case between the economic goals of the antitrust laws, on the one hand, and their social and political goals, on the other. Do you think the right balance was struck?

Suggestions for Further Reading

Armentano, D. T. *Antitrust and Monopoly: Anatomy of a Policy Failure.* New York: Wiley, 1982.

A critique of antitrust laws and policies that concludes that they do more harm than good.

Bork, Robert H. *The Antitrust Paradox.* New York: Basic Books, 1978.

A study of antitrust law that expresses the view that economic concerns merit more emphasis.

Katzman, Robert A. "The Attenuation of Anti-trust." *Brookings Review,* Summer 1984, pp. 23–27.

A brief, clear statement of the view that economic concerns should be balanced with broader social and political concerns in antitrust law.

Posner, Richard A. *Economic Analysis of Law.* Boston: Little, Brown, 1972.

Chapters 6 and 7 examine the connection between the legal and economic concepts of monopoly and antitrust.

Source: *U.S.* v. *Von's Grocery Co.,* 384 U.S. 270 (1966).

Chapter 27

Regulation

WHAT YOU WILL LEARN IN THIS CHAPTER

After reading this chapter, you should be able to

1. Define *natural monopoly* and explain why such monopolies are regulated.
2. Discuss the theory of rate-of-return regulation and the problems it can encounter.
3. Discuss theories that seek to explain the regulation of industries that are not natural monopolies.
4. Give examples of industries in which deregulation has been tried, and describe the results.
5. Describe the main positive and normative issues in health and safety regulation.

Ideas for Review

Here are some terms and concepts that you should review before you read this chapter:

Positive and normative economics (Chapter 1)
Theory of cost (Chapter 21)
Theory of monopoly (Chapter 23)
Price discrimination (Chapter 23)
Cartels (Chapter 23)

"The phone is a necessity, not a convenience."

Spiraling bank and telephone rates, a fallout of deregulation, have triggered demands for so-called "lifeline" service for millions of low-income Americans. The issue is turning into a major public policy debate over what services are essential for survival in today's technological society.

Lifeline accounts—a minimum number of local phone calls at a low price, or a basic, no-frills bank account for a service charge of only a few dollars a month—have become a key political issue for consumer groups, who are using threats of federal and state legislation to pressure companies to provide free or low-cost services to the poor, elderly, and handicapped who they say cannot afford the new, higher rates.

Deregulation has seriously disrupted—and in some cases, removed—a once secure and protective environment for consumers, lifeline supporters say. For example, at a time when the elderly argue that a telephone is more important to them than ever, more than one in five older Americans have been forced to reduce their use of the phone because of higher costs, according to a survey by the American Association of Retired Persons.

"It is important to remember that, in a person's older years, the phone is a necessity, not a convenience," said the AARP's executive director, Cyril F. Brickfield.

Local phone companies defend the higher rates, explaining that they are a result of the breakup of American Telephone & Telegraph Co., the shift from monopoly to competition, and the industry's move toward cost-based pricing.

Before deregulation of AT&T, profits on long-distance phone calls subsidized local rates, according to the telephone industry. Today, AT&T has lowered charges on long-distance calls, but local phone companies—no longer part of AT&T—are applying for, and getting, big increases in their charge for providing a dial tone.[1]

The demands for lifeline services are just one consequence of the changing pattern of economic regulation in the United States—the subject of this chapter. Although this topic comes up at many other points in this book—in the chapters on banking, antitrust policy, farming, labor unions, the environment, and energy, to name just a few—there are some good reasons to have a separate chapter on regulation. For one thing, without a separate chapter some important kinds of government policy would slip through the cracks and escape our attention entirely. Regulation of public utilities, transportation, safety, and health are examples. Also, without this chapter there would be no opportunity to make some points about regulation in general—what it can hope to achieve and what constraints stand in its way.

In what follows, several kinds of regulation will be discussed— regulation of natural monopolies, regulation of competitive industries, and health and safety regulation. (Banking regulation is discussed elsewhere, as part of the study of macroeconomics, but many of the same principles apply.) The last part of the chapter will tie the rest together in the form of some general principles.

---

[1]Sari Horowitz, "Phone, Banking Lifelines Sought for Nation's Poor," *Washington Post*, March 10, 1985, p. G1. © The Washington Post.

REGULATING NATURAL MONOPOLIES

Natural monopoly
An industry in which total costs are kept to a minimum by having just one producer serve the entire market.

A **natural monopoly** is an industry in which total costs are kept to a minimum by having just one producer serve the whole market. Local telephone service is a typical example of a natural monopoly. Gas, electric, and water services are other examples. It is easy for one such utility to hook up more customers once it has run its lines into their neighborhood, but it is wasteful and costly for different companies to run lines down the same street.

Although the term "natural monopoly" is well established in economics, it should be interpreted with care. It is not nature so much as human regulations and technology that determine the conditions for natural monopoly. For example, long-distance telephone service was once considered just as much a natural monopoly as was local telephone service. Today, with optical fiber systems, satellite communications, and microwave relays, it is possible for many long-distance services to compete efficiently with one another. The breakup of AT&T into a long-distance service that faces many rivals, on the one hand, and a number of regional telephone monopolies for local service, on the other, was largely spurred by this technological change.

In this section we will look at the basic principles of natural monopoly and its regulation. In the next section, we will turn to the problem of regulating industries that are not naturally monopolistic.

The Problem

The policy problem raised by natural monopolies is how to keep the firm from taking advantage of its monopoly to raise prices and restrict output. Antitrust policies of the type discussed in the last chapter won't work. Those policies aim to prevent the growth of a monopolistic market structure, but in the case of a natural monopoly no other structure would permit an efficient scale of production.

Consider the example in Box 27.1. The firm shown there, an electric utility, has constant marginal costs and an L-shaped long-run average-cost curve. The demand curve intersects the long-run average-cost curve at quantity Q_1, not far from the minimum efficient scale of production. If this output were divided between even two firms, each of which produced half of quantity Q_1, the cost per unit would be a lot higher—and it would be even more so if there were more than two firms.

If one unregulated firm operates in a market, it can be expected to act like a pure monopolist. Instead of producing Q_1, it will produce Q_2, which corresponds to the intersection of the firm's marginal-revenue curve with its marginal-cost curve. The price that corresponds to this output is P_2, which is far above marginal cost. This is too small an output and too high a price for efficient production.

The Regulatory Solution

The analysis up to this point indicates that in a natural monopoly competition by two or more firms is inefficient, and so is monopoly pricing by a single firm. The traditional solution is to allow just one firm to operate and to regulate the price at which it can sell its output. For example, the firm may be limited to a price no higher than P_1, the price at which the

Box 27.1
Regulation of a Natural Monopoly

This graph shows the cost and demand curves for a natural monopoly such as an electric utility. As an unregulated monopolist, the firm would make the maximum profit by charging price P_2 and selling quantity Q_2. If regulators impose a maximum price of P_1, the firm will find it worthwhile to produce quantity Q_1.

demand curve intersects the long-run average-cost curve in Box 27.1. With this price ceiling in force, the firm becomes a price taker for levels of output up to Q_1, because keeping output below that level no longer enables it to raise the price. The maximum profit is earned under the regulated price by producing Q_1 units of output. This is a larger price and greater quantity than would result either from an unregulated pure monopoly or from dividing production among two or more competing firms.

To make the market perfectly efficient, the price would have to be reduced to the level of marginal cost, which is slightly lower than P_1. At any price less than P_1, however, the firm would suffer a loss. It could survive, in the long run, only if it were subsidized. By allowing the firm to charge price P_1, which is high enough to cover all costs, the regulators avoid the need for a subsidy while giving up only a small degree of efficiency.

Rate of return as a focus of regulation

It is easy to see the correct regulated price in Box 27.1, since the shapes and positions of the demand and cost curves are right there on the page. In the real world, however, regulators do not have complete information about demand and cost. Lacking this information, they must set the price by looking at information that they can observe.

In practice, this means focusing on the **rate of return** earned by the firm. The rate of return is the firm's accounting profit expressed as a percentage of its net worth. Regulators aim to set a price that will make the regulated firm's rate of return equal to the average earned by comparable firms in unregulated markets. This average is assumed to represent the opportunity cost of capital.

Rate of return
A firm's accounting profit expressed as a percentage of its net worth.

Because accounting profit includes the opportunity cost of capital contributed by the firm's owners, setting the rate of return at a "normal" level is equivalent to setting pure economic profit equal to zero—the level of pure economic profit that would prevail under the ideal of perfect competition. If the regulators set the price too high, the firm will earn a pure economic profit. That implies a rate of return higher than the opportunity cost of capital—more than the minimum needed to attract capital from other uses. On the other hand, if the price is set too low, the firm will suffer a pure economic loss. This means that the accounting profit will not be high enough to cover the opportunity cost of capital, so that people will not be willing to invest in the firm. A price just equal to average total cost, then, will permit a rate of return just equal to the opportunity cost of capital. Any lower price will not allow the firm to raise capital, whereas any higher price will permit the firm's owners to earn a pure economic profit by taking advantage of the firm's monopoly position.

Armed with this reasoning, the regulators proceed in five steps:

1. They measure the value of the firm's capital, which for the firm in the box is, say, $1.2 million. This is called the rate base.
2. They measure the average rate of return for the economy, which turns out to be, say, 15 percent per year. (In practice, neither of these two steps is as easy as it sounds, but for our purposes the regulators can be given the benefit of the doubt.)
3. They multiply the rate base by the permitted rate of return to figure out a total cost of capital for the firm—$180,000 per year in this case. This sum should be enough both to make interest payments on the portion of the firm's capital that was acquired by borrowing and, in addition, to give an accounting profit that is high enough to compensate the owners for their investment in the firm.
4. The regulators then ask the firm to propose a price or set of prices that it thinks will allow it to meet its capital costs.
5. As time goes by, they keep track of the firm's actual rate of return, cutting the price if it rises too high and allowing the price to rise if returns fall below the target.

Limits on rate-of-return regulation   For a number of reasons, rate-of-return regulation may not always achieve its goals of lower prices and greater output. One possible reason is that regulators may be guided by goals other than economic efficiency. This may occur, for example, if regulated firms "capture" the regulatory agency by gaining control over the appointment of regulators, or if regulators follow lax policies in the hope of finding well-paid jobs in the industry after their terms as regulators end. On the other hand, regulatory agencies in some areas have been "captured" by groups that represent consumers. They seek the short-run political gains that come from keeping rates low without regard for the regulated firm's long-run capital needs.

Another possible problem is that regulators may not know enough about the industry to control its rate of return. It is by no means easy to measure such factors as the regulated firm's stock of capital, its rate of return, and the opportunity cost of capital. The more the regulators have to rely on guesswork, the less likely they are to be effective.

Finally, there is the fact that regulation, by putting the firm on a cost-plus basis, distorts incentives. If a firm is allowed to earn revenues that exceed its cost by a certain amount and no more, why should it try to minimize its costs at all? Minimizing costs is hard work for managers. Why not relax and take things easy? Why not take Wednesday mornings off for golf? Install new carpets on the boardroom floor? Give a job to the president's nephew? There is no incentive to put effort into keeping costs down.

Distortions caused by the wrong rate of return   For several reasons, then, regulators may set rates of return that are either higher or lower than the opportunity cost of capital. In either case there will be problems. A study by Harvey Averech and Leland Johnson, for example, suggested that in the 1960s regulated rates for electricity tended to be too high. They allowed utilities to achieve a rate of return that was higher than the opportunity cost of capital. This gave the utilities' stockholders an indirect way of taking advantage of their monopoly position. They could raise new capital to build new plants, whether they were needed or not, and add these into their rate base. The regulators then would allow them to raise their rates enough not only to pass along the costs of the new plants but to earn a pure economic profit as well. The outcome—now known as the A-J effect—was that too high a rate of return led to wasteful overinvestment in the regulated industry.

In the 1980s the situation changed. Some economists now are afraid that rates of return are too low. If so, this will cause the A-J effect to operate in reverse. Utilities will avoid investing in new plants even when, from the consumer's point of view, they would be justified. Such a policy of "rate suppression" might keep rates low for consumers for many years before problems became apparent. But as old plants wear out, the quality of service falls. Some writers predict serious shortages of electric power by the end of the century if rate suppression continues.

Some economists do not agree that rate suppression is widespread. It is no easier for outside observers to know whether a utility is charging just the right rates than it is for the regulators to know. It is widely agreed, however, that the A-J effect cuts both ways. Either too high or too low an allowed rate of return is harmful. Thus, in their search for efficiency regulators must walk a narrow line between two kinds of errors.

Distortions caused by average-cost pricing   Even if regulators were able to adjust utilities' rate of return to just the right level, regulation can still lead to inefficiency. One source of inefficiency arises from the use of average-cost rather than marginal-cost pricing. Box 27.1 glosses over this problem by assuming that the marginal cost of producing electric power is constant and that it is not very different from average total cost at the level of output where the utility operates.

In practice, many utilities have plants of different ages that operate at different levels of marginal cost. Regulatory agencies tend to look at the historical costs of these plants in setting prices. Plants built many years ago are listed at the cost that was paid for them at the time they were built, even though this may be far below the cost of replacing them or adding to their capacity. Average cost as measured in historical terms falls far short of marginal cost, since the cost of generating an added kilowatt hour means the cost of generating it in new facilities. Setting prices below marginal cost can lead to wasteful use. It does not provide enough incentive for conservation measures such as insulation and thermostat timers. It also fails to provide enough incentive for shifting electricity use from peak periods, when the least efficient generators must be brought on line, to periods when generating costs are lower. **Cross-subsidization** is another problem that is created by average-cost pricing. Cross-subsidization is the practice of setting prices that cover total costs on the average, but charging some customers more than the cost of their services while charging others less than the cost of their services. Telephone service is a case in point. When AT&T was a regulated monopoly, it charged prices to long-distance customers that were greater than the cost of the service, and charged less than the cost of service to local customers. On the average, telephone costs covered total costs.

Cross-subsidization
The practice of setting prices that cover total costs on the average, but charging some customers more than the cost of their services while charging others less than the cost of their services.

Cross-subsidization is much loved by people who receive the low-cost services. People liked free directory assistance service, which saved them the trouble of reaching to the shelf for the telephone directory; they liked house calls by telephone installers and service people, which saved them the trouble of shopping for phones as they would for hair dryers. But business users did not like having to pay high long-distance rates, and high rates for other business services. They began turning to upstart competitors. Eventually, competition won. Long-distance phone service was extensively deregulated, and local phone companies, newly independent, lost the source of their subsidies.

Can Electric Utilities Be Deregulated?

The increasing need for energy conservation, financial problems, declines in levels of service, and the example of the breakup of AT&T have created interest in a policy that once would have seemed radical—deregulation of electric utilities. Most plans for utility deregulation try to distinguish between areas where a natural monopoly will continue to require regulation and areas where technological change has made competition more feasible.

In the electric-power industry, for example, local service to homes and business firms has many of the features of a natural monopoly. On the other hand, the actual generation of electric power may no longer be a natural monopoly. Rising energy costs and technological advances have combined to make certain types of small-scale generating plants more competitive with large centralized power stations. One example is industrial cogeneration, in which a firm that needs steam for a certain process, such as brewing, may simply install a turbine to extract electric power from the steam before it is used to heat the vats. When the boiler is already in place, it costs relatively little to add the turbine and generator. To make the generator worthwhile, though, the brewery must have a market for any power it produces beyond its own needs.

That is where the idea of deregulation comes in. Local electric service would remain a regulated utility, but it would be able to buy electricity from competing suppliers. Industrial cogeneration would be one such supplier. Large-scale plants, which would be separate from the service utilities, would compete with them. So would other small-scale suppliers, such as small hydroelectric plants and even backyard windmills.

REGULATING COMPETITIVE INDUSTRIES

Electric and local telephone service are industries that, for technological reasons, have long been natural monopolies. There was no pressure to replace regulation with competition in such industries until changes in technology made competition practical. There are, however, many industries that have been regulated despite the fact that their technology has always made them naturally competitive. Transportation industries—trucking, railroads, airlines, and busses—are leading examples. These industries are worth some attention both from the standpoint of the effects of past regulation and from that of recent moves toward deregulation.

Historical Origins

Railroads first came under regulation in the late nineteenth century, but the big surge in transportation regulation came in the 1930s. One tends to think of the Great Depression mainly in terms of high unemployment, but another major feature of the depression was low prices. Between 1929 and 1933 the consumer price index dropped about 25 percent. Today most economists would explain both the high unemployment and the falling prices in macroeconomic terms, blaming them on low aggregate demand, bad monetary policy, and so on. At the time, however, people tended to blame the high levels of unemployment on low prices. If only prices could be raised, business leaders said, it would be possible to put more workers on the payroll.

It is not surprising that competition, which tends to keep prices in certain markets low, was not very popular. In fact, too much competition was seen as a barrier to economic recovery. In 1933 Congress passed the National Recovery Act, which encouraged firms to use cartel-like methods to prop up prices. That act was declared unconstitutional by the Supreme Court, but other legislation that applied only to specific industries survived. Two of the most important industries that were regulated in order to limit competition were trucking, which was brought under the control of the Interstate Commerce Commission (ICC) in 1935, and airlines, which were brought under the control of the Civil Aeronautics Board (CAB) in 1938.[2]

Rate and Entry Regulation in Transportation

The regulation imposed on these industries differed in two major ways from the regulation of natural monopolies. First, it focused on control of entry by new firms. And second, it stressed minimum rather than maximum prices. The traditional argument for regulation of natural monopolies was that without it, prices would rise too high. In the case of airlines and trucking, the concern was that without regulation, prices would fall too low. Both the ICC and the CAB were, however, given the power to set maximum as well as minimum rates.

---

[2]Agricultural marketing orders, another way of limiting competition, date from the same period. They will be discussed in the next chapter.

It is generally agreed that regulation of trucking and airlines achieved the goal of raising prices and limiting the number of firms in those industries. As the years passed, however, many economists began to have second thoughts as to whether high prices and limited competition were the proper goals of government policy. With the advent of high rates of inflation in the 1970s, the doubts about regulation became stronger, and economists turned almost unanimously against the regulation of entry and the setting of minimum rates in competitive industries. Several theories about what the regulation of airlines and trucking has actually accomplished are worth discussion.

The Cartel Theory of Regulation

One well-known theory of airline and trucking regulation holds that regulation is a device that permits rival firms to form cartels. It is easy to see why this theory developed. Chapter 23 showed that two major drawbacks of most cartels are inability to control competition by nonmembers and inability to keep members from cheating on price agreements. The laws that gave the ICC and the CAB authority over trucking and airlines remedied these problems. Both agencies became highly restrictive in terms of entry by new firms. (The CAB did not let in a single new major airline for 40 years, and the ICC was only slightly less restrictive.) And both agencies were granted, and used, authority to prevent carriers from cutting prices below specific minimum levels.

True, the agencies' authority to set maximum as well as minimum limits on prices did not fit in well with the cartel theory of regulation. But proponents of the theory argued that both agencies were soon "captured" by the industries they regulated, so that the power to impose maximum rates was not used fully. And for many years trucking firms and airlines were able to use their influence to ensure that most of the members of the regulatory agencies were friendly to the industry's point of view.

A number of studies seemed to support the cartel theory of regulation. Many of them were based on comparisons of regulated and unregulated markets. One study, for example, showed that unregulated intrastate airline fares in California and Texas were only about half the level of regulated interstate fares for similar distances. Other studies compared regulated freight rates for industrial goods with freight rates for agricultural produce, which had been exempted from regulation. Again, the regulated rates seemed to be quite a bit higher.

The Distributional Theory of Regulation

Not all economists agreed with the cartel theory of regulation, at least in its simple form. Certain pieces of evidence did not fit in. For example, despite the best efforts of the CAB, airlines were not always able to earn high profits. And in the trucking industry the major users of freight service, who should have been hurt most by high rates, rarely complained. In fact, they tended to praise regulation for bringing about a high level of service.

Imperfection in the cartels In trying to explain these puzzling facts, economists began to pay more attention to imperfections in the supposed cartels that regulation had created. The most glaring of these was the fact that although airline and trucking regulations controlled *price* competition, they did not control *nonprice* competition. Both trucking firms and airlines were free to compete for customers by offering more frequent and convenient service, by advertising more heavily, and by engaging in active personal selling. This nonprice competition was very costly. In the case of airlines, for example, adding more flights each day meant that each flight would carry fewer passengers. Nonprice competition thus pushed the cost per passenger up so high that no matter what level of fares the CAB allowed, no more than a normal rate of return could be earned—and sometimes not even that.

Distributional effects   As some of these effects of regulation became better understood, economists began to see that regulation could not be thought of simply in terms of a transfer of monopoly profits from users to producers. The effects of regulation were much more complicated than that. Some producers, no doubt, were able to earn higher profits than they otherwise would have—some of the time. But most of the profits resulting from high fares went elsewhere.

Unionized workers were one group that seemed to benefit from regulation. Controls on entry reduced competition by nonunionized firms and made it possible for teamsters and airline pilots to bargain for higher wages. (Both of these unions strongly favored regulation.) Because nonprice competition sometimes put more planes in the sky and more trucks on the road than were strictly needed, suppliers of trucks and planes may have enjoyed higher sales than they otherwise would have. And at least some customers were able to benefit from nonprice competition by getting a higher level of service than would have been likely without regulation. In particular, small shippers in out-of-the-way points may have benefited from cross-subsidization, in that their rates did not always reflect the higher cost of their service compared to that of larger customers on heavily used routes.

Recent Reforms

In the late 1970s, longstanding criticisms of transportation regulation began to be translated into policy. Through legislation and the appointment of reform-minded regulators, restrictions on competition were eased for passenger airlines, air freight, trucking, and intercity bus service. There was also extensive deregulation of railroad rates and a relaxation of barriers to competition between railroads and motor freight. The CAB was abolished and a few of its former powers were granted to the Federal Aviation Administration, whose main concern is air safety. The ICC stayed in business with a reduced staff and much more limited functions.

The case of trucking illustrates the results of deregulation. One of the first effects was a flood of new entries into the market. In 1980, the first year of deregulation, 1,500 new firms applied for permits. By this time the ICC had reversed its earlier policies, and granted almost all new applications. The number of applications rose to 4,600 in 1981 and 4,900 in 1982. At the same time, under the pressure of competition, many existing firms were forced into mergers or out of business. And the change in the number of trucking firms was only one aspect of increased competition. While new firms were entering the industry, many firms that had been restricted to narrow segments of the market branched out to compete in new regions or new types of freight.

The increased competition put downward pressure on freight rates. By 1982 the rates paid by large shippers had fallen to 75 percent of the average before deregulation.[3] There was also downward pressure on wages—the average wage paid to employees fell by 19 percent. The unionized part of the labor force was hit with widespread job losses. More than 100,000 members of the Teamsters Union lost their jobs.

In some ways the most dramatic effects of deregulation have been on the quality and variety of services available to customers. Regulation had often been viewed as necessary to ensure good service, but the evidence does not support this view. According to one survey, 86 percent of firms that shipped freight by truck found the quality of service to be better or unchanged after deregulation; only 14 percent found it worse. And 47 percent found service to be prompter, while 73 percent found it to be more available.[4] Much of the improvement is due to the truckers' greater freedom to tailor their rates and service quality to the needs of individual shippers.

These results have occurred in most newly deregulated industries: lower prices on the average, but not for all customers; a greater variety of services, including many low-price, no-frills choices that were not available under regulation; new entries, mergers, and bankruptcy for a few firms that were not able to adapt to increased competition. These effects have occurred not only in transportation but also in some areas of banking, stock brokerage, and communications.

But even while some industries were shedding the regulatory framework of the 1930s, the 1970s saw a rapid increase in regulation in the areas of health, safety, and the environment. We turn to these growing areas of regulation in the next section.

HEALTH AND SAFETY REGULATION

Among the fastest-growing regulatory agencies in recent years have been the Occupational Safety and Health Administration (OSHA), the Consumer Product Safety Commission (CPSC), the National Highway and Traffic Safety Administration (NHTSA), and the Environmental Protection Agency (EPA). In addition, some older agencies, such as the Food and Drug Administration (FDA), have become much more active than before. These agencies are not directly concerned with prices and competition. Instead, they are concerned with what kinds of goods are produced and how they are produced. Leaving environmental issues to Chapter 29, this section will look at what economists have to say about health and safety regulation, an issue that provokes much debate.

Some Normative Issues

The goal of health and safety regulation is to make the world a safer, healthier, more pleasant place to live. Since this is a goal that no one can

---

[3]Thomas Gale Moore, "Rail and Truck Reform—The Record So Far," *Regulation*, November/December 1983, Tables 5 and 6.
[4]Ibid., Table 8.

argue with, why are regulations designed to achieve it a matter of debate? Part of the answer is that even when goals are agreed upon, there can be disagreements about the best ways to pursue them. Such disagreements, which belong to the realm of positive economics, will be discussed shortly. Other major sources of controversy are normative. Even though almost everyone believes that health and safety are good in themselves, there are disagreements about the relationship of these goals to other goals that are also worthwhile. Two such disagreements often threaten to overshadow any discussion of the positive economics of health and safety regulation.

Can an economic value be put on health and safety?   The first question is whether one should even consider trade-offs between human health and safety on the one hand and material well-being on the other. Many of those who support strong, strictly enforced health and safety regulations argue that there is no way to measure the value of human life. Regulations, therefore, should be set without regard to economic trade-offs or cost-benefit ratios of any kind.

Others, however, do not share this view. It is not that they belittle the value of human life. Rather, they see no point in condemning something that people do every day. And people do, every day, sacrifice their own health and safety in favor of other goals. People choose the convenience of travel by car over the discomfort of travel by bus, even though buses are known to be many times safer than cars. People take high-paying jobs in cities rather than low-paying jobs in the country, even though city air is known to be many times less healthful than country air. People have medical checkups once a year but not twice a year or once a week because the gain in terms of health is not worth the sacrifice in terms of time and money.

Whose values?   A second normative question remains to be answered even if one concedes that cost-benefit analysis can reasonably be applied in the areas of health and safety. That is the question of whose values should govern any trade-offs that are made between health and safety on the one hand and economic costs on the other. Should policy be guided by the values of the people who receive the benefits and bear the costs? Or should it be reserved to the judgment of experts? In practical terms, this comes down to the question of when people should simply be warned about health and safety hazards and when they should be forced to be safe and healthy whether they want to be or not. Should people simply be warned that tobacco and saccharin could be dangerous to their health, or should use of these products be banned? Should people be allowed to decide for themselves whether to buckle their seat belts, or should they not be allowed to buy cars that are not equipped with air bags or other safety devices?

Strictly speaking, economics as a science has nothing to say about these normative issues. As it happens, though, economists often believe strongly that it is reasonable to consider economic costs and benefits in health and safety decisions and to allow well-informed people to make those decisions for themselves whenever possible. When such an economist discusses health and safety regulation with someone who believes in health and safety at any cost, what takes place is likely to be a fight rather than a rational debate. This is a pity, because there are some things that economics as a science—positive economics—can contribute to the controversy over health and safety regulation.

Positive Issues in Health and Safety Regulation

One area of positive economics that economists and regulators should be able to agree on is that of making sure that regulatory goals, once chosen, are achieved at the least cost. Consider the matter of giving local decision makers the greatest possible leeway in choosing the least-cost means of complying with regulation. One way to do this is to issue regulations in the form of performance standards rather than in the form of engineering controls. *Performance standards* are rules that specify the results to be achieved, whereas *engineering controls* are rules that specify particular techniques to be used or equipment to be installed. A case in point is the regulation of worker exposure to cotton dust, the cause of the brown-lung disease that affects an estimated 150,000 workers in the textile industry. Reduced exposure can be achieved either by installing equipment that reduces cotton dust in the workplace or by requiring workers to wear personal respirators while on the job. OSHA regulations issued in 1978 take the first approach on the ground that it is more effective. Critics have pointed out, however, that once this regulation was in place, it decreased the incentive to develop more effective and easier-to-use personal respirators. If a standard of exposure had been set, there would have been an incentive to develop better respirators.

Another issue on which positive economic can focus is that of comparing the benefits of a proposed regulation with its costs. For example, in 1984 the EPA issued a study that showed that banning lead in gasoline would have benefits totaling $1.8 billion. In the EPA's view, this would more than offset the cost, which it estimated at about two cents per gallon of gasoline. Ethyl Corp., which produced the lead additive that the EPA sought to ban, said that the agency had left out a major cost. According to Ethyl Corp., banning lead would mean that older cars (which had been designed before lead-free gasoline was widely available) would need valve repair much more often. In Ethyl's estimate, the cost of these repairs would be $18 billion per year, far more than the benefits. The point of this case is not that benefit-cost analysis ended the dispute over the proposed ban on leaded gasoline. Rather, the point is that the grounds of the dispute were narrowed and shifted to the plane of positive economics, where some progress toward agreement might be hoped for.

Conclusions

This chapter has covered a lot of ground, including discussions of many regulatory agencies and industries. Everywhere it has turned, however, it has found one constant theme: economists have doubts about regulation. As George Eads, a former member of the President's Council of Economic Advisers, once put it, "The weight of economic evidence has become so great that any economist venturing to support regulation today is apt to find himself in a very lonely position. What only a short time ago was considered heresy now has assumed the status of conventional wisdom."[5]

---

[5]George Eads, "Economists vs. Regulators," in James C. Miller III, ed., *Perspectives on Federal Transportation Policy* (Washington, D.C.: American Enterprise Institute, 1975), p. 101.

When the details are stripped away, why is it that economists are so critical of regulation? It appears that the economic case against regulation can be stated in the form of two basic propositions.

The first proposition is that regulation tends in practice to be dominated by questions of income distribution rather than efficiency. In some cases the goal may be to keep the owners of regulated firms from earning monopoly profits. In other cases it may be to prevent such firms from competing so intensely that none of them can earn a profit. The goal may be to favor one group of customers or suppliers at the expense of others. It may be to give workers higher wages than they would otherwise earn or to give them a different balance between wages and a safe workplace. Economists do not argue with any of these goals; their complaint is that regulation is an inefficient way of benefiting one group at the expense of another. Many dollars in costs are incurred for every dollar in benefits gained by those whom the regulation is intended to help.

The second proposition is that regulation is less efficient than the market as a means of making decisions and using information. Regulators fail to keep rates down because they know too little about the cost and demand conditions under which firms operate. They try to second-guess the market in deciding which firms should be allowed to serve which markets. In this way they end up raising costs for everyone. They leave too little room for innovation and local initiatives aimed to satisfy special needs or suit special circumstances.

These are propositions that we will encounter again in chapters on environmental and energy regulation. And they will continue to influence public-policy debates in all areas of regulation.

SUMMARY

1. A *natural monopoly* is an industry in which total costs are kept to a minimum by having just one producer serve the entire market. This happens when the minimum efficient scale of operation in the industry is as large as or larger than demand when output is sold at a price equal to average total cost.

2. Utility regulators focus on the firm's *rate of return* because they cannot directly observe its cost and demand curves. The idea is that the firm's accounting profit should be held to a level that permits a rate of return just high enough to allow the firm to meet its cost of capital. If the rate of return is set too high, the firm has an incentive to attract more capital than it needs. If it is set too low, the firm may fail to acquire or maintain as much equipment and plant as it needs in order to do its job.

3. Many industries have been regulated even though they are not natural monopolies. Transportation industries are an example. Some economists have seen such regulation as amounting to government-imposed cartels. Others have viewed them as means of redistributing the product of the regulated industry among firms, their workers, and their customers. Efficiency does not seem to be a major reason for the regulation of such industries.

4. A great deal of deregulation has taken place in airlines, air freight, trucking, intercity bus service, and railroads, as well as in some areas of banking, brokerage services, and communications. The results are lower prices, but not for all customers; increased competition, with many new entries and some failures of established firms; and more variety in the products and services offered to consumers.

5. Regulation has been growing in the areas of health and safety at the same time that it has been decreasing in such industries as transpor-

tation, communication, and financial services. Disputes in these areas of regulation raise both normative and positive issues. The normative issues include the question of whether one can place an economic value on health and safety, as well as that of whose values should guide regulatory policy. The positive issues include finding ways of keeping down the costs of regulation and comparing the costs and benefits of regulation.

Questions for Review

1. Define the following terms:
   Natural monopoly
   Rate of return
   Cross-subsidization
2. Draw cost and demand curves for a natural monopoly. What is the connection between demand and minimum efficient scale?
3. List the steps in rate-of-return regulation for a natural monopoly.

4. Why are industries like trucking, airlines, and taxis not viewed as natural monopolies? If they are not natural monopolies, how did they come to be regulated?
5. What industries have been deregulated either wholly or partly since the 1970s? What are the effects of deregulation?
6. Give some examples of positive and normative issues in health and safety regulation.

Problems and Topics for Discussion

1. Compare antitrust law and regulation as ways of dealing with monopoly. When is each type of policy appropriate?
2. In some cities utilities such as electric companies, telephone systems, and gas pipelines are publicly owned. What do you think the advantages and disadvantages of public ownership are compared with both regulated and unregulated private ownership?
3. Before 1980 the ICC limited the number of trucking firms that could serve any given route. Often the only way a new firm could get permission to serve a route was to buy the "certificate" (permit) of a firm that already served it. Some of those permits were worth hundreds of thousands of dollars. After deregulation, the value of such permits fell to zero. Why do you think this happened?

4. How are taxis regulated in the area where you live? Is there free entry into the market? Are minimum or maximum fares set? How easy is it to get a cab if you need one? Would you suggest any changes in regulation?
5. Lowering the speed limit from 70 to 55 miles per hour has reduced the number of people killed on highways. One might expect that a further reduction of the speed limit—to, say, 45 miles per hour—would reduce traffic deaths still further. How would you go about finding out whether such a policy would be worthwhile? Is there any way you could make this decision without placing a value on human life?

Suggestions for Further Reading

Kahn, Alfred E. *The Economics of Regulation*, 2 vols. New York: Wiley, 1971.

A detailed work on the theory of regulation. The author has served as chairman of the New York State Public Service Commission, the Civil Aeronautics Board, and President Carter's Council on Wage and Price Stability.

Miller, James C., III, and Bruce Yandle. *Benefit Cost Analysis of Social Regulation*. Washington, D.C.: American Enterprise Institute, 1979.

A set of case studies in cost-benefit analysis of health and safety regulation, featuring work by the Council on Wage and Price Stability.

Regulation.

A bimonthly journal published by the American Enterprise Institute; contains analysis and commentary on all aspects of regulation.

Viscusi, W. Kip. *Regulating Consumer Product Safety*. Washington, D.C.: American Enterprise Institute, 1984.

A study of the methods and decisions of the Consumer Product Safety Commission.

Chapter 28

Farm Policy

After reading this chapter, you should be able to

1. Describe the market structure of agriculture.
2. Explain the reasons for the instability of prices in agricultural markets.
3. Discuss long-term changes in farming and in the farm population.
4. Discuss *agricultural marketing orders* and their effects on farmers and consumers.
5. Compare *price supports*, *supply management*, and *target prices* as means of raising and stabilizing farm prices.
6. Discuss current trends and issues in farm policy.

Ideas for Review

Here are some terms and concepts that you should review before you read this chapter:

Price and income elasticity of demand (Chapter 19)
Perfect competition (Chapter 22)
Cartels (Chapter 23)
Price discrimination (Chapter 23)

Bryce Neidig and his sons Van and Neal own separate farms near Madison, Nebraska. The father and sons have much in common—and some differences, too. One subject on which the three do not agree is federal farm policy.

"We would all be better off without price supports," says Bryce over coffee and muffins in his kitchen. "There *is* a free enterprise system, and this farmer believes in it."

"You think the market will provide," says Van. "I disagree with that. You never know what's going to happen, especially in farming. We need some subsidies so we don't run out of food [in the United States]."

The disagreement centers on the federal government's longstanding programs of direct aid to farmers, especially price supports. These reached a record level of $20 billion in 1984. But these direct programs are only part of a total farm aid package that costs almost $54 billion a year by some estimates. Included are many "quiet subsidies" from which all three of the Neidigs benefit.

Low-cost credit is one of these programs. The Neidigs' five grain bins were bought with government loans that carry as little as half the market interest rate. Their farms are shaded by black walnut trees bought at low cost from the government. Their irrigation wells are checked free of charge by government inspectors. And, because of a host of special tax deductions, the Neidigs live comfortably without having to report much income on their federal tax forms.

"I may be a free enterpriser," says Bryce Neidig of these quiet subsidies, "but I'm not stupid."[1]

In discussing government policy toward competition and market structure, we have said nothing about policy toward the biggest industry of all—farming. As the case of the Neidigs shows, the government is deeply involved in agriculture, but its farm policies differ from its policies toward industry and services. Some of these policies are aimed at market structure. Others regulate prices and, in some cases, farming practices. All of them are matters of controversy. This chapter will look at the background of U.S. farm policy, the main programs that are now in effect, and the issues these programs raise.

THE MARKET STRUCTURE OF AGRICULTURE

Many agricultural markets come close to meeting the four requirements of perfect competition: large numbers of small firms, homogeneous products, good information flows, and easy entry and exit. In the United States there are almost 2.5 million farms, some 85 percent of which are sole proprietorships—family farms. More than a third of all agricultural output is produced on farms whose annual sales are less than $100,000. Most

---

[1]Based on Jeffrey Birnbaum, "U.S. Farm Programs Come Under Attack as Their Cost Soars," *Wall Street Journal*, November 10, 1983, p. 1. Reprinted by permission of The Wall Street Journal, © Dow Jones & Company, Inc. 1983. All rights reserved.

agricultural products are homogeneous—only rarely do consumers know or care which farm supplied the products they buy. The flow of information in agricultural markets is achieved by means of organized commodity exchanges for major crops, along with the information services of the U.S. Department of Agriculture. The fourth requirement for perfect competition—easy entry and exit—is also met fairly well by agriculture.

As explained in Chapter 22, perfectly competitive markets have some major virtues. Whenever consumers are willing to pay more for a good than its marginal cost, a competitive market will produce the additional supply. If existing firms cannot handle the demand, new firms will enter the market. Likewise, if consumers are unwilling to buy all that is produced at a price at least equal to marginal cost, competition will result in the required reduction in supply. If a long-run reduction in supply is needed, some firms will withdraw from the market. In every case the necessary adjustments occur in response to changes in the market price of the good as determined by supply and demand. No central planner is needed to give orders; Adam Smith's "invisible hand" is at work.

Left alone, agricultural markets really do work in this ideal fashion. But for farmers the ideal is a mixed blessing. Competition means unpredictable prices and unstable incomes as supply and demand curves shift with the weather and with patterns of world trade. In the 1970s, market conditions smiled on the farm sector, and farm income rose. In the 1980s market conditions have turned sour for much of the U.S. farm sector. Competition, including competition from new sources of supply abroad, has sharpened. So partly *because of* the perfectly competitive structure of agricultural markets, there is a farm problem.

The farm problem is a problem for farmers. From the consumer's point of view, and even more so from the point of view of the economist, fluctuating prices and a falling farm population may not be problems at all; they may be merely the healthy functioning of competitive markets. But it is the farmer's point of view that has long dominated the government's farm policy. That being the case, it is worth giving some attention to the cause of the problem in order to evaluate the policies designed to cure it.

Instability and Price-Inelastic Demand

In a competitive market, the response of price and revenue to changes in quantity supplied depends on the price elasticity of demand. This response is shown in Box 28.1. Market A has relatively low price elasticity of demand and market B has relatively high elasticity.

In both markets, we are considering a time period so short that producers cannot make any changes in inputs or outputs in response to a change in price. This is the case in the market for a perishable farm product after the crop is harvested and before farmers have a chance to respond to prices by adjusting their production for the next year.

Suppose that in the first year 100,000 units of each crop are harvested. When that amount of output is brought to market, an equilibrium price of $2 is arrived at for both crops. The next year, because of better weather or increased planting, output in both markets rises to 125,000 units. This is shown in the box by a shift in the short-run supply curve from S_1 to S_2. What happens to price and revenue?

In market A, where demand is inelastic, a large decrease in price is

Box 28.1
Demand Elasticity and Price Instability

The stability of prices and revenues in the face of changing supply conditions depends on the price elasticity of demand for the product. In market A, where demand is relatively inelastic, an increase in supply from 100,000 units to 125,000 units brings the price down from $2 to $1 and revenue down from $200,000 to $125,000. In market B, where demand is relatively elastic, the same increase in supply causes the price to drop to $1.75 and revenue to rise from $200,000 to $218,750.

Market A

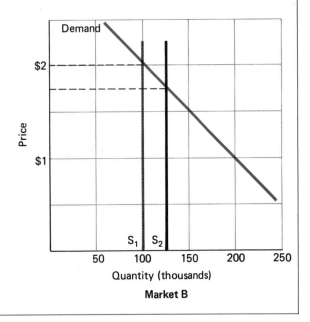

Market B

needed to bring about the required increase in quantity demanded. As the price falls from $2 to $1, total revenue falls from $200,000 to $125,000. In market B, however, a fairly small drop in price, from $2 to $1.80, is enough to raise the quantity demanded to 125,000 units. Because the price falls by a smaller percentage than the output rises, revenue rises from $200,000 to $225,000.

Real agricultural markets appear to be more like market A than market B. Box 28.2 presents some estimates of demand elasticity for farm products. The striking thing about this table is how low most of the estimates are. Except in the cases of calves, sheep, cottonseed, and oats, all the elasticities listed are less than 1.

The Instability of Farm Prices

Because demand for farm products is price inelastic, changing supply and demand conditions result in large year-to-year price changes. The instability of farm prices can be seen in Box 28.3, which shows the historical record of the **parity price ratio**. This is the ratio of an index of prices that farmers receive to an index of prices that farmers pay. The ratio uses the years 1910–1914 as a base period, since they have long been viewed as the best period of peacetime farm prosperity in this century.

As the graph shows, the parity price ratio has had its ups and downs. In the worst period, from 1929 to 1932, the ratio fell from 92 to 58 in just

Parity price ratio
The ratio of an index of prices that farmers receive to an index that farmers pay, using the years 1910–1914 as a base period.

**Box 28.2
Price Elasticity of
Demand for Farm
Products**

This table shows estimates of price elasticity of demand for a number of farm products. Low demand elasticities contribute to the instability of prices of major farm products.

Farm Product	Demand Elasticity
Cattle	0.68
Hogs	0.46
Sheep and lambs	1.78
Chickens	0.74
Eggs	0.23
Milk used for:	
Fluid milk and cream	0.14
Cheese	0.54
Ice cream	0.11
Butter	0.66
Soybeans	0.61
Cottonseed	1.03
Potatoes	0.11
Dry beans, peas, peanuts	0.23
Wheat	0.80
Corn	0.50
Oats	2.00

Source: G. E. Brandow, "Interrelations among Demands for Farm Products and Implications for Control of Market Supply," *Bulletin 680* (University Park: Pennsylvania State University Agricultural Experiment Station, 1961), pp. 59, 64, 80, 81, 96.

over three years. The collapse of demand in those early years of the Great Depression pushed all prices down; but since agricultural demand is so inelastic, farmers were hit worse than anyone else. The index of prices paid by farmers dropped a great deal over this period, from 160 to 112; but the index of prices received fell sharply, from 149 to a mere 65.

Farm prices recovered along with the rest of the economy during World War II. Then, during the 1950s and 1960s, farm prices, as measured by the parity price ratio, declined steadily but without such sharp fluctuations as in earlier periods. Any hope that agricultural markets had become more stable, however, was proved vain by what happened in the 1970s and early 1980s.

In 1973 a combination of factors, ranging from bad weather in the Soviet Union to the failure of the Peruvian anchovy catch, created a worldwide food shortage. Farm prices skyrocketed. The parity price ratio rose to an average of 91 for 1973, and in August of that year it briefly touched the 100 mark for the first time in 20 years. After that, prices collapsed almost as fast as they had risen. By 1985 the ratio had fallen to 58, its lowest point since the Great Depression.

Box 28.3
The Parity Price Ratio

The parity price ratio is the ratio of an index of prices that farmers receive to an index of prices that farmers pay. It is based on prices that prevailed in 1910–1914, a period of unusual prosperity for farmers. Since then the index has been above 100 only in wartime. Even in peacetime, as the record for the 1930s and the 1970s shows, the index can go through wide swings in periods of only two or three years.

Sources: President's Council of Economic Advisers, *Economic Report of the President* (Washington, D.C.: Government Printing Office, 1977); Bureau of the Census, *Statistical Abstract of the United States 1984*, 104th ed. (Washington, D.C.: Government Printing Office, 1983), p.665. U.S. Department of Commerce, *Survey of Current Business*, various issues.

Long-Term Adjustment and the Farm Population

The parity price ratio tells the story of one part of the farm problem—short-term instability. There is a second part of the problem as well—long-term adjustment to rising productivity and the decline in the number of farmers.

The long-term problem too is a result of inelastic demand. Demand for farm products is not only price inelastic but income inelastic as well. As per capita income grows, the demand for agricultural output grows, but not as fast as the increase in income.

The result of slowly growing demand and rapidly growing farm productivity has been a steady decline in the number of farmers needed to meet the demand for agricultural goods. The record of this decline is shown in Box 28.4. As would be expected in a competitive market, the outflow of labor from farming was linked with lower earnings per worker in the farm sector than in the rest of the economy.

Today the farm population is still falling. Official statistics still show lower per capita income for farm families than for nonfarm families, although some observers believe that the standard of living of farm families is higher than their reported incomes imply. But to understand the changes taking place in farming today, it is important to understand the changes that are occurring in the kinds of farms and the sources of farm income.

**Box 28.4
The Decline in the U.S.
Farm Population**

The demand for most farm products is income inelastic as well as price inelastic. Thus, over the years demand has grown much more slowly than farm productivity. The result has been a steady decrease in the number of people required to produce what the nonfarm population consumes. This chart shows the farm population since 1930 as a percentage of the total population. Breaks in the chart represent slight changes in the Census Bureau's definition of a farm family.

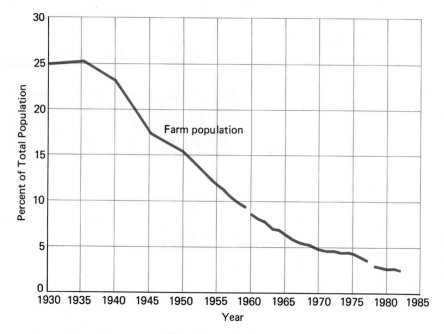

Source: U.S. Department of Commerce, Bureau of the Census, *Statistical Abstract of the United States: 1984*, 104th ed. (Washington, D.C.: Government Printing Office, 1980), p. 649.

It is especially important to understand what is happening to the family farm—the farm with sales in the $40,000–$100,000 range that is the main source of income for the family that owns and operates it. Farms of this type have shaped the image most nonfarmers have of rural life, and they also have strongly shaped farm policy. Yet, as Box 28.5 shows, they do not play as big a role in the total farming picture as they once did. More and more they are overshadowed by two other kind of farms. On the one hand, there are small-scale farms whose operators depend on other jobs for most of their income. (For that matter, even farms in the $40,000–$100,000 range derived most of their income from nonfarm sources in 1982.) On the other hand, there are professionally managed farms with sales of $100,000 or more per year. These tend to be large enough to use the most advanced equipment and techniques. In 1982, just 12 percent of all farms were in this size range, but they accounted for 64 percent of total gross farm income.

Among their other problems, medium-sized farms have suffered a severe credit squeeze in the mid-1980s. During the 1970s, when inflation was rapid, crop prices were high and export sales were strong, the price of

**Box 28.5
Characteristics of
Farms by Size, 1982**

These charts show characteristics of farms of various sizes, classified by total sales. Farms with annual sales of $40,000–$100,000 are the traditional family farms. Chart a shows sources of income. In 1982, farms with sales below $20,000 per year had expenses that exceeded their income from farming, giving them negative net farm income. Nonfarm income outweighed farm income for all but the largest farms. Chart b shows the percentage of farms and the percentage of gross farm income (sales plus government payments) for each size class. Note that just 12 percent of all farms had sales over $100,000, but they accounted for 64 percent of gross farm income.

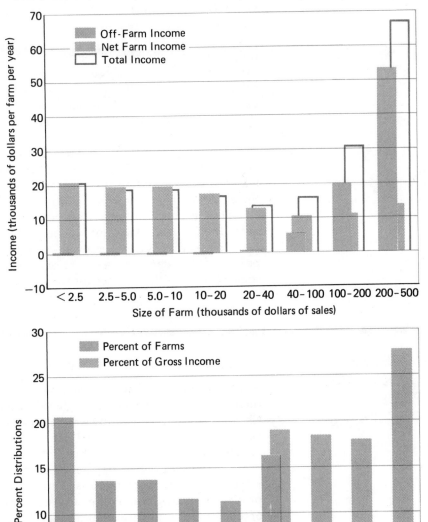

Source: U.S. Department of Commerce, Bureau of the Census, *Statistical Abstract of the United States: 1984*, 104th ed. (Washington, D.C.: Government Printing Office, 1983), p. 665.

farmland rose steeply. Many farmers took advantage of the rising price of their land to apply for increased bank loans, using their land as collateral. They spent the proceeds of the loans to buy new equipment and, often, to buy more land in the hope that its price would rise still further.

In the 1980s, this credit strategy began to unravel. Crop prices and the rate of inflation fell, and the high international value of the dollar hurt export sales. The same factors that pushed up land prices in the 1970s thus pushed them down in the early 1980s. In many cases, land prices fell by so much that the value of the land was worth less than the money that farmers had borrowed against it. When this happened, banks became reluctant to loan the farmers more money, even for essential purposes such as spring planting loans. This drove many farmers out of business. The situation was no picnic for the banks, either. When farmers were unable to repay their loans, the banks took possession of the land that had been pledged as collateral. But if the land was worth less than the amount of the loan, the bank had to take a loss. Losses for many small farm banks were so severe that they, too, were driven out of business.

These four factors, then—price instability, low farm incomes, the decline of the family farm, and the credit crisis—shape the farm problem. To a great extent, the farm problem is an outcome of the structure of farm markets. Understanding this, farmers have naturally tended to wish that these markets were not so competitive.

Their wish has not gone unheeded. Policymakers in Washington have heard the farmers' complaints and agreed that something should be done. Piece by piece, over the past half-century, they have developed a farm policy that has at its heart a set of restraints on competition. We will look at some of these in the next sections.

MARKETING ORDERS AND PRICE DISCRIMINATION

Competition vs. Coordination

Farmers could solve many of their own problems if they could coordinate their actions instead of competing with each other. The theory discussed in Chapter 22 suggests that one way to do this would be to form a system of agricultural cartels. The cartel for each crop could limit the amount supplied to the market and thus hold prices up. It could also hold one year's surplus for sale at a higher price in a year when the harvest was not as good. If there were more farmers than were needed to produce the profit-maximizing output, the cartel could assign each member a fair share of total production while planning for the orderly transfer of capital, land, and labor to uses outside agriculture.

But setting up such a system of cartels on a private, voluntary basis would be a hopeless undertaking. As Chapter 23 showed, cartels have built-in stability problems of their own. To be successful, a cartel must be able to restrict the entry of nonmembers into the industry, and it must be able to enforce its rules. Because the number of farms is so large and the barriers to entry are so few, these problems would soon prove fatal to a privately run agricultural cartel.

Since farmers cannot overcome their problems through coordination, it is not surprising that they have turned to the government for help. The government has one key advantage over any private cartel manager: The rules it sets have the force of law. However, the government is subject to pressure from other interest groups too, so the rules it sets are not always those of a perfect cartel designed with only the needs of the farmer in mind.

Agricultural Marketing Orders

The first farm policies we will look at are set forth in the Agricultural Marketing Agreement Act of 1937. This act, like much of the legislation of the 1930s, reflects the view that the economic problems of the time were caused by too much competition. The solution adopted in the 1937 act was to permit farmers, upon a two-thirds majority vote of producers in a given region, to use marketing orders to coordinate their supply decisions. **Agricultural marketing orders**, which are enforced by the Department of Agriculture, are agreements to control the flows of certain farm products to certain markets. In some cases, only quality is controlled. In other cases, such as dairy products, some citrus fruits, nuts, hops, and cranberries, quantity is also controlled. The following discussion concentrates on marketing orders that include both quality and quantity controls.

Marketing orders can be understood in terms of the theory of price discrimination. Chapter 23 showed that price discrimination can be a profitable strategy for a single-firm monopoly or cartel. For discrimination to be possible, however, there must be two clearly distinguished sets of buyers or markets—one with high demand elasticity and the other with low demand elasticity. Buyers in the low-elasticity market must pay a high price for a restricted quantity, while other units are supplied at a lower price to the high-elasticity market.

The markets for milk, citrus fruit, and many types of fresh produce can be divided in this way. The low-elasticity submarket consists of buyers who intend to consume the product fresh, and the high-elasticity submarket consists of those who intend to buy it for further processing. Thus, the demand for fresh milk by households is less elastic than the demand for milk to be processed into ice cream or dried milk products; the demand for fresh lemons for table use is less elastic than the demand for lemons to be processed into concentrates; and so on.

Being able to divide the market, however, is a necessary, not a sufficient, condition for price discrimination. Price discrimination is not actually possible unless competition among suppliers can be eliminated. Otherwise sellers will try to undercut one another's prices in order to get a share of the high-price market. The voting and enforcement provisions of the 1937 act are designed to prevent this kind of competition.

Assuming that it is enforced, an agricultural marketing order ensures that a profit-maximizing price can be maintained in the low-elasticity market even when a bumper crop saturates the high-elasticity market. For example, in 1981 a larger-than-normal crop of navel oranges was harvested in California. The Navel Orange Administrative Committee, which administers the marketing order for this crop, took action to protect the price of fresh oranges, the low-elasticity part of the market. Under normal conditions, oranges that are not demanded by the fresh-fruit market are turned into juice. In this case, however, the crop was too large for the juice

Agricultural marketing orders

Agreements authorized by the Agricultural Marketing Agreement Act of 1937 that allow farmers to control the flows of certain farm products to certain markets.

processors to handle. To keep the excess oranges off supermarket shelves, the surplus was dumped on abandoned drag strips and in cow pastures.[2]

This episode caused a local Consumer's Union official to dub the Navel Orange Administrative Committee "the OPEC of oranges." But, as in the case of the real OPEC, things do not always go smoothly for agricultural cartels. Many marketing orders have a serious defect. They can control price and the division of a crop between low- and high-elasticity markets, but they cannot control entry of firms into the market or the size of the total crop. To the extent that growers earn a pure economic profit, new entrants are attracted and the market share of the original members shrinks. For example, members of the Sunkist cooperative, who once dominated the navel orange marketing order, have seen their share of the crop fall from 75 percent to just 50 percent. Many of the new entrants are part-time or tax-shelter farmers. But every new entrant means that the cartel's profits from the high-price market have to be split more ways. Sooner or later, some entrants are just breaking even. Here and there a few big growers have come to the conclusion that they might be just as well off in a competitive market.

PRICE SUPPORTS, SUPPLY MANAGEMENT, AND TARGET PRICES

Not all agricultural markets are well suited to price discrimination, and not all crops come under the Agricultural Marketing Agreement Act of 1937. But growers of wheat, feed grains, cotton, rice, peanuts, and a host of other farm products want high prices and market stability just as much as citrus and dairy farmers do. For these markets, government policymakers have devised a different set of restrictive policies to achieve the same goals. These too date back to Depression-era legislation—the Agricultural Adjustment Act of 1933. For wheat, feed grains, cotton, and several other products, the three main policy tools are price supports, supply management, and target prices.

Price Supports

Price support
A program under which the government guarantees a certain minimum price to farmers by offering to buy any surplus that cannot be sold to private buyers at the support price.

One major tool of farm policy is **price supports**. Box 28.6 shows how they work, taking the market for wheat as an example. In this example the competitive equilibrium price is $4 a bushel, and the equilibrium level of output is 2 billion bushels per year.

Suppose that in order to raise farm incomes the government declares a support price of $6 a bushel. At this price farmers will produce 2.5 billion bushels of wheat, but consumers will buy only 1.5 billion. To support the price at $6, then, the government needs to keep the 1-billion-bushel surplus off the market.

The simplest way to do this would be for the government to buy the surplus wheat and put it into storage. In practice, though, the government uses an indirect method that amounts to the same thing. It works like this: Suppose a farmer harvests 100,000 bushels of wheat and cannot find a buyer at $6 a bushel. The farmer can store the wheat and apply for a loan of

[2]See Jay Mathews, "Cows, Not Consumers, See Fruits of Orange Surplus," *Washington Post*, March 24, 1981, p. A6.

**Box 28.6
The Effects of Price
Supports**

This graph shows the effects of price supports for wheat at a level of $6 a bushel, assuming an equilibrium price of $4 a bushel. To carry out the policy, the government agrees to pay $6 a bushel for all wheat that cannot be sold at that price in the open market. Because the support price is above the equilibrium price for a competitive market, this policy will reduce the amount of wheat demanded and increase the amount supplied. The resulting surplus will be bought by the government and put into storage or otherwise disposed of.

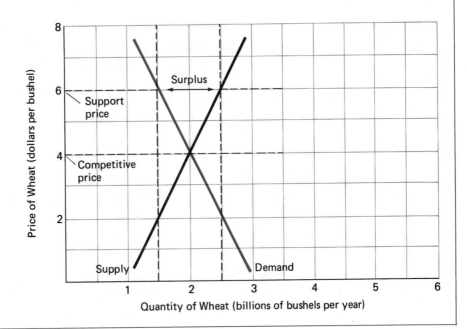

$600,000—the value of the wheat at the support price—from a government agency called the Commodity Credit Corporation. Later the farmer can sell the wheat and repay the loan if the price rises above $6 a bushel. If the price does not rise, the farmer can repay the loan by delivering the wheat itself to the Commodity Credit Corporation, which will take over the problem of storing it. In this way, just enough wheat will be taken off the market by the Commodity Credit Corporation to maintain the market price at the support level.

But what is to be done with the surplus wheat? Government stocks of wheat and other farm products have risen and fallen over the years. Storing them has at times been quite costly. To keep stocks of farm products from growing without limit, price supports have often been combined with two other devices—supply management and target prices.

Supply management
Any of a number of government programs that have as their goal the limitation of farm output.

Supply Management

Supply management refers to any government program whose goal is to limit farm output. In the case of wheat, supply management has most often taken the form of limits on acreage used to grow wheat. Box 28.7 shows how acreage limits work. The demand curve, D, and supply curve S_1 in this box are the same as in Box 28.6. The goal is also the same: to raise the price of wheat from its equilibrium level of $4 a bushel to the desired level of $6 a bushel.

The method of pushing the price up is different this time, however. Instead of offering to buy any wheat that goes unsold at the price of $6 a bushel, the government tries to restrict the amount of wheat produced in order to drive the price up to the desired level. It does this by paying farmers to take some land out of wheat production.

The effect of this policy is to raise the marginal cost of growing wheat. Normally, farmers who want to grow more wheat will reduce their production costs by adding a little more land, a little more labor, and a little more capital (machinery and fertilizer). Now those farmers face a new constraint: They can use more labor and capital but not more land. It is still possible to grow more wheat if the price is high enough to justify the added cost, so the new supply curve, S_2, still has an upward slope. But the increased marginal cost that results from the limit on land use pushes the

Box 28.7
The Effects of Acreage Controls on the Market for Wheat

This box shows the use of acreage controls, a form of supply management, to raise the price of wheat from an equilibrium level of $4 a bushel to a desired level of $6 a bushel. The controls raise the cost of producing any given quantity of wheat, thus shifting the supply curve from S_1 to S_2. The effect is to push up the price of wheat without creating a surplus. However, more resources must be used to produce each bushel of wheat than would have been the case without acreage controls.

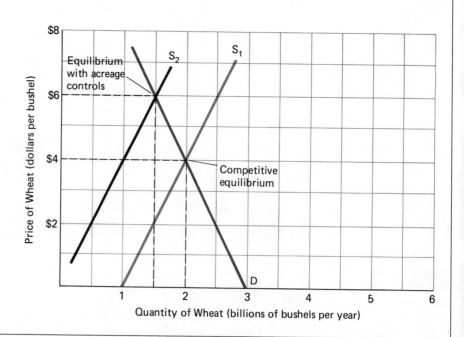

supply curve to a higher level. If acreage is restricted by just the right amount, as it is in Box 28.7, the same price ($6 a bushel) will be reached as was reached through direct price supports in the previous example.

Target Prices

Target price
A price that is guaranteed to farmers by the government; if the market price falls below the target price, the government pays the farmers the difference.

Neither price supports nor supply management offers much to consumers beyond the chance to spend more and get less. A third tool of farm policy, **target prices**, gives consumers a better deal while still supporting farm incomes.

Box 28.8 shows how target prices work. It begins with the same supply and demand curves as before and the same goal of getting the marginal revenue received by wheat farmers up to $6 a bushel. Now, however, the government does not try to control either the amount of wheat produced or the actual market price. Instead, it sets a target price of $6 a bushel and promises farmers a "deficiency payment" equal to the difference between the target price and the market price for each bushel produced. Knowing they will receive $6 a bushel regardless of how low the market price falls, farmers follow their supply curve up to an output of 2.5 billion bushels. When this amount of wheat is thrown on the market, the price falls to $2 a

**Box 28.8
The Effects of Target
Prices on the Market for
Wheat**

Target prices are a third way of raising the price of wheat to the desired level of $6 a bushel. The government sets a target price of $6 a bushel but does not offer to buy any wheat at this price. In response, farmers raise the quantity they supply from 2 billion to 2.5 billion bushels. This drives the market price down to $2 a bushel. The government then makes a "deficiency payment" to farmers equal to the difference between the market price and the target price.

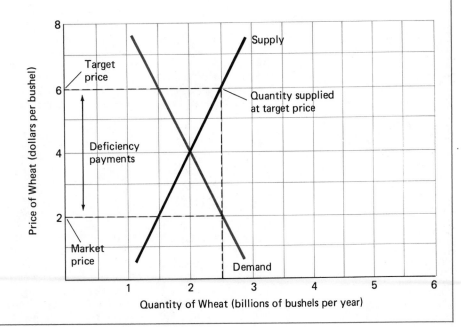

bushel. Consumers get lots of cheap wheat, and the government pays most of the bill.

Combining Policies

Which policy to use is not an either-or decision. In practice, farm policy has made use of all three tools at the same time. The Commodity Credit Corporation is authorized to buy crops at a set support price, but not as high a price as farmers want. To bring farm income to a higher level, a target price is set that is higher than the support price, and deficiency payments are made on that basis. Finally, in an attempt to limit the cost of the programs, limits are placed on supply.

The way these policies are combined varies from year to year and from crop to crop. The ability to mix policies in various ways gives an appearance of flexibility. Despite this flexibility, however, it never seems possible to fine-tune farm policy so that it yields exactly the intended results. The payment-in-kind policy that was tried in 1983 is a case in point—a plan that was clever yet ran into serious problems when it was carried out. The PIK policy is described in Box 28.9.

Box 28.9
The Payment-in-Kind
Program

The basic farm policies of supply management, price controls, and target prices can be combined in many ways. In 1983 the Reagan administration added a new element to the mix in the form of its payment-in-kind (PIK) program. Under PIK, farmers would agree to set aside a certain number of acres of farmland. In exchange, they would be paid not in cash, as under earlier forms of acreage restriction, but in the form of grain that the government had bought as a result of past price support programs. The farmers could store the grain they got under PIK, or they could sell it for cash. Meanwhile, price supports and target prices remained in effect.

The PIK program was supposed to have four helpful effects. First, it was supposed to reduce surplus output by restricting acreage. Second, it was supposed to stabilize farm prices and raise farm income. Third, it was supposed to get rid of government stockpiles, which were becoming costly to store. And fourth, it was supposed to make the federal budget look better, since farmers would be paid with grain, which the government already owned, instead of cash.

As things turned out, PIK revealed the perils of trying to fine-tune the farm economy. For one thing, the payments were too generous. More farmers than expected signed up for the program. As a result, the government ran out of surplus grain to turn over to farmers and had to buy grain for this purpose on the open market. The weather also played tricks. At the same time the program restricted acreage, the midwestern corn crop was hit with a severe drought. The corn crop was lower than normal to begin with, making 1983 not the right year in which to add further output restrictions. Finally, for crops that were not affected by the drought, the reduction in output was less than expected, even though more than the expected number of acres were set aside. In the case of winter wheat, for example, 18 percent of the acreage was set aside, but the crop was reduced by only 8 percent. This happened because farmers, for the most part, set aside only their least productive land and put more effort into the crops they grew on the remaining land.

All in all, the administration was disappointed with the results of PIK, and the program was phased out after its first year.

Comparing Policies

Which of these three policy tools—price supports, acreage controls, or target prices—is the best? The answer depends on whose viewpoint is taken—the farmer's, the consumer's, the taxpayer's, the economist's, or the policymaker's.

From the farmer's point of view, direct price supports and target prices are equally attractive. Both leave farmers free to produce as much as they want, and raise their incomes above the market equilibrium level. Supply management is not as attractive. It causes farmers to change their production techniques in a way that raises costs. Labor and capital are wasted in overly intensive use of some land while other land lies idle. Yet if, as under the PIK program, the rewards for taking part in supply management programs are high enough, farmers will be willing to take part in them.

From the consumer's point of view, target prices are by far the best, with both price supports and supply management much less welcome. Target prices give consumers more of the product at a lower price per unit, whereas the other two policies give them less at greater cost.

From the taxpayer's point of view, the ranking of the three policies depends on the situation. Whether target prices or price supports are cheaper depends on the shape and position of the supply and demand curves. Supply management may be cheaper for taxpayers, since farmers would be expected to accept a smaller payment for not growing crops than for growing them and then selling them. However, if supply management programs result in large payments to farmers to reduce the acreage they plant or the size of their herds, but are offset by higher productivity, they can end up being very costly for taxpayers too.

From the economist's point of view, the policy that is most efficient also depends on the exact shape and position of the supply and demand curves. For example, surpluses caused by price supports are less of a problem when supply is inelastic, whereas supply management works better when demand is inelastic. However, most economists would agree that, other things being equal, the cost required to gain a benefit of a given size should be kept to a minimum, regardless of who gets the benefit.

All three of the policy tools discussed in this chapter involve some costs. All three also distort the use of resources in that they result in the wrong amount of farm output. Under target prices and price supports, output is too high. Under supply management, it may be too low. For price supports there is also the cost of keeping wheat in storage to shore up the market price, instead of letting people eat it. For acreage controls, the cost is the extra labor and capital required to grow each unit of output when land use is restricted. And for target prices or price supports there are excess burdens placed on the rest of the economy by the higher taxes required to make payments to farmers.

The Future of Farm Policy

Throughout this chapter the theme has been the tension between the basically competitive structure of U.S. agriculture and the desire of farmers to shield themselves from what they perceive to be the mixed blessing of competition. The intent is not to condemn farmers for wanting such protection. They owe nothing to the economist's theory of perfect competition. But not all criticisms of farm policy by nonfarmers come down to a simple tug-of-war between contending interest groups, each of which wants more for itself and less for others. In fact, even some farmers are beginning to wonder whether farm policy needs some changes.

First, the critics find that current farm policies are very costly to consumers. And, because of administrative costs and the distortions in resource use that the policies cause, for each dollar in cost to consumers, farmers gain only between 40 and 80 cents in real net profits.

Second, critics claim that farm policies have lost sight of their own goal of short-term price stability. All farm policies involve built-in trade-offs between the goal of stable prices and the goal of higher farm incomes. A pure stabilization policy would raise prices in some years and depress them in others, so that the average price would be close to a competitive equilibrium price. In practice, many farm policies are designed to take advantage of each year's changing supply and demand conditions to raise farm prices as high as possible in that year. That is a major reason why, despite 50 years of activist farm policies, price stability has not been achieved.

Third, farm policies are criticized for failing in one of their main goals: keeping the family farm alive. In 1982, some 45 percent of all federal farm subsidies went to farms with more than $100,000 per year in sales—the large farms that would fare best in a free market. Another 20 percent went to part-time farmers who depended on off-farm jobs for the bulk of their incomes. Only a third of all subsidies went to farms in the $40,000-$100,000 sales bracket. And this was not enough to prevent a steady stream of people from leaving this segment.

It is worth noting that some of the largest and healthiest segments of agriculture in the 1980s are those that operate without price supports, marketing orders, or other market restrictions. For example, soybean, hog, and cattle farmers operate in free markets. Many of them prosper. Although these segments of farming have some bad years, the same can be said of corn, wheat, and dairy farmers, despite all the federal farm programs. It is possible—not certain, but possible—that the late 1980s will see a phasing out of the Depression-era programs and a turn toward freer farm markets. But no one pretends that the transition will be a comfortable one.

Summary

1. The market structure of agriculture meets the basic requirements of perfect competition: There are many firms, all of which are small; products are fairly homogeneous; buyers and sellers are well informed; and entry and exit are easy.

2. Agricultural markets are characterized by inelastic demand and unpredictable shifts in supply curves. Together, these two factors cause prices to vary widely from year to year. They also mean that farm incomes tend to fall when production is high and to rise when production falls.

3. The percentage of the U.S. population that lives on farms has declined steadily for decades and is continuing to do so. Also, changes are taking place in the makeup of the farm sector. The medium-sized family farm is

giving way to large, professionally managed operations, on the one hand, and small part-time operations, on the other.

4. Agricultural marketing orders are cartel-like arrangements that allow growers of many types of fruit and produce to restrict the quantities of their products that reach the market. Often they feature price discrimination arrangements under which higher prices are charged for fresh oranges, lemons, and so on than for the same products when they are to be processed.

5. The three main tools of farm policy for crops that are not subject to marketing orders are price supports, supply management, and target prices. Price supports require government purchases of surplus crops in order to maintain a market price higher than the market equilibrium. Supply management attempts to reduce surpluses by paying farmers to limit acreage planted or herd size. Target prices allow products to be sold at prices that equalize the quantity supplied and the quantity demanded while the government makes up the difference between the market price and a target price.

6. Farm policy changes from year to year as different mixes of the basic policy tools are tried. Opposition to the growing cost of farm programs, plus the fact that these programs have not achieved their goal of preserving family farms, may cause a swing toward free-market policies in the future.

Questions for Review

1. Define the following terms:
   parity price ratio
   agricultural marketing order
   price supports
   supply management
   target prices
2. Left to its own devices, what market structure would agriculture fit most closely? Are most government policies aimed to make agriculture more competitive or less so? Give examples.
3. Why do farm prices tend to be unstable? Discuss in terms of the concept of elasticity.
4. What are some current trends in the size of the farm population and in types of farms?
5. What is an agricultural marketing order? Give examples of farm products that are subject to marketing orders.
6. Sketch supply-and-demand diagrams to show how price supports, target prices, and supply management work.
7. What are the prospects for change in farm policy in the 1980s?

Problems and Topics for Discussion

1. Suppose that the cost of wheat accounts for 10 percent of the retail price of a loaf of bread. Let all the other costs that go into making and selling a loaf of bread—transportation, milling, fuel for baking, retail clerks' wages, and so on—be constant. Under these conditions, would you expect the demand for wheat at the farm level to be more or less price elastic than the demand for bread at the retail level? Why? Does this help explain the instability of farm prices?

2. In this chapter the farm problem is discussed mainly from the point of view of farmers. To what extent are price instability, rising productivity, and the decline of medium-sized family farms also problems for consumers? Discuss.

3. Turn to the table of demand elasticities in Box 28.2. Can you find any examples of the principle that demand will be more elastic for products with close substitutes than for those without close substitutes?

4. Suppose you are a grower of walnuts. This crop is not subject to a marketing order, but you decide to try to form a cartel of fellow walnut farmers in an attempt to increase everyone's profits. Assume that this cartel is *not* challenged under the antitrust laws (in practice, it would be). What problems, if any, would your efforts encounter? What steps could you take to overcome them?

5. Assume that the market equilibrium price of corn is $2 a bushel and that the government wants to raise the revenue received by farmers to $4 a bushel. Draw a set of supply and demand curves for corn that illustrate the possibility that price supports will be less expensive for the government than target prices. Then change the shapes of the supply and demand curves so that target prices will be cheaper.

6. Review the discussion of milk price supports in Chapter 3 (p. 69). What factors made the costs of this program grow? Why was supply management unable to control the cost of the program? What changes, if any, do you think should be made in the program? Bonus question: Using current news sources or government publications, try to find out what changes, if any, have been made in the dairy price support program since 1984.

Suggestions for Further Reading

Council of Economic Advisers. *Economic Report of the President.* Washington, D.C.: Government Printing Office, 1984, chap. 4.

This chapter reviews the background of U.S. farm programs and prospects for change. Check later editions of the report for updates of this material.

Food and Agricultural Policy for the 1980s. Washington, D.C.: American Enterprise Institute, 1981.

The proceedings of a conference on a number of topics related to food and agricultural policies.

Gardner, Bruce L. *The Governing of Agriculture.* Lawrence: Regents Press of Kansas, 1981.

An excellent overview of farm policy.

Chapter 29

Environmental Policy

After reading this chapter, you should be able to

1. Use a production possibility frontier to show the range of possible choices between environmental quality and other goods.
2. Show how marginal analysis can be used to determine the optimal quantity of pollution.
3. Use a production possibility frontier to show the relationship between the goals of optimality and efficiency in pollution control.
4. Use supply and demand curves to illustrate different strategies for pollution control.
5. Discuss the issue of controlling acid rain in terms of the principles of environmental economics.

Ideas for Review

Here are some terms and concepts that you should review before you read this chapter:

Opportunity cost (Chapter 2)
The production possibility frontier (Chapter 2)
Supply and demand (Chapter 3)
Marginal cost (Chapter 21)

"At the lake next to the governor's mansion here, 'no fishing' signs have sprung up."

At the lake next to the governor's mansion in Baton Rouge, Louisiana, "no fishing" signs have sprung up. The Department of Environmental Quality posted them. The governor's lake contains PCBs.

It isn't unusual to find contaminated water here in the state's industrial, oil-refining and petrochemical corridor. Tons of waste containing potentially toxic heavy metals and organic chemicals are generated daily, and have been for decades.

But Louisiana's water problems aren't confined to the industrial zones. In the coastal marshes, areas of heavy oil and gas production, thousands of open waste pits brim with the soup of chemicals poured into the wells during drilling.

Some energy and petrochemical companies in Louisiana have begun to take more care in disposing of wastes. A few are spending millions to clean up their worst dumps. But much waste continues to be disposed of haphazardly.

Meanwhile unusual levels of illness are showing up in much of South Louisiana. No one can demonstrate whether any of the illness is linked to oil and gas activity or to the area's extensive water pollution, but concern is mounting. Statewide, cancer deaths are 9.1 percent higher than the national average, using the figure for white males. And ten counties in the major oil producing and refining region rank in the top 5 percent nationwide for cancer deaths per capita among white males.[1]

The signs by the Louisiana governor's lake warn of a soup of PCBs and heavy metals. They symbolize another soup as well—a pungent blend of politics, industry, and the nation's hunger for energy—that also threatens human health and welfare. In this chapter, the last of four on government regulation of the economy, we turn our attention to the economics of environmental policy.

Before getting down to details, it is worth asking just what economics has to contribute to the ongoing debate over environmental policy. At first glance it might seem that economics can contribute little. It can do nothing to resolve the complex scientific issues of which chemicals pose how much cancer risk, or where underground aquifers carry the wastes from leaking dump sites. It can do little to resolve the political question of how to build a coalition in Congress that can pass sensible legislation. And it cannot do much to resolve the normative issues that arise from the conflicting interests of oil field workers, fishers in Louisiana bayous, and the consumers and taxpayers who bear the burden of cleanup efforts. Still, economists deserve a place at the table where issues of environmental policy are debated. As this chapter will try to show, economics can provide a framework for thinking about the trade-offs and opportunity costs that have to be faced in making decisions about environmental policy. And they can offer guidance on how to avoid policies that needlessly raise the costs of reaching whatever goals are agreed upon through the political process.

[1]Thomas Petzinger Jr. and George Getschow, "Oil's Legacy: In Louisiana, Pollution and Cancer are Rife In the Petroleum Area," *Wall Street Journal*, October 23, 1984, p. 1. Reprinted by permission of The Wall Street Journal, © Dow Jones & Company, Inc. 1984. All rights reserved.

HOW MUCH POLLUTION, HOW MUCH CLEANUP?

In Chapter 2 we used a production possibility frontier to illustrate the trade-offs involved in environmental policy. Such a production possibility frontier is shown in Box 29.1. The horizontal axis of the graph is labeled "environmental quality" and the vertical axis is labeled "other goods."

The upper end of the frontier represents a situation in which all efforts are focused on producing material goods, with no effort made to protect the environment. The lower end represents an uninhabited wilderness in which nothing is produced and the environment is undisturbed. But these extremes are of little practical importance. Instead, we can picture ourselves somewhere along the central part of the frontier, say at point A. From there we can devote somewhat more resources to cleaning up the environment, thus moving toward point B, or we can relax our efforts to protect the environment in favor of more production, thus moving toward point C.

How should we approach the decision of where to move along the production possibility frontier? Economists propose that we approach this problem in *marginal* terms.

Applying the Marginal Principle to Pollution

The trade-off between environmental quality and other goods involves a balancing of two kinds of marginal costs: the costs of putting up with more pollution, on the one hand, and the costs of getting rid of pollution, on the other.

Box 29.1
Trade-offs Faced by Environmental Policy

A production possibility frontier can be used to show the trade-offs faced by environmental policy. A move toward a better environment—for example, from point A to point B—entails an opportunity cost in terms of other goods. A move toward more other goods entails an opportunity cost in terms of environmental values.

Marginal social cost of pollution
The total additional cost to all members of society of an additional unit of pollution.

Marginal cost of pollution abatement
The added cost of reducing a given kind of pollution by one unit.

Box 29.2 represents the first of these costs—the **marginal social cost of pollution**. This means the total additional cost to all members of society of an additional unit of pollution. For each type of pollution—say, sulfur dioxide—the harm done by each additional ton of pollution to each person is summed. Presumably some people are harmed more than others and in different ways than others; the marginal social cost of pollution adds all of these together. As the total quantity of pollution increases, the harm done by each additional unit is also likely to increase. Hence, the curve showing the marginal social cost of pollution slopes upward.

The second factor to be taken into account is the **marginal cost of pollution abatement**, which is the cost of reducing a given kind of pollution by one unit. Other things being equal, the marginal cost of pollution abatement tends to rise as the level of pollution falls. For example, in controlling automobile exhaust emissions, relatively cheap devices can cut pollution by half. Somewhat more complex and costly devices are required to cut the amount in half again, to the level of 75 percent abatement. Very elaborate and costly methods must be installed to cut it in half a third time, to 87.5 percent abatement. Because of this tendency, the marginal abatement cost curve slopes downward, as in Box 29.3.

**Box 29.2
The Marginal Social
Cost of Pollution**

The marginal social cost of pollution is the total additional cost to all members of society that results from a one-unit increase in pollution. At low levels of pollution, those that are within the environment's natural absorptive capacity, the marginal social cost of pollution may be zero. As the quantity of pollution increases, the marginal social cost probably rises for most pollutants.

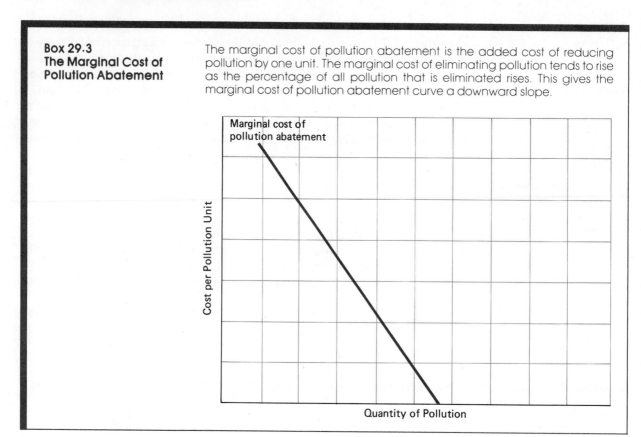

Box 29.3
The Marginal Cost of
Pollution Abatement

The marginal cost of pollution abatement is the added cost of reducing pollution by one unit. The marginal cost of eliminating pollution tends to rise as the percentage of all pollution that is eliminated rises. This gives the marginal cost of pollution abatement curve a downward slope.

The Optimal Quantity of Pollution

In Box 29.4 both schedules appear in one diagram. This makes it possible to identify the point—the intersection of the two curves—where the marginal cost of abatement is equal to the marginal social cost of pollution. As far as economics is concerned, this point represents the optimal quantity of pollution. If pollution is allowed to exceed this amount, the harm done by additional pollution then exceeds the cost of reducing it. (Such a situation corresponds to moving too far up and to the left along the production possibility frontier of Box 29.1.) But if pollution is reduced below the optimal amount, then the marginal cost of pollution abatement exceeds the marginal social cost of pollution. The small gain in environmental quality is more than offset by the relatively large increase in the supply of resources available for other uses. (This situation corresponds to moving too far down and to the right along the production possibility frontier.)

Criticisms of the Optimal Pollution Concept

To economists, the logic behind the choice of the optimal quantity of pollution is no different than the logic behind the choice of the least-cost method of producing running shoes or the choice of the optimal balance of oil and vinegar in making a salad dressing. No one denies that cleaning up the environment entails costs and trade-offs. Few people would advocate choosing either of the extremes—the whole world as a stinking sewer or

**Box 29.4
The Optimal Quantity of
Pollution**

The optimal quantity of pollution is determined by the intersection of the marginal cost of pollution abatement curve and the marginal social cost of pollution curve. To the left of that point, the benefits of further reductions in pollution do not justify the high marginal cost of abatement. To the right of that point, the marginal cost of abatement is less than the cost imposed on society by more pollution.

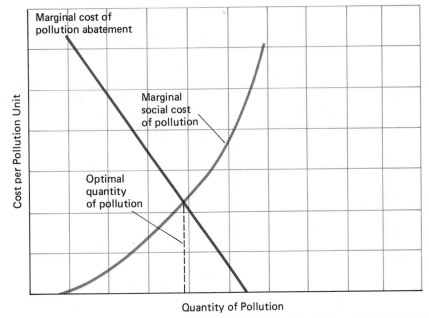

the whole world as an uninhabited wilderness. Therefore, say the economists, there must be an optimal point between the extremes.

Despite the logic of the optimal pollution concept, many critics doubt that it is a useful guide to public policy. The criticisms are of two types, some focusing on problems of measurement and some on problems of rights.

Problems of measurement   Attempts to measure the social cost of pollution usually focus on such things as damage to property, health costs measured in terms of medical expenses and time lost from work, and the value of wildlife and crops killed. These attempts encounter a number of problems. First, data on the costs of pollution are limited at best, and the many gaps must be filled by guesswork. Second, it is difficult to account for purely subjective costs, such as damage to natural beauty and discomforts that do not result in actual damage to health. Finally, estimates of the social costs of pollution rarely give more than the average cost figures. But the marginal cost data, which are much more difficult to obtain, are far more relevant in making pollution policy decisions.

There are also problems in estimating the costs of pollution abatement. One major problem is that the calculations must take into account not only the direct costs of getting rid of one form of pollution but also the social costs of other forms of pollution that may be produced as a result. The measurement of these costs is subject to all the problems of measuring the social costs of any kind of pollution.

Although there are problems in measuring both the social costs of pollution and those of abatement, data on abatement costs seem to be somewhat easier to come by. According to critics, this is a problem in itself. Studies of the costs and benefits of pollution control tend to list dollars-and-cents data on the cost side and subjective claims on the benefit side. This tends to stack the deck against pollution control. Economists often warn policymakers that the fact that the social costs of pollution are hard to measure does not mean that they are small. Even so, the fear that cost-benefit studies tend to be biased in favor of pollution has given the whole idea of the optimal quantity of pollution a bad name among environmentalists.

Problems of rights   The optimal-pollution concept also encounters a quite different criticism. This is based on the notion that environmental policy must respect certain basic rights and should not be guided by economic trade-offs alone.

The idea here is that pollution should be viewed in the same way as crimes like theft, vandalism, or rape. Suppose a vandal breaks into a person's home and smashes a valuable statue. How should a court decide the case? Should it listen to testimony from the owner about the value of the statue, then listen to testimony from the vandal about how big a thrill it was to smash it, and then make a decision by weighing the marginal utility of the vandal against the marginal utility of the owner? Most people would be outraged by such an approach. They would say that the vandal violated the owner's right to enjoy the statue and that the vandal's benefit from the smashing should count for nothing in deciding the case.

Following this line of thought, it is proposed that environmental policy, like criminal law, should be guided by a notion of basic rights. This proposal would place an oil company that poisons the water supply of a Louisiana town on the same footing as an armed robber who holds up the town's banks. The list of environmental rights would include a right to clean air; a right to clean water; a right to enjoy the beauty of unspoiled wilderness areas; and so on. Some environmentalists believe that public policy not only should respect the rights of people but also should respect the rights of other living things; for example, the rights of species to survive. In this view, cost-benefit analysis should enter into environmental policy, if at all, only in determining the least-cost way to protect these rights.

This notion of a rights-based environmental policy is not rejected by all economists. Although cost-benefit analysis continues to dominate environmental economics, there has been serious discussion of the economics of a rights-based policy, as we will see in the next section.

ECONOMIC STRATEGIES FOR POLLUTION CONTROL

In the last section we looked at the question of how much pollution should be allowed. We presented this question as a matter of choosing a point along a production possibility frontier for environmental quality versus other goods. We found that economics can offer a framework for thinking about the trade-offs involved, but not an acceptable, dollars-and-cents answer to the question of where the point of optimal pollution lies. This being the case, it seems likely that economics will continue to play only a minor role in making decisions over allowable levels of pollution.

There are other questions of environmental policy, however, on which economists like to think they have more to offer. These are questions of how to achieve a given degree of pollution control, once it has somehow been chosen as the proper policy goal. This issue too can be presented in terms of the production possibility frontier, as we saw in Chapter 2. Consider Box 29.5. Here the economy starts out at point A, where the level of environmental quality is E_1. It is decided (somehow) to move to a higher level of environmental quality, E_2. If efficient means are chosen to reach this goal, the economy can move along the production possibility frontier from point A to point B. If inefficient means are chosen, however, the economy may end up at a point like C, where the environmental goal is reached, but at a higher cost than necessary in terms of other goods. Worse yet, it may end up at D, where there are no major environmental gains despite high costs.

In this section we will discuss several strategies for pollution control. Our focus will be on the search for efficient means of attaining environmental goals.

Supply and Demand

The tools of supply-and-demand analysis can be applied to the problem of pollution control strategy, as it can to so many other economic problems.

Box 29.5
Efficiency vs. Optimality in Environmental Policy

An optimal environmental policy is one that balances the marginal social cost of pollution against the marginal cost of pollution abatement to pick just the right point on the production possibility frontier. An efficient policy is one that at least gets to the frontier, even if not at the optimal point. In this case a move from point A to point B is efficient. A move from A to C achieves the same improvement in environmental quality, but it is inefficient because it results in too great a loss of other goods. A move from A to D is even less efficient.

Box 29.6 sets the scene. In this box the curve that represents the marginal cost of pollution abatement is given a new name—the demand curve for pollution opportunities. To understand why the same curve serves both purposes, ask how much a firm would be willing to pay for the opportunity to dump an additional unit of untreated waste directly into the environment. The answer is that it would pay any sum smaller (but not larger) than the marginal cost of pollution abatement—that is, the cost of getting rid of a marginal unit of waste products in a nonpolluting way. Thus, the value of pollution to a firm, and hence its demand for opportunities to pollute, is determined by the desire to avoid abatement costs.

Box 29.6 also shows a supply curve for pollution opportunities. The supply curve is a straight line lying right along the horizontal axis. The line shows that unlimited pollution opportunities are available without paying any price at all. The equilibrium quantity of pollution is found where the supply and demand curves intersect. This equilibrium occurs at a level of pollution that is far greater than the optimum, shown by the intersection of the demand curve with the curve representing the marginal social cost of pollution. What can be done to correct this situation?

Command and Control

To date, most pollution control efforts have taken the so-called command-and-control approach. This approach, as embodied in the Clean Air Act,

**Box 29.6
Supply and Demand for
Pollution Opportunities**

The marginal cost of pollution abatement curve can also be called the demand curve for pollution opportunities. The position of the supply curve for pollution opportunities depends on how much firms must pay to discharge wastes into the environment. If they do not have to pay at all, the supply curve will coincide with the horizontal axis, as shown here, and the equilibrium quantity of pollution will be greater than the optimum quantity.

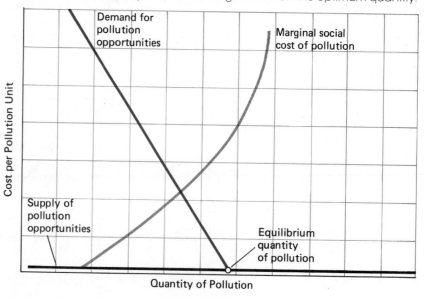

the Clean Water Act, the National Environmental Policy Act, the Noise Control Act, and several other laws of the 1970s, relies on engineering controls and pollution ceilings. Often the law states that a specific pollution control method must be used, without considering its cost compared to other equally effective methods. In other cases a quantitative goal such as 90 percent cleanup is set. Sometimes, in areas where pollution is especially bad, new pollution sources are banned entirely.

The command-and-control strategy has scored some notable successes. Oregon's Willamette River is swimmable again. Sturgeon are coming back to the Hudson. Cleveland's Cuyahoga River no longer catches fire. And many cities can boast of air that is cleaner than it was a decade ago. Even so, the present set of environmental laws is subject to a lot of criticism. The complaints fall into three groups.

First, pollution control efforts have not been as successful as might be desired. The local success stories just mentioned are not mirrored in national statistics. For example, there has been a slight reduction in phosphorus pollution of inland lakes and rivers (phosphorus promotes algae growth) but little increase in the dissolved oxygen needed by fish and little reduction in fecal bacteria counts. In the air, the level of particulate pollutants has fallen a great deal, and local sulfur dioxide concentrations have fallen. On the other hand, little progress has been made against hydrocarbons or carbon monoxide, and nitrogen dioxide pollution has worsened. Perhaps most worrisome of all, efforts to control local sulfur dioxide levels through the use of ultratall smokestacks appear to have caused acid rain hundreds of miles downwind. (We will return to the acid rain problem shortly.)

Second, environmental laws are accused of putting a brake on economic growth. Spending on pollution control has drained away investment funds. Between 1972 and 1979 such spending rose from $34.5 billion to $48.5 billion in constant 1979 dollars—more than 10 percent of gross private domestic investment. (Some economists cite these expenditures as a factor in the slowdown in productivity growth that occurred between 1973 and 1981.) But direct spending is not the whole story. It is also costly to cut through the red tape involved in complying with environmental laws. In many cases it takes two to three years to obtain the environmental permits for building a new plant, roughly doubling lead times for such plants. Of course, many new plants are built despite the red tape. When an industry needs to expand, it has no real choice but to build new plants. However, the problem of meeting environmental standards gives firms an incentive not to replace old plants, even though they may be obsolete and costly to run. And this makes pollution worse, since the old plants do not use new, cleaner technology and since they are exempt from some of the pollution control requirements placed on new plants.

Finally, existing pollution control laws pay very little attention to cost-effectiveness. At the time that the major laws were passed, Congress seems to have expected regulators to find a safe threshold level for each type of pollutant, a level below which pollution would be harmless and above which it would be extremely dangerous. In terms of our diagrams, this threshold concept is equivalent to drawing a marginal social cost of pollution curve that is a vertical line at the maximum tolerable level of pollution. If there were such a threshold, no analysis of cost-effectiveness would be required to find the optimal level of pollution, since the answer would be the same regardless of the height or shape of the marginal cost of pollution abatement curve.

The prevailing view today, however, is that there are no thresholds. At least for many pollutants, cleaner is always safer. The scientific or engineering question of finding a threshold thus is replaced by the economic question of how much safety people want to pay for. And even when standards are set, current law does not pay much attention to cost-effectiveness in meeting them. Requirements to use specific cleanup methods reduce the incentive to discover new, lower-cost methods. No attempt is made to balance the marginal social cost of different kinds of pollutants, with the result that the most serious problems are not always attacked first. Also, different plants are subject to quite different cleanup standards, depending on their age and location.

The high costs and uneven achievements of past policies have created pressure to cut back on pollution control efforts. Economists see this as the wrong response to the problem. Instead, for years they have argued that the cost-effectiveness of pollution control can be greatly increased by using different means to achieve environmental quality. The hope of doing this lies in replacing the command-and-control approach with more flexible approaches based on market incentives. Three such market-oriented pollution control strategies are pollution charges, marketable pollution permits, and rights-based pollution control strategies.

Pollution Charges

One market-oriented strategy for controlling pollution works by shifting the pollution opportunity supply curve. It does this by imposing a charge of a fixed amount per unit of waste on all sources of a given kind of waste. Such charges are, in effect, a tax on pollution. As an example, all sources of sewage might be required to pay a charge of $40 per ton of sewage discharged into lakes and rivers.

Box 29.7 shows that such a charge would shift the supply curve for pollution opportunities upward from its position along the horizontal axis to a position $40 higher. Polluters react to the tax by moving back along their demand curve to a new equilibrium where there is less pollution. They do this because it pays them to use any abatement method that can remove a ton of pollutants from their wastewater for $40 or less.

By raising or lowering the amount of the charge, any desired degree of pollution control can be achieved. Ideally, the charge is set so that the pollution opportunity supply curve passes through the intersection of the marginal abatement cost curve (demand curve) and the marginal social cost curve.

Of course, there are measurement problems to contend with. There is no easy way to tell just where the curves intersect and, thus, how high the pollution charge should be. In the case of water pollution, the damage done is likely to vary from time to time and from place to place, depending on how much dissolved oxygen there is in the water, what the water temperature is, and so on. This would make it difficult to ensure that the charge was always at the right level. However, advocates of pollution charges point out that their plan has advantages even if the charges are not set at exactly the right level. In particular, a charge that was applied uniformly to all sources would apply equal pressure at the margin to all polluters. It would encourage them to eliminate pollution first from

Box 29.7
Effects of a Pollution
Charge

Ideally, a pollution charge could be set just high enough to reduce pollution by the optimal amount. Here the supply curve for pollution opportunities cuts the demand and marginal social cost curves at the point where they intersect. In practice, such fine-tuning of pollution charge would be difficult to achieve.

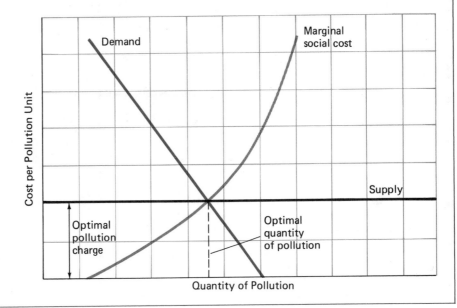

the sources that can be controlled most cheaply. Thus, it would avoid the present situation, in which some sources (for example, industrial plants and municipal sewage systems) pay high marginal costs to meet very strict standards, while other sources (for example, agricultural runoff and urban storm runoff) are almost entirely free from control.

Economists view pollution charges as an efficient means of control, even when problems of measuring costs and benefits make it impossible to calculate the optimal degree of pollution control. In effect, they represent a means of reaching the production possibility frontier, rather than staying inside it, even when the best point on the frontier cannot be identified.

Marketable Permits

A second market-oriented approach to pollution control uses a vertical rather than a horizontal supply curve for pollution opportunities. This is the method of marketable pollution permits. (See Box 29.8.) Like some forms of the command-and-control approach, this one begins by setting a quantitative limit on the amount of pollution allowed. Ideally, this limit corresponds to the optimal quantity of pollution.

Once the limit is determined, however, command-and-control methods are avoided. Instead, a fixed number of permits are issued, each allowing the owner to emit a set quantity of a given pollutant. The permits can then be freely bought and sold. Presumably, the highest bidders will be the plants with the highest marginal cost of pollution abatement. As the market for permits approaches equilibrium, each firm will move upward

**Box 29.8
Effects of Marketable
Pollution Permits**

In a system using marketable pollution permits, policymakers first have to decide what quantity of pollution will be allowed. Ideally, if they can solve the measurement problem, they will set this quantity at the level where the marginal social cost of pollution curve intersects the demand curve for pollution opportunities (that is, the marginal cost of pollution abatement curve). Once the permits have been issued, the supply curve of pollution opportunities will be a vertical line. As the permits are traded from one firm to another, they will end up in the hands of the firms with the highest abatement costs. The effect will be to minimize the cost of attaining the target level of pollution reduction.

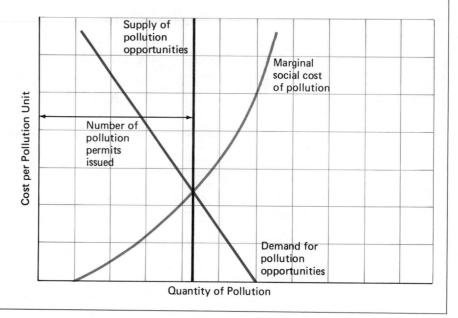

and to the left along its marginal cost of pollution abatement curve by selling permits, or it will move downward and to the right along the curve by buying permits, until the marginal cost of abatement is equalized for all firms. Marketable permits thus are seen as another means of achieving the goal of efficiency.

In recent years policymakers have taken some tentative steps in the direction of marketable pollution permits. For example, the following limited versions of the concept have been tried:

Bubbles. The idea here is to treat all emissions from a given plant as a single "bubble" of pollution. Within the bubble, the plant is permitted to trade off costly control of some sources for less costly control of others. For example, a steel mill might put tighter controls on its blast furnaces to avoid more costly controls on its open-hearth furnaces, while holding total pollution to an agreed upon level.

Offsets. Here the idea is to treat a whole region as a single bubble. A steel mill could get permission to build a new furnace by paying for an offsetting reduction in pollution from a nearby electric power plant.

Banks. Under this concept a polluter that cut emissions below the level required by law could put the credit for the extra pollution control in a "bank." Such credits could later be sold to a firm that wants to build a new plant in the region.

Experiments of this sort have been limited to date, but problems are being worked out and many people find the early results encouraging.

Rights-Based Strategies

Still a third way of introducing market incentives into pollution control is based on the idea that people have property rights to a clean environment. From the viewpoint of owners of property rights, pollution is theft. If you use the air in and around my home as a dumping ground for your unwanted combustion products, you are stealing waste disposal services from me. If you use my living room as a reverberation chamber for noise from your truck or motorcycle, you are robbing me of my right to peace and quiet. If you leak toxic metals into my well water, you are robbing me of my health. As the owner, I should have the right to prevent you from using my property in these ways unless you negotiate with me in advance to buy my permission. If you do not, I should be able to bring civil or criminal action against you in a court of law.

The current legal system is ill equipped to deal with the kinds of harm and sources of harm that are common in pollution cases. The law embodies concepts of proof, causation, evidence, fault, and so on that were developed for other purposes than pollution control. As a result, it is difficult for victims of pollution to win their cases. This is especially true when there are many victims of chronic, low-level pollution—a situation that many people believe to be responsible for the largest share of harm done by pollution.

In recent years many writers have addressed the issue of reforming the legal system to offer better protection of the rights of pollution victims.[2] Some experts believe that such legal reforms, rather than marketable permits or pollution charges, are the best approach to dealing with pollution from toxic substances, especially when the effects are localized and the source can be identified. This approach might, for example, offer the best remedy for residents of some of the Louisiana communities whose wells and surface water have been poisoned by chemical wastes.

What would be the economic effect of laws that allowed property owners to protect themselves from pollution? One possible effect would be the creation of a private market for pollution rights. In such a market people would sell pollution opportunities to firms only if they were offered a high enough price to compensate them for damage done. If everyone sold pollution rights at prices equal to the marginal cost to them of pollution damage, the pollution market would look like the graph in Box 29.9. The pollution opportunity supply curve would follow the marginal social cost curve. The equilibrium quantity of pollution would be exactly the optimal amount.

---

[2]The special issue of the *Cato Journal* listed in the suggested readings at the end of this chapter contains many useful articles and references.

**Box 29.9
Effects of a
Rights-Based Pollution
Control Policy**

If polluters always had to compensate the victims of pollution for damage to person or property, a private market in pollution opportunities would be created. Ideally, the supply curve in this market would exactly coincide with the marginal cost of pollution curve. The equilibrium quantity of pollution then would equal the optimal quantity.

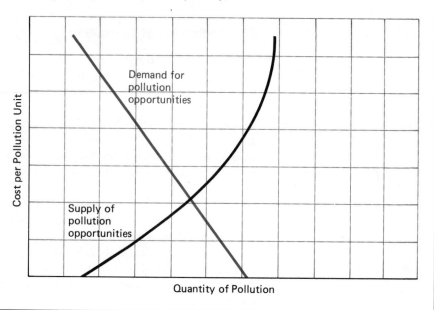

THE PROBLEM OF ACID RAIN: A CASE STUDY[3]

The general principles of environmental economics apply to many types of pollution—pollution of surface water with sewage and farm runoff, pollution of groundwater with toxic metals, pollution of the air with automobile exhaust, noise pollution, and so on. In this section we will illustrate those principles by applying them to one pollution problem—acid rain. How to deal with acid rain is one of the most controversial issues of environmental policy today. We will look first at the chemistry of acid rain, then at the problem of measuring the costs and benefits of control, and finally at the economics of various control strategies.

The Chemistry of Acid Rain

Rain is naturally slightly acid, but there are parts of the world in which it is much more acid than in others. In Germany, Scandinavia, eastern Canada, and the eastern United States, levels of acidity 5 to 20 times that of natural rain, or even higher, are often found. In some areas acid rain is neutralized by natural alkaline substances in the soil, but in the eastern United States many of the areas where the rainfall is most acidic have a low tolerance for

[3]This section draws on Glen E. Gordon, "Acid Rain: What Is It?" *Resources*, Winter 1984, pp. 6–8; Paul R. Portney, "Acid Rain: Making Sensible Policy," *Resources*, Winter 1984, pp. 9–12; Peter Huber, "The I-Ching of Acid Rain," *Regulation*, September/December 1984, pp. 15–65; and Robert W. Crandall, "An Acid Test for Congress," *Regulation*, September/December 1984, pp. 21–28.

acid rain. When acid rain (also acid snow, acid fog, and dry acidic particles) falls on such a region, it can damage plants and aquatic life. There are areas of upper New York State and New England where trees are dying and lakes are crystal clear but devoid of fish. Acid rain is believed to be the cause of much of this damage.

The formation of acid rain begins with the release of sulfur dioxide and nitrogen oxides into the air. These compounds react with oxidizing agents to form sulfuric or nitric acid. Some of the acid that is formed is neutralized by alkaline substances that are also present in the air, such as limestone dust and ammonia gas.

Of all the many sources of sulfur dioxide and nitrogen oxides, by far the largest is combustion of coal. The burning of coal is believed to release some 27 million tons of sulfur dioxide into the air in the United States each year. About two thirds of this amount comes from electric utilities, especially those in the Ohio Valley. The prevailing winds in the eastern United States blow from west to east, so it is this Ohio Valley sulfur dioxide that is thought to be the source of the acid rain of New England and eastern Canada. (Although much acid rain is "exported" from the United States to Canada, some is also "imported" from industrial sources in Ontario.)

On the basis of this reading of the facts, it is proposed that sulfur dioxide emissions from coal-burning industries, especially in the Midwest, be reduced in the expectation that this will reduce the acidity of rain in the East and save eastern lakes and forests from further damage. On the surface this seems simple enough. However, when it comes to measuring costs and benefits, determining an optimal degree of cleanup, and choosing control methods, things turn out not to be so simple.

Measuring the Costs and Benefits

The basic facts of the chemistry of acid rain create a plausible case for controlling sulfur dioxide emissions. According to the logic of environmental economics, once the problem has been identified, the next step should be to estimate the costs and benefits of reducing emissions in order to calculate the optimum degree of reduction. Let's look first at the costs of abatement and then at the benefits, which take the form of reduced damage from acid rain.

Measuring the costs of abatement   The technology and economics of reducing sulfur dioxide emissions from coal-burning power plants have been studied extensively. Many, though not all, of the possible methods have received large-scale, practical trials. As a result, dollar costs for various degrees of reduction can be calculated much more accurately than in the cases of many types of pollution.

The cheapest way of reducing sulfur dioxide emissions appears to be switching from high-sulfur to low-sulfur coal. The most serious polluters among midwestern utilities are located close to sources of high-sulfur coal, which is mined in Illinois, Ohio, and some other states of the Midwest and Appalachia. There are some sources of low-sulfur coal in this region, and larger sources in the West. Taking into account higher transportation costs, the high price of low-sulfur coal, and the costs of converting boilers to burn a different type of coal, the cost of changing fuels is estimated at $250 per ton. It is estimated that about 6 million tons of the total of 27 million tons of sulfur dioxide from coal-burning sources could be eliminated through fuel switching.

The next least expensive method of reducing emissions is to buy dirty coal and clean it before it is burned. The technology for doing this is already in use in some places. It is estimated that an additional 1.5 million tons of sulfur dioxide emissions could be abated through fuel cleaning, at a cost of about $580 per ton.

Instead of cleaning the fuel, or in addition to doing so, it is possible to burn the fuel more cleanly. Several technologies for clean burning of coal have been developed, although none is yet in wide use. At present the costs of these methods are estimated at about $800 per ton of sulfur dioxide abated. The amount of reduction that could be achieved by these methods is not known for certain.

Finally, the most expensive option is to "scrub" the stack gases that come from the boiler after the fuel is burned. This method is in wide use (for reasons that will be explained shortly). Scrubbing costs about $1,000 per ton of sulfur dioxide abated—more when scrubbers are installed on existing plants rather than new ones. Scrubbing also creates a local environmental problem, namely, the disposal of thousands of tons of sludge. It is thought that the use of scrubbing in addition to other methods could bring the total reduction of sulfur dioxide emissions to 10 million tons per year.

This hierarchy of technologies implies a stair-step curve for the cost of pollution abatement, as shown in Box 29.10. In reading this diagram note that the level of pollution increases toward the right and that the degree of reduction of pollution increases toward the left.

Measuring the benefits of abatement   People benefit from the reduction of sulfur dioxide emissions to the extent that the social costs of pollution are reduced. As is the case with many types of pollution, far less is known about the benefits than about the costs. In the case of acid rain, there are three major sources of uncertainty.

One major source of uncertainty concerns the transportation of sulfur dioxide from coal-burning plants in the Midwest to vulnerable areas in the East. It is known that the prevailing winds in this region blow from west to east, but it is not possible at present to say which midwestern boilers emit the sulfur that falls in a given eastern lake. Knowledge of transportation patterns is important, because the greatest control effort should be focused on the sources that cause the most harm. At the other extreme, about a third of sulfur dioxide emissions blow out over the ocean. These are thought to cause little or no harm, since the ocean contains abundant alkaline material to neutralize acid rain.

An even greater area of uncertainty concerns the chemistry of acid rain. There are two possible conditions under which a reduction in sulfur dioxide emissions would fail to reduce the acidity of eastern rain. One possibility is that the formation of acid rain is limited not by the quantity of available sulfur dioxide but, rather, by the quantity of available oxidizing agents. The formation of acid rain is sometimes compared to baking a cake. Suppose each cake requires exactly two cups of flour (sulfur dioxide) and exactly one cup of sugar (oxidizing agents). If you have 20 cups of flour and 4 cups of sugar, you can bake only four cakes. A marginal reduction in your flour supply will not reduce your cake output. At present, scientists

Box 29.10
Marginal Costs of
Pollution Abatement for
Sulfur Dioxide

The costs of reducing sulfur dioxide emissions from coal-burning electric utilities has been studied extensively. As this chart shows, there is a hierarchy of methods—fuel switching, fuel washing, cleaner burning, and scrubbing—each more expensive than the one before. Ideally, pollution abatement policy would provide an incentive to use the least-cost methods first.

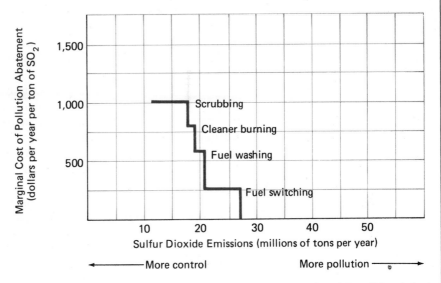

Source: Based on data given by Peter Huber, "The I-Ching of Acid Rain," *Regulation*, September/December 1984, pp. 59–60.

disagree as to whether it is the sulfur dioxide flour or the oxidizing sugar that limit the formation of acid rain. Thus, they are not sure whether a cutback in sulfur dioxide emissions will result in a proportional reduction in the acidity of rain.

Much the same holds true for the natural alkaline materials in the air that neutralize part of the acid rain before it falls. There is some evidence that variations in acid rain from time to time and place to place are associated more with variations in levels of alkaline materials than with levels of sulfur dioxide and nitrogen oxides. Once again, because the recipe for the cake calls for more than one ingredient, the marginal effect of changing the quantity of one of them is not certain.

The third uncertainty regarding the benefits of reducing sulfur dioxide emissions concerns the dollar value of the damage done by acid rain. Even if the chemical and biological effects of a given degree of abatement were known, they would still have to be converted into dollar terms to be compared with the costs of abatement. However, the uncertainties here are enormous. At least six areas of potential benefit have been identified:

Water resources. It is certain that excess acidity of lake and river water can kill fish and other aquatic life. It is likely that acid rain is a factor in the excess acidity of many lakes, especially in the Adirondacks. The economic loss in such cases would be represented by the impact of sport fishing, tourism, and aesthetic values.

Forests. Both in Europe and in the eastern United States, trees have been dying at unusually high rates in many of the areas where acid rain falls. However, these forests have also been exposed to ozone, heavy-metal pollution, drought, and colder-than-average winters. It therefore is not certain how quickly the health of the forests would respond to any given reduction in the acidity of rain.

Farming. In the case of many types of pollution, crop damage is one of the effects that can be assigned a dollar value. However, in view of the heavy treatment of farmland with both acid and alkaline chemicals, it is difficult to sort out the effect, if any, of a change in the acidity of rain.

Materials. Sulfur dioxide and other pollutants can attack a broad range of materials, including stone, metals, and paint. Using reasonable assumptions, it is easy to come up with figures in the hundreds of millions of dollars for pollution damage to materials. However, it is hard to separate the effects of acid rain from the effects of local pollution sources, such as automobile exhaust, that cause similar damage.

Human health. Sulfur dioxide in the air is known to be a health hazard. Thus, any effort to reduce sulfur dioxide emissions would presumably have some health benefits. It is also possible that acid rain causes health problems of its own by dissolving metals from the soil that then become incorporated in drinking water.

Visibility. The same chemicals that cause acid rain also cause the summer haze that hangs over much of the eastern United States. Thus, any effort to control acid rain would probably, as a by-product, improve visibility. This would have an impact on tourism, property values, and aesthetic values.

Striking a balance   Our review of the costs and benefits of controlling sulfur dioxide emissions makes it clear that the costs of abatement are large. The social costs of pollution are large too, but they are much harder to measure. Where does this leave us?

First, it is fair to say that we are nowhere close to knowing enough to determine the optimal quantity of pollution. We just don't know the point where the curves for marginal abatement costs and marginal social costs of pollution intersect. Any decision about how many tons of sulfur dioxide to allow into the atmosphere will have to be made on grounds other than dollars-and-cents comparisons of costs and benefits.

Second, it must be stressed that the fact that we have better numbers for the costs of abatement than for the benefits does not mean that the costs of abatement are larger than the benefits. There is no basis in science, economics, or logic for such a conclusion. It is true that under the too-much-flour-and-too-little-sugar hypothesis, spending $5 billion each year to take 10 million tons of sulfur dioxide out of the air might have no benefits at all. On the other hand, it should be kept in mind that some 50 million people live in the region affected by acid rain. It would take only $100 per person per year in benefits of all types—fish, trees, crops, paint, human lungs, and clear vistas—to justify the $5 billion. Since those same people currently spend thousands of dollars each in an average year on recreation, food, forest products, and home maintenance, $100 doesn't look like so big a number.

In the end, then, policymakers must choose between two arguments. On the one hand, some people say, "We don't know exactly how big a problem we have, so let's study it a little more before we spend billions of dollars trying to solve it." On the other hand, there are those who say, "We can't risk not spending the money now, because by the time we're sure how much damage is being done, it will be too late." Economics can offer only limited help in deciding this matter.

Choosing an Efficient Control Strategy

Economists may sit on the sidelines while engineers and scientists dominate the optimization debate. Once it is decided that an effort should be made to control sulfur dioxide emissions, though, the economists are eager to take the field and start calling the plays. "Whatever we decide to do," they say, "let's do it efficiently." Just what would an efficient strategy for acid rain control look like, and how does it compare with existing regulations and current proposals for change?

The least-cost principle   Economists may disagree about a lot of things, but they agree on one principle: If we are going to reduce sulfur dioxide emissions, less costly methods of doing so are better than more costly methods, assuming that the results are the same. This means starting on the lowest step of the marginal-cost-of-abatement schedule shown in Box 29.10, and then moving upward along it one step at a time. Two economic strategies for pollution control seem well suited to ensuring that this principle will be followed. One is a pollution tax and the other a system of marketable permits.

In Box 29.10 a tax of, say, $400 per ton would produce a 6-million-ton cutback; one of $1,000 per ton would produce a 10-million-ton cutback, and so on. Each plant would choose the combination of fuel switching, fuel cleaning, combustion technology, and scrubbing that was best suited to local conditions. The total cost of reaching the goal would be a minimum figure. If policymakers guessed wrong and set the tax too low, it could be raised later.

As an alternative, marketable permits could be issued that would allow a total of, say, 17 million tons of sulfur dioxide per year—10 million tons less than at present. Firms with clean boilers or nearby sources of clean coal would presumably sell some of their permits to others who could not clean up as cheaply. In Box 29.10 the market price of permits would rise to $1,000 per ton, equal to the height of the marginal-cost curve for pollution abatement at the 17-million-ton limit. Again, costs would be minimized.

If these ideas are too radical for policymakers to accept, economists have a third proposal. Set a specific emission target for each plant, but leave it up to local managers to determine the method of control to use. This would be less efficient than a pollution tax or a system of marketable permits. The reason is that plants that could clean up cheaply would have no incentive to reduce emissions by more than the minimum required amount. However, it would leave cost-cutting incentives in place for managers on a plant-by-plant basis.

Current regulations   Current regulations for control of sulfur dioxide are pretty much the opposite of what economists recommend. In its 1977 amendments to Section 111 of the Clean Air Act, Congress required that any newly constructed electric power plant must meet the emissions limit by scrubbing, the most expensive available technology. The scrubbing requirement applies regardless of how clean or dirty the plant's fuel or combustion technology is. Many old plants, including some of the dirtiest plants that burn the most sulfurous midwestern coal, were not forced to scrub. Instead, they were allowed to meet standards for local pollution by building tall smokestacks—up to 1,000 feet high—that keep the air in surrounding communities fairly clean. Unfortunately, the tall stacks put the sulfur dioxide right up where the chemical mischief is done that turns it into acid rain. They simply turned a local problem into a national one—or, more correctly, an international one, keeping Canada in mind.

Why on earth did Congress choose such a seemingly irrational approach to controlling sulfur dioxide emissions? The answer lies in the nature of the coalition that passed the Clean Air Act and its amendments. The coalition included these elements:

- Environmentalists, who were not able to swing a majority in Congress by themselves and were willing to enter an unholy alliance on the theory that any pollution control measures were better than none.
- Coal-mining interests in the high-sulfur areas of Ohio, Illinois, and elsewhere, which were afraid that fuel switching would mean the shifting of mining jobs from their regions to other parts of the country.
- Politicians from eastern and midwestern states who wanted to stop the flight of industry to western and southern states. By focusing control efforts on newly built plants, the Clean Air Act gives old, dirty plants a few more years of life. And by focusing on scrubbing rather than fuel switching, the act makes sure that coal-burning plants in the South and West are not able to exploit the cost advantage they would otherwise be given by a location close to sources of low-sulfur coal.

This coalition appears still to be alive in the Congress of the mid-1980s. In 1984 Congress considered, but did not pass, several acid rain bills. Those that have the best chance of making it into law continue to call for scrubbing. Don't look for an efficient solution soon.

Summary

1. The trade-offs that must be faced in making environmental policy can be illustrated with a production possibility frontier. The horizontal axis represents environmental quality and the vertical axis represents all other goods and services. An optimal policy puts the economy at a point on the frontier that represents the balance between environmental quality and other goods that best suits the interests of present and future members of society.

2. The task of determining the optimal quantity of pollution can be approached through marginal analysis. The *marginal social cost of pollution* is the total additional cost to all members

of society of an additional unit of pollution. On a graph where the horizontal axis represents the level of pollution, with pollution increasing toward the right, the marginal social cost of pollution can be shown as an upward-sloping curve. The *marginal cost of pollution abatement* is the cost of reducing pollution by one unit. It is shown by a downward-sloping curve. The optimal quantity of pollution is shown by the intersection of these two curves. At that point the marginal social cost of pollution equals the marginal cost of pollution abatement.

3. An efficient pollution control policy is one that puts the economy on its production possibility frontier. A policy can be efficient without being optimal if it puts the economy on the frontier, but at a point that has too much or too little pollution. Given the difficulty of determining the optimal quantity of pollution, many economists think that efficiency is a reasonable goal for policy.

4. The marginal cost of pollution abatement curve can be viewed as a demand curve for pollution opportunities. The shape of the supply curve for pollution opportunities depends on pollution control policy. A pollution charge would result in a horizontal supply curve. A policy of marketable pollution permits would produce a vertical supply curve. And a rights-based policy, under which people could collect damages from polluters through the court system, would produce a supply curve that coincided with the curve that represents the marginal social cost of pollution.

5. The acid rain issue illustrates many of the problems of environmental policy. The costs of abatement are large and fairly well understood. The benefits of controlling acid rain via the reduction of sulfur dioxide emissions are less well understood but may also be large. There appears to be little chance of determining the optimal level of pollution. However, economists recommend that whatever level of pollution control is chosen, it should be achieved efficiently. This means that incentives should be provided to use the least-cost methods of pollution control first. Current policy for controlling sulfur dioxide emissions often results in control costs that are higher than necessary.

Questions for Review

1. Define the following terms:
   marginal social cost of pollution
   marginal cost of pollution abatement
2. Draw a production possibility frontier to represent the trade-off between environmental quality and other goods. What is meant by a movement along this frontier? Under what conditions could the frontier shift outward?
3. Why does the marginal cost of pollution abatement curve slope downward, and why does the marginal social cost of pollution curve slope upward?
4. How can the tools of supply-and-demand analysis be applied to the issue of pollution?
5. What prevents an optimal solution to the acid rain problem? What prevents an efficient solution to the problem?

Problems and Topics for Discussion

1. Draw a production possibility frontier for "energy" and "environmental quality." How can you use this frontier to illustrate the story about pollution in Louisiana? What other uses can you think of for this frontier?
2. Review Boxes 29.2–29.4. Draw a new graph in which the horizontal axis measures "environmental quality" (that is, degree of pollution control) instead of quantity of pollution. What are the shapes of the curves representing the

marginal cost of pollution abatement and the marginal social cost of pollution when plotted on this new set of axes? Which version of the curves do you find easier to explain?

3. Where do you stand on the issue of environmental rights? Do you think people (or other species) have some environmental rights that ought to be upheld regardless of the economic cost of doing so? Discuss.

4. In discussing a tax as a pollution control strategy, we said nothing about what would be done with the revenues raised by the tax. These might be quite large. For example, it has been estimated that a $1,000-a-ton tax on sulfur dioxide emissions would raise some $15–$20 billion. What do you think should be done with these revenues if the tax is imposed? Consider, among others, the following possibilities: (a) using the tax as general revenue to pay for normal government spending; (b) returning the proceeds of the tax to the industry that pays it, so that firms will not have to pass the cost of the tax along to consumers; (c) spending the tax only on environmental projects such as toxic waste cleanup, maintaining national parks, and so on; and (d) spending the revenue to benefit people who are hurt by pollution control measures—for example, miners of high-sulfur coal.

5. Under a system of marketable pollution permits, the market value of permits could be quite high. For example, in the case of permits that limit sulfur dioxide emissions to 17 million tons per year, the permits might have a total market value of about $17 billion. Considering the value of the permits, how should they be distributed to electric utilities and other coal-using firms? Should they be sold by the government? Should they be given away? If they are given away, should they be given away in proportion to current pollution levels? In proportion to electricity output? According to some other rule? Consider both efficiency and fairness in answering these questions.

6. Review the section on public choice at the end of Chapter 5. Comment on the politics of acid rain in the light of public choice theory.

7. **Case for Discussion**

In 1982, during a deep recession, the U.S. Forest Service lost $740 million selling timber from the national forests for lumber, paper, and other wood products. These losses, a result of below-cost timber sales on many forests, confirm what public land experts have long known: National forests are managed uneconomically at best, to the detriment of taxpayers, the environment, and the timber industry. Over the last decade, if below-cost timber sales had been eliminated in both good and bad years, the federal treasury would have netted at least $2 billion more.

While lamentable and contrary to the clear intent of the law, this situation is far from surprising. Born of the need to conserve the nation's timber resources nearly a century ago, the Forest Service has traditionally shunned the use of economic criteria in planning and management decisions. It continues to rely on an obsolete pricing system that often fails to recover the government's cost of growing and selling trees.

As a result, the Forest Service engages in commercial timber harvesting on millions of acres of public land where timber values are so low that profit-oriented landowners would not consider building roads and cutting trees. Several studies show that the most consistent losses are in the Rocky Mountains and in Alaska. Financially unsound logging destroys wilderness values, hindering the growth of recreation industries and the diversification of the local economy.[4]

Questions:

a. What parallels do you see between the problem of pollution and the problem of destruction of the wilderness through logging? Which of the concepts in this chapter apply to the case of logging?

b. What kind of policy would you recommend for logging on public land? Would you try to establish an optimal policy? An efficient one? One based on rights? Discuss.

---

[4]Peter Emerson, Anthony T. Stout, and Deanne Kloepfer, "The Feds Can't See Their Losses in the Trees," *Wall Street Journal*, November 11, 1984. Reprinted by permission of The Wall Street Journal, © Dow Jones & Company, Inc. 1984. All rights reserved.

Suggestions for Further Reading

The Cato Journal, Spring 1982.

This special issue is devoted to articles about rights-based strategies of environmental policy.

Mills, Edwin S. *The Economics of Environmental Quality*. New York: Norton, 1978.

A thorough treatment of environmental policies and problems from an economic point of view, including a historical sketch of environmental policy in the United States.

Stroup, Richard L., and John A. Baden. *Natural Resources: Bureaucratic Myths and Environmental Management*. Cambridge, Mass.: Ballinger, 1983.

The authors stress a public-choice approach to environmental questions. Their book spends much time discussing problems of public land use as well as problems of pollution.

Levin, Michael H. "Building a Better Bubble at EPA." *Regulation*, March/April 1985, pp. 33–42.

An insider's account of progress toward implementing market-oriented pollution control strategies at the Environmental Protection Agency.

In labor markets employees can change jobs or go on strike to seek better salaries or working conditions. This picture shows a strike at Fairleigh Dickinson University.

Part VII
Factor Markets
and Income
Distribution

Chapter 30

Factor Markets and Marginal Productivity Theory

Ideas for Review

Here are some terms and concepts that you should review before reading this chapter:

Marginal utility (Chapter 20)
Consumer equilibrium (Chapter 20)
Marginal physical product (Chapter 21)
Law of diminishing returns (Chapter 21)
Perfect competition (Chapter 22)
Monopoly (Chapter 23)

"At that time the average annual earnings of employed women nationwide were only about 60 percent of those of employed men."

In the early 1970s Governor Dan Evans of the state of Washington became concerned about the fact that the state was paying women employees less, on the average, than men. This situation was not exceptional; at that time the average annual earnings of employed women nationwide were only about 60 percent of those of employed men. But Evans wanted to know why the pay gap existed. Was it because women chose occupations that were worth less to the state than the occupations that men chose? Or was it because the state was paying women less than men even when they held jobs that were worth just as much as those held by men?

In an attempt to find out, Evans hired the consulting firm of Norman D. Willis & Associates to do a job evaluation study for the state. In such a study, points are assigned to each job for such factors as working conditions, risks, education required, problem-solving skills required, and responsibility. Many employers use such studies as an aid to setting pay scales for different job categories.

The study discovered that women, on the average, were found in occupations with lower point scores. However, the difference in choice of occupations was not enough to explain the whole wage gap. Even when adustments were made for differences in point scores, jobs in which 70 percent or more of the employees were women tended to be paid about 20 percent less than jobs in which 70 percent or more of the employees were men. Sometimes women were paid less even when their jobs were rated higher in terms of points. For example, electricians (mostly men), whose jobs were rated at 197 points were paid some $600 more per month than guidance counselors (mostly women), whose jobs were rated at 209 points.

The state did not immediately act to change its pay policies on the basis of the Willis study, partly because it feared that raising women's pay would be too costly. However, in 1982 the American Federation of State, County, and Municipal Employees sued the state over the issue. In 1984 it won the suit. Judge Jack E. Tanner ordered the state to raise the pay of women employees to a level equal to that paid to men in jobs of comparable worth. The case became an instant landmark in a debate over women's pay that has now become nationwide.[1]

Factor markets
The markets in which the factors of production—labor, capital, and natural resources—are bought and sold.

The Washington State pay equity case draws attention to an important set of markets that have been referred to only indirectly up to this point. That set of markets is **factor markets**—the markets in which labor, capital, and natural resources are bought and sold. Factor markets perform two major functions in a market economy: They help determine how goods and services are produced and for whom they are produced. In this chapter and the next three we will look at both functions.

Factor markets are important in determining how goods and services are produced because most goods and services can be produced in more than one way. Wheat, for example, can be grown by means of extensive cultivation of large areas of land with a lot of machinery and little labor, or by means of intensive cultivation of small areas with little machinery and

---

[1]Based in part on Daniel Seligman, "Pay Equity Is a Bad Idea," *Fortune*, May 14, 1984, pp. 133–140.

much labor. The choice of production methods depends on the relative prices of the factors. As those prices change, production methods can change too. Factors that are relatively cheap are used intensively; those that are relatively expensive are used sparingly.

At the same time, factor markets help determine for whom output is produced, because most people earn their incomes by selling whatever factors of production they own. The greatest number sell their labor services. Many also sell or rent capital or natural resources that they own. Because markets determine factor prices, they also determine how much of the total product will go to the owners of labor services, capital, and natural resources.

This chapter and the next three will explore both of these functions of factor markets. The first part of this chapter will outline marginal productivity theory—the foundation of the economics of factor markets. The later part of the chapter will apply the theory of marginal productivity to determining the relative wages of various occupations. Chapter 31 will discuss the role of unions in labor markets. In Chapter 32 we will turn to two other factor markets—those for natural resources and capital—and will also discuss profits as a source of income. Finally, Chapter 33 will take up the problem of poverty. It will show how the operation of factor markets helps determine the incidence of poverty and will discuss government policies aimed at reducing or eliminating poverty.

THE DEMAND FOR FACTORS OF PRODUCTION

The Firm in Factor Markets

In many ways factor markets are much like the product markets we have already studied. The theories of supply and demand and the tools of marginal analysis apply to factor markets just as they do to product markets. But factor markets differ from product markets in one major respect. In factor markets, firms are the buyers and households are the sellers, rather than the other way around. A theory of the demand for factors of production must be based on the same considerations of price, revenue, and profit that determine the supply of products. A theory of factor supply must be an extension of the theory of consumer choice.

In taking the first steps toward a theory of factor demand, we will assume, as always, that firms aim to maximize their profits. Each profit-maximizing firm must take three things into account when it buys factors of production. The first is the amount of output produced by a unit of the factor in question; the second is the revenue derived from the sale of the output that will be produced; and the third is the cost of obtaining the factor.

Marginal Physical Product

Chapter 21 defined the *marginal physical product of a factor* as the change in output that results from a one-unit increase in the input of that factor when the amount of all other factors used stays the same. For example, if using one additional worker-hour of labor in a light bulb factory yields an added output of five light bulbs, when no other input to the production process is increased, the marginal physical product of labor in that factory is five bulbs per worker-hour.

The law of diminishing returns   As Chapter 21 showed, the marginal physical product of a factor varies as the amount of the factor used varies, other things being equal. In particular, as the quantity of a single factor increases, with the quantities of all other factor inputs remaining fixed, a point will be reached beyond which the marginal physical product of the variable factor will decline. This principle is known as the *law of diminishing returns*.

Box 30.1 shows total and marginal physical product curves for a firm that is subject to the law of diminishing returns over the range from zero to 20 units of factor input. (At this point it does not matter whether the factor in question is labor, capital, or natural resources; the principle is the same for all.) As the amount of this factor is increased, with the amount of all other factors used held constant, output increases—but at a diminishing rate. The first unit of the factor yields a marginal physical product of 20 units of output, the second a marginal physical product of 19 units of output, and so on. After the twentieth unit of output, marginal physical product drops to zero. This implies that some ceiling has been reached, so that adding more of the variable factor cannot produce more output unless the inputs of some of the fixed factors are also increased. For example, if the variable factor is labor, it may be that adding more than 20 workers will do nothing to increase output unless, say, the amount of machinery available for use by the workers is also increased. Beyond 20 units of output, where the marginal physical product of the variable factor drops to zero, the total physical product curve becomes horizontal.

Marginal Revenue Product

To determine what quantity of each factor of production it should buy to maximize its profit, a firm must take into account the revenue that will be earned from sale of the output of an added unit of factor input as well as the size of the marginal physical product. Here a new term will be useful. The change in revenue that results from the sale of the output produced by one additional unit of factor input is called the **marginal revenue product** of that factor.

Marginal revenue product
The change in revenue that results from the sale of the output produced by one additional unit of a factor of production.

Marginal revenue product for a competitive firm   What happens to the marginal revenue product of a factor as the amount of that factor is varied depends on what happens to both the marginal physical product of the factor and the marginal revenue earned by selling the product. The simplest case to consider is that of a perfectly competitive firm. Because such a firm is a price taker, as shown in Chapter 22, the amount of output it produces has no effect on the price at which its output is sold. Marginal revenue for the competitive firm thus is equal to the price of the firm's output, which is constant for all quantities of output. To calculate the marginal revenue product of a factor for such a firm, then, we multiply the marginal physical product of the factor by the price of the output.

Box 30.1
Total and Marginal
Physical Product of a
Factor of Production

As the quantity of one factor increases with the quantity of other factors remaining unchanged, total physical product increases, but at a decreasing rate. As part c of this box and column 3 of the table in part a show, marginal physical product decreases as the quantity of the factor employed increases. This decrease is a direct result of the law of diminishing returns.

(a)

Quantity of Factor (1)	Total Physical Product (2)	Marginal Physical Product (3)
0	0	20
1	20	19
2	39	18
3	57	17
4	74	16
5	90	15
6	105	14
7	119	13
8	132	12
9	144	11
10	155	10
11	165	9
12	174	8
13	182	7
14	189	6
15	195	5
16	200	4
17	204	3
18	207	2
19	209	1
20	210	

Box 30.2 gives an example of how marginal revenue product is calculated for a perfectly competitive firm. The marginal physical product schedule is the same as that given in Box 30.1, and a constant price of $1 per unit of output is assumed.

Marginal revenue product for a monopolist

If the firm is not perfectly competitive, the price at which it sells its output will tend to vary as the amount of output varies. Suppose, for example, that the firm is a pure monopolist. As Chapter 23 showed, a pure monopolist must decrease the price at which its product is sold each time it wants to increase the quantity sold, in accordance with the downward-sloping demand curve for its product. Because the price per unit decreases as output increases, marginal revenue per unit of output is always less than price per unit for a monopolist.

To calculate the increase in revenue that results from a one-unit increase in factor input for a monopolist, then, we must take into account changes in both marginal physical product and marginal revenue. Box 30.3 shows how this is done. The box uses the same total physical product schedule as in Boxes 30.1 and 30.2, but this time the firm is assumed to be a monopolist. Column 3 gives the firm's demand curve, showing that the price at which output can be sold drops from $1.40 per unit at 20 units of output to $0.45 at 210 units of output. Multiplying price times total physical product gives the total revenue that corresponds to each quantity of factor input, shown in column 4.

The differences between successive entries in the total-revenue column give the marginal revenue product data, shown in column 5. For example, as the amount of factor input increases from 4 units to 5 units, the total output increases from 74 units to 90 units, while the price falls from $1.13 per unit to $1.05. As column 4 shows, total revenue increases from $83.62 when 4 units of factor input are used to $94.50 when 5 units of factor input are used. This gives a marginal revenue product of $10.88 in the range from 4 to 5 units of factor input.

As the price continues to fall, marginal revenue eventually becomes negative. Beyond that point, additional units of factor input, even though they increase the total physical product, reduce total revenue. In our example, the turning point comes at 10 units of factor input. Beyond that point, marginal revenue product is negative even though marginal physical product remains positive.

At every level of factor input, the marginal revenue product of the factor is equal to the marginal physical product times the marginal revenue per unit of output. This relationship is shown in columns 5–7 of Box 30.3. The marginal-revenue figures in column 7 are expressed in terms of dollars per unit of output, whereas the marginal revenue product figures in column 5 are expressed in terms of dollars per unit of factor input.

Marginal Factor Cost

Marginal factor cost
The amount by which a firm's total factor cost must increase in order for the firm to obtain an additional unit of that factor of production.

The third thing a firm must consider in determining the profit-maximizing quantity of a factor is the cost of obtaining each additional unit of that factor—its **marginal factor cost**.

To keep things simple for the moment, consider only the case in which a firm is a price taker in the market where it buys its factors of

Box 30.2
Marginal Revenue Product for a Typical Price-Taking Firm

For a price-taking firm, the marginal revenue product of a factor is equal to the factor's marginal physical product times the price of the product. This table assumes that the product price is $1 per unit and that marginal physical product is the same as in Box 30.1.

Quantity of Factor (1)	Total Physical Product (2)	Marginal Physical Product (3)	Revenue per Unit (price) (4)	Marginal Revenue Product (5)
0	0			
1	20	20	$1	$20
2	39	19	1	19
3	57	18	1	18
4	74	17	1	17
5	90	16	1	16
6	105	15	1	15
7	119	14	1	14
8	132	13	1	13
9	144	12	1	12
10	155	11	1	11
11	165	10	1	10
12	174	9	1	9
13	182	8	1	8
14	189	7	1	7
15	198	6	1	6
16	200	5	1	5
17	204	4	1	4
18	207	3	1	3
19	209	2	1	2
20	210	1	1	1

production. This will happen if the firm is only one of a large number of firms that are competing to hire that particular factor and if the amount of the factor it uses is only a small fraction of the total used by all firms. For a firm that buys as a price taker, marginal factor cost is equal to the market price of the factor. If, for example, the market wage rate for typists is $7 an hour, then the marginal factor cost for this particular type of labor is $7 an hour for any firm that is a price taker in the market for typists.

Profit Maximization

In order to maximize profits, a firm must hire just enough of each factor of production to equalize marginal revenue product and marginal factor cost. If marginal revenue product exceeds marginal factor cost, hiring one more unit of the factor will add more to the revenue than to the cost and hence will increase profit. If marginal factor cost exceeds marginal revenue product, reducing input of that factor by one unit will reduce cost by more than revenue and hence will also increase profit. Only when marginal revenue product and marginal factor cost are equal will it be impossible for

**Box 30.3
Marginal Revenue
Product for a
Monopolistic Firm**

This box shows how marginal revenue product varies as the quantity of factor input varies for a firm that is a pure monopolist. As column 3 shows, price falls as outputs increase, in accordance with the demand for the firm's product. Total revenue begins to decrease after ten units of input, as marginal revenue per unit of output becomes negative, even though marginal physical product remains positive. Marginal revenue product can be calculated either as the difference between each entry in the total-revenue column or as the product of marginal physical product and marginal revenue per unit of output.

Quantity of Factor (1)	Total Physical Product (2)	Price of Output (3)	Total Revenue (4)	Marginal Revenue Product (5)	Marginal Physical Product (6)	Marginal Revenue per Unit of Output (7)
0	0	—	0			
				$28.00	20	$1.40
1	20	$1.40	$ 28.00			
				22.90	19	1.21
2	39	1.31	50.90			
				18.36	18	1.02
3	57	1.22	69.26			
				14.36	17	.84
4	74	1.13	83.62			
				10.88	16	.68
5	90	1.05	94.50			
				7.88	15	.52
6	105	.98	102.38			
				5.32	14	.38
7	119	.91	107.70			
				3.18	13	.24
8	132	.84	110.88			
				1.44	12	.12
9	144	.78	112.32			
				.06	11	.01
10	155	.73	112.38			
				−1.00	10	−.10
11	165	.68	111.38			
				−1.76	9	−.20
12	174	.63	109.62			
				−2.24	8	−.28
13	182	.59	107.38			
				−2.48	7	−.35
14	189	.56	104.90			
				−2.52	6	−.42
15	195	.53	102.38			
				−2.38	5	−.47
16	200	.50	100.00			
				−2.08	4	−.52
17	204	.48	97.92			
				−1.66	3	−.55
18	207	.47	96.26			
				−1.16	2	−.58
19	209	.46	95.10			
				−.60	1	−.60
20	210	.45	94.50			

Figures in columns 3, 4, 5, and 7 are rounded to the nearest cent.

any change in factor input to raise profit. In equation form, this rule can be stated as

$$MFC = MRP$$

where MFC stands for marginal factor cost and MRP for marginal revenue product. The rule applies both to a firm that is a perfect competitor in its output market and to a monopolist.

Box 30.4 illustrates this profit maximization rule. The box, which contains a table and a corresponding graph, assumes that the firm is a perfect competitor in the output market and that it sells its product at $1 per unit, as in Box 30.2. The firm is also assumed to be a price taker in the factor market, buying inputs of the factor at $5 per unit. Notice that profit

Box 30.4
Profit Maximization for a
Price-Taking Firm

Maximizing profits requires that a firm buy just enough of each factor of production to equalize marginal revenue product and marginal factor cost. Here it is assumed that the firm is a price taker, as in Box 30.2. The point of profit maximization falls between 15 and 16 units of input.

(a)

Quantity of Factor (1)	Marginal Revenue Product (2)	Marginal Factor Cost (3)	Total Variable Cost (4)	Fixed Costs (5)	Total Revenue (6)	Total Profit (7)
1	$19	$5	$ 5	$100	$ 20	−$85
2	18	5	10	100	39	−71
3	17	5	15	100	57	−58
4	16	5	20	100	74	−46
5	15	5	25	100	90	−35
6	14	5	30	100	105	−25
7	13	5	35	100	119	−16
8	12	5	40	100	132	−8
9	11	5	45	100	144	−1
10	10	5	50	100	155	5
11	9	5	55	100	165	10
12	8	5	60	100	174	14
13	7	5	65	100	182	17
14	6	5	70	100	189	19
15	5	5	75	100	195	20
16	4	5	80	100	200	20
17	3	5	85	100	204	19
18	2	5	90	100	207	17
19	1	5	95	100	209	14
20		5	100	100	210	10

(b)

rises as more of the factor is purchased—up to the fifteenth unit of input. The firm just breaks even on the purchase of the sixteenth unit of input, and thereafter profit declines. It is between the fifteenth and sixteenth units of factor input that marginal revenue product becomes exactly equal to marginal factor cost.

Factor Demand Curves

It follows from this analysis that when a firm is a price taker in the factor market, its marginal revenue product curve for a factor is also its demand curve. A demand curve must indicate the quantity demanded at each price, and it has been shown that the quantity of the factor demanded by such a firm will be whatever quantity makes the factor's price (and thus its marginal factor cost) equal to marginal revenue product.

Individual firms' demand curves for a factor of production can be added together to get a market demand curve for that factor. Such a market demand curve is said to be a *derived demand curve*, because the demand for a factor of production does not arise from the usefulness of the factor services themselves. Instead, it is derived indirectly from the usefulness of the products the factor can produce. The market demand for farmland is derived from the market demand for food, the market demand for printers from the market demand for books, and so on.

Changes in Factor Demand

The demand for factors, like the demand for products, changes in response to changes in economic conditions. Look at Box 30.5. Suppose that the demand curve D_0 is the market demand curve for some factor of production. A change in the market price of that factor will cause the quantity of the factor demanded to change. This is represented by a movement along the demand curve. (See the arrow parallel to D_0.) Changes in economic

---

**Box 30.5
Movements Along a
Factor Demand Curve
and Shifts in the Curve**

Changes in the price of a factor, other things being equal, will produce movements along a factor demand curve, as shown by the arrow. Other kinds of changes can shift the curve. An increase in demand for the product produced by the factor might shift the curve from D_0 to D_1. An increase in the price of another factor that is a complement to the given factor might shift the curve from D_0 to D_2.

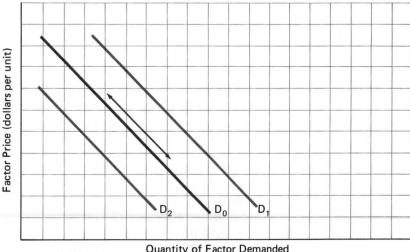

conditions other than a change in the factor's price can cause a change in demand for a factor—for example, a shift in the demand curve from D_0 to D_1 or D_2.

Three kinds of changes are capable of causing shifts in the demand curve for a factor of production. First, an increase in demand for the output that the factor produces will shift the factor demand curve to the right. A decrease in demand for that output will cause the factor demand curve to shift to the left. Second, a change in the price of another factor of production that is used in combination with the given factor can also cause the demand for the given factor to shift. An increase in the price of a factor that is a substitute for the given factor will cause the demand curve for the given factor to shift to the right; an increase in the price of a factor that is a complement to the given factor will cause the demand curve of that factor to shift to the left. Third, any change in technology that increases the marginal physical productivity of a factor will cause its demand curve to shift to the right, other things being equal; any decrease in the marginal physical product of the factor will shift the curve to the left.

SUPPLY AND DEMAND IN THE LABOR MARKET

Up to this point, marginal productivity and factor demand have been discussed in general terms. It is time now to turn to the specifics of markets for particular factors. This section begins the analysis of such markets by looking at the supply and demand for labor. The discussion will be limited at first to the case in which individual workers compete with one another for jobs. The next chapter will take up the case of organized labor markets, in which workers form unions to bargain with employers rather than competing with one another for jobs. Finally, Chapter 32 will look at markets for capital and natural resources.

The Labor Supply Curve

The general analysis of factor demand given in the previous section can be applied to the labor market without major changes. However, we need a labor supply curve to go with the labor demand curve. A look at the labor supply decision for an individual worker will begin the analysis.

Labor supply for the individual   As individuals, people's decisions about how much labor to supply to the market are part of the general problem of consumer choice and can be analyzed in terms of the theory developed in Chapter 20. The best way to approach the problem is to think in terms of a trade-off between two sources of utility—leisure and the consumption of purchased goods and services. Leisure is valued for relaxation, recreation, and the completion of certain household tasks. Time spent at leisure is time taken away from work, however, and thus is time taken away from earning income that can be used to buy goods and services. Within the limits of a 24-hour day, people balance the advantages of work and leisure to achieve an equilibrium in which, ideally, the marginal utility per hour of leisure exactly equals the marginal utility of the goods that can be bought with an hour's earnings.

The hourly wage rate can be thought of as the price—or, more precisely, the opportunity cost—of leisure to the worker in that it represents the dollar equivalent of the goods and services that must be sacrificed in order to enjoy an added hour of leisure. As the wage rate increases, it affects work-versus-leisure decisions in two ways. First, there is a substitution effect; the increased wage rate provides an incentive to work more, because each hour of work now produces more income to be spent on goods and services. That is, purchased goods and services are substituted for leisure. Second, however, the increase in the wage rate has an income effect that tends to reduce the number of hours worked. The higher wage rate, assuming that the prices of goods and services remain unchanged, increases workers' real incomes. With higher real incomes, workers tend to consume more of goods that are normal goods and less of those that are inferior goods. Leisure is a normal good. Other things being equal, people generally seek more leisure, in the form of shorter working hours and longer vacations, as their incomes rise. Taken by itself, then, the income effect of a wage increase is a reduction in the amount of labor supplied by workers.

It can be seen, therefore, that the net effect of an increase in the wage rate on the amount of labor supplied by an individual worker depends on the relative strength of the substitution and income effects. It is generally believed that for very low wage rates the substitution effect predominates, and therefore the quantity of labor supplied increases as the wage increases. As the wage rate rises, however, the income effect becomes stronger. People tend to treat leisure as a luxury good; after they have assured themselves of a certain material standard of living, they begin to consider "spending" any further wage increases on more time off from work. The labor supply curve for such a person has a backward-bending shape like the one shown in Box 30.6. Over the positively sloped low-wage section the substitution effect of wage changes predominates, and over the negatively sloped high-wage section the income effect predominates.

Market labor supply curves   Even though the labor supply curves for individual workers may bend backwards, at least over some range of wages, the supply curve for any given type of labor as a whole is likely to be positively sloped throughout. Consider, for example, the supply of electrical engineers in New York, the supply of typists in Chicago, or the supply of farm laborers in Texas. Beyond some point, each individual engineer or typist or laborer might respond to a wage increase by cutting back on the number of hours worked, but for the market as a whole this tendency would be more than offset by new workers drawn into that labor market from other occupations or areas. Thus, other things being equal, if the wage rate for electrical engineers in New York rose, more engineering students would take up that specialty; if the wage rate for typists in Chicago rose, more people would become typists than, say, filing clerks; and if the wage rate for farm laborers in Texas rose, workers would be drawn in from Arizona, Florida, and Mexico. As a result, for any discussion of the market for a particular category of labor at a particular time and place it is reasonable to draw the labor supply curve with the usual positive slope, as in Box 30.7, regardless of the shape of the individual labor supply curves underlying it.

**Box 30.6
An Individual's Labor
Supply Curve**

On the one hand, a higher wage tends to increase the amount of work that a person is willing to do, since the extra money makes up for time taken away from leisure pursuits. On the other hand, a higher wage allows a person to take more time off from work and still enjoy a high standard of living. Taken together, the two effects tend to give the individual labor supply curve the backward-bending shape shown here.

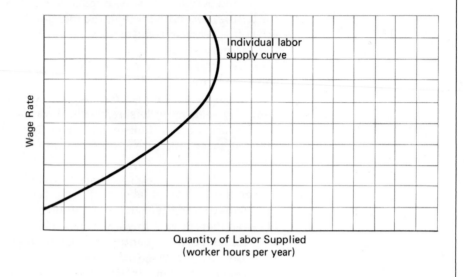

**Box 30.7
A Hypothetical Supply
Curve for Typists**

Although each individual typist may have a backward-bending supply curve, the supply curve for typists in any local market will have the usual upward-sloping shape. As the wage rises, people will be drawn into this occupation from other kinds of work or other localities.

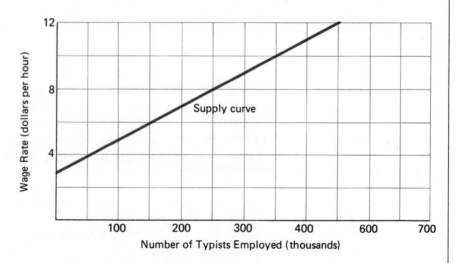

Competitive Equilibrium

Determining the wage rate in a labor market that is fully competitive on both sides is a simple matter of supply-and-demand analysis. Box 30.8, for example, shows supply and demand curves for the labor market for typists in Chicago. It assumes that a large number of typists compete for jobs and that a large number of employers compete for typists, so both are price takers. The demand curve for typists is the employers' combined marginal-revenue curve. The supply curve is the same as that in Box 30.7.

Equilibrium in this market requires a wage rate of $7 an hour, with 200,000 typists employed. If the wage rate were lower, there would be a shortage of typists. Some firms, unable to fill all their job openings, would offer premium wages to workers from other jobs or other regions. The wage rate would thus be driven up to the equilibrium level. If, on the other hand, the wage rate was above $7 an hour, there would be a surplus of typists. Many people would be looking for typing jobs and not finding them. After a long enough search, some would be willing to accept work at lower-than-expected wages, thereby pushing the wage rate down toward equilibrium. Others would drift into other occupations or regions.

In a labor market like this one, where both employers and employees are price takers, the equilibrium wage rate is equal to the marginal revenue product of labor. In the special case in which all employers are price takers (perfect competitors) in the market where they sell their output as well as in the market where they purchase inputs, the equilibrium wage rate is equal to the marginal physical product of labor times the price per unit of output.

**Box 30.8
Determination of the
Equilibrium Wage in a
Competitive Labor
Market**

When both employers and workers are price takers in the labor market, the point of equilibrium is found where the supply and demand curves intersect. Here the equilibrium wage rate is $7 an hour and the equilibrium quantity of labor is 200,000 typists.

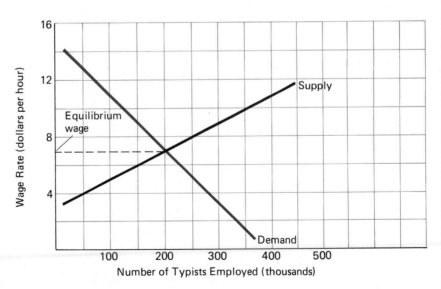

The Marginal Productivity Theory of Distribution

Supply and demand determine how much each worker earns as well as how much labor will be used in making each product. When employers are price takers in the markets in which they buy inputs, profit maximization requires that each factor be used up to the point at which its marginal revenue product is equal to its price. This suggests that each unit of each factor receives a reward that is equal to the contribution it makes to the firm's revenue. The idea that factors are rewarded according to their marginal productivity is known as the **marginal productivity theory of distribution**.

Marginal productivity theory of distribution
A theory of the distribution of income according to which each factor receives a payment equal to its marginal revenue product.

In an economy in which all markets—not only input markets but output markets as well—are perfectly competitive, the marginal productivity theory applies in an even stronger form. In this case marginal revenue product is equal to output price times marginal physical product. In such an economy the reward that each unit of each factor receives is equal to the value of its marginal physical product. If an extra hour's labor in a T-shirt factory produces two extra T-shirts and each T-shirt sells for $5, the wage rate must be $10 an hour—no more, no less.

This principle of distribution, in which every factor receives a reward equal to the value of its marginal product, appeals to some people as being both efficient and fair. The reward of every worker is exactly equal to the contribution of that worker to the productive process. If a worker or a factor owner withholds a unit of productive services from the market, that person will suffer a loss of earnings exactly equal to the value of production that is lost to the economy as a whole.

Monopsony

Monopsony
A situation in which there is only a single buyer in a market.

Not every factor market meets the conditions required for the marginal productivity theory of distribution. The extreme situation in which there is only one buyer in a market is called **monopsony**. Unlike a firm that is a perfect competitor in the market where it buys its inputs, a monopsonist is not a price taker. For such a firm the wage rate is not a given; instead, the wage that must be paid increases as the number of workers hired increases.

Compare the situation of a retail store in Albuquerque that wants to hire a few security guards with that of the U.S. government, which wants to hire soldiers for its volunteer army. The retail store is a price taker in the market for security guards. If the going wage for such guards is, say, $11,000 a year, it can call an agency or put an ad in the paper and get as many guards as it wants at that price. The situation of the government as the employer of volunteer soldiers is very different. Experience with the volunteer army has shown that the success of recruitment efforts depends on the level of military pay. For example, in the late 1970s real military pay decreased slightly as pay increases failed to keep up with inflation. This left some military specialties understaffed. In the early 1980s a combination of military pay raises and slack demand for labor in the civilian economy made it possible to fill many of those positions again.

Normally, if a monopsonist decides to raise its wage offer in order to attract new workers, it must also raise the wages of the workers who are already on its payroll by a comparable amount. To do otherwise—that is, to pay newly hired workers more than those who had been on the job for some time—would be harmful to worker morale. But the need to pay a higher wage to all workers, not just those who are newly hired, means that the monopsonist's marginal factor cost is actually higher than the wage rate paid to the new workers themselves. Box 30.9 shows why, using as an example the supply of typists in a small town where one big employer— say, an insurance company—employs all or almost all of the town's typists.

**Box 30.9
Marginal Factor Cost
Under Monopsony**

Under monopsony, marginal factor cost exceeds factor price. Consider an increase in quantity from 150 to 151 units of labor. The wage rate must be raised from $6 to $6.02 not just for the 151st employee but for all the previous 150 as well. Marginal labor cost in this range thus is $9.02 an hour, not $6.02 an hour.

(a)

Quantity of Labor Supplied (1)	Wage Rate (2)	Total Factor Cost (3)	Marginal Factor Cost (4)
1	$3.02	$ 3.02	$ 3.06
2	3.04	6.08	
3	3.06	9.18	3.10
150	6.00	900.00	
151	6.02	909.02	9.02
152	6.04	918.08	9.06
200	7.00	1,400.00	
201	7.02	1,411.02	11.02
202	7.04	1,422.08	11.06

(b)

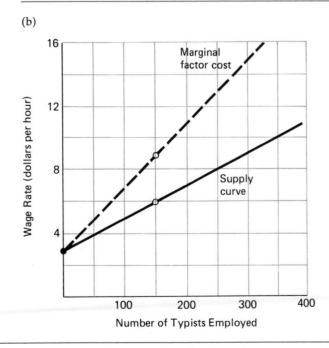

The supply schedule of typists shows that no one will work as a typist if the wage rate is $3 an hour or less. Above that wage, each extra two cents per hour will attract one more worker. Suppose that the monopsonistic employer has hired 150 typists, paying them $6 an hour. The total labor cost for a labor force of this size is $900 an hour. What will happen to the firm's total labor cost if it expands its labor force by one worker?

According to the supply curve, hiring 151 typists requires a wage of $6.02 an hour. That wage must be paid not just to the 151st worker but to all workers. The total cost of a labor force of 151 typists, then, is $6.02 times 151, or $909.02. The addition of one more worker has raised the total labor cost from $900 to $909.02, a marginal factor cost of $9.02. The result is much the same whatever starting point is chosen. In every case the marginal factor cost for the monopsonist is greater than the factor price (in this case, the wage rate).

Part b of Box 30.9 shows a marginal factor cost curve based on the marginal factor cost column of the table in part a. This curve lies above the supply curve at every point. The relationship between the supply curve and the marginal-factor-cost curve for a monopsonist is similar to the relationship between the demand and marginal-revenue curves for a monopolist.

**Box 30.10
Determination of
Wages Under
Monopsony**

Here are a monopsonist's marginal revenue product of labor curve, labor supply curve, and marginal factor cost curve. The quantity of labor required to maximize profits is found at the point where the marginal revenue product curve and the marginal factor cost curve intersect. The equilibrium wage rate is not shown by the intersection of the marginal factor cost and marginal revenue product curves. Instead, the rate is equal to the height of the supply curve directly below that intersection.

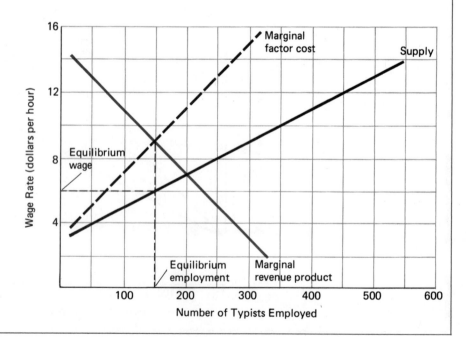

Monopsony Equilibrium

Given the monopsonist's marginal factor cost curve—derived from the factor's market supply curve—determining the equilibrium level of employment for the firm is a routine matter. Box 30.10 shows the monopsonistic employer's marginal revenue product curve along with the labor supply and marginal factor cost curves from Box 30.9. Following the general rule that profit is maximized when marginal factor cost is equal to marginal revenue product, the monopsonist will hire 150 typists at a wage rate of $6 an hour.

When a labor market is in monopsony equilibrium, the wage rate is lower than both the marginal factor cost and the marginal revenue product of labor. In the example just given, the equilibrium wage rate is $6 an hour (which is equal to the height of the labor supply curve), although the marginal revenue product is $9 an hour at the point where the marginal revenue product and marginal factor cost curves intersect. Despite the gap between the wage rate and the marginal revenue product, an increase in the amount of labor hired will not increase revenue by enough to offset higher labor costs. The reason is that the cost of hiring another worker is not just the $6.02 an hour that must be paid to the 151st worker but that sum plus the extra two cents per hour by which the wages of all 150 previously hired workers must be raised. The complete marginal factor cost for the 151st worker thus is $6.02 + $3.00, or $9.02 an hour. We see, then, that the marginal productivity theory of distribution does not apply in a monopsonistic labor market. In such a market workers are paid a wage that is less than their contribution, at the margin, to the employer's revenue.

WHY WAGE RATES DIFFER

Up to this point we have been concerned with the forces that determine the wage rate paid in each particular labor market. Now we turn to the question of what causes wages in one labor market to differ from those in another. Why are typists in New York City paid more than people doing the same job in Goshen, Indiana? Why are people with engineering degrees paid more to work in industry than to teach engineering at a university? And to come back to the story with which this chapter opened, why are many jobs filled mainly by men paid more than apparently comparable jobs filled mainly by women?

Shifts in Demand

We will begin with differences in demand, which are a major cause of wage differences, especially in the short run. Box 30.11 shows the effects of shifts in demand on wage rates. Two closely related labor markets are pictured—the market for typists and the market for word processor operators. As word processors replace typewriters in many offices, the demand for word processor operators shifts to the right and that for typists shifts to the left. The wage rate for word processor operators rises from W_1 to W_2 as this market moves up along the short-run supply curve to a new equilibrium at E_2. At the same time, the wage rate of typists falls.

**Box 30.11
Demand Shifts and
Relative Wages**

Shifts in demand can affect the relative wages of different occupations. This pair of graphs compares the market for word processor operators with that for typists. In the short run, increasing demand for word processor operators shifts that demand curve to the right and pushes wages up. Meanwhile the demand for typists decreases, leading to a fall in wages. In the long run, the supply curves for both types of workers will be more elastic than in the short run. If the demand curves remain in their new positions, then, the difference in pay will disappear.

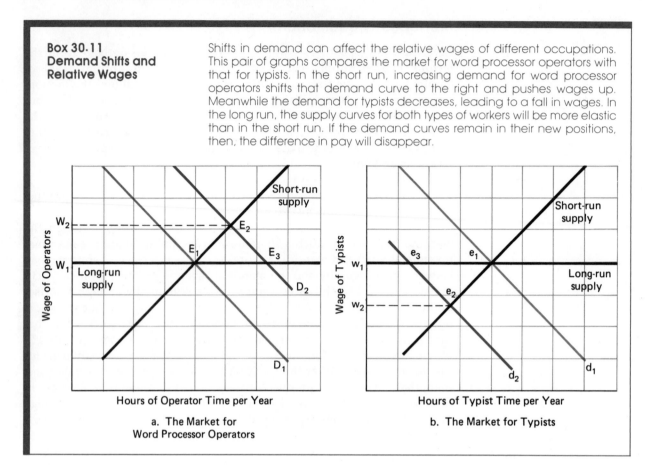

a. The Market for
Word Processor Operators

b. The Market for Typists

This situation cannot prevail in the long run, however. It is no more difficult to learn how to use a word processor than it is to use a typewriter. Not all people who are experienced typists will learn how to use the new machines, but most people entering secretarial occupations will do so. In the long run, then, we expect the supply curve of both typists and word processor operators to be more elastic than in the short run. Here we assume the long-run supply curves in both markets to be perfectly elastic. In this case we can expect the wage differential between word processor operators and typists to disappear in the long run. As that happens, the markets move to long-run equilibriums at E_3 and e_3, respectively.

Earlier in the chapter we discussed various sources of shifts in labor demand curves. In the case of typists and word processor operators, the shifts were caused by a fall in the price of word processors. Word processors are a complement to the labor of word processor operators, so the falling price of the machines shifts the demand curve for those workers to the right. At the same time, word processors are a substitute for the labor of typists, so a decline in their price shifts the demand curve for typists to the left.

Because the demand for factors of production is a derived demand, shifts in labor demand curves can also be caused by shifts in demand for the product. For example, in recent years the demand for restaurant meals has increased faster than the average demand for other goods and services. This has shifted the demand curve for restaurant workers to the right.

**Box 30.12
The Effects of
Discrimination on
Wage Rates and Hours
Worked**

This box shows the effect of discrimination in a labor market that can be divided into a group of workers who are favored by employers and a group that is disfavored. They two groups of workers are assumed to be equal in terms of productivity, but the demand curve for the disfavored group is shifted to the left of the corresponding marginal revenue product curve. If there are no equal-pay laws, the pay of the disfavored group will fall to the level W_2, below the level of W_1 received by members of the favored group. If the law requires equal pay, both groups will receive the wage W_1, but fewer members of the disfavored group will be employed. Many members of the disfavored group who would be willing to work in this occupation at the wage W_1 will be forced into other, less attractive sectors of the job market or into unemployment. With or without the equal-pay law, then, discrimination is harmful to the disfavored group.

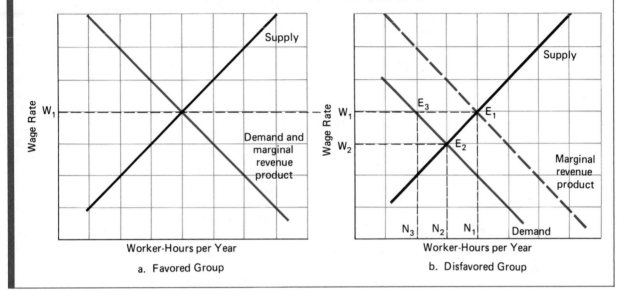

a. Favored Group

b. Disfavored Group

Discrimination

Discrimination is a second demand-related factor that can affect the relative wages of different groups and occupations. Employers can be said to discriminate against a group of workers if they are unwilling to hire them at the same wage rate that they pay to equally productive members of a more favored group.

Box 30.12 shows the effects of discrimination in the labor market. Part a shows the supply and demand curves for workers in the favored group. The demand curve in this market is the marginal revenue product curve, as explained earlier in the chapter. Part b shows the supply and demand curves for workers in the disfavored group. In this market the demand curve is shifted to the left relative to the marginal revenue product curve. This indicates that employers will hire members of the disfavored group only if they are more productive than members of the favored group or if they are equally productive but will work for less.

Equilibrium under discrimination   Two types of equilibrium are possible under discrimination. First assume that there are no legal restrictions on discrimination. In this case the wage rate for the disfavored group will fall to W_2 compared to a wage of W_1 for the favored group. Workers from the two groups will then work side by side, doing the same job, but will receive different pay. All members of the disfavored group who want to work at the wage W_2 will be able to find jobs in this market.

In the second case we assume that the law prohibits paying different wages to members of different groups for doing the same work. This is the situation in the United States since passage of the Equal Pay Act of 1963. In this case employers must pay the wage W_1 to members of both the favored and disfavored groups. As a result, they will employ only N_3 worker-hours per year from the disfavored group.

The effect of the equal-pay law on members of the disfavored group is mixed. On the one hand, members of that group who are employed in this market get paid more than they would without the law. On the other hand, fewer workers from the disfavored group get jobs at the wage W_1. Those who do not get jobs in this market either remain unemployed or are crowded into some other sector of the labor market, possibly one in which employers do not discriminate. However, whether employers in those other markets discriminate or not, wages there will be pushed down by the increased supply of workers who are unable to find jobs in the market shown in Box 30.12.

In the end, then, discrimination lowers the average wage of members of the disfavored group even when the law requires equal pay for all workers doing a given job, and even when there are some markets in which employers do not discriminate. Many women's-rights activists see this as a major factor in the pay gap between men and women. They think that discrimination holds down the number of women employed in high-paying executive and skilled-labor positions. As a result, wages are forced down in such occupations as nursing, teaching, and secretarial work, in which employers are as willing to hire women as men.

Competition and discrimination   Our analysis of discrimination in labor markets is not yet complete. We have looked at the effects of discrimination on workers but not at the effect on employers. At first it might seem that employers gain from discrimination in that it pushes down the wages of members of disfavored groups. However, this is true only to the extent that employers are united in the desire to discriminate. Looking at the matter from the point of view of a single employer, there is a strong incentive not to discriminate.

Consider the case in which there is no equal-pay law. In that case the wage rate for workers from the disfavored group is lower than that of workers from the favored group. Employers who set their prejudices aside and hire only workers from the disfavored group will have a distinct cost advantage over employers who discriminate. This cost advantage will allow them to undercut the prices of their competitors, perhaps driving them out of the market or at least forcing them to change their hiring practices. In the long run competition will tend to eliminate both the practice of discrimination and the pay gap.

Even if there is an equal-pay law, an employer can gain a competitive advantage by not discriminating. In this case, although all employers pay the same wage, the nondiscriminating employer can skim off the most productive members of the disfavored group. The advantage gained by doing so can be seen in Box 30.12 as the vertical gap between the wage rate

W_1 and the marginal revenue product curve at the employment level N_1. Once again, this competitive advantage would tend to bring an end to discrimination.

All in all, the situation of discrimination in the labor market is much like that of a cartel, which was discussed in Chapter 23. Discriminating employers or cartel members can gain as long as they are united. But in practice each has an incentive to cheat on the system. Just as cartel members are pulled by the profit motive to undercut their fellow members, so also are employers pulled by the profit motive to abandon established patterns of discrimination. Box 30.13 looks at these forces in the case of the southern states of the United States in the Jim Crow era. In that case competition and the profit motive undermined discrimination to such an extent that states had to pass laws that, in effect, forced employers to discriminate.

Most economists see competition as a force that tends to break down discrimination, but this does not mean that competition alone will eliminate discrimination. Pockets of discrimination can survive for a number of reasons. In some cases discrimination might originate with the customer, not the employer. If, say, car owners didn't trust women mechanics to fix their cars, there would be no incentive for employers of mechanics to hire women even if they knew them to be competent. In other cases employers might be shielded from market forces. Government employers are one example. It is no accident that some of the major targets of the drive for equal pay for women have been city and state governments. And in Chapter 4 we mentioned the belief of some economists that managers of large corporations do not always share their stockholders' interest in maximum profits. If the head of such a corporation liked to hire only white males even when more highly qualified women or minority candidates were available, he might be able to get away with doing so, at least for a time, provided profits did not fall so low as to trigger a stockholder rebellion or a takeover bid. Finally, it is possible that some employers simply are not aware of the costs of discrimination.

Nonwage Characteristics of Jobs

We turn now to a set of factors that operate from the supply side to cause differences in wage rates. The first of these is the nonwage characteristics of jobs—their interest, safety, prestige, challenge, and so on. Other things being equal, workers are willing to supply their services at lower wages to employers who offer jobs with attractive nonwage characteristics. Many employers know this and try to make the jobs they offer safe, attractive, and challenging.

Of course, not everyone's idea of a good job is the same. Some economists see differences in nonwage job characteristics as one of the reasons for the pay gap between jobs that are held mainly by men and those that are held mainly by women. For example, at least in the past, women, on the average, have entered and left the labor force much more often than men. The desire to do so may lead many women to choose occupations, such as clerical and secretarial work, in which it is relatively easy to enter and leave employment, even though these jobs do not pay as well as some others. Some studies have found that the pay gap between men and women who have never married is much smaller than that

Box 30.13
Exploitation and the Law in the Jim Crow South

In the southern United States in the Jim Crow era (the 1890s through the early 1950s), there was no lack of discrimination against black workers. Especially in the early part of the period, the economy was dominated by white planters who employed large numbers of blacks. As a group, they had an interest in holding down the wages of black farm workers, both to boost their own profits and to maintain the dominant position of the white race.

There was one problem, however: The greed of many white employers overcame racial solidarity. Despite warnings in newspapers that "white men must stick together," the employers competed for black labor. Black workers often left their jobs for higher-paying ones, especially at harvest time, when labor was in short supply. In addition, labor recruiters from the North would appear in the South to entice black workers to come to work in the North's growing industries at wages that, while low by today's standards, were still better than those paid by the southern planters. Something had to be done to protect the traditional system of exploitation against erosion by market forces. The solution was the following set of labor laws, which were passed in most southern states between 1890 and 1910:

Enticement laws made it a crime for white employers to "entice" a worker who had a contract with another employer. The aim was to prevent competition for workers that might bid up wages.

Contract enforcement laws made it a crime for a black worker to break a labor contract with a white employer in order to seek work elsewhere. The standard contract period was one year. The aim was to prevent competition at harvest time, when the demand for labor was strongest.

Vagrancy laws made it a crime for any person who was able to work to "wander or stroll in idleness." The aim was to keep black workers in the labor force and to prevent them from spending time between jobs shopping around for the best wage offer.

Emigrant-agent laws curbed the activities of labor recruiters from other states or even other counties. For example, a law passed by the city of Montgomery, Alabama, imposed a $100 fine or six months in jail on anyone who printed, published, wrote, delivered, posted, or distributed any advertisement that tried to persuade people to leave the city to seek work elsewhere.

Finally, the *convict lease system* allowed black prisoners, including those who had been imprisoned for violating contract or vagrancy laws, to be leased to private employers. Being on the chain gang was worse than being a slave: Since the lease was short term, the employer, unlike a slave owner, did not even have an interest in preserving the worker's health.

The economist Jennifer Roback, in a study of the Jim Crow labor laws, finds that they were effective in keeping wages down and limiting migration. She concludes that without the laws, competition would have undermined the system of exploitation.

Source: Jennifer Roback, "Exploitation in the Jim Crow South: The Market or the Law"? *Regulation*, September–December 1984, pp. 37–44. A longer version of the article appears in the *University of Chicago Law Review*, Fall 1984.

---

between men and married women. This may be in part because the never-married women spend more of their working-age years in the labor force and thus are more likely to choose careers in which steady labor force membership is important.[2]

---

[2]See Walter Williams, "Explaining the Economic Gender Gap," National Center for Policy Analysis, Dallas, November 1983. Among others studies, Williams cites one by Solomon Polachek that found that married women college graduates spend 36 percent of their working-age years in the labor force, compared with 89 percent for never-married women college graduates.

Human Capital and Special Abilities

Special abilities are another factor that affects the supply of labor for certain occupations. Some people are born with special abilities, or at least with unusual potential for developing them. The enormous salaries of professional ballplayers, first-rate opera singers, and so on are a direct result of the scarcity of those abilities.

But abilities that people are born with are only part of the story. Training is a more important factor in the supply of workers for most occupations. The salaries of lawyers, accountants, glass blowers, and hairdressers depend to a large extent on the cost of training. The natural abilities required for these occupations are not very scarce. Many more people could acquire the training needed to practice them than actually do so.

Economists view the costs of training as a form of investment. Taking courses to become an accountant, in this view, is much like buying a dump truck in order to go into the business of hauling gravel. In both cases an expenditure is made now to acquire something that will increase one's future earning power. The main difference lies in the fact that the dump truck operator acquires capital in the form of a machine, whereas the accountant acquires **human capital**—capital in the form of learned abilities.

Human capital
Capital in the form of learned abilities that have been acquired through formal training or education or through on-the-job experience.

According to human-capital theory, the earnings of each occupation that requires special training must be high enough to make up for the opportunity cost of getting the training. In the case of a person going to college to acquire a degree in accounting, the opportunity cost includes both the costs of tuition, books, and so on, and the income that could have been earned if the college years had been spent working in an occupation that did not require a college degree. (See Box 2.2, p. 27, for a fuller discussion of the opportunity costs of a college education.) Other things being equal, we would expect occupations that require longer or more expensive training to pay more than those that call for less training. Thus, we expect doctors to earn more than lawyers, lawyers to earn more than hairdressers, and so on.

Of course, allowance must also be made for factors other than human capital that also affect the supply of people for various occupations. If certain occupations are more exciting or prestigious than others, people may be willing to enter them even if the pay alone is not enough to justify the investment in training. For example, college graduates earn more than nongraduates, but not enough more, on the average, to offset the full opportunity costs of spending four years in college. However, people do not go to college solely for the monetary rewards of doing so. In part, they are motivated by the nonwage characteristics of the jobs they are preparing for. In part also, they may be motivated by the enjoyable nature (we hope!) of the college experience itself.

Formal education is by no means the only way to invest in human capital. On-the-job training is also important. On-the-job training may be specific, such as learning how to run certain kinds of machinery, or it may be general, such as learning good work habits, learning how to work with other people, and learning how to supervise others.

Differences in human capital are believed to be another factor in explaining the pay gap between men and women. For one thing, the large numbers of women who entered the labor force for the first time during the 1970s had less education and experience, on the average, than male workers. Also, the fact that in the past women have spent a smaller percentage of their working-age years in the labor force has affected their human capital. Partly this is because they acquire less human capital on the job. And partly it is because such women, knowing that they will not work full-time for all of their working-age years, have had less incentive to invest in formal education and training.

It is almost certain that the human-capital gap between men and women will narrow in coming years and that the wage gap will narrow with it. Partly this will happen because the large numbers of women who have entered the labor force in the past 15 years will gain in experience and seniority. In addition, young women today appear to expect to be in the labor force for more of their working-age years and therefore are more willing to invest in training and education.

Conclusions

We have looked at a number of things that affect the pay of one job compared with that of another. Some result from choices made by workers themselves—choices based on nonwage characteristics of jobs, choices involving investment in human capital, and choices of whether to remain in the labor force all the time or only part of the time. Other things that affect wage rates are beyond the control of individual workers—shifts in demand, discrimination, and natural abilities. (Two other factors that affect wages remain to be discussed: labor unions, which will be covered in the next chapter, and minimum wage laws, which will be covered in Chapter 33.) What, if anything, can we say in conclusion about the system by which wages are determined? Is it a good one? A fair one?

Economists generally praise wages determined by supply and demand as an efficient solution to the problem of how to produce goods and services. Market-based wages encourage employers to balance the marginal productivity of labor against that of other factors of production in such a way as to choose more efficient methods of production. Market wages give people an incentive to invest in human capital—a major source of growth for the economy. And markets tend, though not always perfectly, to punish employers who waste human resources through discriminatory hiring practices.

There is less agreement about the fairness of a system in which women, on the average, earn only 64 percent as much as men, blacks only 77 percent as much as whites, and Hispanics only 78 percent as much as the average for all workers. Some argue that these differences are largely a result of differences in education, age, experience, career choices, and so on. The important thing, these people say, is to make sure everyone has an opportunity to compete for jobs on equal terms. As long as that is the case, there is no reason to insist on equality of results.

Others, however, do not see formal equality of opportunity as enough. They see women and minority group members as victims of discrimination, often in forms that are too subtle to be dealt with by existing laws. These views have given rise to demands for stronger laws governing the pay practices of both private and public employers. One such demand that is likely to be pushed strongly in coming years is the demand for equal pay for work of comparable worth. In practice, this means pay based on job evaluation studies, as in the Washington State case, rather than pay based on supply and demand alone.

Many economists tend to be critical of these proposals. For one thing, they see them as a threat to the efficient operation of the labor market. Also, they fear that comparable-worth measures, while helping some workers, will crowd others out of the job market. Others, however, see comparable-worth laws as a necessary cure for imperfections in the labor market. The debate is sure to remain a lively one for years to come.

Summary

1. Factor markets play an important role in determining how goods and services are produced. When factor prices change, firms tend to modify their production methods, using less of factors that have become more expensive and more of those that have become cheaper. At the same time, factor markets help determine for whom goods and services are produced, since payments for the services of labor, capital, and natural resources are the main source of income for most households.

2. For a perfectly competitive firm, the *marginal revenue product* of a factor is equal to the factor's marginal physical product times the price of the product. For a monopolistic firm, it is equal to marginal physical product times marginal revenue. In both cases, the firm makes the maximum profit by buying each factor up to the point at which marginal revenue product equals *marginal factor cost*. Thus, the marginal revenue product curve is the factor demand curve.

3. The demand for a factor of production is said to be a *derived demand* because it depends on the demand for the goods or services that the factor produces. An increase in demand for the product shifts the factor demand curve to the right; a decrease in demand for the product shifts the factor demand curve to the left. Changes in the prices of factors that are substitutes or complements for a given factor, as well as changes in technology, can also cause shifts in factor demand curves.

4. Labor supply curves depend on the trade-off that people make between leisure and the goods and services that can be bought with income earned in the labor market. The labor

supply curve for an individual worker and perhaps for the economy as a whole may bend backwards above a certain wage rate. However, the supply curve for a single labor market (say, the supply of typists in Chicago) is positively sloped throughout its length.

5. In a labor market in which employers compete for workers and workers compete for jobs, the equilibrium wage rate will be equal to the marginal productivity of labor. This is known as the marginal revenue product theory of distribution. If employers are also perfect competitors in the market in which they sell their output, then the equilibrium wage rate will be equal to the value of the marginal product.

6. *Monopsony* means a situation in which there is only one buyer of factor services in a given market. The marginal factor cost curve for such a firm lies above the supply curve of labor. Equilibrium is established at the intersection of the marginal factor cost curve and the marginal revenue product curve. In such a market the equilibrium wage is not equal to marginal revenue product.

7. Shifts in the demand for a factor of production can cause wages in one labor market to differ from those in another. Over time, the differences are reduced as workers move from one market to the other. Discrimination against a group of workers can shift the demand for their labor to the left of the marginal revenue product curve. A firm that does not discriminate in hiring tends to have a cost advantage over competing firms that discriminate. This fact limits the extent to which discrimination can be practiced in a competitive market.

8. Anything that affects the supply curve of labor

can affect relative wages. Other things being equal, people will work at lower wages in a job that has attractive nonwage characteristics, such as safety, interest, or status. The supply of employees for some positions, such as professional sports and the performing arts, is limited by the scarcity of natural ability. In other occupations training is a greater constraint on labor supply. The opportunity cost of training for an occupation can be thought of as the cost of an investment in *human capital*.

Questions for Review

1. Define the following terms:
   factor markets
   marginal revenue product
   marginal factor cost
   marginal productivity theory of distribution
   monopsony
   human capital

2. What role do factor markets play in determining how goods and services are produced? In determining for whom they are produced?

3. What is the relationship between the marginal revenue product of a factor of production and the price of the product when the firm is a perfect competitor in the market where it sells its output? When it is a monopolist in the market where it sells its output?

4. What is the factor market equilibrium condition for a profit-maximizing firm?

5. Why is it possible for one person's labor supply curve to have a negatively sloped sec-

tion above a certain wage rate? Why do the labor supply curves for individual labor markets not have such negatively sloped sections?

6. According to the marginal productivity theory of distribution, what is the relationship between the wage rate and the value of the product in equilibrium?

7. In what way is the factor market equilibrium condition for a monopsonistic firm like that for a competitive firm? In what way is it different?

8. List three changes in economic conditions that can cause the demand curve for a factor of production to shift to the left or right. How do such shifts affect the relative wages of different jobs in the short run? In the long run?

9. List three factors that affect the supply of labor to a particular market. How does each affect the relative wages of different jobs?

Problems and Topics for Discussion

1. The chapter discusses only factor markets in which the buyers are firms. Are households ever direct buyers of factors of production? For example, are you the direct buyer of a factor of production when you hire someone to type a term paper for you? How would the theory of factor markets have to be modified to take into account cases in which the buyers of factor services are households rather than firms?

2. For readers who have completed the Chapter 21 appendix on isoquants or wish to read that appendix now: Use an isoquant diagram to derive the demand curve for a factor of production. You may need to refer to the deriva-

tion of a product demand curve in Box 20A.7 (p. 521).

3. In his historical novel *Chesapeake*, James Michener describes the unsuccessful efforts of early European colonists to run their plantations with hired Native American labor. Among the many factors that led to the breakdown of relationships between the planters and local tribes were some economic problems. For example, Michener reports the frustration of a planter who finds that an offer of higher wages does not prevent his native workers from quitting their jobs in the fields after a few weeks of work. In fact, the workers

seem to quit sooner when their pay is raised. Does what you have learned in this chapter shed any light on this problem? Discuss.

4. Is a monopsonist always a monopolist, and vice versa? Try to imagine a firm that is a monopsonist in its factor market but a perfect competitor in its product market. Then try to imagine a firm that is a monopolist but not a monopsonist.

5. Discuss the following statement: "It is a good idea to let factor markets determine how things are produced, but the matter of for whom things are produced should be handled according to need, not according to supply and demand." Is it possible to separate the "how" and "for whom" functions of factor markets?

6. Turn to Box 3.11 (p. 68), which discusses the market for dentists' services. In this case, how have demand shifts affected the earnings of dentists relative to those of other workers? How long is the "long run" in the case of dentists? What evidence do you find in the discussion that a long-run adjustment is taking place? In what way will the short-run and long-run equilibriums in this market be affected by investment in human capital?

7. Between 1973 and 1983 the male-female wage gap narrowed somewhat, and it is expected to narrow further later in this century with or without comparable-worth legislation. Do you think the narrowing of the wage gap has anything to do with the facts that (a) women are more than proportionately represented in service occupations and (b) demand for services is growing more rapidly than demand for goods? Discuss.

8. "Equal pay for equal work is not enough. Employers must also be required to follow affirmative-action guidelines or hiring quotas for members of disfavored groups." Comment on this statement in the light of what you have learned in this chapter.

Suggestions for Further Reading

Goodman, John C., and Edwin G. Dolan. *Economics of Public Policy*, 3rd ed. St. Paul: West, 1985.

Chapter 12 discusses the issue of equal pay for work of comparable worth.

Treiman, Donald J, and Heidi I. Hartmann, eds. *Women, Work, and Wages*. Washington, D.C.: National Academy Press, 1981.

A study of the comparable-worth issue.

Wallace, Mark J., and Charles H. Fay. *Compensation Theory and Practice*. Boston: Kent, 1983.

Discusses issues of pay from a business manager's point of view.

Chapter 31

Labor Unions and Collective Bargaining

After reading this chapter, you should be able to

1. Review the history of labor unions in the United States.
2. Summarize the main elements of labor law.
3. Use supply and demand curves to show the effects of labor unions in competitive and monopsonistic markets.
4. Discuss the impact of unions on wages, fringe benefits, and wage equality.
5. Discuss the impact of unions on aspects of labor-management relations other than wages.

Ideas for Review

Here are some terms and concepts that you should review before you read this chapter:

Opportunity cost (Chapter 2)
Perfect competition (Chapter 22)
Monopoly (Chapter 23)
Monopsony (Chapter 30)

"If I'd had anything I'm really sold on, it's the UAW."

"Everybody has to have something they're really sold on. Some people go to church. If I'd had anything I'm really sold on, it's the UAW [United Auto Workers].

"I started working at Fisher Body in 1917 and retired in '62, with 45 and 8/10 years service. Until 1933, no unions, no rules: you were at the mercy of your foreman. I could go to work at seven o'clock in the morning, and at seven fifteen the boss'd come around and say: you could come back at three o'clock. If he preferred somebody else over you, that person would be called back earlier, though you were there longer.

"I left the plants so many nights hostile. If I were a fella big and strong, I think I'd a picked a fight with the first fella I met on the corner. It was lousy. Degraded. You might call yourself a man if you was on the street, but as soon as you went through the door and punched your card, you was nothing more or less than a robot. Do this, go there, do that. You'd do it.

"We got involved in a strike in Detroit, and we lost the strike. Went back on our knees. That's the way you learn things. I got laid off in the fall of '31. I wasn't told I was blackballed, but I was told there was no more jobs at Fisher Body for me."[1]

In the labor markets discussed in the last chapter, workers competed with one another for jobs as individuals. Many autoworkers, steelworkers, truck drivers, garment workers, and others do not enter the labor market as individuals, however; instead, they do so as members of unions. When Bob Stinson (the former autoworker just quoted) was fired from General Motors' Fisher Body division in 1931, unions were poised for a period of growth. Their membership rose to 35 percent of the nonfarm labor force by 1945. (See Box 31.1.) Union membership has fallen since then, but even though fewer than a fifth of all workers belong to unions today, they still deserve a separate chapter. Partly this is because they are strongest in such key industries as automobiles, steel, and transportation. Partly also it is because wage settlements and labor-management relations in unionized firms strongly influence those in nonunionized firms.

This chapter will examine what labor unions are and what they do. The chapter begins with a brief history of unions in the United States. Next it looks at the effects unions have on wages, and finally it discusses some of the effects unions have on aspects of work life other than wages.

THE HISTORY OF UNIONISM IN THE UNITED STATES

Earliest Beginnings

Unions had their start in the United States toward the end of the eighteenth century. In the 1790s craft workers, including printers, shoemakers, and carpenters, formed local associations to further their economic

---

[1]From an interview with Bob Stinson, former autoworker, in Studs Terkel, *Hard Times: An Oral History of the Great Depression* (New York: Pantheon Books, 1970), p. 129. Reprinted by courtesy of Pantheon Books, a Division of Random House, Inc.

**Box 31.1
Labor Union
Membership in the
United States,
1935–1984**

After the passage of the Wagner Act in 1935, unions began a period of rapid growth. Membership peaked at a little over a third of the nonfarm labor force ten years later. Since then union membership as a percentage of the nonfarm labor force has declined steadily.

*Other than agriculture
**Troy and Sheflin

Source: For 1935–1980, Bureau of Labor Statistics. The official series was discontinued in 1980. Later data are estimates by Leo Troy and Neil Sheflin of Rutgers University.

interests. By the end of the century, printers and shoemakers in Boston, Philadelphia, New York, and other cities of the eastern seaboard were bargaining collectively with employers.

Craft union
A union of skilled workers who all practice the same trade.

These earliest labor groups, called **craft unions**, were organizations of skilled workers, all in the same trade. Their skills and shared interests made it relatively easy for them to work together in union activities and gave their organizations some degree of monopoly power in dealing with employers.

But most of the the early local craft unions were short-lived. They faced many problems. It was not until 1842, for example, that the courts recognized unions as legal. Even after that date the courts were often unfriendly. Furthermore, few of the early local unions were strong enough to survive the frequent business downturns of the period. As soon as business activity declined, they lost most of their bargaining power. They then faded away, to be organized again in the next period of prosperity.

The Knights of Labor

Unionism did not take root on a wide scale until after the Civil War. At that time national unions began to appear, and local unions joined them as chapters. The most prominent of the national labor organizations in the post–Civil War period had the colorful name of the Noble Order of the Knights of Labor. This organization was founded as a secret society in 1869, but its growth began only after it abandoned secrecy in 1878. Membership reached a peak of more than 700,000 workers in 1886.

Many local unions of skilled craft workers were affiliated with the Knights of Labor, but the Knights were much more than an association of craft unions. The Knights welcomed anyone who worked for a living, including farmers, farm workers, and unskilled laborers. Only such "undesirables" as bankers, liquor dealers, Pinkerton detectives, and lawyers were excluded. The Knights' program was not limited to economic concerns. It also stressed worker education and producer cooperatives as ways of combating the "evil of wealth."

The broad scope of the Knights of Labor permitted rapid growth but also led to the eventual decline of the group. After 1886, conflicts between the Knights and its member unions increased, and some of the more discontented unions left the organization. Moreover, public hostility was aroused by the killing of a policeman during Chicago's Haymarket Riot of 1886, although no connection of the Knights with that event was ever proved. From that year on, however, the Knights of Labor lost ground to the American Federation of Labor.

The AFL

The American Federation of Labor, or AFL (first called the Federation of Organized Trades and Labor Unions), was founded in 1881. Its founders included some independent craft unions and some local craft affiliates of the Knights of Labor that felt that the bargaining power of skilled craft workers would be wasted in efforts to win benefits for unskilled workers. Since 1886 the AFL has played a dominant role in union history.

The AFL found strong leadership under Samuel Gompers, its president for all but one year from 1886 until his death in 1924. (See Box 31.2.) Gompers sought to avoid the mistakes that had led to the downfall of the Knights of Labor. The AFL owes its success largely to three features of its organization and philosophy that were prominent from its earliest years.

1. The AFL was based on the principle of craft unionism. Its leaders thought that the dangers of economic depressions and employer opposition could be overcome only by relying on skilled workers who could not easily be replaced during strikes. The AFL itself was, in effect, an umbrella organization of national craft unions.
2. The AFL emphasized business unionism; that is, it devoted most of its energies to bread-and-butter issues of pay and working conditions. Unlike many European labor unions, it was content to work within the capitalist system. It did not seek the overthrow of private property or the establishment of socialism.
3. The AFL limited its political role to that of a lobbyist for labor. Again in contrast to European labor movements, it did not found a labor party. Gompers thought that excessive political involvement would lead to internal conflict within the labor movement and would weaken its ability to achieve concrete economic goals.

The AFL grew slowly at first and then more rapidly. By 1904 it had 2 million members. Membership peaked at about 5 million in 1920 but declined to around 3 million in 1930.

Box 31.2
Samuel Gompers and the AFL

Samuel Gompers (1850–1924)

Samuel Gompers was born in a London tenement; he was the son of a skilled cigar maker. When he was 13 his family moved to the United States and settled on the East Side of New York. Gompers followed his father into the cigar trade.

Although his formal education ended at the age of ten, Gompers was very active in the workers' self-education movement. In the cigar-making shops, jobs were organized on a piecework basis. Groups of workers would have one of their members read to them while they worked. They paid the reader by making his cigars for him. In this way Gompers became acquainted with the works of Marx, Engels, and other European socialists. Often he was chosen as the reader.

The cigar makers' union to which Gompers belonged fell apart during the depression of 1873. Gompers rebuilt it as a craft union like those he was later to unite in the American Federation of Labor. Key features of this union were high membership dues, central control of funds, national officers with control over local unions, and union-organized accident and unemployment benefits for members.

Gompers became disillusioned with radical socialism. The main role of unions, in his view, was to look after the economic interests of their members. He wrote:

Unions, pure and simple, are the natural organization of wage workers to secure their present material and practical improvement and to achieve their final emancipation. . . . The working people are in too great need of immediate improvements in their condition to allow them to forego them in the endeavor to devote their entire energies to an end however beautiful to contemplate. . . . The way out of the wage system is through higher wages.

During the 1890s a socialist faction emerged within the AFL. It adopted a program that called for collective ownership of all means of production and other radical measures. Gompers opposed the group, and in the 1895 election for the AFL presidency he was defeated. He fought back, however, and succeeded in regaining the presidency the next year. He remained president until his death in 1924.

Gompers was an ardent patriot throughout his career. During World War I he opposed pacifism and supported the war effort. In 1918 he said, "America is a symbol; it is an ideal; the hopes of the world can be expressed in the ideal—America."

Early Industrial Unions

Industrial union
A union of all the workers in an industry, including both skilled and unskilled workers in all trades.

Although the AFL dominated the union scene in the decades around the turn of the century, the principle of craft unionism was not accepted everywhere. In some places there were notable early successes in organizing **industrial unions**—unions that included workers of all crafts and skill levels within a given industry. The oldest major industrial union is the United Mine Workers, founded in 1890. After 1900, three successful industrial unions emerged in the clothing industry. The International Ladies' Garment Workers' Union was the strongest of them. Brewery workers also organized successfully. During the same years, though, industrial unionism suffered some major failures. Strike efforts by steelworkers and railway workers were defeated after clashes involving Pinkerton detectives, state troopers, strikebreakers, and the jailing of labor leaders.

On another front, the AFL was challenged by unionists who were unwilling to work within the capitalist system. The most notable of their organizations was the International Workers of the World (IWW), whose members were known as "Wobblies." The IWW campaigned for "one big union" that would embrace all workers of all skills and crafts; it also called for worker management of industry. It was successful in organizing lumberjacks and agricultural workers. However, during World War I the IWW opposed the U.S. war effort—a stand that brought it under intense political attack. Many of its leaders and members were jailed, and the organization faded rapidly.

The 1930s and the CIO

Unionism declined in the 1920s, but during the Great Depression the decline was reversed. In large part, the revival of organized labor was brought about by favorable legislation passed during this period. That legislation (to be discussed in some detail later in the chapter) removed the main legal barriers to union organization and limited the antiunion efforts of employers.

In the improved legal climate there was increased pressure to organize workers in the mass production industries—steel, rubber, automobiles, and others—where earlier attempts had failed. This led to serious conflicts within the AFL, whose old-line craft unionists did not believe that stable unions could be formed in those industries. They also resented the efforts of industrial unions to recruit skilled workers in their industries. The AFL thought that such workers ought to join existing craft unions. As a result of this dispute, an opposition group formed within the AFL, led by John L. Lewis of the United Mine Workers. In 1938 the group was expelled from the AFL and formed the rival Congress of Industrial Organizations (orginally known as the Committee for Industrial Organization), or CIO.

The CIO scored some major successes during the 1930s, the biggest being the unionization of the steel industry. (The industry leader, U.S. Steel, agreed to collective bargaining in 1937.) Successful unionization campaigns were carried out around the same time in the rubber, automobile, electrical, meat-packing, and textile industries, to name just a few.

The successes of the CIO made it clear that craft unionism was not the only workable recipe for labor organization. They also contributed to a rapid growth in union membership—although the AFL also grew quickly during the period. By 1939 union membership had risen to 29 percent of nonagricultural employees, more than double the figure of just four years earlier. By 1945 over a third of nonagricultural workers had been organized.

The AFL-CIO Merger

After World War II unions faced more difficulties. The political and legislative climate began to turn against them. Unionization drives in the South, which had been expected to yield millions of new members, were not very successful. During the 1950s union membership stagnated. At the same time, leadership of both the AFL and the CIO passed into the hands of men who had not been directly involved in the bitter disputes that had led to the split between the two unions. The distinction between craft and industrial unions seemed less important now that it was clear that both types had their place. The outcome was an agreement to merge the two labor federations, which was signed in December 1955.

The Present and Future

The formation of the AFL-CIO did not reverse the decline in union membership or prevent further decline. Many factors have contributed to the problems of union organizers in recent decades. For one thing, blue-collar workers, traditionally the easiest to organize, now make up a much smaller percentage of the labor force than in the past. Women, who make up an increasing fraction of the labor force, have never belonged to unions in proportion to their numbers. Moreover, unions have not successfully followed the shift of jobs from the industrial Northeast and Midwest to the Sunbelt states. Finally, some observers believe that younger workers do not consider unions to be important to their well-being. In sum, despite some success in the organization of state and local government workers and agricultural workers, the prognosis for unionization is continued gradual decline.

PUBLIC POLICY TOWARD UNIONS

Labor unions do not operate in a vacuum. They operate in an environment of law and public policy that has been a topic of heated debate ever since unions began. Some have argued that all unions should be suppressed as illegal restraints on trade. Others have advocated government support for unions to promote industrial stability and high living standards for all. Still others have favored a laissez-faire policy, letting workers and management bargain without government interference. The debate has been clouded by disagreements about the true effect of unions on relative and absolute wages and on industrial efficiency. Without taking a position, the next section will survey the changing course of government policy over time, showing how first one and then another opinion has become dominant.

Early Court Hostility

Unions had trouble with the courts from their earliest days. Under precedents from English common law, they were often treated as illegal conspiracies in restraint of trade. In *Commonwealth* v. *Hunt*, a landmark case decided in Massachusetts in 1842, the court declared that unions were not necessarily illegal in themselves, but it restricted the aims unions could pursue and the means they could use to pursue them.

In the early twentieth century the legal climate grew even more hostile toward unions. In a series of cases from 1908 through the 1920s, the Sherman Antitrust Act was applied to unions. This happened in spite of considerable doubt as to whether Congress had intended the act to be interpreted in this way.

In this period the main legal weapon used against unions was the injunction. If a firm believed that union activities threatened it in any way, it could get an injunction (a court order) barring the union from striking, picketing, publicizing labor disputes, assembling to promote its interests, and just about anything else. Often the courts issued such injunctions without even hearing the union's side of the case.

The Norris–La Guardia Act

As union membership sank to a low point in 1932, the legal climate was changed dramatically by the passage of the Norris–La Guardia Act. This act deprived antiunion employers of the injunction, formerly their biggest weapon. The law declared, in effect, that the government should remain neutral in labor disputes. The courts could still intervene to protect tangible property and prevent the use of violence. As long as they remained nonviolent, however, unions would have the right to strike, picket, boycott, assemble, and persuade others to do these and other things.

The Wagner Act

The growing prolabor climate of the 1930s led to the passage of further labor legislation. The Wagner Act of 1935 came next. This act took government policy out of the neutral position where the Norris–La Guardia Act had left it and put the government squarely on the side of the unions.

The Wagner Act declared that "employees shall have the right to self-organization, to form, join, or assist labor organizations, to bargain collectively through representatives of their own choosing, and to engage in concerted activities, for the purpose of collective bargaining or other mutual aid or protection." The law created its own enforcement agency in the form of a three-member National Labor Relations Board (NLRB). This board was to oversee enforcement of the act, arrange for representative elections, and serve as judge and jury when the act was violated.

The Wagner Act also outlawed a specific list of "unfair employer labor practices." Employers could no longer use lockouts, intimidation, black-lists, or spying. They could no longer force employees to sign contracts that made nonmembership in a union a condition of employment. In some cases employers were even barred from speaking against unions.

The Taft-Hartley Act

The Wagner Act gave such a boost to labor unions that people began to worry about whether it was working too well. Unions became strong and powerful. They could call strikes that could paralyze a region and even threaten national welfare. After a series of damaging strikes in 1946, a Republican Congress passed legislation that amended the Wagner Act.

The Taft-Hartley Act of 1947 tried to move public policy back toward a neutral position on labor issues. It modified the structure of the NLRB and removed its powers as a prosecutor. It kept the list of unfair employer labor practices but added a list of unfair union labor practices. The new list included restraint or coercion of employees by unions, strikes and boycotts aimed at forcing self-employed people to join unions, and secondary boycotts (strikes or boycotts intended to force an employer to cease dealings in the product of another firm involved in a labor dispute). The act limited the closed shop, under which union membership is a condition of employment. It also provided for federal intervention in strikes that threaten to create a national emergency.

The Landrum-Griffin Act

The last major piece of legislation defining government policy toward unions was the Landrum-Griffin Act of 1959. It put government in the business of policing the internal affairs of unions. A series of scandals and congressional hearings had brought several cases of corrupt or criminal practices on the part of union officials to public attention. This legislation was an attempt to clean up unions.

A major provision of the act is a bill of rights for rank-and-file union members. It guarantees their right of free speech, their right to vote in union elections, and so on. The act also requires union reports on finances, regulates the term of office of union officials, specifies election procedures, and strengthens the provisions of the Taft-Hartley Act against secondary boycotts.

COLLECTIVE BARGAINING AND WAGE RATES

From its earliest days through the turmoil of the 1930s and continuing today, unionism has had two faces. One is the economic face. In this respect, unions can be seen as organizations that attempt to exercise monopoly power in order to raise the wages of their members. The other face has to do with unions as the collective voice of workers, bargaining for safety, democracy, and dignity in the workplace, and often campaigning for broader social justice as well. Since this is an economics textbook, we will look first at the effects of unions on wages. Then, at the end of the chapter, we will look at the other face of unionism.

The Union in a Competitive Market

Let us begin with the case of a union that was formed in a competitive market and now seeks higher wages through the threat of a strike. Look at Box 31.3. It shows a labor market in which the competitive equilibrium wage rate is $8 an hour and the equilibrium level of employment is 300,000 worker-hours per year. (See point E_1 in the box.)

Suppose that the newly organized workers tell employers that they want $10 an hour, or else they will go on strike. The strike threat is shown in the graph by a change in the shape of the supply curve. Initially the supply curve had the usual upward-sloping shape. After the strike threat, employers face a supply curve with a kink in it. The horizontal left-hand branch of the kinked supply curve shows that if the employer does not pay at least $10 an hour, no workers will be available. Up to 400,000 worker-hours will be supplied at $10 an hour. To hire more labor than that, the wage will have to be raised above what the union is demanding.

Suppose the employers decide that they have no choice but to accept

Box 31.3
The Effect of
Unionization in a
Competitive Labor
Market

A union formed in a competitive labor market can use a strike threat to bargain for higher wages. Here the union threatens to strike unless the wage is raised from its competitive level of $8 an hour ($E_1$) to $10 an hour. At that point the supply curve of labor becomes horizontal at $10 an hour up to 400,000 worker-hours per year, as shown. A new equilibrium is reached at E_2, where the new supply curve intersects the demand curve. The wage is higher than before, but the quantity of labor employed is smaller.

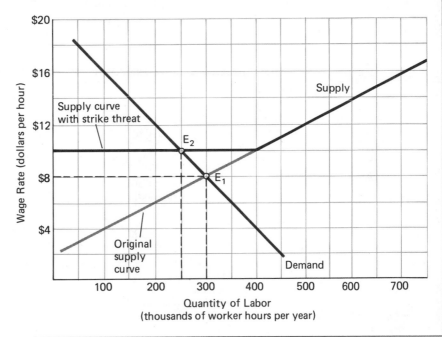

the union's demand. They will react by shifting to a new equilibrium at point E_2 in Box 31.3, where the demand curve and the horizontal part of the new supply curve intersect. There they will hire 250,000 worker-hours per year at $10 an hour. The union will have succeeded in raising the wage of its members, but only at the expense of reducing the amount of work available from 300,000 worker-hours per year to 250,000 worker-hours per year.

What Do Unions Maximize?

In the example just given, we saw that the union could win a higher wage rate only at the expense of jobs for its members. This trade-off raises a question: What do unions maximize? How far up the demand curve should they try to move, if at all, in attempting to serve the interests of their members? These questions have puzzled economists for many years. A number of answers have been proposed, but none has ever been found to apply to all cases. Several of those answers are shown in Box 31.4.

Maximum employment   One possibility is for a union to maximize employment for its members. In Box 31.4 this will require a wage of $8 an hour, as shown by the intersection of the supply and demand curves. At

Box 31.4
The Wage-Job Trade-off

Unions in industries where employers are price takers may choose various ways of dealing with the wage-job trade-off. If the union's goal is to maximize employment, it will not bargain for a wage higher than the competitive equilibrium. If the labor demand curve is inelastic at the competitive equilibrium point, total income of union members can be increased by raising the wage to the point at which the demand curve becomes unit elastic. If unions take the opportunity costs of workers into account, they may want to raise wages higher than the level that maximizes the total wages of members.

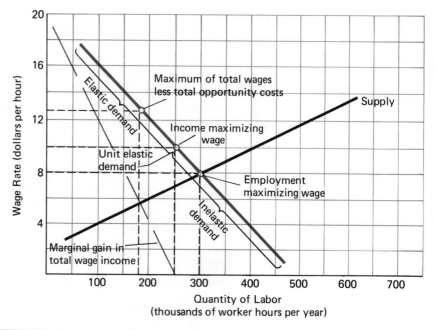

that wage, 300,000 worker-hours per year will be employed. At any higher wage, employers will be unwilling to use so much labor. At any lower wage, workers will not be available. But $8 an hour is the same as the competitive wage that would prevail in a competitive market without a union. An employment-maximizing union thus might represent workers politically or might provide social benefits, but it would be unable to do anything to raise the wage. (An exception is the case in which the union faces a monopsonist, which is discussed shortly.)

Maximum wage bill   A more widely accepted suggestion is that unions seek to maximize the *total wage bill*—that is, the product of the wage rate and the number of hours worked per year. As Box 31.4 shows, the wage bill is maximized at $10 an hour—the point where the elasticity of labor demand is 1. Keeping the wage at this level, however, creates an excess supply of labor. Workers will be willing to supply 400,000 hours per year, but only 250,000 will be required. The union can simply allow workers to compete for jobs on a first-come, first-served basis and not worry about who can get a job. Or it can try to divide up the available work among all the workers who want jobs in the industry. Each worker will be able to put in only a limited number of hours. Whichever route is taken, the union must be well enough organized to prevent nonunion workers from undercutting it—something that is not easy to do.

Maximizing wages less opportunity costs   The wage bill maximization approach has been criticized by some economists for neglecting the opportunity costs that workers face. To any individual worker, the opportunity cost of taking a job is the value of the best alternative use of the workday—usually another job. The height of the labor supply curve at any point can be taken as a measure of this opportunity cost. In Box 31.4, for example, no more than 100,000 labor hours will be supplied at $4, because the remaining workers have other ways of using their time that are worth more than $4 an hour. But if the wage is raised to $6 an hour, another 100,000 worker-hours will be supplied, representing workers whose opportunity costs are more than $4 an hour but less than or equal to $6 an hour.

Using the labor supply curve as a measure of opportunity costs, some economists have reasoned that it would be a mistake for unions to try to maximize the wage bill. Instead, they should permit employment to expand only to the point at which the marginal gain in total wage income for its members begins to fall below the opportunity cost of supplying the marginal unit of labor. The marginal gain in total wage income for members can be represented by a line that is related to the labor demand curve in the same way that, in the product market, a firm's marginal-revenue curve is related to the demand curve for its product. Such a line is drawn in Box 31.4. The point where this line intersects the labor supply curve (which represents the opportunity cost of supplying labor) is the point where total wages less total opportunity costs are maximized.

Union vs. Monopsonist

The problem of what it is that unions maximize stems largely from the trade-off between wages and jobs that most unions face. There is one case in which unions do not face that trade-off, however. That is the case in which a union faces an employer who is a monopsonist. This case is illustrated in Box 31.5.

To begin with, workers are assumed to be unorganized. The equilibrium quantity of labor hired, shown by the intersection of the employer's marginal revenue product curve and the marginal labor cost curve, is 220,000 labor hours per year. The wage rate, shown by the height of the supply curve for that quantity of labor, is $6.50 an hour. This equilibrium point is labeled E_1.

Now consider what happens if the workers unionize and threaten to go on strike if they are not paid $10 an hour. As in Box 31.3, the union's action puts a kink in the labor supply curve. What is more important, along the horizontal part of the new labor supply curve the monopsonist's marginal labor cost is equal to the wage rate. The union says, in effect, that the firm can hire as many workers as it wants at no more and no less than $10 an hour—which means that changes in the quantity of labor hired no longer require changes in the wage rate. One more worker-hour raises total labor costs by no more and no less than $10.

Suppose that the union is strong enough to make the monopsonist accept its wage demand on a take-it-or-leave-it basis. The new equilibrium will then be found where the new marginal labor cost curve intersects the

**Box 31.5
Effects of Unions in a
Monopsony Labor
Market**

When a union faces a monopsonistic employer, it can sometimes raise both wages and employment. Here the initial equilibrium wage is $6.50 an hour, with 220,000 worker-hours per year employed (point E_1). A strike threat changes the shape of the monopsonist's marginal labor cost curve. The monopsonist is now a price taker up to 400,000 worker-hours per year. The new equilibrium occurs at E_2, where both the wage rate and the number of worker-hours employed is greater than at E_1.

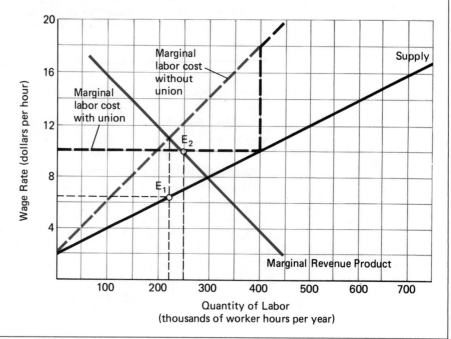

marginal revenue product curve, at E_2. The wage rate there is $10 an hour, and 250,000 worker-hours per year are employed. Both the wage rate and employment are higher than in the previous monopsonistic equilibrium.

However, there is a limit on the power of a union facing a monopsonist to raise wages without losing jobs. This limit is set by the extent to which the original monopsony wage fell short of the competitive wage. Once the wage rate begins to exceed the level at which the supply and marginal revenue product curves intersect, further raises reduce employment. In fact, in Box 31.5 the wage of $10 an hour is already in the trade-off region. Maximum employment is reached at $8 an hour, which is equal to the competitive wage.

Bilateral monopoly
A market situation in which both the buyer and the seller have some monopoly or monopsony power and neither behaves as a price taker.

Bilateral Monopoly

The example just given assumes that the monopsonistic employer will accept the union's demand on a take-it-or-leave-it basis. However, this is not the typical case. Normally the collective bargaining process proceeds through an exchange of demands and offers in which neither party acts as a price taker. This situation is often called **bilateral monopoly**.

The outcome of collective bargaining under bilateral monopoly cannot be predicted by economic analysis alone. Economic analysis can only state a range of outcomes within which a settlement can take place. The actual outcome depends on the relative bargaining strength and skill of the two sides. The headline-making disputes in which "big labor" clashes with "big business" are usually examples of bilateral monopoly.

Evidence on Wage Effects

Economic theory provides grounds for believing that unions have the power to raise wages above the competitive level—but by how much? Theory alone cannot answer this question. The answer depends partly on conditions in the product market. It must be remembered that the demand for labor is a derived demand. The greater the elasticity of demand for the employer's product, the less possible it will be for the employer to pass wage increases along to customers. In the case of an employer that sells its product in a perfectly competitive market, a union would be able to win no wage increase at all.

A union's power to raise its members' wages is enhanced if the entire industry is unionized and the union bargains with employers as a group. This has long been true in such industries as steel, automobiles, and trucking. In such cases it is the elasticity of the industry demand curve that counts, not that of each employer. But even though industry demand tends to be less elastic than the demand of any one firm within the industry, the ability of employers to pass along wage increases is not unlimited. Unions in the steel and automobile industries have learned that high costs, based in part on high union wages, have caused customers to turn to foreign producers. In the trucking industry, the powerful Teamsters Union has been humbled by competition from nonunion truckers in the years since the industry was deregulated. (See Chapter 27.)

In short, the ability of unions to raise wages varies from one industry to another. In a recent study the economists Richard B. Freeman and James L. Medoff concluded that unions raised the wages of their members by somewhat more than 20 percent, and by more than 30 percent in some cases.[2] (See Box 31.6.)

Freeman and Medoff also looked into the impact of unions on fringe benefits. They found these to be more strongly affected than wages. The level of fringe benefits of unionized workers averaged 68 percent higher than those of nonunionized workers. Pensions, life and accident insurance, and vacation pay showed the most significant effects.

Finally, Freeman and Medoff looked at the impact of unions on the distribution of wages. The traditional view has been that unions increase income inequality among wage earners. As we have seen, union wage gains tend to come at the expense of fewer jobs in unionized industries. The reduction in employment in unionized industries increases the supply of workers for nonunionized industries, driving wages down in those industries. If the industries that were most likely to be unionized tended to

---

[2]Richard B. Freeman and James L. Medoff, *What Do Unions Do?* (New York: Basic Books, 1984).

Box 31.6
Estimates of the Impact
of Unions on Wages

Richard B. Freeman and James L. Medoff have estimated the impact of unions on wages, using several data sources and examining several groups of workers. This table gives the results.

Source of Estimates	Year	Number of Observations	Approximate Percentage Gain in Wages Due to Collective Bargaining
Data on Individuals			
May Current Population Survey, Bureau of Labor Statistics	1979	16,728	21
Panel Study of Income Dynamics, University of Michigan	1970–79	11,445	26
Older Men, National Longitudinal Survey, Ohio State University	1976	1,922	25
Younger Men, National Longitudinal Survey	1976	2,335	32
Mature Women, National Longitudinal Survey	1977	1,724	25
Younger Women, National Longitudinal Survey	1978	2,068	21
Data on Establishments			
Expenditures for Employee Compensation Survey, Bureau of Labor Statistics	1972–76	15,574	27

Source: Richard B. Freeman and James L. Medoff, *What Do Unions Do?* (New York: Basic Books, 1984), Table 3–1, p. 46.

be low-wage industries in the first place, this effect might make the distribution of wages more equal. However, the opposite is the case. Unions tend to be strongest among relatively skilled workers, including airline pilots, skilled construction workers, and semiskilled workers such as autoworkers. They tend to be weak among the lowest-paid categories of workers, such as farm workers and retail clerks. In this regard, then, collective bargaining increases the inequality of income between unionized and nonunionized workers.

Freeman and Medoff note, however, that this does not mean that unions make earnings more unequal for the labor force as a whole. For one thing, wages tend to be more equal within unionized firms than within nonunionized firms. In addition, because blue-collar workers are more highly unionized than better-paid white-collar workers, unionization reduces the pay inequality between the two groups. Freeman and Medoff go so far as to claim that these equalizing effects more than offset the tendency of unions to widen the pay gap between their members and nonunionized blue-collar workers.

WHAT ELSE DO UNIONS DO?

To focus entirely on unions' effects on wages would be misleading; unions do many other things besides bargain over wages. This has been true from the earliest days of unionism, when the Knights of Labor campaigned for worker education and self-improvement, to the present, when unions provide social activities, help members with personal and family problems, and serve as a channel for participating in politics. Some of the things that unions do reach beyond the scope of economics. But even on the economic level unions affect more than wages.

For one thing, unions give workers a voice in how the workplace is run. In an economy based on free labor markets, a worker can always seek another job if he or she does not like the way the workplace is run. But unions offer an alternative. They can bargain with the employer over health and safety conditions in the workplace. They can help settle the workers' grievances in matters ranging from job assignments to company policy to conflicts with supervisors. They can bargain over issues of fairness, such as the role of seniority in layoffs and recalls.

Freeman and Medoff point out that these activities of unions can improve labor-management relations, reduce employee turnover and absenteeism, and raise productivity. This chapter began with the comments of a long-time General Motors worker who saw the United Auto Workers as the union that brought an end to an era of hostility, degradation, and "do this, go there, do that." Side by side with this worker's views, it is interesting to quote those of former General Motors chairman Thomas Murphy, who once said of the UAW, "What comes to my mind is the progress we have made, by working together, in such directions as providing greater safety and health protection, in decreasing alcoholism and drug addiction, in improving the quality of work life."[3]

However, there is sometimes a darker side to the ways in which unions exercise their voice in company affairs. Cooperation in improving productivity and quality of work life is not always the rule. Sometimes unions fight new technology that they fear will eliminate jobs; they fight inroads by women, minority groups, and immigrants into what have in the past been jobs for white males; they stir up worker hostility to make the union seem more needed; and they oppose nonunion competition with threats and violence.

Because unions have their negative side as well as their positive side, the managers of nonunionized firms tend not to be enthusiastic about inviting the unions in. Some firms take an openly hostile stance. They fight the unions tooth and nail, sometimes staying within the law and sometimes overstepping it. But today many managers are aware that "do this, go there, do that" is the wrong approach to labor relations, union or nonunion. Instead of fighting the unions, they try to make unions unnecessary for their workers.

According to one study of top nonunion firms, managers see high productivity and better labor relations, rather than lower wages, as the main benefit of not having a union. But low turnover, loyalty, and acceptance of new technology by workers do not come by accident. Box

---

[3]Quoted in Freeman and Medoff, p. 4.

31.7 lists some of the policies followed by the nonunion firms. They include many, if not most, of the major goals of unions.

It may well be, then, that one of the most useful functions that unions perform is that of putting pressure on managers to manage better. Labor-management relations will always be a delicate balance of conflict and cooperation. To some extent, unions have been a means for workers to defend themselves against bad management. Today the power of unions in the United States seems to be on the decline. But if at the same time the quality of management is increasing, the decline of union power need not mean a return of hard times for workers.

Box 31.7
How Top Nonunion Companies Manage Employees

What do managers of top nonunion companies, such as Black & Decker, Eli Lilly, Gillette, Grumman, IBM, and Polaroid, see as the chief benefit of managing in a nonunion environment? Not a lower level of wages but, instead, higher productivity, according to a study by Fred K. Foulkes. The higher productivity comes partly from lower employee turnover and less absenteeism, partly from greater worker loyalty, and partly from greater acceptance of new technology.

Foulkes found that managers of these top nonunion companies made special efforts to give workers a voice in company affairs and to improve the quality of work life. For example:

- Managers work hard to create a sense of equality. Executive status symbols such as exclusive dining rooms and country clubs are avoided. In many firms managers and workers park in the same parking lots and eat in the same cafeterias.
- Many of the firms do everything they can to avoid layoffs. Instead, they handle slack periods by reducing hours or producing for inventory. They handle peak demand with part-time or recently retired workers, rather than with newly hired workers who would have to be laid off when the peak had passed.
- The firms that Foulkes studied tend to promote from within. They post notices of job openings in the plant and offer training to workers who want to upgrade their skills.
- Many of the top nonunion firms offer wages and fringe benefits that are competitive with those in unionized firms. (Exceptions can be found in industries such as steel, airlines, and trucking, where union wage scales are unusually high.) They also tend to pay blue-collar workers monthly salaries rather than hourly wages.
- The managers of top nonunion firms are good listeners, and they keep their office doors open. They are very careful about the handling of grievances. They pay attention to workers' suggestions as well as to their complaints.

Should these practices be viewed as evidence that unions are not really necessary in a well-managed firm? Or should they be viewed as evidence that the threat of unionization causes nonunion firms to treat their workers better? You be the judge.

Source: Fred K. Foulkes, "How Top Nonunion Companies Manage Employees," *Harvard Business Review*, September–October 1981, pp. 90–96.

Summary

1. The earliest labor unions appeared in the United States almost 200 years ago. They were *craft unions*—unions of skilled workers all practicing the same trade. The modern labor movement dates from 1881, when the American Federation of Labor, an association of craft unions, was founded. *Industrial unions*—which include all the workers in an industry regardless of trade—are a later development. Most of the big industrial unions, such as the United Auto Workers and the United Steel Workers, date from the 1930s, although one such union, the United Mine Workers, was founded in 1890. Union membership reached its peak in 1945 at about a third of the labor force.

2. U.S. labor law has evolved over time. Until 1930 the courts were generally hostile to unions, limiting the goals they could pursue and the means they could employ. The Norris–La Guardia Act of 1932 was intended to place the government in a neutral position in relation to unions. Three years later the Wagner Act swung the power of government to the union side. This act created the National Labor Relations Board, set procedures under which workers could form unions, and limited the antiunion tactics that could be used by employers. The Taft-Hartley Act of 1947 limited union powers somewhat and gave the government the power to intervene in strikes that threatened the national interest. Finally, the Landrum-Griffin Act of 1959 gave the government the power to intervene in unions' internal affairs in order to fight corruption and ensure union democracy.

3. A union wage demand, backed by a strike threat, changes the shape of the labor supply curve faced by an employer. The supply curve becomes horizontal at the wage demanded. In a competitive labor market, any increase in the wage brought about by unionization tends to reduce employment. In the case of monopsony, unionization can increase both the wage rate and employment up to the point at which the wage rate reaches the competitive level.

4. Recent research suggests that unionization, on the average, raises relative wages by about 20 percent, although this figure depends on market conditions. Unionized workers tend to receive a higher proportion of their total compensation in the form of fringe benefits. The effect on wage equality is mixed. On the one hand, unionization raises the wages of some workers while crowding others into less desirable markets, where the increase in the supply of labor causes wages to fall. This tends to increase wage inequality. On the other hand, unions tend to reduce wage inequality within firms and to reduce inequality between blue-collar and white-collar workers.

5. In addition to affecting wages, unions give workers a voice in how the workplace is run. Often this voice is used in a constructive way, to improve health and safety conditions, increase fairness in hiring and layoffs, and so on. Sometimes it is used in a negative way, to fight new technology and limit competition. Managers of top nonunion firms recognize that productivity is enhanced when workers have a voice in company affairs.

Questions for Review

1. Define the following terms:
   craft union
   industrial union
   bilateral monopoly
2. When were the earliest unions in the United States founded? The earliest national union organizations? When did union membership as a percentage of the labor force reach its peak?
3. List four major U.S. labor laws and the main provisions of each.
4. Use supply and demand curves to show how a

union affects wages and employment in a competitive industry and a monopsonistic industry.

5. By how much, on the average, do unions raise the wages of their members? How do unions affect the level of fringe benefits? How do they affect equality of wages among workers?

6. What other things do unions do besides bargain over wages?

Problems and Topics for Discussion

1. Just 18 percent of blue-collar workers in the South belong to unions, compared to 38 percent of blue-collar workers in the Northeast. In what way, if any, would union workers in the Northeast gain if unionization became more widespread in the South? Which southern workers, if any, would gain? Which southern workers, if any, would lose?

2. Is the nonteaching staff of your college unionized? Is the teaching faculty unionized? Are any efforts under way to unionize either of these groups? Interview one member of the nonteaching staff and one member of the faculty to learn their attitudes toward unionization.

3. Review the section on cartels in Chapter 23. In what ways do unions resemble cartels? In what ways do they differ from cartels? Do you think that public policy should treat unions and producer cartels differently? Discuss.

4. **Case for Discussion**

Ford Motor Company's Louisville plant used be like a war zone. In one form or another, it had just about every problem of the U.S. auto industry—low productivity, high absenteeism, and poor quality. A consultant found an atmosphere of "deep distrust and alienation" and a "top-down, blame-oriented" management style.

Then Don Baker, a new plant manager, and Ron Gettelfinger, a new local union head, got together and decided that there must be a better way of doing business. They started with small things, such as cleaning up the filthy plant and putting in picnic tables on which workers could eat their lunches. In the improved atmosphere, workers and managers began talking to each other and solving problems. By 1980 the plant was getting high marks from Ford headquarters.

The Louisville plant looked so good, in fact, that Ford chose it as the place to build its new Ranger and Bronco II vehicles. The plant was gutted and an all-new automated assembly line was installed. But before the new machines went in, Ford did something it would never have done in the past: It displayed drawings and mockups of the Ranger and Bronco II in the plant where workers could comment on them and make suggestions about how they should be built. The workers made 749 proposals, of which 542 were adopted. In this way the workers became involved in the success of the new product.

Today the Ranger and Bronco II rate among the best-quality products of the U.S. auto industry. Productivity at the Louisville plant has soared. From a war zone, the plant has been transformed into a showcase.[4]

Questions:

a. Compare this case with the interview with a former autoworker at the beginning of this chapter. How does this case illustrate the functions of unions in areas other than collective bargaining?

b. Compare this case with the discussion in Box 31.6 of the labor relations practices of top nonunion firms. What similarities do you see? What differences?

c. Do this case, the interview, and Box 31.6, taken together, give any insight into the reasons why union membership increased rapidly in the 1930s, whereas it is declining in the 1980s? Discuss.

---

[4]Based on Jeremy Main, "Ford's Drive for Quality," *Fortune*, April 18, 1983, pp. 62–70. Based on material which originally appeared in FORTUNE Magazine.

Suggestions for Further Reading

Freeman, Richard B., and James L. Medoff. *What Do Unions Do?* New York: Basic Books, 1984.

> *A comprehensive look at labor unions and their functions.*

Reynolds, Morgan O. *Power and Privilege: Labor Unions in America.* New York: Universe Books, 1984.

> *A critique of the role of labor unions that addresses some of the points made by Freeman and Medoff.*

Sloane, Arthur A., and Fred Witney, *Labor Relations*, 4th ed. Englewood Cliffs, N.J.: Prentice-Hall, 1981.

> *A respected text that covers all aspects of labor-management relations and collective bargaining.*

Chapter 32

Rent, Interest, and Profit

Ideas for Review

Here are some terms and concepts that you should review before reading this chapter:

Entrepreneurship (Chapter 2)
Price and yield of a bond (Chapter 4)
Incidence and excess burden of a tax (Chapter 5)
Elasticity of supply (Chapter 19)
Pure economic profit (Chapter 21)

"George's ideas were acclaimed world-wide when they were published in 1879—why haven't they caught on?"

In passing out credit for the remarkable urban comeback of Pittsburgh, Pennsylvania, consider the contribution of the nineteenth-century American economist Henry George. Pittsburgh is the only large city anywhere to embrace the Henry George theory of real estate taxation, a theory that says land should be taxed heavily and buildings and improvements on the land not at all.

Pittsburgh has had a modified "land tax" since 1913. Some say the tax was crucial in helping the city grow at the same time that local steel mills were shutting down. Others say Henry George's ideas haven't made a dime's worth of difference in Pittsburgh's renaissance.

The land tax (often called the "two-rate tax" or the "split tax") is widely used in Australia and New Zealand. Pennsylvania, however, is the only state in the United States that has given its municipalities the option of substituting a land tax for the more conventional property tax. And this raises questions. If Henry George's theory is a dud, why have six other Pennsylvania municipalities, including Scranton and Harrisburg, opted for a land tax in recent years? But if it works—and George's ideas were acclaimed world-wide when they were published in 1879—why hasn't it caught on elsewhere in the United States? The genius of the land tax, in the eyes of George's present-day disciples, is that it promotes development and discourages slums and land speculation. Property taxes commonly give great weight to the value of the home or building on a piece of land. Fix up your home, or build a skyscraper on a lot downtown, and what happens? Your tax bill goes up.

But there are skeptics as well as fans. A driver who spends an hour looking for a parking place in downtown Pittsburgh wonders if gridlock is the inevitable byproduct of a tax with a high-rise bias.[1]

The Pittsburgh land tax draws attention to land and other natural resources—factors of production to which we have given little attention in the last two chapters. In this chapter we will complete the story of factor markets by looking at the markets for natural resources and capital. We will also discuss profit and entrepreneurship and how they relate to factor markets.

THE MARKETS FOR LAND AND NATURAL RESOURCES

Pure economic rent
The income earned by any factor of production whose supply is perfectly inelastic.

Pure Economic Rent

The income earned by a factor of production whose supply is completely inelastic is **pure economic rent**. The classic example of such a factor is land, which in this context means the natural productive powers of the earth and the locational advantages of particular sites. It does not include artificial improvements, nor does it include such matters as destruction of the soil through erosion or creation of new land through reclamation.

---

[1]Eugene Carlson, "It's the Land Tax, by George, That Sets Pennsylvania Apart," *Wall Street Journal*, March 12, 1985, p. 33. Reprinted by permission of The Wall Street Journal, © Dow Jones & Company, Inc. 1985. All rights reserved.

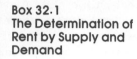

**Box 32.1
The Determination of
Rent by Supply and
Demand**

Pure economic rent is earned by a factor whose supply is perfectly inelastic. This figure shows hypothetical supply and demand curves for Kansas wheatland. No account is taken of the possibility that such land could be created or destroyed, so the supply curve is vertical. As in the case of other factors of production, the demand curve is based on the land's marginal revenue product.

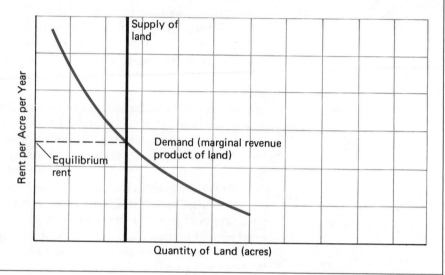

Box 32.1 shows how rent is determined by supply and demand in a competitive market. It considers a specific type of land—Kansas wheatland. The supply curve for Kansas wheatland is a vertical line because the amount of land supplied does not vary as the rent that it earns varies. The demand curve is the marginal revenue product curve for that land as seen by Kansas wheat farmers. The marginal product of land falls as more land is used in combination with fixed quantities of labor and capital because of diminishing returns. The demand curve thus slopes downward and to the right.

The rent that the land earns is determined by the intersection of the supply curve, which represents the scarcity of land, and the demand curve, which represents its productivity. If the rent is higher than the equilibrium shown, not all land will be put to use. The rent will then fall as landowners compete to find tenants. If the rent is lower than the equilibrium rate, farmers will be unable to find all the land they want. They will bid against one another for the limited supply and drive rents up.

Capitalization of Rents

The price paid per year for the use of land is called rent, but much land is used by the person who owns it and therefore is not rented by a tenant from an owner. That fact does not change the way supply and demand determine the value of land. It does mean, though, that it is sometimes useful to speak of the price of land in terms of a lump sum sales price rather than as a rent per month or year.

There is a simple relationship between the value of a piece of land

Capitalized value of a rent
The sum that would earn annual interest equal to the annual rent if it were invested at the current market rate of interest.

expressed as a rent and the price at which that piece can be sold in the market. The market price of a piece of land is said to be the **capitalized value of its rent**—the sum that would earn an annual return equal to the annual rent if it were invested at the market rate of interest.

In fact, the relationship between the market price of a piece of land, its annual rental income, and the market rate of interest is exactly the same as the relationship between the price of a long-term bond, its coupon rate, and the market rate of interest. Consider a piece of land that yields an annual rent of $1,000. A potential buyer will compare the rent to the interest that could be earned on an interest-bearing asset such as a bond or a bank deposit. At a 10 percent rate of interest, the land would yield a 10 percent return if it were priced at $10,000. If the market interest rate rose to 20 percent, the price that buyers would willingly pay for the piece of land would fall to $5,000 in order to bring its yield into line with the yields on other assets. In general, the price of a piece of land with an expected rental income of R dollars per year for the indefinite future, capitalized at the rate of interest r, can be given by the formula R/r. The formula makes it clear that a change in the expected income from a piece of land, other things being equal, will also affect its price. Recent years have seen some dramatic examples of this effect in the case of farmland, especially in the midwestern United States. As Chapter 28 showed, a combination of factors put a squeeze on farm income in the early 1980s. For a farmer, the economic rent of land means the income it yields after allowing for the costs of other inputs, including labor, capital, fuel, fertilizer, and so on. As this rental income fell, the price of farmland also fell. Many farmers had used their land as collateral on bank loans. When the market price of the land fell below the value of the loans, some banks foreclosed on the loans, putting the farmers out of business.

Other Rents

The term rent can refer to the market return earned by any factor of production that is unique or whose supply is perfectly inelastic. Consider the high incomes of people with unique talents, such as singers, actors, and some executives. These incomes can be thought of as rents earned on talents rather than as wages earned for work done. Legal privileges can also be said to earn rents. For instance, part of the earnings of a New York taxicab can be counted as rent earned from the "medallion" (license) that gives it the legal right to operate, because the supply of medallions is limited by city officials.

The hallmark of pure economic rent is inelastic supply. Pure economic rent should not be confused with what is loosely called the rental income earned by assets whose supply is not perfectly inelastic. Take the rental income of an apartment house owner, for example. It may be in part pure economic rent earned by some uniquely convenient site on which the building is located. In addition, though, it includes such things as implicit wages for any custodial work the owner does in the building and implicit interest on the capital the owner invested to build it.

What is pure economic rent and what is not depends in part on the time framework within which the income is considered. In the short run—say, a period too short for new buildings to be built—a case could be made for treating the income earned from buildings as a pure economic rent. In the long run, however, when more buildings can be supplied at a price, such rental income is clearly not a pure economic rent.

Applications of the Theory of Rent

The theory of rent has some useful applications. One such application is tax policy, as in the case of Pittsburgh's land tax. The nineteenth-century economist Henry George, who inspired the land tax, saw the connection between rent and perfectly inelastic supply. He reasoned that if a tax were placed on land, whose supply is perfectly inelastic, the owners would not be able to pass the tax along to their tenants. The entire tax would be borne by the landowners. And if no land were withdrawn from the market, the tax would have no excess burden.

Box 32.2 contrasts the effects of a land tax with those of a tax on buildings or other improvements to land. The supply of buildings and improvements is not perfectly inelastic. A tax on these properties means an increase in costs for their owners. The increase shifts the supply curve

Box 32.2
Economics of the Land Tax

This box explains the logic of a land tax such as is used in Pittsburgh, Pennsylvania. Part a shows the market for land. The equilibrium rental value is $2 per square foot per year. When a tax of $1 per square foot is imposed on this market, the quantity supplied does not change. The entire tax is absorbed by landlords, and the rent paid by tenants remains at $2. Part b shows the market for buildings built on the same land. At first the rental price of buildings is also $2 per square foot. A tax of $1 per square foot is a cost to building owners and shifts the supply curve upward from S_1 to S_2. Part of the tax is passed on to tenants in the form of an increase in the rental price to $2.50 per square foot. The quantity of floor space provided falls by half a million square feet. The shaded area shows the excess burden of the tax.

a. Land Tax

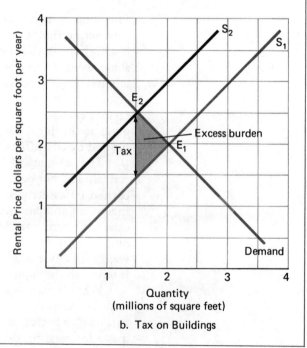

b. Tax on Buildings

upward. As the market price rises, a part of the tax is passed along to tenants in the form of higher rental payments. (Remember that the rental payments on a store or apartment are not pure economic rents.) At the same time, the quantity of improvements and buildings supplied decreases. Some new buildings are not constructed, and some existing buildings deteriorate because improvements are not made and the buildings are not maintained well.

Much the same theory applies in another area of public policy, that of rent control. "Pure" rent control—like a Henry George type of land tax—would apply only to the part of landlords' rental income that could be attributed to land. However, the actual rent control policies of cities like New York and Washington, D.C., limit landlords' income from buildings and improvements as well as their income from the value of the land on which the housing is built. As a result, rent control, like a tax on buildings and improvements, causes a decrease in the quantity supplied. New apartments are not built, old ones are not maintained, and the worst of the old ones may even be abandoned by their owners and tenants. Rent control differs from a tax in one way, though: Although it puts a burden on landlords, the burden is not passed through to tenants in the form of higher monthly payments. As a result, as rent control causes the stock of rental housing to shrink, shortages of rental housing develop. Such shortages are very familiar to apartment dwellers in cities where rent control prevails.

INTEREST AND CAPITAL

The term *interest* is used to express both the price paid by borrowers to lenders for the use of loanable funds and the market return earned by capital as a factor of production. A person who loans $1,000 to another in return for a payment of $100 a year (plus repayment of the principal on a set date) is said to earn 10 percent interest per year on the money. At the same time, a person who buys a machine for $1,000 and earns $100 a year by using the productive services of that machine is said to earn 10 percent interest on the capital.

Consumption Loans

We will begin our discussion of interest and capital by looking at how credit markets work in a simple economy in which households are the only suppliers of credit—that is, of loanable funds. Savers are households that earn income now but consume less than they earn in order to put something aside for future needs. Not all households in the economy are savers, however; some want to consume more than their current incomes permit. The latter may be households that are faced with a temporary decrease in income, or they may be households with steady incomes that are not willing to wait to buy a car or take a vacation. These and other households that borrow are one source of demand for loanable funds. The loans they take out are called consumption loans.

Box 32.3 shows how credit markets look in an economy in which consumption loans are the only source of demand for loanable funds and personal saving is the only source of supply. For simplicity we will assume that no inflation occurs; therefore, the nominal rate of interest, the expected real rate of interest, and the real rate of interest actually obtained are all equal. Under these conditions the willingness of savers to save, at various rates of interest, determines the shape and position of the supply curve. The eagerness of borrowers to borrow, at various rates of interest, determines the shape and position of the demand curve. The intersection of the two curves determines the market rate of interest.

The Productivity of Capital

We have not yet said anything about production or capital. Opportunities to use capital as a factor of production are a second source of demand for loanable funds, in addition to the demand for pure consumption loans. To understand the demand for loans of this kind, we need to understand why capital is productive.

Using capital means using a roundabout method of production rather than a direct method. Consider a person whose business is making bricks. There are two ways to make bricks. The direct way is to form them by hand out of raw clay scooped up from the ground and to bake them over an open fire. Suppose that by using this method a worker can make 100 bricks a month. The other way of making bricks is a roundabout one. The brickmaker first spends a month forming bricks by hand and putting them together to make a kiln. When the kiln is completed, its hotter fire and lower fuel consumption make it possible to produce 110 bricks a month from then on. This method, which uses capital (the kiln), lengthens the period between the time when work starts and the time when finished

---

Box 32.3
The Determination of the Interest Rate for Consumption Loans

If consumption loans were the only kind made, the interest rate would be determined as shown in this box. The supply curve for loanable funds is determined by the willingness of savers to lend their money. The demand curve is determined by the eagerness of borrowers to consume now and pay later. The intersection of the two determines the interest rate.

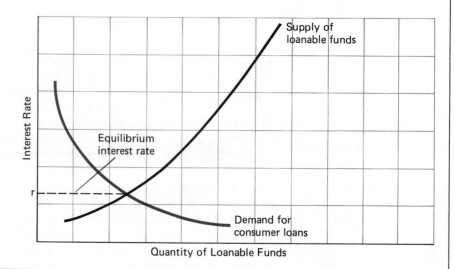

bricks begin to appear. In return, it increases the rate of output. That is the sense in which capital is productive.

The brickmaker's experience is repeated whenever a firm makes a capital investment. Making cars on an assembly line is a roundabout method of production compared to making them one by one with hand tools. Constructing a building in which to hold economics classes is a roundabout method of education compared with holding classes outside under a tree. In both cases time is taken to construct aids to production in order to produce more effectively later on.

Investment Loans

The brickmaker in our example invested directly by actually building the needed capital equipment. However, in a market economy firms do not need to build their own capital equipment. Anyone who sees an opportunity to increase output by using a more capital-intensive (that is, a more roundabout) production process can borrow money and buy capital. The productivity of capital thus creates a source of demand for loanable funds in addition to the demand for consumption loans. Loans that are used to buy capital can be called investment loans.

Box 32.4 shows how the interest rate is determined when the demand for investment loans is added to the demand for consumption loans. The diagram reveals that the interest rate is higher when both types of loan demand are taken into account than it is when only consumption loans are considered. In practice, the investment demand for loanable funds is much greater than the consumption demand, which means that the investment demand is the more important factor in determining the interest rate.

Box 32.4
The Interest Rate with Consumption and Investment Loans

This box shows how the interest rate is determined in a market in which there are both consumption and investment loans. In this case the demand for investment loans is added to the demand for consumption loans to get the combined demand for loanable funds. The equilibrium interest rate R is higher than it would be if only consumption loans were taken into account.

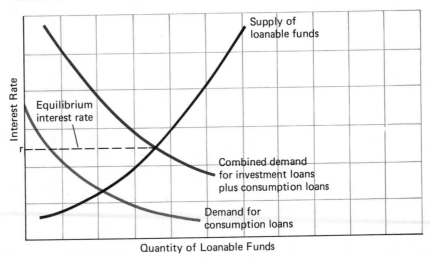

Capital and Interest

We turn now from the determination of the interest rate in the credit market to the link between the demand for loanable funds and the demand for capital as a means of production. Box 32.5 shows the short-run rental market for capital equipment—machines, buildings, and the like. In the short run the supply of capital is fixed by the existing stock of capital equipment, so the supply curve is perfectly inelastic. As in other factor markets, the demand curve is the marginal revenue product curve for the services of capital equipment. The two determine the rental value of capital equipment.

If the short-run rental price of capital equipment is high enough and the expected real rate of interest is low enough, it will pay to build more such equipment. Suppose that a car rental company can buy a car for $8,000 with funds that it borrows at a 15 percent expected real rate of interest. If its expected net income from renting the car, adjusting for inflation and allowing for operating expenses and depreciation, is $1,200 per year or more, it will be worthwhile for the company to invest in expanding its fleet.

Over time, as investment proceeds and capital builds up, the short-run supply curve for capital shifts to the right. In the long run, this tends to drive down the rental price of capital equipment and reduce the incentive to invest. The investment demand for loanable funds decreases and the interest rate falls.

**Box 32.5
The Rental Price of
Capital Equipment**

In the short run, the rental price of capital equipment is determined by the existing stock of capital and the demand (marginal revenue product) curve for the services of capital. In the long run, new investment causes the supply curve to shift to the right. This drives down the rental price, other things being equal. In practice, however, innovations constantly shift the demand curve for capital to the right, and hence the rental price does not fall as much as shown here.

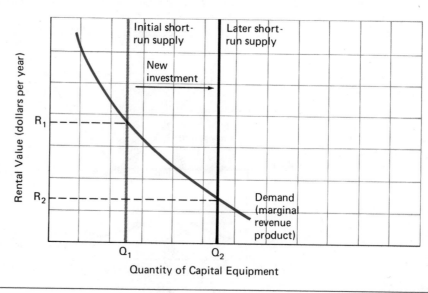

In theory, the economy can end up in a steady-state equilibrium in which all worthwhile investment projects are completed and consumption loans provide the only remaining demand for loanable funds. In practice, the steady state never arrives. Technological change is constantly pushing up the demand curve (marginal revenue product curve) for capital services. The short-run rental value of capital equipment thus is kept high enough to justify investing in new capital equipment year after year.

PROFIT AND ENTREPRENEURSHIP

The term *pure economic profit* was introduced in Chapter 21 to refer to the income, if any, remaining for the owners of a firm after they have deducted all implicit and explicit costs of production. Explicit costs include factor payments to workers, owners of resources, and suppliers of capital, together with the cost of any semifinished inputs that are purchased from other firms. Implicit costs include the opportunity cost of capital supplied by owners of the firm plus the opportunity costs of using natural resources or labor supplied by owners of the firm or owned by the firm itself. What is left over is pure economic profit.

This definition of profit does not answer two important questions: Why does a firm ever earn any pure economic profit? And why is the entire value of the product of all firms not divided up among the owners of the labor, natural resources, and capital used in the production process? These questions have occupied the minds of many great economists, but they have not come up with answers that everyone agrees with. Still, it will be worthwhile to look at some of the answers that have been suggested.

Theories of Profit

Risk and profit   According to one theory, profits are a reward that the owners of businesses receive for bearing risk. Every business venture is subject to the risk of failure. That is the nature of economic life in a world where the future is not known with certainty. People who merely hire out their factor services avoid some of this risk. A new business is usually expected to guarantee its employees that the payroll will be met even if the firm loses money. It is also expected to offer security against default to banks or bondholders who supply it with capital. The owner or owners of the firm (stockholders if the firm is a corporation) bear most of the risk of loss if the firm fails. In return they get the right to keep the profits if revenues turn out to be more than enough to pay off the firm's obligations to hired factors.

Why is it, though, that the profits earned by successful risk takers are not exactly offset by the losses of those who do not succeed? The answer has to do with people's attitudes toward risk. It is possible that some people are indifferent to risk. A person who is indifferent to risk will be indifferent between the opportunity to earn $10,000 a year with absolute certainty and the opportunity to try for $20,000, subject to a fifty-fifty chance of earning nothing. A person who is indifferent to risk will be willing to launch new businesses even when the expected profit if the business succeeds is exactly offset by the expected loss if the business fails.

In practice, though, most people dislike risk. If they know they can earn a secure $10,000 a year, they will not launch a business with a fifty-fifty chance of failure unless that business, if successful, will pay more than $20,000. Because most people dislike risk, somewhat fewer business ventures are launched than would otherwise be the case. That makes opportunities a little more favorable, on the average, for those who are willing to bear some risk. When successes and failures are averaged out over the whole economy, profits more than offset losses. The excess of profits over losses is the reward earned by the people who bear business risks. Factor owners are willing to accept less than the whole value of the product of the firm to the extent that they are shielded from those risks.

Arbitrage
The activity of earning a profit by buying a good at a low price in one market and reselling it at a higher price in another market.

Profits as arbitrage   A second theory holds that profits are the return yielded by *arbitrage*—buying a good at a low price in one market and selling it at a higher price in another. Examples of pure arbitrage can be found in markets for agricultural commodities, precious metals, foreign currencies, and the like, in which standardized goods are traded at different locations. Consider the gold markets in London and Hong Kong. Economic policies, news events, and so forth may affect supply and demand in these two markets differently. A political crisis in the British government, for example, may prompt an increase in demand in the London market, sending up the price of gold there relative to its price in Hong Kong. Before the two prices get very far apart, however, arbitrageurs in Hong Kong will start buying gold at the low Hong Kong price for resale at the higher London price. This activity will raise the demand in Hong Kong and will raise the supply in London until the price in the two markets is equalized. (In practice, because of various transactions costs, the prices will be only roughly equal on any given day.) In the process of acting as a crucial link in the transmission of information through the price system, the arbitrageurs will make a handy profit.

Arbitrage cannot always be seen in as pure a form as in the international gold market. However, Israel Kirzner points out that there is an element of arbitrage in every profit-making transaction.[2] Consider the entrepreneur-owner-manager of, say, a small shoe factory. This person buys inputs in one set of markets at the lowest prices possible and, after combining the inputs to form finished shoes, sells the product in other markets at the highest prices possible. In a world where all markets were in perfectly competitive long-run equilibrium, it would be no more possible to make a profit by buying labor and leather and selling shoes than it would be to buy gold in Hong Kong and sell it in London. In such a world the price of the leather and labor used per pair of shoes would be bid up to just equal the price of the finished shoes. In the real world, though, the entrepreneur can find arbitrage opportunities in a wide variety of markets and earn profits accordingly.

Profits and innovation   A third theory links profit with innovation. This theory has become quite popular as a result of the writings of Joseph Schumpeter.[3] In contrast to the entrepreneur as arbitrageur, taking advan-

---

[2]Israel Kirzner, *Competition and Entrepreneurship* (Chicago: University of Chicago Press, 1974).
[3]Joseph Schumpeter, *Capitalism, Socialism, and Democracy* (New York: Harper & Row, 1942). Schumpeter's theories are also discussed in Chapter 25 of this text.

tage of opportunities to buy low and sell high whenever they occur, the entrepreneur as innovator creates new profit opportunities by devising a new product, production process, or marketing strategy. If successful, the entrepreneur achieves a temporary monopoly that permits pure economic profits to be earned until rival firms catch on or leap ahead with innovations of their own.

Further Comments on the Nature of Profit

Entrepreneurship as a factor of production   It is pointless to argue about which of the three theories of profit just discussed is the correct one. Entrepreneurship is probably best thought of as a blend of risk taking, alertness to opportunities for arbitrage, and innovation.

Because entrepreneurs, like workers, resource owners, and suppliers of capital, earn a reward for their contribution to production, entrepreneurship is sometimes spoken of as a fourth factor of production. Like the other factors, it is scarce. Not everyone is able to organize business ventures and recognize new opportunities to make a profit. Moreover, entrepreneurs earn an income in the form of the profit that remains after all the costs of their firms have been covered. And as is true for labor, natural resources, and capital, production cannot take place without entrepreneurship.

There is a limit, however, to how far the parallel between entrepreneurship and other factors can be pushed. One problem is that entrepreneurship cannot be measured. There is no numerical unit of entrepreneurship and hence no way to determine a price per unit. Applying supply-and-demand analysis to this fourth factor of production just does not work. In addition, there is the fact that profit, the return to entrepreneurship, disappears when the economy is in equilibrium. In equilibrium the entire value of the product of each firm must be paid out to the owners of labor, capital, and natural resources. Profit and entrepreneurship are found only in a state of disequilibrium—a fact that sets entrepreneurship apart from the three other factors of production in a very basic way.

Monopoly profits   This brings us to another point. Up to now no distinction has been made between the profits earned in the short run by a competitive firm (before those profits are eroded by competition) and the profits earned by a monopolist (which, under proper demand conditions, can persist forever). Some writers have suggested that monopoly profits are a separate type of income that cannot be explained either as a reward to labor, capital, or natural resources or in terms of the entrepreneurial activities of risk bearing, arbitrage, and innovation. On close inspection, however, it turns out that most, if not all, monopoly profit can be explained without the need for a special type of income.

Consider the case of a monopoly based on a patented invention. When explicit costs are subtracted from revenue for such a firm, more than enough will be left over to cover the opportunity cost of capital. The firm may be said to earn a pure economic profit, but it is more accurate to say that it earns an implicit rent as the owner of the patent. It can, after all, sell or lease the patent rights to some other firm, in which case the patent owner will earn an explicit rent and the firm using the patent will earn no pure economic profit after paying for the patent. The opportunity cost to a monopolist of not renting the patent to another firm should thus be counted as an implicit cost, not as part of pure economic profit. The same applies to firms with a monopoly based on any other unique advantage whose supply is perfectly inelastic, such as a government franchise, a uniquely suitable location, or a unique natural resource.

If a monopolist does not have some unique advantage, its monopoly will be temporary. Sooner or later other entrepreneurs will enter into competition with the firm and begin the process of reducing its pure economic profit to zero. Temporary monopoly profits of this type are not a separate type of income; they are simply the return earned by the monopolistic entrepreneur who was alert enough to get into the market before any competitors did so.

Windfall profits   So-called windfall profits may appear to be another type of income that we have not yet accounted for. *Windfall profit* is not a well-defined term of economics; rather, it is a popular way of describing almost any kind of unexpected or accidental increase in the income of an individual or firm. Often, use of the term implies that the income in question is undeserved or should not be allowed.

Take, for example, the case of U.S. oil well owners when, in 1979, the Iranian revolution and related events sent the world price of oil up sharply. Through no action of their own, oil well owners reaped great financial gains, which were referred to as windfall profits. (To be technical, they were really windfall increases in rent.) Soon there were widespread demands that this windfall be taxed. These demands were based partly on the normative ground that the income was undeserved and partly on the positive ground that the tax would have no adverse effect on production as long as it was limited to wells that were already in production at the time that the price rose.

It is not always true, however, that taxes on windfall gains have no effect on quantity supplied. It is important to distinguish between windfall gains that arise from events that are entirely unforeseen and those that arise from events that were known to be possible but not certain. Again an example can be taken from the oil industry. After the Iranian revolution sent the world price of oil up from about $15 a barrel to $30 or so, people began to think about what might happen if there were a similar revolution in Saudi Arabia, an even larger producer of oil. Suppose wildcat oil well drillers judged that a Saudi Arabian revolution would send the price up to $40 a barrel and that there was a fifty-fifty chance that such a revolution would occur. If they expected to be able to sell their oil for $40 if the revolution did come, they would drill in somewhat less promising places than if they were sure that the price would stay at $20 a barrel. The U.S. oil supply would therefore be somewhat greater than it would have been if no one had taken the possibility of a Saudi Arabian revolution into account.

If, however, wildcatters got the idea that every time a revolution sent the price of oil up, the government would impose a new windfall tax on existing wells, they would no longer consider it worthwhile to drill in anticipation of a price increase. The oil supply would be smaller than it would have been without the expectation of a windfall tax. This suggests that a tax on windfall gains can sometimes have an adverse effect on supply.

Profits and loot   Another kind of financial gain that is sometimes confused with profit is the acquisition of wealth not through production and voluntary exchange, as in the case of profit and factor incomes, but by force, through the taking of other people's property. Suppose that a service station owner, instead of paying a mechanic the market wage of $10,000 a year, hires a gang of thugs to threaten to burn down the mechanic's house unless the wage is reduced to $6,000. The station's accounting profit will appear to be $4,000 higher. The extra $4,000 is not a pure economic profit, however. Economics lacks an accepted general term for the proceeds of coercive activity, but perhaps the word *loot* can serve as well as any. Looting need not be as crude as in the example just given. If a firm earns money by misrepresenting its product and defrauding consumers, that money is loot, not profit. If it gets rid of industrial wastes by dumping them illegally, part of the firm's apparent profit is really loot. Not only is loot not profit; properly speaking, it is not even a form of income since it is not a payment for newly produced goods or services.

Looking Ahead

Up to this point we have covered the basic economics of factor markets for labor, capital, and natural resources. We have also discussed the economics of profit and entrepreneurship. As we pointed out at the beginning of Chapter 30, these factor markets play a major role in determining the distribution of income in a market economy.

This leaves us with one remaining set of questions: the normative question of whether the market-determined distribution of income is a good or a bad one, and the positive question of what can be done to change the distribution of income if we do not like it. These questions will be addressed in the next chapter.

Summary

1. Pure economic rent is the income earned by any factor of production whose supply is completely inelastic. Land is the classic example of a factor that earns a pure economic rent. The capitalized value of rent determines the market price of land. Rent can also be said to be earned by other factors whose supply is perfectly inelastic, such as the special talents of athletes or performing artists.

2. The term *interest* expresses both the price paid by borrowers to lenders in credit markets and the income earned by capital as a factor of production. The interest rate is determined in credit markets. The supply of credit depends on the willingness of savers to lend. The demand for credit is composed of the demand for consumption loans plus the demand for investment loans.

3. In the short run, supply and demand determine a rental price for the services of capital equipment. If the rental value of newly produced capital equipment (expressed as a percentage of the cost of producing the equipment) is higher than the interest rate, it will be worthwhile for firms to expand the stock of capital. As the capital stock expands, the rental value of capital equipment, other things being equal, will tend to fall. This will reduce the investment demand for credit and drive down the interest rate. In principle, the economy

could reach a steady-state equilibrium in which there was no new investment. In practice, innovation constantly raises the marginal productivity of capital and hence the demand for capital, so the steady state is never reached.

4. There are several theories about the nature of profits. One theory holds that profit is the reward that entrepreneurs earn for bearing risks. Another sees profit as earned mainly through arbitrage. Still another stresses innovation. In practical terms, profit can be thought of as income derived from a mixture of these three sources.

Questions for Review

1. Define the following terms:
   pure economic rent
   capitalized value of a rent
   arbitrage

2. Use supply and demand curves to show the difference between the pure economic rent earned by a factor of production whose supply is completely inelastic and the income earned by, say, the owner of an apartment building.

3. What do we mean when we say that using capital means using a roundabout method of production?

4. Under what conditions will it be worthwhile for a firm to invest in new capital equipment? Under what conditions could the incentive to invest disappear for the economy as a whole?

5. List three theories about the nature of profits.

Problems and Topics for Discussion

1. In 1983, U.S. farmers earned gross revenues of $151 billion. Of this, $135 billion went to cover explicit costs of fuel, fertilizer, equipment maintenance, and so on. This left farmers with a net income of $16 billion. Is that net income best thought of as wages, rent, interest, profit, or a mixture of these? Do you think any farm income ought to be viewed as loot? Discuss.

2. The chapter explains how to calculate the capitalized value of a rent for a piece of land that is expected to yield the same rent for the indefinite future. If you have read the appendix to Chapter 4, or if you want to do so now, you can calculate the capitalized rental price of a factor of production that does not have the same value forever. For example, suppose that you own a professional basketball team. You are negotiating for the services of Carlos Yates, the George Mason University star. You figure that having Yates on your team will bring in $100,000 a year in added income from ticket sales for five years. After that Yates may slow down a bit, but having him on the team will continue to bring in $50,000 in added ticket sales for another ten years. How much would you be willing to pay (in a single, one-time payment) to get Yates for your team if the interest rate is 12 percent per year?

3. This chapter has suggested that part of the income of people with unique talents might be be considered a form of pure economic rent. Suppose you observe that a certain baseball player is paid $1 million a year. How would you distinguish the part of the player's income that is rent from the part that is a return on investment in human capital in the form of training for the sport?

4. Suppose you decide to start a Christmas tree farm. You already own a suitable piece of land. You get seeds from pine cones that you gather in the woods. You plant the seeds with your own hands. Five years later you sell the trees for $30 each. How should your revenue be divided up among wages, rent, interest, and profit?

5. A contractor places an ad for laborers in the

newspaper, offering to pay them $10 per cubic yard for removing rocks and dirt from a cellar hole. Four workers show up and start the job. Alice is a person of average build. She uses a simple shovel and bucket and manages to earn $20 a day. Bill, a giant of a man, also uses a shovel and bucket but is able to earn $50 a day. Charles uses a wheelbarrow and earns $60 a day even though he is no stronger than Alice. Donna uses a bucket and shovel too, and at first she earns only $20 a day. Not satisfied with this income, she takes a month off to complete a muscle-buiding course. When she comes back, she earns $50 a day. How should the income of each worker be classified in terms of wages, rent, interest, and profit?

Suggestions for Further Reading

Baird, Charles W. *Rent Control: The Perennial Folly.* San Francisco: Cato Institute, 1980.

Few economists like rent control. Baird explains why.

Böhm-Bawerk, Eugen von. "The Nature of Round-about Production." In *Contemporary Economics: Selected Readings*, 2nd ed. Edited by Reuben E. Slesinger, Mark Perlman, and Asher Isaacs. Boston: Allyn & Bacon, 1967.

A classic statement of the nature of capital and production by a turn-of-the-century Austrian economist.

Kirzner, Israel. *Competition and Entrepreneurship.* Chicago: University of Chicago Press, 1974.

Kirzner's own theory of profits, which stresses the role of arbitrage in entrepreneurial behavior. The book also contains a critique of other theories.

Scitovski, Tibor. *Welfare and Competition*, rev. ed. Homewood, Ill.: Irwin, 1971.

Chapter 19 discusses capital and entrepreneurship.

Chapter 33

The Problem of Poverty

Ideas for Review

Here are some terms and concepts that you should review before reading this chapter:

Marginal tax rate (Chapter 5)
Progressive and regressive taxes (Chapter 5)
Human capital (Chapter 30)
Economics of discrimination (Chapter 30)

"I'm laughing, but you know, inside I'm busting."

In the sultry air of a public-housing project office in Manhattan, Tessie Russo, a 58-year-old resident in a sleeveless housedress, is seething. Sweat beads dot her upper lip and ring her short gray hair.

Despite the heat, Miss Russo tells the project manager she must give up her window air conditioner. She no longer can afford the $7 monthly extra utility charge, because her monthly apartment rent went up $10 August 1 to $102.75. The former waitress, disabled by cancer, receives $374 in monthly social security payments, her only income.

"I'll just have to learn to live without the air conditioner," she says. "I'm laughing, but you know, inside I'm busting," she adds, her dark eyes, magnified by thick glasses, flashing angrily. "When I drop dead, they can put on my grave, 'Blame it on Ronald Reagan.' "[1]

Tessie Russo's plight illustrates an aspect of factor markets that we have not looked at much so far: the problem of poverty. Not everyone earns enough in wages, rent, interest, and profit to live comfortably. Some of the the poor are too young or too old to work. Some, like Russo, have worked in the past and benefit from the social security program to which they contributed during their working years, but they still find it hard to get by. Still others work part-time or full-time but do not earn enough to pull themselves out of poverty. In this chapter we will look at the pattern of earnings, needs, and transfer payments with which the economics of poverty is concerned. We will see why some people are angered by the fact that the government does not do more, while others, including some within the Reagan administration, think the government's past attempts to deal with the problem of poverty have only made things worse.

POVERTY AND INCOME DISTRIBUTION

Inequality of Income

As we emphasized at the beginning of Chapter 30, factor markets not only determine how goods and services are produced but also help determine for whom they are produced. Workers and owners of capital and natural resources are rewarded according to the productivity of the factors they contribute. Entrepreneurs earn profits or losses according to their degree of success in finding and taking advantage of new opportunities. Since people differ in skills and talents, in the amount of capital and natural resources they control, and in luck and entrepreneurial ability, their incomes also differ. Some earn nothing; others, millions of dollars a year.

On top of the unequal distribution of income that results from the operation of factor markets, it is necessary to take account of taxes and government transfer payments. Each year federal, state, and local governments pay out nearly $500 billion through a wide variety of transfer programs. Some, like the social security benefits that Tessie Russo receives,

---

[1]Joann S. Lublin, "Declining Housing Aid Worsens the Struggle for Many Poor People," *Wall Street Journal*, August 31, 1984, p. 1. Reprinted by permission of The Wall Street Journal, © Dow Jones & Company, Inc. 1984. All rights reserved.

help equalize incomes. But cash payments to the poor account for less than 10 percent of the half-trillion dollars in government transfer payments. Some of the rest goes to provide services in kind for the poor (such as Russo's public housing subsidy), but much of it goes to middle-class and even wealthy people. As a result, even when transfer payments are taken into account, there is a lot of inequality of income. As of 1982 the poorest 20 percent of the population received just 4.7 percent of all income while the richest 5 percent received some 16 percent of all income. Box 33.1 shows how the distribution of income can be summarized in the form of a diagram called a **Lorenz curve**.

Lorenz curve

A graphic representation of the degree of inequality in an economy.

Box 33.1
A Lorenz Curve for the U.S. Economy

A Lorenz curve is a diagram that can be used to represent the degree of inequality in an economy. Such a diagram is drawn in a square, with the horizontal axis representing the percent of the population and the vertical axis representing the percent of all income earned by those at or below each population percentile. In an economy in which income was distributed equally, the poorest 20 percent of the population would earn 20 percent of all income, the poorest 40 percent would earn 40 percent of all income, and so on. In that case the Lorenz curve would be a straight line from one corner of the box to the other. In the U.S. economy, where the poorest 20 percent of the population earns just 4.7 percent of all income while the richest 20 percent earns 42.7 percent of all income, the Lorenz curve sags toward the lower right-hand corner of the box. The degree of inequality can be measured by the shaded area between the Lorenz curve and the line of perfect equality.

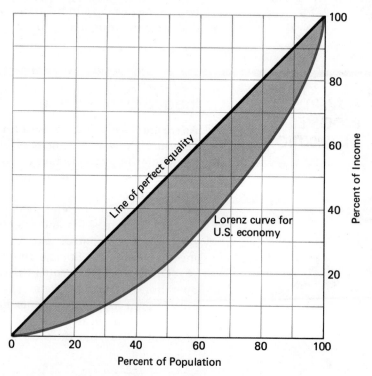

Source: Based on data in U.S. Department of Commerce, Bureau of the Census, *Statistical Abstract of the United States 1984*, 104th ed. (Washington, D.C.: Government Printing Office, 1983), Table 765.

Three Views of the Nature of Poverty

Poverty, obviously, is something that exists at the low end of the Lorenz curve. But just how low an income must a household have in order to be considered poor? There are at least three major points of view on this subject.

First is the view that poverty means not having enough income to provide some objectively defined standard of living. People are poor if they cannot afford the basic necessities of life—food, clothing, and shelter. Implicit in this viewpoint is the idea that people can be raised out of poverty by lifting their incomes above a specific threshold.

A second view also identifies poverty with low incomes, but it holds that what constitutes a low income must be defined in subjective terms, relative to the incomes of other members of the society. For example, it is often suggested that a poverty-level household income should be defined as one that is less than half of the median income for all households. (As of 1985 the median household income was about $25,000; some 20 percent of all households had cash incomes of less than half that amount.) This view makes poverty-level income a moving target rather than an objectively defined threshold. Even so, like the first view, it implies that poverty can be overcome by raising the incomes of the poor.

A third view is somewhat different from the other two. It makes poverty a matter not so much of low incomes as of how people cope with them. Some low-income households are able to make do with what they have, keep the family together, and keep the children out of trouble. Others, including many that, statistically speaking, have been raised above the poverty threshold, are unable to cope. They fall into a pattern of social pathologies ranging from juvenile crime and teenage pregnancy to drug and alcohol abuse. They turn newly constructed public housing into instant slums. In a variety of ways they frustrate the hopes of those who hope to eliminate poverty through generous public spending and giving. Implicit in this view is the idea that no amount of income redistribution can by itself eliminate poverty. If poorly conceived government programs foster dependency and destroy self-respect, they may even make things worse.

Poverty as Officially Defined

Of the three ways of defining poverty, the first is the one used by the U.S. government. The official definition begins with an economy food plan devised by the Department of Agriculture. The plan provides a balanced diet at the lowest possible cost, given prevailing market prices. The cost of the plan varies according to the size of a family. In 1982 the annual cost of a minimal diet was about $3,287 for a family of four.

By itself, a total income equal to the cost of the economy food plan is not enough to keep a family well nourished. Other needs must be met too. To take those needs into account, the government sets the low-income level—the dividing line between the poor and the nonpoor—at three times the cost of the economy food plan. Below that level the pressure of a family's needs for shelter, clothing, and other necessities tends to become so great that the family will forgo the needed food in order to get other things instead. In 1982 the low-income level for a family of four was $9,862.

How Many Poor?

Part of the reason for choosing an objective, need-based official definition of poverty in the first place was to provide a benchmark against which to measure progress toward the goal of eliminating poverty. On the basis of the official definition, the incidence of poverty fell rapidly during the decade after President Lyndon Johnson declared a "war on poverty" in 1964. In 1964, 19 percent of the population was officially classified as poor; by 1973, the figure had fallen to 11.1 percent. During the mid-1970s, however, the poverty rate stopped falling, and in the late 1970s it began to move up. By 1983 the poverty rate had risen to 15.2 percent, its highest level since 1965. And because of population growth the actual number of poor people was as high as it had been 20 years before.

What went wrong? A variety of answers have been proposed. Some observers blame a stagnant economy. Others see the data as evidence that antipoverty programs don't work—or even as evidence that they make the problem worse. Before looking at these claims, however, we need to take a closer look at how poverty is measured.

Box 33.2 compares three ways of measuring poverty. The first is the government's official measure. It is based on a household's *census income*—that is, its cash income from all sources, including wages and salaries, property income, pension benefits, social security benefits, and cash welfare benefits. It shows the pattern discussed earlier: a decline from 1964 to 1973, a flat trend during the later 1970s, and an increase after 1979.

Adjusting the poverty data   Economists who study the poverty problem, however, view the official data as an unsatisfactory mixture of market and government sources of income that in one sense overstates the extent of poverty and in another sense understates it. To indicate the extent of these over- and understatements, two other approaches to measuring poverty are also shown in Box 33.2.

The approach shown in columns 2 and 3 of the table adjusts households' census income to show the effects of government programs other than cash transfers. The most important adjustment is the inclusion of **in-kind transfers**—that is, help given to poor households in the form of free or below-cost goods and services rather than in the form of cash. Medicaid, food stamps, and housing assistance are the three largest in-kind programs. Both column 2 and column 3 take the value of in-kind transfers into account. In addition, the data in column 2 include further adjustments for the effects of taxes and estimated underreporting of income.

When poverty is measured in terms of adjusted income rather than in terms of census income, the picture given by the official data changes greatly. Whereas the official figures show no decline in poverty after 1973, the adjusted data show a continued decline through 1979. The reason for the difference is that in-kind transfers grew much faster than cash transfers during that period. From 1965 to 1981, cash transfers increased from $6.7 billion to $26.9 billion, while in-kind transfers rose from just $840 million to $43.9 billion.

Clearly, if we want to measure the degree to which government programs have succeeded in reducing poverty, we should not use a measure that leaves out the effects of the largest and fastest-growing government programs. The continued decline of the adjusted poverty

In-kind transfers
Transfer payments made in the form of goods or services, such as food, housing, or medical care, rather than in cash.

**Box 33.2
Alternative Measures of
Poverty**

The U.S. government's measure of poverty includes all cash income, both earned income and cash transfer payments. It has been criticized because in one sense it overstates the problem of poverty and in another sense it understates it. Columns 2 and 3 of this table adjust the official data to take into account the value of in-kind transfers. Column 2 includes further ajustments for taxes paid and estimated underreporting of income. These adjustments show that after taking all aid to the poor into account, the poverty rate was lower than shown by the official measure. For some purposes, it is also useful to know how many people would be poor without government aid. Column 4 measures "pretransfer poverty" by subtracting cash transfer payments from the income of poor households. The result is a poverty percentage that is higher than the official figure.

	Percent of Persons			
Year	Official Measure (1)	Adjusted for In-Kind Transfers, Underreporting, and Taxes (2)	Adjusted for In-Kind Transfers Only (3)	Pretransfer Poverty (4)
1964	19.0	—	—	—
1965	17.3	13.4	16.8	21.3
1966	14.7	—	—	—
1967	14.2	—	—	19.4
1968	12.8	9.9	—	18.2
1969	12.1	—	—	17.7
1970	12.6	9.3	—	18.8
1971	12.5	—	—	19.6
1972	11.9	6.2	—	19.2
1973	11.1	—	—	19.0
1974	11.2	7.2	—	20.3
1975	12.3	—	—	22.0
1976	11.8	6.7	—	21.0
1977	11.6	—	—	21.0
1978	11.4	—	—	20.2
1979	11.7	6.1	9.0	20.5
1980	13.0	—	10.4	21.9
1981	14.0	—	11.7	23.1
1982	15.0	—	12.7	24.0
1983	15.2	—	13.0	24.2

Source: Unpublished data, courtesy of Sheldon Danziger, University of Wisconsin–Madison, and Robert Plotnick, University of Washington.

figures throughout the 1970s led some observers to conclude that the war on poverty had, for all practical purposes, been won by 1980. But these declarations of victory turned out to be premature. After 1980, poverty rates began to rise again, even when adjusted for in-kind transfers. (See column 3 of Box 33.2.) To see what was going on, we need to look at yet another approach to measuring poverty.

Pretransfer poverty   Column 4 of Box 33.2 supplies this other approach. This set of data is intended to measure not the government's success in solving the poverty problem, but the size of the problem itself. With this in mind, it adjusts households' census income by subtracting cash transfer payments. What remains is "pretransfer poverty"—a measure of the percentage of the population who would be poor if they did not receive government benefits.

Because pretransfer poverty reflects mainly income earned by households in the labor market, it is very sensitive to the growth of the economy as a whole. Between 1964 and 1969, when economic growth was strong, pretransfer poverty fell from 21.3 percent of the population to 17.7 percent. During the 1970s, when growth was slow, it rose slightly. And during the severe recessions of 1974–1975 and 1980–1982, pretransfer poverty rose abruptly. It was this rise in pretransfer poverty, not any cutback in government programs, that appears to have caused the rise in the other poverty measures in the early 1980s. The four-percentage-point jump in the adjusted poverty rate between 1979 and 1983 is almost exactly matched by the 3.7 percent jump in pretransfer poverty over the same period.

Explaining Poverty Trends

The increase in poverty rates during the early 1980s, however it is measured, has become a subject of widespread debate. True, official poverty figures for 1984 and 1985 are likely to decline because of continued economic growth, although they are not expected to fall below 14 percent. But the real focus of the debate is not over yearly ups or downs in the official figures; rather, it is the enormous contrast between the rapid growth of government transfer payments and the persistence of poverty itself. This contrast is made clear in Box 33.3.

On one side of the debate are those who see the supposed cure for poverty as part of the problem. This view, while hardly new, has recently been popularized by Charles Murray in his book *Losing Ground*.[2] The argument (which we will return to later in the chapter) is that federal transfer programs contain incentives that encourage people to become poor or remain poor in order to qualify for benefits. They do so either by reducing their work effort or by changing the structure of the family units they live in. (For example, unmarried teenagers have children and leave their parents' homes, and elderly people live by themselves rather than with children or other relatives.) As a study by the National Center for Policy Analysis puts it, "Poverty in the U.S. is on the increase, and for only one reason: We are paying people to be poor. . . . The welfare system demands one thing from its clientele: a low money income. In return it offers passage through an entitlements gateway to more than 49 major benefit programs."[3]

It seems to be simple common sense to say that paying people to be poor will increase the number of poor people. Yet economists who have applied statistical methods to the problem have found the effects of poverty programs to be smaller than many critics believe them to be. For example, in a survey of research on the subject Sheldon Danziger, Robert Haveman, and Robert Plotnick concluded that poverty programs appear to reduce the work effort of poor people by just 4.8 percent. This effect can account for only half a percentage point of the 12 percent poverty rate of

[2]New York: Basic Books, 1984.
[3]"Welfare and Poverty," National Center for Policy Analysis, 1984.

**Box 33.3
Trends in Poverty and
Income Transfer
Programs, 1965–1982**

This chart contrasts the growth of spending on major federal transfer programs with trends in poverty. Spending is measured in constant 1983 dollars to adjust for the effects of inflation. The percentage of the population in poverty is based on the official definition. (See Box 33.2.) Despite the more than threefold increase in the real value of transfer payments over the period shown, the percentage of the population living in poverty is only slightly lower today than it was 20 years ago. Even if the official data were adjusted to show the effects of in-kind transfers, they would show an increase in poverty after 1979. Because of population growth, the number of poor people actually increased during the period shown.

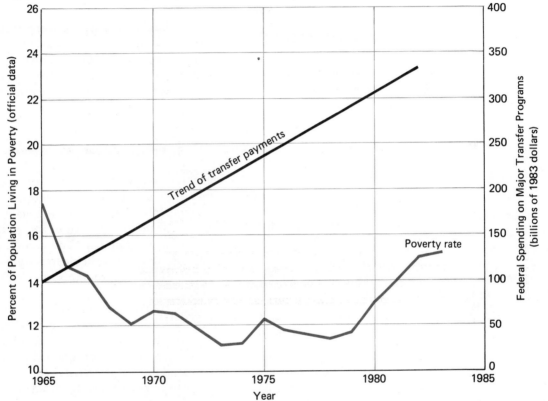

Source: Unpublished data, courtesy of Sheldon Danziger, University of Wisconsin–Madison, and Robert Plotnick, University of Washington.

the mid-1970s. They also concluded that the impact on the living arrangements of the elderly and on the formation of households headed by women is fairly small.

The statistical studies of poverty suggest that two factors other than incentive effects account for most of the rise in poverty rates since 1980. One factor was the back-to-back recessions of 1980 and 1981–1982, which we have already mentioned. The other factor was a pattern of population shifts that moved more people into groups with a high incidence of poverty even while poverty rates within groups fell.

For example, although households headed by nonwhite women have by far the highest incidence of poverty of any population group, the poverty rate for this group has been falling. In 1965 the poverty rate for such households was 80 percent. By 1978 it had fallen to 70.3 percent, and by 1983 it had fallen a bit more, to 68.8 percent. From the point of view of the national poverty statistics, however, the decline in poverty among households headed by nonwhite women has been more than offset by the increase in the number of such families. The formation of such households was boosted, in part, by a rise in the divorce rate among blacks from 92 per thousand to 223 per thousand between 1971 and 1981, and by an increase in the percentage of black children born to never-married women from 41 percent to 55 percent.[4] Data such as these add fuel to the debate over the causes of rising overall poverty rates.

More work needs to be done before the causes of poverty trends can be determined conclusively. However, all the participants in the debate agree that it is disturbing to find that the government's efforts to eliminate poverty have not been more effective. Let's take a closer look at specific programs and policies, and at ideas for making them more effective.

HELPING THE POOR: TRANSFER STRATEGIES

Social insurance
Programs under which transfers are made available to everyone, regardless of income, upon the occurrence of a specified event such as retirement, unemployment, or disability.

Public assistance
Programs under which transfers are made to people who meet some specified low-income standard.

The chief strategies of government aid to the poor emphasize income transfers. These transfers can be divided into two categories. The first, **social insurance**, includes programs in which transfers are made available to everyone, regardless of income, at the occurrence of a specified event such as retirement, unemployment, or disability. The second category, **public assistance**, includes programs that are available to people who meet some specified low-income standard. These programs are also known as *means-tested* programs or *welfare*.

Box 33.4 lists the major income transfer programs. It classifies them as social insurance or public assistance, and also according to whether their benefits are paid in cash or in kind. In addition, where possible, the box shows the percentage of the benefits of each program that go to poor households. This percentage is based on the pretransfer concept of poverty, so households that would have been poor but were raised out of poverty by the benefits they received are included.

Social Security and Related Programs

The Social Security Act of 1935 set up what has become the largest single income transfer program of the U.S. government. Social security is one of the most popular, and in some ways one of the most successful, programs of the federal government. This is especially true when one views the program as a way of reducing poverty among the elderly. In 1960, families headed by elderly people had a poverty rate almost double that of nonelderly families. By 1983, the poverty rate for elderly families was

---

[4]See Gordon Green and Edward Welniak, *Changing Family Composition and Income Differentials,* U.S. Bureau of the Census, Special Demographic Analyses, CDS-80-7 (Washington, D.C.: Government Printing Office, 1982). Between 1971 and 1981 the divorce rate for whites rose from 48 to 100, and the percentage of white children born to never-married mothers rose from 6 percent to 9 percent. The poverty rate for households headed by white women is 50 percent, so to a lesser degree these trends among whites also boosted the overall poverty rate.

lower than that for the nonelderly. Elderly people living alone (mainly widows) still had a higher poverty rate in 1983 than nonelderly people living alone, but the gap had narrowed a great deal since 1960. These improvements in the economic status of the elderly are due in no small part to the fact that social security benefits increased more than twice as fast as the average level of wages and salaries during the second half of this period.[5] But despite this record, social security is the target of many criticisms. It is worth looking at some of them.

Financing problems   One of the biggest problems is that social security has outgrown the method used to finance it. Social security benefits are financed by a special payroll tax, half of which is deducted from employees' gross pay and half of which is paid by employers. (However, most economists believe that all or most of the true incidence of the tax is on employees' wages and salaries.) When the program first began, the payroll tax was a modest one—just 1 percent each for employers and employees on the first $3,000 of income. Over the years, as the program's coverage has expanded and benefit levels have risen, the tax rate and the range of income to which it applies have risen steadily. By 1985 employers and employees were each paying a 7.05 percent tax on the first $38,000 of income—more than 80 times as much as when the program began.

The critics of social security complain not only that the tax is burdensome but also that is is regressive. Because the tax is levied only on earnings below a certain threshold, and because it is levied only on wage and salary income, lower- and middle-income households pay taxes that are higher in relation to their incomes than the taxes paid by higher-income households. Thus, the tax used to finance social security adds to income inequality, partly offsetting the effect of the benefits paid out under the program.

Effects on saving   A second criticism of the social security program is based on the belief that it tends to displace private saving. The program was intended to be a source of saving—workers paid taxes into a trust fund during their earning years and drew on the fund during retirement. The trust fund concept was long ago abandoned in all but name, however, and replaced by a pay-as-you-go system. The proceeds of the payroll tax are now used to pay benefits to currently retired workers, so no saving is involved.

Even though payroll taxes no longer represent saving from the viewpoint of the economy as a whole, they are a substitute for saving from the viewpoint of individual workers. Knowing that they will receive social security benefits upon retirement, workers feel that they can put aside less money to finance their own retirement.

Just how much private saving is displaced by each dollar of promised social security benefits is a matter of debate. But to the extent that there is any displacement of private saving by social security, the economy is left with less saving to finance investment; and with less investment, it is left with slower economic growth. This implies that today's workers will retire into a world where income and living standards will be lower than they

---

[5]For details, see Council of Economic Advisers, *Economic Report of the President* (Washington, D.C.: Government Printing Office, 1985), chap. 5.

would have been if the social security system had not promised to protect those same living standards for future beneficiaries.

Other social-insurance programs   The second-largest of the social-insurance programs is Medicare. This adjunct to the social security program provides in-kind medical benefits to the elderly. The sources of financing and criticisms of the program parallel those of the rest of the social security system. The remaining social-insurance programs are smaller and, as Box 33.4 shows, tend to channel a smaller percentage of their benefits to the poor. For both reasons, then, they do less to alleviate poverty.

Public Assistance

In addition to social security and other transfer programs keyed to specific events, the federal government operates a number of income-conditioned transfer programs for which a low income level is the test for participation. The most important of these are listed in Box 33.4.

Aid to Families with Dependent Children (AFDC)   To most people, "welfare" means Aid to Families with Dependent Children. AFDC provides assistance in covering the costs of food, shelter, and clothing for needy dependent children, generally in single-parent households. AFDC is the largest of the government's cash transfer programs.

The most controversial aspect of AFDC is the incentive that it seems to provide for men to desert their families and for women to bear children. Despite attempts to reform the eligibility rules in many states, and despite the addition of the AFDC–Unemployed Father program at the federal level, these incentives have not been completely eliminated. Defenders of the program are correct in pointing out that there is no hard evidence that these incentives actually operate. As mentioned earlier, statistical studies have not uncovered large effects of AFDC on family structure. Even so, AFDC will be a popular target of reformers as long as households headed by mothers of young children remain a large and growing portion of the poor.

Medicaid   Medical assistance to low-income people under the Medicaid program is the largest in-kind transfer program. Unlike most other public-assistance programs, Medicaid benefits are not reduced gradually as income rises. Low-income families either qualify for full coverage or receive none at all. AFDC families qualify for Medicaid in all states, and in some states families with somewhat higher incomes also qualify.

Food stamps   A third major public-assistance program is food stamps. In some areas where a high percentage of residents are eligible for the program, food stamps have become almost a form of currency. Although they can be spent only on food, they release money for other uses that would otherwise have been spent on food. While there is no doubt that food stamps are important to the budgets of a great many low-income families, it is far from clear that they have a greater impact on nutrition than cash grants of the same value would have.

**Box 33.4
Major Transfer Programs
of the U.S. Government**

This table shows expenditures on the major U.S. transfer programs for 1965 and 1981. Estimates are also given for 1985 where possible. The programs are classified according to whether they are social insurance or public assistance, and also according to whether benefits are paid in cash or in kind.

		Public Expenditures (billions of current dollars)			Percent of expenditures paid to poor people
	Date Enacted	1965	1981	1985 (selected programs)	
Social Insurance					
Cash benefits:					
Social security (OASDI)	1935	$16.5	$137.0	$191.1	57
Unemployment insurance	1935	2.5	18.7	16.8	22
Workers' compensation	1908	1.8	14.8		40
Veterans' disability compensation	1917	2.2	7.5	13.8	55
Railroad retirement	1937	1.1	5.2	5.4	
Black lung	1969	NE	0.9	0.9	
In-kind benefits:					
Medicare	1965	NE	38.4	66.3	60
Public Assistance (welfare)					
Cash benefits:					
Aid to Families with Dependent Children (AFDC)	1935	1.7	12.8	8.9	94
Supplemental Security Income (SSI)	1972	2.7	8.5	9.2	84
Veterans' pensions	1933	1.9	4.1		55
General assistance	NA	0.4	1.5		82
In-kind benefits:					
Medicaid[2]	1965	0.5	27.6	22.9	80
Food stamps	1964	0.04	9.7	11.5	88
Housing assistance	1937	0.3	6.6	10.7	74
Total Expenditures		$31.5	$293.2		
Total Expenditures as a Percentage of GNP		4.6	10.0		

Source: Sheldon Danziger, Robert Haveman, and Robert Plotnick, "How Income Transfer Programs Affect Work, Savings, and the Income Distribution: A Critical Review," *Journal of Economic Literature* 19, September 1981, Table 1. Data for 1985 are from *The Budget of the United States Government, Fiscal Year 1986*.

Income Transfers and Work Incentives

Benefit reduction rate
The reduction in the benefits of a transfer program that results from a one-dollar increase in the earned income of the beneficiary.

All income transfer programs affect the incentive to work to some extent by imposing either explicit or implicit taxes on earned income. The social security payroll tax is an example of an explicit tax. The **benefit reduction rate** built into the AFDC program is an example of an implicit tax: For each $1 of earned income in excess of $30 a month, AFDC benefits tend to fall by about 33 cents. And some transfer programs, such as Medicaid, have all-or-nothing cutoff incomes that also reduce the incentive to work.

Net marginal tax rate
The sum of the marginal tax rate for all taxes paid by a household plus the benefit reduction rates of all transfer programs from which the household benefits.

The percentage of each additional dollar of earned income that a household loses through either explicit taxes or benefit reductions can be called the **net marginal tax rate** for that household. A key principle of the economics of poverty is that marginal tax rates and benefit reduction rates are *additive* in their effects on the net marginal tax rate. For example, a family facing a 7 percent marginal tax rate for the social security payroll tax and a 33 percent benefit reduction rate under AFDC is subject to a 40 percent net marginal tax rate. If, in addition, food stamp benefits are reduced by 20 cents for each dollar of added earned income, the net marginal tax rate rises to 60 percent, and so on.

Box 33.5 shows how the effects of various programs combine to create net marginal tax rates that can exceed 100 percent for households in certain income ranges. Taxes paid by low-income families are, of course, lower than those paid by higher-income families, but when benefit reduction rates are taken into account, the net marginal tax rates for low-income families are actually higher than the net marginal tax rates for high-income families. (See Box 33.6.)

The Negative Income Tax

Negative income tax
A plan under which all transfer programs would be combined into a single program paying cash benefits that depend on a household's level of income.

Economists who are concerned about the undesired effects of transfer programs have long advocated "cashing out" all in-kind transfers and combining them, along with all existing cash transfers, into a single program. Such a program is often referred to as a **negative income tax**. The basic idea is simple. Under a positive income tax people pay the government an amount that varies according to how much they earn. A negative income tax puts the same principle to work in reverse. It makes the government pay individuals an amount that varies in inverse proportion to their earnings.

Box 33.7 shows how a negative income tax could be set up. The horizontal axis of the graph measures the income a household earns. The vertical axis measures what it actually receives after payments from or to the government. The 45-degree line represents the amount of disposable income households would have if there were no tax of any kind. The negative and positive income tax schedules show the disposable income of families with the negative income tax program in force.

In this box the benefit received by a family with no income at all is just equal to the average low-income level, which is assumed to be $10,000. That is necessary if the scheme is to eliminate poverty as officially measured. Starting from zero earnings, benefits are reduced by 50 cents for each dollar earned. When earned incomes reach a level equal to twice the low-income level, a breakeven point where no taxes are paid and no benefits are received is reached. Beyond that point, a positive income tax schedule takes over.

The negative income tax has the advantage of maintaining work incentives for all beneficiaries. The marginal tax rate for poor families is only 50 percent. This rate presumably is low enough to prevent widespread reluctance to work. The cost of the program, however, is much greater than the total amount by which the incomes of all the poor fell below the poverty line to begin with. All but the very poorest families receive more than the minimum they need to reach the low-income cutoff.

Box 33.5
Net Marginal Tax Rates
for a Los Angeles
Family

This table shows how taxes and reductions in benefits affect the monthly disposable income of an inner-city family of four in Los Angeles at various levels of gross monthly wages. Gross monthly wages are the cost of labor to the employer and include both employer and employee contributions to social security. The data on disposable income reflect all payroll and income taxes and assume that the family makes use of the maximum city, county, state, and federal welfare benefits to which it is entitled.

The net marginal tax rate is the sum of the marginal tax rates and benefit reduction rates to which the family is subject. The disincentive effects of benefit reductions and taxes reach a peak just above and below the poverty threshold ($833 a month, based on a low-income level of about $10,000 a year for a family of four). Note that as the family's gross wages increase from $700 a month to $1,200 a month, its disposable income falls from $1,423 to $1,215. This reflects a loss of $385 in AFDC benefits; a loss of $9 in food stamps; a reduction of $23 in the family's housing subsidy; an estimated reduction of $130 in the value of its medical benefits; an $8 increase in state income and disability insurance taxes; $68 in payroll taxes; and $85 in federal income taxes.

Monthly Gross Wages (dollars)	Monthly Family Disposable Income (dollars)	Change in Disposable Income (dollars)	Net Marginal Tax Rate (percent)
0	1,261	NA	NA
100	1,304	43	57
200	1,341	37	63
300	1,366	25	75
400	1,391	25	75
500	1,419	28	72
600	1,429	10	90
700	1,423	−5	105
800	1,418	−5	105
900	1,420	2	98
1,000	1,432	12	89
1,100	1,253	−178	278
1,200	1,215	−39	139
1,300	1,217	2	98
1,400	1,296	39	61
1,500	1,294	38	62
1,600	1,330	37	63

NA = not applicable.

Source: Arthur Laffer, "The Tightening Grip of the Poverty Trap," Cato Institute Policy Analysis No. 41 (August 30, 1984).

What is more, many nonpoor families—those with earned incomes in the $10,000–$20,000 range—also receive benefits. The spillover of benefits to nonpoor families is an inevitable part of the negative income tax scheme. It cannot be avoided without lowering benefits for the poorest families or raising the net marginal tax rate to a level that would destroy work incentives.

Box 33.6
Net Marginal Tax Rates, by Income Decile

This chart shows net marginal tax rates by income decile for the U.S. economy. Marginal tax rates for taxes paid to the government rise as family income rises because of the progressive federal income tax. However, for families in the lowest 70 percent of the income distribution, the progressive nature of the income tax is more than offset by the benefit reduction rate for various transfer programs. As a result, net marginal tax rates—which reduce the incentive to work—are highest for the poorest families and lowest for families in upper-middle income groups.

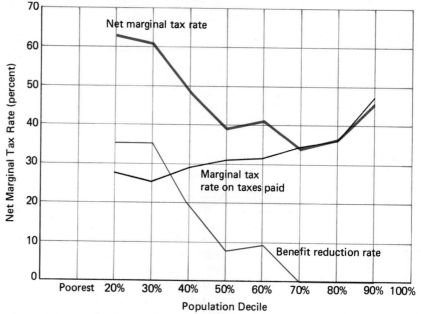

Source: Edgar K. Browning and William R. Johnson, *The Distribution of the Tax Burden* (Washington, D.C.: American Enterprise Institute, 1979), Table 17.

HELPING THE POOR: JOB MARKET STRATEGIES

Transfer strategies for helping the poor are based on the belief that people are poor because they do not have enough money. The implied cure is to give them more resources, either in cash or in kind. A different approach to the problem of poverty is based on the belief that poverty results from a failure of factor markets to allocate human resources properly. This implies that putting wasted labor to work would make many poor households self-supporting.

The view that poverty is a result of factor market failure must be interpreted rather broadly, since relatively few of the poor are adults in households headed by unemployed able-bodied men aged 18 to 65. A narrowly conceived jobs-for-the-poor approach that focused on this group would not have much of an effect on the overall poverty picture. In a broader sense, though, much more poverty is attributable to job-related sources. The number of elderly poor and working poor would be reduced if the market provided higher-paying jobs. The number of families headed by women, where the highest proportion of poor children are concentrated, would be less if it were not for the destructive effect on family life of

**Box 33.7
A Negative Income Tax**

A negative income tax would replace all transfer programs with a single cash transfer based on income. This chart assumes a poverty level of $10,000 for a family of four. A family with no earned income receives $10,000 in benefits from the negative income tax. From $0 to $10,000, benefits are reduced by 50 cents for each $1 of additional earned income. When earned income exceeds $20,000, benefits fall to zero and the family begins to pay income tax. Here a flat 25 percent marginal tax rate is assumed for incomes above $20,000.

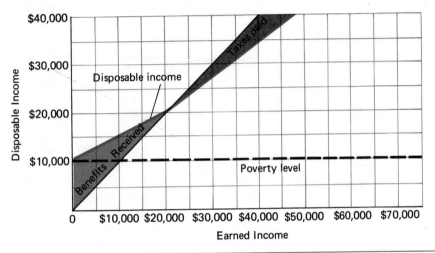

men's inability to get good jobs. In the long run, job market strategies for alleviating poverty could benefit all the poor.

The Dual Labor Market Theory

Job market failure as a source of poverty is not just a matter of unemployment. According to one theory, the problem lies in the existence of a "dual labor market." The primary sector of the labor market contains high-wage jobs at profitable firms. These jobs not only pay more but are more likely to be unionized and to offer opportunities for advancement, and they tend to be less affected by macroeconomic fluctuations than other jobs. The secondary sector of the labor market, in contrast, contains low-paying jobs at marginal firms. These jobs are held by nonunionized workers with unstable work patterns. They are largely dead-end jobs with few opportunities for advancement, and they tend to be strongly affected by cyclical swings in unemployment.

According to the theory, the two parts of the job market are kept separate by a set of interacting factors. Discrimination, coupled with worker attitudes, motivation, and work habits, determines which sector a worker is in. Once in the secondary sector, a worker develops attitudes and work habits that make discrimination more likely. The dual labor market theory clearly implies that antipoverty policy must aim at breaking down the barriers between the two market sectors. The following section looks at some possible ways of doing this.

Education   As we showed in Chapter 30, economists view education as an investment in human capital. By spending money and taking time away from current employment, people can improve their skills and productivity. Later they can sell their services in the labor market at higher wages. One antipoverty strategy, then, is to make good-quality education available to the poor and to the children of the poor in the hope that it will make them self-supporting.

Antidiscrimination programs   Antidiscrimination programs are another job market strategy for aiding the poor. In Chapter 30 we showed that discrimination can lower the incomes of people in the disfavored group. In the absence of laws to the contrary, discrimination is likely to lead to a situation in which workers from different groups doing the same work receive different wages. Today, equal-pay laws prohibit this practice.

However, again as shown in Chapter 30, equal-pay laws by themselves do not benefit all members of a disfavored group if employers' discriminatory attitudes are not changed. Instead, they tend to replace low wages with limited job opportunities. In fact, equal-pay laws, by themselves, can even increase the degree to which minority workers are crowded into low-paying jobs in the secondary sector of the economy. To combat this danger, the equal-pay laws are often supplemented by affirmative-action programs that aim to ensure that minority groups will be treated equally in filling job openings as well as being treated equally in terms of pay.

Public employment   Still another job market strategy for aiding the poor is to have the government employ them directly. The U.S. government has experimented with public-employment programs of various types for more than 50 years. Some people advocate expanding these programs to the point at which the government would become the "employer of last resort" for all people who seek jobs but cannot find them in the private sector.

Public-employment programs have their problems, though. One of the most frequent problems is that the jobs that the government can create most easily are service jobs that require little capital investment, such as park maintenance. Such jobs do not provide the skills and training needed to qualify people for jobs in the primary sector of the private economy. To get around this problem, some economists favor subsidies to private employers who create jobs for the poor rather than direct employment in the public sector.

Minimum wage laws   Minimum wage laws are another approach that is often seen as a means of fighting poverty. Some jobs pay such low wages that even a full-time job held by the head of a household does not bring in enough income to raise a family above the poverty level. (At present, counting 40 hours a week for 50 weeks a year as a full-time job, a wage of more than $5 an hour, disregarding taxes, is needed for one earner to support a family of four at the official low-income level.) It would seem that a simple way to raise the working poor to a more comfortable standard of living would be to legislate a higher minimum wage. In the United States the first federal minimum wage law was passed in 1938 and required employers to pay 25 cents per hour. Since then the federal minimum wage has been raised several times; the minimum wage now stands at $3.35 an hour.

Economists have long been skeptical of the minimum wage as an antipoverty program, however. The reason has to do once again with supply and demand. Although raising the minimum wage does make some low-skilled workers better off, it reduces the quantity demanded of such workers. Each increase in the minimum wage thus means that some people lose their jobs—restaurants remain open fewer hours; automated gates replace parking lot attendants; and so on. Making some low-skilled workers better off while putting others out of work does not do much to reduce inequality.

There are other reasons to doubt the effectiveness of the minimum wage as an antipoverty program. For one thing, according to a study by William R. Johnson and Edgar K. Browning, low-wage workers do not come mostly from low-income households.[6] Instead, over half of all workers at the minimum wage level come from households in the top half of the national income distribution. These workers include students working part-time and living with their families, low-paid spouses in households in which both husband and wife work, and so on. At the same time, low-income households get less than 14 percent of their total incomes from low-wage jobs. More typically, low-income households depend on income from pensions, disability payments, welfare, and other nonwage sources.

All in all, Johnson and Browning conclude, a 22 percent increase in the minimum wage would add just two-tenths of one percent to the average income of households in the bottom 30 percent of the income distribution. And even that slight increase in the average masks the fact that more low-income households would be made worse off because of job losses than would gain.

In fact, some economists are so skeptical of the effects of the minimum wage that they suggest that a reduction in the minimum would help the poor. For example, one proposal would establish a special subminimum wage for teenage workers, for whom unemployment rates are especially high. Even though teenagers would not earn much money working for less than $3.35 an hour, some earnings would be better than none. More important, even a low-paying job might result in experience and improved work habits that would lead to better jobs later. As yet, however, a subminimum wage has not been tried.

Conclusions

Where does all this leave us? In many ways this chapter has struck a gloomy note. Despite billions of dollars a year in transfer payments, more Americans are poor today than was the case 20 years ago. Programs ranging from social security to AFDC are accused of adversely affecting work incentive, saving, and family structure. Economists propose solutions, such as the negative income tax, that look elegant on paper, but the political chances of such reforms are nil. Is there any good news on the poverty front?

At least one recent study shows that poverty, though widespread, is not always a permanent condition. In a recent book, *Years of Poverty, Years of Plenty*, Greg J. Duncan and associates summarize the results of an

---

[6]William R. Johnson and Edgar K. Browning, "The Distributional and Efficiency Effects of Increasing the Minimum Wage: A Simulation," *American Economic Review* 73, March 1983, pp. 204–211.

extensive study of poverty conducted by the Institute for Social Research of the University of Michigan.[7] Duncan and his fellow researchers found that only a little over half of the people living in poverty in one year are still living in poverty in the next year. For example, as we have pointed out, households headed by women with young children are the largest single group of welfare recipients. Yet the University of Michigan study found that at least half of these families were using welfare only as a transitional aid to cope with an economic crisis such as the death or departure of a husband.

In the ten years covered by the study, 25 percent of all families were poor for at least one year. On the other hand, fewer than 3 percent were poor for eight or more of the ten years. In addition, the study found, the children of poor families were not doomed to a life of poverty. Young adults forming households tend to be upwardly mobile, even when they come from families in the lowest or next-to-lowest 20 percent of the income distribution. A significant number move right to the top 40 percent of the national income distribution.

An optimist can take these findings as a sign that initiative and mobility are alive in all sectors of the population, even those that are, in a sense, the victims as well as the beneficiaries of flawed policies for fighting poverty.

Summary

1. Factor markets help determine for whom goods and services are produced as well as how they are produced. Workers and owners of capital and natural resources are rewarded according to the productivity of the factors they contribute. Because skills, ability, and factor ownership are distributed unequally, income also tends to be distributed unequally in a market economy. A *Lorenz curve* is a diagram that can be used to give a graphic picture of the degree of inequality in an economy.

2. The U.S. government measures poverty in relation to a low-income level equal to three times the cost of an economy food plan. In measuring poverty, the government takes into account all cash income, including earned income and transfer payments, but excludes the value of in-kind transfer payments. Economists often use two other measures of poverty. One excludes all transfer payments, and the other includes the value of in-kind transfers along with cash transfers.

3. However it is measured, poverty increased in the United States during the early 1980s. In part, the increase was a result of the recessions of 1980 and 1981–1982. In part, it was a result of demographic shifts that put a higher percentage of the population in groups, such as households headed by women with young children, with a high incidence of poverty. In addition, according to some observers, the increase may have been caused in part by undesired effects of antipoverty programs.

4. The term *social insurance* refers to transfer programs to which everyone is entitled regardless of income. Social security is the largest such program. Veterans' benefits and Medicare are other examples. *Public-assistance* programs are those to which people are entitled only if they meet a low-income test. Aid to Families with Dependent Children is the largest public-assistance program that pays benefits in cash. Medicaid, food stamps, and housing assistance are programs that provide benefits in kind.

5. The *benefit reduction rate* of a transfer program

---

[7]Ann Arbor, Mich.: University of Michigan Press, 1984.

means the amount of benefits lost per dollar increase in earned income. A household's *net marginal tax rate* is the sum of its marginal tax rate for taxes paid plus the benefit reduction rates of all transfer programs to which it is entitled. Net marginal tax rates are higher in the United States for low-income families than for high-income families. Many economists believe that high net marginal tax rates provide a major incentive not to work. A *negative income tax* would convert all transfer programs into cash and subject them to a uniform net marginal tax rate lower than the rate currently imposed on poor families.

6. In addition to transfer programs, there are programs whose goal is to help the poor by improving their ability to earn income and find jobs in the primary sector of the job market. Job market strategies include aid to education, antidiscrimination laws, public employment, and minimum wage laws.

Questions for Review

1. Define the following terms:
    Lorenz curve
    in-kind transfers
    social insurance
    public assistance
    benefit reduction rate
    net marginal tax rate
    negative income tax
2. What is the shape of the Lorenz curve for an economy in which income is distributed equally? How does the Lorenz curve for the U.S. economy compare to this standard?
3. Why do economists often use measures of poverty that differ from the government's measure?
4. What has been the trend of poverty in the United States over the past 20 years as officially measured? List at least three factors that have contributed to the trend.
5. What are the largest federal transfer programs in each of the following categories: cash social insurance; in-kind social insurance; cash public assistance; in-kind public assistance?
6. If a family pays 10 percent income tax on all earned income, loses 25 cents in public housing benefits for each dollar of earned income, and loses 20 cents in food stamps for each dollar of earned income, what is its net marginal tax rate?
7. List four job market strategies for helping the poor.

Problems and Topics for Discussion

1. According to the official definition of poverty, a family living below the low-income level is likely to be unable to afford an adequate diet. Yet a government survey completed in 1977 showed that of families at or near the poverty line, 68 percent owned one or more cars and 12 percent owned two or more; 71 percent owned black-and-white television sets and 37 percent owned color sets; 55 percent owned clothes washers and 25 percent owned clothes dryers; and 38 percent owned air conditioners. Do you find it reasonable that families would begin to give up some food before giving up these durable goods? How do these figures bear on the issue of whether poverty should be measured by an absolute or a relative standard? How do you think these data would be interpreted by a person who lives in a country where cars, color television sets, and so on are luxuries possessed only by the rich? Discuss.
2. What are the relative merits of cash versus in-kind transfers? Review Chapter 20, paying particular attention to the concepts of marginal utility and consumer equilibrium. Suppose that program A gives a family a $1,000 cash benefit and program B gives the family

$1,000 worth of goods in kind—but in proportions that are not chosen by the family itself. Which program would be likely to give the family greater utility? Bonus question: If you read the appendix to Chapter 20, illustrate these two programs for the case of an economy in which there are just two consumer goods, food and clothing.

3. Suppose that an effective negative income tax was in force and that poverty had been eliminated. Would you then be willing to see social-insurance programs such as social security, Medicare, and unemployment compensation abolished? Why or why not?

4. Discussions of "waste" in poverty programs often focus on the fact that some benefits go to families whose incomes are above the poverty line. After reading this chapter, do you agree that it is wasteful to pay benefits to some nonpoor families? Would you favor a program that cut off all benefits exactly when the poverty line was reached? In what ways might such a program itself be wasteful? Discuss.

Suggestions for Further Reading

Bawden, D. Lee, ed. *The Social Contract Revisited.* Washington, D.C.: Urban Institute Press, 1984.

Includes an analysis of the Reagan administration's social policy by Nathan Glazer.

Campbell, Colin D., ed. *Income Redistribution.* Washington, D.C.: American Enterprise Institute, 1977.

The papers in this volume consider not only practical questions but also broad philosophical questions.

Goodman, John C., and Edwin G. Dolan. *Economics of Public Policy*, 3rd ed. St. Paul: West, 1985.

Chapter 14 is devoted to the minimum wage and Chapter 15 to social security.

Murray, Charles. *Losing Ground.* New York: Basic Books, 1984.

Murray argues that antipoverty efforts over the past 20 years have made the problem of poverty worse, not better.

International trade links nations together in a world economy. This scene from Heidelberg, Germany, shows a well-known U.S. export.

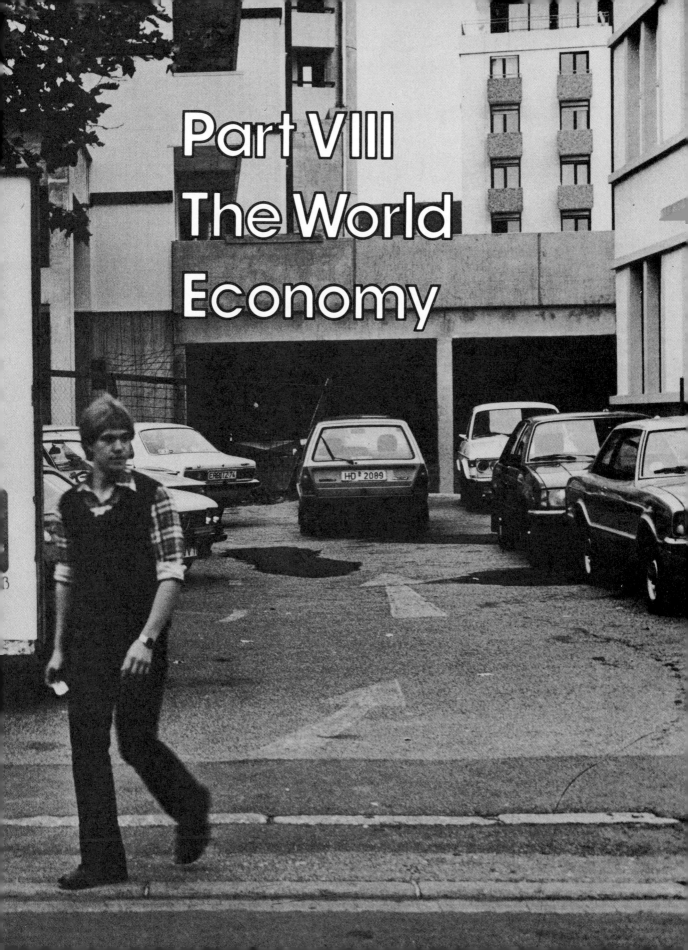

Part VIII
The World
Economy

Chapter 34

International Trade and Comparative Advantage

"You really have to fight for your life if you want to buy an automobile."

Al Stokes of Plymouth, Michigan, waited six months for his new red Pontiac Fiero—and he is a General Motors employee. Carol Derryberry of Falls Church, Virginia, got a "deal" on a Toyota Tercel; she paid only $973 over the sticker price. Michael D. Coleman of Springfield, Virginia, spent almost two months searching for a big Oldsmobile Delta 88 before settling on a demonstrator that "quite frankly had a lot of things we didn't want but we took them because they were there."

That is life in the 1984 seller's market for automobiles. With many models in short supply, the chore of buying a car, often unpleasant even in the best of times, has become a nightmare for many Americans.

"Once you get in there, you really have to start fighting for your life if you really want to buy an automobile," says John Hammond Sr., a travel agent in Annapolis, Maryland, who is shopping for a new car.

Compounding the problem are informal quotas on Japanese car exports to the United States, production-capacity constraints at domestic assembly plants, and Detroit's efforts to combat the Japanese threat by stressing quality over quantity. Despite brisk demand, the Big Three automakers have built fewer cars than planned for much of this year; one reason is parts that didn't live up to Detroit's new, higher standards.

The results: long waiting lists for some models; dealers who won't negotiate at all on price or who add option packages to improve their negotiating position; "availability charges" or "additional dealer mark-ups" of up to $3,000 that some dealers unabashedly put on the sticker and pocket as profit; showrooms where there are no cars on the floor and all the selling is done from brochures.[1]

Up to this point, we have studied micro- and macroeconomics mainly within the context of a single national economy. A whole area of economic theory—the theory of international trade—has received hardly a mention. But as Al Stokes and other consumers' recent experience in the automobile market shows, treating national economies as isolated units can be quite unrealistic. International trade in goods, services, and financial assets increasingly shapes the lives of consumers and producers.

International trade theory has traditionally been divided into two branches. The microeconomic branch, known as the *pure theory of international trade,* deals with patterns of imports and exports, the gains from trade, and policies that affect the international flow of goods and services. That part of trade theory will be covered in this chapter. The macroeconomic branch, often known as the *international monetary theory,* deals with the consequences of the fact that different economies use different currencies. Chapter 35 will cover the monetary theory of trade, including questions of exchange rates between currencies, the balance of payments, and the effects of trade on employment, interest rates, and economic growth.

---

[1] Melinda Grenier Guiles, "Sellers Market: Buying a Car Can Be a Horrible Experience If You Want One Now," *Wall Street Journal*, October 30, 1984, p. 1. Reprinted by permission of The Wall Street Journal, © Dow Jones & Company, Inc. 1984. All rights reserved.

COMPARATIVE ADVANTAGE IN INTERNATIONAL TRADE

The microeconomics of international trade begins with the concept of comparative advantage. In Chapter 2 we introduced this concept in discussing the division of labor within the economy of one country. Now we apply it to the division of labor among countries. This is the context in which David Ricardo first stated the theory of comparative advantage early in the nineteenth century. (See Box 34.1.) Ricardo wanted to show why it would be to England's advantage to maintain active trade with other countries. To do so, he used an example much like the following.

Box 34.1
David Ricardo and the Theory of Comparative Advantage

David Ricardo
(1772–1823)

David Ricardo, the greatest of the classical economists, was born in 1772. His father, a Jewish immigrant, was a member of the London stock exchange. Ricardo's education was rather haphazard, and he entered his father's business at the age of 14. In 1793 he married, abandoned strict Jewish orthodoxy, and went into business on his own. These were years of war and financial disturbance. The young Ricardo developed a reputation for remarkable astuteness and quickly made a large fortune.

In 1799 Ricardo read *The Wealth of Nations* and developed an interest in political economy. In 1809 his first writings on economics appeared. They were a series of newspaper articles on "The High Price of Bullion," which appeared the next year as a pamphlet. Several other short works added to his reputation in this area. In 1814 he retired from business to devote all his time to political economy.

Ricardo's major work was *Principles of Political Economy and Taxation*, first published in 1817. This work contains, among other things, a pioneering statement of the principle of comparative advantage as applied to international trade. With a lucid numerical example, Ricardo shows why it is to the mutual advantage of both countries for England to export wool to Portugal and to import wine in return, even though both products can be produced more cheaply in Portugal.

But international trade is only a sidelight of Ricardo's *Principles*. The book covers the whole of economics as the field was then known, beginning with value theory and progressing to a theory of economic growth and evolution. Ricardo, like his friend Malthus and his later follower John Stuart Mill, held that the economy was growing toward a future "steady state." In this state, economic growth would come to a halt and the wage rate would be reduced to the subsistence level.

Ricardo's book was extremely influential. For more than half a century thereafter, much of economics as written in England was an expansion of or a commentary on Ricardo's work. The most famous of the economists who were influenced by Ricardo's theory and method was Karl Marx. Although Marx eventually reached conclusions that differed radically from any views Ricardo held, his starting point was Ricardo's labor theory of value and his method of analyzing economic growth.

An Example

Imagine two countries called (for the sake of the example) Norway and Spain. Both have farms and offshore fishing grounds, but the moderate climate of Spain makes both the farms and the fishing grounds more productive. The number of labor hours required to produce a ton of each product in the two countries is shown in Box 34.2. For simplicity, only labor costs are considered in this example. Other costs can be thought of as proportional to labor costs. Also, per-unit labor costs are assumed to be constant for all levels of output.

Box 34.2 reveals two kinds of differences in the cost structure of the two countries. First, both fish and grain require fewer labor hours to produce in Spain. Thus, Spain is said to have an **absolute advantage** in the production of both goods.

Second, there are differences in opportunity costs between the two countries. Consider the cost of each good in each country, not in terms of labor hours but in terms of the other good. In Norway, producing a ton of fish means forgoing the opportunity to use 5 labor hours in the fields. A ton of fish thus has an opportunity cost of 1 ton of grain there. In Spain, producing a ton of fish means giving up the opportunity to produce 2 tons of grain. In terms of opportunity costs, then, fish is cheaper in Norway than in Spain, and grain is cheaper in Spain than in Norway. As in Chapter 2, the country in which the opportunity cost of a good is lower is said to have a *comparative advantage* in producing that good.

Pretrade equilibrium   If no trade takes place between Norway and Spain, the fish and grain markets in the two countries will achieve equilibrium independently. Since in this example we are ignoring all costs except labor costs and assuming those costs to be constant, in pretrade equilibrium the ratio of the price of fish to the price of grain in each country will be equal to the ratio of labor inputs needed to produce the goods. In Norway, where a ton of grain and a ton of fish both take the same amount of labor to produce, the price of fish will be equal to the price of grain. In Spain, where a ton of fish takes twice as much labor to produce as a ton of grain, the equilibrium price of fish will be twice the price of grain.

Suppose that each country has 1,000 labor hours available for the production of fish and grain. The way these labor hours are divided between the two products depends on demand and consumer tastes.

Absolute advantage
The ability of a country to produce a good at a lower cost, in terms of quantity of factor inputs, than its trading partners.

**Box 34.2
Labor Hours per Ton of Output in Spain and Norway**

The figures in this table show the number of labor hours required to produce a ton of fish and grain in Spain and Norway. Spain has an absolute advantage in the production of both goods. Norway has a comparative advantage in fish, and Spain has a comparative advantage in grain.

	Spain	Norway
Fish	4	5
Grain	2	5

Suppose that demand conditions are such that in Norway 100 tons of grain and 100 tons of fish are produced, while in Spain 350 tons of grain are grown and 75 tons of fish are caught. The quantities produced and consumed in pretrade equilibrium are noted in Box 34.3.

**Box 34.3
Pretrade Equilibrium
Output of Fish and
Grain in Spain and
Norway**

If Spain and Norway do not engage in trade, each country will have to meet all its needs from its own resources. The quantities of goods that each produces will depend on the strength of domestic demand. The relative prices of the two goods in each country will be determined by their labor costs, as shown in Box 34.2.

	Spain	Norway	World Total
Fish	75	100	175
Grain	350	100	450

The possibility of trade   Now let's consider the possibility of trade between Norway and Spain. A glance at labor costs in the two countries might suggest that there is no possibility of trade. Norwegians might like to get their hands on some of those cheap Spanish goods, but why should the Spanish be interested? After all, couldn't they produce everything at home more cheaply than it could be produced abroad? If so, how could they gain from trade? But a closer analysis shows that this view is incorrect. Absolute advantage turns out, in this case, to be unimportant in determining patterns of trade. Only comparative advantage matters.

To see that possibilities for trade between the two countries do exist, imagine that a Norwegian fishing party decides to sail into a Spanish port with a ton of its catch. Spanish merchants in the port will be used to giving 2 tons of grain, or its equivalent, for a ton of fish. The Norwegians will be used to getting only 1 ton of grain for each ton of fish. Any exchange ratio between 1 and 2 tons of grain per ton of fish will seem attractive to both parties. For instance, a trade of 1.5 tons of grain for a ton of fish will make both the Spanish merchants and the Norwegian fishing party better off than they would have been had they traded only with others from their own country.

Gains from specialization   The opening of trade between Spain and Norway will soon begin to have an effect on patterns of production in the two countries. In Norway, farmers will discover that instead of working 5 hours to raise a ton of grain from their own rocky soil, they can fish for 5 hours and trade their catch to the Spaniards for 1.5 tons of grain. In Spain, people will find that it is no longer worth their while to spend 4 hours to catch a ton of fish. Instead, they can work just 3 hours in the fields, and the 1.5 tons of grain that they grow will get them a ton of fish from the Norwegians. In short, the Norwegians will find it worth their while to specialize in fish, and the Spaniards will find it worth their while to specialize in grain.

Suppose now that trade continues at the rate of 1.5 tons of grain per ton of fish until both countries have become completely specialized. Spain no longer produces any fish, and Norway no longer produces any grain. Norwegians catch 200 tons of fish, half of which are exported to Spain. The Spanish grow 500 tons of grain, 150 tons of which are exported to Norway. Box 34.4 summarizes this situation.

**Box 34.4
Posttrade Production
and Consumption of
Fish and Grain in Spain
and Norway**

This table assumes that Spain and Norway have traded fish for grain at the rate of 1.5 tons of grain per ton of fish. Both countries have become entirely specialized. When this table is compared with the table in Box 34.3, it is clear that the consumers in both countries have the same amount of the product they export and more of the product they import than they did before the trade. Also, total world production of fish has risen from 175 to 200 tons, and total world production of grain has risen from 450 to 500 tons.

		Spain	Norway	World Total
Fish	Production	0	200	200
	Consumption	100	100	200
Grain	Production	500	0	500
	Consumption	350	150	500

A comparison of this table with Box 34.3 reveals three things. First, Norwegians are better off than before; they have just as much fish to eat and 50 tons more grain than in the pretrade equilibrium. Second, Spaniards are also better off; they have just as much grain to consume as ever—and more fish. Finally, total world output of both grain and fish has risen as a result of trade. Everyone is better off and no one is worse off.

A Graphic Presentation of the Theory of Comparative Advantage

The concept of comparative advantage can be illustrated graphically, using a set of production possibility frontiers based on the example just given. This is done in Box 34.5, which shows three production possibility frontiers. Part a is the production possibility frontier for Spain. At 2 labor hours per ton of grain, Spain can produce up to 500 tons of grain per year if it produces no fish (point B). If it produces no grain, up to 250 tons of fish per year can be caught at 4 hours per ton of fish (point D). The combinations of grain and fish that Spain can produce are represented by the line running from D to B.

Part b of Box 34.5 shows the production possibility frontier for Norway. In Norway, fish and grain each take 5 labor hours per ton to produce. If Norwegians devote all their time to fishing, they can catch up to 200 tons of fish per year (point B'). If they devote all their time to farming, they can grow up to 200 tons of grain (point D'). The line between B' and D' represents the Norwegian production possibility frontier.

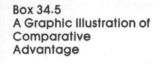

Box 34.5
A Graphic Illustration of
Comparative
Advantage

This box shows production possibility frontiers for Spain, Norway, and the two countries combined. Before trade, Spain produces and consumes at point A and Norway does so at point A'. Together, these correspond to world consumption point P, which is inside the world production possibility frontier. After trade begins, Spain specializes in producing grain (point B) and trades part of the grain for fish, moving to consumption point C. Norway specializes in producing fish (point B') and reaches consumption point C' through trade. As a result, world efficiency is improved, and point Q is attained on the world production possibility frontier.

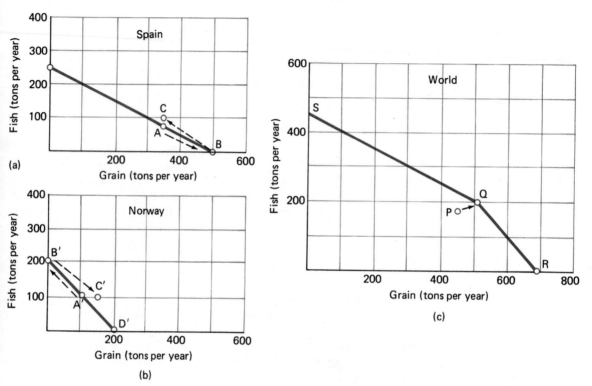

Pretrade production and consumption   According to the example just given, before trade begins Spain produces and consumes 350 tons of grain and 75 tons of fish. This is shown as point A on Spain's production possibility frontier. Norway is assumed to produce and consume 100 tons each of fish and grain. This is shown by point A' on Norway's frontier.

The world production possibility frontier   A production possibility frontier for the world as a whole (consisting of just these two countries in our example) can be constructed as shown in part c of Box 34.5. First assume that both countries devote all their labor to grain. That gives 500 tons of grain from Spain plus 200 from Norway, or 700 tons of grain in all (point R in part c of Box 34.5). Starting from there, assume that the world output of fish is to be increased. For the sake of efficiency it is clear that Norwegian farmers should be the first to switch to fishing, since the opportunity cost of fish is lower in Norway (1 ton of grain per ton of fish) than in Spain (2 tons of grain per ton of fish). As Norwegians switch to fishing, then, world production moves upward and to the left along the line segment RQ.

When all Norwegians have abandoned farming for fishing, the world will have arrived at point Q—500 tons of grain (all Spanish) and 200 tons of fish (all Norwegian). From that point on, the only way to get more fish is to have Spanish farmers switch to fishing. At the opportunity cost of 2 tons of grain per ton of fish, this moves the economy along the line segment QS. When all Spanish farmers are fishing, the world arrives at point S, where 450 tons of fish and no grain are produced. The production possibility frontier for the world as a whole thus is the kinked line RQS.

The effects of trade   The pretrade production point for the world as a whole lies inside the world production possibility frontier. Adding the quantities of fish and grain from A and A' together, we arrive at point P in Box 34.5—450 tons of grain and 175 tons of fish. This is inefficient; the world economy as a whole could produce more of both goods. To increase efficiency, both countries must specialize.

Following our earlier example, suppose that Spain shifts its production from 350 tons of grain and 75 tons of fish (point A) to 500 tons of grain and no fish (point B). It then trades the extra 150 tons of grain for 100 tons of Norwegian fish. Spain's consumption thus ends up at point C while its production remains at B.

At the same time, Norway shifts its production from A' to B', specializing entirely in fish. The extra 100 tons of fish are traded for the 150 tons of Spanish grain, moving Norwegian consumption to point C'.

As a result of specialization plus trade, then, both Spain and Norway have moved to points that lie outside their own production possibility frontiers. As they do so, the world as a whole moves from point P inside its production possibility frontier to point Q on the world frontier. Thus, specialization improves world efficiency, increases world production of both goods, and leaves both countries better off than they would be if they did not trade.

PROTECTIONISM VS. FREE TRADE

Protectionism
Any policy intended to shield domestic industries from import competition.

Tariff
A tax on imported goods.

Import quota
A limit on the quantity of a good that can be imported in a given period.

Our illustration of the theory of comparative advantage has portrayed a very simple trading world, little different from that discussed by Ricardo. In the more than 165 years since Ricardo's time, the theory has been extended many times to cover more complex and realistic situations. The extensions have covered situations in which there are more than two countries, in which there is more than one factor of production, and in which production possibility frontiers are not straight lines, to name just a few. The result of all this work has been to show that the theory of comparative advantage is very general. Regardless of the initial assumptions or the complexity of the situation, international trade, following the principles of comparative advantage, offers all the countries involved an opportunity for mutual gain.

But if international trade is so beneficial, why do free-trade policies so often meet with opposition? Why do governments feel pressure to enact **protectionist** policies, such as **tariffs** and **quotas**, that will restrict the importation of goods from abroad? Why, for example, the restrictions on imports of automobiles into the United States that created the problems for consumers described at the beginning of this chapter? The sources and logic of protectionism will be discussed in the rest of this section.

The Terms-of-Trade Argument

One argument in favor of restrictions on trade concerns the possibility of manipulating the terms of trade. In our example of Spain and Norway we supposed that the terms of trade of grain for fish would be set by competitive bargaining by private traders from each country. Such a process might not always result in the exact 1.5-to-1 trading ratio of grain to fish assumed in the example, but it would not be surprising to see the gains from trade divided fairly evenly.

In the real world, however, a country may want to interfere in the setting of the terms of trade. Suppose, for example, that the United States is the world's leading exporter of wheat and its leading importer of textiles. To take advantage of its partial monopoly in the wheat market, it might restrict wheat exports, hoping to drive up the world price. To take advantage of its partial monopsony in the textile market, the country might restrict textile imports, hoping to drive the world price down. The export and import restrictions would, of course, have the effect of reducing the total volume of trade. Worldwide gains from trade would thus be less than they would be in the absence of protectionist measures. Nonetheless, manipulating the terms of trade might leave the United States with a bigger share of the smaller world total of gains from trade, making U.S. citizens better off, on balance, than under a free-trade policy.

The terms-of-trade argument for protectionism, which has been known for more than a hundred years, has its limitations, however. One of these concerns the possibility of retaliation by trading partners. If other countries react to U.S. trade restrictions by imposing trade restrictions of their own, the attempt to manipulate the terms of trade may fail. The volume of world trade will then shrink even more, and all countries will be left worse off than under free trade.

Income Distribution and Multiple Factors of Production

Although restrictions designed to affect the terms of trade remain a possibility, they are not the main source of protectionist sentiment. To understand the origins of trade restrictions more fully, we need to consider the effects of trade on the distribution of income within each country. This in turn requires an expansion of the analysis to include more than one factor of production. A modification of the Spain-Norway example will serve this purpose.

Assume from now on that fishing requires a relatively large capital investment per worker and that farming requires a relatively small one. Fishing therefore is said to be capital-intensive and farming is said to be labor-intensive. Assume, as before, that in the absence of trade the opportunity cost of fish will be higher in Spain than in Norway. The theory of comparative advantage still applies, regardless of the number of factors of production involved. International trade will still make it possible for total world production of both fish and grain to increase. It will still enable the quantities of both goods available in both countries to increase. But now a new question arises concerning the gains from trade. How will they be distributed within each country?

Internal distribution   To answer this question, we must look at what happens in factor markets as trade brings about increasing specialization in each country. In Norway, production shifts from farming to fishing. As grain production is phased out, large quantities of labor and relatively small quantities of capital are released. The shift in production thus creates a surplus of labor and a shortage of capital. Factor markets can return to equilibrium only when wages fall relative to the rate of return on capital. Only then will fisheries adopt more labor-intensive methods of production. Meanwhile, the opposite process occurs in Spain. The shift from fishing to farming depresses the rate of return on capital and increases the wage rate. This causes Spanish workers to use more capital per worker than before.

These changes in relative factor prices determine how the gains from trade are distributed among the people of each country. Spanish workers and Norwegian boat owners will gain doubly from trade. They will gain first because trade increases the size of the pie (the total quantity of goods) and second because the shifts in factor prices give them a larger slice of the pie. For Norwegian workers and Spanish farm owners, in contrast, one of these effects works against the other. The workers and farm owners still benefit from the growth of the pie, but they get a smaller piece of it than before. They may or may not end up better off as a result of the trade.

Suppose that the comparative advantage in the pretrade situation is large and the difference in factor intensity between the two countries is small. Norwegian workers and Spanish farm owners will still gain from trade in an absolute sense, even though they will lose ground relative to others in their own country. If conditions are less favorable, however, they can end up worse off than before trade began.

The importance of mobility   The preceding section considered only two broadly defined factors of production—labor and capital. What was said there applies even more forcefully to narrowly defined factors of production. If one thinks in terms not of labor in general but of boat owners and tractor owners, then it becomes even more likely that trade will have a very uneven impact on incomes. The more specialized and less mobile the factors of production are, the more factor prices will shift as a result of trade and the more likely it will be that some specific groups will be harmed by trade.

Take an example close to home. Consider the effects on the U.S. economy of increased imports of Japanese cars. The impact of increased automobile imports can be divided into three parts. First, all consumers in the United States will benefit because cars will be cheaper and a wider variety of models will be available than before. Second, the Japanese will increase their purchases of U.S. goods. This will benefit workers in U.S. export-oriented industries.[2] Finally, U.S. autoworkers and manufacturers will face decreased demand for their products.

People with mobile skills or assets can escape most of the impact of decreased demand by moving to other industries. For example, a truck

---

[2]Instead, Japan may spend its earnings from exporting cars to the United States on goods imported from a third country—say, oil from Indonesia, which in turn buys U.S. exports. Such three-cornered trade is common. But whatever the pattern of trade, as we will show again in the next chapter, the dollars that Americans spend on imports come back to the United States in one way or another, as demand for goods, services, financial assets, and so on.

driver working for an automobile company can switch to hauling peaches, or a plant making fabrics for automobile seat covers can switch to making fabrics for furniture. Some workers, however, are less mobile because of their personal situation or specialized skills. They are likely to suffer a loss of income that will more than offset the benefits they receive as consumers from cheaper cars. Imagine, for example, a middle-aged, highly specialized engine technician who has all his savings tied up in a house in a Detroit suburb. He will get little consolation from being able to buy a cheap Japanese car to drive to the unemployment office each week.

In aggregate dollar terms, the loss to the group that is affected adversely is more than offset by the gains to others in the economy. But this fact is not likely to make much of an impression on unemployed autoworkers. They will see free trade as a threat and will campaign for protection. The government then will have a hard political decision to make. Which group of interests should it look after? How much weight should it place on the widespread gains from trade and how much on the complaints of particular groups of people who do not share in those gains? Is there any way to reconcile these conflicting interests?

Balancing gains and losses   These are questions of normative economics. A number of things must be taken into account before a balanced judgment can be made.

First, protection in the form of a tariff or quota on auto imports would benefit autoworkers. Suppose that these workers are relatively low-paid and have lower-than-average mobility. If one's idea of fairness stressed support for the incomes of low-paid workers, the impact of a protectionist policy would be beneficial. On the other hand, if autoworkers earn more on the average than the average car buyer, protecting their high wages would increase inequality.

Second, the tariff or quota would also benefit the owners of other factors of production used in the auto industry. These include stockholders, other investors, executives, and owners of real estate in automaking communities. On the average, ownership of nonlabor resources tends to be concentrated in the hands of people with relatively high incomes. It is hard to say whether these other factor owners would gain more or less from protection than workers would. But it is likely that this part of the impact, by itself, would tend to increase inequality.

Third, protection would hurt consumers by raising car prices. Again, it is hard to be sure about this effect without a detailed study of whether high- or low-income groups tend to spend the greater share of their incomes on cars. But the total impact on consumers could be quite large compared to the gains to producers, as Box 34.6 suggests.

Beyond Tariffs and Quotas

The post–World War II period as a whole has seen a broad movement toward freer trade. Several international organizations were set up after the war to promote freer trade. The International Monetary Fund was set up in 1944 to maintain a stable financial climate for trade. And the General Agreement on Tariffs and Trade (GATT) was created in an attempt to prevent a return of the protectionist policies that were common in the 1930s. GATT rules discourage the use of quotas. And under the so-called most-favored-nation principle, GATT members are supposed to charge the

Box 34.6
The Benefits and Costs of Automobile Import Quotas

The early 1980s were hard times for the U.S. auto industry. A combination of soaring gasoline prices and back-to-back recessions cut demand for new cars by some 20 percent. Because demand for fuel-efficient imported cars held steady during the 1980 and 1981–1982 recessions, the 20 percent drop in total new-car sales meant a proportionately larger drop in sales for U.S.-built cars. Sales of these fell from 9 million units in 1978 to an average of just under 6 million units per year in 1980–1982. Meanwhile, the profits of U.S. automakers, which had averaged 14.9 percent of stockholders' equity in the 1960s and 12.5 percent in the 1970s, turned into a loss in the 1980s. It took a government bailout to save Chrysler, one of Detroit's big three, from bankruptcy.

As the market share of foreign producers soared from around 15 percent in the mid-1970s to nearly 30 percent in the early 1980s, the automakers, the United Auto Workers union, and politicians from car-producing states joined forces to demand protection. The Reagan administration's response was an agreement with the Japanese government to hold Japanese car imports to the United States to 1.68 million units in the year beginning April 1981. This quota was extended for the next two years at the same level, and for the year beginning April 1984 at the level of 1.85 million units. In 1985 the U.S. government withdrew from the agreement, but the Japanese government announced that it would hold Japanese car exports to the United States at 2.25 million units.

The effects of the quotas were dramatic. As the economy recovered from recession in 1983 and 1984, a frantic seller's market developed. Waiting lists for popular models grew. Dealer markups of hundreds or even thousands of dollars replaced the rebates and low-interest loans of previous years. The quotas, which had been accepted quietly as a way of saving American jobs during the recession, became a subject of widespread debate.

Were the gains in terms of jobs saved worth the cost of the quotas to consumers? Probably not, according to Robert W. Crandall of the Brookings Institution.

To evaluate the costs and benefits of quotas, Crandall first had to determine the impact on the prices of cars. The claims were conflicting. Some critics maintained that the quotas had raised car prices as much as $2,000. The automakers themselves said that any increase in prices had resulted from consumers' switching to larger cars after fuel prices started to fall in 1982 and 1983. Crandall used three different statistical approaches to separate the effects of the quotas from those of changes in the size and other features of cars sold. All three methods led to similar conclusions: In the 1981–1983 period the quotas raised the prices of U.S.-made cars by about $400 per unit and those of Japanese cars by about $1,000 per unit. The total cost to U.S. consumers for 1983 was about $4.3 billion.

Next Crandall estimated the number of jobs saved. He estimated that the Japanese market share would have been about eight percentage points higher in 1983 if it had not been for the quotas. If every sale lost to the Japanese had gone to American producers, that would mean 46,000 fewer U.S. jobs without the quotas. But because the quotas also raised the average price of new cars, the total number of units sold declined. Thus, U.S. firms were estimated to have picked up less than one new sale for each two units lost to the Japanese. Taking this effect into account, only about 26,000 auto industry jobs out of a 1983 base of 600,000 were saved by the quotas.

Comparing the $4.6 billion cost of the quotas with the 26,000 jobs saved, Crandall concluded that the cost per job saved was about $160,000 per year. (A separate study by the U.S. International Trade Commission estimated that 44,000 jobs were saved, but it also found a greater price impact. The commission's estimate of the cost per job saved was $193,000, a little higher than Crandall's.)

Was it worth the cost to save these jobs? You be the judge.

Source: Robert W. Crandall, "Import Quotas and the Automobile Industry: The Costs of Protectionism," *Brookings Review*, Summer 1984, pp. 8–16. Conclusions of the International Trade Commission study were reported in "The Cost of Auto Quotas," *Washington Post*, February 21, 1985, p. A18.

same tariff rates for imports from all GATT countries. A series of multinational negotiations sponsored by GATT succeeded in lowering the average rate of tariffs. In addition, the post–World War II period saw efforts to set up regional trading blocs in several parts of the world. The best known of these is the European Economic Community, or Common Market. The aim of the Common Market was to eliminate all barriers to trade among the major European countries, eventually leading to a situation in which trade among these countries would be as free as trade among the states of the United States. The Common Market has not yet achieved this goal, but it has contributed to the growth and prosperity of Western Europe, where standards of living in most countries now are similar to those in the United States.

Even so, some thorny issues of trade policy remain to be faced in the 1980s. These center on what is called the new protectionism—a set of policies that restrain trade even when tariff and quota barriers are removed. The new protectionism focuses in part on such devices as "orderly marketing agreements" and "voluntary export restraints." These involve the use of political pressure—usually backed by the threat of a tariff or quota—to restrain trade in a particular good. A leading example is the complex set of agreements that the United States has negotiated with textile-exporting countries. Although these agreements are referred to as voluntary, their effects on consumers are little different from those of a traditional tariff or quota. Prices go up, and losses in efficiency occur as production moves against the direction of comparative advantage.

The temptation to enter into restrictive bilateral agreements is increased by the fact that they may be less harmful to the exporting country than tariffs imposed by the importer. Again the U.S.-Japanese agreement on automobile exports, which lasted from 1981 to early 1985, is a case in point. This agreement was very costly to U.S. consumers, but a large part of the gains went to Japanese automakers. The effects of the quotas have, in fact, often been compared to those of a cartel of automobile exporters. The United States and Japan agreed on an overall ceiling for sales of Japanese cars in the United States, and then the Japanese government divided the quota among the various Japanese producers. Freed from the pressures of competition, the Japanese companies were able to raise prices and concentrate on larger, more profitable models. The quotas were so beneficial to Japan, in fact, that even after the United States ended the agreement in 1985 the Japanese government announced that it would continue restraints on its own, although at a somewhat higher level than under the bilateral agreement.

Antidumping practices are another device of the new protectionism. A country is said to be "dumping" its goods when it sells them in a foreign market for less than the price it maintains at home or for less than the cost of producing them. Under certain provisions of U.S. law, domestic producers facing competition from imports dumped on the U.S. market can seek tariffs. Steelmakers have recently sought this type of protection. Free-traders object to antidumping laws on two grounds. First, they point out that in times of slack world demand for a product, efficiency requires that firms temporarily sell that product at prices below average total costs. (Chapter 22 explained why this is true for domestic markets; the same holds true for international markets.) Second, they point out that "dumped" imports, like any other imports, produce benefits for consumers that must be weighed against the harm done to producers.

Finally, the new protectionism often takes the form of product standards or procurement practices that have both the intent and the effect of limiting foreign competition. U.S. firms trying to sell their products in Japan constantly complain of such barriers. For example, Japan insists that all electrical products be tested in Japanese laboratories, even if they have passed similar tests in the United States. (U.S. procedures permit Japanese exports to be tested in Japan.) As another example, Japan's huge telephone company has used procurement methods that effectively prevent U.S. manufacturers from bidding on supply contracts. These practices have been a focal point of U.S.-Japanese trade negotiations in recent years, and some progress has been made in opening Japanese markets to U.S. goods. But Japan is by no means the only offender. Import restraints masquerading as quality controls can also be found in the United States in areas ranging from auto safety certification to marketing standards for filberts.

Despite the progress that has been made against tariff barriers to trade, then, protectionism remains alive and free-traders face new challenges in the 1980s.

Summary

1. A country is said to have a comparative advantage in the production of a good if it can produce it at a lower opportunity cost than its trading partner. Trade based on the principle that each country exports goods in which it has a comparative advantage can increase total world production of all goods and services and increase total consumption in each trading country.

2. According to the terms-of-trade argument for protectionism, a single country can gain by restricting exports of any product in which it has a monopoly in the world market and by restricting imports of any product in which it has a monopsony. However, these gains will not be realized if all countries pursue protectionist policies.

3. In a world with two or more factors of production, trade tends to increase demand for factors that are used relatively intensively in producing export goods and to decrease demand for factors that are used relatively intensively in producing goods that compete with imported goods. Thus, although trade benefits a country as a whole, it may not benefit owners of factors that are specialized in producing import-competing goods.

4. The general trend in international trade policy since World War II has been toward a reduction of traditional *tariff* and *quota* barriers to trade. However, recent years have seen increased use of new protectionist devices such as orderly marketing agreements and "voluntary" quotas.

Questions for Review

1. Define the following terms:
    absolute advantage
    protectionism
    tariff
    quota

2. Why are patterns of international trade determined by comparative advantage rather than by absolute advantage?

3. Under what conditions can a country improve its terms of trade by restricting exports or imports?

4. How does international trade affect the demand for factors of production within each trading country?

5. Give some examples of protectionist policies in use during the 1980s (in addition to simple tariffs and quotas).

Problems and Topics for Discussion

1. Look at Box 34.2. Suppose that new, high-yield grains were introduced in Norway and that the number of labor hours needed to grow a ton of grain there was cut from 5 hours to 2.5 hours. What would happen to trade between Norway and Spain? If the labor hours per ton of grain in Norway fell all the way to 2, what would happen to the pattern of trade?

2. Consider the following statement: "The United States may still be No. 1, but I don't think we will be much longer. The Common Market, Japan, all areas of the world are catching up. Soon it will no longer be economical for us to produce anything." On the basis of what you have learned about the principle of comparative advantage, do you think it is possible to reach a point at which it is no longer worthwhile to produce anything—that is, a point at which it becomes economical to import all goods? Discuss.

3. If you, a strong supporter of free trade, were in charge of U.S. international trade policy, would you cut tariffs and quotas or would you negotiate with trading partners, maintaining U.S. trade barriers unless they lowered theirs too? Discuss.

4. The simple trade theory presented in this chapter tells us that countries export goods in which they have a comparative advantage and import goods in which they do not. In practice, countries often import many of the same kinds of goods that they export. For example, countries like France, Germany, and Italy are both importers and exporters of automobiles. Why do you think these patterns of trade exist? Do they invalidate the principle of comparative advantage?

5. **Case for Discussion**
The U.S. Constitution was written partly to prohibit state governments from erecting barriers to trade with other states. Nearly 200 years later, the commerce clause of the Constitution is in desperate need of reinforcement from our courts and legislatures. The system of trade barriers between states is far more extensive than commonly realized, creating enormous economic distortions that result in significant loss of output and jobs.

Agricultural trade suffers from extensive regulation, some of it with legitimate underlying concerns about the spread of harmful disease and insects. However, much of the regulation goes far beyond this. For example, Florida-grown avocados were prevented from being sold in California from 1925 until the law was struck down by state courts in 1973. There have been few if any accusations that the health of consumers has been harmed since. Just last Wednesday a federal judge struck down a New York state law allowing wine coolers made solely from New York state wine to be sold in grocery stores. All other wine coolers could be sold only in the far less numerous package liquor stores. Judge Charles L. Brieant called the law "plain and simple protectionism."

The mobility of professional labor is severely restricted by specific certification requirements by states. One 1978 study found that dentists have 12 percent higher incomes than would be the case if they competed freely, resulting in an economic loss to consumers of $700 million in 1970 (equivalent to more than $1.5 billion today).

State governments themselves engage in protection of their home industries, through in-state purchasing preferences. These preferences allow in-state firms to bid up to 5 percent over out-of-state firms and be awarded state contracts. Twenty state governments have such laws.[3]

Questions:
a. In what ways does trade between the states of the United States resemble trade between countries? In what ways does it differ?
b. Who would gain and who would lose from a

---

[3]Excerpted from Steven G. Craig and Joel W. Sailors, "A Destructive Trade War Between the States," *Wall Street Journal*, February 5, 1985, p. 30. Reprinted by permission of The Wall Street Journal, © Dow Jones & Company, Inc. 1985. All rights reserved.

law preventing the sale of Florida-grown avocados in California?

c. The case lists restrictions on the mobility of professional labor as an example of protectionism. Are such restrictions practiced on an international scale? Could the same argument be given for free trade in labor services as is given for free trade in goods and services? Who would gain and who would lose as a result of free international trade in labor services?

d. Suppose the New York state government buys buses made in New York for 5 percent more than it would have to pay for buses made in Indiana. Who gains and who loses? Would you favor such buy-at-home rules if the cheaper buses were made in Italy rather than in Indiana? Discuss.

Suggestions for Further Reading

Grennes, Thomas. *International Economics*. Englewood Cliffs, N.J.: Prentice-Hall, 1984.

Chapters 1–13 of this text cover the pure theory of international trade.

Mokre, Morris E., and David G. Tarr. *Effects of Restrictions on United States Imports: A Staff Report of the Bureau of Economics of the Federal Trade Commission*. Washington, D.C.: Government Printing Office, 1980.

Contains five case studies of protectionist policies and a chapter on the new protectionism.

Ricardo, David. *Principles of Political Economy and Taxation*. London, 1817. (Available in a modern paperback edition from Pelican Books, 1971.)

Chapter 7, "On Foreign Trade," is generally credited with being the first clear statement of the principle of comparative advantage.

Chapter 35

The Balance of Payments and the International Monetary System

After reading this chapter, you should be able to

1. Classify international transactions into the categories used in the U.S. international accounts.
2. Show how foreign exchange markets determine foreign exchange rates in the case in which only *current account* transactions take place.
3. Explain how *capital account* transactions affect demand in foreign exchange markets.
4. Show how an increase in a country's rate of economic growth, other things being equal, affects its exchange rate, current account balance, and net capital flows.
5. Show how an increase in a country's real interest rate, other things being equal, affects its exchange rate, current account balance, and net capital flows.
6. Explain how *official reserve account* transactions by central banks can be used to affect exchange rates.
7. Discuss systems for managing exchange rates.

Ideas for Review

Here are some terms and concepts that you should review before you read this chapter:

Comparative advantage (Chapters 2 and 34)
Supply and demand (Chapter 3)
Bond prices and yields (Chapter 4)
Protectionism (Chapter 34)

"They used to export construction equipment. Now they export jobs."

Like many two-income American couples these days, Ted and Claudia Lushch have been on something of a buying spree since the economic recovery got under way.

Over the past year and a half, they have bought a microwave oven, a TV set, a camera, a bicycle, an iron, a calculator, a new set of china, a comforter, a fishing rod, a pair of eyeglasses, some games and dolls for their children, and lots of clothing, including a blazer, a jogging outfit, boots and shoes, sweaters and shirts, hats and a scarf.

But the Lushches' burst of spending isn't all helping to sustain the U.S. recovery. The microwave, calculator, camera, china, and blazer were all made in Japan; the iron came from Brazil; the shoes and eyeglasses from Italy; the hats from Britain; the jogging suit and some sweaters from Taiwan; the boots from South Korea; the shirts from France; and the games and scarf from West Germany.

The imports reflect the impact of the superhigh dollar, which has made foreign goods cheaper—and more attractive—here in the United States and has made American products more costly abroad. Since its low point in mid-1980, the dollar made its biggest jump since 1931.

The strong dollar has fundamentally changed life for American corporations and consumers. It has helped keep inflation down and brought consumers a wider choice. It has forced U.S. companies to make badly needed adjustments under pressure from foreign competition. But it has produced a divided economy in which most of the United States is enjoying robust growth while exporters, manufacturers, agriculture, and mining are in a depression, with their profit margins severely squeezed. Some firms, like Caterpillar Tractor, are moving production operations abroad because of the high dollar. Everett Hopkins, president of the United Auto Workers in the area where the Lushches live, laments, "They used to export construction equipment. Now they export jobs."[1]

Of all the economic news that makes the headlines, that involving the value of the dollar and the balance of international payments is probably the least understood. Even well-informed people who have a good understanding of inflation and unemployment may have only the haziest idea of how the international monetary system works.

There was a time when this lack of knowledge about international monetary affairs could be explained by the sheer strength and self-sufficiency of the U.S. economy. This was especially true during the first two decades after World War II, when the United States was less dependent on foreign trade than any of its major trading partners. The country consistently exported more than it imported, and its goods set standards for quality and technology in a broad range of world markets. But in recent years all this has been changing. During the 1970s U.S. readers began to be exposed to the same kinds of economic news that had long been familiar to readers in other countries—ups and downs in the value of their domestic currencies, balance-of-trade deficits, and so on. Policymakers began strug-

---

[1]Art Pine, "Mixed Blessing: Dollar's Rise, a Boon for Many, Also Hurts Major U.S. Industries," *Wall Street Journal*, February 22, 1985, p. 1. Reprinted by permission of The Wall Street Journal, © Dow Jones & Company, Inc. 1985. All rights reserved.

gling to find the right response to these events. In this chapter we will look both at the theory of international financial markets and at the policy response to recent events in those markets.

THE BALANCE OF PAYMENTS

Any discussion of an economy's balance of international payments is complicated by the fact that thousands of different kinds of international payments are made every day. Payments for goods and services exported and imported are likely to come to mind first, but there are many others. Equally important are long- and short-term loans made to finance imports and exports, and payments made in international markets in connection with purchases or sales of assets such as securities or real estate. In addition, governments and private individuals make many kinds of transfer payments to residents of other countries. They include outright gifts, pension payments, and official foreign aid. Finally, the U.S. Federal Reserve System and foreign central banks engage in many kinds of official transactions. Box 35.1 shows a simplified version of the accounts used to keep track of these international transactions for the United States. These accounts make a good starting point for this chapter.

The Current Account

The first section of the international accounts shown in Box 35.1 contains what are called **current account** transactions. These include imports and exports of goods and services and international transfer payments. The current account is, in turn, broken down into several components.

Current account
The section of the international accounts of a country that consists of imports, exports, and unilateral transfers.

Merchandise imports and exports   Imports and exports of merchandise (goods) are the most widely publicized items on the international accounts. During most of the nineteenth century the United States was a net importer of merchandise. Then, from 1894 to 1970, it became a net exporter. Since 1970 it has again become a net importer in most years.

Year A in Box 35.1 is a typical year for the U.S. economy during the 1970s and early 1980s. In such a year the U.S. economy would have a balance or small surplus in trade in manufactured goods, with exports of computers, aircraft, construction equipment, and so on offsetting imports of automobiles, clothing, consumer electronics, and other items. The U.S. economy would also have a strong export surplus in farm products, but this would be more than offset by oil imports, which in some years accounted for as much as one third of all U.S. merchandise imports. Taking all these items together, the **merchandise balance** for such a year would show a small deficit. (News reports often refer to the merchandise balance as the *balance of trade*.)

Merchandise balance
A country's exports of merchandise minus its imports of merchandise.

Services   In addition to trade in merchandise, the United States and other countries carry on a very large trade in services. Chief among these are transportation, tourism, insurance, and other financial services. Net earnings on foreign investment, including interest on financial assets, are also considered an export of services. A high level of net investment income gave the U.S. economy a positive balance on trade in services over these years.

Transfers   The final item on the current account balance consists of transfer payments. This is typically a negative item in the U.S. international accounts because transfers to other countries exceed transfers received from them. This item takes into account both government transfers, such as foreign aid and social security payments to retired workers living abroad, and private transfers, such as private famine relief and church missions.

The current account balance   When merchandise trade, trade in services, and transfers are combined, the result is the country's **current account balance**. (News accounts that refer to the *balance of payments* usually mean the current account balance.)

In year A, the typical year for the U.S. economy in the 1970s and early 1980s, the deficit on the merchandise balance is more than offset by the surplus in services, giving the country a positive current account balance. By the mid-1980s, however, the international payments position of the United States had changed dramatically, as represented by year B in the table. The merchandise deficit grew by leaps and bounds and the services surplus dwindled, giving a series of current account deficits of unprecedented size. We will discuss the reasons for this swing in the current account balance later in the chapter.

The Capital Account

Current account transactions are not the only ones that take place between residents of different countries. International lending and borrowing and international sales and purchases of assets also account for an enormous volume of transactions every day. A U.S. company, for example, might obtain a short-term loan from a London bank to finance the purchase of a shipload of beer for import to the United States. The Brazilian government might get a long-term loan from Citibank of New York to help finance a hydroelectric project. A U.S. millionaire might open an account in a Swiss bank. A Japanese automaker might buy a piece of land in Tennessee on which to build a new plant. All of these transactions are recorded in the **capital account** section of Box 35.1.

Purchases of U.S. assets by foreigners and borrowing from foreign banks and other sources by U.S. firms and individuals create flows of funds into the United States. These transactions therefore are called **capital inflows**. Purchases of foreign assets by U.S. residents or loans by U.S. banks and other sources to foreigners create flows of funds out of the United States and hence are called **capital outflows**.

Capital inflows and outflows can be viewed as a means of financing the current account surplus or deficit. Leaving transfers out of the picture for the moment, there are three ways in which a country can pay for its imports: First, it can pay for them by exporting goods and services on current account. If the country's current account is in balance, it can pay for all of its imports this way. Second, it can pay for them by borrowing from foreign banks or other sources. Many developing countries pay for part of their imports this way. And third, a country can pay for its imports by selling financial or real assets to foreign buyers—corporate stocks, government bonds, real estate, or whatever. The large U.S. current account deficits of the mid-1980s were largely financed in this way.

Current account balance
The value of a country's exports of goods and services minus the value of its imports of goods and services and its net transfer payments to foreign recipients.

Capital account
The section of the international accounts of a country that consists of purchases and sales of assets and international borrowing and lending.

Capital inflow
Purchases of domestic assets by foreigners and borrowing by domestic firms and households from foreign banks or other foreign sources.

Capital outflow
Purchases of foreign assets by domestic firms and households and borrowing by foreigners from domestic banks or other sources.

Box 35.1
Simplified International
Accounts for the U.S.
Economy

This table lists the main elements of the U.S. international accounts in simplified form. Year A shows how the accounts appeared in a typical year of the late 1970s or early 1980s. Year B shows how they had changed by the mid-1980s. The table is divided into three sections: the current, capital, and official reserve accounts. Taken together, these three include all the sources (+) and all the uses (−) of the dollars that are traded in foreign exchange markets. Because every dollar has both a source and a use somewhere in the accounts, the column totals are always zero when the three sections of the accounts are added together. (However, the official accounts do not add up exactly because of errors and omissions in recording international transactions.)

	Year A	Year B
	(billions of dollars)	
Current Account		
Merchandise exports	$250	$225
Merchandise imports	−275	−350
Merchandise balance	−25	−125
Net exports of services	50	15
Net unilateral transfers	−10	−10
Current account balance	15	−120
Capital Account		
Capital inflows	85	225
Capital outflows	−100	−100
Capital account balance	−15	125
Official Reserve Account		
Net change in official reserves	0	−5
Total of current account balance, capital account balance, and change in official reserves	$0	$0

In short, a country that runs a current account deficit can offset the deficit with a capital account surplus, that is, a net capital inflow. For this to happen, loans from foreign sources must exceed loans to foreigners, or sales of assets to foreigners must exceed purchases of assets abroad. Likewise, a country with a current account surplus can use its extra import earnings to make net loans to foreign borrowers or net purchases of foreign assets. This is the situation shown for year A in the simplified international accounts of Box 35.1. In that case the $15 billion U.S. current account surplus is offset by a $15 billion deficit on the capital account, that is, a net capital outflow.

The Official Reserve Account

For completeness, we need to add one more type of transaction to the international accounts. These are transactions by the central banks of various countries—the Federal Reserve System in the United States, the Bank of England for the United Kingdom, and so on. In principle, purchases and sales of assets by central banks are much like private capital flows. However, as we will see later in the chapter, these transactions play

Official reserve account
The section of the international accounts of a country that consists of changes in central banks' official international reserves.

a special role in international economic policy. For this reason, central bank transactions are kept in a special section of the international accounts labeled **official reserve account** in Box 35.1.

In year A there was no net change in holdings of dollar reserves by U.S. or foreign central banks. In such a case a net private capital outflow will just offset a current account surplus, or a net private capital inflow will just offset a current account deficit.

In year B, however, the table in Box 35.1 shows a negative $5 billion on the official reserve account. This indicates either that foreign central banks reduced their holdings of dollar reserve assets or that the Federal Reserve increased its holdings of foreign-currency reserve assets. Either type of transaction would be called a capital outflow if it were carried out by a private citizen. Thus, when the official reserve transactions are added to net private capital flows, the total exactly offsets the current account deficit. This is true not only in year B but in any other year: The sum of the current account balance plus the capital account balance plus the net change in official reserves always equals zero. The reason is that the three parts of the accounts, taken together, include all of the sources and all of the uses of the funds that change hands in international transactions. Every dollar used in international transactions must have a source, so when the sources (+) and the uses (−) are added together, the sum is zero.[2]

FOREIGN EXCHANGE MARKETS

Foreign exchange markets
The set of institutions through which the currency of one country can be exchanged for that of another.

Transactions in international trade differ from payments within a country in one important way: Countries have different national currencies. Because of this, each international transaction involves a visit to the **foreign exchange market**—the set of institutions (including banks, foreign exchange dealers, and official government agencies) through which the currency of one country can be exchanged for that of another. This section will show how supply and demand operate in foreign exchange markets to determine the relative values of different currencies—the number of French francs, West German marks, Japanese yen, and so on that can be bought for a dollar.

Exchange Markets: Current Account Only

To keep things simple, we will begin with a world in which the only international transactions that take place are imports and exports on current account. Suppose that a West German clothing importer wants to buy a shipment of Levis. The importer has West German marks in a Frankfurt bank account, but the U.S. manufacturer wants to be paid in dollars, which can be used to pay workers and buy supplies in the United States. The importer's bank sells the necessary number of marks on the

---

[2]This statement holds true for the simplified international accounts of Box 35.1 and also holds true in principle for the actual international accounts of the United States. In practice, however, government statisticians always miss some items when they tally up imports, exports, and capital flows. As a result, the numbers don't quite add up. In the official accounts this measurement problem is reflected in a line labeled *statistical discrepancy*, formerly called *errors and omissions*.

foreign exchange market, receiving dollars in return. The dollars are then sent to the manufacturer to pay for the Levis.

Meanwhile, thousands of other people in the United States and Germany are also buying and selling dollars and marks for their own purposes. Total activity in the foreign exchange market, like that in any other market, can be viewed in terms of supply and demand curves such as those shown in Box 35.2. This box shows the supply and demand for dollars, with the price (the exchange rate) in terms of marks per dollar. It could equally well be drawn to show the supply and demand for marks, with the price in dollars per mark. The ratios of dollars to marks and marks to dollars are two ways of expressing the same thing; there is just one exchange rate.

The demand curve for dollars   Look first at the demand curve for dollars. If we assume that only current account transactions take place, the shape and position of the demand curve depend on how German demand for U.S. goods varies as the exchange rate varies, other things being equal. Suppose, for example, that Levis sell for $20 a pair in the United States. At an exchange rate of 3 marks per dollar, German consumers will have to pay 60 marks a pair. They may buy a total of, say, 1,000 pairs a day, thereby creating a demand for $20,000 per day in the foreign exchange market. If the exchange rate falls to 2.5 marks per dollar while the U.S. price remains unchanged, German consumers will be able to buy Levis more cheaply—for 50 marks a pair ($20 × 2.5 marks per dollar). At the lower price the Germans are likely to buy a larger quantity—say, 1,250 pairs a day. The demand for dollars created by these sales thus will increase to $25,000 per day.

**Box 35.2
Supply and Demand for
Dollars on Current
Account**

This box shows the supply and demand curves for dollars in the foreign exchange market in which dollars are exchanged for West German marks. Only current account transactions—exports, imports, and transfer payments—are assumed to take place. The slope and position of the demand curve reflect the German demand for exports from the United States. The slope and position of the supply curve reflect U.S. demand for imports from Germany. In the case shown here, U.S. demand for imports from Germany is assumed to be elastic, so the supply curve has a positive slope.

The supply curve for dollars   In a world in which only current account transactions take place, dollars are supplied to this foreign exchange market by U.S. citizens who want to buy West German goods. The supply curve for dollars in Box 35.2 slopes upward, showing that more dollars will be supplied to the foreign exchange market as the price of dollars, in terms of marks, rises. This will be the case whenever U.S. demand for German goods is elastic—that is, whenever a 1 percent change in the U.S. price of German goods causes a greater than 1 percent change in the quantity demanded.

An example will show why the slope of the dollar supply curve depends on the elasticity of U.S. demand for German goods. Suppose that a certain model of the German BMW automobile has a price of 60,000 marks. At an exchange rate of 3 marks per dollar, the car will sell for $20,000 in the United States (not including shipping costs and other charges). If 500 BMWs a day are sold at that price, U.S. buyers will have to supply $10 million per day to this foreign exchange market in order to get the 30 million marks needed to pay the German manufacturer. Suppose that the exchange rate rises to 4 marks per dollar, so that U.S. buyers can get the car for just $15,000 (a 25 percent decrease in the dollar price). Since we are assuming an elastic demand for BMWs, assume that the number of BMWs imported will rise by 50 percent, to 750 a day, as a result of the change in the dollar price. In order to obtain 750 cars at 60,000 marks per car and an exchange rate of 4 marks per dollar, U.S. buyers will have to supply $11.25 million per day to the foreign exchange market (750 cars × 6,000 marks per car × 2.5 marks per dollar). The number of dollars supplied to these markets will have increased in response to an increase in the price of the dollar in terms of marks, as shown in the box.[3]

In Box 35.2 the supply and demand for dollars are equal at an exchange rate of 3 marks per dollar. At this exchange rate the value of imports is equal to the value of exports and the current account is in balance.

Purchasing Power Parity

Purchasing power parity
A situation in which the value of the domestic currency in terms of a foreign currency is just equal to the ratio of the average foreign price level to the average domestic price level.

Why should the equilibrium exchange rate be 3 West German marks per dollar rather than, say, 100, 10, or 0.5 marks per dollar? As we will see in this chapter, there are many factors that can affect exchange rates in the short run, but in the long run exchange rates tend, in at least a general way, to move toward **purchasing power parity**—a situation in which the exchange value of the domestic currency in terms of the foreign currency is equal to the ratio of the foreign country's price level to the domestic price level.

---

[3]If U.S. demand for foreign goods is inelastic rather than elastic, the supply curve of dollars on the foreign exchange markets will have a negative slope. An inelastic demand means that a 1 percent change in the U.S. price of German goods will cause less than a 1 percent change in the quantity demanded. The BMW example can easily be changed to illustrate this. Suppose that when the exchange rate rises from 3 to 4 marks per dollar (bringing the U.S. price of BMWs down by 25 percent, from $20,000 to $15,000), only 50 more cars are sold each day (just a 10 percent increase). To get the German marks needed to buy 550 cars at 60,000 marks per car at an exchange rate of 4 marks per dollar, U.S. buyers will have to supply only $8.25 million per day to the foreign exchange market. An increase in the price of dollars in terms of marks thus will reduce the supply of dollars. However, as long as the negatively sloped supply curve is steeper than the demand curve, the market will function in the usual way. In this chapter we will assume a positive slope for the supply curve.

When the exchange rate is at this level, as the term implies, changing a sum of money from one currency to another does not change its purchasing power. For example, suppose that a selected market basket of goods— so many loaves of bread, so many raincoats, so many theater tickets, and so on—costs $1,000 in the United States and 3,000 marks in Germany. This means that the price level in marks is three times the price level in dollars. If the exchange rate is 3 marks for 1 dollar, an American would neither gain nor lose purchasing power by trading dollars for marks and shopping in Germany instead of in the United States; and a German would neither gain nor lose purchasing power by trading marks for dollars and shopping in the United States instead of in Germany. At any exchange rate higher than 3 marks per dollar, the dollar would be *overvalued* relative to purchasing power parity. It would then be cheaper for Americans to trade their dollars for marks and shop in Germany. At any exchange rate lower than 3 marks per dollar, the dollar would be *undervalued* relative to purchasing power parity, and Germans could gain by trading their marks for dollars and shopping in the United States.

Purchasing power parity serves as a useful benchmark for comparing exchange rates, but before doing so we must note a few qualifications. First, as we have already said, many kinds of economic conditions can cause exchange rates to depart from purchasing power parity in the short run—that is, over a period ranging from a few months to a few years. We will examine several such factors shortly.

Second, the benchmark of purchasing power parity is somewhat inexact because it depends, to some extent, on what market basket of goods is chosen in measuring the price level. Should it be the market basket of goods bought by the typical German consumer? That bought by the typical U.S. consumer? One that includes industrial goods as well as consumer goods? One that includes only goods and services that are exchanged in international trade? A reasonable case could be made for using any one of these bases for measuring purchasing power parity between the German mark and the U.S. dollar, and each would give a somewhat different answer.

Third, it must be stressed that purchasing power parity reflects only the ratio of the *average price level* in the two countries. Major differences in *relative* prices can and do prevail even when exchange rates are equal to purchasing power parity. Thus, an American visitor to West Germany will find certain things relatively cheap—say, a glass of beer, a restaurant meal, or a new Mercedes. But at the same moment a German visitor to the United States will find certain other things relatively cheap—say, a set of towels, an intercity airline ticket, or a new house. These differences in relative prices reflect, among other things, the comparative advantages of each country, and they form the basis of international trade.

Shifts in Supply and Demand—Current Account Only   Changes in economic conditions can cause shifts in the supply and demand curves in foreign exchange markets. Box 35.3 gives an example. For the moment we continue to assume that current account transactions are the only ones that take place internationally.

Starting from an equilibrium at an exchange rate of 3 marks per dollar, suppose that the U.S. Department of Defense places a large order for armored vehicles made in West Germany. To import German goods, it must

**Box 35.3
Effects of a Shift in the
Current Account
Supply Curve for Dollars**

This box shows the effects of a shift in the supply curve for dollars in a world in which only current account transactions take place. The shift in the supply curve is assumed to be caused by a major purchase of German goods by the U.S. government. To buy the German goods, the government must first exchange dollars for marks, thereby adding to the supply of dollars in the foreign exchange market. The excess supply of marks causes the value of the dollar to fall (depreciate). Depreciation of the dollar makes U.S. goods cheaper for German buyers. As exports increase, the market moves downward along the demand curve until the excess supply of dollars is eliminated.

trade dollars for marks in the foreign exchange market. The result, as shown in Box 35.3, is a rightward shift in the supply curve for dollars, from S_1 to S_2.

At first the shift in the supply curve creates an excess supply of dollars, which tends to depress the exchange rate. This surplus reflects the U.S. balance of payments deficit on current account that has resulted from the increase in imports. As the exchange rate falls, U.S. goods become cheaper for Germans to buy, which increases the number of dollars demanded. This situation is shown by a downward movement along the demand curve. At the same time, German goods become more expensive for U.S. buyers, which decreases somewhat the number of dollars supplied. This situation appears as a downward movement along the new dollar supply curve.

In Box 35.3 the supply and demand for dollars come into equilibrium again at an exchange rate of 2.5 marks per dollar. In the new equilibrium the exchange rate is lower than before, and both U.S. imports and U.S. exports have increased. The balance of payments on current account has returned to equilibrium.

In the terminology of foreign exchange markets, the dollar is said to **depreciate** when its price falls in terms of a foreign currency, as in the example just given. Seen from the German point of view, a fall in the price of the dollar in terms of marks is equivalent to a rise in the price of marks in terms of dollars. At the same time that the dollar depreciates, then, the mark can be said to **appreciate** against the dollar.

Depreciation (of a currency)

A decline in the value of a country's currency relative to that of another country.

Appreciation (of a currency)

An increase in the value of a country's currency relative to that of another country.

The Capital Account Demand Curve

Now that we have discussed the current account supply and demand curves for dollars, it is time to consider the capital account. The effects of capital account transactions on foreign exchange markets are illustrated in Box 35.4. This box shows a downward-sloping line that we will call the **capital account net demand curve**. This curve shows the net demand for dollars arising from capital account transactions. If capital inflows to the United States exceed capital outflows, the net demand for dollars on capital account is positive. If capital outflows from the United States exceed capital inflows, the net demand for dollars on capital account is negative. To allow for both positive and negative net demand, the vertical axis is drawn in the middle of the graph.

The slope and position of the capital account net demand curve are determined by the factors that affect international investment, borrowing, and lending. Two of the most important of these are the relationship of the present exchange rate to the expected future exchange rate and differences between countries in real interest rates. Let's look at each of these in turn.

Expectations regarding exchange rates   To see how differences between the present exchange rate and the expected future exchange rate affect the net quantity of dollars demanded, put yourself in the position of a person with a million dollars to invest. You are trying to decide whether to use the funds to buy bonds issued by the U.S. government or similar bonds issued by the West German government. What factors would you take into account in deciding which ones to buy?

You would, of course, look at the interest rates and maturities of the two bonds. We will return to interest rates in a moment; for now, assume that the interest rates on German and U.S. bonds are equal at 10 percent per year, and that both bonds mature one year from the present. What else would you look at? A factor that you would surely want to take into account is any change you expect to take place in exchange rates between the time you buy the bonds and the time they mature.

As a benchmark for this discussion, we can use a situation in which you expect the exchange rate a year from now to be at the assumed purchasing power parity of 3 marks per dollar. Given this benchmark expectation, suppose that today's exchange rate is 2 marks per dollar. If you trade your million dollars for marks now, you can buy 2 million marks' worth of German bonds. When the bonds mature a year later, you will have 2.2 million marks, including the interest you have earned. But by then you expect the exchange rate to have risen to 3 marks per dollar. At that exchange rate you will get only $733,000 for your 2.2 million marks. You would have done better to buy U.S. government bonds. Then you would have come out with $1.1 million at the end of the year, including interest.

Suppose, though, that today's exchange rate is 4 marks per dollar, but that you expect it to fall to 3 marks per dollar over the next year. In that case, you would come out better buying 4 million marks' worth of German bonds for your $1 million. At 3 marks per dollar, the 4.4 million marks you will have at the end of the year will get you $1,466,666 in the foreign exchange market. That is more than the $1.1 million you would have if you had invested in U.S. bonds.

The moral of the story is that, given the same interest rates in two

Capital account net demand curve
A graph that shows the net demand for a country's currency that results, at various exchange rates, from capital account transactions.

countries, you should invest in assets of the country whose currency you think is more likely to appreciate and avoid the assets of the country whose currency is likely to depreciate. The same reasoning applies in reverse if you are a borrower. If interest rates on loans are the same in two countries, you will want to borrow from the one where you expect the exchange rate to fall. That way you will be able to repay the loan in "cheap" marks or dollars or whatever when it comes due.

The effects of expected changes in exchange rates account for the downward slope of the capital account net demand curve. In Box 35.4 the curve intersects the vertical axis at the benchmark exchange rate of 3 marks per dollar. As the exchange rate falls below the benchmark, other things being equal, more investors will expect it to move back up over the life of their investments. Given this expectation of a rising exchange rate, these investors will want to switch their mark-denominated assets for dollar-denominated assets. At the same time, borrowers who expect the dollar to appreciate over the life of their loans will want to switch their borrowing from U.S. sources to German sources. Both the actions of investors and those of borrowers increase the net quantity of dollars demanded on capital account. The farther the exchange rate of the dollar falls in the present, the greater the proportion of investors who will expect it to rise

Box 35.4
The Capital Account
Net Demand Curve

The downward-sloping curve in this graph represents the net demand for dollars on capital account. This demand can be either positive (indicating a net capital inflow) or negative (indicating a net capital outflow). The curve crosses the vertical axis at a benchmark exchange rate of 3 marks per dollar, representing a situation in which the exchange rate is at purchasing power parity and interest rates in the United States and West Germany are equal. The capital account net demand curve has a negative slope because investors are attracted to assets denominated in currencies that they think are undervalued relative to the expected future exchange rate, and tend to avoid assets denominated in currencies that they think are overvalued relative to the expected future exchange rate.

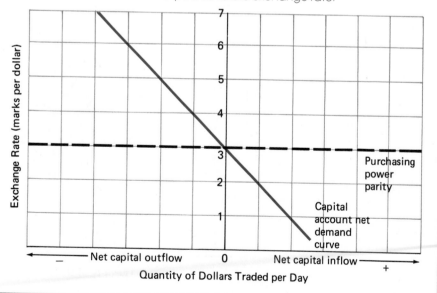

later and who will switch into dollar-denominated assets and the greater the proportion of borrowers who will switch out of dollar-denominated borrowing. The result is shown as a movement downward and to the right along the capital account net demand curve.

When the exchange rate rises above the 3-mark-per-dollar benchmark, the reactions are reversed. As the dollar rises, more and more investors and borrowers judge that the dollar will fall back toward the benchmark over the life of their investments or loans. Hence, they switch their investments out of dollar-denominated assets and switch their borrowing into dollar-denominated loans. The net quantity of dollars demanded on capital account then becomes negative, as the market moves upward and to the left along the capital account net demand curve.

Differences in real interest rates   Now that we have seen how changes in the exchange rate relative to its expected future value cause movements along the capital account net demand curve, we can return to the subject of interest rates. Box 35.5 sets the stage. As before, we assume that interest rates are equal in the United States and Germany and that the exchange rate is at the purchasing power parity level. We also assume that rates of inflation are equal in the two countries and that the marginal investor expects no changes in exchange rates. This puts the capital account in balance at E_1.

**Box 35.5
A Shift in the Capital Account Net Demand Curve**

This box shows the effects of a rise in the U.S. real interest rate relative to the real interest rate in West Germany. An increase in the U.S. interest rate makes dollar-denominated assets more attractive to investors, shifting the curve upward. The upward shift causes the exchange rate to rise. At a higher exchange rate some investors become unwilling to buy dollar-denominated assets because they think the dollar is overvalued relative to the expected future exchange rate. Leaving effects on current account transactions out of the picture, the shift in the demand curve moves the market from its equilibrium at E_1 to a new equilibrium at E_2.

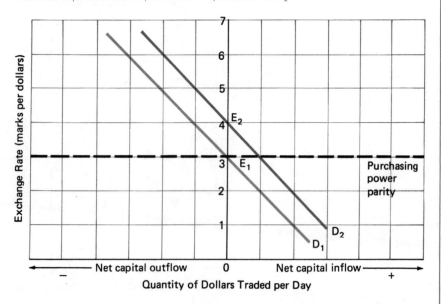

Suppose now that the real interest rate rises in the United States and falls in West Germany.[4] Other things being equal, this difference in real interest rates will encourage people to buy U.S. assets and discourage them from borrowing from U.S. sources. The resulting increase in the net demand for dollars on capital account is shown by an upward and rightward shift in the capital account net demand curve, from D_1 to D_2.

The shift in the demand curve creates an excess demand for dollars in the foreign exchange markets. The excess demand causes the exchange rate to rise above the benchmark level. As the exchange rate rises, investors must begin to take into account the possibility that it will fall again at some time during the life of their investments. Leaving any effects on current account imports and exports out of the picture for the moment, the market will reach a new equilibrium at E_2. At that point the attraction of the relatively higher U.S. real interest rate for the marginal investor is exactly offset by the expectation that the exchange rate will fall. The capital account is back in balance.

Combining the Current and Capital Accounts

Now that we have looked at the current and capital accounts separately, it is time to combine them. Box 35.6 shows how this is done. Part a shows the current account supply and demand curves. As we have seen, these reflect imports and exports of goods and services, plus transfer payments. Part b shows the capital account net demand curve. This reflects international purchases and sales of assets and international borrowing and lending. In this box the net quantity of dollars demanded in capital account transactions is positive when the exchange rate is below the purchasing power parity level of 3 marks per dollar, indicating a net capital inflow. Above 3 marks per dollar, the net quantity of dollars demanded in capital account transactions is negative, indicating a net capital outflow.

In part c of the box the two demand curves are added together. The horizontal distance from the vertical axis to the total demand curve for dollars is equal to the sum of the current and capital account demands. The total demand curve for dollars intersects the current account demand curve at the exchange rate for which the capital account is in balance, that is, at the point where the capital account net demand curve in part b intersects its vertical axis. Thus, at exchange rates below 3 marks per dollar the total demand curve for dollars is greater than it would be if only current account transactions were considered. Above 3 marks per dollar, where the total demand curve lies to the left of the current account demand curve, the total demand for dollars is less than it would be if only current account transactions were considered.

---

[4]In macroeconomic terminology the *nominal* interest rate means the interest rate measured in the ordinary way and the *real* interest rate means the nominal interest rate minus the rate of inflation. For international investors it is changes in the real interest rate that count. An increase in the nominal rate of interest in the United States that is accompanied by an equal increase in the U.S. rate of inflation (thus leaving the real interest rate unchanged) would not make dollar-denominated assets more attractive to foreign investors. The reason is that increased U.S. inflation will begin to change the purchasing power parity ratio between U.S. and German currencies. Investors therefore will expect the exchange rate of the dollar, in terms of marks, to depreciate along with the declining purchasing power parity. The higher nominal return on U.S. assets will thus be exactly offset by the expectation of a lower future exchange rate, leaving the capital account net demand curve unaffected.

Box 35.6
Combining the Current and Capital Account Demand Curves

This graph shows how the current account demand curve for dollars and the capital account net demand curve can be added together to get a total demand curve for dollars. Total demand at each exchange rate is equal to current account demand plus the net capital inflow to the United States. If there is a net capital outflow from the United States, the total demand curve lies to the left of the current account demand curve. Here the market is assumed to be in equilibrium at a benchmark exchange rate of 3 marks per dollar. At that point both the current and capital accounts are in balance.

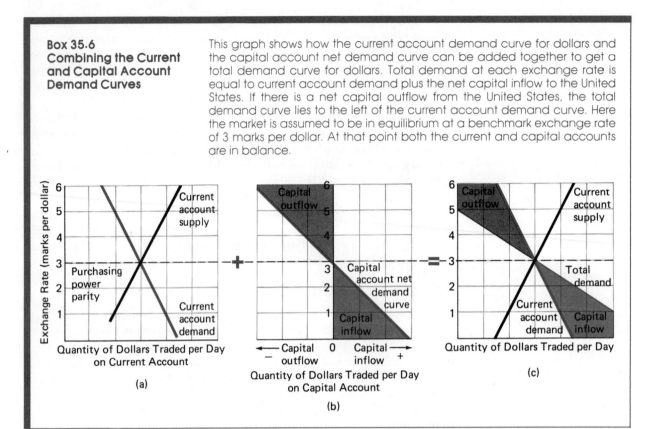

In Box 35.6 the market is in equilibrium at 3 marks per dollar, the exchange rate that corresponds to purchasing power parity. At this exchange rate both the current and capital accounts are in balance. The value of imports is equal to the value of exports plus net transfers, and capital inflows are equal to capital outflows. As we have said, this position of the foreign exchange market provides a useful benchmark for discussing policy issues, and in a general sense it is a position toward which foreign exchange rates tend. However, in practice exchange rates may depart from purchasing power parity and the current and capital accounts can show surpluses or deficits, not only in the short run but often over periods of many years. In the next section we turn to some of the reasons why exchange rates may depart from purchasing power parity.

EXCHANGE RATES AND ECONOMIC POLICY

Every change in exchange rates, whether up or down, helps some firms and individuals and hurts others. When a country's currency appreciates, consumers like the Lushch family benefit from the availability of low-cost imports. They also benefit from efforts by domestic producers to cut costs and improve quality in response to foreign competition. Profits rise and the number of jobs increases in sectors that use imported raw materials and in sectors devoted to marketing and servicing imported goods. On the other hand, a higher exchange rate means trouble for firms and workers in sectors that depend on exports or that compete with imported goods. So while some people gain, others lose.

When a country's currency depreciates, the effects are reversed. Consumers face higher prices. People who sell and service imported goods suffer. But export industries boom, and import-competing industries enjoy a respite from international competition. The former winners become the losers and the losers become the winners.

These effects ensure that exchange rates are a matter of constant concern for policymakers. In this section we will look at the link between exchange rates and economic policy. First we will look at the impact of policies that affect economic growth and interest rates. Then we will look at strategies for managing exchange rates.

Exchange Rates and Economic Growth

Differences among countries in rates of economic growth are a key factor affecting exchange rates. Box 35.7 illustrates this effect. At first the foreign exchange markets are in equilibrium at point E_1. The exchange rate is at 3 marks per dollar, which corresponds to purchasing power parity. Growth rates and real interest rates in West Germany and the United States are assumed to be equal, and both the current and capital accounts are in balance.

**Box 35.7
Effects of an Increase in
the U.S. Rate of
Economic Growth**

An increase in the rate of growth of the U.S. economy increases the demand for imports by U.S. households, firms, and units of government. This shifts the current account supply curve of dollars to the right. As the supply curve shifts, an excess supply causes the dollar to depreciate. As the exchange rate depreciates below the benchmark rate of 3 marks per dollar, some investors shift out of mark-denominated assets into dollar-denominated assets. The resulting net capital inflow, shown as a movement downward and to the right along the total dollar demand curve, brings the market back into equilibrium at E_2. At E_2, the United States experiences a current account deficit, which is shown by the arrow between the current account demand curve and the total demand curve for dollars. This deficit is offset by a net capital inflow.

Starting from this situation, suppose that the rate of growth of the U.S. economy increases. To keep things simple, we will assume that this happens without affecting interest rates or the rate of inflation in the United States. As the economy grows, households and firms in the United States increase their spending on consumer goods, investment goods, and raw materials. Much of this spending is directed toward goods and services produced at home, but a certain fraction of it goes for goods and services imported from Germany. To get the marks they need to buy these imported goods, U.S. households and firms bring dollars to the foreign exchange market. The result is a rightward shift in the current account supply curve, from S_1 to S_2.

Given the position of the demand curve, the increased supply of dollars puts downward pressure on the exchange rate. As the exchange rate begins to fall, both the current and capital accounts are affected. On the current account, the lower exchange rate makes U.S.-made goods cheaper for buyers in West Germany. U.S. exports increase, shown by a movement downward and to the right along the current account demand curve. On the capital account, investors see that the dollar has depreciated to a level below purchasing power parity. This makes dollar-denominated assets more attractive. U.S. real interest rates are unchanged, we assume, and the odds are increased that the dollar will rise back toward purchasing power parity in the future and that U.S. assets bought now when the dollar is low can be sold at a profit later. Thus, the net quantity of dollars demanded on capital account also increases, shown as a movement of the market downward along the total demand curve for dollars.

When the exchange rate falls to 2.5 marks per dollar, the foreign exchange market reaches a new equilibrium at point E_2. At this point the total quantity of dollars demanded has increased by enough to equal the quantity of dollars supplied. Note, however, that although the foreign exchange market is back in equilibrium, the current and capital accounts are no longer in balance. As the arrow in Box 35.7 shows, the current account demand for dollars falls short of the current account supply. This indicates that the value of imports exceeds the value of exports—a current account deficit. The remaining supply of dollars is absorbed by the net demand for dollars on capital account. Thus, the current account deficit is just offset by a net inflow of capital.

To summarize, when a country's rate of economic growth increases, other things being equal, its imports increase, its currency depreciates, and a current account deficit develops, offset by a net capital inflow. When a country's rate of growth slows down relative to that of its trading partners, the opposite effects take place. Imports fall, the currency appreciates, and a current account surplus develops, offset by a net capital outflow.

Exchange Rates and Interest Rate Differentials

Changing interest rate differentials among countries are another major factor affecting exchange rates. Box 35.8 tells the interest rate story. At first the market is again in equilibrium at 3 marks per dollar, which corresponds to purchasing power parity. Growth rates and interest rates are the same in West Germany and the United States, and both the current and capital accounts are in balance. Now we assume that real interest rates increase in the United States but remain unchanged in Germany. To keep things

Box 35.8
Effects of an Increase in the U.S. Real Interest Rate

This graph shows the effects of an increase in the real interest rate in the United States relative to the real interest rate in West Germany. The increase in the real interest rates causes investors to switch into dollar-denominated assets and causes borrowers to switch to mark-denominated borrowing. The result is an upward shift in the capital account net demand curve for dollars and, hence, a shift in the total demand curve from D_1 to D_2. The shift in the demand curve causes an excess demand for dollars, and the dollar appreciates. As it does so, U.S.-made goods become more expensive for German buyers and German-made goods become cheaper for U.S. buyers. The result is a current account deficit, as shown by the arrow. This current account deficit is offset by a net capital inflow into the United States.

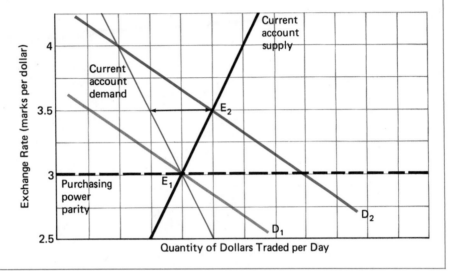

simple, we assume that this happens without any change in the U.S. or German rates of economic growth or inflation.

An increase in U.S. real interest rates relative to those in Germany makes dollar-denominated assets more attractive to investors. At the same time, it makes borrowing from U.S. sources less attractive. These developments are shown by an upward and rightward shift in the capital account net demand curve for dollars. The current account demand curve remains in place, and the total demand curve for dollars shifts from D_1 to D_2.

The increase in demand for dollars by investors puts upward pressure on the exchange rate. As the exchange rate rises, imports become more expensive for U.S. buyers. They supply more dollars in order to obtain the marks they need to buy imports, thereby moving upward and to the right along the current account supply curve. At the same time, U.S. exports become more expensive for German buyers. They demand fewer dollars, thereby moving upward and to the left along the current account demand curve.

The capital account is also affected by the rising exchange rate. The higher the rate rises above the benchmark rate of 3 marks per dollar, the more widespread is the expectation that it will fall again during the time period affecting investors and borrowers. If it were to fall, holders of dollar-denominated assets would suffer a loss. This expectation of an

**Box 35.9
The Rise of the Dollar,
1980–1985**

The first half of the 1980s saw an astonishing rise in the international value of the dollar. In 1979 and 1980 the dollar hit record lows. As the chart shows, it was trading at a level below 90 on a scale that compares the value of the dollar to a weighted average of the currencies of U.S. trading partners. In late 1980 the dollar started to rise. By early 1985 it was trading above 150 on the trade-weighted index.

What caused this dramatic rise in the value of the dollar? First consider the 1981–1982 period. In 1981 and 1982 the U.S. economy experienced a severe recession. Other things being equal, a recession tends to discourage imports and cause a country's currency to appreciate. In addition, as the chart shows, real interest rates in the United States rose above those in other countries by as much as 4 percentage points at some times. This happened because the U.S. rate of inflation fell much faster during the recession than nominal interest rates. Other things being equal, high real interest rates encourage a capital inflow and also cause a country's currency to appreciate. Thus, in 1981 and 1982 current and capital account forces operated together to raise the international value of the dollar.

The continued rise of the dollar after the end of 1982 is not quite as easy to explain. During 1983 and 1984 the U.S. economy entered a rapid recovery from recession while the nation's trading partners continued to grow slowly. This caused an increase in the value of imports relative to the value of exports, which by itself would have tended to put downward pressure on the exchange rate. The fact that the exchange rate continued to rise indicated that the downward pressure of a growing current account deficit must have been more than offset by the upward pressure of rising net demand for dollars on capital account. (The U.S. government intervened hardly at all with official reserve transactions during this period.)

But what was the source of the strong net demand for dollars on capital account? Many observers singled out the large federal budget deficits of 1983 and 1984. Borrowing by the U.S. Treasury to finance the federal budget deficit, they said, kept real interest rates in the United States high, continuing to attract capital inflows. However, this is not the whole story. Although on the average U.S. real interest rates stayed above those in other countries, the gap did not widen, and in some periods it actually narrowed. The combined effects of faster U.S. economic growth and an interest rate gap no wider than in previous years suggest that the exchange rate should have leveled off or even dropped a little. Yet throughout the period the dollar soared to ever greater heights.

Evidently factors other than relatively high U.S. real interest rates affected the capital account net demand curve in this period. European investors may have been increasingly attracted to the relatively free,

exchange rate loss just offsets the attractiveness of relatively high real interest rates on dollar-denominated assets for the marginal investor.

As the higher exchange rate reduces the number of dollars demanded both on current and on capital account, the market moves upward and to the left along the total demand curve for dollars. When point E_2 is reached, equilibrium is regained at an exchange rate of 3.5 marks per dollar. Note, however, that neither the current account nor the capital account is in balance. As the arrow in Box 35.8 shows, the current account demand for dollars falls short of the current account supply, indicating a current account deficit. This deficit is offset by an equal net capital inflow.

It is useful to compare the results of an increase in the rate of growth (Box 35.7) with those of an increase in real interest rates (Box 35.8). In both cases the United States develops a current account deficit accompanied by a net capital inflow. The effects on the value of the dollar are not at all the same, however. In the case of relatively faster U.S. economic growth, an vigorous, and competitive U.S. economy as a place to invest for the long term, despite the leveling off of the real interest rate differential. Other investors may have come to see the United States as a "safe haven" for their funds—an island of political stability in a world of turmoil. Also, third-world countries reduced their rate of borrowing from U.S. banks in this period. A reduction in borrowing from U.S. banks, other things being equal, means an increase in net capital inflows to the United States. Finally, participants in foreign exchange markets seem to have made upward revisions in their expectations regarding the future exchange value of the dollar.

All in all, no single explanation of the "superdollar" of the mid-1980s seems to be enough by itself. It is likely that the matter will continue to be debated for years to come.

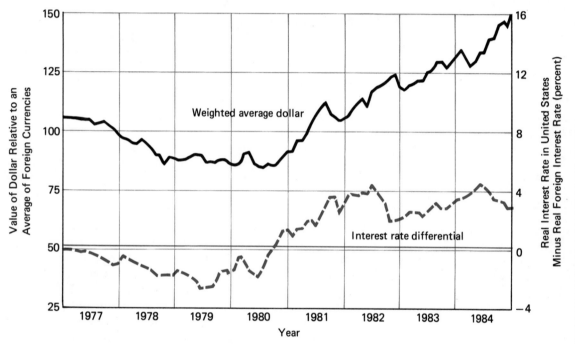

Source: Catherine L. Mann, "U.S. International Transactions in 1984," *Federal Reserve Bulletin* 71, May 1985, p. 277.

increase in the current account supply of dollars produces a current account deficit. It is this deficit that causes the exchange rate to fall. In the case of a higher real interest rate, increased capital account net demand for dollars causes the exchange rate to rise. It is this change in the exchange rate that causes a current account deficit.

An understanding of the effects of changes in relative interest rates and growth rates is useful in interpreting the dramatic changes in the international value of the dollar during the 1980s. However, as Box 22.9 explains, other factors too have been at work.

Intervention in the Foreign Exchange Market

Up to this point our discussion of supply and demand in foreign exchange markets has focused on the current and capital accounts. We have assumed that the official reserve account remains in balance. However, this need not be the case. Governments can and do use official reserve transactions as a means of intervening to affect exchange rates.

We can pick the story up at a point where high real interest rates in the United States have pushed the exchange rate above purchasing power parity to 3.5 marks per dollar. The high exchange rate has been a boon to consumers, but export and import-competing industries are suffering. What can the government do in response to their complaints?

One thing it can do is intervene in the exchange markets by selling dollars in exchange for foreign currency on official reserve account. Such a policy would be set by the Treasury, with the Federal Reserve carrying out the actual sales of dollars through its international trading desk in New York. The immediate impact of the sales of dollars would shift the supply curve of dollars to the right as the dollars sold on official reserve account were added to those sold on current account. Taken by itself, the extra supply of dollars would relieve the upward pressure on the exchange rate. If the drop in the exchange rate were maintained, it would cause the value of exports to rise and the value of imports to fall. The current account deficit would tend to shrink.

However, a shift in the supply curve is not the only result of an official reserve account sale of dollars. In the case of intervention in the foreign exchange market, complications arise from the fact that the dollars sold on official reserve account represent a payment by the Federal Reserve for the foreign currency it buys. This payment ends up as new reserves in the bank where the seller of the foreign currency deposits the funds. The increase in total reserves of the U.S. banking system, in turn, causes the U.S. money supply to expand.

To the extent that the government's goal is to get the exchange rate down, the increase in the money supply is helpful. An increase in the money supply will depress U.S. interest rates. This, in turn, will cause a downward shift in the capital account net demand curve for dollars. The shift in the net demand curve reinforces the rightward shift in the supply curve of dollars and adds downward pressure on the exchange rate.

However, the change in the money supply that results from intervention in the foreign exchange market may conflict with the goals of domestic economic policy. Suppose that before the intervention the Fed had already adjusted bank reserves and the domestic money supply to the level it thinks necessary to serve the goals of price stability, full employment, and economic growth. It will not be happy to see the money supply pushed above the desired level by sales of dollars in the foreign exchange market for the purpose of purchasing foreign currency. Nor, under other conditions, would it be happy to see the domestic money supply pushed below the desired level by purchases of dollars in the foreign exchange market associated with sales of foreign currency.

Sterilization
A process through which a central bank uses domestic monetary operations to offset the domestic monetary effects of official reserve transactions in foreign exchange markets.

If the Fed wants to avoid the monetary side effects of intervention in the foreign exchange market, it can do so through a process known as **sterilization**. This means using domestic open market sales of government securities to absorb reserves at the same time that reserves are being created through intervention in the form of purchases of foreign currency or using domestic open market purchases of securities to provide reserves at the same time that reserves are being absorbed through intervention in the form of sales of foreign currency. However, sterilized intervention has far less impact on exchange rates than simple, unsterilized intervention.

There is still a brief impact on the foreign exchange market supply curve of dollars at the time that official sales (or purchases) of dollars are made. But, the effect, if any, of sterilized intervention on the net demand curve for dollars is quite limited. The volume of foreign exchange market transactions and the world stock of dollar-denominated assets are huge. Trying to make a lasting impact on exchange rates with a few billion dollars' worth of sterilized intervention is like trying to hold back the tide with a teacup.

Systems of Exchange Rate Management

Given these limitations, how, if at all, should governments use their powers to intervene in foreign exchange markets by buying and selling on official reserve account? This much-debated question has received varying answers in the post–World War II period. Sometimes central banks have intervened actively in the foreign exchange markets on an almost daily basis. In contrast, under the Reagan administration the U.S. Treasury and the Federal Reserve System have, with only a few exceptions, followed a hands-off strategy. We will close the chapter by looking briefly at various systems for managing foreign exchange rates.

Bretton Woods and the fixed-rate system   After World War II the major trading nations of the world met under United Nations auspices at Bretton Woods, New Hampshire, to forge a new world monetary system. That system, administered by the newly created International Monetary Fund (IMF), was based on a set of fixed exchange rates—four West German marks to the dollar, five French francs to the dollar, and so on. The member nations of the IMF agreed to maintain these rates through systematic intervention in foreign exchange markets.

For example, suppose rapid growth of the French economy caused the value of the franc to fall relative to that of the dollar. The French central bank would support its currency by buying francs in the foreign exchange markets. To be fully effective, these purchases were supposed to be unsterilized. As a result, they would drain francs from the domestic money supply at the same time that they propped up the exchange rate. Sooner or later, slower monetary growth would slow the growth of the French economy as a whole. This would remove the source of the downward pressure on the franc. Intervention could then stop, and the franc would be back in equilibrium at the agreed-upon level.

This system had both strengths and weaknesses. On the plus side, it controlled variations in exchange rates. Importers and exporters tended to like this situation because it created a stable framework for business planning. However, the Bretton Woods system deprived national governments of a great deal of control over economic policy. They could not use domestic monetary policy to expand and contract their economies, to control inflation, or to create jobs. Instead, domestic economic policy was constrained by the need to maintain exchange rates at a fixed level. Countries whose exchange rates tended to fall below the agreed-upon level had to accept lower growth rates than they wanted. And those whose currencies tended to push upward could be forced to take inflationary steps that they didn't want to take.

In 1973 the Bretton Woods system collapsed. Since then the currencies of most countries have been free to fluctuate or "float" in foreign exchange markets according to supply and demand. (There are exceptions: A group of countries in Western Europe have attempted to maintain exchange rates within a narrow range for their group. And some small countries have pegged their currencies to the U.S. dollar, the French franc, or some other major currency.) What has been the experience with floating rates since 1973?

Experience with floating rates   During its lifetime the Bretton Woods system was criticized by many economists. They viewed the fixed-rate system as a brake on world economic growth and free international trade. They especially resented the fact that many countries used protectionist measures, such as tariffs, quotas, and restraints on capital flows, in addition to simple intervention, as a way of keeping their currencies at the agreed-upon exchange rates. The critics thought that if currencies were left free to respond to the forces of supply and demand, they would gravitate toward a set of natural exchange rate relationships. These would remain stable enough over time to provide a basis for an efficient and growing world economy.

For the most part, the international monetary system has worked well since 1973. Few of the former critics of the Bretton Woods system have concluded that floating rates are a mistake. Even so, there have been some disappointments.

One of these was the worldwide spread of inflation during the 1970s. Fixed exchange rates help restrain inflation by forcing countries with weak currencies to intervene in foreign exchange markets and thereby slow the growth of their domestic money supplies. Floating rates leave the governments of each country open to inflationary pressures from within their own political and economic systems. However, inflation among the major industrial countries has moderated since the early 1980s, so the worst of this problem may have passed.

The volatility of exchange rates has been another disappointment. In the short run, exchange rates have proved to be highly sensitive to any bit of new information that might bear on the expected future levels of exchange rates. And as shown in Box 35.9, the value of the dollar relative to other currencies, and the value of other currencies relative to one another, have also fluctuated over the longer run in the years since 1973—more widely than many critics of the Bretton Woods system expected. These exchange rate fluctuations have produced boom-and-bust cycles in import and export industries. It is hoped that moderation of worldwide inflation may damp exchange rate fluctuations in coming years.

Finally, floating rates have not brought an era of free world trade. True, many governments used Bretton Woods as an excuse to pursue protectionist policies in the early postwar years. Since 1973, however, governments have found many other excuses for protectionism. The danger of a slide back into worldwide protectionism, which did so much damage to the world economy during the 1930s, remains despite floating rates.

For the present, there is no realistic alternative to a floating-rate system. At every international conference on the subject, some speakers urge a return to a fixed-rate system. But the fact remains that national governments are not inclined to give up the control over their domestic economic policies that fixed rates imply. Nor do most economists think that fixed rates are superior to floating rates, despite some disappointments with the latter.

The future, then, will almost certainly see a continuation of the present mixed system. The basis of the system is exchange rates that float against one another. However, the system is modified by exchange rate intervention (used more actively by some countries than by others), by the existence of some currency blocs within which exchange rates are linked to one another, and by protectionist policies that are often inspired by imbalances in current or capital accounts.

Summary

1. The international accounts of the United States list many different types of transactions. Imports and exports of goods and services plus international transfer payments are called transactions on *current account*. International purchases and sales of assets and international borrowing and lending are called *capital account* transactions. (Purchases of U.S. assets by foreigners and borrowing from foreigners by U.S. firms and households are called *capital inflows*. Purchases of foreign assets by U.S. citizens and borrowing by foreign firms and households from U.S. sources are called *capital outflows*.) Purchases and sales of reserve assets by central banks are called transactions on *official reserve account*. If official reserve account transactions are zero, a balance-of-payments deficit on current account must be offset by a net capital inflow, and a balance-of-payments surplus on current account must be offset by a net capital outflow. If official reserve transactions take place, the sum of the current account balance, net capital inflows, and official reserve transactions must be zero.

2. In a world in which only current account transactions take place, the demand for dollars arises from the demand by foreigners for U.S. exports. The supply of dollars arises from the demand for imports by U.S. firms and households. The supply curve will slope upward, provided that the demand for imports is elastic. A shift in either the supply curve or the demand curve will cause the exchange rate of the dollar for foreign currency to rise (*appreciate*) or fall (*depreciate*). In the long run the exchange rate tends toward *purchasing power*

parity—a situation in which it reflects differences in price levels between countries.

3. Capital account transactions can be represented by a *capital account net demand curve* for dollars. The negative slope indicates that, other things being equal, investors are attracted to assets denominated in currencies that they think are likely to appreciate, and avoid assets denominated in currencies that they think are likely to depreciate. An increase in the real interest rate in the U.S. relative to real interest rates abroad will shift the U.S. net capital account demand curve upward. The current and capital account demand curves can be added together to get a total demand curve for dollars in the foreign exchange market.

4. Other things being equal, an increase in the U.S. growth rate will increase the demand for imports. This shifts the supply curve for dollars to the right and puts downward pressure on the exchange rate. As the exchange rate falls, the number of dollars demanded on both current and capital account increases, shown by a movement downward and to the right along the total demand curve for dollars. In the new equilibrium, the exchange rate will be lower and there will be a current account deficit offset by a net capital inflow.

5. Other things being equal, an increase in real interest rates in the United States will cause an upward shift in the capital account net demand curve for dollars and, hence, in the total demand curve for dollars. This puts upward pressure on the exchange rate, and the dollar appreciates. As it does so, U.S. imports increase and U.S. exports decrease. In the new

equilibrium the exchange rate is higher and there is a current account deficit offset by a net capital inflow.

6. Official reserve account transactions by central banks can be used to influence foreign exchange rates. For example, the Federal Reserve System can sell dollars in foreign exchange markets, shifting the dollar supply curve to the right and causing the dollar to depreciate. However, intervention can also upset plans for domestic monetary policy. In order to neutralize the impact of intervention on the domestic money supply, the Fed may *sterilize* the intervention by using domestic monetary operations to soak up the dollars created by its official reserve sales in the foreign exchange market. But sterilized intervention has much less impact on the exchange rate than unsterilized intervention.

7. After World War II the major trading nations met at Bretton Woods, New Hampshire, to set up a new international monetary system. That system featured fixed exchange rates. If supply and demand tended to push the value of a country's currency above or below the agreed-upon exchange rate, the country was supposed to intervene with official reserve sales or purchases. The Bretton Woods system was abandoned in 1973. Since then the world has operated with a system of floating exchange rates.

Questions for Review

1. Define the following terms:
   current account
   merchandise balance
   current account balance
   capital account
   capital inflow
   capital outflow
   official reserve account
   foreign exchange markets
   purchasing power parity
   depreciation
   appreciation
   capital account net demand curve
   sterilization
2. Give examples of the kinds of transactions that appear in the current, capital, and official reserve account sections of a country's international accounts.
3. What determines the slope and position of the demand curve for a country's currency when only current account transactions are considered? What determines the slope and position of the supply curve for its currency?

4. Why does the capital account net demand curve for a country's currency have a negative slope? How is the curve affected by a change in the real interest rate?
5. How does an increase in a country's rate of economic growth, other things being equal, affect its exchange rate, its current account balance, and its net capital flows?
6. How does an increase in a country's real interest rate, other things being equal, affect its exchange rate, its current account balance, and its net capital flows?
7. How can official reserve transactions be used to affect a country's exchange rate? What is meant by *sterilization* of official reserve account transactions?
8. What kind of exchange rate system was established at the Bretton Woods conference after World War II? What kind of system has prevailed since 1973?

Problems and Topics for Discussion

1. Rework the simplified international accounts in Box 35.1 to show a case in which the United States has both a current account deficit and a net capital outflow. What must be the position of the official reserve account in such a case?
2. A current account surplus is often referred to

as a "favorable" balance of payments and a current account deficit as an "unfavorable" balance of payments. Why should it be thought better to have a surplus than a deficit on current account? Other things being equal, whom does a surplus or deficit tend to help? Whom does it tend to hurt?

3. In the mid-1980s the Italian lira was trading at an exchange rate of about 2,000 lire per dollar. The Italian government was discussing the possibility of establishing a new unit of currency, a "strong lira," that would be worth 1,000 old lire. New currency would be issued to replace the old currency; all bank accounts would be changed over to the new unit; and so on. If the Italian currency reform were carried out, how would it affect the purchasing power parity of the dollar compared with the lira? How would it affect the exchange rate?

4. Rework the graph presented in Box 35.7 for a case in which the growth rate in West Germany speeds up while that in the United States stays the same. What happens to the supply curve? The current account, capital account, and total demand curves? The exchange rate? The current account balance? Net capital flows?

5. Rework the graph presented in Box 35.8 for a case in which the real interest rate falls in the United States. What happens to the supply curve? The current account, capital account, and total demand curves? The exchange rate? The current account balance? Net capital flows?

6. In the late 1970s the dollar sank to record lows in the foreign exchange markets. This was a cause of much handwringing in Washington. Great pressure was put on the government to "do something" about the terrible situation of an undervalued dollar. Five years later the dollar was soaring to record highs. This too caused much handwringing and brought forth calls to "do something" about the overvalued dollar. Question: If people are distressed when the value of the dollar is low, why aren't they pleased when it is high? Discuss.

Suggestions for Further Reading

Grennes, Thomas. *International Economics.* Englewood Cliffs, N.J.: Prentice-Hall, 1984.

Chapters 14–24 review the economics of foreign exchange markets and the international monetary system.

Melton, William C. *Inside the Fed.* Homewood, Ill.: Dow Jones-Irwin, 1985.

Chapter 11 of this book by a former official of the Federal Reserve System *covers the relationship between domestic and international monetary policy.*

President's Council of Economic Advisers. *Economic Report of the President.* Washington, D.C.: Government Printing Office, annually.

Each year's economic report contains a chapter on international economic policy.

Chapter 36

Economic Development

WHAT YOU WILL LEARN IN THIS CHAPTER

After reading this chapter, you should be able to

1. Discuss the problem of economic development.
2. Explain the basic relationships on which population growth depends.
3. Describe the demographic transition and the problems that today's less developed countries face in completing the transition.
4. Discuss problems of agriculture in less developed countries.
5. Compare sources of foreign capital.
6. Discuss the role of entrepreneurship in economic development.

Ideas for Review

Here are some terms and concepts that you should review before you read this chapter:

Factors of production (Chapter 1)
Entrepreneurship (Chapter 2)
Comparative advantage (Chapters 2 and 34)
International capital flows (Chapter 35)

Howrah, India: In the black sand in front of his bare feet, a shirtless man named Jaidev is tidying up a capital P, as in Phoenix. Squatting on his heels, he carefully removes what looks like a giant aluminum cookie cutter, then flicks away stray bits of sand with a stick.

Next he dusts the sand with graphite powder and covers it with a box made of molded clay and sand. Molten pig iron is poured in through a hole. When the iron cools, the box comes off, revealing a 200-pound masterpiece entitled "Phoenix Sanitary Sewer."

Jaidev makes manhole covers for America. Around him in a gritty, tin-roofed foundry, hundreds of other workers are molding, chipping, grinding, brushing, polishing, and painting manhole covers labeled "City of Dallas," "Fresno Country Sewer," "Hartford County," "City of L.A.," and so on.

To his government, Jaidev is a small but vital part of India's drive to increase exports and earn foreign exchange. To some of his competitors in the United States, however, he is part of a network engaged in unfair competition.

Where this alleged unfair competition takes place is in an industrial warren of narrow dirt alleys and festering slums clogged with people, cows, goats, pushcarts, rickshaws, trucks, and honking buses. Here, in hundreds of small foundries, workers make from $1 to $3 a day. That's less than a U.S. foundry worker makes in an hour, but it adds up to much more than India's per capita average of $250 per year. Americans say these are slave wages. But workers here are unionized (and strike often), get a base salary plus piecework bonuses, and work from 8 to 5, with an hour for lunch and two tea breaks. Despite their rudimentary conditions, the foundries claim they turn out the best manhole covers in the world.[1]

Jaidev and his employer represent one of many faces of *economic development*, the subject of this chapter. Although Jaidev is far from the poorest of the world's poor, his standard of living is far below what Americans think of as the poverty line. At the same time, Jaidev represents the greatest resource of the developing world: its billions of people, whose ingenuity and willingness to work hard, given the chance, are its hope for the future. This chapter will explore the links among people, opportunity, and economic policy that define the problem of economic development.

THREE FACES OF ECONOMIC DEVELOPMENT

Economic Development as Growth

The less developed countries of the "third world" differ from one another and from the developed countries in many ways, but they have one thing in common—low per capita income. No magic number divides the rich countries from the poor ones; there are many degrees of poverty, as shown

---

[1]James P. Sterba, "The Manhole Cover Is a Thing of Beauty to Howrah, India," *Wall Street Journal*, November 29, 1984, p. 1. Reprinted by permission of Wall Street Journal. © Dow Jones & Co., Inc. 1984. All rights reserved.

Box 36.1
Gross National Product
per Capita, 1977 (in
1977 U.S. Dollars)

$3,001 to more than $7,000

Australia	Gabon	Norway
Austria	Greenland	Oman
Bahamas Islands	Iceland	Qatar
Bahrain	Israel	San Marino
Belgium	Italy	Saudi Arabia
Bermuda	Japan	Spain
Brunei	Kuwait	Sweden
Canada	Libya	Switzerland
Czechoslovakia	Liechtenstein	United Arab Emirates
Denmark	Luxembourg	United Kingdom
East Germany	Monaco	United States
Faroe Islands	Nauru	USSR
Finland	Netherlands	West Germany
France	New Zealand	

$201 to $1,000

Albania	Dominica
Algeria	Dominican
Angola	Republic
Antigua	Djibouti
Belize	Ecuador
Benin	Egypt
Bolivia	El Salvador
Botswana	French Guiana
Cameroon	Gambia
Chile	Ghana
Colombia	Gibraltar
Congo	Gilbert Islands
Cook Islands	Grenada
Cuba	Guadeloupe

$1,001 to $3,000

Andorra	
Argentina	
Barbados	
Brazil	
Bulgaria	
Costa Rica	
Cyprus	
Falkland Islands	
Fiji	
French Polynesia	
Greece	
Hong Kong	Portugal
Hungary	Puerto Rico
Iran	Rumania
Iraq	Singapore
Ireland	South Africa
Jamaica	Surinam
Malta	Taiwan
Martinique	Trinidad and
Mexico	Tobago
Netherlands Antilles	Turkey
New Caledonia	Uruguay
Panama	Venezuela
Poland	Yugoslavia

in Box 36.1. At the very bottom are the poorest countries—those with per capita GNP of less than $200 a year. These countries are found in southern Asia, from Afghanistan to Vietnam, and in a band through central Africa. The box also shows countries with per capita GNP in the range of $201 to $1,000, clearly in the less developed group but a bit better off. A third

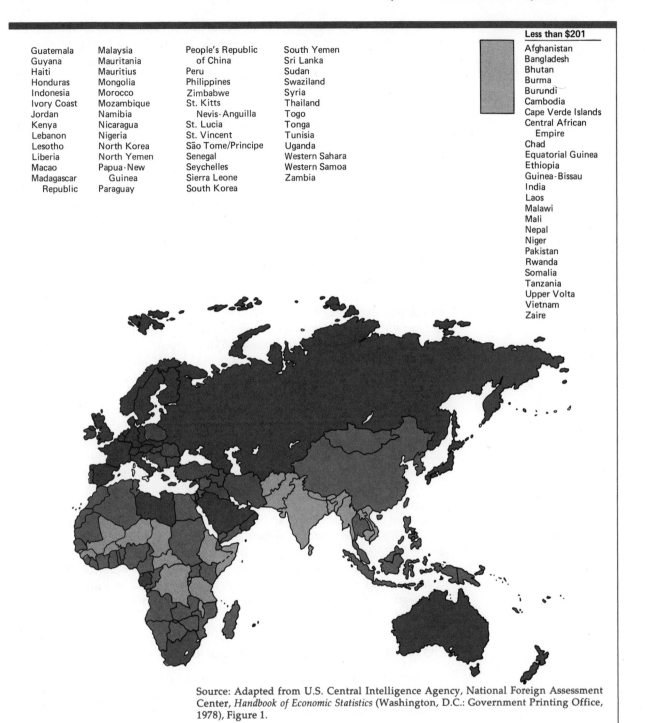

Guatemala	Malaysia	People's Republic	South Yemen	
Guyana	Mauritania	of China	Sri Lanka	
Haiti	Mauritius	Peru	Sudan	
Honduras	Mongolia	Philippines	Swaziland	
Indonesia	Morocco	Zimbabwe	Syria	
Ivory Coast	Mozambique	St. Kitts	Thailand	
Jordan	Namibia	Nevis-Anguilla	Togo	
Kenya	Nicaragua	St. Lucia	Tonga	
Lebanon	Nigeria	St. Vincent	Tunisia	
Lesotho	North Korea	São Tome/Principe	Uganda	
Liberia	North Yemen	Senegal	Western Sahara	
Macao	Papua-New	Seychelles	Western Samoa	
Madagascar	Guinea	Sierra Leone	Zambia	
Republic	Paraguay	South Korea		

Less than $201

Afghanistan
Bangladesh
Bhutan
Burma
Burundi
Cambodia
Cape Verde Islands
Central African
  Empire
Chad
Equatorial Guinea
Ethiopia
Guinea-Bissau
India
Laos
Malawi
Mali
Nepal
Niger
Pakistan
Rwanda
Somalia
Tanzania
Upper Volta
Vietnam
Zaire

Source: Adapted from U.S. Central Intelligence Agency, National Foreign Assessment Center, *Handbook of Economic Statistics* (Washington, D.C.: Government Printing Office, 1978), Figure 1.

group, in the $1,001–$3,000 range—including much of Latin America as well as countries like Portugal, Yugoslavia, and Taiwan—straddles the border between developed and less developed. Countries with still-higher levels of per capita GNP include the truly developed countries as well as the oil-rich countries of the Middle East.

To make such distinctions in terms of per capita income implies that economic development equals economic growth. That is the traditional view, and it has much truth to it. Economic growth can take place without bringing a better life to all, but it is hard to see how a better life for all can come without at least some growth. This is especially true for countries that have less than $200 of GNP per capita.

Much of development economics focuses on ways to help a country grow. Growth-oriented development studies tend to stress capital accumulation. Without capital accumulation, it is hard to put unemployed and underemployed people to work. Without capital, it is equally hard to raise the level of education or use imported technology. Yet, although capital accumulation and growth are important, they are not the whole story.

Development as Industrialization

The developed countries are not only richer than the less developed ones; they are also more highly industrialized. In developed countries between one fifth and one quarter of the population is engaged in industry. In less developed countries the proportion is likely to be 10 percent or less. A second view of economic development, then, is that it means industrializing, just as the advanced countries did in the past.

The view that development means industrialization, like the view that it means economic growth, has much truth to it. The less developed countries have large and growing urban populations. Industrialization gives them opportunities for employment. As incomes rise in a developing country, the need for manufactured goods grows rapidly. It makes sense to meet many of these needs with domestic sources of supply. Many less developed countries have valuable raw materials that they export for processing; they could process those materials themselves instead.

Despite all this, the importance of industrialization should not be exaggerated. For one thing, emphasis on industrialization may cause resources to be wasted on "showcase" projects. Not every country needs a steel mill and an automobile plant. Even small-scale industrial projects may be of little value if they mean building a replica of a plant that was designed for Manchester or Milwaukee, where factor scarcities and other conditions are different. What is more, too much stress on industrialization can lead to the neglect of other development goals. The third fact of economic development shows why.

Development as Depauperization

It is widely believed that a major goal of economic development should be a better life for the poorest of the poor—the people at the low end of the income distribution in the poorest countries. They are the true paupers— lacking enough food, lacking access to medical care, and often lacking even the most primitive shelter.

Development economists once were sure that the benefits of growth and industrialization would trickle down to the poorest of the poor. This view may not be justified, as much recent research has shown. In sub-Saharan Africa and the poorest countries of South America—that is, countries with per capita incomes of $100–$500—development efforts have sometimes made life harder, not easier, for the poorest of the poor. At very low levels of development there appears to be no trickling down at all. The poor begin to benefit only after a certain level of development has been reached.

Sometimes the policies needed to benefit the poor are different from those needed to increase growth rates. The idea of development as growth or industrialization may need to be supplemented with what Irma Adelman and C. T. Morris have called *depauperization*—a matter of providing not only the material basis for life but also access to education, security, self-expression, status, and power.[2] Depauperization stresses social, political, and spiritual deprivation as much as physical deprivation. It has as much to do with equity as with growth.

Two Strategies

The choice of goals strongly affects the strategy that can best promote development. The Soviet Union is at one extreme. For early Soviet planners, development meant industrialization above all else. Through high rates of saving, they sacrificed consumption in order to achieve rapid growth. Through collectivization, they sacrificed growth of agriculture in order to achieve growth of industry. In time the benefits of industrialization began to trickle down to the population at large. At first, though, living standards declined and the distribution of income shifted in favor of industrial workers and against peasants.

Dual economy
An economy that is divided into a modern, Westernized industrial sector and a traditional sector.

Even where industrialization is not a higher goal than overall growth, the benefits of development may be spread unevenly. Many less developed countries suffer from what is called a **dual economy**. In such an economy a modern industrial sector provides high wages for better-educated workers and taxes with which to pay a middle class of civil servants. A secondary sector remains largely untouched. Sometimes the overall growth rate of GNP can be increased by focusing on the modern sector, at least in the short run. Often foreign aid and the investments of multinational corporations are focused on the modern sector of dual economies.

A second strategy puts agriculture, education, and sometimes redistribution first and growth later. Such a strategy includes promotion of small-scale agriculture, sometimes involving land redistribution. Education means mass education in literacy and general knowledge, not just training for work in the modern sector. When this strategy works, it can serve as a basis for rural development and education and for the growth of broadly based, labor-intensive industry. Israel, Japan, South Korea, Singapore, and Taiwan are often cited as countries that have followed this strategy with success.

POPULATION AND DEVELOPMENT

Whatever strategy they choose, all less developed countries include an increase in per capita income as a major goal of development. Because per capita income is a ratio of income to population, it is clear that understanding the challenge of development requires some knowledge of demo-

---

[2]See Irma Adelman and C. T. Morris, *Society, Politics, and Economic Development* (Baltimore: Johns Hopkins University Press, 1967).

Crude birthrate
The number of people born into a population per thousand per year.

Crude death rate
The number of people in a population who die per thousand per year.

Rate of natural increase
The current growth rate of a population, calculated by subtracting the crude death rate from the crude birthrate.

graphics (population science) as well as economics. In fact, as we will see, development economists have been concerned with population from the earliest years of the modern era, when even England was a less developed country. As background for a discussion of this issue, we will begin with a review of some basic population arithmetic.

Population Arithmetic

For a population to grow in a given year, it is obvious that more people must be born than die in that year. (In this section immigration and emigration are ignored.) The number of people born into a population per thousand per year is the **crude birthrate**. The number who die per thousand per year is the **crude death rate**. The difference between the two is the **rate of natural increase**.

Box 36.2 shows the crude birthrates, crude death rates, and rates of natural increase for selected countries. In interpreting data like these, it

Box 36.2
Population Data for Selected Countries

This table shows population statistics for selected countries in 1982, with changes since 1960. The rate of natural increase for a population is found by subtracting the current death rate per thousand from the current birthrate per thousand. If the rate of natural increase is greater than zero, it can also be expressed as the number of years that would be required for the population to double if that rate were to continue.

Country	Crude Birth Rate	Percent Change 1960–82	Crude Death Rate	Percent Change 1960–82	Rate of Natural Increase	Percent Change 1960–82	Population Doubling Time in Years
Bangladesh	47	0.2	17	−24.7	30	24.9	24
Ethiopia	47	−7.0	18	−35.9	29	28.9	24
India	34	−28.3	13	−46.8	21	18.5	34
Tanzania	47	0.8	15	−33.4	32	34.2	22
Haiti	32	−17.4	13	−35.7	19	18.3	37
China	19	−52.8	7	−71.9	12	19.1	59
Kenya	55	0.2	12	−47.9	43	48.1	17
Afghanistan	54	7.4	29	−6.5	25	13.9	28
Bolivia	43	−7.2	16	−28.7	27	21.5	26
Indonesia	34	−23.9	13	−43.2	21	19.3	34
Costa Rica	30	−36.8	4	−51.3	26	14.5	27
Brazil	31	−26.9	8	−37.4	23	10.5	31
Mexico	34	−25.3	7	−41.5	27	16.2	26
Hong Kong	18	−47.2	5	−20.9	13	−26.3	55
Ireland	20	−5.1	9	−18.3	11	13.2	65
U.K.	13	−27.4	12	3.5	1	−30.9	710
W. Germany	10	−42.3	12	0.0	−2	−42.3	—
United States	16	−32.5	9	−9.5	7	−23.0	101

Source: International Bank for Reconstruction and Development/World Bank, *World Development Report 1984* (New York: Oxford University Press, 1984), Table 20.

helps to translate rates of increase into doubling times. This is done in the last column of the table. The faster the rate of natural increase, the shorter the time required for the population to double.

Population Equilibrium

A population that grew at a constant rate would double each time a fixed number of years went by. It would reach 2, 4, 8, 16, 32, 64 (and so on) times its original size, following the same sort of growth path as the value of a sum of money invested at compound interest.

Normally, however, living populations are not able to grow at a constant rate forever. Suppose that bacteria are allowed to multiply in a glass jar of nutrient, or a population of fruit flies is allowed to grow in a glass cage or a room of a fixed size, or a breeding pair of dogs is placed on an island inhabited only by rabbits. Under such conditions the growth of the population of bacteria, fruit flies, or dogs would follow the S-shaped growth curve shown in Box 36.3. At first it would expand at the exponential rate. The biological traits of the species determine the population doubling time under optimal conditions. Sooner or later, though, the population would begin to fill up its jar or cage or island. Then, under more crowded conditions, the time needed to double the population would increase. In the long run, overcrowding would bring population growth to a halt.

Must the growth of the human population also follow this pattern? Many observers have suggested that it must. Estimates of the maximum possible population of the earth vary widely, but no one doubts that there is a ceiling. (One fanciful estimate puts the limit at 20 million times the present world population. This would require people to live 120 to the square meter in a 2,000-story building covering the entire earth. Even that number would be reached in less than 1,000 years at the rates of population growth that prevailed in the 1970s.)

Box 36.3
An S-Curve of
Population Growth

Under laboratory conditions populations of bacteria or fruit flies or other organisms tend to follow S-shaped growth curves like the one shown here. The growth curve for world population also seems to be following an S-shaped curve, which may or may not level off before the absolute carrying capacity of the world environment is reached.

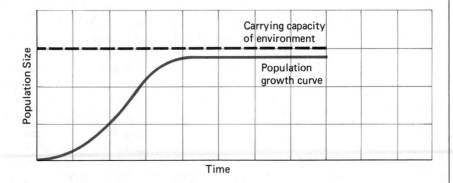

However, the data in Box 36.2 show that population growth patterns are changing. In much of the world birthrates are falling, and in at least some countries the rate of natural increase is falling. (In fact, according to World Bank data the average rate of natural increase for the world as a whole has fallen slightly since the 1960s.) Under what conditions will the rate of natural increase slow enough to bring the population into equilibrium? Will that happen before the absolute carrying capacity of the environment is reached? These questions have interested economists for two centuries.

Subsistence and Population Equilibrium

Imagine a market economy in which people earn money to buy the necessities of life only by selling factor services. The population begins to approach some fixed limit defined by the food supply. Income is distributed unequally. As the population nears the ceiling, the price of food rises relative to the wage rate. The lowest income groups find their standard of living reduced, and this affects their birth and death rates. At some point an excess of deaths over births occurs among the poorest classes. For those living at the margin of subsistence, there is a balance between births and deaths. An excess of births occurs only among the well-to-do. When enough people have been pushed down to or below the margin of subsistence, growth of the population as a whole will cease. The result can be called a marginal-subsistence equilibrium.

This equilibrium assumes a great deal of inequality. It implies wealth for a few against a backdrop of masses of poor people whose numbers are constantly being replenished by the excess children of the rich who are driven down into poverty. If the assumption of inequality is removed, the result is a second type of population equilibrium, which can be called the absolute-subsistence equilibrium. In this case, as crowding begins to lower the living standards of a population, taxes and transfers are used to share the burden equally. This permits population growth to go on longer; no one is starved or crowded to the point of being unable to reproduce until everyone reaches that point. The total number of poor people in the absolute-subsistence equilibrium is greater than in the marginal-subsistence equilibrium.

Population projections like these are what caused nineteenth-century writers to call economics "the dismal science." As long ago as 1798, Thomas Malthus forecast a marginal-subsistence equilibrium that would come about as a growing population caught up with a fixed supply of farm land. (See Box 36.4.) According to Malthus' theory, only the landlords, who owned the means of producing food, would escape poverty. Even the capitalists would be ground down and their profits reduced to zero.

Malthus' prophecy has not come true for Great Britain, the United States, or other advanced industrial countries. These countries have achieved, or nearly achieved, a nonsubsistence population equilibrium with low birthrates, low death rates, and high living standards. The way in which this equilibrium has been achieved is a good example of how economic and demographic processes interact.

The Demographic Transition

In a preindustrial society, birth and death rates are both very high, and the rate of population increase is low. With economic development, per capita

Box 36.4
Thomas Malthus and the Dismal Science

**Thomas Malthus
(1766–1834)**

Thomas Malthus' *Essay on the Principle of Population*, published in 1798, has been the single most influential work in the history of population economics. In it, Malthus argued that population tends to grow in geometric progression (2, 4, 8, 16, and so on) while the means of subsistence grows in arithmetic progression (2, 4, 6, 8, and so on). As population grows, poorer-quality land must be brought into cultivation. Population growth outstrips food production, and wages are driven down to the subsistence level.

Famine, vice, misery, and war can be avoided only if people engage in "moral restraint"—later marriages and fewer children per family. Schemes such as the Poor Laws (the welfare system of the time) were useless, in Malthus' view, because they encouraged population growth.

Malthus' view influenced Charles Darwin's views on the competition among species for food—and hence survival. And his gloomy views on economic development and population were responsible for earning economics the name of the "dismal science." In later editions of his work Malthus modified the conclusions of the *Essay*, but he is still associated with this pessimistic view of the effects of population growth.

Demographic transition
A population cycle that begins with a fall in the death rate, continues with a phase of rapid population growth, and concludes with a decline in the birthrate.

incomes begin to rise. The first demographic effect of a rising income is a reduction in the death rate caused by better nutrition, hygiene, and medical care. Since the birthrate remains high and the drop in the death rate increases the rate of natural increase, the population enters a phase of very rapid growth.

If there are enough natural resources and enough investment in new capital, economic growth can outstrip population growth. Per capita income then rises. This has happened in all the major industrialized countries. There, rising per capita incomes have caused the birthrate to fall. Population growth has slowed, and equilibrium has been approached.

The whole cycle, from falling death rates to rapid population growth to falling birthrates and equilibrium, is called the **demographic transition.** Box 36.5 gives a graphic view of the demographic transition. Part a shows the course of the crude birthrate and death rate over time. Part b shows what happens to the rate of natural increase as it first rises and then falls. Part c shows the S-curve of population growth that results from the demographic transition. The human population growth curve in part c differs in a key way from that of flies in a jar or dogs on an island: It levels off at an equilibrium below the biological ceiling set by subsistence needs.

The crucial part of the demographic transition is the fall in birthrates caused by rapid economic development. Demographers do not fully understand why this decline occurs. In large part, it is probably caused by urbanization. A large number of children is an economic asset to a farm family because they can help out from an early age. In a city, children tend to be an economic burden. There is no guarantee of jobs for them, and their food, clothing, and housing cannot be produced at home. More subtle changes in life-styles and attitudes toward family life, which occur as income rises, also seem to play a role in the demographic transition.

**Box 36.5
The Demographic
Transition**

In a preindustrial society both birth and death rates are high, and therefore population growth is slow. The first effect of economic development is a drop in the death rate. This brings on a period of rapid population growth. As economic development continues, the birthrate begins to fall. Population growth slows and may eventually fall to zero.

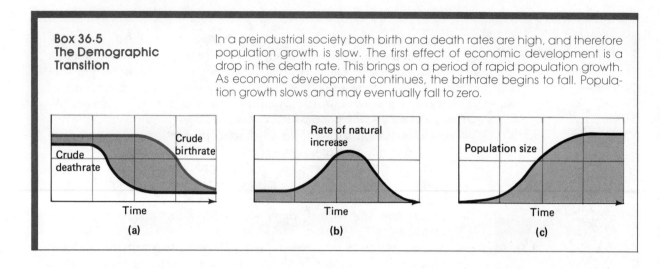

Net Reproduction

Completing the demographic transition and approaching equilibrium takes many decades. To understand why it takes so long, we need to know more about population growth than crude birthrates and death rates can tell us.

Crude birth and death rates can be misleading because they depend on both the reproductive behavior of a population and its age structure. A more direct measure of reproductive behavior is the **net reproduction rate**—the average number of daughters born to each female in the population over her lifetime. If that rate is equal to 1, the population is, in the long run, just replacing itself. If it is greater than 1, the population has a long-run tendency to grow. If it is less than 1, it has a long-run tendency to shrink.

In the short run the rate of natural increase may be positive even when the net reproduction rate is 1 or less. This will happen when population growth has been slowing in the recent past. The United States is a case in point. The U.S. net reproduction rate is less than 1, but it has fallen to that level only recently. The elderly people who are now in high-mortality brackets are members of the relatively small generation who were born around the turn of the century. People in the high-fertility range are members of the much larger generation who were born just after World War II. The difference in the size of the generations causes the crude death rate to be lower—and the crude birthrate to be higher—than will be the case in the long-run equilibrium. If there is no further change in reproductive behavior and the net reproduction rate remains slightly less than 1, it will take some 40 to 60 years for the rate of natural increase to fall to 0. Only at that point will the demographic transition in this country be complete.

Net reproduction rate
The long-term growth rate of a population, measured as average number of daughters born to each female over her lifetime.

A Population Trap?

During the demographic transition a rising level of per capita income first depresses the death rate, causing population growth to speed up, and later depresses the birthrate, causing population growth to slow again. This process is illustrated in Box 36.6. If a constant rate of economic growth is

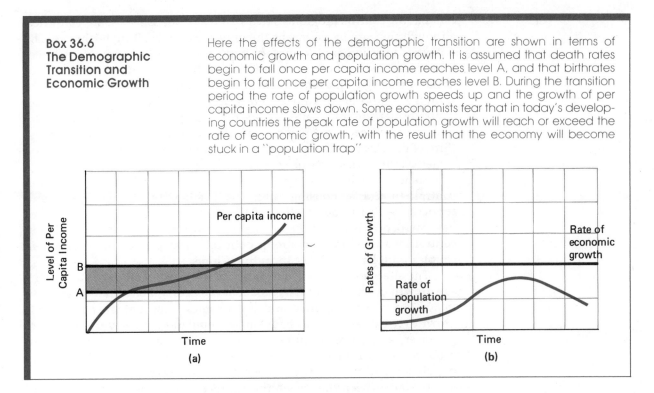

Box 36.6
The Demographic
Transition and
Economic Growth

Here the effects of the demographic transition are shown in terms of economic growth and population growth. It is assumed that death rates begin to fall once per capita income reaches level A, and that birthrates begin to fall once per capita income reaches level B. During the transition period the rate of population growth speeds up and the growth of per capita income slows down. Some economists fear that in today's developing countries the peak rate of population growth will reach or exceed the rate of economic growth, with the result that the economy will become stuck in a "population trap"

assumed throughout the demographic transition, as shown in part b of the box, the growth rate of per capita income will slow during the transition and then speed up again after the transition.

Many observers of developing countries see a danger, however. What if the rate of population growth becomes so rapid during the transition that it outpaces the rate of economic growth? If this happens, the rate of growth of per capita income will fall to zero or become negative and the transition will never be completed. This situation is sometimes called a *population trap*.

The population trap is seen as a real danger, in part, because rates of population growth in today's less developed countries are much higher than they were in Europe and North America during their demographic transitions. In Europe, population growth rates peaked at 1 to 1.5 percent per year; in North America, at about 2 percent per year. In contrast, consider the case of modern Kenya. Between 1960 and 1982 the crude death rate fell from 24 per thousand to 12 per thousand—as low as the rate in Britain. Over this period the crude birthrate remained unchanged at 55 per thousand, resulting in a rate of natural increase of 42 per thousand, or a population growth of 4.2 percent per year. The GNP grew at about 5.5 percent per year over the period as a whole, barely keeping ahead of population, and in the past few years it seems to have slowed. Thus, declining per capita income is a very real prospect.

Escaping the Population Trap

Concern about the population trap has led many governments and international agencies to stress population control as a key to development.

Population control programs have had some success in some countries, although they are by no means the only reason for falling birthrates. The potential for success of voluntary population control measures is sometimes measured by the "unmet need" for fertility control among couples of childbearing age. This term refers to the percentage of couples who do not want more children, or who want to space their children, but are not using contraception or other effective fertility control methods such as prolonged breast-feeding. In many countries as many as one quarter or one third of couples may have an unmet need for fertility control. As this need is met, birthrates can be expected to fall further.

Some countries have gone beyond voluntary methods of population control. In China, housing, jobs, and availability of some goods and services are tied to observation of limits on family size. These measures have helped reduce China's birthrate. However, compulsory population control measures provoke strong political resistance in countries where couples want large families, including China.

The alternative approach to escaping the population trap is to encourage growth of real output. The model of the demographic transition given in Box 36.6 is oversimplified in that it assumes a constant rate of economic growth regardless of what happens to population. However, people are producers as well as consumers. Under conditions in which people can produce as much or more than they consume over their lifetimes, both population and per capita income can rise together. (See Box 36.7.) This has, of course, been the case in the advanced countries over the course of their development. There appears to be a potential for growth in today's developing countries as well. Given proper policies, that growth could carry them through the demographic transition. Let's turn, then, to the policies needed to create a climate for growth.

CREATING THE CONDITIONS FOR GROWTH

Food and Agriculture

Agriculture is a key to economic growth throughout the developing world. It accounts for one third to one half of all output and employment. Food production is also a key factor in the health of the population. Hence, it is a logical starting point for discussing the potential for economic growth.

There are some notable agricultural success stories in the developing world—in some countries of Southeast Asia, in India and Sri Lanka, and in several countries of South America. However, agriculture has stagnated in other parts of the world, notably sub-Saharan Africa. In that region, one of the poorest in the world, food production has hardly increased at all in the past decade; production of export crops has actually fallen in many countries; and food imports have soared. Yet, despite the effects of the much-publicized droughts in the region, there appears to be considerable potential for agricultural growth given the proper policies. A recent report by the World Bank recommended policy changes in several areas, to which we now turn.[3]

_____

[3]*Accelerated Development in Sub-Saharan Africa* (Washington, D.C.: World Bank, 1981).

Box 36.7
The Ultimate Resource

In the Malthusian view, formulating a world population policy is like planning a party when you have a fixed amount of beer in the refrigerator. The more people you invite, the less beer there will be for each guest. If your friends all bring their friends, and they in turn bring other uninvited guests, the beer will run out and the party won't be fun for anyone. The only solution, in the view of many population planners, is to put a strict limit on the guest list and station a big guy at the door to turn away drop-ins.

Julian Simon, a professor at the University of Maryland, is a dissenter from the Malthusian view. To Simon, the world population picture is more like a bring-your-own-beer party. People, says Simon in the title of his book, are *The Ultimate Resource*. They are producers as well as consumers. Given the right economic policies, people can and do produce enough over their lifetimes to support themselves and to give the next generation a start in life. Simon points to densely populated but prosperous countries like Hong Kong and Singapore as examples of what human effort and ingenuity can achieve.

But what of the Malthusian concern about *diminishing returns*? In the Malthusian view, adding more and more people to a fixed amount of potential farmland, fixed quantities of mineral deposits, and so on means that output per worker will fall. In the long run the added people will barely be able to support themselves at the subsistence level, and the whole world will be impoverished.

Simon disagrees. The argument from diminishing returns, he says, holds only if one assumes an unchanged state of human knowledge. But people are entrepreneurs as well as workers. In each generation they find better ways of doing things—ways to get higher crop yields per acre, ways to use lower-quality mineral deposits, and so on. What the Malthusians fail to put into their equations, says Simon, is a term to represent the fact that more people mean more new ideas as well as more new mouths to feed.

Simon does not advocate packing the world with as many people as possible. He supports efforts to help each family have the number of children it wants, and he thinks that as more countries move through the demographic transition the rate of world population growth will slow. He differs from the Malthusian pessimists, however, in believing that the world does have time to complete the demographic transition. Rather than take drastic measures to control population, governments should pursue policies that encourage work effort, saving, and entrepreneurship. If this is done, the world's growing population will be able to take care of itself.

Source: Julian Simon, *The Ultimate Resource* (Princeton, N.J.: Princeton University Press, 1981).

Scale of agriculture Domestic development plans and international aid efforts have stressed agriculture for some time. Between 1973 and 1980 the World Bank and other agencies channeled more than $5 billion into African agriculture. It is now thought that the limited results of that aid are due in part to too great a focus on large-scale, government-run projects. These projects, which involved heavy capital outlays for mechanization and irrigation, did not meet expectations. They were plagued by problems of management, overemployment of staff, underutilization of equipment, and maintenance problems.

In other parts of Africa, Tanzania being a prime example but not the only one, agricultural performance was hurt by programs of rural collectivization. In accordance with ambitious theories of social transformation, the rural population was moved from traditional farms and villages to new population centers. These policies were devastating to the output of small farmers and did not result in enough added output from new, large-scale projects to make up the difference.

Today the World Bank recommends a focus on smallholders as the key to improved agricultural performance. Small farms are seen as the key to providing both food and jobs for the rural population, as well as a surplus for export and for feeding city dwellers. But the success of small-scale agriculture in Africa and elsewhere requires other policy changes as well.

Prices and incentives In many countries the biggest barrier to growth of agriculture is the structure of prices and other incentives. Low food prices, designed to benefit the urban populations that are the base of political support for the governments of many countries, are one part of the picture. Food prices are kept low both by official price controls and, in many countries, by massive imports of wheat, rice, and other staples. With domestic food prices at one half to one third of world levels, farmers have little incentive to produce a surplus above the needs of their own families. A World Bank study of 27 rural development projects highlighted the importance of this factor: Seven out of nine projects undertaken under favorable price conditions met or surpassed their output goals, while 13 out of 18 undertaken under unfavorable price conditions failed to do so.

Prices and incentives are a problem for export crops such as coffee, cocoa, and cotton as well as for food products. Growers of these crops face a double burden in much of Africa. First, sales of these crops are heavily taxed. And second, high exchange rates reduce the proceeds of exports in terms of domestic currency. As a result, farmers typically receive only about 40 percent of what they would have received had they been able to sell their output freely on the world market. Under these conditions exports of coffee, cocoa, cotton, and other crops have fallen steadily.

Marketing and procurement A third major problem facing African farmers has been the lack of effective organizations for marketing agricultural outputs and distributing agricultural inputs such as seeds and fertilizer. In many countries these functions are state monopolies. They are plagued by management problems, overemployment of staff, inadequate budgets for everything other than salaries, and other problems. Under these conditions there are few countries in Africa where farm inputs can be counted upon to be available when needed. As a result, Africa has largely been bypassed by the "green revolution"—new seed varieties, fertilizers, pesticides, and so on—that has benefited small farmers in many other parts of the world.

The keystone of reforming agricultural marketing and procurement, according to the World Bank, is to take advantage of domestic trading systems. These networks of traders already function effectively to supply rural market towns with a wide variety of goods that are not monopolized by state organizations. There is reason to think they could be equally helpful, if given a chance, in distributing farm goods and inputs.

Availability of Capital

Capital is scarce in less developed countries. This is true of all kinds of capital: structures and equipment for industry and agriculture; so-called social-overhead capital in the form of roads, communications networks, and health systems; and human capital in the form of education and training of workers and managers.

Some less developed countries save as large a percentage of their national income as advanced countries do. (See Box 36.8.) In others domestic saving is very low. In any case, because per capita income is low to begin with, even a fairly high percentage rate of domestic saving yields only a limited amount of new capital. As a result, most less developed countries, with the exception of oil exporters, have depended on capital inflows from abroad to help finance development. These capital inflows can take a variety of forms.

Direct foreign investment
Investment in a foreign country that gives the supplier of capital at least partial ownership and control of the project.

Direct foreign investment   **Direct foreign investment** refers to projects in which the investor retains some degree of management control and ownership interest. The construction of an auto parts plant in Mexico by Ford Motor Company would be an example. Potential benefits of direct foreign investment for developing countries include creation of jobs; provision of training for local workers and managers; creation of business opportunities for local firms to supply the foreign-owned firm; participation in ownership and management by local private investors or by the government of the host country; and creation of a source of tax revenue for the host government. In direct foreign investment, the firm that supplies

**Box 36.8
Saving Rates in
Selected Countries,
1982**

This table shows the percentage of gross domestic product devoted to gross domestic saving in selected countries in 1982. In some less developed countries, the share of saving in gross domestic product is as high as in advanced industrial countries. However, because gross domestic product per capita is low in the less developed countries, total savings are low. Many less developed countries find it helpful to supplement domestic saving with capital inflows from abroad.

Country	Saving as Percent of Gross Domestic Product
Ethiopia	3
Nepal	9
India	22
Tanzania	8
China	30
Bolivia	14
Indonesia	19
Jamaica	8
Mexico	28
Singapore	41
Italy	20
Japan	31
United Kingdom	20
West Germany	24
United States	15

Source: International Bank for Reconstruction and Development/World Bank, *World Development Report 1984* (New York: Oxford University Press, 1984), Table 5.

capital retains an interest in the success of the venture. If it fails, the project will generate no profits. The foreign investor thus bears all or part of the risk of failure and has an incentive to see that the project is managed in a businesslike way.

Despite these potential benefits, however, many developing countries raise barriers to direct foreign investment. In some cases the concerns are economic. For example, it may be feared that a project will contribute to a "dual economy" in which a small group of elite workers benefits while the broader needs of the country are not met. In other cases the concerns are political. For example, it may be feared that either the investing firm or the firm's home government will gain undue influence if the economy of the host country becomes dependent on foreign direct investment. Other reasons for barriers to direct foreign investment include nationalist and socialist ideologies, pressure from local business elites, and tendencies toward bureaucracy and state control of all aspects of economic life.

Borrowing   During the 1970s less developed countries turned from direct foreign investment to borrowing, expecially from banks in developed countries. In part, the increase in borrowing represented the "recycling" of oil revenues by oil-exporting countries following the oil price increases of 1973 and 1979–1980. In the recycling process oil-exporting countries deposited revenues in U.S. and European banks, which, in turn, loaned the funds to less developed countries to pay for imported oil.

Bank loans were attractive to many governments because they appeared to avoid some of the problems of ownership and control associated with direct foreign investment by private firms. However, borrowing has drawbacks as well. Borrowing may mean forgoing the benefits of transfers of management skills that come with direct investment. And if borrowed funds are invested in a project that fails, the loan has to be repaid whether there are any profits to repay it with or not.

What is more, less developed countries did not limit themselves to borrowing to finance investment projects. If they had, and if the projects on the average (despite an inevitable percentage of failures) had earned returns that exceeded the rate of interest on the loans, then borrowing would have meant rising living standards in both the short and the long run. However, many countries borrowed to finance public and private consumption rather than investment. For example, many countries borrowed to pay for imported food. This bought political support from urban populations but, as we saw earlier, it had negative effects on domestic agriculture.

When interest rates and the volume of debt rose to new heights in the late 1970s, many countries reached the limit of their capacity to meet interest payments as they came due. This created an international debt crisis that has not yet been resolved. In part, the stockholders of the banks that made the loans have been forced to absorb losses as loan payments were stretched out and interest rate concessions were negotiated. In part, the crisis has been papered over by a process in which new loans are made in order to pay interest on old loans. But in many countries the debt crisis has brought severe cutbacks in imports, public and private consumption, and standards of living. In many cases countries have ended up poorer, rather than richer, than they would have been without the inflows of borrowed capital.

Foreign aid   Foreign aid, in the form of grants and low-interest loans, has been another major source of capital for less developed countries. Millions of people throughout the world are alive or living better thanks to this aid. Even so, foreign aid, like private capital flows, has its critics.

Two criticisms of past aid efforts stand out. First, donors often focused their efforts on projects that were unsuited to the local economies in terms of size or technology. As a result, the poorest countries of the world are studded with factories that stand idle for lack of spare parts, imported materials, and labor and management skills. Second, in too many cases foreign aid made it possible for governments to pursue domestic policies that clearly retarded development. These policies ranged from food subsidies for urban consumers to nationalization of industry and trade to waste of investment funds on "showcase" projects. Box 36.9 illustrates some of these problems in the case of Tanzania, which has received more foreign aid while benefiting less than almost any other country.

Foreign aid will continue to play an important role in development in years to come. Donors appear to have learned some lessons from their mistakes. Much more emphasis is placed on technologies that are suited to the host country, on small-scale self-help projects, and on development of agriculture. If these trends prove to be more than just another fad and if they are accompanied by changes in the policies of the recipient countries, aid may become more effective.

Entrepreneurship

Much of this chapter has focused on population and capital flows. More could be added on the subject of natural resources—oil, for which most less developed countries have to pay too much; natural-resource exports, for which they have received falling prices in recent years; and farmland, which is in short supply in much of the world. But development is not just a matter of having a lucky resource base or getting the right ratio of population to capital. If that were the case, a country like Zaire would be rich and countries like Hong Kong and Singapore would be poor. But the opposite is the case. Something is still missing from our picture of the development equation. In the view of an increasing number of economists, that something is entrepreneurship. Entrepreneurship—the ability to look for new opportunities and find new ways of doing things—is not in short supply in the less developed world. Every country has farmers, traders, and small-scale industrialists eager for a chance to better their lives through their own efforts. What has been lacking in too many countries is the institutional framework needed to encourage such entrepreneurship.

We have already discussed this problem in the case of agriculture. In countries in which farmers have received fair prices for their output and have had access to off-farm inputs and to credit, the green revolution has been a success and per capita food output has risen. The same entrepreneurial drive can be found behind the back-alley steel mill described at the beginning of this chapter. However primitive its technology, any firm that can identify and fill a market need on the opposite side of the globe is not lacking in entrepreneurship.

Box 36.9
Tanzania Symbolizes Failed Growth Model

Like missionaries of an earlier era, they came to Africa bearing a new faith. But instead of the Bible, they preached the gospel of Western technology in an often puzzling argot of industrialization schemes and integrated development plans.

There was one East African nation that attracted them more than any other.

Poverty-stricken Tanzania, once one of the most neglected ornaments in Britain's colonial crown, became the centerpiece of one of this century's great social experiments. The vision of a leader, Julius Nyerere, joined with the funds and expertise of some of the Western world's largest institutions in an attempt to remake a country and lift it out of poverty.

Western countries, led by the World Bank, have poured more than $2 billion into Tanzania since 1970, more than they have given to any other African nation. They hoped to create a model for the third world to follow. Instead, Tanzania has become a symbol of technology and good intentions gone awry, of experts who lost their way, of poor people who became poorer.

A country that once had been able to feed itself and whose farmers had produced surpluses large enough to sell overseas collapsed into chronic dependency on Western grain and emergency food shipments.

Tanzania joined the long list of African nations dependent on food handouts for survival in 1979. It has remained on it ever since.

Africa's food crisis long has been viewed as the result of drought, poverty, domestic politics, and ill-advised government policy. Now, an increasing number of analysts, including international aid workers themselves, have come to the conclusion that Western assistance has also inadvertently compounded the crisis.

In Tanzania, Western donors first emphasized industrial development at the expense of the farming sector. Later, when they turned their attention to rural areas, donors often devised schemes that were too costly and too technologically sophisticated for what the World Bank lists as the fourteenth poorest nation in the world.

The schemes have littered Tanzania's rural landscape with the remains of factories, farm machinery, roadways, and water pumping systems that the country lacks the money, spare parts, and expertise to operate or maintain.

In one case, Canada built a modern, automated bakery in the capital, Dar es Salaam. It is

Yet instead of a climate that encourages entrepreneurship, many third-world governments, often in cooperation with foreign-aid programs, offer state ownership, economic planning, protectionism in foreign trade, and monopolization of domestic trade by overstaffed, underequipped bureaucracies—in short, a climate in which everything that is not authorized is prohibited. No country yet has achieved prosperity through this formula.

There are signs, though, that attitudes may be changing. At the same time that international agencies have become convinced of the need to "think small" in designing aid projects, third-world governments have been taking a second look at the balance between planning and the market. In a number of cases market-oriented reforms have been achieved.

Among the converts, or at least partial converts, to a market-oriented development strategy are the two largest less developed countries of all: China and India. China has encouraged production for profit in the countryside (see Case for Discussion, Chapter 2, p. 41) as well as private trade and even private industry on a small scale. India's new prime minister, Rajiv Gandhi, is leading an attack against the controls, taxes, and designed to turn out 100,000 loaves of bread daily, but it needs new parts and usually operates at less than half capacity. A United Nations consultant has estimated that Tanzania could have built ten smaller, less mechanized bakeries and that they would have produced the same amount of bread while creating four times as many jobs.

Food aid programs provided cheap Western grain that depressed prices that were paid to local farmers for their grain and allowed the government to postpone necessary agricultural reforms. The food aid has contributed to a dual food system in which rural areas grow only enough to feed themselves while the cities live on food from overseas.

Agricultural problems were made worse by the government's policy of "villagization," in which farmers were relocated from scattered homesteads to self-help village communities. When persuasion failed to get them to move, coercion was used. Meanwhile, a series of state-controlled corporations were given legal monopolies to supply credit, tools, fertilizers, and seeds. When they failed to provide supplies on schedule, crops went unplanted.

The fate of the once-thriving cashew crop illustrates the problems of agriculture here. In 1975, Tanzania was the world's second-largest cashew producer, exporting 120,000 tons of raw nuts. But villagization moved many cashew farmers far from their groves, while low government prices for the crop and delayed payments from the state cashew authority gave them little incentive to trek back to the groves to harvest or plant new trees. By 1983, the harvest had fallen to 32,000 tons. Nonetheless, the World Bank loaned Tanzania more than $10 million to expand its cashew-processing capacity. As a result, the country's processing capacity is now three times the size of its crop.

Some officials now admit that aid was a mixed blessing. "It's our fault as much as the donors because, after all, we agreed to their projects," says an aide to Nyerere. "We were nearly always talked into highly sophisticated, ultramodern machinery that we couldn't maintain. We ought to have been firm and said no."

Source: Glenn Frankel, "Tanzania Symbolizes Failed Growth Model," *Washington Post*, November 19, 1984, p. 1.

other policies that have smothered the Indian economy for almost 40 years. Elsewhere, Tanzania's president, Julius Nyerere, appears to be rethinking his policy of African socialism. His government has raised farm prices and has announced that it will return some nationalized estates to private ownership. Meanwhile Zambia's Robert Mugabe peppers his speeches with Marxist rhetoric but maintains a market-oriented agricultural system. This system allows both large-scale white-run farms and African small-holders to prosper, producing one of the few agricultural surpluses in sub-Saharan Africa.

It should not be imagined that a turn toward a market economy will bring prosperity overnight. Still, the idea of tapping local entrepreneurial talent does seem to make more sense than some of the development fads of the past. Market-oriented economies in all parts of the world seem to have performed more strongly, in terms of basic indicators such as food, health, and economic growth, than those that have relied on state ownership and central planning. At any rate, that is the perception of an increasing number of observers both in the West and in the third world itself.

Summary

1. Economic development is a complex process. Economic growth is a big part of that process, but not all of it. Industrialization is a second part, but it is easy to overemphasize industry in the early stages of development. In the view of some experts a process called *depauperization*, which means providing a higher material standard of living and also education, security, self-expression, and power to the poor, is the most important aspect of development.

2. The number of people born into a population per thousand per year is the *crude birthrate*, and the number who die per thousand per year is the *crude death rate*. The rate of population growth depends on the difference between the two, which is known as the *rate of natural increase*. For a population to be stable in the long run, the average number of daughters born per mother over her lifetime—the *net reproduction rate*—must equal 1.

3. The *demographic transition* is a process in which, as per capita income rises, a country's death rate falls, followed by its birthrate. During the transition the rate of population growth accelerates. In some of today's less developed countries, population growth rates are as fast or faster than rates of economic growth. Completing the demographic transition will require either successful population control measures or a speedup of economic growth.

4. Agriculture is a key to economic growth in less developed countries. In some parts of the world the "green revolution," meaning improved crop varieties and farming techniques, has allowed per capita food production to rise. In other regions, notably much of sub-Saharan Africa, food production has not kept pace with population growth. Many observers now think that improving agricultural performance will require greater emphasis on small-scale farming, improved prices and export incentives, and an end to state monopolies of procurement and marketing.

5. Most less developed countries are net importers of capital. Sources of capital include direct foreign investment, loans, and foreign aid. During the 1970s many less developed countries relied too heavily on loans and did not invest borrowed capital as productively as they might have. They are now having trouble repaying the debt.

6. Development requires entrepreneurship as well as adequate supplies of labor, capital, and natural resources. However, state ownership, central planning, protectionism, and bureaucracy have stifled entrepreneurship in many less developed countries. Recognizing this, a number of countries, including China and India, have adopted more market-oriented policies in recent years.

Questions for Review

1. Define the following terms:
   dual economy
   crude birthrate
   crude death rate
   rate of natural increase
   demographic transition
   net reproduction rate
   direct foreign investment

2. What are the links among economic growth, industrialization, and depauperization in the process of economic development?

3. What determines the rate of population growth for a country in the short run? In the long run?

4. Describe the demographic transition in terms of the crude birthrate, the crude death rate, and the rate of natural increase. At what point in the demographic transition does the rate of population growth reach a peak?

5. According to the World Bank, what conditions are needed for growth of agriculture in less developed countries?

6. What are three sources of foreign capital for less developed countries, and what are the advantages and disadvantages of each?

7. What role does entrepreneurship play in economic development? In the prevailing view today, what policies are needed to encourage entrepreneurship?

Problems and Topics for Discussion

1. In what ways are the problems of developing countries today similar to those faced by the United States in the nineteenth century? In what ways are they different?

2. People in the United States eat vast amounts of meat while people in many parts of the world go hungry. It takes about ten pounds of grain to produce each pound of meat. Would poor people in the third world be helped if Americans simply stopped eating so much meat and ate more bread instead? How would the grain released from meat production in the United States get to the countries where it is needed, if at all? Would the world food market do the job? What policy changes might be needed?

3. Rework the graph in Box 36.6 to show the case in which population growth equals or exceeds economic growth at some point during the demographic transition. What happens to the curve showing growth of per capita income in that case? Bonus question: Modify the graph in Box 36.6 to take into account Julian Simon's view that more people mean a higher rate of economic growth. (See Box 36.7.) Is a population trap possible under Simon's assumptions?

4. How would you determine the optimum population for a country? Would it be better to have a situation in which 2 million people enjoy a per capita income of $1,000 or one in which 3 million people enjoy a per capita income of $800? In which situation would total human welfare (whatever that means) be greatest? Discuss.

5. Each year thousands of immigrants come to the United States from the less developed world, both legally and illegally. They benefit by earning far more than they could in their home countries, and they benefit their home countries by sending money to their families. Even though the immigrants often take jobs that are low-paid by U.S. standards, they earn far more than they could have earned in their home countries. What is the effect of this immigration on worldwide income equality? What is the effect on the distribution of income among U.S. citizens? Would you favor or oppose a policy that allowed open immigration from developing countries, provided that the immigrants could prove that they could find jobs once they arrived in the United States? Discuss both positive and normative aspects of this question.

6. **Case for Discussion**

Just when Mexico's commercial future is looking brighter, pressure is building in Washington to upset that country's delicate trade relationship with the U.S.

Late last month, the U.S. and Mexico ended months of stalemate by signing a trade agreement, and Mexican Commerce Secretary Hector Hernandez spoke of establishing "stable market conditions for Mexican exports, based on principles of commercial justice." But some U.S. companies, with supporters in Congress, have other ideas. They contend that a nation's oil, natural gas, timber, minerals—practically any natural resource—constitute a kind of subsidy if that nation's government sells the resources cheaply to domestic manufacturers. Products made with these "resource subsidies," say the Americans, ought to be hit with tariffs at the U.S. border.

Nothing in U.S. trade law defines the price of natural resources as subsidies, but growing efforts are afoot to get the law changed. If they succeed, and the concept of a natural-resource subsidy takes hold, the effects could go far beyond Mexico to include everything from Saudi Arabian petrochemicals to Canadian timber products, all of which compete with American-made goods.

Until now, though, the subsidy argument has been aimed mostly at petroleum-rich Mexico, which supplies its domestic manufacturers with cheap energy and feedstocks. Not surprisingly, Mexico opposes the idea. "The natural resource subsidy [concept] is monstrous," says Petroleos Mexicanos representative in the United States Gutierrez-Kirchner. "It would undermine the whole international trading system."[4]

Questions:

a. Leaving the resource subsidy question aside for the moment, what are the advantages and disadvantages of trade versus aid as a means of helping less developed countries? Do you find it hypocritical for the United States to spend money on foreign aid and at the same time impose tariffs and quotas on imports from less developed countries? Discuss.

b. Suppose for the moment that the low price that Mexican manufacturers pay for oil reflects the true opportunity cost of oil versus other inputs (capital, other raw materials, and so on) within Mexico. In that case, does it make sense for Mexico to export goods made with Mexican oil to the United States, and does it make sense for the United States to import these goods without imposing tariffs? Discuss in terms of the principle of comparative advantage.

c. Now suppose that the Mexican government sells oil to its own manufacturers at a price far lower than the price at which it sells oil on the world market. Suppose, in fact, that although Mexico has a comparative advantage in producing oil, it has no comparative advantage (in terms of true opportunity cost) in producing manufactured goods. In this case who gains and who loses when Mexico exports manufactured goods to the United States? Do these exports help world efficiency? Do you think the resource subsidy policy is a good one from Mexico's point of view? Taking both positive and normative considerations into account, would you favor a U.S. tariff to offset the effects of the Mexican import subsidy?

Suggestions for Further Reading

Bauer, Peter. *Reality and Rhetoric: Studies in the Economics of Development*. Cambridge, Mass.: Harvard University Press, 1984.

This book by a British authority on economic development criticizes the aid efforts of industrial countries and suggests improvements.

International Bank for Reconstruction and Development/World Bank. *World Development Report 1984*. New York: Oxford University Press, 1984.

This volume, part of an annual series of reports issued by the world bank, focuses on population problems of developed countries and stresses the need for population control.

International Bank for Reconstruction and Development/World Bank. *Accelerated Development in Sub-Saharan Africa*. Washington, D.C.: World Bank, 1981.

This report stresses the need for reform of agricultural policy in the countries of sub-Saharan Africa.

Simon, Julian L. *The Ultimate Resource*. Princeton, N.J.: Princeton University Press, 1981.

Simon argues that a growing population does not always mean a lower per capita income in the long run and, by implication, that population control alone will not enrich less developed countries.

Chapter 37

The Soviet Economy

Ideas for Review

Here are some terms and concepts that you should review before you read this chapter:

"Naturally, the long-suffering Soviet carpenters complained."

In a small city in the Soviet Union there was once a factory whose business was to produce nails for use in the construction trade. In a certain year the plant was given the task of producing x tons of nails in a variety of sizes based on the needs of Soviet carpenters. Before the planned year was far under way, the manager of the factory realized that he could not achieve his target for total output if he kept to the planned assortment of sizes. Experience had taught him that the authorities were much more interested in the total output than in the size breakdown, so he came up with a clever strategy. He gave up making little nails, which were a bother to produce and weighed hardly anything, and concentrated on enormous spikes. In that year he turned out far more than x tons of output and was lavishly rewarded for surpassing his quota.

Naturally, the long-suffering Soviet carpenters complained. They had no way to fasten together anything smaller than two railroad ties. A smart planning official hit on a solution. The next year, when the plan was issued, the total output target for the factory was stated not in tons but in number of nails. The reader can guess how the factory manager responded. He gave up entirely on huge spikes, which used up far too much hard-to-procure steel. Instead, he concentrated on producing the tiniest pins and brads, which used hardly any metal and counted millions to the ton.

Naturally, the long-suffering Soviet carpenters complained.

The Soviet Union faces the same economic problems that any other economy does—what to produce, how to produce it, who should produce it, and for whom it should be produced. However, as the story of the nail factory shows, a different method is used in making the decisions. Instead of relying on markets to provide information and incentives about such matters as what sizes of nails carpenters will need, the Soviet economy relies on central planning. Under this system the Soviet economy grew from a very backward one after World War I to an industrial giant. However, the system has problems that have slowed its growth in recent years.

In this chapter we will look at the Soviet economy—its history, structure, and performance. This is worthwhile not only because the Soviet Union is an important country but also because it offers a chance to look at nonmarket solutions to economic problems.

ORIGINS OF THE SOVIET ECONOMIC SYSTEM

Marxism-Leninism

Our discussion of the Soviet economy begins with an explanation of its origins as a system based on the principles of Marxism-Leninism. The extensive writings of Karl Marx are devoted largely to the evolution and structure of capitalism. (See Box 2.7, p. 37.) Marx wanted to pave the way to revolution by showing that capitalism was headed for a breakdown, but he did not try to draw a detailed blueprint for the socialist economy that would replace it. There is little doubt, though, that he viewed the socialist economy in highly centralized terms. Private ownership of nonlabor factors of production would be abolished, and planning would replace the market as the main way of allocating resources.

V. I. Lenin, the leader of the Russian Revolution, was, if anything, more of a centralist than Marx himself. The secret of Lenin's political success was the highly centralized, disciplined structure of the Bolshevik Communist party, which he led. It was natural for him to apply the same methods of administration to the Russian economy. In a book written just before he came to power, Lenin likened the task of running the economy to that of running the post office or any other bureaucratic agency. The important thing would be a strong party leadership that would define economic goals clearly and provide the discipline and willpower needed to carry them out.

War Communism

Within months of the revolution of October 1917 the Bolsheviks were engaged in a civil war with their White Russian opponents. From the beginning of the civil war the market economy was abandoned. Trade between the city and the countryside was replaced by forced requisitioning of farm products. Almost all industry was nationalized, including many small-scale businesses. Retail trade was also nationalized, although a large black market soon emerged. Industrial labor was put under semimilitary discipline, with workers sent to jobs wherever the need was most pressing. As a final blow to the market, a massive outpouring of paper money sent inflation so high that money became useless. Workers in key positions were paid in food or other goods. Party leaders proudly proclaimed that socialism had come to the Russian economy.

Either the civil war or the government's radical policies taken one at a time would have produced chaos. Combined, they were a disaster. Militarily, the Bolsheviks scraped through against the White Russians and Western allies who opposed them. By 1921, however, with the war over, the economy was in sad shape. Agricultural production was down by one third, and industrial workers had fled to the countryside in search of food. It was time for a change of direction.

The NEP

With the threat of war removed, Lenin launched his New Economic Policy, known as the NEP. It was a step backward—taken, as he put it, in order to prepare for two steps forward. Lenin had endorsed the centralist and antimarket policies of war communism, which fitted well with the views he had expressed before the revolution.[1] Now he set those policies aside in order to get production back on its feet. Trade and small industry went back into private hands. Buying replaced forced requisitioning of farm products. The peasants once again found it worth their while to sow their fields. Currency reform put the brake on inflation, and the money economy reappeared. The "commanding heights"—heavy industry, trans-

---

[1]On Lenin's attitude toward war communism, see Paul Craig Roberts, *Alienation and the Soviet Economy* (Albuquerque: University of New Mexico Press, 1971), chap. 2.

portation, banking, and foreign trade—remained in government hands, while the rest of the economy followed its own course. Planning was reduced to the issuance of "control figures," which were not directives but merely forecasts intended to help guide investment decisions.

As a tool of economic recovery, the NEP was a great success. By 1928 prewar production levels had been surpassed in both industry and agriculture. In 1924 Lenin died and Stalin came to power. It was time to take the two steps forward that Lenin had promised.

Collectivization and the Five-Year Plan

The two steps forward taken in 1928 were the Five-Year Plan for industry and the policy of collectivization in agriculture. These steps were designed to overcome two features of the NEP that Stalin saw as serious defects. First, as long as the NEP was in force, central authorities were unable to control the direction of the market economy. Events went their own way while the planners sat on the sidelines and gathered statistics. Second, the NEP provided no mechanism for shifting resources from agriculture to industry. The party needed such a shift in order to pursue its industry-first development strategy. Higher taxes, lower farm prices, or forced requisitioning of grain would result only in a withdrawal of effort by the peasants, as had occurred during the civil war.

In industry, the Five-Year Plan was, for the first time, supposed to set the course of development in advance. Annual plans were to be drawn up in accordance with it. These plans were to assign raw materials to producers on a nonmarket basis. Above all, the Five-Year Plan envisioned a massive program of capital investment.

Industrial growth was to be financed by obtaining more farm produce. Collectivization was the technique used to make sure that the needed grain moved from the country to the city. Between 1928 and 1932 some 15 million peasant households—about two thirds of the rural population—were formed into 211,000 collective farms. On the collectives, land and livestock were owned in common and farm machinery was supplied by independent machine-tractor stations. Land was worked in common too, and a complex system of payment to the farmers was set up. Party control over the peasantry was greatly strengthened. Party policy could be imposed on the collectives in a way that had never been possible while agriculture was in private hands.

Collectivization had limited success. It wreaked havoc with agricultural production. The number of livestock fell by almost half as peasants slaughtered their animals rather than turn them over to the collectives. Grain output also fell sharply, both because of the chaos caused by collectivization and because the incentive structure of the collectives themselves discouraged effort. Despite the disruption of production, though, the flow of goods from the countryside to the city increased; and that, after all, was a major goal of the policy.

The increased flow to the cities occurred partly because collectivization put the grain where party authorities could get their hands on the first share, before the rest was distributed to the peasants, and partly because there were fewer farm animals left to eat it. There were fewer people in the countryside too. Several million died in the turmoil of collectivization and the famine of 1932–1934.

Emerging Outlines

Out of the disorder of the early 1930s emerged an economic system that had most of the major features of the Soviet economy today. Industry, trade, banking, transportation, and foreign commerce were all nationalized. Agriculture was almost entirely collectivized. At the top of the system sat Gosplan, the state planning agency. This agency and the ruling party guided the economy with a development strategy that stressed centralization and planning. The next section of the chapter will look at some details of the structure and functioning of this system. The final section will evaluate its performance.

STRUCTURE

Central Hierarchy

According to the official party handbook, *Fundamentals of Marxism-Leninism*, the Soviet economy functions as a single enterprise directed by a single will. At the top of the economic hierarchy are the highest political bodies of the Soviet government—the Supreme Soviet and its Council of Ministers. Under the Council of Ministers are a number of specialized agencies, including Gosplan, the Central Statistical Administration, and the State Bank. Also under the Council of Ministers are a long list of ministries in charge of specific industries, such as coal, railroads, and ferrous metallurgy. Below these ministries are numerous regional agencies that act as intermediaries between the central government and the firms at the bottom of the hierarchy.

Parallel to the government administrative structure is a Communist party hierarchy that also has major economic responsibilities. One of them is to observe, check, and report to the party leaders what is going on in firms and administrative agencies throughout the economy. A second task is to control appointments to administrative and managerial posts at all levels. A third is to mobilize and exhort the labor force to greater efforts in service of the plan. In addition to these specific responsibilities, local party officials take part in many kinds of managerial decision making at the enterprise level.

Enterprise Status

The operation of individual Soviet firms is governed by a so-called technical-industrial-financial plan. This plan, which is issued annually, is broken down into quarterly and monthly segments. Its most important part is the production plan, which states how much output is to be produced, what assortment of products is to be included, and when the output is to be delivered. Other parts of the plan set forth the quantities of labor and material inputs allotted to individual firms. A financial section sets targets for costs, wage bills, profits, use of short-term credit, and so on. In all, the plan may contain two dozen or more physical and financial targets that a particular firm is to meet.

The plan is binding on the management of the firm. In principle, criminal penalties can be imposed for failure to fulfill the plan, although administrative penalties such as demotion or transfer to less desirable jobs are more common. Positive incentives are also provided. Large bonuses are given to managers who fulfill or overfulfill the various parts of their plans.

Planning Procedures

The heart of the planning process is a set of material balances—summaries of the sources and uses of 200 to 300 of the most important industrial commodities—drawn up by Gosplan. The purpose of each balance is to make sure that the sources (supply) and uses (demands) for each good are equal and that there will be no shortages or surpluses.

In simplified form, the process by which material balances are drawn up works something like this. As soon as Gosplan receives directives from the political authorities telling them the general rate of projected development and the most important priorities, work begins on a preliminary set of balances called control figures. These figures show roughly how much of each good must be produced and how much must be used in each sector of the economy if the overall goals are to be met. The next step is to pass the control figures down through the planning hierarchy, where the main balances are broken down into requirements for each region of the country and then for each firm.

When managers receive these control figures, they are supposed to suggest ways in which they can increase output or reduce inputs in order to achieve more ambitious goals. They also have a chance to complain if they think the plans exceed their capacity for output or do not provide enough inputs. These responses to the control figures are sent back up through the hierarchy to Gosplan.

When the control figures are corrected on the basis of information collected from below, it is likely that the sources and uses of materials will no longer balance. The people who are in charge of carrying out the plans will often have tried to make their jobs easier by asking for reduced output targets or increased supplies of inputs. What follows is a complex process of adjustment and bargaining in which Gosplan tries to avoid material shortages without giving up overall targets. In some cases, shortages may be covered by imports or by drawing down inventories. More commonly, Gosplan responds by tightening the plan—putting pressure on producers to do more with less. If the tightening process goes too far, the result will be a balance on paper only. The plan will contain concealed shortages that will emerge as it is being carried out.

The final balances are then broken down again. In addition to the crucial 200 to 300 materials that are subject to central balancing, individual ministries or regional authorities will have prepared balances on thousands of other goods that are less important. These material balances, when combined, become the technical-industrial-financial plans for all firms throughout the economy. This is a time-consuming process. Often the final plans are not completed until the planned year is several weeks or even months under way.

Labor Planning

The planning process for one key resource needs special treatment. Allocating labor is partly a matter of how goods are to be produced and partly a matter of who is to do any given job. Indirectly, the decisions made on the "hows" and "whos" also affect the distribution of income.

Roughly speaking, the "how" is decided by central planners. Gosplan draws up labor balances for various kinds of work in much the same way that material balances are drawn up. Basic policy on how much labor each firm is to use to meet its goals is set forth in the technical-industrial-financial plan.

The "who" of labor allocation, in contrast, is handled largely by markets. For the most part, workers are free to choose their occupation and place of work. Two methods are used by the authorities to ensure that the right number of workers is available in each sector of the economy. One is to offer large wage differentials, with premiums paid for skilled work or for work that is unattractive. The other is to influence the labor supply through education and training programs.

Individual firms have some control over the wages they pay. They do this both by adding bonus payments to standard wages and by deciding the skill bracket to which any particular worker is assigned. The overall result is a system in which variations in wages are used to ensure a balance between the supply and demand for labor. This is the most important example of the use of the market to allocate resources in the Soviet economy.

The Informal Structure

The formal structure of the Soviet economy fits the model of centralized socialism. Communications follow vertical paths up and down the planning hierarchy. The messages passed to enterprise managers have the force of law. Managers are rewarded or punished on the basis of the extent to which they obey the plan. Only the method of assigning particular workers to particular jobs is a major exception.

A close study of the informal structure of the Soviet economy, however, shows that central control is not absolute. A good deal of informal "horizontal" communication and exchange occurs among firms. Plans are not always treated as binding; sometimes they are treated as only one among a number of factors that influence the actions of managers. And for a Soviet manager the attainment of a comfortable and prosperous life is not merely a matter of obeying commands to the letter.

The safety factor   Soviet managers do not simply wait for plans to arrive from above and then do the best they can to fulfill them. Instead, they put a great deal of effort into making sure that they have a safety factor that will cushion them against the danger of being assigned impossible goals and then being punished for failing to achieve them.

Safety factors often take the form of large inventories of inputs or semifinished products. Inventories have always been a problem in the

Soviet Union. Sometimes, when there are shortages, inventories get so low that any break in deliveries disrupts production. At other times, when a firm manages to get its hands on more of some essential material than it needs, it hoards the extra supply to guard against future shortages.

A rather different safety factor takes the form of concealed productive capacity. By hiding its true capacity, managers hope to get an easy plan. Suppose that when provisional control figures come down to some textile mill, they call for an output of, say, 100,000 yards of fabric in the next year. The manager knows that this is just about all the mill can squeeze out, given the inputs the control figures say will be available. It does not pay to let Gosplan know that, however. Instead, the manager complains that it will not be possible to produce more than 90,000 yards unless the labor force is increased and the firm is given a bigger allotment of synthetic yarn. The easy 90,000-yard plan provides the needed safety factor. The target will be met even if something goes wrong during the year.

Of course, the people in Gosplan know that managers always try to develop a safety factor of some kind. They act on that knowledge when they are juggling their material balances to make them come out even. They do not hesitate to tighten up the plan even when they are told that it cannot be done. The whole thing develops into a sort of game, which greatly increases the degree of uncertainty involved in the planning process.

Procurement   According to the formal structure of the Soviet economic system, managers of individual firms are not responsible for procuring their own raw materials, energy supplies, equipment, or other inputs. As part of the plan, each user of, say, copper tubing is given a schedule of expected deliveries. At the same time, some supplier is given a schedule of deliveries to make. The user and supplier do not even need to communicate with one another. The required plans are all supposed to be set up on the basis of information passed along to higher authorities.

In practice, however, managers who just wait for carloads of copper tubing to roll up to their factory gates are likely to be in trouble. Instead, they must be concerned about the possibility that their assigned supplies are behind the schedule stated in their production plans or that the suppliers are trying to tuck away a hoard of tubing as a safeguard against future demand. Managers use various means to deal with such problems. Among other things, they keep on their payrolls people who are known as "pushers." The pusher's job is to go around wining and dining and wheedling suppliers, in much the same way that the salespeople of a capitalist firm go after potential buyers. Of course, technical-industrial-financial plans do not allow for funds to hire pushers. They have to be worked in under the title of consulting engineer or something of the sort.

Sometimes all that pushers have to do to get supplies moving on time is twist a few arms. Other times they may have to pay bribes. On still other occasions they may have to work out a barter deal in which one firm will come up with a hoarded carload of copper tubing in exchange for a sorely needed crate of ball bearings. All in all, the telephone lines are always busy, despite the fact that such things are not supposed to be necessary in a centrally planned economy.

Selective fulfillment   The plan sets not one but many targets for each enterprise. There are targets for total production, for assortment of production, for cost reduction, for technological improvements, and for many other things. Sometimes the end result of setting so many different targets is to give managers more, rather than less, freedom. This happens when it becomes impossible to fulfill all targets at once and managers must decide which part of the plan is most important. The story of the nail factory at the beginning of this chapter illustrates the problem of selective fulfillment.

Planners' Reactions

Naturally, the central authorities are not unaware of the games managers play. They know that the letter of the law is sometimes broken, that reserves are hidden, and that some parts of the plan are less important than others. They could crack down on the managers, but they don't. They know that the economy could not function if they did. Planners know that the best plans they can make are full of problems and contradictions. They have to rely on local initiative to overcome these defects, even if it means breaking the law. As a result, the authorities take an attitude of selective tolerance toward the behavior of managers. If a manager fulfills the plan, nothing is said. Bonuses are paid, and all is well. Only if illegal methods are used and the plan still is not fulfilled is the manager likely to be called on the carpet. In short, it is recognized that the pushers, the bribes, and the safety factors are the grease that keeps an imperfect machine running.

PERFORMANCE

The Growth Record

Soviet leaders, and Soviet citizens as well, are very proud of one aspect of their economy's performance: its growth record. Within their lifetimes Russia has been transformed from an economic backwater into one of the world's leading industrial powers. In 1917 Russia was clearly a less developed country. It had a small industrial sector set against a backdrop of vast rural poverty. Today Soviet living standards are modest compared with those in Western countries, but they are much higher than they once were. (See Box 37.1.)

However, as Box 37.2 shows, the Soviet economy has grown more slowly in recent years than earlier. Most Western observers expect the rate of growth of total output to be in the 2–3 percent range for the next decade, while the growth rate of consumption will fall to under 2 percent per year. For the first time since World War II, it is likely that the Soviet economy will grow more slowly than that of the United States for a long period. To see what has happened, let's look first at the sources of earlier Soviet growth and then at reasons for the slowdown.

Sources of earlier growth   In the past, the major source of rapid economic growth in the Soviet Union was the ability of the centrally

Box 37.1
Levels of Consumption in the Soviet Union and Selected Other Countries

This table shows levels of consumption in the Soviet Union and a number of other countries. In each case the level of consumption in the United States is equal to 100. By these measures, the Soviet standard of living approaches that of Italy and Japan in some respects but remains short of the United States in all categories.

	USSR 1976	Hungary 1973	Italy 1973	Japan 1973	West Germany 1973	United Kingdom 1973	France 1973
Total Consumption	42.8	49.5	54.0	56.8	68.1	68.6	73.7
Food, Beverages, Tobacco	58.2	75.2	72.1	65.9	77.4	81.1	113.2
Clothing and Footwear	55.9	41.2	50.8	55.2	71.7	66.3	55.3
Gross Rent and Fuel	17.6	27.7	40.2	36.6	59.3	56.2	65.4
Household Furnishings and Operations	29.7	33.8	33.7	52.8	94.6	51.3	63.2
Medical Care	60.1	79.7	92.3	119.6	104.5	82.4	111.1
Transport and Communications	19.4	17.9	32.5	18.4	38.4	50.4	40.8
Recreation	40.4	76.5	44.5	31.2	76.9	97.7	83.3
Education	96.7	66.9	63.0	67.6	64.6	83.7	58.7

Source: Abram Bergson and Herbert S. Levine, eds., *The Soviet Economy: Toward the Year 2000* (London: George Allen & Unwin, 1983), Table 10.4.

Box 37.2
Growth of Output and Factor Productivity in the Soviet Union

This table shows the rate of growth of output, factor inputs, and productivity in the Soviet Union since 1950. The high rate of growth of factor inputs indicates a strategy of extensive growth. In recent years growth has slowed in terms of all three measures.

Period	Growth of Output	Growth of Factor Inputs	Growth of Total Factor Productivity
1950–1960	5.89%	3.95%	1.87%
1960–1970	5.26	3.69	1.51
1970–1975	3.83	3.72	0.11
1975–1980	2.50	—	—

Source: Abram Bergson and Herbert S. Levine, eds., *The Soviet Economy: Toward the Year 2000* (London: George Allen & Unwin, 1983), Table 2.1. Estimate for 1975–1980 supplied by the author on the basis of several sources.

planned economy to mobilize vast new supplies of factor inputs. In the decades just before and after World War II, the number of labor hours employed in the Soviet economy increased at a rate of 2.2 percent per year compared to only 0.5 percent per year in the United States. Even more impressive is the fact that the Soviet capital stock grew at a rate of 7.4 percent per year compared with just 1 percent per year in the U.S.

Extensive growth
Growth based mainly on the use of increasing quantities of factor inputs.

Intensive growth
Growth based mainly on improvements in the quality of factor inputs and in the efficiency with which they are used.

economy. These very rapid growth rates of factor supplies more than made up for the lower dynamic efficiency of centralized socialism. The type of growth experienced by the Soviet Union, based mainly on expansion of inputs, is often called **extensive growth**. The type of growth experienced by the United States, based on better utilization of inputs, is called **intensive growth**.

The second and third columns of Box 37.2 indicate the importance of the growth of factor inputs in the Soviet Union. In the 1950–1970 period increased factor inputs accounted for almost 4 percentage points of Soviet economic growth, while increased factor productivity accounted for the rest. In contrast, increased factor inputs are estimated to have contributed only about 1.6 percent to the growth of U.S. output in this period.[2]

Extensive growth is just as effective as intensive growth in adding to the economic power and prestige of a nation as a political unit, but it has some drawbacks for consumers. For example, a much larger share of GNP has had to be shifted from consumption to investment in the Soviet Union than in the United States—something like 35 percent in the Soviet Union compared with about 15 percent in the United States. As a result, Soviet consumption per capita is only about one third of that of the United States, even though GNP per capita is nearly half. It is also worth noting that Japan, one of the few noncommunist countries to invest as high a fraction of GNP as the Soviet Union, has grown twice as fast in recent years. The Japanese experience shows what can be achieved when rapid growth of inputs is combined with high dynamic efficiency rather than used as a substitute for it.

Explaining the slowdown   As we have seen, Soviet economic growth slowed markedly during the 1970s. In 1979, hit by a bad harvest, the growth rate fell to an estimated record low of 0.7 percent. The slowdown in economic growth appears to be widespread. Industrial output, formerly a leader, grew less than 3 percent in the late 1970s. Actual declines in output were reported in such sectors as ferrous metals and cement. The Soviet energy picture was mixed: A decline in coal production and a slight rise in oil output were at least partly offset by a healthy increase in production of natural gas. As a net oil exporter, the Soviet economy was aided, rather than harmed, by the 1979–1980 rise in the world price of oil, but declines since then have cut into the country's chief source of foreign exchange.

Agriculture remained a problem. As of 1981, grain output had not yet come near its 1978 peak of 237 million metric tons, and per capita meat and milk consumption have fallen.

The slowdown of Soviet growth reflects both slower growth of factor input and a slowdown in productivity. In the energy sector, the growth of investment is falling just as a shift to Siberian sources is making energy production much more capital-intensive. The labor force is not expected to grow at all in the 1980s; the number of people reaching the age of 16 will barely balance a rising rate of retirements. And the population is growing fastest in Soviet Central Asia, the least industrialized region. In the European Soviet Union the labor force is likely to shrink. In principle, declines in investment and in the labor force could be offset by rising

---

[2]For the U.S. estimate, see Edward F. Denison, *Accounting for Slower Economic Growth* (Washington, D.C.: Brookings Institution, 1979), Table 8–1.

productivity, but as Box 37.2 shows, productivity is moving the wrong way. (Adjusted to reflect the increase in average education of the labor force, the rate of productivity growth in the Soviet Union is estimated to have been negative in the 1970–1980 period.)

Pricing and Efficiency

To the extent that it can be measured (which is only roughly), the Soviet economy is inefficient in static as well as dynamic terms. Western estimates indicate that it gets only about half as much output per unit of input as the U.S. economy. There are a number of reasons for this. It may have to do with the incentives of managers, and it may have to do with the motivation and attitudes of Soviet workers. But it is likely that the main source of the Soviet economy's poor record in terms of static efficiency is the lack of a price system that is able to communicate information about opportunity costs to the economy's decision makers.

Consider two functions that are performed by the price system in a capitalist economy. The first is an accounting function. Prices make it possible to add apples and oranges and come up with a total expressed in dollars' worth of fruit. The second is an allocative function. The prices of inputs measure the opportunity cost of doing a certain thing or doing it in a certain way, and the prices of outputs measure the value of doing it.

In the Soviet economy the price system performs the first of these functions but not the second. Industrial and consumer goods are all given prices so that industrial accountants can turn in reports on the number of rubles' worth of output produced. The prices, however, are based on custom and on average cost relationships that have little to do with opportunity costs.

Without knowledge of opportunity costs as reflected in a price system, Soviet planners often have trouble deciding what to produce and how to produce it. In fact, it is impossible for them to make exact calculations. Instead, they can use one of three methods of deciding the what and how of resource allocation. First, they can give up calculations in terms of prices and use rough rules of thumb based on engineering factors. Second, they can do profit-and-loss calculations in terms of their own imperfect prices, even though the answers will be only approximately right. Third, they can imitate Western practices. As Box 37.3 shows, though, none of these methods is foolproof.

Soviet Agriculture

If rapid industrial growth is the Soviet economy's greatest success, agriculture is its worst failure. While Soviet industry grew at a rate of 6.5 percent per year in the first half of the 1970s, agriculture crept ahead at only 2 percent. In 1961, then Premier Nikita Khrushchev set a target of 302 million tons of grain for 1980. In 1975, with three quarters of Khrushchev's allotted time elapsed, output was a mere 140 million tons. That was an especially bad year, to be sure, but even the 1979 peak production rate was only two thirds of the earlier goal.

The roots of Soviet agricultural problems date from the earliest days of collectivization. In the Stalin era agriculture was a cow to be milked for the benefit of industrial development. Now that it has become a serious constraint on industrial development, it is proving difficult to reverse the effects of decades of neglect.

The heart of the Soviet agricultural system is the collective farm, or *kolkhoz*. On paper, the kolkhoz is a cooperative that is run by its members. In practice, three institutions keep a close watch on it from outside. First, the Communist party controls the selection of collective farm managers and guides their decisions. Second, the kolkhoz, like the industrial enterprise, is subject to a plan that sets forth inputs, outputs, production methods, capital investment projects, and dozens of other details. Third, until 1958 collective farms did not own their own machinery. Instead, they depended on rural *machine-tractor stations*. These stations were able to use their monopoly on equipment to control the collective's affairs.

Box 37.3
The Great Dieselization Blunder

During the 1950s Soviet planners were faced with a classic problem in resource allocation. The problem was to decide what proportion of truck and tractor engines should be diesel-powered and what proportion gasoline-powered. The final decision was in favor of massive dieselization. It is revealing to look at the factors that influenced this major decision.

First, from a strictly engineering point of view, diesels seemed attractive. They offer higher mechanical efficiency and are in many ways more technically sophisticated than gasoline engines. Second, the price of diesel fuel in the Soviet economy was low relative to that of gasoline—about 30 rubles a ton for diesel fuel compared with 60 to 100 rubles for gasoline in the late 1950s. Finally, a study of Western experience showed large-scale dieselization of transportation equipment and heavy tractors.

Far from being a wise piece of economic calculation, though, the dieselization program turned out to be a great blunder. For one thing, diesels have higher initial costs. In part, then, the diesel-versus-gasoline decision is a matter of capital budgeting, in which higher initial costs must be balanced against discounted future gains. One defect in the Soviet price system is that the discount rate used by planners in such decisions is too low. Because the discount rate is, in effect, the "price" of future gains in terms of present costs, there is a bias in favor of techniques with high initial costs. This no doubt played a part in the dieselization blunder.

What is more, there is evidence that the official Soviet price for diesel oil was too low compared to that of gasoline in the 1950s. Thus, the price greatly underestimated the opportunity cost of using the heavier fuel. In the United States the refinery price of diesel fuel is not much lower than that of gasoline.

Finally, the program failed to take into account the conditions prevailing in the Soviet economy. The kinds of crude oil available in the Soviet Union are less suitable for making diesel fuel than those available in the United States. In order to provide fuel for all the new diesel engines, refineries were given plans that they could fulfill only by letting the quality of diesel fuel decline. The oil they used to make diesel should have been made into kerosene or furnace oil. Even worse, they allowed the sulfur content of diesel fuel to rise. Cylinders and pistons wore out faster as a result. Under these conditions the operating cost of diesel engines turned out to be higher than that of gasoline engines, not lower. In the 1960s planners realized their mistake and reversed their decision. A program of de-dieselization began, and perhaps the right ratio of the two kinds of engines has now been reached. If so, the discovery was made not as a result of rational economic calculation but as a result of an expensive process of trial and error.

Source: Based on Robert W. Campbell, *The Economics of Soviet Oil and Gas*, Resources for the Future Series (Baltimore: Johns Hopkins University Press, 1968), pp. 164–167.

In the 1930s the whole structure of Soviet agriculture was aimed at a single goal: moving grain from the farm to the city. To that end, delivery targets for the kolkhoz were set not at a percentage of output but at a fixed rate per acre sown. If bad weather brought yields down, the collective farmers bore the entire burden of the shortfall. Although this might seem to create a strong incentive for the collective to work hard in order to avoid shortfalls, the effect was blunted by a complex and inefficient system of distributing collective income among kolkhoz members. The system left them with few incentives to contribute to the common effort.

Khrushchev must be credited with recognizing that the agricultural problem needed a solution. He abolished the hated machine-tractor stations and made major changes in farm work organization and management. However, he diverted much energy and resources into ill-conceived crusades that soaked up resources and offered few long-term results. One such crusade was the *virgin lands* campaign, in which millions of acres of semidesert land was plowed for the first time ever. Twenty years later, massive erosion has cut the productivity of that land. Another of Khrushchev's schemes was an attempt to introduce the growing of corn after his trip to the United States in 1955. Even more than dieselization (which was also touted as a boon to agriculture), the corn campaign was a naive imitation of foreign practice that paid little attention to radical differences in local conditions. In the Brezhnev era, from the early 1960s to the early 1980s, agriculture received more attention. Agricultural investment rose from less than one sixth of total investment to almost one third. However, without other reforms much of the investment seems to have been wasted. For example, from 1976 through 1980 agriculture received 1.8 million tractors, but the stock of tractors at work on the farm rose by only 246,000. Many of the rest sat idle for lack of spare parts and maintenance.

REFORMING THE SOVIET ECONOMY

The Brezhnev era was a time of cautious tinkering with the economic system. Despite steadily slowing growth rates, the system provided political support in the form of a high and stable status for enterprise managers and government officials, and in the form of full employment and slowly but steadily rising living standards for the population. In 1985, after the short terms in power of Yuri Andropov and Konstantin Chernenko, Mikhail Gorbachev came to power facing the need to make major strategic choices. Should the government continue to pursue a conservative course, preserving its political base at the risk of falling still farther behind the West in living standards and technology? Or should it embark on an even riskier course—reform? At this writing, no one knows the answer. However, at least three directions for reform have been suggested.[3]

A Reactionary Course

Nostalgia is a powerful force in any society, and the Soviet Union is no exception. For at least some Soviet citizens, "the good old days" mean the

[3]Writers too many to mention have discussed Soviet economic reform. The classification that follows is supplied by Joseph Berliner. See Abram Bergson and Herbert S. Levine, eds., *The Soviet Economy: Toward the Year 2000* (London: George Allen & Unwin, 1983), chap. 11.

days of Joseph Stalin, when social discipline was strict and the nation was united in the common cause of industrializing or of fighting off the Nazi hordes. Hence, there seems to be some support for a type of reform that would turn back the clock to an earlier era.

In some ways the clock would not have to be turned back far. The basic outlines of the Soviet system of planning and management have not changed very much in the 30-odd years since Stalin's death. Instead of technical tinkering, a reactionary reform would probably stress social and economic discipline. Yuri Andropov, in his short time in power, made some moves in this direction. He began campaigns against absenteeism, drunkenness, and slack labor discipline, and, at a higher level, against official corruption. These campaigns were reported to have resulted in brief spurts of increased output. However, they also seem to have offended some entrenched (and perhaps corrupt) officials. The elderly Konstantin Chernenko, a long-time supporter of Leonid Brezhnev, toned down Andropov's campaigns and returned to a conservative course during his months in power.

Technical Reform

A second possible direction for reform, which is said to be favored by many Soviet economists, would emphasize technical changes in the planning system. Under such a policy decision making would be decentralized, with enterprise managers gaining more authority and central planning becoming less important. Planners would still be involved in forecasting, but their targets for individual firms and sectors of the economy would lose the force of law. In their place, enterprise managers would be expected to respond to strengthened price signals in return for being able to keep a percentage of the profits.

Over the last decade or so, the Hungarian economy has been reformed along something like these lines. The firm has become the center of decision making, and prices have taken on an allocative role in addition to their traditional accounting role. However, the results of the Hungarian reforms have been mixed. There have been major improvements in the quality of goods and in the match between output and consumer needs. But the overall rate of growth has not shot ahead of those of Hungary's neighbors in Eastern Europe.

Decentralization on the Hungarian model would face major obstacles in the Soviet Union. For one thing, decentralization of a planned economy faces an enormous chicken-and-egg problem. If firms are turned loose to make their own plans in response to a profit motive, the results will be efficient only if managers face the right set of input and output prices. This suggests that price reform should come first. However, it is not clear how reformers would be able to determine the "correct" level of prices before decision making was decentralized. After all, if they had the information and the decision-making ability to determine the opportunity costs of all goods and services, they would be able to construct optimal plans in the first place and decentralization would not be needed. This argument suggests that decentralization should come first and then prices should adjust to supply and demand. Whichever way this reform was carried out, the transition would be a jolting one. The reason is that under the present system both prices and output are remote from their equilibrium values under decentralized market socialism.

Besides the technical problem of whether to introduce price reform or decentralization first, a Hungarian-style reform would face serious political opposition in the Soviet Union. It would threaten the power and authority of the bureaucrats who are in charge of transmitting central plans from Moscow to local enterprises. These are the people who have provided key political support for one regime after another in the post-Stalin era. Thus, for both technical and political reasons, it would be hard for the Soviet Union to follow the Hungarian model.

Liberal Reform

A third path to reform would follow a "liberal" model in which a private sector would be allowed to grow up alongside the present centrally planned, state-owned economy. All existing industry would operate as before, but private individuals or cooperatives would be allowed to compete on a small scale. Although individual firms would surely be limited in size under such a reform, the areas of the economy in which they could compete might be large, ranging from agriculture to retail trade to small-scale manufacturing of clothing and other consumer goods to service industries such as auto repair and construction. Such a reform has a number of precedents.

The first and perhaps most important precedent is Lenin's New Economic Policy of the 1920s. At that time small-scale industry, trade, and agriculture were allowed to flourish while the "commanding heights" of industry remained in the hands of the state. Anything that can be given Lenin's seal of approval has a political head start in the Soviet Union.

Second, there are limited precedents within the Soviet Union today. One is the collective farmer's private plot, on which a large percentage of the nation's fresh produce is already grown today. These farm goods are sold legally at prices determined by supply and demand. Also, there is said to be a large "second economy" that consists of illegal or semilegal industrial enterprises. These firms employ moonlighting employees and underused equipment of state-owned firms to turn out consumer goods, for profit, that meet higher standards of variety and quality than those of official enterprises. Simply by legalizing this second economy, the Soviet Union could tap a large reservoir of entrepreneurship and management skill.

Finally, liberal reform of this type has some precedents abroad. By far the best known of these is the case of China. (See Box 37.4.) But Hungary, East Germany, Poland, and Yugoslavia also offer examples of small-scale private enterprise coexisting with large-scale state-owned firms.

Liberal reform would not be free from political risks. Conservatives may fear that allowing even small-scale enterprise would give a power base to political dissidents, independent labor unions, and other opponents of the present regime. However, in some ways liberal reform would be less politically risky than Hungarian-style reform. The main advantage would be that no one's power or job in the present economic system would be directly threatened. On the day the reform went into effect, everyone would come to work and do his or her job as usual. If the reform began with little things such as private taxis, mitten-knitting cooperatives, and back-alley auto repair shops, it would not lead to an immediate revolution.

But it would be a mistake to expect the Soviet economy to be reformed soon. The faults of the Soviet system have been obvious to Western

Box 37.4
Reforming the Chinese Economy

After World War II Mao Zedong led China into the camp of revolutionary communism. For an economic system, Mao turned to the obvious model: the Soviet Union. By the mid-1950s most of the basic features of the Soviet economic system had been transplanted to China—state ownership, central planning, collectivized agriculture, and so on.

Today's top Chinese leader, Deng Xiaoping, was hounded as a "capitalist roader" in the Mao era. The Red Brigades who pinned that label on him seem to have been right, for under Deng China has undertaken the most far-reaching reform ever attempted of a Soviet-type economy. And the outcome, at least in some respects, looks a lot like capitalism.

Today, in place of slogans like "Unlimited Loyalty to Mao Zedong Thought," a Chinese worker is likely to find something like "Time is Money and Efficiency is Life" posted on the factory wall.

Deng's reforms started in the countryside, where four fifths of China's 1 billion people live. Collectivization was largely scrapped, and villagers were given the right to produce what they wanted for whatever market they could find. The result has been a steady rise in average income—an increase estimated at 66 percent between 1980 and 1985.

Small-scale trade and services were the next areas to be reformed. Chinese neighborhoods now are dotted with hole-in-the wall noodle shops, repair shops, and other small businesses. Many of the proprietors were sent to hard labor in the countryside during the Mao era. Now, operating on profit margins of a few pennies per bowl of noodles, they can afford formerly undreamed-of luxuries such as television sets, motorcycles, and refrigerators.

Now Deng's reformers are tackling the biggest challenge of all: large-scale industry. Firms are to be cut loose from the planners' apron strings to find their own markets and sources of supply. They are supposed to sink or swim on the basis of their managers' profit-making skills. Some of the newly liberated plants are working wonders. Entering into partnerships with foreign investors, they are turning out Honda motorcycles, Jeeps, and soft drinks for long waiting lists of eager buyers. But the capitalist road is proving to be a bumpy one in some ways. The government has not yet come to grips with two big problems: prices and unemployment. Most industrial prices are still set by the state, often at levels that are far removed from opportunity costs. As a result, some firms that produce much-needed goods are starved for funds because their output is underpriced. Meanwhile, others grow rich turning out products that command high official prices but cannot be sold. Then there are factories whose plants are so obsolete and whose labor forces so bloated that they have no hope of making a profit at any realistic price. The government has yet to face up to the problem of what to do with the oversupply of workers. Forced unemployment is still out of the question. So there are cases in which workers show up every day and collect a day's pay even though their factories haven't received an order for months.

Recently China's economy has been growing at 8 percent per year. Deng aims to quadruple output by the year 2000. But China is still one of the poorest countries in the world, with a per capita income of under $400 a year. The capitalist road will not be a short one, but then, to borrow one of Mao's favorite slogans, "a journey of a thousand miles begins with a single step."

economists for decades, yet from the viewpoint of Soviet leaders the system's virtues have outweighed those faults. Even if the system is weak when measured in terms of technological progress and economic growth, this does not mean that it is bound to collapse. As long as forward momentum is maintained, there is no reason that the Soviet economy cannot go on forever in a state that is 5 years behind the West in technology and 20 years behind in living standards. A crisis—falling output rather than a mere slowdown, unemployment (currently unknown), inflation (almost unknown)—might force a change. Short of a crisis, betting on reform of any kind seems uncertain.

Summary

1. The origins of the Soviet economic system are found first in Marxist-Leninist ideology and second in the experience of the first years of Soviet rule. After the 1917 revolution an attempt to abolish the market economy all at once (war communism) was followed by a temporary restoration of the market (the New Economic Policy). The main features of what is now known as the Soviet-type economy— central planning plus the collectivization of agriculture—were established around 1928. They were designed to achieve the government's goals of complete political control of the economy and rapid, industry-first economic growth. The combination of planning plus collectivization was effective.

2. In its formal structure, the Soviet economy is a fully centralized hierarchy. Enterprises receive plans that specify inputs and outputs, along with many other targets. These plans are legally binding on firms. In practice, managers of Soviet firms have room to maneuver in fulfilling their plans. They bargain for safety factors, use initiative in procuring scarce inputs, and fulfill plans selectively. The authorities tend to tolerate this as long as it results in the fulfillment of the plan's most important goals.

3. The greatest achievement of the Soviet economy has been rapid growth. However, that growth has slowed since the beginning of the 1970s. The need to switch from a strategy of extensive growth to one of intensive growth has focused attention on the inefficiencies of Soviet industry and agriculture.

4. There has been much talk of reform of the Soviet economy, but as of this writing no decisive measures have been taken. Several possibilities have been suggested. One is a conservative approach in which few reforms are made and the system continues to move ahead slowly. A second approach is a reactionary one that would turn back the clock to the more disciplined days of Stalinism. A third approach is technical reform of the planning system in which state ownership of industry would be retained but firms would be freed from rigid central plans. And a fourth possibility is liberal reform, which would allow small-scale private industry and trade to grow up alongside the centrally planned economy.

Questions for Review

1. Define the following terms:
   extensive growth
   intensive growth
   kolkhoz
2. When did the main features of the Soviet economic system take shape? What was the New Economic Policy?
3. What is the balance between managerial coordination and market coordination in the formal structure of the Soviet economy? In its informal structure?
4. What is the difference between extensive and intensive growth? How does this difference bear on the slowdown in Soviet economic growth?
5. List three possible paths for reform of the Soviet economy. What are the advantages and disadvantages of each?

Problems and Topics for Discussion

1. During the period of war communism in the Soviet Union, some members of the leadership proposed that money be abolished as part of the transition to a centralized economy. Money was restored during the NEP, however, and no further attempt was made to abolish it. Why does even a centrally planned economy find it hard to get along without money?

2. Any economist who has studied the Soviet system can provide many "horror stories" like that of the Soviet nail factory. Does such flagrant waste of resources also take place in the United States? Where would you look for such horror stories? In competitive industries? Monopolies? Regulated industries? Government? Discuss.

3. In what ways do you think a centrally planned economy might be better equipped than a capitalist economy to deal with the problem of pollution? The problem of population? In what ways might it be less well equipped to deal with these problems?

4. If you were a member of the Soviet leadership, what lessons could you learn from the Chinese economic reforms?

5. As of this writing, Soviet leader Mikhail Gorbachev has been in office only a few months and the direction of his economic policy is far from clear. Look through newspapers and magazines in your library for news of recent Soviet economic policies. Has the system moved down any of the paths of reform discussed in this chapter? Has it maintained a conservative course? Has it moved in still another direction? Discuss.

Suggestions for Further Reading

Bergson, Abram, and Herbert S. Levine, eds. *The Soviet Economy: Toward the Year 2000.* London: George Allen & Unwin, 1983.

Contains a series of papers by leading Western experts on the Soviet economy that discuss all aspects of the system.

Johnson, Gale, and Karen McConnell. *Prospects for Soviet Agriculture in the 1980s.* Bloomington: Indiana University Press, 1985.

A comprehensive discussion of the problems and prospects of Soviet agriculture.

U.S. Congress, Joint Economic Committee.

The Joint Economic Committee publishes many reports on the Soviet economy and other centrally planned economies.

Dictionary of Economic Terms

Absolute advantage The ability of a country to produce a good at a lower cost, in terms of quantity of factor inputs, than its trading partners. p805

Accelerationist theory of inflation A theory according to which changes in the inflation rate affect unemployment and real output. p450

Accounting profit Total revenue minus explicit costs. p524

Adaptive-expectations hypothesis The hypothesis that people form their expectations about future economic events mainly on the basis of past economic events. p371

Aggregate nominal demand The total dollar value of all planned expenditures. p136

Aggregate nominal demand curve A graph showing the level of total planned expenditure associated with each level of nominal national income. p212

Aggregate nominal supply The total value of all goods and services produced in the economy, measured in terms of the prices at which they are sold. p136

Aggregate nominal supply curve A graph showing the level of aggregate nominal supply (nominal national product) associated with each level of nominal national income. p216

Aggregate real demand The total planned purchases of all spending units, expressed in constant dollars. p165

Aggregate real demand curve A graph showing the real quantity of goods and services that people plan to purchase at each price level, assuming a given level of aggregate nominal demand. p165

Aggregate real supply The planned level of production of goods and services, expressed in constant dollars, at a given price level. p167

Aggregate real supply curve A graph that shows the connection between the price level and the planned level of production of goods and services, measured in real terms. p168

Agricultural marketing orders Agreements authorized by the Agricultural Marketing Agreement Act of 1937 that allow farmers to control the flows of certain farm products to certain markets. p677

Antitrust laws A set of laws, including the Sherman Act and the Clayton Act, that seek to control market structure and the competitive behavior of firms. p639

Appreciation (of a currency) An increase in the value of a country's currency relative to that of another country. p827

Arbitrage The activity of earning a profit by buying a good at a low price in one market and reselling it at a higher price in another market. p772

Assets All the things to which a firm or household holds legal claim. p85

Automatic fiscal policy Changes in taxes, transfer payments, or government purchases that occur automatically as a result of changes in economic conditions without a change in laws or policies. p247

Automatic stabilizers Programs, such as income taxes and unemployment compensation, that tend to push the federal budget toward surplus as nominal income rises and toward deficit as nominal income falls. p248

Automous consumption The part of total consumption expenditure that is independent of the level of disposable income; for any given consumption schedule, autonomous consumption is equal to the level of consumption associated with zero disposable income. p201

Average propensity to consume Total consumption for any level of income divided by total disposable income. p203

Balance sheet A financial statement showing a firm's or household's assets, liabilities, and net worth. p85

Barrier to entry Any factor that prevents a new firm from competing on an equal footing with existing ones. p602

Base year The year chosen as a basis for comparison in calculating the price level. p155

Benefit reduction rate The reduction in the benefits of a transfer program that results from a one-dollar increase in the earned income of the beneficiary. p789

Bilateral monopoly A market situation in which both the buyer and the seller have some monopoly or monopsony power and neither behaves as a price taker. p754

Bond A promise, given in return for a loan, to make a fixed annual or semiannual payment over a set number of years plus a larger final payment equal to the amount borrowed. p88

Budget line A line showing the various combinations of goods and services that can be purchased at given prices within a given budget. p518

Business cycle A cycle in which periods of growth of real output alternate with periods of falling output, accompanied by high unemployment. p11

Capital All means of production that are created by people, including tools, industrial equipment, and structures. p4

Capital account The section of the international accounts of a country that consists of purchases and sales of assets and international borrowing and lending. p821

Capital account net demand curve A graph that shows the net demand for a country's currency that results, at various exchange rates, from capital account transactions. p828

Capital inflow Purchase of domestic assets by foreigners and borrowing by domestic firms and households from foreign banks or other foreign sources. p821

Capital outflow Purchases of foreign assets by domestic firms and households and borrowing by foreigners from domestic banks or other sources. p821

Capitalism An economic system in which ownership and control of business firms rests with the suppliers of capital. p36

Capitalized value of a rent The sum that would earn annual interest equal to the annual rent if it were invested at the current market rate of interest. p765

Cartel An organization through which several producers cooperate to control the sale of all or most of the output of a product. p577

Change in demand A change in the quantity buyers are willing and able to purchase that results from a change in some factor other than the price of the good; a shift in the demand curve. p55

Change in quantity demanded A change in the quantity buyers are willing and able to purchase that results from a change in the price of the good, other things being equal; a movement along a demand curve. p55

Change in quantity supplied A change in the quantity producers are willing and able to sell that results from a change in the price of the good, other things being equal; a movement along a supply curve. p62

Change in supply A change in

the quantity producers are willing and able to sell that results from a change in some factor other than the price of the good; a shift in the supply curve. p62

Circular flow of income and product The flow of goods and services between households and firms, balanced by the flow of payments made in exchange for the goods and services. p131

Commercial banks Financial intermediaries that provide a broad range of banking services, including accepting demand deposits and making commercial loans. p264

Common stock A certificate of part ownership in a corporation that gives the owner a vote in the selection of the firm's directors and the right to share of dividends, if any. p88

Comparative advantage The ability to produce a good or service at a lower opportunity cost than someone else. p29

Complementary goods A pair of goods for which an increase in the price of one results in a decrease in demand for the other. p58

Concentration ratio The percentage of all sales that is accounted for by the four or eight largest firms in a market. p600

Conglomerate merger A merger between firms in unrelated markets. p643

Constant returns to scale A situation in which there are neither economies nor diseconomies of scale. p536

Consumer equilibrium A state of affairs in which a consumer cannot increase the total utility gained from a given budget by spending less on one good and more on another. p505

Consumer price index (CPI) A price index based on the market basket of goods and services purchased by a typical urban household. p183

Consumption schedule (consumption function) A graphic or numerical schedule that shows how consumption expenditure varies as

disposable income varies, other things being equal. p200

Corporation A firm that takes the form of an independent legal entity with ownership divided into equal shares and each owner's liability limited to his or her investment in the firm. p80

Cost-push inflation Inflation that is caused by an upward shift in the aggregate real supply curve while the aggregate real demand curve remains fixed or shifts upward more slowly. p366

Coupon rate The annual interest payment of a bond, expressed as a percentage of the bond's face value. p92

CPI See consumer price index.

Craft union A union of skilled workers who all practice the same trade. p744

Cross-elasticity of demand The ratio of the percentage change in the demand for a good to a given percentage change in the price of some other good, other things being equal. p494

Cross-subsidization The practice of setting prices that cover total costs on the average, but that charge some customers more than the cost of their services while charging others less than the cost of their services. p658

Crowding-out effect The tendency of an increase in government purchases to increase the interest rate and thereby decrease the level of planned investment. p328

Crude birthrate The number of people born into a population per thousand per year. p850

Crude deathrate The number of people in a population who die per thousand per year. p850

Currency Coins and paper money. p263

Current account The section of the international accounts of a country that consists of imports, exports, and unilateral transfers. p820

Current account balance The value of a country's exports of goods and services minus the value of its imports of goods and services and its net transfer payments to foreign recipients. p821

Current-services budget A version of the federal budget that assumes no changes in laws governing taxes, transfer payments, or government purchases. p236

Cyclical deficit The difference between the actual federal deficit in any year and the structural deficit for that year. p247

Cyclical unemployment The part of unemployment that can be attributed to the difference between the actual level of real output and the natural level of real output. p434

Demand curve A graphic representation of the relationship between the price of a good and the quantity of it demanded by buyers. p53

Demand deposits Non-interest-bearing transactions deposits at commercial banks. p264

Demand-pull inflation An increase in the price level caused by an increase of aggregate demand relative to natural real output. p364

Demographic transition A population cycle that begins with a fall in the death rate, continues with a phase of rapid population growth, and concludes with a decline in the birthrate. p853

Depreciation (of a currency) A decline in the value of a country's currency relative to that of another country. p827

Direct financing The process of raising investment funds directly from savers. p88

Direct foreign investment Investment in a foreign country that gives the supplier of capital at least partial ownership and control of the project. p859

Discount rate The interest rate charged by the Fed on loans of reserves to banks. p299

Discount window The department through which the Federal Reserve lends reserves to banks. p299

Discouraged worker A person who is available for work and has looked for work within the last six months, but is no longer actively looking. p430

Discretionary fiscal policy Changes in laws or policies governing taxes, transfer payments, and government purchases. p246

Diseconomies of scale A situation in which long-run average cost increases as output increases. p536

Disposable personal income (disposable income) Personal income less personal taxes (especially income taxes). p180

Dissaving Negative saving, which occurs when consumption exceeds disposable income. p205

Dual economy An economy that is divided into a modern, westernized industrial sector and a traditional sector. p849

Dynamic efficiency The ability of an economy to increase consumer satisfaction through growth and innovation. p630

Economic planning Systematic intervention in the economy by government with the goal of improving coordination, efficiency, and growth. p38

Economics The study of the choices people make and the actions they take in order to make the best use of scarce resources in meeting their wants and needs. p3

Economies of scale A situation in which long-run average cost decreases as output increases. p536

Efficiency A state of affairs in which, given available knowledge and resources, no change can be made that will make one person better off without making another worse off. p34

Elastic demand A situation in which quantity changes by a larger percentage than price, and therefore total revenue increases as price decreases. p487

Elasticity The responsiveness of quantity demanded or supplied to changes in the price of the good or changes in other economic conditions. p486

Employment rate The percentage of the working-age population that is employed. p156

Entrepreneurship The process of looking for new possibilities: making use of new ways of doing things, being alert to new opportunities, and overcoming old limits. p34

Equation of exchange An equation that shows the relationships among the money stock (M), the velocity of money (V), the price level (P), and the level of real income (y), written $MV = Py$. p292

Equilibrium A condition in which the plans of buyers and sellers exactly match in the marketplace, so that the quantity supplied exactly equals the quantity demanded at a given price. p64

Excess burden An economic burden of a tax, besides the actual burden, that takes the form of lost opportunities for production and consumption. p115

Excess quantity demanded (shortage) A condition in which the quantity of a good demanded at a given price exceeds the quantity supplied. p64

Excess quantity supplied (surplus) A condition in which the quantity of a good supplied at a given price exceeds the quantity demanded. p66

Excess reserves Total reserves minus required reserves. p276

Expenditure multiplier The ratio of an induced change in the equilibrium level of nominal national income to an initial shift in the aggregate nominal demand curve. p222

Explicit costs Opportunity costs that take the form of payments to outside suppliers, workers, and others who do not share in the ownership of the firm. p524

Extensive growth Growth based mainly on the use of increasing quantities of factor inputs. p878

Factor markets The markets in which the factors of production—labor, capital, and natural resources—are bought and sold. p715

Factors of production The basic inputs of labor, capital, and natural resources used in producing all goods and services. p4

Federal funds market A market in which banks lend reserves to one another for periods as short as 24 hours. p299

Federal funds rate The interest rate charged by banks for overnight loans of reserves to one another. p299

Final goods and services Goods and services that are sold to or are ready for sale to parties that will use them for consumption, investment, government purchases, or export. p173

Financial intermediaries Financial firms, including banks, savings and loan associations, insurance companies, pension funds, and mutual funds, that gather funds from net savers and make loans to net borrowers. p88

Finanacial markets Markets through which borrowers obtain funds from savers. p87

Fiscal policy Management of aggregate demand through changes in net taxes and government purchases. p233

Fixed inputs Inputs that cannot easily be increased or decreased in a short time. p525

Fixed investment Purchases by firms of newly produced capital goods, such as production machinery, newly built structures, and office equipment. p134

Flows Processes that occur continuously through time, measured in units per time period. p33

Forecast A prediction of future economic events, stated in the form "If A, then B, other things being equal." p14

Foreign exchange markets The set of institutions through which the currency of one country can be exchanged for that of another. p823

Frictional unemployment Short periods of unemployment needed to match jobs with job seekers

within the mainstream of the economy. p434

GNP See gross national product.

GNP deflator A price index that covers all final goods and services produced in the economy. p181

Government purchases of goods and services (government purchases) Purchases of finished goods by government plus the cost of hiring the services of government employees and contractors. p106

Gross national product The dollar value at current market prices of all final goods and services produced by a nation's factors of production in a given year. p9, 173

Growth recession A situation in which real output grows, but not fast enough to keep unemployment from rising. p385

Herfindahl index An index of market concentration that is arrived at by squaring the percentage market shares of all firms in an industry and summing the squares. p643

Horizontal merger A merger between firms that compete in the same market. p643

Human capital Capital in the form of learned abilities that have been acquired through formal training or education or through on-the-job experience. p737

Hyperinflation Very rapid inflation. p401

Implicit costs Opportunity costs of using resources owned by the firm or contributed by its owners. p524

Import quota A limit on the quantity of a good that can be imported in a given period. p809

Income effect The part of the change in quantity demanded of a good whose price has fallen that is caused by the increase in real income that results from the price change. p506

Income elasticity of demand The ratio of the percentage change in the demand for a good to a given percentage change in consumer income, other things being equal. p493

Indexing Adjusting a value or payment automatically in proportion to changes in a specific price index. p184

Indifference curve A graphic representation of an indifference set. p514

Indifference map A selection of indifference curves for a single consumer and pair of goods. p517

Indifference set A set of consumption choices each of which yields the same utility, so that no member of the set is preferred to any other. p513

Indirect financing The process of raising investment funds via financial intermediaries. p88

Industrial policy A policy under which the government sets an overall framework to promote the growth of new industries and ease the problems of declining ones. p38

Industrial union A union of all the workers in an industry, including both skilled and unskilled workers in all trades. p746

Inelastic demand A situation in which quantity changes by a smaller percentage than price, and therefore total revenue decreases as price decreases. p487

Inferior good A good for which an increase in consumer income results in a decrease in demand. p57

Inflation A sustained increase in the average prices of all goods and services. p8

Inflationary recession An episode in which real output falls below its natural level and unemployment rises above its natural rate while rapid inflation continues. p370

In-kind transfers Transfer payments made in the form of goods or services, such as food, housing, or medical care, rather than in cash. p782

Injections Flows of funds into domestic product markets that do not begin with consumption expenditures of domestic households; included are investment, governnment purchases, and exports. p142

Inside lag The delay between the time when a policy change is needed and the time when a decision is made. p407

Intensive growth Growth based mainly on improvements in the quality of factor inputs and in the efficiency with which they are used. p878

Inventory Stocks of a finished good awaiting sale or use. p64

Inventory investment Changes in the stocks of finished products and raw materials that firms keep on hand; this figure is positive if such stocks are increasing and negative if they are decreasing. p134

Investment The sum of fixed investment and inventory investment. p135

Isoquantity line (isoquant) A line showing the various combinations of variables input that can be used to produce a given amount of output. p544

Keynesian cross A diagram, consisting of aggregate nominal supply and demand curves, that shows how the equilibrium level of nominal national income is determined. p217

Labor The contributions to production made by people working with their minds and their muscles. p4

Laffer curve A graph that shows the connection between the marginal rate at which a tax is imposed and the revenues raised by the tax. p393

Law of demand The principle that, other things being equal, the quantity of a good demanded by buyers tends to rise as the price of the good falls, and to fall as the price of the good rises. p51

Law of diminishing returns The principle that as one variable input is increased, with all others remaining fixed, a point will be reached beyond which the marginal physical product of the variable input begins to decrease. p528

Leakages The parts of national income that are not used by households to buy domestic consumer goods; included are saving, net

taxes, and purchases of imports. p142

Liabilities All the legal claims against a firm by nonowners or against a household by nonmembers. p86

Liquidity An asset is said to possess liquidity if it can be used directly as a means of payment and if it does not vary in nominal value. p263

Long run A time range that is long enough to permit changes in all inputs, both fixed and variable. p526

Lorenz curve A graphic representation of the degree of inequality in an economy. p780

Lump sum taxes Taxes that do not vary with the level of nominal national income (for example, property taxes). p208

M1 A measure of the money supply that includes currency and transactions deposits. p265

M2 A measure of the money supply that includes M1 plus money market mutual fund shares, repurchase agreements, savings deposits, small time deposits, and certain other liquid assets. p266

Macroeconomics The branch of economics that deals with large-scale economic phenomena, especially inflation, unemployment, and economic growth. p7

Managerial coordination A means of coordinating economic activity that uses directives from managers to subordinates. p84

Marginal average rule The rule that marginal cost must be equal to average cost when average cost is at its minimum. p532

Marginal cost The increase in cost required to increase the output of some good or service by one unit. p529

Marginal cost of pollution abatement The added cost of reducing a given kind of pollution by one unit. p691

Marginal efficiency of investment The expected rate of return on an additional dollar of planned investment. p322

Marginal factor cost The amount

by which a firm's total factor cost must increase in order for the firm to obtain an additional unit of that factor of production. p719

Marginal physical product The amount of output, expressed in physical units, produced by each added unit of one variable input, other things being equal. p528

Marginal productivity theory of distribution A theory of the distribution of income according to which each factor receives a payment equal to its marginal revenue product. p728

Marginal propensity to consume The fraction of each dollar of added disposable income that goes to consumption. p201

Marginal propensity to save The fraction of each dollar of added income that goes to saving. p205

Marginal rate of substitution The rate at which one good can be substituted for another without any gain or loss in satisfaction. p515

Marginal revenue The amount by which total revenue increases as a result of a one-unit increase in quantity sold. p553

Marginal revenue product The change in revenue that results from the sale of the output produced by one additional unit of a factor of production. p717

Marginal social cost of pollution The total additional cost to all members of society of an additional unit of pollution. p691

Marginal tax rate The percentage of each added dollar of income that is paid in taxes. p116

Marginal utility The amount of added utility gained from a one-unit increase in consumption of a good, with the quantities of other goods consumed remaining constant. p502

Market Any arrangement that people have for trading with one another. p4

Market coordination A means of coordinating economic activity that uses the price system to transmit information and provide incentives. p83

Market structure The key traits

of a market, including the number of firms in each industry, the extent to which the products of different firms are different or similar, and the ease of entry into and exit from the market. p551

Marketing   Finding out what customers want and channeling a flow of goods and services to meet those wants. p621

Merchandise balance   A country's exports of merchandise minus its imports of merchandise. p820

Microeconomics   The branch of economics that deals with the choices and actions of small economic units, that is, households, business firms, and units of government. p4

Minimum efficient scale   The level of output at which economies of scale stop. p538

Model   A mathematical or graphic version of an economic theory. p13

Monetarism   A school of economic thought that stresses changes in the money supply as a determinant of prices, income, and employment. p338

Money   An asset that serves as a means of payment, a store of purchasing power, and a unit of account. p262

Money market mutual fund   A financial intermediary that sells shares to the public, using the proceeds to buy short-term securities and passing the interest income (less a small service charge) along to shareholders. p265

Money multiplier   The ratio of the equilibrium money supply to the total reserves of a banking system. p285

Monopolistic competition   A market structure in which many small firms offer differing products. p625

Monopoly   A market that is dominated by a single seller. p577

Monopsony   A situation in which there is only a single buyer in a market. p728

National income   The total income received by households, in-

cluding wages, rents, interest payments, and profits. p133

National product   The total value of all goods and services produced in the economy. p133

Natural level of real output (natural real output)   The level of output at which long-run equilibrium with stable prices is possible. p357

Natural monopoly   An industry in which total costs are kept to a minimum by having just one producer serve the entire market. p654

Natural rate of unemployment   The unemployment rate associated with the natural level of real output. p357

Natural real output   See natural level of real output. p357

Natural resources   Anything that can be used as a productive input in its natural state, such as farm land, building sites, forests, and mineral deposits. p4

Negative income tax   A plan under which all transfer programs would be combined into a single program paying cash benefits that depend on a household's level of income. p790

Net exports   Exports minus imports. p147

Net marginal tax rate   The sum of the marginal tax rate for all taxes paid by a household plus the benefit reduction rates of all transfer programs from which the household benefits. p790

Net national product   Gross national product minus an allowance (called the capital consumption allowance) that represents the value of capital equipment used up in the process of production. p177

Net reproduction rate   The long-term growth rate of a population, measured as average number of daughters born to each female over her lifetime. p854

Net tax multiplier   The change in the equilibrium level of nominal national income that results from a $1 change in lump sum net taxes. p242

Net taxes   Taxes paid to government minus transfer payments made by government. p142

Net worth (owners' equity)   A firm's or household's assets minus its liabilities. p86

Nominal   In economics, a term used to refer to data that have not been adjusted for the effects of inflation. p10

Nominal income target   A level of nominal national income judged to be most compatible with progress toward the goals of full employment, price stability, and real economic growth. p236

Nominal interest rate   The interest rate stated in the usual way, in terms of current-dollar interest payments per dollar of principal. p163

Normal good   A good for which an increase in consumer income results in an increase in demand. p57

Normative economics   The part of economics that is devoted to making judgments about which economic policies or conditions are good or bad. p16

Official reserves account   The section of the international accounts of a country that consists of changes in central banks' official international reserves. p823

Okun's law   A rule of thumb according to which each 3 percent by which real output rises above (or falls below) its natural level results in an unemployment rate one percentage point below (or above) the natural rate. p432

Oligopolistic interdependence   The need, in an oligopolistic market, to pay close attention to the actions of one's rivals when making price or production decisions. p604

Oligopoly   A market structure in which there are two or more firms, at least one of which has a large share of total sales. p599

Open-market operation   A purchase (or sale) by the Fed of government securities from (or to) the public. p277

Opportunity cost   The cost of a good measured in terms of lost opportunity to pursue the best alternative activity with the same time and resources. p26

Outside lag   The delay between the time when a policy decision is made and the time when the policy change affects the economy. p407

Owners' equity   See net worth.

Parity price ratio   The ratio of an index of prices that farmers receive to an index that farmers pay, using the years 1910–1914 as a base period. p671

Partnership   An association of two or more people who operate a business as co-owners by voluntary legal agreement. p79

Perfect competition   A market structure that is characterized by a large number of small firms, a homogeneous product, access to information by all buyers and sellers, and freedom of entry and exit. p552

Perfectly elastic demand   A situation in which the demand curve is a horizontal line. p488

Perfectly inelastic demand   A situation in which the demand curve is a vertical line. p488

Personal income   The total income received by households, including both earned income and transfer payments. p180

Phillips curve   A graph that shows the connection between the rate of inflation and the unemployment rate, other things being equal. p441

Planned-investment schedule   A downward-sloping schedule that shows the connection between planned investment and the interest rate, other things being equal. p322

Portfolio   A person or firm's collection of assets. p293

Positive economics   The part of economics that is limited to making statements about facts and the relationships among them. p16

Price discrimination   The practice of charging different prices for different units of a single product, when the price differences are not justified by differences in cost. p589

Price elasticity of demand   The ratio of the percentage change in the quantity of a good demanded to a given percentage change in its price, other things being equal. p487

Price elasticity of supply   The ratio of the percentage change in quantity supplied to a given percentage change in the price of a good, other things being equal. p495

Price fixing   Any action by two or more firms to cooperate in setting prices. p642

Price index   A weighted average of the prices of goods and services expressed in relation to a base year value of 100. p181

Price leadership   In an oligopoly, a situation in which increases or decreases in price by one dominant firm, known as the price leader, are matched by all or most other firms in the market. p606

Price level   The ratio of the average price of goods and services in the current year to the average price of goods and services in a chosen base year. p155

Price support   A program under which the government guarantees a certain minimum price to farmers by offering to buy any surplus that cannot be sold to private buyers at the support price. p678

Price taker   A firm that sells its outputs at prices that are determined by forces beyond its control. p552

Primary financial markets   Markets in which newly issued stocks, bonds, and other securities are sold to investors. p89

Principle of diminishing marginal utility   The principle that the greater the rate of consumption of some good, the smaller the increase in utility from a one-unit increase in consumption of that good. p502

Producer price index   A price index based on a sample of goods and services bought by business firms. p184

Production possibility frontier   A graph showing the possible combinations of goods that can be produced by an economy, given available resources and technology. p25

Progressive tax   A tax that takes a larger percentage of income as income increases. p115

Proportional tax   A tax that takes an equal percentage of income at all levels. p116

Protectionism   Any policy intended to shield domestic industries from import competition. p809

Public assistance   Programs under which transfers are made to people who meet some specified low-income standard. p786

Public good   A good or service that (1) cannot be provided to one person without also being provided to others and (2) once provided to one person can be provided to others at zero added cost. p108

Purchasing power parity   A situation in which the value of the domestic currency in terms of a foreign currency is just equal to the ratio of the average foreign price level to the average domestic price level. p825

Pure economic profit   The sum that is left when both explicit and implicit costs are subtracted from total revenue. p524

Pure economic rent   The income earned by any factor of production whose supply is perfectly inelastic. p763

Pure monopoly   A market structure in which a single firm makes and sells 100 percent of the output of a product. p577

Rate of natural increase   The current growth rate of a population, calculated by subtracting the crude death rate from the crude birthrate. p850

Rate of return   A firm's accounting profit expressed as a percentage of its net worth. p655

Rational-expectations hypothesis   The hypothesis that people form their expectations about future economic events not only on the basis of past events but also on the basis of their expectations about economic policies and their likely effects. p372

Real In economics, a term used to refer to data that have been adjusted for the effects of inflation. p10

Real interest rate The nominal interest rate minus the rate of inflation. p163

Recession A period in which real output falls for 6 months or more. p11

Recovery A period of renewed growth of real output following a recession. p11

Reflation An episode in which policy becomes more expansionary while the expected rate of inflation is still falling. p461

Regressive tax A tax that takes a smaller percentage of income as income increases. p115

Regulation Government intervention in the market for the purpose of influencing the production and distribution of particular goods and services. p38

Repurchase agreement A short-term liquid asset that consists of an agreement by a firm or person to buy securities from a financial institution for resale at an agreed-upon price at a later date, often the next business day. p265

Required-reserve ratio Required reserves stated as a percentage of deposits. p276

Required reserves The minimum percentage of certain deposits that depository institutions are required to hold as reserves. p276

Reservation wage The lowest wage that a job seeker will accept. p438

Reserves Cash in bank vaults and non-interest-bearing deposits of banks with the Federal Reserve System. p267

Saving The part of household income that is not used to buy goods and services or pay taxes. p134

Saving schedule A graphic or numerical schedule that shows how saving varies as disposable income varies, other things being equal. p205

Savings deposits Deposits at banks and thrift institutions from which funds can be withdrawn at any time without payment of a penalty. p265

Say's law The proposition that producing a given level of national product will automatically generate an equal level of aggregate demand. p198

Scarcity A situation in which there is not enough of a resource to meet all of people's wants and needs. p3

Secondary financial markets Markets in which previously issued bonds, stocks, and other securities are traded among investors. p89

Shared monopoly A situation in which the firms in an oligopoly coordinate their activities in such a way as to earn maximum profits for the industry as a whole. p605

Short run A time range within which output can be adjusted only by changing the amounts of variable inputs used while fixed inputs remain unchanged. p526

Shortage See excess quantity demanded.

Social insurance Programs under which transfers are made available to everyone, regardless of income, upon the occurrence of a specified event such as retirement, unemployment, or disability. p786

Socialism An economic system in which business firms are owned and controlled by the people who work in them, or by the government, acting in the name of the workers. p36

Sole proprietorship A firm that is owned and usually operated by one person, who receives all the profits and is responsible for all of the firm's liabilities. p77

Speculation The activity of buying goods or securities in the hope of selling them later at a higher price. p90

Static efficiency The ability of an economy to get the greatest degree of consumer satisfaction from given resources and technology. p630

Sterilization A process thorugh which a central bank uses domestic monetary operations to offset the domestic monetary effects of official reserve transactions in foreign exchange markets. p838

Stocks Quantities that exist at a point in time, measured in terms of units only. p133

Structural deficit The federal budget deficit that would prevail if the economy operated at a constant benchmark rate of unemployment. p246

Structural unemployment The part of unemployment that is accounted for by people who are out of work for long periods because their skills do not match those required by available jobs. p434

Substitute goods A pair of goods for which an increase in the price of one causes an increase in demand for the other. p58

Substitution effect The part of the increase in quantity demanded of a good whose price has fallen that is caused by substitution of the good that is now relatively cheaper for others that are now relatively more costly. p506

Supply curve A graphic representation of the relationship between the price of a good and the quantity of it supplied. p59

Supply management Any of a number of government programs that have as their goal the limitation of farm output. p679

Supply shock An event, such as an increase in the price of imported oil, a crop failure, or a natural disaster, that raises input prices for all or most firms and pushes up workers' cost of living. p366

Supply side economics A school of economics that focuses on efforts to increase the growth of natural real output, especially through the incentive of tax cuts. p391

Target price A price that is guaranteed to farmers by the government; if the market price falls below the target price, the government pays the farmers the difference. p681

Tariff   A tax on imported goods. p809

Tax incidence   The question of who bears the actual burden of a tax, as opposed to who has the legal obligation to pay the tax. p112

Theory   An explanation of how facts are related. p13

Thrift institutions (thrifts)   A group of financial intermediaries that operate much like commercial banks, including savings and loan associations, mutual savings banks, and credit unions. p264

Time deposits   Deposits at banks and thrift institutions from which funds can be withdrawn without payment of a penalty only at the end of an agreed-upon period. p265

Transaction costs   The costs of gathering information, making decisions, carrying out trades, writing contracts, making payments, and other tasks involved in coordinating economic activity. p84

Transactions deposits   Deposits from which funds can be withdrawn by check in order to make payments to third parties. p263

Transfer payments   Payments by government to individuals that are not made in return for goods and services currently supplied. p106

Transitivity   The principle that if A is preferred to B and B is preferred to C, then A must be preferred to C. p517

Transmission mechanism   The mechanism through which monetary policy affects the equilibrium level of nominal national income. p324

Unemployment rate   The percentage of people in the labor force who are not working but are actively looking for work. p7

Unit elastic demand   A situation in which price and quantity change by the same percentage, and therefore total revenue remains unchanged as price changes. p487

Utility   The pleasure, satisfaction, or need fulfillment that people get from the consumption of goods and services. p502

Value added   The dollar value of an industry's sales less the value of intermediate goods purchased to be used in production. p174

Variable inputs   Inputs that can easily be varied within a short time in order to increase or decrease output. p525

Velocity   The ratio of nominal national income to the money stock; a measure of the average number of times each dollar of the money stock is used each year for income-producing purposes. p292

Vertical merger   A merger between firms with a supplier-purchaser relationship. p643

Wage offer curve   A graph that shows the relationship between duration of job search and the best job offer (in terms of wage rate) received to date. p437

Yield (of a bond)   The income received from a bond expressed as a percentage of its current market price. p92

Index

Index of Cases

*These cases are new to the 4th edition.